CHRISTIANITY

CHRISTIANITY

A Social and Cultural History

———

Howard Clark Kee
Emily Albu Hanawalt
Carter Lindberg
Jean-Loup Seban
Mark A. Noll

Epilogue by Dana L. Robert

———

Macmillan Publishing Company
New York

Collier Macmillan Canada
Toronto

Editor: Helen McInnis
Production Supervisor: Andrew Roney
Production Manager: Aliza Greenblatt
Text and Cover Designer: Patrice Fodero
Cover Photo by Howard Clark Kee
Photo Researcher: Barbara Schultz, PAR/NYC, Inc.
Illustrations: Vantage Art

This book was set in 10/12 Janson by Waldman Graphics, and printed and bound by Book Press. The cover was printed by Phoenix Color Corp.

Macmillan Publishing Company
866 Third Avenue, New York, New York 10022

Collier Macmillan Canada, Inc.
1200 Eglinton Avenue East, Suite 200
Don Mills, Ontario M3C 3N1

Library of Congress Cataloging-in-Publication Data

Kee, Howard Clark.
   Christianity: a social and cultural history / Howard Clark Kee
   . . . [et al.]; epilogue by Dana L. Robert.
      p.   cm.
   Includes bibliographical references and index.
   ISBN 0-02-362431-0
   1. Church history.   2. Sociology, Christian—History.
   3. Christianity and culture—History.   I. Title.
   BR148.K38   1991
   270—dc20   90-42146
                                                        CIP

Printing: 1   2   3   4   5   6   Year: 1   2   3   4   5   6   7

PREFACE

The aim of this volume is to offer a fresh analysis and a comprehensive survey of the rise and spread of Christianity, after its two millennia of development from its origins in the remote Roman provinces of Galilee and Judea to its present position as a worldwide religious, social, and cultural phenomenon. The approach to this task by the authors of this book has been to take into account the social and cultural contexts and dynamics out of which Christianity arose and in which it has continued to develop. This method of analysis seems especially important at a time when historical study takes with new seriousness the way in which sociocultural factors shape human thought, including understandings of the past.

This project begins by examining the dynamic changes taking place within Judaism at the beginning of the Common Era, including the changes in Roman policy toward subject peoples. The cultural influence of Greco-Roman culture and imperial policy on emerging Christianity became a two-way factor when, in the fourth century, this religious movement was accepted by Roman imperial leadership as the basis for reshaping the empire. The process continued down through the Middle Ages as Christianity spread geographically and interchanged intellectually with the culture of the late Roman world. The impact on Christianity of the Renaissance and the forces which underlay the Protestant Reformation are assessed, as are the reactions from two different sources: (1) the Roman Catholic tradition, which sought to conserve its authority; and (2) the widening, liberating intellectual spirit of the Enlightenment. The encounters of Christianity with rationalistic and scientific modes of intellectual analysis are described, together with the resulting impact on philosophy, social theory, art, and literature. The role of Christianity in the development of the social, political, and cultural life of Europe and its aggressive expansion into colonial territories is traced, as are the indigenous religious movements in America.

An epilogue sketching the current impact of Christianity in the developing regions of the world brings the book to a conclusion.

The contributors to this volume were chosen because of their ability to examine and interpret the history of Christianity in light of the changing social and cultural context. Since the data differ from period to period, each author was free to offer an analysis of his or her period in what seemed an appropriate style. My own earlier writings have focused on the social setting of early Christianity, while Emily Albu Hanawalt has been a leader nationally in Byzantine studies, and Carter Lindberg has contributed to Reformation studies in Europe and America. Jean-Loup Seban, French in birth and training, now brings to his teaching in America the perspectives and insights of his European background. Mark A. Noll has done important work in analyzing not only the mainline churches in America, but independent and evangelical Christian groups as well. Dana Robert's epilogue gives evidence of her training in the history of worldwide Christianity, demonstrating the impact of Christianity on other cultures and the reciprocal impact on Christianity.

The authors want to express thanks to those who have helped them to bring this project to completion. Colleagues who have helpfully reviewed all or portions of the contents at earlier stages include Daniel Pals, Michelle Saltzmann, Diogene Allen, and Charles Ryerson. Thomas Gillespie provided essential support at crucial points. Helen McInnis, executive editor at Macmillan, offered the initial challenge and opportunity to undertake this project and has offered encouragement and counsel as it has taken shape, for which the authors are grateful.

Howard Clark Kee

CONTENTS

Preface   v

Introduction by Howard Clark Kee   1

Part I: The Context, Birth, and Early Growth of Christianity
by Howard Clark Kee   **11**

Chapter 1:   From Alexander to Augustus: Cultural and Political
       Challenge to Jewish Religious Identity   13
Chapter 2:   Jesus of Nazareth and the Radical Alternative
       for Redefining the Covenant   27
Chapter 3:   Paul: Christian Encounter with the Roman World   44
Chapter 4:   From Charismatic Movement to Institution   62
Chapter 5:   Challenges to Christianity from Roman Culture   75
Chapter 6:   Christian Responses to the Challenges from the Culture   93
Chapter 7:   The Challenges from within Christianity   110
Chapter 8:   Conflict of Church and Empire   128

Part II: The Christian Empire and the Early Middle Ages
by Emily Albu Hanawalt   **145**

Chapter 9:   The Christian Empire and Arianism (324–381)   147
Chapter 10:   Pagan Reaction and Christian Victory (361–476)   157
Chapter 11:   West and East After the Fall: Emergence of Medieval
       Christendom (476–565 East; 604 West)   172

Contents

Chapter 12: The Eastern Empire and the Struggle
with Islam (565–843)   189

Chapter 13: The Medieval Church in the West (481–887)   207

Chapter 14: The Flowering of Medieval Christendom (867–1085)   229

Part III: The Late Middle Ages and the Reformations of the Sixteenth Century by Carter Lindberg   257

Chapter 15: The Bloom of the Twelfth Century   259

Chapter 16: The Harvest of the Medieval Church   283

Chapter 17: "The Haywain," or "All Flesh is Grass"   305

Chapter 18: The Crisis of the Late Medieval Era   324

Chapter 19: The Reformations of the Sixteenth Century   330

Chapter 20: The Radical Reformers   361

Chapter 21: "The Most Perfect School of Christ"—
The Genevan Reformation   372

Chapter 22: Protestant Mission and Evangelism—
The "International Conspiracy"   384

Chapter 23: Catholic Renewal and the Counter-Reformation   406

Chapter 24: Legacies of the Reformation   417

Part IV: European Christianity Confronts the Modern Age by Jean-Loup Seban   425

Chapter 25: The Consolidation of Orthodox Belief   427

Chapter 26: The Reign of the Enlighteners   485

Chapter 27: The Paradox: Ecclesiastical Belief Amidst
Secular Ambiguity   549

Part V: Christianity and Culture in America by Mark A. Noll   601

Chapter 28: Christianity in European America (1492–1740)   603

Chapter 29: The Americanization of Christianity (1720–1820)   627

Chapter 30: The Christianizing of America (1789–1880)   657

Chapter 31: The Passing of Christian America (1861–1925)   689

Chapter 32: Christianity in Post-Christian America (1925–1988)   723

Epilogue by Dana L. Robert   755

Chapter 33: Christianity in Asia, Africa, and Latin America   757

Selected Bibliography   765

Index   777

INTRODUCTION

In the book of Acts of the Apostles, Paul is pictured as standing before the puppet king of Galilee, Herod Agrippa II, defending his activities in the spread of Christianity. He reminds the king that the events that gave rise to the movement could not have escaped the ruler's notice, since "this thing did not happen in a corner" (Acts 28:26). Paul's passing remark to the king is actually a powerful understatement. What he is referring to is that what Jesus did and said, what happened to him, and what his followers were carrying out in his name were matters of public record, not events taking place "in a corner." These public activities that gave rise to the Jesus movement, Paul is implying, are known to the populace at large and have involved the religious and political leaders of Palestine and Syria, of Asia Minor and Greece. Although he could not have foreseen it, the spread of the movement and its message were soon to come to the attention of the emperor Tiberius in Rome, as they already had attracted notice and responses among the civil authorities in cities from Jerusalem northward and westward across Syria and the eastern Mediterranean world. From the second century on, the Christian claims would challenge and enrage some leading intellectuals and persuade others. The Christians would learn to use for their own purposes the artistic and literary styles of the changing eras down through the centuries.

Christianity a Public Event

To keep these public dimensions of Christianity in mind is essential for the study of the origins, development, and subsequent growth of this movement. The death of Jesus, which had such central significance for the message of his followers about

1

him, had taken place on a political charge—that he claimed to be king of the Jews—and was carried out by the Roman military.

From the outset, the conflict of Jesus with the religious authorities had been over his insistence that participation in the people of God was open to all humanity, regardless of ethnic, ritual, or prior religious condition. So rapid was the pace at which this message had spread throughout Palestine, gaining both Jewish and non-Jewish adherents for the new communities, that within a year or two of his death his followers had to interpret the message about him in the language and cultural forms of other Greco-Roman peoples in addition to those of the original Jewish hearers. This inclusive approach to religious identity—how all human beings may be related to God—raised all manner of difficulties for Christians and contributed to the struggles they experienced from the outset.

The social complications and the highly public development of Christianity stand in contrast to the approach of other religions that emphasize private mystical experience and direct divine disclosure to the individual. In some forms of Buddhism, for example, the important aim is the liberation of the self from involvement in the material world. In other religions, there is an effort to become free of the structures of the changing world in order to contemplate eternal good and truth. Although it is true that there are reports in the early Christian writings that Jesus and Paul had direct disclosures of God and his purpose, the events that are central for Christian faith are public and historical. The fact that they happened is confirmed by multiple human witnesses. From the outset, the major goal of the Jesus movement was to call into existence a new kind of inclusive community that might arch over all the ordinary human distinctions of race and religion. Such a movement thrived on public testimony. Beginning with the career of Jesus and on down through subsequent decades, the claims of Christianity were expressed in terms of historical events and in concepts developed in dialogue with the contemporary social and cultural world.

Yet Christianity did later develop important mystical dimensions. From the early centuries of its existence down through the Middle Ages, there were those who claimed to have direct visions of God or Christ. Others said they had been able to see visions of earlier Christian men and women, who because of their special faith or purity of life were known as saints. In the monasteries where pious Christians went to live, withdrawn from the world, there were those who claimed to have direct communion with God. Since the Protestant Reformation of the early sixteenth century, there have been groups throughout the world that claim to have experience of God, visibly and audibly, as they meet together under the power of the Spirit. Some of the better known groups of this ecstatic type are the Shakers, the Quakers, and the Pentacostalists. This claim to experience the outpouring of the Spirit is considered by them to be similar to that described in Acts 2 as occurring on the Day of Pentecost.

Christianity in Conflict with Established Authority

From its beginnings, the early Christian movement was involved in confrontation with the established religious and political leaders. In the gospel accounts of the career of Jesus, the crisis that leads to his death comes when he is called to explain his role and aims to the religious leaders in Jerusalem. He had set aside some of the laws believed to have been given by God to Moses, such as prohibition of work on the Sabbath or the avoidance of contact with non-Jews during meals. This forced the religious leaders to challenge his claims that he was being empowered by God. His assertions of divine support for his actions, his teachings, and for the formation of his band of followers meant that the Jewish leaders saw in him a basic threat to what they regarded as the ground rules for belonging to the Jewish people. Similarly, the fact that he talked so much about the "kingdom" and that his followers spoke of him as king required the political leaders of Palestine to question him and his intentions. This resulted in his execution as a threat to Roman authority in that part of the empire. How could this proclamation about the coming of God's kingdom be compatible with the sovereignty of Rome? For the Jewish leaders, how could his claim that participation in God's people was open to all humanity be reconciled with the traditional view of ethnic, ritually distinct Israel as a chosen people? Political involvement between the emergent church and the empire was inevitable, as was religious conflict and competition with the Jews. Especially hot debate arose over the incompatible Jewish and Christian claims for defining the Covenant People.

This issue of conflict with religious and political leadership has powerfully affected the life of the church throughout its existence. There seems to have been no general persecution of Christians until some time in the second century, but by the late third century there was an organized effort to stamp out the movement. Astonishingly, in the fourth century the Roman emperor Constantine recognized Christianity and identified himself with the church. Immediately, there arose the problem of how the church should be related to the political powers—an issue that subsequently led to the emergence of two centers of churchly power (one in the Rome and one in the eastern Roman Empire), and later to the Protestant Reformation. It is still a source of contention and conflict in Europe and America down to the present day. Church-state issues show up often in the American state and federal courts.

Christianity's Communications Strategy

Because the early Christians were convinced that they had a message for the whole human race, they had from the outset a problem of communication. To convey what they regarded as the Good News to as wide as possible a range of society, both Jewish and Gentile, Jesus and his followers had to employ a variety of media. From the outset, Christians had to be able to use the literary forms developed by people of various cultures in order to get through to them with the Christian story. The reports of what Jesus said and did were orally circulated at first in popular story-telling form. Those who taught and preached in his name simply repeated what they had heard. Only later were these traditions about Jesus brought together in the sequential form that we have in the gospels. Narratives about Paul and his associates were reported a generation after their time in the popular literary style of the late first and second century known as a *romance*. This form of communication was not romantic in our modern sense of the term but was used as a way of attracting readers to the religious figures and experiences that were reported. For example, the popular novel-like tale of the second century, Apuleius's *Golden Ass*, is a fascinating account of a man changed into a donkey and back again, but its main aim is as propaganda for the worship of Isis, the goddess who restores the hero to his true humanity. Through miracles of deliverance and disaster, through journeys by land and sea, the gods guide the lives of those devoted to them. The Book of Acts appears to have employed and adapted this model for communicating its story about the progress of the Christian gospel from Jerusalem to Rome. That is the literary medium by which Acts presents its claim that there had been divine confirmation of this message by miracles and wonders that had taken place through the apostles.

Other traditions in the early Christian writings are recorded in styles that take as their model Jewish hymns and psalms; others imitate formal public addresses or letter-writing patterns of the time. Still other parts of the New Testament and early Christian literature are influenced strongly by such distinctive Jewish writings as apocalypses—documents that claim to be divine disclosures by God to the faithful minority of his people, warning them of conflict and suffering, while promising them ultimate vindication by God. Passages in the gospels and the letters of Paul fit into this literary category, and the Book of Revelation and other early Christian writings are thoroughly apocalyptic in style and substance. Clearly, the early Christians were ready and able to use a variety of forms of communication, employing whatever means they thought were best suited to achieve the end of getting their message through to the intended audience in their contemporary society. We shall see that this same multimedia strategy has been adopted throughout the life of the church. The result was that its message has been conveyed through official decrees, learned philosophical discourses, epistles, and reports of visions and revelations. For centuries after the New Testament writings were finished, various writers produced gospels, apocalypses, and letters purporting to have been written by apostles and other saints. From the outset, the movement was prolific and resourceful in its use of popular modes of communication to reach as wide a public as possible.

Christianity in Competition with Judaism

An essential feature of the early Christian movement was its claim to provide the true and ultimate interpretation of the Jewish scriptures, and to be the heir to the promises God is reported in those scriptures to have made concerning the renewal of the covenant agreement between God and his people. This bold challenge—which has its origins in the teachings and activities of Jesus—led inevitably to mixed reactions from contemporary Jews: Some were persuaded; others fiercely resisted the movement and sought to combat the radical claims that were being made for Jesus on the basis of the biblical tradition. This infighting led for a time to the assumption on the part of outsiders that what we now call Christianity was merely another form of internal debate and conflict within the Jewish religion. That kind of argument also resulted in confusion within and between the Jesus movement and Judaism down into the second century.

In these first centuries of the Common Era (C.E.), Judaism was itself undergoing radical reorganization and rethinking, following the destruction of the temple and the unseating of the priestly leadership that had guided it for centuries. We shall see how the Christians dealt with these issues in a variety of ways in the early Christian writings. Some groups within the early church wanted to emphasize the continuity of the new community with ancient Israel and its traditions, whereas others sought to make a radical break. Still others tried to balance the features retained from Judaism with those rejected.

Christianity's Relation to Secular Wisdom

Similarly, some of the Christians believed that there were features of pagan religions and philosophical insights that were compatible with Christianity or that could be modified and adapted in the interests of communicating the new faith. Others were persuaded, however, that divine revelation and human knowledge were fundamentally at odds. To express God's thought required special holy language and concepts. From earliest times, these tensions between faith and human wisdom were evident within the church and influenced the attitudes of outsiders toward the new movement. In matters of ethics, the new communities could simply take over the basic moral obligations and patterns of behavior from the Jewish tradition, or they could modify them in relation to lofty moral ideas expressed in various pagan philosophical or religious movements. Like other Jews before him, Paul incorporated into his concept of Christian ethics basic features of Stoic philosophy, including the idea of a universal law of nature and the human conscience by which one is aware of this moral law that is at work everywhere in the universe.

Not all Christians shared this approach to ethics, but some—such as the author of the Letter to the Hebrews and the intellectual leaders of the church in Alexandria during the second and third centuries—drew heavily on the philosophy of Plato as well in developing their structures. The great scholar of the middle ages, Thomas Aquinas, developed his elaborate theological system by a synthesis of traditional Christian thought and the philosophy of Aristotle. In the nineteenth century, some German scholars rewrote the history of Christianity by means of a scheme derived from the philosophy of G. W. F. Hegel. Their theory claimed that all human life and thought moved by the tensions between forces and counterforces and that from this emerged new realities. According to this approach, the Jerusalem apostles taught a form of Christianity in which obedience to the Jewish law was essential, whereas Paul taught that the gospel freed Christians from obeying the law of Moses. Out of this conflict developed a kind of Christianity that by the third and fourth centuries had incorporated some of Paul's ideas into a structure of thought and organization that was more like that of ancient Israel, with a fixed leadership and worship structure. In the twentieth century, the attempt has been made to show that the religious insights of Jesus and Paul are closely akin to existentialist philosophy. The essence of Christianity is said to be personal encounter between the individual and God. Obviously, this basic issue of the relationship between Christianity and contemporary intellectual culture has been a concern of the movement from the beginning down to the present day.

As the new insights or claims emerged in the wider culture concerning the nature of human beings, or of the natural world, or of human intellectual or moral capacities, the church has had to face the question of how to react to these proposals. Were they to be rejected, affirmed, or in some way synthesized with earlier Christian beliefs and practices? We shall see that throughout the history of Christianity there has been a range of responses on the part of Christianity to the political, social, and cultural environments that surrounded it. The options have included hostility to the state and prevailing culture, adoption by the church of the basic structures of society and political power, or the effort to transform those modes of human social and political life. Some leaders of the church assumed that their obedience to God demanded that they withdraw wholly from society; hence, they formed monastic communities. Yet even then, the literature produced by monks shows how deeply they were engaged with issues arising from the wider culture. The obligation to make decisions concerning these social, political, economic, and intellectual structures was inevitable and has been a persistent factor throughout the history of the church.

Christianity and Politics

The two chief forms of Roman religion in the imperial age provided both challenge and opportunity for the early Christian movement: the state cult of the traditional gods, and the informal but officially tolerated emergence of shrines and communities devoted to various deities. The Roman emperors and their civilian and military officers insisted that all subjects of the empire honor the traditional Roman gods. This demand served multiple purposes: (1) It gave promise that the deities would look favorably on the Roman state and preserve it from harm. (2) It provided a religious aura around the imperial system and suggested that there was a divine approval for the replacement of the Roman republic by the dictators and their governmental apparatus. The first of these emperors, Julius Caesar, was deified after his death. (3) It gave a common focus of commitment and ritual performance to the whole range of ethnic and cultural backgrounds represented by the peoples across the Mediterranean and middle eastern worlds dominated by the empire.

The Jews and the Christians were faced with the inescapable problem as to whether or not they should share in this official cult. As the issue became more acute in the second century, the resulting conflict between the empire and the noncon-forming Christians appeared to threaten the survival of the movement, because Christianity's refusal to participate in the imperial cult was seen as subversive of the unity or even the survival of the empire. Yet the official approval of Christianity under the emperor Constantine in the fourth century did not remove the issue of the relationship of church and state, as we shall see. In the fourth-fifth century, Augustine was wrestling with this question in his *City of God*, in which he contrasted the divine order with earthly sovereign systems. The issue has surfaced throughout the centuries in various forms of tension between church and political powers. It appeared in conflicts between religious and political authority with the development of the Roman Catholic church in the west and the orthodox churches of the eastern Mediterranean world in Constantinople, Alexandria, Antioch, and Jerusalem. It arose at the time of the Protestant Reformation when the question was raised as to whether the state should support or even control the church. It took new form in modern times when Marxist regimes tried to stifle the church, and it appears in the United States in conflicts over church and state.

The Search for Identity

The ethnic and cultural complexity of the Roman empire was accentuated by the fact that its subjects were often uprooted and forced to move as a result of military, political, and economic changes in the empire. This high mobility stimulated the rise of unofficial voluntary groups throughout the realm so that people could have some local social group with which they could identify. In metropolitan centers, especially in port cities, persons of common cultural background began to develop shrines or centers where devotions could be offered to the traditional deities of the regions from which these people had come. In many cases, these gods and goddesses offered their worshippers a sense of immediate participation in the divine life in a way that the imperial cult did not. Chief among these divinities whose worship centers began to appear across the Mediterranean world as early as the later first century were Isis, the Eygptian goddess, and Dionysus, the Greek god. Through both these divinities renewal of human life was promised. In Greece and the Greek islands, Asklepios, the god of healing, had centers where pilgrims from all over the world came to seek his benefits. Jews, most of whom by the first century of the Common Era lived outside of Palestine in various parts of the world, had also developed local meetings called *synagogues*, where they gathered informally to renew their traditional ties, and for worship and for study of their sacred writings. It was to these gatherings that Paul went as he sought to persuade his fellow Jews that Jesus was the divinely designated fulfillment of their hopes for renewal. The popularity of these spontaneous assemblies of pious peoples throughout the Roman world was an essential precondition of the astonishingly rapid spread of Christianity. Yet no sooner had the church established its identity than there began to emerge small groups of Christians that developed within the larger body of the church or that took up separate existence outside the main structure. Among both pagans and Christians there has been throughout history this unquenchable yearning for group identity.

Christianity Getting Itself Organized

Complicating the inescapable obligation to make decisions about the political powers and about the competing religions of the day were the issues of internal authority within the church. The members of the new movement had to resolve the problems of leadership, authority, and decision-making within the group. As the great sociologist of religion, Max Weber, noted early in the twentieth century, religions typically begin as spontaneous movements launched and expanded through the powerful personality and message of a leader. Although that leader lacks official credentials or even formal training, the *charisma* or special insights and authority he displays are considered by his followers to be manifestations of a divine gift. It is this personal power that gives rise to the movement, attracts its first followers, and provides a focus of aim and identity for its constituents.

Such a movement has no more than begun, however, before those who move into leadership roles begin to develop patterns of authority and increasingly specific guidelines for individual and group decision-making. In Weber's terms, what begins as a charismatic movement soon takes on institutional forms. It must do so if it is to survive, especially as the first generation of adherents begin to die off and the continuation of the group is dependent on a new generation that must be instructed in the group traditions and charged with the range of responsibilities essential for the survival of the movement.[1]

We shall see that before the earliest gospel was written and while Paul was carrying on the mission activity reflected in his letters, the transformation from charismatic origins to institutional forms was already under way in early Christianity. The later books of the New Testament and the literature of the early centuries of

---

[1]This basic position is set forth by Max Weber in "The Sociology of Charismatic Authority," in H. H. Gerth and C. Wright Mills, trans. and eds., *From Max Weber* (New York: Oxford University Press, 1958).

the church reflect the further development of internal structures for providing leadership and establishing the norms to be observed on a range of issues by the members of the movement. Who will be in charge of decision-making about who should be in the group and how its members should behave? These group needs and various solutions that were offered are apparent in the changing forms and concepts that emerged in Christianity down through the centuries to the present day. But the impact of these social and cultural factors is also evident in the opposite direction. From the fourth century on, Christianity moved to assume a major role in the shaping of culture and politics in the western world. We shall trace in detail, therefore, the ways in which Christianity was shaped by western culture, from the days of the Roman empire through medieval and down to modern times, as well as how the movement contributed in fundamental ways to the development of that culture.

Our primary focus in this volume is on the rise of Christianity, its shift to the role of a religion officially sanctioned by the Roman state, and its subsequent development in the western world of Europe and the Americas, where it has experienced a mixture of relationships to the state, ranging from ecclesiastical establishment (as in the United Kingdom) to theoretically total separation of church and state (as in the United States), and the consequent proliferation of religious groups claiming to be the true heirs of the Christian tradition. We also give some attention, however, to the impact of Christianity on other cultures, such as those in Africa and the Far East in later centuries. We take note of the effects of missionary activity in the nineteenth and twentieth centuries on what has come to be called the Third World. We shall also see how Christians at various times and especially in recent decades have perceived their responsibilities to include the use of the earth's resources and the conservation of the environment.

Thus, the insights attributed to Paul in Acts 26 were correct. The Christian movement promised renewal of the world—not merely of human society but also of the whole creation. The terms of admission to the new community were potentially universal, so there was no prior reason why the claims of Christianity should not be heard and heeded by people from any race or culture. This inclusiveness required a variety of strategies and formulas for communicating the message, so that—to borrow another phrase from Acts (2:8)—each person might hear the message in his or her own language. That is, Christianity had to learn how to convey its claims and hopes in the symbolic and verbal modes of communication that could reach persons in spite of basic cultural and social differences. As a result of this attempted universal outreach of Christianity and of the range of responses that its message has called forth down through 2,000 years, the movement has been a diverse phenomenon from the outset.

Although the origins of Christianity were within Judaism, it began at a time when Jews were confronted with a range of theories as to what made them God's special people. Christians offered a radical redefinition of that social identity as God's

9

people. Yet Christianity's own leaders and adherents agreed on the principle of inclusiveness but not on the details of what was to be required of members for admission and maintenance of status. On the following factors there was agreement, however, even though in both details and the descriptive language used by the various groups within Christianity there were wide divergences of interpretation and formulation:

1. That through Jesus, God had announced the renewal of the creation and of his covenant people.

2. That God had chosen Jesus and endowed him with power as the agent and messenger through whom this goal of renewal was to be launched and accomplished.

3. That through the crucifixion and resurrection of Jesus God had dealt decisively with the two basic human problems of sin and death.

4. That through the followers of Jesus and their successors, the people of the new covenant were being called into existence, and through them the power was already operative for the renewal of humanity and of the creation.

5. That the nucleus of this new community consisted of those who trusted in Jesus as the agent of God, who affirmed the message that he proclaimed, and who took on the responsibilities that he assigned to his followers.

The detailed implications of these claims were understood in a variety of ways by those who came to be part of the Christian movement. At times, the leaders of the church seemed to be more concerned with setting straight those who claimed to be members but who disagreed with them in their perceptions of matters of faith and practice than with addressing those outside Christianity who ignored or scorned its claims. There was wide divergence as well on the questions of the attitude of the Christians toward the political and cultural structures and norms of any particular era in the life of the church. But given the way in which Christianity appears from its origins to have involved the basic issues of social identity, of cross-cultural communication, of ultimate political power, it was inevitable that there would be a range of responses by the Christians to these issues. From the outset, therefore, Christianity was fundamentally required to react (1) to the issues of identity and responsibility for those who saw themselves as God's people, and (2) to the challenges that this new community faced in its relation to the wider world. Paul's observation concerning Christian origins that we noted earlier is wholly appropriate therefore: "This thing did not happen in a corner!"

Part One

The Context, Birth, and Early Growth of Christianity

—————

Howard Clark Kee

Chapter 1

FROM ALEXANDER TO AUGUSTUS:

Cultural and Political Challenge to Jewish Religious Identity

―――――

To understand how Christianity began as a movement within Palestinian Judaism and then spread so quickly throughout the world requires three kinds of information: (1) concerning the political changes that brought Jews under the power of a series of world empires; (2) concerning the pressures of Jews to conform to the culture and customs of the dominant power; (3) concerning the efforts of Jews and their Gentile contemporaries in the midst of these social and political changes to find meaning in life and a sense of group identity. What did it mean to be a Jew and to claim to be a member of a people who claimed a special relationship to God? All these factors had a powerful influence on Judaism, but they also set the stage for the rise and spread of Christianity, which had to deal with them as well. The various ways in which these issues were posed by Jews and the answers were sought continued to have direct effects on the shaping of Christianity. It is essential, therefore, that we look at the experience of the Jews after the time of Alexander the Great to see how this experience shaped the problems and pointed toward solutions among the early Christians.

The tensions under which Jews lived in the three centuries before the rise of Christianity were in large measure the result of Alexander's change of policy from that of the Persians toward conquered peoples. Alexander wanted to control the world militarily and politically and to force it to conform to Greek culture. As a young man, he had studied philosophy with one of Greece's greatest, Aristotle, and was convinced that this view of the world was the greatest imaginable. He wanted to conquer the world for Greek culture. Historians refer to this process as *Hellenization*, a term that derives from Hellas (the Greek name for Greece): to Greek-ize the world. His culturally aggressive approach became apparent after he took over the eastern Mediterranean territories from the Persians, who had governed it since they seized control of the Babylonian territories in the late sixth century B.C.E. Persian strategy had been to allow subject peoples dislocated from their lands during the Persian takeover of the Middle East to return to their native regions and to live and worship there with a considerable degree of local freedom. The Jews were among those who benefited from this policy. One of their prophets went so far as to acclaim Cyrus, the king of Persia, as Messiah, or "annointed of God" (Isa. 45:1). The very fact that this pagan ruler was described as someone commissioned by God to perform a special act in behalf of Israel shows that the Jews perceived themselves to stand in a special relationship to God, both in the past and in the present. But the new situation in which the Jews now found themselves after the rise of Alexander was very different from the time when they lived in their own land, before they were carried off to Babylon as captives. Earlier they had had their own leaders: judges, kings, and priests. Now the king was a pagan, helpful as he had been in allowing them to return to the land and reinstitute the temple and its priesthood. The unavoidable question was: What does it now mean for Israel to call itself the people of God?

Who Are the People of God?

The Jews, as we noted, had been taken to Babylonia as captives in the early sixth century but had been permitted by the Persians to return to their land, to resume the worship of their God, and to reconstruct both the temple and their capital city, Jerusalem. That this had taken place is reported in Ezra 1–6, with details of the official support by the Persian rulers. When Ezra went back to Palestine as leader of the exiles returning from Babylon, his first concerns were to reestablish the priesthood in the temple and to see to it that Jews who had remained in the land and married Gentiles divorced their non-Jewish wives. Thus, the purity of Israel as God's people was to be recovered, both through the priestly rites performed in the central shrine and through the regaining of strictly defined ethnic identity by intra-Jewish marriages (Ezra 7–10).

The Old Testament book of Nehemiah (which is actually part of Ezra) describes the coming to Jerusalem of a Jewish governor appointed by the Persians—Nehemiah—and the mixture of support and opposition he met from the inhabitants of the land. The program for reawakening group identity among the people of Israel is described in Nehemiah 8–9, where Ezra is pictured as reading the Law of Moses to the people, and they respond by confessing their sins and assuming responsibility to meet their obligations as a people in convenant relationship with God. What is commonly known among Jews as the Law of Moses, comprising the first five books of the Bible (Genesis, Exodus, Leviticus, Numbers, Deuteronomy), had achieved its present form through an extended process of editing and revision, which probably began during the exile in Babylon and was not completed until a century or more after Israel's return to the land. Although the whole of the Law is traditionally attributed to Moses, it is this reworked version of the history and laws of Israel as they appear in our Bibles that was, and continues to the present day to be, normative among the Jewish people.

Although interpreters down through the centuries have disagreed as to how details of the law were to be interpreted as binding on Israel in its changing circumstances, there was a wide consensus that the nation had been given special knowledge of God in three ways: (1) through the patriarchal figures such as Abraham, Isaac, and Jacob, (2) through Moses, under whose reported leadership the law was given and the exodus from Egypt to the land of Canaan began, and (3) through the kings, wise men, and prophets to whom God continued to disclose his purpose to and for his people. The perennial question was: What must Israel do to preserve its purity and integrity as God's people? A second basic issue for Jews was: Who will be the agent—or agents—through whom God's purpose for his people and for the creation will be brought to fulfillment? Both these issues were to have profound importance for Christianity.

The Jews of subsequent centuries had no uniform solutions for these basic questions, and the actions of the pagan powers that dominated them enormously complicated these problems of religious and social identity for those like the Jews who were convinced that they were in a special sense the people of god. We must examine the forces that bore in upon the Jews, as well as the attempts they made to deal with these problems.

The Challenge of Forced Conformity to Pagan Culture

Alexander the Great, son of King Philip II of Macedon, had at age fifteen begun broad and intensive study of literature, the arts, and the sciences under Aristotle, and he acquired from this great philosopher not only a vast knowledge of the world but also a profound appreciation for Greek culture. When, at age twenty-one (336 B.C.E.), Alexander took over from this father the military and political subjection of all Greece, he also set out to achieve both military and cultural domination of the regions to the east, where the Persians were still in control. In a series of brilliant military successes, he quickly conquered Asia Minor, with its many cities of Greek tradition. The decisive battle was at Issus, on a narrow strip of land between the mountains of Cilicia and the Mediterranean Sea north of Syria. Once past that strategic point, the way was open for him to invade and occupy Syria, Palestine, and Egypt, as well as to conquer vast territories farther east: Mesopotamia, Persia, and parts of India.

As Alexander traveled on this relentless world-conquering expedition, he visited ancient sites and called at shrines of various deities, with some of whom he seems to have identified and even communed, treating them as manifestations of the traditional gods of Greece. In Egypt, for example, he took time to visit the oracle of the local god, Ammon, whom he regarded as one with Zeus. There he was reportedly told that he was a son of the god. Also in Egypt he founded a metropolis to which his name was given—Alexandria—which became a great center of learning, rivaling or even eclipsing such ancient intellectual and artistic cities as Athens itself. It is clear that one of his major aims was to spread not merely political domination but Greek culture. This was to pose a major problem for Jews. How could they maintain their special identity if they conformed to such pressures?

When Alexander died in Babylon in 323 B.C.E., his generals divided his empire among themselves, competing for control of various territories with varying degrees of success. Two of the generals who were able to establish enduring realms for themselves and their heirs were Seleucus in Syria and Ptolemy in Egypt. The district that lay midway between these two centers of Hellenistic power was Palestine, the land of the Jews. It was at first controlled by the Ptolemies and then by the Seleucids. Under both dynasties, the Jews were subjected to pressure to adopt Greek ways of life and thought—and religion. Theaters, gymnasia, and public baths were built, as well as shrines to the Greek gods. The coinage in use in these kingdoms pictured Greek gods and addressed the rulers with divine titles. Greek was the official language, and acceptance by the ruling powers was contingent on conformity to the manner of life and the values of Greek culture. Education and intellectual communication were dominated by the Greek way, and many Jews adopted with enthusiasm the Hellenistic modes of life and thought. Other Jews were only partially open to the pagan influences, and still others stoutly resisted the acculturation process. In the first half of the second century B.C.E., however, the issue of religious and cultural domination came to the crisis stage for the Jews.

The Effort to Regain Jewish National Identity

The Seleucid king Antiochus IV (ruled 175–164 B.C.E.) was particularly eager to coerce his subjects, including the Jews, into conformity to the Greek way. He went so far as to identify himself as divine and to insist that his subjects acclaim him as "Epiphanes," which means a manifestation of deity. Faced with understandable and mounting opposition from certain Jews who called themselves Hasidim ("pious ones"), in 168 B.C.E. he decreed that worship of the God of the Jews was no longer to be permitted and ordered the erection of an altar of Zeus in the temple at Jerusalem. Altars were also constructed throughout the land, and the military was instructed to enforce the worship of the Greek gods and to require that all subjects offer the appropriate sacrifices. A priestly member of the purity group of Jews, Mattathias, killed a fellow Jew in the village of Modin who was making the sacrifice decreed by Antiochus the king. Mattathias then fled to the hills with his five sons to organize opposition to Hellenistic rule. One of this sons, Judah (or Judas)—whose nickname, "hammer" (Maccabee) was adopted by the nationalist movement—assumed the leadership of the movement, which drew large numbers of supporters and took the form of guerilla warfare, achieving astonishing results. By 165 B.C.E. the Maccabees had gained military control of much of the land and of the Temple, which was cleansed and rededicated. Political control of the land of the Jews was established in the years immediately following, and the brothers of Judah (whose family name was Hasmonean) assumed the dual roles of priestly and royal leadership.

Because the Maccabean rulers and their successors became increasingly secular and oppressive, however, and because they had taken the title of king even though they were not descended from David's royal line, there was growing disillusionment with them. At one point the Maccabean dynasty turned for support to a rising power in the west, Rome. In 63 B.C.E., Roman forces under Pompey—claiming to offer assistance to their ally but actually taking over political control—invaded Palestine, establishing the region as a Roman province. The domination of the land by Roman authority continued throughout the subsequent centuries until the Islamic rule was established there in the first half of the seventh century C.E. As was their policy in all the provinces under their control, the Romans allowed Jews a considerable degree of autonomy with regard to local social and economic life. The Roman governors resident in Palestine worked closely with the high priests, who had to gain approval from the Romans for their appointment and who accordingly collaborated with the Roman governmental authorities. At the same time, the Romans controlled parts of Palestine and the adjacent areas through local puppet kings, of whom the best known was Herod, who ruled from 37–34 B.C.E. His mother was Jewish, and his non-Jewish father had helped the Romans first establish themselves in power in this land. Herod not only rebuilt the temple in Jerusalem on a grander scale than ever; he also built Hellenistic centers throughout the land, including a city on the Mediterranean coast that he called Caesarea in honor of his Roman benefactors. It contained all the features of a Hellenistic city: theaters, temples, and gymnasia. At his death, his sons were placed in control of various parts of the region, including Galilee, Samaria and the strongly Hellenized territories east of the Jordan River. One of them, Archelaus, who was put in charge of Judea and Jerusalem, was so incompetent that he had to be replaced by Roman-appointed governors, of whom the best known was Pontius Pilate (C.E. 26–36).

The Range of Responses to the Challenge of Greco-Roman Political and Cultural Domination among First-Century Jews

As has been noted, Jews in the time of Jesus were wrestling with the question of group identity. Rephrasing the basic questions Jews had to face in these two centuries before the birth of Jesus, they were asking:

Who is the agent(s) of God through whom he will work to achieve his purpose for his people?

What are the criteria for participation in the people of God?

Influencing the responses to these questions were such factors as how one viewed the political and cultural forces represented by Rome and its imperial rule. Should Jews accept what seemed inevitable and accommodate themselves politically and culturally to their Roman overlords? Or was it the Jewish people's destiny to be distinct from all other peoples? If so, in what way were they to be distinctive? If not, where were the areas of permissible and defensible overlap with Gentile culture and values? How was Jewish identity to be affirmed and its continuity guaranteed?

The Conformist Jews

The easiest answer to these questions was to conform to the prevailing Greco-Roman modes of life and thought in the political, cultural, social, and personal spheres. Many Jews did, taking Greek names, sending their children to the Hellenistic schools, attending theaters and sports events, and adopting the philosophical concepts of the Hellenistic culture. A radical example of this kind of cultural adaptation is a writing known as IV Maccabees,[1] which retells the struggles of the Maccabees for freedom in terms of the Stoic notion of suffering as disciplinary and morally purgative. Some Jewish males went so far as to have the marks of circumcision surgically removed, so that they could take part without embarrassment in the nude gymnastics of the contemporary Hellenistic society. They participated by the thousands in the other features of Hellenistic culture, such as theaters and the forms of often bloody public entertainment.

Combining Hellenistic and Biblical Wisdom

Far more subtle than the popular conformity to Roman culture, but of profound significance for the future of Judaism and, by extension, of Christianity was the thoughtful incorporation of Hellenistic ideas into the religious traditions of Israel. One of the clearest evidences of this form of intellectual impact of Hellenistic thinking on the Jews of this period was the strong emphasis in Jewish literature of the period on wisdom. Two examples indicate how wisdom was employed by Jewish writers wishing to come to terms with Hellenistic philosophy and science.

---

[1]This is included among the *Pseudepigrapha*. Compare J. H. Charlesworth, ed., *The Old Testament Pseudepigraphia*, Vol. 2 (Garden City, NY: Doubleday, 1985).

The Wisdom of Ben Sira (the book is also known as Sirach and as Ecclesiasticus) is a conscious response to the Hellenistic claims to knowledge of the universe. The writer asserts that true wisdom comes from Yahweh, the God of Israel, and that it existed before the creation, through which it became visible to discerning human beings. Those who perceive it show that they have access to wisdom by the purity and moral responsibility of their lives. The embodiment of this wisdom is the Book of the Covenant—Israel's scriptures. And the evidence of God's accomplishment of his wise purpose in human life is to be seen in the leaders he has raised up to establish and guide his people, Israel. The culmination of this process of divine ordering of the life of God's people has recently appeared in Simon the High Priest (ca. 220–195 B.C.E.), who restored the temple and its ritual, and thereby became the supreme instrument of blessing of Israel by the Most High God. For the writer of this work, Jewish identity is to be found in three resources: (1) the reading and appropriation of the Bible; (2) the celebration of God's historical guidance of Israel; (3) participation in the official worship of God in the temple. Yet in making his case for the uniqueness of Israel's relationship with God, the author draws subtly on the language and insights that came from Hellenistic wisdom.

That development is even more clearly the case in a Jewish work produced in the late first century B.C.E., the Wisdom of Solomon. Although it is attributed to Solomon (tenth century B.C.E.), the work unmistakably comes from the epoch of domination of Jews by Hellenistic culture. The book is written in quite sophisticated Greek and uses the technical terminology of Hellenistic philosophy and science. Its literary style is that of the Hellenistic diatribe, in which the author publicly debates issues, raising questions and offering solutions. The virtues that wisdom instills in her devotees are those of Stoic philosophy: temperance, prudence, justice, and fortitude. As in Ben Sira, the history of Israel is retold, but here it is recounted, not so much as a celebration of the past but as a kind of parable or metaphor of the journey of the soul that leads one to knowledge of God and his purpose. Even the Exodus of Israel from Egypt is not so much a historical account as a model of God's creative activity in the world. There is extensive denunciation of the pagan deities, especially the star gods, since those who engage in the worship of these follies honor what God has made rather than the One who created the world.

Similarly, Philo of Alexandria, a Jewish scholar and leading figure in the large Jewish community in Alexandria in the first half of the first century C.E., retells the stories of the Jewish patriarchs and interprets the details of the Law of Moses in allegorical fashion: as models of the journey of the soul from ignorance to revealed truth concerning God and his purpose for his people. Philo was a faithful member of the Jewish minority in Alexandria and journeyed to Rome to protest hostile actions toward Judaism on the part of the emperor Gaius Caligula (ruled C.E. 37–41). But this learned Jew saw Hellenistic philosophy as a resource for the fresh appropriation of the Jewish biblical tradition. In the Old Testament, God gave instruction to Moses (Exod. 25:40) to build the portable sanctuary and its equipment where God was to dwell in the midst of Israel and to do "according to the pattern which was shown [to Moses] on the mountain [of Sinai]." Philo interpreted this reference to the "pattern" as a statement of the Platonic notion that in the heavens there were perfect patterns or ideal models of which all earthly phenomena were imperfect, temporal copies. In this way he perceived a complete compatibility between biblical teachings and Platonic idealistic philosophy. Philo's allegorical interpretation of the Jewish scriptures saw intellectual concepts to be represented by the persons and events in the biblical stories. For example, Moses going up to Mt. Sinai to meet God was a symbolic way of describing the ascent of the soul of the philosopher to the point at which it could behold the Supreme Being. Based as it was on his adaptation of features of Greek philosophy, this method provided an important precedent for the early Christians as they sought to demonstrate the compatibility of some of these philosophical notions with what they believed God had revealed through Jesus.

Collaboration with the Roman Authorities

Another way of coming to terms with Greco-Roman culture—and especially with Roman political power—was adopted by the members of the Jewish priestly families. They cooperated with Rome through the structures of local government in order to retain control of the operation of the temple and to maintain a role in guiding Jewish public life. The natural strategy for the maintenance of a significant function in Jewish life throughout the region was for the priests and other aristocrats to take on roles in the local councils that Rome authorized to be established throughout its subject territories. In Jerusalem, members of these leading families met regularly in what was called (there as elsewhere in the Roman world) a *synedrion*, the responsibilities of which were to guide the life of their people, to settle disputes, and to maintain the norms of Jewish society, while leaving to the Roman administrators fiscal and political issues. The public symbol of Jewish identity for this leadership group, as well as for large numbers of Jews of this period, was the temple. Jewishness was affirmed and reinforced by the required participation in the temple's ritual and celebrations. Because the temple was believed to be the place where God dwelt among his people, carrying out the proper approach to Israel's God was a guarantee of maintaining that special relationship.

Jewish Identity Through Voluntary Groups

Since the days of the Maccabees, however, many Jews had become disillusioned by the priesthood and by the national leaders, both those who operated before the Romans took over and those who collaborated with the Roman authorities. Jews who perceived that their religious and social leaders' collaboration with Rome was compromising the distinctiveness of Israel's relationship with God became persuaded that their identity as the people of God was dependent on their maintaining their personal ritual purity in spite of the social and cultural pressures to conform to Hellenistic and Roman patterns of life.

Some withdrew into small private groups, where their study of the scriptures and their refusal to adopt the manner of life that their rulers sought to force on them enabled them to remain true to their convictions. They were persuaded that God had revealed to them that in the near future he would act decisively in human affairs, crushing the pagan powers and those who collaborated with them, and then vindicating and establishing in positions of power the small remnant who had remained faithful to the Jewish traditions. Scholars have given to this view of God and his people, and to the revelatory style of literature through which these insights are conveyed to the community that shares these convictions, the designation *apocalyptic*. Derived from the Greek word for "revelation," the term refers both to this revelatory type of writing and also to the convictions that God is said to have conveyed to his chosen few about the nearness of his action in the world to defeat his enemies and to vindicate the remnant of his people who have remained faithful to his purpose. This is the point of view expressed in the Book of Daniel, where the obedient community sees itself as the "saints of the Most High" through whom God will establish his rule in the earth (Dan. 7:11–18). There one may read how God will destroy the evil political powers, which are depicted as horrendous beasts and to which misguided persons have yielded in obedience. To the small community that has endured the threats and schemes of the pagan rulers and remained faithful to God's will, he has given insight concerning the victory he is soon to achieve, as well as assurance of the vindication of its faithful members, who now see themselves as the true people of God.

One such group, which arose in the later second century B.C.E., of which only a few details were known through ancient historians, came into the clearer light of contemporary historical knowledge some forty years ago when portions of its library and the basic structure of its community center were discovered on a bluff overlooking the northwestern end of the Dead Sea in an area known by the local Arabs as Qumran. The Dead Sea Scrolls, as they have come to be known by scholars, included copies of various books of the Jewish Bible and detailed commentaries on the biblical prophets, as well as rule books for the members of the community that had its center there and writings that predicted how God would defeat their enemies. The promised process of divine triumph would result in the defeat of the Romans and their collaborators and in driving out the official priests and leaders of Judaism—whom this community regarded as hopelessly corrupt and misguided. God would enable them to rebuild the temple and would establish them in Jerusalem as the true and pure people of God.

Jewish Identity Through Nationalist Revolt

Another alternative for dealing with the political and cultural domination of Palestine and its Jewish inhabitants by the Romans was to follow the example of the Maccabees and take up arms against them. In the 60s of the first century C.E., and again in 132, there were such surges of Jewish nationalism, with the aim of establishing once again a politically autonomous Jewish state. Unfortunately for these nationalists, the attainment of their objectives was severely hampered, not only by the superior military might and skills of the Roman forces, but also by the fact that among the Jews themselves there were various factions competing for control of the uprising. These fiercely rival groups were contesting among themselves for power even before they had achieved independence form the Romans. As a result, the Roman military reaction to the revolts destroyed these attempts to gain political freedom for the Jews. We shall consider some of the details of these revolutionary efforts when we examine the gospels in light of their historical backgrounds, but it is sufficient here to note that the option of political independence was not taken up until decades after the death of Jesus. Although he was accused of nationalistic aims, there is no evidence from the early Christian writings or from the Jewish sources that such an effort was launched until the late 60s of the Common Era

The Pharisaic Answer to the Jewish Identity Question

The one strategy for gaining and maintaining Jewish covenantal identity that survived the failures of the others and flourished after the destruction of Jerusalem and its temple was that of the Pharisees. In the first century B.C.E., as disillusionment with the Maccabean rulers set in, a group calling themselves the Pure Ones (*perushim*, or Pharisees) initially hoped to transform the ruling dynasty and the priesthood into more worthy lines of succession. After the Roman takeover, however, they turned their energies to developing a way in which they could celebrate their identity as God's people that would not make them dependent on the priestly and aristocratic collaborators with Rome, that would not require them to withdraw physically from their homes and towns, and that would not be viewed by the Romans as a challenge to their political control of the land and the people. It was essential that they and their offspring know and identify with the biblical traditions, and that the relevance of this heritage to their lives in the present circumstances be clear and compelling. How could these aims be achieved effectively without rousing the suspicions of the Romans that subversive or nationalistic schemes were being perpetrated?

The Pharisaic movement that developed was based on voluntary and informal gatherings in homes. There the study of the law and the honoring of God could go on wholly apart from the corrupt, collaborating religious officials. Instead, the Pharisees interpreted the laws, especially those dealing with the purity of God's people, in such a way as to transfer to the members of their groups the regulations and requirements that the scripture imposed on the priests. Although initially they did not have anything like our modern distinction between laity and clergy, by the later first century, leaders of the movement came to assume the title of *rabbi* and to take on authoritative roles in the development of the movement. Up until the rabbinic movement began to assume organizational shape, there seems to have been a spontaneity in the informal worship and in the study of the scripture in these gatherings in homes. Following the pattern developed somewhat earlier among Jews in Egypt and the Greek cities, they called their meetings simply, "gatherings," which in Greek is *synagogē*. If a home was not available or adequate for these gatherings, a meeting place was chosen in a public hall or other area where assembly was feasible. In some parts of the Roman empire, such a location for the gathering of these Jewish communities was called simply a *proseuche*, a "place of prayer." Inscriptions from the cities of Greece and Asia Minor and literature from this period (such as that of Philo of Alexandra and of the Jewish historian, Josephus) designate them in this way. In addition to whatever prayer, worship, and instruction went on in these meetings, the high point of what occurred there was a shared meal in which the common identity of the group was celebrated.

By the time the gospels and Acts were being written—toward the end of the first century C.E.—certain formal patterns and practices had come to be associated with the synagogues. Yet the simple, informal origins of the movement have become apparent in those Palestinian cities where synagogues of the third and later centuries C.E. have been excavated. Beneath these later structures with their evidence of set patterns for seating and designated space for worship and instruction are private houses, which give evidence of having been only slowly adapted to serve as increasingly public meeting places. The changes in architectural evidence from informal to formal styles correspond to the institutional development of the synagogue and the rabbinic roles.

In ways that follow closely the pattern of change in religious movements traced by Max Weber—from spontaneous origins under self-authorized lay people to carefully delineated structures of leadership and fixed patterns of instruction and worship—Judaism in the second half of the first century C.E. began to undergo major transformation. The program of instruction in the interpretation of the Law to demonstrate its contemporary relevance began to take on formal procedures and strategies. Schools came to be developed in connection with the synagogues. Instead of the earlier impulsive and unstructured exposition of the scriptures carried on in someone's living room, the methods of interpretation came to be specified and eventually written down. As the form of the meeting-room developed, the role of the interpreter was provided with a dramatic symbol in the form of the Seat of Moses, from which the person designated to expound the text offered his sermon or instruction.

The results of these developments are to be seen most readily in the weighty literature produced through the synagogue movement in the period from the second to the sixth centuries. Included are records of debates between representatives of various points of view among the rabbis. The title *rabbi* came to be assigned to these leaders who devoted the major portion of their time and energies to these interpretive and institutional developments. The initial collection of these scriptural interpretations was called the *Mishnah*. It was supplemented by collections of discussions of legal questions, one assembled in Babylon and the other in Palestine, which are known respectively as the Babylonian and Palestinian Talmuds and which are arranged topically, primarily on purity issues. Together they provide the guidelines, not merely for scriptural interpretaion, but through this process, for the gaining and maintaining of purity for those who see themselves as God's people. Supplementing these analyses of the law were the Targums, collections of paraphrases in Aramaic (a Semitic language in wide use throughout the Middle East in the ancient world) of the Jewish scriptures, which were nearly all in Hebrew.

This body of literature became the basic interpretive supplement to the Jewish bible and has continued down to the present to provide the strategy by which the biblical tradition is appropriated and its relevance for the Jewish community is understood. The events of Jewish history, perceived as the acts of God in behalf of his people, came to be celebrated in a series of feasts, through which the present members of the community shared in the common heritage and gained a sense of continuity with their ancestors in the covenant people. The Passover meal, for example, recalled God's act of deliverance of Israel from slavery in Egypt and looked forward to the future fulfillment of God's purpose for the nation. In a similar way, the sacred meal described in the supplement to the Scroll of the Rule found in the Dead Sea caves was not only an experience of present unity among this group who regarded themselves as the true and pure people of God. It was also a corporate expression of the conviction that God would in the future act through his chosen agents (the priestly and the kingly Messiahs) to fulfill the destiny of the covenant community. Both in these ceremonial meals and in the increasingly structured system of instruction of the younger generation, effective means were adopted to ensure the transmission of the tradition of those who would take the place of the present leaders and the people. The forms of meeting, worship, and study had profound influence on the early Christian movement.

These developments within what was to become rabbinic Judaism had their roots in earlier Jewish experience, both in Palestine and in the lands where Jews had been dispersed. They began to take more specific shape, however, in the second half of the first century C.E. With the fall of the temple in 70 C.E., the Roman authorities, who dreaded the collapse of one of their subject people or the emergence of another nationalist movement, seem to have encouraged the Pharisees to take a leading role in the reconstitution of their people. With the disappearance of the temple, there had to be a new center of focus and identity for Jews, and Pharisaism apparently provided the solution.

It is impossible to determine how systematic the process of development of rules, patterns, and guidelines was, although later Jewish tradition reports that there was an extended planning council that convened in the later first century C.E. at Yavneh (Jamnia) near modern Tel Aviv. All that one can be certain of is the result: the emergence in the second to sixth centuries C.E. of the basic patterns and structures, conceptually and organizationally, that were to make possible Jewish reappropriation of the biblical tradition in a way that would ensure continuity for Jewish identity following the crises created first by Antiochus Epiphanes and then by the Roman rulers. The climax came with Titus's destruction of the temple. The second attempt by the Jews at establishing a politically independent state in 132–135 was better organized than the effort in 66–70, but the empire was far more securely unified under Hadrian than it had been under Titus. The revolt was crushed, and Jerusalem for some time was off limits for Jews. On the site of the temple, a shrine to Zeus was erected, and the city was given a Roman name, Aelia Capitolina. In spite of this second total defeat of the nationalists, the continuity of Jewish identity and commitment was effectively carried out through the emergent rabbinic pattern of interpretation and practice of the tradition.

The Context of the Christian Alternative for Covenantal Identity

In the first century C.E., before the disastrous failure of these two Jewish attempts at achieving political independence as a way of fulfilling the aspirations of Israel as God's people, the issues that had come to a focus during the period of Hellenistic and early Roman domination of Palestine remained unresolved, and multiple solutions were being offered. We have noted that the two major questions were: Who is the one through whom God is at work in behalf of his people? And, what does God require of those who are members of his Covenant People?

Answering the second of these questions was complicated in this period because of the considerable number of Gentiles who were attracted to Judaism and who wanted in some way and to some degree to identify with it. They were drawn by its strictly monotheistic base and by its rejection of any physical representation of the gods in the form of idols or statues. They admired its strict ethical stance, with the moral demands—especially in the Pharisaic movement—that were placed on its adherents. In the midst of social and cultural conflicts that pervaded the ethnically and economically complex empire, those who had been uprooted from their ancestral environment or who felt adrift in the changing atmosphere of the emergent empire were attracted to groups like the informal Jewish gatherings, where there was the possibility of gaining and reinforcing group identity. Here was a nonpolitical group movement tolerated by the Romans. Was it possible for Gentiles to become part of such a group?

As we shall see, there were two ways in which Gentiles could become affiliated:

(1) by becoming worshippers of Israel's God; (2) by proselytism, a process by which male Gentiles were circumcized, baptized, and received as members (proselytes) of the community. It is difficult to know by what stages these procedures of Gentile inclusion were developed, but inscriptions from the eastern Mediterranean show that there was a significant segment of non-Jews who wanted to participate to some degree in the life of these Jewish groups, and therefore in God's people. Inevitably, the issue arose in this connection as to how completely these converts to Judaism—or Gentiles on the fringe of Judaism—were to be obliged to obey the Law as the Pharisees interpreted it.

These are precisely the issues on which Jesus challenged his Jewish contemporaries. In what sense did he appear as the agent of God to prepare for the renewal of the covenant? What evidence could he or his followers adduce for their claim that God was the source of his power and purpose? Who were the potential candidates for sharing in his reappraisal of the covenant tradition? If outsiders were to become part of the community, to what extent was it obligatory for them to obey the Law of Moses? What attitude should be taken toward the Roman state? Was it to be accepted and its demands fulfilled, or was it to be overthrown? And if overthrown, by what agency? These issues, which we have seen to be at the heart of the identity crisis of ancient Israel, were the ones addressed by Jesus and the early Christians as they sought to define his role and the grounds he offered for participation in God's new people.

Chapter 2

JESUS OF NAZARETH AND THE RADICAL ALTERNATIVE FOR REDEFINING THE COVENANT

Who Jesus was, what he said and did are described in a variety of ancient documents from Christian and non-Christian sources. The most useful of these date from the first and second centuries and include both Roman and Jewish writings. About many details, however, there is a regrettable lack of information, or even some conflicting evidence. Yet the basic picture is clear, and there emerges an outline of Jesus as an independent critic who claimed to be the agent of God but who challenged the values, the leadership, and the institutions of his Jewish contemporaries. Through the early Christian writers who preserved and edited the Jesus traditions, it is also possible to discern how his followers and their successors shaped those traditions about him in ways that were appropriate to their own changing interests and needs. That process of adaptation of the Jesus tradition has gone on from the beginning of the movement down to the present, starting with the presumed sources of the gospels as we now have them. Through awareness of the modification of the material about Jesus, it is possible to achieve two useful historical goals concerning him: (1) to see how certain features of the Jesus tradition are confirmed and illuminated by sources from outside the New Testament; and (2) to trace the development of that tradition within the New Testament period. Through this approach one can see how in the course of the early history of Christianity, the movement that began with Jesus took the forms and adopted the tactics that shifted the action from the cities and villages of Palestine to the centers of Greco-Roman culture in the wider Mediterranean regions and eventually throughout the world, both culturally and geographically.

The Chief Sources for Knowledge about Jesus

Christianity had a powerful and enduring impact on the Roman Empire, most decisively and dramatically in the fourth-century conversion of the emperor, Constantine. One might expect, therefore, that there would be abundant evidence about the origins of the movement in the writings of historians of the first and second centuries. But this is not the case, largely because the impact of Jesus and his followers was initially so limited in scope that the historians might have regarded it as beneath their concern. There are references to Christianity in ancient secular historical documents, however, and they offer sufficient detail to shed light on or to confirm evidence that we have from the Christian and Jewish sources.

Jewish Sources

The fullest report we have concerning Jesus from outside the Christian sources comes from Josephus, a Jewish writer who shifted his role from leader of the nationalists in the revolt of 66–70 C.E. to subsequent collaborator with the Romans. Born in the decade following the death of Jesus, he spent his later years in Rome, where his extensive writings served the dual purpose of reporting the history of the Jews for Roman readers and presenting it in such a way as to propagandize in behalf of his co-religionists. Much of his material was drawn from ancient sources that otherwise would have been lost to us, so that in spite of his apologetic aims and because of his extensive cribbing from other historians, his work is invaluable as a historical resource.

In the ancient copies of Josephus's *Antiquities of the Jews* (18.63), he wrote (in Greek) as follows:

> About this time [during the term of office of Pontius Pilate, Roman governor of Judea A.D. 26–36], there lived Jesus, a wise man, if indeed one ought to call him a man. For he was one who wrought surprising feats and was a teacher of such people as accept the truth gladly. He won over many of the Jews and many of the Greeks. He was the Messiah. When Pilate, upon hearing him accused by men of the highest standing among us, condemned him to be crucified, those who had in the first place come to love him did not give up their affection for him. On the third day he appeared to them, restored to life, for the prophets of God had prophesied these and countless other marvelous things about him. And this tribe of Christians, so called after him, has still to this day not disappeared.[1]

As the passage stands, it sounds as though Josephus were a Christian. Some scholars have insisted that the paragraph is an interpolation by some early Christian writer into the original text of *Antiquities* (18.63–64). L. H. Feldman, a Jewish scholar who translated and edited this document, thinks, however, that the only added words

[1]From L. H. Feldman, ed. and trans., *Antiquities*, Loeb Classical Library (Cambridge, MA: Harvard University Press, 1965).

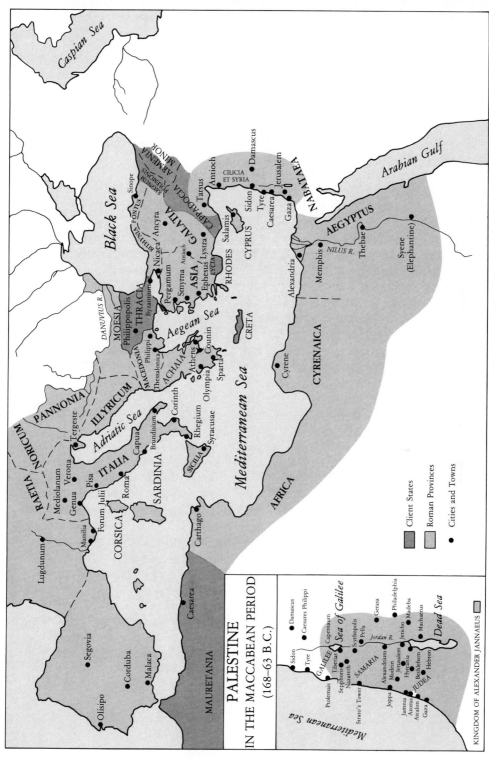

Client States
Roman Provinces
● **Cities and Towns**

PALESTINE
IN THE MACCABEAN PERIOD
(168–63 B.C.)

KINGDOM OF ALEXANDER JANNAEUS

Figure 2.1 The Roman World at the Time of Jesus

are "He was the Messiah." The rest of the statement is merely a report of what the early Christians *claimed* about Jesus. But as such, it is extremely important. It highlights the unusual capacities that Jesus had, which are reported in the gospel accounts of his healings and exorcisms. It conveys the sense of the power of his teaching and the loyalty he evoked from his followers. And it is specific about the circumstances of his death, both the method (crucifixion) and the identity of the one who condemned him (Pilate). Also reflected are the claims of his adherents that what he did was in fulfillment of the Jewish scriptures and that God had vindicated him by raising him from the dead. The phrase, "if one ought to call him a man," sounds as though Josephus is implying Jesus's divinity. According to the gospels, however, Jesus's opponents insisted that he had these extraordinary powers because he was in league with Satan (Mark 3:22; Matt. 9:34). Perhaps it is this accusation that lies behind Josephus's remark. In any case, there is a series of useful parallels between what this Jewish historian reports and the evidence from the gospels.

When the Dead Sea Scrolls and the community center where they were produced were discovered in the late 1940s near the northwestern end of the Dead Sea, there was speculation and even hope that in some way these documents from the first century B.C.E. and first century C.E. would shed some light on Jesus and the origins of Christianity. The fact that John the Baptist and his followers, like this group, were based in the Jordan Valley, practiced ceremonial washings, and claimed to be preparing the faithful for a renewed covenantal relationship with the God of Israel suggested there might be direct links between these movements and, therefore, with Jesus. The literary finds and the archaeological evidence point to the following parallels between the groups:

> The followers of Jesus and the members of the Dead Sea sect participated in a community meal of bread and wine, eaten in expectation of the coming of God's agent (or agents) in final triumph.
>
> Both groups were persuaded that their respective founders had given them the key to interpreting the scriptures.
>
> Both had their own collections of writings that provided the insights for understanding God's purpose for and through the new community.
>
> Both were critical of the official religious leadership and expected God to replace the then-existing temple.
>
> Both believed God would soon intervene in their behalf, defeat their enemies, and establish his rule in the world.

Apart from these general principles, however, the basis for participation in God's people for the Dead Sea community was utterly different from that of the Jesus movement. The former group was severely critical of the religious leaders because they were not sufficiently strict in holding their people to obeying the ritual and purity requirements of the Law of Moses. Jesus, however, is accused of permitting or even performing actions violating the Sabbath and purity laws, and of welcoming into the fellowship of his people those who by birth or manner of life would be excluded by Jewish legal norms. The Dead Sea community had formal regulations for temporarily or permanently denying access to its group to those who violated its stringent regulations. If Jesus ever had associated with the Dead Sea community, his break with them on requirements for admission and maintenance of status was radical.

The rabbinic sources, written in the second to the sixth centuries C.E., refer on occasion to Jesus, although usually without direct mention of his name. His followers are alluded to as *Minim*, which means "deviants" or "heretics." He is at times identified as "the son of Ben Stada," or "of Ben Pantheros." His mother is depicted as a disreputable person, and his father is said to be a Roman soldier. There is apparently a kind of pun here; Pantheros is close to Parthenos, the Greek word for virgin. Instead of having been born to a virgin (who did not have intercourse with a human father), as the Christians claimed, Jesus was—according to these sources—the illegitimate son of a Roman soldier. In one of the rabbinic sources, the so-called Eighteen Benedictions, which may go back to the late first century C.E., there is a curse invoked on the *Minim*, those who consider Jesus to have been the Messiah of God.[2] All that this rabbinic material tells us, therefore, is that the Christian movement was regarded as a perversion of the concurrently developing Jewish principles of the covenant people. As we examine the gospels, we shall see what specific form these competitive claims assumed.

Roman Sources

Three Roman writers of the early second century refer in passing to the Christian movement and its origins. Tacitus (53–120 C.E.) mentions in *Annals* (15:24) that the fire which destroyed a large segment of Rome during the reign of the emperor Nero (54–68 C.E.) was thought by many in the city to have been set by Nero's order. To shift the blame from himself, Nero decided to hold the Christians of the city responsible. Tacitus writes as follows:

> Neither human help, nor imperial munificence, nor all the mode of placating heaven could stifle the scandal or dispel the belief that the fire had taken place by order [of Nero]. Therefore to scotch the rumor, Nero substituted as culprits and punished with the utmost refinements of cruelty, a class of men, loathed for their vices, whom the crowd styled as Christians. Christus, the founder of the

---

[2]Although the date of these Benedictions (and curses) is disputed, it is most likely that this indirect attack on the Christians dates from the period after 70 C.E.

name, had undergone the death penalty in the reign of Tiberius [14–37 C.E.], by sentence of the procurator, Pontius Pilate, and the pernicious superstition was checked for a moment, only to break out once more, not merely in Judea, the home of the disease, but in the capital itself, where all things horrible or shameful in the world collect and find a vogue. First, then, the confessed members of the sect were arrested; next, on their disclosures, vast numbers were convicted, not so much on account of arson as for hatred of the human race. And derision accompanied their end: they were covered with wild beasts' skins and torn to death by dogs; or they were fastened on crosses, and when light failed were burned as lamps by night. Nero offered his gardens for the spectacle, and gave an exhibition in his circus, mixing with the crowd in the garb of a charioteer, or mounted on his chariot.[3]

Apart from the gruesome fascination of the story itself, there are a number of important historical implications in the brief account. The death of Jesus was not an isolated incident in the life of a single individual but was a climactic moment in a movement that began with his public activity and continued far and wide beyond his death. So serious were its social and political dimensions that the Roman authorities sought to stamp it out, first in Jerusalem and later in Rome. On the basis of information elsewhere about Pontius Pilate, it is possible to fix the probable date of Jesus's death to the year C.E. 29. A little more than thirty years later, the movement had spread to the capital of the Gentile world, where there were "vast numbers" identified with it. The charges against them are not specified, except "hatred of the human race" and that they were "loathed for their vices." The first accusation probably was the result of two factors: (1) their refusal to participate in honors to the Roman gods and the deified emperors, which would have been understood by the Romans as adding to the risk of national calamities sent by the gods; (2) the conviction of the members that they were the people of God, distinct from the rest of the human race. Even the principle of inclusive membership, which was characteristic of both Jesus and his followers, would not offset this sense of a favored, elect community. Their claim that they alone would survive the divine judgment that was to bring to an end the present age of the world would confirm this impression of them as hostile to the rest of humanity. The depiction of the movement as a "pernicious superstition" may reflect the claim of the Christians that through Jesus there was among them the power to heal, to expel demons, and to raise the dead by what they called the Spirit of God. There is no hint that their membership was limited to Jews or was primarily Jewish: They are set aside by the historian as a sect, a class, "whom the crowd styled as Christians."

The designation of the group as Christians is echoed by one other Roman his-

---

[3]Tacitus, *Annals* (15.44), J. Jackson, trans., Loeb Classical Library, Vol. 4, (Cambridge, MA: Harvard University Press, 1931).

torian, Pliny, and possibly by a third, Suetonius. About the year C.E. 110 Pliny was serving as governor of Bithynia, a Roman province on the south shore of the Black Sea. It was a sensitive post, since over the centuries the Romans felt threatened by the Parthians, the people to the east of this district who had periodically invaded Bithynia. In one of Pliny's letters to the emperor Trajan, he reports that the Christians, who earlier had had groups in the cities, had now become numerous even in the rural districts. As a result, there had been an alarming drop in participation in the worship of the traditional deities in the official temples. And furthermore, even under threat of execution, the Christians were refusing to offer the appropriate sacrifices to the image of the emperor—thus adding to the threat of waning popular support and divine benefactions to the Roman state.

There is a deep ambivalence in Pliny's assessment of the movement. Although he denounces it as a "depraved and excessive superstition," his investigation of the practices of its members showed that they were harmless. Their custom was to gather early in the morning to sing a hymn to Christ as a god. Their sacred meal involved only ordinary food. Their common oath required them to avoid adultery, fraud, deceit, and theft. Their leaders included women known as deaconesses. They were guilty of no crime against the state except their refusal to honor the traditional gods and the deified emperor. This, however, was sufficiently serious to lead to the execution of those members who, even under pressure, refused to renounce their allegiance to Jesus, the Christ. The designation of the group as Christians shows that central to their existence and identity was this affirmation, and in making it, as well as in sharing the common meal, they took a firm stand as to their identity as God's people. In Chapter 5 we consider more fully the social and political import of this movement as the Romans perceived it.

The evidence from Suetonius (69–140 C.E.) is ambiguous. His *Lives of the Twelve Caesars* records an incident that occurred during the reign of Claudius (41–54 C.E.). Suetonius describes a serious conflict that developed within the Jewish community in Rome "at the instigation of one Chrestos." The response of Claudius was to drive all the Jews out of Rome. In Acts 18:1–4 there is an account of Paul's having met in Corinth a Jewish couple who had been driven out of Rome by Claudius. Originally from Pontus (like Bithynia, on the southern shore of the Black Sea), these two worked at the same craft as Paul: tentmaking. The fact that they were already Christians when Paul met them, even though they had been expelled from Rome as Jews, suggests that the source of trouble in Rome was not an otherwise unknown person named Chrestos (a common name of that day, meaning "worthy," "respectable") but the arrival there of the message about *Christos*. The result of the proclamation of Jesus as Messiah (i.e., Christos) among the Jews in Rome had been violently divisive, so that the repercussions were known to the public. Claudius had reacted in a firm way by expelling the whole lot of them, both those who affirmed Jesus as Christos— which was confused with Chrestos—and those who did not. This is a significant piece of evidence, because if this reconstruction is correct, it means that the message about Jesus was being proclaimed in Rome within twenty years after the death of Jesus and perhaps two decades before Paul reached there (about 60 C.E.).

Another indirect bit of evidence from a Roman historian comes from a somewhat later period—the end of the first century. Dio Cassius (150–235 C.E.) reports that Domitilla, a niece of the emperor Domitian (81–96), was exiled from Rome because she had adopted "Jewish customs" and "atheism." These two accusations would seem to be contradictory, unless we assume that the movement that attracted her was one with Jewish roots that required its adherents to refuse to participate in honors to the state gods. This description fits Christianity, and that inference is confirmed by the existence in Rome of a catacomb (underground Christian burial chamber) named in her honor. If this reading of the evidence is correct, then by the end of the first century, the Christian movement had penetrated not only Rome but the imperial household itself.

Paul as a Source for Knowledge about Jesus

In the letters of Paul, there is a heavy emphasis on the importance of the death of Jesus. For example:

> God put forth [Jesus] as an expiation by his blood, to be received by faith. (Rom. 3:25)

> While we were still weak, at the right time Christ died for the ungodly. (Rom. 5:6)

> Have this mind among yourselves which is yours in Christ Jesus, who, though he was in the form of God, did not count equality with God a thing to be grasped, but emptied himself, taking the form of a servant, being born in the likeness of human beings. And being found in human form he humbled himself and became obedient unto death, even death on a cross. (Phil. 2:5–8)[4]

Paul also makes the point that God sent Jesus into the world in human form to accomplish the salvation of his people (Gal. 4:4; Phil. 2:8). Jesus's life was one of complete obedience to the will of God. Although he does not attribute the insight to Jesus, Paul perceives the centrality of the laws to lie in the command to love one's neighbor, just as Jesus did (Cf. Rom. 13:8–10; Mark 12:31). Similarly, although Paul reports none of the miracles and healings attributed to Jesus in the gospels, he repeatedly refers to these acts as signs that confirm the message about Jesus that he preaches (I Cor. 12:9–10; II Cor. 12:12). Indeed, Paul reminds his readers that through him and his associates, events similar to Jesus's miracles had frequently

---

[4]Unpublished translation by H. C. Kee.

taken place wherever they traveled to proclaim the gospel (Gal. 3:5; Rom. 15:18–19). The evidence about Jesus is concrete in that Paul takes for granted the life, miracles, and death of Jesus. But it is also indirect in that he merely assumes that his readers see continuity between the miracles that God did through Jesus and those that are happening through himself and his co-workers.

Another important link between Paul and the gospel traditions about Jesus is the common conviction that God raised Jesus from the dead. Paul is persuaded that if this had not taken place, then the faith of his readers would be futile, and he and his associates "are of all men most to be pitied" (I Cor. 15:16–18). Thus, even though Paul's emphases are different from those of the writers of the gospels, he shares with them three basic convictions: (1) that Jesus lived a life in full obedience to God; (2) that the authorities put him to death; (3) that God raised him from the dead.

Our Oldest Gospel Source

A careful reading of the Gospel of Matthew and the Gospel of Luke shows that they used a common source. It consisted mostly of the sayings of Jesus, which each of these writers has incorporated into his gospel with some modifications. Although no copy of this source (which scholars call *Q*, from the German word for source, *Quelle*) has survived, it can be reconstructed with a high degree of certainty. And it gives a remarkably clear picture of who Jesus claimed to be and what he taught his followers, especially in Luke's use of the source, from which the quotations in the following paragraphs are drawn.

As in the Gospel of Mark (our oldest account of the career of Jesus), Jesus is associated with John the Baptist, who went out into the desert region adjacent to the Jordan River. There John called his fellow Jews to be baptized as a public expression of their concern to be identified with the pure and obedient people of God (Luke 3:3). In *Q* John denounces his contemporaries as the offspring of snakes in his warning to them of the divine judgment that is about to fall on the world. They are not to assume that their being descended from Abraham guarantees participation in God's people; God is able to create his community of the faithful from unlikely sources (Luke 3:7–9). Jesus, however, differentiates himself from John, who seems to have become disillusioned with Jesus when Jesus began eating and spending time with people who by Jewish regulations could not share in the worship of God: the blind, the lame, the deaf, and lepers. This practice contrasted sharply with that of John, who was ascetic and strict. Jesus acknowledges that his opponents call him "a glutton and a drunkard, a friend of tax-collectors and sinners."[5]

[5]In the various parts of the Roman empire, local individuals would contract to help Rome collect taxes, including those on goods transported through the region. This collaboration with the pagan rulers, in addition to the inevitable contact of the tax-collectors with ritually impure substances, made them extremely unpopular and caused them to be regarded as traitors to the integrity of the Jewish people.

In the gospel tradition, Jesus was denounced as being in league with the devil ("Beelzebub, prince of demons") when he performed exorcisms. In the *Q* source, Jesus responds by claiming that the source of his power to cast out demons is God himself (Luke 11:19–20), so that through these actions of his, God's rule over the creation is becoming a reality in their midst. Yet Jesus will not perform miracles on request as a means of proving that God is with him (Luke 11:29–32). The only "sign" that will be given is the call to his contemporaries to change their ways, just as Jonah of old had called the Gentile people of Nineveh to repent (Jonah 3:5). Jesus's wisdom will attract a favorable response from Gentiles as well, just as Solomon's wisdom brought the Queen of Sheba to come "from the ends of the earth" to hear the truth from Solomon. Jesus is a greater prophet than Jonah, he declares, and as a messenger of God's wisdom, he is greater than Solomon. The religious leaders of his day, however, are more concerned with ritual purity than with inward moral purity, Jesus maintains, and as a result, they will reject him and his message, just as their ancestors rejected the prophets of old (Luke 11:37–53). Those who acknowledge him as God's agent, on the other hand, will be acknowledged by God, and those who reject him will be judged in the presence of God (Luke 12: 8). Through Jesus, who stands in a unique relationship to God as "son," God's purpose and truth have been disclosed to those regarded by the religious leaders as immature and ignorant—as "babies." And these insights have been hidden from those who think themselves to be wise (Luke 10:21–22). Already, a new era has come in the history of God's people: The epoch of the Law and the prophets ended with John the Baptist. Since then (that is, in the words and works of Jesus), the good news of God's rule is being preached, although those prepared to enter the kingdom must be prepared to experience violence and conflict (Luke 16:16). This new age is not something to be awaited in the future but is already a reality in the midst of God's people (Luke 17:20–21). The rest of the human race, however, continue to live life as usual and will do so until the divine judgment falls on the world (Luke 17:22–37).

The new people of God are called to a new mode of life in which the traditional human and religious values are overturned. It is the poor, the hungry, the excluded, the sorrowing who are to see themselves as blessed by God. The treatment they suffer at the hands of their proudly, ostentatiously pious contemporaries resembles that accorded to the prophets in ancient times. Instead of retaliation in kind to those who mistreat them, they are to love their enemies, to give generously to those who beg or even try to steal from them, acting in love toward all other humans as they would themselves like to be treated. In this way they will show graphically that they are indeed the children of God (Luke 6:27–36). Living in obedience to these norms of human relationships is like building a structure that will endure in spite of the conflicts and judgments to come (Luke 6:47–49). Their daily petition to God honors the divine name and the authority it embodies, hopes for the coming in fullness of God's rule in the world, and asks only (1) for the daily supply of basic needs, (2) for divine forgiveness, which is to overflow into forgiveness toward others; and (3) for deliverance from the time of testing that will befall the world at the end of the age (Luke 11:1–4).

To enter the life of discipleship is costly in terms of ordinary human values: For the disciples there is to be no certainty of a dwelling place, no time to fulfill such basic obligations as burying one's parents, no place for reflecting on what one has done in the past (Luke 9:47–62). When they are proclaiming the good news of God's rule, they can expect to meet rejection, just as Jesus did (Luke 10:16). They are not to fear those who seek to kill them but those who try to corrupt and disqualify them for the task in which they are engaged (Luke 12:4–5). They can expect to be brought to trial before religious and political leaders, just as Jesus was, but God will sustain them in their times of testing, just as he supported Jesus (Luke 12:11–12). They are to live their lives free of anxiety, in confidence that God will care for his own people as he cares for the creation (Luke 12:22–34).

Who is to share in the life of this new community that Jesus is calling into existence by his message and activity? Building on the familiar image of a banquet as a representation of the new era when God and his people will be united, Jesus compares the invitation to share in the kingdom of God with a host who sends advance notice of a great festivity he is planning. Those first invited are too busy with ordinary, respectable responsibilities (getting married, acquiring property) to accept the invitation. It is then extended to a most unlikely segment of humanity: "the poor, the maimed, the blind, the lame," and then to the homeless living outside the city in lanes and hedges. The ailing and the outsiders do accept and share in the banquet (Luke 14:15–24). Here in a vivid parable is an indication of the criterion for sharing in the life of God's new people, both now and in the age to come: to be in need, and through Jesus, to look to God to fill that need.

God's side of this enterprise to which Jesus has been called and to which he commits his followers is depicted by Jesus in the Parable of the Seeking Shepherd (Luke 15:4–7). In this symbolic story, the owner of the flock goes out to find and recover the lost sheep—a clear image of God, who through Jesus takes the initiative in uniting the outsider and the needy as members of his Covenant People. In what was likely the conclusion of the *Q* source (Luke 22:28–30), Jesus addresses his followers as "those who have stayed with me in my trials," and promises them a share in the kingdom of God. This participation will include the exercise of authority over God's people, as well as eating and drinking with Jesus in the New Age.

Our Oldest Gospel: Mark

The oldest surviving narrative account of the career of Jesus is an anonymous document known since the second century as the Gospel of Mark. Since Peter figures prominently in this gospel, and since someone named Mark is associated with Peter and the other apostles in the New Testament (Acts 12:12, 25), Mark's name came to be linked very early with this report of Jesus's words and acts. Mark's gospel is not simply a biography; it tells us nothing of the birth and early life of Jesus. Rather, it is what anthropologists call a "foundation document"—that is, an account of the life and activity of the founder of a religious movement, which serves to give purpose, direction, and future orientation for the members. Specifically, it serves as a source of concrete examples of what Jesus said and did along the lines indicated but not described directly in the *Q* source: to prepare Jesus's people and to define their role in preparation for the coming of the kingdom of God.

In Mark there are compact, vivid accounts of the healings and exorcisms Jesus performed. When Jesus expels an unclean spirit from a man in a synagogue, the demon is aware that Jesus is God's agent who has come to destroy him and these powers of evil associated with him (1:24). Jesus is able to heal the relatives of his disciples (1:29), as well as throngs that follow him, seeking health or freedom from demonic control (1:32–34). At times, he links his acts of healing with the grant of forgiveness, as in the healing of a paralytic who was lowered on a pallet through the dirt roof of Jesus's house in Capernaum on the shore of the Lake of Galilee (2:1–12). For this, Jesus's claim to being authorized by God is challenged by the religious leaders who are observing him. Ironically, the demonic spirits he expels acknowledge him to be the "Son of God" (3:7–12). The question of the source of Jesus's extraordinary power to heal and to control the demons is raised by the scribes, the authoritative interpreters of the Jewish tradition, who have come to Galilee from Jerusalem to observe him. It is their conviction that he has these powers because he is in league with Satan, the adversary of God (3:22–30). His own family thinks that he is crazy and try to remove him from public view (3:19–21, 31–35). He repeats to them and to his followers that in the new people of God, the family is radically redefined.

After initially centering his activity in Jewish towns and synagogues (Mark 1:39), Jesus begins to attract crowds that include some people from Gentile territories (3:7–8). He goes into these pagan regions and performs healings and exorcisms in the Hellenistic cities and in Syrian territory to the north of Galilee (5:1–20; 7:24–37).

One of the most vivid of these stories (Mark 7:24–30) describes a persistent Gentile woman in the Syrian territory visited by Jesus. She had a daughter who was under the control of a demon. Even though Jesus was then trying to find some privacy after his extended public appearances, the woman came directly to him, urging him to help her child. Jesus's response is to put her off by drawing a sharp distinction between "children" (Jews, who have a traditional right of access to God and his benefits) and "dogs" (Gentiles, who have been denied this relationship). Her reply is vivid and powerful: "Yes, sir, but even the dogs under the table eat what the children drop." He responds favorably to her challenge, and she returns home to find her daughter cured. The traditional distinctions about access to God by Jews and Gentiles are no longer valid.

In addition, Mark tells us that Jesus makes or allows physical contact with the dead, with a woman with a bloody flux, with epileptics, lepers, and the blind—all of which would render him impure by the Pharisaic standards of ritual cleanliness (5:21–43; 6:53–56; 7:24–37; 9:14–29; 10:46–52). Similarly, he welcomes among his inner circle of followers and pupils (the disciples) a tax-collector named Levi (2:13–17).

The challenges and responsibilities Jesus places on the disciples are spelled out in detail in Mark: His followers are to serve as witnesses of what he does and, on this basis, to proclaim the message of God's Rule on earth; in preparation for it, they are to expel demons (3:14–15), just as Jesus has done. Jesus sets them the example of placing human need above the venerable Jewish laws of Sabbath observance when he defends his disciples' having rubbed the husks from grain and eaten some of it as they passed through a field on the Sabbath day (Mark 2:23–27).[6] The later rabbis attest that this was considered work and was therefore unlawful on the holy day of rest. Mark reports Jesus as declaring that the Sabbath was made for human beings, not the reverse, and that he as Son of Man is "Lord of the Sabbath." Similarly, on the Sabbath Jesus heals a man with a withered hand, which serves as the occasion for his opponents to organize a coalition of the pious (the Pharisees) and the collaborators with Rome (the Herodians) to find a way to destroy him (Mark 3:1–6).

Jesus's basic view of God and his people as it appears in the gospel tradition is closely related to Jewish apocalyptic writings. The common features include both unhappy and happy prospects for Jesus's followers. On the one hand, these prospects involve the need for suffering by the faithful, the opposition to the movement from the ruling authorities, and the expectation that history will lead to mounting catastrophes. On the hopeful side are the special revelations of God's purpose that have been given to the faithful community, the reassurance that God will triumph over evil, and his provision of the agent through whom his purpose is being disclosed and will come to fulfillment.

Accordingly, Jesus warns his followers that their persistence in following him may lead to their death (Mark 8:34–37). Yet he assures them that he will return to vindicate them, supported by God and his angels, and in the context of the fulfillment of their hopes of the coming kingdom of God (8:34–9:1). That event will be preceded by the coming of Elijah, the prophet of God, whose return was foretold in Malachi (4:5–6), and who in the gospel tradition was linked with both John the Baptist and with Jesus (Mark 1:2; 6:15; 8:28). Mark reports Jesus as repeatedly informing his disciples of his own impending death, which is to take place on the initiative of the religious leaders but will be carried out by the Gentile rulers (8:31; 9:31; 10:33–34). An experience of Jesus in the presence of the inner core of the disciples, in which his outward appearance is changed, recalls that of leaders of Israel who were granted

---

[6]The Law of Moses permitted someone passing through a field or vineyard to help himself to grain or grapes, though not to collect them systematically (Deut. 23:24–25).

visions of God (Moses, Elijah, Isaiah, Daniel) to give them assurance that the difficult road they had taken was to end in divine vindication (9:2–8). Meanwhile, the disciples must be prepared for suffering, rejection, and martyrdom (8:34–35).

Jesus's bold action in riding an ass into Jerusalem and entering the temple courts is implicitly in fulfilment of the prophetic promise of the coming of Israel's king (Mark 11:1–10; cf. Zech. 9:9).[7] Accordingly, his followers link him with the renewal of the kingdom of David. His subsequent bold actions in Jerusalem include disrupting and denouncing the selling of sacrificial animals in the temple and the changing of money into appropriate coinage for temple offerings (Mark 11:15–19). His Parable of the Wicked Tenants (Mark 12:1–12) is a kind of allegory of the infidelity of those in charge of God's people (depicted under the familiar image of a vineyard; cf. Isa. 5) and a foreshadowing of his own impending death. The outcome will be the replacement of those in charge of the "vineyard" by others: the new community Jesus is calling together.

God's judgment on those whom Jesus portrays as his disobedient people will be dramatically symbolized by the destruction of the temple (Mark 13:1–4), which will be preceded by its desecration (Mark 13:14). Apparently the desecration will come through the Romans, as it had through Antiochus, the Hellenistic king in Maccabean times. Jesus's followers must expect persecution and betrayal by their own families (Mark 13:9–13), but if they remain faithful, God will soon vindicate them by sending his agent, the Son of Man, to defeat their enemies and gather them together (Mark 13:21–27). All this is announced as taking place within the lifetime of the present generation, even though the precise date is known only to God (Mark 13:30–32). The temple was destroyed in 70 C.E. without the other promised events of divine deliverance occurring. But the confidence that this vindication would come and that Jesus would return as the triumphant Son of Man continued to be expected and affirmed by the church down through the centuries.

At the same time, Mark reports Jesus as laying down some basic rules for the life of the community of his followers. Those who fail to remain faithful to him when they undergo persecution and suffering for his sake will be put to shame by him when he comes in judgment (Mark 8:34–38). His followers must be willing to accept subservient roles within the community (Mark 9:33–35), caring for others and strictly disciplining themselves (9:42–48). The community is to include children (9:36; 10:13–16), who are to serve as models of trust for all. The wealthy will find it difficult to meet the obligation of renouncing their riches (10:17–31), just as they must resist the temptation to strive for positions of power (10:35–45). There are to be no divorces and remarriages among the members (10:1–12). Far from seeking to subvert the empire, they are to pay their taxes to the Roman state (12:13–17). The overarching commandment is twofold: to love God and to love one's neighbor as

---

[7]This link is made explicit in Matthew's version of this story (Matt. 21:5).

oneself (12:28–34). God will reward their fidelity by giving them a share in the resurrection (12:18–27).

Meanwhile, the disciples must accept the fact that Jesus's impending death is part of the divine plan (Mark 8:31; 9:31; 10:33–34); his crucifixion will serve to liberate many from the powers of sin and evil that dominate their lives (10:45). That death is prepared for symbolically by the anointing of Jesus for burial in advance (14:3–9) and, above all, by the meal in which the broken bread and poured wine represent his death in the disciples' behalf (14:22–25).

To a casual observer, this last meal of Jesus would have seemed routine. Some of the gospel evidence pictures it as a Passover meal (Mark 14:12), whereas John states that it was before the Passover celebration (John 13:1). In any case, there is mention of bread and wine, which would have been standard fare for a simple meal, rather than the specially prepared Passover lamb. The meal takes place in a large upper room of a house in Bethany, a village not far east of Jerusalem. Meals like these were celebrated by families and friends, but they also served as fellowship meals to unite members of groups that met for prayer and Bible study, as was the case with the Pharisees. Reclining around a common bowl of food placed on the floor or a low table, the participants broke off pieces of pancake-shaped bread to use in dipping out bits of the common food. A common cup was passed among them to provide drink but also to reinforce the sense of belonging. All these were standard features of group meals among Jews in this period. But Jesus added important significance to this meal by linking the symbolism of the shared bread and wine with his own impending death.

The continuing reenactment of that meal by Christians down through the subsequent years serves to remind them that their association with Jesus will be renewed and fulfilled in the New Age that is soon to dawn. In the gospel tradition, another important image for this rite of renewal of the new community is that of Jesus feeding the hungry crowd in the desert. A related story is important in the Old Testament, when through Moses God feeds Israel in the barren wastes of Sinai. Mark tells two similar stories (Mark 6:30–44; 8:1–10), one symbolizing the participation of Jews in the new people, and the other that of Gentiles. A significant detail in these accounts is the use of what was to become the technical language of the shared meal of the Christian communities, which is variously known as the communion or the eucharist down to the present day: "He took, he blessed, he broke, he gave." The similar story of miraculous feeding told in Mark 8:1–10 takes place in predominantly Gentile territory, apparently in anticipation of the response that Jesus's movement was later to find among non-Jews. Thus, the ritual of the meal has three temporal dimensions: It looks back to the death of Jesus, it serves as a fellowship and renewal in the present, and it anticipates the final achievement of God's purpose for his people in the future age.

The closing chapters of Mark (14:26–16:8) recount in vivid detail Jesus's arrest by the authorities, his hearings before the Jewish leaders, and his being sentenced to death by the Roman procurator, Pontius Pilate. There is evidence in the narrative of Jesus's own inner struggle and of the inability of his disciples to understand what is happening and why Jesus yields to these earthly powers. His execution is by the civil authorities and is based on a civil charge: his claim to kingship of the Jews (Mark 15:9, 18–20, 26, 32). Just before death comes, Mark reports two symbolic incidents: the tearing of the curtain in the temple, which suggests that access to the presence of God is now open; and the acclaim of Jesus by a Roman military officer as "son of God" (15:38–39).

A pious member of the Jewish council receives permission to have the body of Jesus placed in his own rock-hewn tomb. Two women followers of Jesus see the place of burial, but because nightfall is about to usher in the Sabbath, they cannot then make the traditional preparation of the corpse (Mark 15:42–47). The first opportunity for them to return and carry out this process is at dawn on what is now called Sunday. To their astonishment, the large, round closing stone has been rolled away from the opening of the tomb, the body of Jesus is gone, and a young man instructs them that Jesus has been raised from the dead and will be reunited with his followers in Galilee, where he first called them and commissioned them to carry forward his work of preparing for the coming of the kingdom of God (Mark 16:1–8). Although the oldest copies of Mark end at this point, some manuscripts go on—as the other gospels do—to describe Jesus's post-resurrection reunion with his disciples (Matt. 28:11–15; Luke 24:13–35; John 20–21).

From the *Q* source and from Mark, therefore, we have four major lines of tradition, as follows:

1. The basic portrayal of the career of Jesus and of his words and works, which both announce and demonstrate the coming age in which God's Rule will triumph and describe the radical way in which he defines God's people as an inclusive community.

2. The formation of the nucleus of the new community commissioned by Jesus to spread his message and to do what was necessary to enlarge the size and scope of the new covenant people.

3. The precedent for conflict between this activity and the authority of the Roman state.

4. The radical approach taken by Jesus on the issues of purity that were taking shape within the Pharisaic Jewish community and that set the stage for conflict between these two emergent movements—rabbinic Judaism and Christianity—both of which claimed to have the true way of reappropriating the Jewish biblical tradition.

The basic pattern for the subsequent development of Christianity is discernible through these earlier forms of the gospel tradition about Jesus. In the case of the Gospel of Mark, that tradition is already in process of modification in light of the conflict developing between the incipient church and the Pharisaic efforts to define the covenant people in terms of ritual purity and careful observance of the Jewish law. Jesus's precedent in reaching across those boundaries in his invitation to socially and ritually unacceptable people to share in the community awaiting God's rule has already created serious conflict between Jews and Christians and among the Christians by the time the Gospel of Mark is written. The tensions become more serious after the fall of Jerusalem and the destruction of the temple, however, when the process of redefinition of the covenant becomes more intense and unified among both Jews and Christians.

A major factor heightening the tension between Jews and Christians and even among Christians in the first century was the movement that began shortly after the death of Jesus to take the initiative in inviting Gentiles, as well as nonobserving Jews, to share in the life of the new community. On the basis of his own testimony, preserved in his letters, the man who was transformed from a violent opponent of the inclusiveness of the Jesus movement to the primary instrument for opening covenant participation to Gentiles in the major cities of the eastern Mediterranean was a Jew whose Semitic name was Saul, commonly known by his Greek name, Paul. He did not set the precedent for Gentile inclusion, but he became its most effective agent. It is to his letters preserved in the New Testament and the biographical information that they provide about his launching of Christianity into the wider Mediterranean world that we now turn.

Chapter 3

PAUL:

Christian Encounter with the Roman World

Half the books of the New Testament are attributed to Paul, and more than half of another distinctive New Testament writing—the Acts of the Apostles—is devoted to a description of his career in spreading the Christian message from Damascus in Syria to Rome. Paul clearly served as the model figure in the activity that made possible the transition of Christianity from its original context in Judaism to the wider Greco-Roman world. Some of the writings claimed to be by Paul come from the next generation of his followers.[1] The Acts of the Apostles includes material that seems to tell us about the church's image of Paul in the late first century as well as providing us with traditions about Paul himself. The importance attached to the role of Paul in this crucial period of transition from Jewish to Gentile constituency is heightened by these later literary representations that claim Paul as the effective agent of these changes within Christianity. Also apparent in these writings attributed to Paul is the evidence for the gradual transformation of the church from a spontaneous movement to an institution with organizational forms and defined leadership roles. Yet Paul's role in reaching out to the wider Roman world was not wholly without precedent in the Jesus tradition, as we shall note.

[1] The letters of Paul in the New Testament may be grouped as follows:

1. Those almost certainly by Paul: Romans, Galatians, I and II Corinthians, Philippians, I Thessalonians, Philemon.
2. Those probably not by Paul but close to his style and perspectives: Colossians, II Thessalonians.
3. Those almost certainly not by Paul: Ephesians, I and II Timothy, Titus.

Over the centuries, the Letter to the Hebrews has been attributed to Paul, but it is an anonymous writing, very different in style and approach from any of those in the three categories just mentioned.

44

Paul's Jewish Roots

Fortunately for modern historical interests, Paul includes in his letters some information about his own life and the background from which he came to Christian faith. His credentials are solidly Jewish. He declares in his Letter to the Philippians (3:4–5) that he was born within the people of Israel and that he was descended from the Israelite tribe of Benjamin. He indicates the faithfulness of his parents to Jewish law in that he was circumcized on the eighth day after his birth, as prescribed in the Law of Moses. In Genesis 17:9–14, this ritual act on a male infant is set out as the basis for participation in the covenant of God with his people. There is no mistaking the strict tradition with which Paul was born and reared.

Paul goes on to mention that his way of understanding the Jewish law was that of the Pharisees (Phil. 3:5). This meant that a primary concern was the observance of ritual purity for all the members of the covenant community, not merely for the priests. Paul's commitment to this principle was so strong that he was zealous in his determination to stamp out any movement that laid claim to the covenantal tradition while failing to observe the ritual requirements differentiating the true people of God from those who falsely claimed such membership. In describing his devotion to the principle of ritual purity in his letter to the Galatians (1:13–14), Paul notes that he exceeded the zeal of many of his contemporaries by his determination to destroy what he regarded as a wholly illegitimate group calling itself the *ekklesia* (the "gathered community") and claiming to be the divinely redefined Covenant people. Although Paul does not specify where this group is located, he mentions that following his conversion experience he "*returned* to Damascus." This wording clearly implies that it was in that important Hellenistic city that there was a Christian group of sufficient size and vigor to attract his attention and set off his zeal to put it out of commission.

Scholarly reconstruction of the chronology of the career of Paul indicates that his conversion to Christianity probably took place within one or two years after the crucifixion of Jesus. Therefore, the basic pattern in the earliest Christian communities of including those who were ritually or ethnically *impure* by Pharisaic standards had been set by Jesus and was being carried out by his followers. We must infer that their activity in persuading people about Jesus and his redefining of the covenant people was not limited to predominantly Jewish villages or cities but was being carried forward in the thoroughly Hellenized cities, of which Damascus was the largest. The Hellenistic rulers had developed model cities, which the Romans continued to expand, complete with all the typical features: temples, baths, theaters, hippodromes, and colonnaded public marketplaces. There was a loose federation of ten of these cities known as the Decapolis, stretching from the seacoast to beyond the Sea of Galilee, and from Syria down into Palestine and east of the Jordan. That there was a Christian community in such a city as Damascus suggests that Paul was not an innovator in preaching the gospel to Gentiles or in inviting them to share in the new community. Indeed, it must have been this feature of the movement in the year or so before his conversion that attracted his wrath and persuaded him to destroy it before it spread further.

Paul's links with the Jewish tradition go beyond his having identified with the Pharisaic reinterpretation of the Law of Moses along the lines of personal purity. It is obvious from his letters that he was strongly influenced by Jewish apocalyptic writings as well. The importance Paul attached to the return of the triumphant Christ at the end of the present age and the defeat of the powers of evil Christ will accomplish in subjecting all the creation to the will of God (I Cor. 15:20–28) shows how central to Paul's thinking was this feature of Jewish tradition.[2] Similarly, in I Thessalonians he describes the return of Christ and the resurrection of the faithful that will then take place (4:13–18).

Related to the apocalyptic expectation of triumphant divine intervention in history that would usher in the New Age was a form of mysticism in which it was believed that certain faithful individuals were granted permission to see the throne of God as a way of assuring them that God would reward their faithfulness and that their hopes would be fulfilled. In the biblical tradition, God's dwelling place among his people was associated with a chariot (I Kings 7:27–33), and God's throne is pictured as wheeled (Ezek. 1:15–21; 10:1–19). Therefore, the experience of being taken up into the presence of God was called *Merkavah* ("chariot") mysticism. Paul describes such an experience of mystical transport, which he was persuaded had been granted to him to reassure him when he was experiencing personal difficulties (2 Cor. 12:1–10).

Clearly central to Paul's thinking, both before and after his conversion, was the question of how human beings could enter a right relationship with God. Most English translations of the letters of Paul have obscured this major factor in his understanding of God's purpose for his people by translating a crucial term in his letters as "justification" or "righteousness." In the argument advanced in Romans 3:19–28, for example, when Paul is contrasting faith and works, we read of the manifestation of God's righteousness (3:21), as though the abstract divine moral qualities were on display and have now been transferred to true believers (3:22). Legal imagery seems to be involved in Romans 3:28, where we read in some versions that someone may now be "justified by faith," as though a judicial case has been made in defense of the believer. These Greek terms Paul uses in Romans and Galatians 3 are his attempts to offer equivalents for the Semitic concepts that describe how God works to bring his covenant people into right relationship with himself. As a thoroughly committed Pharisee, Paul had been convinced that for him and other Jews to achieve full obedience to the Law of Moses as the Pharisees interpreted it would result in the establishment of God's Rule in the world and in the maintenance of the covenantal relationship that God intended for his people.

---

[2]An excellent development of this theme is that of J. Christiaan Beker, *Paul's Apocalyptic Gospel: The Coming Triumph of God* (Philadelphia: Fortress Press, 1982).

Through the experience of meeting Jesus raised from the dead (Gal. 1:15–16), however, Paul becomes persuaded that the sacrifical death of Jesus on the cross is God's way of freeing human beings from the assumption that conformity to the Law is the essential requirement for participation in God's people (Gal. 3:10–14). In the purpose of God, the Law had an interim function: to keep immature human beings under control, like a schoolmaster or baby-sitter (Gal. 3:23–25). But now Paul becomes convinced that the religion of maturity had been revealed by the life, death, and resurrection of Jesus. Through trusting in God's dealing with human sin and seeking to reconcile all humanity to himself by the death and resurrection of Jesus, God has put into operation this new understanding of who his people are and how one becomes a member of this new community. The sole requirement for admission is trust in what God has done in Christ to establish this new community. Within that new covenant people, all the old human distinctions are transcended: "There is neither Jew nor Greek . . . slave nor free . . . male nor female; for you are all one in Christ Jesus" (Gal. 3:28). Thereby this new community fulfills the promise to Abraham of a transethnic covenant people with the potential for including people from all the nations of the earth (Gen. 12:3; cf. Gal. 3:8). Furthermore, what God has done through Jesus to set human beings in right relationship to himself is not a novelty but is the fulfillment of what God intended from the beginning of the human race. That purpose, Paul declares, as well as the means of achieving it, have now been made known through what God has done in the death and resurrection of Jesus.

Hellenistic Features of Paul's Background

The fluency of Paul in Greek and his familiarity with literary conventions of the Greek world are evident in his letters. Not only are they forceful and subtle in style; they also disclose his knowledge of modes of argumentation developed in Greek literary circles. One such is the diatribe, in which the speaker anticipates and answers the counterarguments of his opponents. The fact that Paul's abundant quotations from the Jewish scriptures are based on the Septuagint (the common Greek translation of the Jewish Bible) rather than on the Hebrew original confirms this impression of him as strongly influenced by Hellenistic culture.

That impression is strengthened by details of Paul's arguments at several points. For example, when he wants to show that all humanity stands condemned before God because of its disobedience and its foolish reliance on its own corrupt self-seeking impulses, he feels obligated to show that his indictment falls not only on Jews, who had the revealed law of Moses, but on Gentiles as well. How could non-Jews know what God expected of them? Borrowing from Stoic philosophy the concept of a universal human capacity to recognize and respond to the natural laws that pervade the universe, Paul speaks of Gentile possession of *conscience*. The word means literally *co-knowledge*, or the universal human capacity to discern these natural laws and to obey them. Paul asserts that parallel to Jewish access to the revealed law of Moses, Gentiles have the capacity of conscience to convey to them what God expects of human beings (Rom. 2:13–16).

When Paul describes how the Spirit that God sends upon his people gives them both insight and strength to live obedient lives, he details the moral qualities that the Spirit produces. Among them are "kindness, goodness, gentleness, self-control" (Gal. 5:22–23), which are terms familiar from comparable recitations of virtues in Stoic writers of the first century. What is evident is that in addition to subtle and perhaps unconscious influence of Hellenistic thought and culture, Paul is able to exploit these insights and concepts from the Gentile culture of his time and to adapt and synthesize them with the basic orientation that came to him from his Jewish Pharisaic tradition.

Paul's Conversion Experience and Its Consequences

Although Paul does not offer in his letters an elaborate description of the experience that transformed him from a fierce opponent of the Jesus groups to the most significant agent for spreading the movement into the wider Gentile world, he does give significant details. He believes that Jesus appeared to him risen from the dead (I Cor. 15:8) or was revealed to him by God (Gal. 1:15–16). He is persuaded that his experience of having seen "Jesus our Lord" is as real and concrete as that of those who were Jesus's disciples and who were convinced that the risen Jesus had commissioned them to spread his message to the world. They, like Paul, considered themselves to be "sent ones," that is, apostles, as their self-designation in Greek, *apostolos*, indicates. When Paul "saw the Lord" he did not go to the other apostles to confirm his experience, but instead, leaving Damascus, he went off to the desert regions east of the city ("into Arabia") before returning to launch his work there. His sphere of activity soon included the wider area of the Roman province of "Syria and Cilicia," which stretched northward from Palestine to the southern coast of Asia Minor. The chief city of Cilicia, Tarsus, which is designated in Acts (9:11; 21:39) as Paul's native city, was an important center of Greek learning, rivaling Athens and Alexandria. This reported place of Paul's origin and education may help to account for his incorporation of Greek concepts into his interpretation of the Christian faith.

The basic conviction that arose from Paul's encounter with the risen Christ was that God was now fulfilling through Jesus what he had promised to Abraham: the establishment of an inclusive covenant community. The requirement for participation in this new people was not conformity to the requirements of the Jewish law, since failure to obey even a single statute could lead to disqualification. Rather, that potentially universal curse on humanity had been assumed by Jesus, whose sacrificial death made access to God's blessing possible for all who trusted in this divine remedy for the human situation. Trust in God's promise as the ground of right relationship with God had been established as the sole basis of human acceptance in the time of Abraham. The giving of the Law to Moses some 400 years later did not set aside the prior and primary principle for human acceptance before God (Gal. 3:9–17).

Now that this right relationship with God has been established through the sacrificial death of Jesus, Paul asserts, the Spirit of God is at work among his people to free them from slavery to the law and to other powers in the universe that seek to entrap and dominate human beings (Gal. 4). The member of the community of faith is freed from the Law and from the wicked forces that work to distort and corrupt human life. Instead, the life of trust becomes the channel through which the Spirit of God produces the moral qualities of love, joy, peace, goodness, and self-control, against which there is no law (Gal. 5:16–23).

The same themes are sounded in another autobiographical passage in Paul's letters (Phil. 3:4–11), as we noted earlier. In addition to his depiction of his firm roots in the Jewish legal tradition, Paul describes there his basic shift of trust regarding his relationship with God: from his former reliance on his conformity to the requirements of the Law to his present trust in the one who suffered and died in his behalf, and was raised by God from the dead. Now he, Paul, seeks to share in those sufferings through his own obedience to the purpose of God, and rests his hope that, like Jesus, he too will be delivered from death.

Paul's Career as Apostle to the Gentiles

After his initial brief and private visit with Peter and James in Jerusalem, Paul spent fourteen years preaching the message of Jesus to Gentiles in his native province of Syria and Cilicia. As a result of what seem to have been inner doubts, he returned once more to Jerusalem for a session with a wider segment of the apostles there. Their reaction was to affirm Paul's role as an apostle but to recognize a division of labor: Paul would go to the Gentiles; in proclaiming the message of Jesus, they would concentrate on Jews. When Peter (or to use the Semitic form of his nickname, Cephas, meaning "rock") visited Antioch in Syria, he at first met and ate freely with the Gentile converts. After associates of James arrived there, however, Peter withdrew from social contact with these uncircumcised Gentile Christians (Gal. 2:11–13). In response to this divisive attitude, Paul insists that none of the Law—not even circumcision—was a prerequisite for sharing in the life of God's people. In spite of this disagreement, Paul continued to send contributions to the Jerusalem apostolic community, which seems to have chosen a term used by Jesus, "the poor" (Luke 4:18; 5:20) as a designation of its members. That commitment of tangible support as an expression of common life within the wider community appears in one of Paul's later letters in which he describes a collection he has taken up among the churches of Asia Minor that he is going to carry back to Jerusalem (Rom. 15:25–29).

Paul's letters were written in response to the specific immediate needs of the communities addressed in cities across the Mediterranean world. It is impossible, therefore, to arrange them in an assuredly systematic or chronological way. Although the Acts of the Apostles traces the journeys and activities of Paul in a more nearly orderly way, it is selective in what it includes, and at some points is in tension with what Paul reports in his letters.[3] It may be assumed, however, that the basic pattern of Paul's career is accurately described in Acts, moving him from city to city, reaching from his native Syria and Jerusalem to the capital of the empire in Rome. It is also highly likely that the typical strategy of Paul in his mission to the Gentiles is accurately pictured in Acts. His initial approach was to go to places where Jews met regularly in the cities of the Roman world, to give special attention to Gentiles who had been drawn to the God of the Jewish scriptures, and on occasion to address directly pagan worshippers or intellectuals. The author of Acts is careful to describe many occasions when Paul and his associates have opportunity to explain their work and their message in the presence of religious, military, and political powers as well.

As is evident from Paul's letters, the disciples of Jesus remained primarily in Jerusalem, although some of them—Peter, for example—traveled to visit other cities in the eastern Mediterranean. Peter went to Antioch, as Paul notes (Gal. 2:11), and was apparently associated with other communities of Christians in Asia Minor as well (I Pet. 1:1–2). Tradition links Peter with the church in Rome, although there is no direct reference to this in the New Testament material. The author of Acts, however, is careful to point out that from the very beginning in Jerusalem the intention of God was to extend the good news to all humanity and to witness to the truth to the ends of the earth (Acts 1:8). The multitude depicted as converging on the house in Jerusalem when the outpouring of the Spirit of God on the disciples occurs in such a dramatic fashion (Acts 2:1–6) includes Jews and devout seekers "from every nation under heaven." The miracle by which these Jews and proselytes are able to hear the disciples' message in their own language, regardless of their land of origin, is a symbolic way of showing that the good news is going to reach out to people of whatever linguistic or ethnic origins. Divine confirmation of this phenomenon is offered in the address of Peter reported in Acts. The address is based on an extended quotation from the Hebrew prophet Joel, who announced that God's Spirit would be poured out on all humanity (literally, *flesh*), and that whoever called on the name of the Lord would be saved (see Joel 3:1–5 and Acts 2:17–21). The concluding line of this sermon of Peter incorporates themes from the Hebrew scriptures to make the point that the invitation to share in God's people goes out to those who are geographically or ethnically far off from Israel and includes all who respond to the call of God (Acts 2:39). It is this potentially universal invitation to share in the

---

[3]For example, in Galatians 2, there are no legal obligations placed on Gentile converts by the Jerusalem leaders of the church. But in Acts 15, a consultation between Paul and the Jerusalem-based apostles results in the imposing of minimal ritual food laws on Gentiles (abstinence from eating what has been killed by strangling or what contains blood; see Leviticus 17:10–14).

covenant that is depicted in Acts as originating with the original apostles, so that Paul's mission to the Gentiles is a logical development, not a dubious innovation.

The inclusive feature is developed in the early chapters of Acts, in which a lame man is healed by Peter at the gate of the temple (Acts 3). Lameness disqualified anyone from serving as a priest, and no lame animal could be offered in the temple.[4] In the Dead Sea Scrolls, the lame and any otherwise deformed were to be forbidden to enter Jerusalem in the new age of the restored temple. The disciples' special attention and careful justification for the healing help extended to this man underscore the theme that we saw in the teachings of Jesus: It is the outsiders and those on the fringe of the covenant people who are to be the special concern of the new covenant community. In Acts 6 and 7 the role of Greek-speaking Jews is highlighted by the selection of seven men—all with Greek names!—to handle the daily distribution of food to the members of the community. It is one of this group, Stephen, who articulates the theme that God does not dwell in houses, not even in the temple. This theme fits with Jesus's regret-free prediction of the destruction of the temple (Mark 13:2). Stephen goes on to denounce the leaders of Israel who have persistently persecuted the prophets God has sent to them, and who have now connived to have Jesus put to death (Acts 7:44–53). The council rises up to have Stephen put to death by stoning, which takes place outside the city. The leader of this mob action against one who, in the name of Jesus, challenges Israel's special relationship to God through the law and the temple is Saul—that is, Paul (Acts 7:54–60). Acts proceeds to describe in vivid, dramatic detail the conversion of Paul and the stages that lead to his acceptance by the Christians in Damascus and then in Jerusalem, after which he goes back to Syria (Acts 9).

Alternating with the early stages of Paul's career as told in Acts are further indications that the Christian community is being extended to include non-Jews. Acts 8 recounts the conversion of Samaritans and of a eunuch from Ethiopia, whose ethnic origins and whose physical condition would have disqualified them from participation in the covenant of Israel. Through a series of visions, Peter is brought together with a Roman military officer stationed in the Hellenistic coastal city built by Herod and named Caesarea. Peter is instructed not to allow the ritual food laws to separate him from other potential members of the new community, since there is no partiality with God. All who will may enter the covenant. After Peter tells Cornelius, the Roman centurion, about Jesus and what God was doing through him, this Gentile receives the Spirit and is baptized (Acts 10). Peter's subsequent report of this event to the church in Jerusalem makes explicit the principle of Gentile participation in the new people of God, and it is then confirmed by the church leaders (Acts 11:18).

It was in Antioch, however, that Acts reports the first systematic effort to bring Gentiles into the community of faith (Acts 11). Barnabas was sent by the Jerusalem

---

[4]Leviticus 21:18; Deuteronomy 15:21.

church to assess the situation in Antioch and recruited Paul to assist him. The results were large numbers added to the community, whose members (we are told) were for the first time called *Christians* (Acts 11:26). As in the letters of Paul, Acts tells us of the financial support offered to the Jerusalem community by these predominantly Gentile churches in the urban centers of the wider Mediterranean world. It is the Antioch community that commissions Paul and Barnabas to launch a mission to such regions beyond Syria as the island of Cyprus and the Roman provinces in central and southern Asia Minor (Acts 13).

Paul's strategy in each city is to go first to the Jewish meeting places where he explains from the Jewish scriptures Jesus's role in the purpose of God, and how through Jesus the promises of covenant renewal are fulfilled. The reactions are a mixture of acceptance of the message and violent rejection of it and its bearers. The cities where this activity is carried out include Antioch in Pisidia, Iconium, Lystra, and Derbe. In each case, the basic pattern is to approach Jews first in their meetings and then to turn to interested Gentiles, especially to those who are on the periphery of Judaism ("the devout").

An important stage in the spread of Christianity is described in Acts 16. In response to a vision, Paul crosses from Troas to the mainland of Europe.[5] His first reported activity is at Philippi, the leading city of the province of Macedonia, which had been named by and for Philip, the father of Alexander the Great. Again, the symbolism of Paul's first European convert is significant: Lydia is a Jewish woman with a Greek name. Her livelihood is the business of selling luxury items made with the enormously expensive purple dye extracted from a type of sea shell. She is a pious person, as is evident from her going to the place of prayer where she met with a group of women. It is women, including those of means and power, who were to comprise an important part of the early Christian communities. Another revealing detail of this story is that when Lydia was converted and baptized, the members of her household were baptized as well (Acts 16:15). Conversion was not a purely individual matter but involved one's larger social context.

Another story in Acts 16 that is indicative of the ways in which Christianity was to penetrate the structures of Roman society and politics is that of the conversion of the jailer in charge of the prison at Philippi. This city had been established as capital of his expanding realms by Philip, the father of Alexander the Great, and it was named in his honor. Paul was placed in prison there after he reportedly exorcized a demon that was credited with enabling a slave girl to foretell the future and read fortunes. Her owners were so furious that she had lost her fortune-telling skills that they appealed to the local judge, who ordered that Paul and his companion, Silas, be put in prison. They were stripped of their clothing, severely beaten, and thrown

---

[5]Troas was a district on the Aegean coast of Asia Minor, of which the chief city was Troy, famed through the poetry of Homer and regarded by the Romans as the place from which the first settlers of Rome came, as reported by the Roman poet, Virgil, in his epic, the *Aeneid*.

into prison. To guarantee that they would remain in jail, the jailer put them in an inner cell and placed their feet in stocks. Far from being discouraged by this treatment, the two Christian prisoners sang and prayed aloud on into the night while the other prisoners listened. But God was at work, the Acts narrative tells us: A great earthquake shook the prison to its foundations, the doors of all the cells swung open, and all the fetters of the prisoners were released at once. On realizing what had happened, the jailer was ready to commit suicide for his failure to keep imprisoned those in his charge. Entering the prison with lights, the jailer fell down before Paul and Silas, asking how he might get out of the predicament. With a pun on his question how he might be "saved" (Acts 16:30), Paul tells him how he and all in his household might be "saved" through coming into right relationship with God. Paul declares that the jailer and all those in his house must trust in "the Lord Jesus" if all are to be "saved" (16:31). During the night the jailer washes the wounds of Paul and Silas while the latter explains God's message to him and all his household. At once, the jailer and all his family are baptized as evidence of their trust in the God whom Paul preached. On the next day the local magistrate decides to release Paul and Silas, but since they are Roman citizens they should not have been treated so harshly, and especially without a proper trial. After the judge apologizes, Paul and Silas agree to leave Philippi. This vivid story is an example of the way that the Christians from the outset of their reaching out to the wider Roman world for converts were confronted by and in debate with the civil authorities of the empire. It also shows the attraction that the movement had for people at large, including government officials.

Different kinds of encounter are depicted in Acts 17. In Thessalonica the local Jewish leaders were enraged by the success of Paul and his co-worker Silas in persuading not only some Jews but also many devout Gentiles and leading women who had been associated with the synagogue that Jesus was God's agent to reconstitute his people. The leaders accused the apostles before the civil authorities of politically subversive claims about the kingship of Jesus. Paul and Silas were permitted to leave the city, but their antagonists followed them to Beroea when they heard of the similar effectiveness of the preaching of Jesus there. In Athens, however, Paul's public arguments in support of his claims about Jesus were depicted as carried on not only in the synagogue but also in the public market place, the Agora, where philosophers of various sorts addressed the crowds that passed through (Acts 17:16–18). Because Paul had a theme in his public lectures that was new to the city, he was called before the local council, which had jurisdiction over what was taught and proclaimed there. He seized the occasion of the hearing before the council, which met on the Areopagus overlooking this vast public area of the city, to make the point that the unknown god to whom a local altar was dedicated had revealed himself, not only in the ordering of the universe and in the divine presence within human hearts, but specifically through this man, Jesus, whom God had raised from the dead and who was to be judge of the world (Acts 17:19–33). In the course of Paul's speech as reported in Acts, he quoted Greek poets and affirmed several basic ideas that Greek philosophers affirmed: the inner presence of God and the future judgment of human deeds, for example. The response was one of mixed scorn and interest, but a few members of the council believed what Paul had to say. Once more, Acts presents us with a symbolic incident that points to the continuing engagement between the messengers of Christianity and the intellectual leaders of the Greco-Roman world.

In Acts 18, there is an account of a mixed reaction at Corinth to Paul's message about Jesus that was delivered to the Jewish community. The leader of the synagogue was converted, but the hostility of the Corinthian Jews as a whole was so vehement that Paul announced his intention to concentrate on winning Gentiles to faith in Jesus, using as his base of operations a house adjacent to the one where the synagogue met. The accusations against Paul brought by the Jews before the Roman governor were rejected by the governor on the ground that the issue was not one of Roman law but of the interpretation of the Jewish traditions. Gallio, the governor, is known from Roman historical sources to have been in that post during the latter part of the reign of Claudius as emperor (A.D. 41–54), so that this detail in Acts provides a valuable chronological reference point for reconstructing the career of Paul.[6]

In Ephesus Paul encountered two kinds of problems that must have characterized the Christian movement as a whole in the first century and subsequently. The first difficulty came from the instruction offered to the Christians in Ephesus by a man named Apollos, a Jew originally from Alexandria, whose knowledge of the scriptures and ability to interpret them was impressive. He did not know, however, of the resource of the Spirit of God that was available to members of the new community. Paul set Apollos straight when he visited Corinth, and then went back to Ephesus himself. There the growth of the Christian community was so rapid that local merchants and craftsmen began to fear that the spread of this movement would endanger the enterprise that was the chief attraction of the city and the major source of their revenue: the temple of Artemis, the fertility goddess, for whom statues and offerings were locally prepared and sold. At a public confrontation in the city theater, where Jews, Christians, and devotees of Artemis were locked in verbal conflict, the town clerk finally quieted the masses and told them that there was no basis for their charge against Paul and his associates. These reported accusations against Paul anticipated and exemplified the two major sources of opposition that the growing movement experienced in the second and subsequent centuries: (1) the charge of subversion of both Roman religion and civil authority brought by pagan opponents; and (2) the hostility from Jewish leaders who rejected the early Christians' claim that Jesus was the fulfillment of the covenant promises of their scriptures.

A brief return visit to the churches of mainland Greece and a farewell address to the leaders of the Ephesian church in which Paul is described as anticipating his

---

[6]An inscription found early in this century at the Temple of Apollo in Delphi makes possible the determination of the precise period when Gallio (who was the brother of the famous Roman philosopher, Seneca) was serving as governor in Corinth: between 51 and 53 C.E.

own arrest and martyrdom are related in Acts 20. There follows a description of his return to Syria and then to Jerusalem. In the extended accounts of the various hearings and trials to which he was subjected in the presence of religious and civilian officials, Paul repeatedly makes a case for the following propositions: (1) that the message about Jesus that he proclaims is rooted in the Jewish scriptures and embodies the fulfillment of the hopes expressed in them; (2) that God has repeatedly shown through miracles his support for what Paul is doing and saying; (3) that nothing which Paul and his associates proclaim is in conflict with Roman law. Accordingly, as a Roman citizen, Paul makes an appeal directly to Caesar to rule on the charges brought against him.[7] The appeal is granted, and Acts describes in vivid detail the voyage to Rome, with abundant signs of special divine protection for Paul. The narrative ends with Paul awaiting trial in Rome but engaged in missionary activity and in debate with the Jews, operating from his own rented quarters in the capital city.

Although the author of Acts includes many important historical details that have been corroborated by modern scholarship, his work as a whole is selective, stylized, and symbolic in its approach.[8] Its overall scheme of the spread of Christianity is probably historically reliable, and there is surely much detail found only in Acts. But we are on far safer ground historically if we regard Acts as a schematic survey of these events, written from the perspective of the late first century. More certain is the evidence that comes from the first-hand reports of Paul in his letters. Not surprisingly, the issues discussed in Acts are the very ones that Paul deals with in his letters to the various churches.

Paul's Communications with the Gentile Churches

It is clear from the letters of Paul preserved in the New Testament that he wrote more of them than we now possess and that he received letters from the churches, to which he sent replies. In the letter known as I Corinthians, for example, he mentions his earlier letter to the community there (5:9) and the letter they had written to him inquiring about some issues within the group (7:1). Among the preserved letters of Paul are references to places and incidents reported more fully in Acts, such as the difficulties he had experienced in Philippi (I Thess. 2:1) and his stay in

---

[7]Citizenship in the Roman empire was by no means universal but was instead a highly prized status that involved commercial and property rights and that was transmitted by heredity to natives of Rome and parts of Italy. In addition, it was conferred on persons born in other lands who had in some way served or supported the cause of Rome.

[8]An attempt to demonstrate the historical reliability of Acts is by Martin Hengel, *Acts and the History of Earliest Christianity* (Philadelphia: Fortress Press, 1979). A standard reference work on Acts and its historical setting is an older series of volumes by F. J. Foakes-Jackson, K. Lake, and H. J. Cadbury, *The Beginnings of Christianity: Part 1, The Acts of the Apostles*, 5 vols. (London: Macmillan, 1922–1932).

Athens (I Thess. 3:1). In the closing sections of each of the letters, there is a series of personal notes to persons in the community from which he is writing, or a recommendation of someone who is going to visit the community that is addressed in the letter. As a result of these personal notes, the reader obtains a vivid picture of the relationships within individual communities and the surprising extent to which members moved from one city to another, as was so common for a large segment of the populace as a whole in the Roman world of the first and second centuries.

I and II Corinthians give us the fullest picture of the problems and the resources for dealing with them in the first generation of Christian churches. In I Corinthians, each chapter or group of chapters deals with a major issue that confronted a community of Gentiles who were persuaded that, through Jesus, God's purpose outlined in the Jewish scriptures was being fulfilled. The first two chapters deal with the conceptual or intellectual question whether the message Paul preached was compatible with human wisdom. Some members were siding with certain leaders in the church against the others, claiming superior wisdom. Paul seeks to combat this development by declaring that Christ is both the power of God and the wisdom of God. There is no place in the community for these claims for having access to superior knowledge. This issue anticipates the struggles in the late first and early second centuries of the church's intellectual leaders to discern the relationship between the gospel that the apostles preached and the lofty intellectual traditions of the Greco-Roman world.

Besides the claim to superior wisdom, some members regarded one or another of the leaders as fulfilling the most significant role in the life of the community. Paul's response in I Corinthians 3 was to declare that each leader had a distinctive task to perform and that all were essential to healthy growth of the community. Together they comprised the temple of God, who by the Spirit dwelt within the community. Some members, however, were grossly proud of their individual accomplishments within the community, whether intellectually or in terms of the roles they performed in the church. Paul seeks to show that the humiliation and suffering that he and the other leaders had been subjected to were analogous to the rejection that Christ had to suffer in the plan of God (I Cor. 4). Also causing major antagonisms within the Christian community was the practice of some members to turn to civil courts in settling legal disputes with other Christians—a procedure Paul denounced (I Cor. 6).

In this letter Paul addresses the specific issues of behavior of the Christians, especially those who have gone to excess in trying to show how free they are from the obligation to obey the Law of Moses. Some are living in an incestuous relationship (I Cor. 5). Other questions relating to marriage are also dealt with in I Corinthians 7. These questions include such problems as whether Christians can divorce and remarry, whether Christian couples should abstain from sexual relationships, whether the unmarried and widows should maintain their status, and whether someone who is converted should continue to be married to an unconverted spouse. On only one question does Paul have a Jesus tradition to which he can appeal: Jesus's prohibition of divorce and remarriage (I Cor 7:10–11; Mark 10:1–12). On the other matters, Paul can offer only his own opinion. A special question is raised because Paul has no wife, although the other apostles are accompanied by theirs. The answer is that in each case the welfare and image of the community as a whole must be taken into account, as well as the distinctive roles and dispositions of the individuals involved. Some members tried to display their freedom by buying and eating meat that had originally been offered in sacrifice to pagan deities. These people should have known that the gods were shams, and so should have scoffed at pagan religion. Paul reminds them, however, that new converts have only recently been liberated from these pagan cults and will not understand the seeming participation in these idolatrous rites by those who claim to be Christians (I Cor. 8).

I Corinthians 9–14 deals with problems that arise from the varieties of leadership and function within the community, including the question whether the apostles should receive financial support from the members. Paul asserts that he has a right to receive financial support from the community, as the other apostles do from their communities, but that he chooses not to do so. He prefers to work for a living (I Cor. 4:12; 9:6) so that he can be free of any sense of obligation to any members of the community. He addresses a whole range of social issues as follows:

The subservient role of women in the churches.

The fact that at the eucharistic meal of the community (the Lord's supper, as Paul calls it; I. Cor. 11:17-22) some are drunk and some go hungry.

The diversity of origins of the members: Jew and Gentile, slave and free (I Cor. 12:13).

The diversity of roles to be performed by the members of the community and the range of values attached to those roles: apostles, prophets, teachers, miracle workers, healers, those gifted with ecstatic speech and the interpreters of those who "speak with tongues" (I Cor. 12:27–29).

Paul's advice with regard to the divisive factors within the community at Corinth is to recognize that, like the parts of a human body, the role of each member is essential for the welfare of the whole. And the quality that is to pervade and facilitate the functioning of the "body" is love (I Cor. 13–14). What is clear in all this counsel from Paul to the community at Corinth is that there had not yet developed in the churches either a clear pattern of leadership for decision-making or a set of guidelines that each community was expected to observe. It appears that Paul had different standards for different communities, since he refused to accept financial support in Corinth but did so in Philippi (Phil. 4:15). It is not that Paul was simply inconsistent but that his policies were adjusted to the specific conditions of each of the communities where he lived and served. The institutional norms of structure and behavior are yet to come in the life of Christianity. On one question, however, Paul does have a firm tradition: how the Lord's Supper is to be conducted. Here is one of the few issues on which the Jesus tradition is known and is appealed to explicitly (I Cor. 11:23–26). On the other questions he seems to have been guided by what he thought would foster the common life of the community as a whole.

Two issues on which he has a consistent point of view are (1) How will the present age come to an end? and (2) How are the Gentile churches to give tangible expression to their spiritual debt to the Jerusalem-based apostles and the earliest Christian community there?

As for the coming of the end of the age, Paul shares with Jewish apocalyptic thought the belief that the present age is dominated by the powers of evil, although he is confident that the rule of God over the creation has already begun to be established through Jesus. When that work of subjugation of evil is complete, then Jesus will return in triumph. The church's ground of confidence that this victory will take place is that God has already raised Jesus from the dead as a kind of down-payment on the resurrection of all the faithful (I Cor. 15:23–24). The result will be the triumph of the power and purpose of God over the whole of the universe. In his earlier letter to the Thessalonians, Paul expresses the same basic expectation (I Thess. 4:13–18), making clear that he expects to be among those who are alive when this cosmic event takes place. In his later letter to the Philippians, which may have been written from prison in Rome, there is a clear indication that, since he is now subject to Roman governmental authorities, the outcome of his circumstances may be his execution by the Romans.[9] The perennial issue of when and in what mode Christ will return in triumph is dealt with in a variety of ways in the New Testament and in the ensuing centuries.

The instructions for taking the collection for the Jerusalem Christians and for conveying the gift are quite explicit. Since this was a major factor in Paul's agreement with the Jerusalem apostles, he was determined to see that it was carried out. In doing so, as we have seen in the account in Acts, he confronted the Jewish authorities, whose charges before the political powers in Palestine led to his being taken as prisoner to Rome.

The overarching theme in Paul's letter to the Galatians and in his most systematic letter, Romans, is how God through Jesus constitutes his new covenant people. Participation in the new community is not by human achievement through conformity to the requirements of the Law of Moses but through trusting in the sacrificial death of Jesus on the cross and his having been raised from the dead as God's means of effecting reconciliation with a disobedient and alienated human race and of overcoming the powers of evil and death. This theme dominates the first five chapters

---

[9]Paul's reference to the Praetorian Guard (Phil. 1:13) is a possible indication that he was imprisoned under the elite imperial troops in Rome itself, although it could also refer to the special forces of a provincial governor in Palestine or elsewhere.

of the letter to the Romans. The inward commitment of faith in what God has done is given outward expression in the rite of baptism "into Christ Jesus" (Rom. 6:1–4). In this new group relationship, all of life is renewed, members are freed from a sense of obligation to obey the legal requirements as a means of gaining or maintaining status with God, and the power of the Spirit of God renews life in an atmosphere of freedom and love (Rom. 6–8). From this community of love, no power can separate the members of God's people (Rom. 8:38–39). God has not abandoned his historic people, Israel, but now they too have the opportunity to share in the life of this reconstituted covenant people (Rom. 9–11).

Jesus and Paul as Models for the Outreach of the Church to the Graeco-Roman World: Luke and Acts

As we have seen, the two-volume work known as the Gospel of Luke and the Acts of the Apostles is far more than an ancient archive of information about Jesus and the apostles. From the opening words of Luke's gospel to the dramatic account of Paul's voyage to Rome in Acts, the author uses the literary devices and modes that were common features of popular literature of the late first and early second century of our era. The formal, stylized introductory lines of Luke are echoed in the opening of Acts. The frequent references to rulers and officials of the Roman system enable the reader to locate in time the events that are being described and also to place these occurrences on the larger stage of the early Roman empire. Although Luke's gospel is developed on the basis of an earlier Christian model (the Gospel of Mark), the literary style and strategy of Acts reflect what literary historians call the *Hellenistic romance*, which was a narrative type developed in this period to serve as propaganda for a religious movement or a divinity.[10] Since the author of Luke and Acts is concerned to show the continuity with, as well as the transformation of, Judaism that occurred with the coming of Jesus, he also employs some of the literary styles of the Jewish traditions, such as the hymns and prophetic utterances that accompany the story of the birth of Jesus in Luke 1–2.

In passages unique to Luke, the aged Simeon foresees that Jesus will be the instrument of God's revelation to Gentiles as well as Jews (Luke 2:32). John the Baptist announces that all humanity will see God's salvation (Luke 3:6) and demonstrates this by welcoming into his group those who would be rejected by Jewish standards: tax-collectors and soldiers (Luke 3:10–14). Similarly, Jesus's sermon in Nazareth not only announces that God's good news is intended especially for the "poor"—that is, the deprived and excluded—but recalls the precedents for non-Israelite participation in God's healing benefits through the prophets Elijah and Elisha

---

[10]An example of this narrative religious propaganda is the *Metamorphoses* of Lucius Apuleius, written in the mid-second century C.E., which describes participation in the cult of the goddess, Isis.

(Luke 4:16–30). Luke reports Jesus as sending out not only twelve of his followers to spread his message, but seventy others as well (10:1–20). Twelve is the number of the tribes of Israel, and seventy is the symbolic number of the nations of the world. Jesus's actions and his parables point to the inclusiveness of the community as part of God's purpose:

> The Parable of the Good Samaritan, in which there is praise for the concern and kindness of a member of a religious group despised by pious Jews (10:29–37).
>
> The Parable of the Pharisee and the Publican, in which the pride of the former is contrasted with the humble reaching out for forgiveness by the latter (18:9–14).
>
> The Parables of the Lost Sheep, the Lost Coin, and the Lost Son, in which the point is that God and his agents take the initiative to restore the alienated (15:1–32).
>
> The story of Zacchaeus, the tax-collector, to whose house Jesus invites himself as a public demonstration of his message that God welcomes into his people all true seekers (19:1–10).
>
> The Healing of the Ten Lepers, whose physical condition precluded their participation in Jewish common life or worship (Luke 17:11–19).

Women, whose role in the life of the Jewish religious community and in Roman society as a whole was often peripheral, are pictured in Luke as having a central place in the new community. This is apparent from their role in the birth and infancy stories, the special attention Jesus gives to meeting their needs (as in the healing of the widow's son, 7:11–17), the insight of the woman who anoints Jesus for his burial (7:36–50), the support that women provide for Jesus and his associates (8:1–3; 10:38–42), and their faithful presence during his crucifixion and in preparation of his body for proper burial. Similarly evidencing Jesus's challenge to the social patterns of his day, Luke pictures him throughout the gospel as stressing the blessing that is to come to the poor and the judgment that is to fall on the rich.

The ongoing life of the community is anticipated by Luke in his unique stories of the followers of Jesus after his resurrection from the dead. They meet with him on several occasions, including meals, on the basis of which they observe that he was made known to them as he showed how the scriptures prepare for his coming and as they shared the common meal (24:35). Thus the community's study of the Jewish scriptures and their participation in the Lord's Supper are the major resources for their sustenance and understanding.

In at least two ways, the author of Luke prepares the reader for the possibilities and problems that will confront the community after Jesus has been taken from them. First, in his expanded version of the hearing of Jesus before the political authorities, Luke notes that neither Herod Antipas (the Jewish regional ruler) nor

Pilate can find Jesus guilty of any crime against the Roman state (Luke 23:6–16), which becomes a central theme in the Acts of the Apostles. Second, Jesus is described as promising his followers that they will be empowered by the Spirit for the work they will do in his absence (Luke 24:48). In Acts, the fulfillment of that promise occupies the center of interest for the first two chapters, the outpouring of the Spirit is portrayed as a microcosm of the world-wide role of the church in the years to come. Throughout Acts, the apostles are brought before the civil authorities, and in each case they are exonerated from any charge. One of the aims of the author of Acts is to show that neither Jesus nor Paul (or any other disciple) was guilty of anti-Roman words or actions. This point would be especially important in the later first and early second century as Christianity became a sufficiently large and aggressive movement to be a concern to the Roman authorities. But Jesus and Paul are the models for effective outreach with the good news of what God has done and is yet to do. Luke and Acts offer vivid detail to make that basic point. The reworking of the tradition in each case helps to underscore the strategy that the community is to employ in following its mission to the wider world.

Chapter 4

FROM CHARISMATIC MOVEMENT
TO INSTITUTION

The process of transformation of the early church from a spontaneous religious movement that emerged in various parts of Palestine and the wider Mediterranean world into an organized enterprise is evident when we compare earlier with later forms of the New Testament writings. For example, this change is apparent when we contrast older and later forms of the gospel tradition—specifically, Mark with Matthew—and authentic letters of Paul with those subsequently written in his name. Analogous kinds of structural changes in the early Christian movement and of adaptation to the wider Roman culture may be discerned by analysis of other writings of the New Testament as well.

From Apocalyptic Sect to Authoritarian Community:
The Gospel of Matthew

Unlike the Gospel of Mark, which is written in a breathless style, moving quickly from one event in the life of Jesus to another and emphasizing throughout the imminent end of the present age, Matthew is deliberative in style and manifests many features of a structured, ordered community lying behind and addressed by his account of Jesus. The intensity and frequency of Matthew's contrasts between prevailing Jewish practices and Jesus's instruction to his followers are best accounted for as arising from the grave tensions between Matthew's community and that of emergent rabbinic Judaism in the later decades of the first century C.E. (see Chapter 1). Just as the Jewish leaders were engaged in drawing the boundaries for their conception of the covenant people, so this group of second-generation Christians was countering that activity by defining its own community as the people of God.

This definitional activity is evident in both positive and negative ways in the Gospel of Matthew. From its opening lines, the author keeps making the point that the birth of Jesus and each aspect of the accompanying events was in fulfillment of the Jewish scriptures (Matt. 1:22; 2:5, 15, 17, 23; 3:3; 4:14, etc.). When Jesus is reported as offering his followers a summary of his teachings, the parallel with Moses's giving the law to Israel on Mount Sinai is explicit (Matt. 5:1–2), as are the direct contrasts between what Moses taught and what Jesus teaches (Matt. 5:17, 21, 27, 31, 33, 38, 43). This inference about the conscious contrast between Judaism and Matthew's Christian community is confirmed by the structure of this gospel, which is divided into five sections, just as the law of Moses is.[1] Equally sharp are the differences specified between Jewish piety (alms, fasting, and prayer) and that which Jesus urges his followers to exemplify (Matt. 6:1–18). Much of this material is found only in Matthew, which underscores how important for his community these contrasts and controversies are. The most vehement attack on Judaism in Matthew is the denunciation of the Pharisees in Matthew 23, which has no counterpart in the other gospels and which ends by blaming the Jews for the murder of all God's messengers throughout biblical history (Matt. 23:32–36) and warning that divine judgment is going to fall on them. That event of divine censure is linked explicitly with the destruction of the temple, which is a prelude to the coming of the end of the age (Matt. 24:1–3). At several points in Matthew's distinctive account of the trial and crucifixion of Jesus, the blame for his death is placed on and accepted by the Jewish leaders, and at the same time Pilate declares his freedom from responsibility for the sentencing of Jesus to death (Matt. 27:24–25).

Throughout Matthew, the writer pictures Jesus and his followers as engaged in discussion of precisely those issues in the appropriation of the biblical tradition that were central for Judaism in this period, to an extent and with an intensity that is not matched in the other gospels. Furthermore, Matthew reflects an instructional program and a decision-making process within the community that has no counterpart in the other three gospels. Jesus's commissioning of the disciples in his appearance to them after the resurrection includes his telling them to go throughout the world making disciples from all the nations (Matt. 28:19). The term translated "make disciples" means to give instruction, or to promote the learning process—which is precisely the practice that was being developed by the rabbis of this period to train adherents in the emergent forms of Jewish life and thought. The fundamental importance of the instructional program is made explicit in the final verse of Matthew (28:20), in which the disciples are told to teach the new members of the community to observe all the commandments given to them by Jesus. What is needed, therefore,

---

[1]The phrase "when Jesus had finished" occurs five times in Matthew (7:28; 11:1; 13:53; 19:1; 26:1), in each case at the end of a major teaching section of this gospel. The only item in Matthew that does not fit this scheme is Matthew 23, which is probably a polemical feature added to the gospel after its original fivefold structure had already been established.

is not merely converts but trainees to learn the truths and requirements of this new community.

Analogously, Matthew 18 describes a decision-making process within the community by which the appropriate behavior of the members can be determined. Disputes are to be settled between the individuals involved, but if that is not possible, officers of the church or the congregation as a whole are to hear the issues and render a decision. This process may result in expelling a member: "If he refuses to listen to the church, let him be to you as a Gentile or a tax-collector" (Matt. 18:17). The church's decisions are confirmed by God in heaven (Matt. 18:18–19). Furthermore, in Matthew 16 the disciples as leaders of the community are given the right and responsibility to determine the standards for admission to or exclusion from the membership of the group: "I will give you the keys of the kingdom, and whatever you bind on earth will be bound in heaven, and whatever you loose on earth will be loosed in heaven" (16:19). The terms, "bind" and "loose" used here (in 16:19 and 18:18) are precisely those that the Jewish sources of the time employ for the comparable process within the rabbinic community. Only in Matthew is there explicit reference to the community as "church" (Matt. 16:18; 18:17). The church is not an informal community to be gathered but a structure to be built.

Further evidence of the movement toward fixed patterns in the life of this community is to be found in the formalization of some of the basic practices of the earlier community. For example, the simple direct prayer of Jesus in Luke 11:2–4 ("Father, hallowed be thy name, they kingdom come") appears in Matthew 6:9–15 with the balanced lines and formal phrasing of the Lord's Prayer as it is used in Christian liturgical form down to the present day:

> Our Father who art in heaven,
> Hallowed be thy name.
> Thy kingdom come,
> Thy will be done,
> On earth as it is in heaven.

Similarly, the widespread practice of baptism as initiation into the community is linked in Matthew 28:19 with a trinitarian formula ("in the name of the Father, and of the Son, and of the Holy Spirit") absent from all the other gospel tradition.

What is apparent in Matthew is that his community has developed patterns for liturgy, prayer, administering the sacraments, instruction of members, decision-making within the membership, polemics against the emergent forms of rabbinic Judaism, and assignment of responsibility to its leaders. It is not in the least surprising, therefore, that Matthew was assigned by the early church the place of honor at the head of the New Testament, since his gospel addresses so directly the needs of the Christian movement as it moved beyond the first generation of spontaneity into a period of consolidation, definition, and organization for both leaders and members. The urgency of these needs was heightened by the fact that, concurrent with these developments within Christianity, Judaism was taking shape in a movement that shared with it the claim to be the true heir to the promises of the God of Israel to his future covenant people.

The Community of Mystical Participation in the Life of God: The Gospel of John

Although the mystery religions, with their promise of direct participation in the life of the gods, had flourished in the Mediterranean world for centuries, it was in the late first and early second centuries C.E. that popular interest in them surged. The earlier policies of Greece and Rome to suppress these popular religious movements are evident in the classical Greek play *The Bacchae* by Euripedes (480–406 B.C.E.), in which ecstatic women devotees of this god of wine and fertility think they have been divinely enabled to kill a wild animal with their hands, only to find that they have dismembered the son of their leader. In the early part of the second century B.C.E. another group of women was discovered to be engaging in orgiastic rites in honor of Bacchus (or Dionysus, as he was known to the Greeks) and was forbidden by the Roman senate to continue this worship, which was outlawed by this official action. Yet by the second century C.E. milder forms of worship of deities such as Osiris and Isis (Egyptian divinities linked with the fertility of the land through the annual overflow of the Nile) attracted a wide following, including both the simple and the sophisticated of the Roman world. Osiris, the god of the Nile, was depicted in the popular Egyptian myth as put to death by his enemy when the flow of the Nile subsided each year. His consort, Isis, was instrumental in restoring him to life. Later she was worshipped as the divine agent through whom her devotees could share in eternal life. The appeal of these mystery cults included the belief that through divinities one might in this present life perceive the divine ordering of the universe, gain the protection of the gods, and experience direct encounter with them. Although the details of the mystery religions were mostly secret, Plutarch (46-120 A.D.) wrote an informative account of the cult of Isis, and a mid-second-century writer, Lucius Apuleius, offered a vivid story of the transformation of a man who devoted his life to her service. In this highly symbolic narrative, a man who had been turned into an ass through dabbling in magic was restored to his true humanity by Isis, who gave him purpose and fulfillment in his new life. In other writings of this period, Isis is identified with cosmic wisdom, so that the knowledge she provides her followers gives them understanding of themselves and of the world in which they live.

This reworking of ancient traditions along symbolic lines, with allegorical interpretations of early myths, was engaged in not only by worshippers of the pagan gods, such as Isis, but also by Jews. In Alexandria, for example, the prolific writer and leader of the Jewish community, Philo, interpreted the biblical laws and narratives in such a way as to picture the experiences and legal requirements of ancient Israel as symbolic vehicles of participation in the life of God through mystical visions and spiritual understanding of the Law of Moses. Abraham's journey from Ur of the Chaldees to Hebron, where God met him and commissioned him, is a symbolic picture of the journey of the soul from the material realm into the realm of the divine, where direct encounter with God occurs. The distinctions between matter and spirit, as well as the concept of discernment of ultimate reality beyond the physical world, derived from the Platonic philosophical tradition in which Jews in Alexandria were obviously being trained in this period (early first century A.D.). Philo weaves together these philosophical and mystical features with his own upbringing in the Jewish biblical heritage to produce this remarkable synthesis of symbolic transformation and renewal of older tradition.

The Gospel of John is an analogous reworking of the gospel tradition. Jesus is the divine agent through whom the world was made, as well as the instrument through whom God's true people come to understand his purpose and to share in the true life he offers them. Instead of the feminine Greek word for wisdom, *sophia*, which is used in connection with Isis, John identifies Jesus with *logos*, a masculine Greek word meaning word, or reason, or rationale. Unlike the Isis mythology, however, in which she dwells in the mythical realm except in moments of mystical disclosure, Jesus is pictured as living among his own people and within the world that was created through him, bringing light of the knowledge of God to those ready to receive it (John 1:1–14).

The story of Jesus's career and the accounts of his teaching are cast in forms that distinguish them from the other gospels. Jesus's miracles are described as "signs" that manifest his divine glory (John 2:11; 20:30–31). In each case, the literal content of the narrative is intended as a vehicle of symbolic meaning for the community to which this gospel is addressed. The stories and the images used derive from the Old Testament accounts of God's dealings with his people in Israel. The changing of water into wine at a wedding feast (John 2:1–11) is a symbol of the time of fulfillment and consummation of God's purpose for his people. The feeding of the 5,000 represents God's provision for his people during the time before that purpose is accomplished (John 6). The restoration of sight to the blind man is contrasted with the blindness of Jesus's Jewish contemporaries who cannot see in him the instrument of God's healing purpose for them (John 9).

Similarly, many of Jesus's teachings in the Gospel of John are placed in the framework of declarations by Jesus that begin with the phrase, "I am." That phrase in Greek is used in the Greek translation of the Jewish Bible as the special name of God (usually transliterated into English as Jehovah, or Yahweh). Jesus declares his oneness with God, therefore, not in the abstract but in terms of his role as God's agent to reconstitute God's people. As in the signs, the images are drawn from the biblical tradition: Jesus is the bread of life who feeds God's people (John 6:35); he is the light of the world (8:12); he is the "I am" whose call to the covenant people transcends God's call to Abraham (8:58); he is the door through which one enters the flock that is God's people (10:7), and he is the shepherd who cares for them (10:11); because he is the embodiment of the resurrection, he brings eternal life to his followers (11:25); he is the way to God, the truth about God, and the life God has prepared for his people (14:6); he is the living organism through which God's people are nourished and enabled to be productive (15:1–5). When the crowd who came to seize him in the Garden of Gethsemane asked if he was Jesus of Nazareth, he responded, "I am," and they fell back in the presence of this divine majesty (18:1–6). In a mixture of narrative, discourse, and symbolism based on the Old Testament, Jesus's oneness with God and his central role in God's purpose for his people are sketched by John.

As in Matthew's gospel, John pictures Jesus in conflict with the Jewish leaders, who are excluding his followers from their synagogue meetings (9:22, 34). The crucial issue is the identity of Jesus as manifestation and agent of God. The decision about Jesus is determinative of one's destiny (9:35–41), as John pictures it. The only indications of moral requirements on the members of this new community are that they are to love one another (13:35), to bear fruit—that is, to work the works of love, even to the point of dying for others (15:1–11). The only ecclesiastical role assigned to the disciples is to pronounce forgiveness (20:22–23). There is in John's gospel no hint of leadership roles or of ecclesiastical structure. The major concern is with harmony and mutuality within this new community to whom Jesus has revealed God's purpose through the symbolic reworking of the biblical and the earlier gospel traditions. This document probably was written near the end of the first century A.D., and represents a segment of early Christianity that had kinship with mystical religious movements, both Jewish and pagan. It is more concerned about insight into the purpose of God and concord within the group than with organization or outreach into the wider society.

Toward Organizational Order and Structure

When we move from the Gospel of John to the Letters of John, there are some continuities but also some significant changes. The vocabulary and writing style of these letters are much the same as in the Gospel of John, even though the content has shifted from reports of what Jesus said and did (in the gospel) to guidelines for the internal life of the Christian community (in the letters). There is still an emphasis on love within the group, but now there is a warning about hatred of other members as well (I John 2:7–11; 4:7–12). There is a new feature: warning about impending divine judgment and the need to prepare oneself for this fearsome event (I John 2:13–3:3). The symbolic language of the Gospel of John is evident in passages like I John 5:6–8, where the references to Spirit, water, and blood could refer to the baptism and the death of Jesus, but they probably also are allusions to the Christian rites of baptism (when the Spirit comes on believers) and the Eucharist (when the body and blood of Jesus are symbolically shared by the community). This is in contrast to the Gospel of John, in which there is no account of the bread and wine at the Last Supper, but it also resembles John's admonition that sharing in the life of God's people requires eating the flesh and drinking the blood of the Son of Man (6:52–58). The sacraments of the church seem to have become somewhat more explicit by the time I John was written.

In II John, there is also a reminder of the commandment of love, but the question of correct doctrine is also raised. Apparently there were some within the Christian movement who were ready to affirm the divinity of Jesus but who considered his humanity to have been only a guise or an appearance. The author of this letter insists that one must affirm that Jesus came "in the flesh"—that is, in fully human form. To affirm a false doctrine of Christ is to forfeit one's place in God's people. Those who adopt these false views of Jesus are to be excluded from the fellowship and denied even a greeting (II John 7–10). A similar development in the Johannine wing of early Christianity is apparent in III John. Someone named Diotrophes does not acknowledge the authority of the author of this letter and does not offer hospitality to welcome his associates, but goes so far as to put them out of the church (II John 9–10). Clearly, this segment of Christianity that came to be identified with the name of John—even though all four of these writings are anonymous—has moved from the earlier atmosphere of mutuality and a minimum of ethical or doctrinal guidelines toward a structure of authority and a definition of correct doctrine.

The later letters attributed to Paul (Colossians, Ephesians, I and II Timothy, and Titus) represent an even more dramatic shift toward defining true doctrine and creating a hierarchy of both leadership and membership within the Christian community. In the opening lines of the Letter to the Colossians (attributed to Paul, but probably written by one of his successors), the gospel is presented as "the word of truth," and its aim is to fill Christians "with all knowledge." The goal of this process of instruction is that Christians may be "rooted and built up and established in the faith" (Col. 2:6–7). Faith is no longer primarily trust in Jesus as God's agent; rather, the emphasis falls on correct *belief* concerning Jesus. There is accordingly a solemn warning against vain and deceitful philosophy that rests on human ideas rather than on divine wisdom (2:8), and that fosters a false notion of piety based on ascetic rules rather than on concern for the common life of the church (2:16–23). To seek for wisdom that comes through the Christ, now exalted in heaven, is to experience true renewal in knowledge (3:1–10). In the so-called Letter to the Ephesians (which in its oldest copy has a blank rather than an address to a specific church), there is a comparable emphasis on sound doctrine, which discloses "the manifold wisdom of God" (Eph. 3:10). The readers are warned against deceitful and faddish teachings that are opposed to the eternal truths disclosed to the church (4:13–14) and that provide the ground of its unity in faith and practice (Eph. 2:11–12; 4:3–6). Similarly in the Letters of I and II Timothy (also attributed to Paul but dating from the later first century), there is insistence on teaching the one true doctrine and on recognizing and denouncing those who peddle false teachings within the church (I Tim. 1:3–7; 2:4; 6:3). This doctrine is preserved in the church through its system of instruction (Titus 1:9; 2:1), which must be guarded against infiltration by teachers of error. The educational program begins with children, continues through later life, and is based on a body of sacred scriptures (II Tim. 3:14–16), which presumably include not only the Jewish Bible but also the earlier writings of the New Testament.

In all these letters in the later Pauline tradition, there are two types of ranking according to authority. The first is represented within Christian households, where wives are to be subject to husbands and slaves are to be subject to masters (Col. 3:18–4:1; Eph. 5:21–6:9; Titus 2:3–10). The fancy clothes and jewelry of the women (I Tim. 2:9) and the fact that members of the churches own slaves show that the Christian movement by the end of the first century has penetrated the higher levels of Roman society. The second structure within which authority is to be defined and assigned is that of the church leadership. In contrast to Paul, who regards the various roles that are served in the communities as gifts of the Spirit—ecstatic speech, working miracles, utterance of prophecy, teachers, healers, helpers (I Cor. 12:27–30)—and as essential for the functioning of the whole organism that is the church, these letters describe the levels of authority of the officials of the church as an organization. The bishop, or overseer, is the highest officer of the local or regional church. Under him are elders and deacons (i.e., "servants"), who have a more menial role in the life of the community (I Tim. 3; 5:17; Titus 1). In addition, there may have been a special function for widows, perhaps resembling that of nuns in the later church (I Tim. 5:9.16), although their enrollment by the church could have been to qualify them for support from the Christian community. In either case, these details evidence the emergence of the church as a structural institution for which the architectural and priestly image in Eph. 2:11–12 is wholly appropriate: a holy temple in the Lord.

Social and Political Attitudes within the Church

Because Paul expected the imminent end of the present age and the establishment of God's rule over all the world, he was not concerned for political revolution. Accordingly, he urged his readers in the Letter to the Romans (13:1–7) to obey those in political power because he believed it had been established by God and would be replaced in God's own time. The later Pauline tradition goes a step further and instructs Christians to pray for kings and other rulers because their maintenance of law and order makes it possible for the faithful to lead quiet, respectable lives. Titus 3:1 enjoins submission to these authorities and the avoidance of an evil speaking concerning them or anyone else. This same attitude of subjection to and honor of the Roman powers, as well as the effort to sustain a good reputation as law-abiding persons, is encouraged in I Peter 2:11–17). The public image of the Christians and their freedom from charges of insurrection are seen by these authors as essential goals for the Christians at the dawn of the second century. To assure that they will be regarded by outsiders as morally upright, orderly people, I Peter echoes many of the injunctions found in the later Pauline material about Christians' acceptance of places of submission and subservience within their communities, especially wives and slaves (I Pet. 2:18–3:6).

The author of I Peter (which is also a pseudonymous and later document) expects the outbreak of divine judgment and warns the Christians of trials and suffering—even martyrdom—that they may be called on to undergo before the final revelation of the triumphant Christ occurs and the rule of God is established on earth (I Pet. 4:12–19). Yet they are to remain law-abiding until the end. Another Christian writing from about this same time is the Revelation of John, which also expects the inbreaking of God's judgment but which regards the Roman empire as the agency of Satan and eagerly awaits its destruction by God's power. There is no hint of political insurrection in Revelation, but John depicts in an elaborate series of apocalyptic visions the events that will lead to the final cataclysm that will bring human empires to an end. The faithful are to be prepared to endure suffering, confident that God will vindicate them and establish his rule over the universe.

Toward a Cultural Synthesis with the Roman World

Two of the New Testament writings at the opening of the second century display the desire of some early Christians to state their convictions in the intellectual style of the Roman world. The Letter of James shows the influence of Cynic and Stoic philosophy, and the Letter to the Hebrews employs concepts and perspectives derived from the Platonic tradition. The precedent is set for the policy of Christian thinkers to employ the ideas and the modes of expression of Greek and Roman philosophy in their interpretation of the Christian faith, a policy that was operative throughout the Roman and Byzantine periods, during the Middle Ages, and from the Enlightenment to the present.

The author of the Letter of James identifies himself by that name, which is the English equivalent of Jacob. It was also the name of one of Jesus's first disciples and of his brother, who became the leader of the church in Jerusalem after Jesus's death. The sophisticated language of this letter makes it unlikely that it was written by a Galilean villager, however. Whoever the author was, he knew well the style of communication developed by the Cynic philosophers, whose approach was to pose questions and then provide answers in such a way as to challenge the reader and force rethinking of standard positions or easy assumptions. The issues with which

James is dealing are not those of Paul and the gospel writers: ritual purity, circumcision, Sabbath observance, the cosmic struggle between God and the powers of evil, the relationship between Judaism and the New Covenant people. Indeed, he addresses the church as "the twelve tribes" (1:1) or simply as "Israel" (5:13) and builds on quotations from the Jewish scriptures to make his points. Even when he refers to the commandment to love one's neighbor, he derives it from the Old Testament, with no mention of Jesus's use of this precept (2:8).

For James, the primary goal of the leader of the church is as teacher, and the goal is to develop wisdom (3:1–7). The good works produced by wisdom include the standard Stoic virtues of steadfastness and endurance (1:2–4). In Stoic sources, such as the third century B.C. Hymn of Cleanthes and the writings of Seneca (4 B.C.–46 C.E.), the basic principles are (1) the universal divine plan for the world, (2) human kinship with the gods through reason (*logos*), and (3) happiness attained by living in accord with the natural law inherent in the universe. This point of view is evident in James's call to his readers to be serious of purpose, to recognize the beneficence of God, and to live in accord with the perfect law (1:5–25). Questions of leadership roles or rank within the community are never discussed. Life in accord with wisdom will give stability and safety from political involvement and economic difficulties. The writing seems to have been addressed to intellectuals for discussion among themselves and with pagans who are oriented toward kindred philosophical outlooks.

The so-called Letter to the Hebrews, an anonymous writing, is an intellectual discourse, probably intended for oral presentation. It is based on the Old Testament, especially on two themes: What is God's purpose for his people? How can Israel have access to the presence of God? The answers are given in terms of a philosophical position similar to that adopted by Philo of Alexandria in the early first century A.D.: Platonism. The Platonic view of reality was that in the heavens there was an eternal sphere in which a master image or an eternal model exists for every object, concept, and relationship found in the earthly sphere. The earthly counterparts are time-bound, transitory, and multiple, whereas the heavenly ideal forms are single and eternal. The history of Israel, including the accounts of her leaders and the description of her sanctuary, is the disclosure of the time-bound copies of God's purpose for his people. Jesus, who has now entered heaven, is the revelation to faith of the eternal realities. His once-for-all sacrifice is a world removed from the repeated rites in the Jerusalem temple (8:1–13), which were only a shadow of what God planned for his own (10:1–22). The goal set forward is to enter that New Covenant people (12:22–24), although in the interim before that transport to the heavenly reality takes place, the members are to show mutual love and to manifest the qualities of the heavenly ideal. There are no ecclesiastical titles in the writing and only one possible reference to a community rite: the Eucharist (13:9). This imaginative work was a forerunner of the efforts of the theologians of the church to synthesize insights from the biblical and Christian traditions with those of the wider intellectual world.

The Move in the Second Century Toward Structural Unity and Conceptual Uniformity

At least three major factors impelled the leaders of Christianity in the early second century to clarify its identity and its goals for itself and for the Roman society it was penetrating. These were as follows:

1. The distinction between Christianity and Judaism, with which Christianity shared so many views and resources.

2. Christianity's attitude toward the Roman state; much standard Christian terminology had political implications (e.g., king, kingdom, universal rule).

3. The diversity of perceptions of Christian faith that had emerged in various parts of the empire.

From the founding of the Jewish state under the Maccabees in 168 B.C., its leaders had sought and gained the support of the Romans. The Romans responded by excusing Jews from certain obligations such as offering divine honors to the emperor, and granted them a degree of autonomy over their territories in Palestine. This was in part an effort to develop a sense of obligation toward Rome, since the Parthians (in what is now Persia and Iraq) were a constant threat of invasion of the Roman territories from the east. The two Jewish revolts against Rome—in A.D. 66–70 and 130–135—had failed, and the leadership of the Jewish people had passed to non-political religious leaders who fostered piety among Jews rather than fomenting revolution. So long as the Christians were considered to be a group within Judaism—since they shared the same scriptures and many of the historic and conceptual traditions—the Roman authorities were only occasionally active in repression of the Christian movement. Nero had had some Christian leaders killed during the latter part of his reign (A.D. 54–68), and there may have been some repression of Christians under Domitian (81–96). By the later years of Trajan's reign (98–117), however, the Christians had spread so widely throughout the empire and were defining themselves over against Judaism (as we have noted earlier in this chapter) that the Romans established the policy that Christians must publicly acknowledge the divinity of the emperor or be executed. The preserved correspondence between Trajan and Pliny, governor of provinces in northeast Asia Minor, make this explicit. Trajan and his successors would use this practice of divine honors as a way of symbolizing and enforcing loyalty.

The break with Judaism after A.D. 70 required the Christians to emphasize the beliefs that differentiated them from the Judaic tradition and that offered a potential for the inclusion of people from any ethnic or cultural background in the New Covenant community. The fact that the earlier expectation of Christians that Jesus would soon return in triumph did not take place led them to face the intellectual and organizational tasks of formulating goals for the movement and providing unifying organizational structures for the scattered Christian communities. Since they all claimed the Jesus tradition as the ground of their existence as a people of God, this tradition had to be interpreted in ways that would foster a sense of unity in the midst of their diversities. Similarly, if they were to survive in the face of mounting official and intellectual opposition, they had to be able to formulate their ethical norms and theological convictions in a coherent and effective way. The body of writings that emerged from this transition period of Christianity has come to be called by scholars as the writings of the Apostolic Fathers,[2] who in the period from about 100 to the middle of the second century were giving intellectual and organizational leadership to Christianity and doing so with a claim of continuity that reached back through the apostles to Jesus. These preserved works include the First and Second Letters of Clement; letters of Ignatius (bishop of Antioch) to several Greek and Roman churches; a letter of Polycarp (bishop of Smyrna in Asia Minor); an allegorical treatise, the Shepherd of Hermas; the Letter of Barnabas (whose name is linked with Paul); the story of the Martyrdom of Polycarp. In the nineteenth century a writing known as Didache (the teaching of the apostles) was found that showed close kinship with the writing of the Apostolic Fathers; it seems to have used a source—the Two Ways (to life and to death)—that lies behind the Letter of Barnabas.

Five themes run through these documents: (1) the prospect of martyrdom, (2) obedience to the church leaders, (3) differentiating Judaism from Christianity, (4) a pattern of behavior for Christians, and (5) true Christian doctrine. All these motifs are mixed with the issues of confrontation with Rome and the expectation of the end of the present age. The Martyrdom of Polycarp obviously emphasizes the first theme. The theme of martyrdom also appears in the Letter of Polycarp, in II Clement, and in Ignatius's letter to the Romans, in whose midst he was to be martyred under Trajan. The earliest full account of a martyrdom is the Martyrdom of Polycarp, which is a communication from a church in Smyrna (in Asia Minor) to another Christian community in Philomelium. It was written about the year 155. There is vivid description of the ghastly tortures that Christians experienced if they refused under pressure from the Roman authorities to renounce their faith in Christ. Some were beaten until their veins and arteries were exposed. The authorities told them that if they publicly denounced Christ and acknowledged Caesar as Lord they could go free. Polycarp, a bishop, had a vision that led him to expect death by burning at the hands of the Roman authorities. When caught by them, he refused to recant his faith and offered to instruct them in the Christian way. When preparations were made for putting him to death by fire, he asked that he not be fastened, promising to remain in the fire until his death. The account says that he was filled with courage and joy, and as the burning began he uttered public praise to God for

[2]Kirsopp Lake, trans., *The Apostolic Fathers*, Loeb Classical Library (Cambridge, MA: Harvard University Press, 1912–1913).

the knowledge he had received through Christ and for the opportunity to present himself as a living sacrifice to God. After his peaceful death in the midst of such horror, his followers were permitted to collect his bones to remember and honor his faithful witness.

As bishops, both Ignatius and Polycarp emphasized obedience to the two kinds of church leaders: the bishops (who are appointed by God) and the presbytery (the group of elders who make corporate decisions for the church). Didache mentions the role of apostles and prophets in the churches, in addition to that of the bishops and deacons (those who assume more workaday tasks in the churches). The importance of differentiating Christian faith and practice for that of the Jews is stressed by Ignatius in his letters to the Magnesians and the Philadelphians. The Letter of Barnabas and the Shepherd of Hermes, however, solve the problem of this interreligious relationship by interpreting the Jewish scriptures allegorically, on the assumption that they foreshadow the fuller disclosure of God's purpose through Jesus.

The writings that incorporate the Two Ways source (which may go back to the later first century A.D.) reflect the needs and procedures of the Christian communities. The Way of Life emphasizes love of God and neighbor, in addition to a long series of prohibitions. It then turns to advice for those who are receiving instruction as they join the churches, including how they are to live and how they are to accept responsibilities within the Christian community. Significantly, these moral instructions, like those found in I Clement and Ignatius (to the Ephesians) show the strong influence of Stoic ethics, which is evident in Christian writings as early as the letters of Paul. The effort to define and maintain true doctrine is evident in the Letter of Polycarp but especially in the letters of Ignatius, even though the details are not spelled out. Although most of the injunctions are to affirm the truth and reject heresy, one specified theme is docetism, which is the denial of the full humanity of Jesus: He merely seemed to take on human form. Ignatius directly denounces this view in his letter to the Smyrnaeans. It remained for the theological leaders of the church in the later first and subsequent centuries to make these issues more precise, but the attention drawn to them this early shows how important for Christian identity and community these questions were. Compounding the pressures from these matters were the growing confrontation between the church and the empire, the spontaneous movements within the church that attracted attention and followers while splitting the communities, and the small but significant attack on the credibility of the Christian claims by pagan intellectuals. It is to the specifics of these challenges and the Christian responses that we now turn.

Chapter 5

CHALLENGES TO CHRISTIANITY FROM ROMAN CULTURE

The Diversity and Vitality of Religious Options in the Empire

As Christianity began its spread across the Mediterranean world, it was moving into areas of competition, rather than filling a religious vacuum in an irreligious world. The religious movements of the early empire included a wide range of options, from ecstatic cults to staid philosophical groups wrestling with religious issues, from the imperial cult offering the emperors divine honors to small and large gatherings of devotees of various deities. Contrasting with the grand scale of those movements fostering the divinity of the emperor and celebrating the state—which he headed with the blessings of the gods—were myriad gatherings that met for the announced purpose of worshipping a deity or deities but that in the process provided a community in which participants could find meaning for life, mutual support, and the joys of social interchange. Both church and synagogue, which were launched along planned, organized lines in the second and subsequent centuries, were examples of this social phenomenon as well as beneficiaries of the widespread yearning for these forms of group identity.

The Imperial Cult

With the bestowing of divinity on the emperor Julius after his death, there was a growing disposition to treat the emperor as a manifestation of the divine, especially in the eastern Mediterranean, where the tradition of the divinity of kings reached back into earliest antiquity. Although Nero seems to have made some effort to promote his own status as divine, it was not until Domitian (81-96) that an emperor

75

announced that he was to be addressed as *Dominus et Deus* ("Lord and God"). That policy continued to develop until the time of Diocletian (284–305), when the imagery of the worship of the sun was associated with the emperor. In this role, the ruler of the empire became the symbol of truth and righteousness, and his function was to bring universal light to his subjects. Rather than merely promulgating such a policy, the emperors built grand structures in Rome and elsewhere throughout the empire to symbolize this universal authority and to provide the setting for solemn assemblies of the peoples of the Roman realms to link the power of the state with the celestial gods.

It is in keeping with these strategies that Trajan (98–117), in response to an inquiry from Pliny, the Roman governor of Bithynia and Pontus (provinces in north-eastern Asia Minor), confirmed a policy for dealing with Christian groups, as noted in Chapter 2. These groups were springing up or thriving throughout the provinces in numbers large enough to diminish participation in the prescribed ceremonies and sacrifices through which subjects of Rome were to give public expression to their devotion to the emperor and gratitude to the traditional Roman gods for the peace and prosperity they enjoyed. In one of the larger cities of the area, Nicomedia, Trajan had constructed a great Temple of Rome and Augustus. Yet throughout the provinces, those who prepared the appropriate animal sacrifices were running out of customers. What was to be done? Were the Christians, with their seeming disregard or even hostility toward Roman power and its divine sources, to be sought out, apprehended, and executed? Pliny's inquiry and Trajan's reply have both been pre-served.[1] The governor had found nothing evil or subversive about the practices, worship, or food of the Christians, or even that they were engaged in illegal political activities. The crucial test came when members of this group refused to repeat an invocation to the Roman gods and to offer "adoration, with wine and frankincense" to the image of the emperor, and to curse Christ. Those who refused to perform these religious acts were executed. Trajan confirmed Pliny's policy, adding that the Christians were not to be sought out or seized without proper evidence, but when they were exposed and persisted in taking a position that put them outside of Roman society—what Pliny called "a depraved and excessive superstition"—they were to be put to death. The link between religious performance and loyalty to the state was firm. Christians, by identifying themselves with another community—the people of the New Covenant—and by their refusal to honor either the gods who had blessed the Roman state and the agent they had designated to preside over it, demonstrated that they were its mortal enemies. The seriousness with which the consequences of this principle were applied by subsequent emperors varied widely, but it culminated in fierce conflict (Chapter 8).

[1]Available in "Pliny's Correspondence with Trajan." Greek text and English translation in *Pliny* (sec. 96–97), W. M. L. Hutchison, trans., The Loeb Classical Library (Cambridge, MA: Harvard University Press, 1952).

Popular Associations and Cults

As noted at the opening of this chapter, in the ethnically, geographically, socially, and culturally complex world of the Roman empire, people with similar backgrounds, interests, or occupations banded together in clubs or voluntary associations to find or to preserve a sense of identity and common interests. These groups met in homes, taverns, or club rooms. Drawn mostly from the lower classes (which constituted the vast majority of the population of the empire), they would designate some deity or deities as their patrons and honor these gods in formal ways as their protectors and helpers. The rallying point might be area of origin or occupation (like the guilds of a later era). Borrowing the term that was used for the lounging areas in the public baths, their meeting places were called *scholae*. There the members shared their common concerns and ate common meals.

Other social groupings that flourished in the second century were those devoted explicitly to honoring a deity—usually one not in the traditional Roman pantheon but readily adaptable to Roman social and cultural patterns. One of these was Asklepios, the god of healing. He was venerated chiefly at Epidauros in Greece and at Pergamum in Asia Minor. In addition, there were centers in honor of this god at Alexandria in Egypt and on the Greek island of Cos, where human anatomy was studied and training was offered for those interested in the practice of medicine. At the shrines of Asklepios, however, the sick and the wealthy—of the sort that in our time spend long periods at health resorts and spas—took up residence for extended stays during which they would visit the shrine, hoping for evidence of the god's presence and of his healing powers. From the third century B.C. down to the late second century A.D., there have survived inscriptions and texts that tell of the healings said to have been performed by Asklepios at Epidauros, including recovery from blindness, broken limbs, extended pregnancies, leeches, dropsy, tuberculosis, and disfigurement from various kinds of physical attack.

The shrines functioned like modern outpatient clinics, where the ailing came to regain their health through the kindness of the healing god, as the testimonies left behind affirm. An important additional factor in reports of those who stayed at these healing shrines is also similar to what may be found at modern spas: Persons spending long periods there were at least as much interested in the social connections they made and in the time for self-examination as in recovering physical health. For example, in the middle of the second century, Aelius Aristides, who had inherited great wealth and had made an enviable reputation as a public orator in Athens and Rome, became ill and went to Pergamum, presumably in search of health. But he lingered long at the Asklepion in Pergamum and recorded his thoughts, observations, and experiences of the divine in that situation. What he found was not so much restoration of the body as renewal of the soul, great happiness in his new-found sense of the god's presence with and interest in him. In dreams and direct visions, he claimed that the god appeared to him, giving him assurance and comfort, new meaning and purpose in life.

Similarly, Isis (whose earlier roles among the Egyptian deities we have already noted) came to be viewed in the Roman period as the benefactress of those stricken with disease or injury. Diodorus Siculus wrote of Isis in the first century B.C.,

> For standing above the sick in their sleep she gives aid for their diseases and works remarkable cures upon such as submit themselves to her; and many who have been despaired of by their physicians because of the difficult nature of their malady are restored to health by her, while numbers who have altogether lost the use of their eyes or some other part of the body, whenever they turn to help to this goddess are restored to their previous condition.[2]

By the middle of the second century, however, her role as healer had been matched by the experience of her in mystical self-disclosure that her devotees reported.

In Lucius Apuleius's *Metamorphoses*, the author reports how, following years of wandering about the world and the catastrophe of having been changed by magic into an ass, he recovered both his true humanity and a sense of purpose in the world through an appearance to him of Isis in one of her temples. He addresses her directly as follows:

> O holy and blessed dame, the perpetual comfort of human kind, who by thy bounty and grace nourishes all the world, and bears a great affection to the adversities of the miserable as a loving mother. You take no rest, night or day, neither are you idle at any time in giving benefits and succouring all humans on land as on the sea; you are the one who puts away all storms and dangers from human lives by stretching forth your right hand, by which also you unweave even the inextricable and tangled web of fate, and appease the great storms of fortune, and keep back the harmful course of the stars; you make the earth turn; you give light to the sun, you govern the world. You tread down the power of hell. By means of you the stars give answer, the seasons return, the elements serve; at your commandment the winds blow, the clouds nourish the earth, the seeds prosper, and the fruits grow. Birds of the air, beasts of the hills, serpents in their lairs, and fish of the sea tremble before your majesty. But my spirit is not able to give you adequate praise; my possessions are unable to provide adequate sacrifices; my voice lacks the power to utter what I think of your majesty— no, not even if I had a thousand mouths and as many tongues and could continue forever. Even so, as a good religious person, I shall do what I can: I shall always

[2]Diodorus Siculus, *Library of History* (1.25.3), R. M. Geer, trans., Loeb Classical Library (Cambridge, MA: Harvard University Press, 1944).

keep your divine appearance in my remembrance, and within my heart I shall enclose your most holy divinity.[3]

The mixture of personal adoration, gratitude for renewal of life, and sense of the inner presence are powerfully conveyed in this hymn to Isis. The conclusion of the story tells how Apuleius became a priest in her temple, thus locating the core of his life in the community of her followers.

Obviously, as individuals and in groups, many persons were finding meaning and a shared, enriched existence through their dedication to a beneficent deity. This growing and pervasive concern to attune one's life to the will and purpose of the gods is evident in the simplest to the highest levels of Roman society in the second and subsequent centuries. Even the emperors are reported as consulting astrologers when important matters of state were to be decided. In the upper classes there was widespread belief, not only in the miracle-working gods and goddesses, but also in magic. To gain certain benefits, as well as to protect oneself from the attacks of personal enemies, magical rites were performed and magical formulas recited as a way of guaranteeing the desired results for one's own benefit or for the detriment of one's foes. Among documents of this period found in Egypt (known to scholars as the *Greek Magical Papyri*) is the following, which shows how invoking the name of a god guarantees the results desired by the one making the request:

By your name, which I have in my soul and which I invoke, there shall come to me to be in every way good things, good upon good, thoroughly, unconditionally you shall grant me health, salvation, welfare, glory, victory, strength, contentment. Cast a veil on the eyes of all who oppose me, male and female, and give me grace in all my activities.[4]

This is not a request to the god but a demand based on the use of the divine name. Magicians claimed to know the right names and formulas that would guarantee the desired results.

Literary figures of the time were reviving and offering fresh, often symbolic, interpretations of the traditional myths and legends of the Greek and Roman deities. For example, Plutarch (46–120) prepared an elaborate edition of the myths of Osiris and Isis that was intended to serve as information and guidelines for contemporary worshippers of these gods, rather than as an archive of a dead past. The question was not historical—What were the ancient gods like?—but contemporary: What can these gods do for me now? The fact that Plutarch's approach was right for his time

---

[3]Lucius Apuleius, *Metamorphoses* (XI.25), W. Adlington, trans., Loeb Classical Library (Cambridge, MA: Harvard University Press, 1915).

[4]This quotation is from *Greek Magical Papyri* (XIII, 788–809), in H. C. Kee, trans., *Medicine, Miracle and Magic in New Testament Times* (New York: Cambridge University Press, 1988, p. 108).

is attested by the popularity of his work over subsequent centuries. Groups of seekers were reaching out for direct experience of the gods as a way of orienting and fulfilling their own lives.

Popular Philosophical Movements

At the highest intellectual levels in the second century, there was a surge of interest in philosophy that took as its aim the recovery and fresh appropriation of older traditions. Much of the effort took the form of a rebirth of the philosophical traditions of ancient Attica, of which Athens was the political and intellectual center. Assigning a name derived from *sophos*, the Greek word for "wisdom," scholars designate this period of cultural development as the Second Sophistic. Dio Chrysostom (45–115), for example, sought to replace what he regarded as the cheap commonplaces of ideas, practices, and modes of communication of his day by a recovery of Attic culture. Similarly, Herodes Atticus (101–178), an extremely wealthy Athenian philosopher, worked hard at reviving the heritage of Greece in philosophy, literature, and above all in rhetoric, the speech art that could engage and inform crowds of listeners. Even though Lucian of Samosata (120–200?) developed a delightful and effective style of comic dialogue by which he scoffed at wealth and power, belittling the gods, caricaturing the ancient myths and the great events of the past, the very fact that he chose these areas as his battleground shows how important these factors were in the culture of that era. His own goal was to enable his readers to rise above human fears and follies; his tactic was to expose what he regarded as the pretentions and uncertainties in the shifting religious and philosophical trends of his time.

The seriously developed philosophical movements of this period sought to reclaim Platonic, Aristotelian, Pythagorean, and Stoic concepts and perspectives. The original Platonic preoccupation with metaphysical questions—such as how ultimate reality can be discerned behind and beyond the varied, changing, decaying physical world—was overshadowed in this period by ethical and human issues. The Stoic principle of natural law as pervading the universe and being operative in the human conscience (that is, shared awareness of this universal law) was combined with the Aristotelian interest in analyzing all reality by classifying it into appropriate intellectual categories. The result was a new synthetic philosophy focused on the natural world and the place of humanity within it. The Stoics of this period were moving beyond their earlier major interest in describing the natural world and then depicting humanity's place within it to consider directly personal religious longing and experience of the gods. This shift is evident in the historical examples of individual and social moral responsibility set out by Seneca (4 B.C.–65 A.D.?). Already in Seneca there is emphasis on the pervasive presence of God, not only in the natural realm but within personal experience. In his *Moral Epistles* (41.1) he wrote: "God is near you, he is with you, he is in you."

The philosophy of Pythagoras (582–507? B.C.E.), with its major emphasis on the mathematical structures of the physical world, was also revived in this period, but the emphasis shifted overwhelmingly from the structures of nature to this philosopher's discussion of the human soul, which Pythagoras had taught was released from the body at death to take up residence in another body, human or animal. The new version of this theory regarded the body as the prison of the soul and saw philosophy as the means of purifying the soul so that it could understand its origin and destiny, and could ascend ultimately to the celestial realms. A similar view was developed by Plutarch (46–120), who taught that there were *daimones*, beings intermediate between the gods and humans, through whom the gods act in human affairs, communicating through visions and oracles. The discerning human may at death take up new existence as a *daimon* and eventually ascend to the realm of the gods.

In the same period, many persons shared these philosophical ideas, but some were more skeptical about the possibilities for human happiness. The aim of the great Stoic philosopher, Zeno (336–264 B.C.?), to seek the good was replaced by the philosophy of Epictetus (50–120?) who wanted to avoid everything in life which is not subject to our control, except the attempt to achieve our own moral aims. Thus, one should avoid anger, desires, sorrow, and anxiety. To achieve this style of life, Epictetus recommended that philosophers should gain true freedom by divesting themselves of family, wealth, and permanent residences and should wander about the earth, challenging the almost universally accepted values, living on the basis of the generosity of those who received and cared for these itinerant critics of society, bearded and dressed in ragged clothing. Epictetus characterized himself in this way: "Look at me! I am without house or city, property or slave. I sleep on the ground. I have no wife, no children, no official residence, but only earth and sky and my bit of a cloak. Am I not without distress or fear? Am I not free?"

At the other end of the socioeconomic scale, the philosopher-emperor, Marcus Aurelius (161–180), while affirming the essential goodness of Providence, was painfully aware of human sin and widespread wickedness in the world. He longed for a life of freedom but expected to find it only beyond death. Yet so deep was his despair of human existence that he was ready to accept extinction if that is what lies beyond life as he experienced it in all its frustrations and cruelty. The issues of the meaning of life, of understanding human evil and natural disaster, of ultimate human destiny were the dominant questions in popular consciousness, from simple handworkers to the head of the empire.

Direct Challenges to Christianity

Was Christianity ready to give adequate responses to these profound and universal problems that dominated popular consciousness in the second century? Answers

81

ranging from flat dismissal of Christianity to qualified criticisms of it were offered by central thinkers in the Roman world of this period.

Included among the works of Lucian of Samosata, whose critique of his contemporaries we noted earlier, was a story called, "The Death of Peregrinus." Peregrinus is depicted as a wanderer in both the literal and the ideological sense. As he roamed the eastern Mediterranean world, he tried out a series of religions and philosophies, one of which was Christianity, which he encountered in its birthplace, Palestine. He met some Christians there and "picked up their queer creed" (Sec. 11–16). He succeeded in convincing them of his superior qualifications as a member of their group, with the result that he became a prophet in their movement, then an elder, and finally a ruler of one of their meetings. He not only expounded the Christian writings but wrote some of his own for them. They accepted his guidelines and made him leader of their sect. Lucian notes in passing that the Christians even to his own time continued to worship the man who had introduced their peculiar rites and ended by being crucified. Peregrinus was imprisoned by the local political authorities (the Roman rulers of the land) and was cared for in prison by the Christians who, while seeking to have him released, visited him regularly, took him food, and even bribed the jailers to be allowed to stay in the cell with him. Others, including some widows and orphans, were imprisoned because of their sympathy for him. Christian delegations were sent in support of him from as far away as the cities of Asia Minor. Lucian remarks, "The activity of these people in dealing with any matter that affects their community is something extraordinary: they spare neither trouble nor expense." It is because "these misguided creatures" believe that they are forever immortal that they scorn death and manifest the voluntary devotion that is so common among them. From the moment of conversion to this religion, they deny the gods of Greece, worship the crucified sage, and live according to his laws. They despise all worldly goods, regarding what each possesses as the property of the whole community. Some of them have adopted the garb of the philosophers: long hair, shabby cloak, philosopher's handbag and staff. Their support for Peregrinus continued until he discredited himself among them, perhaps by eating some kind of forbidden food. Lucian's scornful portrayal of the gullibility and strange values of the Christians builds on his low estimate of their beliefs, but it also betrays a kind of unconscious admiration of them for their devotion and courage.

A more reasoned criticism of the Christians is to be found in the extensive writings of Galen (129–199), a major figure in the development of ancient medical tradition. In his treatise *On Medical Experience*, he rejected the belief in creation shared by Jews and Christians: If God waited in time to create the world he was either holding back from the establishment of the greatest good, and therefore morally irresponsible, or unable to accomplish the creation, and therefore limited in power. Galen deplored the degeneration of the philosophical schools of his day into warring factions that adopted fixed, exclusivist positions, rather than engaging freely in the common search for truth. Among the worst offenders on this score were the schools of Moses and

Jesus: Judaism and Christianity. Galen felt that his fellow physicians who made decisions on the basis of prior theory rather than being open to trial-and-error methods of experimentation were like these Jewish and Christian dogmatists. Since only a small number of human beings had the capacity to develop or follow logically consistent arguments, most people turned (as did the Jews and Christians) from rationality to myths and parables, appealing to miracles to support their truth claims. Rhetoric and poetry could lead people to conviction but not to truth. Ironically, Galen acknowledged that the Christians, in spite of the major flaws in their logical methods, did attain as high a level of morality as the philosophers but they could not be considered true philosophers because of their irrational base and procedures. As he stated it:

> [The Christians'] contempt of death and of its sequel is patent to us every day, and likewise their restraint in cohabitation. For they include not only men but also women who refrain from cohabiting all through their lives; and they also number individuals who in self-discipline and self-control in matters of food and drink and in their keen pursuit of justice have attained a pitch not inferior to that of genuine philosophers.[5]

Their assumptions were unreasonable, he said, and their methods logically deplorable, but they did exhibit one of the highest of human virtues in the Greek philosophical tradition: *sophrosune*, which means "moderation, rationality, self-control."

More negatively critical of Christians was Celsus.[6] Celsus was a Roman philosopher of the later second century, whose work is known only through the extended quotations preserved in the rebuttal by the great Christian scholar and biblical interpreter, Origen of Alexandria (185–254) in his huge work, *Contra Celsum* ("Against Celsus"). The elaborate nature of Celsus's attack on Christianity shows that the movement was sufficiently broad and visible—and appealing—to come to the attention of intellectuals. It is clear that Celsus knew the New Testament writings, as well as the claims that were being made in the second century by various competing Christian groups, such as the Gnostics and the followers of Marcion. His tactic was that of a scornful critic, alternating between exposing the follies of his opponents and offering his own alternative points of view. Five themes run throughout the work:

1. The Christians relied on miracle and magic. The miracles Jesus is reported to

---

[5]Quoted from the translation of an Arabic version of one of Galen's treatises, in Richard Walzer, *Galen on Jews and Christians* (London: Oxford University Press, 1949), p. 65.

[6]Celsus's writing, *The True Doctrine*, is mentioned by Eusebius in his *Ecclesiastical History* (6.36.2) as having evoked a half century later the detailed response of Origen. This Celsus, whose orientation is clearly Platonic, is not to be identified with Celsus the Epicurean mentioned by Lucian.

have performed, including the feeding of the multitudes, are evidence that he practiced sorcery. Jesus made this accusation against his opponents, but it is applicable to him as well. He invented the story of his virgin birth and went to Egypt to learn magic. Celsus believed that if miracles of healing occurred anywhere, it was at the shrines of Asklepios, which were open to all who sought to have their needs met. These powers were not limited to Jesus, in whose behalf his followers made the preposterous claim of the resurrection of the body—his and ultimately theirs. There was abundant public testimony, on the other hand, to the healing powers of the Greek god Asklepios.

2. Christianity was a low-class movement. From the outset, Jesus appealed to the ignorant and the gullible among his contemporaries, having chosen ten or eleven infamous men of wholly undistinguished background to form the inner circle of his followers. Christianity was primarily interested in sinners, rather than in the educated or the intelligent strata of society. It failed to rely on cumulative human wisdom, treating it, rather, with scorn. Healing and prophecy, with which the Christians were obsessed, were trivial factors in human existence as compared with the life of the mind, which Christians ignored or demeaned. As for the boastful attitude Christians took toward Jesus and the martyrs of the early church, those who suffered and died in the cause of philosophical truth were far more noble and admirable. In this connection, Celsus tells the story of the Epicurean philosopher, Epictetus, who was being tortured by those opposed to his philosophical views. When they twisted his leg, "he smiled gently and said, 'You are breaking it.' And when [his tormentor] had broken it, he said, Did I not tell you you were breaking it?' "[7] For Celsus, this was true wisdom and humanity.

3. Jesus could not have been divine. Celsus raised a series of questions that he was convinced completely discredited the Christian claim that Jesus was God in human form. If Jesus had really been God, he should not have had to flee to Egypt to escape his attackers or have allowed himself to be put to death. Indeed, if he was God, why did he need someone to open the tomb to let him out? When he arose from the dead, as his followers claimed, why did he show himself only to them and not to the power figures who had conspired to put him to death? The prophecies it is said that he fulfilled are so general as to be applicable to a number of other human beings. In fact, Celsus insisted, the contradictory features of the gospel showed that his followers were trying to cover up the disparities between what they claimed for him and his actual competence. He was simply powerless before the authorities of his day. Accepting a charge made by Jewish critics of Christianity in the second century, Celsus asserted that Jesus was really not the Son of God but the illegitimate offspring of a Roman soldier, Pantheros. The Christians unwittingly betrayed the emptiness of their claim about Jesus's divinity in that they worshiped a corpse.

4. The Jewish-Christian view of God is preposterous. If the God of the Jews and

---

[7]Henry Chadwick, trans., *Contra Celsum* (7.54) (New York: Cambridge University Press, 1965).

Christians created the world, and did so in the realm of time, why did he wait so long to reveal himself? The result was that many human beings never had an opportunity to know him. And why when he chose to reveal himself through Jesus did he do so in such a limited sphere, thereby excluding from participation the majority of the human race? Why did the Jews and Christians claim that God created the universe for the benefit of human beings, rather than recognizing the interdependence that characterizes every feature of the cosmic order? Why did this God create the serpent as the embodiment of evil and turn it loose on humanity if he was going to hold men and women responsible for their misdeeds? Celsus was convinced that the basic difficulties of this view of God were evident in the fact that Jews and Christians differed between their groups and even among their own kind as to how the world was created and who was responsible for it. Both Jews and Christians adopted the subterfuge of covering up the difficulties in their view of God by resorting to allegorical interpretation of their scriptures, which saved them from affirming the obvious meaning of the texts.

5. Celsus's alternative: One God behind the many names. Celsus affirms that there is and always has been a single god accessible to humanity through reason. The name assigned to this deity is inconsequential because it derives from local factors, rather than from the cosmic source of reality. Plato's view of the world as consisting of an eternal sphere of unchanging being, of which the material universe is an imperfect and ever-changing copy, was to be affirmed and taken as the base for understanding god. God is known through the mind, rather than the body of flesh, as the foolish Christian claim about God incarnate in Jesus assumed. There were, he acknowledged, some admirable moral truths affirmed by the Jews and Christians, such as love of one's neighbor. But these ethical insights were already present in the writings of the Greek philosophers, just as there were oracles and prophecies at work in other religions as well. The Christians were so foolish as to employ the human, fleshly Jesus as their base for understanding God and his purpose for the cosmos. What Celsus longed to see was all human beings acknowledge the one god behind and beyond the language, images, and modes of worship by which various segments of the human race approached and worshiped him. All must recognize that all were serving the one ultimate deity of the universe.

In setting out these stinging criticisms of Judaism and Christianity, Celsus made two charges that were especially important within the wider Roman culture of that time. The first was that the Christians were seditious, in that they separated themselves out from the rest of the human race, instead of affirming and working toward the basic unity of humanity. The second accusation was that the Christians, by their refusal to acknowledge and honor the traditional gods of Greece and Rome, were raising the possibility of a divine retaliation that could work harm on the human race as a whole and on the Roman empire in particular. The security and the prosperity of the empire and its people were linked with the popular celebrations and expressions of gratitude to the god behind the gods, in which the Christians refused to participate even under threat of execution.

The most powerful and carefully reasoned attack on Christianity came in the later third century through Porphyry, a pupil of Plotinus and a leading figure in the Neoplatonic philosophical movement in this period. A prolific writer, he produced a work in fifteen volumes, *Against the Christians*. Although this work was later officially destroyed when in the fourth century Christianity became the dominant religion in the empire under Constantine, quotations from it have survived in Eusebius's *Church History* and in other Christian writings in subsequent centuries. Attacking what he regarded as an antiintellectual streak in Christianity, Porphyry observed that what Moses is reported to have said includes riddles, which are treated by Jews and Christians as divine oracles, full of hidden mysteries. He considered this way of treating the puzzling passages from the Bible as a trick to avoid the intellectual difficulties involved: "[They] bewitch the mental judgment by their own pretentious obscurity," and through this tactic put forward their own interpretation. They treat the prophecy of Daniel as a document from the sixth-century exile of Israel in Babylon, whereas it is actually from the Hellenistic period and was written during the reign of Antiochus Epiphanes, who was pagan ruler of Syria and Palestine in the early second century B.C. Modern scholarship would agree with Porphyry's shrewd perception, but his charge was intended to display the gullibility and antiintellectual qualities of Jews and Christians who regarded the book of Daniel as being actually from the earlier period. On the question of the intellectual level of the Christians, Porphyry acknowledged the brilliance of Origen of Alexandria, probably the leading scholarly figure of the first four centuries of the church, but sought to expose him as what today would be called a charlatan and a schizophrenic. Although Porphyry admitted Origen's enormous range of linguistic competence and breadth of learning in history, science, and philosophy, as well as his repute and attractiveness as a teacher sought out by pagans and Christians alike, he claimed that Origen was intellectually completely in the Greek tradition, yet he lived a Christian way of life that was contrary to Greek learning as well as Roman law.

As for his view of Jesus, Porphyry heaped scorn on the defenselessness of Jesus on trial before Pontius Pilate. If he truly possessed all the learning and insight that the Christians claimed for him, Porphyry asked, why did he not make a case for himself before Pilate? His behavior was personally and intellectually cowardly. Porphyry found detestable the notion that a divine being took up residence in the womb of Mary, "that it became an embryo, and after birth was wrapped in rags, soiled with blood and bile, and even worse." His estimate of Christianity as a whole was forcefully expressed in a passage quoted by Augustine. A man whose wife had turned from traditional pagan religion to Christianity sought counsel from the oracle of Apollo as to how he might recover her from her present commitment to Christianity, to which Apollo replied:

You may perchance more easily write in lasting letters on water, or spread wings and fly like a bird through the air, than recall to her senses an impious wife who has once polluted herself [through conversion to Christianity]. Let her continue as long as she pleases, persisting in her empty delusions, and lamenting in song one who, as a god, died for delusions, who was condemned justly by judges whose verdict was just, and executed by the worst death in iron shackles.[8]

The Issue between Christianity and the Empire: What Shapes the Destiny of Rome?

The strategy of Porphyry's attack on Christianity sounds like the in-fighting that was going on generally among philosophers of this period. What is surprising is that a leading intellectual would see Christianity as such a challenge that he would devote fifteen volumes to the effort to discredit it. These fragments quoted from Porphyry show how scornful many pagan intellectuals were of the claim made for Christ by his followers but also how the movement was penetrating Roman society and culture at many different levels. What was at stake was not only the future of the church but also the fate of the empire. How were the leaders and the people of the Roman world to perceive the future of the empire? Was the possibility a real one that, if the populace in growing numbers abandoned the traditional rites and sacrifices in honor of the ancient gods of Greece and Rome, the latter would exact penalties, sending political or natural catastrophes? To guarantee the future of the empire, was it essential that its leaders forcefully require all its subjects to observe the ceremonies carried out to ensure peace and prosperity, or would the decline of the official cults lead to Rome's barbarian neighbors to the north and east taking over the imperial lands?

Or was the continuing threat to the empire and the pervasive movement that refused to participate in the traditional state cult an indication that a new epoch in the life of the empire was in store? If the Christians were right, God was at work in history to fulfill his purpose for and through his people and to create a new, potentially universal community. Was that going to take place, and if so, by what stages? Before an answer to such fundamental questions could be reached, the power of the Roman state felt obligated to try to eradicate this movement (Chapter 8). Meanwhile, however, the Christians were having to develop a rational defense for their faith in the face of possible martyrdom (Chapter 6). And they were also having to strive for some kinds of uniformity within the movement in light of the radical ways in which the Christian tradition was being interpreted (Chapter 7). It is to this series of responses to challenge that we now turn.

[8]Augustine, *The City of God* (19.23), in *The Fathers of the Church*, Vol. 1 (Washington, D.C.: Catholic University Press of America, 1947).

The site of the Dead Sea
community at Qumran, where the
Dead Sea Scrolls were produced.
(Howard C. Kee)

The ruins of Sebaste,
the capital of Samaria,
where descendants of
the northern tribes of
Israel lived, worshipping
God in their own
nearby temple on
Mount Gerizim.
(Howard C. Kee)

The site of the temple in
Jerusalem from the
Mount of Olives. Only
the massive retaining
wall remains of this
monumental structure
built by Herod the Great.
(Israel Government
Tourist Office)

The Tholos at Delphi in Greece, to which seekers came from all over the Mediterranean world to obtain answers to their problems through the oracle of Apollo there. (Howard C. Kee)

The Acropolis at Athens, with the Parthenon (temple of Athena) above and the Areopagus (Hill of Ares) in the foregound, where Paul addressed the Athenian council. (Agora Excavations, Athens)

A fourth-century C.E. synagogue pavement in Galilee, which shows by the Greek inscriptions and the signs of the zodiac how heavily influenced Palestinian Judaism was by hellenistic culture. (Israel Government Tourist Office)

A Christian sarcophagus portraying Jesus being baptized by John the Baptist, with the Spirit descending as a dove. (Howard C. Kee)

The sacred treasures, which are being carried in triumph from the Jerusalem temple following the fall of that city to the Romans in 70 C.E., is portrayed on the Arch of Titus in Rome. (Howard C. Kee)

The Roman forum was the seat of imperial power; the senate met in the rectangular, nearly windowless building. (Howard C. Kee)

A portrait of Christ as a triumphant figure from the Catacomb of Domitilla, the underground burial chambers which were named after a convert to Christianity who was a member of the family of the emperor Domitian. (Howard C. Kee)

A reconstruction of a third-century C.E. Christian baptistry at Dura Europos in eastern Syria, which was found in proximity with a Jewish synagogue and a shrine of the god Mithra. (Howard C. Kee)

An illuminated manuscript of the Bible, Codex Purpureus (sixth–seventh century C.E.) picturing the wise and foolish virgins described in Jesus' parable (Matthew 25). (Giraudon/Art Resource)

Chapter 6

CHRISTIAN RESPONSES TO THE CHALLENGES FROM THE CULTURE

By the middle of the second century C.E., the leadership and the attitudes of the church toward the Roman culture and the empire had changed significantly. In Jerusalem, where the movement had had its center under James, the brother of Jesus, and the other apostles, the Jewish-Christian leaders had fled at the time of the first Jewish revolt against the Romans in 66–70 C.E. They took up residence in Pella, on the eastern side of the Jordan Valley south of the Sea of Galilee.[1] Their fate is not reported, but the Jewish-Christian leadership in Jerusalem was replaced by Gentiles during the reign of Hadrian in 120, as Eusebius notes.[2]

The Christians continued their claim to be the true heirs of the biblical traditions of the Jewish Bible, but the issues of Christian attitude toward the Jewish cultic laws died out with the destruction of the Jerusalem temple and the emergence of rabbinic Judaism, with its exclusive claim to be the heir of the biblical tradition. Although Jerusalem continued to be an important center of the church in the eastern Mediterranean, it was at Caesarea by the sea and at Alexandria in Egypt that the vitality of the cultural life of the church was most clearly evident. Both these cities were centers of Greco-Roman culture and learning, and in both of them the Christians took on the challenge of coming to terms with that culture in ways that were both constructive and critical. In each place, the Christians developed schools for the instruction of their leaders that became major factors in shaping the life and thought of Christians for subsequent centuries.

Like the Jewish intellectual activities in Alexandria in the early decades of the

---

[1]Eusebius, *Church History* (3.5). Quotations throughout from an edition of *Church History*, Kirsopp Lake, trans., Loeb Classical Library (Cambridge, MA: Harvard University Press, 1926, 1965).
[2]Eusebius, *Church History*, 4.5.

first century C.E., as represented by Philo, there was a major effort by the Christian leaders there to correlate the higher learning from the Greco-Roman world with the special insights into the nature and purpose of God in the biblical tradition. In contrast to the Jews, however, the Christians claimed that God had brought this fuller and final disclosure of his plan for the human race through Jesus. In Rome and Carthage, which were the major centers of Roman culture in the western Mediterranean world, the issues that dominated the thought of the church were different:

> What were the criteria for gaining and maintaining membership within the Christian community?
>
> How were the sacraments of baptism and the eucharist to be understood, and who was qualified to administer them and to participate in them?
>
> What were the true teachings of the Christian church, and who was authorized to define these doctrines?

Stated in more traditional terms: How was Christian orthodoxy to be defined?

Equally as important for the church as the adjudication of these internal issues was the developing attitude toward the Christian movement on the part of both the political and the intellectual leaders of the Roman world. Among those who spoke for Christianity were some who had been trained in the best that the Greco-Roman intellectual tradition had to offer. These persons offered reasoned explanatory justifications for what the Christians believed and taught. The Greeks called this strategy an *apologia*, which means "defense" or "rationale," rather than "apology" in the modern sense of providing an excuse. Hence, these leaders of the church have come to be known as the Apologist Fathers. Their skills and self-confidence were such that they addressed their declarations to the emperor and to their non-Christian intellectual contemporaries, rather than limiting their audience to members of the movement. Jesus was portrayed as primarily a teacher, who gave instructions to his followers that they, as apostles, passed on to successive generations. For example, the effort was made by Melito of Sardis (died ca. 177 C.E.) to show that Christianity had been free of conflict with the empire and that it had flourished since the days of Augustus, except during the mad reign of Nero and briefly under Domitian. Hadrian (117–138) had set the example of declining to take negative action against what Melito terms "our philosophy."

Theophilus of Antioch (died ca. 185) claimed to be the sixth to have succeeded Peter in leadership of the church there, and he presented the Christian program as primarily one of instruction, including the weeding out of false or inappropriate teaching. By 180 a catechetical school had been established in Alexandria for the intellectual training of potential leaders of the church. Led first by Pantaenus, it was headed subsequently by two of the early church's greatest scholars, Clement and Origen, whose work we examine later. The major concern of these leaders of the church in the second century was to answer constructively the intellectual and political charges that were being made against developing Christianity. As early as 125, a Christian thinker from Asia Minor named Quadratus addressed an apology directly to Hadrian. In the second half of the second century, Athenagoras of Athens wrote to the emperor Marcus Aurelius (161–180) to reject the charge that Christians were atheists and to defend their claims that God had spoken through the prophets and definitively through his Son. On the latter point, he asserted that Jesus was "the First-begotten of the Father, not as having been produced through human birth processes—for from the beginning God had the Word in Himself, God being eternal mind and eternally rational—but as coming forth to be the model and energizing force of all material things."[3] The three Christian thinkers whose extensive writings provide the fullest picture of this effort to defend and commend the Christian faith to the wider Roman political and intellectual world are Justin, Clement of Alexandria, and Origen.

Justin Martyr (100–165 C.E.*)*

A pagan native of the Hellenistic Palestinian city, Flavia Neapolis (modern Nablus), Justin explored the major philosophical options of his day—those of the Stoics, Aristotle, Pythagoras, and Plato—before turning to an investigation of Christianity. He wandered about the Mediterranean world as a Christian philosopher, finally settling in Rome, where he founded a Christian school. His two major writings that have survived are both apologies, one addressed to Jews and the other to Gentiles.

    The first of these is an apology addressed to a Jew, Trypho, but one can infer from Justin's way of dealing with what Christians came to call the Old Testament that his line of argument is as important for showing Christians how to understand this history and literature as it is to convince Trypho about the Christian claims derived from the Jewish scriptures. Justin claims that the new covenant disclosed through Jesus, and for the establishment of which Jesus is the agent of God, has displaced the successive covenants with Israel described in the Bible and is now God's instrument to bring the light of knowledge of him to all nations. Jesus was attested in this role by his works, and especially by the miracles he performed, and is now the embodiment of the new law and the new covenant. Christians are the true heirs of the patriarchs of Israel, many of whom lived and died before such rites as circumcision and such rules as abstinence from work on the sabbath had been instituted through Moses. Jews have abandoned the everlasting, inclusive covenant promised through David and the prophets, but it is now open to all through Jesus. It is Jesus to whom the Jewish scriptures point, Justin maintains. Even details of the

---

[3]Quoted from William A. Jurgens, trans. and ed., *The Faith of the Early Fathers*, Vol. 1 (Collegeville, MN: The Liturgical Press, 1970), p. 70.

ritual requirements may rightly be understood allegorically or metaphorically as pointing to Christ. This way of understanding the Jewish scriptures proves that Jesus is one with God, and the Christians are the true Israelite race, the authentic offspring of Abraham.

In his "Apology to the Gentiles," which is addressed to the emperor Antoninus Pius (138–161) and to the Roman senate and people, Justin describes Christianity as a rational search for truth and invites dialogue or debate about it on philosophical grounds. In connection with his appeal to philosophy, he quotes approvingly Plato's wish that philosophers would be the rulers of society. Indeed, the truth that Plato conveys is derived from Moses, who preceded Plato in time, and from whom the philosopher borrowed his ideas of the creation of the world. Justin goes on to depict Jesus as primarily a teacher who, as the divine Logos, is the embodiment of reason. Whether Jews or pagans, people before Jesus's coming who lived in accord with reason are now a part of the new community Jesus is gathering through the apostles and their successors. That he is the divinely designated instrument of Wisdom is evident from the ways in which the prophecies of ancient Israel are fulfilled in him. That predictive confirmation has likewise been apparent since his coming, in that his warnings of the destruction of Jerusalem and of the unbelieving response of most Jews to him have recently come to pass.

In reply to the charges that Christians are morally perverted and politically subversive, Justin declares that they are law-abiding citizens, grateful for the order and stability of life that the emperors maintain, and willing to pay taxes to support the Roman state. He speaks of Hadrian (117–138), for example, as "the greatest and most illustrious emperor." Jesus's teaching is compatible with that of the ancient philosophers, and his predictions are similar to those of the Greek and Roman sibyls and the oracles of Hermes, messenger of the Greek gods. Both these types of prophecy were relied on by the Roman populace as well as by its intellectuals and its rulers. The members of the Christian community have experienced moral and social transformation:

> We who formerly delighted in fornication now cleave only to chastity. We who exercized the magic arts now consecrate ourselves to the good and unbegotten God. We who valued above all else the acquisition of wealth and property now direct all that we have to a common fund, which is shared by every needy person. We who hated and killed one another, and who, because of differing customs, would not share a fireside with those of another race, now, after the appearance of Christ, live together with them. We pray for our enemies, and try to persuade those who unjustly hate us that, if they lived according to the excellent precepts of Christ, they will have a good hope of receiving the same reward as ourselves from the God who governs all.[4]

[4]"First Apology" (14), from W. A. Jurgens, *The Faith of the Early Fathers*, Vol. 1, p. 52.

The philosophers have only a partial view of the Logos. It is fully disclosed in Jesus, as Justin asserts: "Christ, who appeared on earth for our sakes, became the whole Logos, body and soul. Everything that the philosophers and legislators discovered and expressed well they accomplished through their discovery and contemplation of some part of the Logos. But since they did not have a full knowledge of the Logos, they often contradicted themselves." Paraphrasing Plato, Justin quotes Socrates that it is not easy to find the Father and Creator of all things, nor when he has been found, is it safe to announce this to all humanity. He concludes, "Yet our Christ did all this through his own power," as the Logos who is in everyone, who assumed human nature, and has taught these truths about the nature of reality.

A second apology of Justin (which is only a later appendix to the earlier one) is addressed to the Roman senate. In it Justin points out the falsity of the charges of cannibalism and sexual excesses that have been brought against the Christians. He is confident that God will vindicate the faithful believers in the future day of judgment, and so he and all true Christians refuse to obey the official orders of the empire to renounce their allegiance to Christ and participate in divine honors to the emperor. Indeed, he notes that the bravery of the Christians in this regard had been an important factor that attracted him to that faith. At the same time, he did not have to repudiate the philosophy of Plato, since he regarded it as part of the divine preparation for God's full and final disclosure of Reason (Logos) in Jesus Christ.

In a document that is very likely authentic, *The Martyrdom of the Holy Martyrs*, there is a report of how Justin and other brave Christians of this period were put to death by the Roman authorities for their refusal to sacrifice to the traditional Roman gods and to honor the emperor as divine. All those Christians who were interrogated by the Roman officials were threatened with execution by beheading. The Roman officer asked Justin, "Do you suppose that you will ascend to heaven to receive some recompense?" Justin replied, "I do not suppose it, but I know and am fully persuaded of it!" All the others on trial joined him in expressing assurance that God would take them into his presence. It was in this confidence that all of them were put to death.

Clement of Alexandria (150–211 C.E.)

Born in Athens of pagan parents, Clement was converted to Christianity and visited the major centers of Christian learning in the eastern Mediterranean world. In Alexandria, he became a pupil of Pantaenus, who was head of the catechetical school there, and about 200, succeeded him in this post. During the persecution of Christians under the emperor Decius (193–211), Clement was forced to flee Egypt, and he died in eastern Asia Minor (Cappadocia) about 212 C.E. His three major works are *The Exhortation to the Greeks*, *Paidagogos* ("Instructor of Children"), and *Stromateis*, which means "miscellany" or "patchwork." The strategies of these writings are (1) to challenge the Greek intellectuals on their own ground; (2) to offer instruction for

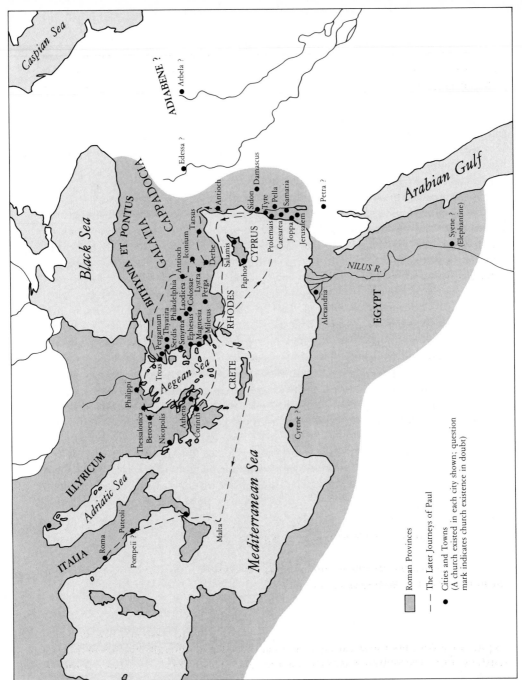

Figure 6.1 The Church at the End of the First Century A.D.

leading Christians from child-like to mature faith; (3) to provide deep and challenging insights to serious Christians, behind the intentionally misleading and innocuous title "Miscellany." In the *Exhortation* Clement declares that the Logos has become a human being: he had formed us in creation; he has now appeared as our teacher; and in the future he will provide us a new life with God. To all humanity a divine emanation has come to enable one to recognize and affirm the unity and eternity of God. As Instructor, Jesus brings enlightenment to human life and thought, enabling one to attain self-knowledge and to live according to steadiness, beauty, and obedience to God. In *Stromateis* Clement declares that faith is superior to knowledge, that it leads from what cannot be demonstrated to the universal. Yet God cannot be taught or expressed adequately in words; rather, knowledge of God is possible only through the capacity that God provides. Similarly, the thoughts of virtuous men and women are produced by divine inspiration. Faith is a comprehensive knowledge of the essentials about God and the universe, but knowledge is the firm and strong proof of what has been accepted by faith. The participants in the people of God stretch back through human history:

> The true church, which is ancient, is one; and in it are enrolled those who, in accord with the [divine] design, are just. . . . In substance, in concept, in origin and in eminence, the ancient and universal church is alone, gathering as it does into the unity of the one faith which results from the familiar covenants—or rather, from the one covenant in different times, by the will of the one God and through the one Lord [Jesus]—those already chosen, those predestined by God who knew before the foundation of the world that they would become right with God.[5]

Origen (185–253)

Although Origen was named for the god of the Nile (Origen means "offspring of Horus"), his father was presumably a Christian, since he was killed during the persecution of the church by the emperor Severus (193–211) when Origen was ten years old. He wanted to follow his father in martyrdom, but his mother kept him safe in the house by hiding his clothes. Trained in both secular and Christian learning, he quickly excelled, developing special competence in the languages and contents of the Jewish and Christian scriptures, so that at age eighteen he began to preside over the Christian school in his native city, Alexandria. He was extremely ascetic, sleeping on a bare floor and eating a minimal diet. Taking literally the injunction of Matthew 19:12 (becoming a eunuch for the sake of the kingdom of God), Origen

[5]Paraphrased from the translation in *The Fathers of the Church*, Vol. 1. (Washington, D.C.: Catholic University of America, 1947). p. 185.

castrated himself. In spite of what was regarded by many as a physical disqualification, he was ordained as an elder by the bishops of Jerusalem and Caesarea. He had so many pupils that he was busy morning to night and decided to divide his teaching responsibilities with a colleague who handled the beginners while Origen worked exclusively with the advanced students. Among his technical accomplishments was the preparation of a set of versions of the Bible in various languages and translations, so that the reader could compare them in the finest detail. One of these ancient copies of the Bible that he used was found near Jericho. It was perhaps a part of the library of the Dead Sea sect that was discovered only in the middle of the present century. Even the anti-Christian philosopher Porphyry acknowledged the vast range and depth of Origen's learning. By means of allegorical and figurative interpretation of the scriptures, Origen was able to show the correlation, as he saw it, between Greek philosophy and the Bible. In 232 he moved to Caesarea, where he was not only a teacher but was also constantly being consulted by local and regional leaders of the church. At the age of sixty his program of teaching and writing was so enormous that he had stenographers on hand during his lectures to record his discourses. He was among those tortured during the persecution of the church under Decius (249–251). He died from these injuries in Tyre in 253 or 254.

In addition to Origen's parallel version of the biblical texts, his greatest contributions were his detailed commentaries on various parts of the Bible and an extended apologetic response to an earlier attack on Christianity by Celsus (as we noted in Chapter 5). His commentaries were on the Jewish biblical writings—Genesis, Isaiah, Ezekiel, the twelve minor prophets, and Song of Songs—as well as on the Gospel of Matthew and the Gospel of John. His interpretations of the text concerned more its relevance for his contemporaries than its historical context. Accordingly, much of the commentary is allegorical or philosophical in nature. For example, the study of the Song of Songs uses the erotic themes and language of the book as a vehicle for conveying the possibilities of sharing in the love of God that has been disclosed through Christ. The appearance of terms in the Gospel of John that are significant in the Greek philosophical tradition provides Origen the occasion for developing deep and highly intellectual connotations for the seemingly simple language and style of the Gospel of John. For example, the opening phrase of John, "In the beginning," is interpreted by Origen through his showing that the Greek word, *arche*, can mean chronological beginning but that it also implies divinely intended purpose, eternal principles inherent in the universe, and the rule or standard by which the cosmos operates. The entire first book of this commentary is taken up with the unfolding of the meaning of that simple phrase. Origen's interpretive method begins with the basic meaning of the original text, and that serves as a launching platform for far-reaching flights of philosophical and theological inquiry and insight.

In his extended response to Celsus's intellectual attack on Christianity in *The True Doctrine* (which we examined in Chapter 5), Origen notes with some reluctance that he had complied with the request of his patron, Ambrose, to prepare a full-scale counterargument to what Origen considers to be an ill-informed and intellectually irresponsible string of charges against the faith. Nevertheless, he did reproduce much of the original document from some seventy years earlier, preparing this massive counterattack just before the middle of the third century, during the reign of Philip the Arabian (244–249). Two factors seem to be significant in the belated appearance of this response to the pagan intellectual's attack on Christianity: (1) it was only in the subsequent century that the challenge to the intellectual integrity of the church's teaching was seen to be important and demanding a rejoinder; and (2) it was only then that the church had produced a scholar like Origen of sufficient learning to be able to respond effectively to this challenge.

Because Greek religion and philosophy were the base from which Celsus was operating, Origen began his argument by reminding his readers of the basic disagreements and contradictions among Greek philosophers and of the morally debased practices of the Greek and Roman gods and goddesses. The power of Jesus is evident in the spread of Christianity throughout the Roman world in spite of official opposition to it. Although the beginnings of the movement were among the unlearned, judged by ordinary human standards, its message has penetrated the world, geographically and intellectually. Origen's own learning is evident in the linguistic distinction he makes between the gospel account of Jesus' birth to a virgin (in Greek, *parthenos*; Matt. 1:23) and the Hebrew text of Isa. 7:14 referred to by Matthew, where a "young woman" (*almah*) is predicted to bear a son who will redeem God's people. Origen notes but dismisses the Jewish charges that Jesus had been the illegitimate son of a Roman soldier named Pantheros. The interpretation of any historical event, Origen observes, is a mixture of the literal and the figurative, as the various Greek legends of the Trojan wars evidence.

The inclusion of miracle stories in the reports of Jesus's birth and public career, and earlier in the life and work of Moses, is essential for communicating with the intellectually uncritical masses who are not reached by sophisticated arguments. The fulfillment of prophecy is in Origen's view a powerful element in the credibility of Christianity and one that Celsus has largely avoided. These prophecies must be seen as pointing to two advents of Jesus: one in lowliness and humiliation and one in triumph and divine vindication that is yet to come. Likewise, Celsus too quickly dismisses the report of the star that led the Magi to the cradle of Jesus, since the appearance of new heavenly bodies may be shown to accompany important historical events. The failure to distinguish the lofty, admirable aims of Jesus in his healings and exorcisms has led Celsus to compare them with the self-serving magical stunts that professional magicians perform.

The lowly and unpretentious origins of the followers of Jesus are not an embarrassment to the Christian movement, as Celsus implies, but instead testify to the marvelous power of this religion to transcend human boundaries, both ethnic and intellectual. Similarly, that Jesus had a human body does not deny his divine role or reduce his stature intellectually but points to the reality of the incarnation of God in human form. No ordinary human being could have converted so many and have influenced so many human leaders, among them kings, rulers, Roman senators, as well as the common people. It is true that some of what Christians believe has been more elegantly expressed by the philosophers, but if Christianity is to constitute a new human community, it cannot limit itself to the tiny intellectual elite. It must be accessible to, and understandable by simple people.

The goal of God's creation of the universe has been the welfare of human beings. God cares for all rational beings, although he holds them accountable for their way of life when they go against human nature. He warns them of divine judgment as an inducement to them to live in accord with the divine purpose. They are ever in need of divine healing and correction, which has been provided through Jesus. Celsus rightly praises the wisdom of philosophers and of other religious leaders, but he ignores the gross immorality the deities of these religions practice, such as incestuous marriages. God has left his creatures with the ability to make decisions, with the result that the demonic powers in the universe have used their capabilities to oppose God, for which they will be called to account. As for the ancient prophetic promises of wealth and prosperity, Celsus takes them literally, thereby missing the spiritual meaning by which they become promises to God's people to supply their deepest needs, both personally and within the community of faith. In their role as those who are seeking to prepare humanity for the coming of God's Rule in the earth, they avoid accepting civil responsibilities, since these structures and systems will be replaced by the eternal order of the cosmos that Jesus announced and for which he is preparing his people through the transformation of human society.

Origen neatly epitomized what he saw as his role in life: "It is our task to try to confirm men's faith by arguments and treatises." He sought thereby "to handle rightly the Word of Truth" (II Tim. 2:15).[6] That his role in Christianity of the middle third century would be thus conceived and that it would be supported by ecclesiastical leaders and used by those seeking significant places in the life of the church shows the extent to which this movement had perceived its task in the Roman world as both challenging and transforming the intellectual and cultural forces of the Roman world. With the spread of Christianity and the inevitable diversity of institutional form and doctrinal substance that emerged in these early centuries, it was of equal importance for its major thinkers not only to challenge the intellectual critics from without but to cope with basic differences in perception of Christian faith and life within the church. It is to some of the major figures in this phase of the church's development that we now turn.

Irenaeus

One important challenge from the culture of the second century was indirect but came to have an ongoing and divisive influence on developing Christianity. There

---

[6]Paraphrased from Henry Chadwick, trans., *Contra Celsum* (8.75) (New York: Cambridge University Press, 1965).

were regional differences between the eastern and western parts of the empire on social and political aspects of human life that led the church in the east to adopt different institutional structures as well as different strategies for trying to unify and systematize what the church affirmed to be the truth. How was the church to organize itself to withstand mounting political, cultural, and intellectual pressures from without? How could it maintain its integrity while responding to these forces, both external from the political powers and internal from the society of the region?

A major figure among the Christians of the second century who worked on the problem of inner consolidation of faith and practice was Irenaeus. Born at Smyrna in Asia Minor (about 140), he was made bishop of Lyons in Gaul (France) in 178, succeeding the first bishop there, Pothinus, who was martyred. It is possible that Irenaeus was descended from the Gauls (or Celts) who had invaded Asia Minor in the third century B.C.E. and that he was returning to his ancestral territory when he went to Lyons as bishop. In any case, he sought to make peace between Victor, the bishop of Rome, and Polycrates, the bishop of Ephesus in Asia Minor, over the issue of the date of Easter (discussed later). So severe was the controversy that Victor wanted to excommunicate all who failed to celebrate Easter only on a Sunday, but Irenaeus urged him and the other western bishops to withdraw this excommunication decree in recognition of the great antiquity of the eastern churches' custom of linking the remembrance of Jesus's death with the Jewish dating of the Passover.[7] What is clear from this ecclesiastical dispute between East and West is that the western bishops were deeply concerned about order and uniformity, whereas the eastern churches were committed to continuity with tradition. The emergence within certain Christian groups of teachings regarded by the majority as incompatible with the New Testament writings made it seem essential to the bishops and leading Christian scholars that proper doctrine and practice be defined for the churches. It is to this task that Irenaeus set himself in his *Against Heresies*, also known as *The Detection and Overthrow of What Is Falsely Called Knowledge.* In Chapter 7 we consider some forms taken by this teaching, which has been referred to in ancient and modern times as *gnosis*, Greek for "knowledge." What Irenaeus presents in this major work is not merely an attack on false teaching but a full setting-forth of what he considered to be the essence of authentic Christian faith. It is illuminating to consider his compact summary of the faith that appears early in his treatise:

> For the church, although dispersed throughout the whole world even to the ends of the earth, has received from the apostles and from their disciples the faith in one God, Father Almighty, the Creator of heaven and earth and all that is in them, and in one Jesus Christ, the Son of God, who became flesh for our salvation; and in the Holy Spirit, who announced through the prophets the dispen-

---

[7]The controversy is described in detail by Eusebius, in his *Ecclesiastical History*, 5.23–24.

sations and the comings,[8] and the birth from a virgin, and the passion, and the resurrection from the dead, and the bodily ascension into heaven of the beloved Christ Jesus our Lord, and his coming from heaven in the glory of the Father to reestablish all things; and the raising up again of all flesh of all humanity, in order that to Jesus Christ our Lord and God and Savior and King, in accord with the approval of the invisible Father, every knee shall bend of those in heaven and on earth and under the earth, and that every tongue shall confess him, and that He may make just judgment of all; and that he may send the spiritual forces of wickedness and the angels who transgressed and became apostates, and the impious, unjust, lawless and blasphemous among men, into everlasting fire; and that he may grant life, immortality, and surround with eternal glory the just and holy, and those who kept His commands and who have persevered in his love, either from the beginning or from their repentance.[9]

In this statement are combined the affirmation of the oneness of God, the divinity of Jesus and of the Holy Spirit, the formulation and preservation of the faith through and from the apostles, the continuities of God's purpose with the past through the prophets, the miraculous birth, the death and resurrection, the ascension and coming triumph of Christ as God's agent for the renewal of the created world. Also involved are the solemn warnings of judgment for those who reject or stray from the faith, and the assurance of support and eternal blessing for those who stand firm in the faith. Like the philosophical insights about the Logos of which Origen wrote, faith has an intellectual content that is being defined with increasing clarity.

This faith has penetrated the whole world, Irenaeus reminds his readers, and has done so in spite of important cultural and linguistic differences among various human societies. Yet this unity of faith is being threatened by those who are denying various aspects of the basic creed that he has just summarized. In Gaul there have appeared those who teach Gnosticism, including the denial that the creation is good or that the God of Jesus is the Creator of the universe. Those influenced by Marcion rely only on their expurgated version of the Gospel of Luke for their depiction of Jesus as one whose break with Israel was complete, and they share with the Gnostics the absolute break between the God of creation and the God of human redemption. For Irenaeus, God is the Designer, Builder, Inventor, Maker, and Lord of the universe. The continuities between the Old Testament and the New are essential for Christian faith: the divine act of creation; the existence of the human race; the opening of the covenant with God to non-Israelites; sacrifice as essential to the maintenance of a relationship between God and his people; the prophetic insights and utterances as prime factors in God's self-disclosure to his people. In reaction to those who perceive

---

[8]Presumably these refer to the various ways in which God manifested himself to his people in the past, now reaching their climax in the coming of Jesus.

[9]Quoted from W. A. Jurgens, *The Faith of the Early Fathers*, pp. 84–85.

Jesus as a divine being masquerading as a human, Irenaeus insists on his full humanity, including his birth, his growth to maturity, and his literal death.

The Gnostics reject the essential features of biblical faith: creation as the work of God; the incarnation of Jesus Christ in full identification with humanity; the eucharist as the shared symbolic meal that effects continuing renewal of the covenant people. Access to the truth of God disclosed through Jesus is possible only through the apostolic witness to Jesus in the gospels. To know the truth, therefore, one must contemplate the apostolic tradition. As Irenaeus summarizes it:

> The true gnosis is the teaching of the apostles, and the ancient organization of the church throughout the whole world, and the manifestation of the body of Christ according to the succession of bishops, by which successions the bishops have handed down the church which is found everywhere; and the very complete tradition of the scriptures, which have come down to us being guarded against falsification, and which are received without addition or deletion; and reading without falsification, and a legitimate and diligent exposition according to the scriptures, without danger and without blasphemy; and the preeminent gift of love which is more precious than knowledge, more glorious than prophecy, and more honored than all the other charismatic gifts.[10]

Thus the unity and truth of the church are provided by the apostolic witness, the succession of leadership from the apostles through the bishops, and the fidelity to the accepted collection of scriptures, especially the four gospels. Unlike the heretics who take only one gospel as their norm, Irenaeus insists that there are four, just as there are four winds and four corners of the earth. The one gospel message rests on four pillars, "breathing immortality on every side and enkindling life anew in human beings."[11] The guidelines for faith and ethics are being drawn, as are the fixed principles and authorities for determining what is an authentic part of Christian faith and what is to be rejected as error.

Tertullian

Another kind of response to the mounting political and cultural pressures on Christianity in the later second century was to promote the idea that God would intervene directly in current affairs to destroy the opposition and to vindicate his own people. One Christian leader who came to share this point of view was Tertullian. Born in Carthage of pagan parents about 155 and trained as a lawyer, Tertullian was converted in 193. Thereafter he devoted his legal skills to the defense of Christianity.

---

[10]Quoted from W. A. Jurgens, *The Faith of the Early Fathers*, Vol. 1, p. 97.
[11]From ibid., p. 91. Quotations throughout the remainder of this chapter are from this volume.

His writings were in Latin, which was a new feature in Christian literature. Until that time Greek had been the literary language of the Christians, and Latin was the vernacular of the masses in the western Mediterranean world. In spite of his linguistic shift, Tertullian's primary concerns were to foster instruction of Christians and to affirm the continuity of the Christian tradition in the face of new interpretations of the faith that were emerging. It is the more ironical, therefore, that in his later years he was himself strongly influenced by a speculative, charismatic movement that claimed to have received prophetic revelations which supplemented and modified the New Testament writings. The leader of this movement, Montanus, appeared in Phrygia in Asia Minor in the middle of the second century, claiming to have the revelation of the Spirit that the present age was soon to end and that the New Jerusalem would descend from heaven to a valley in Asia Minor. Even though the prediction obviously was not fulfilled, the movement spread to the West and strongly influenced Tertullian in his later years. (We examine Montanism as an example of the resurgence of apocalyptic expectations in Chapter 7.) It was not until the opening years of the third century, however, that the attraction for Tertullian of this ecstatic and rigorous religious style became evident.

In the initial phase of his work, Tertullian addresses the two major charges that are brought against the Christians: that they do not worship the traditional gods (which is sacrilege), and they do not offer the sacrifices for the emperor (which is treason). Christianity is not subversive, he asserts in his *Apology*, but offers divine instruction. Jesus is the Teacher of God's grace and the Enlightener and Trainer of the human race, who came to renew our receptivity toward the truth. Jesus is the embodiment of reason and power. Through him all things were fashioned, and through him the divine purpose will be brought to fruition. This movement has already spread across the world, filling "cities, islands, fortresses, towns, market-places, the military camps, tribes, companies, the palace, the senate, the forum"— every place except the temples. Christians are the enemies of human error, not the enemies of the human race.

Tertullian is concerned to show that the charges made against him and other Christians that they are antisocial are simply unfounded and perverted. Instead of accepting the charge that Christians are morally and politically subversive groups, he describes in detail what they do, thereby providing the modern reader with a vivid picture of life in the churches of the second century. They gather to pray to God for strength and guidance and for the welfare of the emperor and the state, for the triumph of peace in the world. They are also concerned for the illumination of the community through the Scriptures and for calling to moral account the members of the group, to the extent of excommunicating members adjudged guilty of grievous sin. Their affairs are presided over by elders (presbyters), and the modest resources of the members are shared. Support is provided for burial of the poor, for orphans, for the aged confined to their homes, and for those deprived as the result of a shipwreck or of service in mines or imprisonment. They are ready to die for each other and share all that they have—except their wives! Their basic group rite is the Eucharist, or *agape* (from a Greek word for love), which begins and ends with prayer, includes songs, and celebrates the origins of the movement through Jesus's last meal with his followers and the symbolic anticipation of his death in their behalf.

In his *Guideline Against the Heathen*, Tertullian addresses the intellectual problems that the church faces from pagan detractors as well as from those who consider themselves Christians but are opposing or basically altering parts of the apostolic tradition. To both types of opponents he declares that there is no need to search for truth because the gospel has been fully disclosed through Christ, and the rule of faith has been established. As he phrases it, following a summary statement of the essence of Christian faith, "This rule . . . was taught by Christ, and admits of no questions among us, except those which heresies bring in and which make men heretics" (13.1). The apostles have preserved this truth. Even the replacement of Judas among the apostles was confirmed by lot and by scripture.[12] The apostles founded churches, preached true doctrine. From the one primitive apostolic church all others are derived, and in them only what Christ revealed to the apostles may be preached. It is churches thus established that alone can decide what is true, and decisions about doctrine can be made only by those who succeeded the apostles: the bishops of the apostolic churches. Conversely, where true doctrine appears, one can be sure of apostolic origins and links. In his treatise *On Baptism*, Tertullian asserts that membership in the church is to be confirmed by baptism, which is to be performed in the apostolic tradition, preferably by a bishop. The rite should be delayed in the case of the unmarried or of children, pending their having received proper instruction in the apostolic tradition.

In his later writings Tertullian gives increasing evidence of speculation about the future and of an increasingly rigorous view of Christian morality. For example, in his treatise *Against Marcion*, he reports on an event—"attested even by pagan witnesses"—that in Judea a heavenly city was visible suspended in the sky every morning for forty days, which would vanish later in the day. This was a foretaste of the New Jerusalem coming down from heaven that John depicted in Revelation 21:9–27. Tertullian is persuaded that the fulfillment of these promises of renewal of heaven and earth is about to take place. In *Against Praxeas*, he declares that there is already occurring a new epoch of the Spirit in which special revelation of God's purpose has been disclosed—an apparent affirmative reference to the prophecies of the Montanists. Tertullian's growing moral strictness is evident in his *On Monogamy*, in which he extols the chaste and eunuchs, as against those who have married, and in his treatise *On Modesty*, in which he says that adulterers should be permanently excluded from the community. This denial of restoration, even to repentant sinners, he seeks

---

[12]The reference here is to the incident reported in Acts 1:15–26, when the choice of a successor to Judas is authorized by an appeal to Psalms 109:8 in the Greek version, where what is taken over is someone's *episkope* (that is, overseer or leader).

to justify by an appeal to a new message from the Spirit and to Hebrews 6:4, which denies readmission to apostates.

In *Apology*, Tertullian deplores the fact that any natural disaster that occurs is blamed on the Christians and that they are imprisoned simply because they bear Christ's name, even though they are fully law-abiding. Ultimately, his views are optimistic: The more the Christians are hewed down, the more numerous they become. Or, as he puts it in a vivid and oft-quoted phrase, "The blood of the martyrs is the seed of the church" (50.12).

Cyprian of Carthage

Cyprian's personal experience as well as his writings point up the issues faced by the third-century church. Born of wealthy pagan parents in the opening years of that century, by 250 Cyprian had been converted, had entered the priesthood, and had been made bishop of Carthage just about the time of the outbreak of the persecution of the church under Decius (249–251). Cyprian was severely criticized because he fled to the hills, where he carried out his episcopal duties during the persecution. One of his major concerns was, accordingly, the restoration of those who had lapsed from the faith. In his letters to other bishops and clergy, he warned against easy restoration on terms dictated by the lapsed, and stressed penitence as the essential requirement, with forgiveness to be bestowed by the bishop. He insisted that it is the bishops alone who provide continuity of faith and practice in the churches and are the ground of unity. His treatise *On Unity of the Church Universal* has survived in two versions. This in itself is an indication of the range and depth of the issue of whether authority in the church was collegial among the bishops as a group or centralized in the bishop of Rome, who was regarded as the successor of Peter, the rock on which Christ was to build the church, according to Matthew 16:18.[13] As for membership in the church, Cyprian affirmed that infants should be baptized, although the rite administered by heretics was valueless. There is only one baptism into the people of God, and it is available only in the universal church. Cyprian's claim to the exclusive efficacy of baptism through the apostolic succession of the bishops and the churches and clergy they authorized was affirmed at the seventh council of the church in Carthage, over which Cyprian himself presided in 256.

Competition for Episcopal Authority in Rome

The continuing problem of the Christians who, faced with the prospect of martyrdom, caved in under pressure and took part in divine honors to the emperor continued

---

[13]Some Protestant interpreters of Matthew argue that it is Peter's confession of Jesus as Son of God that is the rock, not Peter in his apostolic role.

throughout the third century. Hippolytus, a prolific theolological writer of the first decades of the third century, was vigorous in his attacks on other Christians—on those whom he regarded as heretical in their views on the deity of Christ and on the church leaders in Rome who tolerated the heretics. But he was especially critical of the bishop of Rome, Callistus (217–222), for his policy of easy readmission of members of the church who had yielded to pressure from the empire and publicly renounced their faith. For a time he was bishop of a separatist wing of the church, having been elected to the position by his supporters and he was subsequently martyred about the year 235 C.E. The theological ideas in the surviving fragments of his extensive writings affirm what had come to be regarded as the apostolic faith, so that his break with the main body of the church was not the result of his heretical theological ideas. Furthermore, in *Apostolic Tradition* he provides details of the process by which bishops, presbyters, deacons, and other church officials were to be ordained and of the responsibilities that they were to carry out, as well as the process by which members were to be added to the church and how the sacraments of baptism and the Eucharist were to be administered. It is the more surprising, therefore, that he would have taken such a radical step in having a small group of dissidents designate him as bishop. But the issue involved—readmitting those who had taken part in the emperor cult—serves a reminder of the unresolved questions of church and state.

Midway in the third century another Roman clergyman had himself elected bishop of Rome. Details in Eusebius's *Ecclesiastical History* (6.43) tell how a prominent clergyman in Rome named Novatian was so eager to be bishop that he enticed three bishops to Rome from remote parts of Italy. He managed to make them drunk, and in their stupor, he led them to lay hands on him as bishop. The issues between Novatian and the official bishop were focused by this dissidence on strictness of requirements for Christians and especially on the question of readmission of the lapsed. Like Hippolytus, Novatian had no significant doctrinal differences with the mainstream bishops. But also like him, he insisted that Christians could not marry the second time and that under no circumstances were those who had violated their devotion to Christ through participation in the emperor cult to be accepted back into the Christian community. Although in common consciousness, the immediate issue was the restoration of the lapsed, the fundamental questions were the authority of the bishop and the basis of the unity of the church. In Chapter 7 we turn to a consideration of some of the detailed challenges to church unity, both institutionally and conceptually, that emerged in the third century.

THE CHALLENGES FROM WITHIN CHRISTIANITY

Who Is in Charge?

Because Christianity began as a spontaneous movement and in the expectation that its hopes of a New Age were soon to be fulfilled, at the outset there was no set pattern of leadership and no well-defined process for decision-making within the group. The tradition apparent in the gospels and the letters of Paul, which promised power and authority by the Holy Spirit at work among and through Jesus's twelve followers, did not point to any specific organizational structures or assigned leadership roles by which direction and specific guidelines were to be established. The only indication of a centralized leadership was the implicit role of the group of apostles based in Jerusalem, with whom Paul conferred as he carried out his mission to bring Gentiles into the community of faith. He consulted first with their leader, James the brother of Jesus, and later with the apostolic circle as a whole (Gal. 1:18–2:10). They had given corporate approval to what he was doing, they "shook hands with us on it," which symbolized their support of Paul's program of outreach beyond Judaism.

The term *apostle* is simply a transliteration of a Greek word that means "sent" or "commissioned." The group of twelve who had been Jesus's disciples (literally, "learners," as they are designated in the older gospel tradition) during his lifetime believed that he had appeared to them after his resurrection and had commissioned them to carry forward the movement he had launched with their cooperation. It was to Peter that he had appeared initially, followed by appearances to the remainder of the twelve. That was the basis of their claim to be "sent ones" (i.e., apostles). Then, as Paul put it, "last of all, he appeared also to me" (I Cor. 15:5–9). Although in the latter passage, Paul speaks of himself as "unfit to be called an apostle" because of his persecution of God's people, he does in fact regularly identify himself at the opening of his letters as "apostle." He believes he has been commissioned and empowered by God to carry out his work of calling Gentiles to faith and participation in the new community.

Originally, the term *apostle* did not have a technical meaning, as is evident from its use by Paul on occasion to refer to messengers or emissaries (Phil. 2:25; II Cor. 8:23). But in the final editing of the gospel tradition (Mark 6:30; Matt. 10:2; Luke 11:49), the disciples are also called apostles during Jesus's lifetime. In one text (Luke 22:30), there is an implicit link between the number of the apostles and the number of the tribes of Israel. With few exceptions, the term is limited to the circle of twelve based in Jerusalem.[1] In his letters and in Acts, it is to the Jerusalem apostles that Paul and others appeal for confirmation of policy questions such as the basis for Gentile participation in the New Covenant people (Gal. 2; Acts 15). Paul elsewhere declares that the apostles are at the head of the list of those whom God has appointed for leadership roles in the churches, followed by prophets, teachers, workers of miracles, healers, helpers, administrators, and those who spoke in ecstatic languages (I Cor. 12:28). Most of these roles seem to be functions essential for the ongoing life of the church rather than official positions.

In the later New Testament writings, however, the apostolic role is represented as fundamental for the church, which is described as having been built on the foundation of the apostles (Eph. 2:20). That image is given vivid expression in the picture of the New City of God that comes to earth from heaven in the new age. The New City of God that comes to earth from heaven in the new age. The New City has twelve gates, each bearing the name of one of the tribes of Israel, and twelve foundation stones, each with the name of one of the twelve apostles (Rev. 22:10–14). The authoritative role of the apostles is heightened in Acts, where they are depicted as making the basic policy decisions that guide the life of the whole church. It is astonishing, therefore, that following the fall of Jerusalem to the Roman armies in 67–70, nothing more is heard of the apostolic circle other than otherwise unsubstantiated reports in Eusebius's *Ecclesiastical History* (3.5.3; 4.6.4) that the church fled to Pella east of the Jordan and that the original Jewish bishops of Jerusalem were replaced in the second century by those of Gentile origin.

The word *bishop* derives from the Greek term, *episkopos*, which means "overseer." Paul mentions it only once (Phil. 1:1), but in the later letters produced in his name there are detailed guidelines for selecting a bishop (I Tim. 3:1–7; Titus 1:7–9). These guidelines include fidelity in marriage and parental responsibilities, being temperate in drinking, being amiable and free of greed, as well as having an aptitude for teaching and being orthodox in doctrine. The qualification that a bishop must not be a recent

---

[1]Paul identifies himself as an apostle at the opening of nearly all his known letters. This identification is also found in the later letters attributed to Paul (Eph. 1:1; I Tim. 1:1; II Tim. 1:1), as well as in Acts 14:4, 14).

convert shows that these texts deal with a considerably later stage in the development of Christianity.

Although Acts does not mention bishops, Paul's farewell to the leaders of the church of Ephesus (20:17–35) is addressed to the elders (*presbyteroi*), who are instructed to serve as overseers (*episkopoi*) of the church, which is God's new flock. What seems to have happened is that the elders replaced the apostles as the policy-making council in the churches. They are associated with the apostles in the decision-making function in Acts 15 ("apostles and elders"), even though the term *elder* is never used in Paul's own letters.

Another leadership role in process of development in the first century and a half of the church was that of deacon (*diakonos*). The word means "servant" and is used by Paul to refer to secular civil servants (Rom. 13:3–4) and to Christ's role in fulfilling the purpose of God to form a new inclusive Covenant People (Rom. 15:8), as well as to his own role in carrying out the ministry to which God has called him and his co-workers. Yet in Paul's letters there are references to those persons who have provided financial support for him and the churches as deacons, including a woman, Phoebe, in one of the churches near Corinth (Rom. 16:1). In the later material attributed to Paul, however (I Tim. and Titus), qualifications and responsibilities for both elder and deacon are spelled out. The elders are to be in charge of the churches, even while they are to be responsible heads of their families, but they are subject to trial and expulsion if they misbehave. Deacons, who may be male or female, are to be morally upright and fiscally responsible. Emphasis on good management tends to confirm the inference that may be drawn from the brief mention of the apostles' appointment of seven "who serve (*diakonein*) tables" in Acts 6 when there was a problem of unequal distribution of common funds: A deacon was someone with financial and physical responsibilities for the life of the community.

Clearly, there was no set, uniform definition of these leadership roles in the church during the first century of its existence. From the later first century onward, the bishops of major metropolitan centers, such as Antioch, Alexandria, Carthage, and Rome, not only had large constituencies but also derived prestige from the fame and fortune of their seats of power. Obviously, those powers were modest and limited at the outset, becoming increasingly significant as the size and influence of the movement grew. Fortunately, literature has survived that reflects and even characterizes the episcopal role in the early centuries. Like the New Testament sources, it also evidences significant changes that took place in the leadership patterns within early Christianity.

One of the earliest bishops of whom direct knowledge is available is Ignatius, bishop of Antioch in the opening years of the second century. He wrote letters to the churches of Asia Minor and to Rome as he passed through on his way to martyrdom in Rome in the latter years of the reign of the emperor Trajan (98–117). In each letter he calls for submission by the members to the bishop and the elders and requests respect for the deacons. In poetic imagery he writes to the Ephesian church that the bishop and the presbytery are attuned like strings of a harp so that Christians led by them may sing with one voice to God and Jesus Christ. There is to be unity of faith and practice of the Eucharist under the presidency of the bishop. In his letter to Polycarp, bishop of Smyrna in Syria, Ignatius says flatly, "Let nothing be done without your approval." The members are to be subject to the bishop, the presbyters, and the deacons. A council convened at Smyrna will elect the successor to Ignatius for the church in Antioch.

Also surviving from the early second century is a letter from Polycarp to the church at Philippi in northern Greece. In it he offers counsel to the deacons and the elders, much of which consists of quotations from the gospels, the letters of Paul, and other parts of both the New and Old Testaments. This practice indicates how basic for Christian belief and behavior the Bible had become by this time. Significantly, the apostles are referred to as venerated figures from the past. Even so, other writings from the second century evidence the eagerness of churches in various parts of the empire to claim continuity with, or even establishment by, one of the apostolic figures. Thus Peter is associated with Rome, Mark with Alexandria, John with Ephesus, and Matthew with Antioch. There is no firm evidence to establish or to refute these claims. What are significant are the foundational role of the apostles in this later tradition and the efforts to guarantee continuity of belief and practice by establishing legitimating links with the apostolic period of the past through the presiding roles of the bishops in the present.

Additional evidence for the appeal to the authority traced back to the apostles is *The Teaching of the Twelve Apostles*, which we have already examined (Chapter 4). Dating from the second century, it may incorporate earlier Christian moral tradition. The ongoing development of these traditions is evident in Hippolytus' *Apostolic Tradition*,[2] written about 215, where he describes ways in which Christian charity may be practiced, how nuns are to be chosen and supported, what attitudes are to be assumed toward Judaism, how the Eucharist is to be celebrated, and what is the essence of Christian character. That the sanction for these guidelines claims to be the teaching of the apostles shows how important the legitimation process was by which important and inevitable later developments in Christianity are given authorization by alleging that they have apostolic roots.

The Relationship of Christianity to Emergent Rabbinic Judaism

The failures of two attempts by Jewish nationalists to establish an autonomous Jewish state (in 66–70 and 130–135 A.D.) were concurrent with the moves within Judaism toward institutionalization of the synagogue movement and the emergence of its

---

[2]Excerpts appear in W. Jurgens, trans. and ed., *The Faith of the Early Fathers*, Vol. 1 (Collegeville, Minn.: Liturgical Press, 1970).

rabbinic leadership. We have already examined this development (pp. 29–34) which began a process of reinterpreting the Law of Moses with the aim of transferring the requirements for cultic purity from the priests and the temple to the pious laity and the houses or halls where they gathered for prayer and worship, for study of their scriptures, and for table fellowship. Gaining and maintaining group identity were central for the adherents of the movement. Nationalistic hopes, or even specific messsianic expectations of a divinely endowed deliverer, were absent. Accordingly, there was an abandonment of the prophetic traditions announcing God's intervention and of the apocalyptic literature in which the elect community was warned of the sufferings through which it was to pass and was assured of its impending vindication by God. The importance of this Jewish move toward definition of community identity was heightened by the appearance and remarkable growth of a group claiming to be the heirs of the covenantal tradition and to have the correct clues for interpreting the biblical heritage: the Christian church.

These developments within Judaism, which we have seen to be reflected in the New Testament writings and which continued until the completion of the Talmuds in the sixth century C.E., presented some serious internal dilemmas for the Christians in the second and third centuries. In the churches of the eastern Mediterranean world, there were two conflicting reactions to this problem of the relationship with Judaism. The first reaction was the strategy of Marcion, which (as we have noted) was to repudiate the Jewish scriptures, as well as those parts of the New Testament evidencing Jewish influence. The church was to regard itself in a wholly new way as the people of God. Second, within the church in these centuries there were also those who wanted to affirm the continuity between Israel and the church in claiming that Christians were the true heirs of this biblical tradition.

Given the anxiety that pervaded the church in Asia Minor as the result of the martyrdoms resulting from Trajan's policy of forcing the Christians to take part in the imperial cult, it was natural that the church there would be drawn to a Jewish resource that dealt with the problems arising when a community of one faith lives under the threat of destruction by a state of another faith. That resource was the Jewish apocalyptic literature, the earliest forms of which went back to the time of the Jewish exile. It took its definitive form in the Hellenistic period (third and second centuries B.C.) when a small group of opponents of the paganization of their temple and their people were convinced that beyond the suffering or martyrdom they might experience, God had revealed to them that the pagan rule would be destroyed and that through the Jews God would exercise control over the creation. This mixture of hope and private disclosure to the faithful few, which scholars have come to call *apocalyptic*, is most fully documented in the Book of Daniel. Writings of this type served no important purpose for rabbinic Judaism when it was consolidating its position after 135. The Jewish apocalyptic writings produced in the period before the destruction of Jerusalem and its temple in that year were thus taken over by the Christians, who edited and adapted them for their own purposes. The Revelation of

John is the most fully developed instance of this literary style and outlook on the world within the New Testament, but apocalyptic elements are also present in the gospel tradition and in the letters of Paul, as we have observed. We examine some of these adapted Jewish documents and some early Christian parallel documents in the next section.

In the western churches, however, the reaction to this apocalyptic tradition was for the most part to assert that, because the Jewish prophecies had been fulfilled through Jesus Christ, the present task of the church was to concentrate attention and efforts on developing a well-defined community with a recognized structure of leadership. This duty was seen as essential if the church was to survive for the forseeable future, especially in light of the hostile pressures from Roman political and intellectual powers. An issue that arose between the eastern and western churches during this period may seem to the modern reader to be insignificant, but it exemplifies the eastern leaders' eagerness to keep continuity with Jewish tradition and the western churches' sense of the importance of Christian distinctiveness and ecclesiastical order. The issue concerned the date of Easter. Because the Last Supper of Jesus as reported in the gospels was linked with the Jewish Passover—the date for which is set on the basis of phases of the moon—it could occur on any day of the week. In the western churches there had developed a pattern of forty days for the observance of Lent, a period of pious self-examination that culminated in Good Friday as the day of penitence, which commemorated Jesus's death. This was followed by Easter Sunday as the celebration of his resurrection. The moveable Passover adopted in the eastern churches spoiled this ecclesiastical symmetry and led to a denunciation of that policy. A cynical reader of the extensive surviving literature on the subject might conclude that the controversy was more of a power struggle than a substantive issue. In any case, it was a symptom of the ambivalence of the church about its relationship to Judaism.

Predicting the Future: Oracles and Revelations

As we have noted, paralleling the aim of the apologists of the second and third centuries to demonstrate the rationality of Christian faith and its freedom from political subversion was the conviction of some church leaders that the tensions between church and empire in recent history disclosed to the discerning observer signs of cosmic conflict that were leading to a climax that would bring divine judgment on the wicked and vindication of the faithful community. The resources on which the Christians drew to make this case were not only the apocalyptic writings indigenous to Judaism but also the traditions of oracles that had been operative in Hellenistic times and continued in public and official favor down into the republican and imperial periods of Roman history.

Characteristic of Jewish apocalyptic writing are the convictions that all history

115

and the whole creation are ultimately governed by God, but that the powers of evil that have seized control in the present are to be defeated in the age to come. Meanwhile, the faithful must suffer during the transition but will be vindicated by God when his rule triumphs. Insight into this process and the outcome has been reserved for the faithful and is now being conveyed in the veiled, symbolic form of the apocalypse. The messenger through whom this divine wisdom is provided for the community is in each case someone reported in the Jewish Bible to have had direct personal relationship with God—for example, Enoch, who walked with God and was taken by God (Gen. 5:24); Isaiah, who saw God enthroned (Isa. 6:1); Elijah, who did not die but was taken up to God (II Kings 2:1)—or someone who was closely associated with God's disclosure of a new status for Israel. Examples of the latter are the prophet Baruch, the scribe of Jeremiah, who announced the new covenant (Jer. 36:32) and Ezra, who prepared Israel for a new kind of life on their return from exile in Babylon. To each of these biblical characters, a newer secret revelation has been given of God's purpose for his people that is embodied in an apocalyptic writing preserved down to the present. From the first century A.D., certain early Christians simply took over these apocalyptic writings, interpreting them in relation to God's people in a Roman-dominated world. In some cases others supplemented the writings by minor additions or modifications. In other cases, they composed new works that they attributed to these ancient messengers of God to Israel.[3] At the same time, the production of some mystical writings about these biblical characters who communed with God went on in Jewish circles as well.

Two prime examples of the ways the apocalyptic literature grew are in writings attributed to Ezra and Enoch. In addition to the biblical book of Ezra (or two books of Ezra that are found in some versions of the Old Testament), there are later Christian additions, so that modern scholars distinguish six stages of the books of Ezra (sometimes known as Esdras). Furthermore, there are also a Greek apocalypse of Ezra, the Question of Ezra, and the Vision of Ezra. In the versions of this material known as Fourth Ezra, there are explicit references to Jesus as Son of God, as well as the pronouncement of judgment on those who formerly considered themselves to be God's people: the Jews. The imagery in the Ezra Apocalypse points unmistakably to Rome as the enemy of God's people. Similarly, the Enoch literature includes sections from the period before Christ, parts of which were found in manuscripts among the Dead Sea Scrolls. One part of the literature (the Similitudes of Enoch) dates from about the time of the birth of Jesus and speaks of "that son of man" who will be God's agent to defeat the powers of evil and to establish the New Age. It was inevitably picked up by the early Christians and linked with the role of Jesus. Enoch 1:9 is quoted as though it is scripture in Jude 1:14. Yet a document known

---

[3]These writings are conveniently translated and edited, with introductions, in J. H. Charlesworth, ed., *The Old Testament Pseudepigrapha*, Vol. 1 (Garden City, NY: Doubleday, 1983); vol. 2 (1985).

as III Enoch seems to have been written in the fifth or sixth century A.D. and is filled with esoteric speculations about God and visions of God that probably originated within rabbinic Judaism of that period. The schematic view of history found in the apocalyptic writings, which divided time into a series of ages under the control of various earthly powers, resembles and may even derive from the scheme of the successive ages of humanity sketched by Hesiod in his poem, *Works and Days*, (ca. 700 B.C.). The golden age, followed by the ages of silver, bronze and iron, is the period of the ideal human community, to which the wise and moral are called to aspire. The impact of this apocalyptic tradition on both Christianity and Judaism in the early centuries of the common Era—whatever its origins may have been—was thus deep and varied.

The projection of hopes and fears about the future was by no means limited to Christians of Jewish origin or orientation, however. The Greco-Roman phenomenon of the oracles consulted by commoners and rulers for insight in making important personal and national decisions clearly influenced both Judaism and Christianity in this same period. Two examples of this cultural influence are the *Shepherd of Hermas* (mentioned in Chapter 4) and the Sibylline Oracles. In these Jewish-Christian oracles the woman through whom the revelation comes concerning the future deliverance and blessedness of God's people seems to have been modeled after the Cumean Sibyl. Over the centuries at a cave in Cumae, an ancient Greek colony on the coast of Italy north of Naples, women known as "the Sibyl" who were said to be inspired by Apollo, gave answers in poetic form to questions addressed to them concerning personal affairs or matters of state. In a poem known as the *Fourth Eclogue* by Virgil, the Sibyl predicts the unprecedented prosperity of Rome that will take place as the result of the birth of a child who will become the agent of renewal.[4] Jews in Alexandria, followed by Christians, claimed to have a similar resource that produced the Sibylline Oracles. The Christian Sibyllines announced the coming of Christ, the spurning of him by the Jews and the acceptance of him by the Gentiles, the judgment that will fall on Rome, and the coming of God's reign over the world.

The most dramatic manifestation of the apocalyptic view of Christianity in the second and third centuries came through Montanus of Phrygia, in a section of Asia Minor referred to in the only complete apocalypse in the New Testament, the Revelation of John. Apparently that type of thinking flourished on the soil of that region. Montanus and his two associates, the prophetesses Priscilla and Maximilla, claimed to be the instruments of the Holy Spirit. Some time after 170 they announced that the return of Christ was about to occur and that the New Jerusalem predicted in the Revelation of John was going to descend near some villages a dozen miles outside Philadelphia on the Aegean coast. In spite of fierce opposition by the ecclesiastical

---

[4]The translation of the complete text of the Fourth Eclogue of Virgil may be found in H.C. Kee, *The New Testament in Context: Sources and Documents* (Englewood Cliffs, NJ: Prentice-Hall, 1984), pp. 162–163.

authorities and the failure of this prediction to come true, Montanism took hold in the villages of Asia Minor. It also spread to the churches of the West, where it took root in Gaul but especially in North Africa.

This opposition on the part of the church leaders fits well with the apocalyptic tradition evident in Daniel: The official religious leaders were regarded by the Montanists as part of the political coalition that opposed God's real work. This official opposition served only to encourage the enthusiasm of the supporters of Montanus's prophetic pronouncements. As we have observed, it was Tertullian who in his later years adopted the Montanist point of view, especially concerning the central role of the Spirit in the life of the church, which he regarded as not a structure ruled by the bishops but a free community of those guided and empowered by the Spirit. He viewed the Spirit's work as leading to a strict moral life for clergy and laity alike, including the refusal to readmit those put out of the church on moral or political charges. In Tertullian's hands, the details of apocalyptic interest in prophetic fulfillment were eclipsed by insistence on the purity of God's people.

Knowledge of the Truth: Gnosticism

One way by which the early Christians came to understand the continuing power of evil in the Roman world, at both the personal and the political level, was to assume that an evil dimension was inherent in the created order of the universe. The truly discerning person could recognize this and be freed from its power through the acquisition of knowledge of reality. In contrast both to the nationalist movements that had set the Jewish people against Rome and to the apocalyptic groups that awaited God's intervention in history to destroy the empire, which was regarded as a cultural and political enemy, and to establish God's rule over the earth, there arose among the Christians of the second century groups that sought liberation from the world through knowledge. They came to be known as the Gnostics, from the Greek word for "knowledge," *gnosis*. For them the goal of faith was not God's triumph over the created world and the history of humanity but the escape from the material world into the eternal realm.

It was the Gnostics's conviction that the essential struggle in which they were engaged was at the metaphysical level, not the historical. Unlike the survivors of the apocalyptic struggle, whose fidelity and courage during the period of conflict with the demonic powers would qualify them for deliverance in the Age to Come, the Gnostics saw themselves as characters in a cosmic drama beyond the physical world of appearances. Proper knowledge of ultimate reality would enable them to escape from this material realm of deceit and apparent reality and to return to the eternal sphere from which they had originally come. The ability to understand this origin and destiny came through a special kind of knowledge of God: gnosis.

The two components from which the Gnostic view of human origin and destiny was formed were the philosophical concepts of Platonism as they had been reformulated in this period and an allegorical understanding of the creation stories in the opening chapters of Genesis. Similarly, in the first century A.D. Philo of Alexandria had drawn heavily on Plato's *Timaeus* for his interpretation of creation. In the fourth century B.C., Plato had made a sharp distinction between the eternal world that was knowable and unchangeable and the physical world that could be known only imperfectly and tentatively, since the latter was an ever-changing and temporal copy of the former. God had formed the world at a point in time, and in it human souls were a mixture of immortal and rational elements, which came from God, and material, temporal features. The human body was created by lesser gods (i.e., the stars). God was the intelligent and efficient cause of the structured world, which is always in a state of change. Thus, Being (God in his changeless essence) is the cause of Becoming (the world in its constant condition of change and decay). Although Plato asserted that God was able to overcome an apparently intractable element in the world, necessity, the Platonists of the first century A.D. and later subsequently came to regard necessity as equivalent to matter, which they considered to be inherently evil.

It is this basic view of God and the world, woven in with details of the Genesis stories of creation, that lies behind the myth set forth by the Gnostics to account for the creation and for evil.[5] It also articulates the substance of the Gnostic hope of deliverance from the present world. The literature in which the myth is found reports the origins of the world and of the Gnostics in particular, for whom is provided a sense of group identity, an esoteric style of expression that communicates to the inner members, and indications of the ritual by which that identity is gained or maintained. The specifics of the myth can be reconstructed from two kinds of sources: (1) the criticisms of the Gnostics in the writings of the leading teachers and writers of the church, such as Justin Martyr, Irenaeus, Clement of Alexandria, Origen, and Hippolytus of Rome; (2) the Gnostic writings that have been preserved, especially the manuscripts from a Gnostic library found in Upper Egypt in 1945 at Nag Hammadi.[6] The fullest account of the Gnostic myth is in "The Secret Book According to John,"[7] in which four stages of the scheme of cosmic redemption are depicted, as follows:

1. The eternal, solitary principle expands into a spiritual universe filled with divine power.

---

[5]This sketch of the Gnostic myth and the following summary of the Gnostic teachings that follow depend on the illuminating analyses of Gnosticism by Bentley Layton in his study and annotated translations of the basic texts, *Gnostic Scriptures*. (Garden City: Doubleday, 1987).
[6]These writings in Coptic, a form of ancient Egyptian still used among Christian groups there, have been analyzed by an international group of scholars and are available in an English translation, James M. Robinson, ed., *The Nag Hammadi Library* (San Francisco: Harper & Row, 1977).
[7]See Bentley Layton, *Gnostic Scriptures*.

2. Out of this spiritual universe is created the material universe, including the stars, the planets, Earth, and hell. In the process of formation of the material world a nonspiritual being, Ialdabaoth, steals divine power and uses it for his own purposes.

3. In the creation of Adam and Eve and their begetting of children, the thieving Ialdabaoth is deceived, so that in spite of the death of Abel and the corruption of Cain, Seth is imbued with spirit, and thus becomes the progenitor of the Gnostics, in whom the spirit can work.

4. Gradually the divine recovers power in the universe when the Gnostics are summoned by a savior and return to God and to their destined place in the spiritual universe. Wisdom is the agent through whom this knowledge is dispensed and the renewal accomplished.

In the elaboration of this myth in other Gnostic writings, it is Ialdabaoth, who stole the divine power, who is responsible for the material universe. In the *Egyptian Gospel* the myth is retold by the Great Invisible Spirit in preparation for the baptism of the Gnostics and their reception into the community of the elect and enlightened. In the *Gospel of Truth*,[8] creation is corrupted by error and therefore is unable to discern its origins. Jesus, who is God within and exists within God the Father, comes as a teacher, and by suffering on the "tree" (the cross) overcomes the produce of the tree of the knowledge of evil. He discloses God to the members of the elect community, who are the only ones able to discern the truth in his parabolic teachings. He reveals to them that the material world will vanish. Their duty is to care for the enlightened group, who alone have access to knowledge of the truth. The Father gave the secret name to the Son whom he produced to be the messenger of truth to the elect; only those who possess this great name can utter it and have access to reality. All who came from the place of eternal repose will return to it, having escaped sorrows and hell and attained truth and perfection. Yet it is in that state, spiritually speaking, that the true children of God already dwell.

Valentinus, born in lower Egypt about the turn of the second century A.D. and educated in Alexandria, migrated to Rome around 140 where he became the intellectual leader of the Gnostic-oriented Christians. The school of thought that arose in his name flourished in both the eastern and western churches down to the seventh century. By using the allegorical method of interpreting scripture, Valentinus and his followers were able to remain within the church even though the substance of the Gnostic teachings was incompatible with the New Testament claims that the God of Jesus was also the God of the creation of the world and that Jesus would return to restore and renew the world. Examples of the allegorical interpretation appear in the Gnostic Gospel of Thomas, where eating flesh and drinking blood are

---

[8]For both the *Egyptian Gospel* and *Gospel of Truth*, see Bentley Layton, *Gnostic Scriptures*.

perceived as partaking in the Word and Spirit. In the Gnostic writings, Jesus does not invite to the eucharistic meal: He *is* the Eucharist. As God anointed Jesus, so he anointed the apostles, and the elect are anointed through the Spirit and the light, which Jesus brings to his own and which is essentially self-knowledge.

A parallel development of Christianity along Gnostic lines took place in Syria, where the central figure for conveying the hidden truth to the elect was the apostle Thomas, who was portrayed as the twin of Jesus. This may have been meant literally or figuratively, but the point was that the relationship between Jesus and Thomas was a model of the links between Jesus (who was thought to dwell within his own people) and the inner life of the faithful. Other writings from this tradition include the Acts of Thomas, the Book of Thomas the Contender, and the Gospel of Thomas. The basic features of the Gnostic myth appear in the Hymn of the Pearl,[9] which builds on Jesus's parable of the man who seeks for the costly pearl (Matt. 13:45–46) to describe the journey of the soul. The soul enters the physical body but gains release following a series of inner experiences leading to heightened self-knowledge and comes finally to the eternal repose. Similarly, the formless collection of sayings of Jesus in the Gospel of Thomas are a summons to the elect to free themselves from family ties or sexual identity, from physical bonds or obligations, in order to gain unity and enlightenment from within through true self-knowledge. Jesus is the All; his kingdom is spread over the earth but is discernible only to those who through him have found the light of true knowledge.

Simon Magus was credited by some ancient critics of the Gnostics with having founded the Gnostic sectarian movement. He is mentioned briefly in Acts 8 as a Samaritan magician who was converted to Christianity but who tried to buy the rights to the bestowal of the Holy Spirit that was accomplishing such wonders according to the Acts narrative. There are reports in the writings of Justin, Irenaeus, and Hippolytus of Rome that during the reign of Claudius (41–54 A.D.) Simon Magus went to Rome, where he lived in association with a Phoenician woman named Helen. It is told in these Christian sources that he died in a failed attempt to duplicate Jesus's experience of death, entombment, and resurrection. From these later sources we hear that Simon claimed to be the supreme god, with Helen as the primary concept emanating from him. She had appeared in history as Helen of Troy and was rein-carnated as Simon's companion of the same name. Simon had taken on bodily form to rescue her and symbolically to redeem all the elect from involvement in physical existence and the material world. Trust in him—or them—assures salvation. Al-though the second- and third-century Christian writers thought that the historical person, Simon, had taught these claims about himself and his cosmic role, it is much more likely that the stories of Simon and the claims made in his behalf were created well after the New Testament period. They consist of a combination of features of Greek mythology, the religion of the Samaritans, New Testament narratives, and

[9]See again Bentley Layton, *Gnostic Scriptures.*

magic. It is difficult to know whether it arose as competition with, or a caricature of the claims Christians were making for Jesus. But the extent to which it was taken seriously shows how ready segments of the populace in these early centuries of the Christian era were to accept claims of celestial visitors and heavenly messages.

In at least two ways, Gnosticism offered a serious challenge to Christianity. At the intellectual level, it represented a basic alternative to the Platonic philosophical tradition used by Philo and drawn on by Clement and Origen to provide a rationally coherent framework in which to understand the origins of the world, the human race, God, and the future. For Plato, the material world was the divinely made image of the eternal world of the forms or patterns. Philosophers in that tradition, such as Plotinus, sought to maintain the notion that the eternal model of the world was discernible in the imperfect, transitory copies comprising the material world. Later Platonists, however, assumed that an independent principle of evil was responsible for this world, subject to corruption and decay. The Gnostics not only took this position about the material universe but denied that knowledge of God was attainable by humans apart from the special revelations granted to the elect. Although rejecting the proposals of the Gnostics, Christian thinkers in this and subsequent centuries—most notably Augustine in the later fourth century—were going to have to deal with these twin issues of how God may be known and how one can account for evil.

At the level of social identity, Gnosticism posed the problem of how one might find identity as a member of God's people. The apparently widespread positive responses to Simonian, Valentinian, and other forms of Gnosticism among Christians and others served to show the mainstream Christian leaders and writers that they must emphasize the full humanity of Jesus and the earthly, human sphere in which they were persuaded God was now at work and in which God's purpose for the creation would achieve the divinely intended goal of the establishment of his rule on earth. The fact that the Gnostic movements grew by claiming to have access to secret insights conflicted with the older Christian tradition of evangelism, according to which all were invited to faith in Jesus as the Messiah regardless of ethnic, social, financial, or intellectual status. Was Christianity ready to become an esoteric, intellectualistic movement like the Gnostics? If not, what were the alternatives for its mode of group identity? What was required was a clear image of the church as a human society, complete with guidelines for admission and maintenance of membership and with defined structures of leadership. Down to the present, those have continued to be the perennial issues the church has faced.

Which Are the Authoritative Scriptures?

By the turn of the first century A.D., the rabbinic leadership in Judaism had made a firm decision that defined its movement over against Christianity and increased the urgency for the church to make comparable decisions. Both the Jews and Christians had to deal with the issue of which of the writings they used for study and instruction were to be regarded as authoritative for depicting their respective histories, formulating their present obligations, and sketching their views of the future. According to later tradition, at Yavneh in the last decade of the first century, the Jewish leaders designated as authoritative the Hebrew writings known by Christians as the Old Testament. The version of the Jewish scriptures in most common use among Christians in this period and subsequently was the so-called Septuagint, the Greek translation of the Jewish scriptures used by Jews throughout the Greco-Roman world. It included several writings originally composed in Greek or translated early into that language. With slight variations, this form of the Jewish bible remains as standard for many Christians, either in the ancient Greek or in the Latin or other translation.[10] It is from the Septuagint that nearly all the quotations from the scriptures are to be found in the New Testament. Because the various parts of the New Testament were produced in sites scattered across the Mediterranean world, and because some of its parts had not yet been written by the end of the first century, there was no immediate possibility or necessity to create a Christian counterpart to the official list of Jewish scriptures.

That necessity began to emerge, however, as the result of several factors in the life of the church in the second and third centuries.[11] One of these, which we have noted earlier, was the proposal by Marcion to recognize only his version of Luke and the letters of Paul as authoritative for Christians. He rejected the Old Testament and purged from Luke any favorable references to it. Christianity became for Marcion the antithesis of Judaism. Montanus, as we have observed, sought to supplement the basic Christian teachings through the prophetic utterances he and his associates claimed had been given them by the Spirit of God. The church had to face the possibility of ongoing supplements to the gospels and other early Christian writings that would alter or even supplant the older documents. The Gnostics, as we have seen, effectively transformed the Jewish scriptures by means of their allegorical interpretation of them, which they derived from their reading of Plato. For the church to tolerate these movements in diverse directions would make it impossible to define the church, the criteria for membership, or the ground of its faith.

By the middle of the second century, therefore, there began to appear among various Christian writers lists of writings from what we now call the New Testament that were declared to be based on the teachings of the apostles and therefore to be authoritative. The effective list came to be known as the canon, which derives from a Greek word meaning "rule", or "authoritative measurement." It included the four

---

[10]Protestant Christians, following the lead of Martin Luther, adopted the rule of Jewish orthodoxy, which recognizes only the scriptures written in Hebrew as authoritative. Calling them the Old Testament, their list of Scriptures omit the other documents, which have come to be designated as the Apocrypha.

[11]The finest survey of the origins of the New Testament canon is that of Bruce M. Metzger, *The Canon of the New Testament: Its Origin, Development and Significance* (New York and Oxford: Clarendon Press, 1987). The analysis offered here is dependent on Metzger's work.

gospels and the letters of Paul, as can be inferred from the quotations of these books in the writings of the church fathers from this period.

The New Testament writings referred to by three Christian writers from different parts of the Roman world at the end of the second century illustrate this emerging consensus. Theophilus of Antioch, who died about 190, quotes as scripture from the four gospels, the letters of Paul (including I and II Corinthians, Romans, Philippians, Colossians, and the so-called Pastorals).[12] Clement of Alexandria specifies the authority of the four gospels, the fourteen epistles of Paul (among which he includes the letter to the Hebrews), Acts I, Peter, I John, and Revelation. He expresses doubts about the other so-called Catholic Epistles,[13] however. More significant for the fluid state of the question about the New Testament canon is that Clement refers to some non-New Testament writings as "inspired," and that he states that there are three versions of the Gospel of Mark: the canonical, the spiritual, and the secret, which was supposed to be accessible only to a small Christian group. Only the canonical version has survived, Clement asserts. Similarly, earlier in the second century Justin (100–180) had spoken of the gospels as the "memoirs of the apostles." He expressed preference for the first three gospels, while using in his theological constructions the Logos or "Word" that appears only in the Gospel of John. It is Irenaeus of Lyons, however, who discussed directly the importance of what he regarded as the core of the New Testament: the four gospels, the number of which he compared with such basic features of the world as the four winds, the four points of the compass, and the four elements. Furthermore, he stated that the unchanging faith of the church rested on scripture and tradition, and by scripture he meant these authoritative New Testament writings in addition to the Jewish scriptures, for which the Christians now claimed to have the key for proper understanding. His list of "scripture" included not only the Revelation of John but also the Shepherd of Hermas.[14]

One of the earliest and most important evidences of the development of a canon of the New Testament is an eighth-century copy of a document from the late second century found in Rome in the eighteenth century. It is called the Muratorian Canon, in recognition of Muratori, the Italian scholar who found and published it. There is a discussion of the Canon on the basis of "what is recognized and received"—thus highlighting the consensus of the churches and their leadership on this issue of the canon. By the early fourth century, Eusebius (whose *Ecclesiastical History* we have repeatedly referred to and whose role in the establishment of the church through the emperor Constantine we shall consider later), prepared a list that included the four gospels, Paul's epistles, I Peter, and I John. Eusebius gave differing opinions on Revelation but admitted it to the canon. He debated the inclusion of James, Jude, II Peter, and II John and rejected a whole series of writings that were apparently

---

[12]The Pastorals include I and II Timothy and Titus, all of which purport to be written by Paul.
[13]II and III John, II Peter, and Jude.
[14]See discussion on p. 72–73, 114.

being taken as authoritative or being used in various parts of the church, which he grouped as follows:

- **Spurious works which are orthodox but not canonical include:**
  Acts of Paul; Shepherd of Hermes, Apocalypse of Peter, Barnabas, Teachings of the Apostles (Didache), Gospel according to the Hebrews.
- **Fictions by heretics include:**
  Gospel of Peter, Gospel of Thomas. Gospel of Matthias, Acts of Andrew, Acts of John.

Similar confirmation of the central core of agreed-on writings for the New Testament canon and the items over which uncertainty continued may be found in two of the oldest (fourth century) manuscript copies of the Bible: Codex Sinaiticus and Codex Vaticanus. The former contains the four gospels, fourteen letters of Paul (including Hebrews), Acts, seven catholic epistles, and Revelation. But Barnabas and the Shepherd of Hermes are also in these copies of the "New Testament." By the last third of the fourth century, an attempt was made to close the canon by Athanasius of Alexandria, who in an official communication to the diocese under his supervision listed the present twenty-seven books of the New Testament as canonical. In subsequent centuries, however, various individual and corporate decisions differed in some details, even though the common core remained as it had been since the middle of the second century.

As significant as the official actions about the canon of the New Testament, however, is the evidence for the enduring popularity in certain regions of the church of writings that never gained canonical status. Examples of these may be grouped as follows:

- **Letters and reports of preaching:**
  The Preaching of Peter
  Correspondence between Paul and Seneca (Roman philosopher and advisor to emperors)
- **Acts of the individual apostles:**
  Acts of John, Peter, Paul, Andrew, Thomas
- **Gospels addressed to special groups:**
  Gospel of the Nazoreans, of the Ebionites, of the Hebrews
- **Gospels linked with an apostle or early follower:**
  Gospel of Philip, of Thomas, of Nicodemus, of Bartholomew
  Gospel of Mary
- **Secret revelations:**
  Sophia Jesu Christ (Wisdom of Jesus Christ)
  Pistis Sophia (Faith-wisdom)

- **Infancy Gospels:**
  Protevangelium of James (Early Gospel); Infancy Gospel of Thomas[15]

Other apocryphal gospels and acts have been described in our analysis of the apocalyptic and Gnostic developments of Christianity within the early centuries, of which the Gospel of Thomas and the Gospel of Truth are noteworthy examples. The writings just listed vary widely in content and style. Some claim to offer additional revelations about Jesus, often along Gnostic lines. The acts type of writings seek to highlight the supernatural features of the experiences of the apostles. This interest is identical with what was occurring in the literary and conceptual development of second- and third-century Roman literature, which sought to highlight and expand the miraculous features of wise men and philosophers.[16] For example, in Philostratus's *Life of Apollonius of Tyana*, there is a vivid portrayal of the journeys of an itinerant philosopher across Syria and Persia to India. Astonishing events are depicted in connection with his travels and teaching, with the clear aim of suggesting divine approval of the content of his teachings. Jesus and the apostles are similarly portrayed in these apocryphal writings as performing astounding public actions as a way of proving that God is behind their message. In some of them, Jesus strikes down his detractors, as when (in the Infancy Gospel of Thomas) he puts to death one of his playmates who mocks him. Peter outdoes Simon Magus in public stunts before crowds in Rome. As the membership of the Christian communities grew in numbers and rose in cultural status, there was felt to be a place for their equivalent of the romantic novel-like stories of their founder and his original associates. The apocryphal gospels and acts filled this need. Only rarely and in scattered places did any of these documents come to be treated as authoritative, except in cases like the Gnostic gospels in which the perspective of a writing like the Gospel of Truth was held by the Gnostics to be essential for understanding the whole of the Jesus tradition.

The Canon as a Primary Instrument of Unity

By the end of the third century, there was as yet no center of authority for the churches scattered across the Roman empire. The high mobility of the populace (including the Christians), the mounting pressure on the Christians from the empire on political grounds and from philosophers on intellectual grounds, as well as from

---

[15]These noncanonical materials from the early Christian centuries are conveniently brought together in English translation in the two volumes of W. Schneemelcher, ed., English ed. by R. McL. Wilson, *New Testament Apocrypha*, Vol. 1 (Philadelphia: Westminster, 1963); Vol. 2 (1965).

[16]Philostratus, *Life of Apollonius of Tyana*, F.C. Conybeare, ed., Loeb Classical Library (Cambridge, MA: Harvard University Press, 1918, 1960).

groups within the church who were espousing ideas incompatible with those held by the majority of Christians, made it essential to develop fixed norms on the basis of which decisions could be made about Christian faith and life. One of the important possibilities seized by the Christians in this period was the effort to formulate the official list of sacred writings that could be appealed to for settling these burning issues.

Before there was any firm consensus on this issue, however, the growth of the Christian movement and the clear threat of a split within the Roman Empire between centers of power in the eastern and the western Mediterranean led to mounting pressures against the church. The shaky state of the imperial system led many to revive the charge that it was the reaction of the gods against the Christians' refusal to participate in divine honors to the emperor that was causing the profound unrest and uncertainty about the future of the empire. By the second half of the third century, this state of affairs had resulted in major periods of persecution of the Christians. It is these developments and the unforeseen outcome of the empire's turning to Christianity for unity and stability that we discuss in Chapter 8.

Chapter 8

CONFLICT OF CHURCH AND EMPIRE

In spite of Nero's attack on the Christians in the 60s, the issue of the relationship of Christians to the Roman empire did not come into clear focus until well into the second century. Until that time the Christian movement had been widely regarded as a Jewish sect, and its disputes with Judaism were seen by the Roman authorities as intra-Jewish. The Jews had long benefitted from imperial policies that classified their religion in the officially permitted category, and Christians throughout most of the first century seemed to be a variant version of that tolerated group. Major factors in the respect Judaism enjoyed among the Romans were the antiquity of its laws and the fidelity with which its adherents sought to obey them. There were, however, hostile attitudes toward Jews as well. The first century B.C., author and senator, Cicero, said of the Jews that "The practice of their sacred rites was at variance with the glory of our empire, the dignity of our name, and the customs of our ancestors."[1] Earlier, Jews had been regarded as allies of Rome, but by the later first century A.D., the nationalistic uprising of the Jews in Palestine, followed by the revolt under Bar Cochba in the second century, made them suspect in official Roman eyes. As a result, the early Christians benefited from the officially favorable policy toward the Jews, but at the same time there was an ongoing suspicion of possible subversion or political revolt they might instigate.

Christianity Regarded as a Branch of Judaism

The confusion of Christians with Jews in the first century is readily understandable. Judaism was highly diverse, both in Palestine and in the wider Roman world in

---

[1]Cicero, *In Defense of Flaccus* (28.69), from Louis E. Lord, tr., *Cicero, Marcos Tullius, Speeches*, Loeb Classical Library (Cambridge, MA: Harvard University Press, 1937).

which Jews had lived for centuries. Although nearly all Jews identified with the cult that was carried out in the splendid Jerusalem temple of Yahweh, the physical remoteness of that shrine had led Jews to develop the practice of holding meetings in homes or public halls where they could gather to read their ancient writings, to worship, and to study the implications of these scriptures for their own lives. Until the late second century, when the interpretations of the law began to be organized into the collection known as the Mishnah, the pattern of synagogue worship and study seems to have been informal, with local peculiarities. In some areas—such as Egypt, for example—there had been efforts to bring together insights from pagan philosophy and the biblical tradition as exemplified by the extensive writings of Philo of Alexandria. Elsewhere, the intellectual level was more modest, with the primary concerns being for fostering social identity for Jews in a pagan environment. Outwardly, the Christians' gatherings for reading the scriptures and informal worship must have seemed nearly identical to those of the Jews. Both groups studied the Jewish scriptures and prayed to the God of Israel; both were concerned to define their relationship to God as his covenant people; both declared the universal power of God over the universe and over human history.

In the first and second centuries, the Jewish apocalyptic tradition, with its denunciation of worldly powers as demonic and doomed and its parallel hope of divine deliverance, was shared by many Jews and Christians. The political criticism of Rome and the potential for hostility toward the empire in this apocalyptic literature were apparent and could be regarded by the Roman authorities only with profound suspicion. The fact that the Jews had twice revolted against Rome in this period and on other occasions had sided with Middle East nations determined to regain from Rome control over the eastern provinces of the empire increased suspicion of the Jews. As we shall see, the Christians' steadfast refusal to take part in the sacrifices to the Roman gods in behalf of the empire and its leaders became the major issue between the church and the Roman state.

By the middle of the second century, several factors helped to set Christianity apart from Judaism in the eyes of the Romans. The Jews, following the crushing defeat of their forces under Bar Kochba in the second revolt against the Romans, abandoned the nationalist cause and turned instead to sharpening the definition of themselves as God's covenant people. The criteria for separating themselves from the Gentiles were strict observance of circumcision and of food and sabbath laws and the maintenance of ethnic purity through marriage within their community. The Christians did not observe these requirements, and their numbers included a growing majority of Gentiles, including those from intellectual circles and even some from families involved in the Roman political structure. The burials of Christians in the catacombs of Rome began to display distinctive Christian art at this time. Just as Judaism was organizing itself into what became the rabbinic system, the Christians were developing regional hierarchical structures that were presided over by a bishop, with presbyters (elders) and deacons under his supervision. There was no mistaking that this movement was different from Judaism. The major distinction, however, was that whereas the Jews, as a substitute for offering sacrifices in the name of the emperor, agreed to pay to Rome the equivalent of the tax they had paid to the temple in Jerusalem before its destruction, the Christians would not under any conditions share in the emperor cult which the Romans saw as both symbol of loyalty on the part of the citizens and guarantee of divine support for the empire on the part of the gods. To bear the name of Christian, therefore, was evidence of attitudes hostile toward Rome.

The Central Issue: Christian Nonparticipation in the State Cult

The expectation that there would be universal participation in the rites in behalf of the emperor became increasingly important at the turn of the second century. The first clear evidence of this expectation is in the famous correspondence between the emperor Trajan and Pliny, governor of the province of Bithynia in Asia Minor. There is further evidence of the importance of the state cult in the policies of the emperors. As said earlier, Domitian (81–96), for example, insisted that he be addressed as *dominus et deus* ("Lord and God"). Most of the peoples conquered by the Romans were polytheistic and seemed to have recognized the similarities between the roles of their gods and those of the Romans. It was possible for them to find Roman equivalents for the deities of their own religions. Accordingly, these subject peoples were quite willing to take part in the divine honors in behalf of the emperor. Because the Romans believed that the maintenance of political, social, and moral order was directly dependent on continued devotion to the gods by the Romans and all those subject to Rome, the refusal of the Christians to participate in this politico-religious rite was seen as subversive.

The Christians' acclamation of Jesus as Lord (in Greek, *kyrios*; in Latin, *dominus*) forced them to decide which person was to be acknowledged by them as Lord: Christ or Caesar? Failure to offer a libation to the genius, or guardian spirit, of the emperor was a clear sign of disloyalty. The belief in the divinity of rulers that was widespread among the Greek kings combined with the Roman concept of divine support for rulers to construct an idea of sacrifice in behalf of the monarch. This idea was almost universally accepted in this period, and it served to bind the diverse peoples ruled by Rome in support of the emperor. The refusal of the Christians to share in this mixture of devotion and patriotism set them apart as suspect and despicable. The Christians' interpretation of the fall of empires, past and future, as signs of God's activity in history only heightened the suspicion that Christianity was a subversive movement. Both Christian apocalyptic writings and the Christian Sibylline oracles foretold in cryptic, symbolic language the downfall of earthly empires before the establishment of God's Rule in the earth. Jewish opponents of Christianity drew to the attention of the officials the import of these predictions of doom promulgated by the Christians.

Yet the Christians from the beginning had insisted on their gratitude for the order that Rome maintained and on their commitment to obey Roman law. Paul advised the Roman Christians to be subject to the governing authorities as having been placed in power by God (Rom. 13:1), to pay taxes, and to honor the rulers as "ministers of God" (13:6–7). The author of Acts makes the point repeatedly that neither Paul nor the other Christian leaders were ever guilty of violation of Roman law. The author of the First Letter of Peter calls his readers to be subject to human institutions, including governors and emperors, who are to be honored by Christians (I Peter 2:13–17). Yet Christians remained under suspicion because of the more or less secret nature of their gatherings and the implicitly anti-Roman nature of their hopes for the triumph of God's kingdom over the earthly powers.

One of the few serious political problems for the emperors in the first four decades of the second century was the Jewish revolt, which was put down in 135 with the defeat of the nationalists and the transformation of Jerusalem and its temple site into a fully Roman city with a shrine to the chief Roman god, Jupiter. Nerva (96–98) seems to have reversed the anti-Christian policy of Domitian. The policy of Trajan (98–117) as outlined in his response to Pliny was to allow the Christians to continue their movement, so long as they were not called before the Roman authorities, in which case they could choose between making the sacrifice in behalf of the emperor or death. Similarly, Hadrian (117–138) ruled that action was to be taken against Christians only as lawbreakers, and that they were to be protected against informers or unfounded accusations against them.

The Christian engagement with Roman intellectuals continued, and the Christian apologists of the second century sought to show that their teachings were in harmony with true philosophy of the Greek tradition (Plato and the Stoics, especially), and that Christians were the soul of the world, devoted to the service of humanity. In an anonymous treatise of this period addressed to someone named Diognetus, its author declares that "What the soul is in the body, that are the Christians in this world." They preserve the body, and even though hated by the body, as flesh hates the spirit, they love and preserve the body.[2] By the second half of the second century, however, the success and increased visibility of Christianity resulted in its heightened vulnerability, with the result that a number of its leaders were challenged by the imperial authorities and executed.

The oldest and most detailed report of these martyrdoms describes the death of Polycarp, bishop of Smyrna in Asia Minor. He is reported by ancient tradition to have been a disciple of John the Apostle and to have lived from about 70 until his martyrdom in 155 or 157. The Roman proconsul offered to release him on condition

---

[2]Epistle to Diognetus (6), in K. Lake, trans. *The Apostolic Fathers*, Loeb Classical Library (Cambridge, MA: Harvard University Press, 1912–1913).

that he would acclaim the emperor as lord and offer sacrifice, to which he replied, "I have served God eighty-six years, and he has never done wrong to me. How, then, could I blaspheme the King who saved me?"[3] He insisted that he was a Christian and therefore could not swear by the guardian spirit of the emperor. When he was about to die, he looked up to heaven and praised God for the knowledge of himself and his people that God had provided and for the privilege of being granted a place among the martyrs. His final petition was that his death might be a sacrifice acceptable to God.[4] The author of this account of Polycarp's martyrdom notes that he was the twelfth in that region to die for his witness as a Christian.[5] An ancient and probably reliable account of the death of the second-century leader Justin and several of his Christian associates reports that the crucial issue in their interrogation by the Roman officer was that they declared themselves to be Christians and therefore refused to offer the required sacrifice to the emperor. All were forthwith beheaded.[6]

The growing tendency in the Roman Empire to combine features of various religious traditions at the turn of the third century was evident in the highest place: the imperial family. Septimius Severus (193–211), of African origins, had sought to legitimate his role as caesar by claiming that Marcus Aurelius (161–180) had adopted him as son. But he also was eager to lend an aura of divine sanction to himself by having himself identified in ceremonies and on coins with Sol, the god of the Sun, and his wife, Julia Domna, as the Moon. It was further claimed that Julia Domna was Cybele, a deity in Asia Minor known as the mother of the gods. Her son, Caracalla (198–217), called himself "Lord" and "Ruler of the World," and sought to unite all humanity religiously in devotion to the Egyptian god, Serapis, who combined features of Zeus and Osiris as sovereign and healer. A little later, Julia Mamaea, mother of Severus Alexander (222–235), was designated as mother of all the gods. In these circumstances, the refusal of the Christians to adopt any kind of synthesis between their religion and those of the rest of the empire seemed to the authorities all the more odd and annoying.

In spite of the efforts of some emperors, such as Commodus (176–192), to relax the opposition to Christians and even though there was a significant number of conversions of women within the imperial establishment, pressures against the church continued to mount. In 202 Septimius Severus decreed a prohibition of conversions to Christianity. Empire-wide persecution of the Christians began, with reports of martyrdoms from Antioch, Corinth, and Alexandria in the east to Rome and Carthage in the west. On occasion there was sufficient curiosity about this religion and sympathy toward it to lead members of the imperial establishment to

---

[3]Martyrdom of Polycarp (8–9), in William Jurgens, trans. and ed., *Faith of the Early Fathers* (Collegeville, MN: The Liturgical Press, 1970), pp. 30–31.
[4]Martyrdom of Polycarp 14.
[5]Martyrdom of Polycarp 19.
[6]Martyrdom of the Holy Martyrs, in *Ante-Nicene Fathers*, Vol. 1 (Grand Rapids, MI: Eerdmans, n.d.), pp. 305–306.

inquire about or even quietly to support Christianity. For example, although many political leaders were scornful of the movement, Julia Mamaea, the mother of Severus Alexander (222–235), set up an extended conversation with the great Christian scholar, Origen (185–254), the outstanding intellectual figure in the church at that time. A later Roman historian reported that in Severus Alexander's imperial chapel there were statues of great religious figures of the past, including Orpheus (the mythical Greek musician), Abraham, and Christ. Severus Alexander, whose origins were in Syria, was killed on the banks of the Rhine by Maximinus (235–238), who tried to combat the imperial policy of quiet support for the church by a campaign of martyrdom for its leaders. The reasons given for this imperial scorn of Christianity were that it was attracting to its membership the lowest levels of society, that it was engaging in shameful secret rites, and that it was thereby ignoring the great Roman religious traditions.

A Latin writer of the late second or early third century, Minucius Felix, reports the description of Christianity by one Caecilius as the pronouncement about the universe and its powers by "people ignorant of learning, unlettered, unacquainted with even the meanest arts" and as a "sham philosophy." He calls the Christians "a gang of discredited and proscribed desperadoes . . . gathered together from the lowest dregs of the populace." They are "ignorant men and credulous women—and women are naturally unstable—and have formed a rabble of impious conspirators; at their nocturnal gatherings, solemn fasts, and barbarous meals; the bond of union is not any sacred rite but crime. They are a secret tribe that lurks in darkness and shuns the light, silent in public, chattering in corners."[7]

Intensification of Roman Opposition to Christianity and the Christian Response: Martyrdom

Apocalyptic pronouncements about the end of the age and the destruction by God of the earthly regimes persisted in the churches of Syria and Asia Minor. In the middle of the third century, this view of the impending overturn of the present order had a resurgence in the West as well. Tertullian (150–230) in Carthage became more and more interested in the pronouncements of self-styled New Prophets and their revelations about the future. In his later years he became persuaded by the visions and predictions of the end proclaimed by Montanus and later developed his own version of the apocalyptic expectation of the destruction of the present order and the establishment of the Kingdom of God. Hippolytus of Rome (170–230?), who was probably originally from Antioch, also emphasized the themes that Christians had borrowed from Jewish apocalyptic writing, with the result that the Roman authorities

[7]Quoted from J. Stevenson and W.H.C. Frend, eds., *The New Eusebius* (London: SPCK, 1987), pp. 177–178.

suspected that subversion of the state was being secretly organized by the leaders of the church.

Instead of the martyrdoms cooling the fervor of the Christian movement, however, this violent imperial effort at suppression succeeded in increasing the zeal and commitment of its members. Irenaeus, although eloquent and learned in combating what he believed to be the heresies taught by his contemporaries in the name of Christianity, continued to affirm his expectation of the New Age and saw the death of the Christian witnesses as evidence that it was soon to come. Although Origen did not share the apocalyptic expectation of Irenaeus, he wrote a treatise, *Exhortation to Martyrdom*, in which he described anyone who died for the faith as entering mystical union with Christ in his suffering and death.[8]

Origen prized martyrdom because it showed publicly who the true believers were; only the martyr was the authentic follower of Christ.[9] Quoting extensively from the Psalms and the Old Testament prophets and even more from the gospels and the letters of Paul, Origen developed the case that God has already stored up in heaven a reward for those who have shown their fidelity to Christ by accepting death as his followers. Just as God ordered Abraham to leave his native land to journey to the unknown land of promise, so Christians are called by God to leave this world and prepare to enter the kingdom of heaven. Belief in the heart is not enough: It must be matched by confession in public. From the days of Trajan onward, this public affirmation or denial of oneself as a Christian had been the crucial factor in deciding whether one accused of membership in the movement was in fact a Christian and therefore doomed to be executed by the Roman authorities. As we have noted, refusal to take part in the imperial rites, and especially the failure to take an oath by the fortune or genius of the emperor, was seen as a subversive act because it was considered to jeopardize the support of the empire by the gods. The true Christians rejected any conformity or even compromise on this issue, Origen insisted. Central for identification of the individual as a member of God's New Covenant people was the passage in the gospels in which Jesus calls his disciples to take up the cross and follow him (Matt. 16:26–27). God will render to each according to his or her response to that demand. The faithful will be enthroned and will receive multiple awards in the presence of God. True blessedness is to affirm this basis of the covenant in spite of scorn of neighbors and officials, because it will be acclaimed by the heavenly throngs of the saints and the angels. Jesus's call to his disciples to "drink the cup" was a reference, not to the Eucharist, but to martyrdom. The special significance of such a death is "that it is endured for the sake of Christianity and piety and holiness," according to Origen. The first baptism was with water; the second is with the blood

---

[8]Origen, "Exhortation to Martyrdom," translation in Henry Chadwick, ed., *Alexandrian Christianity* (Philadelphia: Westminster, 1954).
[9]Henry Chadwick and J. E. Oulton, eds., *Alexandrian Christianity* (Westminster: Library of Christian Classics, 1977), p. 391.

of martyrdom. Jesus's instructions about accepting death at the hands of the authorities are addressed to the inner core of his disciples rather than to the masses. Accordingly, no one should be surprised that large numbers of professing Christians submit to imperial pressure and offer the required pagan sacrifices, and thus avoid martyrdom.

Origen says further that steadfastness in one's profession of faith in Christ must take precedence over even family obligations and loyalties. The world will hate the martyrs, but God will ultimately vindicate them. Meanwhile, there is to be no compromise or rationalization on the issue of officially required participation in divine honors to the emperor. Instead, although longing to depart this life and be with Christ, Christians are to follow the counsel of Jesus's parables: to stand firm like the house on the rock, resisting the erosive forces that seek to undermine faith in Christ alone; to continue to bear the true fruit of faith, while others are producing the worthless products of deceit and compromise. In this way the faithful will be enabled to stand unshaken in the stormy attacks by the evil powers because they recognize (with Paul, II Cor. 4:17–18) that the sufferings of the present time are but a prelude to the glory that is to be revealed for and through the true witnesses to Christ. The pain and death are merely transitory to the situation of glory in God's presence that is to come.

After the murder of Severus Alexander in 235, the empire was for thirty-five years torn by competing claimants to the imperial title and by ongoing threats to the borders of the empire on the Euphrates, the Danube, and the Rhine. It was through the efforts of a series of military-oriented emperors in the seventies and eighties of the third century that order and firm borders were restored, but the result was to heighten the issue of the unpatriotic and seriously nonconformist attitude of the Christians. Yet interest in Christianity continued to flourish across the spectrum of economic and cultural strata of Roman society. Celsus had remarked that if everyone wanted to be a Christian, the Christians would no longer want them.[10] To this Origen responded:

> So far as they are able, Christians leave no stone unturned to spread the faith in all parts of the world. Some, in fact, have done the work of going round not only cities but even villages and country cottages to make others pious toward God. One could not say they do this for the sake of wealth, since sometimes they do not even accept money for the necessities of life, and if ever they are compelled to do so by want in this respect, they are content with what is necessary and no more, even if several people are willing to share with them and to give them more than they need. I admit that at the present time perhaps, when on account of the multitude of people coming to the faith even rich men and persons in positions

---

[10]Quoted by Origen, in *Contra Celsum* (3.9), Henry Chadwick, trans., (New York: Cambridge University Press, 1965).

of honor, and ladies of refinement and high birth favorably regard adherents of the faith, one might venture to say that some become leaders of the Christian teaching for the sake of a little prestige. Yet at the beginning when there was great risk attached particularly to teachers, no such suspicion could reasonably be entertained. Even now, however, the disgrace among the rest of society is greater than the supposed reputation among fellow-believers.[11]

Even when Origen's reminder that there are more who profess Christian faith is balanced against the fact that there are fewer willing to put their lives on the line as a witness, it is clear that he perceived and welcomed the range of persons who were drawn by the Christian message, which he regarded as at least theoretically universal in its appeal. Origen's positive attitude toward Greek philosophical tradition, which was shared with such leaders as Cyprian, bishop of Carthage (200–258), disposed him to affirm many of the traditions and intellectual values of Greco-Roman culture. On the question of Christian participation in pagan rites or oaths in behalf of the emperor, however, he was adamantly negative.

The Growing Strength of Christianity and the Mounting Imperial Opposition

In the imperial power struggle of this period, the emperor Philip (244–249) seems to have been sympathetic with the Christians. His attempts to reshape the army and the administration of the provinces failed, however. His successor, Decius (249–251), proceeded with ruthless vigor to attack these problems, and he sought to support the attack by a reassertion of traditional Roman religious values and practices. Accordingly, his attack on Christians as deviants was severe. It was probably Decius's decree that there be universal participation in the sacrifices in behalf of the emperor that provoked Origen's treatise on martyrdom. Ironically, Origen was not executed as a confessor, but the torture and sufferings he underwent were so severe that they led to his death in 254. Martyrdoms are reported from Rome to Antioch, and tactics to enforce this decree were adopted across the empire from Spain to Egypt. Everyone was required to sacrifice, and those who complied were given a certificate. Failure to possess such a credential was a capital crime. Eusebius reports that many Christians fled to remote areas or simply yielded to the empire's demands.[12] Reports of those who lapsed from the Christian faith extend in rank from simple believers to the bishop of Smyrna, and geographically from Rome to Egypt. Lists of the faithful martyrs have been preserved, but there is no way to determine the actual numbers involved. The victims were probably in the hundreds—a small percentage of those

[11]Origen, *Contra Celsum*, 3.9.
[12]Eusebius, *Ecclesiastical History*, 6.40.10.

who had professed faith or were associated with the Christian communities. Among those put to death in this purge were members of groups regarded as heretical, such as the Montanists in Asia Minor. The resulting problem for the Christians of how to deal with those who defected under pressure was to haunt the church for decades to come (see the next section).

The mixture of astonishing courage of convictions on the part of many Christians with the intellectually impressive defense of the faith offered by brilliant thinkers of the caliber of Origen forced many thoughtful Romans to reassess their attitudes toward this strong and surging religious movement. There is no hint of an official attitude that assumed, "Just keep quiet about Christianity and it will go away." Instead, the emperor Valerian (253–260) renewed the attack on the Christians, going so far as to prohibit them from gathering in their places of worship or even in cemeteries for burial of their members. The antagonism toward the church was heightened by the fact that, at precisely this time when the empire was undergoing major financial and military crises, the churches were stable and economically prosperous even though some bishops and ordinary Christians alike were driven into exile or put to death. Typical of the range of responses of Christians to the crisis created by the emperors is that of Cyprian, the bishop of Carthage. As noted earlier, at first, he simply fled from Carthage while maintaining communications with the Christians in the provincial capital. For this escape he drew criticism among the more radical opponents of Rome, but he seems to have justified his action on the ground that he was providing stability and leadership for the faithful in a time of crisis. Later, however, he was exiled by the authorities and in 258 he was beheaded in Carthage, the first bishop there to undergo a martyr's death.

The Climax of Imperial Hostility to Christianity and the Beginning of Transformation of the Empire

At the end of the third century, Diocletian (284–305) made another attempt to regain order in the empire. In the more than 100 years before his accession to power, major social, political, and economic changes had occurred. The once-dominant military and political roles of the senators (the traditional elite with respect to wealth and power) were shifting increasingly to the *equites* (or "knights"), a group whose economic status and political power were far below that of the senators. It was now a frequent occurrence that persons of low position in the Roman social order proved effective in the military or in an administrative role and were designated as knights and given central posts under the emperors. The emperors divided the provinces so that the number of persons to whom the emperor could assign the role as head of a province was doubled and hence the circle of the emperor's personal power was enlarged. The military system dominated the empire, and it was controlled by the emperor.

As an aid to fostering stability and tranquility in the realm, Diocletian adopted the practice of having titles and names of the Greek and Roman gods and mythological figures applied to himself and to his major officials. Accordingly, he took the name of Jupiter for himself. Because the extent of the empire was so vast that no one leader could effectively administer it all, Diocletian adopted a policy of dividing the provinces into smaller units that could be directly governed by his designated officials. At the same time, he imposed men of his choice to control both the eastern portion of the empire where he was resident and the western provinces as well. To preserve the old tradition of heredity in the imperial rule, he adopted two men as "caesars" and married his daughters to them: Constantius to share with Maximian (Diocletian's chief colleague) responsibility for rule in the West, and Galerius as his own major aide in the East. Maximian was identified with Hercules, who in mythology was the strong man who triumphed over beasts that symbolized the powers of evil. Then in 305, Diocletian and Maximian abdicated, after naming as "caesars" Severus in the West and Maximin in the East. Constantius and Galerius were designated by Diocletian as "augusti," and to them he assigned the two new caesars and designated assigned territories for them to control: Africa and Pannonia (Severus), Egypt and Syria (Maximin). Constantius was in charge of Spain and Gaul, but he took the initiative in suppressing a rebellion in Britain. Galerius had commanded the armies along the Danube, where the threat of invasion by Germanic tribes was recurrent, but in 298 he had shifted to the eastern borders when the Persians tried to regain control of the Syrian and Asia Minor provinces of the Roman empire that had once belonged to Persia. Further evidence of the effort to exploit Roman religious traditions to achieve unity and order is reflected in the coins Diocletian issued, which honored "The Genius of the Roman People." These imperial figures also adopted the practice of wearing clothing or displaying symbols, such as the radiant crown of the Sun God, which implied their links with the gods.

A major tactic for channeling the populace of the empire into participation in public commitment to the empire was Diocletian's decree requiring everyone to offer the sacrifices and oaths in behalf of the emperor. All the Christians, whether civilians or in the military, were required to perform these state rites. When an omen consulted by the emperor failed to give an unambiguous response, Diocletian concluded that it was the consequence of the nonparticipation of the Christians, with the result that the gods were showing their displeasure. In the spring of 303, the church in Nicomedia, a leading city on the neck of land that joins Europe and Asia Minor, was destroyed in the presence of civilian and military officers. Apparently Diocletian hoped to establish a major city there to serve as the capital of the eastern empire, or even of the empire as a whole. Although he did not live to see the fulfillment of this hope, a city in the same vicinity, Byzantium, was to become the center of the empire and to be named in honor of the one who made it the seat of Roman power: Constantinople. Diocletian's decree ordered that all churches were to be destroyed throughout the empire, as well as all copies of the Christian scriptures. Any Christians who served in governmental posts were to be dismissed, and any who had special legal privileges were to lose them immediately. They could not serve as witnesses in the courts in most types of civil cases. The only concession was that there was not to be mass murder of all adherents to this faith. Yet in Nicomedia alone, 268 Christians were put to death as a consequence of this decree. Similar purges of the Christians took place in other eastern provinces as well. Although Diocletian shared control of the realm with other "caesars" in the West, the attack on the Christians was not matched in those provinces where the movement was not perceived as so great a threat to Roman control. But the basic issue was posed for the Christians: Could Christianity and the empire co-exist?

In the early years of the fourth century, Constantius was taken ill in York (in what is now England). He sent for his son, Constantine, who was with Galerius in the eastern empire. Described by some ancient Roman sources as the child of a commoner or even of a prostitute, Constantine's intelligence and administrative skills continued to stand him in good stead when the army in Britain proclaimed him ruler of the western provinces. In 307 Severus was deposed and fled to Ravenna, where he was soon put to death. Maxentius, who succeeded him, had himself declared *princeps* ("leader") and assumed control of Rome and southern Italy. Meanwhile, Constantine had married the daughter of Maximian and took from him the title of Augustus. The coalition between Galerius and Maximian in the East was broken by the latter's defection. Galerius's efforts to impose order on the empire failed, as can be inferred from the fact that at one point there were six who bore the imperial title. Initially, Galerius sent a colleague, Licinius, to try to regain control of the northwestern provinces from Constantine, but soon these two were allied against Maxentius. In 312 Constantine led his troops across the Alps into northern Italy where, in spite of fierce opposition from Maxentius's army, he was victorious and found that city after city opened its gates to him. The Milvian bridge, north of Rome, was the scene of the final decisive battle in which the vastly more numerous Roman troops were defeated by Constantine, who entered Rome as victor.

Various legends have come down from this time that may or may not have a basis in fact. One tells that Constantine had sought the help of the God of the Christians when he undertook his invasion of Italy and that it had been promised to him. There are reports of his use on the shields of his troops an X or a ✶, which consists of the first two letters in the Greek word, Christos, and was a symbolic representation of Christ. When Constantine was declared emperor in Britain, he released all the Christians in the province under his control, granting them full freedom of worship. Conversely, Maxentius is reported to have been told by a Roman oracle that the real enemy of Rome would perish in the battle at the Milvian Bridge. Only in retrospect was it clear that, according to this legend, the divinely supported victor was Constantine. In Rome he was confirmed as senior Augustus by the Roman senate. His policies of freedom were extended to the Christians in these regions, including the restoration of property the government had seized from them. Licinius, who controlled the eastern provinces, gave a similar grant of freedom to the Christians there. Even Maximin (309–313), who came to power in the east, agreed to religious freedom for the Christian subjects there as well.

The Beginning of the Transformation of the Church under Constantine

In many ways Christianity had been victorious in this struggle for power and popular commitment within the far-flung empire. But in gaining imperial support—or as some cynics might say, through being used by Constantine to take over the empire— the Christians were confronted with a series of problems and more severe responsibilities than would have been clearly defined a century earlier. Foremost was the relation of church and state. How were the lines of responsibility to be drawn between the ecclesiastical and the political authorities? A prior question was: Who will now make the decisions about the leadership of the churches? About the defining of areas assigned to a bishop? About the exercise of authority within that framework? Since the new emperor had claimed support of the God of the Christians in gaining victory over his enemies, was he to be the center of decision-making within the church? If not, how and by whom were these crucial decisions to be made? Who would control the property of the churches?

A major problem within the church that we have mentioned earlier was how to treat those who, under pressure from the pagan leaders of the empire, had violated their Christian obligations by offering prayers or sacrifice to the Roman gods. Were these lapses on the part of formerly professing Christians simply to be forgiven or overlooked? Was there some purging process by which they could be purified and regain their status within the church? Some members proposed that the solution for restoring to their faith those who were regarded by the faithful as traitors was a repetition of their baptism. What did that imply about the efficacy of their original baptism if they now needed to pass through the cleansing waters again?

These kinds of issues did not originate in the time of Constantine. They had been more or less submerged within the church for some time as it sought to present a united front against its antagonists. Once that pressure from the central government was removed, however, the unresolved intra-Christian issues rose rapidly to the surface. The matter of restoring or excluding those who had betrayed their Christian commitment under pressure came to a head in North Africa, specifically in Numidia, the province to the west of Carthage. The leaders of the church there had a mixed record on the issues of betrayal of the faith and surrender of the scriptures. When Constantine, on advice of an ecclesiastical counselor, supported Caecilian to become bishop of Carthage, immediately the stories surfaced about this man's having yielded to pressure from the Romans during the period of persecution. In Numidia the

140

church leaders had compromised to the extent of turning in copies of the scriptures, although one of those involved, Menurius, claimed that he had fooled the officials into thinking he had done so. In any case, the Numidians, led by one Donatus, denounced Caecilian and the bishops who had consecrated him, on the ground that they had all been traitors to the Christian faith and that they had refused to provide food for those Christians imprisoned by the Romans. Donatus went so far as to begin rebaptizing the clergy who had defected. At a council convened in 312, the Numidians formally rejected Caecilian and those who had installed him as bishop. The furore that resulted from this local action involved accusations against several of the leaders of the church in Rome itself, so that the integrity of various bishops and archdeacons was called into question. Yet as troublesome as the basic issue of dealing with these who were regarded as traitors was the larger question of with whom responsibility rested to adjudicate such disputes. In 316 in Milan, Constantine took a step of grave consequences when he ruled that Caecilian was properly the bishop and ordered the confiscation of the property of the followers of Donatus. This action not only raised doubts about the emperor's earlier proclamation of freedom of conscience in religious matters; it also failed to remedy the situation of the church in Numidia, which continued to reject Caecilian. At a council of the church convened in Arles in France, an effort was made to force clergy to accept the appointments and assignments made through these theoretically universal conventions of clergy. The powerful hand of the emperor could no longer be ignored, however. The church-state issue was not resolved but intensified.

The high esteem in which the martyrs continued to be held by the church following the assumption of imperial power by Constantine had two major effects. It produced a large body of material in which the martyrs were depicted in vivid narrative style, including details of their courage, suffering, and death. Known to modern scholarship as *The Acts of the Martyrs*, this material is readily available in various translations. Although the details are no doubt heightened and even romanticized, they still give a clear picture of the issues that confronted Christians under pressure from the empire and of the enormous faith and strength that enabled martyrs to refuse to conform to the demands of the political authorities. A vivid example of this type of literature is the *Letter of Phileas*. This man, who was noted for his vast secular learning, wrote a letter describing the martyrdoms that took place in Alexandria in the early years of the persecution under Diocletian. He noted the precedents from the lives of earlier martyrs and the instructions given in the sacred writings. The martyrs followed the example of Christ who "humbled himself unto death, even death on a cross" [Phil. 2:8]:

> What words could be adequate to the courage and the heroism they showed under every torture? Everyone was allowed to insult them as he liked: some beat them with cudgels, some with rods, some with scourges, some again with thongs, some with whips of rope. And though the spectacle of their indignities kept

changing, it constantly involved the utmost viciousness. Some were affixed to wooden horses with their hands tied behind them, and then had their limbs torn apart by pulleys. Then the torturers at a signal got to work on their entire bodies, and then not merely on their sides (as in the case of murderers), but they tormented them with instruments on their belly, the thighs, and the cheeks. Others were fastened by one hand and hauled up from the portico, and no pain could have been more intense than the stretching of the joints and limbs. Others were tied to columns facing inwards with their feet on the ground, the weight of the body forcing the bonds to tighten.[13]

After describing additional forms of torture to which the martyrs were exposed, Phileas goes on to depict the results of this treatment at the hands of the civil authorities and the hostile populace:

> In this way some passed on under the tortures, putting their adversary to shame by their courage; others were locked up in prison semi-conscious, and not many days afterwards, overcome by their agony, attained perfection. Others with care and a sojourn in prison recovered their health and became ever more confident. At any rate, the order was given that they had a choice either of participating in the unholy sacrifice and going free, and thus obtaining from their persecutors a tainted liberty, or else not sacrificing and paying the penalty of death. Here they did not hesitate, but gladly went to their death. For they were aware of what the sacred scriptures had prescribed for us. It said: "Whoever sacrifices to other gods shall be utterly destroyed, and you shall have no other gods before me" [Exod. 22:20; 20:3].

The editor of this letter notes that Phileas, whom he characterizes as a "lover of wisdom as well as a lover of God," had sent this message to fellow members of his diocese while he was in prison, urging them to be faithful unto death, even while his own martyrdom was about to be accomplished.[14]

This type of literature effectively served the aims of those within the church who wanted to give a primary focus to the saints. The saints in both life and death embodied total commitment to the Christian faith and values and therefore came to be regarded not as only models for the faithful in any era, but also as those whose works of love and grace in some way benefited their less worthy followers of the time. The cult of the saints and martyrs can be seen as already developing in this collection of stories about those committed even to death.

Another kind of literature that emerged in this period came from the hand and

---

[13]Quoted from Herbert Musurillo, ed. and trans., *Acts of the Christian Martyrs* (Oxford: Clarendon Press, 1972).

[14]Quoted, with some modifications, from Herbert Musurillo, *Acts of the Christian Martyrs*, pp. 260–265.

archives of Eusebius of Caesarea in Palestine. Born in Caesarea, which by that time was an important center of Christian learning and of Roman culture, Eusebius took as his second name that of his teacher, Pamphilus, who had succeeded to the post held earlier by Origen of Alexandria. During the years before and after the accession to power of Constantine (300–325), Eusebius wrote *Ecclesiastical History*. This encyclopedic work is not only the first of its kind; it contains hundreds of quotations—many of them fairly extensive—from ancient pagan and Christian writers whose works would otherwise have been lost. It describes the origins, growth, and spread of the church, with detailed references to leading figures from the first to the early fourth century. As was appropriate and politically timely, this historical account of the church sees the hand of God at work through what has occurred, and portrays its own epoch as one in which a new purpose of God is about to be achieved. Modern critics of Eusebius think it was to benefit his own standing with Constantine that he shaped his account of the church's transformation from a beleaguered sect to an instrument for achieving imperial power. What is certain is that this weighty work served the emperor as an apologetic for his power role in relation to the new circumstances of the church and that it has served scholars since the fourth century as a rich resource of knowledge of the development of Christianity in the first three centuries.

By the time that Constantine had first assumed power in the west, however, his one-time ally, Licinius, was in control of the imperial regions to the east. It was to this military and cultural challenge that he had now to direct his attention.

Part Two

The Christian Empire and
the Early Middle Ages

Emily Albu Hanawalt

Chapter 9

THE CHRISTIAN EMPIRE AND ARIANISM (324–381)

The Greco-Roman World in 324

In 324 the rival emperors Constantine and Licinius declared war on each other, with the victor to win sole lordship of the Roman Empire. Religion and politics were inextricably linked in this contest. Licinius stood for the ancestral gods of pagan Rome, the gods who had protected and nurtured the state throughout its illustrious history. Before the campaign, Licinius performed the time-honored sacrifices to these gods, and he carried their images into battle as Roman emperors had done for centuries. Constantine's standard-bearer, in vivid contrast, held the golden banner with the new Christian symbol at its top, a jewel-encrusted wreath surrounding the Chi-Rho monogram signifying Christ. The two armies met at Adrianople in Thrace (see Figure 9.1). In the fierce combat Constantine himself was wounded in the thigh before his well-disciplined forces finally defeated their more numerous enemy. The Christian victors credited their standard, called the *labarum* in late fourth-century sources, with miraculous aid against the pagan foe.

Licinius fled and holed up in the ancient city of Byzantium on the Bosphorus, an impregnable fortress that Constantine failed to take in a two-and-a-half month siege. Losses at sea forced Licinius to leave this haven and risk a land battle at Chrysopolis, where once again the labarum presided over his defeat.

Constantine was now master of the empire that he would rule until his death in 337. What was his empire like? In the early fourth century, the Greco-Roman world was very different from the old realm of Augustus or even of Marcus Aurelius, which was swept away by the chaos of the third century. Devastating plagues, military revolts, and civil wars had produced nearly a hundred years of political instability, massive inflation, and fiscal collapse. Germanic and Persian invasions had

147

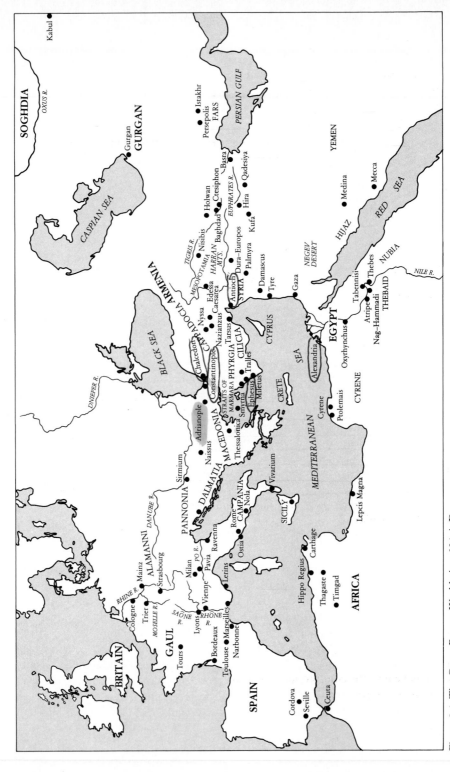

Figure 9.1 The Greco-Roman World circa 324 A.D.

capitalized on a weakened state. This instability on the frontiers strangled trade. To push back the invaders and control civil unrest, emperors had nearly doubled the size of the army. Only an oppressive taxation could support this expanded army as well as a growing central and provincial bureaucracy. The principal financial support came from the land tax levied against the free and slave tenant farmers who had now replaced the old slave plantations. But there were no longer enough peasants to till the soil. Perhaps one-third of North African fields went out of cultivation, and the remaining farmers were tied to the land to assure a continuing supply of produce and taxes. In an increasingly rigid society, tenant farmers everywhere felt the oppressive burden of their proscribed lives and increasing taxation. Did they also sense the widening gap between themselves and the wealthy? The senatorial aristocracy may have been as much as five times wealthier in the fourth century than in the first century C.E. If the century of chaos did not precisely represent a class war, as some historians have claimed, at the very least it exposed heightened social tensions and a rejection of old Roman values. The breakdown was more than military or economic; it was spiritual as well.

The old empire was distinguished by its urban life, and this had not entirely changed. The great cities of the East (including such venerable centers as Alexandria, Ephesus, Antioch, and Jerusalem) were still especially strong, even if civic responsibility was declining as men of wealth and privilege attempted to renege on their old civic duties and withdraw from public life or transfer allegiance from the town to the imperial power. Private spiritual quest replaced civic duty for some; for others, personal greed and the acquisition of vast wealth seemed to cut them off from the celebrated old Roman virtues.

Out of the third-century disorder came the rigid political, economic, and social policies of Diocletian and Constantine, radical revisions of the Roman Empire. Arguably the most profound changes were yet to appear with the creation of a new capital, a new wave of barbarian invasions, and perhaps especially with a thorough Christianization of the society. In an age of anxiety, religious fervor ran high. Transformed by Christianity, this passion would create a new society. If the year 324 saw the restoration of *pax Romana*, the celebrated Roman peace, still there would be no return to old Rome.

Having finally conquered the eastern provinces with his victory over Licinius, Constantine entered into the center of this empire's wealth and resilience, a significantly Christianized Asia Minor. Who were the Christians in 324, and where did they live? Christianity was still largely an urban movement. Christian communities existed in most of the towns throughout the empire, where the poor, manual workers (including slaves) and merchants were the major converts. As early preachers had traveled from city to city, they had founded urban churches, and the parish system had yet to move into the countryside. For this reason, the *pagani*, the country people, came to mean non-Christians. Many peasants, conservative by nature, offered passive resistance to the new religion they confronted only in the towns and whose preachers

149

spoke only Greek or sometimes Latin but not the native languages of the countryside. The army, recruited from the peasantry, was predominantly pagan as well, although soldiers wrenched from their native communities seem to have converted rather easily to the prevailing religion of their commanders and colleagues. Wealthy and powerful families, meanwhile, and particularly the senatorial aristocracy remained largely devoted to ancestral rituals.

The typical Christian, then, was an urban resident of modest means. Geography still played an important role, too. Christianity was strongest in the eastern provinces, closest to the land where Christianity was born and where Greek-speaking missionaries would have the greatest impact. Christian communities were already flourishing in North Africa and Egypt, but some towns in the western provinces (notably in Gaul, Illyricum, and Spain) were still without bishops. And Rome itself remained a hotbed of aristocratic devotion to traditional deities.

In the newly won East, Constantine could witness, more dramatically than in the West where paganism was dominant, the power of the Christian community in an otherwise alienated world. While pagans were withdrawing from the civic life in towns all over the empire or transferring their loyalty from the local town to the imperial power, Christians were shifting their allegiance to supporting the church and nurturing the poor and needy. The bishops of these cities were building local organizations with stable and potent administrations destined to survive the collapse of the imperial structure in the West and to exercise considerable power and influence in the East throughout the Middle Ages. Christianity had its own distinctive flavor in the East, too, where Greek rather than Latin was the common tongue that linked peoples of various native languages and dialects and where traditions of ancient philosophy and law, of Hellenic literature and culture were still strong. Christianity was absorbing this culture and its ideals and forging a moral unity that would create the sensibilities of a new age.

Constantine's Christian Capital

To celebrate his victory over Licinius, Constantine at once began plans for a new Christian capital untainted by pagan rites and dedicated to the Christian God. Rome and its rowdy populace had become a liability to recent emperors. Impossible to defend against a siege, the venerable city was also strategically unimportant, far from the empire's eastern heartland. For Constantine, Rome's connection with pagan ritual provided additional problems, especially since the pagan senators, so wealthy and powerful, could continue to thwart his majesty just as they had acclaimed the rival emperor Maxentius during the civil wars.

Constantine chose the old city of Byzantium to replace Rome. The new capital would soon attract stories about its foundation that were modeled on the myths of Rome's creation. Like Aeneas, the legendary Trojan hero whose gods guided him to

Italy, Constantine is supposed to have been advised by oracles that protected him from choosing the wrong site. He allegedly looked at Thessalonica, Chalcedon, and even Troy itself, Rome's mythic parent, before turning to Byzantium. Within about seventy years, the residents would discover that the city was situated on seven hills, like Rome, and they would divide it into fourteen regions, also in imitation of Rome. Constantine modestly named the city after himself, Constantinople, and gave it the title "New Rome."

Constantine's city was a brilliant choice that would assure the survival of the Christian empire. Strategically placed close to both the Danube and eastern frontiers, it straddled Europe and Asia and also commanded the sea routes that linked East and West. For its fleet and merchant ships, it boasted a calm inland harbor, the famed Golden Horn. Although easily accessible, its position along the Bosphorus was highly defensible as well, requiring land walls on only one of its three sides. Constantine pillaged the empire, including Rome, for antiquities befitting the new capital. The imperial city needed a senate, too, mostly as an adornment rather than a potential rival. Some senatorial families were induced to move from Rome with gifts of property in the new city. Late sources even report that Constantine used clever coercion, sending some Roman senators away on campaign against the Persians and, in their absence, moving their wives and families to Constantinople where the senators eventually joined them. Much of the senate, however, came from families of recent wealth, the new group of administrators unfettered to senatorial traditions and so ripe for social and religious change. Many doubtless converted as an act of conscience; for all who did, conversion to Christianity proved a good career move.

Constantine consecrated his Christian capital on May 11, 330, the anniversary of the city's principal martyr, Saint Mocius. Constantinople would become the greatest city in Christendom and the monastic center of the empire, throughout its history housing 325 monasteries and nunneries in city and suburbs. The city was a Christian reliquary that would boast the tool that Noah used to build his ark, the head of John the Baptist, the stone of Jesus' tomb, the crown of thorns, the Virgin Mary's belt and robe, and countless other precious remains. Constantine himself commissioned the great church of Holy Wisdom, Hagia Sophia, and many other sacred buildings, including the Church of the Holy Apostles, with its twelve symbolic tombs and a thirteenth for himself.

The Arians

Constantine's city would be a monument to Christian victory over paganism, but could the emperor forge harmony within the Christian community itself? This question haunted Constantine's days and nights when a struggle among Christians threatened the faith as pagan persecutions never had.

United in the promise of salvation, early Christians had not troubled to hammer out coherent doctrine, but communities in different regions of the empire were developing their own theological concepts and beliefs that sometimes conflicted with the assumptions made by other Christians. How should these conflicts be resolved? Each urban center, with its own bishop, was more or less autonomous. Churches boasting descent from apostolic founders claimed special authority, but there was still no firm hierarchy of administration for settling disputes or determining and enforcing incipient doctrine. The Arian controversy would compel the Church to move toward creating both universal dogma and government.

Arius (ca. 250–336) was a Christian priest in Alexandria, Egypt, which had long been the cultural center of the Hellenized, intellectual East where Christianity was forging an alliance with Greek philosophy. In attempting to understand the nature of Jesus, Arius began with the Platonic idea of God's eternal oneness. Since there cannot be two gods, he reasoned, Jesus the Son must be a creation of the Father and not co-eternal with him, therefore not fully god. "There was a time," Arius preached, "when he [Christ] was not." Nor is he fully human, but he is a bridge between God and the world of human beings. Arius took his ideas directly to the people, working his dogma into popular ballads that were sung, his opponents claimed, "on the sea, at the mill, and on the road."

His bishop, Alexander, and the young deacon and future bishop Athanasius were alarmed by the number of supporters Arius attracted. "Ario-maniacs," they called them, stricken with an "Arian plague." If Christ was not fully human, how could he suffer and die on the cross? If he was not god, how could he promise salvation? Neoplatonism had led to a disdain for the physical world, but the essence of Christianity was the affirmation of God's presence in the created order and among men and women. The Christian God became man and intervened in history to save humankind. If Christ was less than fully god or fully human, the sacrifice was meaningless. Behind Athanasius stood the people of Asia Minor, whose doctrine supported the complete equality of God the Father and God the Son.

The church lacked a structure for resolving such a fundamental conflict. And so it was the emperor who summoned the first general council of bishops to Nicaea in 325. Constantine seems mainly to have longed for consensus, an end to dissension that threatened the unity of his empire and of Christendom. Awed by the emperor's presence, the bishops allowed him to dominate the council and agreed to the solution that Constantine's western advisors offered him. The council produced the Nicene Creed, which affirms that Jesus Christ is fully god and fully human, consubstantial (*homoousios*) with the Father. A term current in the unphilosophic West, the homoousion was distasteful to the intellectual sensibilities of the East, including Constantinople and the territories of Asia Minor, Syria-Palestine, and Egypt, but the emperor's advocacy assured its promulgation.

If the decisions of this first ecumenical (i.e., general) council were important, equally critical was the emperor's role at Nicaea. He convened and chaired the council, he proposed a doctrinal formulation that the council felt obliged to accept, and he authorized civil penalties for the parties deemed heretical, banishing Arius and his unreformed partisans. Under Constantine's domination, the church was subsumed by the jurisdiction of the Christian empire. By permitting imperial dominance, the council set a crucial precedent for the future relationship between church and state, forming the foundation for the Eastern Roman Empire.

Constantine died in 337, having recently been baptized by the Arian bishop Eusebius of Nicomedia. The Roman senate decreed him a god; posterity would call him a saint, the Great, and peer of the apostles. He deserves the last title at least, because his conversion assured the survival of Christianity and its place as a world religion. The eventual success of Christianity may seem inevitable to us today, but comparative evidence suggests otherwise. In fourth-century Persia there were many Christian churches; the exotic appearance of one Persian bishop even created a stir at Nicaea. Yet no Persian king ever converted, and Christians remained a minority there. On the other hand, Christian territories in Syria, Egypt, and North Africa became predominantly Muslim after a few centuries of tolerant Muslim rule. Within the Roman Empire imperial protection, which began under Constantine, offered the Christian religion a safe haven and open encouragement. Some critics have argued that this was ultimately bad for the church because self-interest and inertia brought nominal and indifferent converts and undermined the ethical and religious fervor of the church. But the church flourished under Roman emperors after Constantine, and the Roman Empire soon became nearly synonymous with Christendom.

At Constantine's death the empire was divided among his three sons, who took opposing sides in the Arian controversy. The Arian Constantius ruled in the east, surviving his brothers to become sole emperor from 353 to his death in 361. By the time the Arian Valens ascended the eastern throne in 364, Arianism was the dominant religion in the East, at least among the wealthy and powerful families.

The most charismatic leaders of the day, however, were devoting their energies to the orthodox cause. Arius's old opponent, Athanasius, bishop of Alexandria off and on (whenever the orthodox were in power) until his death in 373, used his considerable strength in vigorous support of the Nicene doctrine. He galvanized public opinion with a blockbuster saint's life, the *Life of Antony*, the first work in this genre that would be so popular throughout the Middle Ages.[1] In Athanasius's pages, the Egyptian ascetic becomes a champion of orthodoxy and a mighty spokesman against the Arian heresy.

Three leading figures, who came to be known as the Cappadocian Fathers, inherited Athanasius's cause and assured its intellectual victory. In the fourth century, Cappadocia in eastern Asia Minor was not a wild and barren place; rather, it was a center of considerable culture. Basil of Caesarea, his friend Gregory of Nazianzus, and his brother Gregory of Nyssa used their knowledge of Greek philosophy to

---

[1] See H. Ellershaw and A. Robertson, trans., in P. Schaff and H. Wace, eds., *A Select Library of Nicene and Post-Nicene Fathers of the Christian Church* (Grand Rapids, MI: William Eerdmans, 1976).

Hellenize Christian tenets and to reconcile Nicene doctrine with Greek learning. Gregory of Nazianzus, bishop of Constantinople for a brief but critical moment in 381, won the capital to orthodoxy with his eloquent preaching. Basil was a capable administrator as well as an intellectual, and he worked to elevate orthodox priests to bishoprics and to buttress the orthodox structure of ecclesiastical organization. He also created an influential monastic Rule, the code under which monks would live, that stressed restraint, order, and obedience. Monastic movements in Egypt and Syria, more and more linked to the orthodoxy of Basil and Athanasius, became passionate foes of the Arians.

In the West, too, the most dynamic religious leader, Bishop Ambrose of Milan, lent his support to Nicene orthodoxy. Arianism attracted no such advocates in this critical period, and when the ardently orthodox Theodosius came to the throne in 379, the time was ripe for outlawing Arianism altogether and seeking peace and unity within the church and empire. Theodosius first made Christianity the only official religion of his realm. After banning pagan sacrifices, he closed famous pagan monuments where the ban had been ignored. During his reign, zealots took a violent offensive against paganism. The archbishop of Alexandria rounded up a posse of monks to demolish the great Serapeum, shrine of the Egyptian god Serapis and one of the wonders of the ancient world. Theodosius congratulated the perpetrators, who had also destroyed the temple's magnificent library. In 381 the emperor convened the second ecumenical council. This Council of Constantinople affirmed a modified Nicene Creed. Theodosius promptly disestablished the Arians and handed over all their church property to the orthodox. Without official sanction or brilliant supporters, Arianism limped along for a half century or more, its numbers of adherents gradually but steadily declining. Forced to hold clandestine services outside the city walls, split into sects that haggled over the minutiae of their doctrine, and harried by orthodox emperors, Arians slowly disappeared from the Roman Empire.

The Arian Germans

It is perhaps ironic that just as these Arians were dying out, the heresy was winning fresh converts on the Gothic frontier. For centuries the German presence had been building along the northern borders of the empire. When pressure from the Mongolian Huns forced the Visigoths to cross the Danube into Roman territory in 378, these Germanic tribes would confront the orthodox Romans with their own brand of Arian Christianity.

It was a meeting of two very different societies. The Germans did not live in cities, nor did they have a written culture that linked various peoples to a common heritage. Instead, the Germanic tribes were kinship groups united by blood and custom. Most Germans lived by hunting and herding. Many farmed the land, settling in small villages separated from one another by dense forests. The men were warriors who valued women strong enough to tend the land and to maintain the home while the warriors were off fighting, perhaps as soldiers in the Roman army. By the fourth century, many tribes had significant contact with Rome, not only through military service but also by exchange of German slaves for prestigious Roman wares. Increasingly familiar with Roman civilization, Germans came to admire its handiwork, its grand architecture and art, its ceremony and luxury, and the religion they associated with that culture—Christianity.

We know little about the native religion of the Germans. It seems to have been tribal, with kinship groups functioning as religious communities united by memories of ancient cult practices and by a profound sense of the spiritual powers both favorable and dangerous that were present in their world. A pessimism permeated this religion and the views of life associated with it. This dark outlook produced incantations, spells, and charms meant to influence and control gods and spirits dwelling among the people and able to inflict harm unless thwarted. Germanic magic and superstition would linger to influence popular Christianity throughout the Middle Ages and beyond. As tribal organization weakened, however, the tribal cults themselves surrendered to Christianity within a generation of settlement in Roman territories.

Before these invasions many Goths knew of Christianity not only from Roman military service and commerce but also through Roman Christians who lived among them. One such family was that of Ulfila, who claimed descent from Roman prisoners captured during a mid-third-century raid on their village in Cappadocia. When Ulfila was born about 311, the family was still Christian, and so he was raised Christian in a pagan society. Still he also grew up as a Goth who spoke the Gothic language. Dispatched to Constantinople as a hostage or ambassador, he espoused the Arian Christianity that was dominant there in the final years of Constantine's reign. It was almost certainly the Arian leader Eusebius of Nicomedia, the same bishop who baptized Constantine, who consecrated Ulfila bishop to serve the Christians in Gothia, the old Roman province of Dacia (now Romania). For seven years Ulfila preached Arianism there, until a persecution of Christians forced him to flee with his community to Roman Moesia. He probably was never able to return to Gothia, but at his death in about 383 he left behind a tradition of Gothic Arianism and a translation of the Bible into Gothic, for which he first had to devise a Gothic alphabet. One fifth-century source claimed that Ulfila refrained from translating the Books of Kings (that is, I and II Samuel; I and II Kings) because he was unwilling to expose the savage Goths to bellicose scripture that might seem to condone warfare. In fact we do not know if he translated the Old Testament at all, since only later fragments remain of Old Testament books in the Gothic Bible. Still, this assertion provides early testimony for the expectation that Christianity ought to play a significant role in civilizing the barbarians.

The process was slow. To train priests and to preach Christian doctrine, to eradicate or Christianize pagan customs in the countryside, and perhaps especially to inculcate Christian ethical values were complex tasks. Like the Christianizing of the Roman peasantry, genuine conversion of German farmers and villagers would take centuries of effort. The nobles, on the other hand, quickly declared themselves and their tribes to be Christian. German kings saw the immediate advantages in adopting a religion that could unify their people by diffusing tensions among tribes, eradicate the power of tribal priests and chiefs, affirm divine authority for their rulership, and also win Roman military aid. Arianism made a further political and social statement by asserting independence from the Huns, who rejected Christianity, and also from the orthodox Romans. Christianity was the religion of Roman civilization, but Arian Christianity was distinctively German, too. The theological niceties were lost on Germans who did not ponder the nature of the Trinity or the divinity of Jesus. Arianism simply became the new supratribal religion that allowed Germans in Roman territories a separate communal identity until they could assimilate with the native inhabitants and eventually replace Arianism with orthodoxy. Their Arianism was Christianity with a distinctively Germanic flavor, imbued with ancestral pride and lingering pagan practice. Over time it would influence western Christianity even as the two strains merged to create medieval Catholic Christendom.

Chapter 10

PAGAN REACTION AND CHRISTIAN VICTORY (361–476)

The Pagan Reaction

In the second half of the fourth century, Greco-Roman paganism was by no means dead. Constantine might embrace Christianity; Theodosius might even outlaw polytheism. Still, many subjects of the Roman Empire considered paganism to be interconnected with all elements of their ancient heritage. For some of the old aristocracy, paganism *was* the traditional and civilized way of life, and they actively resisted any loss of this integral part of the social fabric. Unwilling to abandon their art and literature, these patriotic Romans further argued that to abandon pagan rituals within state ceremonies could imperil the Roman state.

Pagan rivals challenged the authority of Constantine's sons to rule. In 350 Constans died fighting the pagan usurper Magnus Magnentius, who was finally defeated by Constantius in 351. At Constantius's death ten years later, the Christian future of the empire must have seemed secure until his cousin and successor, Julian, cast off the pretense of being a Christian and sacrificed oxen to the gods in public thanksgiving for his accession to the throne.

The last pagan emperor of Rome, Julian was also the first emperor to have been born at Constantinople, his uncle Constantine's new capital. No opulent and carefree youth was in store for this child of the imperial family. Soon after his birth, his mother died; when he was only six, in the uncertain period following the death of Constantine, his father and most other family members were massacred. Julian always held Constantius accountable for the murders. Indeed, the ultimate beneficiary of the dynastic battles was this same Christian cousin, who later (in 354) executed Julian's half-brother Gallus for treason. Small wonder that Julian finally moved against Constantius in 360 and that civil war was averted only by the emperor's death by fever in 361.

Even if Julian had personal, philosophical, cultural, and patriotic reasons for loathing Christianity, he could not escape the influence of a religion whose success he attempted to emulate in restoring paganism. He saw clearly that the high moral tone of Christianity attracted converts from the old cults and that the organizational structure of the church nurtured Christians and promulgated the faith. He attempted, therefore, to create a pagan church with its own structure and hierarchy, and he tried to enforce pagan charity and a morally pure priesthood in imitation of Christian virtue. Understanding that persecution had only strengthened the church, he promulgated a policy of official tolerance while eliminating any advantages for Christians. Still, his idiosyncratic and archaic movement failed to attract converts, in part because his strange personality repelled potential allies. Bitterly disappointed by this failure, he led a reluctant army on campaign into Persian Mesopotamia, hoping that a stunning victory would dazzle his subjects and bring them around to paganism. At about age thirty-one, Julian might have expected that a long lifetime of persuasion would turn the tide against Christianity. Instead, he fell victim to a fatal lance during a skirmish with Persian forces and was buried at Tarsus. The great pagan rhetorician of Antioch, Julian's admirer and ally Libanius, pretended that the people revered Julian after his death as if he were a kind of pagan saint. In the oration to the emperor's memory, Libanius asserted that the late emperor was answering prayers directed to him. In fact, Julian seems to have been virtually unmourned, and his quirky personal vision of restored paganism died with him.

Julian had been preaching his philosophy in the Christianized East, but from a distance even the more pagan West had virtually ignored his attempts. Enormously wealthy, Roman senators devotedly pursued *otium*, the cultivated leisure that they could enjoy on their country estates far from the bother of Rome. Much as they cherished *otium*, however, they valued tradition even more and willingly pursued the active civic careers and weighty responsibilities that their ancestors had shouldered, accepting government office or acting as emissary between emperor and senate. Many still held to classical paganism, which enjoyed a venerable link with Roman ceremony, power, and social habit. Among the leaders of this senatorial class, the patrician Symmachus provides a noble example of these powerful men. Governor of Lucania and proconsul of Africa, in 384 he held the title of urban prefect of Rome. His father, grandfather, and father-in-law had all been urban prefect before him. Well born and well connected, he was a superbly cultivated pagan and an excellent spokesman for the senate.

During his prefecture, he clashed with the emperor and especially with the powerful and brilliant Ambrose, bishop of Milan where the imperial court was residing. The immediate cause of the dispute was the Altar of Victory, gift of Augustus to the senate of Rome. Christian emperors beginning with Constantius had removed the altar from the senate house, only to see it returned in answer to the senators' pleas. On behalf of the senate, Symmachus drafted a respectful plea that the emperor once more return the altar on which the senators made their prescribed sacrifices, the traditional rituals that assured the survival and political success of the Roman Empire. The response came from Ambrose, himself born to secular power in the senatorial ranks. Drafted as bishop, he became a tough and fervent Catholic. The fiery and brilliant preacher who would convert Augustine demanded that the emperor refuse Symmachus's plea. The unyielding bishop, the Christian emperor he controlled, and the pagan aristocracy were on a collision course.

Rome witnessed the last hurrah of pagan spring rites in 394, when forbidden cult rituals were revived and performed with ostentatious opulence. Once again Rome saw processions for Magna Mater and Isis along with sacrifices to Jupiter and Saturn, Mithras and the Unconquered Sun, Ceres and Proserpina. With all the ancestral rites, the younger Nichomachus Flavianus, scion of a great pagan family, married a daughter of Symmachus, further allying two families at the head of the revolt. Then the Roman senatorial pagans rode out under pagan standards to defend their antiquarianism, patriotism, and the old ways. With statues of Jupiter looking down from the cliffs above and the image of Hercules paraded among the troops, the last Roman army to march under pagan standards met defeat at the Frigidus River when (the Christians under emperor Theodosius reported) a miraculous wind blew up, tearing the shields from the hands of the pagan soldiers and hurling their spears back against them. The same wind at Theodosius's back drove him down from the mountain pass where he was trapped and on to victory. In purely political terms, the results were clear: Imperial forces had smashed an insurrection of the Roman aristocracy. Christian writers interpreted the contest from another perspective: In their eyes, divine forces had crushed the last pagan resistance along the Frigidus.

Christianity and Classical Culture

Symmachus and his friends closely associated paganism with Greco-Roman culture. Their Christian neighbors agreed. Must these Christians therefore abandon classical literature and art as incompatible with their religion? Must they abandon the only culture they knew? Julian the Apostate had been savvy enough to argue that they must, and he even forbade Christians to teach pagan literature, thus removing Christians from influential contact with young students while also cleverly divorcing Christianity from Greco-Roman culture. What would have happened if he had succeeded in enforcing a separation between the two? Given the necessity of choosing, would a Roman aristocrat abandon Christianity or cultural heritage? There was some danger that Christians themselves might force that choice. Tertullian had asked, "What has Athens to do with Jerusalem?" Jerome feared that a passion for Ciceronian rhetoric, which sometimes seduced him away from biblical study, would lead to his eternal damnation. In a nightmare the heavenly judge charged him with this sin. To Jerome's desperate defense, "I am a Christian," the terrifying answer came back: "You are a Ciceronian, not a Christian!"

Augustine (354–430), the famous North African bishop with whom Jerome carried on a meticulously civilized and sometimes rancorous correspondence, convinced the West that Christians could use pagan learning so long as they granted scripture the foremost importance in this synthesis. There need be no conflict if the Christian used Ciceronian eloquence in defense of the faith. In the Hellenized east, the three Cappadocian Fathers had already envisioned a Christian culture that accepted and transformed their ancient intellectual heritage. Basil of Caesarea, Gregory of Nyssa, and Gregory of Nazianzus—the champions of orthodoxy—encouraged use of pagan philosophy and literature, the best products of ancient Greece, which Christianity was absorbing as part of its own culture.

Cities and Bishops in Late Antiquity

As demonstrated by the struggles with paganism and classical culture, the emerging leaders of both church and society were influential bishops such as Ambrose at Milan (374–379), John Chrysostom at Antioch and Constantinople (398–407), and Augustine at Hippo in North Africa (391–430). Although they might be unwillingly conscripted, despite initial resistance such men earnestly and capably filled the vacuum created by the withdrawal of the old aristocracy and the great landowners, who abandoned the responsibility of onerous public service. The bishop tended to his Christian flock, preaching, overseeing the distribution of alms, and caring for the needy. His tireless work in the community deserted by civil authorities made a great impact on contemporaries. After cataloguing the many volumes of Augustine's works, his biographer Possidius reflected on the man himself: "Yet I think that those who gained most from him were those who had been able actually to see and hear him as he spoke in church, and, most of all, those who had some contact with the quality of his life among men."[1]

Increasingly, as civil administration failed, the bishop was called to more and more duties, becoming arbiter of private quarrels and patron of people in the town and surrounding countryside. In 387, for instance, the people of Antioch rioted to protest an increase in taxes. When they reflected on the nasty consequences of their civil disobedience, it was the bishop whom they dispatched to Constantinople to plead (successfully) for the emperor's forgiveness. In a violent age, it was the bishop who could win mercy or dispense justice, even when the adversary was the emperor. In 390 the bishop Ambrose excommunicated Theodosius for his angry massacre of 7,000 people in the circus at Thessalonica after the citizens there had assassinated a

[1] Peter Brown, *Augustine of Hippo: A Biography* (Berkeley: University of California Press, 1967), p. 433.

barbarian military commander. Before Theodosius could receive communion again, Ambrose forced him to accept public penance. Cowed by the bishop, the emperor stood before all without imperial regalia, admitting the superior authority of the church. It was a precedent that theologians would not forget. To decide cases involving clergy or ecclesiastical matters, Theodosius further permitted the church to create its own courts, which would begin to develop their own law, called *canon law*.

Inevitably there arose a tension between spiritual and civic duties. The bishop became courtier and administrator within a complex hierarchy. How could he reconcile this worldly sophistication, the social influence and status, with the simple faith of Jesus and the Apostles? Indeed, although Christianity had grown as an urban religion, some Christians were asking if any person could live an upright life amid the cares and decadence of the city. Perhaps the only way to salvation lay in radical asceticism divorced from civilization.

Monasticism and Holy Men and Women

A young Egyptian, Antony (ca. 250–356) heard the messages of the gospel: "If you will be perfect, go and sell all you have, and give it to the poor, and you shall have treasure in heaven: and come and follow me" (Matt. 19.21). So he gave away his inheritance and fled to the desert, becoming one of the first Christian hermits ("hermit" comes from the Greek *eremos*, meaning "desert"). Antony lived to the ripe old age of 105, attracting a famous biographer, Athanasius, and countless imitators.

How did he live? According to Athanasius, he struggled with himself daily, seeking to make the body subject to the soul. If he could not suffer actual martyrdom, which was the most desirable lot, at least he could deny the body its physical wants and thus become as spiritual as possible. Loathing the physical world, he sought to free himself of it and come closer to God. Augustine was impressed by the willpower of a man who was profoundly embarrassed whenever he gave in to hunger and ate, or even when he had to witness someone else eating. Moving deeper and deeper into the desert, Antony confronted and wrestled with the devil, whose presence in his world was very real. Once he experienced mystical ecstasy, as his soul fought its way upward to a blinding beam of light. People sought him out, and it was increasingly difficult for him to be alone. By his hard-won holiness, he performed socially valuable acts of exorcism, casting out demons and healing physical and spiritual wounds, as Jesus had done. He spoke only Coptic, so his religious dogma was inscrutable to most observers. The passionately orthodox Athanasius, however, assured his readers that Antony loathed all heretics—Meletians, Manichaeans, and especially Arians. Even the emperor Constantine heeded Antony's teachings of the ascetic life that Antony had learned from scripture.

Antony's own example and Athanasius's influential *Life of St. Antony* led many people to conversion and imitation. Translated from Greek into Latin, the *Life* reached a large audience. Many of its readers felt compelled to follow Antony's example, prompting the famous quotation from Adolf von Harnack, an unsympathetic modern critic: "If I may be permitted to use strong language, I should not hesitate to say that no book has had a more stultifying effect on Egypt, Western Asia, and Europe than the *Vita S. Antonii.*" To be sure, the *Life* encouraged a dramatic rejection of the classical ideal of an educated, rational mind in a healthy, athletic body. Antony expressed a radical anti-intellectualism, as when he confronted smart aleck philosophers with the taunt: "The person who has a sound mind doesn't need to know how to read and write." By a brutal denial of the physical world with its profane knowledge and by a punishment of the body, Antony simply turned his soul to the perception of God, actively rejecting pleasure in this life in the hope of winning salvation after death. Antony's life looks ahead to a powerful strain in medieval Christendom.

Antony's ideal had many imitators, often poor and simple folk who found this a dramatic way to defy society and seek personal salvation. In Syria and Mesopotamia ascetics became particularly notorious for their extreme mortifications. Some wore heavy iron chains; others wore almost no clothing and lived like animals in the open air, grazing on grass and avoiding shelter; still others lived in trees or in tiny cages, depending on neighbors for meager food and support. Near Damascus, Symeon the Stylite (389–459) lived for forty years on top of his narrow pillar, sixty feet high. There he performed brutal acts of self-punishment, such as touching his feet with his head 1,244 times in a row or standing for hours on end with his arms outstretched in prayer while crowds gathered to venerate him and even to worship the worms that fell from his body. Though he was illiterate, his advice was sought by country people, bishops, and the emperor himself. The government required his ratification of the ecclesiastical councils of Ephesus (431) and Chalcedon (451).

The austere sanctity of such men dazzled the late antique world. People felt that these holy men performed acts of value to the whole society by praying for ordinary Christians and healing their bodies and spirits and by keeping the demons at bay. People who saw Symeon high on his pillar believed that, through their hero, they were glimpsing the divine.

Such passions presented a dilemma for the church and for the bishops whose authority the hermits rivaled and sometimes defied. The hermits were following biblical injunctions thoroughly compatible with a messianic, apocalyptic community. While these solitaries scorned the world, however, the bishops were busily organizing within the world a Christian community that they themselves would order and control. Could they expand this community to embrace even its most antisocial members? At the same time, could they place ascetics firmly within the hierarchical structure of the organized church? Hermits like Antony often claimed direct mystical experience of God, without the mediation of priest or church. Could such men disregard the church or even replace priests and bishops as spiritual leaders for Christendom?

The solution came through the creation of monastic orders where men and women could lead ascetic lives in common under the authority of abbot or bishop. When other hermits sought him out, Antony himself had organized hermits' colonies into semimonastic communities. The true founder of Christian monasticism was another Egyptian nearly contemporary with Antony but living far to the south in the district around Thebes. Pachomius (ca. 292–346) was a soldier who brought to his task the ideal of strict discipline and military obedience. A convert at about age twenty, at his death he left ten monasteries in Egypt, including a convent for women, all governed by his brief written rules for a life of common prayer and strenuous manual labor. The great austerity of Pachomian monasticism, bred in the desert in an age of heated religious controversies, provided a harsh standard that individuals were free to exceed. By the end of the fourth century, 7,000 monks were living in his monasteries. After Jerome translated Pachomius's Rule into Latin in 404, Pachomian monasteries began to spring up in the West.

A wide variety of monastic arrangements soon evolved in various parts of the Christian world. Asia Minor saw a relaxation of austerities, with greater emphasis on communal activities and charitable works. After himself living six years as a hermit, Basil of Caesarea wrote the *Long Rules* that have influenced eastern monasticism until the present day. Persuaded by his sister Macrina to renounce his chair of rhetoric, Basil embraced the ascetic life and traveled to Egypt where he experienced austere Pachomian monasticism. Still, he did not altogether abandon his philosophical training, which had taught him to seek virtue through disciplined moderation, avoiding extremes of asceticism. Swearing poverty, chastity, and obedience to the bishop who was charged with their care, monks under Basilian Rule devoted fixed hours to liturgical prayer and to work. Basil stressed the principles of a common life that allowed for both correction of the errant and charity toward others. A central feature of the Basilian Rule is its insistence that the ascetic life should serve not only the individual who practiced it but also the church and community. Basilian monks operated hospitals, orphanages, and schools for both boys and girls. By working for the Christian community, these ascetics provided an active example of the Christian life.

His Rule earned Basil the title Father of Eastern Monasticism, which was developing a strong tradition already in the fourth century. In the West, meanwhile, the appeal of asceticism was considerably weaker, and the monastic movement was slow to emerge. Cold and snowy winters deterred people from living the hermit's life in the wilds of northern Europe, where fierce animals prowled dark forests, and Germanic tribes also threatened. Irish ascetics gained notoriety by flaunting their disregard for the elements. In his *Ecclesiastical History* (early eighth century), the Venerable Bede wrote of Brother Drycthelme of Melrose, who habitually broke the ice over a nearby river so that he could stand in its chilly waters, answering stunned onlookers with a laconic, "I've seen colder." For most of the West, however, only a moderate and protected monastic life could assure survival.

Various models appeared. Fashionable senators and aristocratic ladies converted their palaces or country estates into ascetic communities. About 540, for instance, the Roman senator Cassiodorus turned his Italian villa into a cultural center called the Vivarium, where men of learning copied religious and secular texts. Bishops such as Augustine housed their clergy in communal centers. Martin of Tours in Gaul (ca. 335–397) and Patrick in Ireland (early fifth century) combined asceticism with missionary activity. Amid this great variety, it was Benedict of Nursia (ca. 480–ca. 547) who created the Rule that would become the standard for the West.

Benedict wrote his Rule for his monastery at Monte Cassino, founded in 529, but it soon spread through the West. Here was a Rule ideally suited to its age, offering humane and simple regulations for ordinary country people. Roman in its emphasis on order and organization, obedience and respect for law, Benedict's Rule stressed moderation and self-discipline. The day and night were organized around periods of common prayer, called the Work of God, chanted in choir. There were times for private Bible study, and monks were taught to read. Benedict also prescribed daily manual labor that balanced the hours of prayer and devotional reading, because he believed that idleness was the enemy of the soul. All the monks should have adequate sleep, however, and two good meals a day so that no one indulged in extravagant self-punishment. The Rule allowed flexibility for adaptation to various climates and seasons, for women as well as for men, for scholars or farmers. Within a self-sufficient monastery in Gaul or Italy or Britain, all monks of varied skills and abilities might find a home where they could live their whole lives through, without wandering from place to place, a practice Benedict roundly condemned. In times of war, pestilence, and famine, medieval men and women would find a haven of peace, stability, and order in the Benedictine cloister, where the abbot was enjoined to treat his tightly knit community as if he were the father of this family.

With ascetics safely in their monastic communities, the early institutional church had to face a similar problem with spontaneous popular cults centered on the tombs of local martyrs. Just as people venerated the holy men, so they also worshipped local saints as human beings whose devotion and courage had brought them into direct contact with the divinity. They could thus intercede with God on behalf of a suppliant, or the saint's relics could work miracles and heal the sick. Some scholars have suggested that the rise of the cult of saints demonstrates popular resistance to the solidifying power of the bishops and emperor: The people wanted to maintain personal access to spiritual authority. Others have speculated that these cults represented a survival of the traditional Roman patron-client relationship: The people still needed a private protector in treacherous times. Whatever the impulse that produced these popular movements, the church acted quickly to absorb this phenomenon, as it had the ascetic movement. In the fourth century, cults of the saints were becoming institutionalized under the strict control of ecclesiastical authorities who channeled into the mainstream of the church those passions aroused by admiration for the saints.

By the early fifth century, this was a church whose institutional hierarchy was already complex and carefully defined. In each city a bishop held authority over local priests, including those of the surrounding countryside. The bishop of a larger city was called a *metropolitan* (known in the west today as an archbishop) and exercised authority over all clergy of his province. The highest rank belonged to the patriarchs, bishops of the most venerable Christian cities—Rome, Constantinople, Jerusalem, Antioch, and Alexandria. Quite distinct from the clergy, the laity were expected to follow the teaching of their priests and bishops and obey the precepts of the institutional church.

Women's Roles in the Chain of Command

Attitudes toward laymen and women were shaped by the prevailing attitudes of the society in which Christianity was flourishing. The bishops accepted the social, political, and economic order more or less without questioning and generally agreed that the church should authorize and protect that natural and God-given order. Augustine argued this view most coherently:

> The Catholic Church, most true Mother of Christians. . . . it is You who make wives subject to their husbands . . . by chaste and faithful obedience; you set husbands over their wives; you join sons to their parents by a freely granted slavery, and set parents above their sons in pious domination. You link brothers to each other by bonds of religion firmer and tighter than those of blood. You teach slaves to be loyal to their masters . . . masters . . . to be more inclined to persuade them than to punish. You link citizen to citizen, nation to nation, indeed, You bind all men together in the remembrance of their first parents, not just by social bonds, but by some feeling of their common kinship. You teach kings to rule for the benefit of their people; and You it is who warn the peoples to be subservient to their kings.[2]

It was a tidy and compelling system. Although Roman women, especially aristocratic women, had won a measure of legal rights and social prominence, the Fathers preferred a more restrictive model, often citing precedents from the Hebrew bible or the example of Jesus and his male disciples. Following this standard, women were forbidden to hold the priesthood or other positions of authority within the church. Yet Christianity did open new doors to women even if the hierarchy of the church was keeping some firmly closed. Wealthy women found a prestigious vocation in patronage to the bishops and the urban poor. They might win both honor and salvation by supporting ecclesiastical and monastic institutions. Religious vows of

[2]Brown, *Augustine of Hippo*, p. 225.

celibacy could free them from family obligations and bestow greater independence than they had enjoyed before.

Imperial women provided role models for Christian women, and the church voiced strong approval of their dutiful piety. In the official paean at the death of Flacilla, first wife of Theodosius I, Gregory of Nyssa praised her acts of charity to the poor and needy, to widows and orphans. Another author testified that she visited the sick and maimed in the hospitals of Constantinople, personally feeding them soup and giving them medicine.

Men like John Chrysostom, archbishop of Constantinople from 398 to 404, continued to assail women as the heiresses of Eve, vain and dangerous snares for men, unfit in God's eyes for spiritual leadership. He approved of only the modest and obedient women who served God by donating their fortunes to the church. He did support the right of one recent widow, the heiress Olympias, to resist the new marriage arranged for her by the emperor Theodosius II. Chrysostom ordained her a deaconess in order to thwart the emperor's plan. In the bargain Olympias won autonomy, and the bishop became trusted advisor for the disposition of her wealth. Theodosius's own sister, Aelia Pulcheria Augusta (413–453), proclaimed perpetual virginity for herself and by her asceticism assured that she would share her power with no husband and his ambitious kin. In her last years, she concerned herself with the rights and care of holy women.

Ordinary women had constrained and limited options. Enjoined to become subservient wives and devoted mothers, many poured their energies into these traditional roles. Syrian saints' lives reveal other women empowered by their faith to explode societal stereotypes, shunning marriage, family, or even religious community to become solitaries in men's clothing or pilgrims to the holy shrines. A few women found voices of their own, like the fourth-century pilgrim Egeria (or Aetheria), who left an enthusiastic and distinctively personal journal of her tour to biblical sites.

Articulate Christianity

Egeria's Latin itinerary joined growing volumes of Christian literature. Although Greek and Latin were the languages of the urban upper classes, we must not forget the diversity of early Christendom and the variety of cultural influences at work. Outside the cities, farmers and laborers spoke their own native languages. The old Roman Empire had made little effort to integrate these people into the political structure, and Christianity was slow to preach to them in their own tongue. Early records do substantiate such efforts in the eastern Mediterranean, where Syriac had become the language of Christian communities during the first and second centuries A.D. and developed a rich Christian literature. When the eloquent John Chrysostom preached in Greek to a packed congregation in the cathedral at Antioch, a bilingual deacon would offer simultaneous translation to the farmers and humble workers who knew only Syriac.

By Chrysostom's time, a Christian rhetoric had already been developing for several centuries in both Greek and Latin. In the Latin West, Jerome (ca. 340–420) combined rigorous training in classical thought and literature with biblical scholarship and Christian asceticism. His crowning achievement was the translation into Latin of both the Hebrew Bible and the Greek New Testament. Jerome's Latin Bible, usually called the Vulgate version, became the authoritative text for the European Middle Ages.

Jerome's correspondent, Augustine of Hippo (354–430) also used pagan learning to support Christian teaching. His supremely influential spiritual autobiography, *The Confessions*, explored the moral struggles within the developing soul of a man living in the last years of Roman North Africa. Converted to philosophy through Cicero's *Hortensius*, then to dualist Manichaeism, and finally to orthodox Christianity through bishop Ambrose of Milan, Augustine was a contemplative conscripted into the priesthood. As a bishop who had to act as patron and protector of his flock, he came to accept coercion as a proper ingredient in opposition to heresy and defense of the social order. He had used every power at his command to crush the Donatists, rigorists who wanted to restrict the church to the elect alone and banish sinners who had denied their faith when persecution threatened. In his later years, Augustine similarly opposed Pelagius, the British or Irish monk who came to Rome about the year 400 and attempted to demolish the social habits of the Roman world and enforce a stern morality. Pelagius inherited the old moral ideal, as seen for instance in Stoicism, of the autonomous human mind and spirit. He held that original sin did not condemn humans to imperfect lives; on the contrary, all could draw on their own willpower to lead perfect lives if only they would. Those who did not should be exiled from the Christian community. Augustine, on the other hand, found the human race essentially weak; only through divine grace could any men or women find salvation. This idea was taking hold in late antiquity and anticipated the medieval spirit. Augustine's victory over Pelagianism, confirmed at the Third Ecumenical (or universal) Council at Ephesus (431), assured that ordinary good Christians had a place within the fold. Christianity was not to be a tiny sect of righteous ascetics within a pagan world but a religious community that embraced all sinners and worked within the imperfect world in which it grew.

Christianization of Late Antique Art

As Christians were finding a distinctive Greco-Roman voice, so too Christian art was developing its own style, evolving from its classical heritage. By the fifth century, the wealth that used to go to public buildings and then in the fourth century had been channeled into imperial palaces and aristocratic estates now went into the construction of magnificent basilicas adorned with shimmering mosaics, silk tapestries and vestments, silver candelabra and liturgical vessels, and perhaps an ivory throne for the bishop.

Mosaics made of stone paved floors in ancient buildings and porticos. Late antique artisans discovered that lighter and more brilliant glass cubes could be fitted into wall mosaics perfectly suited to the new architecture. Rough-cut or smooth, dyed a rich purple or even made of gold, set at various angles to catch and reflect the light, mosaics seemed to expand the sacred space and to radiate a divine essence. The so-called Mausoleum of Galla Placidia at Ravenna, dating from the middle of the fifth century, has preserved the earliest surviving mosaic decoration in complete harmony with its setting. Over the entrance door of this tiny space, the Good Shepherd is a traditional bucolic figure from the Hellenistic age transformed into a potent symbol of regal and spiritual glory. Christian art had found its ideal medium.

Council of Ephesus, 431

Only a generation earlier than the construction of the Mausoleum, the council at Ephesus (431) had hammered out a formula for defining the relationship of human and divine natures within Jesus Christ. The story behind this controversy illustrates social struggle within the fifth-century Church—a struggle of bishop against bishop, and of bishop against monks and imperial women.

On a purely theological level, the arguments seem relatively straightforward. Nestorius, patriarch of Constantinople (428–431), claimed that two *separate* natures co-existed in Jesus, the divine and the human. Here he was following the rationalist school of Antioch, which contended that God could not suffer in the flesh; Jesus the man was only the chosen vessel of the godhead. Cyril, patriarch of Alexandria, adhered to the Alexandrian mystical teaching that the divine and human natures united in Jesus, who was God become man. There were important theological reasons for Cyril's argument. If Jesus did not suffer on the cross as God, could his sacrifice truly bring salvation? What meaning could his death hold if only the man Jesus died? Cyril found support from Rome, from the empire's growing number of monks, and from another unexpectedly powerful source, the women of Constantinople, led by imperial and aristocratic women who were not influenced by doctrinal reasons alone.

The contentious Nestorius had alienated the people by assailing their much-loved circus races, theater, and mimes. In other attempts to enforce order, he demanded that monks leave their public ministry and stay in the monastery, where they could no longer encourage the populace to resist the oppression of unprincipled authorities. A hard line against heretics and various dissidents brought him headlong against Cyril, raising again the question of the relative authority or independence of their respective bishoprics. Could the patriarch of Constantinople overrule the patriarch of Alexandria? Finally Nestorius met his match in Pulcheria, sister of the reigning emperor Theodosius II and a woman dedicated to holy virginity. Cyril saw that with her support he could bring Nestorius to defeat.

Like Chrysostom before him, Nestorius was eager to put women in their proper place. Women had traditionally attended evening psalms and prayers as well as night vigils for the dead. In Nestorius's view, these were plainly invitations to promiscuity, and he acted swiftly to lock women out. The prominent women of the imperial city did not submit meekly to his will. Down from the women's gallery of the Great Church rained shouts of anger from Heleniana, a noble woman whose piety and benefactions were beyond dispute. The bishop had already alienated the most powerful and influential lady in the city in a confrontation only five days after his ordination. The empress Pulcheria was accustomed to take communion with her brother and priests of the Great Church, but that Easter Sunday Nestorius personally blocked her entry into the sanctuary, proclaiming that "only priests may walk here." Seeing only a daughter of Eve, he could not bear the sacrilege of a woman's presence in the Holy of Holies. Considering herself to be living the life of a religious virgin in the footsteps of Mary, the empress asked: "Why? Have I not given birth to God?" Nestorius drove her away with the incensed charge: "You? You have given birth to Satan!"

The lines were drawn. Strongly implying that Pulcheria had not kept her vow of chastity but had been sexually promiscuous, the new bishop refused to honor Pulcheria as the bride of Christ in his prayers for the imperial house and systematically withdrew other dignities from her. The attack broadened to an assault on the Virgin Mary, and here Nestorius made a fatal mistake. He canceled a popular Mary festival that had become an occasion during the liturgical year when virgins and religious women were honored. Mary was not the mother of god, claimed Nestorius, but only the mother of Jesus the man, *christotokos* but not *theotokos*.

To decide the question, Theodosius summoned the bishops to the Third Ecumenical Council at Ephesus in 431. The emperor expected that his bishop would be vindicated, but he may well have been outsmarted by his sister, who may have chosen the battleground. Ephesus was not only a haven for pro-Cyril forces but also the ancient cult center of the virgin goddess Artemis/Diana and now devoted to the cult of the *theotokos*. Cyril's allies packed the city with supporters, including dissident monks from Constantinople. It took only a day for the overwhelmed council, meeting in a church dedicated to the Virgin Mary, to excommunicate Nestorius and declare Jesus fully God and fully human. Proclaiming victory for the *theotokos*, women swinging censers led the crowd that escorted Cyril from the council. A reluctant Theodosius finally ratified the council's decision, yielding to his sister's influence and Marial piety.

Nestorian churches survive to the present day in Turkey and India. Throughout most of the fifth-century Roman Empire, however, a reaction set in against Nestorianism, a reaction so potent that many Christians moved to the opposite extreme expressed by monophysitism, a Greek term meaning "a single nature." Whereas

Nestorians believed that Jesus had two separate natures, human and divine (with an emphasis on the human), monophysites stressed his predominantly divine nature.

Council of Chalcedon, 451, and Chalcedonian Orthodoxy

Monophysites were strongest in the eastern provinces, Syria and Egypt, where Semitic tradition reinforced visceral reactions against any multiplicity of gods or divisions within the godhead. The doctrines of the Trinity and the incarnation were difficult enough. To divide the nature of Jesus further fragmented and diluted God, in the view of eastern Christians who inherited their biblical tradition and cultural orientation directly from the Jewish communities out of which they arose. The Greco-Latin churches to the west, on the other hand, responded to the Christian message through their own background in the thought-world of classical antiquity. The texture and tone of the distinct communities were bound to be different, although they shared a common faith. Monophysitism emphasized the cultural gap. Rapidly it broadened that gap even further, as it became an outlet for the cultural and political separatist tendencies of Egypt and Syria.

Far from the world that bred monophysite ideas, the bishop of Rome could not understand the fuss, and he was unsympathetic. In Constantinople, bishop and emperor had to be more sensitive to the spirituality that produced monophysitism. At the Fourth Ecumenical Council, held at Chalcedon in 451, monophysitism was nonetheless condemned. Chalcedonian orthodoxy adopted a doctrine of salvation through a savior who is perfect man and perfect God.

The decision brought rebellions in Egypt and Syria and talk of secession. Indeed, some scholars have argued that these provinces yielded easily to Islam in the seventh century because of their continuing disaffection with Chalcedonian orthodoxy imposed by Constantinople. In the intervening years, some emperors would attempt to find consensus or compromise; others would persecute the recalcitrant or exile them to Persia. None of these tactics succeeded, and most Syrian and Egyptian Christians remain non-Chalcedonian to the present day.

Barbarians and the Fall

The Nestorian and monophysite controversies of the fifth century raged in a world radically transformed by the unforeseen collapse of the imperial government in the West. On the death of Theodosius I in 395, the empire had been irreversibly split in half, with one son (Arcadius) holding the East and the other (Honorius) taking nominal control of the West. Although the concept of imperial unity survived, the division emphasized differences of language, military and material resources, and social custom. The East survived the barbarian threat, but the West fell prey to

Germanic tribes that crossed the Rhine and Danube frontier and ravaged the provinces. In 378 the emperor Valens fell to the Visigoths at Adrianople; Vandals ravaged North Africa. Finally in 476 the last Roman puppet emperor, Romulus Augustulus, was deposed as an unnecessary nuisance, and the fragmented West was in the hands of various Germanic kings and princes.

The powerfully symbolic end of Roman imperium in the West was the pillaging of Rome by Alaric's Visigoths in 410, a cataclysmic event that sent shock waves throughout the Mediterranean world. Rome had stood inviolate since a Gallic sack 800 years before. Why, asked the Roman world, had their ancient capital fallen so soon after the conversion to Christianity? Were Christians to blame because they had abandoned civic duties, preferring the monastery to the army or the farm, endowing churches instead of public buildings? Had the Christians sacrificed civilization in selfish folly while looking only to their lives in the next world? Had they alienated the ancestral gods who had protected Rome, and was Rome's destruction the sign of divine vengeance?

The brilliant and visionary Christian response came from Augustine, who would live to see a tribe of 80,000 Vandals cross Gibraltar and descend upon his native North Africa like a virulent plague, besieging his city of Hippo even as he lay dying in 430. Augustine's *City of God* looks beyond ruined Rome and doomed Hippo, beyond Babylon and the corrupt cities of this earth, to describe a celestial Jerusalem, the heavenly city where the chosen people would at last find a home.[3] All human history has inexorably led to the grandeur of the Christian community on earth, destined to be united by God's grace and love. Into his vast scheme, Augustine absorbed both the Jewish and the Roman past. Adam's fall has condemned human beings to experience the woes of this life; Christianity has in fact blunted evil in the world, even touching the barbarians and making them (Augustine claimed) remarkably merciful in their destruction of Rome as they spared churches and Christians who sought haven in them. The people's propensity for sin has made the Roman state essential for the preservation of an orderly environment in which people may pursue their quest for the City of God. The bonds of human society have their useful place because the state controls its sinful people through laws divinely revealed and vigorously enforced.

The *City of God* systematically demolished paganism and in the process came to terms with the classical heritage as a building block for a Christian future. Augustine's Christian masterpiece moves with epic grandeur from the ancient world into a new Christian age, throughout the voyage articulating the sensibility that would define and shape medieval society.

---

[3]See Henry Bettenson, trans., *Concerning the City of God against the Pagans* (Baltimore: Penguin, 1972).

Chapter 11

WEST AND EAST
AFTER THE FALL

Emergence of Medieval Christendom (476–565 East; 604 West)

West and East after the Fall of Rome

What did the map of the Mediterranean world look like after the fall? Two distinct cultures emerged out of the vast migrations that shook the late antique Roman world (Figure 11.1).

The eastern empire survived intact. It would in fact endure another thousand years, until the Ottoman Turks stormed Constantinople in 1453. Boasting healthy cities with thriving trade and industry, the more populous East could gather sufficient wealth in taxes to support a strong army and to pay off barbarians. The East also had energetic leaders who acted decisively to protect the capital. Alarmed by Alaric's sack of Rome in 410, men at the court of Theodosius II began in 413 to construct new walls that would protect the city from Attila's siege. Because the population had outgrown Constantine's walls, the Theodosian walls extended the city limits to the west as well as guarding the coastline. Later in Theodosius's reign, a second land wall was added, so that there were two land walls fortified with towers and separated by a terrace. Just beyond the outer wall workers dredged a deep ditch that could be filled with water when enemies threatened, altogether making Constantinople the most defensible city in Christendom.

The city's hard-pressed empire, surrounded by enemies, would need all the defenses it could muster. To its east were the Persians, ancient rival of Greco-Roman peoples. To the north, groups of Alani, Indo-Iranian nomads, joined forces with assorted Goths and Huns for an attempt on Constantinople that was repelled at last by the new walls. Vast numbers of Slavs swarmed along the Danube frontier, occupying what is now eastern Europe and southern Russia, and swept into the Balkans. In the sixth century, Slavs and Bulgars raided the countryside around the

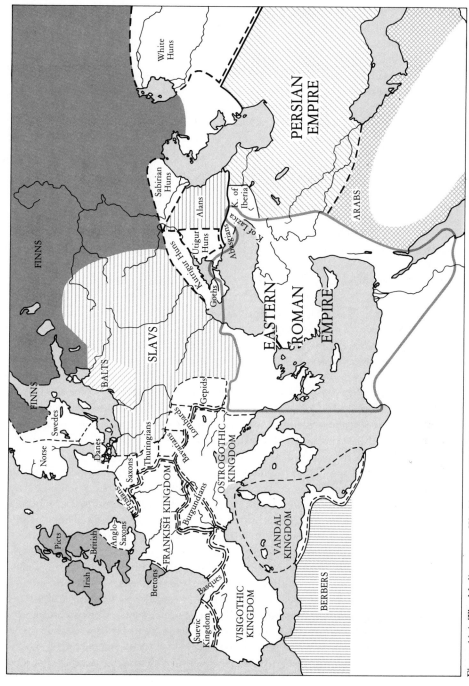

Figure 11.1 The Mediterranean World circa 528 A.D.

capital, to be stopped only by the massive walls. When 100,000 Avars (an Asian people related to the Huns and Turks) arrived in 558, their sophisticated political development under a strong khan allowed them to subjugate millions of Slavs and ultimately to engineer the great Avar-Slav-Persian siege of Constantinople in 626.

The battered eastern empire survived all these assaults because the capital remained untaken and the succession of emperors unbroken. Eastern sources, however, dated the fall of the western empire to 476, when the last formally designated emperor was deposed. To the eastern imperial view, this marked the significant breaking point. Modern observers tend to see an ongoing process of invasion, instability, and fragmentation into various Germanic states after the breakup of the Hunnic realm at the death of Attila in 453.

Of all the Germans, the Vandals earned a reputation as the most violent and fearsome. Crossing the straits from Spain into North Africa, Vandals took the rich farmlands of the coast, breadbasket of Rome. In an instant they disrupted that critical source of grain and also destroyed the intellectual primacy of North Africa within the western church. From their capital at Carthage (439–533), they persecuted Catholics and ruled a defiantly Arian state, even building a fleet through which they controlled the Mediterranean Sea along with western Sicily, the Balearics, Corsica, and Sardinia. Not content to shatter Roman hegemony over the Mediterranean, they assailed Rome directly in 455, committing atrocities much more brutal than those of Alaric in 410.

Other Germanic peoples established less destructive kingdoms in old Roman territory—a Visigothic realm in Spain, Ostrogothic in Italy, Burgundian in the valleys of the upper Rhone and Saône rivers (the region still called Burgundy), and Frankish in Gaul, while Anglo-Saxon tribes took control of Britain. When Germans settled in Roman provinces, they followed varying models of *hospitalitas*, the system by which chiefs and armies received a portion, usually one-third, of revenues from land. Gradually chiefs and kings claimed the land itself. Because Germans settling on Roman territory composed a small share of the total population—perhaps as low as 5 percent—slowly assimilated Germanic chiefs and Roman elite tended to preside as landlords over peasants who were largely native "Romans." Many peasants saw few changes in their lives under the new regime. Perhaps a Germanic landlord replaced their old Roman master and armed Germanic forces patrolled their lands. The newcomers usually absorbed the language and much of the culture of the natives, with whom they intermarried. The great cultural change occurred beyond the countryside, with the demise of cities that had controlled the economy and distinguished the culture of Mediterranean antiquity. Besieged and pillaged by invaders, then shunned by Germanic farmers and herders who preferred their habitual village life, cities virtually disappeared from the West. With them went the cosmopolitan society of the ancient world along with its characteristic economic and cultural life, to be replaced by the predominantly peasant society that marked the medieval West.

This new society emerged from the combination of three elements: Roman cultural heritage, Germanic customs, and Christianity. The most influential of these was Christianity, which molded divergent cultural elements and offered a common world view and model for behavior. Many factors allowed for diversity of time and place, including such variables as geography or the relative strength and numbers of the indigenous peoples and Germans. To study one specific example, let us look at the Ostrogothic kingdom of Italy, where Theodoric dreamed of a glorious civilization of cultured Romans and virile Goths coexisting and complementing one another's strengths. But religious antipathy between Catholic and Arian became the lightning rod for cultural and ethnic animosities that would blow the society apart.

Ostrogothic Italy

When the boy emperor Romulus Augustulus was deposed in 476, the army in Italy proclaimed their leader Odoacer as his replacement. He ruled for seventeen years until defeated in 493 by Theodoric's Ostrogoths, dispatched to Italy by the eastern emperor Zeno, who was eager to rid himself of rowdy and dangerous guests. Technically, Theodoric assumed power as subject-king of Byzantium, formally acknowledging his allegiance to the emperor in Constantinople and receiving in return an authentication of his own rule. In fact, Theodoric exploited this prestigious connection in his grand experiment—to create, quite self-consciously, a new composite civilization of Germans and Romans. For a brief time, the experiment seemed destined for brilliant success, but charges of Roman treason triggered Gothic reprisals before Theodoric's death in 526. When the Roman emperor of the east, Justinian, found a pretext for intervention, his armies fought to wrest Italy from Ostrogothic hands. By the time the last sizable Gothic force surrendered in 553, Italy lay in ruins, easy prey for barbaric Lombards. The promising Ostrogothic reign had lasted only sixty years.

While Theodoric ruled, he was zealous to preserve the best of Roman culture, which he greatly admired. He courted the favor of the Roman senate; in his theoretical separation of Roman and German, the senate played an honorable and useful role. Theodoric celebrated this survival and transmission of culture by carrying out an impressive program of building and repairing palaces and amphitheaters, aqueducts and baths and city walls. His mausoleum stands today in Ravenna, a monument to a grand program. A mid-sixth-century source, the Anonymous Valesianus, praised Theodoric for bringing peace and prosperity, offering the traditional games and grain dole for the people, keeping the laws of former Roman emperors like a new Solomon, offering gracious treatment to pope and catholics, and choosing from the old Roman senate such fine statesmen as Boethius and Cassiodorus to assist him.

Cassiodorus (ca. 485–ca. 550) was a particularly fine example of a talented and immensely learned Roman aristocrat in Gothic service. Secretary to Theodoric by 514, he was to hold office under three Ostrogothic kings. By about 538 he withdrew from the court, at first with the ambition of founding a university of Christian studies at Rome, but then he retreated to his country estates, where he lived in monastic seclusion until his death at an advanced age. Profoundly conscious of the old culture that was fast dying, he lamented the loss of books burned during barbarian incursions. To save, even in epitomized form, whatever knowledge he could rescue, he wrote works fusing Greco-Roman wisdom with Christian piety—works that would inspire learning throughout the Benedictine monastic houses in the medieval West. In the face of declining literacy, Cassiodorus stimulated generations of monks to spell correctly by insisting that "every word of the Lord written by the scribe is a wound inflicted on Satan." He praised pragmatic knowledge such as grammar and rhetoric as the products of a world created by God and so linked to the Creator. But he believed that theoretical study is also valuable in drawing the mind away from carnal affairs to the world of the spirit. So, for instance, he praised music, which leads the ear and soul to the divine, and astronomy, which draws the human mind to contemplation of the celestial realm.

The learned and pious Cassiodorus, philosopher/theologian/monk, was the last of his kind, his works a precious and tantalizing remnant of the old erudition and culture nourished within the Gothic-Roman synthesis. How did this promising civilization die? According to an anonymous contemporary source, the devil entered Theodoric and made him suspicious and cruel. Modern critics are tempted to make a similar assessment by reckoning that religious tensions in Italian society finally erupted into violence.

The native Romans were orthodox Christians. The Ostrogoths, on the other hand, cherished their Arianism as an important element of their culture. Like their long hair and distinctive jewelry, it made an essential statement about their heritage and special character. Their institutional lives focused on Arian churches in the center of Gothic communities. Few Goths cared about or understood the fine points of dogma that separated their churches from the orthodox. Rather than discourses on the Trinity, Goths showed a fondness for stories of the Old Testament featuring warriors and battles. To most Goths willing to abandon their pagan ways, Arianism was simply the new tribal region or perhaps the national religion of their Gothic state—Christianity grafted onto Germanic rituals and beliefs. Had it been given the time, political Arianism may well have died out in the long run since its theological base among Goths was not intellectually or spiritually firm. As they were assimilated into Christian Roman society, individual Ostrogoths (even Theodoric's mother, Hereleuwa) were converting to orthodoxy, just as their Visigothic kin were doing in Spain.

Most Ostrogoths seem quite deliberately to have seen Arianism as a version of Christianity that bound them to their kin and set them apart from the Romans. A natural consequence of this distinction was further hostility between the two peoples as religious differences exacerbated other tensions. Romans who hated a second-class status in their homeland concentrated their animosity on the heretical status of their rulers. The Goths, for their part, feared treason motivated by religious passions.

Religious change in the eastern empire triggered the feared explosive reaction. So long as the monophysite Anastasius held the imperial throne (491–518), the orthodox Roman aristocracy had neither reason nor opportunity to join cause with the East. In those years, Theodoric acted as protector of the orthodox church. When the militantly orthodox Justin succeeded to power, however, influential senators at Theodoric's court entered into an incriminating correspondence with Constantinople. Were the two parties joining to foment revolution against Theodoric? Soon Justin began to harry Arians in the East, and the suspicious Theodoric snapped. One famous victim of his rage was the aristocrat Boethius, who wrote the *Consolation of Philosophy* while in prison awaiting execution for treason. Like Cassiodorus, Boethius had sought to preserve classical culture as he witnessed the demise of the ancient world. He had labored diligently to translate Greek works into Latin and to write handbooks and commentaries. His final philosophical treatise, the *Consolation*, is heavily informed by Christianity's message that human beings must seek fulfillment not in earthly pleasure or wealth but in pursuit of God. Boethius's final legacy inspired readers throughout the Middle Ages, including Dante, and provoked numerous commentaries. King Alfred translated the *Consolation* into Old English in the ninth century, and Notker translated it into Old High German in the tenth.

The execution of Boethius signaled the end of Theodoric's dream of Gothic-Roman synthesis. Literature produced at his court had praised Theodoric as a Christian king who united two peoples in harmony before God. In his capital at Ravenna, the great church of St. Apollinaire Nuovo featured mosaics celebrating this harmony. The west end of the nave showed a procession of Theodoric and entourage; balancing this on the east was Christ enthroned in company with his angels. On both sides of the nave, stately processions of martyrs and saints linked the earthly and heavenly kings. Images of Christian rulership blessed with peace and prosperity dominated the church. But this fragile culture disappeared in Theodoric's persecutions and the long Gothic–East Roman wars that followed. Only the persistent myth of Theodoric as ideal Christian/Germanic/Roman ruler would survive to influence another Christian prince of like vision, Charlemagne.

Justinian and the Eastern Empire: Dreams of a Single Empire (527-565)

Perhaps the Gothic Wars were inevitable, given Roman-Gothic tensions and Theodoric's violent reprisals. They were also an integral part of the program of Justinian, the tireless East Roman emperor driven by the conviction of his sacred mission to free Roman territories from barbarians and Arian heretics and to restore the frontiers of a single Roman and orthodox Christian empire.

Justinian inherited an empire that had weathered the storms of the fifth century, from barbarian incursions to religious controversies. Thanks to the prudent fiscal policies of the emperor Anastasius (491–518), the imperial coffers were full. The prospects for this state seemed limitless to Justinian, nephew of the emperor Justin (518–527). A Macedonian swineherd turned soldier, Justin had come to power through the army. Justinian too hailed from the westernmost territories (modern Yugoslavia). Latin, not Greek, was his native language. His eyes were trained west, so that he was determined to restore the ancient boundaries of a Roman Empire united by a single faith.

To pursue his dream, he first had to buy peace with the Persians, whose heartland had recently shifted from Iran and Central Asia to Mesopotamia, the borders of Justinian's empire. The Persians also had a new ruler, the formidable Chosroes I. Religious tensions heightened the rivalry of strong neighboring foes, as the Persians embraced a zealously intolerant Zoroastrianism led by a powerful priesthood. Byzantine diplomacy, on the other hand, had brought Christianity into Lazica and Caucasian Iberia, creating spiritual and hence political allies at Persia's doorstep. Yet Justinian chose to pay increasing tribute to Persia rather than exploit potential eastern inroads because he was willing to accept peace at any cost in the East so he could direct all his military resources to western reconquest.

At first the gamble seemed remarkably successful. Justinian's troops crushed the Vandal kingdom by a surprise attack in 533 and then took the Spanish coastline from the Visigoths. Ostrogothic resistance, however, was crushed only after more than twenty years of costly campaigns that depleted Justinian's resources of men and provisions. The destruction in Italy was devastating. During successive sieges, the aqueducts serving Rome were cut, closing down the great public baths that were prominent features of classical civilization. Surrounding territories reverted to marshes that would be drained only in the twentieth century. The price of reuniting Christendom was indeed dear. Nor would the union last. Depopulated and economically ruined, Italy proved easy prey for the Lombards, who swept down the peninsula only three years after Justinian's death. Its wealth exhausted, the eastern empire could not hold the hard-won lands.

If Justinian dreamed of removing Arians from the West, he also longed to rout out heresy from the eastern provinces and support orthodoxy as the state religion. More than any of his predecessors, he exercised control over the church, and he aimed at absolute domination. Here Justinian's background and instincts as a westerner impeded him. When left to his own devices, he exhibited a personal intolerance for monophysites. This theological aversion was reinforced by political considerations: Abandoning monophysitism would encourage renewed contacts with Roman senators and assure their support in the Gothic war. Actions against monophysites, however, risked dangerous consequences in the eastern provinces. With this thorny problem, as with many others, Justinian was immeasurably assisted by his wife Theodora, daughter of a bearkeeper in the circus and former prostitute and exotic performer. Theodora was savvy in the ways of the world. When a lover abandoned her in Alexandria, she had reportedly been rescued by monophysite leaders, who persuaded her to give up her scandalous life. She became a monophysite supporter, perhaps out of appreciation for their help in her survival and rehabilitation but also because, unlike her husband, she had lived in Egypt and Syria and understood both the religious temperaments of the East and the importance of respecting eastern religious expression if these valuable territories were not to be irretrievably alienated. To Theodora it seemed self-evident that the orthodox emperor must find some accommodation with monophysites.

Under Theodora's influence, Justinian duly suspended the persecution of monophysites and attempted conciliation. In 533 he reverted to the emperor Zeno's policy. Zeno's *Henoticon*, or "Edict of Union" (482) had recognized the rulings of only the first three ecumenical councils and avoided expressions of "one nature" or "two natures," thus trying to skirt the burning issue. In 533 Justinian issued his "new *Henoticon*" allowing monophysites to preach their doctrine. He even permitted a monophysite, Anthemius, to assume the patriarchate in 535. Hoping to mollify the anti-Nestorian monophysites, in 553 he convened the Council of Constantinople to anathematize the Three Chapters, pronouncements of Chalcedon that had approved three Nestorian-leaning theologians. Despite such conciliatory moves, the orthodox emperor failed to find a compromise that would satisfy any of the parties in the dispute, orthodox or monophysite. Disaffection only increased.

Even while he dictated various compromises, Justinian ever remained the complete autocrat. A devout student of theology, he successfully championed the imperial claim of supremacy over ecclesiastical powers. But not all the bishops surrendered quietly to his demands. The Italian West provides a particularly interesting example of this resistance.

Once Justinian reclaimed Italy, he sought to express his sovereignty there through imperial portraiture, as Roman emperors had customarily done. In the great church of San Vitale in Ravenna, as elsewhere, he wiped out traces of Theodoric's presence and replaced them with emblems of his own power. This plan produced the famous mosaics of Justinian and his court, and opposite them Theodora and her entourage. Justinian wears silks with Persian motifs signifying the absolute autocracy of a Persian king of kings, while his consort appears equally regal in her diadem and jewelry heavy with pearls, emeralds, and sapphires. They occupy a place of honor in the church, on facing sides of the apse, linked by the apse mosaic of Christ, angels, and saints. Here is a potent association of imperial power and religious devotion expressed by an iconography that fuses sacred and imperial powers and serves to sanctify the imperial ideology. Such a political statement in a sacred building might shock a twentieth-century American Christian raised in the tradition of church-state separation, but it seemed entirely appropriate to a Christian emperor for whom empire and church were mutual protectors, with the emperor styled as Christ's regent on earth.

This mosaic is often admired as the most beautiful and dramatic expression of Justinian's imperial domination, but does the bishop who consecrated the church in 547 or 548 in fact have the last word, challenging Justinian's primacy? The scene is a grand procession, a notable moment in the liturgy. Does not the bishop, Maximian, at least seem to be jockeying for position with the emperor? Their dark robes set the two apart from the other central figures. Although Justinian's robe overlaps Maximian's slightly, the bishop's feet are plainly farther forward than the emperor's, and so the bishop appears to be standing ahead of Justinian. Only Maximian is identified with his name inscribed over his head. The emperor who would be supreme autocrat in the church as well as in the society at large must unwittingly share prominence with the local bishop who oversaw the mosaic's workmanship.

But this was after all distant Ravenna, for decades at war with Justinian, naturally offended by his policy of autocracy from afar. Were there signs of disaffection in the East as well? Indeed, no one has attracted extremes of adulation and vituperation more than Justinian. Perhaps the examples best known today come from the pen of Procopius, who sang the emperor's praises in works describing foreign wars (*History of the Wars*) and magnificent monuments to God's glory (*Buildings*) and who vilified him in the *Secret History*.[1] The *Secret History* describes a mad, demonic Justinian, a hypocritical devotee of assassination and robbery, who looked and acted like the notorious Roman emperor Domitian. This Justinian is a demon who stalked the imperial palace by night, his severed head tucked under his arm, and a monster who extorted taxes to hand out as bribes to barbarians. Such wild charges express the frustration of a man disillusioned by Justinian's policies, maybe personally harmed as well, and seething at the impossibility of open criticism against an autocratic regime.

Procopius was not alone in his anger. The civil unrest that had plagued Roman cities escalated during the fifth and sixth centuries and erupted with great violence during Justinian's reign. Procopius described the hooliganism of skinheads in the Circus Factions, associations of sports fans that had survived from the earlier Roman period. Young men affected Persian-style beard and mustache, shaving their hair to the temples and then wearing it long in the back in the Hunnic fashion. They affected Hunnic clothing, too, with long flowing sleeves that concealed the weapons they used to rob and kill, terrorizing the city. An anonymous sixth-century dialogue, *On Political Science*, blames the Circus Factions for corrupting the youth of the empire and ultimately weakening the army; instead of hooliganism (or, incidentally, monasticism as well, which harbored vast numbers of draft resisters, according to this same source) young men should expend their energies in armed service to their state.

---

[1] See Averil Cameron, trans. and ed., *History of the Wars, Secret History, and Buildings* (New York: Washington Square Press, 1967).

Rebellion came to a head with the Nika Revolt of January 532 when the Circus Factions united to protest hated officials and extortionate taxation. Nerves were on edge in Constantinople because the disorganization of transport and economic uncertainty in the provinces had caused temporary disruption of the food supply to the capital. Amid the riots and fires, it was Theodora who persuaded Justinian to fight back and not to flee. In a surprise sally, his soldiers entered the hippodrome to slay 30,000 demonstrators and put down the rebellion.

The factions had burned great stretches of the city. Before the embers were cool, Justinian resolved to turn this tragedy into a brilliant opportunity. He had already embarked on an empire-wide program of building fortifications, monasteries, palaces, bridges, cisterns, aqueducts, baths, hospitals, and especially churches, like the monastery of St. Catherine on Mt. Sinai. But the Nika revolt offered the orthodox emperor the grandest stroke of all: to rebuild Hagia Sophia, the Great Church that would reign over orthodox Christendom for nine centuries. More than 100 feet across and 180 feet high, the Great Church's vaulted interior would be much more massive than churches of Europe, and would soar to heaven (so witnesses marveled), reaching even the choirs of the stars. At its dedication only five-and-a-half years later in 537, Justinian exclaimed: "Solomon, I have surpassed you!" The architects were master mathematicians and theoreticians who perfected the dome style. Under the spellbinding influence of Hagia Sophia, this element would be a characteristic feature of eastern churches for the future, along with a near indifference to the exterior appearance of the building. In contrast with classical temples such as the Parthenon, with graceful exteriors fitted to their own peculiar landscapes, eastern churches would follow the example of Hagia Sophia in emphasizing the interior space, which was a model of God's universe and was intended to guide the worshipper to contemplation of the divine. Byzantine sources are quite explicit in identifying the church's interior with the Christian universe. In the seventh century, for instance, Maximus the Confessor wrote: "The whole church by itself is the symbol of the entire cosmos as perceived by sense alone, since it has a sanctuary like the heavens and a beautiful nave like the earth."

The majestically decorated interior of Hagia Sophia perhaps best exemplified this concept, and the whole decoration of the interior of the building was conceived to support it. The surviving capitals and marble floors convey something of the former grandeur. Because the interior decorations are lost except for post-Justinianic mosaics, we must imagine the total effect of the spacious interior gleaming with silver altar screen and silk draperies, and smoky with incense and hundreds of candles and lamps. On a rare sunny day along the Bosphorus, light would stream down from the row of windows in the dome, which (in Procopius's words) "seems not to sit upon solid masonry but to cover the space beneath as if suspended from heaven by a golden chain."

The people of Constantinople crowded eagerly into Hagia Sophia just as they did into their other churches, even pressing against the sanctuary barrier. Only the sanctuary itself was inaccessible to the masses, but the church otherwise invited all initiates to the full revelation of the mysteries. Some modern scholars have assumed that women were relegated to special balconies. It seems, however, that instead special aisles on the left of the nave were reserved for women. Men sat separately on the right. One gallery above was reserved for the empress and her entourage. The emperor had his own throne in Hagia Sophia, located in the southern aisle where he could witness the grand, public celebration of the liturgy. In Justinian's day, a series of processional movements structured the liturgy, beginning with the First Entrance of clergy and congregation singing together with the bishop as they streamed into the church. The Ravenna mosaics of Justinian and Theodora are meant to portray just such a procession.

The Great Church was Justinian's legacy to the grandeur of his empire but also to God and the people of Christendom. To restore order to his realm, he planned the reorganization and preservation of the legal code, which had fallen into a confusing disarray. The laws were written in Latin, which by the sixth century almost no one in the East could read. As a concession to his Greek-speaking people, Justinian was compelled to order all new laws written in Greek. An even worse problem than the language barrier was the tangled mass of the law. Under the pagan jurist, Tribonian, Justinian's commission organized the vast code into manageable form, resolving inconsistencies. The old Roman law was pagan, but its principles of justice were not fundamentally at odds with Christianity. Only occasionally do we see in Tribonian's Code a softening of penalties, which may reflect the influence of Christianity. In Justinian's New Laws (the Novels), however, is expressed more clearly the merging of the traditional pagan legal system with the Christian ethic of the medieval empire. New laws, for instance, restricted the death penalty, often substituting mutilation, which was considered more humane. Other laws improved the position of slaves so that they could more easily win emancipation. This was not an especially courageous stand because slavery was not very important in the sixth-century empire. Laws improving the lot of women may be more telling. Perhaps Theodora's influence, as much as that of Christianity, is felt in Justinian's laws reclaiming and protecting prostitutes, granting women the right to keep the property that had been their dowries, and allowing them guardianship of their children. The law increasingly intruded into the most private lives of imperial subjects, inspired by a Christian ruler eager to regulate the morality, conduct, and orthodoxy of his people.

The presence of non-Christians in his realm particularly incensed Justinian. He abused the few surviving Samaritans in Palestine until they rebelled, then crushed their revolt. Jews he treated a little better. After two centuries of Christian rule, there were still pagans throughout the empire, even among the court at Constantinople, as Tribonian attests. Justinian destroyed the last pagan temples in Egypt, and he struck at the intellectual core of paganism by closing the Platonic Academy of

Athens, whose scholars fled to the Persian king. In western Asia Minor alone, an early center of Christian communities, the emperor's emissary Bishop John of Ephesus found 70,000 pagans, mostly in the countryside. Despite great efforts at conversion, paganism would persist there into Arab times, when they took the name Sabians to win status as "people of the book." Evidence from the later sixth and seventh centuries proves the continuing activities of pagan magicians, diviners, and rainmakers. Canons of the Council in Trullo (691–692) mention pagan festivals of the Brumalia and the New Moon. In the eighth century, the cult of Kybele still lived in Caria, and a sacred stone outside Melitus was venerated into the tenth century.

Justinian's law stressed obedience to a Christian code of right belief and right conduct. The emperor wanted to control all people and institutions within his realm, including the church itself, and so he regulated clerical and monastic life in addition to the administration and privileges of the church. Justinian was generally successful, setting the pattern for eastern Christendom. Resistance to his caesaropapism surfaced, however, taking various forms. The depiction of Maximian in the Ravenna mosaic may be one subtle example. Another comes from North Africa, where the church was still stunned by recent persecutions of the Arian Vandals, and the bishops were in no mood to tolerate interference from Constantinople in their ecclesiastical affairs. When Justinian attacked the Three Chapters, African bishops led the defense. The dissidents were promptly summoned to the capital. Among them was the last Christian poet of North Africa, the learned bishop Verecundus of Junca (now Bordj Younga in Southern Tunisia), who fled to the Church of St. Euphemia in Chalcedon, where he died. His only surviving poem, *De satisfactione paenitentiae*, begs for God's mercy in the cataclysmic end of the world, which he felt was at hand. Verecundus's intensely personal conviction, heavily influenced by apocalyptic literature and contemporary apocalypticism, represents an idea not uncommon in the sixth century. Gregory the Great, for instance, saw the Lombard invasions as presaging the end of the world. Could civilized Christendom survive the waves of violence or, for that matter, the repression of despots?

Under Justinian, the eastern empire was overtaxed and ruled autocratically, its emotional and financial reserves stretched to the breaking point. Drought, swarms of insects, and bubonic plague also took their toll. In Constantinople alone during one three-month bout of plague in 543, as much as one-third of the entire populace died—as many as 1,000 a day. (Procopius says that 10,000 perished daily.) Plague recurred in waves; by the year 600 the population of the eastern empire may have been only 60 percent of its preplague figures. It seemed an empire ill-equipped to handle the stresses that lay ahead. Despite pockets of resistance to autocracy, however, the empire had a strong spiritual center and a consistent sense of itself as the God-given Christian empire, ruled by a sacred emperor who was God's regent on earth. This certainty of communal identity and sacred mission would play a monumental role in its survival.

Rome: from Episcopate to Papacy

Whereas Justinian and his successors dominated the eastern church, a radically different situation prevailed in the West, where the collapse of Roman civil authority left the bishops in charge. Within this highly visible episcopal structure, the bishop of Rome held nearly uncontested power and prestige. No emperor resided in Rome, as in Constantinople, to challenge his political or spiritual control, nor were there western patriarchates to compete with Rome.

Medieval tradition traced the lineage of the Roman bishop (called pope from the Latin *papa*, meaning "father") back to Peter and the scriptural authority of Matthew 16:18.

> And I tell you, you are Peter and on this rock I will build my church, and the powers of death shall not prevail against it.

The doctrine of the Petrine Succession, the belief that subsequent Roman bishops inherited Peter's authority and importance, was first cited by the bishop Damasus (366–384). The prestige of Leo I (440–461) moved the papacy to greater heights. As early as 445, the western emperor Valentinian III ordered all western bishops to submit to Leo's authority. Although this order applied only to the West and even there not all complied, reverence for Leo was so great that the predominantly eastern bishops at Chalcedon in 451 greeted his legates with the salutation: "Peter speaks through Leo." His courage and leadership became legendary; according to tradition, he won mercy for Rome from two barbarian armies, the dread hordes of Attila the Hun and the Vandal Gaiseric.

Leo consistently stressed the principle of Petrine Succession, and later popes followed his eminent example. In the early centuries papal power was limited mainly to Italy, and popes did not even attend the first eight ecumenical councils, although they would convene and preside over all later ones. Growing papal prestige found a worthy recipient in Gregory I (ca. 540–603), known as Gregory the Great, whose influence extended far beyond the borders of Italy.

Born in Rome during the Gothic wars, Gregory lived through the brief east Roman imperial dominance and the Lombard invasions. These were nasty and violent years for Italy. As a member of a senatorial Christian family, Gregory received the aristocratic education of the day, but there was much less classical culture available to him than to Boethius and Cassiodorus only two generations earlier. In these few intervening decades, Italy had entered the Middle Ages. Although he learned Latin grammar, law, and music, Gregory never bothered to learn Greek, even though he spent six years in Constantinople as a papal envoy. This ignorance, even disdain, illustrates the breach between East and West as surely as it marks the gap between Gregory's world and classical antiquity.

Gregory began a civil career and rose to become city prefect of Rome, but like many of the best men of his day, he was drawn to the church. In 575 he converted his palace into the monastery of St. Andrews, one of seven monasteries he would found out of his ancestral inheritance, and withdrew to the life of a Benedictine monk. In such troubled times, a man of Gregory's practical talents could not remain in seclusion, however, and he was reluctantly drawn back into active affairs, this time under the church's auspices. In addition to his experience in Constantinople, Gregory served as deacon, managing the church's estates and charities. Conscripted as pope, he stepped in to fill the void at a moment when the city was threatened by plague, famine, and Lombard invasions. The civic administration of Rome had collapsed, and so it was Gregory who concluded the truce of 598 with the Lombards. Ransoming captives, providing food and water, founding hospitals for the sick, he organized the church to meet the social and political needs of his people, who came to consider the church their state. Not surprisingly, Gregory's claims of Roman primacy carried great weight in the West, where there were no rival patriarchates, and helped transform the Roman episcopate into the medieval papacy. But this only sharpened discord with the East, where the Patriarch of Constantinople countered by taking the title of Ecumenical or Universal Patriarch.

Meanwhile, Gregory became recognized as one of the four fathers of the western church, along with Ambrose, Augustine, and Jerome. Gregory's much-loved *Dialogues*, lives of Italian saints and martyrs written in a simple, conversational style, enthralled medieval audiences with credulous accounts of wonders. He was an influential interpreter and popularizer of Augustine for the Middle Ages, following his master especially in creating a distinctively western theology of penance and purgatory. The latter became another of the issues dividing western and eastern Christendom, the emerging catholic West and orthodox East.

According to legend, Gregory also created a dynamic Latin liturgy, the Gregorian chant. This plainsong remains an important part of Roman Catholic ritual to this day as one of the elements that distinguishes it from the eastern rites. A prominent feature of the eastern service was the *kontakion*, developed in Justinian's day by the monk Romanos from sources in Syriac hymns and Greek rhythmic prose homilies. Chanted by a cantor, with choir or congregation singing the refrain, these rhythmical sung sermons, full of dialogue and drama, paradox and word play, were popularly used in many services until the Council in Trullo (691–692), whose Canon 19 made the preaching of a *prose* homily mandatory at all major liturgical functions.

In fact, Gregory did not invent western religious song, as tradition held, but merely initiated some liturgical reforms. In another respect, however, Gregory's true influence ranged far beyond Italy. Through his patronage of Benedictine monks, he helped the young order survive rough times to become, for centuries, the West's only monastic order. When Gregory commissioned Benedictine monks to extend the bounds of Christendom far to the north, he gained not only souls for the faith but also loyal supporters for the papacy. Gregory's friend, the monk Augustine, and thirty companions traveled to the Anglo-Saxons in Britain, where little of Roman culture, including Christianity, had survived nearly two centuries after the Roman retreat in 406–407. At Kent, Augustine converted King Ethelbert, whose Christian Frankish wife had perhaps prepared the way. Then Augustine set up his own see at Canterbury, beginning the slow and not altogether steady process of Christianization from the top reaches of society downward. With Christianity came Latin learning, writing, and law, altering the society of medieval Britain even as it changed the social expression and spirit of Christianity in the West.

Christian Culture: Christianity as a Central Expression of Medieval Life

In important ways, late sixth-century Christendom was no longer the classical world. On the one hand, conversions had extended the bounds of Christendom beyond the frontiers of the Roman Empire, from Britain to Armenia, Georgia, and Albania. Abyssinia converted in the early fifth century, Nubia in the early sixth. Arians such as the Spanish Visigoths gradually embraced Roman Christianity. As the physical horizons of the Christian world expanded, on the other hand, so its cultural sensibilities simplified into the nonclassical views of medieval life.

In the West, a rather uniform Roman high culture disappeared with the creation of tribal societies, virtually erasing the boundaries between aristocratic and popular culture. The despoiled capital, its ancient monuments ruined and decaying, had a population of perhaps only 30,000, reduced from several hundred thousand. Where once cultured aristocrats fostered the classical tradition of Greek and Roman literature and learning, now bishops and monks read the scriptures and wrote biblical commentaries and saints' lives in Vulgar Latin. But Gregory the Great embodied the vision of the papacy and the new vigor of medieval Christendom.

Major cities of the East, especially the capital, nurtured the survival of a secular elite who studied ancient Greek literature and wrote elegant letters for their cultivated friends or histories modeled on Thucydides (for example, Procopius's *History of the Wars*). These archaizing works, in imitation of an archaic style, had a very limited audience. Even in the East, society was being redefined by its Christian outlook as the church absorbed the culture and made it its own. New kinds of literature appeared, naturally steeped in Christian language and values, and accessible to people whose secular education was modest.

One such work from the age of Justinian is the *Chronicle* of John Malalas, an Antiochene who spent his last years in Constantinople.[2] The *Chronicle* owes much to Eusebius's Christian chronicle and is itself an extraordinarily influential representative of the genre of popular historical writing: the world chronicle. Malalas

---

[2]See E.M. Jeffreys, M.J. Jeffreys, and R. Scott et al., *The Chronicle of John Malalas: A Translation*, Byzantina Australiensia 4 (Melbourne: Australian Association for Byzantine Studies, 1986).

wrote in a simple style close to that of the spoken language, a Greek dialect with some Latin and eastern expressions.

Malalas's view is Christian and apologetic, showing much Biblical influence on language and content. Like others of its genre, the *Chronicle* begins with Adam and Eve, assuming that all peoples were descended from Ham, Shem, and Japheth and that all events of this world, directed by God, led inexorably to Christ's incarnation and the Last Judgment. The great events of world history are structured within the framework of Hebrew history as recorded in the Hebrew bible. Beginning with Augustus, chronology is organized around the reigns of Roman emperors continuing through the reign of Justinian.

Malalas is famous for his errors, such as having Nero die of illness at the age of sixty-nine. Mostly, however, he tells us information we would love to have for all periods and places of the Middle Ages—gossip, fiction, anecdotes, and historical details—all as the average sixth-century east Roman of fairly good education viewed them. Imagine a twentieth-century tabloid with a primitive Christian overlay, and you will understand the tone, value, and limitations of the *Chronicle*. Malalas was determined to entertain, and the *Chronicle* shows what fascinated the ordinary east Roman. Malalas recorded portents, signs of Persian-Roman tensions, riots among the Circus Factions in Antioch, flooding in Edessa. In this partisan provincial view, the great fire in Antioch, with its subsequent earthquake and banditry, receives a disproportionate emphasis. The *Chronicle* is an excellent source for social history. For example, there are valuable tidbits about Justinian, like the confession that he "did not speak the Roman language [that is, Greek] correctly." From Malalas we learn that the emperor was always more comfortable with Latin. The *Chronicle* reveals how a sixth-century Antiochene viewed the world: when it lists rulers elsewhere, it gives the ominous sense of God's people being surrounded by potentially dangerous aliens. In such a world, Malalas's credulous piety remains the ordering principle.

Another interesting example from the age of Justinian is the superstitious and otherwordly *Christian Topography*, written in about the 530s by Cosmas Indicopleustes (i.e., sailor to India). Cosmas probably hailed from Alexandria where he settled in a monastery upon retiring from the life of a merchant who had sailed throughout the Mediterranean, Red Sea, and Persian Gulf. His book is a precious work, the only Christian topography extant, which combines descriptive geography, cosmography, and scriptural exegesis. Much of the geography is quite accurate, based on personal observation in lands as far-ranging as Ethiopia and Christian Abyssinia, and from the Sinai Desert to India. For all his practical experience, Cosmas cheerfully confessed his lack of formal education, and in fact he considered the absence of rhetorical training an asset, since rhetoric would be out of place in a book "for Christians, who had more need of correct notions than of fine phrases." The resulting grammar is loose and colloquial but usually clear and forceful and even eloquent when Cosmas was writing about his faith.

Cosmas ordered his experience and beliefs from a Christian worldview. As he rejected "pagan" grammar, so he also rejected pagan science. Like many pious Christians of his day, he assumed that the universe created by God could be understood only through the interpretation of Christian scripture. So he refuted the Ptolemaic concept of the earth as a globe and deduced instead that the earth must be shaped like the sanctuary of the tabernacle of Moses, which was a copy of the earth; the tabernacle itself was modeled on the universe, which had the earth as its base and God's heaven at its vaulted top. Ancient Jewish and Akkadian concepts of the universe had clearly influenced Cosmas. He tells the reader that he got his ideas on creation from Mar Aba, who was then the Nestorian Katholikos (metropolitan bishop).

The views of Cosmas and Malalas nicely illustrate the changing tastes and passions that we identify as medieval. Christianity became an essential, inextricable part of the culture of medieval men and women, east and west. These people created their own evolving Christian mythologies to express their worldview. From the second century onward, they venerated martyrs and their relics, looking back to the time of the persecutions as a heroic age when martyrs were the athletes of Christ. By the end of the fourth century, the popular imagination revered martyrs as protectors and healers, intercessors with God. The remains of a holy man or anything the saint had touched remained sacred. The passion for relics increased as did the enthusiasm for pilgrimages to places where they were preserved, especially to the Holy Land or to Rome.

The apostles continued to be revered, too, and by the fifth century the angels were also, especially Michael. Both Rome and Constantinople built churches in his honor, and Michaelmas, his feast day on September 29, became one of the most popular in the medieval West. When the Third Ecumenical Council at Ephesus authorized the title Mother of God for Mary, she could with official sanction receive much of the fervor once granted the old mother goddess worship, as Christianity absorbed and modified some of the pagan impulses it could not obliterate. With Christendom entering the Middle Ages, the religion was secure in its position as the central expression of medieval life. It was Christianity that was molding all the elements of society into the distinctive tastes and passions that identified the medieval world.

Chapter 12

THE EASTERN EMPIRE AND THE STRUGGLE WITH ISLAM (565–843)

Byzantium after Justinian

Justinian's failed attempt at reunion only served to separate western and eastern Christendom and alienate each from the other. In the generations after Justinian's death in 565, his empire seemed less and less Roman, less and less classical. By the time of his death, it is appropriate to call the eastern empire by the name now commonly used for its medieval continuator: Byzantium.

It is important to remember that the people we call Byzantines recognized no radical break from their Greco-Roman heritage. They continued to call themselves *Romaioi*, "Romans." Their empire they called *Basileia ton Romaion*, "Empire of the Romans." They spoke these names in Greek, having lost virtually all contact with the Latin language. Modern historians have seen this change as but one sign of a new era that began with Constantine's conversion to Christianity and his movement of the capital to old Byzantium/new Constantinople and ended when the city fell to the Turks. Many historians thus date the Byzantine empire from 330 to 1453. Others count Justinian as the first Byzantine emperor; still others begin with Heraclius (610–641). Far-reaching transformations marked the century from Justinian's accession to Heraclius's death. The eastern empire had to make radical adaptations to survive and flourish once again, and religious issues played a dominant role in these changes.

Justinian had not been able to resolve the religious tensions of the Christological controversies. From its earliest years, Christianity had attempted to be ecumenical, to be inclusive. But in an age of religious fervor, the prevailing Greco-Roman heritage within Christianity could push into heretic status those people whose radically different cultures had developed outside the Roman mainstream.

189

The continuing Nestorian and monophysite disputes illustrate this problem. Late antique Syria harbored many monophysites, and a Nestorian community survives there even now. The Armenian church, originally reacting against the Nestorianism of its ancient oppressor, Persia, embraced monophysitism and remains monophysite today, as does the Coptic church of Egypt and Ethiopia.

Religious dissatisfaction, as in Armenia, sometimes had political roots. So it could also have political consequences. Three of the five great patriarchates (Alexandria, Antioch, Jerusalem) were lost to Islam in the seventh century. Did the religious alienation of Egyptians and Syrians from Constantinople incline them to capitulate first to the Persians, then to the Muslims, rather than resist? That is the standard view, although in fact we have little historical data from that period of chaos.

Heraclius and His Tragedy

Shaken by natural disasters, religious controversies, and foreign invasions, the eastern empire was vulnerable to lawlessness and revolution. In 602, for the first time in 300 years, a usurper had successfully snatched the throne. This emperor, Phocas, seems to have inaugurated a reign of terror, although we must use contemporary sources with great caution because nearly all the accounts that survive come from his enemies, supporters of the man who dethroned him eight years later. Heraclius (610–641), son of the governor of Africa, sailed from Carthage to Constantinople and founded a dynasty that would last for five generations. He rescued an empire fallen into dire straits. Lombards had overrun Italy; Avars and Slavs had swept across the northern frontier into the Balkans; in the East, the Sassanid Persian empire was gaining strength. These pressures would culminate in 626 with a combined Avar-Slav-Persian siege of Constantinople.

Enmity between Greeks and Persians had a long history stretching back 1100 years to Darius and Xerxes and the Persian Wars recorded by Herodotus. Under a strong Sassanid king, the Persians might have found victory at last and crushed the Byzantine empire if it had not been for the energy and military brilliance of Heraclius. He built up the fleet, strengthened and reorganized the army, radically altered provincial administration, and counted heavily on the religious passions and convictions of his Christian subjects. Without a doubt, Heraclius and his people viewed their Persian Wars as a religious crusade. Standing firm in their collective assumption that they lived in a God-given Christian empire, Byzantines shared a potent religious-political theory: the belief that their Roman Empire was the last of the world empires and would survive until the apocalypse, to surrender only to God. Until that moment, God would protect their city and their empire from ultimate harm, although they stood poised on the brink of disaster.

In fact, even as Heraclius wrested his empire from Phocas, the two superpowers were preparing to fight to the death. The year 611 marked the beginning of Persian

190

aggression aimed at the Byzantine heartland. In lightning campaigns, the Persians took Antioch and Damascus and held all Syria. They set their sights next on Palestine, and after a twenty-day siege, they took the holy city of Jerusalem. There it became clear that the Persians saw this as a religious war. With determined ferocity, they destroyed Christian monuments, including the Church of the Holy Sepulchre built by Constantine and his mother Helen, which was despoiled of its treasures and then burned. Eager to be free of Christian domination, the Jews of Jerusalem took the Persian side. Some sources report that 60,000 Christians were slaughtered in the melée, and the patriarch of Jerusalem, Zacharias, was taken prisoner to Persia. One of the most precious relics of all Christendom, the Holy Cross on which Jesus was believed to have died, was also carried off to Ctesiphon. The loss of the holy city with its sacred monuments and relics was a disaster beyond reckoning.

In 618 or 619 (the records for this chaotic period being extremely spare and confusing), a third patriarchate fell as a Persian army stormed Alexandria, exposing all Egypt to Persian domination. This was a severe economic loss because Egypt supplied the grain for Constantinople. Of the four eastern patriarchates, only that capital city was not yet in Persian hands, and the disappearance of its provisions considerably weakened Constantinople's defenses. In 626 the Persians reached the Bosphorus, took Chalcedon, and camped opposite the capital. By chance, a great Avaro-Slav horde had also reached the city on a raid from the north and began a siege with Persian support.

Since 622 the emperor Heraclius had been on almost constant campaign, allied with Caucasian tribes and the Khazars, waging distant battles on the old frontiers and into the heart of Persia. For this crusade, the patriarch had finally surrendered the church's treasures, lending them to the state at interest. Heraclius was winning dazzling victories, but he was obliged to leave the capital with few defenders, and the Persians resolved to imitate Heraclius's tactics and strike at the enemy's vital core. The siege of 626 presented the double assault by land and sea that Heraclius had most feared. For eleven days the patriarch Sergius sustained the religious fervor of the people with passionate sermons, night vigils, and solemn processions. In this desperate moment, when all might have seemed lost, the Byzantine navy was able to turn the tide. Byzantine maritime supremacy overwhelmed the Slav fleet, compelling the land army to retreat in complete disarray. Although historians have ascribed victory to the naval forces, the inhabitants of Constantinople credited the direct intercession of the Virgin, who defended her people and her shrine at Blachernae.

Heraclius had sent forces to the city, but he himself remained at the eastern front. There he struck the final blow, virtually annihilating the Persian army in a battle near ancient Nineveh in 627. The following year the Persian king Chosroes was deposed and murdered. His successor sued for peace, returning the lost provinces of Egypt, Syria, and Palestine. The Byzantine victory was complete. Never again would Persia threaten Byzantium.

After a six-year absence, Heraclius returned to Constantinople in triumph. The patriarch Sergius met him on the coast of Asia Minor, leading senate, clergy, and people, who greeted their victorious emperor with olive branches and lighted candles, hymns and acclamations of joy. After a brief respite, Heraclius cleared Asia Minor of Persians, and then in 630 he traveled with his wife, the empress Martina, to Jerusalem, where he restored the Holy Cross to its place of glory amid great celebration. A contemporary Armenian historian, Sebeos, has left an eyewitness account:

> There was much joy at their entrance to Jerusalem: sounds of weeping and sighs, abundant tears, burning flames in hearts, extreme exaltation of the emperor, of the princes, of all the soldiers and inhabitants of the city; and nobody could sing the hymns of our Lord on account of the great and poignant emotion of the emperor and of the whole multitude. The emperor restored [the Cross] to its place and returned all the church objects, each to its place; he distributed gifts to all the churches and to the inhabitants of the city and money for incense.[1]

These joyous ceremonies symbolized the victorious conclusion of the first great holy war of Christendom. Flush with God's evident approval of Christian Byzantium and angry with the Jews for their support of Persia, Heraclius ordered all Jews of the empire baptized. His realm would be a true city of God, untainted by non-Christians or heretics.

The intoxicating joy was brief. Even as Heraclius celebrated, his victory was being duly recorded in the Koran, the holy book of the emerging religion that would nullify Heraclius's triumph in the emperor's own lifetime. It was Heraclius's tragedy to live as a contemporary of Muhammed (ca. 570–632), prophet of Islam. In 622, the very year when Heraclius began his counterattack against the Persians, Muhammed fled from Mecca to Yathrib, later called Medina, "the city of the prophet." This marks the Muslim year of the Hegira (or *hijrah*), Year One in their reckoning of time.

Welcomed in Medina, Muhammed began to establish a community there and to lay the foundations for a religiously based state. He then returned to Mecca as conqueror and set about destroying its idols and all remnants of polytheism. His religion he called Islam, "submission" to God, its essential character revealed in the Koran. Monotheism and discipline characterize Islam, showing the influence of Judaism, Christianity, and even Persian Zoroastrianism. Muhammed may have been reacting in part to monophysite teachings about Christ when he stressed the unity of the one god Allah, whose prophets (himself included) were holy men but not themselves divine. By the time of Muhammed's death, the diverse Bedouin tribesmen and wealthy merchants of all Arabia had accepted his creed of submission to Allah.

---

[1]A. A. Vasiliev, trans. (following K. Patnikov and F. Macler), *History of the Byzantine Empire*, Vol. 1 (Madison, WI: University of Wisconsin Press, 1952), p. 198.

The social and political effects of this union were enormous, as the hostile energies formerly directed against one another were channeled outward in holy war, the Islamic jihad.

Desperately exhausted by their wars, Persia and Byzantium proved easy prey for Arabs united in a fresh religious passion. Within ten years of the Prophet's death in 632, Persia and the eastern provinces of Byzantium had yielded to Islam. Syria succumbed in 636 after the decisive military defeat at Yarmuk. Jerusalem surrendered following a two-year siege in 637 or 638, although only after Christians succeeded in removing the Holy Cross to Constantinople. Mesopotamia was conquered along with Persia. Devastated by the relentless and completely unanticipated Arab advance, Heraclius died in 641, a pathetic and broken man. Within a year or two, Muslims occupied Alexandria, burning the famous libraries, with irretrievable loss of ancient learning and literature. The disorganization of the Byzantine army in Egypt and the apparent weakness of its resistance to Islam have provoked continuing speculation that religious disaffection with Constantinople was taking a political toll. Imperial intolerance of religious diversity can only have undermined the will of both Egypt and Syria to defend their ties to the orthodox empire.

Never again would a Roman Empire hold Egypt. Once the Arabs claimed that rich province, they moved into North Africa and assailed Mediterranean islands, working irreparable damage to many remnants of classical civilization. The Colossus of Rhodes, a statue of Helios that was one of the wonders of the ancient world, was sold to Jewish merchants who carted it away on 900 camels. Arabs crossed the Straits of Gibralter in 711 and swept across Spain in a mere seven years, passing over the Pyrenees into the kingdom of the Franks, where they would finally be stopped by Charles Martel at the battle of Tours (732). Meanwhile, a contemporary proverb proclaimed the Mediterranean—once a Roman sea—now a Muslim lake.

The Aftermath: Crisis of Church and Society

Very limited sources have survived from the troubled seventh century, making it difficult to assess that period. The documents that do exist are predominantly religious in orientation, written by men attempting to find a spiritual interpretation of the catastrophe. Just as the Byzantines believed that good fortune or success demonstrated divine approval of the empire, so they felt that disasters were signs of God's wrath, perhaps even signifying the impending end of the world. One Mesopotamian monk, horrified not only by the Muslim conquest but also by the easy accommodation some Christians made to Muslim rule, wrote the so-called *Revelation of Methodius of Patara*, which argued that recent events fulfilled New Testament prophecies; very soon the Antichrist would come, followed by the Son of Man and the Last Judgment. Greek and Latin translations of the Syriac *Revelation* brought these ideas to a large and receptive audience. With the unforeseen tragedies of the

Muslim advance, Byzantium became a society in turmoil, questioning its identity as God's chosen realm and the very survival of its civilization.

There are numerous signs that the empire had changed significantly since the age of Justinian when it was still characterized by its thriving urban life. As late as the sixth century, the East was dotted with cities that were self-administering units with control over the surrounding countryside. For 200 to 300 years, since the barbarian threat, these cities had been walled towns, small by our standards. But the walls enclosed wide streets laid out in a regular pattern, with shops under colonnades, a forum ringed by public buildings and decorated with statues and fountains, public monuments, a theater, and perhaps a hippodrome if the city was large enough. And of course there were churches throughout the city, so many churches, in fact, that their upkeep was becoming a financially oppressive responsibility.

Only in the Balkans had cities collapsed under assaults from Huns and Ostrogoths, and later from Slavs, who had learned to storm walls but had no interest in living within them. Ruined cities dotted the landscape. Elsewhere in the eastern empire, people continued to enjoy the amenities and culture of Greco-Roman urban life. Everyone—women, men, children, even clergy—seems to have spent plenty of time at the baths. Although amply criticized by the church, the theater and hippodrome and wild beast fights remained popular. City folks lived very public lives, lingering with friends in taverns or listening with admiration to the speeches of rhetoricians.

With the disruptions of the sixth century, city life declined. Drought, plague, locusts, earthquakes, and urban violence all took their toll. In Asia Minor the Persian invasions further weakened cities, and the Arabs delivered the final blow. Archaeological evidence suggests that Byzantine cities surviving into the seventh century were greatly reduced in size and population. Nearly every remaining city (*polis*) was transformed into a *kastron*, a heavily walled fortress. Most cities centered around a hill (*acropolis*, the high city) withdrew to the hillside alone, abandoning territory outside the old *acropolis*. Even a once flourishing coastal city like Ephesus saw its harbor silt up and let its baths fall into decay, becoming a tiny and isolated settlement, walled and landlocked. By the seventh century, when Byzantines spoke of "the city," they usually meant Constantinople. Only in Constantinople did the hippodrome still exist, and even there it operated no more than a few days a year for imperial ceremonies.

The capital produced imperial art; elsewhere art became notably provincial in style. Much of public life disappeared with the loss of theaters and civil basilicas that housed both courts of law and commercial centers, with the colonnades where the people had gathered. Public activity continued almost exclusively in the church, which became more and more important as the site of social contact, ritual, and entertainment. Otherwise, social intercourse contracted to focus on private life within the family.

The extent of this fortification and ruralization of the empire is still being debated among scholars, but beyond doubt the character of Byzantine society changed radically during this period. With the collapse of civic life in the provinces, intellectuals clustered in Constantinople where the bureaucracy demanded men with a classical education in ancient Greek letters. Outside the capital, secular training at the primary school level continued, so that basic literacy survived. Even in public schools, children first learned to read the Psalter, and echoes of the Psalms resound throughout Byzantine literature.

The church took over more and more aspects of education, just as it accepted an increasing role in other aspects of Byzantine life. Public doctors of Greco-Roman cities, for instance, were no longer paid by the city in which they practiced but instead were supported by the church and worked in church-supported hospitals, where the sick might stay and receive round-the-clock care, clean beds, and good meals. These philanthropic institutions were an original creation of Byzantine Christianity. Tensions often arose between the monks' twin goals of loving both God and neighbor. To resolve this conflict, the *typika* (foundation documents) of some monasteries specifically forbade the monks themselves from serving as physicians or servants in contact with the patients. Hospitals outside the monastery's inner walls, however, might be staffed by doctors and other caretakers supported by the monastery.

The Icon and Iconoclasm

Rapid changes in the society and challenges from threatening enemies brought a crisis of identity and faith. Various signs point to this spiritual conflict. It was marked, on the one hand, by a rising number of anti-Jewish texts, which were really expressions of Christian self-doubt. The documents featured staged debates between Christians and Jews, in which the Christian answered various arguments against their religion and defended it from attack. In these texts, the Jews were inevitably confounded or even converted, but the real audience was Christian, and the real successes lay in alleviating anxieties and resolving uncertainties of Christians.

The most far-reaching sign of this societal tension lay in the attack on and defense of icons. Icons are images or pictures of Jesus, Mary, or saints. They portray the holy person in a distinctively stylized pose, as a frontal image of an isolated figure hovering in empty space. Typically, the saint faces the worshippers with both eyes visible so that viewers can have full access to the holy person, the prototype the images lead them to emulate. Icons are meant to be symbols rather than realistic representations—symbols of divinity and spirituality, richness and power. As representations of a holy person, they attracted the veneration of Christians. They are still venerated by the faithful today. Even for persons outside the orthodox tradition, Byzantine icons provide a unique and compelling entry into the spirituality of Byzantine society.

Byzantine Iconoclasm: Icon Smashing

At the moment when Byzantium needed to concentrate all its resources against Islam in order to survive, the empire began diverting energies to an internal battle over the icons. In fact, this conflict proved both symptom of crisis and provocation of further tensions that reached dangerous proportions. Just as monophysitism had done in previous centuries, so iconoclasm threatened to tear Byzantine society apart.

Iconoclasm (icon smashing) was the imperial policy during two periods, 726–787 and 815–843. The struggle pitted the Greco-Roman love of figural representation against Old Testament prohibitions of idolatry. These ideals represented two very different sensibilities. Often displaying a visceral antipathy to icons, iconoclasts accused iconophiles (icon lovers) of worshipping idols, and they called them iconodules (icon slaves). Iconophiles vigorously denied this charge and insisted that they were simply venerating holy images of the divinity and saints; to destroy the images was to assail the saints themselves.

At least as early as Clement of Alexandria (ca. 150–ca. 215) and Tertullian (ca. 160–ca. 240), some Christians had expressed a theological distaste for pictorial representations of divinity, from time to time exciting outbursts of violence against holy pictures. Yet the cult of the images flourished during the sixth and seventh centuries, perhaps in part because people cherished intercessors with God during particularly difficult times as popular piety increased. In 691–692 the Quinisext Council (so-called because it continued the work of the fifth and sixth ecumenical councils, but sometimes also called the Council in Trullo, or Trullan, from the domed hall where it met) debated the issue of images and the popular depiction of Christ as a lamb, encouraging the representation of him in his human form. Canon 82 concludes: "Through his figure we perceive the depth of the humiliation of God the Word and are led to remember his life in the flesh, his suffering and his saving death, and the redemption which comes from it for the world." In encouraging the production of icons, the council decreed that the image of Christ in his human form helps the viewer understand the full impact of the incarnation, of God's suffering and death for humankind.

Almost simultaneously with this decree, the emperor Justinian II made a very public show of support for this idea. In a daring move, he replaced the imperial portrait on the obverse (front) of an issue of gold coins with a portrait of Christ, inscribed "King of Kings." Justinian relegated his own portrait to the reverse, with the inscription "Slave of Christ." Since such a valuable gold piece was not likely to be seen by ordinary Byzantines but by wealthy traders who might well circulate it beyond the borders, this new coinage may have been partly intended as a provocative act against Islamic neighbors. In fact, the coin instigated a chain reaction in the Arabic world, ultimately resulting in the removal of the caliph's image from coinage, to be replaced by religious slogans in Arabic script.

Evidently Justinian's successors, too, were taken aback by such a bold image, for they dropped his controversial design and returned to a traditional portrait of the emperor on coinage. Does this rejection point to the questioning of images in imperial circles? If so, this supports a recent thesis that labels iconoclasm an "imperial heresy," initiated and supported primarily by the emperor. At any rate, the iconoclast impulse, which had been smoldering for centuries, erupted with Leo III in 726. Some Byzantinists have felt that Leo was stimulated by the actions of the Caliph Jazid II, who may have initiated an iconoclast policy in 723–724, ordering all Christian churches in the caliphate to remove their icons. The evidence points to mutual influence as well as hostility within the iconoclast movements of the caliphate and the Byzantine empire. In Leo's own day, enemies charged that he was semi-Muslim. Although Leo persecuted Jews and fought Arabs, both these Semitic peoples had an impact on his thought. He seems to have grown up in Syria and lived for many years in Asia Minor, where he learned Semitic prejudices against images, prejudices that would be nurtured under Islam. Should Christianity adopt these widespread religious impulses or maintain a distinctive alternative? For Leo and other Byzantines, iconoclasm paradoxically attempted a kind of accommodation to Islamic ideals alongside the fierce competition with this religion that was Christianity's most threatening competitor. Islam claimed to be the legitimate heir to Christianity and to supersede it, just as Christians believed that their religion had inherited and superseded the traditions and special role of Judaism. Military victories appeared to confirm Islamic claims to God's favor. The challenge to Byzantine identity was profound. It is only natural that Christian society would be influenced by Islamic ideas while it struggled to redefine itself as a religious people and political entity in the wake of enemy successes and natural catastrophes.

Leo III began cautiously, encouraged by the bishops of Asia Minor, who opposed the iconophile tendencies of the patriarch Germanos I. The people of Asia Minor harbored strong iconoclast sentiments, whereas support for icon veneration came from European provinces of the empire. While Leo wavered, a providential earthquake persuaded him that the persistence of icons in his realm was angering God. The emperor lay the groundwork for his revolution by delivering sermons against the icons; but when he ordered his agent to remove the mosaic figure of Christ from its honored place above the Chalke Gate, the ceremonial entrance to the palace in Constantinople, a riot ensued and the imperial agent was killed. Women, rather than the usual adolescent males of the old Circus Faction riots, made up the large majority of rioters. A protest erupted in Greece, where a rival emperor even emerged to dispatch a fleet to attack Constantinople.

The emperor easily defeated the usurper, but he could not win over the patriarch or the pope, Gregory II. In letters to Rome, Leo explained that as God's designated chief pontiff, he himself must take the responsibility for executing this policy. Gregory found himself in a bind. The iconoclast agenda did not sit well with him, but he could not afford to lose imperial protection needed against the Lombards. The best defense of icons came from outside the Byzantine empire, but from the East rather than the West. The greatest theologian of the age, John of Damascus (ca. 675–ca. 750), argued on behalf of the iconophiles. A Christian Arab who was treasury official for the caliph, John wrote three treatises in defense of images, maintaining that they were not idols but symbols, mediators between heaven and earth, like the saints themselves. He employed a Neoplatonic argument that the appreciation of visible beauty leads necessarily to the appreciation of absolute beauty, that is, to the true knowledge of God. The incarnation justifies the material form of the image. It might even be argued that the incarnation makes the icon a uniquely Christian object of veneration, as suitable for Christianity as it is inappropriate for Judaism or Islam.

Led by the emperor Constantine V (ruled 741–775), the brilliant military man and theologian who succeeded his father Leo III, the iconoclasts responded with subtle theology of their own. From the primitive, instinctive attack on images as idolatry, they moved to Christological arguments, declaring that iconophiles were either Nestorians or monophysites. Either the artist was portraying only the human nature of Christ and thus sliding into Nestorianism by separating the inseparable divine and human natures of the divinity, or the artist was pretending to portray both the human and divine, confusing them into one as the monophysites did. In fact, iconophiles were successful in throwing this theological argument back on Constantine, seeing an element of monophysitism in iconoclasm that emphasizes Christ's divinity and distant majesty.

In 754, Constantine summoned a council he called the seventh ecumenical council, which ordered icons destroyed and prohibited their veneration. In Hagia Sophia as throughout the empire, images were smashed or plastered over, often replaced by mosaics of the cross or pictures of the emperor and his family. Constantine initiated vigorous persecutions, especially against monks, and even some executions. Scholars are not in full agreement that these persecutions were direct retribution against iconophile monks; some insist that Constantine's personal aversion to the monastic ideal must be considered a separate issue. But it is likely that there was a link between the veneration of the holy man and the veneration of the icon that individualized and privatized worship and salvation, threatening imperial authority. Monks may well have played a considerable role in the support of icons, thus contributing to the hostility of a military emperor who resented the large numbers of monks (perhaps 100,000 monks at the time), who drained the potential ranks of soldiers and farmers, defied the usual Byzantine social order of the nuclear family, and resisted imperial control. Constantine confiscated some important monasteries in Constantinople and turned them into army barracks. To humiliate monks, he commanded some to be paraded in the hippodrome, each forced to hold the hand of a woman while the crowd shouted insults. At Ephesus the provincial governor summoned all the monks and nuns of his territory and ordered them to choose either marriage or blinding and exile. To escape persecution, pious people fled to the Caucasus or the north shore of the Black Sea, or even to Rome.

It was a woman who restored icon veneration to Byzantium. Constantine V had arranged for his son and heir Leo IV to marry the Athenian Irene, perhaps as a conciliatory gesture to European territories. She was herself an iconophile, like most of her Greek compatriots. Under compulsion, before her coronation and marriage in 768, Irene swore a solemn oath never to accept icons. She was under suspicion, however, when her husband died suddenly in 780. A much later source reported that Leo had found two images hidden under cushions in Irene's apartments.

Irene carefully prepared the way for the true Seventh Ecumenical Council, which met at Nicaea in 787. Its full acts are extant. The bishops found few biblical endorsements of icons, and so they relied heavily on unwritten tradition and quotations from the Church Fathers, using the arguments articulated by John of Damascus. To the charge that images were pagan idols, they replied that Christians worshipped only the personalities represented in the images; iconophiles offered the icons not worship but veneration and honor. To the charges of Nestorian or monophysite tendencies in the creation of the icon, they answered that the artist paints just the body, but the soul and personality are reconstructed only in the mind of the viewer.

For her role in the restoration of icons, the orthodox church still reveres Irene as a saint. She also coveted the secular designation as emperor. After years of rivalry with her son Constantine VI, she had him blinded in 797 and took for herself the masculine imperial title, *basileus*, becoming the first woman to rule Byzantium in her own right, not as co-ruler or regent. Her ambitions ranged far. She negotiated a brief engagement to Charlemagne; his envoys were in Constantinople when Irene was deposed in 802.

The forces of iconoclasm were by no means spent. Military disasters under iconophile emperors (especially Irene) seemed convincing signs of God's disfavor with the icons. Iconoclast emperors on the other hand, most notably Constantine V, had won stunning victories against the Arabs. In reinstating the decrees of 754, a second iconoclast council of 815 protested that "female simplicity" had restored the adoration of "dead figures" and "lifeless icons." The synod inaugurated a second period of vigorous iconoclasm linked to internal reform of the empire. In 843 this period, too, ended with icons being restored by a woman, the empress Theodora, regent for her six-year-old son after his father the emperor Theophilus died in 842. During her regency, Theodora imitated Justinian II by striking gold coins with a bust of Christ on the obverse. From that time on, Byzantine coins always contained some image of Christ, the Virgin, or a saint.

Can it be coincidental that icons were both times restored by women? Some Byzantinists have argued that the significant operative factor was not the woman herself but rather the weak imperial control during a regency. These critics see iconoclasm as a statement of imperial dominance over the church and society, a dominance shattered without a strong man at the helm. Others believe that women were more often than men the ardent venerators of images, and so it was natural that a woman in power would restore the images. According to this view, women sought out sacred mediators (often Mary and female saints) to intercede with a God of overwhelming power and majesty. There is evidence that mothers encouraged their daughters to kiss and fondle icons just as some children today play reverently with dolls. Family icons seemed almost like honored family members, even being named occasionally as godparent to a child, and women might feel a special intimacy with these images.

On this particular question of female support for icons, the debate still rages. It seems likely, however, that the icon question did polarize Byzantine society along certain lines, pitting women and monks against the army and the emperor, and setting the Greek religious and cultural outlook against the Asian and Semitic. Later iconoclasm at least developed antimonastic tendencies and served as an outlet for antimonastic sentiments. Although both sides developed theological arguments to support their views, the controversy over icons was primarily a societal issue, one symptom of a clash of cultural values and the resulting struggle for dominance during a period of great stress.

The course of the controversy reveals a great deal about Byzantine society, including the depth of Byzantine piety, the lingering intensity of the Christological conflicts, and the complexity of their philosophical underpinnings, as well as the inseparability of religion, politics, and culture. We can see that the emperor usually exercised great control over the patriarch and the religious policy of the empire, but it is also clear that some forces were beyond even the emperor's control. Despite obvious hostilities toward monks, in the end the monks held the people's confidence, so that they could prevail against the throne and the army and the central authorities of the church. Despite the considerable constraints on women, they too could stand against imperial will and even become the agents of the restoration of the icons. Finally, this conflict illustrates the intricate workings of a Christian society that was by no means monolithic or unchanging.

Iconoclasm exacted a heavy toll in its destruction of Byzantine art. To grasp what was lost to icon smashers in Constantinople and Asia Minor, we need only look at the dazzling late antique and early Byzantine art of Ravenna, which was beyond the range of icon smashers. Some media never recovered from the long hiatus in production; the techniques for sculpting statues disappeared among Byzantines forever, and religious statuary never returned to the empire. Political repercussions were equally far-reaching. Iconoclasm weakened the empire by magnifying internal dissent at a time when all resources were sorely needed to combat the major external threat: Islam. The conflict also strained relations with the West, motivating the pope to turn elsewhere for support. As central Italy was wrenched away from the Byzantine sphere of influence, Byzantium's field of vision narrowed to ignore the West; the concept of universal empire receded into the background.

The consequences of iconoclasm were not all bad, however. Out of that period came a renewed consensus of Byzantine self-definition as a Christian empire where distinctively Christian art and sensibilities could flourish. Constantinople was clearly the cultural, economic, and political core of this Christian realm. Abounding in relics rescued from Syria and Palestine, the capital attracted pilgrims unwilling to risk the dangers of visiting sacred sites under Muslim domination. By the late ninth century, pious visitors to Constantinople could also witness the relics of new iconophile martyrs and miracle-working images that had multiplied to counteract iconoclasts' claims. Constantinople had become the world's greatest Christian treasury—a holy city.

Schism between Eastern and Western Christendom

The iconoclast controversy struck another in a series of blows against the unity of Christendom. Constantinople was once again trapped between eastern and western religious convictions. Even during the Persian campaigns, Heraclius had tried to find a compromise that would mollify the monophysite provinces over which they were struggling and yet not alienate the West. His solution was monothelitism, the concept of "one will" for Jesus Christ. He wanted monophysites to agree that Jesus had two natures if the orthodox would concede that he had one will. But by the time Heraclius published his statement of this dogma, the *Ekthesis* (or "Exposition of Faith") in 638, Syria and Palestine were already unexpectedly lost to the Arabs, with Egypt soon to follow suit. The *Ekthesis* only succeeded in alienating the pope, who condemned monothelite teaching as heresy. This act naturally resulted in great hostility between pope and emperor. Constantinople was caught between a rock and a hard place. It is doubtful if any compromise could have mollified either East or West, or reconciled them to the center, represented by Constantinople. The religious sensibilities were profoundly different, and the breach was widening.

Heraclius's successor continued his monothelite policy but also tried a new tack in search of harmony in the church and peace with the pope. Constans II proclaimed the *Typus* (or "Type of Faith"), forbidding "all Orthodox subjects being in immaculate Christian faith and belonging to the Catholic and Apostolic Church, to dispute and to quarrel with one another over one will or one energy or two energies or two wills." In other words, the topic was banned without exception; even written discussions were removed from public view—including Heraclius's *Ekthesis* from the walls in the narthex of Hagia Sophia. What was the papal response to the imposed ban? At the Lateran Synod, in the presence of Byzantine clergy, Pope Martin condemned "the most impious *Ekthesis*," and the "vicious *Typus*," and proclaimed as heretics any people associated with those documents. A furious Constans II, himself of course included in that attack, ordered the imperial authority in Ravenna to arrest Martin and deliver him to Constantinople, where he was convicted of attempted sedition, humiliated, and imprisoned. Later exiled to far-off Cherson, on the south coast of the Crimea, Martin soon died there after dispatching pathetic pleas for bread.

Despite the animosities aroused by that incident, the emperor and patriarch negotiated successfully with Martin's successors to end the schism. Peace seemed assured with the Sixth Ecumenical Council of 680 in Constantinople, where monothelitism was condemned and Chalcedonian orthodoxy affirmed. Byzantium was writing off the eastern provinces lost to Islam. In 691 the emperor Justinian II summoned the Quinisext, or Trullan, Council and charged it with completing the work of the Fifth and Sixth Councils. Its decrees contained provisions that the pope protested— for example those forbidding fasting on Saturdays and allowing priests to marry. These tenets were unacceptable in the West, and Pope Sergius I refused to sign. Justinian tried to follow earlier tactics and have Sergius arrested by imperial forces in Italy, but the plan backfired when the army protected the pope. An honorable meeting in Constantinople between Justinian and a later pope, Constantine, seemed once again to forge a peace.

An increasing number of issues, however, divided eastern and western Christendom. Not the least of these were the tensions surrounding the icon question. Pope Gregory II had tried to sustain cordial relations despite his firm disapproval of imperial iconoclast policy, but Leo's iconoclast edict of 730 and his deposition of the iconophile patriarch compelled Gregory's successor, Gregory III, to condemn Byzantine iconoclasm. Leo responded by imprisoning the papal legates, and religious dissension led to political enmity. The popes finally made a complete break from Byzantium to find new supporters in the Franks (754). Popes such as Paul I (757–767) routinely referred to the Byzantines as *nefandissimi Graeci* ("most villainous Greeks") in asserting papal claims to autonomous spiritual and political power.

It is a tragic irony for Christianity that the onslaught of Islam did not unite Christendom against a common religious and political enemy; instead, the Arabic expansion only exacerbated hostilities between the eastern and western churches. Increasing isolation, combined with prejudice on both sides, bred contempt. Finally in 1054, a theological disagreement and severe personality conflicts led the bishop of Rome and the patriarch of Constantinople to excommunicate each other. The outcome was a permanent schism between the Roman Catholic and the Greek Orthodox churches.

Mutual animosities prevented the West from acknowledging the important role played by Byzantium in the struggle against Islam. The long-standing goal of Muslim armies, Constantinople proved the roadblock to Mediterranean conquest. The turning point in the Muslim advance came after fifteen years of annual raids in Asia Minor when the Muslims besieged the city by sea (674–678). The city was saved by the fleet's secret weapon, Greek fire, a liquid probably containing naphtha, sulphur, and saltpeter, that was so potent it ignited spontaneously and burned even on water. Along with the defeat of Arab forces in Asia Minor, this victory checked the Muslim advance and prevented Arab armies from taking the direct northern route to the West along the famous and efficient Roman roads that had linked Rome to her provinces for more than 700 years. Byzantium thus sheltered the West from the full brunt of the assault until the Franks were strong enough to withstand a weakened Arab onslaught. Charles Martel's victory near Tours (732) was made possible by the Byzantine stand, which arguably preserved Christendom from usurpation by Islam.

Sarcophagus from the Lateran Palace in Rome, featuring the labarum. (Alinari/Art Resource)

A gold plaque from a sixth-century reliquary, showing Symeon the Stylite on his pillar confronting the devil in the form of a monstrous snake. (Reunion des Musées Nationaux)

Twelfth-century mosaic from Hagia Sophia in Constantinople, with Constantine I (right) presenting his newly consecrated capital to the Virgin Mary and Justinian I offering the great church. (Hirmer Fotoarchiv)

Majestic and austere Christ Pantocrator from the dome of the eleventh-century church at Daphni in Greece. (Marburg/Art Resource)

A ninth-century mosaic from Hagia Sophia, showing the enthroned Mother of God and Child. (Courtesy of Dumbarton Oaks Center for Byzantine Studies, Washington, D.C.)

Christ crowning King Roger II of Sicily, from the Martorana Church, Palermo, twelfth century. (Scala/Art Resource)

Chapter 13

THE MEDIEVAL CHURCH IN THE WEST (481–887)

The Franks and Merovingian Gaul

In contrast to the sophistication of Byzantium's theological debates and the epic importance of its struggles with Persia and Islam for the very life of Christian civilization, the story of Frankish Christianity seems small and secondary—a minor episode set in the backwoods. Yet out of this savage Germanic society would develop a durable and mighty medieval realm. It is customary to credit the Franks with the salvation of Christendom from the invading Muslims. As we have seen, this victory was possible only because the Byzantines provided such a formidable defense in the East. Still, the Frankish resistance was critical to the survival of Christian Europe. How did the Franks assume this role of leadership in Christendom? How did the longing to forge a moral Christian society culminate in the renaissance under Charlemagne? The answers to these questions reveal much about the bridge between late antiquity and medieval Christendom.

The Franks were a confederation of tribes first attested in the mid-third century, with their homeland in the lower Rhine valley (most of modern Belgium and southern Holland). Historians must rely heavily on archaeological data to piece together bits of their past because written materials for the early period are so spare. We have only two major primary documents. The Salic Law, the first written Germanic code, issued by the Frankish king Clovis in the early sixth century, provides ample evidence of the violence of the age. Near the end of the same century, the remarkable historian, Gregory, nineteenth bishop of Tours, completed a *History of the Franks* that confirms this picture in lush and terrifying detail.

Gregory of Tours (538 or 539 to 594 or 595, not to be confused with his notable contemporary, Pope Gregory the Great) belonged to the Gallo-Roman aristocracy.

207

Among his distinguished ancestors were senators, bishops, saints, and even an early Christian martyr of the year 177. Gregory claimed that all but five of the previous bishops of Tours were his relatives. In Gregory himself we can see how the old Gallo-Romans and the Franks were merging into one Christian people. The bishop of noble lineage had no contempt whatsoever for the upstart Franks, although he scorned Arian Germans.

Thoroughly orthodox, Gregory was a man who shared the religious sensibilities of his contemporaries, both Frankish and Roman. At his mother's urging, he wrote saints' lives filled with miracles, including some he had supposedly witnessed himself. His most famous biography, a *Life of St. Martin of Tours*, inspired readers throughout the Middle Ages with tales of Gregory's fourth-century predecessor, whose tomb attracted pilgrims seeking miraculous cures for their ailments. This same spirit pervades his *History of the Franks*, which was so shaped by religious convictions that some critics have called it *The Ecclesiastical Histories*.[1] The work begins like any good chronicle with the creation of the world, revealing debts to the earlier church histories of Eusebius, Jerome, and Orosius. Gregory brought the account up to his own day, stopping only a few years before his death.

Gregory had received the best education available in sixth-century Gaul, but this modest training did not prepare even so talented a man to write a taut and coherent narrative. On the contrary, the chaos of his Latin syntax mirrors the chaos in his society. Nevertheless, despite a confused chronology and episodic style, a certain coherence comes from Gregory's profound belief that the church and its bishops were working tirelessly to civilize the Franks and their brutal princes. The *History* gives us an invaluable view of a vicious age for which the bishops were beacons of light in ominous darkness. Life in such a world was wholly unpredictable, although astrological portents could foretell a tyrant's death and relics might heal an ailing Christian. Very much a man of his time, Gregory believed deeply in these signs and cures.

It is a telling fact that a bishop would be virtually the only recorder of the horrors of that age, as well as the one person struggling to elevate morals and relieve the suffering of those around him. From Gregory we glean precious details about the early Merovingian kings, descendants of King Merovech for whom the royal dynasty is named. A son of Merovech, Childeric I, helped the Romans against Visigoths and Saxons. He also worked with the Gallic church, although he and his kin were still pagan. In this way, Childeric set the stage for his son Clovis (ruled 481–511), who founded the Frankish state through military victories against other Germans and assassinations of rival Frankish kings and through his conversion from paganism to Christianity. In an immensely significant move with far-reaching consequences, Clovis converted to Catholicism instead of Arianism. If Gregory was correct, the king finally surrendered to the influence of his Christian wife Clotilda, a Burgundian

---

[1] See Lewis Thorpe, trans., Gregory of Tours, *The History of the Franks* (New York: Penguin, 1974).

princess, who wanted their firstborn son to be baptized. Writing nearly 100 years later, Gregory credited her with this argument to woo Clovis away from paganism:

> The gods whom you worship are useless. They haven't been able to help themselves, let alone others. They are carved out of stone or wood or some sort of metal. The very names that you have given them were the names of men, not of gods. Take Saturn, for instance, who is supposed to have slipped away in flight from his own son so he wouldn't be exiled from his kingdom; and Jupiter, that really foul perpetrator of all sorts of lewd acts, who defiled other men and enjoyed humiliating female relatives and couldn't even refrain from sleeping with his own sister, as she herself said: . . . *Jovisque/et soror et coniunx*
>
>   ("Both sister and wife of Jupiter"). [*Aeneid* 1, 46-7]
> What could Mars and Mercury ever do? They may have been endowed with magic arts, but they certainly didn't deserve to be called divine. You should instead worship him who created at a word and out of nothing heaven and earth, the sea and all that therein is [*Ps.* 146, 6]; who made the sun to shine; who adorned the sky with stars; who stocked the waters with fish, the earth with beasts, the sky with birds; at whose nod the fields are graced with fruits, the trees with apples, the vines with grapes; by whose hand the human race was created, and by whose dispensation all that creation in compliant devotion serves the man whom He created.[2]

The rhetoric is obviously Gregory's own. He had read selections from the *Aeneid* when he was a student, whereas Clotilda surely was a stranger to classical literature. Would Clotilda have mentioned the Greco-Roman deities and not the Germanic gods? Whatever her real arguments may have been, Clotilda's pleas slowly took effect until, again according to Gregory, the king remembered them in the midst of a difficult battle with the Alamanni, and swore fealty to the Christian god if only he would provide victory as a sign of his power. After routing the enemy, Clovis was baptized along with 3,000 Franks by Bishop Remigius of Reims (St. Rémi). It is difficult to overemphasize the impact of that conversion on medieval Christendom. Clovis's Catholicism provided a convincing pretext for warring against rival Arian Germans and conquering their territories. From distant Constantinople, the emperor Anastasius dispatched an embassy in 507, apparently sending his Christian brother the insignia of an honorary consul. The Byzantine emperor could not have known that Clovis was forging a close union with the papacy that would eventually rival and then replace Byzantine protection of papal territories and privileges.

At the death of Clovis, his four sons ruled together, crushing the Burgundian kingdom and winning Provence from the Ostrogoths in exchange for military aid. Within a half century, the Merovingian kings were the most powerful monarchs of

---

[2]Gregory of Tours, *History of the Franks* (II.29). Unpublished translation by Emily Albu Hanawalt.

the West, despite continuing migrations of Germans and the arrival of Avars into the middle Danube region (Hungary) and Slavs into the Balkans, Bohemia, and Moravia. The sons of Clovis ruled most of Gaul and some of Italy and Germany, held power over other tribes in Germany, and claimed control over southeast England. Clovis's last surviving son, Chlothar I, died in 561. Gregory of Tours reported the words of this proud ruler as he lay on his deathbed: "Wa! What kind of king is it in heaven, who kills off great kings like me?"

The Merovingians left an important legacy. Other Germans fell under the influence of the Franks and renounced Arianism to embrace Catholic Christianity. The Bergundians converted in 517, a few years before they became part of the Frankish kingdom. Throughout the sixth century, while Justinian was assailing Arian kingdoms of the Ostrogoths and Visigoths, individuals in Italy and Spain continued to abandon Arianism at a steady rate. King Recared of Visigothic Spain converted in 587, confirming this act at the Third Council of Toledo in 589. By the mid-seventh century, the process was complete. The last to convert were the Lombards, and their tardiness provided a political opening for the Franks. When Arian Lombards in Italy threatened papal territories, the Franks became champions of popes, eventually ousting the Lombards from papal lands.

Paganism in Gaul

The west became nominally catholic, but paganism was slow to die, especially in the countryside. In his *Liber in gloria Confessorum*, Gregory of Tours described pagan rites attested from late fourth-century Gaul, outside Autun:

> They say that in this city there was a statue of Berecynthia [Cybele, the great goddess] as the history of the passion of the holy martyr Symphorian explains. When they were drawing her about in a cart, according to the wretched custom of the pagans, to assure the salvation of their fields and vineyards, the bishop Simplicius was nearby. Not far away, Simplicius saw them singing and dancing before this statue. And groaning to God for the people's folly, he said: "I entreat you Lord: enlighten the eyes of these people so that they know that the idol of Berecynthia is useless." And when he made the sign of the cross against it, at once the statue fell down to the earth. And the animals that were drawing the cart in which the statue was carried were cast down on the ground and could not be budged. The huge crowd was stupefied and the whole throng exclaimed that the goddess had been hurt. Victims were sacrificed and the animals were beaten, but they could not be budged. Then four hundred men of that foolish multitude, gathered together, said to one another: "If the statue of the deity has any power let her stand herself up without any help, and order the oxen, who are immobilized on the ground, to get moving. Surely, if she cannot move herself it is

clear that there is no divinity in her." Then, approaching and sacrificing one of their animals, when they saw that their goddess could by no means move, they abandoned their error of paganism . . . and they were consecrated by baptism.[3]

Despite dramatic confrontations like this one and the continuing vigorous protests of the Christian clergy, pagan rites associated with the protection of crops survived into Gregory's own lifetime and long after. A seventh-century sermon by Saint Eligius of Noyen (588–659) warned his congregation against pagan practices they were still observing, such as wearing charms to ward off evil, consulting the moon's phases for auspicious times to undertake a new venture, or engaging in ancient ceremonies at temples or sacred rocks, fountains, trees, or crossroads. It seems that Eligius's parishioners, too, were purifying the crops with magic rites.

The protection of the crops was so central to the existence of the medieval peasantry that ancient rituals were abandoned only with greatest reluctance. Sometimes they were merely transformed into Christian rites. An excellent example comes from the legend of Radegund, who was a historical figure from Merovingian Gaul, wife of Clovis's son, Chlothar I. We glean some information about her life from Gregory of Tours and from the poet Fortunatus, who had come from Italy to visit the tomb of Martin of Tours and stayed, eventually to become bishop of Poitiers. Gregory reports that Chlothar took the Thuringian princess Radegund as part of the booty after he invaded her land and massacred the Thuringian army. His eventual marriage to the princess did not stop Chlothar from arranging for her brother to be murdered by assassins. Radegund turned to God, took the habit of a religious, and built a nunnery for herself in Poitiers. For her prayers, vigils, and charities, she became so famous that the common people looked upon her as a saint.

Later folklore wove a dramatic tale of her desperate flight from Chlothar and his angry pursuit. During her escape, it was said, the queen came upon a peasant sowing his field. She urged him to tell anyone who inquired that no woman had passed through that field since he had sowed the oats. At once the oats grew so tall that the queen could hide in the grass. When the king arrived and interrogated the farmer, the peasant's truthful answer tricked him into abandoning the chase. The Christian saint Radegund, venerated for bringing miraculous fertility to the field, came to replace the ancient grain goddess. In modified form, the ancestral rites connected with the February sowing continued, with worshippers carrying to church little sacks of grain dedicated to Radegund. Finally in 1627 the bishop of Poitiers authorized a festival for February 28, dedicated to Saint Radegund of the Oats.

In such ways some irradicable pagan habits survived among the Franks, assimilated into Christianity. While churchmen were often willing to accommodate these customs, they saw no satisfactory compromise with the notoriously bad behavior of

---

[3]Gregory of Tours, *Liber in Gloria Confessorum*, chap. 77, in Joannes Zwicker, *Fontes Historiae Religionis Celticae* (Berlin, 1934), p. 180. Unpublished translation by Emily Albu Hanawalt.

Merovingian princes, who had readily accepted the name of Christian but were slow to adopt Christian morality. It was a vexing problem for bishops such as Gregory of Tours, who understood the civilizing role the church should play and tenaciously worked for its success.

Of all the vile Merovingian princes whom Gregory chronicled, the worst was Chilperic, son of Chlothar I by his third wife Aregund. Gregory found him monstrously cruel, so greedy and arrogant that he proclaimed him "the Nero and Herod of our time." Chilperic's domestic affairs were as violent as his public crimes. He repudiated his wife, whom he later had murdered, in order to acquire the rich dowry of a second wife, the young Spanish princess Galswintha. Soon he had Galswintha strangled so that he could keep her dowry and marry his favorite concubine, Fredegund. Chilperic himself was murdered in 584, after a life of unimaginable evil. By Gregory's admission, he was a man of stunning contradictions. This murderer of wives, for instance, also championed the rights of women to inherit land on occasion, against the restrictions of the Salian law. He also fancied himself a theologian and opposed the dogma of the Trinity, arguing vigorously with Gregory that no one should speak of three persons when describing God. Gregory's firm insistence on the orthodox formulation, backed by other eminent churchmen, finally persuaded Chilperic to rescind his decree outlawing trinitarian language.

The domain of Chlothar I and Chilperic seems an unlikely center for a Christian renaissance, but the Church relentlessly stressed Christian values of a kinder and gentler morality. Gradually, these teachings had an impact until committed and strong Carolingian rulers (the dynasty named for Carolus Magnus, or Charlemagne, who ruled 768–814) would create a Christian empire out of the chaos their Merovingian forebears had wrought.

The Carolingians: Pepin of Heristal, Charles Martel, Pepin the Short

This emerging Christian realm was far different from the old Roman empire, with its urban centers and Mediterranean commerce (Figure 13.1). In the seventh century the Arabs had come to control the sea, holding many islands, the southern Mediterranean shore, and Spain. Like all of northwestern Europe, Gaul lost most ties with Roman ways of urban commerce and sea trade and turned to agriculture instead. To support this agrarian life, the Franks needed some political stability, but at the same time as Muslims were extending their control, the kingdom of the Franks was deteriorating and any central authority was collapsing. The administrative agencies of Merovingian kings slipped into the hands of household officials, called mayors of the palace, who were wooing the Frankish aristocracy to their side.

One of these mayors of the palace, Pepin II of Heristal (635/655–714), consolidated Frankish power under himself. Pepin's son Charles Martel (ca. 688–741), fa-

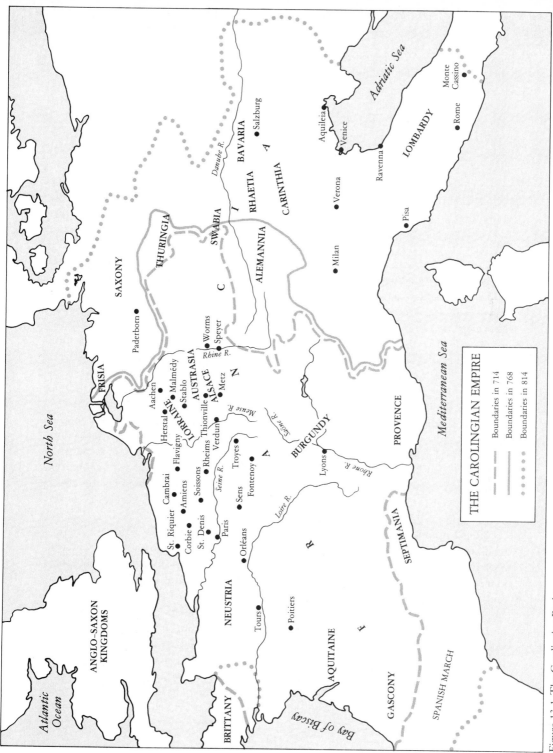

Figure 13.1 The Carolingian Realm

mous for his victory over the Arabs in 732, extended this authority while also tightening his grip on church and society. Charles's policy replaced local control of the church with a centralized, hierarchical episcopal structure that he kept firmly and openly under his thumb. It was Charles who appointed and deposed bishops. When he needed revenues or when he wanted lands to distribute to his followers as their reward for service, he systematically confiscated ecclesiastical holdings. The pope scolded him for these impertinences but never terminated the mutually beneficial alliance.

Martel's son, Pepin III the Short (747–768), finally used this alliance to remove from the throne the last Merovingian, Childeric III. He dispatched two envoys, the abbot of St. Denis and the bishop of Wurzburg, to Pope Zacharias I (reigned 741–752) to ask "concerning the kings in Francia who had no royal power, and whether this was fitting or not." The pope agreed that this situation did not promote order and justice, and he sent a papal legate, the Anglo-Saxon Benedictine Boniface, to anoint Pepin as king in 751 before an assembly of Frankish nobles at Soissons. No Frankish king had ever been anointed before. This remarkable act signified divine approval of the king's rule and, at the same time, granted him a kind of priestly authority. In return, Pepin deeded to Zacharias's successor, Pope Stephen II, the estates in central Italy that the papacy would hold for more than 1,000 years until the kingdom of Italy absorbed them in 1870. Pepin personally conducted campaigns in Italy to wrest these lands from the Lombards and present them to the pope. This so-called Donation of Pepin alienated not only the Lombards, who had been allies of Pepin's family in the common struggle against the Arabs, but also the Byzantines, who still claimed Italy as part of their Roman Empire. In distant Constantinople, however, the emperor Constantine V was too preoccupied with Byzantine iconophiles and Arabs to intervene in the West. He had been unable to protect the pope from Lombard threats, and to make matters worse, his iconoclasm made him a heretic in the pope's eyes. When the Franks offered aid against the Lombards, therefore, Pope Stephen formally broke with Byzantium and declared Pepin "protector of the Roman church" (754).

About this time (ca. 754–767), the Donation of Constantine was forged. It pretends to be a charter issued by the fourth-century emperor Constantine I when he moved the capital to the East in 330. It granted to the papacy spiritual and temporal power, including specifically named authority over Rome and Italy. Ever since Lorenzo Valla exposed the document as a fake in 1440, critics have claimed that the Donation's forger had a broad political motive. Most scholars placed the document in the context of the papal-Frankish alliance, assuming that the forger's primary goal was to discredit Byzantine claims to Italy and to pave the way for the deal between Pepin and the pope. Some historians argue that it was created especially for the occasion of Pepin's anointing. Most recent research, however, suggests that the forgery had a more private and localized purpose. Because it features the supposed endowment of the Lateran Palace to Pope Sylvester, it may well be the invention of a lower cleric of the Church of the Savior (St. John Lateran). Frustrated because the rival church, St. Peter's in the Vatican, was siphoning off pilgrim business from his own church, he merely wanted to produce a dramatic confirmation of the historical importance of St. John Lateran. This anonymous cleric could not have foreseen the larger implications of the controversy exacerbated by his forged document, which successive popes used to authenticate their claims to secular rule in Italy.

The Celtic Church and English Monasticism

Thanks to Pepin's ousting of the Lombards, the pope became an influential temporal prince, sometimes more important as a politician than as a theologian or spiritual leader. English Benedictine monks played a critical role in forging the powerful alliance that strengthened both popes and Frankish kings. Each of these three parties allied with the others in various permutations to create a dynamic interchange that had far-ranging results for the history of Europe and the history of the church.

By the third century, Christianity had reached the Celts of Roman Britain and spread from there to Ireland (Figure 13.2). This Celtic church outlived the departure of Roman troops in 407. Its history is difficult to trace in detail, but its center gradually shifted from England to Ireland, which the Roman Empire had never dominated. Just as Celtic culture in Ireland had evolved independently of the Roman, so the Celtic church developed in its own way, although it never lost contact with the church on the continent or severed ties with papal Rome. Throughout the Mediterranean world, Christianity had been growing as an urban religion, governed by bishops in cities. The church had a distinctively different development in the rural, tribal communities of England and especially Ireland. Like the pastoral society it penetrated, the Celtic church remained decentralized.

Rural monasteries held special importance in this nonurban church. Leaving their own foundations, significant numbers of monks traveled great distances to create new outposts of Christianity among the pagans. In his sixth-century missions to Scotland, for example, St. Columba (ca. 521–ca. 597) established a monastery on the island of Iona, which in turn sent out other missions to christianize Northumbria. One of these missions reached the island of Lindisfarne, founding a bishopric and a monastery that became the core of English religious life. St. Columbanus (died 615) spread Celtic monasticism in the opposite direction, taking it to the continent. His foundations include Luxeuil in Burgundy and Bobbio in northern Italy.

Monks directed the monastic Celtic church, and abbots ruled over it, even holding authority over the bishops, who fulfilled liturgical functions but had little administrative control. Other peculiarities of this Celtic church included retaining the old method for calculating the date of Easter and dictating a unique tonsure for monks. The common "tonsure of St. Peter" was a shaven head with only a circle of hair shaped like a crown. The Celtic tonsure seems to have been a semicircle of hair at

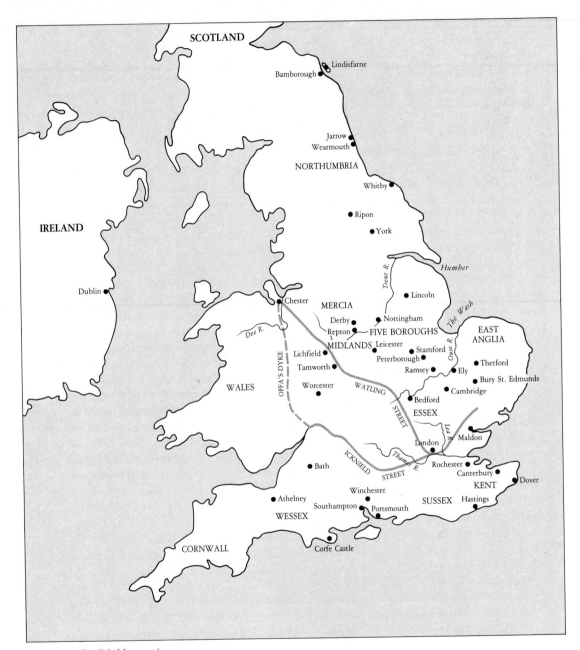

Figure 13.2 English Monasteries

the top of the head from ear to ear, with the hair behind it growing long. This unique tonsure may have been a remnant of old practices; it was the ancestral hairstyle of elite males such as the Druids in Celtic society. Celtic monks became famous for their idiosyncratic and extreme behavior, for mortifications such as flagellations and fasts lasting as long as four days. Some lived their lives as hermits, like their Syriac brothers in the spirit, and others accepted voluntary exile and wandering. This custom of aimless pilgrimage may also recall Irish tradition; banishment from the tribe had been the prescribed punishment for the most offensive crimes. Monks continued this custom as penance for their sins or as a dramatic sign of their love of Christ.

Celtic monks often demonstrated a flair for the dramatic. They developed a strange and bombastic Latin style that matched their sometimes flamboyant lives. They also contradicted Christian practice elsewhere by allowing great power to abbesses, including Brigid of Kildare and Hilda of Wearmouth-Jarrow, two who ruled over double monasteries of women and men.

When Pope Gregory I dispatched Benedictine monks as missionaries to England, some conflict with Celtic monasticism was inevitable. The Synod of Whitby in 664 resolved the major disputes, with the Roman tradition winning a complete victory over the Celtic. Although this decision suppressed traditions with ancient roots, it also brought some advantages to English monks, who found that papal ties could help free them from unwelcome constraints of local barons. The two traditions met in their shared passion for pious learning and classical culture, and the disagreements between them stimulated further scholarship. The dynamic marriage of cultures produced scholars of great energy and brilliance, such as Benedict Biscop, born Biscop Baducing, an Anglo-Saxon nobleman turned monk, who founded St. Peter's monastery at Wearmouth (674) and St. Paul's at Jarrow (682). Staunchly Benedictine, he introduced Roman liturgical practice in his religious houses and nurtured the Northumbrian cultural renaissance by risking five journeys to Italy to collect manuscripts, art, and relics. Biscop's accumulated treasures immediately influenced the impressive manuscript production of Northumbrian monasteries, including missals for the celebration of the mass, books of psalms and prayers, biblical commentaries, and collections of laws, letters, and sermons. Perhaps the finest of these creations is the richly illustrated Gospel book of Lindisfarne. Produced around 700, the Lindisfarne Gospels contain portraits inspired by eastern and western Mediterranean art, from Byzantium to Greece and Italy. This is a brilliant manuscript, but it is not really an anomaly. The northern monasteries quickly repaid the cultural debt they owed to Roman contacts. When the stern and able abbot Ceolfrid of Wearmouth and Jarrow died en route to Rome (713?), he was bearing a deluxe manuscript of the scriptures, copied by his monks for the pope.

The resources of Ceolfrid's monasteries were well spent on their greatest alumnus, the Venerable Bede (672/673–735). His parents brought him as an oblate (offering) to Wearmouth when he was only seven years old. Later he moved to nearby Jarrow.

He seems never to have traveled more than seventy-five miles from that neighborhood, although his contemporaries were accustomed to range far and wide. Thanks to the collecting of Biscop and others, Bede had no need to leave Northumbria in search of knowledge. With access to perhaps 200 books and 100 authors in his monastic library, he became the greatest scholar of his day, so far above the others and so influential that some scholars have called the years from Pope Gregory I to the coronation of Charlemagne (604–800) the Age of Bede.

Bede's vast literary output encompasses a variety of writings, including scriptural studies, prayers, and hymns in Latin verse, as well as textbooks to instruct scribes on proper spelling, grammar, and even handwriting. Bede's learned biblical commentaries drew on the works of great predecessors whom he admired and knew well, including Augustine, Ambrose, Jerome, and Gregory the Great. Bede also had a creative mind of his own. He popularized the idea of reckoning time from the birth of Christ, instead of from the foundation of Rome or from the regnal year of German kings, and he introduced the term *anno Domini*, "in the year of the Lord," abbreviated A.D. He is best remembered, however, for tracing his spiritual and cultural heritage in two works, the *History of the Abbots of Wearmouth and Jarrow* and his masterpiece, the *Ecclesiastical History of the English People*.[4] The *Ecclesiastical History* delivers more than its title promises, for it contains much secular information on early Britain, culled from many sources, which Bede conscientiously identified for his audience while he compared and analyzed them for their reliability. His critical judgment earned him the titles Father of English Scholarship, History, and Literature.

No author was more widely read throughout the western Middle Ages than the Venerable Bede, and few were as deeply admired as Bede was in his own lifetime and beyond. He lived a simple and pious life. Finding holiness, humility, and scholarship utterly compatible, he would not let his talents and revered status exempt him from the usual duties of monks. Alcuin (a student of Bede's disciple, Egbert) reported Bede's disclaimer: "I know that angels visit the congregation of brethren at the canonical hours, and what if they should not find me among the brethren? Would they not say, 'Where is Bede?' "

Bede's gentle holiness seems all the more remarkable when viewed in the context of his own day. The warrior ideal of Germanic society had by no means disappeared. It is useful to remember that the Lindisfarne Gospel and Bede's *History* are roughly contemporary with *Beowulf*. Set in the period of the Germanic migrations, this heroic poem glories in the splendid halls of great princes and in the blood of combat. Although scholars point out its Christian allegories and theological themes, the poem testifies to the persistence of the pagan spirit in Bede's day and beyond.

The Anglo-Saxon passion for missionary work, however, continued the Chris-

---

[4]See James Campbell, ed., *The Ecclesiastical History of the English People and Other Selections from the Writings of the Venerable Bede* (New York: Washington Square Press, 1968).

tianization of England which would result in a tenth-century renaissance, the Anglo-Saxon monastic revival. Meanwhile, Anglo-Saxon teachers carried the learning of Wearmouth, Jarrow, and Bede to the Frankish realm where the close attachment of the English Benedictines to Rome would have far-reaching consequences.

An early missionary to the continent was the Northumbrian monk, Willibrord, who crossed the English Channel to Christianize pagans on the Frisian Islands and in the territory that is now the Netherlands, Belgium, and Luxembourg. With the support of the Frankish king Pepin II and the pope, he became the first bishop of Utrecht. One of Willibrord's assistants in Frisia was another Anglo-Saxon Benedictine, Wynfrith, who had been raised in English abbeys and baptized as Winfrid (ca. 675–754). When he was ready for his own mission, Winfrid traveled to Rome to receive the blessing of Pope Gregory II, who gave him the new name of Boniface (719) after the Roman martyr. In Thuringia, Frisia, Bavaria, and Hesse in central and southern Germany, Boniface won many converts among the poor through his emphasis on Christian charity. On another sojourn in Rome in 722, Boniface was consecrated bishop, swearing fidelity to the pope. His enthusiastic support of papal authority continued the English Benedictine tradition. When he founded the monastery of Fulda, which would be his base, he even put it under papal control.

Meanwhile, the widespread missionary activity of Boniface met continuing success. When he chopped down the famous Oak of Thor at Geismar, a pagan cult center, Boniface won new converts among pagans who were impressed that such a courageous act of sacrilege brought no retribution from their gods. Boniface continued to demolish pagan temples and replace them with Christian churches. He founded the bishopric of Mainz, which would become the chief see of Germany. As he organized southern Germany into Christian dioceses, he planted numerous Benedictine monasteries throughout the countryside, all with links to England and reverence for papal authority. Gregory II made him archbishop in 732 and papal legate in 739.

It was the pope who arranged Boniface's connection with Charles Martel, Carolingian Mayor of the Palace. The alliance fit nicely with Martel's plans to expand eastward into Germany; religious and political expansion could work hand in hand. After Martel's death in 741, his successors, Carloman and Pepin III, invited Boniface to reform the Frankish church. With their encouragement and under their protection, he held reforming councils, confronted heretic priests, ousted worldly bishops, and regularized monastic rule, using the Roman model for uniformity in liturgy and religious practice. At the same time, he also preached peace and Christian obedience to the civil authorities—the Carolingian princes and their agents. As papal emissary in 751, Boniface anointed Pepin king, with divine sanction. (His brother Carloman had become a monk.) Pope Stephen II crossed the Alps in winter to repeat the consecration, anointing Pepin, his queen, and his sons.

These two anointings, taken together, represent an important stage in the alliance of papacy, English monasticism, and Frankish kings. To Boniface belongs the greatest credit for cementing this bond and for influencing each of the three related elements: a strengthened papacy controlling a reformed and reorganized Church; Benedictine foundations that shared a single Rule—indeed, after the work of Boniface, the only Rule in Britain, Italy, France, and Germany; and the Carolingian dynasty, now advanced to royal status. On his missions to monastery and court, Boniface never wavered in loyalty to the Roman pope and the Roman cultural heritage. Thanks in large part to Boniface, with the Christianization of northern Europe came its Romanization as well. Under the united western church fostered by Boniface, the cultural and religious groundwork was in place for the creation of the Carolingian renaissance.

On June 5, 754, in a dawn attack by a group of pagans, Boniface was martyred in Frisia with his companions. Having devoted the last thirty-five years of his life to conversion and the organization of the church, he left behind a remarkable legacy as a brilliant evangelist, statesman, and administrator. Boniface well deserves to be remembered as Apostle to Germany; in truth, he was one of the most important people of the early Middle Ages.

The letters of Boniface reveal a great deal about Germanic social customs, which were at variance with Christianity, and show how far the two had to go before they could meet on common ground. He wrote about the Germans' love of extravagant dress, the dangers women pilgrims faced on their pilgrimages to Rome, the survival of pagan practices, and sacrifices to the pagan gods. Boniface reported that Christians among the Germans were even selling slaves to pagans for use in human sacrifice. He found it necessary to persuade the people not to eat horsemeat. He lamented the laxity and immorality among clergy. Pope Gregory III urged Boniface to forbid widowers to remarry "if you are able." The question of remarriage was minor compared with other domestic issues on which the two cultures clashed. German and ecclesiastical law were worlds apart in matters of polygamy, incest, and divorce— all of which were accepted elements in German society. A half century after Boniface's martyrdom, Charlemagne finally forbade incest and decreed penalties for both men and women who committed adultery. Royal pronouncements did not put an immediate stop to old customs, but the values of state, church, and society were slowly moving toward conformity.

Charlemagne and the Carolingian Renaissance

Charlemagne (ruled 768–814), son of Pepin III and grandson of Charles Martel, was the Frankish king whose vision and energy converted the legacy of Boniface into Europe's first medieval renaissance. For a century Charlemagne's family had been leaders in the political, economic, and religious revitalization of the West. These efforts culminated in the reign of Charles the Great, who fashioned western Europe into a single Christian empire.

When Pepin III died in 768, Charlemagne and his younger brother Carloman shared the kingdom uneasily until Carloman's timely death in 771. Charles proved himself a brilliant monarch. His military conquests of northern Spain and of Lombards, Saxons, and Bavarians more than doubled the size of the realm. The subjugated territories yielded rich booty for the royal coffers, giving Charles a measure of independence from his barons. At the same time, the campaigns offered the center of the kingdom a period of stability and recovery essential for an agrarian economy. Charlemagne lavished loving attention on the details of governing, controlling the forces of anarchy, the warrior chiefs with their rich estates and violent ambitions. In this way, he worked to establish a unified central administration and to create a civilized state. To him this meant a Christian state, with church and state mutually supportive of each other.

With Charles's imperial coronation by Pope Leo III in Rome on Christmas day 800, the western church renounced its ancient dependency on Byzantium. No longer did the papacy acknowledge the Byzantine emperor as nominal master and protector of Italy. The eastern empire responded with outrage, but the pope's recognition of Charles as Holy Roman Emperor sealed the bond of the ecclesiastical and political units in the west. The coronation explicitly linked old imperial Rome and new Christian Rome, with the authority of both devolving on Charles.

It was no easy matter for Charlemagne to Christianize his empire. Christian ideals linked to Roman traditions merged slowly with Germanic ideals, but the impact of this union on the Germanic peoples and on western civilization was to prove immense. Pagan Germans lived in forests of Europe, which separated one tribe from another and kept the society fragmented. These pagans considered it an act of terrible impiety to cut down trees, which were sacred, and to offend the gods and spirits of the forests. Likewise, they would not build bridges or mills over rivers for fear of disturbing the river spirits. The rivers' power remained unharnessed, just as the land remained uncleared. Christianity changed all that. Christian saints' lives repeatedly report the cutting down of some sacred tree or another as proof of the pagan spirit's inefficacy and sign of the power wielded by the Christian god and his agents. Charlemagne's first campaign against the pagan Saxons saw the felling of Irminsul, the sacred oak tree. When the pagans realized that no ill consequences befell the Christian perpetrators, many accepted baptism. The course of western history changed dramatically when the Germans came to believe that God had given mankind dominion over the earth. At last the Germans could use rivers and forests; all people could graze animals in the forests, burn logs on the hearth, and build homes of wood. Men no longer had to wander as nomadic hunters; they could enjoy a settled economy instead. As the forests were destroyed, so agriculture increased. Until very recently, the western world has viewed this as a uniformly positive step in the progress of civilization. Now, of course, new questions about the global effects of deforestation have challenged the conviction that human beings own natural resources, and so may exhaust them at will. Civilization as we know it, however, was unthinkable among the Germans before Christianity overcame their pagan prohibitions.

Conversion of the Germans to Christianity produced dramatic consequences, yet the assimilation of Christian ideals of poverty and humility proceeded slowly. Once tribal chiefs were baptized, the entire tribe was expected to follow. Charlemagne himself seems to have regarded baptism as a mandatory sign of loyalty to him. He even decreed in 785 that conquered Saxons who refused baptism (or violated Christian law in any way, for instance by eating meat during Lent) should face the death penalty. Charlemagne's ecclesiastical advisor, Alcuin of York, argued against this policy, but his master would not back down. Still, baptism was only a first step.

German warriors might accept Christian baptism, but would they adopt Christian beliefs and values? The ideals of poverty and love of enemies, for instance, are difficult for many people to accept even now after two millenia of Christian tradition; these concepts were virtually incomprehensible for fierce warriors whose status came from bloodshed and the spoils of war. The Christian emphasis on poverty, universal brotherhood and sisterhood, and love of enemies was nearly impossible for German warriors to understand. The concepts of sin and repentance were equally difficult for them to grasp.

Charlemagne understood what few of his contemporaries could. His genius lay in envisioning a Christian society made over in the image of Augustine's *City of God*. He followed a deliberate program of religious and moral renewal, consciously inaugurated and supported by earlier Carolingian kings, especially by his own father, Pepin III. Under Charles these policies bore succulent fruit. The program aimed at no less than a spiritual regeneration of the entire society, the creation of a truly Christian community. Moved by this religious and moral impetus, Charles initiated specific and pragmatic policies. As a first step, he wanted to improve literacy so that people could read the scriptures. He especially wanted to provide basic education for the clergy. This required a school system for parish-level education for men on the front lines of teaching and preaching. The priests needed to understand their responsibilities and their faith; for their own study and for teaching others, they also needed adequate libraries with liturgical and biblical texts.

From this simple goal came far-ranging results: Schools were founded throughout the kingdom and manuscripts were copied to fill their libraries. Carolingian scribes created a new style of writing, the Carolingian minuscule, from which our modern typefaces come. It was a uniform and highly legible script that all literate people could decipher. It was a lowercase script (hence, the word minuscule) that was compact and therefore made economic use of precious vellum.

Once Latin had been the common tongue of the West, but the people of Charlemagne's day spoke a variety of vernacular languages. By the late eighth century, Latin posed a problem not only for native speakers of German but also for those in

Gaul whose spoken language was developing away from classical Latin and toward what we know as Old French. It was difficult for both groups to understand the Bible and the Latin liturgy. In his missionary efforts, Boniface had encountered a Bavarian priest who did not know the simplest word endings for Latin and so was mistakenly baptizing "in the name of the Fatherland and the Daughter and the Holy Spirit." Anglo-Saxon and Irish monks of Charlemagne's court had texts for teaching Latin to non-native speakers. Through accurate Latin, priests could teach true doctrine, and the various peoples of the Carolingian empire could communicate with one another. Uniform and correct Latin, comprehensible to all who knew the language, was therefore an important priority. With a common Latin education and manuscripts available to many, once again there arose a whole class of people who could write and also read each others' writing, creating their own literature that rivaled the production of the ancient world. Scholars compiled biblical commentaries and collections of canon law, and some also wrote secular verse and epics.

Charlemagne's modest beginnings of scholastic renewal led to a classicizing revival, as scholars turned to ancient texts in order to understand standards of correct grammar, spelling, and style. Inevitably, some also found literature they wanted to preserve and imitate. This effort rescued classical learning, which was by then in danger of extinction as existing manuscripts decayed or were burned in monastery fires or otherwise lost. Carolingian manuscripts are critical links in the transmission of Latin literature. Without this renaissance, much of our precious legacy from antiquity would have been lost. The phenomenon has often been studied through the eyes and sensibilities of classicists, who have focused on the new literature created in imitation of classical style and on the preservation of ancient culture. This was an incidental result, however, of the renewal whose primary impetus was the desire to infuse society with Christian sensibilities and to mold Christian behavior. Although the study of Latin benefited from this revival, definite losses counterbalanced the gain. By forcing ecclesiastical Latin back into the classical mold, Carolingian scholars unwittingly assured the artificiality of that Latin and the demise of Latin as a living vernacular language.

To set in motion the phenomenon he envisioned, Charlemagne wooed learned men from all over Europe to his court at Aachen (Aix-la-Chapelle), where Anglo-Saxon, Irish, Italian, and Visigothic scholars found some stability, refuge from Muslim (and later, Viking) incursions, and the promise of royal patronage. The brightest men of the age became enthusiastic supporters of this self-conscious religious movement aimed at purifying society. From Visigothic Spain came Theodulf, distinguished theologian and a talented poet. From the Lombard district of Italy came Paul the Deacon, who later returned to the monastic life at Monte Cassino, where he wrote a *History of the Lombards*, which remains our primary source for understanding the rise and success of his people.[5] From the abbey of Fulda came Einhard, who

---

[5] William Dudley-Foulke, trans., *History of the Langobards* (Philadelphia: University of Pennsylvania, 1907, 1974).

wrote the famous biography of Charlemagne modeled on the work of the ancient Roman historian Suetonius.

The most influential figure in the transfer of learning to the Carolingian centers was the Anglo-Saxon missionary, Alcuin of York (ca. 730–804), student of Bede's disciple Egbert. Born in Northumbria and educated at the cathedral school in York, Alcuin became teacher, then headmaster there. When he was about fifty years old, he met Charlemagne on one of his visits to the continent. Charles persuaded him to head the palace school at Aachen, where Alcuin became religious and educational advisor to Charles. Alcuin's students at Aachen were scholars and courtiers, even Charles himself and his family. The academic program at the school under Alcuin encompassed the trivium and elements of the quadrivium, with the emphasis always on biblical and ecclesiastical application of this learning. It would be difficult to overemphasize the Christian orientation of the program Alcuin oversaw. Christianity was its core; the service of Christianity was its purpose. Alcuin and his school assisted the Christian program, for instance, by editing and correcting biblical and liturgical texts and by creating a uniform lectionary. The aim was not merely to educate people of the secular and ecclesiastical court but to provide tools for clerics and parish priests throughout the realm.

As we have seen, the educational reforms Alcuin oversaw had modest aims: to enable people to read Latin, write the Psalms, know correct grammar and the rudiments of mathematics, master the chant, and understand Christian texts. The pursuit of these goals nonetheless brought Roman Christianity to the people of northern Europe. Alcuin thus completed the work of Boniface and the other Anglo-Saxon missionaries. For the last eight years of his life, he retired from the court to oversee the Abbey of St. Martin at Tours. There he wrote his own epitaph: *Alchuine nomen erat, sophiam mihi semper amanti* ("Alcuin was my name and wisdom always my love"). For Alcuin, as for Charlemagne, this wisdom was Christian.

The Carolingian renaissance nurtured art and architecture as well as literature. The court school produced beautifully illuminated manuscripts, including masterful gospels. This Carolingian art, like its literature and learning, adapted classicizing forms in the service of Christian sensibilities. To rival Roman grandeur, Charlemagne imported marble columns and bronze statues from Rome and Ravenna and displayed them in his royal capital. Not content only with pillage, he set up a foundry at Aachen that cast bronze doors and gallery railings, and he patronized mosaicists and painters. Such artists could decorate the grand public art of Charles's ambitious building program. As we might expect, the most important public buildings of the period were churches. Carolingian princes built many palaces; scholars have counted 100 in the period from 768 to 855, but in those same few decades at least 27 new cathedrals and 417 monasteries were produced.

Classicizing monuments looked to the past for their inspiration and sometimes achieved a timeless majesty. Still, it is important to keep in mind the fundamentally Germanic character of the Carolingian realm. Charlemagne himself worked assiduously to learn Latin. His biographer, Einhard, poignantly described the emperor's habit of keeping writing tablets under his pillow so that he could practice his letters on nights when he could not sleep. The art of writing Latin did not come naturally to a Frankish king, even if he was the author of the Carolingian renaissance. In his later years, Charlemagne appreciated the Germanic cultural heritage of his people and collected songs celebrating the Franks.

The greatest masterpiece of the Frankish epic tradition in fact arose from legendary material surrounding Charles's own exploits. Composed as late as 1100, the *Song of Roland* contains some memory of Charlemagne's struggle against the Muslims of Spain. Crossing the Pyrenees on their return from one campaign, the rear guard of Charlemagne's army was surprised by an enemy ambush, and many Franks were massacred. Three hundred years after the event, the epic still held the remembered consciousness of the close proximity and threat of the Muslim world. Of Charlemagne's many campaigns, some checked Muslims in Spain by the establishment of strongly fortified borderlands known as marches.

These enemies who were kept at bay by Charles and who were remembered by later generations as treacherous infidels were in fact the heirs of a rich cultural tradition. Centuries earlier, monks and scholars had fled from Africa to escape the Vandal threat. The North Africans had exercised a strong influence on Visigothic kings, converting them to Christianity. The cultural mix had produced the most learned man of the early seventh century, Isidore of Seville, bishop of that town and thus head of the Spanish church. Isidore wrote a vast collection of historical and theological works and became an important transmitter of ancient thought to the Middle Ages. Until the twelfth century, the western Church used his statements of doctrine, collected in the *Book of Sentences*, as its principal theological textbook. Isidore's *Origins* or *Etymologies* was an encyclopedia that summarized Greco-Roman wisdom for the medieval world. Isidore and others produced a lively intellectual heritage that was permitted to survive and even flourish under the Arabs. Latin, Greek, and Arabic learning intermingled in this cosmopolitan society in which ancient philosophy, science, and medicine prospered. Although not nearly as brilliant as that of the Ummayad emirate to the south, Christian and Islamic Spain nevertheless proved to be civilized compared to its Frankish neighbor.

Feudalism and the Dissolution of the Frankish Realm

In the Frankish realm, a social revolution was occurring with the evolution of feudalism. The disappearance of the Roman imperial structure and the centralized state had left a power vacuum. Local lords, no longer checked by the imperial administration, rose to fill the void. Without governors to shield them from mayhem, free farmers had to surrender to local lords who offered defense in exchange for property and service. Lesser lords swore fealty to greater lords, granting them military service in return for patronage and protection. The *Song of Roland* illustrates the values of this military elite who prized loyalty, courage, and martial prowess. When abbots or bishops were the property holders, the church became part of the feudal process, which it hoped to civilize. In the feudal ceremony itself, when one man swore allegiance to another in the presence of priests and holy relics and the Bible, all the people in the community witnessed the visible and inextricable connection between religion and politics in feudal society.

By the year of Charlemagne's coronation, the process of feudalization was well under way. Scholars have estimated that by 800 perhaps as many as 60 percent of the people in western Europe were serfs bound to the land and their feudal lords. Increasingly, free people were submitting to more powerful military men. Charlemagne could manage the feudal lords, but his grandsons could not. During the ninth century, weak control by Carolingian kings left the land vulnerable to attack by Muslims, Magyars, and Vikings.

Viking pirates sailed in their long boats from the fiords of their mountainous homeland and terrorized Europe from the eighth to the eleventh century. Unleashed by domestic upheaval and a land too poor to sustain a growing population, expert sailors who traded in fish, wine, salt, metals, and furs turned to more profitable brigandage. The east-facing Swedes raided the Black Sea, conquering Slavs and founding a monarchy at Novogorod and Kiev. In the west, the Danes and Norwegians ranged as far as Iceland and beyond. They repeatedly assaulted France and the British Isles, sailed around Spain, and entered the Mediterranean in 859. Even Italy knew the wrath of these marauders. Viking ships penetrated rivers, threatening inland towns and especially the monasteries and cathedrals whose wealth held special attraction for hostile pagans.

The first recorded Viking attacks were against the great northern monasteries at Lindisfarne (793), Jarrow (794), and Iona (795). Some scholars have suggested that Vikings were especially attracted to monasteries, not so much for the treaures they yielded as for the opportunity to express their fanatical paganism and hatred of Christianity. They pillaged monasteries with systematic violence, stripping them of their treasures, sometimes burning the libraries, and exercising particularly bloodthirsty vengeance on monks.

Even Viking terrorism yielded some advantage for the larger Christian community. Vikings chased scholars and their rescued books to the Carolingian court, where Charlemagne nurtured the resulting convergence of resources. In 911 a descendant of Charlemagne, the French king Charles the Simple, ceded the land at the mouth of the Seine to a Viking named Rollo, who accepted baptism as a sign of loyalty to the king. This territory—the land of the Northmen, Northmannia, or Normandy— served as a buffer against rival pagan bands and attracted others who readily accepted Christianity as a condition of settlement. Ultimately, the Viking raids brought Scandinavia into closer contact with Christian Europe. This meeting of hostile worlds would eventually Christianize the last outposts of northern European paganism.

Meanwhile, Muslims to the south of the Frankish realm began a fresh assault, invading Sicily and southern Italy. They attacked St. Benedict's abbey of Monte Cassino and forced the monks to flee for their lives. Arab raiders even made a foray up the Tiber in 846, threatened Rome, and sacked the basilica of St. Peter, still outside the city walls. From bases in Muslim Spain, Saracens plundered the southern coast of Gaul and sent raiding parties as far inland as Burgundy. By the end of the ninth century, the Asian Magyars, or Hungarians, threatened from the east. Soon they were raiding Lombardy, Bavaria, Saxony, and Burgundy. They ravaged villages and monasteries, selling their prisoners as slaves across the eastern frontiers.

All these raids of Vikings, Muslims, and Magyars took their toll on the Carolingian kingdoms, increasing their instability and giving further impetus to the feudal forces that were fragmenting the realm. The empire began to collapse almost at once upon Charlemagne's death, because only the tremendous personal strength of the great king had held it together. The military barons were not the only ones who imperiled the unified state. Churchmen did so as well. Abbots and bishops vied with other lords to seize authority over vast estates. Feudal struggles and enemy raids tore Frankish society apart from within and without.

The disintegration of the Carolingian empire proceeded apace under Charlemagne's only surviving son and heir, Louis the Pious (814–840), and grandsons. Louis was deeply religious and well educated, but no soldier. At Louis's death, the empire was divided among his sons, Charles Lothair and Louis the German, who embarked upon a course of fratricidal warfare.

Given the swift decay of the Carolingian kingdoms, it is no wonder that later generations venerated the memory of Charlemagne. For a while, he had fashioned a uniform Christian culture for western Europe. True, his program provoked some idiosyncratic responses, pedantic treatises, and quarreling among intellectuals. Still, his vision resulted in a remarkably uniform and radiant culture. Carolingian scholars created a virtual canon of authors to be read for a Christian education, including Roman poets and grammarians, who were considered a critical element in the preparation for biblical study but also of powerful and enduring influence on liberal learning in western culture. This canon linked Christian European culture with the ancient Roman world. The Church Fathers also occupied a cherished place in that canon, and Charlemagne's schoolmen adapted their writings for medieval readers. The legacy of this Carolingian tradition—classical and Christian—was a shared language and script, a literate class enjoying the vitality of cathedral and monastic schools, and a tradition of royal patronage of Christian culture. At the same time, the culture that came to flower in Carolingian schools differed significantly from that of the classical world it emulated. Pope Leo's coronation of Charlemagne in the year 800 signifies the shift of power from the Mediterranean to the North. At the very least, this event symbolizes the end of the ancient world. As Charlemagne's realm fragmented into localized communities, it marked the final step in medieval European civilization.

Was Charlemagne's program a success? How Christian was the society he inspired? The scriptural, Christian view from Charles's court and schools reveals the determination to initiate a Christian renaissance. At the same time, aristocratic warriors and rustic peasantry present a different picture, marked by a lively persistence of magic, sorcery, and paganism. Still, Charlemagne's program produced notable results. Under his aegis, church and state were acting together to order Christian education and preaching. The state undoubtedly benefited directly because this process produced literate clerics who could assist with the secular administration. On the other side, even as clerics learned to manage the church's vast resources, the church also became more civilized through monastic and educational reform.

Later centuries revered Charlemagne as the archetypal Christian ruler. In legend he became a pilgrim who returned from Jerusalem laden with holy relics and a victorious warrior in the crusade against the Saracens of Spain. Admiring the power of his image and myth, many European princes strained to trace their descent from Charlemagne, the ultimate Christian hero of the Middle Ages and the creator of a Christian European culture.

Chapter 14

THE FLOWERING OF MEDIEVAL CHRISTENDOM (867–1085)

Byzantium after Iconoclasm

While the Carolingian empire was fragmenting and disintegrating under Charlemagne's heirs, the Byzantine East was entering a period of political expansion and cultural renaissance in the wake of the iconoclast controversy. The battle over the icons had threatened to tear apart Byzantine society. The dangerous intensity of the crisis, however, stimulated intellectual and religious ferment that led to a revival sometimes called the Macedonian Renaissance (from the dynasty that ruled from 867 to 1057, whose founder was born in a province of Thrace called "Macedonia" by the Byzantines). Through this struggle, Byzantium reclaimed its classical heritage and gave definitive shape to its Christian identity.

When Irene became Empress-Regent in 780, she set about defending the icons with the assistance of her learned iconophile patriarch, Tarasius. The two encouraged research and the copying of theological manuscripts that would provide textual support for icon veneration and evidence of the icons' power. The iconophile authorities published new sources, including sermons and correspondence of Tarasius and the lives of iconophile saints and martyrs. The educated elite rallied around the defense of icons. During the second iconoclast period (813–843), animated debate between the two sides led to vigorous scholarship. Enthusiasm spilled over from theological into secular interests such as mathematics, astronomy, and grammar. In Constantinople, the center of this revival, perhaps 2,000 or at most 3,000 men at any given time constituted the intellectual elite. Although only these few were highly educated, the general literate public expanded dramatically. In the monastic schools monks received a good education, and women of elite families were taught at home by private tutors.

229

The revival owes its inspiration to the iconoclasts who unwittingly provoked this response. Once the icons were restored, the victorious iconophiles found that they had inherited yet another treasure from the struggle: Although they had destroyed countless works of irreplaceable art, the iconoclasts had also recovered the Greco-Roman tradition in art and literature. Byzantium had never abandoned the classical past, but the iconoclast emperors adopted a secularizing policy that increased classical influence. As icon smashers struggled to extricate themselves from religious images, they replaced the images with ancient models whose proportion and restraint they admired. Under the emperors' patronage, scholars revived classical learning. This revival gained a momentum that did not end with the restoration of icons. Byzantium would always remain a distinctly Christian state. After iconoclasm, however, the classical influence gave order to the intense religious inspiration. Classical decorum and Christian passion combined to produce the greatest art of Byzantium.

With the controversy resolved in favor of the icons, the production of religious art resumed throughout the empire. Hagia Sophia and other churches were adorned with lavish mosaics, and new churches were built and decorated according to schemes rooted in Late Roman art. Most of these new churches were small. Travelers from the West were continually surprised to see that major eastern churches were considerably smaller than the cathedrals they had seen back home. Hagia Sophia remained the exception. Aside from this one glorious monument, the Byzantines preferred a church whose interior could be grasped as a whole and viewed as a single icon, with images of God, the Virgin, angels, martyrs, prophets, and saints hierarchically arranged on its various surfaces.

The eleventh-century monastery church in Phocis, Greece, dedicated to Hosios Loukas, shows the typical scheme. The floor plan exhibits the usual Byzantine pattern from the post-iconoclastic period that was known as the Greek cross or cross-in-square. It is a cross with equal arms, inscribed in a square. A dome crowns the intersection of the arms. The plan boasts structural integrity and balance, having no need of external supports or buttresses. Most Byzantine churches do not look remarkable from the outside, but the interior is a different matter altogether. To walk into such a church is to step into a holy space and see a miniature of the larger universe. The dome is the heavenly realm, adorned with Christ Pantocrator (Ruler of All), who looks down on the faithful. The dome mosaic from Hosios Loukas is lost, but the mosaic from the church of the virgin at Daphni, also in Greece, presents a contemporary masterpiece. On nearby ceilings stand the archangels, and the twelve apostles support the dome. The worshippers look up, straining to see heavenly figures. Dominating their view, straight ahead on the vault of the apse, sits the loving intercessor between the congregants and God, the Virgin Mary holding the baby Jesus. Scenes from the life of Christ occupy the curved corners where the dome meets its square base. The saints, martyrs, and prophets line the walls, each in his or her proper place, signifying the church on Earth. All these holy images announce the presence of the divine at the liturgy, which daily represents Christ's Passion.

The Holy Liturgy, like the sacred building and its icons, became stabilized in the period after iconoclasm. Religious life revolved around the liturgy, and Byzantines became devoted to its unchanging form, with liturgical cycles imitating the temporal cycles in endless repetition. In the fifteenth century, when the city was threatened by Ottoman Turks, Byzantines rejected union with the western church and possible rescue from Islamic invaders in no small part because this earthly salvation required them to adopt the western liturgy and abandon their own.

Byantium had emerged from the icon controversy a strong empire, sure of its identity as a Christian state. The icon worshippers won a clear victory with the restoration of the icons so important to the people. The imperial attack on the images had proved unsuccessful, and it seemed that the icon-loving monks had defeated the imperial power. The social and cultural principles of the iconoclasts prevailed, however. Although monks had controlled intellectual life in the earlier period, in the ninth and tenth centuries Byzantine culture became more secular. The emperor retained his power as a sacred figure, God's regent on earth and the authority who appointed patriarchs and dominated ecclesiastical affairs. Monks could pray for mankind and mediate between humans and their God, perform the sacred liturgy and administer the sacraments, even deliver social services, but the emperor was master of the Byzantine church, patriarch, and monks.

The so-called Macedonian dynasty capitalized on the unified purpose and culture of Byzantium. Macedonian emperors nurtured the cultural renaissance. Constantine VII (913–957) himself was a notable scholar who directed various important compilations including a precious record of court ceremonial and a treatise on the neighbors of Byzantium, friend and foe. The revived empire produced warriors as well as monks and intellectuals. With the aid of talented generals and disciplined armies, Byzantium embarked on an aggressive foreign policy. Constantinople was then the greatest city of Christendom, the site of the imperial and patriarchal courts and center of international trade controlled by the emperor and his agents. The capital, with its elaborate state bureaucracy, stood utterly without peer in the empire. Since the seventh century, the empire had shifted from an urban to a rural economy. Provincial cities had disappeared, and the society moved from a monetary economy to one based on barter. On the one hand stood the bureaucratic elite of Constantinople and on the other, the independent peasants of the countryside and villages. No stable class mediated between the civil aristocracy in Constantinople and the peasants who had by then replaced slaves as the basis of countryside economy. Although the empire was almost continuously at war from the seventh through the ninth centuries, Byzantium employed no professional army, so the free farmers were soldiers, too. Barely better off than the poorer peasants, these soldier-farmers had to supply horses and fight in long campaigns as well as farm.

This post-iconoclast Byzantine state had a very different social structure from that of the old Roman Empire. The public life of urban civilization had disappeared, replaced by village society. Rural society had simplified with a temporary decline of large estates and the provincial elites who owned them. In medieval Byzantium the most important social units were the nuclear family and the *oikos*, the household. Religous life was increasingly isolated as well, as smaller establishments replaced large monasteries. In general, smaller social units tended to benefit the emperor, whose power met no rival until the early tenth century when the provincial aristocracy began to rise again. This occurred when the peasant-warriors agreed to accept serfdom under wealthy neighbors in exchange for protection from burdensome taxes and military service. This tendency presented an unwelcome danger to the emperor and the central administration, who could not condone the alienation of taxes and manpower or the dangerous rivalry of feudal lords. The church, too, began ceding monastic lands to local aristocrats who were to administer them on behalf of the church.

As the aristocracy was rising to challenge imperial authority, external threats continued to exert pressure on the Byzantine state. Strong Macedonian emperors such as Basil II the Bulgar-Slayer (976–1025) devoted their lives to the state's defense, but still the seeds of troubles to come were sown during the period known as the Macedonian Renaissance. The growing struggle between the landed military aristocracy of the provinces and the civil aristocracy of the capital would produce disastrous consequences after Basil's death. The navy, proud victor over Arab ships in the seventh century and the terror of Arab and Russian fleets in the tenth, was replaced by Italian mercenaries. Essentially, rural Byzantine society put little stock in maritime ventures and lost valuable commercial control to Jewish, Muslim, and especially Italian merchants. Potentially the middlemen in the booming commercial revival of the twelfth century, Byzantium instead lost revenues to enemies who gained tax concessions and harbor rights in exchange for naval protection.

During the Macedonian period of military expansion and glory, all this was in the dark future. Meanwhile, Byzantium was winning military victories, most notably over the Bulgars, along with religious victories in the conversions that would bring the Slavs into the spiritual and cultural sphere of Byzantium.

Byzantine Missions to the Slavs

The ninth-century missionary successes of the Byzantines owe much to two brothers, Constantine (who took the monastic name Cyril just before his death) and Methodius. Growing up in Thessalonica, they received a bilingual education in Greek and Slavic. Since the migrations of the fifth and sixth centuries, the Slavs had been scattered widely over Eastern Europe: west to the Elbe River, south into the Balkans and Greece, east beyond the Dnieper River and into the northern forests of Russia. West Slavs would come under the influence of the Latin and Germanic West, while east Slavs and most south Slavs would enter the sphere of Byzantium, in no small part thanks to Constantine and Methodius.

The rivalry between Byzantine and western Christendom for the souls of central Europe both exemplified and aggravated tensions between the two. Constantine and Methodius began their mission with Patriarch Photius and Pope Nicholas in a conflict that climaxed with mutual excommunications between the two leaders (863–867). In a meeting place between East and West, Franks and Byzantines were vying with one another to convert the Slavs. The territory was variously called Moravia or Bohemia; the natives called their land Čechy and themselves Czechs (Češi). In 845 fourteen of their nobles journeyed to Regensburg to accept Christian baptism from their western neighbors. It looked as if Bohemia/Moravia would soon be drawn into the western religious alliance.

The Moravian prince Rastislav (846–870), however, soon sought Byzantine ties to counter the Frankish-Bulgar alliance against his realm. Enter Constantine and Methodius, sent on a cultural and diplomatic embassy by the Byzantine emperor. For their mission into still un-Christianized territories, Constantine had created a new Slavonic alphabet, now called Glagolitic. (Today most Slavic peoples use the Cyrillic alphabet, named after Constantine-Cyril but composed later.) He had also translated both the bible and the liturgy into the vernacular language of the converted. To defend this translation, Constantine invoked the biblical precedent of the apostles preaching in many tongues on Pentecost (Acts 2:5) and also St. Paul's teaching (I Cor. 14:19):

> Since you have learned to hear, Slavic peoples,
> Hear the Word, for it came from God,
> The Word nourishing human souls,
> The Word strengthening heart and mind. . . .
> Therefore St. Paul has taught:
> "In offering my prayer to God,
> I had rather speak five words
> That all brethren will understand
> Than ten thousand words which are incomprehensible."[1]

The distinctive feature of Orthodox missions was this concession that the Word of God, the Logos, must be heard and understood by the believer. Sometimes the Byzantines enforced the use of Greek when they controlled Slavic lands, but the principle articulated by Constantine remained the church's official stance. At the same time, the Christian West remained adamant in the conviction that the vernacular was not an acceptable medium for preaching the gospel. During their mission to Moravia and their stay in Venice, Constantine and Methodius debated with Franks, who held what Byzantines called the "heresy of the three languages," that is, the

[1] Roman Jakobson, trans., in "St. Constantine's Prologue to the Gospel," *St. Vladimir's Seminary Quarterly* 7, No. 1 (1963), 17–18.

conviction that the gospel could be communicated only in the three languages used in Pilate's inscription on Jesus' cross: Hebrew, Greek, and Latin. By contrast, Constantine and Methodius affirmed that in the East Slavs and Armenians, Persians and Egyptians, Georgians and Arabs, all properly praised God in their own languages.

By this policy of translation, Orthodox Christianity became profoundly settled in people's lives and part of the indigenous cultures. The Slavic liturgy has continued among eastern and southern Slavs until the present day, and in Moravia until the eleventh century when the lingering influence of Latin Christendom finally prevailed. This vernacular tradition reaped a rich harvest. A literature in Slavonic developed within 100 years of the conversion, whereas vernacular literatures appeared only later in the West. But there were problems for Orthodox Christians, too. The use of various languages created national churches and further threatened the unity of Christendom, already divided into East and West. Without learning Greek, Eastern European Christians had no direct access to the classical heritage. A common use of Latin gave the western church greater cohesion along with the precious bonus of accessibility to Latin classical culture.

Because they permitted native peoples to retain their own languages for the liturgy, Constantine and Methodius enjoyed an advantage over their rival missionaries from the West. In their mission the brothers also received support from a surprising quarter, the papacy. While they were in Venice, Pope Nicholas I invited them to visit Rome. They took with them the alleged relics of St. Clement of Rome, a first-century martyr. When they presented these relics to Nicholas's successor, Adrian II (867–872), he threw the weight of his support behind the Slavonic liturgy. Constantine-Cyril died in Rome shortly thereafter, but Adrian consecrated Methodius as archbishop of Sirmium and granted him jurisdiction over much Slavic territory, including Moravia, Pannonia, and Slovakia. There Methodius met continued resistance from Frankish missionaries, who promoted a Latin liturgy and also a Latin version of the Nicene Creed to which they had added the controversial *filioque*. By the interpolation of this word, the revised creed affirmed that the Holy Spirit had proceeded from the Father *and the Son*. The Eastern Church maintained that the Holy Spirit proceeded only from the Father. Methodius's new protector, Pope John VIII (872–882), indicated his disapproval of the *filioque* clause, but the Frankish missionaries ignored the pope's views.

Byzantine Christianity exercised a lasting influence on the East Slavs, called in medieval times the *Rus*, whose modern heirs are the Russians, Ukrainians, and White Russians. In their movements from the sixth to the ninth centuries, these peoples had pushed east as far as the Volga River and north almost to the Baltic Sea, establishing important settlements at Novgorod and Kiev. Viking invasions in the early ninth century brought the Scandinavians into contact with the East Slavs, who called them Varangians. Their contact produced the first East Slavic state, which Oleg (873?–913) founded by uniting Kiev and Novgorod under his rule. In 988 the ruler Vladimir converted to eastern Christianity and forced his people to accept baptism.

Under Vladimir's son Yaroslav (1015–1054), the principality of Kiev achieved its greatest power and brilliance. Yaroslav extended the boundaries of the Kievan state and also established the independence of the Rus church from Constantinople. The Rus church had its own leader, called a metropolitan, who reigned from Kiev, the political and ecclesiastical capital of the state. Yaroslav imported Byzantine artisans to decorate the many churches he built, including St. Sophia Cathedral at Kiev, modeled on Hagia Sophia of Constantinople. Attempting to imitate in wood the domes of Byzantine churches, the builders of Kiev created the onion domes that characterize Russian churches. Byzantine influence is also visible in the painted or enamel icons that decorate these churches.

Byzantine clergy dispatched to Kiev established schools for training priests, but these schools also trained young men from the Kiev aristocracy, and convents educated some women. Missionaries translated parts of the bible and other ecclesiastical writings. These influenced Kiev writers, who produced a native literature featuring sermons, saints' lives, and religious treatises. The Kiev masterpiece is the *Primary Chronicle*, which focuses on the conversion of the Rus to Christianity and their struggles against the pagans surrounding them. Through this treasure of medieval literature, the East Slavs expressed their national identity within a Christian framework.

Despite religious links to Constantinople, the Rus of Kiev maintained political links with the West as well. Yaroslav's daughter Anna married the French king Henry I. (She may have been the only literate layperson at the French court during her day.) Yaroslav's family also had marriage ties with the ruling families of England, Germany, Norway, Poland, and Hungary, as well as with Byzantium. Although Kiev declined after Yaroslav's death, eastern Christianity continued to influence the civilizations of the East Slavs.

The spectacular expansion of Byzantine Christianity after the ninth century brought cultural advantages to the Slavs in Russia and the Balkans. The Cyrillic alphabet made possible the birth of Russian literature, and Russian art and architecture were inspired by Byzantine models. So great was the influence that Moscow eventually became known as the Third Rome, after the New (second) Rome, Constantinople.

Byzantine missions to the Slavs brought those peoples within the realm of eastern Christian influence, but ironically these same missions helped the Bulgars challenge Byzantine claims to universal supremacy. A mighty Bulgarian empire had taken command of the Balkans in territories wrested from Byzantium. This empire boasted an administration rendered more efficient by the introduction of Greek and then Cyrillic as the official written language. Its unique Slav-Bulgar culture was dominated by warlord khans who aspired to Byzantine grandeur. Byzantium and Bulgaria engaged in a bloody struggle that finally ended in victory for the last ruler of the male Macedonian line, Basil II, called the Bulgar-Slayer (975–1025).

In 866 the Bulgar khan Boris accepted a Christian mission founded by Constantine and Methodius, and Bulgaria soon became a Christian state. In the tenth century,

Bulgaria hatched a native-born Christian heresy, Bogomilism. Perhaps influenced by Armenian Paulicians dispatched to the area around Philippopolis, this sect was the creation of a Bulgarian called Pop Bogomil. Byzantines connected the heresy with Manichaeans, followers of the fourth-century Mani, who had taught that two creative urges, good and evil, were at work in the world. Like Mani, the Bogomils claimed that this physical world was entirely the work of the devil. The human spirit, an angel imprisoned in the flesh, longed to escape the Earth and flee to God. Since matter is evil, Christ could not have been truly material and born of a human mother (so Bogomils rejected the cult of Mary), but he will return at the Last Judgment to overturn Satan and his agents, who include all those who have wealth or power, either temporal or religious. In this Bogomil scheme, the church and its prelates are agents of the devil. Our information comes mostly from the tenth-century orthodox Bulgarian priest, Cosmas, who has Bogomils hurl the following challenge to orthodox priests:

> If you are holy, as you claim to be, then why do you not lead lives in accordance with the letter of Paul to Timothy: A bishop must be "above reproach, the husband of one wife, temperate, honest, dignified and hospitable . . . not a drunkard, not quarrelsome and no lover of money, but gentle . . . and must manage his own household well." But you priests do the opposite; you indulge in secret vices, of which no one may reform you.[2]

Cosmas insisted that the Bogomils had a political and social agenda as well as a spiritual one: "They teach their own people not to obey their masters, they revile the wealthy, hate the king, ridicule the elders, condemn the boyars, regard as vile in the sight of God those who serve the king, and forbid every serf to work for his lord."[3]

If it was in fact a movement of social protest against authority, Bogomilism seems to have condemned especially the claims of Byzantine ecclesiastical supremacy. It may thus have provided a spiritual ideology to support the national movement of Bulgars against Byzantium, though many modern scholars are quick to point out that Bogomil leaders do not seem to have supported militant acts against the enemy. Still Bogomils expressed the national Bulgar animosity to Byzantium. For example, while church buildings are the work of Satan and the places where devils dwell (and therefore the good Bogomil must never go to church), it is significant that Satan himself lives in the grandest church of all, Hagia Sophia in Constantinople.

Bogomils sent missionaries to neighboring peoples. Their priests even ventured into the heart of enemy territory. In a famous confrontation, Basil the Bogomil

---

[2]Janet Fraser, trans., from Martin Erbstösser, *Heretics in the Middle Ages* (Leipzig, 1984), p. 48.
[3]Robert Browning, trans., *Byzantium and Bulgaria: A Comparative Study across the Early Medieval Frontier* (Berkeley: University of California Press, 1975), p. 164.

entered the imperial palace in Constantinople and tried to convert the emperor Alexius Comnenus (1081–1118), who finally burned the heretic before a huge crowd in the hippodrome. In their native Bulgaria, Bogomils seem to have attracted only a small following. By their aggressive apostolizing, however, they eventually influenced twelfth- and thirteenth-century dualist heresies of the Cathars, Albigensians, and Patarins.

Photian Schisms: Rome Versus Constantinople

Meanwhile, an arguably greater threat to Christianity was the widening rift between eastern and western Christendom. The last ecumenical council accepted by both churches was the seventh, in 787. Even before this, councils had produced important rulings rejected by one part of Christendom or another. For example, the West refused to confirm the rulings of the Council in Trullo (also called *Quinisext* Synod because Byzantines considered it a complement to the fifth and sixth councils), which met in Constantinople in 692. Its official acts affirmed the Chalcedonian position that Constantinople enjoyed equal privilege with Rome. The council also permitted deacons and presbyters to marry, condemning the Roman prohibition of these marriages. In Orthodoxy today, priests still may marry. The council further attacked Roman customs, such as fasting on Saturdays in Lent, and the artistic depiction of Christ as a lamb, which was popular in the West. The *Quinisext* Synod insisted that Christ be shown in human form to emphasize the incarnation. These points of difference may not indicate major doctrinal divisions, but the acts of the council demonstrate insensitivity and hostility to western practices. When the pope rejected these decrees, Justinian II dispatched a legate to Rome with orders to deliver him to Constantinople to stand trial. In both Ravenna and Rome, the local militia was so incensed by the legate's mission that soldiers would have lynched him had the pope not urged clemency.

In fact, the doctrinal distinctions remained minor. Could priests marry, or should they remain celibate? Must the liturgy be in Latin, or may it be celebrated in vernacular languages? There was, of course, the *filioque* dispute, and only the western church believed in purgatory, an intermediate state between heaven and hell where souls cleansed themselves of lesser sins before they could enter heaven. All these were issues fiercely debated. But cultural, sociological, political, and personal differences (more than doctrinal ones) led to schism. Although Byzantines remained devoutly Christian, the Byzantine church enjoyed limited political and economic influence. The emperor ruled in Constantinople, where he selected the patriarch and could sometimes depose him. The Roman church, on the other hand, filled the vacuum left by the collapse of the western Roman Empire. The papacy developed a centralized government over which the pope exercised strong authoritarian control. He often claimed secular power and could rival secular rulers.

Tensions arose from Roman claims to universal primacy and also from arguments about influence over newly Christianized eastern Europe. A mutual intolerance and distaste for rival cultures intensified existing hostilities. Finally, of course, easterners and westerners simply could not speak with one another. The language barrier aggravated the many cultural barriers. Only an elite handful of Byzantines knew Latin, and few westerners understood Greek.

Liudprand, bishop of Cremona, left a diary of a famous encounter between the rival cultures during his embassy to Constantinople. Sent by Otto I to the court of Emperor Nicephorus I (963–969), Liudprand loathed all aspects of the civilization he encountered, from the resinated wine to court ceremonial, from the "piglike" emperor to customs officials who confiscated the silks he tried to smuggle out of the empire. For their part, the Byzantines told him that they were the true Romans. "Listen!" insisted one imperial official. "The silly blockhead of a pope does not know that the sacred Constantine transferred to this city the imperial sceptre, the senate, and all the Roman knighthood, and left in Rome nothing but vile slaves, fishermen, confectioners, poulterers, bastards, plebeians, underlings."[4]

Reciprocal disaffection and lesser religious differences led inexorably to the schism of 1054. Disagreements arose in southern Italy, where eastern and western claims met head on. Arguments focused on the old dogmatic and liturgical problems—the *filioque*, Roman fasting on Saturdays, married versus unmarried clergy, questions of primacy and jurisdiction, and especially the use of leavened or unleavened bread for communion services. Hoping to foster understanding and cooperation, Pope Leo IX dispatched Cardinal Humbert of Silva Candida to Constantinople. The rigid personalities of the papal legate and the imperious patriarch Michael Cerularius assured disastrous results. Failing to wring concessions from the patriarch, the legates deposited a bull of excommunication on the high altar at Hagia Sophia. Michael Cerularius responded in kind, and the Latin envoys barely escaped with their lives. Only in 1965 was the mutual excommunication lifted by pope and Greek patriarch.

Western Christendom: The Ottonian Empire and the Church

While Byzantium flourished in the ninth century, western Europe was reeling from the attacks of Vikings, Magyars, and Muslims. Without the unifying power of Charlemagne, Carolingian principalities disintegrated, but the Carolingian ideal of a Christian state did not die. In Germany, where Charlemagne's line ended in 911, the Ottonian dynasty succeeded the Carolingian as protectors of Christianity. In 919 Henry the Fowler, duke of Saxony, was elected king by the German nobles and greater clergy. Beginning with Henry's reign, the kingdom of Germany rose to supreme importance in western Europe for much of the next three centuries.

[4]F. A. Wright, trans., *The Works of Liudprand of Cremona* (New York: E. P. Dutton & Co., Inc., 1930.)

Henry's son, Otto I (936–973), checked feudal anarchy by using the financial and military resources of the church. He waged successful campaigns against the Hungarians/Magyars and moved into Italian territories, where he seized a rich stash of holy relics and also won royal power in 951. To symbolize his role as Charlemagne's heir, he had himself crowned king in Aix-la-Chapelle (Aachen). At Rome in 962, Pope John XII crowned him emperor. To express the mutual dependency between pope and emperor, Otto I and John XII drew up an agreement, the *Ottonianum*, suggesting papal duties to the emperor and imperial protection of papal interests. Otto held control over the church by his power to appoint bishops and abbots who owed him feudal homage. This process came to be called *lay investiture*, and it produced a crisis between church and state in the eleventh century. Initially the *Ottonianum* brought back the potent union of church and state that Charlemagne had nurtured. Otto I confirmed the vital importance of that union: "We believe that the protection of our Empire is bound up with the rising fortunes of Christian worship." [Tardif, *Cartons des rois*, no. 357; *Diplom. regum et imperatorum Germaniae*, I, Otto I, no. 366.] Otto and his heirs brought peace to northern Italy, resulting in the revival of cities, notably Venice.

A contemporary, probably a relative, of Otto has left us a precious literary record of the era. Hrotsvitha lived in the convent at Gandersheim, whose history she wrote. Her account describes visions and prophecies that inspired the foundation of the convent by the Lady Oda and her husband Duke Liudulf, great-grandparents of Emperor Otto I. Pope Sergius provided precious relics for the new foundation, the intact remains of two bishops of Rome, Anastasius and Innocent. Borrowing imagery from the gospels, Hrotsvitha described how humble swineherds saw a "dazzling radiance" of lights from the woods, pointing out the spot where the convent should be built. Her narrative here owes some inspiration to the biblical account of shepherds and the starry light that guided the wise men to the site of Jesus' birth. The pristine wooded spot, home to fauns and monsters, also borrows elements from Vergil's account of the site where Rome would rise. Such a mingling of classical and biblical elements characterized Carolingian literature, and the Ottonians inherited this tradition.

Gandersheim's cofounder, Liudulf, was an aristocrat in military service to Charlemagne's grandson, Louis, king of the Franks. Louis married a daughter of Liudulf and Oda. From its beginnings, therefore, aristocratic and royal connections set Gandersheim apart from the usual convent. Its abbesses came from the ruling family. In 947 Otto I invested the abbess with complete authority, free from episcopal or royal control. Gandersheim enjoyed direct protection of the papal see and had a representative at the imperial assembly. The convent and its properties comprised a small principality with its own courts, army, and mint. There unmarried royal women could wield power and meet intellectual challenges while living spiritually satisfying lives. The dynasty benefited, too, because these women did not marry princes whose new kinship to the royal family might make them dangerous rivals to the throne.

Except for the servants, all the women at Gandersheim were of noble birth. Some were nuns who had surrendered their fortunes and taken vows of perpetual chastity. Others, perhaps including Hrotsvitha herself, were canonesses who could keep their wealth and even maintain their own servants and libraries. Canonesses were free to entertain guests and to come and go as they pleased; they could even leave the nunnery to marry without penalty or disgrace. Hrotsvitha had perhaps spent some time at Otto's court. She had literary aspirations and wrote plays that are the first to survive after the demise of ancient classical theater. Hrotsvitha claimed that she was inventing Christian dramas to rival the sublime Roman playwright, Terence.

Hrotsvitha was a talented woman, and she enjoyed rare advantages of education and birth. For most women with monastic ambitions, the tenth and eleventh centuries were a difficult age. In this period, few convents were endowed, and women's religiosity received little encouragement. The great monastery at Cluny, itself created in the tenth century, founded dozens of monasteries for men but only one for women, a retreat for wives whose husbands had become Cluniac monks. Gandersheim provided a unique refuge for women of privilege.

The Ottonian line ended with the premature death in 1002 of Otto III, son of a Byzantine princess, at age twenty-one. Powerful nobles opposed the troubled succession of his cousin, Henry II of Bavaria (1002–1024), who also died without heir. His successor, Conrad II (1024–1039) inaugurated a new dynasty. Conrad's son Henry III (1039–56) died leaving the infant Henry IV as his heir. A minority invited difficulties; enemies felt free to flex their muscles and test the authority of regents and young ruler alike. The reign of Henry IV spawned the so-called investiture conflict, which challenged the theocratic basis of imperial power and ultimately weakened the German throne.

Meanwhile, the lands farther west, ravaged by Viking raiders and reduced to feudal estates designed for self-defense, were edging toward a revival that would later be called the last medieval renaissance or the renaissance of the twelfth century. Rapid changes occurred after 1000, as population increased, land was cleared, commerce revived, new settlements arose, and urban life reappeared. Serfdom almost vanished in France, Spain, Italy, and western Germany. Women and men enjoyed the freedom to travel on pilgrimage or crusade. Philosophers scrutinized Christian theology, and the church entered into major reform.

Normandy, France, England

While the German empire was thriving, Carolingian France suffered from Muslim and Viking threats. In 911 a desperate Carolingian king, Charles the Simple, ceded land to a Viking chief named Rollo. Charles hoped that Rollo and his Northmen would protect Paris from raids by rival Viking bands. For his part, Rollo received land that would form the core of the future duchy of Normandy, along with its principal city, Rouen. In return, Rollo and his Vikings accepted Christian baptism. Within a few decades, the versatile and highly adaptive Northmen/Normans had abandoned their old customs, language, and religion, and had become nearly indistinguishable from their French neighbors whose language they spoke and whose institutions they adopted. For an increasingly sophisticated administrative machinery, their courtiers issued documents written in the Latin of France. Men who had pillaged monasteries and cathedrals and destroyed their relics saw their sons and daughters fervently embrace Christianity. According to Norman legend, Rollo's own son, Duke William Longsword, piously harbored monastic ambitions. Rollo's great-great-great-grandson, Duke William I (1035–1087), controlled the feudal system in his duchy and limited warfare while supporting the church-sponsored peace movement. He took an active role in church councils and ecclesiastical appointments.

This William became known as the Conqueror after he took England in 1066. Like France, England had suffered from the chaos of the Viking incursions, with the attendant damage to culture and religious tradition. Under Alfred the Great (ruled 871–899) Britain finally began its revival. Alfred engineered military and political successes as well as cultural, spiritual, and religious reforms. It was Alfred who molded Britons and Anglo-Saxons into a united people, but the reconciliation of Vikings and Anglo-Saxons fell to Cnut, king of England (1016–1035) and from 1030 until his death king of Norway, too. Cnut fashioned a strong state. Despite some abuses in the English church, Christianity flourished in pre-Conquest England. Benedictine monasteries fostered learning and provided educated men for both church and government. The conquest of 1066 returned the island state to the European realm and to greater western Christendom.

The Pornocracy and the Reform Movement

By the time of the Conqueror, Christendom had seen hard times and then a brilliant revival. Under St. Nicholas I (858–867) the papacy was a powerful institution. Within twenty-five years after his death, it had plummeted to a debased condition sometimes called the *pornocracy*. When a pope died, Italian nobles and whatever Roman faction happened to be in control chose his successor. The papal office might be sold to the highest bidder. Other bishoprics throughout Christendom often suffered similar fates, being considered by local nobles as prizes available to the best schemers. In the case of Rome, because of its claims to supremacy, the scandals had broad consequences. The outrageous behavior of some popes shocked the sensibilities of Christians far and wide. Consider, for instance, the case of Pope John XII (955–964), who succeeded his father at age eighteen. A contemporary chronicle alleged that he wore himself out with sexual excesses before he turned twenty-eight. When King Otto found it politically expedient to depose John, he found no dearth of moral pretexts, including the charges that he had castrated a cardinal, toasted the devil's health, and called on Venus and Jupiter to help the dice fall in his favor.

Reform began in the monasteries. In the early Middle Ages, Benedictine monasteries had been precious centers of Christian living and education. Monasteries such as Bobbio in northern Italy, St. Gall in Switzerland, Luxeuil in France, and Wearmouth and Jarrow in England were beacons of civilization that preserved both classical and Christian learning. Charlemagne protected monasteries, but after his death, Viking, Magyar, and Muslim raids took a deadly toll. The invaders destroyed some establishments, and others fell into the hands of feudal lords who used monastic resources and sold offices to men without spiritual commitment. No longer havens of religious observance and intellectual efforts, the surviving monasteries often exploited the very societies that the prayers of devout monks were supposed to protect.

In 909 William the Pious, duke of Aquitaine, established the abbey of Cluny near Mâcon in Burgundy. In his charter of endowment, Duke William declared that Cluny should enjoy complete independence from all feudal or secular lordship. Only the pope would have authority over the new monastery; no lay lords or bishops could interfere in its affairs. The duke then renounced his own possession of and influence over Cluny. This independence and freedom from secular control would soon catapult Cluny into the center stage of the monastic reform movement.

The monastery and its foundation charter came to exert vast influence. The first two abbots, Berno (910–927) and Odo (927–942), set high standards of religious behavior. They stressed strict observance of the Rule of St. Benedict, the development of a personal spiritual life by the individual monk, and the importance of the liturgy. In the church as a whole, Cluny gradually came to stand for clerical celibacy and the suppression of simony (the buying or selling of offices or sacraments). Within a generation, neighboring monasteries sought Cluny's help and were reformed along Cluniac lines. Even Monte Cassino, the mother Benedictine monastery, entered Cluny's sphere of influence. Cluny's fifth abbot, Odilo (994–1048), established the right of Cluny's abbot to appoint and oversee the abbots of all Cluniac foundations. This made Cluny almost an order. Cluny's rise to power and influence culminated in the sixty-year reign of Abbot Hugh (1049–1109). At his death, from England to Spain and Italy, from France and Germany even to the Holy Land, hundreds of monasteries submitted to the jurisdiction of Cluny. The list grew to include nearly 1,200 houses. Sometimes the monks themselves objected to the unwelcome discipline, but support came from powerful secular rules such as Alfonso VI of Leon-Castile, who was married to Constance of Burgundy, a niece of Abbot Hugh. With such mighty allies and reforming zeal, the Cluny movement expanded beyond monasticism; it became a voice for the improvement of clerical life and for larger issues of church reform.

Cluny itself was showered with gifts, and wealth led to corruption. Late in the eleventh century, Cluniac monks adopted opulent lifestyles, threatening spiritual passion and monastic discipline. Abbots traveled with huge retinues, like the great feudal lords they were; the monks wore only the finest clothes and ate sumptuous meals. Men who became disillusioned with Cluniac decadence created new monastic orders. The Cistercians best exemplify the reforming spirit of the twelfth century. In 1098 monks fled Molesme in Burgundy and founded a new monastery in the swamps of Cîteaux. There they sought a simple and austere life on the frontiers of civilization, far from the feudal bonds of secular society and the ostentatious liturgy and luxury of Cluniac houses. Cistercian monks dedicated themselves to working uncultivated soil and living lives unencumbered by feudal gifts. By searching out wilderness, they led the way in the land reclamation of the twelfth century. In the Low Countries, Cistercians built dikes and reclaimed land from the sea. In the eastern reaches of the German empire they drained swamps. In Burgundy they planted vineyards, and on England's rocky soil, they built sheep runs.

The first Cistercians faced a difficult life of deprivation and illness. In 1112, however, Bernard of Clairvaux entered Cîteaux with thirty of his noble friends and kinsmen, and their entry gave great impetus to the movement. In the twelfth century, Cîteaux founded hundreds of monasteries and exercised great influence on European society, nurturing the high ideals of the age. The Cistercians formed a closely knit organization that could wield considerable influence, although by the end of the century wealth began to corrupt Cistercian monasticism as it had done Cluniac.

How did monks live? Monastic life varied considerably according to time and place. The early Cistercians, for instance, placed great emphasis on the physical labor of bare survival. For all monks, the liturgy held central importance. Seven times daily and once during the night, monks met to chant the psalms and offer prayers for benefactors and deceased abbots and the monks' relatives, for the welfare of the people and the blessing of the crops. To pray for God's blessings—this was a critical function of the monks in medieval society. Because the liturgy played such a crucial role in monastic life, monks invested great wealth in liturgical art and vestments and sacred vessels. They cherished precious reliquaries, gospel books, and thuribles for burning incense.

When they were not in prayer, monks performed various roles. One monk, the cellarer, supervised the peasants or lay brothers who tilled the soil. The aristocratic choir monks did not cultivate the fields themselves until the early Cistercians insisted on doing their own work. Monks kept herb gardens and prepared medicines from them. The almoner fed and cared for the neighboring poor. The cantor sang the liturgy and cared for the liturgical repertory. The sacristan looked after the sacred vessels, candles, altar cloths, vestments, and incense. The novice master trained the recruits. And a few monks copied manuscripts and wrote their own works. We know a great deal about some of these men—for example, the celebrated Norman historian Ordericus Vitalis (1075–ca. 1142). Ordericus was too extraordinary to be considered an average monk, but his recruitment is typical. He tells us that when he was only ten, his parents sent him to the abbey of St. Evroult, where he lived the rest of his life. Some men entered monasteries as adults, but until the thirteenth century, parents usually presented their children as child-oblates. The monastery offered careers for younger children of the feudal aristocracy; in turn, it served the kings and feudal lords by training administrators and scribes.

In a society that lacked the concept of governmental responsibility for social welfare, monks performed social services and ran schools and hostels. Rarely did Benedictine monasteries provide services for sick laypersons. Only in the mid-twelfth century did hospitals come to be commonly found in most western towns and many villages. Laypersons built and staffed some hospitals; others were supported by bishops or monasteries. In this period, religious orders arose specifically to assist pilgrims and provide nursing care. The Knights of St. John of Jerusalem (also known as the Knights Hospitalers) organized a huge hospital for pilgrims and crusaders in the Holy Land. Although this development came late to westerners, Byzantine hospitals were part of the philanthropic system supported by state, monastery, and bishopric from the fourth century on. At one time Constantinople alone had forty hospitals, including the well-documented institution at the Monastery of the Pantokrator, staffed by male and female physicians trained in various medical specialties.

In yet another area, the monastic influence on society moved beyond prayer to action. Monks inspired the peace movement of the church. According to the monastic theory of the Three Orders—those who work, those who pray, and those who fight— each order provided services for the others. In his biography of St. Gerard of Aurillac, Abbot Odo of Cluny expounded the belief that warriors were duty-bound to defend the helpless and the church. The idea was expanded by bishops in a series of councils, beginning near the end of the tenth century in Burgundy. There in southern France, part of the old Carolingian Empire, chaos reigned, with local lords even attacking churches and peasants in their fields. The council put under ecclesiastical protection the poor, priests, and monks; it safeguarded places too, peasant fields and sacred buildings. Any men who attacked these persons or places were anathematized, that is, they were denied any contact with Christians. In 1027 another council enjoined warriors to observe the Truce of God and refrain from fighting during specified periods, or suffer excommunication. To keep the Lord's Day holy, no one could attack an enemy from Saturday evening until Monday morning. Soon councils increased the days of truce, adding Thursday, Friday, and Saturday in commemoration of Christ's Passion, then including major saints' days, the seasons of Advent (the four weeks before Christmas) and Lent (the six weeks before Easter). By the mid-eleventh century, Duke William of Normandy had thrown his support to the Peace of God and Truce of God, forcing his vassals to support the movement.

These precepts may not have held up often in practice, but they influenced public opinion of Christian behavior. In advancing ideals of a just society, the church also moved to limit slavery by opposing the enslaving of Christians. This was a rather late and fitful development, however. Early Christians inherited the justification for slavery from the Greco-Roman past. Slaves (along with women and children) were considered intellectually inferior to free men. Following Aristotle, St. Augustine argued in *The City of God*: "The justice of masters dominating slaves is clear, because those who excel in reason should excel in power." Slavery thus continued into the early Middle Ages. In fact our word "slave" comes from the name "Slav," suggesting the widespread trading of war captives from Slavic territories. Monasteries kept slaves, including sometimes female weavers and domestics. The numbers declined in the later Middle Ages, however, partly in response to condemnations of the church, such as that of a ruling by a London council in 1102, forbidding "the ignoble trade whereby men are sold like beasts."

The religious revival of the eleventh century, begun in monastic reform, finally reached the papacy itself. Some support came from Otto I and his successors in the German empire, who fought against simony and clerical marriage and protected church lands from lay lords who would usurp them, but they would not threaten their own interests by surrendering lay control. The monks and reforming bishops would have to turn to the pope for leadership.

After a century of decadence, the papacy responded to the spiritual movement. Some evidence suggests direct influence from Cluny. There was, for instance, the friendship of Abbot Odilo of Cluny (994–1048) and the German Emperor Henry III, who supported the reforms. The reforming Pope Gregory VII (1073–1085) seems to have been a monk, and he expressed an empathy for Cluniac reforms. Urban II (1088–1099) had himself been a Cluniac monk and prior. In any case, Cluny and the papacy shared similar reforming goals that included providing moral leadership and leadership in codifying church law and doctrine, strengthening the hierarchy of bishops and authorizing the college of cardinals to elect as well as to advise popes, and enforcing priestly chastity and excluding women from the priest's household as wives or concubines.

It is likely that a majority of priests were married or living with women in the eleventh century, despite papal condemnation. These priests were called *nicolaites* from a passage in the Book of Revelation condemning Christians who practiced pagan sexual customs. To compel priests to be celibate, reform propaganda focused on the sacramental argument that priests who celebrated the Eucharist should not profane themselves by engaging in sexual activity. Privately, the popes had pragmatic material concerns that married priests were using church resources to care for their wives and children, and even bequeathing churches to them. Priest's sons often inherited the parish ministry of their fathers. Compelled to care for their families on stipends meant to support only one man, some parish priests sold sacramental services, so that people had to pay for baptisms, masses, marriages, and absolution of sins. The reformers felt they could remove the need for this simony by eliminating married priests. For their part, many clergy resisted the papal commands, claiming marriage as their ancient right. Some angry priests even threatened to murder bishops who were trying to enforce the papal decree.

Pope Leo IX (1049–1054) began the reforms in earnest. As bishop of Toul and a kinsman of Emperor Henry III (who had appointed him to the Holy See), he could safely flout the Roman factions. During his procession to Rome to accept the papal staff, he had dressed as a pilgrim. As pope, Leo traveled throughout Italy, Germany, and France, holding synods condemning injustice to the poor, simony, nicolaitism, and violence. People came to call him the "Apostolic Pilgrim." He was a humble man whose high moral character lent authority to his decrees. During his reign, Leo prepared the *Collection of Seventy-Four Titles*, a compilation of ecclesiastical law based on papal letters and decrees of councils emphasing papal authority.

Leo IX bequeathed the reform movement to his successors. Under Nicholas II (1058–1061), a council met in the venerable church of St. John Lateran in 1059 to preserve papal independence from Roman factions and lay interference. The Lateran Council of 1059 authorized the college of cardinals as sole body to elect new popes. The college still has that power today. In the Middle Ages the cardinals were about twenty-five priests of major churches in and around Rome. They served as papal assistants and advisors as well as electors. In 1586, their number was set at seventy, and in the 1960s, Pope Paul VI expanded their ranks to include an international body.

The Lateran Council asserted the independence of the papacy from quarrelling Roman factions. This was not entirely a popular view with nobles or with young Emperor Henry IV, who believed it his own duty to protect the governance of the church. German emperors had encouraged monastic and clerical purity, but the success of the ensuing moral reform gave Nicholas II and Gregory VII the commanding respect that enabled them to take political power to themselves. Emperor and pope, once allies, would find themselves locked in a struggle for authority and control.

The papal reform movement of the eleventh century is often named Gregorian after Pope Gregory VII (1073–1085). This is not a precisely accurate title, because the movement was well along when Gregory ascended the papal throne and it continued after his death. Gregory was a critical figure in sustaining the reform, however, and directing it to a new revolutionary phase. His passionately held ideas and bold acts produced substantial political and social consequences.

We know little about Gregory's early life. He was born to an obscure family in Tuscany and christened Hildebrand. Scholars have sometimes focused on his social origins to explain his views and actions. Most other medieval popes came from the aristocracy and felt close bonds with their aristocratic and royal kinsmen. Hildebrand, on the other hand, spent his youth in a Roman monastery and then lived in the entourage of reform popes, beginning with Leo IX. He became such a prominent papal advisor that, on the death of Alexander II (1061–1073), an enthusiastic Roman crowd enthroned him pope without bothering to wait for a canonical election. As Gregory VII, he swiftly moved the papacy from moral and clerical reform to political action. Gregorian reform was based on the assumption that people can attack the evil practices of this world and make the world closer to God's wish for humankind; it held the faith that the world can be the home of good and moral actions. Gregory believed that to produce this ideal society, the Christian world must acknowledge the pope as supreme ruler, who could summon secular lords, even kings and emperors, to do his bidding in the service of this higher good. This concept of papal responsibility and power directly challenged the authority of kings and princes.

Gregory held the deeply felt conviction that God commanded people through the pope, who was God's regent on earth, free of all judgment except God's. In Gregory's view, only a pope could wear the Roman imperial insignia or have his feet kissed by all princes. For their part, secular princes had a sacred duty to maintain peace and order and in this way to facilitate the Christian journey to the heavenly city. Kings were obligated to act righteously; if they did not, the people need not obey them. This presented a revolutionary theory, especially along with its corollary: that God granted to popes the duty to oversee the kings' behavior and depose them if necessary.

In March 1075, Gregory promulgated his ideas in a document known as the *Dictatus papae*. For centuries popes had articulated this ideal of kingship, but Gregory determined to put it into practice. Gregory's decree meant the end of lay investiture (i.e., the selection of churchmen by secular authorities), a practice the church had often protested. The so-called Investiture Conflict focused on a single privilege, but investiture represented the larger struggle between papal and secular authority.

The feudal structure had given some pretext for lay investiture. Throughout feudal realms, secular lords typically numbered among their loyal vassals the bishops or abbots whose land fell within their domain. It seemed natural to lords that they should appoint their own vassals, especially when these same churchmen were critical members of feudal administrations. Where else could lords find literate men to keep their records and write documents? Furthermore, the secular princes were the chief patrons of local parish clergy. Should they not enjoy religious privileges in exchange for their patronage? Kings had even more potent arguments against papal claims. Anointed by God and reigning by divine right, the king symbolized Christ the King; by his consecration, he represented in himself both Christ's divine nature and Jesus' human nature. Because of this, the king demanded the right to be both spiritual and temporal ruler.

From the pope's viewpoint, on the other hand, the western tradition of lay domination compromised the sacred church. When secular landlords controlled church property and appointed priests, they often profited at the church's expense, selling offices or giving away lands to their family and friends. Church property and revenues disappeared, and unsuitable men accepted offices for which they had no spiritual inclination. Honorable priests might even resort to simony to keep the church operating once the resources were depleted.

Did the king have power over his subjects, or did the pope? In 1075 Gregory convened a council at Rome that published decrees against nicolaitism and simony and issued the first decrees against lay investiture, with penalties for all parties in the transaction. Guilty clerics were to lose their office, laymen to face excommunication. The most powerful rulers of the Christian West rebelled: the French king Philip I, the German emperor Henry IV, and William the Conqueror, king of England and duke of Normandy. Henry responded with the greatest anger. Although he and his predecessors had strongly supported the reform movement, this latest step threatened his Holy Roman Empire, a huge realm governed only with the administrative help of churchmen, most of whom he had chosen and invested. He could ill afford to relinquish this right or the authority over his subjects. He flaunted his intransigence by appointing three bishops to Italian sees over which the pope claimed authority.

Gregory and Henry exchanged angry letters. Gregory upbraided the king for disobeying God by disobeying the pope. Henry responded in a letter beginning, "Henry King not by usurpation, but by the pious ordination of God, to Hildebrand, now not Pope, but false monk." In January 1076 at the Diet of Worms, Henry and most of his bishops withdrew allegiance from the pope.

The lines were drawn. Gregory excommunicated Henry and the bishops loyal to him. He released the German nobles from obeying their king and encouraged insurrection. Pleased to display their piety by ridding themselves of a mighty lord, the nobles eagerly supported the pope's wishes. They even elected a new king, the German prince Rudolf of Rheinfelden, whose authority Gregory confirmed. Threatened with the defection of his princes, Henry played out the drama brilliantly in his famous journey to the northern Italian castle at Canossa, where the pope had taken refuge. In the middle of a bitter winter (1076–1077) Henry crossed the Alps and then waited before the castle gates, seeking forgiveness. According to tradition, Henry stood barefoot in the snow for three days. This scene of Henry's submission is commonly interpreted as a victory for papal power. In fact, the king outmaneuvered the pope, whose priestly duty compelled him to forgive the penitent sinner and lift the sentence of excommunication. This freed Henry's allies to rally around him again and angered the pope's German supporters, who felt betrayed.

On the one hand, the papacy had demonstrated its power over secular rulers, who would rarely venture serious rebellion for another 200 years. On the other hand, the questions of lay investiture and the rights and duties of Christian kings remained an open wound. Successive popes and Henry's heirs continued to quarrel. Gregory even excommunicated Henry a second time, in 1080, but now public opinion shifted to support Henry, who kept the loyalty of his lords. This enabled the emperor to invade Italy and take Rome. Gregory VII died in exile in 1085, and his successors retaliated by pressing Henry's sons to rebellion.

The quarrel with the German emperor took center stage in European affairs, but the papacy struggled against the kings of England and France as well. William the Conqueror practiced lay investiture in England and relied on bishops as crucial barons. His sons, William Rufus and Henry I, continued to quarrel with the papacy until 1107. The French king, Philip I (1060–1108), profited from the sale of church offices and also feared an independent church in his realm. Philip's adulterous marriage, however, provoked his most bitter contest with the papacy, consigning investiture to a less conspicuous role.

The English king, Henry I, agreed to terms in 1107. At last in 1122 the papacy and the German emperor—then Henry V, son of Henry IV—reached the same compromise with the Concordat of Worms. According to this agreement, canon law would dictate the selection of bishops by the clergy, but the emperor or his delegate won the right to be present. Although lay rulers would no longer invest the bishop with the episcopal ring and staff, they would continue to invest a bishop or abbot with the symbols of their temporal power. The emperor's continuing right to accept or refuse feudal homage from the new bishop offered some power of veto. This compromise failed to resolve whether king or pope ruled supreme, but it brought a formal end to the contest.

Fifty years of struggle created serious social and political consequences. In Germany the winners were the feudal aristocracy, who gained vigor while the emperor and pope feuded. Along with acquiring rights from the emperors, the nobles also came to exercise tighter control over the peasants and serfs in their domains. The investiture controversy was directly responsible for the localism and feudal independence that weakened and divided Germany in the late Middle Ages. Not until the nineteenth century did a strong, united Germany emerge. In France the consequences were quite different. Because each cathedral chapter (the organization of priests who administered the cathedral) claimed the right to elect its own bishop, the great nobility found it increasingly difficult to award these posts to their relatives. Bishops tended to come more and more from the minor nobility, who posed a smaller threat to the French crown.

The papacy emerged a winner from the long struggle. It was apparent that popes could humble even emperors. More than that, the contest had compelled the papacy to centralize church government in a brief time, consolidating papal rule over the ecclesiastical organization. This same consolidation and reform had a dark side: a hardening of attitude and practice toward dissent, whether by defiant king or noble or cleric, or by heretic or Muslim or Jew. In no part of Europe did Jews make up more than 5 percent of the population, but even these small numbers threatened medieval concepts of a homogeneous Christian society. Jews were easy scapegoats in times of trouble; when religious passions rose, Jews could become their victims. So, for instance, in 1096 unruly mobs of German crusaders systematically slaughtered Jews in one Rhineland town after another before heading east. Some bishops tried to protect the Jews but to no avail.

For good or ill, the controversy energized all of western Christendom, as laity were drawn into the pamphlet war and compelled to take sides in matters of Christian policy and belief. This broad participation awakened an intense piety that found expression in the First Crusade (1095–1099) and in the religious enthusiasm of the twelfth century, with its focus on love as the ultimate worthy pursuit. In the new emotionalism of the twelfth century, troubadours sang of "new love" or "true love," which we sometimes call courtly love, a passion that could be both carnal and spiritual. Religious passion produced outpourings of love for God and a rebirth of the cult of the Virgin.

Popular Religion

Even before the Third Ecumenical Council had authorized her title as Mother of God (431), Mary had enjoyed special honor with Christians. The cults of other saints arose or flourished near their relics, but all Christendom venerated Mary. It is true that Constantinople claimed to possess her robe, and Chartres, the nightdress she wore when she gave birth to Jesus. Other sites displayed for pilgrims fragments of her veil and even drops of her milk. Christians came to believe, however, that she had been assumed into heaven, leaving no relics. Her universal appeal made cult centers spring up everywhere.

The eleventh century saw increasing interest in Jesus the man, and so in his human mother. Prayers addressed him as "God, son of Mary." The movement met resistance from ecclesiastical leaders who had inherited the deep-rooted notion that woman was Eve and that feminine influence was treacherous. But in popular expressions of piety, Christian worshippers sometimes elevated Mary to a loftier emotional level than the masculine Trinity, inspiring Gautier de Coinci (ca. 1177–1236), a Benedictine friar who wrote fanciful and pious songs to Mary, to proclaim, "God changed sex!" Twelfth-century monks began insisting on her own immaculate conception. The influential Bernard of Clairvaux (1090–1153) attacked this new idea but without success. The people praised Mary as queen of heaven, *Regina coeli*, and by the early twelfth century, artists were depicting her as crowned by her son. The thirteenth century was yet to witness the climax of her cult, when Mary aroused spiritual passion just as the courtly lady inspired her lover's devotion. In the metrical patterns of Latin church hymns, Peire Cardenal (1180–1278) wrote a song to the Virgin, using words commonly heard in troubadour lyrics to a beloved lady:

Vera vergena, Maria,
vera vida, vera fes,
vera vertatz, vera via,
vera vertutz, vera res,
vera maire, ver' amia,
ver' amors, vera merces;
per ta vera merce sia
qu'eret en me tos heres!

True virgin, Mary,
true life, true faith,
true truth, true way,
    true virtue, true thing,
true mother, true friend/lover
    true love, true mercy:
grant by your true mercy
    that your heir inherit me![5]

[5]René Lavaud, ed., *Poésies Complètes du Troubadour Peire Cardenal* (Toulouse, France: Edouard Privat, 1957). Unpublished translation by Emily Albu Hanawalt.

The church was compelled to embrace this enthusiasm. Within Bernard's own Cistercian order, all churches came to be dedicated to the Virgin.

Great church festivals arose to commemorate events in Mary's life: the Annunciation, the Visitation (to her cousin Elizabeth, mother of John the Baptist), Candlemas (recalling the Virgin's purification; the day when candles are blessed for sacred use), the Assumption, and eventually, the Immaculate Conception (celebrating Mary's freedom from the taint of original sin). Interest spread to include her family, notably embracing the cult of her mother, St. Anne.

Eastern Christians revered Mary with increasing enthusiasm, too. Daily liturgical acclamations declared her "More honorable than the Cherubim, and more glorious beyond compare than the Seraphim." After the demise of iconoclasm, Byzantines took a fresh look at the Virgin, stressing her humanity and accessibility. Beginning in the tenth century, the theme of her intercession finally found a distinctive iconography that is more passionate and more loving than earlier static forms. The earliest known images in the new style are votive icons from tenth-century Cappadocia in central Asia Minor, where they are frequently found on the south wall of churches. The pose became common. The famous Vladimir icon of the twelfth century shows this maternal sentiment as human love meets the divine.

The increased spirituality of the age, along with broadened horizons and commerce, encouraged pilgrimage. Western Christians found a new incentive to visit holy sites, which began to offer indulgences to shorten the time the pilgrim would have to spend in purgatory. The first recorded pilgrim to the northern Spanish shrine of St. James, Santiago de Compostella, arrived in 950. St. James came to symbolize the *Reconquista*—the gradual reconquest of Spain from the Muslims—and became a popular pilgrimage goal, along with Italian sites of Rome, the Church of St. Nicholas at Bari, and Gargano. Westerners even risked the journeys to relic-laden Constantinople and Jerusalem.

Relics were precious sacred items and also valuable assets to a shrine or church. A vigorous trade developed in inventing, altering, and stealing relics. Sometimes duplicate relics caused embarrassment or confusion. Toulouse already claimed the body of St. James when a Spanish bishop found the saint's bones in the early ninth century. To counter conflicting assertions, a twelfth-century guidebook to Compostella insisted that the bones proved to be immovable, so the high altar of the cathedral was built above the intact remains. In another case, three monasteries claimed to hold the body of the Welsh St. Teilo, who had ruled them all. It was decided that each had genuine relics because the saint had prevented violence among his communities by producing three authentic sets of himself.

Saints and their relics, pilgrimage and hope of heavenly reward worked their way deep into the consciousness of medieval men and women. Christianity offered hope for the life to come and meaning in their harsh and precarious earthly lives, touching virtually all elements of their everyday existence. From birth to death, the lives of peasants revolved around the village church, where infants were baptized, couples were married, and the bereaved prayed for the souls of their dead, who were buried in the church cemetery. The central event in religious experience was the liturgy of the Eucharist, the re-creation of the Last Supper. In the medieval West, people called this service the mass, from the priest's dismissal at its close, "ite, missa est" ("go, [the meeting] is dismissed"). Every Sunday and holy day, all the people in the village stood at mass. Especially pious folks might attend daily, though they did not necessarily stay for the entire service in Latin, a language understood by few. Great Christian festivals—Easter, Christmas, Pentecost—and the numerous saints' days dominated the calendar and defined the passing of time.

Village social life revolved around the church building. Inside, people met to reconcile differences, solemnize oaths, or ratify treaties. Circuit judges held court on the church porch. Fairs, usually opened on church festivals, flourished in the church-yard, as did feasts to celebrate baptisms, weddings, and funerals. The priest was an important member of the community. Often the only literate person in the village, he played a critical role as protector of the peasants by making their contracts with merchants and tax collectors.

The culture of medieval people was Christianity. Christianity gave them a sense of security, belonging, and meaning. But most could not read and so had scanty exposure to details or subtleties not preached by clergy in vernacular homilies. In a traditional society that passed on beliefs and customs from one generation to the next, most of Christendom shared a profound faith but one that had regional variation in folk practices and often significant variation from official teachings. The rituals of popular religion sometimes preserved and cherished elements of pagan rites. For instance, folks often put salt on the tongue of a child at baptism in order to chase away demons; pagan Roman sacrifices had used salt, which had also symbolized purity to the Jews. And though clergy often repeated the statement of Pope Gregory I permitting a woman to enter the church immediately after childbirth, ancient superstitions and Old Testament laws of purification conspired to keep the "unclean" woman away for forty days; only then could she enter for the ritual of "churching" or the "benediction of a woman entering church after childbirth." Sometimes magic and ritual directly challenged Christian practice, as when young people defied interdict to perform masked dances in the village cemetery.

Economic Recovery of Europe: The Rise of Towns and Commerce

Village life in medieval Christendom changed only slowly from one generation to the next. In the eleventh century, however, Europe was entering a period of revolutionary social change leading to the rise of towns and the origins of a new commercial class. From the tenth to the fourteenth centuries, no major plague assailed Europe. In the century after 1080, mild weather blessed England, France, and Germany. The more hospitable climate led to prosperity and growth in population.

Some of the new towns grew up around cathedrals or monasteries to offer services to the religious establishments. Whatever the original reasons for the town's origins, it began to attract peasants seeking respite from the burdens of their old lives. Gradually a law evolved promising freedom for the serf who stayed in the town for a year and a day. In addition to freedom, towns offered more diversity than the countryside. By the late eleventh century, many towns had Jewish residents who settled near one another and near their synagogue. Merchant guilds and craft guilds appeared, offering men and sometimes women the opportunity for commercial profit. As might be expected, hostilities often developed between the peasants and townspeople, and the church might have been wary of the town at first, too. But early Christianity had been an urban phenomenon, and the church proved it could adjust to the changing social setting. No longer were nobles and princes the only ones who could provide generous endowments for buildings and acts of charity. The growing wealth from crafts and business provided new benefactors.

The Meeting of Christians, Muslims, and Jews in Spain, Norman Sicily, and the Holy Land

While the Christian flock was expanding from within, the borders of Christendom were growing, too, with the *Reconquista* in Spain. This heroic era demanded military men, and it catapulted some like El Cid (Rodrigo Diaz de Vivar, 1043–1099) to fame and glory. The expectation of military expansion provided only a small part of the motive for fighting. For Christian Europe, the Spanish reconquest offered an exhilarating crusade, forerunner of the crusades to Jerusalem. Troubadour lyrics promised a "washing place" nearer than the Holy Land, a battleground where sins were washed clean in the blood of Christian struggle against the infidel.

The Spanish frontier provided the opportunities for social mobility that traditionally accompany a frontier society. Throughout the Islamic occupation, Spain had also enjoyed a long history of tolerance among Mozarabs (Arabized Christians) for their Muslim lords. The Christian liberators brought a zealous hatred for the infidel, however. With the capture of Toledo in 1085 by Alfonso VI of Castile (1065–1109) and the end of Muslim rule in most of Spain and Portugal by 1200, Mozarabs pleaded for toleration but to no avail. The invading conquerors transformed the chief mosque of Toledo into a cathedral. Active Cluniac influence led the newly arrived Christians to substitute the Roman rite for the native Mozarabic liturgy, which was condemned. The attitudes of Christian and Muslim hardened.

Indigenous Spanish traditions suffered, but still the Iberian peninsula remained fertile soil for the meeting of Christian, Muslim, and Jewish culture. Islamic intermediaries preserved Greek learning for the Latin West. An important school of translation flourished in Toledo, giving special attention to scientific and mathematical documents. A famous abbot of Cluny, Peter the Venerable, commissioned Spanish scholars to make a Latin translation of the Koran and other Muslim texts. Important contributions also came from Jewish scholars, who knew Latin, Hebrew, and Arabic. Until his family was forced to wander to escape persecution, the greatest commentator on the Torah, Moses Maimonides (1135 or 1138–1204) spent his childhood in Cordoba. The fertility of the Spanish cultural mix, where the three major religions of the medieval West had intimate contact with one another, enriched even European music. Spanish Moors introduced to western culture new song forms and new instruments.

In southern Italy and Sicily, Normans nourished similar cross-cultural contacts, with similar results. The Norman kingdom of Sicily imitated Byzantium and imported Byzantine artisans to build churches and create mosaics. Sicilian kings ruled and even dressed not like the dukes of Normandy but like the Byzantine emperors they aspired to be. Eastern and western Christendom, Judaism, and Islam met in Sicily, and their meeting further expanded the mental and cultural horizons of western Europe and stimulated intellectual and cultural awakening, theological development, the rise of the universities, and enlightenment. Shipwrecked on Sicily in 1184, a Spanish Muslim named Ibn Jubayr marveled at the varieties of religious expression freely tolerated at the court. He reported that all the pages were Muslims, who prayed to Allah without royal reprisals. When Roger II found his concubines and pages praying to Allah after a frightening earthquake, he allegedly said, "Let each of you pray to the God he adores; he who has faith in his God will feel peace in his heart."[7]

At the end of the eleventh century, a revitalized western Christendom exuded energy and self-confidence. Cluniac and Cistercian reforms had made monasteries the cultural centers of Europe, nurturers of spirituality and rich ceremony, art, and architecture. The moral revival of the papacy had bred a political resurgence that strengthened the church bureaucracy and centralized authority. In 1095 Pope Urban II summoned both his moral and his political authority to call for a crusade to recover Jerusalem from the Turks. Knights and princes, peasants and churchmen mustered to take the cross.

Crusaders to the east found a Byzantine empire weakened by the civil unrest that followed the reign of Basil the Bulgar-Slayer (1025) and the subsequent death of Basil's brother, Constantine (1028), who left no male heir. Shattered by internal quarrels, in one year (1071) Byzantium lost Bari, the final outpost in Italy, to the Normans and suffered a more ominous defeat against Seljuq Turks on the eastern frontier. Following their victory at Manzikert, Turks overran Asia Minor, the heartland of Byzantium, and camped across the Bosphorus from Constantinople. A ca-

---

[7]R. J. C. Broadhurst, trans., *The Travels of the Jubayr* (London: Jonathan Cape, 1952). This work is the chronicle of a medieval Spanish Moor, who journeyed to the Egypt of Saladin, the holy cities of Arabia and Baghdad, the city of the Caliphs, the Latin kingdom of Jerusalem, and the Norman kingdom of Sicily.

pable military ruler, Alexius Comnenus (1081–1118), finally ascended the throne by coup d'état and methodically began to push the frontier back across Asia Minor. When Alexius requested the aid of western mercenaries, however, he got—against his will—the First Crusade. In battles to restore the Holy Land to Christendom, East and West would meet again, intensifying old hostilities.

Part Three

The Late Middle Ages and the Reformations of the Sixteenth Century

Carter Lindberg

Chapter 15

THE BLOOM OF THE TWELFTH CENTURY

Even today, some seven centuries after they were begun, the cathedrals of Europe continue to fascinate, awe, and inspire almost everyone who sees them. It is not just tourists or romantic lovers of the past who find these monuments so capturing. Students of medieval life and society find in them the figurative as well as the literal centerpiece of medieval culture in bloom. It is not just that the cathedral symbolizes the identity of the church with the whole of medieval society. The harmonious proportions of length and width and height; the brilliantly colored windows and the light they allow to play upon the frescos, statues, and carved stonework; the interior space, the graceful lattices of flying buttresses, and not least of all, the soaring towers—the whole a symphony in stone—make these reactions possible. All these characteristics of the cathedral symbolize the blooming of medieval society's aspiration toward the heavenly city.

By the late twelfth century, the storm and stress that had marked the struggles of western Christendom's pilgrimage from St. Augustine's fifth-century penning of *The City of God* to the age of the cathedrals had abated. The violence and chaos of the first feudal age with its spasmodic social order, internal cruelties exacerbated by Viking invasions, hardscrabble existence of high and low in the great forest wildernesses, and declining population had sown the seeds for this second feudal age. Medieval life was now not only beginning to hold its own but even had a quickened pulse. What seem to us to be simple, technological advances—such as iron farm implements, the balanced and sharp scythe, the horse collar, and the iron plowshare—spurred agriculture and consequently population among the people of that time. The water and wind mills, as well as an effective harness for draft animals, relieved some of the strains on human muscles. And knowledge of building techniques led to increased number of masonry structures such as bridges and buildings

259

with windows. But lest we wax too romantic about the high Middle Ages, we need only recall that as late as the seventeenth century, Thomas Hobbes (1588–1679) described life as "nasty, brutish, and short." On a superficial level, we might recall that soap did not come into much use until the twelfth century. Camelot was more smells and garbage than sanitized fairy tale. Kings and nobles traveled from castle to castle not only because without effective communication systems they had to personally appear in their lands, but also because they and their retinues used up an area's produce and left piles of refuse. Most people did not have the luxury of moving on. They lived mainly on cereals and cabbage. Their homes, such as they were, were small, dark, and damp. An open fire for cooking provided some heat in the winter, but mostly it provided smoke that filled the chimney-less huts from the roof down to about head height. Infant mortality was astoundingly high. Most medieval people never had the opportunity to contemplate having a "midlife crisis" because they had fully shouldered adult responsibilities of family and work by the time in life at which our present-day youth are asking to learn how to drive. The key to survival was strength. By our standards, most lives were extremely insecure, marginal, impotent, and brief.

This brings us back to our opening image of the cathedral and the churchly culture it symbolizes. The attraction of the cathedral was that it broke into the threatening space and time of this world of feeble struggle and pointed beyond it to the security and stability of the heavenly city. It is not surprising that medieval humankind at the mercy of natural and social forces largely beyond its control and understanding should yearn for peace and rest. The great architect of medieval mentality, the north African bishop, St. Augustine (354–430), had already expressed this in his *Confessions* when he wrote of God: "You made us for yourself, and our hearts are restless until they rest in you." Augustine had continually hammered home the theme that this world is not our true home and that we are pilgrims on the way to the heavenly city. Thus the great medieval theme of pilgrimage carried within it seeds of alienation and introspection that easily took root in a harsh world. If this world was at all to be outfitted to be a suitable vehicle for human pilgrimage to the beyond, it would have to be linked and patterned on the heavenly city. Thus in ritual, art, architecture, and both political and religious thought, people strove to create an image of an eternal world within a world of change.

The Cathedral of the Intellect

Difficult as it may be for us to understand, one of the most exciting discoveries for the medieval thinker was logic. Logic became *the* exciting intellectual discipline because it was an instrument for imposing order on a chaotic world. The medieval person perceived nature as a realm of supernatural forces, demonic and otherwise, over which he or she had no control. The worlds of politics, economics, law, language, and society itself were similarly disordered and intractable to comprehension. But logic, however little at first, began to open a window to an orderly and systematic view of the world. The whole process of simplification and arrangement of material was a revelation of the powers of the mind. And it provided a sense that there was order residing behind the bewildering complexity of apparently unrelated observations and experiences.

The man reputed to be the first teacher of logic in medieval Europe was Gerbert of Aurillac (ca. 940–1003), later Pope Sylvester II (999–1003). Gerbert became a master at the cathedral school in Reims and there set forth a substantial part of the logical works of Aristotle and Boethius. From Gerbert through the twelfth century, the major intellectual task was the digestion of Aristotle's logic. By the thirteenth century, Aristotelian logic had become the main feature of undergraduate studies at both Paris and Oxford. This ideal of ordering all knowledge into a coherent whole was the stimulus for the development of universities, comprehensive expositions of knowledge known as *summae*, and a particular method of thinking that came to be known as scholasticism because it was developed in the schools.

There was such an incredible blossoming of creative thinking in this period that it is often termed the renaissance of the twelfth century even though the period included is from about 1050 to 1250. Three men in particular personify the intellectual and cultural ferment and contributions of this period: St. Anselm (1033–1109), Peter Abelard (1079–1142), and St. Bernard of Clairvaux (1090–1153). Each in his own way was vitally involved in every aspect of his culture, and all three forcefully put the lie to the modern prejudice that scholasticism was an ivory tower abstraction from "real" life.

St. Anselm

Anselm was born in the small town of Aosta, at the foot of the St. Bernard pass on the Italian side of the Alps. Little is known of his family other than that they appear to have been nobility of declining fortune. After the death of his mother in his early twenties, Anselm, who had some quarrel with his father, left Aosta and never returned. After some time in southern France, Anselm was drawn to the monastery of Bec in Normandy by the intellectual renown of its prior, Lanfranc. He did not go to Bec to become a monk but to learn the new disciplines of grammar and logic. His conversion to the Benedictine Rule (the norm for medieval monasticism derived from St. Benedict of Nursia in the sixth century) did not at all diminish his questing mind. At the age of twenty-six, Anselm became a monk at Bec, where he stayed until he was sixty. The last sixteen years of his life were in public and political service as the archbishop of Canterbury, a service he had desparately tried to avoid.

Anselm became archbishop of Canterbury in circumstances obviously beyond his control in every respect. He was visiting England on business for his monastery.

His reputation for piety and knowledge was well known. The most secular ruler of England up to that time, William Rufus, had kept the archbishopric open as a means of using its revenues for his own purposes. At this time of Anselm's presence in England, however, William Rufus believed he was mortally ill and that in light of an impending eternity it was time to make amends with the church and appoint an archbishop. Anselm was the choice of the bishops and the king's councillors, but he refused. A great scene ensued in the king's chamber with councillors, friends, bishops, and the king alternately entreating and threatening Anselm to consent. Finally, at the end of their patience, they thrust the bishop's staff into his hand, but he refused to hold it. Failing to wrench open his hand, they held the staff by force against his closed hand and literally carried him off to the church. Anselm later described the scene in a letter to his monks at Bec: "It would have been difficult to make out whether madmen were dragging along one in his senses, or sane men a madman, save that they were chanting, and I, pale with amazement and pain, looked more like one dead than alive."[1] The king, by the way, recovered only to be assassinated a few years later.

Anselm is not remembered because of the unusual story of his entry into the episcopacy, however. Rather, the story is remembered because of Anselm. Anselm was a thinker and logician of unparalleled power and originality in his time. Ever since, he has been known as the "father of scholasticism." The static mentality and the social holding operations, the "survival mentality," of previous generations were replaced by him with a rousing search for new avenues and possibilities for understanding and living life. To be sure, peasants in their huts, knights on their chargers, and many of his fellow monks in their cells did not know, or if they did, could not follow all his logic. But he symbolized a new energy and a new questing that vitalized succeeding generations. This is apparent in his theological program: *fides quaerens intellectum* ("faith seeking understanding").

This quest to know and to understand is expressed in Anselm's arguments for the existence of God and for the necessity of the incarnation. His originality and power are evident in his dissatisfaction with his own first effort to prove logically the existence of God, his *Monologion*.[2] Even here in his first work, two qualities set Anselm apart from his predecessors. One is that he departs from the medieval slavishness to the process of collecting, arranging, examining, and harmonizing authorities. The task of science is not merely to repeat the words of others. The other, related development is that science, in this case theology, is rooted in meditation. Anselm's emphasis on theology as meditation promoted a certain freedom in inquiry because it allowed mental exploration without scholastic debate.

The long, clumsy, and complicated argument of the *Monologion* failed to satisfy

[1]R. W. Church, *Saint Anselm* (New York: Macmillan & Co., 1870), p. 102.
[2]For this and Anselm's other writings mentioned below, see S. N. Deane, trans., *St. Anselm: Basic Writings* (LaSalle, IL: Open Court Publishing Company, 1962).

Anselm's desire for a logical and esthetic exposition, just as theoretical physicists today sense that an argument or theorem remains unrefined and inadequate if it is not esthetically simple. Anselm's desire for a simple argument that did not need other proofs for its support was fulfilled by a sudden inspiration after much meditation. In the words of his biographer: "Behold, one night during Matins, the grace of God shone in his heart and the matter became clear to his understanding, filling his whole being with immense joy and jubilation."[3]

The *Proslogion* ("ontological argument") is simply the brief exposition of the conception provided by faith that God "is that than which nothing greater can be conceived." Even the fool (Ps. 14:1) who says there is no God understands this statement. Thus, what is understood must exist at least in his understanding. But "that than which nothing greater can be conceived" cannot exist merely in understanding, for then it would not be that than which no greater can be thought, for it is greater to exist in fact and not merely in the mind. Hence, that than which no greater can be conceived exists both in the mind and in reality. The subtle simplicity of this argument is that conceptions of God that do not include God's existence are inferior conceptions. Although this argument has been criticized on various grounds ever since it was proposed, it has never ceased to fascinate logicians and philosophers.

Theology also includes biography. Anselm's arguments for the existence of God develop in the context of his meditative life as monk and teacher in the monastery of Bec. His famous treatise on why God became incarnate in a person, *Cur deus homo*, was begun just before he went into self-imposed exile in 1097 because he would not consent to William Rufus's exploitation of the church. While in Italy, waiting for papal support, Anselm withdrew to a mountain village to escape the summer heat and there finished his treatise.

In the years after becoming archbishop of Canterbury, Anselm had been wrenched out of his meditative monastic environment and thrust into the midst of the political and social world of feudalism. A key concept in this feudal society of hierarchy and subordination was that an offense is commensurate with the status of the person offended. Thus an offense by one peasant against another was proportionately magnified if the peasant turned it against his lord, a knight, a baron, or the king. To impugn or deprive a person of his or her honor was extremely serious in Anselm's society; it was a fundamental crime against the social order. In feudal language, honor included a person's estate, lands, title, and status.

For feudal society, the absolute head of the social hierarchy was God. If the maintenance of a king's honor was necessary for the preservation of his kingdom, of a baron's honor for his barony, and so on down the social scale, how much infinitely more important for the preservation of the entire social world was the maintenance of God's honor. An offense to the king could be satisfied and his honor restored if

---

[3]Cited in R. W. Southern, *Saint Anselm and His Biographer: A Study of Monastic Life and Thought, 1059–c. 1130* (Cambridge: Cambridge University Press, 1963), pp. 58.

there were a punishment up to death commensurate to the offense. But how and who could satisfy the offense to God caused by human sin? The difficulty of this question was exacerbated by the Jewish criticism in Anselm's time that the traditional Christian answer concerning God's incarnation in Jesus was itself dishonorable to God because the indignity of Jesus's life and his shameful death were incompatible with the majesty of God. The art and piety of this time further sharpened the issue because it focused on and elaborated the sufferings and indignities of Christ.

The logic of Anselm's response was to locate the satisfaction of God's honor within God Himself. For this reason, his theory of the atonement is sometimes called "theocentric." For God merely to forgive the offenses of humankind would diminish his justice and honor and thereby undermine the stability of the universe itself. For God to reclaim his honor by just punishment of humankind's offenses would annihilate humanity and condemn all to eternal punishment. The solution to the maintenance of both God's honor and mercy was for God himself to become a human being and thereby to satisfy the offenses of humankind.

Without venturing into the complicated and controversial issues of the extent to which theological expressions of doctrine both reflect and form the aspirations, fears, and hopes of an era, some aspects of Anselm's thought appear to express new perspectives for his time. The feudal imagery of his *Cur deus homo* has been noted. The work is also of interest for its omission of a mainstay of the religious thought of prior generations: Satan's legal claim on humankind. Since the famous "cosmocentric" theory of the atonement set forth by Gregory the Great (d. 604), humankind had understood itself to be engaged in a constant, mortal struggle to atone by heavy penances and abundant alms the devil's claim on it. The constant conflict and battle within feudal society against the forces of chaos and evil were not limited to the warrior class; those who prayed (i.e., the monks) were understood to be the front line in the struggle for life against death. So burdensome was this religious orientaton that rigorous monasticism was believed to be the preferred path to salvation. Anselm's religion, too, is severe, but it opens the door to a more relaxed and hopeful religion. God himself has made the offering to himself that remits all human sins. Redemption is no longer only for the few elite, the spiritual knights of monasticism, but is available for all. This should by no means be mistaken for the heady liberation that came with the sixteenth-century Reformation's proclamation of salvation by grace alone apart from works. There is, however, a new hopefulness now. And it is probably not an accident that it was at this very time that the indulgence practice (ecclesial remission of the temporal penalties of sin) arose. As abused and venal as the indulgence practice became, it nevertheless expressed the sense that the treasury of grace is available to all.

Abelard

The new hope and humanism of the twelfth century are expressed in the stormy life and thought of Abelard, so poignantly expressed in his autobiography, *History of My*

Calamities (*Historia Calamitatum*). Born in Brittany, the eldest son of a lower noble, Abelard gave up his inheritance to pursue the studies that were now attracting so many of the younger generation. From the beginning he was recognized as both exceptionally brilliant and extremely difficult to get along with. For example, he irritated his teachers in Paris by setting himself up as a lecturer in competition with them and attracting their students. The relationship for which Abelard is most famous—or infamous, as the case may be—is his relationship with Heloise. Abelard was commissioned by her uncle and guardian, Fulbert, a fellow priest with Abelard at the Cathedral of Notre Dame, to teach the apparently attractive and intelligent young woman philosophy and Greek. By the time Uncle Fulbert realized that more was being conjugated than Greek verbs, Heloise was pregnant. Fulbert's rage found expression through a gang attack on Abelard that in Abelard's words, "cut off those parts of my body with which I had done that which was the cause of their sorrow."[4] This event also cut short his teaching career at Paris. Following the birth of their son, Heloise became a nun.

Abelard retired to the monastery of St. Denis where he assumed the office of abbot. There he incurred the wrath of ecclesial authorities by his teaching on the Trinity. His opponents condemned him unheard at the Council of Soissons (1121) where he was forced personally to burn his condemned book. Soon after this he was forced to flee the monastery owing to the anger of the monks over his argument that the patron saint of the monastery was not Dionysius the Areopagite, convert of St. Paul (Acts 17).

Abelard next established a small house of prayer outside of Paris dedicated to the Paraclete (i.e., the Holy Spirit as aide and comforter) that attracted large numbers of students. He then was appointed to the spiritual care of the nunnery of Argenteuil where Heloise was prioress. About 1135, Abelard once again began teaching philosophy and theology in Paris. In the following years, he wrote a number of important treatises on Christian theology, ethics, and methodology. St. Bernard's formidable opposition to his theological contributions led to Abelard's second condemnation in 1141 at the Council of Sens. By now, Abelard had had enough of "calamities," and he retired, a sick man, to a monastery under the jurisdiction of Cluny. There he died in 1142. Heloise was buried next to him in the Paraclete cloister on her death in 1164.

As even this very brief sketch suggests, Abelard was out of step with contemporary authorities. The rest of his age fell into step with him, however, or perhaps it was that he perceived before others the steps they yearned to take. At any rate, Abelard's life and theology manifested a new understanding of love that was destined to dominate Western thought until its banalization in Hollywood movies and "true confessions" journalism: romantic love. In fact, it was Heloise who did not want the marriage pushed on her by Abelard. "God knows," she wrote to him later from her

---

[4]Henry Adams Bellows, trans., *The Story of My Misfortunes: The Autobiography of Peter Abelard* (Glencoe, IL: The Free Press, 1958), p. 30.

nunnery, "I never sought anything in you except yourself; I wanted simply you, nothing of yours. I looked for no marriage-bond, no marriage portion."[5] Heloise shared with Abelard his low view of marriage as no more than the legalization of the weakness of the flesh, a view transmitted to their time from early Church Fathers such as Jerome and Augustine. They also shared the "ethic of intention" set forth in Abelard's *Scito te ipsum* ("Know Thyself"). For Heloise, marriage could add nothing to their relationship but would indeed detract from it, for she believed it would interfere with Abelard's true calling as a philosopher. She wrote to him: "Wholly guilty though I am, I am also, as you know, wholly innocent. It is not the deed but the intention of the doer which makes the crime, and justice should weigh not what was done but the spirit in which it is done."[6]

It may be suggested that Abelard's experience of the love of Heloise, with both its heady joy from which he composed love songs as well as its profound pain and loss, was influential on his understanding of the Atonement. The significance of the incarnation now is not in satisfying the claims of either the devil or God, but in the example and teaching of love manifest in Jesus, and the renewed love of humankind for God and others that Jesus's example stimulates. This so-called moral-influence or anthropocentric theory of the Atonement became widely popular in nineteenth-century Protestant liberalism. The monastic and feudal inspirations of Anselm's theology are displaced by worldly and humanistic inspirations in Abelard. As we have already noted, the guardians of the old order were not ready for this attention to personal fulfillment.

Abelard and Heloise typify one of the important cultural developments of the period—the discovery of the individual. Although few of their contemporaries were as self-conscious about self-knowledge, there was a flowering of vernacular poetry and song concerned with friendship and romantic love as well as with religious introspection.

Before turning to St. Bernard, the self-appointed judge, jury, and prosecutor of Abelard, it is necessary to note the contribution by which Abelard most influenced his contemporaries and their successors: his philosophical and theological method. Abelard's *Sic et Non* ("Yes and No") is remembered as his greatest contribution in furthering rational and dialectical argument and thought. It is certainly a milestone on the road leading away from unexamined reliance on past authorities. The *Sic et Non* is the first comprehensive exposition of theology as a science instead of a meditation. What Abelard did was to propose a series of 156 questions in doctrinal theology with quotations from the Fathers of the Church in support of both a "yes" and a "no" to the questions. His approach to contradiction among and even within these authorities was to propose a critical methodology for determining the authenticity, reliability, intentionality, and historical context of the text in question. When

---

[5]Betty Radice, trans., *The Letters of Abelard and Heloise* (New York: Penguin Books, 1983), p. 113.
[6]Ibid., p. 115.

resolution of contradiction by these means was not possible, then the strongest witness with the greatest support was to be preferred. This was a strong impulse toward the systematization of the faith on an intellectual foundation, which was carried forward by Peter Lombard's (d. 1160) *Sententiarum libri quatuor* ("Four Books of Sentences"). The book gave the opinions (*sententiae*) of various authorities on the subject under discussion. Lombard's *Sentences* became the basic instructional text in theological studies for the next few centuries.

This new theological orientaton sought to comprehend all of life by means of intensive rational reflection. As such, it corresponded to contemporary themes of personal responsibility, ethics of intention, personal and subjective interpretations of doctrine, reason, and centralization attendant on the beginnings of urban and commercial development.

At this time there was also an expanding awareness of the world that was stimulated by contact with Jewish and Islamic culture and thought, both in Spain and by the return of Crusaders. It was through the scholars of Muslim Spain that Christian thinkers became aware of aspects of Aristotelian philosophy that had been lost to the West. The works of Islamic philosophers such as Avicenna (lbn Sina, 980–1037) and Averroës (Ibn-Rushd, 1126–1198), and the great Jewish philosopher Maimonides (Moses ben Maimon, 1135–1204) were translated into Latin. The Latin translation of the Koran (1141–1143) was commissioned by the abbot of the monastery Cluny, Peter the Venerable (ca. 1092–1156). The preservation of classical philosophical writings by Arabic and Jewish thinkers provided a crucial impetus for learning and the development of universities in the West. On the other hand, the first Crusade, initiated at Clermont by Pope Urban II in 1095, created a reservoir of mutual antagonism between Christianity and Islam that has lasted to today.

In spite of the great cultural and intellectual contributions to Western culture by Islamic philosophers and scholars, Christians reacted to Islam with profound fear, anxiety, and hatred. To a great extent this reaction was rooted in the Christian perception that Islam was the first serious challenge to the Christian faith. The early church had explained away the religious challenge of pagan religions and Judaism by claiming that they were forerunners and only partial expressons of the final revelation of God in Jesus Christ. Islam came into existence well after the rise of Christianity, however, and therefore could not be explained away as a forerunner of Christianity. To medieval Christians, Islam was an even further scandal because it incorporated elements of Judaism and Christianity into its faith. Christians, unwilling to give up their claim to superiority over all other religions, thus resorted to attacking Islam militarily and theologically as the incarnation of the devil and all heresies. The purpose of the Latin translation of the Koran was to provide material to refute rather than to understand Islam. Unfortunately, the medieval Christian response to Islam has strongly biased western understanding of Islamic peoples up to the present.

St. Bernard

It is ironic that St. Bernard, who pursued and hounded Abelard with a fervor worthy of later inquisitors, refined further than Abelard himself the introspective conscience that St. Augustine bequeathed to the western church. Bernard (1090–1153), born in a noble family near Dijon, seemed destined to be a religious giant from his youth. By the age of twenty-two, he had persuaded thirty other young noblemen, including his brothers, to join the Benedictine renewal movement that had just recently developed into an order in its own right: the Cistercians (named after its foundaton in Cîteaux). The rigor of the Cistercians had already brought the order to the edge of extinction when Bernard's impact so transformed it that the Cistercians became known as the "Bernardines" also. It was the most renowned order in the twelfth-century church. Bernard played such a role in the affairs of his time—selecting popes, haranguing kings, preaching crusades, advising clergy, reforming the church, and rooting out heresy—that he has been called "the uncrowned ruler of Europe." It is as the "father" and doctor of medieval mysticism, however, that Bernard was to be known to his age and the following generations. Thus two centuries later Dante (1265–1321) in his *Divine Comedy* has St. Bernard, as the representative of mystic contemplation, lead him in Paradise to the Virgin Mary.

The meditative literature that flowed from the Cistercians under the dominating influence of Bernard emphasized personal experience, appealed to the individual conscience, and delved into the spiritual interior of humankind. This was not a departure from the love of logic that continued to stimulate this age but was, rather, its reflection in the self-conscious and systematic searching of the soul. The Cistercian program, expressed in the words of one of Bernard's followers, William of St. Thierry, was:

> When body and soul and spirit have each been ordered and disposed in their rightful place, each esteemed according to their merits and distinguished according to their qualities, a man may begin to know himself, and by progress in self-knowledge may ascend to the knowledge of God.[7]

The ascent to God is presented in terms of logical steps of an intelligible development beginning with self-love and moving through self-knowledge to union with God. Logic is now used to investigate the internal movements of the soul and states of mind. This "psychologizing" of theology is already present in Bernard's reworking of St. Benedict's treatise on the twelve steps of humility.

Bernard's tremendous spiritual influence derived not only from the power of his personality and perception but also from the readiness of his age to look inward, a readiness that also informed and received Anselm's emphasis on meditation and

---

[7]R. W. Southern, *The Making of the Middle Ages* (New Haven: Yale University Press, 1974), p. 229.

Abelard's call to know one's self. The romanticism and humanism of this twelfth century renaissance were graphically expressed in its changing art. Images of the crucifixion shift from representatons of divine power and majesty to depictions of extreme human suffering. The heroic images of Christ the king, a crowned and royally clothed warrior on the cross with head erect and open eyes expressing power, slowly changed to images of a humiliated, dishonored man, eyes closed, whose head and arms slump under the pain, and whose naked body shows his wounds. Likewise, the Virgin and Child images changed from the enthroned Byzantine images of *theotokos*, Mary the God-bearer, whose child holds up his right hand in benediction and clasps a symbol of dominion such as an orb or book in his left hand. Before this time, Christians could not conceive of Jesus as a baby but depicted the child Jesus as a miniature adult. The new art depicted a mother feeding her child who no longer clasps symbols of authority. Maternal tenderness and infant vulnerability began to come to the fore. The stage was being set for the Christian romance incarnated in St. Francis. Anselm's faith seeking understanding, Abelard's quest for self-knowledge, and Bernard's love seeking spirituality in the person of Francis focused on the symbolism of the wandering homelessness of the unsheltered beggar. The virtue of poverty was to be transmuted from the vigor of Benedictine renunciation of pride to the romantic embrace of material impoverishment. The prelude to this story is the transformation of social life in relation to urban and commercial development.

Church and Society

Sociologists of knowledge may provide a helpful clue to our understanding of the church's role in the development of the hierarchical social structure of medieval society. In *The Sacred Canopy* (1967), Peter Berger posits that every human society is involved in an ongoing task of structuring and/or maintaining a meaningful world for itself.[8] In the face of the precariousness of personal and social life, society strives to shield itself from chaos, formlessness, meaninglessness, and the terror of the void by structuring a meaning that can deal with the marginal situations of life. The Viking, Magyar, and Saracen invasions from without and the knightly raids and brutality within contributed greatly to the natural marginality of medieval life. Faced by the constant possibility of personal and cultural collapse into lawlessness, humankind has perpetually grounded social structures in the cosmos and thereby given ontological status to institutions. Religion provides a cosmic frame of reference with answers to the questions of origin, identity, purpose, meaning, and destiny.

This model of religion as world-building is fruitful for understanding the church's contribution to a political order that derives peace and justice in the world from the

[8]See Peter Berger, *The Sacred Canopy: Elements of a Sociological Theory of Religion* (Garden City, N.Y.: Doubleday & Company, Inc., 1967).

sacred and that legitimates and sanctifies social structures through the sacraments and the jurisdiction of the church. The church, through the agency of its pope, bishops, priests, and monks, is the agency through which divine order is brought into human order and divine law finds expresson in historical legal codes. From this perspective, the long development from the Middle Ages into the Europe we know today is the fruit of this struggle to construct a world in the face of the chaos and pressures in the West, beginning with the collapse of the Roman Empire and then the collapse of the Carolingian (from the reign of Charlemagne, d. 814) Rule.

The biblical image of the Christian community as a body (e.g., I Cor. 12; Eph. 4; Col. 3) informed the medieval sense of the *corpus Christianum*, the total Christian society. A body without its head, or whose limbs were uncoordinated or in conflict with each other could not survive. Medieval prelates developed this image into a metaphor for society. Their Latin word *ordo* signified the immutability of human social existence grounded in God's created order. Deviation from this divine order was sacrilege. By the tenth century, this concept of social order was refined by dividing it into three orders: workers (*laboratores*), prayers (*oratores*), and warriors (*bellatores*). In France, Bishop Alderberon of Laon dedicated a political poem to King Robert in which he wrote:

> But the city of God, commonly thought to be a single whole, has in reality three Orders: the men who pray, the men who fight and, thirdly, they who work. All three Orders coexist; none can dispense with the others; the services of each enable the others' tasks and each in turn assists the others.[9]

About the same time (ca. 1030), Bishop Gerard of Cambrai stated: "From its very origin the human race had been divided into three classes, all of which aid each other: the men who pray, the fighting men, the tillers of the soil."[10]

Theologians, politicians, and moralists emphasized the cooperation and harmony among these three orders under the rubric that there can be no order (*ordo*) without the orders. After all, this social organization was sanctioned by a Godhead believed to be a Trinity. The complementary functions of the social orders (spiritual welfare, defense, supply and maintenance) assisted all in their earthly life to conform to the divine plan, the ultimate end of which was, in the words of Thomas Aquinas, "the enjoyment of God." On the other hand, it is not difficult to imagine how this design impressed upon the collective consciousness contributed not only to a static view of society but also to the sanctioning of social inequalities and all forms of exploitation. "For the knight and learned clerk live by him who does the work." In the sixteenth century, this darker side of the orders of society was expressed in the fables of Adam

---

[9]Quoted in Georges Duby, *The Making of the Christian West* (Geneva: Editions d'Art Albert Skira, 1967), p. 61.
[10]Ibid.

and Eve's children who were assigned their social status by God on the basis of their beauty and ugliness or goodness and badness.

The three orders, or estates, as they are sometimes called, formed the "feudal" foundation for social relations that lasted in varying degrees up to the French Revolution. The quotation marks around the word "feudal" are to indicate that the term itself is the invention of modern historians to describe a social pattern more complicated than the three orders would suggest. The term itself derives from the Latin *feudum*, meaning a fief: something over which one has rights and control. Nearly all wealth in the agrarian Middle Ages rested on land holdings and their produce. And the granting of the fief by a lord to a vassal was everywhere the backbone of the social structure. However, common phrases such as "feudal system," "feudal law," and "feudal custom" are misleading if they are read to mean that the European Middle Ages were uniformly organized everywhere. With this caveat in mind, it is possible to make some observations about the feudal system.

Feudal relationships arose to facilitate cooperation in war. The lord was responsible for protecting his vassals and their lands, and his vassals were obligated to serve in his army. The vassals were also obligated to provide counsel to the lord when they were summoned to the lord's court. This latter feature of feudal custom is also present in the monastic rules that directed an abbot to seek the advice of his monks before embarking on a matter of interest to the whole community. The relationship between lord and vassal was expressed through swearing fidelity and doing homage. In this ceremony, the vassal placed his hands between the lord's hands, swore to be faithful, and to carry out the services required of him. Eventually, vassals could fulfill their obligations by substituting money for actual service in person. The church was fully involved in the feudal system both in terms of its own fief holdings and lordship, and in the obligations of bishops to provide men and material to their lords, both secular and religious, when needed. This helps to explain why monasteries sought exemption from obedience to the local bishop through direct relationship to the pope. The monasteries were attempting to avoid their feudal obligations. The word "lord" was also a term of address to God; thus the French *seigneur* was used of the feudal lord and is still used to address God. The posture of prayer with the hands held together that is so common today is a development from the posture of a vassal doing fealty. Portrayals of covenants with the devil used the same posture. These ideas of lordship and vassalage began from the twelfth century on to be used to describe relationships to women. In courtly literature, the man as vassal pledged his service to his lady (lord). Hymns written to both God and the Virgin Mary also began to use this language.

The Rise of Cities

The hierarchy of the three orders and the language, customs, and relationships of feudalism in which function determined social classification had a place for everyone and everyone for a place. Almost! By the twelfth century, a new "class" was arising: the merchants. That feudal structure, society, custom, theology, and ethics had no place for the merchant is epitomized in the dictum of canon law that "a merchant is rarely or never able to please God."

The rise of a merchant class was not an anomaly for feudalism, however. Feudalism itself was a response to the social disintegration occasioned by Viking and Magyar invasions. This disintegration was augmented by the decline of centralized authority, which brought in its train political fragmentation, shrinkage of long-distance trade, and the displacement of cities by castles and monasteries as cultural and political centers. Europe would continue to be primarily agrarian into the early modern period, but the relative peace and the agrarian developments in the wake of feudalism allowed the development of population, roads, trade, and cities. In turn, the initially itinerant merchants began to congregate for both protection and the increase of commerce. Whether traders and merchants settled near fortified places for protection, or built up areas around an already existing town nucleus that was favorably situated for their trading patterns, or settled around existing centers of learning and administration to cater to the needs of the populace, there is no doubt that the symbiotic development of towns and a new commercial class constituted a social revolution that formed the basis for Europe's gradual transition from a rural, agricultural society to the urban, industrial society we know today.

For the medieval person and community, however, this transition was fraught with anxiety as well as promise. The town exemplified the shift occurring at this time from an exchange economy to a money and profit economy. The development, already underway by the eleventh century, of money as a tool to be used for the creation of more money and goods rather than just a treasure to be displayed created changes in every aspect and corner of society. The anxieties accompanying these changes were directly related to the impersonalism and moral uncertainty involved in a profit economy.

The impersonalism was related directly to the growth of the towns. The quality of interpersonal relationships experienced in the small village, where common tasks and dialect undergirded solidarity and identity, was diminished markedly as a town grew in size and the number of specializations related to a market economy. Anonymity may be heady at first, but the initial euphoria evaporated when needed personal and material support was lacking. Anonymity was a function not only of the size of towns and cities but also of the use of money, an impersonal medium of exchange. The rise of both formal education and prostitution in the cities may be related to this anonymous, impersonal medium of money used by youth away from family, home, priest, or village. Since up to half of any given urban population consisted of immigrants from the countryside, personal encounter with urban complexity and impersonalism was widespread. The loosening of social ties and the relaxation of traditional and religious systems of constraint and supervision in the towns and cities became a matter of increasing concern.

Those peasants able to move to the cities discovered that they were not welcome. They were excluded from the guilds, the medieval equivalent of modern professional associations and building trades. They were almost always excluded from citizenship. If they found work, it was generally as a day-laborer subject to whoever hired them. Since laborers had no "safety net" of social security or savings, they were always on the edge of poverty, an edge over which they quickly fell when sick or when work was not available. It has been ventured that by the late Middle Ages 75 percent of the population suffered severe nutritional deficiencies, poor clothing, and miserable housing. It is not surprising that there were outbreaks of peasant violence that finally culminated in the Peasants' War of 1524–1525. But this gets ahead of our story.

The immediate problem as cities began to develop was the fact that it took money to live in a city. At the same time, the cities grew because they were the places where early capitalism could thrive. That made the cities attractive to outsiders because they hoped to make their fortunes there. But this new money economy was as unsettling as it was attractive. Instead of trading goods crafted or grown by a neighbor, one exchanged money for something from a stranger. And with enough money, anything could be had—privileges, positions, prostitutes, and even penance to make one feel better about whatever had been bought. The city and money combination did not make everyone feel better, however. It left many feeling uneasy and guilty. The traditional morality valued humility and attacked pride, and it found idealized expresson in the monastic striving for spiritual poverty. The traditional morality was not yet prepared to cope with the avarice and real poverty that were beginning to grow up alongside the cities.

The religious reaction to the new profit economy was twofold: severe judgment of those engaged in urban and financial life, and projection of this judgment with its attendant guilt and anxiety on the only available outsiders to the Christian community—the Jews. Already by the twelfth century, avarice had displaced pride in popular perception as the chief vice infecting both society and church. This is reflected in the satirical version of the traditional acclamation, "Christ conquers, Christ reigns, Christ rules the world," which substitutes money for the place of Christ. In art, avarice is depicted as a person, usually accompanied by demons, desperately clutching money bags and burdened by the terrible weight of money hanging from his neck or pressed on his back. Merchants are described as fraudulent liars who will do anything for gain. Indeed, Peter Lombard (d. 1160) made it clear that a merchant could not carry out his work without sinning.

The profound ambivalence toward the new profit economy was related not merely to the vice of avarice associated with it but also to the fact that a profit economy necessitates using money as an instrument of growth. Throughout the Middle Ages, loaning money at interest (termed *usury*) had been rejected by Christian moralists. The only people immune to the moral and religious outrage of the preachers against usury were the Jews. And in fact a high percentage of Jews became moneylenders and did the "dirty work" prohibited to Christians. This is the source for the laws forcing Jews to wear yellow badges and six-pointed stars that were initiated by the Fourth Lateran Concil in 1215. The consequent pogroms against Jewish communities were not only expressions of religious bigotry but were also projections onto the Jews of Christian anxiety and self-hatred concerning the new use of money. The Jews served as scapegoats for Christian difficulties with the new profit economy.

The Church and Poverty

The rise of cities and a profit economy along with the aspirations and values they created collided head-on with the fundamental religious values of the prior millenium. For a thousand years, the church had posited poverty as the favored path to salvation. The gospel's obvious bias toward the poor was succinctly stated in Jesus's words that it is harder for a rich person to enter heaven than for a camel to go through the eye of a needle. Clement of Alexandria's (ca. 150–ca. 215) famous sermon title "How is the rich man to be saved?" is only one of the many expressions of the early church's wrestling with the problem of salvation for the middle- and upper-class people entering the church. The answer to Clement's question was almsgiving to the poor and needy. This simple answer drew on a selection of biblical and early church texts to form an ideology of poverty that had profound social as well as theological significance for the Middle Ages. This ideology served as a cognitive and ethical map for society until the rise of the urban profit economy.

The architect of the theological perspective dominant through the Middle Ages was St. Augustine (354–430). His doctrine of charity became the heart of medieval theology. Charity or love directed to God is "motion of the soul to enjoy God for his own sake and one's self and the neighbor for the sake of God."[11] Cupidity, that is, love directed away from God, is the "motion of the soul bent upon enjoying one's self, the neighbor, and creatures without reference to God."[12] For Augustine, love not only makes the world go 'round; love sustains the entire cosmos and is the essential ingredient even in sin, which is misdirected love. Thus his famous definition of the two cities—the heavenly and the earthly: "Two cities have been formed by two loves: the earthly by the love of self, even to the contempt of God; the heavenly by the love of God, even to the contempt of self."[13]

At the risk of oversimplification, the complex theology of Augustine may be thought of diagrammatically in terms of ascent. For Augustine there is a hierarchy of being, the apex of which is God, the highest good and being itself. This meta-

---

[11]Augustine *De Doctrina Christiana*, in J. P. Migne, ed., *Patrologiae cursus completus, series latina*, Vol. 34 (Paris, 1844–1855), p. 72.
[12]Ibid.
[13]Marcus Dods, trans., Augustine, *The City of God* (New York: Random House, 1950), p. 477.

physical scheme conceives of God as the eternal, absolute, immutable being, and thereby conceives of all beings below God as relative, temporal, transient, and incomplete. This theology of ascent is graphically expressed in his metaphor of the traveler journeying to his or her homeland who is in danger of enjoying the journey itself and thereby forgetting the destination. The world, in other words, may be used as an aid on the way of love up to God; but it will become a hindrance if enjoyed, for then our misdirected love directs us down and away from God to the earth. The earthly city is a foreign land; here we are pilgrims, travelers on our way to the heavenly city, our true homeland. Here is the root of the great medieval themes of pilgrimage, renunciation, alienation, and asceticism. Thus alienation and order are intimately related in the fundamental theology of the West. And the story of medieval development may in a real sense be described as the history of the efforts to realize in society the right relationship of alienation and order.

Love of the earthly city leads to disaffection from the heavenly city, and love of the heavenly city frees one from the earthly city. Here the biblical suspicion of riches (e.g., Mark 10:25; Matt. 5:3 and 19:24; Luke 18:25; James 5:1–3) receives systematic theological articulation. Pride and covetousness are the major vices; humility and almsgiving are the major virtues. "It is enough," says Augustine, "if riches do not destroy their possessors; it is enough if they do them no harm; help them they cannot."[14] Although this is a modification of Tertullian's (d. ca. 225) earlier claim that God always justifies the poor and damns the rich, it does elevate poverty over wealth as the favored status for the Christian. This precept found its most startling expression in St. Francis of Assisi (1181–1226), whose life was not merely an imitation of the real poor of his time but, rather, his own stylization of this apostolic model.

The human condition of pilgrim and wayfarer was both interiorized and projected upon society by the monastic movement. The genius of the earlier Benedictine rule was its emphasis on stability. The monastic community in its ascetic withdrawal from this world provided a glimpse of divine order through its highly ordered life and liturgy. In response to the social tensions of the early Middle Ages, the monasteries posited that every pilgrim who appeared at the door of the monastery must be received as though he or she were Christ himself. Beyond this hospitality to individuals, the Benedictine effort was oriented to the tension between the powerful and the weak—a predominant phenomenon in pre-urban, agricultural, and feudal society. The major vice was perceived to be pride associated with power and status. The Benedictines, themselves largely from the noble, fighting class, sought protection from the sin of pride through spiritual warfare against worldly power. Their emphasis on voluntary poverty was thus not material but spiritual in nature. In fact, Benedictine monasteries were frequently comfortable and occasionally magnificent.

---

[14]Augustine, *Enarrationes in Psalmos* (85.3), in Migne, *Patrologiae*, Vol. 36–37, p. 1083.

This was not seen as a contradiction because their function was prayerful struggle against the violent forces of their age. Knightly violence was ritualized and thus restrained by the monastic liturgy that spiritually sanctioned Christian warfare.

In the eleventh century, economic and social changes began to influence Christian ideals. The major vice was now seen as avarice rather than pride, and material poverty was more highly regarded than spiritual poverty. Thus the mendicant movements associated with men such as Waldo and Francis (to be discussed later), both from the new merchant class, emphasized the abandonment of material wealth, and literal rather than spiritual pilgrimage. As the Benedictines sought protection for themselves and their society from pride, so the mendicants sought protection for themselves and their society from avarice. As the Benedictines sought within a feudal context to develop a moral theology in response to power and violence, so the Franciscans and mendicants sought within an urban context to develop a moral theology in response to the profit economy, and to aid townspeople toward a vision of Christian citizenship. The future of the monastic movement belonged to the Franciscan and mendicant movements because instead of withdrawal from the world into monasteries outside the cities, as was the case with the Benedictines, they established themselves in the cities and moved about with the people.

The ideology of poverty was a theological construct that made charity a condition of salvation. Later scholasticism gave this ideology an epigrammatic formulation in the phrase, "faith formed by charity." Even before such theological precision, the early church was developing a theological and social perspective that included a symbiotic relationship between rich and poor. In the second-century writing called "The Shepherd," the relationship between rich and poor is portrayed by analogy to the relationship between a vine and an elm tree. The huge elm itself bears no fruit. And the vine, when limited to the ground, bears only poor fruit that is easily crushed underfoot. But when the elm supports the vine, the vine is able to bear rich fruit for both of them. Biblical passages, especially from the popular apocryphal books, Tobit and Sirach, provided support for the redemptive significance of charity.[15] In these passages, almsgiving and charity are presented as not only a kind of investment in heaven but even as a remedy for sin. Tobit advocates almsgiving as a way of "laying up a good treasure for yourself against the day of necessity. For charity delivers from death and keeps you from entering the darkness."[16] Sirach, which by the third century was so esteemed by the Latin church that it came to be known as Ecclesiasticus, provided what must certainly be one of the more memorable passages on the subject of alms: "As water extinguishes a blazing fire: so almsgiving atones

---

[15]The Apocrypha ("the hidden things") are those books excluded by the Hebrew Bible but included by the Greek-speaking Jews in the Septuagint (LXX). The apocryphal books were included in the old Latin Vulgate Bible but rejected by the Reformers of the sixteenth century. A modern edition of the Apocrypha is in *The Oxford Annotated Bible with the Apocrypha*, Revised Standard Version (New York: Oxford University Press, 1962).

[16]Tobit (4.9–10).

for sin."[17] This promise of almsgiving is colorfully set forth in the oft-used sermon illustration that medieval preachers believed came from Gregory the Great (d. 604). There was an unchaste man who was also generous to the poor. On his death he, like all the unchaste, had to cross a slippery bridge suspended over a bottomless sea of sulphur and brimstone in which the devil swam like a frog in a filthy pond. It had been determined that the unchaste would slip on this bridge, and so this man, too, fell toward the horrible abyss below. But two angels quickly grasped his hands, which had given alms, and drew him upward, while the devil at the same time grabbed him elsewhere and attempted to pull him down. The sermon illustration wisely does not conclude the story, but it is clear that wealth is an even greater danger to salvation than lack of chastity. The only effective antidote is almsgiving, by which the rich atone for their sins and receive in return the intercessory prayers of the poor.

This theology of poverty to a certain extent associated its victims with a sort of spiritual order that is inconceivable apart from an economy of salvation in the community of saints. Thus poverty acquired, through its function of suffering, a social dimension otherwise reserved for the rich. This is the key to the thoughts and attitudes of the twelfth century with regard to poverty and the poor. Most of the authors of the time appear to consider the poor to be in service to the rich. The poor appear to be created and put in the world for their salvific function. Thus the works of mercy under the generic name of *alms* are the constant subject of letters, tracts, and sermons. The role of the poor is to receive because the gift is an obligation.

Thus the poor is a privileged creditor, a born intercessor with God, and finally even the image of Christ. Alain of Lille summarized this view in a sermon in 1198. Christ cannot live among the prelates who dwell in simony, and he is refused refuge among the knights who are concerned only to shelter their plunder. There is no lodging for Christ among the citizens because their usury has already taken his place, and the merchants are so dominated by lies that they reject him. Where then, Alain asks, shall Christ dwell? Only among the poor of whom it is said, "Blessed are the poor in spirit."

It is of interest in light of the developing profit economy that medieval preachers and theologians did not hesitate to refer to the relationship of the rich to the poor in terms of a commercial transaction. The poor carry the riches of the wealthy on their backs to heaven! This concept was given graphic expression by the funeral rituals developing at this time. The wealthy drew up wills that left major funds for clothing and feeding the local poor on the condition that they participate in the funeral procession. The last will and testament now became an expression of individualism, a last show of ostentation, and a means of associating one's personal wealth with the working of one's personal salvation. A favorite means for attaining the latter goal was to establish ecclesial foundations and endowments that supported priests who

---

[17]Sirach (3:30).

said masses for the souls of the dead benefactor. This was the source for the prolif-eration of altars, which so influenced medieval church architecture. Another means by which the rich could gain salvation was the establishment or support of hospitals, which had the added advantage of requiring all the inhabitants of the hospital to pray for the benefactor. Furthermore, alms had a penitential role not only for the militant church on earth; they also mitigated the purgatorial torment of the suffering church. Thus twelfth century testaments and charters were marked by what became a legal formula: "For the salvation of my soul and the souls of my ancestors and successors."

This symbiosis of rich and poor expressed in terms of alms and intercessory prayer allowed begging to become a recognized, even religious, form of life in medi-eval society. Thus from within the perceived immutability of the feudal structure, the powerful ninth-century archbishop of Reims, Hincmar, subscribed to the formula recounted in the *Life of St. Eligius:* "God could have made all persons rich, but he willed that there be poor in the world so that the rich would have an opportunity to atone for their sins."[18] Obviously, such perspectives created an obstacle to what we might consider realistic understandings of poverty and its sources.

Popular Piety

In spite of arising outside the feudal structures of society, the medieval merchant began to carve a niche for himself in the *corpus Christianum* by relating to the existing theology of poverty. The cities and guilds also created space for themselves by direct expressions of community building through sacred oaths and charters that would be ritually commemorated in festive anniversaries. All these new expressions of medieval life found rootage and sustenance in their understanding of human community origi-nating in Adam and Eve and renewed in Christ. Thus the kinship of the *corpus Christianum* transcended individual genealogies. This Christian family was shaped and channeled by the theology and piety of sacraments, the saints, and an eccle-siology that transcended space and time in encompassing the suffering church in purgatory, the militant church on earth, and the triumphant church in heaven. Because piety (*pietas*) means dutiful conduct toward the family and relatives as well as toward God and country, the church's sacraments covered the major rites of passage in human life, from birth to death, and related them to the maintenance of the whole society.

The church's intensive interest in the sacraments began very early in its history even though the number of sacraments was not doctrinally limited to seven (baptism, confirmation, penance, eucharist, marriage, orders, extreme unction) until the Coun-

---

[18]Michel Mollat, *The Poor in the Middle Ages: An Essay in Social History,* Arthur Goldhammer, trans. (New Haven & London: Yale University Press, 1986), p. 44.

cil of Florence in 1439. Already in the twelfth century, however, Peter Lombard assumed that there were only seven sacraments. The word "sacrament" is from the Latin *sacramentum*, which in turn is a translation of the Greek term for "mystery." The Latin term is of significance because it originally meant an oath, in particular a soldier's oath of allegiance and its accompanying tattoo of identification. Thus in the early church, the language itself conveyed the sense that the nonrepeatable sacraments (baptism, confirmation, and ordination) impressed an indelible mark (*character indelebilis*) on the soul.

Whereas baptism initiated a person into the community, the sacrament that nourished the community as it progressed in its pilgrimage toward the heavenly city was above all the Eucharist. The early church had expressed its understanding of the Eucharist in both realistic and symbolic terms. That is, even before missions to the West, there was a sacramental realism that could speak of converted Jews drinking the blood (of Christ) they had once spilled, and of communicants eating and drinking the real body and blood of Christ. At the same time, the Eucharist was understood symbolically as the church's perpetuation of the memory of the once-and-for-all sacrifice of Christ. During the Carolingian era, the realistic understanding was strengthened and intensified by a popular piety and crude faith in miracles until it became generally accepted that the bread and wine are somehow changed into the body and blood of Christ as the result of their consecration by the priest.

There were a number of influences on this development. Whereas on the one hand, in conjunction with the hierarchical, feudal, and social orientation, the divine was conceived as increasingly in the realm of the unreachable, the ordinary life of the western Christian was surrounded by myriads of mysteries and miracles. Thus there was popular pressure to develop the sacred act of the Lord's Supper into the wonder of wonders so that it would not be diminished by comparison with common miracles. In this period there was so much emphasis on God as the omnipotent, mysterious, arbitrary power that even the incarnation of God in Jesus was perceived in terms of divine majesty and judgment. Thus the proclamation of the incarnation that God had become a real, human person in Christ faded into the background, and the institutional church was perceived to be the safest means to apprehend God. The growing perception of Christ as the divine judge had a number of ramifications: Contact with God was increasingly focused on the point at which the mystery of Christ's incarnation and death was most present and palpable—the Eucharist. Sociologically as well as religiously, the clergy gained power as those who alone could make Christ present in the Eucharist. And there were increasing hope and reliance placed in those who might be able to mediate between the Mediator and the community—the saints and especially Mary.

A series of eucharistic controversies from the ninth to the eleventh centuries led to the supremacy of the realistic view of the Eucharist. The Synod of Rome in 1079 stated that "the bread and wine, which are placed on the altar, through the mystery of the sacred prayer and the words of our Redeemer are substantially changed into the true, proper, and life-giving flesh and blood of our Lord Jesus Christ."[19] Although the concept of transubstantiation was not yet developed, the church now asserted the real change of bread and wine into Christ's body and blood. Popular piety was so awed by the sacrament that there developed both adoration of the host and the withdrawal of the cup from the laity. The latter practice was not enforced by clerical fiat but by popular demand because of the great fear of dishonoring the sacrament by spilling the consecrated wine. By the time of Thomas Aquinas (1225–1274), lay communion using only the bread was a widespread practice that found its explanation and legitimation in the doctrine of "concomitance." This doctrine asserted that the whole body and blood of Christ are present in either consecrated element. A decree of the Council of Constance in 1415 officially established the centuries-old desire of popular piety to abstain from the consecrated wine and commune by using only the consecrated bread.

While baptism incorporated a person into the pilgrim community of the church, which was always in process of traveling to its true home with God in the heavenly city, and the Eucharist nourished the pilgrims during their voyage, the danger of shipwreck on earthly delights was omnipresent. The church's response to this danger was to offer what medieval theologians called the "second plank after shipwreck," the sacrament of penance.

The sacrament of penance was the subjective side of the objective sacrament of the Mass. Through the sacrament of penance, the church provided not only the absolution of guilt but also the means for satisfying the socially disruptive and religiously offensive actions of persons. Although historians have suggested Germanic and feudal roots for this idea of atoning for crimes by rendering satisfaction commensurate to the station of the person offended, the theological basis for penance is also important. The theologians of the early church had conceived of penance as a way of making satisfaction to God, and this concept was incorporated into the understanding of the sacrifice of Christ in Anselm's (d. 1109) *Cur Deus Homo* (discussed earlier).

The significance of penance for medieval life and religion cannot be underrated. The term itself derives from the Latin *poena*, which not only means punishment but also compensation, satisfaction, expiation, and penalty. Already, St. Augustine had spoken of the necessity of punishment for sin that will be satisfied either here through human acts or hereafter by God. On the basis of these assumptions, there developed the doctrine of purgatory and its purifying fire, the pastoral and disciplinary life of the church, and the indulgence system for commuting penitential impositions too severe for completion outside the monastic regimen. Thus when the austere eleventh-century reformer, Cardinal Peter Damian (1007–1072) imposed a 100-year penance

---

[19]Hubert Jedin and John Dolan, eds., *The History of the Church, III: The Church in the Age of Feudalism,* Anselm Biggs, trans. (New York: Crossroad, 1987), p. 468.

on the Archbishop of Milan for simony, he also indicated how much money would commute each year of penance. Although the intent of the indulgence system was to adjust satisfaction for sins to changing social conditions, by the late Middle Ages it became such an abused instrument for clerical social control and revenue raising that it evoked Luther's *Ninety-five Theses* on penance and indulgences and thus contributed to the Protestant Reformation.

By the twelfth century, the norm was a private penance before a priest that consisted of three parts: heartfelt repentance (*contritio cordis*), oral confession (*confessio oris*), and satisfactory work (*satisfactio operis*). A further development in the easing of the sacrament was to make attrition (i.e., fear of punishment) a possibility when contrition was lacking. The close connection of penance to the sacramental means of grace, the Mass, was codified by the Fourth Lateran Council in 1215, which mandated that every Christian had to make private confession and partake of the Eucharist at least once a year. As a rule the penitential works were expressed in terms of the triad of almsgiving, fasting, and prayer. Here, once again, with the emphasis on almsgiving, may be seen the intimate connection between social conditions, ecclesial social control and revenue raising, and the symbiotic relationship of rich and poor.

The critical role that the sacrament of penance played in the Middle Ages and the Reformation explosion against it is also related to the ascetic role penance played. Here, where the medieval church most intimately affected the lives of the laity, the church was unable to move much beyond a piety that was monastic and clerical. The superiority of clerical over lay life posited by the clerical asceticism of poverty, celibacy, and obedience did not allow the development of lay piety but instead imposed upon the laity the piety of the clergy. In the course of the Middle Ages, the originally inspiring piety of the monastic life became an increasingly oppressive subject of criticism.

In fact, this burden of individual and collective acts of satisfaction for sin became focused in collective rituals of asceticism. In some cases, these efforts skirted heresy— for example, the penitential bands of men known as flagellants who spread through Italy in 1260 scourging themselves. In other cases, ascetic movements such as the Franciscan and Dominican mendicants became institutional organs of the church. But the collective ritual of ascetic penance par excellence was Lent. Its collective ascetic rigor was such that it spawned a wild collective prelude of oral confession known as "carnival." The term derives from the *dominica carnevalis*, "farewell to flesh Sunday," which marked the transition to the meatless asceticism of Lent. Carnival consisted of the days or week preceding Shrove Tuesday, the day before Ash Wednesday, which is significantly termed in French, "fat Tuesday," *Mardi Gras*.

The object of carnival was to expose the collective sins of the community. This period when the world is turned upside down represented carnality as a fat figure carried in procession and then tried, condemned, and executed by fire at the end.

The obligatory overindulgence in food and drink is vividly expressed by the dedication of Shrove Tuesday in Nantes to St. Dégobillard—St. Vomit! Sexuality and obscenity were equally on display:

> Prostitutes, whatever their status during the rest of the year, were essential; bears, cocks and other symbols of lechery abounded in the iconography; massive representations of the penis, plain in Naples or disguised as enormous sausages in Königsberg, were carried in procession through the streets. Since the object of the performance was to expose that which was concealed, it was natural that conduct to which shame was attached should be a favorite target for exposure.[20]

Violence and hostility were also displayed, more or less symbolically and more or less anonymously through mask and costume. Even today, one is liable to assaults by rotten eggs and bags of flour in parts of France during Mardi Gras. This was also when the hierarchical and patriarchal culture could be overturned, at least momentarily, and women ruled and beat men.

[20]John Bossy, *Christianity in the West 1400–1700* (Oxford & New York: Oxford University Press, 1985), p. 43.

Chapter 16

THE HARVEST OF THE MEDIEVAL CHURCH

The bloom of the twelfth-century church and culture began to be harvested in the thirteenth century. As the cathedrals were beginning to be topped off by their remarkable spires, the papacy reached the heights of its power and influence, and universities were extending the frontiers of human understanding and knowledge. There were protest movements arising, too, but they in turn stimulated responses such as the Franciscan and Dominican movements, which became generators of social, spiritual, and intellectual renewal.

Innocent III and the Zenith of the Papacy

Innocent III (reigned 1198–1216) was clearly the ablest of the medieval popes. It is equally clear that his great personal, intellectual, and political acumen and skills were effectively realized because of the centuries-long development of papal ideology. A brief review of this development will indicate the basis from which Innocent proceeded to rule Europe.

Constantine's fourth-century recognition of the church as a legal corporate body within the terms of Roman law set the stage for the perennial medieval conflict between rulers and the bishops of Rome. Emperors conceived of themselves as divinely ordained rulers of a Christian commonwealth in which the bishops were members. On the other hand, the bishops of Rome understood the state to be coterminous with the church of which the emperor was a member. The Petrine basis (Matt. 16:15–19) for the Roman church was also being expressed at this time by both emperor and pope. One of the first papal decretals, addressed to Spanish bishops in 385, referred to the pope as the heir of St. Peter. And the famous "dogmatic letter"

283

of Leo I to the Council of Chalcedon in 451 regarding the person of Christ was unanimously acclaimed with the words, "St. Peter has spoken through Leo."

Although the Petrine Succession as the basis of the papacy was generally acknowledged in the areas around Rome by the late fourth century, there was as yet no documentary basis for it. Documentation was accomplished by the translation and embellishment of a Greek document, the Epistle of Clement. Purported to be a letter by Pope Clement I written to St. James, brother of Jesus, this spurious letter claimed that St. Peter himself passed his authority on to Clement. This letter traced to Peter both the succession of Roman bishops and the juridical usage of the Matthew 16 passage regarding the binding and loosing of sins. On this foundation Leo I, himself a superb jurist, used the Roman law of inheritance to assert that the pope is Peter's heir in regard to his powers though not to his personal merits. This Roman tradition that the heir legally takes the place of the dead person in terms of estate, assets, rights and duties Leo expressed in the formula of the pope as "the unworthy heir of St. Peter."

Leo further developed papal primacy by applying the Roman legal term for imperial monarchy to the papacy. He distinguished imperial and papal claims by positing that the papal monarchy was the result of a unique divine act, whereas imperial monarchy was a historical development of human organization. The imperial monarchy as a result of historical, human work was thus divinely willed only in a secondary sense. It was Pope Gelasius I (reigned 492–496) who gave classic formulation to Leo's program. The Gelasian theory, sometimes called "the great charter of the medieval papacy," distinguished sacred power from royal power by use of the Roman distinction between *auctoritas* and *potestas*. The authority of the church was *auctoritas* ("legislative"), whereas the authority of the emperors was *potestas* ("executive"). In Roman law, legislative authority was superior to executive authority. Thus Gelasius implied that the church as legislative institution gave power to the emperor as executive. This political theology received further confirmation by the conversion of Clovis (496), the king of the Franks, and the developing relationship between the papacy and the Franks.

By the mid-eighth century, the Frankish Merovingian (from Merovech, grandfather of Clovis) dynasty had a reached a low point, and in Italy the Lombards (sixth-century invaders of northern Italy) were making substantial inroads upon the empire. Pope Stephen II (reigned 752–757) used the former situation to resolve the latter. In 754 he arrived in Frankish lands and negotiated with the king, Pepin, whose usurpation of the Merovingian rule had been legitimated by the church only three years earlier. In return for papal prohibition of the choice of a Frankish king outside the line of Pepin, Pepin was to drive the Lombards out of papal territory. At St. Denis in 754, the pope anointed Pepin as patrician (i.e., supreme magistrate) of the Romans.

Pepin fulfilled his part of the bargain by crushing the Lombards and donating the lands to St. Peter (i.e., to the papacy) in a solemn document, the Donation of Pepin, deposited at the tomb of St. Peter. The "documentary" basis for the Donation of Pepin was the Donation of Constantine, which itself rested on a novelistic product of the late fifth century, the so-called Legend of St. Sylvester, which portrayed the conversion of Constantine and legitimated the superiority of Rome over Constantinople, the new capital of the empire. The legend vividly portrays the emperor lying prostrate without imperial garments and emblems before the pope in contrition for his sins. In gratitude for papal absolution, Constantine gives the pope his imperial insignia, the lands of the empire, and the right to create consuls and patricians. The pope then returns the imperial regalia to Constantine and allows him to establish a new seat of government in Byzantium; the pope will keep Italy as a papal patrimony. The story thus accounts for the rise of Constantinople as a direct result of papal permission and also for the papal right to make emperors. The importance of Pepin's Donation was that it confirmed that of Constantine and manifested Frankish veneration for St. Peter and Peter's successors.

It was Pepin's son Charlemagne who from his accession in 768 fully lived up to the role of patrician of the Romans. He added more territory to the papal patrimony and came to the defense of Pope Leo III (795–816) when Leo was charged with lechery and perjury by the Roman aristocracy. The latter was one of two significant events relating to papal primacy that took place in 800. Charlemagne went to Rome where Leo took a solemn vow of innocence of all charges against him. The reason for Leo's oath was the ancient but hitherto unused principle based on I Corinthians 2:15 that the pope could not be judged by anyone. ("The spiritual man judges all things, but is himself to be judged by no one.") This principle, one of the most frequently quoted mottos of the Middle Ages, had first been set forth in the early sixth century by the so-called Symmachan forgeries, which included the story that Pope Sylvester had issued a decree that "Nobody can sit in judgment on the first apostolic see which distributes rightful justice to all. Neither the emperor nor the whole clergy nor kings nor people can judge the supreme judge."[1]

The second event was that at this time, Leo took the initiative to crown Charlemagne as the Roman emperor. This was a highly orchestrated event that Leo had worked out partly in collusion with Charlemagne but also partly to his surprise. Before the celebration of the Christmas mass—held at St. Peter's rather than at the customary Santa Maria Maggiore because of the pope's sensitivity to the great Frankish veneration of Peter—Charlemagne had agreed to take the title of emperor. He understood this to mean king over several nations, at best a parity with the emperor in the East. But the coached crowd responded to Leo's crowning with the acclamation, "Emperor of the Romans." With one stroke, Leo extricated the papacy from the East and placed the center of the Christian world in Rome rather than either Constantinople or Aachen, Charlemagne's capital. The Roman empire was now identified with the papal ideology of a Christian empire held together not by ethnic or

---

[1] Walter Ullmann, *A Short History of the Papacy in the Middle Ages* (London: Methuen University Paperback, 1974), p. 39.

historic ties but by the faith enunciated by the church of Rome. The further significance of the papal crowning of an emperor was that the pope could either withhold the crown until a candidate pleased him or take it away if the emperor displeased him. This was of great significance throughout the Middle Ages because popes more or less successfully exerted authority over the emperors of the Holy Roman Empire. It also explains the symbolic political significance in the nineteenth century of Napoleon's snatching the crown from the hands of Pope Pius VII in order to crown himself.

Papal supremacy was further strengthened by the mid-ninth century collection and invention of doctrines, decretals, and laws—including the Donation of Constantine—known as the Pseudo-Isadorian Decretals. This exhaustive and able collection, forerunner of canon law, was attributed to Isador of Mercator, a Spanish archbishop contemporary with Gregory I (d. 604). The Pseudo-Isadorian Decretals expressed a papal ideology of supreme judicial authority, limited archiepiscopal rights, clerical freedom from secular control, and the right of clerical appeal to the pope. This collection supplied what the papacy had up to now lacked: ancient laws in the form of decrees allegedly issued by the papacy in the first centuries. The first pope to make effective use of the Decretals was Nicholas I (858–867), who bent Lothair II, king of Lorraine, to his will by threat of excommunication. Nicholas also used this threat to depose archbishops and the patriarch of Constantinople.

Following Nicholas, there was a succession of weak and corrupt popes, and the church became increasingly dependent on secular powers. The consequent renewal movement in the church came to be called the Gregorian reform after one of its leading exponents, Hildebrand (ca. 1021–1085), who became Pope Gregory VII in 1073. After becoming pope, Gregory proceeded with vigor against immorality and lay interference in ecclesial appointments (the investiture struggle). His most famous stand was against Emperor Henry IV, who finally submitted to the pope in 1077 at Canossa.

Gregory's theoretical contribution to the concept of papal monarchy rested on his knowledge of the Pseudo-Isadorian Decretals and his ecclesial administrative experience prior to being elected pope. He declared the universal monarchy of the papacy in his famed *Dictates*, which summarized papal rights as they could be identified in tradition. The following selections indicate the self-perception of the papacy at this time:

1. That the Roman church was established by God alone.

2. That the Roman pontiff alone is rightly called universal.

3. That he alone has the power to depose and reinstate bishops.

8. That he alone may use the imperial insignia.

9. That all princes shall kiss the foot of the pope alone.

18. That his decree can be annulled by no one, and that he can annull the decrees of anyone.

19. That he can be judged by no one.

22. That the Roman church has never erred and will never err to all eternity, according to the testimony of the holy scriptures.

24. That by his command or permission subjects may accuse their rulers.

26. That no one can be regarded as catholic [that is, as part of the whole, true church] who does not agree with the Roman church.

27. That he has the power to absolve subjects from their oath of fidelity to wicked rulers.[2]

Gregory in both theory and praxis exceeded the prior ideology of papal supremacy. He moved beyond the power to bind and loose sins to the power to depose rulers; he connected the power to open and close the gates of heaven to the right to judge on earth.

Innocent III also believed that the whole world is the province of the pope and that Peter had been commissioned by Christ to govern not only the universal church but also the secular world. A gifted administrator and leader, Innocent was also an able canon lawyer and theologian who was convinced of the hierocratic theory of the spiritual sword over the earthly sword, which he expressed by his image of the monarchy being related to the papacy as the Moon is to the Sun. Innocent III was the first to employ the title Vicar of Christ, and he proceeded to actualize his vision of a centralized Christian society under papal jurisdiction.

To impress this image on Europe, Innocent levied the first general income tax on European churchmen to provide for papal diplomatic and military ventures. To be free for European involvement, Innocent first secured his power and authority in Rome and the papal states. The death of Emperor Henry VI in 1197 and the consequent struggle for the throne between rival claimants gave him the opportunity to intervene and arbitrate. In his bull (a papal edict so-called because of the lead papal seal, *bulla* attached to it) *Venerabilem*, he claimed that although an emperor is elected by the imperial electors, the appointment of the emperor comes within the sphere of papal authority *principaliter* (principally) and *finaliter* (finally). *Principaliter* because the translation of the empire from the Greeks to the Romans was owing to the pope, and *finaliter* because the blessing, coronation, and investiture of the emperor came from the pope. Innocent allowed the German feud over the election to continue for three years in order to deplete the power of the German crown. Then in 1200 he decided in favor of Otto IV. Otto in turn recognized the boundaries of the papal

[2]Ray C. Petry, ed. *A History of Christianity. Readings in the History of the Early and Medieval Church* (Englewood Cliffs, N.J.: Prentice-Hall, 1962), pp. 236–237.

states, surrendered the remnants of royal authority over the German church, and promised not to intervene in Italy.

However, once Otto was without rivals in Germany, he again took up the perennial policy of the German kings to claim Italy for himself as patrician of the Romans. In turn, Innocent recognized the only son of Henry VI, Frederick II, as Otto's replacement. He then organized a great coalition of the papacy, Frederick II, and Philip Augustus of France against Otto and his ally, King John of England. This is the first great example of the clash of international alliances in European history. Otto was crushed at the battle of Bouvines in 1214.

Innocent paralleled his triumph in the "imperial business" with his relations with the English and French kings. In a dispute concerning traditional English royal authority over the English church, Innocent forced King John to accept the papal appointee to the see of Canterbury and to become his vassal, thus making England a fief of the papacy. One of the interesting sidelights of this story is that John accepted Innocent's conditions in 1213 because he was unsure of the support of his barons. When in 1215, these rebel barons compelled John to issue the *Magna carta libertatum*, which restricted the crown's feudal and sovereign rights, Innocent stood by the king and declared the *Magna carta* null and void. Even Innocent's appointee to Canterbury, Archbishop Langton, disregarded Innocent's judgment and as a result was removed.

Innocent also placed France under interdict (cessation of the administration of the sacraments) to compel its king, Philip Augustus, to be reconciled with his wife, Ingeborg of Denmark. Innocent's authority was also felt beyond England, Germany, and France, extending as far north as Scandinavia, south and west to Spain, and east to Cyprus and Armenia.

In general however, Innocent's relationship to Philip was beneficial to Philip's monarchy. Philip's expansionist policy in the South of France was cloaked in the dubious morality of a crusade against heretics. The occasion for this crusade was Innocent's efforts to win the hearts and minds of the heretical communities in southern France who were known as the Albigenses or Cathari (cf. the later discussion on page 291). Missions to them of outstanding preachers had little effect, and when in 1208 a papal legate was murdered, a crusade was launched against the heretics.

The shift of the crusading mentality from infidels to heretics was facilitated by the capture and sack of Constantinople during the Fourth Crusade. This sorry spectacle of "holy war" of Christian against Christian poisoned relations between East and West for generations to come. But if a crusade could turn against Christian allies, then certainly it could be directed against heretics, the cancer within that threatened not only the unity but the faith of Christendom. Innocent had already been energetically attacking heresy with all the spiritual and secular means at his disposal. As with the political issue, so with the heretical issue: Innocent began in his own territory. This is the context for his famous decretal *Vergentis in senium* of March 1199, which for the first time equated heresy with the *crimen laesae maiestatis* ("lese majesty," a crime against the sovereign power) of Roman law.

The French barons responded enthusiastically to Innocent's preaching of a crusade against the Albigenses. The consequence was a great bloodbath and land grab. The resistance of the southern nobility was broken in 1213 at the battle of Muret, and by the 1220s the French crown had assimilated the wealthy Languedoc lands of southern France. Because the papacy did not trust the local officials in southern France to purge the remnants of heresy, Innocent sent papal legates to establish courts to deal with the heretics. It was from this context that the Inquisition (ecclesial courts for the discovery and punishment of heresy), officially established in 1233, developed.

Although Innocent reorganized the church, humiliated kings, and took up the sword against heretics, it is not the least of his accomplishments that he realized the importance of law and piety for the well-being of Christendom. He commissioned a collection of canon law that was the first since Gratian's *Decretum* (ca. 1140). It included the decretals of his own first twelve years in office. Completed in 1210, it was sent to the University of Bologna to be the authentic text for teaching. Innocent recognized the value of piety in the religious movements of Dominic (the Dominicans) and Francis (the Franciscans) for the renewal and reform of the church. The institutionalization of asceticism through the papal approval of their orders was a major factor in the development of the thought, religion, and culture of the thirteenth and later centuries. Finally, his summoning the Fourth Lateran Council in 1215 established one of the most important conciliar meetings between Nicaea (325) and Trent (1545–1563). Among this council's accomplishments were the following:

- Setting the number of sacraments at the seven still recognized.
- Making transubstantiation the orthodox doctrinal teaching on the Eucharist.
- Limiting confirmation and ordination to bishops.
- Mandating at least annual penance and Eucharist for all Catholics.
- Legislating moral and educational reform.
- Placing limits on the cult of relics (i.e., the veneration of the bodies or parts of the bodies of saints and of objects that had touched them) and pilgrimages.
- Legislating against the Jews to prohibit their appearance among Christians during Holy Week and to mandate their wearing of yellow identification badges.

Tares Among the Wheat: Heretical and Protest Movements

Compared to his predecessors, Innocent alone was able to realize in practice the papal ideology that had developed up to his time. More than any other before him he focused the power and wealth of the church on the goal of a centralized Christian society. It may be, however, that his very success added to the growing unease and anxiety of some elements of this society, which for some time now had been wondering how the wealth and power of the church correlated with its founding Lord who had said: "My kingdom is not of this world."

Influenced by the renewal movements exemplified in the Cluniac and Gregorian reforms, the increasing marginalization of the poor by a series of famines, urban development, and the rise of a profit economy, more and more people were influenced by preachers who identified the apostolic life with actual poverty.[3] Innocent inherited a series of radical poverty movements that explicitly as well as implicitly criticized the church for its wealth and power: the Humiliati, the Waldenses, the Beguines, and the Cathars or Albigenses. The Humiliati originated in Milan and spread to other cities of Lombardy. The Waldenses originated with the religious conversion of Peter Waldo (Valdez), a wealthy merchant of Lyons, who embraced apostolic poverty. They spread quickly throughout southern France, northern Italy, the Rhineland, and southern Germany. The Beguines formed a movement of pious women active in the cities of the Low Countries, the Rhineland, and northern France. The Cathars, attractive to noblewomen among others, were numerous in the Rhineland and northern Italy and were especially strong in southwestern France. The geographical pattern of these groups roughly corresponds to the map of Europe's most advanced commercial areas. The cloth industry had a key place in the rising commercialization of this time that was pitting a growing pool of poorly paid and dependent workers against the few entrepreneurs who controlled all the resources. It is not accidental that the term *weaver* became associated with social dangers and heretical dissent. All these movements were constituted by lay groups who were particularly sensitive to the profit economy. Although contemporary accounts of these movements were intended to discredit and destroy heresy, the adherents themselves were protesting what they perceived to be the growing greed and corruption in public life.

The Humiliati of the late twelfth and early thirteenth centuries recruited members from the monied, favored class who then embraced the apostolic life of poverty. They exercised poverty in moderation but also in explicit opposition to the new lifestyle of well-being around them. They opposed ostentation, prohibited every kind of usury and interest taking, and distributed their surplus income to the needy. They were decisively opposed to every form of what they perceived to be avarice and greed.

---

[3]The abbey of Cluny in France was founded in 910 and under a series of exemplary abbots soon became the major force in monastic renewal. The Gregorian reform movement takes its name from Gregory VII (pope from 1073–1085) although it was already underway by the 1050s. The Gregorian reform was characterized by forceful disciplinary action against both simony (the buying and selling of church offices) and Nicolaitism (the disregard of clerical celibacy). The Gregorian popes thus became involved in a series of conflicts with secular rulers over simony and with the lower, especially rural, clergy who not infrequently were married or cohabited with women.

The Waldenses originated in the small circle known as the "poor men of Lyons," which gathered about Peter Valdez in the twelfth century. Valdez was a rich merchant of Lyons who some time around 1173 was moved by the story of St. Alexis (a favorite medieval tale about a fifth-century wealthy Roman who gave up everything for a life of mendicancy and almsgiving) and by Jesus's counsel for perfection in Matthew 19:21 ("sell all you own, give the proceeds to the poor, and follow me"). Valdez then provided for his wife, placed his daughters in an abbey, distributed his wealth, and became an itinerant and mendicant preacher. His lifestyle and his preaching against both clerical worldliness and the Cathars soon gained him a following. They produced vernacular translations of parts of the bible for preaching purposes, embraced voluntary poverty, and sought ecclesial recognition at the Third Lateran Council in 1179. The papacy granted them preaching rights only on condition of local clerical approval. This approval was not forthcoming, but the Waldenses began preaching anyway and thus incurred excommunication in 1184. They then organized themselves apart from the church, appointed their own ministers, and developed a theology and piety at variance with the church, including donatist tendencies (the validity of the sacraments depended on the worthiness of the minister). Viciously persecuted through the centuries, they survived to become what is today the Waldensian Church.

The Beguines were groups of women who led a semireligious, communal life and who were active in philanthropic activities in service to the sick and needy. Their male counterparts, the Beghards, were mainly from the cloth industry in which they were weavers, dyers, or fullers. The Beguines did not reject private property, but the Beghards did but held a common purse to support their activities. Their names supposedly derived from that of Lambert le Bègue, a revivalist preacher at Liége. Their social doctrines, religious mysticism, and especially their sympathy toward the Spiritual Franciscans led to their condemnation by the Council of Vienna in 1311.

The most notorious of all these groups were the Cathars (from *katharos*, meaning "pure") or Albigenses (after the town of Albi), whose opponents associated them with the ancient heresies of dualism and the Manichaeans. Their origins are obscure. They were regarded as a major threat by the church both for their heretical theology and for the austerity of their lives. The latter gained adherents for them by its sharp contrast to the laxity of the clerical life of the time. Their theology seems to have been strongly dualistic in positing the evil of the physical world, which caused them to abandon all material possessions and to abstain from sexual relations and from all foods that were products of sexual intercourse. The purpose of redemption was liberation of the soul from the flesh, and thus the end of the "mixed state" of human life brought about by the devil. Their moral doctrine was extremely rigoristic and thus too austere for most followers. They distinguished between two classes of persons: the "perfect" and ordinary "believers." The "perfect" received the *consolamentum* (i.e., baptism of the Holy Spirit by imposition of hands) and then kept all the ethical

291

precepts. The ordinary "believers" were allowed to lead normal lives but promised to receive the *consolamentum* when in danger of death. If they recovered, they were obliged to lead the life of the "perfect" or die by starvation, the *endura*. The Albigenses believed that they, not the church, were truly following in the footsteps of Christ. They believed they were the true *pauperes Christi*, the true imitators of the apostolic life, because they did not possess houses, land, or any personal possessions just as Christ and his disciples had nothing. They charged that the Catholic clergy sought only the things of this world, adding house to house and lands to lands. They charged that even the most high-minded clergy were fallen because individual poverty practiced within a wealthy corporation was no poverty at all.

It is interesting that some of the tenets of the Albigenses parallel those of Catholic Christianity. Their strictures against sexual relations, eating meat, and accumulating possessions had a long history in monastic spirituality. All these themes were embodied in a widespread and fervent revival of the apostolic life as the model of the ideal Christian existence. It was a model that stressed scriptural literalism, simplicity, and poverty. It is also of interest that the frequent orthodox charges that the Albigenses were usurers and sexually licentious reflect behaviors forbidden to orthodox Christians and may be a projection on a marginal social group.

The Albigenses were condemned by successive councils in 1165, 1184, and 1215. After Innocent III's unsuccessful attempt to convert them, a crusade was mounted against them, and in 1233 Gregory IX charged the Dominican inquisition with their final extirpation. They had largely disappeared by the end of the fourteenth century.

Why did peasants, workers, merchants, and nobles, including women, join the Albigenses? For the poor there may have seemed the chance to exchange their corrupting and distressing involuntary poverty for a morally and spiritually sanctioned voluntary poverty. For women, whether prostitutes or noblewomen, there was the offer of a sense of equality that the patriarchal and priestly Roman church could not make. For others there may just have been the comfort of an ultimate spiritual security. It seems that economic insecurity and social friction contributed to religious heterodoxy, for the unorganized and unprotected poor flocked to the antichurch of the Albigenses. This movement also seems to indicate that more and more laity were pressing for a more spiritually responsive clergy as well as desiring for themselves a greater share of participation in Christian spirituality. The more successful participants in the new commercial society, both businessmen and usurers, tended to remain faithful to the traditional church.

Weeders before the Harvest: Franciscans and Dominicans

Francis (ca. 1181–1226) and Dominic (1170–1221) responded in innovative ways to the social crises of their time that had stimulated the rise and attraction of the various heretical movements we have mentioned. The social construction of reality to which the early medieval church had contributed so much was now showing ever more dangerous signs of stress. The theology of the church had worked to legitimate and reflect a culture based on a patrimonial peasant economy that was almost totally agricultural. The population had remained fairly stable, and kinship and social communities were the norms for stable personal relationships. At all social levels, roles were indicated and prescribed by sex, age, and hierarchical position. Cooperation was the norm for such settled agrarian communities. Church and state were closely related and even in their antagonisms shared the vision of a Christian commonwealth. The center of the system was the king, who controlled mobility and preserved balanced relations. The church provided the ideology for the king's role by pronouncing and affirming the values of stability, tradition, and order in the doctrine of the three estates or orders (workers, prayers, warriors, as discussed earlier). The monastery was itself the ideal and incarnation of *stabilitas*. Theology and ritual maintained the equilibrium between the earthly and heavenly cities through the sacrifice and penance of the people and by the proxy of monks and priests.

The social changes that began around the eleventh century were stimulated by population growth, technological improvements, urban growth, and the profit economy. The changes that accompanied these developments were in kind as well as degree. Personal roles as businessman, citizen, and worker became increasingly differentiated. These new roles were less all-embracing than the groupings of village and kindred, and the keynote of life shifted from cooperation to competition. An increasing number of people, deprived of kin and community, faced the need to prove themselves rather than play assigned roles. They were now exposed to new kinds of social experience for which their religion offered no meaningful patterns. Their disorientation was not merely material suffering but a cognitive dissonance; that is, it became increasingly difficult to coordinate personal and social experience with the teachings of the church. That is why the newly rich such as Valdez and Francis suffered disorientation as much as the poor. Mobility in any dimension— horizontally in space or vertically in a social hierarchy—raises new problems for the displaced person. Such significant changes called into question the religious construct of society. Religious authorities faced adaptation or obsolescence.

The urban, economic development led then to social experiences for which the church provided no meaningful patterning. What relevance had a religion of stability to a life of mobility, competition, and uncertainty? If God is the reinforcer of social order and conformity and of the unity of religious and political structures, then what happens to those who fall between the cracks of the new social realities? How can God have any regard for the marginal person who is in physical and social transition?

The church's response to these issues tended toward reaffirmation of traditional practices such as the piety of pilgrimage, church building, monastic patronage, eucharistic ritual (the doctrine of transubstantiation arose in 1215), and indulgences to meet the new social scene. Furthermore, the Cluniac and Gregorian renewal movements were intent on purifying, not changing, the church and its theology. In contrast, the heretical movements were antistructural and thus raised a crucial note of disobedience in the promulgation of their new apostolic lifestyle. The resolution of crisis was sought in a renewed search for community and for identification with the divine through personal commitment to asceticism. Both Francis and Dominic were able to incorporate contemporary concerns into their commitment to apostolic poverty as the means of reaching a new communion with God. Whereas the Benedictine monasteries of the earlier Middle Ages were rooted in the land and spurned towns as iniquitous, the mendicant orders of the Dominicans and Franciscans rooted themselves in the centers of urban development. The Benedictine movements had emphasized humility and obedience and stability; poverty to them was understood in terms of poverty of the spirit. The mendicant orders, as their name indicates, lived by begging and emphasized material poverty. As a consequence of their desire to imitate the early church and the wandering, preaching, poor Christ as a response to the erosion of feudalism by urban and economic developments, they understood their place to be in the cities and towns. Their effectiveness was owing in no small part to the fact that they displaced the older monastic ideal of rural stability by urban itinerancy; they were able to go to where distressed people longed for their message of the life and poverty of Jesus. The nontheological and nonspiritual factors in this development included the fact that since poverty was a natural element in the rural medieval society, the renunciation explicit in the *vita apostolica* could not be clearly manifested. Poverty is clearly an issue only when it is contrasted with the wealth present in the cities. That is why to a Benedictine monk in his rural cloister, poverty took the form of the denial of self-will, but to the urban mendicant, poverty was destitution. The cities were also the locus for the mendicant movements not only because they were the places where people were most beset by the cognitive dissonance between the feudal order and religion on the one hand, and new experiences of wealth and poverty on the other hand, but also because it is possible for groups of people to beg only in cities. One or two persons might survive by begging in the countryside but not whole groups of people. An organized community of beggars can survive only within a larger population that has enough disposable income to support them. Although the Dominicans and Franciscans shared these factors, they differed in their origins and development.

The Dominicans, or Order of Preachers, were founded by the Spanish priest, Dominic Guzman (1170–1221). His inspiration to found an order whose primary function would consist of itinerant preaching of the gospel derived from his accidental confrontation with the Albigensian movement. In 1203 Dominic accompanied his bishop Diego on a royal mission to Scandinavia to arrange a marriage for the king's son. On the way they stayed in Toulouse where Dominic engaged the Albigensian innkeeper in a nightlong religious conversation that converted him back to the Catholic faith. This experience made Dominic aware of both the prevalence of the Albigensian heresy and the need for persuasive preaching to counteract it. Soon afterward, Dominic met some Cistercians who had been sent by the pope to combat this heresy but who were totally unsuccessful in their endeavors. Dominic pointed out that they would never be able to converse with the heretic so long as they embodied the ecclesial wealth and power that the heretics were rebelling against. Only by equaling the ascetic austerity of the heretics would it be possible to preach the true doctrine with credibility. Thus began a new style of Catholic evangelizing that embraced voluntary and absolute poverty as a means of promoting an itinerant preaching mission. The difference between Dominic and his contemporary, Francis of Assisi, is that Dominic embraced poverty as a tactic to get a hearing whereas Francis embraced poverty as an end in itself.

Dominic's years of preaching in southern France bore little fruit because in the meantime the pope decided to restore order and true religion by means of a crusade rather than preaching. In 1215 Dominic went to Toulouse where he received the support of the bishop and also attracted followers. In 1216 the successor to Innocent III, Honorius III, officially recognized Dominic and his followers as an order according to the Rule of St. Augustine, which was more flexible than the Benedictine Rule. In the next years Dominic traveled tirelessly, establishing friaries (from *frater*, "brother") and organizing the order. He urged his preachers to live entirely by alms in their own communities as well as on the road; everywhere the gospel was to be preached in itinerant poverty. Furthermore, by example and by argument he insisted that the order always remain flexible so that it could respond to needs as they arose. In 1220 Dominic set out to preach to the pagans in Hungary, but he became ill and on his return to Bologna died.

Dominic's original impetus to preach the gospel to the Albigensians had convinced him of the necessity for a learned ministry. Heresy was to be combated by preaching that was reinforced by the example of the apostolic life of the primitive church. The establishment in Dominic's own lifetime of his order in the intellectual centers of Paris and Bologna was significant for his goal of academic discipline to support preaching. The intellectual prowess of the Dominicans (by 1228 three years of theological study were required for permission to do public preaching) was soon recognized by the papal appointment of the Dominicans as inquisitors in 1232 by Gregory IX and exemplified by its outstanding scholars such as Albertus Magnus (ca. 1200–1280) and Thomas Aquinas (ca. 1225–1274).

The most radical exponent of the new evangelical piety of the twelfth and thirteenth centuries was Francis of Assisi (1181 or 1182–1226). More than any other of his time, and perhaps since, Francis lived out the ideal of "naked, following the naked Christ" (*nudus nudum Christum sequi*) and "poor, following the poor Christ" (*pauper pauperum Christum sequi*). These twelfth-century formulas, adapted from ancient tradition, associated the individual Christian with Christ in a common nakedness, or poverty, of both worldy goods and worldly cares.

Francis vividly enacted this ideal when, nearly twenty-five years of age, he stood before his angry father and the bishop's court of Assisi and stripped himself naked, gave his clothes to his father, and declared that from now on he would speak only of his Father in heaven.

Whereas for Dominic poverty was a means for gaining an audience for preaching, for Francis poverty was the goal and expression of the imitation of Christ. Francis's emphasis on a life of the utmost poverty confounded not only his merchant father but others as well. Francis rejected the new merchant world of profits and accumulation of wealth, the world of his father, as something so corrupt that he henceforth refused even to touch money, which he regarded as excrement. He urged his followers to flee money as if it were the devil. The 1223 Rule of St. Francis strictly commanded all friars "never to receive coin or money, for themselves or for any other person." This attitude is graphically illustrated by the story in the thirteenth-century work, *The Mirror of Perfection*, in which Francis commanded a friar who had absent mindedly touched money to pick up the coin with his mouth and to place it with his mouth upon a pile of dung.

Although this attitude toward money would at first seem unlikely to enhance the recruitment process, it nevertheless worked wonders. Whether Francis touched some deep emotional springs of piety or the nerves and anxieties of the urban, profit-oriented society, his ideal of nakedly following the naked Christ stimulated a remarkable response from his contemporaries. Francis soon became the reluctant head of an organization that, in perceiving the whole world as its parish, grew by the early fourteenth century to encompass all Europe with numbers reaching perhaps as high as 28,000. Francis also established a female branch known as the Poor Clares, after Clare of Assisi, the first woman converted to the poverty ideal by Francis. For those who were unable to embrace the full rigor of Franciscan poverty, a third order was established that permitted remaining in secular life while practicing certain elements of the ideal.

Why were Francis and his mendicant order so appealing? Certainly it is clear that the medieval person was deeply concerned about achieving salvation and that, since the early church, poverty had been presented as the preferred path to nearness to Christ. Francis himself was reputed to have received the stigmata, the very wounds of Christ, the highest expression of medieval piety. It is, however, possible to surmise other motives as well. Large numbers of people in the cities were forced to subsist on begging, and the Franciscan movement offered a transition from secular to religious begging accompanied by security and respectability. After all, if one has to beg to survive to begin with, why not join a movement that will not only enhance one's receipts but add heavenly bread to one's daily bread? And rebellion against fathers and the rejection of social respectability were not limited to Francis (or to his age!). The fact that well-to-do families supported the friars but were horrified by the prospect of their children joining them may have imbued the poverty of the friars with the appeal of high romance. And for the intellectuals and aspiring teachers of the time, the friars, both Dominican and Franciscan, offered an escape from the heavy debts and obligations incurred even then by a university education, as well as escape from the rat race for promotions and financial support. The desire of scholars to live and work in a university community dovetailed nicely with the needs of friars to have scholars to educate their new recruits.

Dominican and Franciscan scholars addressed the social and ethical problems confronting urban life. They legitimated private property as necessary and good for the development of an ordered state. They applied their new moral theology to economics and developed a theory of just price in relation to supply and demand, and they conceived of money as a rational medium of exchange rather than an attractive evil. These contributions as well as their work on business ethics in general made it possible for the urban Christian, previously marginalized by feudal social mores and religion, to be reintegrated into Christian society. Furthermore, as mendicant orders, the Dominican and Franciscans provided merchants with a meritorious subject for philanthropy. This was not only a key to the justification of profits but also an honorable and much preferred option to the penance and opprobrium that earlier had accrued to businesspersons.

The mendicant friars not only supplied the city dwellers with a new ethic and an outlet for charity but also with an urban ideology which explicitly recognized and praised the city as an integral part of the well-ordered society. The city's contributions to the whole society rested on wealth. This urban ideology was then crowned by the creation of not only urban but *merchant* saints, and thus was "marked the coming of age of Europe's commercial economy." The paradox is that the great despiser of money, Francis of Assisi himself became such an urban merchant saint. In the 1260s, in one of his annual sermons to his city, the archbishop of Pisa, Federigo Visconti, exclaimed: "How pleasing it must be for merchants to know that one of their cohorts, St. Francis, was a merchant and also was made a saint in our time. Oh, how much good hope there must be for merchants, who have such a merchant intermediary with God."[4]

The Rise of the Universities

The development of universities was closely tied to the urban and mendicant developments we have sketched. Organized studies had earlier depended on the monasteries and cathedral schools, and they were rooted in their everyday tasks of calculating liturgical calendars, composing books on the lives of the saints, hymns, and lectionaries, and the daily needs of computation and correspondence regarding rents, crops, and lands. The foundational studies for the development of a "free man," the seven liberal arts, had long been established. Even with the development of the

[4]Lester K. Little, *Religious Poverty and the Profit Economy in Medieval Europe* (Ithaca, N.Y.: Cornell University Press, 1978), pp. 213–217.

professional curricula of theology, medicine, and law in the universities, the arts faculty continued to emphasize the *trivium* (grammar, dialectic, and rhetoric) and the *quadrivium* (arithmetic, music, geometry, and astronomy). We have already mentioned the excitement generated by the discovery and use of logic and its impetus to early scholasticism. By the twelfth century, there was growing enthusiasm for ordering knowledge into a coherent whole, a *summa*. In theology, the great example is Peter Lombard's *Four Books of Sentences* which, endorsed by the Fourth Lateran Council in 1215, became the leading theological textbook until replaced by the *Summa theologica* of Thomas Aquinas in the sixteenth century. Lombard's contemporary, Gratian, working in Bologna, initiated the science of canon law with his *Decretum* (ca. 1139), which sought to harmonize critically the legal resources of the time. Gratian's "Concordance of Discordant Canons" (*Concordantia Discordantium Canonum*) dealt with nearly 4,000 texts and with conciliar and papal decrees. The advances in the study of theology and law symbolized by these two major works began to attract students from all parts of Europe to those places, initially Bologna and Paris, where these subjects had the most and the best-known teachers (Figure 16.1).

The cities were not only conducive for the development of universities but strove to attract universities. The cities provided a freedom of life and intellect not possible in the rural monastic schools. The cities provided living possibilities for the increasingly large numbers of teachers and students flocking around renowned masters. And the urban social arrangements of charters and guilds provided models for the first university corporations. Indeed, the word *universitas* can mean "corporation" or "guild." Thus for their mutual support and protection, students formed corporations (student unions) and were granted monopolies by the city government similar to those of other guilds. Teachers later followed their example. A student who completed a satisfactory apprenticeship to a teacher received a certificate of membership in the guild of teachers (i.e., became a "master"); hence the degree system.

Cities, and rulers too, solicited the founding of universities because they realized the practical value of centers of learning. Scholars not only provided an attractive aura to a town; they also provided technical know-how and advice for merchants, and a pool of servants for government and the church. Nevertheless, then as now, the pursuit of education was not without cost and frequently involved the accumulation of substantial debt. Graduates faced an uncertain and insecure future, and far too many masters had only marginal incomes from the fees of their students. Thus there was a constant search for patrons and benefices for support, and this meant having to make oneself useful as a clerk or administrator. As mentioned, the mendicant orders provided welcome relief from the economic distractions suffered by these scholars and teachers. Theologians freed from the necessity to keep a sharp eye out for advancement and favors could now live fully in an academic community and pursue the new ideas that were being introduced to Europe by Jewish and Islamic philosophers and scientists.

Figure 16.1 European Universities (12th–16th centuries)

The Discovery of Aristotle

The core of the new ideas flooding into the Latin West in the thirteenth century was the discovery of the complete writings of Aristotle. Renewed contact with Aristotle's philosophy was occurring in Syria, Constantinople, Sicily, and above all in Spain. In all these areas, the mixed population of Christian, Muslim, and Jew stimulated intellectual exchange. Toledo exemplified these developments as the leading center for the translation of ancient Greek writings into Latin. This was a sensational event because the full body of Aristotle's philosophy had implications for every facet of medieval life from esthetics to politics to theology. The incompatibility of Aristotle and traditional Augustinian Christian thought soon became apparent in many spheres of life. For example, the traditional ecclesial claim of superiority over the secular world based on the Augustinian view of the state as a consequence of sin was challenged by the Aristotelian view of the state as a positive and creative force. Not surprisingly, rulers wanted to hear more about this. In the realms of philosophy and theology, Aristotelian thought brought new challenges to everything from epistemology to sacramental theology. In short, Aristotle—whose influence was so great that it became commonplace to refer to him simply as "The Philosopher"—affected nearly everthing people thought and experienced about God, the world, and humankind.

Once again, the mendicant friars contributed excitement and innovation, in this case to the universities. The Dominicans and Franciscans, with their vision of the world as their parish and of education as the tool for its conversion, unleashed an intellectual energy that transformed universities from trade schools for clerks into centers of intellectual ferment and creativity. Such intellectual giants as Albertus Magnus (ca. 1200–1280), Thomas Aquinas (ca. 1225–1274), and Meister Eckhard (ca. 1260–1327) among the Dominicans, and Bonaventure (ca. 1217–1274), Duns Scotus (ca. 1265–1308), and William of Ockham (ca. 1285–1347) among the Franciscans made theology the "queen of the sciences."

Thomas Aquinas and the Cathedral of Intellect

Aquinas has long been regarded as one of the most brilliant and clearest thinkers of the Middle Ages, indeed even of western Christianity. The range of his thought and the phenomenal synthesis he achieved in relating reason and revelation give his architectonic system an esthetic quality. "St. Thomas's thought has often been likened to a Gothic cathedral, and at the risk of banality, their common sweep and proportion, balance and harmony, may be reiterated."[5]

And yet Thomas was no disembodied intellect. By all accounts, he was of massive

[5]Gordon Leff, *Medieval Thought: St. Augustine to Ockham* (Baltimore: Penguin Books, 1965), p. 213.

physical proportions, although the story that a semicircle had to be cut out of the table to accommodate his girth is only legend. It was undoubtedly his stature along with his quiet and gentle nature that led his fellow students to dub him "the dumb ox." His teacher, Albert the Great, was far more perceptive than Thomas's fellow students when he told the class: "You call him a Dumb Ox; I tell you this Dumb Ox shall bellow so loud that his bellowings will fill the world."[6]

Albert was right, although Thomas's "bellows" would not be measured in decibels but in a sort of Richter scale of conceptual intensity. One occasion when both occurred was during a great court dinner given by King Louis IX (St. Louis, 1214–1270). Attending the dinner out of respect for the authority of the king and the command of his Dominican superiors, Thomas soon became absorbed in his own theological reflections in the midst of the glitter and hubbub of the royal dinner. Suddenly, during a lull in the conversation, goblets and plates jumped and crashed in response to Thomas's huge fist smashing down on the table accompanied by his bellow, "And *that* will settle the Manichees!" King Louis's response was to send two of his secretaries to Thomas's place to take notes of his refutation of the heretical community Dominic had set out to convert by theological argument a generation earlier.[7]

Thomas was born into the great feudal family of Count Landulf of Aquino, whose castle was near Naples and who was related to the emperor and to the king of France. In consonance with his family's position and prestige, Thomas was sent at the ripe old age of five to the famous Benedictine monastery of Monte Cassino, where he was to be trained to become its abbot. As a teenager, however, Thomas decided to enter the newly formed begging order of the Dominicans. His father and warrior brothers were furious that Thomas would turn away from a respectable ecclesial career customary for the younger sons of nobility. No doubt the family concern was not just for what they perceived to be an immature decision by Thomas but also for their good name, which they did not want to see connected with ecclesial riffraff. The family response was as straightforward as it was feudal: They imprisoned him in the family castle for fifteen months. As if this were not enough, his brothers attempted either to dissuade him from his decision or to render it impossible by scandal. This they did by putting a beautiful courtesan in his room. The story is that Thomas sprang up, snatched a burning log from the fire, and chased the poor woman out of his room, slamming and barring the door after her and burning a huge black cross into the door with the blazing brand.

Thomas's determination to become a Dominican was not weakened, and he joined the order in April 1244. He studied under and with St. Albertus Magnus (Albert the Great) at both Paris and Cologne. It was Albert who introduced Thomas to the newly discovered philosophy of Aristotle. In 1252 Thomas returned to Paris to

---

[6]G. K. Chesterton, *Saint Thomas Aquinas* (Garden City, N.Y.: Image Books, 1956), p. 71.
[7]Ibid., pp. 97–101.

301

become lecturer at the Dominican convent of St. Jacques. In 1259 he was sent to lecture in various Italian cities until he was recalled to Paris in 1269. Soon on the move again, he went to Naples in 1272 to set up a Dominican school. He died in 1274 at the Cistercian monastery of Fossanuova on his way to the Council of Lyons. Several of his propositions were condemned in 1277 by the archbishops of Paris and Canterbury, but in 1278 his teaching was officially imposed on the Dominicans by its General Chapter. He was canonized in 1323 and declared a Doctor of the Church (i.e., official teacher) by Pope Pius V in 1567. In 1879 Leo XIII's encyclical *Aeterni Patris* made Thomas's works mandatory for all students of theology. In 1923 on the sixth centenary of Thomas's canonization, his teaching authority was reiterated by Pope Pius XI.

Thomas was and continues to be so influential in the life and thought of the church not only because he addressed clearly and forcefully the crisis of intellectual faith of his time but also because he did so in a way that opened faith to dialogue with philosophy, revelation with empirical reason, religion with science. Thomas slaked his contemporaries' great thirst for reality without giving in to their influential cries that one could drink at only the bar of reason or only the bar of faith but not both. For Thomas, there is only one truth, not two mutually exclusive truths. This conviction is expressed in his watchword that grace does not destroy nature but fulfills it. Put another way, there is a continuity between reason and revelation:

> The gifts of grace are added to nature in such a manner that they do not remove it but perfect it. So it is with the light of faith that is infused in us gratuitously; it does not destroy the light of natural knowledge with which we are by nature endowed. Now, although the natural light of the human mind does not suffice for the manifestation of the things that are made manifest by faith, yet it is impossible that what is divinely taught to us by faith be contrary to the things with which we are endowed by nature. For the one or the other would then have to be false, and, since both come to us from God, God would be to us an author of falsehood, which is impossible. Rather, the situation is this. Since within the imperfect there is a certain imitation of what is perfect, though an incomplete one, in what is known through natural knowledge there is a certain likeness of what is taught to us by faith.[8]

Like Anselm before him, Thomas also began from the position of faith seeking understanding. Both insisted on the importance of reason. But whereas Anselm developed the rational necessity of concepts already given by revelation, Thomas thought there are some truths, such as the existence of God, that can be developed

---

[8]P. Mandonnet, ed., *S. Thomae Aquinatis Opuscula Omnia*, vol. III, (Paris: P.Lethielleux, 1927), p. 50f. Cited by Anton Pegis in his introduction to *Saint Thomas Aquinas: On the Truth of the Catholic Faith, Summa contra Gentiles. Book One: God* (Garden City, N.Y.: Image Books, 1955), p. 24.

by applying reason to the data provided by sense experience. Thomas began with what is and reflected on what that means for faith. And for Thomas, what *is* in reality is not first in the mind but, rather, what is in the mind first *exists* in reality. In Thomas's words, "Everything that is in the intellect has been in the senses."[9]

On this basis, Thomas regarded Anselm's ontological argument as invalid and put in its place rational proofs for the existence of God that began by examination of nature. His arguments for the existence of God are heavily indebted to Aristotelian philosophy, especially the relationship between effects and their causes. Everything that exists has a cause, except the cause behind the series of causes. This Aristotelian reasoning enabled Thomas to conclude that there is a first unmoved mover, God. This argument in turn allows a certain knowledge of God's being as eternal, without matter and without composition. Thus God is his own essence and being. That God is a personal Trinity is, however, not a knowledge achievable by reason but granted by revelation. Here, again, revelation does not destroy reason but fulfills it.

Thomas applied his conviction of the continuity of nature and grace, the natural and the supernatural, to all areas of life. Here we can only sketch how this continuity influenced his understanding of human nature and salvation.

Thomas accepted the Greek philosophical tradition's understanding of human nature as being oriented to self-fulfillment. The Greek term for this is *eudaemonism* and is sometimes translated to mean "happiness," but it should not be interpreted to mean that the purpose and meaning of life is simply to have fun. Rather, when the term is broken down, it is seen to mean the driving divine power (*daemon*) toward the well (*eu*)—that is, health, wholeness, the fulfillment of one's essential nature. For Thomas, the Christian, this pagan beginning really finds its true fulfillment only in the blessedness of knowing not just one's self but God. Thus the God-given supernatural or theological virtues of faith, hope, and love are necessary to complete the natural virtues of courage, moderation, wisdom, and justice and thereby enable the blessedness of knowing God.

Following the common sense philosophy of Aristotle, Thomas agreed that virtues are acquired through practice and thus become a "habit." The supernatural virtues, however, unlike the natural virtues, are not innate to humankind but have to be infused into the person through the grace of God mediated by the church's sacraments. Once infused, the supernatural virtues are, analogously to the natural virtues, to be "acquired" or "realized." In this sense, the person who is in a state of grace does good works that please God and thus cooperates in his or her salvation. The scholastic phrase that expresses this process is *facere quod in se est*—that is, to do what is within oneself. The significant point about this order of salvation is that salvation is understood as occurring within one through the actualization of faith formed by acts of charity. Thus the person who did his or her best to cooperate with the aid of grace would receive the reward of eternal life as a just due. Later scholastic

[9]Chesterton, *St. Thomas Aquinas*, p. 162.

theologians would be even more optimistic about human capability to cooperate with God in salvation and would suggest that good works done in the state of nature would also be rewarded by God with an infusion of grace as an appropriate due.

Although Thomas's synthesis of reason and revelation and his conviction that faith could not be endangered by reason provided a certain intellectual freedom to medieval thinkers, the sixteenth-century reformers would regard this accomplishment as the source of the fundamental distortion of faith into human moral efforts. From a historical point of view there is also a sense that the age of Thomas was the watershed of the medieval era. The greatest of the medieval popes, Innocent III, had died in 1216. The ideal Christian monarch, Louis IX of France, died in 1270, and three years later so did Henry III, the English servant of the papacy. The close friend of Thomas, the great Franciscan theologian and mystic St. Bonaventure, also died in 1274. The creative synthesis constructed in this period covered all realms of life including not only revelation and science but sacerdotal authority and individual religious experience. The hierarchical church authority, the sovereign state, and the links between them could not be maintained, however. Even the advances in the development of canon law, reinforced by the Thomist claim that the state is subject to an eternal and absolute order of values, could not stand before the growing view that the law has no other sanction than the absolute will of the state. This would be graphically expressed in little more than a generation after Thomas when Philip of France turned the Thomist hierarchy upside down in his subjugation of Pope Boniface VIII. Perhaps partly because of the tremendous intellectual achievement of Thomas and partly because of the later Roman Catholic endorsement of Thomism, it has become a common fallacy to regard thirteenth-century thought as the age of Thomism.

Chapter 17

"THE HAYWAIN," OR
"ALL FLESH IS GRASS"

The long-striven-for medieval aspiration of the *corpus Christianum*, the Christian commonwealth, appeared to reach fulfillment in the great Thomist synthesis. As discussed in Chapter 16, this achievement was short-lived if not illusory. A brief review of the innumerable factors that contributed to the religious and moral hardening of Christendom's arteries will provide the context for the attacks on the heart of the church's authority: the papacy.

Charles of Anjou, the brother of Louis IX of France, had invaded southern Italy under papal auspices and had the grand scheme of creating a new Mediterranean empire. His plan, however, was frustrated by the rage of the Sicilians against the oppressive French occupation and rule. This rage erupted in the massacre of the French garrison of Palermo on Easter Monday, 1282. The revolt, known as the Sicilian Vespers because it began at the hour of vespers, led to a protracted war involving France, Sicily, Naples, Aragon, and the papacy. Of all the parties involved, the papacy lost the most by siding with the French (Pope Martin IV, 1281–1285, was himself French and a former servant of the crown) and overusing to ill effect the powers of excommunication, interdiction, deposition of rulers, and preaching crusades.

Papal authority also suffered from abusing its power in other financial and territorial issues. The contemporary Christian doubt and even open criticism of papal activity, further enhanced by the critical spirit of inquiry arising in the arts and law faculties of the universities, reached an intensity previously unknown. Furthermore, the laity in the new towns and urban areas who were now also increasingly part of a new social class began to perceive the papacy with a new suspicion and even animosity. This new laity, the nucleus of the Third Estate, was further liberated from traditional understandings of papal authority by the recent acceptance of Aristotelian thought. Members of this social group began to conceive of themselves as citizens with intrinsic rights and duties and not simply as subjects of papal authority. The Aristotelian orientation of the age also redirected the attention of scholars and citizens from preoccupation with the heavenly city to interest in the earthly city, the natural, and the human. The obvious disparity between the theoretical exposition of the *corpus Christianum* and the reality of papal activity further prepared the way for the development and reception of new political theories. The papacy's claim to be an institution of government rooted in the supranatural began to be challenged by an emerging concept of the state as a body of citizens.

This statism (nationalism was a later development), frequently attributed to the spread of Roman law and Aristotelian philosphy, included the appearance of assemblies of estates (representatives of church, nobles, and towns) and was one of the first signs that people were beginning to put their own particular interests above those of Christendom as a whole. The erosion of the ideal of the *corpus Christianum* was further abetted by the displacement of Latin by vernacular literature. Latin as the universal language was a potent aspect of the idea of a universal European Christian community. Now the Latin monopoly was being broken by the rapid rise of vernacular literature of every type, including hymns and songs and the translation of the bible into the vernacular. Although this development was not a direct consequence of the declining credibility of the papacy, it was a process that impinged on the universalism represented by the papacy as a universal government.

The credibility of the papacy was, however, directly affected by another development of the time: the growth of subjectivism. From the beginning, papal ideology had distinguished person and office. Popes were always acknowledged to be "the unworthy heir" of St. Peter; what was crucial was the objective and universal validity of the institution of the papacy itself. Now there was growing concern about the person of the pope himself. This subjective assessment of the personality of the pope was, ironically, the basis for the Franciscan argument for papal infallibility.

In the latter half of the thirteenth century, the Spiritual Franciscans, a minority group of the Franciscan order, vehemently upheld Francis's ideal of absolute poverty in opposition to the more lax interpretations of the Conventual Franciscans, who were allowed the use of property and money held in trust for them. This so-called *usus pauper* was embodied in Pope Nicholas III's decretal *Exiit qui Seminat* (1279). Influenced by the apocalyptic theology of history advanced by Joachim of Fiore (d. 1202), the spokesperson for the Spiritual Franciscans, Peter John Olivi (d. 1298), proclaimed that the final age of history had begun with Francis. Olivi and others harshly criticized the wealthy church and its existence as a state. They called for a return to the poverty of the primitive church and warned that the Antichrist would appear in the papacy. The argument for papal infallibility was designed to *limit* the power of future popes and thus to prevent the prophesied Antichrist from altering the endorsement of the Spiritual Franciscans by Celestine V (1294). This zealous revival of the ideal of absolute poverty to the point of Christian anarchy against all institutions, including the papacy, was influential in stimulating a mood of apocalyptic suspicion about the total ecclesial institution.

Boniface VIII and the Decline of the Papacy

Hailed by the Spiritual Franciscans as "the angelic pope" because of his reputed goodness and piety, Celestine V was the compromise candidate of the College of Cardinals. Following the death of Pope Nicholas IV in 1292, the College of Cardinals had been deadlocked for twenty-seven months because of the conflicting factions within the college of the powerful Roman noble families of the Orsini and the Colonna. This compromise candidate was from outside the college. He was the esteemed pious and ascetic hermit, Peter of Murrone (ca. 1215–1296). At the time of his election, he was nearly eighty years old and yielded to the pleas of the Cardinals with great reluctance. It was immediately apparent to all, including Peter himself, that he was unequal to the responsibilities thrust on him. He was crowned pope on August 29, 1294, and abdicated on December 13 the same year. His abdication was a sensation at the time and earned him a place in Dante's Vestibule of Hell—the place of futility:

> And when I'd noted here and there a shade
> Whose face I knew, I saw and recognized
> The coward spirit of the man who made
> The great refusal.[1]

Clestine V was said to have heard heavenly voices urging him to abdicate. After consulting with Cardinal Benedict Gaetani, Celestine declared the legal validity of papal resignation and laid down his office. The fact that Gaetani was then chosen to be pope prompted the rumor that Celestine's "heavenly voices" were really the whispers of Cardinal Gaetani while he slept. Gaetani, now Boniface VIII (1294–1303), fearing that both his own opponents and the adherents of Celestine would unite against him, had Celestine placed in custody until his death in 1296.

Boniface, born about 1240 at Anagni, was of Roman noble lineage. He had studied law at Bologna and went into the service of the Curia, eventually being made a cardinal and a legate to France. Although an able administrator and canon lawyer, he was vain (he distributed statuettes of himself and claimed, "I am pope, I am Caesar"), arrogant, extremely ambitious for increasing his own family fortune, and temperamental. By experience and temperament, Boniface represented the papal legacy of Gregory VII and Innocent III that political facts could and should be

---

[1]Dorothy Sayers, trans., *The Comedy of Dante Alighieri. Cantica I: Hell*, III, 58–61 (Baltimore: Penguin Books, 1957), pp. 86–87.

altered by papal ideology. Unfortunately for both Boniface and the papal office, the world context had shifted markedly since Innocent's triumphs.

When Boniface attempted to increase his family's estates at the expense of other noble houses, in particular the Colonna, he ran into his first difficulties. The Colonna raided the convoy transporting Boniface's (actually, the papal treasury's) funds. In return Boniface preached a crusade against the Colonna, destroyed their castles, dispersed their lands among his relatives, and forced the Colonnas to flee to the French court. Two of the Colonna family were cardinals, and although now deposed by Boniface, they continued to call for a general council to try the pope for his ostensible part in removing Celestine from the papacy.

Boniface proved to be equally adept at alienating the kings of England and France. In 1295 Philip IV of France (1285–1314) and Edward I of England (1272–1307) were preparing for war over the duchy of Gascony. The duchy was a continuing source of friction between the two countries that finally led to the outbreak of the Hundred Years' War in 1337. Both kings moved to supplement their war chests by taxing the clergy. In 1296 Boniface challenged both kings by his bull *Clericis Laicos*, which forbade clergy to give up ecclesial revenues or property to any ruler without prior consent of the pope. The bull further forbade the laity, princes, or officials to exact or receive taxes from the clergy. Neither Edward nor Philip was intimidated. Philip responded by banning the export of precious metals from France, thus cutting off the flow of money from France to the papal court. Philip also expelled all foreign merchants from France, which affected those who handled the papal finances in France. Boniface had met his match. He began to try to mend relations with the king by explaining that the bull did not invalidate feudal clerical obligations and that certainly "voluntary" gifts could be made to the king by the clergy upon the king's "friendly suggestion." And if there was a case of necessity, then the king who was the judge of such things could proceed to taxation without papal permission. Finally, to appease Philip's anger and show his strong affection for the French monarchy, Boniface canonized Philip's grandfather, Louis IX, in 1297.

Boniface's next miscalculation was stimulated by the great jubilee year, 1300. On the basis of the popular belief that special graces and indulgences could be gained in Rome at the turn of a century, Boniface proclaimed the first jubilee indulgence in February 1300. This afforded Boniface a means of putting on a great show of papal pomp and salvaging his damaged reputation. Huge crowds flocked to Rome, but Boniface failed to notice the singular absence of princes and rulers in these crowds. Thus he mistook appearances for reality and assumed that universal support for the papacy was undiminished. Boniface's renewed self-assurance was once again shattered by the French king, however.

Informed in 1301 that Philip had imprisoned the bishop of Pamiers, Bernard Saisset, on charges of defamation of the crown, treason, sedition, simony, and heresy, Boniface charged the king with violating the freedom and immunity of the church and reinstituted the bull *Clericis laicos* for France. Furthermore, Boniface summoned the French bishops to Rome to take measures to reform the king and the kingdom. The bull *Ausculta fili* ("Listen, son") of December 1301 summoned Philip himself to Rome to answer charges. Undaunted, Philip had *Ausculta fili* destroyed and a forgery, *Deum timi*, put in its place that distorted the papal claims. Philip ("the father of the big lie") executed a brilliant propaganda coup by circulating the forged bull along with his response to the pope that began, "Your utter fatuity may know that we [the king] are not subjected to anyone." The royal chancery also drew up a list of charges against Boniface that included blasphemy, simony (the buying and selling of church offices), heresy, the murder of Celestine V, and fornication. At the same time, public opinion was fanned by popular pamphlets and academic treatises attacking Boniface in particular and the papacy in general.

Boniface's response was to issue on November 18, 1302, one of the most famous and debated decrees of the medieval papacy, *Unam sanctam:*

> The true faith compels us to believe that there is one holy catholic apostolic church, and this we firmly believe and plainly confess. And outside of her there is no salvation or remission of sins, . . . Therefore there is one body of the one and only church, and one head, not two heads, as if the church were a monster. And this head is Christ and his vicar, Peter and his successor; . . . If therefore Greeks or anyone else say that they are not subject to Peter and his successors, they thereby necessarily confess that they are not of the sheep of Christ. . . . Both swords, therefore, the spiritual and the temporal, are in the power of the church. The former is to be used by the church, the latter for the church; . . . (S)piritual power surpasses any earthly power in dignity and honor, because spiritual things surpass temporal things. . . . For the truth itself declares that the spiritual power must establish the temporal power and pass judgment on it if it is not good. . . . Therefore if the temporal power errs, it will be judged by the spiritual power, and if the lower spiritual power errs, it will be judged by its superior. But if the highest spiritual power errs, it can not be judged by men, but by God alone. . . . We therefore declare, say, and affirm that submission on the part of every man to the bishop of Rome is altogether necessary for his salvation.[2]

One of Philip's royal ministers is said to have remarked: "My master's sword is of steel, the pope's is made of verbiage."

Philip was no slouch at verbiage either. He focused his wrath on achieving the deposition of Boniface. The French king and his advisors now used the new ideas of representation and participation of the Third Estate in important public matters.

[2]Ray C. Petry, ed., *A History of Christianity. Readings in the History of the Early and Medieval Church* (Englewood Cliffs, N.J.: Prentice-Hall, 1962), pp. 505–506. Only the concluding sentence received dogmatic significance by confirmation by the Fifth Lateran Council in 1516.

In June 1303, all three estates met in a large assembly that was marvelously stage-managed to include speeches against the pope by eminent leaders and the king himself. The assembly resolved that the pope should be tried by a general council. This resolution was then disseminated throughout France. The result was that now Boniface was not opposed by the king only but by the entire French people. Against Boniface's papal ideology, the king had forged new weapons of government propaganda and the claim to be executive spokesperson for the nation.

Philip knew that now Boniface's only remaining weapon was excommunication, and he moved quickly to prevent its publication. A troop of soldiers led by William Nogaret, the king's advisor, and Sciara Colonna stormed the papal palace at Anagni the night of September 7, the night before the excommunication decree was to be published. Boniface refused to resign and offered instead his life. This was acceptable to Colonna, but Nogaret's wisdom prevailed; a dead pope was of little use to him or his master. The pope was liberated the next day by the local populace, but he soon died a broken man.

"*Unam sanctam* was the sonorous, proud and self-confident swan song of the medieval papacy."[3] The centuries-long development of the ideal of a universal Christian commonwealth within the confines of the church, the ark of salvation captained by the papacy, had run aground on the particularist rocks of language, culture, and statism. Papal ideology since the Donation of Constantine had focused exclusive attention on the empire and the emperor and neglected those rulers whom Gregory VII had called mere "kinglets" *(reguli)*. These kinglets had become aware of a new national sense and outlook for which the papacy had little or no ideological means of control, however. Philip's triumph over Boniface concluded one phase in the history of the papacy and initiated another.

Avignon and the Western Schism

Traumatized by the shocking attack on Boniface, the papacy now attempted both to appease France and to restore its own shattered prestige and role. Boniface's successor, Benedict XI (1303–1304), revoked the papal censures of Philip but demanded the punishment of Nogaret, the king's servant. Benedict, however, died before this plan could proceed. The next pope, Clement V (1305–1314), the archbishop of Bordeaux and thus a subject of the English king Edward I, was French by upbringing and outlook. Thus he was supposedly not a partisan in the conflict between England and France, or a partisan of the papacy because he was not a member of the Curia. This politic choice, whether or not it was influenced by Philip, foundered on the

[3]Walter Ullmann, *A Short History of the Papacy in the Middle Ages* (London: Methuen University Paperback, 1974), p. 275.

personal weakness of Clement, who was a sickly hypochondriac. Unwilling to expose himself to the rigors of crossing the Alps, Clement continually put off his journey to Rome. He soon ensconced the papacy at Avignon, which although on the empire's side of the Rhone river, was under the influence of France. Thus began what became known in Petrarch's phrase as the "Babylonian captivity" of the church (1305–1377), during which all the popes were French. Clement himself created twenty-eight cardinals, twenty-five of whom were French. France was declared exempt from *Unam sanctam*. A French pope with a French curia lived in a French-speaking city on the French frontier. The papacy, which under Innocent III had subdued kings and emperors, was now widely perceived to be captive to the French.

The reign of Clement had an ominous beginning. At his crowning at Lyons, a wall collapsed during the solemn procession and killed several dignitaries; Clement himself was knocked from his horse and lost the most precious jewel from his tiara, which had been knocked from his head. More fateful than this, however, was Philip's desire to gain even more from his conflict with Boniface VIII. Philip demanded that Boniface be exhumed, put on trial, and publicly burned for all his supposed heretical and immoral activities. Not surprisingly, the papacy wanted to avoid such a public humiliation at nearly any cost.

Philip's price was a high one: the dissolution of the Order of Templars and the transfer of their immense wealth to the royal coffers for "safekeeping." From the time of the crusades, this order of knights had acquired many privileges, immunities, and great wealth, especially in France. Philip's propaganda experts once more earned their keep. They charged that the order had become a den of iniquity based on obscene rites with the devil and that its members were sodomites and blasphemous heretics. The Templars in France were arrested and after sufficient torture confirmed the charges against them. The tendency to retract such extorted testimony when questioned by papal commissioners was effectively minimized by burning some fifty Templars. Clement V avoided the threatened trial of Boniface VIII by congratulating Philip on his zeal in pursuing the Templar heresy and by dissolving the order and distributing much of its wealth to the French treasury.

In hindsight it might be assumed that the humiliation of the papacy from Boniface VIII to Clement V would have sobered papal claims and tempered papal efforts to subordinate rulers. It seems, however, that the inertia of papal ideology was greater than the recent roadblocks thrown in its way. Pope John XXII (1316–1334) became embroiled to the further detriment of the papacy in conflicts with the claimant to the imperial throne, Lewis the Bavarian, and with the Franciscans. In the former case, Lewis ignored papal strictures, invaded Italy, had himself acclaimed emperor by the Roman people and crowned by their representative Sciarra Colonna—the very man who had assaulted Boniface in Anagni twenty-five years earlier. In the latter case, John "settled" the dispute between the Franciscans and other orders over the absolute poverty of Christ and the apostles by declaring the Franciscan claim heretical. Among the more noteworthy and influential Franciscans who rejected the pope and fled to Lewis the Bavarian for protection was the English philosopher William of Ockham (ca. 1285–1347).

One of the consequences of all these events was the first critical study of the concept of the church and its theological and legal bases. Already about 1302, the French Dominican, John of Paris (ca. 1250–1306), had argued in his treatise *On Papal and Royal Power* that secular government was rooted in the natural human community, and that therefore not only was royal authority not derived from the papacy, but that the popes had no authority to depose kings. A far more radical expression of such secularism was the 1324 work *The Defender of the Peace* by Marsilius of Padua (ca. 1275–1342). Marsilius, who had been rector of the University of Paris (1311–1312), made it clear that it was the papacy which was destroying world peace. The solution was to limit the executive authority of the papacy by the laws governing all human institutions, laws that derived from the whole community. Marsilius not only stressed the principle of popular consent as the basis for legitimate government; he also denied that the papacy was divinely established. These attacks on the papacy, which went to the heart of its legitimacy as an institution, used arguments from Aristotle and Roman law. William of Ockham, who wrote numerous tracts supporting his defender, Lewis of Bavaria, concluded that Pope John XXII was a heretic because of his rejection of the Franciscan theology of poverty. Thus Ockham went beyond reviving older canonistic arguments regarding the possibility of deposing a heretical pope to posit that no ecclesial institution, not even a general council, could claim to define with certainty the faith of the church. To claim that the whole church could not err meant, according to Ockham, only that the true faith would survive in unspecified individuals even when popes and councils denied the truth. The great Italian poet, Dante Alighieri (1265–1321), who had been exiled from Florence in 1301 for supporting the opponents of Boniface VIII, assailed the papacy and popes not only in his *Divine Comedy* but also in his treatise *On Monarchy*. In the latter he argued that the papacy should abandon all temporal authority and possessions and that temporal peace required a universal monarchy under the emperor. Papal condemnations and excommunications could no longer either control rulers or silence critics.

The Avignonese papacy further alienated Christians throughout Europe by a building craze that left splendid palaces and monuments in Avignon for modern tourists but severely taxed the faithful in order to build them. The luxury and worldliness of the papal court were described by the poet Francesco Petrarch (1304–1374), who had lived in and around Avignon for some years, as "the sewer of the world." The spiritual vision of the papacy was clouded not so much by its materialism as by its bureaucratic mentality. Instead of responding to the philosophical, theological, and literary critiques against it, the papacy turned to developing increasingly efficient administrative machinery for collecting more and more taxes, shuffling its thousands of pages of documents concerned with benefices and indulgences and politics, and administering its webs of patronage. Pastoral work was displaced by work for creating greener and greener pastures.

The damage Avignon was causing to the papacy and hence to the faithful was noted by many, and calls increased to return the papacy to its home in Rome. It was Gregory XI (1370–1378) who heeded these calls. On January 17, 1377, the papacy re-entered Rome and took up official residency at the Vatican. It remains a disputed question how much influence the entreaties of St. Catherine of Siena (d. 1380) and St. Bridget of Sweden (d. 1373) had on Gregory's decision. He is reputed to have sought mystical enlightenment for difficult problems, and thus they probably at least strengthened his resolve to return the papacy to Rome.

Ironically, the end of the "Babylonian captivity" of the church led almost immediately to the great western schism of the church. Gregory XI died on March 27, 1378. His body was barely cold when Romans began rioting in the streets to make clear their demand that the papacy remain in Rome and that a Roman or at least an Italian be chosen pope. While the cardinals were in conclave struggling to resolve their own internal factions regarding the papal election, Roman mobs milled around outside shrieking their will. It was not a pleasant scene. All but four cardinals voted for the efficient, hard-working bureaucrat who was administrator of the Avignonese curia, Bartolomeo Prignano. He was neither a Roman nor an Italian nor a Frenchman but a Neopolitan (Naples was closely related to France through the house of Anjou). Although a respected administrator, he was essentially a civil servant with no experience in policy making. He took the title Urban VI (1378–1389). In spite of the riotous behavior during the election process, there is no indication that the cardinals were intimidated by the mobs. Indeed, the very choice of Prignano may indicate the cardinals' resistance to threats. This is important to note because soon after the enthronement of Urban, the cardinals decided they had made a serious mistake and used the supposed pressure of the mobs to claim that the election was invalid.

In the weeks following his election, Urban exhibited a behavior that was extreme even in the context of the behavior of his immediate predecessors. He was a tactless, rude, megalomaniac with an uncontrollable temper. The cardinals soon came to the conclusion that Urban was unfit to be pope. Their solution was to impugn their own election process on the basis that it had taken place under conditions of duress and fear. One by one they slipped out of Rome and gathered at Anagni where they declared to all Europe that Urban had been uncanonically elected and that the papacy was to be considered vacant. In September they elected Cardinal Robert of Geneva, who took the title of Clement VII (1378–1394). Urban did not accept the cardinals' request that he abdicate. Instead, he excommunicated Clement, who in turn returned the favor. The sorry spectacle of pope excommunicating pope and vice-versa would continue for nearly forty years (1378—1417).

There had been antipopes before in the history of the church, but this was the first time that the same legitimate College of Cardinals had legitimately elected two popes within a few months. Urban VI and his successors [Boniface IX (1389–1404),

Innocent VII (1404–1406), Gregory XII (1406–1415), Martin V (1417–1431)] remained in Rome. Clement VII and his successor [Benedict XIII (1394–1423)] returned to Avignon. It is difficult today to appreciate fully the depth of the religious insecurity and the intensity of institutional criticism this schism caused. If, as decreed by *Unam sanctam*, salvation itself was contingent on obedience to the true pope, it was crucial to know who was the true vicar of Christ. But how could this be decided? And now not only were there two popes, each claiming to be the sole vicar of Christ, there were also two colleges of cardinals, and so on down the line even to some parishes that had two priests. Europe itself split its allegiance. Clement VII was followed by France, Scotland, Aragon, Castille, and Navarre; Urban VI was followed by much of Italy, Germany, Hungary, England, Poland, and Scandinavia.

Public opinion was hopelessly confused. Even the learned and the holy clashed over who was the true pope. St. Catherine of Siena worked tirelessly to secure universal recognition of Urban. She called the cardinals who elected Clement "fools, liars, and devils in human form." On the other hand, the noted Spanish Dominican preacher, Vincent Ferrar, was equally zealous for the Avignon popes and labeled the adherents of Urban as "dupes of the devil and heretics."

The major victim of this protracted struggle was the church. The prestige of the papacy sank to a new low; belief in the necessity of papal primacy was called into question and thus also the universality and validity of the church's sacraments. The rise of renewal movements in England under Wyclif and in Bohemia under Hus further complicated efforts to restore the credibility of the church. John Wyclif (ca. 1330–1384) was an English philosopher and theologian whose concern for reform of the church led to his condemnation by synods of the English church and finally by the Council of Constance in 1415. He was for a time in the service of the English crown, and his claim that the state could lawfully deprive corrupt clergy of their endowments was certainly of interest to the crown but was condemned by Pope Gregory XI in 1377. He further argued that papal claims to temporal power had no biblical warrant, and he appealed to the English government to reform the whole church in England. The extent to which he was an influence on the Lollard movement for a biblically based Christianity and on the English Peasants' Revolt (1381) is problematic.

Wyclif's ideas were widespread among the lower English clergy and spread to Bohemia after the marriage (1382) of Richard II of England to Anne, the sister of King Wenceslaus IV of Bohemia. The Bohemian reformer John Hus (ca. 1372–1415) translated some of Wyclif's writing into Czech. Hus, rector of the University of Prague, was a fiery preacher against the immorality of the papacy and the higher clergy in general. In spite of a safe-conduct from the Emperor Sigismund, Hus was condemned and executed at the Council of Constance in 1415. Both Wyclif and Hus were signs of growing national consciousness. After his execution, Hus was declared a martyr and national hero by the University of Prague.

The maintenance of two papal courts and their related expenses increased the ecclesial tax burdens on the Christian community. And the disputing popes' appointments of partisans to bishoprics and ecclesial benefices served to spread the disputes everywhere. A result of all this was increased corruption and relaxation of ecclesial discipline with a concomitant growth of state influence on the church because the popes were obliged to offer various concessions to gain the favor of princes.

Conciliarism

From the beginning of the schism, there were efforts to find a solution to it. It was proposed that both popes abdicate to allow a new election. Neither the Roman nor Avignonese lines favored this. Other solutions included the establishment of a tribunal with each pope to acknowledge its verdict and the proposal that government supporters of the popes withdraw allegiance and thus prepare the way for a new election. The solution favored and advanced by the universities was the recovery of the ancient principle that in an emergency (e.g., the case of a heretical pope) the papacy was to be subordinated to a general council that would decide what to do. This royal way of the ancient church had already been suggested at the beginning of the schism by two German professors at the University of Paris, Henry of Langenstein (d. 1397) and Conrad of Gelnhausen (d. 1390). Their writings promoting this solution were augmented by the concurrence of others coming from the many new universities founded at this time.

The actions of the popes themselves gave urgency to finding a solution. The conflict between Urban VI and Joan I of Anjou, Queen of Naples (1343–1382), is a case in point. Urban excommunicated her, deposed her, and gave her crown to her cousin Charles of Durazzo because she supported Clement VII. It was reported that Joan attempted to poison Urban. Charles then had Joan strangled in prison. Soon Charles and Urban had a falling out, and Charles was excommunicated and deposed. Then Charles and six cardinals planned to imprison Urban. When the plot was discovered, the cardinals were imprisoned, tortured, and put to death. When Urban died (October 15, 1389), it is said that even his followers experienced a certain amount of gratification.

Finally, in June 1408, cardinals of both popes met and resolved to summon a general council to meet at Pisa. Both popes were invited to attend, but they refused. The Council of Pisa (March to July 1409) met anyway and was well attended by cardinals, bishops, hundreds of theologians, and representatives of almost every western country. Among the participants were distinguished scholars of conciliarism such as Pierre d'Ailly, chancellor of the University of Paris and Jean Gerson, his successor. Their argument that supreme ecclesial power was located in the council was accepted. The council proceeded to depose both popes as notorious schismatics and heretics and then elected a new pope, Alexander V (1409–1410), archbishop of Milan and a

315

cardinal of the Roman line. The deposed popes refused to recognize the validity of the Pisan council, however, and thus there were now three popes.

This scandalous situation was further aggravated after the death of Alexander V by the election to this new Pisan papacy of a man reputed to have engaged in piracy during his previous military career. Baldassare Cossa had been such a successful commander of papal troops that Boniface IX had made him a cardinal in 1402, and then a papal legate. Cossa took the title John XXIII and reigned from 1410 until 1415 when imprisoned and deposed by the Council of Constance. His title and efforts to manipulate the Council of Constance were redeemed approximately 450 years later by John XXIII (1958–1963) and Vatican II.

Without being unduly concerned about the means used, John was able to achieve his initial goal of expelling the pope of the Roman obedience from Rome. However, political and military events in central Italy forced him to take shelter with his curia in Florence and to seek for a protector. He turned to the king, later (1433) emperor, of Germany, Sigismund.

Sigismund had already endorsed the Pisan line of popes established at the Council of Pisa and thus was a natural source of assistance for John XXIII. However, Sigismund was also greatly concerned for the unity of the church. He had been persuaded by the writings of conciliarists, especially that of Dietrich of Niem (1340–1418), who had asserted that in ecclesial emergency the emperor should follow the model of the ancient Christian emperors and convoke a general council. Dietrich further argued that a general council had plenary powers, including the rights to depose a pope and reform the church. Although not yet emperor, Sigismund decided to act on the arguments that a general council is superior to the pope and that the emperor as first prince of Christendom and protector of the church has the duty to call a council when needed. He successfully arranged to organize such a council on German soil at the city of Constance. John could not afford to jeopardize Sigismund's support and oppose his plans.

The Council of Constance (1414–1417) was convoked in 1414 by John. The council was to deal with three main issues: the great schism, extirpation of heresy, and reform of the church in "head and members" (the ecclesial metaphor for the whole church). The council was one of the greatest ecclesial assemblies of the premodern church. The active participation of Sigismund not only stimulated a large and representative attendance; it also stabilized and overcame threats to its validity. By early 1415 the attendance included twenty-nine cardinals, thirty-three archbishops, three patriarchs, more than 300 bishops, numerous abbots, priors, theologians, canonists, and representatives of rulers. The council vindicated conciliarism and defeated the papal-hierocratic system.

Pope John initially hoped that the council would depose the popes of the Roman and Avignonese obediences and legitimize him. He soon discovered that there was a consensus that all three popes should resign. John's own plans for the council were further jeopardized by the conciliar decision to vote by nations rather than by persons, with each nation having one vote. This procedure counterbalanced the preponderance of Italian prelates on whom John was counting.

It is important to note that the decision to vote by nations had a significance that extended beyond the immediate politics of John's efforts to win conciliar endorsement. It was a democratizing event because in the separate deliberations of the nations it was now not only the prelates but also representatives of cathedral chapters and universities, theologians, canonists, and representatives of princes who had a voice. Furthermore, the idea of a nation as a unit, an idea taken over from the universities, contributed to the already developing sense of nationalism that was undermining the old idea of a universal Christian commonwealth under the headship of the papacy. The further consequences of this nationalism will be seen in the Reformation and the rise of national churches.

John soon perceived that the polity of the council was not in his favor. His concern was heightened by a lengthy document that began circulating that detailed charges against him. Hoping to get away to a safe haven in order to dissolve the council, John fled at night in disguise. Sigismund not only rallied the confused council; he also managed to have John captured and held in protective custody in the vicinity of Constance.

An important consequence of John's flight was that in his absence as papal convenor, the council thought it necessary to give itself judicial standing. This is the context for the famous decree *Haec sancta* (1415), which clearly placed the authority of the council over that of the pope.

> This holy synod of Constance . . . has authority immediately from Christ; and that to it everyone of whatsoever estate or dignity, even the papal, is bound to obey, in matters pertaining to the faith, to the extirpation of said schism, and to the reformation of the Church in head and members.[4]

Haec sancta sanctioned conciliar theory as the official teaching of the church. The character of a general council was set forth as a lawful assembly representing the universal church, whose power was directly from Christ and whose authority therefore extended over every office holder in the church, including the pope.

John XXIII was then deposed for abetting schism by his flight from the council and also for notorious simony and a disgraceful life. The Roman pope, Gregory XII, agreed to resign on the condition that the council allow him to reconvoke it and authorize it as a council. This was accepted without the council's acknowledging any prior illegitimacy nor implying that Gregory was the true pope. The Avignonese pope, Benedict XIII, was adamant in his determination to remain pope. Gradually, however, his Spanish support was eroded, and in 1417 he too was deposed as a schismatic, perjuror, and heretic. He continued to claim to be the legitimate pope

---

[4]B. J. Kidd, ed., *Documents Illustrative of the History of the Church*, III (New York: Macmillan, 1941), p. 209.

until his death in 1423 even though he no longer had any significant following. On November 11, 1417, Cardinal Odo Colonna was elected pope by the college of cardinals and six representatives of each of the five nations present at the council. He took the title of Martin V in honor of the saint of the day. The great western schism was over.

The council declared heretical the renewal movements of the time led in England by Wyclif and in Bohemia by Hus. Wyclif (ca. 1330–1384) escaped the punishment of the council by having already died. Hus (ca. 1372–1415) was executed at the stake, an action that ignited fires in Bohemia still burning by the time of the Reformation.

Concerned that reform of the church would falter without conciliar direction and support, the council passed the important decree *Frequens* in 1417. In unmistakable language, the council stated:

> The frequent assembling of General Councils is a principle means for tilling the Lord's field for it uproots the brambles, thorns and thistles of heresies, errors and schisms, corrects excesses and reforms what is amiss, and restores the vineyard of the Lord to rich and fruitful bearing.[5]

The decree then provided for frequent general councils. The next one was to be held in five years, a second in seven years, and thereafter every ten years "in perpetuity." It ended by stating that it is lawful for the pope to "shorten" the period but on no account to put it off."

Martin V closed the council in April 1418. He did not, however, confirm or approve it, an omission probably little noted because of the profound relief over resolving the schism. His successor, Eugene IV (1431–1447), however, approved it in 1446 insofar as it was not prejudicial to the rights, dignity, and supremacy of the papacy. Pius II (1458–1464) in his bull *Execrabilis* (1460) prohibited any and all appeals to a council over the pope; such an appeal was to be regarded as heresy and schism. This principle would later be applied against Luther, who initially hoped for reform of the church through an ecumenical council.

Some of the decrees of the Council of Constance became parts of special agreements between Martin V and particular nations. This was the first time papal agreements with nations were called *concordats*. The significance of this development apart from the specific subject matter of the concordats is the further indication of the displacement of the ideal of a universal Christian commonwealth by the independence of individual nations. The papacy, hitherto claiming sovereignty over all peoples, was now reduced to one government among many national governments, and it bound itself in a contractual manner to them. This too was to have significance a century later in the Reformation.

[5]Kidd, *History of the Church*, pp. 210–211.

The Councils of Basel (1431–1449) and Ferrara–Florence (1438–1445)

The immediate aftermath of the Council of Constance may perhaps be best described in terms of battle fatigue. The spiritual and physical anxiety and stress occasioned by the long schism and the energy required for its resolution left an inheritance of confusion and uncertainty. The church was now entering a period of transition in which the old hierocratic papal institution had not yet become merely a memory, and the new conciliar orientation was still an innovation. Was the *corpus Christianum* to be reformed and renewed from below or from above?

While the weary participants in the conciliar-papal struggle were understandably hoping for a respite, a new problem was thrust on them. The eastern empire was seriously threatened by the Islamic expansion. In 1371 Bulgaria became a vassal state of the Turks, and by 1389 the entire Balkan peninsula was under their mastery. The seriousness of the Greek situation is indicated by the circuit around Europe made by the Byzantine emperor, Manuel II Palaeologus (1391–1425) in an effort to arouse support from the West. Byzantine representatives were invited to the Council of Constance by Sigismund, but the combination of the death at the council of Manuel's major representative and the press of western issues precluded help for Byzantium. Desperate for western political and military assistance, Byzantine envoys approached Martin V requesting a council of union between the Roman and Byzantine churches. It was suggested that the East was even willing to accept the Roman papal primacy, faith, and ritual. Conciliarists and the papacy now competed with each other to court Byzantine favor.

In the meantime, Martin V, in accordance with the decree *Frequens,* convoked a council at Basel for 1431. By December only a few participants had arrived, and in February Martin died. His successor, Eugene IV (1431–1447), was against the council from the start and dissolved it on the basis of insufficient attendance and the argument that the appropriate setting for reunion discussions with the Greeks was an Italian city. Because the ideal city for papal leverage, Rome, was in too much disorder for a council, Eugene convoked a council to meet in Bologna in 1433. By now, however, the Council of Basel had already had its first session, and, offended by the action of Eugene, sharply protested the action of the pope. Those at Basel were soon supported by Germany, England, France, Scotland, and Burgundy and now threatened to depose the pope. In 1433 Eugene formally recognized the Council of Basel, which by now had become practically a European parliament. Basel reaffirmed the superiority of a council over the pope and then further alienated Eugene by a number of decrees, including curtailing papal finances.

The mutual hostility between Eugene and the council was increased when Eugene transferred the council to Ferrara for the purpose of advancing his agenda regarding reunion with the East. A minority of the council acceded to the pope's decision; the majority declared Eugene deposed. In turn, the pope declared those remaining at Basel heretics and schismatics. The election of an antipope, Felix V (1439–1449) had little significance because he received little or no support from the nations. The French had already embodied no less than twenty-three decrees of Basel into national law in the Pragmatic Sanction of Bourges (July 7, 1438), an action that supported the older claims of the French national church to a privileged position in relation to the papacy. This Gallicanism, so-called from those *libertés de l'Eglise gallicane*, continued to assert the autonomy of the French church until the definition of papal infallibility at Vatican I (1869–1870).

A local epidemic in Ferrara prompted the move of the council to Florence where a union with the East was negotiated and signed in 1439. It was signed and supported by the Byzantine emperor himself and all members of the legation. But it was not acceptable in Constantinople where, in spite of the Turkish threat, the centuries of East-West strife were indelibly etched. Byzantium fell to the Turks in 1453, and its legacy was appropriated by Russia. Tsar Ivan III (1462–1505) had married the niece of the last eastern emperor and claimed succession to the "Roman" empire, arrogating the imperial double eagle as the symbol of its continuation. The Tsars and Russia also inherited the eastern antipathy to the papacy that has continued to today.

Meanwhile, the authority of the Council of Basel was eroded when its leading spokesmen deserted their own camp and joined the forces of the very papacy they had vigorously attacked. One of these men, the secretary of the council, later became a hard opponent of conciliarism when he was elected pope: Pius II. These one-time conciliarists were now sensing what the representatives of rulers were also seeing in the conciliar movement—the danger that the governed everywhere would become the masters of their kings and princes as well as of their pope. Now that the papacy had been demoted to the status of one monarchical government among others, it dawned on other monarchs that conciliarism was a two-edged sword. As rulers came to realize that the means developed to control the papacy could become a weapon used against them, they raised gloomy predictions of sedition and anarchy. Thus, as never before, the papacy and monarchs were now disposed to conclude concordats with each other. The possibility of democracy drove all theocratic monarchs, including the papacy, toward cooperation for the sake of mutual preservation. Hence, Felix V was the last antipope, and his role was negligible because now monarchs saw that any short-term benefit in supporting him would be outweighed by the long-term costs. The papacy's own effort to overcome the challenge of conciliarism and to consolidate its patrimony in Italy diverted its energy and attention from the widespread cry for reform of the church in head and members.

In less than a century, this cry would become the full-throated roar of the Reformation that blew away the last vestiges of the ideal of the *corpus Christianum* and the papal efforts to realize a universal headship over Christians. Although that roar would include a cacophony of voices, the first sighs of those alienated by poverty, the profit economy, and the stress of urban growth were now to be augmented by terrors of famine, plague, and war, the anger of the frustrated renewal movements of Wyclif and Hus, and the individualism of the Renaissance. Altogether, by the end of the Middle Ages, people were in one way or another being thrown back on themselves while the external supports of their Christian commonwealth were undermined.

Famine, Plague, and War

Western Christendom's spiritual insecurity, uncertainty, and anxiety during the papal schism had already been initiated by the famines and plagues that swept through Europe by the mid-fourteenth century. The increased food production of the twelfth and thirteenth centuries was a major factor in a steady population growth, but the population outgrew the agricultural output that had made its growth possible. By 1320 nearly all of northern Europe suffered under a terrible famine precipitated by a conjuncture of major crop failures caused by years of unusually bad weather, considerable price inflation, and urban dependence on the immediate countryside for food owing to the lack of long-distance transportation. Weak and malnourished, the population was hit by an outbreak of typhoid fever that in 1316 killed an estimated 10 percent of the population of Ypres within a few months. The malnourished population of Europe was ripe for the Grim Reaper, who soon appeared in the form of the bubonic plague.

The spread of the bubonic plague to Europe was facilitated by design improvements in Italian ships that enabled them not only to sail faster and farther but to sail year-round even up the dangerous Atlantic coast of Europe. The rats that carried the fleas that bore the disease were thus able to reach all of Europe's ports. Originating in the Far East, the plague brought by Genoese ships reached Sicily in October 1347. Within months nearly all Italy was infected; by late spring 1348 the disease was attacking southern Germany; and in June 1348 it entered England. The dense and filthy urban environments provided breeding grounds for the black rat that carried the disease-bearing fleas, and the thatch roofs of so many houses made fine launching pads for the fleas to jump on persons below. The lethal nature of the plague was not limited to transmission by flea bites, however. The pneumonic form was transmitted from person to person by inhaling bacilli-bearing coughs and sneezes:

> Infections of the lungs contracted in this fashion were 100 per cent lethal in Manchuria in 1921, and since this is the only time that modern medical men have been able to observe plague communicated in this manner, it is tempting to assume a similar mortality for pneumonic plague in fourteenth-century Europe.[6]

Mortality rates in modern times for the bubonic form transmitted by flea bites ranged

---

[6]William H. McNeill, *Plagues and Peoples* (Garden City, N.Y.: Anchor Books, 1976), p. 147.

from 30 to 90 percent before the discovery of antibiotics. Because there are no population figures for fourteenth-century Europe, it is not possible to give an accurate account of the mortality rate of the plague. It is estimated that 30 percent of the population was killed. Local variations must also be taken into account; some areas were passed over, whereas others were completely wiped out. The horror of such devastation was increased by the gruesome nature of the disease itself: first a large, painful boil *(buba)* followed by black spots or blotches caused by bleeding under the skin, and then the last stage of violent coughing up of blood. A more graphic description reads: "All the matter which exuded from their bodies let off an unbearable stench; sweat, excrement, spittle, breath, so fetid as to be overpowering; urine turbid, thick, black or red."[7] Family and friends deserted the sick, leaving them to die alone and in agony.

It is difficult for us today to realize the profound personal and social impact the plague had on those who survived. The plague was inexplicable and swift. People did not know where it came from or what it was; at its height, it could strike down a healthy person in twenty-four hours. The widespread and intense fear of imminent death broke down customs and norms. The result was often panic, bizarre behavior, and the projection of guilt and fear upon others outside the group. Groups of people began flagellating themselves—sometimes to death—in frenzied orgies of penance for the personal and communal sins believed to be the cause of the plague. A variation on the theme was to blame the Jews for the plague, with the consequence that thousands of Jews were murdered across Europe. It was not unusual for survivors of the plague to lose all confidence in their tradition and faith that had not prepared them for a disaster of such magnitude. A profound pessimism ensued that was graphically illustrated by the dance of death motif that entered art as well as by more realistic representations of suffering. For example, the rational view of the world and the confidence in theological system-building exemplified by the age of Thomas Aquinas was severely tested, if not destroyed, by such an experience of arbitrary disaster. If God acted in such intense, arbitrary, and inexplicable ways, then perhaps the way to God was not through rational theology and the sacramental, institutional church but through direct, intensely personal mysticism. At this time there arose widespread efforts to achieve personal rather than institutionally mediated access to God. The other side of this coin of the loss of traditional meaning was the attempt to lose oneself in gross sensuality. In short, the plague left the survivors with guilt and insecurity compounded by a crisis of faith.

As if natural disaster were not enough, the human community managed to turn on itself through the Hundred Years' War (1337–1453), which was both a dynastic struggle between the English and French monarchies and a feudal struggle within France itself. The expansionist policy of the French king, Philip VI (1328–1350),

---

[7]John McKay, Bennett-Hill, John Buckler, eds., *A History of World Societies*, Second Edition, I (Boston: Houghton Mifflin, 1988), p. 430.

sought to absorb the English duchy of Aquitaine. Edward III of England (1327–1377), the eldest surviving male heir of Philip IV (his mother Isabella was Philip's daughter, whereas Philip VI was Philip IV's nephew), decided that his rightful sovereignty over Aquitaine could be achieved by assuming the title King of France. The feudal or civil war aspect in France was the consequence of the French barons' attempt to thwart the centralizing policy of the French crown by alignment with Edward on the basis that he was a more legitimate overlord. Economic factors also played a role in terms of the wool trade between England and Flanders, a fiefdom of the French crown. The disruption of the wool trade threatened the prosperity of the Flemish citizens, and thus they supported Edward. The war, really a series of sporadic raids and sieges, was fought almost entirely in France, with England winning most of the battles.

The turning point for the French came through the action of an obscure peasant girl, Joan of Arc (1412–1431). As a child, she had claimed to hear the voices of saints who revealed to her her mission to save France. She convinced the uncrowned king, Charles VII, to support her relief of the besieged city of Orleans in 1429, and soon thereafter she accompanied Charles to Reims for his coronation. These events marked the turning point in the war, although soon afterward Joan was captured and sold to the English by the Duke of Burgundy. She was accused of witchcraft and heresy and burned at the stake in the marketplace of Rouen. She was canonized in 1920 and is the second patron saint of France. The rallied French forces slowly reconquered the English areas until, at the end of the war, only the town of Calais was controlled by England.

War was in a real sense another plague of the times. Although the natural disasters of famines, epidemics, and plague claimed more victims than war, war brought vast destruction and the disintegration of economic and social life. The French taxation for the Hundred Years' War was a tremendous burden on the peasants, who exploded in rage and rampage in 1358. Mobs swept through the countryside murdering nobles, raping their wives and daughters, and destroying their estates. The nobles' revenge was an even more vicious suppression of the peasants that mercilessly slaughtered thousands, guilty and innocent alike. A similar revolt in England in 1381 was a huge uprising that combined economic and religious grievances against noble and clerical rulers. Its revolutionary sentiment of social equality was immortalized in the famous couplet of the popular preacher John Ball (d. 1381): "When Adam delved and Eve span; Who was then the gentleman?" In England, too, the revolt was ferociously crushed. Similar rebellions occurred in Italy, some of the north German cities, and parts of Spain.

The "Babylonian captivity" of the church and its consequent schism accompanied by famine, plague, and war combined to plunge late medieval Europe into crisis. In place of the old Augustinian order of the City of God embodied in the ideal of a universal Christian commonwealth, the *corpus Christianum*, headed by the papacy, there now appeared to be only universal disorder, death, and devastation.

Chapter 18

THE CRISIS OF THE
LATE MEDIEVAL ERA

The incessant repetition of epidemics, famines, plagues, natural catastrophes, and wars in the late medieval era gave birth to the idea, frequently expressed in the fifteenth century, that the universal work in creation is death. Embittered by the crises they had gone through, many contemporaries described life as a kingdom of death and desolation. The *Apocalypse* woodcut cycle of 1498 (based on the biblical book Revelation) by the German artist Albrecht Dürer (1471–1528) provided the age with a graphic symbol of its distress and fear. The best-known woodcut of this series is *The Four Horsemen* representing pestilence, war, famine, and death. Under the command of an angel, the horsemen dash over the helpless people, who are thrown to the ground under the hooves of the horses and are already being drawn into the jaws of hell. In *The Seven Trumpets* the angels receive their trumpets heralding judgment from God, and as they blow them an eagle flies across the sky crying "Woe to all who dwell on earth." The effects of the judgment—a storm of hail and fire "mingled with blood," swarms of locusts and scorpions ravaging the land, the earth in flames, the sea set afire by a flaming mountain, and wells poisoned by the star "Wormwood"—are depicted in the lower third of the picture.

The rupture of social and personal life that occasioned these images and that was so horribly experienced had actually already begun in the demographic movements to the cities of the twelfth and thirteenth centuries. The derangement of human relations was initiated by this new urban environment and was so accelerated by the mass death and destruction of the fourteenth century that it called into question the medieval Christian conviction that death is not an end of life but a passage to a new life. In the mass death of the plague, when parent deserted child and child deserted parent, when the sick were abandoned by friends, neighbors, and servants, and when public authorities knew not what to do, the worst experience was not death itself

324

but the death of the self. The traditional religious rites and customs of death that, in the funeral procession and meal enacted the separation of the dead from the living while symbolically reconstituting the family and the continuity of society, collapsed totally in the face of the plague. The old rules of mourning that channeled and reduced the trauma of death rarely endured during the mass death of the time. The socialization and "domestication" of death by common custom that provided a certain rapport with the past and with one's ancestors was ruthlessly uprooted by the new fear of the dead. The terror before the decomposition of the body was linked to the terror before the loss of individuality. As a consequence of the plague as well as migrations, it was no longer possible in the towns to mourn the dead according to traditional rules. If one was fortunate enough even to have a deathbed, there certainly would be no relatives and friends gathered around it. Nor would there be, after death, rest among ancestors in the cemetery or the church. The dead no longer earned continuity with their forebears but only darkness. The survivors more and more understood themselves to be like orphans. The end of the Middle Ages is characterized by widespread melancholy—today we call it depression—that has been interpreted as an unconscious protest not just against the horror of death but against the solitude and abandonment that death thrust on the townsfolk of the fourteenth and fifteenth centuries. Townsfolk were increasingly conscious of having lost their roots and their ancestors and were anguished by the reality of being thrown back on themselves.

A consequence of this shock to faith and to feudalism was a new search for the self that ranged from the egoism manifest in Boccaccio's *The Decameron* to personal and national narcissism.[1] The disturbing discovery of the death of the self is nearly contemporaneous with the development of new funeral practices and the writing of wills, or testaments. In the hierarchy of contributions to the price of passage from this world to the next, the earlier emphasis on charity to the poor is displaced by a concern to endow as many Masses as possible for oneself after death. This "mathematics of salvation" exalted the multiplication of intercessions that directly favor the passage of the deceased into the beyond.[2] This shift is an indication not only of the church's ability to adapt to a new situation but also of the growing influence of a market mentality with its orientation toward the calculation of accounts. Between the mid-fourteenth century and the beginning of the sixteenth century, the Mass became the essential preparation for this journey. At the moment when the relations between the living and the dead were interrupted, the Mass ritually established the powerful bonds between this world and the next.

The development of Masses for the dead, the essential ritual action providing

---

[1]Published in 1353, these one hundred tales of romance, humor, and intrigue are set in the context of ten days of story-telling by upper-class refugees from the Florence plague. The *Decameron* established Boccaccio as the "Father of Italian prose."

[2]This insightful phrase is the subtitle to the second part of Jacques Chiffoleau's fascinating study of death in the late Middle Ages: *La Comptabilité De L'Au-Delà* (Rome: École Francaise de Rome, 1980).

direct and efficacious aid to the deceased, were complemented by the development of the doctrine of purgatory and increasing emphasis on the saints and the Virgin Mary. The multiplication of Masses for the dead popularized purgatory as a place for those snatched from life without benefit of time to amend their ways or prepare for death. These abandoned or orphaned souls found in purgatory a refuge with a new family. Purgatory also offered a mitigation of the fear of damnation by the opportunity it offered to purge the offenses incurred during life and to benefit from the prayers and intercessions of the Mass.

Likewise the cult of the saints and the Virgin of Consolation increased during this time when people were losing their relatives on a soul-numbing scale. In the communion of saints a new family was recognized, and heaven became populated with a multitude of familiar intercessors. It has been suggested that the appeal to Mary was basically a quest for protection against misfortune on the basis of some iconography presenting her cloak as a shield against the arrows of the plague. Equally if not more important was the appeal of Mary as the Great Mother and Consoler at whose feet those bereft of family might find a tender welcome.

The Renaissance Papacy

Humanists among the new orphans created by the disasters of famine, plague, and war sought new ancestors among the ancient Greeks and Romans, thus seeking to provide a rebirth, a renaissance, of society. The focus on the individual that arose from the matrix of the disasters, fears, and anxieties of the late Middle Ages led to a new awareness of the human as a natural, even secular, phenomenon to be developed and praised. This new attitude toward humankind and the world may be characterized as individualism. The initial sparks of self-consciousness present in Abelard's quest for self-knowledge had been dampened by his sucessors but were now again fanned to life. This new life was characterized by a driving ambition to realize to the fullest every aspect of human potential. The humanist advocates of this new individualism viewed the foregoing 1,000 years as a barbaric suppression of the human individual and sought new models for being human in a revived form of Greco-Roman culture.

Classical culture was not only mined from newly accessible literature but literally unearthed in Italy when the foundations dug for new buildings revealed ancient tombs, statuary, and mosiacs. This recovery of classical art stimulated realistic artistic expressions of life. Whereas Abbot Suger (d. 1151), a contributor to the development of Gothic architecture, believed that art was to lead people through the visible world to invisible certainties, Albrecht Dürer (1471–1528) could write: "Above all else we are pleased to see the image of a beautiful human being."[3] Artists now began to

---

[3] Karl-Adolf Knappe, *Dürer: The Complete Engravings, Etchings, and Woodcuts* (Secaucus, N.J.: Wellfleet Press, nd.), p. xxxiii.

portray people as they appeared in real life—right down to wrinkles and a man's "four o'clock shadow." The new realism also included critiques of human folly such as the extremely influential *Ship of Fools* (1498) by Sebastian Brant (1457–1521) and the satirical attack on the church, the *Praise of Folly* (1509) by Erasmus (ca. 1469–1536). Brant himself represents the development of German literature for the educated laity.

This new individualism, with its emphasis on obedience to one's own conscience and on responsibility to make one's own judgments, was already manifesting itself in the conciliar movement with its criticism of the papacy and its questioning of the papacy as an institution of public government. The popes themselves were now drawn into this same orbit of individualism. By virtue of individualism, the office-holder began to take the place of the office. That is, the papacy itself as an office or institution of government began to recede behind the personal character of the individual pope.

The personal characters of the Renaissance papacy raised more issues than they resolved, however. Sharp and tough-minded, they set out to smash the conciliar movement's strictures on papal authority. Their success in this endeavor may be seen in that, apart from the Council of Trent (1545–1563), which was held to counter the Reformation, there was not another council until Vatican I (1869–1870), which in its declaration of papal primacy and infallibility was the final answer to the Council of Constance. Late medieval people, of course, could not see that far ahead. What they could see, however, was the great gulf between the biblical image of the shepherd guiding the flock toward the heavenly city and the series of Renaissance popes who exploited the flock for their own advancement in the earthly city. A satirical woodcut of the sixteenth century graphically portrayed the mercenary spirit of the papacy by picturing the pope and curia counting money in one panel and Jesus driving the moneychangers from the temple in the other panel. The papacy became an Italian Renaissance court, and the pope was increasingly perceived to be nothing more than an Italian prince whose problems and interests were now local and egoistic rather than universal and pastoral. Two particularly notorious popes exemplify the depths to which the papacy sank at this time: Alexander VI (1431–1503, pope from 1492) and Julius II (1443–1513, pope from 1503).

A Spaniard by birth, Rodrigo Borgia was made a cardinal by his uncle, Pope Callistus III in 1456 and won the papacy largely through bribery. It is no surprise that Alexander VI's reign, rooted in nepotism and simony from its beginning, was determined by continuing familial and financial concerns. He is one pope to whom the title "father" if not "holy" may be literally applied. His many mistresses bore him at least eight known children, the most famous of whom are Cesare Borgia and Lucrezia Borgia. The former is infamous for his ruthless exaction of total obedience as his father's military leader, as well as for his immorality, murders, and possibly the assassination of his brother. He is the model for Niccolo Machiavelli's *The Prince* (1513). Lucrezia served her father's plans by a series of ambitious political marriages marked by extravagant wedding parties in the Vatican palace. One of her husbands was murdered by order of her brother Cesare. At one point, when absent from Rome for a political military campaign, Alexander appointed his daughter regent of the Holy See.

Alexander's own involvement in sexual promiscuity, alleged poisonings, and intrigue made the name Borgia a synonym for corruption. He was denounced in his own time by the influential and fiery Dominican preacher Girolamo Savonarola (1452–1498). When Alexander could not persuade Savonarola to discontinue his attacks by offering him a cardinal's hat, he proceeded against him and was at least partly responsible for Savonarola's execution in Florence. Alexander's political efforts to strengthen the papal state abetted French intervention in northern Italy, which helped initiate a new period of power politics with Italy as the focus of international struggles. Ironically, the sordidness of Alexander's life aside, he also patronized great artists whose legacy may still be enjoyed by the visitor to Rome.

Julius II continued patronage of the arts by his support of Raphael, Michelangelo, and Bramante. As a result of Julius's generosity, we still have among other works, Michelangelo's statue of Moses, the paintings in the Sistine Chapel, and Raphael's frescos in the Vatican. Julius's enthusiasm for rebuilding St. Peter's led to the indulgence that later occasioned Martin Luther's *95 Theses*. In his own time, the art by which Julius was primarily known was the art of war; Raphael painted Julius mounted and in armor.

Julius continued the political and military efforts of the Borgias to control the Papal States and to expel all foreigners from Italy. He himself led his troops with such strength and drive that he became known as *terribilita*, the terrible man. So much of his reign was involved in warfare that more and more of the laity began to wonder in disgust what this pontiff had to do with the Prince of Peace. The great humanist, Erasmus, who had witnessed Julius's triumphal martial entry into Bologna, angrily criticized and satirized Julius in the *Praise of Folly* (1511), *The Complaint of Peace* (1517), and *Julius Exclusus* (1517).[4] In dialogue form, *Julius Exclusus* spread rapidly all over Europe and portrays Julius appearing before the gates of heaven on his death. For all his threats and bombast, Julius cannot force his way into heaven. In response to Julius's demand that Peter recognize him as the Vicar of Christ, Peter says:

> I see the man who wants to be regarded as next to Christ and, in fact equal to Him, submerged in the filthiest of all things by far: money, power, armies, wars,

---

[4]Erasmus (1469–1536) contributed to the Reformation not only by his satires that exposed ecclesial corruption but also by his celebrated edition of the Greek New Testament (1516), which profoundly influenced theological studies. The most renowned scholar of his age, Erasmus was deeply concerned for the moral renewal of the church but could not share Luther's demand for theological reform. In 1524 Erasmus and Luther publicly split over the issue of human freedom to cooperate with God in the process of salvation.

alliances—not to say anything at this point about his vices. But then, although you are as remote as possible from Christ, nevertheless you misuse the name of Christ for your own arrogant purposes; and under the pretext of Him who despised the world, you act the part of a tyrant of the world; and although a true enemy of Christ, you take the honor due Him. You bless others, yourself accursed; to others you open heaven, from which you yourself are locked out and kept far away; you consecrate, and are execrated; you excommunicate, when you have no communion with the saints.[5]

On the eve of the Reformation, the question was not whether the church should be reformed, but when. The successor to Julius II was a son of the famous Florentine political and banking family, the Medici. He took the title Leo X (1513–1521) and was pope during the early years of the Reformation. The words with which he reputedly opened his reign indicate how little prepared he was to respond to the widespread desire for reform of the church: "Now that God has given us the papacy, let us enjoy it."

---

[5]Paul Pascal, trans., *The Julius Exclusus of Erasmus* (Bloomington, Ind.: Indiana University Press, 1968), pp. 46, 87–88.

Chapter 19

THE REFORMATIONS OF
THE SIXTEENTH CENTURY

———

Little did Leo X know, as he was preparing to enjoy his spoils, that his papacy would soon be the lightning rod for a reform movement unleashed by a young student struck to the ground by a lightning bolt in 1505. The thunderstorm that prompted Martin Luther (1483–1546) to become a monk was but a foretaste of the storm that would shake late medieval Europe to its foundations and permanently alter western Christianity. These destructive and constructive energies were fed by the highly charged atmosphere of life on the eve of the Reformation.

Aspects of Everyday Life on the Eve of the Reformation

Everyday life in the sixteenth century was difficult at best. The infant mortality rate was extremely high. In Renaissance Florence, for example, 61 percent of the children did not live beyond six months. Poor diet, little sanitation, repeated outbreaks of the plague as well as various other diseases, not to mention everyday violence, feuds, and warfare, prompted people to think of themselves as old if they reached the age of forty. Although the population of Europe was recovering from the terrible plague devastations of the mid-fourteenth century, the plague was still a real danger. The Swiss reformer, Ulrich Zwingli (1484–1531), nearly succumbed to the plague, and in 1527 the plague struck Luther's area. In Wittenberg those who could, fled; the others died or were cared for in Luther's home, which he turned into a sort of hospice. This was the occasion for Luther's tract, *Whether One May Flee from a Deadly Plague.*[1] The fear of this disease is practically unimaginable to us today. Even love could not close a person's eyes to the omnipresence of death in the midst of life, for this was

[1] Jaroslav Pelikan & Helmut Lehmann, eds., *Luthers' Works*, 55 vols., (St. Louis: Concordia Publishing House, and Minneapolis: Fortress Press, 1955–1986), vol. 43, pp. 113–138. Hereafter cited as LW.

the period when syphilis appeared on the continent. The shortness of life was never far from peoples' minds.

The causes of disease were little understood; it was not until the early eighteenth century that people began to understand the relationship between sanitation, hygiene, and health. Physicians, if available, understood little about curing those who were sick. Luther himself is a good example of the physical health of the time. He was perpetually in ill health. Throughout his reforming career he suffered from attacks of vertigo, severe and sometimes incapacitating headaches, hemorrhoids, constipation, and stones of the kidneys, bladder, and urinary tract. In later life he suffered from an ulcerated leg that, on medical advice, was kept open as a running wound. He also had heart problems, sinus infections, and a middle-ear infection. Luther lived in a time when illness was endemic and hospitals were not for therapy but for solace and shelter.

Yet Luther's living conditions were better than those of most of the population. His prince gave him the Augustinian monastery for living quarters, and he and his family had meat, fish, and fruit to supplement the medieval staple of life, bread. Luther's wife—by his account—made the best beer available. The vast majority of the population, however, were usually engaged in a daily struggle for survival. This struggle became critical when there was a crop failure or shortfall owing to any number of natural causes such as drought, too much rain, or early frost. Although the larger towns constructed granaries for storing surpluses from good harvests, there were opportunists who would hoard food and inflate prices in times of need. Furthermore, surplus food in one area was not readily available to another area in need because transportation networks, especially apart from rivers, were still primitive. Grain prices could fluctuate as much as 150 percent in a year. Speculators who profited from these events were the targets of vigorous sermons and tracts by Luther and other churchmen who condemned such "usury" and called for increased government control of commerce.

Most people in the sixteenth century were peasants who toiled on the land from sunrise to sunset. Their life of labor was occasionally relieved in the festivities of major holy days and the ritual breaks occasioned by marriages and funerals. In some areas, the peasant was a virtual slave, whereas in others he was a small landholder. Peasant diet and housing were sometimes adequate and sometimes inadequate. The diversity of conditions in the German area alone makes generalization about peasant life difficult. In any case, the life of the peasant was hard and not infrequently hardening. The upper class frequently depicted the peasant as stupid, coarse, loathsome, untrustworthy, and prone to violence. For the nobles, such self-serving descriptions rationalized and legitimated oppression of the peasants.

Not all writers and lawyers supported such prejudice against the peasants but reproached lay and ecclesial nobility with the adage that true nobility derives from virtue not from blood. Nevertheless, long before the Reformation, the adverse economic and social status of the peasant was legitimated by blaming the victim. It is of interest that the Noah story (Gen. 9:20–27) was used in medieval Germany for the same purposes as in slaveholding America: to explain that subjugated people bore the curse of God.

When pushed to extremes, the normally conservative peasant could react violently. Usually peasants acted out their rage against their conditions by turning against each other, but a picture from the period shows four peasants slaughtering an armored knight with axes. Far more serious than individual acts of violence were the outbreaks of communal peasant rebellion against the oppression of their lords. There were peasant uprisings in 1493, 1502, 1513, 1517, and the great Peasants' War was in 1524–1525. The nobility believed these were orchestrated conspiracies; in fact they began as spontaneous revolts generated by much the same kind of rage and frustration that stimulated the African-American riots that swept through American cities in the 1960s. This long-repressed peasant anger against the lords, including the ecclesial lords who were great landholders, helps to explain the enthusiastic reception of Luther's early writings that attacked church authority and extolled Christian liberty.

It is estimated that only 10 percent of the population lived in the cities and towns. However, some areas in Germany and the Netherlands had a higher percentage of urban population. In Saxony, Luther's area, as many as 20 percent lived in its many small towns. In this period there was a very rapid growth of towns and cities, some even doubling in size. Augsburg and Cologne had populations of about 30,000. The population growth in the urban areas was stimulated by the new money economy, which made urban centers places of both creative change and opportunity and of social conflict. The feudal economy was being displaced by an early form of capitalism, which in turn undermined the traditional idea of society as a sacred corporation, the *corpus Christianum*, wherein each person was ethically responsible to all others.

One of the major social problems stimulated by these urban and economic developments was poverty. Then as now there were numerous causes of urban poverty. It is estimated that as much as two-thirds of the population of any given city consisted of the working poor who struggled to live on a minimum wage that was at or below the poverty level. These daylaborers received their income on a daily basis. Because they received only enough to live day to day, an illness, accident, or decision by their employer could plunge them into a catastrophic situation. These people were politically powerless and economically marginal.

The social and economic problems of the urban population were increased by the influx of peasants from the countryside seeking a better life in the cities. Despite the fact that the cities and towns actually offered little possibility for an improved life, they continued to attract peasants throughout the century. And during periods of social and religious conflict, the cities were a haven to refugees fleeing conflicts and persecution. In the mid-sixteenth century, the city of Strasbourg, for example, was strained by an annual entrance of dispossessed people equal to 6 percent of its population that caused severe social problems. Even the small town of Wittenberg, with a population of only about 2,500, felt the pressure of the begging poor as well as the begging religious orders. Luther's colleague, Karlstadt, described the poor as everywhere, "begging for bread on the streets, before the houses, or sitting before the churches."[2]

In spite of all these social problems, this was also a period of expanding lay education. By the eve of the Reformation, the number of European universities had risen from twenty to seventy as a result of the efforts of monarchs, princes, and wealthy merchants. The University of Wittenberg, for example, was founded by Prince Frederick the Wise in 1502. Perhaps 3 to 4 percent of the population could read by the beginning of the sixteenth century. The thousands of published Reformation pamphlets and sermons were thus designed to be read to the illiterate as well as by the literate. "Faith," as Luther stressed, "comes by hearing."

The educational system that Luther encountered as a youth was certainly effective in his case even though he did not find it at all edifying. Knowledge was literally beaten into the students. Luther started school before he was quite five years old. The techniques by which he was forced to learn Latin as the basis for later studies included coercion and ridicule. Unprepared students were forced to wear a dunce cap and were addressed as an ass. A student speaking German rather than Latin in class was beaten with a rod. Even music, Luther's favorite subject, was presented in a utilitarian fashion to train youths for church choirs. In short, the education of children was at best dull and at worst barbaric. Luther later recalled that one morning he was caned fifteen times for not mastering the tables of Latin grammar.

Those who finally mastered enough Latin went on to more advanced education. At thirteen, Luther went to the town of Magdeburg, where he lived and studied at a school run by a pious lay religious organization, the Brethren of the Common Life. From there he went to study in Eisenach. All the students literally had to sing for their suppers. After classes they roamed the streets in childrens' choirs to beg for food. Toward the end of his studies in Latin school, Luther was fortunate to find some teachers who stimulated him and also recognized his abilities. He was introduced to the Latin classics and history, which made a lifelong impression on him and gave him great pleasure. In later life, Luther translated Aesop's fables into German and insisted that everyone should study the classics and history.

It was a university education, however, that opened doors for commoners to careers in medicine, law, and the church. Luther's father was eager for Martin to improve the family status by going to university and becoming a lawyer. Thus Luther attended the University of Erfurt, where he received both his Bachelor of Arts and Master's degrees.

---

[2]Carter Lindberg, " 'There Should Be No Beggars among Christians': An Early Reformation Tract on Social Welfare," in Carter Lindberg, ed., *Piety, Politics, and Ethics: Reformation Studies in Honor of George Wolfgang Forell* (Kirksville, MO: Sixteenth Century Journal Publishers, 1984), 160.

The late medieval university consisted of an arts faculty and the three professional faculties of medicine, law, and theology. *The* authority, "the father of those that know," was Aristotle. Students were taught how to think by emphasizing Aristotle's writings on logic. The typical mode of educating the students in logical thinking was the disputation. The teacher would assign a set of theses to the students who were then required to defend them according to the rules of logic. The disputation was also the form for the final examination for a degree. Today's oral examination of Ph. D. students in our universities, during which they have to defend their dissertation or thesis, is but a pale reflection of the rigorous exercises common to the medieval university. It is of interest that the disputation is precisely the form in which Luther cast his *95 Theses*[3] (see pp. 339f.) as well as many other of his Reformation writings. In many ways, the Reformation was a movement from within the universities.

By all accounts, the late medieval period was a time of insecurity prompted not only by the physical difficulties of the time but also by the rapid social changes that called into question the values and traditional truths people had lived by. The church further irritated these insecurities by promoting a type of pastoral care designed to make people uncertain about their salvation and thus more dependent on the intercessions of the church. Visitors to medieval cathedrals and churches can still see today the representations of Christ on the throne of judgment with a sword and a lily on either side of his head. The lily represented resurrection to heaven, but the sword of judgment to eternal torment was more vivid in the minds of most people.

Everywhere in everyday life the medieval person was surrounded by images serving to remind him or her of eternity and how to achieve it. As the early medieval pope, Gregory the Great (d. 604) had said, "images are the books of the laity." Medieval churches presented the bible and the lives of the saints in stone, stained glass, and wood carvings. The medieval person had no sense of the modern compartmentalization of life into sacred and secular spheres. Thus "the books of the laity" were evident at the town fountain, the town hall, carved in the doorways, and painted on the walls of homes and public buildings. Where people walked, worked, and gathered for news and gossip, there were religious reminders of their origin and destiny.

A whole set of practices and exercises were developed to assist people to avoid hell. As if people needed reminders of their omnipresent sense of mortality, the art work of the day graphically presented the theme of the "dance of death," complete with a skeletal Grim Reaper, and literarily presented manuals on the "art of dying." Saints and their relics were avidly collected and venerated with the conviction that they were efficacious in reducing sentences to purgatory. Luther's own prince had one of the largest relic collections of the area—more than 17,000 pieces. And the Wittenberg Castle Church was dedicated to All Saints.

[3]LW, Vol. 31, pp. 17–33.

The place where every real or imagined sin was ferreted out was the confessional. The laity were expected to go to confession frequently. There the priest pried into every aspect of their lives, especially their sexual lives. The list of sexual sins in the confessional manuals of the day was so complete that even sexual thoughts were categorized according to their particular danger of damnation. Whether sexual relations within marriage were serious sins was debated, but there was agreement that at least in principle they were sins. Part and parcel of this orientation was the elevation of celibacy and the cloister as the supreme form of a God-pleasing life. The corollary to this view was a demeaning of marriage and family as necessary evils for the propagation of the community. It is no wonder that the Reformation attack on mandatory celibacy for the clergy and its renewed appreciation of the human value of sexuality was so well received by the laity.

Everyday life on the eve of the Reformation also included elements regarded today as superstitions: belief in witches, magic, and astrology. But before we look too quickly down our collective modern nose at late medieval superstitions, we might recall that most of our daily newspapers include horoscopes, and that the "health and wealth" gospels using contemporary media appeal to the same fears and desires that motivated the medieval person to seek out supernatural healers and diviners of the future.

Martin Luther and Reformation Beginnings

Luther's reform movement was not initiated by the righteous and moral indignation of a Savonarola or an Erasmus directed against the Renaissance papacy. Luther's movement was rooted in his own personal anxiety about salvation—an anxiety that, if the popular response to him is any indication, was widespread throughout Europe. This anxiety was an effect of the crises of the late medieval period already discussed. The crises of famine, plague, and war were further enhanced by the rapid and confusing social changes caused by technological developments, urban growth, the accelerating displacement of the feudal economy by the profit economy, and the perceived corruption of the church. Cynics played on the traditional image of the church as the ark of salvation by comparing it to Noah's ark without benefit of shovelled stalls. Reynard the Fox, from the medieval animal epic of the same name, stated succinctly: "Little crooks are hanged; big crooks govern our lands and cities." Explaining his own dishonesty and immorality to his nephew, Grimbert the Badger, Reynard goes on to say: "Sometimes I think that, since everybody does it, this is the way it ought to be." The fable ends with the moral, "Money counts, and nothing else."[4] Reynard's point is that if you want to get to the top, you should imitate him.

[4]Gerald Strauss, ed., *Manifestations of Discontent in Germany on the Eve of the Reformation* (Bloomington, IN: Indiana University Press, 1971), pp. 91, 96.

By the late fifteenth century, the population had largely recovered from its decimation by famine and plague, but the social effects were still being felt. The initial labor shortage in the cities and towns owing to the plague lured many peasants who hoped to make better lives for themselves. But this flight from rural areas jeopardized the livelihood of the landowners who therefore took whatever steps they could to keep their workers on the farms. In many cases these steps were very oppressive. Serfdom was established or, where already present, strengthened. Laws such as the English Statutes of Laborers arose throughout Europe mandating that laborers were not to abandon their employers. These laws prescribed severe punishments for vagrancy and begging. In southern Germany especially there was a movement to replace local laws and customs by Roman law in order more efficiently to squeeze as much labor and goods as possible out of peasants and day laborers. The ecclesiastical landlords were particularly adept at this practice because they were already familiar with Roman law in the form of canon law. This is one of the reasons for the widespread anticlerical anger on the eve of the Reformation.

Technological developments also stimulated the insecurities of the age. The invention of moveable metal type, inexpensive paper, and good ink led to a media explosion. More books were printed between 1460 and 1500 than had been produced by scribes and monks throughout the entire Middle Ages. The printing press made possible the rapid and reliable dissemination of new ideas, including religious ideas. Luther himself was a prolific author. Before 1520 he had already produced eighty-two writings that appeared in 607 editions. Assuming a printing of 1,000 copies each, more than 500,000 pieces were in circulation. This was only the beginning of a flood of writings that, thanks to the printing press, allowed Luther and then other reformers to transmit their messages.

The development of sump pumps and smelting led to a boom in mining and metallurgy. One effect of this technology was a massive increase in silver production that in turn stimulated inflation because much of the silver was made into coins. Another effect in combination with the invention of a stable gunpowder mixture was the development of guns and cannon. Indiscriminate death and destruction were now possible beyond the medieval person's wildest dreams. When this technology was coupled with national and religious fanaticism, these dreams became a devastating nightmare. Thus the Spanish cavalry was wiped out by French artillery in the battle of Ravenna in 1512. There was money to be made in arms, and so this fledgling military-industrial complex grew and bore its deadly fruit. In turn, these developments made an entire medieval class of people, the knights, obsolete. This along with other factors led to the Knights' Revolt of 1523.

All these various crises found their focal point in the crisis of the church, or in broader modern terms, the crisis of the society's fundamental values. The erosion of security in so many aspects of late medieval life came to a head in the loss of certainty about the meaning and goal of life itself. The church had been the guarantor of the symbols of certainty, but now the many late medieval vicissitudes of the church contributed to the perception that the church itself was in crisis.

Because of the crisis of the church, the credibility of religion in every area of piety and theology was also in crisis. Scholars have sometimes puzzled over the great surge of popular piety in the late Middle Ages. Why did people throw themselves into such a piety of achievement? Perhaps because in times of crisis people tend to yearn for the "good old days," and try harder to emulate what they think they were. No other period celebrated so many religious festivals and processions, or threw itself so wholeheartedly into church construction. Mass pilgrimages, frequently sparked by some perceived miracle usually associated with the Lord's Supper, caught on like wildfire. The dark side of this devotion erupted in mass attacks on Jews and persons thought to be witches. Miracles seemed to multiply everywhere in the empire. The veneration of saints reached its peak and changed its form. Saints were depicted life-size, individualized, and garbed in contemporary dress. Saints were now aligned with the arrangement of society and were made patrons for every human exigency. The practice of giving children saints' names became so widespread that the old German names all but disappeared. Insecure about salvation, people attempted to guarantee it by capturing mediators between themselves and God.

Death seems never to have been more realistically considered than in this era and hardly ever so anxiously feared. Even today we are still fascinated by the bizarre paintings by the Dutchman, Hieronymous Bosch (ca. 1450–1516), with their weird, rapidly breeding hybrid creatures associated with lust and fertility but which in the end symbolize sterility and death. Artistic realism also blossomed with popular manuals on the art of dying, depictions of the dance of death, and deeply moving representations of Christ's passion. Relic collections abounded. Luther's contemporary, Cardinal Albrecht of Brandenburg believed his collection was worth 39,245,120 years off purgatory. The extraordinary prosperity of the indulgence trade was fueled as much by the desires of believers as by the financial interests of the church. If this seems surprising, think of the similar appeal and success of modern media evangelists who promise to satisfy modern desires to control God and conquer insecurity. Late medieval Christendom has been characterized as having "an immense appetite for the divine."[5]

Theological and Pastoral Responses to Insecurity

A characteristic of late medieval theology and pastoral practice was that its very effort to provide security led an insecure world only to more insecurity and uncer-

---

[5]Lucien Fèbvrés' phrase, which is cited by Bernd Moeller, "Piety in Germany Around 1500," in Steven Ozment, *The Reformation in Medieval Perspective* (Chicago: Quadrangle Books, 1971), p. 59.

tainty about salvation. One of the key scholastic ideas that led to this uncertainty about salvation was expressed in the phrase *facere quod in se est* ("do what lies within you"). That is, striving to love God to the best of one's ability—however weak that may be—will prompt God to reward one's efforts with the grace to do even better. The Christian's life of pilgrimage toward the heavenly city was increasingly perceived, literally and not just theologically, as an economy of salvation. As mentioned earlier, this "mathematics of salvation" concentrated on achieving as many good works as possible in order to merit God's reward. It may be suggested that this theology reflected the new social, political, and economic developments of the times. In religion as in early capitalism, contracted work merited reward. Individuals were to be responsible for their own life, society, and world on the basis and within the limits stipulated by God. The concern of the theologians was to provide an avenue to security through human participation in the process of salvation. The result of this theology was, however, to enhance the crisis because it threw people back upon their own resources. That is, no matter how grace-assisted their good works were, the burden of proof for these works fell back on the performers, the more sensitive of whom began asking how they could know if they had done their best.

As Thomas Aquinas was fond of saying, grace does not do away with nature but completes it. So the famous scholastic phrase, "do what lies within you," means that salvation is a process that takes place *within* us as we perfect ourselves. Put another way, we become righteous before God as we do righteous acts, as we do good works. But to an anxious and insecure age, the question became: "How do I know if I have done my best?"

The answers to such a question came primarily from the parish priests who were frequently unversed in the subtleties of academic theology. The most common answer was to try harder. This answer is the clue to that great surge in popular piety mentioned earlier. When in doubt about your salvation, examine yourself to determine if you have done your best, and then put more effort into achieving the best you can. To encourage more effort, pastoral practice consciously stimulated anxiety and introspection by citing the church's translation of Ecclesiastes 9:1, "No one knows whether he is worthy of God's love or hate."

An important clue to the religious sensibilities of the people and the lower clergy is provided by catechisms—simplified expositions of basic theology, usually in question and answer format, used by the priests in daily pastoral practice. Widely popular, catechisms were translated from Latin into the vernaculars to reflect the spiritual needs of the people. Dietrich Kolde's (1435–1515) *Mirror of a Christian Man* indicates the deep religious fear and anxiety of the people up to the eve of the Reformation and thereby provides the context for understanding Luther's reform movement.

Kolde's *Mirror* was very popular. First printed in 1470, it appeared in nineteen editions before the Reformation and continued to be reprinted afterward. Translated into various European vernaculars, Kolde's work was probably the most widely used Catholic catechism before and during the early years of the Reformation. The significant point of this catechism for our purposes is the author's expression of the peoples' widespread lack of certitude about salvation. Kolde summed up this anxiety when he wrote:

> There are three things I know to be true that frequently make my heart heavy. The first troubles my spirit, because I will have to die. The second troubles my heart more, because I do not know when. The third troubles me above all. I do not know where I will go.[6]

Luther's first steps on his own quest for certainty about his relationship to God were not unlike those of many before him and countless others since—he entered "seminary." In Luther's case it was the Augustinian monastery in Erfurt. Again, not unlike countless other seminarians past and present, Luther's decision greatly upset his father. His father was by this time making a decent living at what we might call the medieval equivalent of a mining engineer. He had sent Martin to Erfurt University with the ambition that he would earn a law degree, return home to the town of Mansfeld, and perhaps eventually become mayor. Luther had barely begun his law studies when his father's dreams were shattered by the same lightning bolt that knocked Martin to the ground as he walked to Erfurt after a visit home. In terror, Martin implored St. Anne, the patron saint of miners, for help, shouting, "I will become a monk."

And become a monk he did. In July 1505 he entered the Black Cloister (so-called because the monks wore black) of the Observant Augustinians in Erfurt. The Black Augustinians were known for their rigorous pursuit of spiritual benefits that more than matched in intensity the pursuit of material benefits practiced by Luther's father and other budding entrepreneurs in the world. It was no less the business of monks to earn spiritual currency for themselves and others than it was the business of the early capitalists to earn material currency.

In the monastery, Luther threw himself wholeheartedly into efforts to achieve salvation. Between the six worship services of each day, which began at 2:00 A.M., Luther sandwiched intense prayer, meditation, and spiritual exercises. But this was just the normal routine that Luther in his zeal to mortify his flesh and make himself acceptable to God soon surpassed. It has been suggested that his long periods of fasting, self-flagellation, and sleepless nights in a stone cell without a blanket against the damp cold characteristic of the area, all contributed to the continual illness that plagued him for the rest of his life. Later in life, Luther remarked: "I almost fasted myself to death, for again and again I went for three days without taking a drop of water or a morsel of food. I was very serious about it."[7] Luther could not believe,

[6]Denis Janz, *Three Reformation Catechisms: Catholic, Anabaptist, Lutheran* (New York & Toronto: The Edwin Mellon Press, 1982), p. 127.
[7]LW, Vol. 54, pp. 339–340.

however, that God was placated by his efforts to do what lay within him. And so, Luther came to hate "the righteous God who punishes sinners. . . . Nevertheless, I beat importunately upon Paul at that place, most ardently desiring to know what St. Paul wanted."[8]

"That place" is the passage in Romans 1:17, "For in it [the gospel] the righteousness of God is revealed through faith for faith; as it is written, 'He who through faith is righteous shall live.'" Up to this point Luther like so many of his contemporaries had heard the gospel as the threat of God's righteousness and wrath because medieval theology and pastoral care presented the righteousness of God as the standard that sinners had to meet in order to achieve salvation. Years later, Luther wrote: "But every time I read this passage, I always wished that God had never revealed the gospel—for who could love a God who is angry, judges, and condemns?"[9]

What Luther discovered through his intense study of the language and grammar of the bible and assisted by the linguistic tools provided by the Renaissance humanists was that the righteousness of God is not a demand to be met by achievement but a gift to be accepted by faith. This discovery is the source for the Reformation watchwords of *sola gratia* ("grace alone") and *sola fide* ("faith alone"). Luther's conversion was the realization that salvation is not the goal of life but the foundation of life. It is an indication of the power of this discovery that the theology faculty at the University of Wittenberg, which he had joined in 1512, instituted a curriculum reform. In the spring of 1517, Luther wrote to a friend in Erfurt:

> "Our theology and St. Augustine are progressing well, and with God's help rule at our University. Aristotle is gradually falling from his throne, and his final doom is only a matter of time. . . . Indeed no one can expect to have any students if he does not want to teach this theology, that is, lecture on the Bible or on St. Augustine or another teacher of ecclesiastical eminence.[10]

The authority of Aristotle was displaced by the authority of the bible, hence the other major Reformation watchword: *sola scriptura* ("scripture alone").

What Luther discovered and what so moved his faculty colleagues and students was an understanding of God and salvation that overthrew the anxiety-ridden catechetical teachings of priests such as Kolde. Luther's biblical study led him to the conviction that the crisis of human life is not overcome by striving to achieve security by what we do, but by the certainty of God's acceptance of us in spite of what we do. Luther now never tired of proclaiming that the burden of proof for salvation rests not on a person's deeds but on God's action. This conviction delivered Luther from what he called "the monster of uncertainty."

[8]LW, Vol. 34, pp. 336–337.
[9]LW, Vol. 5, p. 158.
[10]LW, Vol. 48, p. 42.

This monster of uncertainty is worse than all the other monsters. . . . [I]t is obvious that the enemies of Christ teach what is uncertain, because they command consciences to be in doubt. . . . Let us thank God, therefore, that we have been delivered from this monster of uncertainty and that we now can believe for a certainty that the Holy Spirit is crying and issuing that sigh too deep for words in our hearts. . . . And this is why our theology is certain: it snatches us away from ourselves and places us outside ourselves, so that we do not depend on our own strength, conscience, experience, person, or works but depend on that which is outside ourselves, that is, on the promise and truth of God, which cannot deceive.[11]

Luther to the Diet of Worms

Luther was propelled into the public arena by the indulgence controversy initiated by his *95 Theses*. The popular mind, abetted by some preachers, had twisted the meaning of indulgence from that of the church's remission of a temporal penalty imposed because of sin to that of a ticket to heaven. The hard-sell medieval indulgence sellers such as John Tetzel, whom Luther attacked, offered direct access to heaven even for those who were already dead and in purgatory. One of Tetzel's sales jingles was, "As soon as the coin into the box rings, a soul from purgatory to heaven springs." Would you buy a used car from this man? Well, crowds of anxious contemporaries believed they could buy salvation from him. He was good at his job, but then he was also rewarded handsomely.

Tetzel's routine would have been the envy of Madison Avenue, had there been one. His advance men announced his arrival some weeks before he came to town. They also compiled a special directory of the town that listed the financial resources of its citizens. Tetzel's entrance into the town was accompanied by a fanfare of trumpets and drums and a procession complete with the flags and symbols of the papacy. After a vivid sermon on hell and its terrors in the town square, he proceeded to the largest church and gave an equally vivid sermon on purgatory and the sufferings not only awaiting the audience but presently endured by their dead relatives. After the next sermon picturing heaven, his audience was sufficiently prepared and eager to buy indulgences. There was always something for everyone because Tetzel had a sliding scale of prices depending on the person's financial resources.

It is interesting that Tetzel was not allowed in Wittenberg because Luther's prince, Frederick the Wise, had his own relic collection with its associated indulgences and he did not want competition from Tetzel. Luther's parishioners overcame this inconvenience by going out to Tetzel. Luther was appalled when they returned

---

[11]LW, Vol. 26, pp. 386–387.

and said they no longer needed to go to confession, penance, and the Mass because now they had tickets to heaven.

This was the immediate context for the *95 Theses* of October 31, 1517, the traditional date of the beginning of the Reformation. What Luther attacked in these theses was not the church's doctrine of indulgences but the abuse of that doctrine so evident in the activities of Tetzel. In fact, the *95 Theses* were a typical academic proposition for debate among university colleagues. They were written in Latin, and most Wittenbergers could not even read German. Thus the popular image of Luther as the angry young man pounding incendiary theses to the church door is far more romantic fiction than reality. Then how did this document for debate cause such an uproar? Luther sent it to Tetzel's superior, Albrecht, the archbishop of Mainz, with the naive thought that Albrecht did not know that his hireling was abusing the authority of the church. Someone in the archbishop's office sent the document on to Rome. The result was an explosion that startled and frightened Luther as much as anyone else.

Luther had unknowingly touched the nerve of a far-reaching political and ecclesiastical scam. Pope Leo X was short of funds but wanted to build St. Peter's to impress his secular rivals. Albrecht was legally under age to hold an archbishopric and was not even ordained, but he was of the ambitious House of Hohenzollern. The Hohenzollerns wanted to gain the archbisopric of Mainz because it included membership in the electoral college that elected the Holy Roman Emperor. This electoral college, constituted by the Golden Bull of 1356 (which remained in effect until 1806), consisted of seven electors: the archbishops of Mainz, Trier, and Cologne, the Count Palatine of the Rhine, the Duke of Electoral Saxony (Luther's Prince Frederick), the Margrave of Brandenburg (Albrecht's brother!), and the King of Bohemia. With two votes of their own, the Hohenzollerns reasoned that they might be able to swing the impending imperial election. Thus the Hohenzollern's "bought" the archbishopric for Albrecht. The special papal dispensation that allowed Albrecht to become archbishop cost a very substantial amount of money, which was borrowed at an exorbitant interest rate from the famous Fugger banking house of Augsburg. To pay back this huge loan, Albrecht, now archbishop, was given the right by Leo X to sell indulgences with half the proceeds going to finance the building of St. Peter's in Rome. It is no wonder that Albrecht hired the best indulgence salesman he could find: Tetzel.

Events accelerated rapidly. In the summer of 1518, Luther was informed by the papacy that he was a heretic and was cited to Rome. Local pride and German law, however, saved Luther from what would surely have been his execution had he gone to Rome. Prince Frederick by this time realized that student enrollment had increased markedly at Wittenberg University, his pride and joy that he himself had just founded in 1502. He was not about to let his prize professor and academic drawing card go off to be burned at the stake. Besides, German law said its citizens should be tried in its own courts. Arrangements were made to have Luther interviewed by papal representatives in Germany, but the outcome of Luther's interview with Cardinal Cajetan in Augsburg in October 1518 was unsatisfactory to all concerned. Luther would not recant, and the cardinal would not discuss the theological issues.

The next step in what was rapidly becoming the Luther affair was a debate in Leipzig in July 1519. Surrounded by armed students and colleagues, Luther journeyed to Leipzig University, where he confronted one of the most clever debaters of the day, Johann Eck. Eck prodded Luther with charges that he was a Hussite and a Bohemian, tantamount to being called a communist in the 1950s. After some consideration, Luther burst out that many of Hus's views condemned by the Council of Constance were indeed Christian, which indicated that a church council as well as the pope may err. The audience was shocked. Luther was now confronted by the implications of the teachings he had been developing over the past years: Christ alone is head of the church, and when the institution of the papacy usurps this headship it is the Antichrist.

Luther, now on center stage, had gained the attention of humanists and German nationalists as well as clergy and theological professors. In June 1520 the papal bull *Exsurge Domine* gave Luther sixty days to recant or to be excommunicated. If Luther failed to recant, his very memory was to be erased. Easier said than done, for by now much of Germany had rallied to his side. When the bull was posted in Germany, it was defaced. When the book burnings that normally accompanied such a bull were to take place, gleeful students gave papal and scholastic writings to the illiterate enforcers of the bull who then burned them as Luther's works. Eck himself added fuel to the fires by adding his own private "enemies list" to the bull's list of those condemned.

The sixtieth day of grace granted Luther by the bull fell on December 10, 1520. On that day Luther's colleague, Melanchthon, led the faculty and students out of the university for a truly revolutionary act. They publicly and solemnly burned the constitutional foundations of medieval Europe: the books of canon law. Luther himself threw the papal bull on the fire. After singing the *Te Deum*, the faculty returned to the university. The students, however, carried on boisterous demonstrations against the pope for the next few days until the town authorities stopped them. The actual bull of excommunication, *Decet Romanum*, was published on January 3, 1521.

The papacy now urged the recently elected emperor, Charles V—a Hapsburg, in spite of Hohenzollern machinations—to issue a mandate against Luther. But the German constitution and Charles' coronation oath upholding the right of Germans to trial by an impartial panel of judges forced Charles to promise Luther a safe passage to the Diet (the German parliament) to be held at Worms for a hearing. In spite of the friendly reminders that Hus, too, had been given a safe-conduct to Constance where he was then executed, Luther made a triumphal journey to Worms. There, before the emperor, princes, and lords—a whole world away from his monastic cell and dingy classroom—Luther did not receive the hearing he had hoped for. Rather, he was presented with a pile of his writings and asked to recant their errors. Luther's brief answer included the memorable lines:

> Unless I am convinced by the testimony of the Scriptures or by clear reason (for I do not trust either in the pope or in councils alone, since it is well known that they have often erred and contradicted themselves), I am bound by the Scriptures I have quoted and my conscience is captive to the Word of God. I cannot and I will not retract anything, since it is neither safe or right to go against conscience. I cannot do otherwise, here I stand, may God help me. Amen.[12]

The evening the Diet closed, the emperor gathered a rump Diet of conservative princes and bishops, and issued the Edict of Worms (1521), which proclaimed Luther an outlaw. All subjects were forbidden to have any dealings with him but were instead to seize him and deliver him to the authorities. Luther's followers and supporters were to be treated likewise, and their property was to be confiscated and given to the one carrying out the edict. Fortunately for Luther, he now had a number of powerful supporters including his own prince, Frederick the Wise.

The Reformation and Social Change

Medieval people, and Luther among them, considered the church and the human community to be coextensive. Although they certainly made distinctions between ecclesial and civil rights and responsibilities, they had no conception of the modern separation of church and state. It was taken for granted that theological change would have social implications and consequences. It is not surprising that Luther's translation of the bible into German was so influential that it contributed significantly to the development of the modern German language, but his translation of the bible had other social and political effects as well. Coupled with Luther's theological emphasis that all baptized Christians are equally priests before God, his emphasis on making the Word of God accessible to all deprived the elite class (the priests and some rulers) of control over words as well as the Word. This challenge to authorities was facilitated by the printing press.

Furthermore, Luther's emphasis on the normative religious authority of the Scriptures led to his conviction that all Christians should be able to read the bible, preferably in its original languages. This was a first step toward universal education. Luther also made it clear that Christians should be educated not only for deepening their faith but also for serving the community. Luther was confident that God would preserve the church, "but in the worldly kingdom men must act on the basis of

---

[12]LW, Vol. 32, pp. 112–113.

reason—wherein the laws also have their origin."[13] Therefore, Luther maintained that the government should compel its subjects to send their children to school "so that there will always be preachers, jurists, pastors, writers, physicians, schoolmasters, and the like, for we cannot do without them."[14] Luther's address to municipal authorities has a contemporary ring to it:

> My dear sirs, if we have to spend such large sums every year on guns, roads, bridges, dams, and countless other items to insure the temporal peace and prosperity of a city, why should not much more be devoted to the poor neglected youth . . . ?[15]

Luther was no less hesitant to appeal to religious and civil leaders to reform the structures of social welfare. As mentioned earlier, the late medieval society was faced by extensive and often severe poverty. Pre-Reformation laws to compel able-bodied beggars to work were largely ineffective because the medieval church had developed an ideology of poverty as a virtue. This ideology compounded the new social problem of widespread poverty because the picture of the poor person as blessed by God and as an object for the meritorious work of almsgiving prevented the society from seeing poverty as a social problem related to the new social and economic developments. This ideology of poverty also provided a large and cheap labor pool. All this was undercut by Luther's rejection of charity as a means of salvation. Because salvation was now understood to be a free gift apart from works, there was no longer any need to have poor people as God-given objects for the practice of charity and the benefit of businesses. In attacking the theological idea that poverty is a virtue as well as an opportunity for the rich to do good works of almsgiving, Luther and other reformers such as Zwingli and Calvin were able to expose the social roots of poverty and to contribute to the development of social welfare programs directed to systemic and not merely individual change.

In Lutheran areas, this social welfare program was linked not only to education but to what became known as the common chest. In nearly every town that adopted the Reformation, legislation was soon enacted that included provision for this common chest. The common chest was literally a large chest kept in the town's major church and usually fitted with four different locks. The chest contained funds for relief of the poor, account books, and lists of the area poor. The funds initially came from the large endowments of the church that had accumulated during the Middle Ages. These funds were supplemented by offerings of money and goods; later they were regularized by taxation. Elected representatives, usually one from each quarter of the town, would each have a key to one of the locks on the chest. Every Sunday

[13] LW, Vol. 46, p. 242.
[14] LW, Vol. 46, p. 256.
[15] LW, Vol. 45, p. 350.

these representatives along with the pastor and the church deacons would meet to assess the needs of the town's poor and to provide for distribution of money and goods to them. The funds were to be used for relief of the poor, low-interest loans to poor workers and tradesmen, subsidy of education for poor children, and dowries for daughters of the poor. The legislation establishing the common chest was concerned not only with such important remedial work but also with developing social structures and policies, such as job training, to try to prevent poverty. The first common chest was instituted in Wittenberg in 1522, and it soon became a model for similar programs in the major cities of Germany and the Scandinavian areas. The organizational genius for this social welfare program in the Lutheran areas was Luther's co-worker, Johannes Bugenhagen (1485–1558). Bugenhagen traveled tirelessly throughout northern Germany and Scandinavia developing legislation for reform of the church that included educational and welfare policies.

As these examples suggest, Luther never advocated that Christians withdraw from the world. Indeed, the very point of his understanding of the gospel was that because salvation is the foundation rather than the goal of life, the Christian is free to redirect to service to others the time and energy previously expended on achieving salvation. That is, trust in God's promise of salvation included liberation from constantly checking one's spiritual pulse. The Christian was allowed to turn his or her attention from otherworldly achievements to this-worldly activities.

This is the reason Luther vigorously distinguished between the kingdom of God and the kingdom of the world. He hammered incessantly on this distinction because he wanted to call Christians to political action in an age that conceived of religion primarily as withdrawal from the world—even kings preferred to spend their last days in a monastery. The medieval person could not conceive of having a vocation in the world because vocation had a narrow religious meaning and politics was "dirty." Luther hoped to free Christians for service in a world that is always shrouded in political ambiguity by distinguishing between human, civil righteousness measured by justice and equitable laws and the righteousness before God that is a free gift.

Luther's distinction, but not separation, between life in the world governed by reason, law, and works and life before God governed by grace alone was put to the test by a contemporary radical reformer, Thomas Müntzer (ca. 1489–1525). Initially influenced by Luther, Müntzer came to believe that the civil authorities should play a central role in christianizing society. In his famous "Sermon Before the Princes" (1524) preached to the Duke of Saxony and his advisors, Müntzer exhorted the princes to act as the servants of God's wrath on all the ungodly. "For the godless person has no right to live when he is in the way of the pious. . . . The sword of the rulers is bestowed on them for the retribution of the wicked as protection for the pious."[16]

---

[16]George H. Williams & Angel M. Mergal, eds., *Spiritual and Anabaptist Writers*, The Library of Christian Classics, Vol. XXV, (Philadelphia: Westminster Press, 1957), p. 66.

It was soon clear that the princes not only were not convinced by Müntzer's message but considered it dangerous. Müntzer then fled from one city to another. When he returned to Saxony, he became involved in the Peasant's War not because he was a social revolutionary but because he saw the war as the occasion for the final battle of God against all the ungodly. Thus he exhorted others to join the battle crying, "The time has come, the evil-doers are running like scared dogs . . . show no pity. . . . Don't let your sword grow cold . . . It is not your fight, but the Lord's."[17] By this bloody purification of the world, Müntzer hoped to usher in a genuine theocracy that would realize completely the medieval aspiration for a Christian commonwealth. In May 1525 Müntzer preached encouragement to the peasant troops at Frankenhausen before their bloody slaughter by the troops of Duke George of ducal Saxony. But his utopian exhortations were no match against the duke's firepower. Müntzer himself fled but was found hiding in a bed feigning illness. Under torture he recanted and was executed.

The Müntzer episode further convinced Luther that the world must be governed by reason and law, not by any religious ideology. From Luther's point of view, all efforts to govern the world by the gospel of free forgiveness would lead either to unrestrained chaos and destruction or to a demonic crusade against all perceived "evil empires." To Luther, the identification of any political program, regardless of its intrinsic merit, with the will of God is to subvert both politics and the gospel. The political process is subverted because the claim to absolute righteousness precludes the ambiguity present in all social life as well as the art of compromise necessary in social relations. Group and national self-righteousness lead people to see political opponents as followers of the devil (i.e., the "ungodly") who have no right to live. The gospel is subverted when identified with a political program because then all citizens are forced to conform to a religious norm, and salvation is made dependent on a particular political affiliation and program (i.e., in theological terms) on the good works of politics. For Luther, faith alone granted the security to live within the human insecurity of relative political structures and to avoid the defensive sanctification of past, present, or future goods and values. For Luther, faith alone was the enabling ground of the person content to be human and to let God be God. Luther's efforts to improve education, social welfare, and the political process reflected his conviction that all systems of justice and politics are only relative and instrumental for the humanization of persons. He attempted to de-ideologize politics by declaring that God, not the party and not the church, is sovereign in history.

The Peasants' War

The Peasants' War had presented Müntzer with what he believed was the context for the coming divine separation of the elect from the godless, but Müntzer was by

---

[17]Peter Matheson, trans. & ed., *The Collected Works of Thomas Müntzer* (Edinburgh: T. & T. Clark, 1988), pp. 141–142.

no means the instigator of the war. Neither was Luther, although he was blamed for it after the defeat of the peasants. In Germany the peasant protest against political and economic injustice coalesced in a peasant league known as the *Bundschuh*, after its logo of the peasants' laced shoe as a contrast to the nobles' fancy boots.

By the eve of the Reformation, the image of the peasant had changed markedly from the earlier picture of a stupid, nasty, obscene, scheming, drunken subspecies of humankind. The Renaissance humanists with the aid of the printing press began to promote a romanticized image of the peasant in the terms of classical poetry. Now the peasants were presented as the noble children of the soil whose closeness to nature made them superior to the urban and upper classes. Religious coloring was given to these images by suggesting that the peasants were of all people best suited to interpreting the bible because they were simple folk just like the apostles. Woodcuts and poems idealized the peasants as Christ's own sheep in contrast to the clergy who were wolves. Early Reformation pamphlets picked up on this imagery and presented the peasants as biblically astute and godly defenders of the Reformation against the superstitious and corrupt clergy. Luther's own pamphlets and sermons on Christian freedom and his attacks on Roman law and authority reinforced widespread anticlericalism and peasant ideals of an egalitarian society based on biblical principles. It is not surprising that the peasants appealed to Luther and other reformers to support their cause for social and economic justice.

A Lutheran pastor was one of the authors of the moderate peasant appeal known as "The Twelve Articles of the Peasants" (1525). Addressed to the "Christian reader," the articles present such themes as the godly common persons wanting only such legitimate rights as community authority to choose, appoint, and depose if necessary, their pastor; proper and biblically regulated taxation; abolition of serfdom; common access to game and fish; free firewood from the forests; release from excessive services; cessation of oppression by the lords; equitable rents; return to the old laws of custom in place of the new imposition of Roman law; the return of expropriated "meadows and fields which at one time belonged to the community;" and abolition of the "death tax" that oppresses widows and orphans. The twelfth, concluding point is the willingness to retract any of the foregoing articles if it can be "proved to be against the word of God by a clear explanation of the Scripture."[18]

Luther's reply to "The Twelve Articles" was a tract titled *Admonition to Peace* that called on the rulers to amend their ways before a rebellion arose that would destroy all Germany. He wrote as follows:

> We have no one on earth to thank for this disastrous rebellion, except you princes and lords, and especially you blind bishops and mad priests and monks, whose hearts are hardened, . . . [Y]ou do nothing but cheat and rob the people so that

[18]"The Twelve Articles," in Lowell Zuck, ed., *Christianity and Revolution* (Philadelphia: Temple University Press, 1975), p. 16.

you may lead a life of luxury and extravagance. The poor common people cannot bear it any longer. The sword is already at your throats, but you think you sit so firm in the saddle that no one can unhorse you. . . . Well, then, since you are the cause of this wrath of God, it will undoubtedly come upon you, unless you mend your ways in time.[19]

Luther also insisted to the peasants that rebellion is never justified and most especially not when identified as a Christian action. This was a position he had publicly expressed years earlier, and it was widely understood.

However, Luther was no more effective in stopping the rebellion than Müntzer was in leading it to victory. Peasant rage exploded in a number of areas, but once the princes recovered from the initial shocks of the war they ruthlessly crushed the peasants. As many as 100,000 peasants may have been killed in Germany in 1525! In spite of this great tragedy, the Reformation did not lose peasant support. Evangelical preachers continued to go out to rural areas, and the Reformation continued to spread in Germany.

The Swiss Connection: Zwingli and the Reformation in Zurich

Whereas the German Reformation was sparked by Luther's academic theological disputation over the sacrament of penance and indulgences, the Swiss Reformation went public with the Affair of the Sausages.

During Lent of 1522, Zwingli was at the house of Christopher Froschauer, a printer who was laboring over the preparation of a new edition of the epistles of Paul. To refresh his tired workers, Froschauer served sausages. This public breaking of the Lenten fast flouted medieval piety and ecclesial and public authority. The Zurich Town Council arrested Froschauer but not Zwingli, who himself had not eaten the meat. Zwingli, who held the eminent post of peoples' priest at the Great Minster in Zurich, could have smoothed everything out. Instead, he made a public issue out of this incident by preaching a sermon, "On the Choice and Freedom of Foods," that was soon enlarged into a printed pamphlet. Almost certainly influenced by Luther's earlier (1520) treatise on Christian freedom, Zwingli argued that Christians are free to fast or not to fast because the bible does not prohibit the eating of meat during Lent.

How had Zwingli reached this point of public opposition to ecclesial and political authority? A precocious farmboy from an alpine village, Zwingli was already studying the classics in Basel at age ten. He then went on to the universities of Vienna and Basel where he studied theology, philosophy, and the new humanistic studies. He received his master's degree from Basel in 1506. He then became the parish priest

[19]LW, Vol. 46, p. 19.

at Glarus in the Swiss canton of the same name. Here he had time for his passionate interest in the classics, the church fathers, and the bible with enough time left over for his avocational interest in women.

However, his growing tensions with the magistrates of Glarus were not over his personal morality but his public denunciation of the mainstay of the Swiss export business—the mercenary trade in professional soldiers. Swiss pikemen were renowned for their skill and ferocity and were sought after by the French, Spanish, and the papacy for their armies fighting over Italy. As chaplain to the Glarus contingent of soldiers, Zwingli witnessed the carnage of battle. In 1516 he saw an estimated 10,000 Swiss killed by the French at Marignano. He also experienced the pain of informing familes of the dead on his return. Both Zwingli's pastoral concern and his patriotic nationalism motivated him to oppose the mercenary practices he believed were eroding the moral and social fabric of the Swiss, not to mention their very existence as a people as they killed each other in the pay of opposing armies.

The magistrates of Glarus were willing to grant Zwingli's request to transfer to the nearby parish of Einsiedeln in April 1516, where he functioned as a chaplain to the many pilgrims who flocked to its shrine of the Black Virgin. In his off hours he was absorbed in the newly published Greek New Testament compiled by Erasmus. Zwingli soon became a celebrity for his expositions of the bible in worship and sermon. His Erasmian erudition and biblical fervor served him well in his denunciation of the Franciscan indulgence seller, Bernard Samson, the Swiss counterpart to Tetzel. Zwingli preached Samson right out of town.

Zwingli's reputation for biblical preaching led to his nomination for the post of peoples' priest at the Great Minster in Zurich in 1518. Detractors raised the issue of Zwingli's womanizing, but their changes were finally ineffective because the other priest vying for the post lived openly in concubinage and had six children. In light of this specific example and the generally widespread practice of priestly concubinage in the late Middle Ages, it is not surprising that one of the first reforms initiated in the Swiss Reformation was the right of the clergy to marry. Only months after the Affair of the Sausages, Zwingli, then living with the widow Anna Reinhart, led ten other Swiss priests in a petition to the Bishop of Constance *To Allow Priests to Marry, or at Least Wink at their Marriages* (July 1522). The priests signing this petition declared that chastity is a rare gift of God, and that they hadn't received it. Zwingli married Anna in a public ceremony in 1524 shortly before the birth of their child. In 1525 the Zurich magistrates instituted a marriage ordinance mandating clergy living in concubinage either to end the relationship or to marry. A marriage court was also established that clarified marital relationships by expanding grounds for divorce to include extreme incompatibility, desertion, physical and mental illness, and fraud.

The reform principle that Zwingli was formulating on the basis of his humanist and biblical studies was that everything was to be judged by scripture. What did not conform to biblical teaching did not command obedience. The test was whether traditional ceremonies and teachings promoted the gospel of redemption by Christ.

This test quickly raised questions about all areas of life beyond sex and sausages. The effort to provide biblical norms for all of life also led to "neighborly" spying and court-enforced attempts to oversee the city's moral life.

The town magistrates called for a public disputation between the advocates and opponents of reform in the Zurich town hall in January 1523. This was the occasion for Zwingli's preparation of his *Sixty-seven Articles,*[20] the charter of the Zurich Reformation. The articles affirmed salvation by grace alone, insisted on the full and final authority of scripture, and rejected the pope, the Mass, good works for salvation, monastic orders, a celibate clergy, penance, and purgatory. Zwingli's proposals meant nothing less than the dismantling of medieval ecclesiology. Zwingli carried the day against the old order, and the Zurich clergy were ordered to confine their preaching to scripture. A second disputation held in October, which was directed to those in the reform party who wanted more radical reform, will be discussed later in the section on the Anabaptists.

Zwingli's reform movement now began to spread rapidly throughout Switzerland and south Germany. Congregations in Constance, Ulm, Frankfurt, Augsburg, Lindau, Memmingen, and Strasbourg were won over to the Zurich Reformation. The conversion of the Swiss canton (i.e., a state in the Swiss confederation) of Bern in 1528 to the Zwinglian cause was particularly important not only for the immediate establishment of Zwinglianism in the Swiss Confederacy but for the future reform of Geneva under the auspices of William Farel and John Calvin. Basel, also of political importance, followed Bern into the Zwinglian fold.

In the meantime, however, the rural and conservative Catholic cantons of Switzerland were allying to oppose the Reformation. In 1529 the threat of Zwinglian expansion pushed the Catholic cantons of Uri, Schwyz, Unterwalden, Zug, Lucerne, and Fribourg into an alliance with the ancient enemy of the Swiss Confederacy, Hapsburg Austria. The execution of a Zwinglian preacher as a heretic in Schwyz led to a military confrontation at Kappel. The obvious strength of the Zurich forces, however, and the common Swiss distaste for Hapsburg meddling in the affairs of the Swiss Confederacy prompted an armistice in June 1529. At least temporarily, Swiss nationalism superceded religious differences.

Religious friction continued, however, and Zwingli was convinced that the southern cantons were still allied with Austria. At the same time, the German Lutherans were also menaced by Charles V, who had by now greatly reduced the French and Turkish threats and felt free to turn his attention to the Luther affair. He intended to eliminate heresy from his lands. At the Diet of Speyer in April 1529 the emperor demanded that the previous Diet's (1526) allowance of territorial and urban discretion regarding the Lutheran question be rescinded. This in turn prompted four evangelical states and fourteen free imperial cities to submit a formal *Protestatio* (hence the name

---

[20]Samuel M. Jackson, ed. & trans., *Ulrich Zwingli (1484–1531): Selected Works* (Philadelphia: University of Pennsylvania Press, 1972), pp. 111–117.

"Protestant") that decreed that the 1526 religious agreement be maintained until a national assembly and ecumenical council could be convoked to settle the religious issues. The signatories to the *Protestatio* included Lutheran (e.g., Electoral Saxony) and Zwinglian (e.g., Strasbourg) areas. The German Lutheran prince, Philip of Hesse, was convinced that the time was ripe to create an international political and military alliance between the Lutherans and the Zwinglians for their mutual protection against the emperor, and for the spread of the Reformation.

Philip was a convinced and theologically articulate Lutheran who realized that his dream of a Protestant alliance was unrealizable unless the mutual antagonisms of Luther and Zwingli over their respective understandings of the Lord's Supper could be reconciled. This is the context for Philip's invitation to the two sides to meet for a religious colloquy at his Marburg castle in October 1529.

It is a tragic irony that the Lord's Supper, the sacrament of Christian unity, has served in various periods of the history of Christianity to divide rather than to unite Christians. This was especially the case in the sixteenth century: to be right about the sacrament was to be right about God and salvation. Neither Luther nor Zwingli thought the other was right about the sacrament. Although they agreed in rejecting both the mass as a sacrifice and the doctrine of transubstantiation, they disagreed—vehemently!—over their understanding of what the Lord's Supper is.

By 1524 Zwingli had begun to interpret the "is" of "this is my body" as "signifies." This interpretation was influenced by the Platonic dualism of flesh and spirit earlier advanced in connection with the sacrament by Zwingli's humanist hero, Erasmus. In his 1503 *Enchiridion*,[21] which went through numerous editions and translations, Erasmus developed a spiritual or memorial understanding of the Lord's Supper that strongly influenced Luther's former colleague, Karlstadt, and through Karlstadt influenced Zwingli. One of their favorite biblical verses was John 6:63: "It is the spirit that gives life, the flesh is of no avail." Karlstadt and those he influenced used this verse to justify differentiating between the bread eaten by the communicant and the Christ received by faith. Indeed, Karlstadt's interpretation of the words of institution of the Lord's Supper posited that when Jesus said "This is my body" he was pointing at himself. This led one contemporary wag to suggest that when Jesus said "This is my blood," he must have had a nosebleed.

After the falling out between Luther and Karlstadt, Karlstadt not only had five tracts on the Lord's Supper printed in Switzerland; he also visited Zwingli. Erasmus had also attacked Luther in 1524. Thus Luther's view of Zwingli was strongly colored by his controversies with Karlstadt and Erasmus. Luther's insistence that Christ is really present in the sacrament appeared to Zwingli to be a relapse into the Catholic doctrine of transubstantiation. A further sense of the magnitude of Philip's task in

[21]Matthew Spinka, ed., *Advocates of Reform: From Wyclif to Erasmus*, The Library of Christian Classics, Vol. XIV (Philadelphia: Westminster Press, 1953), pp. 295–379.

reconciling these two reformers is provided by an overview of their writings on the subject prior to 1529.

By 1525 in Zurich, the Mass had been discontinued. Discussions about the Lord's Supper were heatedly carried on throughout the German and Swiss lands. As the divergence between Luther and Zwingli became more apparent, each reformer was anxious to convince the world that he had not read the other's writings. With the common Protestant rejection of transubstantiation, innumerable theologians (Karlstadt, Oecolampadius, Bucer, Schwenkfeld, Althamer, Billican, Stigler, Bugenhagen, Brenz, to name only the better known) were floating alternative theories and analyses of this central sacrament of the church. It became apparent then that Wittenberg and Zurich were competing for the spiritual—and therefore political—allegiance of the south German cities such as Basel, Strasbourg, Augsburg, Nördlingen, Biberach, Memmingen, Ulm, Isny, Kempten, Lindau, and Constance. Without them, especially while Bern remained officially Catholic, Zurich would be isolated. With the help and allegiance of these cities, however, the German lands might be won over to Zwingli's movement. The Luther-Zwingli debate was not merely personal or conceptual.

In 1525 Zwingli published a major statement of his position, *Subsidium sive coronis de eucharistia* in which he developed his distinction between the "natural" body of Christ before the crucifixion, the "glorified" body of Christ ascended to heaven, and the mystical body of the church. In this work, Zwingli's humanist linguistic work comes to the fore. He argued that only the recognition of the bible's figurative use of words (*trope*), in particular the metaphorical explanation of the Last Supper, could make the bible plain, reasonable, and humanly intelligible. Christ's own words were intelligible only if the bread and wine were symbols to which the recipient brought faith and hope in God. To Luther this meant that Zwingli had shifted the focus of the Lord's Supper from God's promise of salvation present in the eucharistic action to the active memory of the congregation. Luther saw this shift as another expression of putting the burden of proof for salvation on the believer rather than on God.

In the fall of 1525, fourteen south German Lutheran pastors had subscribed to a basically Lutheran confession of faith, the *Swabian Syngramma*, which Luther endorsed while also declaring Zwinglian views to be the work of Satan. Zwingli's response in 1526 was that Luther had taken the "simple words of Christ" and made them obscure and incomprehensible, thereby allowing the reintroduction of extreme papal claims. Here Zwingli raised what would become a central theme: the ubiquity (omnipresence) of Christ. Launching into a discussion of the early church's doctrine of the two natures of Christ, Zwingli asserted that Christ's divine nature never left heaven because, being one with God, the divine nature could not ascend to heaven as Christ's human nature did. The divinity of Christ is and always has been everywhere, but after the ascension the bodily Christ remains in heaven at the right hand of God until the Last Day. Those who claimed that Christ's body was eaten in the

Last Supper must believe (with Marcion) that Christ was not sensible of his sufferings on the cross or that the disciples did not eat in human fashion since Christ had not yet risen when he instituted this meal. Thus, Zwingli argued, "this is" can only mean "this signifies."

Luther saw in Zwingli's theology the reappearance of the Nestorian heresy of the early church that had separated the divine and human natures of Christ. To Luther, this clearly meant that how one understood the Lord's Supper was related intimately to how one understood salvation and God's activity in the world. Thus, in a parallel to the early church's controversy over the person of Christ, Luther advocated the position set forth by Cyril of Alexandria that emphasized a personal union in Christ of the divine and human natures, known as the *communicatio idomatum* ("communication of properties"). The Council of Chalcedon in 451 had asserted that "the divine and human in Christ are united unchanged and unmixed, but undivided and unseparated." In advancing this doctrine against Zwingli, Luther emphasized that God had genuinely condescended into the depths of human existence (Luther was fond of saying that Christ cannot be dragged too deeply into the flesh) and that in Christ there is a genuine transmission of God's full divinity and majesty.

This Lutheran argument against Zwingli found expression in the phrase that "the finite is capable of bearing the infinite." This meant for Luther not only that ordinary bread and wine may communicate the presence and promise of God but that all creation may serve the Creator. This is the theological foundation for Luther's profound appreciation of nature and art as vehicles for communicating the gospel. Luther's love and use of music, for example, continued to be expressed among his theological descendants, among whom Johann Sebastian Bach is well known.

Those reformers who so emphasized the transcendence of God that they did not accept that the finite is capable of the infinite began the process toward the modern world's exclusion of the sacred altogether. The first steps in this process may be seen in the iconoclastic reactions of reformers from Karlstadt to Zwingli and in part on into Calvin, who strove to purify the church by removing as much art as possible. These reformers stripped the churches of all images and color, and in Zurich they literally nailed shut the organs. This trend was later to be expressed by the word *puritan*. Some theorists think that these reformers struggled so successfully against the possibility of idolatry that the Holy was transformed into the morally good and that righteousness was given ascetic connotations—all of which was finally banalized in the phrase that "cleanliness is next to godliness."

In early 1527, Zwingli completed his *Amica exegesis* ("Friendly Exposition") in which he tried to combine independence and conciliation. This tract, which Zwingli sent to Luther, warned that Luther was perilously close to the Catholic doctrine of transubstantiation. But let the conflict end, wrote Zwingli, for the future could be bright if Luther would only recognize his mistakes. Luther's response against "this insolent Swiss," as he called Zwingli, appeared in his April 1527 tract, *That these words of Christ, "This is my body" still stand fast against the Fanatics.*[22] His opponents, Luther wrote, were both crazy and possessed by the devil, not to mention blasphemous in their appeal to reason and common sense. In May, Zwingli responded in his "Friendly Answer" that among other things Luther had incorrectly read the scripture and had conceded too much to Rome, and that God had not revealed to Luther the meaning of the Lord's Supper. So it went!

The antagonism between Zwingli and Luther was aggravated by what we may call nondoctrinal factors. One was Zwingli's humanistic fascination with classical figures of speech. Luther was convinced that Zwingli's biblical interpretation suffered from his use of such figures of speech deriving from classical studies as trope, allegory, ellipsis, metathesis, aposiopesis, hyperbole, prolepsis, synechdoche, and alloeosis. The latter, one of Zwingli's favorite allusions to the transposition of attributes, allowed him to argue that Christ's humanity could sometimes imply his divinity and vice versa.

Another nondoctrinal factor that contributed to mutual misunderstanding was that Luther lived in an absolutist state under a benevolent and sympathetic prince, whereas Zwingli lived in a city governed by a representative style of government. This meant that for Zwingli to carry out his desired reforms he had to persuade and convince the people and the magistrates. Therefore, with regard to the Lord's Supper, Zwingli had to explain his position in a way that would be intelligible to ordinary people. This plus Zwingli's humanistic leanings help to explain why Luther saw him as a rationalist. On the other hand, for Zwingli to agree with Luther's understanding of the Lord's Supper, which many Catholics saw as basically orthodox, would have been a political disaster.

The Marburg Colloquy opened on October 1, 1529. By October 4 the Lutherans and the Zwinglians had agreed to fourteen of fifteen articles prepared by Luther. They could not agree on the Lord's Supper. Both sides repudiated transubstantiation as well as the belief that the Eucharist is a sacrifice for the living and the dead, and they insisted on communion in both kinds (bread and wine). But the Lutherans continued to hold that Christ is really present in the Eucharist for all recipients, whereas the Zwinglians maintained Christ's presence is only in the hearts of believers. Although the two parties left Marburg with the intention to practice Christian charity toward each other, they failed to achieve either a confessional or a military alliance.

In less than a year, the Imperial Diet met at Augsburg, where the Lutherans presented their confession of faith, the Augsburg Confession, which remains to this day the basic confessional document of Lutheran churches. The Zwinglian confession, written mainly by the Strasbourg reformer Martin Bucer and known as the Tetrapolitan Confession because it was subscribed to by the four cities of Strasbourg,

[22]LW, Vol. 37, pp. 3–150.

Constance, Memmingen, and Lindau, was also presented at Augsburg. Zwingli, himself not invited to Augsburg, was determined to be heard and thus sent his hastily composed *Fidei Ratio*. Since this writing had no effect on Charles V, Zwingli composed a pamphlet, *Fidei Expositio* for Francis I in the hope of winning the French king's support against the Emperor and Rome. There is no evidence that Francis ever read this more impressive defense of Zwingli's faith, and the pamphlet had no influence on the course of events.

A Zurich-inspired economic blockade of the Catholic cantons that refused to admit Protestant preachers increased Protestant-Catholic tensions. In retaliation, the Catholic cantons surprised Zurich with a vastly superior military force. Zwingli, himself armed, accompanied the Zurich forces into this second battle of Kappel in 1531. During the rout of the Zurich forces, Zwingli was seriously wounded and left on the battlefield. Later recognized by the Catholic forces, he was given a mortal blow, and the next day quartered (the punishment for traitors). Then the parts of his body were burned with dung so that nothing of Zwingli would be left to inspire other Protestants.

Unlike Zwingli, the Swiss Reformation was not exterminated; where established it was allowed to remain. Catholic minorities were not to be disturbed in Protestant lands, whereas Protestant minorities were not to be tolerated in Catholic lands. The division of Switzerland offered a foretaste of the fate of Europe. Almost a quarter century later, in 1555, the Peace of Augsburg legally ratified the confessional divisions of the empire by aligning the religion of an area with that of its ruler. Later this would be described by the motto *cuius regio, eius religio* ("whose reign, his religion"). This included the safety valve of allowing persons to emigrate to territories amenable to their confession of faith.

The medieval ideal of the *corpus Christianum*, the union of all Christians in one body, one community, is illustrated by this twelfth-century fresco in the church St.-Pierre-le-Jeune in Strasbourg. Known as "The Procession of the Nations to the Cross," this fresco presents the solidarity of the European peoples in spite of all past conflicts. Contrast this with the fifteenth century procession of "The Hay Wagon" by Bosch, the last figure in this grouping. (Bildarchiv Foto Marburg/Art Resource)

Christ, the Judge of the World. The fourteenth-century stone relief (left) was originally on the outside wall of the Wittenberg parish church. (Bildarchiv Foto Marburg/Art Resource) Before he came to understand the righteousness of God as a gift to persons, Luther was terrified by this image of God's judgmental severity. He later recalled that he would shield his eyes as he hurried past it. The same image of Christ as Judge is portrayed in the late fifteenth-century woodcut (right). Under the lily, the word "come" (VENITE) invites the faithful to salvation; under the sword, the word "go" (ITE) commands the damned to enter the jaws of hell.

"Death and the Maiden" is from the so-called Heidelberg Dance of Death series of woodcuts (fifteenth century). Death is portrayed as a dancer whom every person has to follow. Woodcuts of the Dance of Death were widely circulated and served preachers of repentance and judgment who emphasized the transitoriness of life. Here Death claims the maiden who herself confesses that she has been preoccupied with the world and its pleasures, to the neglect of God's commandments. The popularity of these woodcuts on the eve of the Reformation is also due to their social–critical aspect: All are equal before Death, who removes the human masks of beauty, wealth, and status. At the same time, these images also express the late medieval church's hostility to life and creatureliness.

In the later Middle Ages the clergy was increasingly criticized for perceived wealth, drunkenness, and lechery. (By permission of the British Library, MS Sloane 2434, fol.44v [left]; MS Roy.10. E. IV, fol. 187r [right].)

The fourteenth-century Pieta expresses the period's emphasis upon the real, bodily suffering of Christ. Painted wood, less than life-size. German, c. 1370. (Marburg/Art Resource, NY 6.807)

"Knight, Death, and the Devil" engraving by Dürer (1513). Art historians have suggested that this engraving expresses the old theme of the Christian knight revived in humanist circles by Erasmus's *Manual of the Christian Soldier* (1504). The knight has also been identified with the martyred Dominican preacher of repentance, Savonarola (1452–1498), who thought of himself as a knight of Christ. (Fogg Art Museum, Harvard University. Bequest-Francis Calley Gray Collection)

The intense religiosity of the Catholic Baroque expression of the Catholic Reformation is superbly captured by Bernini's (1598–1680) sculpture of the Spanish Carmelite nun and mystic, Saint Theresa of Avila (1515–1582). Bernini depicts Theresa's vision of an angel who repeatedly pierced her heart with a golden arrow, producing a "pain so great that I screamed aloud; but simultaneously I felt such infinite sweetness that I wished the pain to last eternally." (Alinari/Art Resource)

Francois Dubois's depiction of the Saint Bartholomew's Day massacre. (Musee Cantonal des Beaux Arts, Lausanne)

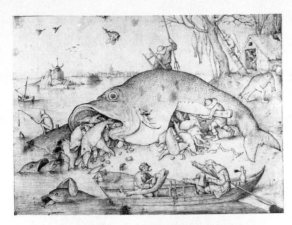

Pieter Bruegel the Elder's
(c. 1525–1569) copper engraving in
the style of Bosch is a variation on
the theme that the big crooks hang
the little crooks. The engraving also
utilizes symbols of false prophets
(fish), infidelity (mussel shells), and
punishment of evil (knives).
(Marburg/Art Resource)

The fame of Albrecht Dürer (1471–1528) continues
to rest on his graphic works such as the woodcut
series, *Apocalypse*, which includes the "Four
Horsemen." Dürer's *Apocalypse* series appeared the
same year (1498) that the Dominican preacher
Savonarola was burned at the stake. People
everywhere were expecting the imminent end of the
world, and these prints captured and expressed this
fear. The "Four Horsemen" of pestilence, war,
famine, and death, which are commanded by an
angel, are trampling the people before them.
(Marburg/Art Resource)

"The Hay Wagon" by Hieronomous Bosch
(c. 1450–1516), the central panel of a triptych now
at the Prado Museum in Madrid, illustrates the
Flemish proverb, "The world is a pile of hay and
everyone takes from it whatever he can grab."
Bosch was a moralist, here attacking greed, but his
"Hay Wagon" also echoes the famous words of
Isaiah (40:6): "All flesh is grass." The hay wagon,
drawn by weird monsters, is headed for hell (the
third panel of the triptych) while the members of a
wild mob seek to grab their share of the hay,
fighting and killing each other in the process. The
world's powerful, kings and bishops, follow the
wagon. The other groups illustrate the seven sins.
Atop the wagon, amorous couples seem oblivious to
their impending destruction. (Anderson/Art
Resource)

Chapter 20

THE RADICAL REFORMERS

The radical reformers were and continue to be a difficult group to define and describe. From the beginning, these reformers and their adherents have been lumped together under labels that nearly always are pejorative. Their contemporaries called them enthusiasts (from *en theos*, "God-withinism"), spiritualists, fanatics, and Anabaptists (or rebaptists). The latter label was applied to these people because they believed that only adults able to make a profession of faith could be baptized. Because the first generation of these reformers had been baptised as infants, an adult baptism was literally a rebaptism. Discussion of the radical reformers, or Anabaptists, is complicated by their heterogeneous origins, leaders, and visions of reformation. Under the labels mentioned, such disparate groups and persons have been lumped together as the Zwickau prophets, who apparently rejected infant baptism and who initiated the Wittenberg disturbances of 1521–1522; Karlstadt; Müntzer who called for the execution of the godless; the equally if not more disruptive leaders who took over the city of Munster and precipitated a bloody debacle there; the dissenters in Zurich who were a thorn in Zwingli's side; and such men as Menno Simons whose heirs form the still-existing peace church known as the Mennonites. (See Figure 20.1.)

A number of outstanding Anabaptist leaders contributed substantially to the vitality of the movement, but none of them enjoyed the widely acknowledged leadership positions of reformers such as Luther, Zwingli, and Calvin. The Anabaptist groups also lacked a clear confessional norm or statement aside from the brief Schleitheim Confession of 1527, which was not generally accepted by all of them. All this ambiguity surrounding the Anabaptist groups both dismayed and delighted their contemporaries (and modern historians) who picked and chose among the multiplicity of opinions, groupings, divisions, and leaders to form their own judgments. These judgments, whether formed by Lutheran, Zwinglian, Calvinist, or Catholic,

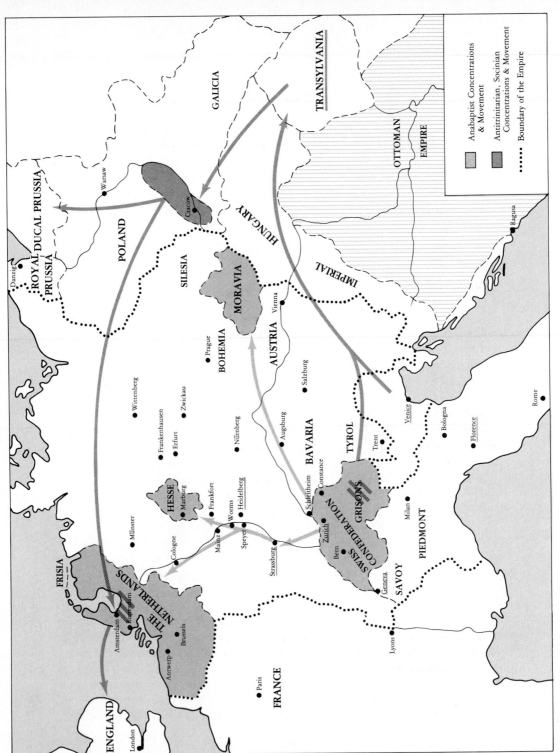

Figure 20.1 The Left Wing of the Reformation

were united in perceiving the Anabaptist groups as a threat to sixteenth-century society.

A major locus of the Anabaptist development was Zwingli's Zurich. We have already seen that Zwingli's reform program depended on persuasion of the authorities and existed in the face of the threats of Catholic cantons. In the sixteenth century it was obvious to nearly everyone that a community without a common ideology was not only at the mercy of one that was united (e.g., the Turks) but was also subject to a civil war that could imperil the very existence of the state.

In Zwingli's eyes the rise of the Zurich Anabaptists was therefore a clear and present danger. He regarded these evangelicals as quarrelsome, envious, backbiting, and hypocritical extremists who lacked charity and undermined the government. Their opposition to infant baptism, their open-air preaching, and their constant street discussions and harangues were bringing the gospel into disrepute. Indeed, Zwingli saw these people as social revolutionaries whose teaching would overthrow society and religion alike.

The immediate controversy centered on infant baptism, but behind it lay a very different view of world Christianity. Other reformers such as Luther and Calvin agreed that there was but one catholic (i.e., universal) church with one creed. They understood that the visible church is coextensive with the local community wherein the people must live and worship in harmony. The Anabaptists focused not on the whole community but on local congregations of voluntary members who regarded themselves as altogether set apart from the state. For them, the one true church consisted only of true believers, who could be ascertained by tests of conduct and belief. Those not meeting their standards for church membership were to be expelled and banned. The Anabaptists posed a radical alternative to the state churches of Lutherans, Zwinglians, and Roman Catholics, who believed that the visible church embraced all professing Christians. The alternative churches of the Anabaptists scrutinized members to eliminate the unworthy, and worshipped and associated in separate, voluntary communities.

The Anabaptist development in Zurich is instructive for understanding the widely held perception of this reform movement. Zwingli and the Zurich magistrates perceived a threefold danger in the Anabaptist movement. First, they were seen to be deliberately and consciously disruptive of the social and religious tenets of the town and therefore a danger to both Swiss unity and the success of Zwingli's reform. In Zurich, as elsewhere, the success of the reform movement was seen to depend on the support of the magistrates, the government. Fearful of possible aggression from the Catholic cantons, Zurich and other reformed cantons believed that only a community united in religion could defend itself and maintain its freedom. Thus, insofar as the Anabaptists hindered this union they were seen as abetting the Counter-Reformation.

Second, the Anabaptists turned Zwingli's own weapon, scripture, against him, much as had Karlstadt and Müntzer against Luther. Much to their chagrin, the reformers were beginning to discover that the lay assertiveness and independence they encouraged against the Catholic Church could be turned against them as well. The dissidents insisted that they were only carrying to its logical conclusions Zwingli's own commitment to the bible as the norm for faith and life. When the Anabaptists read the bible, they could find no warrant in it for infant baptism but only for baptism as a sign of adult faith and regeneration. When these dissidents read the Sermon on the Mount, they believed it literally meant believers must separate from the world. Zwingli, just as had Luther, experienced the shock of having his own followers read very differently the biblical text he had so labored to make available to all. Both Zwingli and the Anabaptists accepted the same bible and agreed that tradition and human authorities must give way before the Word of God. And they agreed that the bible was perfectly clear if read under the guidance of the Holy Spirit in faith and love. Of course, when their followers did not agree with them, Luther and Zwingli insisted that this was precisely what the "fanatics" did not do. So Zwingli viewed the Anabaptists' alternative reading of scripture as an expression of ignorance, malice, and contentiousness.

Third, the Anabaptists were viewed as being politically as well as religiously exclusivistic and thus a civil liability. In refusing to accept the normal obligations of citizenship [oaths, taxes (the tithe), military service], the Anabaptists were seen to be forming states within the state. Their refusal to take oaths was a very serious element in this perception because for late medieval society the oath was a major part of the glue that held the society together. Citizens swore oaths to the common good and defense of the town, to the guilds to which they belonged, and to the truth. Perjury, with its assumed certainty of divine punishment, was abhorred. Without the public oath, indispensable in any court of justice, the ordinary daily administration of public life was in danger of breaking down. The Swiss confederation itself was traditionally dated from an oath-swearing in 1291 that was renewed by its annual repetition.

The refusal to bear arms was equally serious. In sixteenth-century Switzerland, there was no paid standing army. Every man was responsible for defense and was expected to appear armed and ready when called on by the government. The citizen-soldier was the support and guarantor of public order and independence. The walls of the towns were to be guarded according to a set pattern. The towns had their own cannon and armory, and they held regular crossbow and shooting matches. Every male was liable for military service, and military preparation was a normal, expected masculine duty for which boys were trained from an early age. For a man to refuse military service was, in effect, to renounce citizenship. Townsmen resented Anabaptist pacifism as a shirking of indispensable duty and as a placing of extra burdens on themselves. A further fear was that if the Anabaptist movement spread, there would be no one to shoulder arms for defense.

The Anabaptist refusal to pay tithes and interest was similarly seen as a rejection of civic responsibility. The Anabaptists made it clear that the tithe was refused not primarily because it was an economic imposition but because it was perceived as an instrument of control by the Zurich government over the parishes within its jurisdiction. For Zwingli, the tithe was a key to the centralized territorial church that he wanted to reform but not to dissolve. The refusal of tithes, like iconoclasm and attacks on the Mass, represented the disintegration of the old religious order. To some at least, this rejection of tithes and taxes appeared very similar to the Catholic Church's unpopular insistence on exemption from taxation and from civil law courts. Similarly, the Anabaptist insistence on a church of true believers, and thus the institution of excommunication and the ban, also led people to associate the Anabaptists with elements of Catholicism.

Zurich Beginnings

In Zurich in 1522 a group of future Anabaptists began to meet in the home of Klaus Hottinger for bible study. The most attractive and influential member of this group was Conrad Grebel (1497–1526), the reputed founder of Anabaptism. Grebel came from a patrician family and was educated at Vienna and Basel. In 1522–1523, Grebel actively supported Zwingli in Zurich, but then he became one of Zwingli's ablest and bitterest critics. After the second Zurich disputation (October 26, 1523), Grebel became deeply disappointed by the magistrates' slowness in "cleansing" the churches and by the fact that the Mass was still being said. Grebel acknowledged that Zwingli had pointed the way to reform, but now he called Zwingli a false prophet because of his program of compromise and his "hastening slowly" in instituting change. By December 1523, Grebel had written to his brother-in-law, Vadian, "Zwingli, the herald of the Word, has cast down the Word, has trodden it underfoot, and has brought it into captivity."[1]

After Christmas 1523, the Anabaptist movement began to take form. Grebel's calls for changes in society and religion soon led to an uproar. The dissidents interrupted sermons, became involved in iconoclasm, and ended up smashing the baptismal font in the Zollikon church. A public discussion was held on January 17, 1524, that was dominated by Zwingli. The outcome was that the majority in Zurich felt Zwingli had answered the dissidents' charges and objections. An order was given to baptize all unbaptized children within the next eight days under penalty of expulsion from Zurich. Furthermore, all unauthorized preaching was to cease, and the broken baptismal font was to be repaired.

In response to these orders, a small group of dissenters gathered on January 21 at the house of Felix Mantz (ca. 1500–1527). Among them were Grebel and George Blaurock, a married ex-priest who was later martyred in Innsbruck in 1529. The company joined in prayer, and then Blaurock called upon Grebel to baptize him.

[1]Cited in George H. Williams, *The Radical Reformation* (Philadelphia: Westminster Press, 1962), p. 96.

After this, Grebel and Blaurock baptized fifteen others at what was the first recorded adult baptism. At this very time, the city was drawing up an order requiring Grebel and Mantz to abstain from further propaganda for their cause. A couple of days later, Grebel followed his continued preaching by distributing bread and wine—a clear act of defiance because no town decision had yet been made concerning the Mass. These incidents multiplied in the following days so that by the end of January it was reported that eighty adults had been baptized.

Zwingli and the Zurich magistrates warned and threatened the dissenters and then proceeded to imprison a few and expel some others. Nevertheless, the new teachings spread with remarkable rapidity. Soon a small group was parading through Zurich with ropes around their waists and willow rods in their hands, crying, "Woe to you, Zurich," and "Freedom to Jerusalem," and calling Zwingli "the old dragon." These new prophets proclaimed that only forty days remained for Zurich to repent. Blaurock went so far as to call Zwingli the Antichrist. In early November a debate was held on baptism during which Grebel, Mantz, and Blaurock were confronted by Zwingli and others. The debate soon degenerated into a shouting match. At one point a local farmer shouted: "Zwingli, I adjure you by the living God, tell me but one truth," to which Zwingli replied: "You are the worst specimen of a trouble-making, discontented farmer that we have in the neighborhood."

The town magistrates now decided to deal more severely with those they regarded as "the wild men in the streets." Hubmaier was arrested, tortured, and allowed to leave upon recanting. Others were imprisoned. Grebel, Blaurock, and Mantz reappeared in March 1526 to renew their attacks on Zwingli as a false prophet and to demand separatist worship. Because threats did not silence them, they were imprisoned. They were soon free, however, because someone had left a window open in the prison.

At this same time, Zwingli's dream of a reformed Swiss Confederacy was evaporating before the advances of Catholic opponents. Convinced that the Anabaptists were weakening the cause of the reform, Zwingli and the magistrates moved against the dissidents with new severity. Grebel missed martyrdom by dying of the plague in August 1526. His father, Jacob Grebel, a town councilor who symbolized both the Anabaptist opposition to Zwingli and the patrician resistance to the more democratic guilds on which Zwingli depended, was less fortunate. On October 30, 1526, Jacob was beheaded on charges of treason. By mid-December, Mantz and Blaurock had been recaptured and delivered to Zurich. By this time, rebaptism was mandated punishable by death by drowning—a grim parody of a believer's baptism. Mantz and Blaurock were steadfast during their hearings and professed the divine ordinance of adult baptism. Since Blaurock was not a citizen of Zurich, he was whipped out of town. Mantz was executed by drowning on the day he was condemned, January 5, 1527, thus becoming the first Protestant martyr at the hands of Protestants. The Anabaptist understanding of themselves as the continuation of the early suffering church led them to rejoice in martyrdom and to neglect or refuse opportunities to leave quietly when possible.

Anabaptist Multiplicity

Zwingli may have been one of the first, but he was certainly not the last to learn that the sparks of dissident evangelicalism could not be extinguished by drowning people. Both Protestant and Catholic authorities soon were confronted by a variety of Anabaptist movements in Switzerland, Austria, the Netherlands, and Germany. Popular Anabaptist preachers and leaders continued to arise from both evangelical and Catholic clergy and laity. Their professions in word and life of brotherhood and egalitarianism appealed to the oppressed both during and after the Peasants' War. They touched a neuralgic aspect of late medieval life not only by their communal lifestyles but also by their millennial prophecies rooted in the biblical books of Daniel and Revelation. These aspects of the dissident movement spawned radically different expressions of the ideal of restoring the early church that ranged from an absolute pacifism to an apocalyptic crusade to usher in the kingdom of God. In every case, however, the establishment authorities perceived the Anabaptists as seditionists, underminers of social order.

It is easy to understand the nervousness of the authorities when confronted by those radical dissident movements and persons such as Thomas Müntzer and the Anabaptists at Waldshut under Hubmaier, who linked up with local expressions of the Peasants' War and who appeared to be able to stimulate mass revolutionary loyalties. The teeth of the authorities were put on edge even by the more representative Anabaptist teachings expressed by Michael Sattler (ca. 1490–1527).

Sattler was an exemplary leader of the Swiss and southern German Anabaptist movements who moved from being prior of a Benedictine monastery in Breisgau to become an Anabaptist in Zurich. After his expulsion from Zurich, he took refuge in Strasbourg and then moved to the Black Forest to continue missionary work. He was so esteemed by the dissidents that he was chosen to preside at the 1527 conference at Schleitheim on the German-Swiss border that developed perhaps the most representative statement of Anabaptist principles, the Schleitheim Confession.

In seven articles, the Schleitheim Confession set forth a consensus on baptism contingent on repentance and amendment of life; the ban or excommunication of brethren who do not keep the commandments; the Lord's Supper as a memorial meal for the baptized; a radical separation of believers from the evil world, for "truly all creatures are in but two classes, good and bad, . . . and none can have part with the other;" the pastor as the model of the godly life; absolute rejection of bearing arms and holding civic offices because the Christians' citizenship is in heaven and their weapons are spiritual; and the prohibition of oaths.[2]

For his leading role in developing this confession, Sattler was arrested, tried, horribly tortured, and executed by the Austrian authorities. The historical context of this Austrian Catholic tribunal does not excuse their action but does provide some insight into the rulers' anxieties about the spread of Anabaptism. At this time Austria

---

[2]Zuck, ed., *Christianity and Revolution*, pp. 71–75.

was confronted by a Turkish advance that threatened to enter the whole empire through the gates of Vienna. At his trial, Sattler stated:

> If the Turks should come, we ought not to resist them. For it is written [Matt. 5:21]: Thou shalt not kill. We must not defend ourselves against the Turks and others of our persecutors, ... [I]f warring *were* right, I would rather take the field against so-called Christians who persecute, capture, and kill pious Christians than against the Turks. . . .[3]

The suspicion that even the pacifist Anabaptists were really only wolves in sheep's clothing and potentially radical revolutionaries was confirmed, if it ever needed confirmation, in the minds of the authorities by the wild events at Münster in 1533–1535.

The Münster Debacle

The conjunction of Anabaptist aspirations for the restitution of the pure church they found in the bible and the social unrest epitomized by the Peasants' War found explosive expression in the episcopal city of Münster, located in Westphalia near the Dutch border. There was already a widespread religious dissident movement in the Netherlands. Influenced by the extravagant visions and prophecies of Melchior Hofmann (ca. 1495–1543), these people were known as Melchiorites. Sometimes called "the father of Dutch Anabaptism," Hofmann, a furrier by trade and a lay preacher by conviction, had preached that everyone should accept baptism into the pure church of Christ in preparation for the return of Christ and the end of the world in 1533. Proclaiming himself to be the prophet Elijah, Hofmann went to the city of Strasbourg, which he prophesied would be the New Jerusalem. The magistrates of Strasbourg declined the honor of being the locus for the end of the world and imprisoned Hofmann until his death in 1543. Nevertheless, Hofmann's preachings and writings continued to influence people in the Netherlands, some of whom transposed his prophecy of the New Jerusalem from Strasbourg to Münster. Hofmann's central ideas about the triumph of the godly were written while he was in prison and smuggled out in his tract *Concerning the Pure Fear of God* (1533). His vision was that the ungodly would be exterminated *before* the end of the world, that *before* the return of Christ the saints would rule the earth through cooperation between the prophet (the second Jonah) and a pious ruler (the second Solomon), and that the "apostolic messengers" could not be hurt or defeated. In one way or another, these themes found expression in the Anabaptist takeover of Münster.

By 1532, Münster itself had focused its own social and religious unrest against

---

[3]George Williams & Angel Mergal, eds., *Spiritual and Anabaptist Writers*, Library of Christian Classics, Vol. XXV (Philadelphia: Westminster Press, 1957), p. 141.

the prince-bishop of the city, and under the fiery leadership of Bernard Rothmann, a priest turned Lutheran preacher, had become an "evangelical city." This news stimulated thousands of Anabaptist refugees to flock to the city in search of haven from persecution in the Netherlands and areas surrounding Münster. The townspeople divided into three factions: a small number of Catholics who still supported the expelled bishop, conservative Lutherans who were the majority in the town council, and the Melchiorites who won the backing of the town guilds. In the summer of 1533, simmering tensions in the alliance of the guilds with the magistrates boiled over. Rothmann, under the influence of the Melchiorites, was becoming increasingly radical in politics and religion, and both opposed infant baptism and innovatively celebrated the Lord's Supper with unconsecrated bread. The strength of the radicals was such that the town council no longer had sufficient authority to expel or even discipline Rothmann. Alarmed Catholic and Lutheran families began to flee the city, but this population loss was more than made up by the influx of Anabaptists.

In the February 1534 elections, the radical party won the town council. Münster had already been declared the New Jerusalem by Jan Mathijs, a baker from Haarlem, who believed as had Müntzer that the godless had no right to live. On February 25, Mathijs announced his intention to put to death all who refused to join the new rebaptismal convenant. Persuaded by a colleague to allow people to leave rather than to execute them, Mathijs announced he had received another revelation allowing the expulsion rather than the death of the godless. All who remained were forcibly rebaptized in the marketplace. A blacksmith who dared to challenge Mathijs was killed instantly by Mathijs himself. Not too long after this, Mathijs himself was killed when he led a sortie against the army assembled by the bishop besieging the city. It seems that Mathijs had received a vision that God would make him invulnerable to the weapons of the godless.

During the six weeks Mathijs ruled Münster, he instituted the ideal of Anabaptism everywhere—a society based on the life of the primitive church as recorded in Acts and an early church writing, the Pseudo-Clementine Epistle IV, which claimed that all things should be held in common. The property of the expelled citizens was confiscated; food was made public property; real property was declared to be in common, although people could continue using what was theirs with the stipulation that all house doors had to be kept open day and night; the use of money was outlawed; and twelve elders were appointed to oversee the stockpiling of goods and their distribution to the needy.

After Mathijs's death, the prophetic mantle was assumed by Jan of Leiden, who assumed he was the voice of the Lord. After a major attack by the bishop's army on the city in May was repelled, there was a strong feeling of being God's chosen people. After another major victory in August, Jan had himself anointed and crowned "king of righteousness" and "the ruler of the new Zion." He not only stated that to oppose him was to oppose the divine order; he enforced his statement by ruthlessly crushing his and thus the Lord's opposition. Church, state, and community were now to be one and the same regenerated body. This regenerate church could consist only of the righteous; sinners were to be punished by death. Sinners were identified by their blasphemy, seditious language, disobedience to parents and masters, adultery, lewd conduct, backbiting, spreading scandal, and complaining!

Jan's most controversial and notorious innovation was the introduction of polygamy. Some two hundred townsmen were killed or executed for resisting Jan's vision of the New Jerusalem rationalized as an emulation of the Old Testament patriarchs. Although Jan found justification in the Old Testament for his mandate of polygamy, nonbiblical factors were also operative in his decision. Although already married, Jan wanted to marry the beautiful young widow of Mathijs to bolster his own claim to leadership. Furthermore, there was a disproportionate number of women to men in the city as a result of male attrition from battle and expulsion. Polygamy provided the means of not only increasing the population in preparation for the return of Christ (the eschatological number of the saints according to Rev. 7:4 was to be 144,000); it was also the means of subjugating all women to male authority. In his book on the restoration of the primitive church, *Restitution* (1534),[4] Rothmann added that sexual dependence on one woman lets her lead a man about "like a bear on a rope" and that women for too long have "everywhere been getting the upper hand" and now should submit to men as men submit to Christ, and Christ to God. In political perspective, what Jan was doing was ensuring control over the majority of the population.

As might be expected, many women did not respond warmly to this new state of affairs. Those women who dissented from the new rule of polygamy were imprisoned. And Jan himself beheaded and trampled the body of one of his fifteen wives in the marketplace in front of the rest of them. That seems to have quieted their murmurings!

In spite of Jan's proclamation of the New Jerusalem and his accompanying revelations, the siege of the city inexorably took its toll of the bodies and spirits of its inhabitants. Appeal after appeal to Anabaptists outside the city to bring armed relief were frustrated by the besiegers. The people in Münster were reduced to eating vermin and finally even the dead. In June 1535 the city was betrayed by two deserters who revealed to the army the weakest gate. After a fierce battle, the city was taken on June 25 and nearly all the inhabitants were slaughtered. Rothmann was apparently killed in the battle, but the other three leaders including Jan of Leiden were condemned and then tortured with red-hot irons. Their bodies were then suspended in an iron cage from the tower of St. Lambert's church as an example to all. The Anabaptist kingdom of Münster was materially destroyed, but it spiritually lived on in the minds of religious and political authorities as the logical consequence of Anabaptist dissent. The tragedy of Münster was a consequence not only of the leaders' megalomania but also the followers' conviction that the bible was to be

---

[4]Zuck, ed., *Christianity and Revolution*, pp. 98–101.

literally followed. In the minds of the establishment, whether Protestant or Catholic, it was now clear that there was a revolutionary continuum from Thomas Müntzer to the city of Münster.

The Anabaptist aspiration was to communal solidarity as a holy people defined by believers' baptism and celebrated by the community-constituting act of consensus in the Lord's Supper. The effort to expand this theocratic ideal to the limits of the urban space in Münster led, however, not to the peaceable kingdom but the annihilation of the community itself. The result was the discrediting of militant millenarian (the belief in a 1,000-year reign of blessedness; Rev. 20) communalism. After this there was not another Anabaptist attempt to restore the world to primitive Christianity. Rather, future Anabaptist developments were marked by withdrawal from the world. Under the leadership of Menno Simons (1496–1561), whose brother was killed in the Münster debacle, the Anabaptist remnants were gathered into voluntary communities separate from the established civic and religious world.

What Menno did for the Dutch and northern German Anabaptists, Jacob Hutter (d. 1536) did for the disparate Anabaptist refugees in Moravia who had sold house and goods to form communistic colonies. Hutter was able to develop and stabilize the faltering communalism expressed by the Anabaptists in Zurich, Münster, and elsewhere into a Christian communism that shared goods and production. In this development we may see a certain continuity with the aspirations of medieval monasticism as well as an advance beyond it. Medieval monasticism was marked by an ascetic contempt for the world that, until the Franciscan movement, contrasted with the corporate wealth of the order itself. Furthermore, although the monastic movement shared a common life and a common goal, each monk was primarily concerned for his own salvation. The Mennonite and Hutterite Anabaptist advance beyond medieval religious asceticism and individualism consisted in developing a covenanted community of families that claimed to be *the* church itself, outside of which there is no salvation. This household of faith was marked by a communism of love and production, pacifism and suffering, separation from the world, trust in their ultimate vindication as the true household of faith, and confidence that until the final end of the world, human freedom and fulfillment are possible only in the brotherly love of evangelical communism.

Persecuted throughout Europe, the Mennonite and Hutterite Anabaptists eventually found homes in North America. Their faithfulness and perseverance under dreadful tortures and oppression contributed to the gradual development of the idea of religious toleration and liberty. And their insistence on a voluntary, separate church contributed to the modern development of religious pluralism and constitutional separation of church and state.

Chapter 21

"THE MOST PERFECT SCHOOL
OF CHRIST"—
THE GENEVAN REFORMATION

In 1556 the fiery Scottish reformer John Knox (1513–1572), having taken refuge in Geneva from the wrath of Mary Tudor, wrote to a friend: "[Geneva] is the most perfect school of Christ that ever was in this earth since the days of the Apostles. In other places, I confess Christ to be truly preached; but manners and religion to be so sincerely reformed, I have not seen in any other place." About the same time, another Marian refugee in Geneva wrote: "Geneva seems to me to be the wonderful miracle of the whole world. . . . Is it not wonderful that Spaniards, Italians, Scots, Englishmen, Frenchmen, Germans, disagreeing in manners, speech, and apparel . . . being coupled with only the yoke of Christ, should live so lovingly . . . like a spiritual and Christian congregation."[1]

The extravagant praise of Geneva as a "holy city" guarded by "legions of angels" indicates that this "new Rome" of the Reformation was not only a refuge for Protestants expelled from other lands for their faith; it was also a mecca for adherents to the new faith. As we shall see, Geneva as the model of a Christian commonwealth was not built in a day but was the result of a long and often bitter struggle. Furthermore, in this process, Geneva not only welcomed refugees; it created them. In the center of all the praise and blame that swirled through and around Geneva stood John Calvin, himself a displaced person from France.

John Calvin (1509–1564)

John Calvin (Jean Cauvin) was born in Noyon, a cathedral city about sixty miles northeast of Paris. His father, an attorney for the cathedral chapter and a secretary

---

[1]Both citations in John T. McNeill, *The History and Character of Calvinism* (New York: Oxford University Press [A Galaxy Book], 1967), p. 178.

to the bishop, obtained a modest church benefice for John that subsidized his education. At fourteen, Calvin set out for Paris, where he engaged in general studies at the Collège de la Marche and then theological studies at the Collège de Montaigu, where Erasmus had preceded him and Loyola was to follow. In 1528 at eighteen, Calvin received his Master of Arts degree. Calvin's mastery and skill in the prevalent forms of Latin argumentation as well as his religious and ethical seriousness may be behind the legend that his classmates nicknamed him "the accusative case." A somewhat more friendlier description of Calvin's student days comes from his friend and biographer, Theodore Beza (1519–1605), who explained Calvin's penchant for lying in bed in the mornings as time for reflecting on his diligent late-night studies.

In 1528 Calvin moved from Paris to Orleans and then to Bourges, where he completed a degree in law in 1532. This shift from preparatory theological studies to law was at the insistence of his father who had become involved in a controversy with the clergy of Noyon and who may well have believed that law would provide a better career. At Bourges, Calvin had the opportunity to pursue his lively interest in the classics, including the study of Greek. That Calvin's pursuit of law was largely a matter of filial obedience is evident in the fact that on the death of his father, Calvin returned to Paris to study humanism. In 1532 he published his first work, a learned commentary on Seneca's *On Clemency*. This commentary, contrary to some suggestions, is not an indication of a move toward the Reformation or a plea for religious toleration but an expression of his enthusiasm for the classics.

In fact, Calvin himself provided scant autobiographical information regarding his conversion to Protestantism. He certainly shared the humanists' desire to return *ad fontes* ("to the sources") of culture, including the scriptures. Late in his life, Calvin did speak of his "sudden conversion," which scholars posit took place sometime in 1533–1534. This conversion was publicly attested by his return to Noyon in May 1534 to surrender the ecclesial benefices he had held since he was twelve. Unlike many French reform-minded humanists who remained publicly in the Roman church, Calvin made a clean break. Throughout the rest of his ministry, Calvin would sharply criticize these "Nicodemites" (after Nicodemus in John 3:1–10), who could not bring themselves to live publicly what they believed inwardly.

Journey to Geneva

Calvin left Paris because of the Cop affair. Nicholas Cop, a friend of Calvin's from their days together at the Collège de Montaigu, was elected rector of the Sorbonne. In his inaugural address, delivered on November 1, 1533 (All Saints' Day), Cop attacked the theologians of the Sorbonne, citing as his support not only the works of French Humanists and Erasmus but also a sermon of Luther's. The theologians responded by charging that Cop was a Lutheran propagandist, and the king called for the arrest of the Lutherans. Calvin, suspected of being a coauthor of the address because of his close association with Cop, fled. Cop managed to escape to Basel. Calvin found security at a friend's home in Angoulême, where he began to write what would soon become the most significant single statement of Protestantism, the *Institutes of the Christian Religion*.[2]

Calvin completed and published the first edition of the *Institutes* in 1536 in Basel, where he had sought refuge in January 1535 from the intensifying French persecution of Protestants. Originally intended as an evangelical catechism for the education and reformation of the churches, this work quickly earned Calvin an international reputation. Analogous to Luther's catechisms, the first edition consisted of chapters on the law, the creed, the Lord's Prayer and the sacraments of baptism and the Lord's Supper, arguments against the remaining Roman sacraments, and a discussion of Christian liberty. In great demand, the *Institutes* were repeatedly republished, expanded, and also translated into French. By the 1539 edition, Calvin conceived of the work as a text for the training of ministerial candidates. Calvin's final revision of 1559 extends to more than 1,500 pages in modern English translation. The *Institutes* was prefaced by a letter to Francis I, the king of France, pleading for a fair hearing of the evangelical faith. This letter is a defense attorney's masterpiece of vindication for French Protestantism, and it clearly exhibited Calvin's leadership qualities to Protestants everywhere.

The letter did not prompt a change of heart in Francis, however. His brief general amnesty for French religious exiles was prompted rather by his need for support on the eve of his third war with the emperor, Charles V. Taking advantage of this opportunity for a safe return, Calvin made his way back home to settle family affairs. Then, with his brother Antoine and his sister Marie, Calvin set out for the free imperial city of Strasbourg, where he intended to settle down to a life of scholarship. On the way to Strasbourg they were forced by imperial troop movements to detour via Geneva. It turned out to be one of history's most remarkable detours.

Calvin arrived in Geneva in July 1536. He planned to stay only overnight before continuing his trip to Strasbourg. But someone recognized Calvin and tipped off an old acquaintance of his from Paris, William (Guillaume) Farel (1489–1565). Farel, a fiery preacher, had been laboring for some months to bring Geneva to the Protestantism already espoused by Bern, Basel, and Zurich. Farel saw Calvin as literally a godsend to the cause and exhorted Calvin to stay and join in the work of reforming Geneva. Calvin refused, explaining that he was a scholar, not an administrator or preacher, and that he lacked the temperament for such a task because he generally did not get along well with people. As Calvin later wrote of himself: "Being of a rather unsociable and shy disposition, I have always loved retirement and peace. So I began to look for some hideout where I could escape from people. . . . My aim was always to live in private without being known."[3]

---

[2] John T. McNeill, ed., Ford Lewis Battles, trans., *Calvin: Institutes of the Christian Religion*, 2 vols., Library of Christian Classics XX and XXI (Philadelphia: Westminster Press, 1960).

[3] B. A. Gerrish, "John Calvin," in B. A. Gerrish, ed., *Reformers in Profile: Advocates of Reform 1300–1600* (Minneapolis: Fortress Press, 1967), p. 151.

Undeterred by Calvin's refusal, Farel thundered out an angry denunciation of Calvin's selfish desires and proclaimed that God would curse Calvin's scholarly life if he did not stay in Geneva and carry out God's assignment. Calvin was overcome by this "dreadful adjuration." As he said of this event: "Farel kept me at Geneva not so much by advice and entreaty as by a dreadful adjuration, as if God had stretched forth his hand upon me from on high to arrest me."[4] Thus Calvin yielded to a responsibility he had neither sought nor wanted. "In spite of my disposition [God] has brought me into the light and made me get involved, as they say."[5] This "God-frustrated scholar," as Calvin has been called, devoted the rest of his life to Geneva, except for a short exile in Strasbourg.

The Reformation in Geneva

The Reformation in Geneva was intimately allied with the political emancipation of the town. Geneva, more than many other Reformation areas, exemplified the revolutionary potential of the Reformation, a fact not lost on the French crown, which later would always suspect Protestants of political subversion.

In the early sixteenth century, Geneva was struggling for independence from the House of Savoy, the dominant power south of Geneva between France and Italy. The traditional ruler of Geneva was a prince-bishop who by this time was little more than an extension of the House of Savoy. To the north of Geneva were the powerful Swiss cantons of Catholic Fribourg and Protestant Bern, both of which politically wanted to draw Geneva into a Swiss alliance. In 1525 Savoy lost its satellite Lausanne to an alliance with Bern and correctly surmised that Geneva might follow. Although Duke Charles III of Savoy coerced reaffirmation of Genevan allegiance to their bishop and the House of Savoy, Genevan exiles negotiated a treaty with Fribourg and Bern that brought Geneva into the Swiss orbit in February 1526. The Genevan supporters of the Swiss Confederation were called Eidguenots (*Eid*, "oath"; *Genosse*, "associate"). It has been suggested that this name was conflated with that of a Genevan exile leader, Besançon Hugues, to form the name "Huguenot," which was later applied to French Protestants and refugees. In 1527 the Genevan Council of the Two Hundred was instituted; it formally assumed the legislative and judicial powers previously exercised by the duke of Savoy. Executive functions were exercised by the Litte Council, which consisted of twenty-five members, sixteen of whom were appointed by the Council of Two Hundred; the others (four syndics, the city treasurer, and four from the previous year's Little Council) were elected annually by the General Council of the citizenry.

---

[4]Williston Walker, *John Calvin: The Organizer of Reformed Protestantism, 1509–1564* (New York: Schocken Books, 1969), p. 158.
[5]B. A. Gerrish, "John Calvin," p. 152.

Geneva was attacked by Savoy in 1530 but was rescued by the intervention of Bern and Fribourg. In 1533 Bern energetically missionized Geneva for Protestantism, and the resultant religious riots, iconoclasm, and rise of "heresy" in the city collapsed its alliance with Catholic Fribourg. Through public disputations and fiery sermons, Farel led the vanguard of Protestants against the old church. He gained the pulpit of the cathedral and persuaded the Council of Two Hundred to suppress the Mass on August 10, 1535. By December 1535, the magistrates gave the Catholic clergy the choice of conversion or exile. In May 1536 a general assembly of citizens ratified reform measures and affirmed their will "to live according to the gospel and the Word of God." Bern had defended and liberated Geneva from Savoy, but Geneva resisted Bernese attempts to substitute itself for the ousted prince-bishop and the House of Savoy. Genevan sovereignty was formally recognized by Bern in August 1536, although Bern continued to be a power for Geneva to respect.

Thus when Calvin arrived in Geneva at the age of twenty-seven, Farel and his colleagues were just beginning to try to implement the recent mandate for the Reformation. The Roman church had been expelled, but a new Protestant structure was yet to be created. It was for this task of firmly establishing and consolidating Protestantism that Farel believed Cavin had been divinely sent to Geneva. Apparently not everyone was privy to Farel's insight, for in formalizing Calvin's appointment as reader in Holy Scripture, the secretary of the Little Council missed his name and wrote down, "that Frenchman."

Calvin's first attempts to reform Geneva not only failed but led to his expulsion from the city. It was axiomatic to him that church worship and discipline belonged in the hands of the leaders of the church, not the hands of the politicians. This was a departure from the polity of other Swiss Protestant cities, including that of Bern, Geneva's defender. The citizenry, which still included a large population of Catholics, was not pleased with the discipline and doctrinal uniformity that Calvin and Farel sought to impose. In November 1537, the general council refused to enforce the confession of faith to which Calvin insisted the whole population must adhere. Next the Council of Two Hundred denied Calvin and Farel the right to excommunicate. The town had not gotten rid of a Catholic prince-bishop in order to replace him with Protestant ones! And in February 1538 the annual election put syndics in office who were hostile to Calvin. In mid-March the Council of Two Hundred warned Calvin and Farel not to meddle in politics but to stick to religion. This religion included the liturgical practice sanctioned by Bern that unleavened bread must be used in the Lord's Supper. On Easter Sunday 1538, Calvin and Farel preached in the two main Geneva churches but refused to administer communion in defiance of the order of the magistrates. In short, they excommunicated their entire congregations. They were not against the use of unleavened bread per se, but against the right of the civic authorities to dictate ecclesial matters. There was an uproar, and the Genevan council immediately dismissed Farel and Calvin and gave them three days to leave Geneva.

Farel settled in Neuchâtel, and Calvin at the urging and Farel-like threats of Martin Bucer (1491–1551), the leading reformer of Strasbourg, settled in Strasbourg. Having finally arrived at his original destination, Calvin spent three of his happiest and most productive years (1538–1541) as a university lecturer and pastor to a French refugee church there. While in Strasbourg, Calvin learned a great deal about church organization from Bucer, a former Dominican, who himself had received his initiation into the evangelical movement from Luther at the Heidelberg Disputation in 1518.

From Bucer, Calvin learned and experienced how civic and religious life were integrated through the church offices of doctor or teacher, pastor, lay elder, and lay deacon. By this time, Strasbourg had become signatory not only to the semi-Zwinglian Tetrapolitan Confession but also to the Lutheran Augsburg Confession. Bucer's irenic and ecumenical leadership included Calvin in international Protestant-Catholic ecumenical efforts to avoid the division of Christendom that finally happened with the Council of Trent.

Calvin also learned from the humanist Jean Sturm (1507–1589), whose educational labors made Strasbourg one of the foremost educational centers in Europe, and whose *Gymnasium* (a secondary school to prepare students for advanced studies) continues to this day under his name. Sturm's humanist ideals, which included learning Greek, Latin, and the classics as well as religious and moral education, informed Calvin's own later educational efforts in Geneva.

Not least of Calvin's joys in this marvelous reformed city was his marriage to Idelette de Bure, the widow of an Anabaptist he had been instrumental in converting. In response to the efforts of Farel and Bucer to push him toward marriage, Calvin made it clear that his model of womanhood focused on modesty, thrift, and patience with his ill health rather than on a "fine figure." But Farel, whose priorities in such matters did not exactly coincide with Calvin's, mentions that she was also beautiful. Farel himself married a young refugee widow when he was 69, much to the disapproval of Calvin. In any case, Idelette remained Calvin's faithful companion until her death in 1549.

During his stay in Strasbourg, Calvin reworked his *Institutes* and expanded the original six chapters to seventeen. He also compiled a book of French psalms and a liturgy for his congregation, and wrote an exposition of Paul's letter to the Romans as well as a treatise on the Lord's Supper. Most important of all, he responded to Cardinal Jacopo Sadoleto's appeal to the people of Geneva to return to the Roman church.

The expulsion of Farel and Calvin from Geneva had created disarray in the evangelical community of Geneva. Factions arose among the evangelicals, and the numerous Catholics still in Geneva had hope that the reform could be overthrown. Sadoleto was a humanist and a distinguished cardinal who had participated in the drafting of a famous Catholic report calling for thorough moral reform of the church in preparation for a reform council. He took advantage of the unstable situation in Geneva to affirm Roman authority and tradition against Reformation innovations.

Sadoleto's long entreaty was addressed to the Little Council. The magistrates could find no one capable of making a suitable reply to this dangerous challenge to Geneva, and thus appealed to Calvin. Calvin responded to Sadoleto with one of the most noteworthy defenses of the evangelical faith. On the two major issues of the Reformation, Calvin fully sided with Luther in arguing that the ultimate authority in the Christian life and community is scripture not the church, and that justification is by faith and trust in a merciful God alone, apart from human achievements.

Calvin's eloquent defense of the evangelical faith won him new respect in the city. This plus internal political developments concerning concessions to Bern led to the ouster of the anti-Calvin party among the magistrates. In mid-1540, the new magistrates pled with Calvin to return to Geneva and resume his work of reformation there. Calvin's response was that he would rather die a hundred times than go back to Geneva. Once again, Farel, who was not invited back, threatened God's wrath on Calvin if he did not accept this call. Calvin yielded and was back in Geneva in September 1541. This time the secretary noted not only his name but that he was "to be forever the servant of Geneva." He was appointed the pastor of the ancient cathedral of St. Peter, provided with a decent salary, a large house, and annual portions of 12 measures of wheat and 250 gallons of wine.

Geneva under Calvin, 1541–1564

Although it was the Geneva government that implored Calvin to return, Calvin's progress in winning the town to his vision of the church rightly constituted and truly reformed was neither smooth nor rapid. His eventual triumph by 1555 over numerous opponents and his creation of a model of Protestantism that continues to influence churches the world over are remarkable because he worked solely by moral suasion. Calvin never enjoyed the political power and material resources of the deposed Catholic bishop of Geneva. Nor did Calvin have at his side the hundreds of priests, monks, and canons available to the old church. By Calvin's death, there were only nineteen pastors in Geneva, all employees of the municipal government. To an astute observer of Geneva in 1541, it would have appeared highly unlikely that Calvin could carry out a thorough reform of the city. Yet Calvin's reform of this recalcitrant city was so thorough it may legitimately be called a revolution. How did he accomplish this reform?

The clue to Calvin's success in Geneva is that he wrote the rules for the city's political and ecclesial games. He had not been trained as a lawyer for nothing! As one of the conditions for his return from exile, he had bargained for the right to draft the institutional and legal form of the church. Within six weeks of his return, he submitted to the magistrates his *Ecclesiastical Ordinances*.[6] With a few minor amend-

---

[6]See Robert M. Kingdon, ed., *Transition and Revolution: Problems and Issues of European Renaissance and Reformation History* (Minneapolis: Burgess Publishing Company, 1974), pp. 97–103.

ments, the government enacted them into law. Within the next two years, two further sets of laws regarding justice and political offices were enacted that further formed the constitution of the Geneva city-state. Whether or not Calvin was the author of these later laws, as some scholars believe, there is no doubt that the magistrates looked to Calvin as a legal and moral resource for drafting them. In short, Calvin's success in Geneva was related to his firsthand and intimate knowledge of who made decisions and how these decisions were made.

The *Ecclesiastical Ordinances* organized the Genevan church by setting forth four categories of ministry—doctors, pastors, deacons, and elders—and creating institutions for the work of each. The doctors were to study scripture and to teach. Their theological scholarship was to serve the maintenance of doctrinal purity and the preparation of ministers. Pastors were to preach the Word of God, administer the sacraments, and instruct and admonish. Candidates for the office of pastor were examined in doctrine and conduct, and they had to be approved by the ministers and the Little Council. The pastors of Geneva and its dependent villages met weekly for discussion of theology and doctrine. The deacons were responsible for the supervision of charity, including relief of the poor and overseeing the hospitals. They were elected once a year in the same manner as the elders.

The doctors and the pastors together constituted the Geneva Company of Pastors, also known as the Venerable Company. The Company of the Pastors met quarterly for purposes of administration and mutual discipline. Although of limited legal authority, the Venerable Company held a notable place in the moral structure of Geneva.

The elders were laymen whose function was to maintain discipline within the community. Against Calvin's wishes, the elders were political appointments chosen from and by the magistrates. In all, there were twelve elders, of whom two were chosen from the Little Council, four were chosen from the Council of Sixty, and six were chosen from the Council of Two Hundred. Selected for their wisdom and piety, they represented different parts of the city. They were to watch over the lives of the people, to admonish the disorderly, and when necessary report erring people to the Consistory.

The Consistory, a kind of ecclesial court, was the principal organ of church discipline; it included the twelve elders and the pastors. Its presiding officer was ordinarily one of the syndics. The main concern of the Consistory was the systematic supervision of the morals of the people of Geneva, including the enforcement of the moral laws. This was the source of Geneva's reputation for austerity and puritanism. The Consistory had the power to excommunicate those who in its eyes had committed serious offenses.

It is not surprising that the Consistory was the most controversial institution of the Reformation in Geneva. It soon became the focal point for the opposition against Calvin, but it was also for Calvin a crucial vehicle for expressing his authority. This latter point warrants emphasis because those living in contemporary pluralistic and secular societies easily forget how threatening the charge of unauthorized innovation was to the Reformers. From the early church to the early modern period, innovation was equivalent to heresy. The very reason Calvin had been implored to return to Geneva was that the Genevans were threatened by Sadoleto's accusation of innovation and his appeal to traditional authority. The Consistory thus was Calvin's means for instilling respect for his authority even if at times this approximated a moral reign of terror.

Calvin's Consolidation of His Authority

Opposition to the not-so-secret ecclesiastical police in Geneva crossed class and economic lines to include magistrates as well as common citizens. In turn, the Consistory did not shrink from judging prominent citizens. In January of 1546, Pierre Ameaux, a member of the Little Council, publicly criticized Calvin. Calvin perceived this not as a personal attack but as an attack on his authority as a minister. He persuaded the Council of Two Hundred to impose on Ameaux the punishment of a public penance that included a walk around the town dressed only in a penitential shirt and beginning for God's mercy. The effect was a public proclamation of Calvin's authority.

More serious threats to Calvin's authority came from the patrician families of the Perrins and Favres, respected Genevan families who had been among the strongest advocates for bringing Calvin back to Geneva. Neither Ami Perrin nor Francois Favre, his father-in-law, was in favor of the Consistory's inquisitorial practices. When Calvin censured Francois's wife for lewd dancing at a wedding and excluded Francois himself from the sacrament for immoral behavior, Ami Perrin publicly questioned the competence of the Consistory. The Favres fled town, and Ami left on a diplomatic mission to France. When they returned to Geneva, both Francois and Ami were imprisoned, the latter because he was also suspected of being in collusion with France to invade Geneva. Bernese intervention obtained the release of Favre, and Perrin was acquitted. Calvin now labeled Perrin and his followers "Libertines," alleging that they did not want discipline because it would expose their loose living and faithless lives.

One of these Libertines, Jacques Gruet, who was also from an old Genevan family, not only criticized Calvin but was found to have appealed to the French king to intervene in Geneva. Believing Gruet to be part of an international plot against Geneva, the magistrates tortured and then beheaded him with the consent of Calvin. In December a Libertine mob gathered to intimidate the Council of the Two Hundred. Calvin himself ran into their midst proclaiming, "If you must shed blood, let mine be first." Unnerved, the mob subsided.

The continuing influx of religious refugees into Geneva provided a source of political support for Calvin, for they were generally of high social and intellectual status and were obviously grateful for the haven Calvin provided them. Not all of these newcomers agreed with Calvin's theology, however. A famous example of such opposition was Jerome Bolsec, who although generally sympathetic to reformed theology sharply criticized Calvin's doctrine of predestination. Consequently, he was banished for life. Bolsec's revenge was to publish in 1577 a scurrilous biography of Calvin that continued to be an arsenal for anti-Calvinist polemics for the next two centuries.

The Servetus Case

The growing opposition to Calvin was the context for the infamous Servetus case. Michael Servetus (ca. 1511–1553) was born in Aragon and became a public figure by the publication of his *Seven Books on the Errors of the Trinity*[7] in Strasbourg in 1531. Protestant and Catholic theologians alike joined in condemning Servetus's attack on the fundamental doctrine of the Trinity. The next year, Servetus responded with his *Two Dialogues on the Trinity*, which maintained that in its doctrinal development the church had fallen away from Jesus. Although Servetus was not renowned for his discretion, he did at this time realize that the better part of valor incuded anonymity and a different profession. Thus he went to Paris, where he studied medicine and anatomy. In the annals of medicine, he has a certain fame for being one of the first to discover the pulmonary circulation of the blood, a discovery probably prompted by his concern to show that the Spirit entered the blood system through the nostrils.

Servetus could not abstain from theological publication and controversy, however. He began a pseudonymous correspondence with Calvin, who recognized him from his writings. When Servetus sent Calvin his newest endeavor, *The Restoration of Christianity*, Calvin sent back his own *Institutes*, which Servetus promptly returned filled with insulting marginal comments. Calvin then sent all this correspondence to a friend in Vienne who passed it on to the Inquisition in Lyons to assist in the capture of Servetus. In August 1553, Servetus managed to escape from the Catholic Inquisition and fled toward Italy. On the way to seeking asylum in Naples, he stopped in Geneva.

In his writings and in his correspondence with Calvin, Servetus had presented infant baptism as diabolical, had denied original sin, and had likened the Trinity to a three-headed Cerberus. Jesus was not the eternal son of God but a human become divine. Servetus presented himself as another archangel Michael, leading an angelic

---

[7]For bibliographical information on Servetus's writings, compare A. Gordon Kinder, ed., *Michael Servetus* (*Bibliotheca Dissidentium, X*), in André Séguenny, ed. (Baden-Baden: Koerner, 1989).

host against the Antichrist. To Calvin, this was the "impious ravings of all the ages," and he wrote that should Servetus ever appear in Geneva he would not leave alive. In Geneva, Servetus disguised himself and attended Calvin's church. He was spotted and immediately arrested.

The trial of Servetus on charges of heresy was seen by the libertines as a chance to embarrass Calvin, who was the expert witness for the prosecution. But Servetus's fate was sealed by the Genevan magistracy even before the unanimous denunciations of Servetus poured in from Basel, Bern, Schaffhausen, and Zurich. Servetus was found guilty of spreading heresy and sentenced to death by burning. On the morning of October 27, 1553, Servetus was burned to death. He died with the prayer, "Jesus, Son of the Eternal God, have mercy on me." To the end, Servetus would not pray in trinitarian language to "the eternal Son of God."

Calvin had sought, in an unsuccessful humanitarian gesture, to commute this punishment from burning to beheading. Farel rebuked Calvin for such undue leniency! Following the execution of Servetus, Calvin wrote his *Defense of the Orthodox Faith* in which he declared that in cases of heresy the glory of God must be maintained regardless of all feelings of humanity. But Sebastian Castellio, the Genevan schoolmaster forced out of town in 1544 by Calvin, wrote in his *Concerning Heretics, Whether They Are to be Persecuted* (1544): "To burn a heretic is not to defend a doctrine, but to kill a man." However, Castellio was far ahead of his time, for Calvin and Geneva received congratulations and applause from all quarters for execution of the archheretic. Now the modern world reserves its wrath and persecution for political heretics.

The Servetus affair was a turning point for Calvin. His opponents were unable to use the Servetus case against him, and those leading Libertines who tried were discredited. Soon Geneva was firmly in Calvin's control. As a consequence, restrictive and disciplinary elements in the city were enhanced; the Consistory became more of an ecclesiastical court; and the ministers were now consulted on the choice of elders. This development was not without personal trials for Calvin; his sister-in-law was discovered in adultery with his own servant, and later his stepdaughter Judith was also caught in adultery. (Both women were expelled from Geneva.) Nevertheless, Calvin's influence continued to grow with the combined circumstances of the defeat of his enemies and the continuing influx of religious refugees. In 1559 Calvin founded the Geneva Academy, now the University of Geneva, which attracted students from all areas of Europe and became the training ground for the Protestant leadership, that became influential throughout Europe. In the same year, Calvin was made a citizen of Geneva.

It is a mistake to conclude that Calvin turned Geneva into a theocratic police state. Rather, for most of Calvin's career he had to struggle to maintain authority. Indeed, there were times when Calvin's authority was so fragile that Genevans even called their dogs "Calvin." Calvin, in common with other Reformers, recognized that the success of his reform movement rested in no small part on respect for his leadership and authority. What is remarkable is not his efforts to consolidate authority, but that in this process he did not succumb to favoritism to win support. Neither prominent citizens nor his own family were allowed to be above the law. In this, Calvin provided a model of democratic equality under the law that modern states would do well to emulate.

Chapter 22

PROTESTANT MISSION AND EVANGELISM— THE "INTERNATIONAL CONSPIRACY"

Nearly 5,000 religious refugees flocked to Geneva, attracted by the stature of Calvin and driven by persecutions of Protestantism in their homelands. They were from nearly every province in France as well as from England, Scotland, Holland, Italy, Spain, Germany, Poland, and Bohemia. When they returned home, they took Calvinism with them. Furthermore, the Academy in Geneva trained missionaries for work in other countries. These pastors traveled in disguise, frequently as merchants, into countries where Calvinism was outlawed, and established churches patterned after the church in Geneva. The Geneva church functioned as the international headquarters for this missionary movement, a kind of Protestant Vatican. Foreign theological disputes and questions were sent to Geneva for resolution and clarification. The missionary churches were also served by an extensive news bureau and communications network centered in Geneva. Calvinism ultimately prevailed in England and Scotland, whereas it survived only in a minority status in France.

The Reformation in England

Historians have sometimes portrayed the English Reformation as an act of state. In the words of the English historian, A. G. Dickens:

Altogether, the English Church during the period 1500–30 stood poorly equipped to weather the storms of the new age. It was a grandiose but unseaworthy hulk, its timbers rotted and barnacled, its superstructure riddled by the fire of its enemies, its crew grudging, divided, in some cases mutinous, its watchmen near-sighted and far from weather-wise, its officers lacking in navigational skill. If in this situation the King decided to take personal command, most Englishmen— even most churchmen—would be likely to applaud rather than object. And few would stop to consider that the kings of England bore not a little of the responsibility for the problems of the Church![1]

These storms of the new age included an endemic anticlericalism that was fed by anger over the corruption and sexual lapses of the clergy. This attitude was sharply expressed by the notorious *Supplication for Beggars* (1529) by the London lawyer, Simon Fish: The clergy "truly [do] nothing more but apply themselves . . . to have to do with every man's wife, every man's daughter, and every man's maid, that cuckoldry and bawdry should reign over all. . . . These be they that have made a hundred thousand idle whores in your realm."[2] Lawyers in general were jealous of the privileges exacted by canon lawyers and focused their wrath on Thomas Wolsey (ca. 1474–1530), the mighty upstart who as lord chancellor and papal legate seemed to monopolize all ecclesial and civil power in the realm. The public's indignation exploded into a series of measures against the church when Wolsey fell from power in 1529.

These endemic English resentments were fertile ground for Lutheran preaching and doctrine, which entered England about 1520. The first group of Lutheran sympathizers began meeting about this time at the White Horse Inn in Cambridge, whose university would provide most of the future leaders of English Protestantism. From Cambridge the movement spread to Oxford. Lutheran ideas were also influencing London merchants and their colleagues in the English business colony in Antwerp. Here, outside the control of the English king and his bishops, Protestant bible translators and publicists worked with enthusiasm. Largely through the influence of Thomas Cromwell (ca. 1485–1540), the chief political agent behind Miles Coverdale's first complete English translation of the bible (1535) and Archbishop Thomas Cranmer (1489–1556), the king was persuaded to put the bible in all the churches—a step that could not be retracted.

Even Henry VIII's Catholic reaction of his last years could not halt the Protestant advance. The religious phraseology in middle-class wills of the time indicate the decline of saint worship and the advance of Protestant convictions. These Protestant convictions were present even in the court and among the tutors of Henry's son, Edward VI. With the death of Henry in 1547, the English Reformation had six years for development under Edward VI and his advisors. During this time, Cranmer presented the English people with his prayer books (the first in 1549, the second in 1552), the second of which was a distinctly Protestant expression of worship and theology.

---

[1]Joel Hurstfield, ed., *The Reformation Crisis* (New York: Barnes & Noble, 1966), p. 48.
[2]Hans J. Hillerbrand, ed., *The Reformation: A Narrative History Related by Contemporary Observers and Participants* (New York: Harper & Row, 1964), pp. 307–308.

The preceding sketch of Protestant influences and development in England cannot be divorced from the energetic reign of Henry VIII (1491–1547), who became king in 1509. His father, Henry VII, had victoriously concluded the English civil war, the War of the Roses, and established the Tudor dynasty. Like his father, Henry VIII took his Catholicism very seriously and in 1521 published a tract against Luther titled *Assertio Septem Sacramentorum* for which Pope Leo X awarded Henry the title "Defender of the Faith." Henry's defense of the seven sacraments is an indication not only of his lifelong zealousness for the Catholic faith but also of a theological and literary skill rare among contemporary heads of state.

Henry's break with Rome was not theological but personal and political. There are indications that Henry was a sexual athlete but probably no more so than many other monarchs. Henry VII was concerned to provide stability, prestige, and power to the fledgling Tudor house. He pursued this through long diplomatic wrangling for an alliance with Spain that was cemented by the marriage of Catherine of Aragon to his first son, Arthur. But five months after the marriage, the young Arthur died. In order not to lose his new connection to one of the oldest and most powerful houses of Europe, Henry immediately proposed that his second son, Henry (VIII), marry the young widow. Since Leviticus 18:6–18 prohibited marriages within close relationships, a special papal dispensation for the marriage of Henry and Catherine was obtained from Pope Julius II.

Henry and Catherine were married in 1509. Of Catherine's numerous pregnancies, only one child survived—Mary Tudor, born in 1516. By 1525, the queen was forty and there appeared no hope for further children. In the meantime, Henry was involved with a variety of mistresses and then became infatuated with Anne Boleyn, one of the ladies at court and sister to one of his earlier mistresses. His growing desire to be rid of Catherine and to remarry, however, was motivated not just by his intense attraction to Anne Boleyn but primarily by a hope for the stability of the Tudor reign and England itself. He needed a son to succeed him in order to avoid the specter of civil war over the succession and the many problems foreseen if his daughter succeeded him.

Henry appealed to Pope Clement VII to annul his marriage to Catherine on the basis that it was invalid to marry a deceased brother's widow (Lev. 20:21). This appeal put the pope in an extremely difficult situation. Doctrinally it would be awkward, to say the least, for the pope to grant Henry's request because that would impugn the decision of a prior pope to allow the marriage and raise the question of papal fallibility, already sharply put by Luther. Perhaps more to the point in explaining the pope's hesitation was that at this time (1527) the pope was the virtual prisoner in Rome of the Emperor Charles V, who happened to be Catherine's nephew.

Henry's rage at Cardinal Wolsey for failing to persude the pope to his cause led to Wolsey's downfall and his replacement by Thomas More (1478–1535) in 1529 as lord chancellor. It was Thomas Cromwell who finally achieved the king's desire by appealing to the universities of England and Europe for a decision on the case and by suggesting that the pope be displaced from headship of the church in England by the crown. The dispensaton for Henry's annulment was granted by the English court in 1533. The pope responded by annuling the annulment and excommunicating Henry. In turn, Henry replied in 1534 with the Act of Supremacy, which appointed the king and his successors "Protector and only Supreme Head of the Church and Clergy of England." This was the decisive break of the English church with Rome and was accompanied by a loyalty oath to the king, which led to the beheading of Thomas More in 1535 for refusing to sign it. The Act of Supremacy was a constitutional break from papal authority, not an introduction of Protestantism. Although Henry used the anticlerical, especially the antipapal, sentiments of his people to his advantage, he reaffirmed Catholic dogma in the Statute of Six Articles in 1539. The Six Articles maintained transubstantiation, communion under one kind for the laity, clerical celibacy, sanctity of monastic vows, necessity of auricular confession, and private masses; and it declared the denial of any of these to be heresy.

Henry further consolidated his position as head of the English church by suppressing first the smaller and then the larger monasteries in 1536 and 1539. The dissolution of the monasteries, while certainly leading to the destruction of some art and architecture, effectively eliminated the last refuge of papalism and thus to some degree smoothed the way for Protestant development. Furthermore, it enriched the king's treasury, and the sale of monastic lands to wealthy laity ensured the self-interest of the laity against reintroduction of monasticism.

Passions, Politics, and Piety

Although in many ways, Henry's passions provide raw material for plays and movies, few historians would explain the English Reformation as being caused by them. Nevertheless, Henry's wives and their children have a legitimate place in the story of the development of English Protestantism.

On January 25, 1533, Henry secretly married Anne Boleyn, now pregnant with Elizabeth, who would be born in September. It was crucial to Henry that his expected heir be born legitimate. In March the statute restraining appeals to Rome was passed, and this made possible Henry's divorce from Catherine. Anne was crowned queen on June 1, 1533. Unfortunately for her, Henry's passion rapidly waned because their child was a girl, and future pregnancies ended in miscarriages. As long as Catherine lived, Anne was secure as queen, because the repudiation of her marriage would imply the validity of the marriage to Catherine. Catherine died in 1536. On May 17 Cranmer declared Anne's marriage void, and on May 19 she was beheaded on charges of adultery.

On May 30, Henry married Jane Seymour, a lady of the court. In October, Henry at last had a son—Edward—whose birth cost his mother's life. Henry next married Anne of Cleves on January 6, 1540, at the prompting of Thomas Cromwell to establish a political alliance with the duchy of Cleves against the emperor and on the basis of an all too flattering portrait of her painted by Holbein. When she arrived in England, Henry was immediately displeased with both her and Cromwell. By the end of June, Henry had divorced her, and Cromwell was on the way to the scaffold for this and other advice the king did not like. In August 1540, Henry married Catherine Howard, who seems to have lacked discretion about her behavior in the court. Her adultery was the cause for her beheading in February 1542 on the charge of treason. Catherine Parr, the king's last wife, whom he married in June 1543, had the good sense to remain in both his political and marital beds and thus she outlived him. Henry himself died on January 27, 1547, and the Tudor succession according to earlier legislation and the king's will passed to his children Edward, Mary, and Elizabeth in that order.

Edward VI came to the throne at the age of nine; always sickly, he died in 1553. Under Edward, or more accurately his advisors, the Reformation was established in England. His uncle, Edward Seymour, the earl of Hertford, appointed lord protector and duke of Somerset, immediately ended all persecution of Protestants and led the Parliament in repealing most of the treason and heresy laws, including the Six Articles. This in turn stimulated not only the return of those Protestants who had fled under Henry VIII; it also attracted continental reformers, most of whom were of Zwinglian persuasion. Such prominent reformers as Martin Bucer of Strasbourg and Peter Martyr Vermigli of Italy were invited, respectively, to Cambridge and Oxford universities.

The architect of English Protestantism, however, was Henry's archbishop of Canterbury, Thomas Cranmer, whose Protestant orientation found significant expression under Edward. Clerical marriage now flourished. Cranmer himself had been married since 1532 to Margaret Osiander, niece of the German Lutheran theologian, Andreas Osiander. Cranmer's first prayer book of 1549 was revised in 1552. The *Book of Common Prayer* set the tone of an English Protestantism that avoided extremes in doctrine and liturgy. Likewise in 1553, Cranmer produced a statement of faith for the English church that represented a compromise between the Lutheran and Calvinist theologies. These Forty-two Articles were the foundation for the later Thirty-nine Articles that defined the Church of England under Elizabeth I and that continue to inform the Anglican Church today. Catholic bishops were replaced by Protestants, some of whom, such as John Hooper at Gloucester, were proto-Puritans and some of whom were more radical Protestants, such as John Knox. The reform of the English church moved rapidly, perhaps too rapidly, for it depended on the continuing health of Edward.

The anxiety that Protestant reforms would be undone after Edward's death by the ascent to the throne of Mary Tudor, a staunch Catholic, led Edward and Somerset's successor, John Dudley, the duke of Northumberland, to conspire to exclude Mary from the succession on the grounds that, as the daughter of Catherine, she was illigitimate. In her stead they proposed Lady Jane Grey (1537–1554), the Protestant grandniece of Henry VIII and daughter-in-law of Northumberland. Unfortunately for the innocent, youthful Jane Grey, this plan ran aground on the passionate loyalty of the English to the Tudor succession. Queen for a day, or more precisely nine days, this plot cost Jane Grey and the leadership of Edwardian Protestantism— Hooper, Coverdale, Latimer, Cranmer, and Ridley—their lives. Knox fled to Geneva, where he bided his time for a fiery return.

Mary Tudor and the Catholic Reaction

The accession of Mary Tudor to the English throne severely threatened the English Reformation. Yet, ironically, Mary's overwhelming concern for the Roman Catholic faith served to strengthen the Protestant cause. By her marriage to Philip of Spain, she identified Catholicism with the unpopular, foreign Spain; by her reliance on her cousin Reginald Cardinal Pole and his efforts to introduce the Counter-Reformation, she became more unpopular; by attempting to restore monastic lands to the church, she alienated the landed class that had bought them; by persecuting Protestant leaders without proceeding to eradicate Protestantism itself, she created an army of martyrs who were celebrated in the influential book by John Foxe, *Acts and Monuments*; and by the exile of some 800 leading Protestants to Frankfurt, Geneva, and Strasbourg, she created an army of zealous Protestants trained in continental Protestantism and eager to return and recapture England for the evangelical faith.

Mary Tudor was queen only five years (1553–1558), but her brief reign left an indelible antagonism in English minds toward all things Catholic and Spanish. The daughter of Catherine of Aragon, she was reared Catholic and, from a purely non-theological perspective, had to be Catholic to be the legitimate heir to the throne. She became queen solely because she was Henry's daughter, and the English were loyal to the Tudor crown. She failed to understand this, and the consequences were disastrous. Ironically, Mary's personal traits were the most attractive of all the Tudors. She was personally gentle and inclined to mercy and generosity—remarkable traits in light of the treatment of her mother and herself by her father and brother. Her failings consisted primarily of her obsession with her Catholicism and her Spanish descent. Initially welcomed by her people, she died hated by nearly all.

From Mary's perspective, her vocation was to save her people from mortal sin by restoring them to papal obedience. She chose to accomplish this by a foreign policy that allied England with Spain. The Hapsburg emperor Charles V was more than willing to help and decided that his son, Philip II of Spain, should do his bit for the empire and Catholicism by marrying Mary and bringing England into the Hapsburg orbit. The English were not at all pleased, for although they were by no means wedded to the recent Edwardian turn to Protestantism, they hated foreign intervention and still retained a residual dislike of papal and clerical rule. Thus as

Mary's plans advanced, she and her counselors were always sniffing conspiracy and rebellion in the air. In the first months of 1554, Sir Thomas Wyatt led a rebellion of some 3,000 men into London. They were overcome and the leaders executed. Elizabeth Tudor almost suffered the same fate but was instead imprisoned in the Tower.

Since Parliament balked at Mary's plans to restore Catholicism, she proceeded, ironically, to use her father's break from Rome to restore Rome to England. She acted as supreme head of the church to remove Protestant clergy from their churches, usually on the grounds that they had broken the vow of celibacy. The Mass was restored, and with the return of Cardinal Pole, the old heresy laws were reinstated, accompanied by ferocious new treason laws. Parliament at last agreed to repeal all the antipapal and anti-Roman legislation passed since the days of Henry. Thus a legal basis was provided for the Marian persecutions.

Ironically, the Spaniards, including Philip II and Charles V, were against persecution for policy reasons. But Mary and Cardinal Pole, perhaps sincerely believing that they were saving English souls from damnation, inspired heresy trials that led to the burnings of nearly 300 dissenters, who became martyrs for the Protestant faith.

In September 1555, Philip returned to Spain, leaving Mary childless and disconsolate. War between Spain and France broke out, and in providing assistance to Philip Mary ended by losing Calais, the last remnant of England's medieval empire on the continent. From a practical point of view, Calais was no loss, for it had been expensive to maintain and served no purpose to the English. From a symbolic point of view, however, its loss was a blow to English pride and eroded the last vestiges of loyalty to Mary. In November 1558, Mary died. Cardinal Pole died twelve hours later. With their deaths, the Catholic reaction was over. Mary had succeeded in destroying the two things most dear to her: the old religion and the Spanish alliance. Elizabeth learned from her sister's failure.

Elizabeth I

The reign of Elizabeth Tudor (1558–1603) may well be described as a forty-five year love affair between the queen and her people, for it was a rare correspondence of purpose and program between a monarch and a people. Under Elizabeth, England turned Protestant, became a leading nation of Europe, won a world empire, and experienced a cultural renaissance.

Elizabeth came to the throne at the age of twenty-five, already wise beyond her years. Just as Mary had to be Catholic to be a legitimate ruler, so Elizabeth had to be Protestant because she was the daughter of Anne Boleyn. Her diplomatic skill, evident in all she did, was at times tested by the pressure on her to marry for the sake of the realm, a pressure exerted not only by various lovers but by Parliament as well. Her brother-in-law, Philip II, offered his services, but Elizabeth was too smart to repeat Mary's mistake. Her passionate lover, Robert Dudley, earl of Leicester, was not only spoiled and undependable but was surrounded by public scandal that included the death of his wife under mysterious circumstances. Elizabeth was strongly attracted to him but ruled her heart with her head, putting her reign above her personal feelings.

Elizabeth could speak French, Latin, and Italian and was equally skilled in double-talk. She was able not only to keep many ambitious men living in hope and in her service but also to control the factions in her court and countryside. To Protestants, the "virgin queen" was a heroic Judith; to Catholics she was a Jezebel, a servant of infamy, and the refuge of evil men.

Elizabeth's closest advisors were always Protestants and nearly always more Protestant than she. William Cecil, later Lord Burghley, was a moderate Protestant who served first as secretary of state and then as treasurer for nearly all of Elizabeth's reign. Her secretary of state from 1573–1590, Sir Francis Walsingham, followed a policy of active support for Protestants on the continent, especially the Dutch Reformed and the French Huguenots. He was also energetic in ferreting out Roman Catholic plots against Elizabeth, and he developed an elaborate counterespionage system directed particularly against the Spanish and the Jesuits.

Elizabeth's religious policy sought a middle way between the religious extremes that not only wracked England but were erupting in wars of religion on the continent. Her pursuit of moderation was intended to provide England the peace necessary for development after the Edwardian and Marian upheavals. She knew by both experience and observation the dangers inherent in rapid religious change. She claimed she would rather hear a thousand Masses than be guilty of millions of crimes done by some who suppressed Masses. Thus Elizabeth held both Catholics and radical Protestants in check by fostering an Anglican settlement in doctrine and discipline. This is what prompted John Knox to observe that Elizabeth was "neither good Protestant nor yet resolute papist."[3]

Elizabeth appointed Matthew Parker, a moderate, as archbishop of Canterbury. Parker had been a follower of Martin Bucer, was married, and knew well many of the Marian exiles who were now returning to England. It was from these Marian exiles that Elizabeth had to choose most of her bishops, all of whom were more radical in religion than Elizabeth.

It was Parliament that guaranteed the success of Elizabeth's policy. In April 1559, Parliament passed an act of supremacy that recognized the queen as head of the English church. All royal officials, judges, and the clergy, on pain of losing their office, had to take a loyalty oath acknowledging the supremacy of the crown over the church. To uphold the authority of any foreign prince or prelate was high treason,

[3]Lewis W. Spitz, *The Renaissance and Reformation Movements* (Chicago: Rand McNally & Company, 1971), p. 525.

punishable by death. Mary's Catholic legislation was rescinded, and Edward VI's second *Book of Common Prayer* was reintroduced with some modifications. The retention by the prayer book of images, crucifixes, and vestments made it more palatable to Catholics but offended the more radical Protestants. Those clergy who refused to conform were replaced, so that eventually appointees amenable to Elizabeth filled the ecclesial sees.

The second Parliament of 1563 reaffirmed the Act of Uniformity and passed measures for its strict enforcement. The Forty-two Articles were revised to become the Thirty-nine Articles. Elizabeth was involved in this revision. The articles were designed to accommodate the major evangelical theologies by denying transubstantiation on the one hand and Zwinglian symbolism on the other hand and remaining open to the range of Lutheran and Calvinist interpretations. The scriptures were declared the source and norm of faith, and the creeds were accepted because they could be proved by scripture. General or ecumenical councils were declared not to be infallible in themselves. The article on predestination was presented in a masterfully ambiguous way.

This Elizabethan settlement offended the more radical Protestants who desired to purify the church of all Roman Catholic vestiges. Those Protestants who remained within the Church of England while advocating removal of Catholic ceremonies and forms (vestments, sign of the cross, saints' days, etc.) came to be known as Puritans. The Puritans should not be thought of in terms of the later Victorian morality; they were not "puritanical" in the word's popular contemporary sense of moralistic. Those Protestants who rejected episcopal church polity and argued for clerical equality were called Presbyterians. And those who wanted all religious authority to be in local hands came to be called Congregationalists, Separatists, or Independents.

The first systematic statement of Anglicanism was presented by John Jewel (1522–1571), consecrated bishop of Salisbury in 1560, in his *Apology for the Anglican Church* published in 1562. Jewel's person and work were influential on one of the poor boys he patronized, Richard Hooker (ca. 1554–1600), who became the apologist *par excellence* for the Elizabethan settlement of 1559. Hooker's masterful *Treatise on the Laws of Ecclesiastical Polity* places him among the most important theologians of the English church. In response to the Puritan conviction that whatever was not expressly commanded in scripture was unlawful, he elaborated a theory of ecclesial and civil law resting on reason and natural law that was influential on future political writers such as John Locke (1632–1704).

Another very important Elizabethan was John Foxe (1516–1587), who under Mary had been a religious refugee in Strasbourg, Frankfurt, and Basel. His history of Christian persecutions was first written in Latin and published in Strasbourg in 1554. An English translation in 1563 was titled, *Acts and Monuments of matters happening in the Church* and is commonly known as "Foxe's Book of Martyrs." Officially approved by the Elizabethan bishops, this work went through four editions in Foxe's lifetime. The book praised the heroism and endurance of Protestant martyrs under

Mary and papist tyranny, and it soon ranked next to the bible in popularity. It is here we read that when the fire was lit under the Protestant martyrs, Ridley and Latimer, Latimer said: "Be of good cheer, Ridley; and play the man. We shall this day, by God's grace, light up such a candle in England, as, I trust, will never be put out."[4] Foxe's crimson martyrology helped to create a specifically Protestant anti-Roman Catholic consciousness that blended with the nationalistic sentiment of the Protestant English-speaking world.

Although by the end of Elizabeth's reign, Roman Catholics were a small minority of mainly conservative upper nobility in England, the years from 1569 to the destruction of the Spanish Armada in 1588 were filled with perceptions of a Catholic menace. There was a Catholic uprising in 1569 in the north instigated by the duke of Norfolk to advance the cause of Mary Stuart that was quickly put down. And the papal bull excommunicating Elizabeth in 1570 stimulated perceptions of internal and external conspiracies to overthrow the crown. Pope Pius V made it clear that his power extended over all nations and that since Elizabeth was a slave of vice, a usurper of the pope's office, and a "Calvinist," she was cut off from the body of Christ and all subjects were absolved from oaths of allegiance to her. It was the menace of Spanish invasion in 1587 that led Elizabeth finally and reluctantly to execute her cousin Mary Stuart, who had been under house arrest for nineteen years.

Elizabeth's course between the extremes of Catholicism and Calvinism was politically motivated because the former denied her legitimacy and the latter abolished the episcopacy that she believed supported monarchy. But she was not without religious sensibility herself. In her youth she had translated Marguerite d'Angoulême's *Mirror of a Sinful Soul* and was appreciative of the liturgy. She held that as long as her subjects openly observed the laws of the land, their consciences should not be examined. When she banished the Jesuits in 1585, one of her motives was to temper public outrage against foreign conspiracies and thereby to minimize public attacks on English Catholics. Like her father, Elizabeth determined the course of the Reformation in England in light of the dominant Tudor concern for royal supremacy. This concern necessitated denial of the ultramontane papacy and shaped the course of events up to the Act of Toleration in 1689.

Mary Stuart (1542–1587) and the Reformation in Scotland

The Tudor struggle for royal supremacy is exemplified in the story of Mary Stuart, queen of Scots. Mary was the daughter of James V (Stuart), king of Scotland. James's mother was Margaret Tudor, daughter of Henry VII and sister of Henry VIII. James's wife, the mother of Mary, was Mary of Lorraine from the powerful and very

[4]*Fox's Book of Martyrs; or The Acts and Monuments of the Christian Church*, revised and improved by the Reverend John Malham (Philadelphia: J. J. Woodward, 1830), p. 334.

conservative French Guise family. These dynastic relationships explain the threat that Mary Stuart posed to the reign of Elizabeth.

When the English defeated the Scots at the battle of Solway Moss in 1542, Henry VIII attempted to cement Scotland to England by arranging a marriage between Edward and the infant Mary Stuart. Not surprisingly, this was rejected. In 1548 Mary was sent to France, the traditional enemy of England, where she was married to the dauphin, soon to become Francis II. When Francis died in 1560, the queen mother, Catherine di Medici, did not want the rivalry of Mary, whose relationship to the duke of Guise and his brother, the powerful cardinal of Lorraine, gave her too much power. The Guises themselves were in favor of Mary's returning to Scotland to take up her crown because they believed she could also claim the throne of England and thus restore Catholicism there. In the meantime, a number of Scottish lords together with John Knox, who had returned to Scotland in 1559, rose up and expelled the French from Scotland.

Unwelcome in France and suspect in Scotland, Mary Stuart returned to Scotland to take up her crown. She created partisans then, and she does even now among historians. Of her, the English historian G. R. Elton wrote the following:

> It remains impossible so to speak about Mary Queen of Scots that all are satisfied; she had to the utmost the Stuart ability of attaching men's loyalties to herself despite the most outrageous and the most foolish of deeds. Of her famous beauty her surviving portraits provide little evidence. She was passionate, willful, intelligent, given to violent moods of exaltation and depression, and entirely without common sense—one might say, entirely without moral sense. It was too much to expect that this young woman, reminder of the recently overthrown French domination and ardently catholic, should bring peace to the land.[5]

Mary's immediate concern was not religion but dynastic politics. The cardinal of Lorraine had even suggested she turn Protestant in order to achieve her claim to the English throne. And, indeed, for a while she was conciliatory toward the Protestants, a stance no doubt difficult in light of the tactless preaching Knox directed at her. This was the man who had called her mother, Mary of Guise, who was regent when Mary lived in France, an "unruly cow saddled by mistake." No doubt Knox's hatred of all things French and Catholic was probably increased by his nineteen months as a French galley slave after the defeat of the Scottish uprising at St. Andrews in 1547. But Knox's opposition to Mary Stuart included also the fact that she was a woman. In his 1558 Genevan writing, *First Blast Against the Monstrous Regiment of Women*, Knox had declared that to "promote a woman to have rule above any realm is repugnant to nature, contumely to God, a thing most contrarious to

---

[5]G. R. Elton, *England Under the Tudors* (London: Methuen, 1969), p. 279.

His revealed will and approved ordinance, and finally it is the subversion of good order, of all equity and justice."[6]

In 1564 Mary moved both to mollify the Scots' distaste for the rule of a woman and to strengthen her claim to the English throne. She married Henry Stuart, Lord Darnley, and a grandson of Mary Stuart's own Tudor grandmother. Furthermore, since Lord Darnley had been born on English soil, as Mary Stuart had not, English law enabled him to inherit England. Even better for Mary, she fell madly in love with this strikingly handsome man whose contemptible character was not yet in evidence.

Soon after the marriage it became apparent that Darnley was unsuited not only for rule but even for normal human relationships. Alienated from her husband, Mary began to put her trust in her secretary, an Italian named David Riccio. Whether or not their relationship was innocent, Darnley became enraged with jealousy and with a gang broke into the queen's chamber and stabbed Riccio to death. Mary, then pregnant with her son James, resolved to be avenged. In February 1567, Mary took her then-ill husband to the house of Kirk o' Field near Edinburgh. She managed to be conveniently away when the house was blown up, and Darnley, who survived the explosion, was murdered.

The conspiracy to kill Darnley was led by the Protestant James Bothwell, who took Mary to Dunbar, where they lived together until he was divorced and they could be married in a Protestant rite in May. Catholic Europe was horrified, and the Scots were thoroughly fed up with a murderous and adulterous queen tainted with Catholicism. In June she was imprisoned in Loch Leven and forced to abdicate in favor of her son. Bothwell, himself not noted for constancy, deserted her and fled to Denmark. Although she managed to escape Loch Leven, she was unable to regain her crown. She then fled to England and appealed to Elizabeth for help against the "rebels."

Mary Stuart thus put Elizabeth in an untenable position that even she could not temporize about indefinitely. Obviously, regicide was frowned on by all monarchs of the time. Restoration of Mary to her throne would alienate Scots allies, but not to restore her would provide a focus for Catholic disaffection in England, as well as alienate other monarchs who, regardless of religion, did not wish to see people depose rulers. Elizabeth put Mary under house—rather, castle—arrest until finally in 1586 the Elizabethan secret service produced documents that implicated Mary in a plot against the queen. Mary, queen of Scots, was beheaded on February 1, 1587. She went to her death with great courage. Holding her crucifix high and dressed in the red of martyrdom, she prayed for her enemies, for mercy for Elizabeth, and for grace for England. Her dynastic ambition was realized by her son, James VI of Scotland, who on the death of Elizabeth became James I of England.

[6]L. W. Spitz, *The Renaissance and Reformation Movements*, p. 465.

France

Until the late 1520s, reformers and reform-minded humanists in France were shielded from ecclesial censure and punishment by the king, Francis I. The king's motivation was not evangelical but political. Since the thirteenth century, French theologians and conciliarists had argued that the French church held a privileged position in relation to the papacy. The supposed liberties of *l'Église gallicane*, hence the term Gallicanism, were reinforced in 1516 by the Concordat of Bologna between the king and Pope Leo X. This treaty increased the already considerable power of the crown over the church by, among other things, conceding the nomination of bishops and other ecclesiastics to the king. In effect, this meant that ten archbishops, eighty-two bishops, and more than 500 lesser clergy owed their appointments to the king. By 1516 Francis I had everything from the church that Henry VIII broke with the church to get.

We have already seen, however, that the tolerance of Francis I for reform turned to hostility when radicals indulged in violence and iconoclasm. Both ecclesial and royal authorities blamed the teachings of reformers for the actions of radicals. The results were that men like Calvin fled abroad or went underground to escape repression. Francis's persecution of evangelicals vacillated between imprisonment and execution, stimulated by outrages such as the affair of the placards, and moderation necessitated by alliances with German Lutheran princes to assist him against the emperor.[7]

Nevertheless, by the mid-1530s it was clear that evangelical reform of the French church could not be carried out from within France but would need external support. The source of this support was the Reformed church of Geneva. Once Calvin's leadership was firmly established in Geneva in 1555, he and other French exiles set up a very effective propaganda machine directed at France. Calvin was soon besieged by requests from French towns and noble families to provide them with pastors trained in Geneva.

As noted previously, the first evangelical congregations in France were called Huguenot, but these Calvinists preferred the term, *Réformés* ("the Reformed"). Catholic satires of the time called them *la Religion Déformée*. Early congregations at Meaux (1546) and Nîmes (1547) were dispersed by persecution. The martyrdom of the Fourteen of Meaux for celebration of an evangelical communion was particularly vicious. All underwent extraordinary torture but refused to reveal the names of other Protestants. At the stake six did submit to confessing to a priest in order to escape the penalty of having their tongues cut out, but the others remained firm even before this last mutilation.

---

[7]Placards titled "True Articles on the Horrible Abuse of the Papal Mass" were posted in Paris and other cities on October 18, 1534 by radical Protestants. The king was particularly outraged to discover that one had been tacked to his bedroom door in Amboise.

The son of Francis, I Henry II (1547–1559), unbiased by humanist sympathies or the need to conciliate German Protestant allies, was even more severe than his father. He issued edicts decreeing harsh punishment for such heretical practices as eating meat during Lent and attending unauthorized assemblies. He also instituted a special court for heresy cases appropriately named *la Chambre Ardente* ("the burning-chamber"). Those accused of disseminating heresy through books or preaching were often sentenced to cruel deaths such as being drawn and quartered while still alive. Thus before Genevan pastors were smuggled into France, they frequently signed their property over to their families because they knew they probably would not live to return.

By 1567 Geneva had sent 120 pastors into France to organize congregations, which because of persecution usually led a covert existence. Nevertheless, the Reformed church spread rapidly throughout France. A key to its success was the organizational genius it borrowed from Calvin's Genevan church. The first national synod of the Reformed church in France met in Paris in 1559. It set forth a confession of faith, the Gallican Confession, the first draft of which was written by Calvin. A modified form of this confession of faith containing forty articles, ratified at the synod of La Rochelle in 1571, continues to serve the French Reformed church to this day. By 1561 the national synod of France represented more than 2,000 congregations.

Calvinism in France appealed to particular social groups. A major source of adherents were skilled artisans, independent shopkeepers, and middle-class businessmen such as bankers. It is this phenomenon that has led some scholars to associate "the Protestant ethic" with "the spirit of capitalism" (usually under the heading of the "Weber thesis"). There is no doubt that the Calvinist virtues of hard work and thrift motivated by a theology of vocation dovetailed nicely with a capitalist economy. As with similar theories about the Jews, however, there is also a variety of other historical factors involved in Calvinist business success.

The social group that was most significant for the Reformation in France was the nobility, especially the houses of Bourbon (after the Valois, next in line for the throne) and Montmorency. Gaspard de Coligny (1519–1572, Montmorency), the admiral of France and a major influence on the young king Charles IX, became an outstanding Huguenot leader. Other important noble families in the west and southwest of France also joined the Reformed church, and lesser nobles and peasants followed their lead with the consequence that this area of France became the military bastion of the Reform movement.

The north and east parts of France were in the control of an ultra-Catholic faction of the nobility led by the Guise-Lorraine family. This powerful family held a strong position under Henry II and included cardinals who pressed for setting up a Spanish-style inquisition to exterminate all Calvinists. In response, a military and political Huguenot party arose to defend their power and privileges as well as their faith. The rivalry between noble families was sharply escalated by their opposing religious commitments.

397

Although Henry II and his wife Catherine de Medici, niece of Pope Clement VII, detested Protestants, their major energies were preoccupied with perpetual rivalry with Charles V in the Hapsburg-Valois wars. Furthermore, Henry did not seem to realize until the end of his reign how extensive the religious defection of his people had become. With the treaty of Cateau-Cambrésis (1559), which ended the Hapsburg-Valois wars, the king was now free to direct his attention to eliminating heresy in his lands. But within the year Henry died of a wound suffered during a joust. His accidental death created a crisis in royal authority that set the stage for a rapid growth of Protestantism and a long, bitter religious conflict.

The eldest of the four Valois princes was Francis II, who was only fifteen at the death of his father. During his brief eighteen-month reign (1559–1560), the ultra-Catholic party came to the fore through the domination of the government by the Guise uncles of Francis's wife, Mary queen of Scots. Their repressive measures against the Protestants caused such widespread resentment that more nobles joined those already committed to the Reformation because they both hated the Guises and had designs on the wealth of the Catholic church. The queen mother, Catherine, also sought ways to weaken the Guise faction that not only treated her disdainfully but was trying to displace her own sons in its effort to establish its own dynasty to rule France.

The intensity of anti-Guise feeling was evident in the Conspiracy of Amboise (1560), a bungled attempt led by a group of Huguenot nobility to kill the Guises and remove the king from their influence. Some of these nobles were executed. The Bourbon prince Louis de Condé was implicated in the plot and sentenced to death but released after the death of Francis. The Conspiracy of Amboise foreshadowed the coming wars of religion, which had the nature of civil wars. Various groups, including some Calvinist pastors, were beginning to come together in common opposition to the government, but such a negative basis for agreement was an unstable basis for cooperation and led to confusion and failure. The suggestion by some Reformed leaders such as Knox and Bullinger (the successor to Zwingli) that subjects had the right to revolt against idolatrous (i.e., Catholic) rulers was firmly rejected by Calvin, who wrote to dissociate himself from the Amboise conspiracy. The involvement of Calvinist pastors in the plot has been nicely phrased by N. M. Sutherland: "faced with a choice between resistance and extermination, they desired some solution less sublime than that of prayer alone."[8]

When Francis II died, Catherine's second son, Charles IX (ruled 1560–1574) succeeded as a minor at the age of ten. Legally the regency could go to either the queen mother or to the first prince of the blood (i.e., whoever was first in line to the throne after the reigning king's sons). The first prince of the blood was Anthony of Bourbon, king of Navarre, a leader of the Huguenots. His wife Jeanne d'Albret, a

---

[8]N. M. Sutherland, "Calvin's Idealism and Indecision," in J. H. M. Salmon, ed., *The French Wars of Religion: How Important Were Religious Factors?* (Lexington, MA: D. C. Heath, 1967), 19.

convinced Calvinist, was a leader of the Huguenots who corresponded with Calvin and participated in the national synod of La Rochelle. Catherine was able to out-maneuver Anthony in the struggle for the regency, but that triumph entailed developing a policy favorable to the Huguenot party as a counterweight to the Guise faction.

The Colloquy of Poissy

Catherine, assisted by her chancellor Michel de L'Hôpital, created a policy of moderation toward the Protestants that suspended persecution, released Condé and other Huguenot prisoners, allowed Huguenot nobles at court to have their own services, and appointed new, liberal-leaning Catholic tutors for the young king. Anthony of Bourbon renounced his claim to the regency and accepted the title of lieutenant-general of France. As a further effort to pacify her lands and, not incidentally, to provide a Gallican alternative to the Council of Trent, Catherine called for a public Protestant-Catholic debate and dialogue. The Colloquy of Poissy, which met in September and October 1561, was a significant royal recognition of the reality and growth of Protestantism.

The Colloquy of Poissy was the high-water mark of the Protestant Reformation in France. Chancellor L'Hôpital opened the colloquy with a speech concerning the king's gracious purpose to resolve the religious crisis by summoning this national council. It was the royal hope that a mutually respectful exchange of theological views between the Catholic and Huguenot representatives might preserve peace in the Gallican church. The colloquy, he went on to state, was not a place of judgment but of dialogue.

In immediate response, the archbishop of Lyons and primate of France, Cardinal Tournon, leaped to his feet to protest the very nature of this assembly. The some fifty bishops present, for all their gallicanism, despised a government-imposed assembly that raised heretics to their level. Heretics were to be judged, not debated.

Catherine was not interested in ultimatums and anathemas; her new policy was accommodation. At her motherly prompting, the king indicated to the chagrin of the bishops that the meeting would go on as scheduled. The signal was given and the Huguenot delegation—eleven ministers in their black Genevan robes and twenty lay representatives from various Calvinist congregations in France—was ushered into the assembly hall. Cardinal Tournon broke the tense silence with his stage whisper, "Voici ces chiens genevois!" ("There are those Genevan dogs!").

The "Genevan dog" who now stepped forth to present the Huguenot position immediately impressed his audience as a "purebred." Theodore Beza (1519–1605), born to an established Burgundian family, was a Calvinist's Calvinist and a scholar's scholar. During his thirteen-year exile in Switzerland, he had become Calvin's close friend, confidant, heir apparent, and professor of biblical studies at the new Genevan

Academy. His work on the Greek New Testament is still remembered by the naming of the fifth-century Graeco-Latin manuscript of the gospels he discovered and presented to the University of Cambridge in 1581, the Codex Bezae, and for the first critical edition of the Greek New Testament that he published in 1565. His background of family wealth and position, similar to that of his audience, and his years of theological reflection and writing precluded any sense of intimidation from this assembly of royal and ecclesiastical dignitaries. To the astonishment of all, he opened his remarks with a prayer at which his delegation fell to their knees: "Lord God, Father eternal and all-powerful, we confess before your majesty that we are poor and miserable sinners."[9]

Then for the next hour Beza eloquently and learnedly presented the Calvinist position. The queen mother was filled with hope, and even the bishops were not unmoved as Beza pledged himself to concord and elegantly surveyed doctrinal agreements between the antagonistic churches, such as the Trinity and the Incarnation. And he discussed such matters of disagreement as authority with a sweet reasonableness. Only at the end of his speech did he make the fateful slip of stating that in the Eucharist Christ's body "is as far removed from the bread and wine as is heaven from earth."[10] The hitherto polite reception of Beza's address was now shattered by shouts from the prelates—"He blasphemes!" Catherine later called Beza's simile "absurd and offensive."

The colloquy went on for another month, but the neuralgic nerve that had already sent waves of pain through previous colloquies at Marburg (1529) and Regensburg (1541) had been inelegantly exposed by Beza. The mode of Christ's presence in the Eucharist was the rock on which accommodation foundered. For the Catholic theologians, the Mass was the Christian community's supreme good work of offering and receiving the corporeal Christ, whereas for the Calvinist theologians, the Mass was an idolatrous and blasphemous denial of the true gospel. Furthermore, the Calvinists knew as did other Protestants that the Mass was only the tip of the Catholic iceberg. The mass was upheld by a whole hierarchical priesthood whose ability to perform the Mass was linked to an ordination process rooted in the successor to St. Peter and whose caste was endowed with special powers and prerogatives. From Luther on, the Mass was the focal point of the Protestant Reformers' attacks on the establishment because they knew that if the Mass went, the whole papal church would crumble. Throughout Europe a generation of iconoclasts had desecrated churches and trampled and urinated on holy objects, including the consecrated sacramental bread, in ritualistic reversals of Catholic ritual.

Thus the Catholic laity did not need refined theological rebuttals of Calvinist

[9]Marvin R. O'Connell, *The Counter Reformation, 1560–1610* (New York: Harper Torchbooks, 1974), p. 121.
[10]Donald Nugent, *Ecumenism in the Age of the Reformation: The Colloquy of Poissy* (Cambridge, MA: Harvard University Press, 1974), p. 100.

heresy in order to recognize it. They saw it in the actions of those who refused to honor a Corpus Christi procession and defaced sacred objects. When the Spanish Jesuit theologian Diego Lainez obtained permission to speak, he made it clear to the queen mother that her intentions for conciliation failed to understand that the Calvinists are "serpents, wolves in sheep's clothing, and foxes." The remedy against Calvinist "venom" was not this national council of dubious ecclesial legality but, rather, the Council of Trent already in session and presided over by the pope not the crown. Lest she did not get the point, Lainez insinuated that her crown as well as her soul were at stake in these matters.

The Wars of Religion: 1562–1598

The Colloquy of Poissy failed to create religious accommodation, but it did prepare the way for the first Edict of Toleration in January 1562, which provided a measure of freedom to the Huguenots. Huguenot leaders like Beza continued to have access to the court and strove for the conversion of the royal family. Huguenot public worship was allowed in private homes in towns and outside the towns' walls. This was the watershed for French Protestantism. It seemed that at the least France might go the way of England under Henry VIII a generation earlier and adopt a national church under the control of the state.

Within a month of the Edict of Toleration, however, the situation for the Calvinists was radically altered. By mid-February, Catherine was fully cognizant of the wrath of the Guise family and of the Spanish. She now came to believe that the unity of the nation and the royal future of her sons was more threatened by the hostility of the Spanish than by the Huguenots and their allies. Her balance-of-power policy therefore shifted toward the Catholic faction. Anthony of Bourbon sensed the shift in the wind and defected from the Huguenot party for the sake of his own personal and dynastic ambitions. The Huguenot politial and military resources were not sufficient to bring France into Protestantism, but they were strong enough to ensure their existence as a rebellious minority. Under these conditions civil war was inevitable. (See Figure 23.1)

On March 1, 1562, the duke of Guise went on a hunting trip with 200 armed men. At Vassy in Champagne they came across a large congregation of Huguenots gathered in a barn for worship and set upon them. Some fifty Huguenots were killed and many more wounded. The incident sparked more massacres, and the religious wars were on. For more than thirty years, Huguenots and Catholics murdered and assassinated each other with increasing barbarity. In some regions (e.g., the southwest), the war was endemic; elsewhere it was sporadic or almost nonexistent and punctuated by truces. The most infamous event of all this bloodshed was the St. Bartholomew's Day Massacre (August 24, 1572).

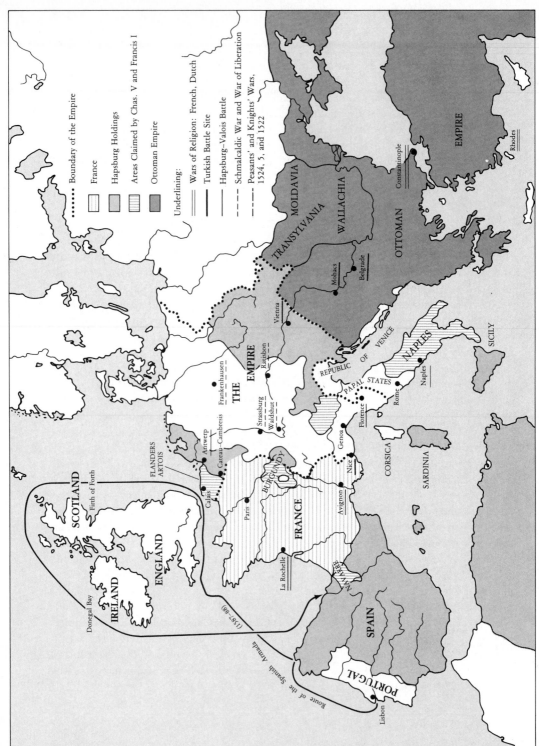

Figure 23.1 Major Battles of the Reformation Era (16th Century)

The St. Bartholomew's Day Massacre

During one of her shifts from repression to moderation, Catherine appointed the Huguenot leader Coligny a member of the royal council. He soon became a strong influence on Charles IX, who was now of age. This aroused both the political and maternal anxieties of Catherine. When Coligny convinced Charles to reverse traditional foreign policy to support Protestant resistance to Spain in the Netherlands, thus risking a disastrous war, Catherine decided that Coligny must go.

Knowing that her son would not agree to a legal execution, Catherine opted for an assassination. She convinced herself that Coligny was an impenitent rebel who had to be killed for the peace, if not the glory, of France. In 1563 Coligny had condoned the assassination of Duke Francis of Guise. The Guise family, convinced that Coligny had ordered this deed, had long demanded revenge. Catherine conceived the cunning idea that if it appeared that the admiral was killed by the Lorraine-Guise family, then Protestant wrath would turn against the Guises, neatly eliminating both the Coligny and the Guise threats to the state. With Coligny dead and the Guises massacred by the Protestants, the king would have a clear field. The plot had a certain brilliance and would have left the queen untouched but for one flaw—the assassin was a poor shot and only wounded Coligny.

It is said that for the first time in her life Catherine panicked. Charles was enraged that his esteemed father-figure and counselor had been shot, and Catherine feared that Charles would learn who was behind the attack. All her concerns were now in jeopardy—the interests of state, her passion for power, and potential peril to her other son Henry, who had participated in the attack. The way out of her dilemma came with the accusation that Coligny was now plotting with the Huguenots to kill the queen and her children. Whether or not the accusation was true and whether or not Catherine believed it are not known; what is known is that here was the means for influencing Charles to take steps to thwart a new Amboise conspiracy.

Catherine's argument to Charles was that rebels had to be executed. The crown must act quickly before the Huguenot forces were ready to strike the crown, and, more important regarding Catherine's position, before the inquiry into the attempted murder of Coligny discovered anything. Catherine perceived Coligny to be the king's master and believed that if she did not strike first, she would be executed and Catholic France would rise up against her son who, they believed, was allied with the Protestants. It was kill or be killed. The Spanish ambassador summed up the situation: "As the musket shot was badly aimed and as the admiral knew whence it came, they determined to do what they did."[11]

The context for the murder of Coligny and the massacre of his "rebels" was the

---

[11]Jean Héritier, "The Massacre of St. Bartholomew: Reason of State and Ideological Conflict," in J. H. M. Salmon, ed., *The French Wars of Religion* (Lexington, MA: D. C. Heath and Company, 1967), p. 51.

marriage of Margaret of Valois, Catherine's daughter, and Henry of Navarre, first prince of the blood since the death of his father. This marriage, negotiated as a means for creating peace between the warring religious factions by uniting the royal princess and the titular leader of the Protestants, took place in Paris on August 18. The marriage festivities had filled Paris with prominent nobility, including most of the Huguenot leadership. Coligny had been shot on August 22. The plot was planned for the early morning of August 24.

Charles now had the opportunity to prove himself to his mother and brother. The bell of the Palace of Justice gave the signal at three in the morning. To maintain order, the gates of Paris were closed, locking the Huguenot troops outside the city in the suburbs. The king's militia was deployed in the city. One of the militia leaders, however, was Claude Marcel, a fanatical Catholic and one of Guises' men. He took it on himself to proclaim to his men that the king's orders were to kill all heretics. Lists of heretics were provided to facilitate a methodical massacre. At the signal given by the king, the unsuspecting Huguenots were slaughtered in their beds, beginning with the finishing off of Coligny, whose body was tossed from the window of his apartment and then mutilated.

A conflagration of savagery fueled by religious hatred was now unleashed. A description by a contemporary follows:

> The streets were covered with dead bodies, the rivers stained, the doors and gates of the palace bespattered with blood. Wagon loads of corpses, men, women, girls, even infants, were thrown into the Seine, while streams of blood ran in many quarters of the city. . . . One little girl was bathed in the blood of her butchered father and mother, and threatened with the same fate if she ever became a Huguenot.[12]

About 6,000 people were killed in Paris, and thousands killed in lesser cities as the massacre spread through the land. By the time the frenzy subsided about 20,000 in all France had been murdered. Catherine had unleashed state terrorism.

European reactions to the massacre were mixed. Protestant leaders and royalty mourned but took no major steps against France. Queen Elizabeth of England wore mourning to show her grief, but a few months later she agreed to serve as godmother to the daughter of the French king. The Poles ignored the massacre and elected Charles's brother Duke Henry of Anjou their king. Pope Gregory XIII prescribed an annual Te Deum as a special thanksgiving service that was celebrated for many years. He also had a special commemorative medal struck, *Ugonatorum Stranges, 1572,* that depicted an angel upholding the cross as prostrate Protestants are being slain. It was said that the Spanish king, Philip II, laughed publicly for the first time in his

---

[12]Clyde Manschreck, ed., *A History of Christianity,* II (Englewood Cliffs, N. J.: Prentice-Hall, 1965), p. 144.

life and ordered his bishops to celerate the event with Te Deums (a Latin hymn of thanksgiving) and other ceremonies. Charles IX, however, seems to have been overcome with grief and guilt for his part in the massacre. He died less than two years later and was succeeded by his brother, now king of Poland, as Henry III, who reigned 1574–1589.

Henry III was the last of the Valois line. He refused to side with either Catholics or Protestants and moved toward a third party, the *politiques*, so-called because they placed national unity before religious uniformity. Nevertheless, his ongoing conflicts with the Bourbons and Guises, known as the War of the Three Henrys because each leader had that name, led to the murders of both Henry of Guise and Henry III. In 1589 the Bourbon, Henry of Navarre, came to the throne as a Huguenot. It took Henry IV five years to subdue the Catholic League and its Spanish allies. In 1594 he converted to Catholicism under pressure from the Catholic League, which threatened to declare his succession invalid. The popular story is that Henry said, "Paris is worth a Mass." His conversion had the desired effect of securing both the legitimacy of the Bourbon succession and the unity of the nation. Since Pope Clement VIII did not insist that the decrees of the Council of Trent be enforced in France, Henry responded to the anxieties of his former coreligionists by setting forth a policy of limited toleration, the Edict of Nantes, in 1598.

The Edict of Nantes made the Catholic church the official state church with its former rights, income, and possessions. The Huguenots, about 15 percent of the population, were granted religious rights to worship on Protestant estates and in many areas but not within five leagues of Paris. They were also granted civil rights, such as their own courts for legal protection and eligibility to hold offices, as well as political rights that included 200 fortified places. The edict did not work perfectly, but it did bring an end to the religious wars. It was revoked by Louis XIV in 1685.

Chapter 23

CATHOLIC RENEWAL AND THE COUNTER-REFORMATION

Following Leo X's initial dismissal of the Reformation as nothing more than a drunken brawl among German monks, there was a growing realization even in the papacy that renewal and reform of the church could not be lightly brushed aside. Indeed, the rapidity of the reform movements throughout Europe raised apocalyptic visions in more than one curial mind. Pope Clement VII, who suffered the trauma of the sack of Rome in 1527, had a medal struck that depicted Christ bound to a column with the inscription *Post multa, plurima restant* ("After many things, even more remain"). And just before his death, he commissioned Michelangelo to portray the Last Judgment on the front wall of the Sistine Chapel.

It is important to note, however, that the Catholic renewal movement was not merely a reaction, a Counter-Reformation, to the Reformation. Before Luther, there was already sharp criticism of the church that may be illustrated by the Italian proverb that the person who goes to Rome will lose his or her faith, and by the acrostic for Rome, *R[adix] O[mnium] M[alorum] A[varitia]* ("love of money is the root of all evil"). Persons concerned about the renewal of the church included not only leading humanists such as Erasmus but cardinals such as Gian Matteo Giberti (1495–1543), who as bishop of Verona strove to upgrade the education and morality of his clergy, sponsored a printing press that issued editions of the Greek fathers, and developed a platform for the restoration of church discipline that was influential on the Council of Trent.

As is all too often the case, these early renewal efforts were too little and too late to forestall the Reformation. For example, Emperor Maximilian had called for a reforming council in 1509. He was outmaneuvered by Pope Julius II, who held the

Lateran Council in 1512 that reaffirmed the full power of the pope, condemned conciliarism, and denounced the tendency toward independence of the national churches. Furthermore, the gravity of the church's situation was not fully grasped by Rome until Leo's death in 1521. The cardinals then elected a Dutch cardinal of spotless reputation, Adrian Dedel of Utrecht (1459–1523), as Pope Adrian VI.

Adrian VI had studied with the Brethren of the Common Life and taught theology at Louvain, where he had received a doctorate in 1492. He was a friend of Erasmus, tutor of the young Charles V, and had been a bishop and inquisitor in Spain. An earnest and zealous reformer, he moved quickly after his election toward his goals of checking Protestantism, reconciling European princes, and reforming the curia. But the times were against him. The Italians looked down on him for his rude Latin and lack of Renaissance sophistication. He was elected in January 1522 and died in September 1523. His epitaph read: "Alas! How the power of even a most righteous man depends upon the times in which he happens to live!"

Adrian was succeeded by another Medici, a cousin to Leo X, who took the title Clement VII. He was personally of blameless character, but instead of devoting himself to official duties, he was an easygoing, urbane patron of the arts. His inability to deal with Henry VIII's drive to divorce Catherine was characteristic of his ineffective efforts to conciliate all parties. He sent the moderate Cardinal Campeggio to the Diet of Nürnberg in 1524 with the offer to the Lutherans of "Wine and women"—communion with both wine and bread and clerical marriage—without realizing how deep the doctrinal divisions had already become. In 1532 he consented to call the ecumenical council the Protestants had been requesting for the last twelve years but died in 1534 without convoking it.

The next pope, Alexander Farnese, Pope Paul III, was a typical Renaissance prelate. He immediately made two of his teenage grandsons cardinals in order, as he put it, to provide for his old age. He did encourage dialogue with Protestants such as Melanchthon and Bucer and made a number of humanists cardinals. In 1536 he proclaimed that the long-desired council would meet in Mantua in May 1537. In preparation for this council, he appointed a commission of nine cardinals to prepare a report for reforming the church. After two months of solid work, this commission issued the report *Advice . . . Concerning the Reform of the Church*, which scored the abuses of nepotism, simony, pluralism of benefices, absenteeism, and clerical immorality and venality. When the Protestants got hold of the report, it only confirmed and substantiated their criticisms of the church. Furthermore, the commission's emphasis on *moral* reform of the church indicated that they were unable to come to grips with Luther's explicit call for *theological* reform. Luther himself published a German translation of the report with his own ironic glosses in the margins.

Nevertheless, there were Roman Catholic theologians who not only understood but even shared some of the religious concerns of Luther. An outstanding example of these so-called mediating theologians was Gasparo Contarini (1483–1542). Contarini had been present at the Diet of Worms in his capacity as Venetian ambassador to the imperial court. Later (1528–1530) he was ambassador to the papal court in Rome, where his deep piety and his diplomatic ability to negotiate and compromise differences led to his elevation to the cardinalate (1535) while still a layman. He sought to reconcile Protestant and Catholic differences and advocated an ecumenical council to heal the divisions in the church. He and his Lutheran counterpart Melanchthon did reach agreement on some significant theological issues such as justification at the Regensburg Colloquy in 1541. But their mutual efforts were rejected by both sides as compromises at the expense of the truth. With the death of Contarini, the liberal Catholic reform movement also suffered a mortal blow prior to the Council of Trent.

One thing after another prompted the postponement of the council, and in 1542 war broke out again between Charles V and Francis I. The council, which we shall treat separately later did not actually convene until 1545—twenty-five years after Luther's first calls for a council! Paul III died in 1549. After the brief reigns of Julius III and Marcellus II, Cardinal Caraffa (1476–1559) became Pope Paul IV in 1555.

Paul IV is sometimes termed the first of the Counter-Reformation popes for his dogmatic rigidity and determination to eliminate Protestantism. It was during his pontificate that the Catholic renewal movement centered on repression and earned the label Counter-Reformation. Two of its tools were the *Index of Prohibited Books* and the Inquisition.

Lists of prohibited books had been circulated since 1521, mainly by the theological faculties of Paris and Louvain. It became clear to Paul IV that effective thought control included not only burning authors but also their writings. Thus it was Paul IV who promoted a complete list of heretical works to be universally prohibited. The *Index librorum prohibitorum* was fist published in 1557 by the Congregation of the Inquisition under Paul IV. It was modified in 1564 by the Council of Trent. The list proscribed not only heretical Protestant works but also humanist classics thought to be injurious to morals, such as Boccaccio's *Decameron*. Even the works of Erasmus, who had once been offered a cardinal's hat, were forbidden and then later pubished in bowdlerized versions. The great majority of editions of the bible and the fathers were also prohibited. In 1571 Pius V established a special Congregation of the Index whose duties were transferred to the Holy Office (now titled the Congegation for the Doctrine of the Faith); the *Index* itself was abolished in 1966.

The Inquisition, juridical persecution of heresy by special ecclesial courts, has roots going back to the thirteenth-century proceedings against the Catharist heresy when the church secured the assistance of the secular powers. The Spanish Inquisition was closely tied to the state. In 1478 the pope granted the Spanish sovereigns the right to set up and direct the Inquisition. Inquisitors had power over all religious orders and (after 1531) even over bishops. It has been suggested that the militant orthodoxy and fanatical spirit of the Spanish church resulted from the centuries of combat with Islam. Ferdinand and Isabella established powerful institutional controls against any form of deviation. By 1508 Cardinal Ximénez had not only strengthened the Spanish hierarchy by a kind of rigid moral rearmament but had himself served as Grand Inquisitor. By the 1530s the Inquisition was directed against Erasmians and Lutherans.

Even before becoming pope, Paul IV had been favorably impressed by the Spanish Inquisition's effectiveness and suggested that it be introduced in Italy. Paul III, fearing popular hostility, was less than enthusiastic about the idea but reluctantly allowed the then Cardinal Caraffa to introduce the Inquisition because moderate reform efforts were failing to curb the growth of Protestantism. Caraffa was so eager to begin that he set up interrogation chambers in his own house and exclaimed: "If our own father were a heretic, we would carry the faggots to burn him!" On another occasion he stated: "No man is to lower himself by showing toleration toward any sort of heretic, least of all a Calvinist!"[1]

So the Roman Tribunal was organized. The judges were the customary Dominicans, who were subordinated to six cardinals appointed by the pope to serve as inquisitors general. One of these six men was Cardinal Caraffa. On July 21, 1542, Paul III formally sanctioned the Roman Inquisition and extended its authority to all Christendom. It was an effective instrument so long as the monarch cooperated with it. It was also during this period that the defensive weapon of the Inquisition was supplemented by the offensive weapon of the Jesuits.

Loyola and the Society of Jesus

In his person, Ignatius Loyola (1491–1556) was the embodiment of both the Roman Catholic church and the Counter-Reformation. The youngest of twelve children born to a Basque family of noble lineage, Loyola was trained from his youth in the ideals of the nobility. Although he was much taken by the romances of chivalry, his life as a courtier was less than edifying. Although it may be too harsh to characterize his life in courts and barracks as dissolute, it is not too extreme to say that his life took an abrupt about-face as the result of his volunteering to help defend the city of Pamplona against an advancing French army. At the siege of Pamplona in 1521, during the first of the Hapsburg-Valois wars, a cannonball broke Loyola's right leg and wounded his left. His leg was set by a doctor of the victorious French army, and he was taken back to the family castle to recuperate. There, doctors found that the leg had been badly set and Loyola insisted that the leg be rebroken, reset, and a protruding bone sawed off! The ensuing discomfort and nine months of convalescence gave Loyola occasion for reflection about his life. His physical pain was compounded by his anguish at realizing that his crippling wounds also had crippled his knightly ambitions. Influenced by the reading available to him in the castle, translations of Ludolf of Saxony's *Life of Christ* and *Flowers of the Saints*, Loyola came

[1] L. W. Spitz, *The Renaissance and Reformation Movements*, p. 477.

to the conviction that God wanted him to become a spiritual knight. Loyola's shattered military ambitions found a new outlet: the defense of the church.

In March 1522, on the feast of the Annunciation of the Virgin Mary at Montserrat near Barcelona, Loyola offered his sword to the service of Mary, exchanged clothes with a beggar, and, as he put it, clothed himself "with the armor of Christ." His intention to set out on a pilgrimage to Jerusalem was frustrated by an outbreak of the plague, and he remained for most of the year in ascetic retreat at the nearby cave of Manresa. It was during this period of intense prayer, extreme mortification, and rigorous introspection that he developed the basis for his later famous and influential *Spiritual Exercises.*[2] Although not published until 1548, this guide for developing conformity to God's will was already in use in 1527.

The *Spiritual Exercises* are a four-part series of meditations and rules designed to strengthen and discipline the person's will to conform to and serve the will of God. The first part of the discipline is a systematic consideration of sin and its consequences. The second part presents the significance of the life and kingdom of Christ. The third part focuses on the Passion story, and the fourth part culminates the exercise by meditation on the risen and glorified Christ. The original intention was that the *Exercises* extend over four weeks. Through his exceptional insights into religious psychology, Loyola created a discipline by which he and his followers could direct themselves through progressive resolutions to detest sin, join the ranks of God's disciples, test and confirm their commitment, and actuate their wills toward the pursuit of perfection. This systematic reasoning and meditation included daily self-examination that focused on cultivating a single virtue or attacking a single sinful inclination. This schedule allowed one problem area after another to be conquered in the intended process for reform of the person's life. In a sense, Loyola and his followers anticipated the approach of the eighteenth century Methodists under John Wesley (discussed later).

In contrast to Luther, Loyola perceived the problem of the church not as doctrinal aberration but as personal aberration from the teaching and tradition of the institution. The key to reform of the church, then, for Loyola was the reform of individuals. And the reform of individuals was to take place through the self-mastery of the person's will. By complete self-mastery, the person could then avoid extremes in pursuit of service to God and salvation of self and others. This orientation combined the Renaissance conception and esteem of the individual personality with the late medieval intentionality of the mystics for the perfection of the soul, which in Loyola's military mind meant unquestioning submission to Christ and the church in the person of the pope.

From Manresa, Loyola set out in 1523 for Jerusalem to convert the Muslims but discovered in the process that his intentions needed a solid educational foundation. At thirty years of age he returned to Barcelona and enrolled in a school for boys.

[2]Ignatius Loyola, *Spiritual Exercises*, Anthony Mattola, trans. (Garden City, N.Y.: Doubleday, 1964).

He then went on to the University of Alcalá, where the first group of followers gathered around him. Ironically, he was here suspected of heresy and twice imprisoned by the Spanish Inquisition. Acquitted, he went on to study at Paris in 1528 after a brief sojourn at Salamanca.

In Paris (1528–1535), Loyola earned his Master's degree. Here he also laid the foundations for the Society of Jesus, the Jesuits, with some of his companions who included Diego Lainez, who was to be the next general of the order, Alfonso Salmerón, and Francis Xavier, the great missionary to the Far East. With an oath reminiscent of the medieval Spanish crusades, they swore to dedicate themselves to go to the Holy Land to convert the Muslims.

In 1537 Loyola and his companions met in Venice, were consecrated as priests, and prepared to set out for Jerusalem. These plans were foiled by war between Venice and the Turks, and so they decided to "seek their Jerusalem in Rome." The life of service to the church that Loyola and his small group of companions envisaged was sanctioned by Pope Paul III in 1540. As the last major medieval monastic order, the Society of Jesus was a distinct development that embodied Loyola's appreciation for military organization. The older monastic ideals of contemplation and withdrawal from the world were replaced by Loyola's emphasis on action in the world. This emphasis on the active life required well-educated priests, which in turn led to the well-known long and rigorous training that candidates for the Society went through. This extra training was to interiorize monastic discipline because the Jesuits were not to be isolated in a monastery but active in the world in mission and evangelism. Another distinctive element of the Society of Jesus was that the candidate took not only the three regular vows of poverty, chastity, and obedience, but also a fourth vow: a special vow of obedience to the pope.

It is this special fourth vow of obedience to the pope that starkly highlights Loyola's distance from Luther on reform. To Loyola, the church was the hierarchical church. The authoritarian character of Loyola's understanding of personal relationship to the church is expressed in this vow to go without question or delay wherever the pope ordered for the work of the church. The celebrated thirteenth rule of the *Spiritual Exercises* reads as follows:

> If we wish to proceed securely in all things, we must hold fast to the following principle: What seems to me white, I will believe black, if the hierarchical church so defines. For I must be convinced that in Christ our Lord, the bridegroom, and in his spouse, the church, only one Spirit holds sway, which governs and rules for the salvation of souls.[3]

Loyola's understanding of reform was the epitome of the papalism soon to be defined by the Council of Trent (see Figure 23.2).

[3]Robert McNally, S. J., "Ignatius Loyola," in B. A. Gerrish, ed., *Reformers in Profile*, p. 249.

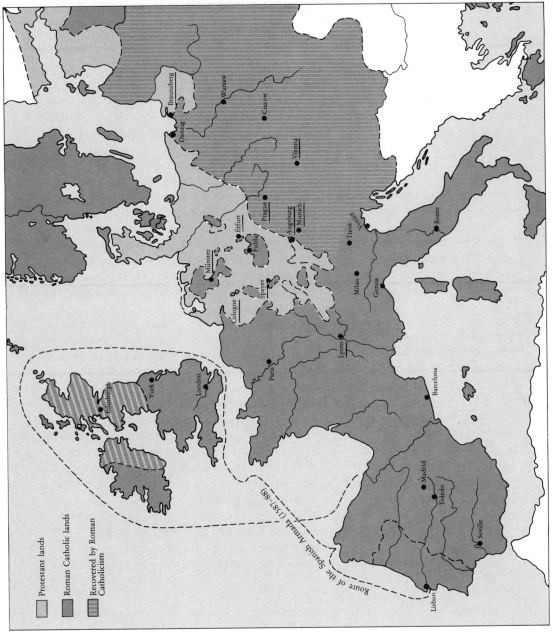

Figure 23.2 The Counter-Reformation (to 1648)

Protestant lands

Roman Catholic lands

Recovered by Roman Catholicism

Route of the Spanish Armada (1587–88)

Braunsberg
Warsaw
Danzig
Cracow
Vienna
Prague
Erfurt
Fulda
Augsburg
Munich
Münster
Speyer
Cologne
Trent
Venice
Rome
Milan
Genoa
Lyons
Paris
Edinburgh
York
London
Barcelona
Madrid
Toledo
Seville
Lisbon

In response to the Reformation, the Jesuits sought to extirpate heresy and win Protestants back to Rome by means of political influence and effective education. Jesuit political influence grew as members of the order gained access to the courts of Europe as confessors to influential persons. In this way, they were effective in inducing political rulers to suppress Protestantism. The Jesuits also placed great emphasis on education, which coupled with their military discipline, promoted both advanced learning and strong devotion to the authority of the church. Loyola himself founded grammar schools and both the Roman College (the Gregorianum) and the German College in Rome and established missions in India, Malaya, Africa, Ethiopia, Brazil, Japan, and China. By Loyola's death in 1556, the order included more than 1,000 members, and by 1600 there were more than 8,000 Jesuits throughout the world.

The Council of Trent (1545–1563)

Loyola's understanding of reform animated the Council of Trent in both its spirit of individual renewal as the key to church renewal and in the fact that members of the Society of Jesus played key roles in the council as papal theologians. The council, as did Loyola himself, illustrated the twin concerns of the Catholic church: self-renewal and opposition to what it regarded as Protestant heresy. The council was convoked in 1545 in a theoretically still-united Christendom; the council closed in 1563 with a Christendom rent by divisions that still affect world Christianity today.

The Council of Trent, sometimes regarded as the most important council since the Council of Nicaea (325), definitively ended medieval hopes for conciliarism. Indeed, Trent was so influential on the mind-set of modern Roman Catholicism that until Vatican II (1962–1965) the church was known as the *Tridentine* (from the Latin for Trent) church. It is with the Council of Trent that the intrinsic contradiction of linking the specific and the universal in the name Roman Catholicism received meaning as a denominational term in contrast to the varieties of Protestant churches. Following the adjournment of the Council of Trent, there was not another ecumenical council for 300 years and that was Vatican I (1869–1870), which concluded one of the problem areas Trent did not resolve—papal authority and infallibility. The other problem area not treated by Trent, the person of Mary, was defined by papal decrees in 1854 (the doctrine of the Immaculate Conception: from conception Mary was free from original sin) and 1950 (the doctrine of the Assumption: on her death Mary was assumed bodily into heaven).

The Council of Trent itself was only reluctantly convoked after numerous delays. Papal reluctance to agree to an ecumenical council was rooted in political and theological concerns. The conciliar movement of the fifteenth century had strongly challenged papal authority when it tried to place the pope under the authority of councils. And Luther's call for a free, Christian council meant a council free of papal domination, with the scriptures rather than tradition as the norm—a demand that the pope obviously found offensive. The long delay in convening this council was also related to the desire of every party to have the council meet in its own territory in order to better control it. The town of Trent in northern Italy was finally chosen because it was technically on German soil and therefore appeased the emperor. Political events also influenced the fact that the council as a whole did not actually meet for the entire period (1545–1563). Instead, there were three distinct assemblies: 1545–1547, 1551–1552, and 1562–1563.

The council opened on December 13, 1545, in the midst of commercial scalpers whose inflated prices for lodging and food (the price of wine increased 30 percent!) expressed their delight at the presence of such an august gathering. Initial attendance at the council was low and included only three legates, one cardinal, four archbishops, twenty-one bishops, and five generals of orders. Most participants were Italians, although there were enough Spanish clergy sensitive to the emperor's wishes to provide difficulty for the curia. On the initial crucial issues of voting and agenda, it was decided that voting would be by individuals and that dogmatic and disciplinary reform issues would be treated concurrently. The voting decision was a specific departure from the practice of the fifteenth-century councils, which had voted by nations. This decision gave the papacy a distinct advantage because Italians at the council outnumbered participants from other nations.

Some of the council fathers favored far-reaching reforms of the church and conciliation with the Protestants. However, the Jesuit papal theologians, Salmerón and Lainez, effectively countered this desire both through their influence as theological advisors and as preachers at the council.

Although the council did not condemn Luther in a formal, judicial sense, its doctrinal decisions were clearly intended to counter the Reformation understanding of the gospel. Against the Reformation watchword of "scripture alone," the fourth session (April 1546) decided that the apostolic traditions must be accepted with the same reverence as scripture: "This truth and teaching are contained in the written books *and* in the unwritten traditions."[4] Thus arose the controversial theological issue of whether scripture and tradition are two equal sources of revelation. The significance of Trent's decision is that the Magisterium, the teaching authority of the Roman church, is the final interpreter of tradition and thus of scripture.

> [T]he council decrees that no one should dare to rely on his own judgment in matters of faith and morals affecting the structure of Christian doctrine and to distort Sacred Scripture to fit meanings of his own that are contrary to the meaning that holy Mother Church has held and now holds; for it is her office to judge about the true sense and interpretation of Sacred Scripture.[5]

[4]John F. Clarkson, S. J., et al., eds. & trans., *The Church Teaches: Documents of the Church in English Translation* (St. Louis: B. Herder, 1955), p. 45. My emphasis.
[5]Clarkson, *The Church Teaches*, p. 46.

This decision was complemented by decreeing Jerome's Vulgate (old Latin) edition of the bible as normative for dogmatic proofs.

In response to the Reformation watchword of "grace alone," the council affirmed the role of human cooperation with grace for salvation. The sixth session, January 1547, set forth the Catholic teaching on justification in sixteen doctrinal chapters and thirty-three canons condemning errors. It is of interest that in affirming the free human cooperation with God's grace in salvation, the council used the very proof text of Zechariah 1:3 ("Return to me, . . . and I will return to you") that Luther had identified as a support of salvation by human activity in his 1516 "Disputation Against Scholastic Theology."

In response to the Reformation emphasis on baptism and the Lord's Supper as the two sacraments of the Christian faith, the seventh session of the council reaffirmed the seven sacraments of baptism, confirmation, Eucharist, penance, extreme unction, holy orders, and matrimony. These sacraments are objectively efficacious, i.e., they effect grace by virtue of their administration (*ex opere operato*). With regard to the Protestant communion with both bread and wine, "Holy Mother Church . . . approves of the custom of communicating under one species [i.e., the bread] and declares that this custom has the force of law." Later, in the thirteenth session (1551), the council reaffirmed the doctrine of transubstantiation.

Emperor Charles V was by now disturbed that the council was ignoring his demands for thoroughgoing reform and was passing decrees that would imperil his concern for Protestant-Catholic reconciliation. To avoid imperial pressure on the council, Pope Paul III took advantage of the presence of a few cases of plague in Trent to induce the majority of prelates to move the council to Bologna in March 1547. Charles made it clear that he thought this was an illegal move, and he proceeded to try to settle the religious controversies in Germany on his own through the Augsburg Interim of 1548. Paul III died in 1549.

In 1551 Pope Julius III recalled the council to Trent. Protestant delegates arrived in January 1552, but they were obviously too late for any influence on the decrees already formulated against the central concerns of the reformers. A Protestant military rally against Charles led to Catholic fears that the Protestants would invade Trent, hence this second assembly was suspended.

The third assembly of the Council of Trent, 1562–1563, met under the skillful diplomacy of Pope Pius IV. By this time, all hope of conciliating the Protestants had evaporated. This assembly took the earlier dogmatic decrees for granted and thereby avoided battles over whether this assembly was a legitimate continuation of the first two assemblies. The bitter debates of this period revolved around reform proposals, especially the obligatory residence of bishops in their sees. Tendencies by the Spanish, the French, and the imperialists to decentralize the church and thus diminish the powers of the papacy were overcome by skillful diplomacy that won the monarchs over to the pope's position. The basis for the ultramontanism (the centralization of authority and influence in the papacy) that culminated in the declaration of papal infallibility in 1870 was thus established. The council itself became a means for renewed rejection of conciliarism by this papal triumph. Although no decree described the power and functions of the papacy, the council submitted the decrees to the pope for his confirmation. On January 26, 1564, the pope issued the bull *Benedictus Deus* confirming the canons and decrees of the Council of Trent. The bull stated that the pope alone had the right to interpret them.

Although the Council of Trent failed to achieve all its goals of reformation of the faith, restoration of morality, and reunion of all Christians, it certainly restored spirit and energy to the Roman church. The decades following the council witnessed renewed theological scholarship and education, moral reform, and spiritual growth as Catholicism responded to Protestantism. Disciplinary decrees of the council stimulated biblical preaching and the establishment of seminaries to provide an educated clergy for pastoral work. A variety of moral reforms was also carried out with regard to clerical celibacy and chastity and the residency and faithfulness of bishops.

The Catholic reform movement was essentially personal. The church was to be transformed by transforming its members, and its members were to be transformed by a transformed elite leadership. The emphasis on personal spiritual renewal was the emphasis of both tridentine reforms and Loyola's Jesuits. But this renewal of prayer, penance, and spiritual and corporal works of mercy, important as it was, neglected liturgical reform. The heroic stature of individuals such as Loyola could not substitute for the centrality of public, corporate worship that Luther and other Protestant reformers had recovered. Liturgical reform and hymnody were crucial to the Protestant reformers, but the Catholic reformers remained liturgically indifferent. Late sixteenth-century Catholic worship still preserved the highly clerical complexion it had received in the Middle Ages. Of course, Catholic worship did not lack festival, drama, and artistry, but the corporate biblical emphases revived by Luther, Zwingli, Calvin, and others remained in the shadows. The spirituality of Catholic reform was the ascetical, subjective, and personal piety exemplified by such mystical athletes as Teresa of Avila (d. 1582) and John of the Cross (d. 1591) and their baroque artistic expressions exemplified by Bernini's striking sculpture "St. Teresa in Ecstasy" (1646) and the paintings "Christ on the Cross" and "Resurrection" by El Greco (d. 1614). Indeed, it may be argued that baroque art expressed the triumph of the tridentine Counter-Reformation, for in its form it manifested control over seemingly turbulent forces, and in its content it focused on the emphases of the Counter-Reformation: Mary, the saints, Corpus Christi processions, and regnant popes with the keys of St. Peter.

Chapter 24

LEGACIES OF THE REFORMATION

One of the consequences of the Reformation in general and the Council of Trent in particular was the splintering of western Christendom. The legacies of this fragmentation of the medieval *Corpus Christianum* have affected every aspect of modern life and thought. Because the rest of this book discusses these legacies, the following survey is intended to be suggestive rather than definitive.

Theology

The decisions of the Council of Trent on justification, scripture, and the sacraments made so definitive the divisions that had arisen in the Reformation that hopes for a reunited Christian church would not begin flickering again until the ecumenical movement of the twentieth century. By the conclusion of the Council of Trent, there was a second generation of reformers whose memories of the "one, holy, catholic, and apostolic church" had receded behind the vivid present impressions of the martyrs and confessors of their own particular communities. Loyalty to the "fathers" of the church now came increasingly to mean loyalty to the confessions of faith of the previous generation. Conversations between and even among the churches consisted largely of mutual condemnations and anathemas. The intensity and rancor of these theological and ecclesial conflicts is reflected in Philip Melanchthon's sigh on his deathbed that finally he was being delivered from the *rabies theologorum* (the "madness of the theologians").

The competitiveness of the churches led to both an "edifice" complex and a kind of siege mentality. Protestant theologians became so involved in constructing theological systems to protect their churches and to wall off alternatives that the late sixteenth and early seventeenth centuries came to be known as the period of Protestant Orthodoxy, or Scholasticism. Both Lutherans and Calvinists developed theories of verbal and plenary inspiration to safeguard the sole authority of scripture against the Catholics' use of tradition on the one hand and the dissidents' use of experience and "inner light" on the other hand. The reformers' original understanding of faith as trust and confidence in God's promise shifted in the heat of battle to understanding faith in terms of intellectual assent to correct doctrine. The resulting highly rationalized schemata of salvation are exemplified by the Elizabethan Puritan, William Perkins's (1558–1602) chart of election and reprobation. This rationalistic and creed-bound Protestantism contributed to the developments of rationalism, Deism, and Pietism that fed the Enlightenment of the eighteenth and nineteenth centuries.

Politics

The Reformation introduced into western culture the problem of pluralism—religious, social, and cultural. The modern world is still struggling with this legacy in its classrooms and courtrooms and on its streets and battlefields. It should not be surprising that the people of the sixteenth century found it exceedingly difficult to live with alternative and competing commitments. The first response was to compel conformity, but religious commitments were not easily swayed by laws and force. In some cases Protestant triumphalism contributed to the development of a "chosen nation" syndrome. England's overcoming of the threats of the Spanish Armada (1588) and the recusant (English Catholic rejection of the Anglican church) conspiracy to blow up the houses of Parliament and the king (the Gunpowder Plot, 1605) were interpreted in terms of God's election and blessing of the nation, and subsequent centuries contributed to the messianic sense of the United States as a "city set on a hill" with a "manifest destiny."

Another response was to assert the rights of the individual conscience. In various ways, Luther's statement to the emperor at the Diet of Worms in 1521 has had political echoes ever since: ". . . [M]y conscience is captive to the Word of God. I cannot and will not retract anything, for it is neither safe nor right to go against conscience. I cannot do otherwise, here I stand, may God help me, Amen."[1] Later Luther was equally adamant in defending the freedom of faith against both the theological right (the pope) and left (Karlstadt and Müntzer): "I will constrain no man by force, for faith must come freely without compulsion."[2] Soon Lutheran jurists and theologians were developing constitutional and theological arguments for the resistance of lesser magistrates to the emperor's coercion of the faith of his sub-

[1] LW, Vol. 32, pp. 112–113.
[2] LW, Vol. 51, p. 77.

jects. Political resistance was also defended in the Lutheran Madgeburg Confession (1550–1551), which in turn influenced French Calvinist political thought. Huguenot arguments for a constitutionalism that limited royal power and defended individual conscience were advanced by Francois Hotman's *Franco-Gallia* (1573), Theodore Beza's *Right of Magistrates* (1574), and Phillippe du Plessis-Mornay's more radical *Vindication Against Tyrants* (1579), which authorized individual rebellion on the explicitly religious grounds that God may "raise up new liberators" outside the constitutional framework. The authority of kings became relative before God, the king of kings.

The Reformation legacy to politics was rooted not merely in the defense of conscience against compulsion, however. Many of the doctrinal positions of the Reformation contributed to the rise of a democratic ethos. Luther's translation of the bible and his emphasis on universal education to facilitate reading it, a path followed by other reformers as well, was a step toward depriving the elite of exclusive control over words as well as the Word. The doctrine of the priesthood of all the baptized proclaimed that the ordained priest or minister is distinguished from all other Christians only by office. For Luther, the church is no longer a hierarchical institution but a community of believers in which "no one is for himself, but extends himself among others in love." Thus he translated *ecclesia* not as "church" (*Kirche*) but as "community" (*Gemeinde*), "congregation" (*Gemeine*), and "assembly" (*Versammlung*). The Calvinist idea of the church as a covenanted community contributed to the idea of social contract. These antihierarchical, leveling processes were corrosive of political as well as ecclesial structures. Politically, the Reformers' goal was the social experience of communion. As John Knox declared: "Take from us the freedom of assemblies and [you] take from us the evangel."[3]

Culture

The Reformation touched every aspect of culture: work, economics, art, literature, and music. The doctrine of justification by grace alone through faith alone released energy for this world that had hitherto been devoted to achieving the next world. With their new ethos of vocation or calling, the Reformers undercut the medieval dualism of sacred and secular. In the medieval world, only the religious (priests, monks, nuns) had a sacred vocation or calling from God. Those who worked in the secular world were understood by all to be on a lower and less God-pleasing plane. The Reformers now emphasized that whatever a person did in the world that served the neighbor and helped build up the human community was pleasing to God. All mundane tasks from changing diapers to changing laws were now imbued with religious significance not because human works are salvatory but because God intends

[3]L. W. Spitz, *The Renaissance and Reformation Movements*, p. 552.

neighbors to be served. As Luther once explained his own ministry: "A cow does not get to heaven by giving milk, but that is what she is made for."[4]

Nowhere was this understanding of vocation applied more explosively to medieval life than in the area of sex and marriage. According to the historian Steven Ozment: "No institutional change brought about by the Reformation was more visible, responsive to late medieval pleas for reform, and conducive to new social attitudes than the marriage of Protestant clergy. Nor was there another point in the Protestant program where theology and practice corresponded more successfully."[5] The Reformers vigorously criticized the Roman church's imposition of celibacy on priests, monks, and nuns because men and women were thereby removed from service to the neighbor, the divine order of marriage and family was contravened, and the created goodness of sexuality was denied. Marriage was not just the legitimation of sexual fulfillment but above all the context for creating a new awareness of human community with all its pains and joys. So Luther declared: "Marriage does not only consist of sleeping with a woman—anybody can do that—but of keeping house and bringing up children."[6] Thus the Reformation not only saw in marriage a new, joyous appreciation for sexual drives but also a new respect for women as companions.

Perhaps the point at which the Reformers' proclamation of vocation has received the most attention in the modern world is where religion and economics intersect. Since the publication in 1904–1905 of Max Weber's *The Protestant Ethic and the Spirit of Capitalism*, it has been popular to associate capitalism with Calvinism. The Weber thesis is that Calvinist theology so stressed predestination that anxious believers began to seek signs of their election in their success in vocation. In response to this thesis, it should be noted that the profit economy or early forms of capitalism clearly antedated the Reformation and that Calvin did not associate material success with the individual's standing before God. Calvin's understanding of predestination and providence was not individualistic but communal and world-historical. The doctrine of predestination is an affirmation that despite evil and suffering the ultimate destiny of the world and history rests in the good and infallible hands of God.

Calvin's theology was communal not individualistic. Therefore, he could perceive riches as a divine blessing not in terms of endorsement of the individual but rather as a blessing to be shared with the whole community. Conversely, poverty is an expression of the wrath of God not toward the individual but toward the whole community for sin and thus to be borne by the whole community by its alleviation of the plight of the poor. The "blame the victim/praise the achiever" ideology of modern times is a secularized and individualized kind of covenant theology. The biblical answer to this form of "Deuteronomic history," which attributes failure and poverty to intrinsic character flaws and success to moral quality, is the Book of Job.

---

[4]Roland Bainton, *Here I Stand: A Life of Martin Luther* (New York: Mentor Books, 1957), p. 299.
[5]Steven Ozment, *The Age of Reform 1250–1550* (New Haven, Conn: Yale University Press, 1980), p. 381.
[6]LW, Vol. 54, p. 441.

The Reformation answer is to recall the vigorous attacks Luther and Calvin made on capitalism as unrestrained greed, as well as their continual calls for government control of capitalism. On the other hand, Luther and Calvin both contributed to the development of modern social welfare. Urban and state welfare programs were instituted that were sensitive to structural causes of unemployment and underemployment, job training, and civic responsibility for preventing as well as alleviating poverty.

Education and Science

The Reformation doctrines of justification and vocation also had an impact on the development of education and the sciences. Building on the contributions of the humanists, the Reformers stressed education as the resource for preparing persons for service to the whole community. It was not accidental that universal literacy was first achieved in Scotland and the Protestant areas of Germany. As Melanchthon declared, "the ultimate end which confronts us is not private virtue alone but the interest of the public weal." And by 1560 Knox and his colleagues had drawn up a vision for a natural system of education in Scotland.

It may be argued that Luther's greatest contribution was not his tracts on such practical subjects as that towns should establish schools and public libraries and that parents should make sure that their children went to school but his initiation of a new way of thinking. In our time it has become fashionable to call a major shift in thinking a "paradigm shift." Luther's thorough rejection of Aristotle and classical "authorities" is no less than a paradigm shift from medieval epistemology (theory of knowledge) based on deduction from textual authorities to an epistemology of induction and experience. In his theological context, Luther stated: "It is not by understanding, reading, or speculation that one becomes a theologian, but through living, dying, and being damned."[7] Less dramatically, he also said: "None of the arts can be learned without practice. What kind of physician would that be who stayed in school all the time? When he finally puts his medicine to use and deals more and more with nature, he will come to see that he hasn't as yet mastered the art."[8] This shift from deduction to induction was recognized by contemporaries who called the maverick physician Paracelsus (1493–1541) "the Luther of the physicians." The point was that Paracelsus shared Luther's view of authority. Similarly, the English thinker Francis Bacon (1561–1626) compared Aristotle to Antichrist and indicted Greek philosophers for conjuring scientific knowledge out of their heads instead of seeking it in nature.

Institutionally, Luther and Melanchthon were instrumental in the development

[7]*D. Martin Luthers Werke*, Vol. 5 (Weimar, 1883), p. 163.
[8]LW, Vol. 54, pp. 50–51.

of the medical faculty at the University of Wittenberg. Melanchthon's son-in-law Casper Peucer (1525–1602) was a physician as well as a theologian. By the seventeenth century, the University of Wittenberg had a renowned medical faculty. The turn away from the old authorities was evident in the important contributions of Salomon Alberti (1540–1600) in anatomical studies and the contributions of other colleagues to botany.

Ironically, the theological controversies after the death of Luther also contributed to the development of science. For example, Johannes Kepler (1571–1630) was not accepted for ordained ministry because his theology of the Lord's Supper was not regarded as orthodox. He then became an assistant to the Danish Lutheran astronomer Tycho Brahe (1546–1601). In spite of his disappointment over rejection for the ministry, Kepler wrote in his first publication, "I wanted to become a theologian. For a long time I was restless. Now, however, observe how through my efforts, God is being celebrated in astronomy."[9] Kepler went on to influence Newton and to contribute to the triumph of the Copernican over the Ptolemaic theory of planetary motion.

Similarly, the Royal Society of London focused on scientific studies because they were free from both dogmatism and scepticism. Yet Kepler spoke for many of his scientific colleagues when he described scientists as "thinking God's thoughts after him."[10] By and large these were religious men zealous to discover and admire the works of God in nature.

Literature and the Arts

From the beginning of the Reformation, historiography played an important role. Luther used history to argue that the papacy of his day was an aberration from the early church, martyrologists such as John Foxe selectively used history to present their case for the truth and witness of Protestantism, and the dissidents argued that the entire church had fallen when it became the establishment under Constantine in the fourth century. The first comprehensive history of the church was not only equally biased but dull to boot. In thirteen volumes the *Magdeburg Centuries* under the general editorship of the Lutheran theologian Matthew Flacius (1520–1575) covered the first thirteen centuries of the church from the viewpoint that the pope was the Antichrist whose empire of the Roman church had constantly opposed the work of God. The Catholic response was the equally biased and dull *Ecclesiastical Annals* by Caesar Baronius (1538–1607), which appeared in numerous volumes between

[9]Bruce Wrightsman, "Lutheranism and the Protestant Synthesis: Religion and Science in America", in John E. Groh & Robert H. Smith, eds., *The Lutheran Church in North American Life* (St. Louis, 1979), p. 66.
[10]L. W. Spitz, *The Renaissance and Reformation Movements*, p. 588.

1588–1607. Although these histories were designed to make history serve their respective theologies, they did stimulate the development of historical criticism.

National literatures were influenced by their respective great reformers. There are too many major contributions even to list them here, other than to mention the Elizabethan dramatist William Shakespeare (1564–1616), whose literary brilliance and insight into humankind remains unequaled. In music, too, the Reformation stimulated compositions that continue to enrich modern life. The Reformers' concern for making the liturgy accessible to the people was supplemented by their love for music as a glorious gift of God. Many of Luther's hymns continue to be well known and sung today, especially "A Mighty Fortress Is Our God," which informed later works by Bach and Mendelssohn. The scope and complexity of the legacies of the Reformation prompt appreciation for Thomas Carlyle's disclaimer: "Listening from the distance of centuries across the death chasms and howling kingdoms of decay, it is not easy to catch everything."[11]

[11]Cited by Lewis W. Spitz, *The Renaissance and Reformation Movements* (Chicago: Rand McNally & Company, 1971), p. 547.

Part Four

European Christianity Confronts the Modern Age

Jean-Loup Seban

Chapter 25

THE CONSOLIDATION
OF ORTHODOX BELIEF

———

European Politics at the Turn of the Seventeenth Century

The Ottoman Empire from 1571 to 1683

The destiny of Christendom was closely related to that of its powerful neighbor, the Ottoman Empire, which spread over three continents from Algiers to Baghdad and from Mecca to Budapest. The sultan reigned over 14 million subjects, and his capital Istanbul, with 800,000 souls, was by 1650 the world's largest city. The Turks represented a threefold threat to Christendom: (1) religiously, by competition through the propagation of Islam; (2) economically, by controlling the Mediterranean Sea; and (3) politically, through an expansionist policy supported by a powerful army. For geopolitical reasons the papacy, Spain, Venice, Austria, and Moscovia were at the forefront of the action. The naval victory of John of Austria over Turks at Lepanto in 1571 had far-reaching consequences for the political, religious, and intellectual life of Christendom. Besides securing the borders of a small, compact Christendom, it also released Spain from being the European watchdog, thereby enabling her to concentrate her efforts on the internal European scene. Indeed, the Castillian monarchy, the most archaic of all feudal societies, had accidentally risen to world power through the exploitation of American silver and had become the champion of the Counter-Reformation. On the whole, the Spanish leadership in the Roman Catholic strategy for political and religious reconquest met with success in Mediterranean Europe. It failed, however, against the English, against the secessionist Dutch who freed themselves from Spanish rule in 1587, and against the German Protestant principalities.

A third consequence of the victory of Lepanto was a change in frame of mind.

427

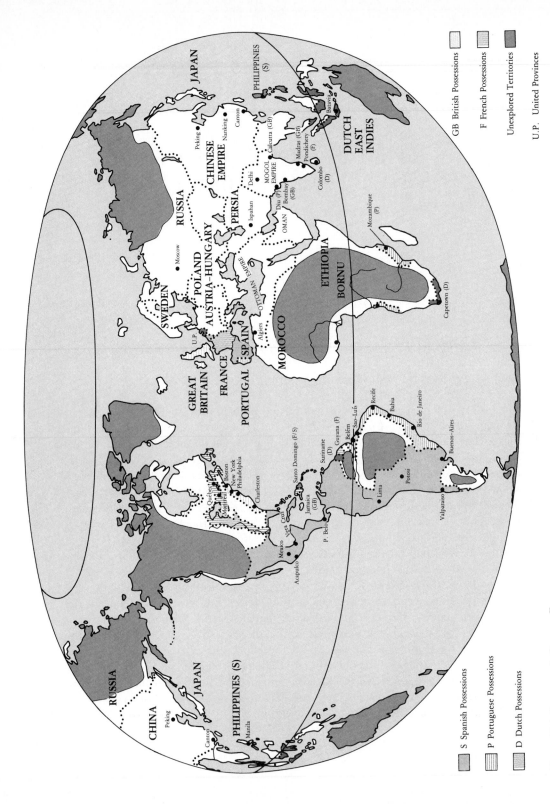

Figure 25.1 Seventeenth Century Europe

Life in a compact Christian world, currently secure yet permanently threatened by the infidels, aroused a siege mentality. Quite understandably, Christian Europeans strove to preserve their cultural and spiritual heritage and, as expected, turned to authoritarian systems of government and belief. The venturesome, cosmopolitan, and hedonistic spirit of the Renaissance gave way to a doctrinaire, parochial, and Stoic spirit that crystallized in seventeenth-century orthodox belief, rationalist world views, and absolutist regimes. Similarly, another victory over the Turks a century later propelled European minds in the opposite direction. The reintegration of Danubian Europe into Christendom after the battle of Kahlenberg, near Vienna in 1683, marked the beginning of a new way of thinking, the enlightened mentality. Among other causes, the territorial expansion of Christendom to the east brought about a new idea: that of ongoing progress. The spiritual and cultural values of the Renaissance therefore benefited from a second birth, and the constraining and conservative frame of mind of the seventeenth century was superseded by cosmopolitanism, toleration, and libertinism. Just as the spirit of the Reformers triumphed in the seventeenth century, so also the mentality of the Renaissance triumphed in the eighteenth century in the form of an enlightened mentality.

The World Powers

During the first decade of the seventeenth century, two world powers were falling into political decline: the Ottoman Empire, which suffered from the inability of the sultans, and Spain, whose cities were progressively depopulated and whose trade monopoly was lost for the most part to northern European countries, although Spain still administered to an immense colonial empire. In western Europe, the powers on the rise were, first and above all, France, which finally emerged from eight internecine religious wars. The recently enthroned Bourbon dynasty was centralizing political decision-making while pursuing a politics of conquest. The second was England, which had gained maritime domination after having defeated the Spanish armada in 1588. Third were the United Provinces (northern Low Countries), the merchant fleet of which was by far the largest.

In northern Europe, the Swedish crown controlled the Baltic Sea, and in central Europe the Austrian Hapsburgs were expanding their territorial possessions eastward and strengthening their political hold over the religiously and politically divided Holy Roman Empire. Finally, in eastern Europe, Moscovia (Russia) was beginning a long and difficult recovery owing to the accession to power of the Romanovs in 1613, while Poland's golden age was slowly fading away. At the outset of the seventeenth century, there were two major players on the European political chessboard: Spain and France. And at its close there were three: France, England, and Austria.

The Rise of the Absolutist State

At the turn of the seventeenth century, throughout Europe the princely state of the Renaissance had consolidated its hold and considerably expanded its sovereignty. The monarch commanded the armed forces, imposed and spent taxes, controlled public life, and set public policy by enacting laws. The strengthening of the monarchic principle was part of the general growth of the national identity. However, it aroused resistance that occasionally turned into open revolt. Provinces, ethnic groups, feudal families, chartered royal or imperial cities, representative institutions (assemblies, diets, estates) and above all, the church as a quasi-autonomous power, all experienced the erosion of their autonomy by monomonarchism. Therefore, social and political rebellions multiplied by the midseventeenth century. The victory of the crown over the rebels and representative institutions (Cortes, Diet, Parliament, Estates General) evolved in most cases to the unrestricted advantage of the monarch. Except for England, Poland, and the United Provinces, absolutism became the standard European form of government. Political theorists provided the doctrinal basis for absolutism through a modified theory of the divine right of kings, and the churches either rallied or coerced the moral and spiritual support for the absolutist state.

Socioeconomic Life

Demography between 1600 and 1740

The period between 1600 and 1740 was characterized by demographic stability. Europe no longer suffered catastrophic losses of population, as was the case during the great plague of the fourteenth century, nor had Europe yet experienced a population boom comparable to that of the second half of the eighteenth century. Warfare, such as the Thirty Years War, and occasional plagues, both of which continued to drain Europe of manpower, still did not exhaust its population as in previous centuries. One can venture a rough estimate of European population: 80 million by 1500; 105 million by 1600; and 115 million by 1700. The population of some states decreased. For example, Spain underwent massive emigration to its American colonies and began an irreversible economic decline. Others such as England almost doubled their population between 1500 and 1700. Of all European countries, France was the most heavily populated, with about 21 million. The Holy Roman Empire of the German nation followed with 15 million; the Italian peninsula with 13 million; and Poland with 10 million. The Hapsburg states (Austria, Bohemia, and Hungary) totaled 8 million. Spain, which had expatriated its Morisco population, numbered 6 million. The United Provinces rose to world economic power with no more than 2 million inhabitants. Scandinavia counted 3 million, and England had 5 million inhabitants at best. And in the far east, Moscovia extended its empire to more than 18 million people by 1700. Why was there no significant increase in population during that period? The European demographic system was regulated by four factors: (1) low nuptiality due to a high celibacy rate for religious, social, or economic reasons; (2) collective marital asceticism on either economic (England) or religious (neo-Augustinianism in France) grounds; (3) the delay in the age of marriage, which reached 25 years for women and 27 for men; and (4) the high rate of infant and child mortality.

Commerce

After steady economic growth since the close of the fifteenth century, European economies were passing through a period of pause at the turn of the seventeenth century. Besides, colonial trade was beginning to profit northern European states. Maritime routes, which up to this time had been controlled by the Portugese, the Spanish, and the Venetians, were progressively passing under Dutch, English, and French control. By the 1620s, the spice trade was mostly in the hands of the Dutch. Amsterdam had become the European center of the East and West Indies trade, and the Bank of Amsterdam, founded in 1609, was now the leading European banking institution. The shift of economic power from the south to the north of Europe meant that the Protestants had the means to withstand the huge effort of the recatholicization of Europe championed at first by picaresque and theocratic Spain and later by the Austrian Hapsburgs.

Social Transformations

The expansion of the princely state produced a new social class of courtiers, administrators, and officers who operated the centralizing process at every level of government. Ministers such as Thomas Cromwell (England), Richelieu and Colbert (France), Oxenstierna (Sweden), Perez and Olivares (Spain), and Pombal (Portugal) epitomized the new sociopolitical pattern. All of them were at the origin of the modern statism. However, of all social classes the bourgeoisie was the true beneficiary of the economic, social, and political mutations. They increased their wealth, became landowners, provided lawyers and magistrates to the crown, and sought peace and prosperity. In Catholic Europe, the bourgeoisie gave its generous contribution to charitable work. In Protestant Europe, it encouraged a pious, austere, puritan religion. On the whole, the bourgeoisie valued comfort, manners, and learning. One of its achievements was the promotion of the dignity of women. The women of the bourgeoisie were well mannered, well read, and often tenacious businesswomen. They took their destiny into their own hands more than in other social classes.

The Religious and Cultural Climate

The Religious Fronts

In the wake of the religious explosion of the sixteenth century, Christendom was divided into four major fronts: the Roman Catholic, the Lutheran, the Anglican, and the Calvinist. One could add a fifth front formed by the variegated and diffuse sectarian movements. On the strength of the successful reaffirmation of traditional belief at the Council of Trent (1545–1563), the Roman Catholic church had begun during the last decades of the sixteenth century a comprehensive process of internal reorganization, reinforcement of discipline, and reconquest of lost ground in France, Austria, Bohemia, and Poland. In the Italian and Iberian peninsulas and in southern Germany, the Roman Catholic church consolidated its hold. The Book of Concord (1580) defined doctrinally the Lutheran front, which covered central and northern Germany and the Scandinavian countries. Elizabethan England finally enforced the peculiar English way of combining Catholic liturgy and piety with reformed theology by the adoption of the Thirty-Nine Articles of Religion in 1572, which became the "Charter of Anglicanism." As regards the Calvinist front, which spread over western and central Europe—Geneva, the Rhine, the United Provinces, and Scotland, with pockets in France, Hungary, and Poland— and which had produced numerous confessional documents, it gave itself a strong identity in 1580 with the Discipline and in 1618 with the Canons of Dort. One of the most fascinating of the religious phenomena of the age was without a doubt the revival of the sectarian movements. Besides the long-established Bohemian Hussites, who refused catholicization and Germanization altogether, there were movements that formed either communities, like the "Unitas Fratrum" or Bohemian Brethren, the Polish Brethren, the Dutch Anabaptists, the English Puritans, Independents, and Baptists, or associations such as the Rosicrucians and the mystics of Germany, who cultivated close relations with alchemists and pantheist theosophers. These sectarian movements questioned the tenets of orthodox belief and therefore, in most instances, were subjected to inhumane repression.

Compared with the macrocosm of Tridentine Catholicism, secessionist Protestantism resembled a mosaic of antagonistic microcosms. Lutheranism, Calvinism, and Anglicanism asserted their respective orthodoxies at each others' expense and at the cost of sectarian movements, united only in their common anti-Romanism and hatred for freethinkers. Like Tridentine Catholicism, seventeenth-century Protestantism blossomed on a soil of religious intolerance.

Cultural Mutations

One of the aims of the reformers of the sixteenth century was to bring the laity closer to the bible. By providing translations in contemporary languages or vernaculars, they contributed to the birth of national literatures. England with Marlowe and Shakespeare, and France with Clement Marot, Ronsard and Rabelais offer two outstanding examples. Owing to Luther's *Bible*, a Germanic dialect became the German language. In the Iberian peninsula, where the Catholic Reformation triumphed religiously and culturally, Cervantes and Lope de Vega propelled Spanish literature to its zenith. Further developments in mathematics and astronomy, especially the rejection of the official Aristotelian astronomy for the Copernican heliocentric astronomy, brought about a scientific revolution that later modified the picture of the world and engendered the so-called crisis of European consciousness. Scientific studies were stimulated by the foundation of Gresham College in London in 1597 and the creation of the Accademia dei Lincei in Rome in 1603. The initial impetus had been given by late Renaissance Italian naturalist philosophers. In northern Europe, it was Francis Bacon's *Advancement of Learning* (1605) that directed the inquiring mind along the experimental track. René Descartes's *Discourse on Method* (1631) thus became the philosophical manifesto of the age. In a now famous passage, the German romantic philosopher Hegel hailed Descartes as the originator of the intellectual revolution that gave birth to the modern age.

The furthering of such a new knowledge was not without risk. By dismantling the medieval Aristotelian-biblical synthesis, most innovators were indeed challenging some tenets of orthodox belief and thereby jeopardizing the credibility and authority of the church. Giordano Bruno's death at the stake in Venice in 1600, Galileo's notorious trials, and the fate of both the Dominican Tommaso Campanella (1568–1639), an empiricist, and the Moravian bishop Comenius (1592–1670) remind us of how repressive the alliance of religious superstition, cultural prejudice, and political faction can be. An advocate of Copernican astronomy, the Dominican Bruno (ca. 1548–1600) was bold enough to contemplate the possibility of innumerable worlds and to lean toward pantheism. As for Galilei Galileo (1564–1642), who stands as a martyr to the cause of free scientific inquiry, his life would have ended the usual way had he not enjoyed the protection of the enlightened pope, Urban VIII. As his accusers, Cardinal Bellarmino and the Jesuits, rightly perceived, Galileo's heliocentric astronomy and corpuscular physics sapped the authority of the church in matters of astronomy and eucharistic theology. Galileo's atomist physics led to the denial of the distinction between substance and accidents, so essential to the doctrine of transubstantiation. Galileo's retraction saved the church's image. Yet, it was a Pyrrhic victory, because by the close of the seventeenth century scientists and freethinkers had won the war in northern Europe. In southern Europe, however, the cost of the church's triumph was heavy. Any significant cultural development was halted for more than a century.

Fine Arts and Music

In the domains of both fine arts and music, the Italian city-states remained in the lead. The dome of St. Peter's of Rome was eventually completed in 1593 by Giacomo della Porta, just in time for the jubilee of 1600. By that time, two new trends had made their debut.

While in Rome, Caravaggio (1569–1609) was launching the naturalist style in painting, in opposition to the mannerism of the age. In Florence the Camerata—a group of musicians—advocated a novel style (*stile moderno*) which emphasized the emotional and the dramatic by contrast with the constraining polyphony of the late Renaissance. Caravaggio's realistic approach inevitably aroused a polemic with the Carracci family, whose mannerist style continued painting grandiose and magnificent scenes aimed at inspiring noble virtues. The Caravaggio-Carracci controversy, which was echoed throughout Europe, prefigured the long-lasting quarrel between the classicists and the advocates of the baroque.

With Palestrina (ca. 1525–1594) at St. Peter's of Rome (*Missa Papae Marcelli*), Cabezon (1510–1566) and Victoria (1548–1611) at Madrid, Hofhaimer (1459–1537) at Salzburg, the Flemish Lassus (ca. 1530–1594), the Anglicans Tallis (1505–1585) and Byrd (1543–1623), the Lutheran Praetorius (1571–1621), and the Calvinist Goudimel (ca. 1514–1572), the late Renaissance marked undoubtedly the golden age of polyphony. Owing to Guillaume de Machault (ca. 1300–1377) and Josquin des Près (1440–1521), polyphony had superseded the homophony of the Gregorian chant by the fifteenth century. Because the Camerata Fiorentina intended to apply the rules of rhetoric to music, a novel music genre was devised to that end. Polyphony was thus replaced by monody. In the year 1598 the Camerata Fiorentina released its first production: the first opera ever composed, *Daphne*, by Corsi and Peri. Three years later Caccini (ca. 1545–1618) unfolded in *Nuove Musiche* the principles of the so-called representative style (*stile rappresentativo*), a forerunner of the bel canto, which was successfully promoted by Claudio Monteverdi (1567–1643). Besides composing madrigals, laments, and operas, Monteverdi devoted much of his creative genius, at Mantua first and later at Venice, to sacred music, assimilating and refining both styles, the antique (polyphony) and the modern (monody), and embellishing the Roman Catholic liturgy with Masses, motets, psalms, and other vocal pieces of incomparable beauty (*Madrigali spirituali*, 1583; *Vespro della Beata Virgine*, and *Selva morale et spirituale*, 1610).

Catholics, Anglicans, and Lutherans all benefited, although differently, from another musical genre also born in the Italian peninsula in the 1620s, namely the cantata. Cognate with the opera, although unstaged, the cantata is a profane or sacred poem for one or several voices combining arias and recitatives. During the baroque period, which spanned 1600–1750, the cantata was the most successful genre of vocal chamber music. Giacomo Carissimi (1605–1674), Alessandro Scarlatti (1660–1725), and Antonio Vivaldi (1678–1741) excelled in this genre. In Lutheran Germany, the *Kantate* became an integral musical component of the service. Dietrich Buxtehude (1637–1707), Johann Sebastian Bach (1685–1750), and Georg Philipp Telemann (1681–1767) were the sublime masters of German sacred cantata.

Meanwhile, in the Italian peninsula, the followers of Filippo Neri, the Oratorians, had adopted the sacred cantata as a means for the propagation of their moralizing religion. The extended sacred cantata, usually based on a nonliturgical text and named after them "oratorio," became a predominant genre of vocal sacred music from the time of Carissimi, who composed about sixteen of them, to that of Joseph Haydn (1732–1809), the representative of Viennese classicism with Mozart and Beethoven. A profuse composer, Haydn left about twelve Masses, a *Te Deum* (1800), a few oratorios (*The Seven Last Words*, 1796; *The Creation*, 1798), as well as innumerable symphonies. With the supreme masters of baroque music, J. S. Bach and George Frederick Handel (1685–1759), the oratorio genre reached its peak. Among the thirty-one oratorios composed by Handel, *Esther* (1718), *Athalia* (1733), *Saul* (1739), *Messiah* (1742), *Solomon* (1749), *Jephtha* (1752), and *The Triumph of Time and Truth* (1757) stand out as incomparable masterpieces. Bach's oratorio-passions (*St. John's Passion*, 1724; *St. Matthew's Passion*, 1727) and the *Christmas Oratorio* (1734) magnify Lutheran piety.

Superstition and Witchcraft

In the seventeenth century, the Christian churches were more than ever confronted with a twofold phenomenon: on the one hand the skepticism of the learned freethinker that dared to come into the open, and on the other the credulity of the ignorant that exploitation by baroque piety tended to stimulate. By mid-century, witchcraft cases proliferated in England, the Rhineland, Burgundy, and southern Germany. The drowning of alleged witches in rural areas and exorcisms of the demon-possessed in urban convents were common practices of the age, which freethinkers were first in denouncing. Because of the supernatural component of every religious belief, of practices such as processions and veneration of relics, and of the specific function of Satan in Christian doctrine and iconography, the struggle that Tridentine Catholicism—the form of Catholicism shaped by the Council of Trent— and Protestant orthodoxy waged against every form of superstition was ambiguous and largely unsuccessful. The downfall of superstition eventually resulted from the diffusion of the enlightened mentality.

The Jesuits' Spectacular Success

No religious order has been more spectacularly successful in its undertaking than the Society of Jesus; none has aroused more envy and hatred throughout Catholic and Protestant Christendom alike than those soldiers of Christ who were so daring as to penetrate the Forbidden City, Peking, the heart of the Celestial Empire. The militant church, as they defined themselves in their constitution, waged a theological and political struggle against the Protestant heresy in the parts of Europe already won over or still under threat. In competition with the Dominicans, Franciscans, and Capuchins, the Jesuits started new mission fields on the maritime routes opened up by the Portuguese and the Spanish. Missionaries were sent to the Americas, the Congo, India, Japan, China, Indochina, and the Philippines. The Spaniard Francisco de Xavier (1506–1552), Loyola's companion, took Christian belief to Nagasaki at a time when Buddhism was declining, and the Italian Matteo Ricci (1552–1610) established the first Christian community in Peking in 1601. The martyrdom of the French Jean de Brebeuf, who was tortured to death by the Iroquois in New France (Canada) in 1649, illustrates the heroic determination of the militant church. As a result, two opposite patterns of Christianization were competing: the American pattern based on the practice of the *tabula rasa*, or erasing of indigenous beliefs, and the Asian pattern, devised by the Jesuits, which consisted in adapting Christian belief to local cultural traditions.

By the time of Loyola's death in 1559, the Society was already 1,000 members strong and possessed about a hundred houses or foundations. When Pope Clement XIV suppressed the Society in 1773, the Jesuits were divided into thirty-nine provinces and administered 800 colleges caring for more than 200,000 students. Of the 23,000 existing Jesuits, 15,000 were teachers. Their influence on European culture had been paramount.

What are the reasons for such success? There are basically three: the structure of the institution, the doctrine, and the educational policy. Organized almost militarily, with a general in command of the whole order and provincials supervising regions, and endowed with a discipline stressing obedience to the general and absolute submission to the pope, the Society of Jesus had the most effective pyramidal structure to carry out its militant task. Unlike the democratic and autonomous system that regulated the foundations of medieval religious orders, decision-making was centralized after the manner of the current monarchies. More than any other order, the Society of Jesus had assimilated the sense of organization that was beginning to prevail in the European mentality.

As regards its doctrine, it can best be characterized as a combination of mysticism with activism, of meditation with the work ethic. While in Venice, Ignatius of Loyola (1491–1556) was conceiving of his clerical society based on the model of the Theatins, mysticism was coming back to life: in Catholic Spain, with Teresa of Jesus and John of the Cross; and in Lutheran Germany with Johann Arndt and Jakob Böhme, who followed the exalted spiritual path cleared by the great Flemish and Rhenish mystics of the fourteenth century (Eckhart, Suso, Tauler, and Ruysbroek). In spite of initial troubles with a suspicious Inquisition, the Spanish movement of *Illuminati*, to which Loyola belonged in his youth, eventually gained respectability and became an essential component of the monastic revival. At the turn of the seventeenth century, Catholic Christendom was full of contemplatives and mystics. Teresa's *Autobiography* 1587), which relates her illnesses, dreams, and hallucinations, was widely published and avidly read. Her analysis of the four degrees of prayer inspired many a mystic writer from François de Sales to Madame Guyon and Zinzendorf. Better than any other mystic, John of the Cross (1542–1591) expressed the will to deprive oneself of everything but God through the "night of the senses" in order to ascend Mount Carmel. Loyola, who had endured visions and spiritual illuminations, understood the importance of disengaging the believer from everything but God. Thus he turned mysticism into a method. The illustrious *Book of Spiritual Exercises*, written in 1522–23, was aimed at strengthening the devotion of the believer to God. In the introduction to the *Spiritual Exercises*, Loyola defined his purpose as follows:

> By the title *Spiritual Exercises* is meant every method of examining the conscience, of meditating, of contemplating, of praying vocally and mentally, and of other spiritual activities which will be mentioned later. For just as strolling, walking and running are bodily exercises, in just the same way all methods of preparing and disposing the soul to free itself from all disordered attachments and, after their removal, of seeking and discovering God's will regarding the disposition of one's life for salvation, are called spiritual exercises.[1]

After fifteen years of intensive spiritual training, a Jesuit's loyalty to the general of the order and the Pope was unassailable.

The doctrine of justification by divine grace and human works, adumbrated by the Jesuits Lessius and Fonseca, that every Jesuit preached, was given a normative expression by Luis de Molina (1536–1600). In his 1588 *On the Concord of Freewill with Gifts of Grace, with Divine Presence, Predestination and Reprobation*, Molina upheld the belief that sufficient grace becomes efficacious grace by assent of the free will, and he replaced strict predestination by a provisional predestination based on merits. Molina's position was challenged twice in spite of its growing success, first by the Dominicans, then by the Jansenists. The classical Thomist Dominican, Dominic Bañez, retorted that sufficient grace becomes efficacious by divine will and that in the process God is always operating, whereas the human being is merely cooperating. Against Molina, Bañez reaffirmed the more predestinarian views of Augustine and Thomas Aquinas. In addition, the dispute focused on the eligibility for receiving absolution. Whereas the Jesuit confessors advocated a rather lenient attitude, called Probabilism, the Dominicans stood in favor of a stricter attitude, called Probabiliorism. The Probabilism, two opinions may be probable, neither of them being decisive. By contrast, Probabiliorism denies any subjective interpretation of the moral law unless there is a strong probability for it. By the mid-seventeenth century, the controversy with the Dominicans was overshadowed by the rising argument with the Jansenists, which also had cultural and political overtones. Cornelius Jansen propounded an extreme Augustinian understanding of grace and predestination, which denied free will and asserted the efficacy of all grace.

---

[1] Elisabeth Meier Tetlow, *The Spiritual Exercises of St. Ignatius Loyola* (Lanham, MD: The College Theology Society, University Press of America, 1987), p. 3.

The third reason for the Jesuits' unprecedented success was their decisive option in favor of education. Loyola perceived that the struggle against the Protestant heresy could be won only by preaching and teaching. Hence, the Jesuits multiplied colleges, especially in the Holy Roman Empire of the German Nation, France, and the Low Countries, where the heresy had gained a strong hold. They devised an elitist educational program for the cream of society that was codified in 1584–1586 by their general, Father Acquaviva (*Ratio atque Institutio Studiorum Societas Jesus*). The Jesuit rule or pattern of education consisted of teaching the humanities, pagan and Christian alike, classical and national as well, and the new sciences—mathematics, cosmography, and geography—and of training in religion, rhetoric, and good manners. The youths of the upper classes—nobility and bourgeoisie—were taught the basic religious and social values of the perennial Catholic world view, mainly embodied in the Old Regime type of society.

The Jesuit curriculum soon became a model widely imitated, even by Protestant pedagogues. By shaping the minds of the youths of high society, the Jesuits contributed largely to the furthering of baroque culture throughout Europe and even in the Americas. In the Spanish Low Countries, for instance, the Jesuits invigorated cultural life remarkably. The painters Rubens, Teniers, and Van Dijck, who in 1632 emigrated to England and shaped the English School of Portraiture, and the neostoic moralist Justus Lipsius (1547–1606) belonged to local Jesuit "communities." Peter Paul Rubens's (1577–1640) altarpiece, "The Assumption of the Virgin," of 1626 in Antwerp cathedral epitomizes the Jesuit's conception of religious decorative art as a celebration of the supernatural, cosmic, and divine order. Colorful, sensuous, imaginative, and ostentatious, that particular brand of baroque decorative art and architecture, known as "Jesuit Style," was intended to overwhelm the senses with a feeling of beauty and thereby to remind the believers that they belonged to a triumphant Christendom. In church music, the French composer Marc Antoine Charpentier (?1645–1704), a pupil of Carissimi and a follower of Jean-Baptiste Lully's sense of grandeur, best embodies what the Jesuits believed religious music should be. His numerous Masses and Magnificats, and his famous *Te Deum* communicated the overpowering feeling of a magnificent God. It also was the Jesuits who familiarized Europeans with Confucianism in the 1680s. However, Chinese moral philosophy became influential only a century later when it was promoted by the enlighteners (Wolff, Diderot, and Rousseau). Moreover, by giving a substantial place to the humanities, the Jesuits unwittingly assured the transition from the Renaissance to the Enlightenment. Both Descartes and Voltaire were educated by the Jesuits. The Society gained such a pedagogical reputation that after its suppression a Protestant monarch, Frederick II of Prussia, who badly needed to educate his people, invited Jesuits to pursue their educational task in his realm. So did Catherine II of Russia. Nonetheless, crippled by routine by the mid-eighteenth century, the Jesuit colleges underwent the same decline that had affected medieval universities when the Jesuits took over.

Two Jesuit luminaries deserve mention. First was the Spaniard scholar Francisco Suarez (1548–1617), who taught at Rome, Alcala and Salamanca in Spain, and Coimbra in Portugal, and wrote monumental commentaries on Thomas Aquinas. By the time of the Council of Trent, the University of Salamanca under the influence of the Domincan Francisco de Vitoria played the role in Catholic Christendom that the Sorbonne of Paris had played in the thirteenth century. It functioned as a theological referee. Second was the Italian Cardinal Roberto Bellarmino (1542–1621), who taught at Louvain, in the Low Countries, and at the *Collegium Romanum* established in Rome in 1550 by Loyola. A pugnacious anti-Protestant polemicist (*Disputations Against the Heretics*, 1595) and pertinacious apologist of the Tridentine Reformation, Bellarmino unfolded in *On the Prime Office of the Supreme Pontiff* (1600) a doctrine of the church centered on the primacy of the Holy See. He asserted that the church would stand firm as long as the pope was at its head; without him, the church would collapse. Bellarmino formalized what came to be known as "Ultramontanism." Against the Calvinist doctrine of the church, Bellarmino emphasized the function of the hierarchy and made a stand of the apostolicity, visibility, immutability, and timelessness of the church in its communion with the bishop of Rome. Bellarmino's theory, which prevailed in Jesuit circles, was contested mainly in France. Under the influence of Edmond Richer's Gallican views, even some French Jesuits leaned politically toward Gallicanism, divorcing themselves from the Society's Ultramontane mainline.

The "Gallican Liberties" were given a normative expression in a libel, or printed statement, of 1611 by Edmond Richer (1559–1631), the syndic of the Sorbonne of Paris. On the strength of the conciliar theses of the fifteenth century, Richer combined Presbyterianism with Gallicanism into a democratic and nationalist doctrine of the church. His theory was framed in response to Roberto Bellarmino's view that the unity of the church lay "beyond the mountains" (i.e., Ultramontanism) in Rome.

Simplicius Simplicissimus's Delusion, or The Thirty Years' War

Seventeenth-century European Christendom was convulsed by the last two counteroffensives of Tridentine Catholicism: the Thirty Years' War and the repealing of the Edict of Nantes. In the empire, the Peace of Augsburg of 1555 had delineated the religious borders between Catholics and Lutherans on the basis of the *cujus regio, ejius religio*, without, however, actual papal sanction. The principle, later known as *Jus Reformandi*, meant that only the prince or head of state decided what the religion of his subjects was to be. The Peace of Augsburg had thus introduced a rudimentary form of pluralism. Fanaticism and distrust, enhanced by an aggressive Tridentine spirit, upset the delicate balance of power in both instances.

439

What Set Europe on Fire?

The conflict between Catholics and Protestants that historians labeled the Thirty Years' War broke out in May 1618 in the province of Bohemia. The outbreak of hostilities was predictable. The tension between the religious fronts had hardened since the creation in 1608 of a Protestant Union by the Calvinist Prince Christian of Anhalt for the purpose of "self-defense" and the formation in response of a Catholic League a year later by the Duke Maximilian of Bavaria. An unfortunate imperial decision augmented the resentment among Protestant princes. In the eastern part of the empire, in Bohemia and Moravia, Lutherans, Calvinists, and Hussites alike had built up a stronghold of Protestantism. Catholicism had shrunken noticeably to the annoyance of Ferdinand, the Catholic Hapsburg who in the meantime had inherited western Hungary (eastern Hungary was still Ottoman), Bohemia, and Moravia. To gain the loyalty of the Bohemian and Moravian people, the emperor Rudolf II, a great patron of the arts, had readily granted a charter in 1609 (*Majestätsbrief*) that guaranteed freedom of worship, and he had instituted a dual Diet (one Hussite and one Catholic) and a college of Defensors to mediate.

When Ferdinand of Hapsburg was elected to the Bohemian crown in 1617, he transferred the chancellery to Vienna in Austria, leaving behind in Prague a small regency of ten lieutenants. Ferdinand's intention was obviously to force the Bohemian people back into the Catholic fold. He thus took the controversial decision to repeal the right of the Defensors to conduct Protestant affairs. A violent argument arose between the Defensors and Ferdinand's lieutenants at a meeting in the castle of Prague that concluded dramatically with the Defensors losing their temper and throwing two of Ferdinand's spokesmen out a window. That grotesque episode came to be known as the Defenestration of Prague. The infuriated Defensors called a meeting of the Diet, formed a provisional government, and levied an army. In 1619 the insurrectionists elected a Calvinist, Frederick V of Palatinate, as their new king. A week later Ferdinand was elected emperor of the Holy Roman Empire of the German Nation in Vienna. The new emperor resolved to subdue the rebellion in order to retrieve his kingdom. He sent an army that was paid by the Catholic Duke Maximilian of Bavaria and commanded by the Belgian Tilly. The Bohemians and their allies were defeated at the battle of the White Mountain in 1620. A fierce repression was then carried out in Bohemia by Lichtenstein and in Moravia by Cardinal Dietrichstein. Twenty-seven members of the rebellious Diet were executed. Protestants were hunted down throughout both countries. Landowners were expelled; their estates were sold at discount prices to Catholics. As a consequence, a massive immigration took place between 1620 and 1648.

Meanwhile, missionaries from Catholic countries flocked to the former heretical provinces. Dominicans, Franciscans, Carmelites, Augustins, Barnabites, and of course Jesuits—who staffed the University of Prague founded in 1357 by Charles IV of Bohemia—undertook the labor of recatholicization. Catechism and attendance at the Mass became compulsory. A new constitution declared Catholic faith the state religion in 1627. Frederick V of Palatinate had lost his throne, the Palatinate, and the electorship, which was transferred to the Duke of Bavaria. The imperial electoral college comprised now a Catholic majority. The balance of power was broken. Moreover, Tilly's and Wallenstein's victorious campaigns throughout Germany were seriously threatening the Protestant party, while the ascending power of the Hapsburg was alarming foreign rulers on either religious or geopolitical grounds. Hence, the conflict became an international one. It passed through three phases: the Danish phase from 1625 to 1629—essentially marked by the military reverses of Christian IV of Denmark; the Swedish phase from 1629 to 1635, which successfully halted the imperial advance; and the French phase from 1635 to 1648, which concluded the war to the advantage of Louis XIII of France.

How did the general warfare that troubled Europe in the 1630s come to its conclusion? First and above all, both Catholics and Protestants had experienced the limit of their respective expansion in the empire. Next, almost all initial protagonists had met their death. Maximilian, Christian IV, and Philip IV, who pursued the war with France until 1659, were the sole survivors. Then, the Holy Roman Empire, the largest battlefield of Europe, was desolated, its population decimated and its civilization ruined. As early as 1640 Pope Urban VIII, who had eased Galileo's ordeal, had proposed a meeting of belligerent powers. Eventually, negotiations began in December 1644. In January 1648, the Peace of Münster was ratified by Spain and the United Provinces. Later, in October, the Peace Treaties of Westphalia were separately signed by the empire, Sweden, and France.

The Settlement

The Treaties of Westphalia settled political and religious matters as well. The political settlement dealt on the one hand with the empire and on the other with concessions to foreign powers. The legislative and executive structures of the Holy Roman Empire of the German Nation, which lasted until the Napoleonic era, were finalized. The so-called *Constitutio Westphalia* confirmed the sovereignty of each independent state and declared the Diet perpetual. The division of the Diet into three colleges (electors, princes, and free imperial cities) was sanctioned. The composition of the electoral college was modified: the son of the late Frederick V of the Palatinate recovered both the Palatinate and the electorship, and Maximilian of Bavaria kept his electorship. Territorial modifications favored the Hapsburgs, Catholic Bavaria, and Protestant Brandenburg. The independence of the Swiss cantons (small states) was formally recognized. Sweden retained its possessions on the North Sea and the Baltic. France gained Alsace. And the legal existence of the United Provinces was finally recognized by Spain. France, the United Provinces, and Sweden were the political winners. The second half of the seventeenth century was marked by a

441

threefold hegemony: the French political and military hegemony that prepared for her cultural hegemony in the eighteenth century; the Dutch maritime and financial hegemony crystallized by an unprecedented artistic, scientific, and philosophical prosperity; and the Swedish hegemony over northeastern Europe under the reign of Queen Christina, one of the most learned women of the age. The religious settlement sanctioned the division of Christendom adumbrated at Augsburg in 1555 and filled in some gaps. The rights of German Calvinists were formally recognized, and both Calvinists and Lutherans considered themselves to form one party over against the Catholics. Free worship was granted yet restricted. The Edict of Restitution promulgated in 1629 by Ferdinand II, which had canceled the secularization of ecclesiastical property since 1532, was abrogated. The enforcement of the *Jus Reformandi*, though substantially amended, confirmed the head of state in Lutheran states in his function as head of the church, and he was advised in this capacity by a consistory. What had been a temporary measure became institutionalized by habit. In spite of the political accord between Lutherans and Calvinists, Protestant syncretism did not follow suit. Lutheran orthodoxy proved to be adamant to anything other than mere toleration of Calvinism, even in spite of the efforts of William IV of Hesse (1532–1592) and of the Lutheran divine Georg Calixt (1586–1656), a "Philipist" theologian (Melanchthon's brand of Lutheranism). It was the dynamism of Calvinism that aroused anti-Calvinist sentiments within Protestant ranks.

What was the European religious geography like halfway through the seventeenth century? Tridentine Catholicism had manifested unexpected vigor, and Lutheranism had shown enough resistance to withstand the tide. The cause of the Protestant Reformation had lost ground in southern Germany and failed in the Spanish Low Countries (Belgium) and in Bohemia. Catholicism had strengthened its hold in the Iberian and Italian peninsulas, Bavaria, and Austria. Before the close of the century, Poland and France returned *in toto* to the Catholic fold. The largest part of the Holy Roman Empire, all of Scandinavia, the United Provinces, the Swiss cantons, a sizable portion of western Hungary, Scotland, and England were definitely gained by Protestantism. Sectarians and heterodox movements were the actual losers; they paid the price for the strengthening of Catholic, Lutheran, Calvinist, and Anglican orthodoxies.

A series of drawings by Jacques Callot, entitled *The Miseries and Ills of the War*, dating from 1633, and the *Adventures of Simplicius Simplicissimus*, a satirical novel published in 1668–1669 by Hans von Grimmelshaussen, an Alsatian, drew a moving portrait of the devastating effects of the Thirty Years' War on the populations. After the manner of the Flemish Till Eulenspiegel and the Spanish picaresque hero, Simplicius experiences the vanity of the world and the unfairness of destiny, and, disillusioned, eventually seeks the knowledge of God. Grimmelshaussen's tale accounts on a sarcastic note for the rebirth of personal piety in late seventeenth-century Germany. The war had profoundly affected the moral fiber of the survivors who had an overwhelming sense of irretrievable disaster that they attributed to the excesses of religious intolerance. Religious fanaticism coupled with the will for power had shattered the foundations of Christian civilization. Several generations were needed to recover the losses. Permanent warfare and the proliferation of epidemic diseases (plaque, typhus, venereal diseases) reduced rural populations by 33 percent and urban populations by 40 percent. The total population had dropped from 16 million to 10 million. Nefarious military groups and ravenous hordes of refugees had plundered the country. Farming lands were ravaged. Whole cities, such as Magdeburg, were sacked. The commerce of the Hanseatic cities on the North Sea and the Baltic had shrunken to a third. Minefields were abandoned, manufacturing industries were demolished. Notwithstanding, the war had been profitable for the Austrian armament industry. Owing to the wise economic policy of the elector of Saxony, Leipzig rose to be the central European trade center. In northern Germany, the city of Hamburg not only passed through the whole conflict unaffected; it also prospered so that the mercantile and lettered middle-class could meditate on the advantages of political neutrality and religious toleration.

Calvinism in Crisis

Orthodox scholasticism, be it Calvinist or Lutheran, departed substantially from the experiential and practical character of the sixteenth-century reformers' theologies. In both traditions, orthodox theologians had their hearts bent on speculative thought. Using Aristotelian logic and Thomistic categories, they unfolded precise systems that presented Christian belief from the divine perspective. Whereas Lutheran scholasticism, from Leonhard Hütter (1563–1616) to Andreas Quenstedt (1617–1688), focused its attention on the issue of Christ's ubiquity, Calvinist scholasticism was obsessed by the question of predestination. Was redemption meant for all human beings or reserved to a preselected few? In the *Institutes of Christian Religion*, John Calvin dealt with predestination within the context of salvation. Following Theodore de Beze, Calvin's successor in Geneva, orthodox divines of the like of Turretini and Cocceius wrote extensively on the external decrees of God and included predestination in the doctrine of God. This dramatic departure from Calvin radicalized an idea originally meant to ensure that God was in control. In short, Calvinist orthodoxy revolved around the biblical notion of covenant, as the theologies of William Perkins (*A Golden Chaine*, 1590) and William Ames (*The Marrow of Theology*, 1629) exemplify. Orthodox Calvinist divines usually upheld biblical inerrancy, complete human depravity, unconditional election, and restricted atonement.

In the United Provinces

In the recently independent republic of the United Provinces, at the University of Leiden (founded in 1575 by the father of the nation, William of Orange), a bitter controversy burst out. Jacob Arminius (1560–1609) taught during his brief tenure that election was conditioned by faith and that grace could be resisted. Thus, Arminius denied the Bezan doctrine of predestination and as a result incurred the hostility of his orthodox colleague, Franz Gomar (1565–1641), who advocated current supralapsarism (the view that predestination was in force prior to the fall). The dispute would have ended had it not turned into a domestic sociopolitical issue. For some time, Dutch Calvinism had been divided between a majority who acknowledged the Belgian Confession of 1561 and the Heidelberg Catechism of 1563, and a liberal minority. The conservatives sided with Gomar. The Stathouder Maurice of Nassau, the nobility, most ministers, and the lower classes formed a powerful conservative party. Although considerably smaller, the liberal, or Arminian, party had nevertheless outstanding advocates and won sizable support among the merchant oligarchy. As the Gomarians connived at ousting their rivals from their positions, a group of Arminian ministers, led by Simon Episcopius, submitted a remonstrance to the state of Holland in 1610. The document comprised five articles:

1. God has appointed Jesus Christ as Redeemer of humanity and has decreed to save all believers.

2. Christ died for all, yet only believers benefit from forgiveness of sin.

3. The human being must be regenerated by the Spirit.

4. Divine grace is not irresistible.

5. Perseverance in faith is granted, yet one can relapse into sin.

The Gomarians retorted with a strictly orthodox counter-remonstrance.

The dispute raged throughout the whole country in spite of conciliatory efforts by the famous Arminian humanist, Hugo Grotius. City councils took sides: Amsterdam with Gomar, Rotterdam and Utrecht with the Arminians. Eventually, the Gomarians obtained from the Estates General of the United Provinces the convocation of a synod to crush the heresy. When the synod convened at Dort in November 1618, repression against the Arminians had already begun. The Dutch were joined at Dort by delegates from the Swiss cantons, the Palatinate, Nassau, Hesse, Bremen, Scotland, and England. The French delegates were not given permission from their government to attend. The synod was composed of an overwhelming orthodox majority. At the close of the 163rd session, in May 1619, the Five Remonstrant Articles were officially refuted by the promulgation of five canons:

1. God's eternal decree of predestination is the cause of both election and reprobation.

2. Christ died for the elect only.

3. By nature the human being is unable to seek God.

4. Grace is irresistible.

5. The elect persevere in faith to the end.

Basically, two kinds of voluntarism clashed at Dort: an exclusively divine voluntarism and an inclusively human one. Orthodox Calvinism triumphed at the cost of religious freedom. Two hundred Arminian ministers were suspended, and eighty were exiled to England. In spite of this, Calvinist intolerance could hardly last very long in a country of tradespeople. The United Provinces had more in common in this respect with the relatively tolerant Republic of Venice than with the intolerant Swiss cantons. After the death of Maurice of Nassau, the Stathouder allowed the Arminians to return home and resume their activity. Pluralism had triumphed and had become the landmark of a small and powerful country that welcomed freethinkers and sectarians of all sorts. In 1634, Simon Episcopius established a dissenting church and created an Arminian seminary at Amsterdam.

What was the aftermath of the Arminian controversy? In the United Provinces, orthodox uniformity was short-lived, and despite some conservative measures against the new philosophical school (Cartesianism), plurality and toleration became increasingly common practices. The orthodox divine Voetius and the mild neo-Arminian Cocceius professed both theologies at rival Calvinist universities. By the mid-seventeenth century, foreign travelers observed that religious indifference had grown into a component of Dutch mentality. In the rest of Protestant Europe, the Huguenots of France, the Puritans of England, and most Swiss Reformed had espoused Gomarism, whereas Arminianism was echoed at the Academy of Sedan, in France by Moise Amyraut, and among the Polish Brethren, the Laudian Anglicans, and in the eighteenth century, by the Methodists. Arminian voluntarism triumphed in the theologies of the Enlightenment as well as in nineteenth-century liberalism.

In France

Soon the affair rebounded in France. Cardinal Mazarin, in effect the French "prime minister," unexpectedly held a Huguenot poet, moralist, and theologian in very high esteem, namely Moise Amyraut (1596–1664). He was, however, less admired by his correligionists. Trained at the Academy of Samur, a Reformed school, by the Scot Cameron, Amyraut endeavored to change the legalistic course of Calvinist orthodoxy by reinterpreting covenant theology. In Calvinist dogmatics, covenant theology provided the framework of the divine-human relationship. Thus, Amyraut made a distinction between an unfathomable absolute covenant and a debatable conditional covenant. Only the latter was an issue for theological discussion. Far more historical than speculative, Amyraut propounded a threefold covenant theology that depicted the divine revelatory process. Each covenant expressed a type of divine-human relationship. The latest, that of the New Testament, is the covenant of mercy. Two of Amyraut's numerous works deserve mention: *The Brief Treatise on Predestination* (1634) and *Christian Ethics*, which unfolds the first comprehensive Calvinist set of ethics.

What did Amyraut teach that almost prompted a trial for heresy at the synods of the French Reformed Church of 1637 and 1645? Against orthodox divines, Amyraut held that the purpose of a doctrine of predestination was not to account for the justice of God but, rather, to explain why some people were saved and others were not. Confuting the current thesis of limited atonement, Amyraut asserted that God had intended Christ's sacrifice to be a universal one. Redemption is universal, provided there is first belief. He then explained that some people have no part in universal salvation because of a divine desire to limit participation to a select few. Amyraut had recourse to the idea of a paradoxical divine will, universalist and particularist at the same time. Almost all French, Dutch, and Genevan Calvinist academics detected in Amyraldism the marks of Pelagianism and Arminianism. So they strove to silence the heretic. Yet, why was Amyraut only reprimanded and not anathematized as Arminius had been? The French Reformed Church could not afford a schism. The Huguenots were a small minority who had lost their political autonomy and military power. A schism would have facilitated the Tridentine reconquest. A certain degree of toleration was the price for ecclesiastical unity.

When Arminianism and Amyraldism reached the motherland of Calvinism, the Genevan Company of Pastors reacted as expected. They erected a dogmatic dam to protect their flocks from the heretical flood. Francis Turretini (1623–1687), rector of the Academy of Geneva, persuaded the Genevan Company of Pastors to require that every minister sign a statement denying both universal redemption and conditional predestination. As liberal views were gaining strength in Geneva, the conservative party produced a document in 1674, the *Consensus Helveticus*, which condemned both heresies. Quite similar to the course of events in the United Provinces, doctrinaire orthodoxy lost ground in the eighteenth century mainly because of general tiredness with theological bickering.

Flamboyant Catholic Piety and Letters

In 1566 Teresa of Avila wrote on perfect love as follows:

> Now it seems to me that, when God has brought someone to a clear knowledge of the world, and of its nature, and of the fact that another world exists, and that there is a great difference between the one and the other, the one being eternal and the other only a dream; and of what it is to love the Creator and what to love the creature; . . . I say that he whom the Lord brings thus far possesses this love. Those whom God brings to this state are, I think, generous and royal souls;

they are not content with loving anything so miserable as these bodies, however beautiful they be and however numerous the graces they possess. . . . Those who are perfect, however, have trodden all these things beneath their feet—the blessings which may come to them in this world, and its pleasures and delights—in such a way that, even if they wanted to, so to say, they could not love anything outside God, or unless it had to do with God. . . . Do you think that such persons will love none and delight in none save God? No; they will love others much more than they did, with a more genuine love, with greater passion and with a love which brings more profit; that, in a word, is what love really is. And such souls are always much fonder of giving than of receiving, even in their relations with the Creator Himself. This [holy affection], I say, merits the name of love, . . .[2]

Whereas the Iberian and Italian peninsulas dominated the Catholic scene in the sixteenth century, it was France that took the lead in the seventeenth century. The "elder daughter of the church" was by then the most dynamic Catholic country. The Catholic cause was triumphing over the Calvinist, and the Tridentine renewal was pervading the entire social structure, changing social behavior, animating literary circles, and stimulating philosophical and theological inquiry. New developments, as defined later, included Salesianism, Berulism, and Quietism (which continued Spanish mysticism in a less excessive form), and of course Jansenism, which took over the debate on grace and free will where the Council of Trent had left off. All these sought to rejuvenate the Catholic Church and thereby to bring the Tridentine reformation to its spiritual and cultural completion.

Devout Humanism

Salesianism is best understood as devout humanism. In many respects François de Sales (1567–1610), bishop of Geneva in residence at Annecy in the Alps, was the heir of Picco della Mirandolla, Erasmus, and the Jesuits, Maldonado, Molina, and Bellarmino. After Loyola's *Book of Spiritual Exercises*, Sales's *Introduction to the Devout Life* (1609) and posthumous *Treatise on the Love of God* (1616) were among the most influential books of their day. In the seventeenth century, books of piety were often best-sellers. Sales's *Introduction* proposed a simple method of leading a personal spiritual life. The union of the soul with God was to be achieved in three stages: (1) a purgative stage—by cleansing the soul of sins and evil desires; (2) an uplifting stage—through meditation, prayer, and communion; and (3) a final stage in which the union with God is certified. This method became very popular, mainly because it was

---

[2]E.A. Peers, trans. and ed., Teresa of Avila, *The Complete Works*, Vol. 2, 4th Ed. (London and New York: Sheed and Ward, 1957), pp. 27–29.

available to all people regardless of their occupation. For Sales had claimed in the beginning of the *Introduction* that "true devotion does no injury to any vocation or employment, but on the contrary it adorns and beautifies it."[3] Sales urged the believer not to be ashamed of being a devout and concluded the *Introduction* on the following note of encouragement:

> As the philosophers publicly called themselves philosophers in order that they might be allowed to live like philosophers, so must we profess ourselves to desire devotion in order that we may be allowed to live devoutly.[4]

Somewhat reminiscent of Bernard de Clairvaux (1090–1153), love was the motto of Sales's second work. The bishop of Geneva in exile declared that charity was the reason for existence (*raison d'être*) of the human being. Sales made many disciples, among whom the most notable were Jean-Jacques Olier, who established the Congregation of Saint-Sulpice in Paris; Monsieur Vincent, who also founded the French Lazarists; and Cardinal Pierre de Bérulle, who introduced in France the Spanish Carmelite and the Italian Oratorian ideals.

Cardinal Pierre de Bérulle (1575–1629) was a critical figure in seventeenth-century Catholicism. He was not merely a founder of religious orders but also a prolific writer whose profound pessimism regarding human nature prefigured another towering figure, Blaise Pascal. Bérulle was also responsible for the Augustinian revival of the early part of the century that left a permanent mark on European Catholicism. Like Sales, the starting point of Bérulle's thought was human nature, yet he stressed the misery of the human condition far more than Sales. Bérulle formalized the incongruity between the nothingness of human nature and the greatness of the transcendent God.

It is significant that since the middle of the seventeenth century the diocesan priesthood of the Gallican church was trained in seminaries that were both created and staffed by Sulpicans, Lazarists, and Oratorians. These orders also founded colleges for the education of the youth. Along with the Jesuits, and sometimes in competition with them, they successfully carried out the Tridentine educational policy so essential to Catholic restoration.

Mysticism and Quietism

At the close of the seventeenth century, Spanish mysticism and Salesianism were flamboyantly echoed by a widow of affluence and demonstrative piety, Jeanne-Marie

---

[3]John K. Ryan, trans., St. Francis of Sales, *Introduction to the Devout Life* (New York: Harper & Brothers, 1950), p. 6.
[4]Ibid., p. 230.

Guyon du Chesnoy (1648–1717). Even by the standards of the devout ideal of the time, Madame Guyon's *Autobiography* describes a life very much out of the ordinary. Young Jeanne-Marie, of poor health, was educated by nuns and at the age of sixteen was married off to a much older businessman. This unhappy union intensified her early mystical aspirations. From her fervent reading of Sales, she learned that love was the heart of Christianity and that the love of God was the threshold of pure love. She wrote:

> As soon as the soul has died in the embraces of the Lord, it is united to Him in truth and without any intermediate; . . . It is then, from that moment, united to God immediately, but it does not recognize it, nor does it enjoy the fruits of its union, until He animates it and becomes its vivifying principle. A bride fainting in the arms of her husband is closely united to him, but she does not enjoy the blessedness of the union, and may even be unconscious of it; but when he has contemplated her for some time, fainting from excess of love, and recalls her to live by his tender caresses, then she perceives that she is in possession of him whom her soul loves, and that she is possessed by him. . . . The soul thus possessed of God finds that He is so perfectly Lord over it, that it can no longer do anything but what He pleases and as He pleases; and this state goes on increasing. Its powerlessness is no longer painful but pleasant, because it is full of the life and power of the Divine Will. . . . The soul is thus . . . gradually changed and transformed into Him, as food is transformed into the one who has partaken of it. . . . The soul then becomes a partaker of the ineffable communion of the Trinity. . . . The soul acts and works in this Divine Will, which is thus substituted for its own, so naturally, that it cannot tell whether the will of the soul is become the will of God, or the will of God become the will of the soul.[5]

She found a model in the exemplary lives of Teresa of Avila, Catherina of Genoa, and Jeanne de Chantal, the mother superior of the Visitation of St. Mary. As a widow, she felt called by God to a special ministry. Like the Spanish mystics, she underwent many ecstatic experiences, which led her to believe that she was the cornerstone of the Celestial Jerusalem.

Contrary to the customs of her time, she neither took the veil nor cloistered herself in a religious community but became an itinerant preacher. With her devoted friend, Father La Combe, she toured southern France and northern Italy, preaching mystical conversion. She healed, prophesied, and financially supported missionary work. She gained access to the highest Parisian society and animated devotional meetings attended by members of the French court and relatives of Louis XIV. She

---

[5]*Concise View of the Way to God and of the State of Union by Madame Guyon*, in James W. Metcalf, ed., *Spiritual Progress, or Instructions in the Divine Life of the Soul* (New York: Dodd & Mead, 1976), pp. 324, 326, 330, 333.

befriended François de Fénelon, a luminary of the Gallican church, whom she inspired. Because of her considerable success and lay status, she antagonized an envious Roman Catholic hierarchy. She was twice arrested and incarcerated on the alleged charge of immoral behavior and doctrinal heresy. After many hardships, she finally retired to a small, uninteresting town in the Loire Valley and ended her life dispensing her pious counsels and completing her writings.

She left behind a collection of mystic *Poems*, a spiritual commentary on the *Song of Solomon*, and testimonies of her ecstatic love for God in her turbulent *Spiritual Torrents*. Above all, she is remembered for having developed an uncomplicated manner of prayer in *A Short and Very Simple Method of Prayer* (1685). According to Guyon, there are three degrees of prayer: (1) contemplative reading in the divine presence; (2) prayer of simplicity in silence and abandonment to God; and (3) active contemplation while receiving divine grace. In spite of her excessive enthusiasm, which aroused much criticism, this uncommon laywoman exerted a notable influence even beyond the Catholic church. Her works found a place among the devotional readings of pietist Lutherans and English Methodists.

Madame Guyon's downfall had followed the condemnation of Miguel de Molinos (1640–1697), a Spanish revivalist priest, by the Inquisition in 1687. Quietism, as Molino's practical theology came to be known, offered an alternative to the Jesuit doctrine of works of righteousness. In his *Spiritual Guide* (1675), Molinos placed an overriding stress on the need for contemplation in absolute passivity and self-denial. The Jesuits were quick in sensing the impending danger and instigated the condemnation of Molinosism, which in the meantime had spread among the Roman and Parisian lower clergy. Molinos ended his life in prison in Rome.

The Quietist affair stirred up, in the late 1690s, a bitter controversy between two prominent figures of French Catholicism: Bishop Jean Bénigne Bossuet (1627–1704) and Archbishop François de la Mothe Fénelon (1651–1715). Both ecclesiastical courtiers symbolized a different kind of Tridentine catholicism at the classical age. Bishop Bossuet, from a down-to-earth bourgeois family, stood for strict orthodox Catholic belief (*An Exposition of the Doctrine of the Catholic Church*, 1670), and gave his unwavering support to royal absolutism (*Politics Drawn from Scriptures*, 1709). He advocated the "Liberties" of the Gallican Church and waged a merciless struggle against every heresy, particularly against Protestantism (*Treatise on the Communion in Both Kinds*, 1682, and *History of the Variations of the Protestant Churches*, 1688). Bossuet was a man of reason and order, but he also left his mark as the most celebrated sacred orator of his age. His funeral orations for royal figures rank among the masterpieces of French literature.

By contrast, Archbishop Fénelon, a fine humanist scholar of aristocratic stock, tended toward mysticism and Quietism (*Explanation of the Maxims of the Saints on Inner Life*, 1697), castigated Louis XIV's absolutism (*Letter to the King*, 1695), wanted to reform the systems of justice, trade, taxation, and the army as well as the church (*Examination of the Duties of Kingship*, 1734). He resuscitated the old ideal of humanity, justice, and virtue in his pedagogical odyssey, the *Adventures of Telemachus*, written in 1699 for the heir to the French crown. On an educational journey under the guidance of Mentor, Telemachus discovers that bad kings inhabit the lowest part of hell whereas great kings enjoy the rewards of Elysium. He learns that an ideal king is like an architect who competently presides over the realization of a project. A conscientious monarch is greater than a tyrant, even a glorious one.

Whereas Bossuet exemplified the grandeur and inflexibility of doctrinaire Catholicism and embodied the social and political patterns of the absolutist monarchy, Fénelon typified the social and political reformer, the loving and caring pastor, and the virtuous nonconformist, thereby anticipating the Romantics at the end of the eighteenth century. Fénelon's 1687 *Treatise on the Education of Young Women* prefigured Jean-Jacques Rousseau's 1762 *Émile*. As a man of heart, Fénelon foreshadowed François-René de Chateaubriand (1768–1848), who was an enthusiastic singer of the beauty of Christian theology and literature (*The Genius of Christianity*, 1801). The Catholic revival of the early nineteenth century had more affinities with Fénelon and Pascal than with Bossuet.

In spite of the differences, both dignitaries shared a common taste for the new European philosophy, Cartesianism. In the 1644 *Principles of Philosophy*, René Descartes (1596–1650) unmistakably severed human reason from divine revelation, arguing that the mysteries of the Incarnation and Trinity ought to be believed because they are beyond the grasp of our inquiring minds. Truly Cartesian, Bossuet always kept reason and faith separate. In a *Treatise on the Existence of God*, posthumously released in 1712, Fénelon inferred the existence of God from the observation of the laws of nature. It was a kind of Augustinian reinterpretation of Descartes essentially aimed at refuting an Oratorian priest and follower of Descartes, Nicholas Malebranche, who was suspected of Spinozist or pantheistic leanings.

Malebranche

Concerned over the rise of the ethical naturalism, materialism, and atheism, Nicolas Malebranche (1638–1715) unfolded a new Catholic philosophy that combined Cartesianism with the Augustinian legacy. In 1674 he published a *Treatise Concerning the Search after Truth*, which continued Descartes's 1637 *Discourse on Method*. This was followed by a *Treatise on Nature and Grace* in 1680 and the famous 1688 *Dialogues on Metaphysics and on Religion*. At the request of missionaries to China, he later wrote an apology of Christian belief, which was a disguised attempt at defending himself against the charge of pantheism: *Dialogue of a Christian Philosopher with a Chinese Philosopher on the Existence and Nature of God* (1708).

Malebranche's metaphysics crowned the Cartesian method of reasoning and physics with the Platonic doctrine of ideas and with the Augustinian doctrine of grace. Emphasizing the dependence of nature on God and the union of the soul to God,

Malebranche asserted that God was the principle of both knowledge and being. God is not merely eternal truth, but also necessary and immutable order. Thus the final purpose of philosophy and religion alike is ethical: the actualization of the divine order. Beyond their cultural differences, the Christian and the Chinese philosopher address the same fundamental issues. Chu-Hsi (1130–1200), the neo-Confucian philosopher in the *Dialogue*, defines God as the Great Ultimate who is the neutral principle and totality of all things. Malebranche contrasted Chu-Hsi's Great Ultimate, which reminded him of Spinoza's pantheism, with the Christian understanding of a personal and living God. Malbranche's God was actually closer to Chu-Hsi's and Spinoza's than to the biblical God. Besides God, the dialogue between the philosophers focuses on the problem of evil, a burning issue at the time, and on the dogma of creation out of nothing. If there is a beneficent God, asks the Chinese philosopher, how does one then account for the presence of evil? If the matter is eternal, how can there be a creation out of nothing? As expected, the dialogue ends with the triumph of the Christian point of view. However, Malebranche drew attention to Asian religions just as Herbert of Cherbury had revealed the beauties of Greco-Roman religion (*Of the Religion of the Gentiles*, 1663).

As a rational mystic who framed one of the most significant Catholic metaphysics of modern times, Malebranche taught that the capital virtue—the law of God and of all intelligences—was the love for union with God, which requires freedom, courage, and obedience. All humans strive for happiness, which comes only through the knowledge of truth and the love of good. Malebranche belongs with Pascal, Spinoza, and Leibniz as the prominent defenders of the cause of God in an age of rising belief in nature and humanity.

A Celebration of Divine Magnificence: The Baroque

Cradled in the Italian peninsula, the Baroque style developed in Catholic Europe in the period from 1600 to 1750. The Baroque calls for seven observations. First, Tridentine Catholicism gave birth to a new style that visually proclaimed the greatness of the Creator and the triumph of the church and that was made dominant in Europe and in the colonies by the Jesuits. The motto of the Society of Jesus, *Ad Majorem Dei Gloriam* ("for the greater glory of God"), encapsulates the religious and cultural ideals of the Baroque. Second, the Baroque emerged in a hierarchical society based on the feudal system at the time of the rise of state centralization and royal absolutism. Third, the Baroque was a response to the scientific hypothesis of an infinite universe devoid of supernatural essence, of a mathematical world reduced to its physical laws (Mechanism). It was the response of those who believed that God reveals truths by supernatural means. Though not denying the rational and natural aspects of reality, the Baroque reminded believers of another aspect of reality, namely the metaphysical and supernatural. Fourth, the spread of Baroque culture caused the demise of traditional, local, and popular cultures. From Rome and Paris to Saint Petersburg and Budapest, an almost uniform style leveled the hitherto variegated physiognomy of Europe. Fifth, Baroque Europe may be divided into three varieties: (1) the dazzling Baroque of Italy, Spain, Catholic Germany, and Danubian Europe (Austria, Hungary, and Transylvania); (2) the poised Baroque of France or "Classicism"; and (3) the occasional and temperate Baroque of England, the United Provinces, and Scandinavia. Less affected by the Baroque, Protestant Europe held longer to the Gothic and High Renaissance.

Sixth, as an offspring of the High Renaissance, the Baroque style—in architecture and in decorative and plastic arts—bloomed in the period between Giorgio Vasari's (1511–1574) Mannerism and the eighteenth-century French-born Rococo style, whose colorfulness, lightness, playfulness, and sensuousness are illustrated by the painters Boucher and Fragonard. As a style, the Baroque was not truly innovative; it kept the classic patterns of Renaissance art and aimed at creating an atmosphere of grandeur and loftiness. Thus, dynamic, emotional, and imaginative forms were added to the proportionate forms of the Renaissance in order to manifest the overpowering sense of the unfathomableness and overwhelmingness of divine sublimity.

As a style that can express itself only on a huge scale, the Baroque specialized in the erection of flamboyant churches and palaces: the Palazzo Odescalchi by Gianlorenzo Bernini and the Church of San Carlo alle Quattro Fontane by Francesco Borromini in Rome; the Karlskirche and the palace of Schönbrunn by Johann Bernhard Fischer von Erlach in Vienna; the church of the Invalides in Paris and the palace of Versailles by Jules-Hardouin Mansard; Saint Paul's Cathedral in London by Christopher Wren; Blenheim Palace and Castle Howard in England by John Vanburgh; the Austrian Abbey of Melk by Jakob Prandtauer; the Residenz at Würzburg in Bavaria by Balthasar Neumann; the Royal Palace of Berlin by Andreas Schlüter; the Peterhof Palace by Jean-Baptiste Leblond and the Winter Palace by Bartolomeo Rastrelli, both in Saint Petersburg; the Palace of Caserta near Naples by Luigi Vanvitelli; the Palace-Monastery of Mafra near Lisbon by Ludwig; and the west front of the Cathedral of Santiago de Compostela in Spain by de Casas y Novoa. As for Baroque painting, the Venetian Giambattista Tiepolo (1696–1770), who created sumptuous altarpieces and ceilings (the Apotheosis of Spain in the Royal Palace of Madrid), the Spaniard Francisco Zurbarán (1598–1664), whose austere and meditative portraits of monks and saints associate naturalism with mysticism (the Carthusian Saints in the Cadix Museum), and the Flemish Rubens stand out as supreme masters.

Seventh, Baroque music began with the Camerata Fiorentina in the early 1600s and ended with the birth of Viennese Classicism in the late 1750s. The main features of Baroque music were expounded by the doctrine of affections. Baroque music was meant to move the listener's emotions (affections) by associating particular musical means with particular emotions. The belief in contrast, a predilection for vocal music—the birth of the opera—and a preferential use of the harpsichord (by Couperin) and the organ (by J. S. Bach and Handel) characterized the Baroque era.

Among the masterpieces of Baroque church music we may single out are Jean-Baptiste Lully's *Miserere* (1664) and *Te Deum* (1677); Antonio Vivaldi's *Gloriae* and *Magnificat;* Domenico Scarlatti's and Giovanni Battista Pergolesi's *Stabat Mater* (1715; 1736); Handel's *Chandos Anthems* (1720) and *Dettingen Te Deum* (1743); and J. S. Bach's motet *Jesu, meine Freude* (1723), *Magnificat* (1723), *Saint John Passion* (1724), and *Christmas Oratorio* (1734). Bach's *Great Mass in B Minor* (1737) best portrays his subjectivist Lutheran religiosity. With Handel in Anglican England and Bach in Lutheran Germany, the musical expression of Protestantism reached unparalleled heights.

The Divided Heart of the English Church

William Ames wrote in 1629 as follows:

> Scripture is not a partial but a perfect rule of faith and morals. And no observance can be continually and everywhere necessary in the church of God, on the basis of any tradition or other authority, unless it is contained in the Scriptures.[6]

When Elizabeth ascended the throne of England, three options were open to her: continued obedience to Rome, restoration of Henry VIII's schismatic Catholicism, and restablishment of the Edwardian church. She chose the latter option.

Conciliatory and innovative though it was, the Elizabethan settlement failed to rally the staunch Catholics and the radical Protestants. Henceforth, English Christianity swung from one extreme to the other for more than a century, often following the religious preference of the political leaders.

Puritanism emerged as a major religious trend in reaction to the Elizabethan settlement. The term, which was coined in the 1560s, applied first to Presbyterians and later to miscellaneous sects such as the Ranters, Seekers, Quakers, Diggers, Levellers, Family of Love, and Fifth Monarchy Men. Under the influence of continental reformers from Geneva, Zurich, and the Rhineland, some English Protestants who had fled during Mary's reign to these parts returned to the homeland with the unwavering belief that the bible contained the basis for the new religious, social, and political order that was to replace the Catholic medieval system. The bible was to serve as a final referee in all matters of personal and public religious practices, family life, morals, education, civil government, and international affairs. Religiously, the Puritans stood for a more thorough reform of worship and ceremony and manifested an obsessive hatred for sin only matched by their aversion to Rome. Theologically, they held Calvin in the highest estimation, framed the doctrine of the

[6]John D. Eusden, trans. 2nd ed., William Ames, *The Marrow of Theology*, 1629 (Durham, N.C.: The Labyrinth Press, 1983), p. 187.

two covenants, one of works and the other of grace, and sustained a rigorous conception of predestination. Their major theologians were William Ames (1576–1633), John Preston (1587–1628), William Perkins (1558–1602), Richard Baxter (1615–1691), and John Cocceius (1603–1669). None of them actually produced a doctrine of noticeable originality. Politically, they resuscitated a concept of authority founded on natural law and social contract that had some currency in medieval English thought, and, after having experienced numerous misfortunes, they called into question royal sovereignty by divine right. Culturally, the Puritans were bible readers and sermon-tasters and, apart from Bunyan and Milton, produced no outstanding literary figure. In every aspect of life, the Puritans denied the values of patrician culture. They dreaded visual beauty, dressed plainly, praised restrained indulgence, and believed in virtuous and frugal domestic life. The Puritan and the Baroque person stood at the poles of the cultural spectrum of the seventeenth century.

It was the issue of the revised *Book of Common Prayer* that prompted the constitution of a Puritan party. The garments worn by the priest in the celebration of the Mass reminded Protestant zealots of Roman Catholic vestments. Furthermore, the eucharistic liturgy could be interpreted in the sense of the Catholic doctrine of transubstantiation. Thereafter, the Presbyterians began to worship God privately as in Queen Mary's days. The reform of church discipline became the bone of contention between the Presbyterians and the Anglo-Protestants. A Lady Margaret Professor of Divinity at Oxford, Thomas Cartwright (1535–1603), devised a Calvinist church discipline at the cost of his career. In the year 1571, John Field and Thomas Wilcox submitted to Parliament an *Admonition for the Reformation of Church Discipline*, which proposed to substitute eldership for episcopacy. A second and more offensive *Admonition*, written by Cartwright as a rejoinder to Bishop John Whitgift's stern reply, failed to impose Presbyterian polity in English ecclesiastical affairs. Field and Wilcox were incarcerated, and Cartwright was sent into exile. As soon as John Whitgift, archbishop of Canterbury, was enthroned, the Elizabethan settlement was drastically enforced. His predecessor, Archbishop Edmund Grindal, had nonconformist sympathies. Archbishop Whitgift ordered all clergy in the realm: (1) to observe strictly the prescriptions of the *Prayer Book* and the wearing of vestments, (2) to accept the Royal Supremacy, (3) to acknowledge that the *Book of Common Prayer* contains nothing contrary to the Word of God, and (4) to subscribe to the *Thirty-Nine Articles of Religion*. So many Puritan clergymen—about 400 of them—refused to abide by the ruling that the archbishop had to compromise and make allowance for some limited form of nonconformism. On the strength of their partial victory, the Puritans resumed their attack on the bishops. Their tracts, signed Martin Marprelate, were so acrimonious that the enraged bishops responded by having suspected authors prosecuted and by increasing their repression of the Puritan movement.

The last two decades of the seventeenth century witnessed the political, economic, and cultural rise of England on the European scene. London merchants were opening new markets. Elizabethan literature was reaching its climax. The Spanish threat was contained by the defeat of the Great Armada in 1588. And soon the colonizing movement was to begin.

The year 1602 closed with the death of Queen Elizabeth. The son of Mary Queen of Scots, James VI of Scotland, mounted the throne of England as James I (1566–1625). Because the new king came from a Presbyterian country, the Puritans assumed that he would lend a sympathetic ear to their requests. Hence the Puritans presented James I with a moderate plea for church reform known as the *Millenary Petition*, which expressed the desires of about 1,000 clergymen. At the Hampton Court conference in January 1604, James I scornfully rejected the Puritan plea: "No bishop, no king," he replied. Although he was an ardent Calvinist, he believed in the need for absolutism and episcopalism. King-theologian, James revealed his conception of Protestant absolutism in two works: *True Law of Free Monarchies* (1598) and *Royal Gift* (1599). His political theory consisted of extending Calvinist predestination to the state, so that the king ruled by divine right. He promoted three main politico-religious ideas: (1) the primacy of the bible (a new translation was published under his patronage in 1611); (2) the right of the state to prescribe religious observances unnecessary to salvation but socially useful (e.g., vestments); and (3) the accountability of the monarch to none but God, which excludes the Parliament. King James cherished two biblical figures: David, king and priest at the same time, and Solomon, the king-legislator. Both symbolized for him what royal duty was all about.

In due course, the subscription to the Thirty-Nine Articles was imposed on the universities. Eventually, in 1610, James I established a Scottish Episcopal church in Glasgow much to the irritation of the Presbyterians. In spite of the conciliatory efforts of George Abbot, archbishop of Canterbury, James I's intransigence bred religious separatism. The fate of the Gainsborough-Scrooby congregation is a typical instance of what the Puritans had to endure. The Gainsborough portion fled to Amsterdam, where under the leadership of John Smyth it formed the earliest English Baptist church. The Scrooby portion emigrated to Leiden under the leadership of John Robinson. From there some parishioners left for the New World and established the Plymouth Colony. Reluctant to break away from the established church, many Puritans compromised, adopting a middle position called nonseparatist congregationalism. William Ames propounded a doctrine of the church that emphasized the congregational character of the Church of England. According to this doctrine, the Puritans were justified in creating independent congregations, when necessary, without renouncing fellowship with the established church. It is worth noting that nonseparatist congregationalists founded the Massachusetts Bay Colony in 1629.

The Puritan Interregnum

With the coronation of Charles I in 1625 and the consecration of William Laud as archbishop of Canterbury in 1633, a new page in the history of the Puritan movement was written—a tragic one. Archbishop Laud implemented rigorous measures to enforce conformity: Puritan libelers were persecuted; the press was censored; preaching was strictly controlled; and recalcitrant ministers were sacked and exiled. Royal absolutism and ecclesiastical intolerance aroused political opposition. It all started in Scotland. The extravagance of Charles I's coronation as king of Scots in Edinburgh in 1633 had shocked the Presbyterians. Anti-episcopal feelings grew out of all proportion. In February 1638, several thousand Presbyterians subscribed to a new covenant in one of Edinburgh's graveyards and committed themselves to defend Scottish religious freedom. Thereafter, at Glasgow an assembly of ministers and elders suppressed episcopacy, forcing the archbishop-primate into exile. Charles I found himself in an awkward predicament. He wanted to crush the rebels, yet lacked financial backing. He then turned to Parliament. When Parliament convened in 1640, political unrest was rife in London. In both the Short (1640) and the Long Parliament (1640–53), the majority rejected episcopalism. Archbishop Laud was subsequently arrested in 1641.

Inevitably, civil war broke out in 1642. The war between the crown and the Scots on the one hand, and the revolt of Ireland on the other—8,000 Englishmen were massacred in 1641—eased the coming of the first English revolution. The year 1643 turned out to be crucial. The English anti-episcopalians joined forces with the Scottish Presbyterians; the Parliament appointed a committee, whose task was to draft a new constitution for the Church of England, and abolished the episcopal system, the *Prayer Book*, and the Anglican liturgy. The committee on church reform, called the Westminster Assembly, met from July 1643 to February 1648 and produced a new confession of faith in thirty-three articles. The Confession of Westminster, as it was called, replaced the Thirty-Nine Articles. Unlike the Elizabethan Confession, the Westminster Confession was more genuinely Calvinist. The state was expected to protect the church, yet not to interfere in matters of belief and sacraments. Furthermore, greater emphasis was placed on predestination, which was extended to the angels. Most Anglicans had espoused Arminianism in the wake of the Council of Dort. The Westminster Confession became the charter of the Church of Scotland until 1910.

Meanwhile, Cromwell's victories at Marston Moor (1644) and Naseby (1645) had consolidated the Presbyterian political and religious takeover. A severe anti-Anglican repression followed. Archbishop Laud was executed in 1645, and 3,000 loyalist ministers who were considered too ignorant and unworthy were suspended. In October 1647, the Parliament legislated that Presbyterianism should become the state religion within one year. This legal enforcement of religious uniformity met with opposition from the separatist Puritans or Independents. Although they were a minority in Parliament, these independents formed a majority in Cromwell's army. By the close of 1648, the army had arrested Charles I and purged Parliament. After an expeditious trial and despite the protests of the Presbyterians, Charles I was beheaded on January 30, 1649. The regicide, which horrified European dynasties, was as much a political as a religious act. After all, to all Christians, Catholics, and Protestants alike, Charles was within his own realm God's temporal lieutenant. The Puritan regicide confirmed Catholics' opinion that Protestantism was seditious at heart. As a result, in some Catholic countries, France for instance, the condition of Protestants worsened in the second half of the seventeenth century.

Just as Hugo Grotius had written an apology for the Dutch secession in 1610, so the poet John Milton defended the rights of the English people. First in *The Tenure of Kings and Magistrates* (1649) and later in *Pro Populo Anglicano Defensio* (1651), Milton maintained that kings and magistrates are accountable to the people and argued that the free people possess the right to depose and to punish tyrants. Milton's political views were drawn from the bible as well as from history. Proclaimed lord protector in 1653, Oliver Cromwell (1599–1658), who tamed both the Scots and the Irish, cleansed the state, purified the church, and was believed by his partisans to have started the millennium.

The World View of the Puritans

The Puritan interregnum may be characterized by the following six main features:

1. Political innovation.
2. A shift of mentality.
3. Social concern.
4. Religious toleration.
5. Moral rigor.
6. Capitalism.

The *political novelty* was undoubtedly the establishment of a republican government (commonwealth) with the support of the army and the Parliament. The monarchical principle had been legally abolished. The son of Charles I, the future Charles II, was not proclaimed king after his father's death.

The *shift of mentality* accounts for the ultimate failure of the Puritan interregnum. In seventeenth-century England, Christian eschatology and sociopolitical theory became intertwined once again. The belief in a period of a 1,000 years of Christ's rule (the millennium) was nurtured by most Puritans. They were confident that true religion (*religio purissima*) was overcoming decadence and that owing to Cromwell's army history had taken an eschatological turn. The idea of historicoreligious progress, certified by the triumph of Puritanism, significantly modified people's social and political attitudes.

Fascinating *social reforms* were promoted by some radical groups of Puritans. The Levellers emerged as a political force in 1645–1646 and won considerable support among the lower ranks of the army. They came from the left wing of the Independent coalition in Parliament. They were democrats who demanded the reform of guilds of justice and local governments. They addressed the economic, social, and moral issues of pauperism (*The Large Petition* and the *Agreement of the People* of 1647). In March 1649, Leveller leaders were arrested and incarcerated. Cromwell and the council of state had no sympathy for an egalitarian society. In April 1649, True Levellers, or Diggers, established a kind of communist colony on a wasteland in Surrey. Within a year, ten Digger colonies were founded under the protection of the army. Voicing an old medieval claim, the Diggers maintained that wastelands and commons belonged to the peasants. In spite of the collapse of these colonies, one of the Digger leaders, Gerrard Winstanley (ca. 1609–1676), drafted in 1652 a program for the creation of a communist society (*The Law of Freedom in a Platform*). Winstanley's communism was inferred from the bible. He stood for an inner and this-wordly religious life. He believed that private property caused the fall of the human race and that the restoration to Adamic innocence required its abolition. He attacked the clergy in a manner that prefigured the Enlighteners and the left-wing Hegelians. Winstanley denounced the clergy's comfortable and pleasurable existence, while the poor were told to expect a reward in heaven only. A radical reformer, Winstanley rejected any state church and every ecclesiastical ordinance. He pled for an egalitarian society guided by the spirit of God. He ended his life as a member of the Society of Friends (Quakers).

The crushing of he Levellers brought another group of radicals to the forefront: the Ranters. One of them, Abiezer Coppe (1616–1672), advocated an internalized form of religion and maintained that "perfect freedom and pure libertinism" was all that God expected from us. Coppe was forced to recant by Parliament. In 1661 Lodowicke Muggleton (1609–1698) reissued John Reeve's (a former Ranter) *Divine Looking-Glass*, thereby starting Muggletonianism, which consisted of a thoroughly this-wordly biblical religion. A fifth group of radicals, which came into existence in the 1650s and found its main support among the Londoners of the lowest classes, was known as the Fifth Monarchists. On the whole, Fifth Monarchism was formed from a combination of millenarian theology and Leveller social theory. The Fifth Monarchists held that the actualization of the kingdom of God had to be prepared by "the rule of the saints."

The lord protector, the council of state, the generals of the army, and the majority of the members of Parliament entertained social views that were progressive yet were by no means revolutionary. The gentrified bourgeoisie, on the rise since Henry VIII, was the victorious class. The aristocracy had lost political power, and the masses, dreaded for their capacity to incite disorder, were given minimal satisfaction and kept in subservience. The revolution, the successful furthering of the Puritan world view, and the creation of independent congregations facilitated the dissolution of the feudal system on the one hand and on the other stimulated an interclass conscious- ness. Furthermore, the Protectorate implemented a policy of laicization: civil mar- riage was introduced.

In this period, *religious toleration* was on the rise. With the exception of Roman Catholics and Anglicans, Christians of all persuasions and Jews enjoyed unprece- dented freedom of worship and propaganda. Jewish merchants and bankers returned to London after Rabbi Menasseh ben Israel's successful negotiations with Oliver Cromwell. Presbyterians, Congregationalists, Baptists and the like prospered. New sects, such as the mystical Seekers and Finders and above all the Society of Friends, emerged. Launched in the 1650s by George Fox (1624–1691), the Quakers, who successfully spread in the New World, believed in personal spiritual truth (inner light) and rejected current ecclesiastical structures. The Puritan interregnum was a period of passionate theological debate. Infant baptism and the pastoral ministry were among the most disputed matters. On these issues, the Baptists and the Quakers divorced themselves from mainstream Protestants. So lax was censorship that, for a decade, all kinds of utopias and heterodox religious views were printed and even diffused throughout continental Europe. Puritan England had become the cradle of subversive religious and political theories.

Tolerant though it was, Puritan England had no sympathy for libertinism. In this respect, the Puritans were closer to Pascal and the Jansenists than to the Jesuits and the Enlighteners. They established a well-deserved reputation for *moral rigor*. Morality was legally enforced in the commonwealth on religious and social grounds. The Puritans closed the houses of ill repute, severely punished adultery and drunk- enness, disapproved of dancing and licentious plays, and imposed strict observance of the Sabbath.

Several theories claimed to account for the fact that the first industrial revolution took place in Sweden, England, and the United Provinces in the period that spans 1540–1640. How does one explain, for instance, that first Amsterdam and later Geneva rose as European financial centers? What made it possible for the Dutch and English merchants to become the wealthiest European communities? Was there any reason for Richard Steele, an English clergyman, to publish the *Tradesman's Calling* in 1685? In *The Protestant Ethic and the Spirit of Capitalism* (1901) the sociologist Max Weber argued, against Karl Marx, that *capitalism* was a fruit of Protestantism. As Weber explained it, to develop capitalism needed a shift of attitude toward profit. This change of mentality was brought about by the Lutheran conception of calling and the Calvinist doctrine of predestination. Both doctrines stimulated religious in- dividualism, which in turn modified social and economic patterns. Because good works and devotion no longer secured salvation, professional life provided the new standards for the measurement of a person's divine election. Basically, the Protestant

Reformation had secularized religious life and had thereby put people back to work. Protestantism drew the people away from vain and useless contemplation. Seventeenth-century Protestants, whether Dutch Calvinist, English Puritan, or French Huguenot, read the sign of divine election in their professional success. The Calvinist reconciliation of money with religion, coupled with asceticism, generated a new frame of mind: the capitalist mentality. Weber's thesis was refuted by the historian H. Trevor-Roper in *The Gentry 1540–1640* (1955), who understood modern capitalism to be the continuity of medieval capitalism. Other thinkers contributed to the debate. Whereas Ernst Troeltsch slightly altered Weber's view, Werner Sombart argued in 1902 in *Modern Capitalism* that the origin of modern capitalism lay in Judaism and not in Protestantism.

Monarchic, Religious and Cultural Restoration in England

Lasting no longer than a decade, the Puritan "millennium" proved to be a political delusion. The collapse of the protectorate after Oliver Cromwell's death in 1658 brought disenchantment and bitterness in the Puritan ranks. Milton magnificently lamented the fall from paradise in *Paradise Lost* (1667), and Bunyan pedagogically depicted the ordeal of the Calvinist faithful and the fate of the apostate in *Pilgrim's Progress* of 1678. Incapable of overcoming internal divisions and of withstanding a strengthening royalist and Anglican party, Richard Cromwell, the son of the Lord Protector, was forced to step down in favor of Charles I's son. Charles II was crowned in May 1660. The restoration of the Stuart dynasty put an end to the rule of the Puritan oligarchy and to Presbyterian preponderance. In spite of the royal commitment to religious freedom (the *Declaration of Breda*), the Cavalier Parliament took a firm stand and uncompromisingly reinstated full-fledged Anglicanism. The *Prayer Book*, liturgical vestments, and episcopacy were restored. A new Act of Uniformity was passed through Parliament in May 1662. Thereafter, an extensive purge followed: Some 1,760 ministers who refused to conform were suspended without pay. Dissenters moved underground and emigrated, while Romanists were gaining strength at the court. The Stuarts had definite crypto-Catholic leanings.

The Cavalier Parliament fought on two fronts: on one side against nonconformism and on the other against Romanism. Thus, the Parliament legislated the Five Mile Act (1664) and the Conventicle Acts (1664, 1670) against the Dissenters, and the Test Act (1673) against both nonconformism and Romanism. The aim of the Test Act was to keep Catholics and Nonconformists out of public affairs. All public office holders were required to subscribe to Anglicanism.

In their capacity as primate of all England, Archbishops Sheldon and Sancroft attempted to restore the true Anglican tradition with beauty. The restoration brought secular and religious cultures to a new zenith. In architecture, Christopher Wren adopted continental church Baroque styles to the English taste, and Inigo Jones transformed English homes by importing classical and Palladian architecture from Italy. The Great Fire that swept London in 1666 gave Wren the opportunity to rebuild St. Paul's Cathedral on the model of St. Peter's of Rome. In painting, the Flemish Anthony van Dijk launched the much-celebrated English school of portraiture. In music, a disciple of John Blow carried the English school to its summit.

Henry Purcell (1658–1695), kapellmeister first at Westminster and at the court afterward, combined the Venetian style (chacone and lamento) with the French (chorus) in a vigorous and passionate manner that also integrated some subtle dissonances. His delicate, harmonious, and elegant use of the counterpoint paved the way for his illustrious successor: Georg Friedrich Handel. Besides cantatas, anthems, odes (*On St. Cecilia's Day*), symphonic interludes (*The Fairy Queen*), and a *Te Deum*, Purcell composed two famous operas: *Dido and Aeneas* (1689), of amazing modernity, and *King Arthur* (1691), his masterpiece, on a libretto by John Dryden.

Political philosophy was flourishing in an unstable English state and society. Just as the strengthening of the Florentine princely state had produced Nicolo Machiavelli (*The Prince*, 1513), so the convulsions of the revolution inspired Thomas Hobbes (1588–1679) and James Harrington (1611–1677). Hobbes's initial political reflections, *The Elements of Law, Natural and Politic*, circulated in 1640 while absolutism was under attack in Parliament. During the Puritan interregnum, Hobbes sought refuge in Paris, where he associated with friends and disciples of Descartes. A part of his threefold philosophical system, *De Cive* was issued in London in 1642 (the remaining parts—*De Corpore* and *De Homine*—came out in 1658). The successful release in 1651 of his masterpiece, *Leviathan*, incurred the hostility of the Parliament. Against Hobbes and in defense of the Puritan ideals, James Harrington published a political utopia in 1656, derived from Plato, Machiavelli, and Bacon: *The Commonwealth of Oceana*.

What political view did Hobbes advocate? He was a classical humanist and mechanical philosopher, an analyst of power in a bourgeois society, and an advocate of peace. Hobbes unfolded a political theory that departed from the current rival doctrines. Indeed, Hobbes denied both the feudal doctrine of the divine right of kings, upheld by the royalists, as well as the bourgeois principle of revocable contract of sovereignty, advocated by the Parliamentarians. By applying a geometric method to political science (the Galilean resolutive—composite method), Hobbes framed a mechanical theory of human nature that concluded with the human being's innate, competitive, and harmful desire for power. To prevent the savagery and anarchy of the law of nature, civilized human beings must transfer their natural powers and rights to the sovereign whose omnipotence they acknowledge without restriction. The sovereign is all and is accountable to no one. As the ultimate principal of natural authority, the sovereign guarantees security and comfortable living. Too excessive, Hobbes's original view annoyed both the crown and Parliament, although a grateful Charles II eventually allocated a pension for him.

Philosophical trends appeared and prospered under the Stuarts's reign: Christian

Platonism, deism, and empiricism. At Cambridge, a circle of dons reacted against scholasticism and dogmatic Puritanism. Benjamin Whichcote (1609–1683), the initiator, who asserted that "reason was the candle of the Lord," and Ralph Cudworth (1617–1688) and Henry More (1614–1687), the followers, promoted a reasonable Christianity based on the compatibility of faith and reason and expressed by the exercise of virtue. The Cambridge Platonists, as they came to be known, showed the influence of neo-Platonism, Florentine academic Platonism, Arminianism, and Cartesianism. To preserve human freedom, Cudworth refuted all forms of fatalism: Calvinistic predestinarianism, Hobbesian materialism, and Stoicism. Because they denounced intolerance, these Cambridge Platonists were called "Latitude-men." Their actual aim was to find a middle ground between Puritanism and Laudian Anglicanism. Cambridge Platonism failed, however, to spread beyond the confines of the academic world.

Born in Renaissance Italy, deism found its home in England in the seventeenth century after a tour through France. It reached its heydey between the 1690s and the 1740s and returned again to France. From there, it pervaded the German culture. Voltaire, Rousseau, and Lessing were all indebted to English deism, the initiator of which had been Edward Lord Herbert of Cherbury (1581–1648).

The advancement of experimental learning progressively liberated scientists from all pre-established authority. Since the days of Bacon, Galileo, and Kepler, knowledge—whether it was astronomical, mathematical, physical, or medical—was no longer solely inferred from the scholastic tradition. Comenius, Mersenne, and Descartes endeavored to establish the conditions of this new knowledge. Crucial discoveries in physics and chemistry by Robert Boyle and Isaac Newton propelled England to the summit of the scientific community. Newton's 1687 *Mathematical Principles of Natural Philosophy* and Locke's 1690 *Essay Concerning Human Understanding* were the crowning achievements of the rapidly spreading novel intellectual mentality.

The accession to the throne of James II in 1685 crystallized anti-Catholic and antiabsolutist sentiment. To many Englishmen, James II's Romanism and the revocation of the Edict of Nantes in France in 1685 seemed to be the omen of a Catholic reconquest of England. After all, Catholicism was certainly conquering France and Poland. As the new head of the established church, James II made some initial conciliatory statements. However, his real ambition soon became unmistakably clear. Failing to gain Anglican support, James II tried to lure the Dissenters. By the Test Act of 1673, service in the army and the state was prohibited to both nonconformists and Catholics. The kings' Declaration of Indulgence in 1687, which indirectly revoked the Test Act, failed to win him the support of the Dissenters. This act only increased their suspicion of him. The king then made a foolish miscalculation by bringing Archbishop Sancroft to trial for refusing to support his Declaration of Indulgence. Outraged Anglicans and suspicious Dissenters joined forces to withstand Catholic despotism, as the very basis of English religious and political life was being sapped. Mary, Charles II's and James II's sister, had married a prince of Orange.

Called to the rescue by Parliament, her son, William of Orange, landed on the English shore in November 1688. The Glorious Revolution brought with it religious toleration and parliamentary monarchy. England served as a model; as in the United Provinces, Protestantism was proven capable of securing religious and political liberties.

Poland's Return to Rome

Poland, the so-called sick man of Europe, relapsed into serious illness in the second half of the seventeenth century. It partly recovered in the 1680s under the guidance of John III Sobieski, only to be thrice amputated by his imperialistic neighbors in the eighteenth century. Tragedy indelibly stains Polish history. In the first place, Protestants and dissidents paid the cost of the national ordeal. The fatal geopolitical encirclement of Poland by expansionist powers favored the cause of the Counter-Reformation. It aroused nationalistic sentiments interwoven with religious feelings. Surrounded to the north and west by Protestantism (Sweden, Saxony, Brandenburg), to the east by Orthodoxy (Moscovia), and to the south by Islam (Ottoman Empire), the Polish crown, from Sigismond III Vasa to John III Sobieski, was able for a time to gather national forces under the Catholic flag with the benediction of Rome and the support of the Hapsburgs.

After 1648, Dominicans, Benedictines, Lazarites, Sisters of Charity, and Jesuits very successfully carried out the Tridentine reconquest and reform. The victorious resistance of the fortified monastery of Czenstochowa in 1655, besieged by Charles X Gustav of Sweden, prompted the queen of Poland, Louisa Mary of Gonzague, to place her kingdom under the special protection of the Black Virgin. Quite expectedly, the enthusiastic populace began to persecute non-Catholics. In 1658 the Diet of Warsaw condemned the antitrinitarians. The precarious condition of Lutherans, Calvinists, and Polish Brethren worsened after John III Sobieski's decisive victory over the Turks at Kählenberg in September 1683. Vienna was no longer threatened. On the whole, European Christendom was not, either, for the reflux of the Ottoman ebb from eastern Europe had begun irreversibly. In the aftermath, Tridentine intolerance culminated in Poland at the Diet of 1717, in which non-Catholics were denied their rights.

The religious situation was extremely complex in Poland. The Catholics were divided between the Roman, the Uniat (churches of Byzantine rite yet in communion with Rome), and the Orthodox rites, and the Protestants between the Calvinists and the Lutherans in addition to the Polish Brethren. Several attempts to enforce uniformity had been made in each camp to little avail.

Protestantism and heterodoxy had found in Poland a receptive soil and had prospered. Lutheranism and Calvinism had penetrated the country from East Prussia through Lithuania by the mid-sixteenth century. In the 1560s the dissenters (Antitrinitarians, Arians, Socinians, etc.) dissociated themselves from other Protestant churches and formed a "minor church." Meanwhile, the Consensus of Sendomir provided the Protestant churches with a solid theological basis by the adoption of Henri Bullinger's Second Helvetic Confession as the Polish Confession in 1570. At the turn of the eighteenth century, Catholicism had reclaimed its unchallenged position of state religion, sectarianism had been crushed, and Protestantism merely subsisted in pockets along the Polish borders. In the Hapsburg province of Silesia, for instance, Lutheranism suffered greatly from Emperor Leopold II's policy of Catholicization (by the creation of a Catholic university of Breslau in 1702). Leopold II had ignored provisions of the Treaty of Westphalia. Resentment was so strong that the population welcomed the annexation of the province by Frederick II of Prussia, a Protestant monarch, during the war of the succession of Austria (1741–1748).

Socinus and Comenius

Two foreign scholars who contributed uniquely to the rise of heterodoxy in Poland were the Italian Fausto Sozzini (1525–1562), known as Socinus, and the Bohemian Jan Amos Komensky (1592–1670), whose Latinized name was Comenius. Faustus Socinus found himself in possession of his late uncle's manuscripts, which unveiled rationalist views of sin and of Jesus Christ. After having been at the service of Francesco de Medici in Florence and a sojourn at Basel, Faustus Socinus joined the Polish Anabaptist movement in 1579. Soon he became the leader of the "church free from mysteries," which was to gain wide repute throughout seventeenth-century Europe, from Krakow to the United Provinces and England. Faustus Socinus unfolded his doctrine in *De Statu Primi Hominis Ante Lapsum* (1578), *De Jesu Christo Servatore* (1594), and in the *Catechism of Rakow*, which defined the beliefs of the Polish Brethren and was posthumously released in 1605. Socinus claimed his doctrine to be deduced from the bible. It consisted mainly of a rationalization of ideas once put forth by radical reformers such as Servetus. Socinus denied the Trinity, the divinity of Christ, and special Providence. Jesus Christ rose above mere humanity by his holiness and therefore was given divine authority by God. For this reason, and although his death was never a sacrifice, he deserved to be worshipped. As a Zwinglian, Socinus also held the sacraments to be merely symbols. However, he was not a libertine; Socinus insisted that faith demanded a congruent conduct of life. In many respects, Socinus's rationalistic belief heralded the Enlighteners and prefigured neo-Protestantism.

Because of his incomparable genius and unorthodox opinions, Comenius led a nomadic existence. He began his career as a minister of the Hussite Church of Bohemia and, following the disaster of the White Mountain and the ensuing Catholicization of Moravia and Bohemia, fled to Poland and in 1628 settled at Leszno.

There he subsequently became bishop of the church of the Polish Brethren. The war between Poland and Sweden determined the course of his destiny. Because Charles X Gustav had set Leszno on fire in 1656, Comenius was forced into exile once again and sought refuge in the United Provinces. He died in Amsterdam in 1670, the very year in which another outcast, a Dutch-Portuguese Jew, was turning the religious and political world upside down by merely publishing a short political treatise. His name was Baruch Spinoza. Like René Descartes, Comenius had caught the attention of Queen Christina of Sweden. This energetic and lettered woman invited him to settle in her kingdom. Like Descartes, he declined the offer. Three contemporary minds shared a common interest: Chancellor Bacon, Descartes the philosopher, and Bishop Comenius were obsessed by scientific methodology. In an age still under scholastic influence, they refuted the current arguments founded on the authority of Aristotle and propounded a new method based on observation and experimentation—a method Galileo and Kepler were successfully implementing.

Three works established Comenius's reputation as the leading pedagogue of the age: *The Gate of Tongues* (1631), *The Great Didactics* (1632), and the *Pansophiae Prodromus* (1630). Comenius believed in human goodness and in the final victory of good over evil. He put great hope in the progress of humanity and therefore devised a program of a superior kind of education. The pansophic school was meant to be the threshold of wisdom. The youth would be trained in letters, sciences, and religion in order to fathom and apply the truth. However, the purpose of education was not restricted to the fulfillment of one's humanity; it was also ordained to a higher goal, that of changing the world for the better. Having suffered the terrible ills of the age, Comenius had his heart set on improving the human condition. Because he was a scholar, he believed education was the surest path. Comenius anticipated Lessing and Rousseau. The movement of the Bohemian and Polish Brethren had produced in Comenius an educational reformer of world stature, whose works were translated into many languages and who today is celebrated as one of the fathers of modern pedagogy.

From the Paraná to Peking

Two experiments, one political and the other cultural, brilliantly carried out by Jesuits at each pole of the civilized world, gave Tridentine Christendom its note of originality. In 1609 Father Acquaviva, the general of the Jesuits, obtained from Philip III of Spain a concession on the Paraná River between Paraguay and Brazil. The territory was inhabited by the Guaranis, who were sociable and industrious Indians although less civilized than the Incas or the Aztecs. The first autonomous community or "reduction" was established in 1610. Reductions multiplied as the concession expanded. By the mid-eighteenth century, the Christian Communist Republic of the Guaranies numbered sixty-six reductions with a total population of

350,000. After a century and a half of existence, the republic was destroyed by the joint efforts of the Truly Catholic kings of Spain and Portugal.

What were the ingredients of the Jesuit success with the Guaranies? On the whole, missionary labor had been rewarding in the American colonial empires, first in the Spanish and later in the Portuguese regions. However much Mexico represented the jewel of the crown, the Guaranian experiment was so unusual that it won the praises of the great philosophers of the eighteenth century. Montesquieu, Voltaire, and d'Alembert, who could hardly be suspected of pro-Christian leanings, admired the dream of Antique and Renaissance philosophers taking shape among the savages. The Jesuits had established an ideal republic whose citizens benefited from equal rights, education, and social and medical care, while financial disparity and the death penalty had been suppressed. Each town, often totaling several thousand inhabitants, was endowed with a church, a school, an infirmary, a cemetery, shops, and a town hall. The economy of each reduction was essentially agricultural, although the Guaranies proved to be good clocksmiths, weavers, and printers. A council of elected notables, assisted by two Jesuits, governed each reduction. The system worked because it was self-governing and preserved from contamination by the corrupt Spanish empire. What caused the disruption of the experiment? In 1750 Ferdinand VI of Spain conceded some reductions to the Portuguese. Dreading the settlers' greed and cruelty, the Guaranies engaged in armed resistance. Six years of war ensued. Increasingly subjected to criticism in Europe, the Jesuits were furthermore accused of fomenting rebellion by Charles III of Spain and were subsequently expelled from the Spanish colonies in 1767. The most beautiful page of the history of the Society of Jesus had been abruptly turned.

A different page, though no less fascinating, was written in the Far East by Francis Xavier and his disciples. When Xavier discovered Japanese culture in the 1560s, he understood that missionary tactics had to be adapted. Prior to his arrival the Portuguese had practiced the traditional "tabula rasa." Instead, Xavier sought acceptance by the religious and political elite. The Daimyo of the south was so impressed that he received the baptismal water in 1567. Within two decades, many powerful feudal lords had given their support to the missionaries. An unfortunate nationalistic and Buddhist reaction disrupted the progress of Christianity in 1614. After the massacre of Kyushu in 1637, Japanese Christendom moved underground. As a result of the same method of adaptation to cultures and traditions, the Chinese Ming dynasty and its intellectual elite looked favorably on Christianity. At the turn of the seventeenth century, China had a population of about 80 million, of whom merely 200,000 had been drawn to Christian belief. The fall of the Ming dynasty in 1644 momentarily halted missionary advance. The Manchurian dynasty and its elite were strongly nationalistic, Buddhist, Confucianist, and xenophobic. Notwithstanding, Emperor K'ang Hi, "miraculously" healed by a Jesuit who had administered to him a certain drug (quinquina), permitted in 1692 the preaching of the gospel throughout the Celestial Empire.

The reason for the Jesuits' success, despite political upheavals, lay in their attempt to de-westernize Christianity. After a fashion, the Jesuits imitated early Christian apologists who sought to win over the Greco-Roman culture. The Jesuits adapted Christian practices to Chinese culture and thereby horrified the Dominicans, Franciscans, and Augustinians, all of whom stood for the uncompromising power of divine grace. The so-called quarrel of the rites, which ensued between Europe and the Far East from 1645 to 1744, opposed two conceptions of what evangelizing should be. Whereas the Jesuits appeared forward-looking, cosmopolitan, and tolerant, their detractors sounded backward, parochial, and intolerant. Again nonconformism was brought to trial by conformism. During the whole affair, Rome equivocated, while the Sorbonne of Paris, having been drawn into the dispute, was divided. The matter was largely complicated by the inconclusive struggle that orthodox belief and mentality were still waging against resilient pagan beliefs and rites on European soil. At the beginning, the Jesuits seemed bound to win the case. The Congregation for the Propagation of Faith produced an amazing statement in support of the Jesuit initiative in 1659. Yet their adversaries finally obtained in 1704 the condemnation by the Holy Office of any accommodation of Christian belief to local customs.

Rome had outrageously blundered. Emperor K'ang Hi, who had sided with the Jesuits, was so offended that he withdrew his support for the Christian cause. The fatal blow came in 1742, when Benedict XIV, a pope hostile to the Jesuits, promulgated the bull *Ex quo singulari*, which condemned the Chinese rite. The bull remained in force until 1939. The quarrel of rites gave sarcastic Voltaire the opportunity to scoff at Rome for daring to censure the emperor of China. The abandonment of the Chinese rite increased Chinese distrust of Christianity. In Peking and elsewhere, the Lazarists took over after the suppression of the Society of Jesus and the subsequent departure of Laimbeckhoven, Bishop of Nanking. By 1720, the Chinese Christian community numbered 300,000; by 1815 it had shrunk to 220,000. The community was left with only eighty-nine local priests and eighty missionaries. In 1811 all Christian churches were closed in Peking by imperial order, and in 1814 the presence of the foreign missionaries in the Celestial Empire was declared illegal.

The Jansenist Threat

Two Friends: Cornelius Jansen and St. Cyran

In the sixteenth and seventeenth centuries, many a theologian, whether Catholic or Protestant, held Augustine to be infallible. His pessimistic view of human nature was more fascinating than ever, as the Gomarian triumph over the Arminians in the United Provinces shows. The Tridentine pronouncements on free will and grace, which confirmed Thomist intrinsicalism (internal grace) against Lutheran extrinsicalism (external grace), appeared to many to be lacking in precision. Henceforth, the unsettled matter of efficacious grace became a topical bone of contention between Jesuits and Dominicans. The Catholic church was divided between attritionists and contritionists. Meanwhile, a devotee of Augustine, Baius, was teaching total depravity at Louvain in the Spanish Low Countries. Suspicious of all forms of crypto-Lutheranism, the Roman Congregation of the Holy Office had already censured Baius's works in 1567. Notwithstanding, Baism did not fall into utter oblivion in the Low Countries, despite a harassed Holy See's successive prohibitions in 1611 and 1623 of any further discussion on matters pertaining to grace. The Jansenist affair commenced in 1623 and annoyed the French monarchy for 150 years. It all began when two friends, who read theology together at Louvain and Paris, met again and devised the grand scheme of compiling a *summa* of Augustine's thought. Both clergymen were committed to restoring the Catholic church to its primeval simplicity and purity. One was a Dutchman teaching Holy Scriptures at Louvain, Cornelius Jansen (1585–1638), and the other was a Frenchman, Jean-Ambroise Duvergier de Hauranne (1581–1643), abbot of St. Cyran. Jansen did all the scholarly work, which he barely completed before dying from the plague at his episcopal see of Ypres in the Low Countries. St. Cyran, as he was commonly called, cared for the diffusion of this new strain of Augustinianism, particularly at the Bernardine convent of Port Royal of Paris, where he was in charge of spiritual needs after 1633.

How was it possible for a 1,300-page, double-column folio that treated in Latin an abstruse scholastic topic to stir up a controversy that aroused French Catholicism like no other issue between the Huguenot dissension and the Revolution of 1789? First and above all, because the Jansenists were able to influence public opinion; second, because some of the greatest minds of the age, Blaise Pascal and Jean Racine, gave their support; third, because the initial issue developed into matters of piety, morality, and ecclesiology; and finally, because at a time of the antiabsolutist rebellions (Frondes), the affair embodied social and political aspects.

What was the theological argument of Jansenism? Commonly named *Augustinus*, Jansen's compilation unfoled a rigid system drawn from Augustine's anti-Pelagian stand. the basic teachings of the *Augustinus* may be summed up in six points as follows:

1. Before the fall, Adam needed sufficient grace to fulfill the divine commandments.

2. After the fall, sufficient grace no longer sufficed: Efficacious grace was necesary.

3. Efficacious grace is all-powerful and irresistible.

4. Efficacious grace is not bestowed on all people because atonement is limited to the predestined.

5. Since the fall, only the elect escape divine punitive justice.

6. The "massa perditionis" deserves its fate because freedom is unconstrained.

Having failed to prevent the publication of the *Augustinus*, the Jesuits of Louvain appealed to the Holy Office. After a close scrutiny of the denounced work, Cardinal Barberini ruled in favor of the Jesuits. Drafted in March, 1642 the papal bull was not promulgated until 1643, however. Jansen was condemned, but Augustine's doctrine of irresistible grace was not. The Jesuits had victoriously prevented what they dreaded most, namely, a resurgence of the Calvinist doctrine of election, and had salvaged their controversial doctrine of attrition.

The whole affair could have died out then, had St. Cyran not shifted the focus of the dispute to matters of piety and morality. As an eloquent preacher and erudite theologian, particularly versed in Patristics, St. Cyran, who had been attached to Cardinal de Bérulle for a while, had built a solid reputation in Parisian circles for his moral rigor and his stand on contrition. Two years before the publication of the *Augustinus*, St. Cyran was arrested by order of Cardinal Richelieu, the prime minister, on theological and political grounds, and was incarcerated at Vincennes, where he remained until Richelieu's death in 1642.

Arnauld, Pascal, and Port Royal

At Vincennes, St. Cyran, who reluctantly agreed to sign a document of retraction after two years of pressure, made the acquaintance of Antoine Arnauld (1612–1694), brother of Mother Angélique and Mother Agnès of Port Royal. The new friendship launched Jansenism as a sectarian movement. It became on the one hand a family affair, that of the Arnaulds, and on the other the religious flagship of a learned and gentrified high magistracy. Jansenism crystallized the factious spirit of a rising social class against the church and the crown, both of which embodied aristocratic privileges and medieval ideals. Like the Dutch Arminians and the English Puritans, the French Jansenists belonged to the upper-middle class. Early Jansenism set episcopalism against Ultramontanism, and later Jansenism advocated presbyterianism (church governed by elders or presbyters as in early Christianity). The absolutist monarch par excellence, Louis XIV is reported to have literally charged the Jansenists with republicanism. Linking them with the Puritans was not ill-founded.

Antoine Arnauld took the solemn oath of a doctor of the Sorbonne in 1643. Shortly afterward, Arnauld released his first Jansenist work to the public, entitled *On Frequent Communion*. This volume met with immediate success and stirred up a controversy with the Jesuits on sacramental practices. In the line of St. Cyran, Arnauld spoke out against the "seducers of souls," denouncing the leniency of some Jesuit confessors and calling for strict observance of penitential discipline before communion. Backing the Jesuits, who demanded that the book be censured, Cardinal Mazarin, Richelieu's successor, vainly appealed to Rome. Discomfited, the Jesuits changed tactics. In 1643 and 1645, Arnauld wrote two *Apologies* for Jansen, whose major work was still on the Index. Thereafter, in 1649 the Jesuit Nicolas Cornet of the Sorbonne submitted his Five Propositions allegedly drawn from the *Augustinus* to the judgment of his peers. Owing to influential friends, Arnauld obtained a ruling from the Parlement of Paris, which was a judicial institution, forbidding examination of the case. With the support of the ninety-four French bishops, Nicolas Cornet eventually requested from the Holy Office an examination of the Five Propositions in 1651. Like the blade of the guillotine, fate struck on May 31, 1653. Pope Innocent X formally condemned the Five Propositions with the bull *Cum Occasione*.

The indefatigable Arnauld again attempted to clarify the Jansenist position and made some concessions. Nevertheless, the papal condemnation was reiterated in 1656, and Arnauld was subsequently ousted from the Sorbonne. At this stage, the whole debate was brought before the public with unprecedented success by a physicist, mathematician, and Christian philosopher and apologist who brilliantly espoused the Jansenist cause: Blaise Pascal (1623–1662). The *Letters to a Provincial*, which appeared separately between March 1656 and January 1657, struck a stylish blow against the Jesuits. With humor and contempt, Pascal ridiculed the practices and maxims of the Jesuit confessors, and in the tenth letter scoffed at attritionism. As expected, the *Provincial Letters* were censured and duly burnt.

In the same year, Pascal planned an apology for Christian religion that he never completed. His jottings were collected posthumously and published under the title, *Thoughts* (Pensées). Taking a Berullian and Jansenist stand, stressing the hiddenness of God, and focusing on the paradox of the human condition, which was both great and miserable at the same time, Pascal denounced moral laxity, indifference, libertinism, and free thinking. Like the Port Royal circle of learned devouts, Pascal intended to use the new science, to whose development he contributed, in the service of faith. In the meantime, the anti-Jansenist repression had been organized. The French bishops decided to force all clergy in the realm to sign a formulary repudiating the incriminated Five Propositions. After papal sanction, the decision was enforced in 1661. What ensued was a shameless violation of the freedom of Christian conscience: The nuns of Port Royal were forced into subscribing. The austere Mother Angélique of St. John, proud abbess of Port Royal, withstood pressure from the archbishop of Paris and the chief of police, who were in the forefront of the enforcement. With inflexible courage, she braved the pope, the Roman Curia, the Jesuits, most French bishops, almost all other religious orders, and above all the monarch, Louis XIV, who demanded religious uniformity. Finally, in August 1664, the secular arm subdued passive resistance. The recalcitrant nuns were transferred by force to separate convents, the "solitaries" who formed a literary and scientific elite were dispersed, their schools were closed, and any further recruitment was prohibited. When all the signatures throughout the French Catholic Church had been collected, a truce began in 1669 and lasted a decade; it is commonly called "the peace of the church." Officially, Jansenism had been crushed. All its protagonists were either dead or in hiding. Naturally, the Jesuits savored their triumph, although only for a short period because fortune soon turned away.

Under the growing influence of moral rigor, Pope Innocent XI censured a considerable number of Jesuit maxims, and in 1700 the French clergy warned believers against the Jesuits' lax practices. The implacable hatred aroused among most religious and secular authorities by the Jesuits' political intrigues resulted first in their expulsion from Spain, Portugal, and France, and later in their eventual suppression. But had Jansenism actually been crushed? The disbanding of the Port Royal group put an end to a small, although prestigious, cultural community that was withdrawn from the world and that had produced in addition to Blaise Pascal and the dramatist Jean Racine, a fine thinker, Pierre Nicole (1625–1695). Nicole took part in the conception of the famous *Logic* of Port Royal, which steered a middle course between Descartes's *Discourse on Method* and Malebranche's *Search for Truth*. He also contributed to the publication in 1696 of the vernacular bible of Port Royal, which Arnauld and his nephew Le Maitre de Sacy had undertaken during their Belgian exile. Above all, he is to be remembered for his *Moral Essays*, released between 1671 and 1678, which were among the best-sellers of the time along with Epictetus' *Handbook* (*Encheiridion*) and Michel de Montaigne's *Essays* (1580–1588).

Had Jansenism then been wiped out? Its moral rigor had appealed to a large portion of the Parisian lower clergy and had impressed the Italian clergy. In Rome, some members of the Curia welcomed its Augustinianism. After the truce of 1668 between France and Spain, Jansenism found a favorable reception in the southern Low Countries and even in Roman Catholic circles in the United Provinces. In point of fact, Jansenism survived outside France, rearming for a counterattack.

This offensive was launched by Pasquier Quesnel (1634–1719), a former Oratorian who had joined the exiled Arnauld in Brussels and published his *Moral Reflections on the New Testament* in 1699. Known as "second Jansenism," the movement propagated by Quesnel differed substantially from early Jansenism. It was less Augustinian and more rigorist and stood for Presbyterianism and Gallicanism. Quesnel's *Reflections* were condemned by the bull *Unigenitus* that Clement XI promulgated in 1713. In spite of the enforcement of the papal ruling throughout the realm by Louis XV in 1730, Jansenism subsisted clandestinely until the French revolution, embodying all sorts of grievances against absolutism and Ultramontanism. More than ever, it expressed social and political discontent in the form of religious dissidence. Beyond all differences, the Jesuit-Jansenist dispute crystallized the incompatibility between two mentalities: one that complies with the reality of the world, and the other that refuses to acknowledge the world as it is.

The Heights of Lutheran Mysticism and Pietism

In seventeenth-century Lutheranism Alsatian Spener encapsulated the pietist experience as follows:

> It is not enough that we hear the Word with our outward ear, but we must let it penetrate to our heart, . . . Nor is it enough to be baptized, but the inner man . . . must also keep Christ on and bear witness to him in our outward life. Nor is it enough to have received the Lord's Supper externally, but the inner man must truly be fed with blessed food. Nor is it enough to pray outwardly with our mouth, but true prayer . . . occurs in the inner man. . . . Nor, again, is it enough to worship God in an external temple, but the inner man worships God best in his own temple.[7]

Lutheran Mysticism

Pre-Reformation German mysticism found a renewed expression in Lutheranism with Johann Arndt (1555–1621), Valentin Weigel (1533–1588), and Jakob Böhme (1575–1624). Their foremost spiritual progenitor was a physician, jurist, and theologian who knew about everything, wrote about everything, led a sometimes secluded, sometimes wandering life, and whose name is now forever associated with alchemy: Theophrastus Paracelsus (1493–1541). A contemporary of the learned Dr. Faustus, whose life fascinated Marlow and Goethe, Paracelsus revealed his mystical vision of the relatedness of nature and God in his *Philosophia Sagax*. His optimistic view of nature and life resulted not only from bookish learning but also from experimental and magical knowledge. Paracelsus claimed to possess the key to a new all-encompassing knowledge.

As much as orthodox dogmaticians, such as Johann Gerhard (1582–1637), whose anti-Roman Catholic polemics and stand on the authority and divine inspiration of scripture had made famous, acknowledged Johann Arndt as a true Lutheran, they reproved Valentin Weigel's heterodox views. Resuscitating Johannes Tauler's *Theologia Deutsch* and offering a fresh translation of Thomas à Kempis's *Imitation of Christ*, Arndt called for an interiorized personal piety. Daily penitence, illumination by prayer and meditation, and mystical union in love are the levels of one's inner life. Arndt's *True Christianity* (1606–1610) comforted many evangelical Christians during the Thirty Years War and inspired those who worked for the improvement of religious life in seventeenth-century Germany. Arndt was the Lutheran equivalent of François de Sales. Without Arndt's mystical pietism, Lutheranism would have suffocated in the utter confinement of its scholastic intellectualism.

---

[7]T. G. Tapert, trans. and ed., Philip Jacob Spener, *Pia Desideria* (Phil.: Fortress Press, 1964), p. 117.

Valentin Weigel lived and preached all his life like any other Lutheran country pastor. After his death, however, his writings revealed him to have been a heretic of incredible stature. In *Dialogues des Christianismo* (1570), Weigel reduced every aspect of Christian belief to a dimension of the self. Heaven and hell are inward, and not outward, realities. Only the indwelling of Christ in us can arouse faith; neither the sacraments nor the preaching of the gospel can do so. Faith is the work and the light of God, whence all knowledge streams. The believer achieves the unity of the human with the divine by following an inner gaze the grace instilled by God into the heart. By overemphasizing Christ-in-us at the expense of Christ-for-us, Weigel dismantled the cornerstone of Lutheran theology, namely, the doctrine of justification by faith alone. By casting sharp criticism on the visible church, he jeopardized the vital concept of Christian community (*Gemeinde*). And finally, by focusing on the exclusive interdependence of God and the self, he inclined toward pantheism. Unlike Arndt's mysticism, Weigel's pantheistic subjectivism sapped the very essence of Christian belief. It is no wonder that the Weigelians were hounded by the Lutheran churches.

With the cobbler and poet Jakob Böhme, Geman Protestant mysticism reached its zenith. As mystic and philosopher of nature, Böhme shows the influence of neo-Platonism, gnosticism, cabalism, Paraclesian pansophism, the spiritualism of Caspar Schwenckfeld, and the humanistic illuminism of Sebastian Franck. Yet he remained a Lutheran at heart, even in spite of the hostility that he endured from the established church. His own influence has been considerable. Descartes, Spinoza, and Newton all read his works. Böhme formulated the identity of God with nature half a century before Spinoza's *Deus sive Natura* (*God or Nature*). His theosophy delighted the Romantic poet and novelist Hardenberg-Novalis and his friend Ludwig Tieck. Böhme even interested Goethe. The philosopher Hegel celebrated him as the first true German philospher, and Schelling owed his philosophy of identity to him. Böhme also influenced numerous theologians, among whom was the English devotional writer William Law, and he had an ecclesiastical following in the United Provinces (The Invisible Church of the Angel's Brothers) and in England (The Philadelphists).

When Böhme's first work, *The Dawn* (*Aurora oder die Morgenröte im Aufgang*), fell into ecclesiastical hands in 1612, Böhme was urged to refrain from writing. He kept his promise five years and then released the *Description of the Three Principles of the Divine Essence* (1618–1619) and *The Great Mystery* (*Magnum Mysterium*, 1623). What was so appealing and at the same time controversial about Böhme's theosophy? Like Weigel, Böhme starts from the self. Unlike Descartes, who attains the certitude of a thinking and existing self by applying a universal methodological doubt, Weigel and Böhme deduced the self as the source of all knowledge from a universal feeling for life (*Lebensgefühl*). Weigel and Böhme saw themselves as prophets, as agents of the Spirit. Therefore, it was the Spirit and not reason (as for Descartes) that gave the impetus to Böhme's process of self-understanding that culminated in the inner vision of a universally present and active Christ. At the core of the human self and the divine essence lies the will, the ultimate principle of the universe. Böhme's

474

voluntarism is coupled with the dualism of light and darkness, good and evil, love and hatred, grace and wrath. And history precisely unfolds the struggle for life that Böhme described as a fight between good and evil, as the place where the decision for God or Satan is taken. What is God then? Böhme defined God as the *Abyss* (*Urgrund*), the "ground of all things," the natureless eternal Nothing that lies at the foundation of everything. What is the Trinity? The unfathomable will of the Father creates for all eternity the fathomable will of the Son, while the mirror of the Spirit reflects both the Father and the Son. What is nature? It is the image of God. Where is meaning to be found? In Christ. The purpose of life is to overcome the dualism by letting the fire of love, Christ's heart, embrace everything.

What characterizes Protestant mysticism? Unlike Tridentine mysticism, Lutheran mysticism leaned strongly toward separatism. It was a sectarian movement at heart. It reacted against rigid worship, rite, and dogma and offered an alternative to institutionalized religious life. Individualistic, it contributed to the development of the bourgeois society. Anti-intellectual, it countered the strengthening of orthodox belief.

Spener

When the Alsatian Philipp Jakob Spener (1635–1705) came on the ecclesiastical scene, a debilitated German Lutheran church was in urgent need of invigoration. In the aftermath of the Thirty Years' War, Lutheran orthodoxy, stifled by a rigid confessional process, had little to offer people other than scholastic discourses on true doctrine. How did Spener inflate life into such a fading body? Realizing the extent of the skepticism and depravity of many self-styled Christians, Spener undertook at Frankfurt in the late 1660s a new form of ministry that focused on ethical, spiritual, and social dimensions. Spener instructed the youth, introduced confirmation, stigmatized debauchery, organized regular visits to parishioners' homes, and created small groups who prayed, fasted, and meditated on biblical and mystical writings. One of Spener's innovations was to give religious initiative to laypersons by letting them run these so-called colleges of piety.

In 1675 Spener published a new edition of the works (*Postillen*) of Johann Arndt, for which he had written an introduction. The introduction became so popular that it was later reissued separately under the title *Pious Longings* (*Pia Desideria*). Spener denounced the evils of the time, lamented the corruption of the clergy, deplored the lack of spirituality of official Lutheranism, and drafted a program of reform. He put forth six practical proposals as follows:

1. Focus on the Word of God and its explanation.
2. Implement the priesthood of all believers.

3. Put the commandment of love into practice.

4. Relinquish vain doctrinal polemics and concentrate on prayer and moral life.

5. Give priority to exegetical theology in the training of ministers.

6. Deliver morally and spiritually edifying sermons.

This sixfold program was meant to fulfill the Reformation of the sixteenth century, which had been left incomplete according to Spener. Pietism was the goal of such a completion. An inborn shyness, a scrupulous conscience, a sheltered upbringing in a devout milieu, and a soul nourished by mystical and devotional literature had predisposed Spener to this form of religious creativity.

On a study-journey, Spener met in Geneva in 1695 the much celebrated ex-Jesuit Jean de Labadie (1610–1674) and was impressed by his mystical-pietistic ministry. Labadie had developed the concept of a small community of true saints after the model of the primitive church. After an initial ministry at Strasbourg, Spener was offered the deanship of Frankfurt. Already his oratorical talents had earned him wide repute. At Frankfurt and later at Dresden, his reforming ministry aroused so much envy and hostility among his conservative colleagues that his enterprise would have been jeopardized had not the Elector of Brandenburg, the future King Frederick I of Prussia called him to Berlin to fill the vacant pulpit of St. Nicholas. There he pursued his mission until his death. In his capacity as ecclesiastical superintendent of Brandenburg, he created in 1694 the divinity school of Halle, which soon became the mecca of pietism under the leadership of August Hermann Francke (1663–1727).

What were the roots of Spener's pietism? First, pietism can be traced back to some Anabaptist circles at the outset of the Reformation, which required the true rebirth of the soul in the Spirit, and to Caspar Schwenckfeld's evangelical spiritualism, which focused on religious feeling and experience. Second, it echoed the spiritual and ecclesiastical dimensions proper to the Bucerian reformation at Strasbourg. Third, it inherited the ascetic, yet joyful form of belief of the Moravian and Bohemian Brethren. Fourth, it was substantially indebted to English Puritanism for its reforming ideas. Spener had read Lewis Bayly's *Practice of Pietie*, which set forth devotional exercises for daily use and offered meditations on fasting and communion. Fifth, it was the nonspeculative heir of the German mystical tradition. Sixth and last, pietism also grew out of a large body of devotional literature written by pious Lutheran parsons.

What kind of effect did Spener's pietism have on German religious life and mentality? In spite of an attempt by the University of Wittenberg, the flagship of orthodox Lutheranism, to discredit pietism on the charge of heresy—283 allegedly unorthodox views were denounced—Spener's movement prospered and reached its heyday between 1730 and 1750. The scope of pietism expanded. The denial of the world and the overwhelming appeal of the experience of conversion was increasingly accompanied by a social and missionary commitment. Missionaries trained at Halle labored in India and translated the bible into the Tamil language. August Hermann Francke, often seen as the true leader of the movement, not only directed pietism toward social and charitable work but also founded a college for the biblical instruction of laypeople at Leipzig (Collegium Philobiblicum). A Württembergian pietist theologian, Johann Albrecht Bengel (1687–1752) was among the first to lay the principles of biblical criticism. By the mid-eighteenth century, pietism prevailed over Lutheran orthodoxy in the Protestant states of Germany. Generations of Lutheran parsons came out of the divinity schools of Halle and Jena. They spread pietism among the Prussian aristocracy and in the army and thereby contributed to the shaping of a national identity. Religious introversion, biblical learning, lay emancipation, social concern, and the repudiation of the transitional Caesaro-papalism of the Lutheran heads of state impregnated German culture. Franckean pietism was one of the most crucial ingredients of Prussian mentality. Ludwig von Zinzendorf, who created the Herrnhut community, the Swedish theosopher Emmanuel von Swedenborg, the Anglican revivalist John Wesley, the Swiss spiritualist and occultist pastor Johann Gaspar Lavater, and the "father of modern theology," Friedrich Schleiermacher, were all indebted to Spener, each in his own special way.

The Revocation of the Edict of Nantes

At Fontainebleau, in the southeast of Paris, on October 15, 1685, the Sun King, Louis XIV, at the zenith of his glory made the most controversial decision of his reign. He abrogated the perpetual Edict of Nantes of 1598 under the pretext that most of his subjects had embraced Catholicism. The Edict of Nantes had been in force for the last eighty-seven years and was now believed to be redundant. Of all the prominent Catholics of the realm, only a sarcastic memorialist, the duke of Saint-Simon, whose *Memoirs* (1788) throw a deprecating light on the reign of Louis XIV, sincerely disapproved of the royal intolerance.

Why did Louis XIV resolve to erase Protestantism from his realm? First, like Emperor Ferdinand II and Gustavus II Adolphus of Sweden, Louis XIV was a fervent believer, whose moral turpitude, however, often caused him remorse and guilt, and thereby an intense craving for absolution. Accordingly, the clerics at his court at Versailles, in the outskirts of Paris, wielded considerable power over his conscience. Second, the king thought that if the eradication of the heresy could be a personal spiritual gain, it could also enhance his prestige so that European Catholics might celebrate him as a new Theodosius. Because the Emperor Leopold II seemed to have forestalled Louis's design by the Austro-Polish victory of 1683 over the Turks, crushing the heretics at home was now a matter of urgency. Third, the affair of the *Regale* and the adoption of the Four Gallican Articles by the French clergy in 1682, with the support of the crown, was damaging the king's image among the Ultramontane curia. Fourth, the Puritan regicide—the beheading of Charles I of

England in 1649—had increased the distrust of a monarch who in his youth had endured the revolts of the nobility and the Parlement, known as *Frondes*. Fifth, the monomonarchic principle—one king, one law, one religion—that guided Richelieu's home policy had borne its fruits so that the absolutist monarch par excellence could now put the finishing touch by suppressing the still-existing duality of religion. Sixth and last, after the conclusion of the Franco-Spanish war sealed French dominance in 1678–1679, Louis XIV was at leisure to deal with neglected home affairs.

The provisions of the Edict of Fontainebleu, which replaced the Edict of Nantes, left no room for the free exercise of the "religion allegedly reformed" apart from a clause pertaining to private devotion. The institutions—churches, academies, schools, and synods—were dismantled; ministers were forced to recant or to leave the realm without their children; emigration was forbidden to laypeople; Catholic baptism and marriage were made compulsory. To justify this string of measures and the ensuing persecution, the regime adduced Augustine's advice to compel the Donatists to return to the fold of the Catholic church (*Compelle intrare*). A schismatic North African movement, the Donatists believed that they were specially guided by the Holy Spirit and cultivated a secessionist sense of purity and a zeal for martyrdom. What had been understood as a mere concession by the Catholic party and as a starting point by the Protestants—a tactic that had created a unique situation throughout Europe enabling both confessions to coexist side by side—was brought to an end by a triumphal Counter-Reformation. The Tridentine reconquest had reached its zenith. Ironically, however, from this time on Catholicism receded in France under the growing pressure of libertinism, deism, and anticlericalism. Just one century after the revocation of the Edict of Nantes the situation was completely reversed; the French revolutionists hounded the "oppressors of the people" and "agents of superstition."

In spite of the Edict of Nantes, anti-Huguenot persecutions had resumed in the aftermath of Louis XIV's assumption of power. A quarter of a century before the revocation of the Edict of Nantes, Protestant areas were flooded with Catholic missionaries. Huguenot children were abducted and raised in convents. The poor and the needy were bought off. Royal dragoons were lodged in Huguenot homes, forcing conversions at gunpoint. How did the Huguenots react? So resigned to their fate were they that the expression "patient as a Huguenot" entered common parlance. The irony of the matter was that unlike their Swiss, English, or Dutch counterparts the French Calvinists were staunch royalists. Raised in the theocratic ideal of the Old Testament, they naively believed that an empathetic sovereign was all they needed. They practiced democracy but were as antiliberal and antirepublican as the Roman Catholics.

What was the aftermath of the revocation? In France, the religious and political consensus around the Catholic absolutist monarchy was solidified, but in the long run the country was impoverished. About 200,000 skilled Huguenots fled clandestinely to England, the United Provinces, Switzerland, Scandinavia, and Brandenburg. Under the charismatic guidance of a young baker, Jean Cavalier, the revolt of the "Camisards" burst out in the south of France in 1702, forcing the royal dragoons into two years of guerilla war. Unrepentant Huguenots were sent to the royal galleys and their wives to convents. A couple of months after Louis XIV had taken a further step by prohibiting all freedom of conscience, a Huguenot peasant, Antoine Court, gathered all the preachers in hiding in the Cevennes and Lower Languedoc (southern France) and held the first clandestine synod on August 21, 1715. Ordained as a minister, Court began to organize prayer meetings in waste lands (in the desert) and gradually restored the Calvinist tradition. He left a *History of the Troubles in the Cevennes or the Camisards' War* (1760). During the eighteenth century, the remnant of the Calvinist church survived underground. Voltaire, who never missed an opportunity to strike a blow for toleration, denounced the trial for heresy of the Huguenot merchant Jean Calas in 1762. The abuses of the Roman Catholic church had become so intolerable that it fueled anticlerical sentiments among the Enlighteners.

Outside France, the revocation was an economic and cultural gain to the Protestant nations that offered asylum to Huguenot refugees, for the Huguenots formed an elite. England and the United Provinces welcomed the largest contingent. In London, Soho became a French borough adorned with several Calvinist churches, and the Rainbow Coffee House became a European center of antiabsolutist and proliberal propaganda. From Rotterdam, Pierre Bayle (1647–1706), a Huguenot man of letters, stigmatized Roman Catholic intolerance, the scandalous violation of people's conscience, in *A Philosophical Commentary of the "Compelle Intrare"* (1686). Another Huguenot refugee, Pierre Jurieu (1637–1713), a former professor at the Academy of Sedan in northeastern France, who had polemicized against both Arnauld and Bossuet, launched from the United Provinces a virulent antiabsolutist campaign between 1686 and 1689 (*Pastoral Letters*). The exiled Huguenot community produced a rich literature of opposition and significantly contributed to the formation and diffusion of enlightened ideals. With the migration there of about 14,000 Huguenot refugees, Berlin lost its Teutonic character and became a center of French culture, despite its promotion to capital of the new kingdom of Prussia in 1701. Under the reign of Frederick II, the king-philosopher, Berlin was often hailed as the "Athens of the North."

Galileo Galilei (1564–1642), Italian scientist who was harassed by the Inquisition because of the theological implications of his heliocentric astronomy and corpuscular physics. (The Bettmann Archive)

A Chinese mandarin. In the wake of the missionary involvement in the Celestial Empire, Confucianism was much debated among Christian theologians and philosophers. (Bibliotheque Nationale, Paris)

The Abbey of Melk, a masterpiece of Austrian
baroque architecture built on a hill overlooking the
Danube by Jakob Prandtauer between 1702 and 1714.
(© Wim Swann)

Gottfried Wilhelm Leibniz (1646–1716), a
German mathematician, philosopher, jurist,
and polymath, who pioneered the ecumenical
dialogue. (The Royal Society)

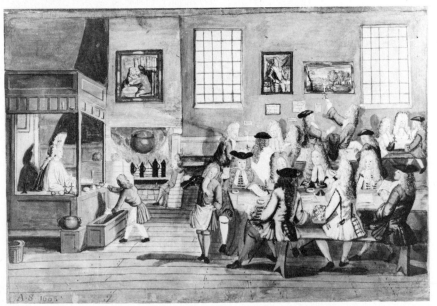

A London coffeehouse
around 1700. A typical
place where freethinkers
gathered to debate new
ideas. (By permission of
the Trustees of the
British Museum)

A page of William Blake's grand symbolical poem, *Jerusalem: The Emanation of the Giant Albion*, written and etched between 1802 and 1820. (The Pierpont Morgan Library)

Frederick the Great of Prussia, the enlightened despot and "king-philosopher," in the company of his mentor, the French philosopher Voltaire, in the garden of Sans Souci in Postdam in the early 1750s. (The Bettmann Archive)

Vladimir Ilyich Lenin (1870–1924), the prominent Bolshevik leader, speaking in public from a motorcar. (UPI/Bettmann Newsphotos)

The bishops' procession at the installation in 1934 of the primate of the German Evangelical Church, Ludwig Müller, a leader of the German Christians and a devotee of the Führer, Adolf Hitler. (National Archives)

Friedrich Nietzsche (1844–1900), a German classical scholar and eminent philosopher, who proposed a new human type, the "superman," in *So Spoke Zarathustra* (1883–1885). (The Bettmann Archive)

Count Leo Tolstoy (1828–1910), a Russian prose writer and utopian moral and religious thinker, photographed in 1908 at his ancestral birthplace, Yasnaya Polyana. (Library of Congress)

Chapter 26

THE REIGN OF THE ENLIGHTENERS

From a tour of London in 1729, Charles de Montesquieu, a French political theorist, happily reported how poorly attended church services were in that city and praised the Londoners for being so enlightened. At the outset of the eighteenth century, a host of mutations reshaped the European mentality, bringing into question the truths and the standing of orthodox belief. The reign of the upholders of the Enlightenment, or Enlighteners, had begun.

European Politics in the Enlightened Age

European Expansion to the East

The Austro-Polish victory over the Turks at Kahlenberg near Vienna in 1683 and the peace treaty of Karlowitz in 1699 marked the decline of the Ottoman Empire and at the same time the takeoff of a new European civilization. Danubian Europe was reintegrated into Christendom. Europeans had the exhilarating feeling of gaining more space. Henceforth, Baroque culture expanded eastward.

Already in the early eighteenth century, the Austrian Hapsburgs had ceased to be the dominant dynasty in central and eastern Europe. They were rivaled by the Hohenzollerns of Prussia and the Romanovs of Russia. The coronation of the elector of Brandenburg as Frederick I of Prussia at Königsberg in 1701 and the accession to the Moscovite throne of Czar Peter I in 1689 changed the balance of power and the state of civilization in these parts of Europe. The steady rise of Prussia and Russia took place at the expense of Sweden, Austria, the smaller German principalities, the Ottoman Empire, and above all Poland, which in the process lost two-thirds of its

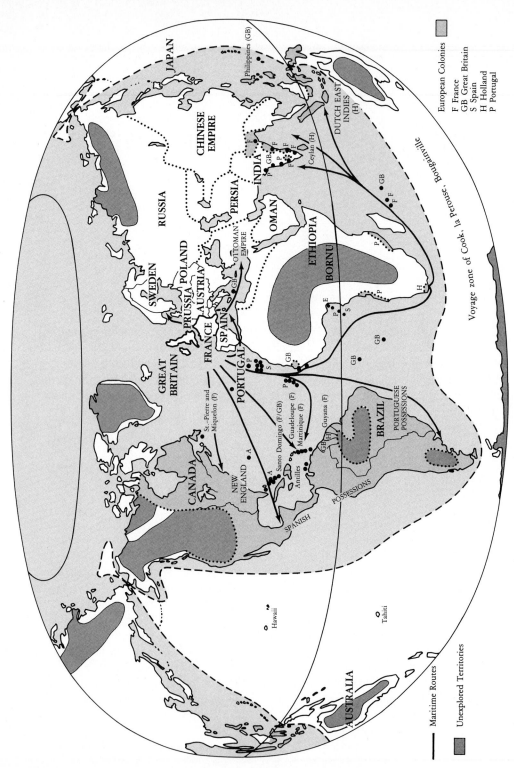

Figure 26.1 World Trade in The Eighteenth Century

territory. By the end of the century, there were five major players on the European political chessboard: England, France, Austria, Prussia, and Russia.

Which power assumed European hegemony? It was France and England alternatively: Louis XIV's France at the outset of the century and revolutionary and Napoleonic France at its close, and Georgian England in the meantime. The history of the time is dominated by the momentous Franco-English rivalry. The duel between the leading Protestant nation and the leading Catholic nation set in opposition two religious, cultural, and political systems.

Constitutional Monarchism, Absolutism, and Enlightened Despotism

There were three types of monarchies in eighteenth-century Europe: the English parliamentary system, the French absolutist regime, and the Prussian enlightened despotism. Each served as a model.

In the United Provinces, Poland, and England, the political system reflected the social predominance of the wealthiest class, which was composed of moneyed men (United Provinces), landed men (Poland), or both (England). In England the Glorious Revolution of 1688 and the Bill of Rights of 1689, which laid down the right of parliamentary free speech, dispelled the fear of both absolutism and Romanism. Moderate Anglicanism was enforced, and the constitutional monarchy was consolidated. With the establishment in 1714 of the Hanoverian dynasty (George I) and under the leadership of outstanding majority leaders (Robert Walpole, William Pitt the elder and the younger), Parliament became the main organ of British economic, political, and religious decision-making, even in spite of George III's attempts to upset the balance of power in favor of the crown in the 1760s.

To those who, like the French political theorist Charles de Montesquieu, saw the flow of absolutism, the British parliamentary system, which separated the legislative from the executive power, seemed an ideal model of modern government. The French professional and lettered upper class increasingly fancied the British form of constitutional monarchism.

Absolutism became the hallmark of the French Bourbon dynasty. Seventeenth-century religious warfare and social upheavals had underscored the general conviction that the absolutist monarchy had salvaged society from disintegration. Continuing the centralizing policy set forth by Richelieu, Louis XIV tamed the nobility, made religious belief (Catholicism) uniform, delimited the role of the Parlements (courts of justice), restricted the powers of the provincial estates (local representative assemblies), and above all built up a highly structured and professional administration. Absolutism turned out to be a model of government because of its successful economic strategy (i.e., mercantilism, or Colbertism), its administrative efficacy, its well-equipped regular armed forces, and its cultural policy.

The seat of government and lavish symbol of royal supremacy, Louis XIV's palace of Versailles, a masterpiece of Baroque architecture on the outskirts of Paris, served as a means to impose both political and cultural hegemony, at first over the entire realm and then over continental Europe. Under Louis XIV, French culture attained its golden age: Classicism. Owing to temporary political hegemony, French Classicism spread throughout Europe, overshadowing Italian influence. The French language began to replace Latin in courtly and lettered central and eastern European circles.

A form of absolutism adapted to the various needs of states whose bureaucracy was less advanced (Prussia and Russia), complex (Austria), or rigid (Spain, the Italian states), enlightened despotism lasted half a century from the accession to the throne of Frederick II of Prussia in 1740 to the death of Emperor Joseph II of Austria in 1790. The idea was put forth in 1739 by Frederick II in his political treatise *Anti-Machiavel*. The notion of social contract served as a foundation for the principle of royal sovereignty. Fascinated by French culture, the "king-philosopher," who befriended the untamable Voltaire, transformed his father's militaristic kingdom into a modern state and a European power. This exemplary achievement, celebrated by French philosophers, was the pride and envy of Europe, and it was soon imitated by monarchs from the Iberian peninsula to the Baltic Sea. Continuing Peter the Great's westernizing and centralizing policy and adapting it to modern ideas, Catherine II of Russia made an oriental replica of Prussia. Both Prussia and Russia gained most from enlightened despotism. They were able to catch up with the rest of Europe politically, economically, and culturally.

What did enlightened despotism consist of? Its substance may be summed up in the following seven points:

1. By contrast with absolutism, which originated from an alliance of politics with theology, enlightened despotism resulted from an alliance between political theory and rational philosophy.

2. Enlightened despots took the nascent public opinion very seriously into account, inasmuch as newspapers and the correspondence between women and men of letters affected their public image.

3. Enlightened despotism kept the administrative aspect of French absolutism yet disposed of the coerciveness of its monolithic religious structure.

4. Enlightened rulers enacted religious toleration. In Berlin, for instance, Lutherans, Calvinists, pietists, Catholics, Rationalists, and Freemasons all had equal rights. As for the Jews, the edict of 1750 granted them certain rights. The emancipation of the Jews in central and eastern Europe expressed a crucial shift of mentality.

5. In economic affairs, enlightened despots adopted mercantilism (Colbertism) from the French.

6. Their cultural strategy consisted mostly of a massive literacy program and a huge sponsoring of the arts and sciences.

7. By focusing on the institution and not the ruler, enlightened despotism tended to deify the state. Instead of identifying themselves with the state, as Louis XIV did, enlightened despots understood themselves as first of all servants of the state.

It was the French Revolution, a by-product of the Enlightenment, which because of its extremisms put an end to half a century of this moderately successful utopianism.

Eighteenth-Century Socioeconomic Life

Demography Between 1680 and 1800

The period between 1680 and 1800 witnessed an exceptional demographic growth. At the eve of the French Revolution in 1789, European population totaled 187 million. Europe was not equally populated throughout. Central western Europe was more populated than Mediterranean Europe, and Mediterranean Europe more than eastern and northern Europe. France numbered 26 million, the Italian peninsula 18 million, and England 9 million. Spain, Sweden, and Prussia had almost doubled their population, while Russia and Hungary had, respectively, nearly tripled and quadrupled theirs.

Without what has now been termed the Vital Revolution, the enlightened mentality would never have arisen. Taking place between 1670 and 1730, the Vital Revolution was crucial in the formation of a new cutural ideal. Several baby booms, the fall of infant and child mortality rates, the limited devastations of lesser plagues, and the extension of the average life expectancy by ten years caused the doubling of the European population in the period that spans 1680 to 1800. In the seventeenth century, average life expectancy did not exceed 25 years; it rose to 35 years in the eighteenth century. This gain resulted from momentous progress in housing, nutrition, hygiene, and medicine. Alarmed at the prospect of an overpopulated earth, Thomas Robert Malthus (1766–1834) devised an ingenious scheme to control the birth rate in *An Essay on the Principle of Population* (1798). Malthus denied the poor the right to sexual intercourse and generation.

The Economy

In the eighteenth century, the European economy was still predominantly agricultural. With the exception of England, the Low Countries, and Lombardy (northern

Italy), peasants made up to 85 percent of the total European population. Technical innovations and the creation of larger estates helped to improve quality and to increase productivity. New crops such as corn, potatoes, and rice appeared.

On the whole, from Lisbon to Nijni-Novgorod, Europe benefited enormously from a booming colonial trade. The new maritime routes to northern America, the Antilles, the west coast of Africa, the Mogul Empire of India, and Indonesia opened up by the English, the Dutch, and the French in the previous century brought unprecedented wealth and created a modern industrial, commercial, and financial infrastructure. Trading companies multiplied, grew powerful, and competed mercilessly. The triangular trade—between Europe, Africa, and America—became a considerable source of wealth. Competition turned into a permanent sea warfare. The rising colonial powers waged war against the old colonial empires and among themselves.

The prosperity of colonial trade brought about the following six changes:

1. It necessitated the modernization and expansion of communications and of commercial and industrial infrastructures.

2. The monetary supply rose to unprecedented heights and facilitated credit. Whereas in the seventeenth century, the European economy ran on a monetary shortage, in the eighteenth it ran on a surplus. Just as Venice gave way to Antwerp as the European financial center, and Antwerp to Amsterdam, so Amsterdam was supplanted by London, though the Bank of Amsterdam still remained Europe's largest lending institution.

3. The trade boom opened new markets, raised domestic consumption, and boosted manufacturing production.

4. The boom also generated two new social classes, one at the top of the scale and the other at the bottom. Merchant bankers, financiers, shipowners, manufacturers, and large retailers formed an extremely wealthy bourgeoisie who entered the ranks of the landed aristocracy. In harbors and industrial areas, a proletariat proliferated and was often degraded by alcoholism (gin mania) and prostitution.

5. The boom transformed culinary art and changed people's drinking habits. The variety of exotic products, the quality of the local produce, and a choosier clientele gave birth to gastronomy.

6. The trade boom largely contributed to Britain's rise to economic hegemony until 1880. Profits from trade and industrial production and a steady pound sterling enabled Britain to keep an impressive fleet, to support armies engaged on several fronts, and to subsidize political allies heavily, with the aim of imposing its rule on the world. Political hegemony followed economic hegemony.

The Social Structure

In spite of economic prosperity and political mutations, the medieval, pyramidal structure of society remained on the whole unchanged. The "Old Regime" or feudal system—clergy, nobility, bourgeoisie, peasantry—was variably in force, less in the most advanced societies like England and the Low Countries, more in lesser developed and predominantly agrarian societies such as Spain, Austria, Prussia, and Russia.

The hereditary aristocracy highly retained its social preponderance, having, however, generally lost its political autonomy. In most advanced countries, it was overshadowed by a new rural and urban patriciate whose fortune came from moneymaking or service to the crown: the gentlemen in England, the "regent" class in the Low Countries, the "nobility of the robe" in France.

As the main instrument of economic prosperity and instigator of social and political change, the bourgeoisie were able to transform their economic superiority into political power in Britain, the Low Countries, the Hanseatic cities of Germany, and the city-states of Genoa and Venice. In France, northern Italy, and the rest of Germany, the bourgeoisie who did not move into the nobility felt deprived of the influence normally corresponding to their wealth and ability, a resentment that explains their subversive inclinations. However, the bourgeois values (industriousness, frugality, decency, family life, and orderliness) increasingly pervaded urban civilization (as shown by the erection of austere townhouses, creation of cultural facilities, and urbanization), transforming business centers into cultural centers, affecting literary genres (bourgeois novel and theatre), and refining the lifestyle of towndwellers (artisans and shopkeepers). The impact of the bourgeois culture on eighteenth-century civilization cleared the path for the nineteenth-century political takeover by the bourgeoisie, which resulted in liberalism and democracy.

Nowhere in Europe was the fate of the peasantry enviable, and it was certainly far less so in eastern Europe, where serfdom was still in force, than in western Europe, where peasants sometimes owned their land. In general, peasants were illiterate, superstitious, ill-housed, ill-fed, and ill-clothed. Their existence was basic and often depended on a year's harvest. However, they were better off in advanced countries such as England, the Low Countries, and France than in less developed states such as Spain, Austria, Prussia, and Russia. The growing humanitarian conscience of government officials led to several attempts at agrarian reform in central and eastern Europe. Joseph II, for instance, abolished serfdom in 1781. Both Frederick II and Catherine II tried to improve the inhuman conditions of their peasantry, but none of these reforms actually changed the peasantry's life substantially.

In mining and manufacturing areas, underpaid and exploited journeymen began to form a distinct lower social class, which gained importance and power in the nineteenth century: the proletariat.

An Intellectual and Cultural Earthquake

Cultural Aftermath of the Vital Revolution

The Vital Revolution had a fourfold effect on European civilization. Above all, it revealed that children were lovable and worth educating. Parents increasingly involved themselves in the nurturing and raising of their children. In this respect, the English upper class served as a model. By mid-century, pedagogy had become one of the favorite topics of physicians, men of letters, and clerics, as Rousseau's *Emile* (1762) exemplifies. Next, the Vital Revolution pushed the frontier of illiteracy further away. The literacy rate rapidly rose throughout Europe, yet at a variable pace. Northern Europe was ahead of southern Europe, and western Europe ahead of eastern Europe. As a result of the diffusion of vernacular bibles, Protestant Europe had a comfortable lead over Catholic Europe. Between 1700 and 1800, the literacy rate rose in Scotland from 45 to 85 percent, and in England from 45 to 63 percent. In Catholic Europe, France was largely ahead with merely 50 percent. In eastern Europe, owing to an extensive literacy program, Prussia caught up with the rest of Europe by the end of the century. Despite remarkable progress, Russia still stood far behind with 10 percent. The Vital Revolution also demystified the popular perception of death. In medieval times, death commanded awe and silence. The Renaissance and the Baroque transformed death into a theatrical performance. In the eighteenth century, death was restricted to a private event. Finally, along with the scientific and technical revolutions and European geopolitical expansion, the Vital Revolution aroused public confidence in endless progress.

Scientific and Technological Advances

The scientific discoveries and technological innovations of the eighteenth century were prepared by the double scientific revolution of the seventeenth century. The Cartesian mathematization of the universe and Newton's three laws of motion laid the foundations of a mechanistic world view that pervaded the eighteenth century from London and Paris to St. Petersburg and New England. Since Bacon's 1605 *Advancement of Learning*, scientific interest had progressively eclipsed speculative and religious considerations among the European intellectual elite. Natural philosophy, as the sciences were called, fascinated men of letters, clerics, and fashionable ladies. Kepler, Galileo, Newton, and Toricelli were enthusiastically discussed in salons. As it had been customary for Renaissance princes to keep a cabinet of antiques, it was now common for the wealthy to possess a cabinet of physics or chemistry. Both state and society encouraged and financed scientific pursuit because it was thought to contribute to the general welfare.

Because continental universities firmly held to their outdated Aristotelianism, it was the newly created learned societies which promoted experimental knowledge and facilitated international collaboration. Academies of science were founded in Berlin (1710), St. Petersburg (1724), Stockholm (1737), and Copenhagen (1745) on the model of the Florentine Accademia del Cimento (1657), the Royal Society (1662), and the Academie des Sciences of Paris (1666). To diffuse and exchange information, scientific journals were also started, such as the *Philosophical Transactions of the Royal Society* and the *Journal des Savants* of Paris (both in 1665), and the *Acta Eruditorum* of Leipzig (1682). Just as printers had propagated otherworldly and devotional ideals in the previous century, so they now furthered the current predilection for life and nature. Scientific, technical, travel, and artistic subjects formed the bulk of the book production, 90 percent of which originated in England, the United Provinces, France, and Protestant Germany.

From the vantage point of science, the eighteenth century was less revolutionary than either the seventeenth or nineteenth. In the period that spans the second and third scientific revolutions (1680s and 1820s–1840s), scientists organized their discipline, improved methods, made inventories, completed earlier experiments, and searched for technological implements. Descriptive geometry, astronomy, chemistry, biology, cartography, hydrography, mineralogy, meteorology, all grew into mature sciences. The eighteenth-century thirst for conquest and adventure could not be quenched so long as a last domain still remained unmastered and the unfortunate mythical Icarus unavenged. A precursor of Jonathan Swift, the French burlesque poet Cyrano de Bergerac (1619–1655) had narrated an imaginary eccentric voyage to the moon in his *Comical History of the States and Empires of the Moon and the Sun* (1656). Cyrano later became the main character of Edmond Rostand's famous play (1897). Was space travel to remain a poet's illusion? Two venturesome brothers, Etienne and Joseph de Montgolfier, proved the contrary by launching the first aerostatic balloon in June 1783. Later in December, a balloon filled with hydrogen, launched by the physicist Charles and the engineer Robert, spectacularly ascended 10,000 feet. The conquest of space had begun.

Did scientific and technological progress have any bearing on the European mentality? Yes. It reduced the world to its phenomenal reality, and it enthroned mathematics as queen of the sciences. The mathematician enjoyed the same standing that the logician had held in the fifteenth century and the theologian in the thirteenth century. It emancipated the sciences from philosophy, fragmenting knowledge. It gave priority to methodology and epistemology (i.e., theory of knowledge). It evidenced that the focus of the human mind on nature was rewarding, inasmuch as it fulfilled the destiny of the human race. It legitimized the crucial shift of the 1680s from transcendence to immanence, from faith to reason, from speculative discourse (metaphysics) to empirical account (physics), from the absolute truth to relative truths.

A Reversion of Perspective

The seventeenth-century mentality predominantly apprehended the world from the vantage point of the otherworldly reality: Nature was divine creation, society was a mirror of divine will and order, and the human being was in the image of God. Undisputed, revelation set the standards universally. General lassitude and intellectual emancipation deflected most eighteenth-century people from the coerciveness of authoritarian systems, whether they were religious, political, or social. Negatively, liberation meant a disengagement from the utopian, Augustinian City of God, a disinterest in transcendence and the absolute, and a denial of hierarchy, discipline, and obedience. Positively, liberation meant a belief in the progress of humanity, a love for nature, a sense of reasonableness and relativeness, and a desire for freedom of conscience and earthly happiness. Therefore, new standards needed to be established in every field of knowledge and in all spheres of life. Such a momentous task could be achieved only through epistemology and methodology, two of the age's main concerns. The reversion of perspective transformed a duty-oriented into a justice-oriented civilization. The businessman and freethinker replaced the lord and the priest as norm-givers. The reign of critique superseded the reign of apology, as Voltaire, the anti-Pascal, cast pearls of secularized wisdom to a bemused world.

No philosophy of history more authentically mirrored the eighteenth-century confidence in the "indefinite and infinite progress" of humanity than Condorcet's posthumous *Sketch for a Historical Picture of the Progress of the Human Mind* (1795). A mathematician-turned-revolutionary and an anticlerical philosopher, Antoine-Nicolas Caritat de Condorcet (1743–1794), the prestigious secretary of the Paris Academy of Sciences, completed his most influential treatise in the winter of 1793–94 at the height of the French Revolution, during the bloodthirsty Terror which claimed his life. On the strength of an unwavering faith in the human capacity to know the truth, to achieve the good, and to attain happiness, Condorcet demonstrated that the progress of the natural sciences secured the progress of the moral sciences, and he vigorously argued that the progressive emancipation of humanity from the evils of both nature and society opened the future to a free and rational society. The *Sketch* became the manifesto of the upholders of the values of the Enlightenment in the nineteenth century. It inspired the educators who were in charge of the French school system and the thinkers who founded the social sciences—Claude de Saint Simon and Auguste Comte.

Basically, the "long" eighteenth century (1680–1815), a long time span that crosses over the traditional chronological divisions, can be divided into four periods: (1) an initial, brutal awakening from dogmatic slumber and the subsequent identity crisis (from 1680 to 1715); (2) a period of systematic demolition, or the reign of criticism (from 1715 to 1750); (3) a time for systematic reconstruction or the renovation of the moral and social realms (from 1750 to 1790); and (4) the final attempt at concretizing the enligtheners' utopianism and the cruel disillusionment (from 1790 to 1815).

The enlightened spirit took form in England and in the United Provinces, and gained France and Italy about two decades later. From Paris, it spread eastward. It conquered Brandenburg-Prussia first, and Russia afterward by the mediation of Prussia. In Leipzig, Berlin, and Königsberg, enlighteners distilled a moralized and bible-oriented blend of enlightenment: the *Aufklärung*.

Freemasonry

> When virtue and justice
> strew the path with fame,
> then is the earth a kingdom of heaven,
> and mortals like the gods.

This Masonic hymn concludes the first act of Mozart's 1791 *The Magic Flute*. It celebrates the new moral and political ideals.

As an outgrowth of religious wars, absolutism—be it fully fledged or enlightened—used and rewarded the bourgeoisie for its expertise and enterprising spirit, yet denied it a political voice. Moreover, by subordinating morality to politics (following Hobbes and Bossuet), absolutism deceived the ethically oriented bourgeoisie and indirectly favored the constitution of a moral counterweight in the form of a secret society, a humanist and humanitarian brotherhood, a secularized and dechristianized church: the Masonic lodge. The bourgeois debated religion and politics in coffeehouses, clubs, salons, literary societies, academies, and lodges, but it was above all in the Masonic lodges that the bourgeois political ideal took shape. In the lodges, the feudal system, obsessively present in church and state, was leveled out; there were freedom of expression and social equality. In the cocoon of the Masonic lodge, the talented and learned bourgeoisie formed a moral tribunal to whose evaluation the state, the social structure, and religion were subjected.

The English and French Masons, the German Illuminati, all waged the war of nature and reason against all forms of evil in society and in the world at large. All of them believed in a virtuous, brotherly, and perfect bourgeois order from which the state was almost precluded. Although they claimed to be neutral and apolitical, the Freemasons' moral verdict on the Old Regime had a subversive political effect in the long run: It contributed to the demise of the current political and religious order.

Matrimony, Sexuality, and Eroticism

A new pattern of marriage developed in the eighteenth century. From the late Middle Ages to the seventeenth century, matrimony was essentially a matter of economic and demographic survival. Marriage was predominantly a kin and community business. In the upper class it was property-oriented, whereas in the lower class it was intended to help increase productivity. Basically, the marital condition was not meant to provide a sexual and emotional outlet. On the model of the hierarchical, patriarchal, and authoritarian structure of society, the head of the household claimed unchallenged obedience and kept wife and children at a respectable distance. By contrast, psychological closeness within the family nucleus was gaining currency during the seventeenth century. It was mostly a bourgeois phenomenon, which variably spread among the aristocracy and the lower class. Based on mutual affection, matrimony became more conjugal, private, sexual, child-oriented, and self-fulfilling. Several theories account for this cultural shift. It was not likely a product of industrial capitalism but, rather, reflected the passage from a traditional, feudal, and agrarian society to a predominantly liberal, professional, and merchant society.

In the seventeenth century, moral rigor and heightened piety reproved premarital sex, regulated marital sex, and severely repressed extramarital sex. Vindicating the permissiveness of the Renaissance, the eighteenth century liberated human sexuality. Adolescent onanism was judged less harmful. Although it was outlawed by church and state, male homosexuality was considered an aristocratic penchant best left unnoticed. It was common for upper class men and clerics of high rank to keep one or several mistresses. In large cities like London, Paris, Naples, or Vienna, prostitution was a booming industry. Concerned, the churches vainly tried to curb the trend. Government officials were divided between abolitionists and regulationists. The latter, more pragmatic opinion, eventually prevailed, and prostitution was kept under close police surveillance. If the emotional and sexual liberation dignified sexual passion, thereby anticipating the Romantic movement, it also encouraged sexual libertinism and generated a permissive society as a result.

Puritanism and pietism in Protestant countries and neo-Augustinianism in Catholic countries had erased eroticism from life and culture. By contrast, the eighteenth century transformed eroticism into an alternative way of life. Eroticism pervaded literature, the fine arts, and music. Something of the sexual license and cynicism of the age is suggested in the posthumous *Memoirs* of Giacomo Casanova (1725–1798) and in Pierre Cholderos de Laclos's *Dangerous Liaisons* (1782). Prefiguring Nietzsche and Freud, the Marquis de Sade's *Justine* (1791) turned hedonism into boundless perversity. Of all the painters of the time, Francois Boucher's pastoral and mating scenes rendered best the current ideal of refined eroticism. As an omen, Mozart's most famous opera *Don Giovanni* (1787) concluded with the damnation of the lawless, godless, and womanizing libertine whose life motto had been "to be faithful to one, is to be cruel to the others." Such was the verdict of bourgeois moralism on a leisurely society that Napoleon's leading diplomat, Prince Talleyrand, celebrated as the apex of civilized life.

The World Overturned

The subversion of seventeenth-century orthodox belief and the sociopolitical order originated from two Protestant countries, England and the United Provinces, where freedom of opinion was far less hazardous for historical reasons. In a way, this was the revenge of northern Europe over southern Europe, where the Renaissance had started; of Protestantism over Catholicism, which had launched Baroque culture; of the dissenting mind and the expatriate over the establishment and the community; of peripheral cultures over imposing centers of civilization. From the fringes of the post-Reformation order, to which freethinkers and outcasts had been consigned, came a succession of earthquakes that eventually shattered the "best possible" world. The first seismic forewarnings of these epochal earthquakes go far back into the early seventeenth century.

The Rise of Deism

In the year 1624, His Britannic Majesty's ambassador to Louis XIII's court in Paris, Edward Lord Herbert of Cherbury, administered the first consequential blow to orthodox belief and especially to the joint rule of revelation and tradition. Like Francis Bacon, whose *Novum Organum* had just been published, Herbert disdained the authority of tradition and the deductive methods of scholastic reasoning, and propounded a divorce of philosophy from Christian doctrine. The twofold issue Herbert dealt with had grown in importance since the rediscovery of Greco-Roman philosophy, the division of Christendom and the subsequent religious wars, and the recent awareness of other world religions like Islam (Ottoman Empire). Herbert investigated the relationship between faith and reason, and the relations between the various religious beliefs and within divided Christianity. Adopting an inductive approach, Herbert isolated the essential core of true, universal religion, from the singularities of each religion. His 1624 *De Veritate* concluded with the exposition of the five universal innate ideas or common religious notions that constitute the essence of natural religion:

1. There is a Supreme Being.
2. He must be worshipped.
3. True worship involves the proper use of the human faculties and results in virtue.
4. Sin is conditioned by experience and must be expiated by repentance.
5. Because of divine justice, there are both rewards and punishments after this life.

On the strength of this philosophy of religion Herbert then endeavored to show, in what is perhaps the first attempt at comparative religion, *The Ancient Religion of the Gentiles* (*De Religione Gentilium*, 1663), that these five common notions were shared by all world religions.

How much of an innovator was Herbert of Cherbury? This question calls for several observations. First, Herbert adumbrated a new theory of religious knowledge that cleared the path for the study of the religious phenomenon. Second, he discovered and emphasized the undisputed universal validity and the advantages of natural religion. Herbert's disaffection with Christian revelation anticipated Lessing and Kant. Third, against the fideists (those who uphold "faith only") on the one hand and the skeptics, agnostics, and atheists on the other, he demonstrated the compatibility of reason with faith. Fourth, rising above seventeenth-century religious partisanship, Herbert advocated a spirit of mutual understanding and toleration that reached far beyond the confines of Christianity. Fifth, prefiguring Toland's, Voltaire's, Holbach's, Feuerbach's, and Marx's anticlericalism, Herbert blamed the clergy for the decline of religious belief. Sixth, civic and moral as he was, Herbert pled for virtue instead of devotion, for morality instead of mere piety. And seventh, often called the father of deism, Herbert ensured the liaison between the naturalism of Italian Renaissance philosophers of the like of Pietro Pomponazzi (1462–1525) and the philosophical theology of the Enlightenment from Newton to eighteenth-century philosophers such as Voltaire and Rousseau. Above all, Herbert ought to be remembered for having inspired those whose controversial views caused the deist controversy that convulsed the Church of England from the last decade of the seventeenth century to the mid-eighteenth century.

The Birth of Biblical Criticism

The second consequential blow to orthodox Christianity was struck by three audacious biblical scholars. The Academy of Sedan was a reputed center of Calvinist theological education in seventeenth-century France. A professor of Hebrew, Louis Cappel (1585–1658), established in the *Secret of Punctuation Revealed* (1624) that the punctuation of the Hebrew text of the Bible was not of divine origin but had been invented by the Masoretes sometime in the fifth century A.D. Furthermore, in *Critica Sacra* (1650), Cappel showed that the Old Testament text had been altered several times, and he attempted to reconstruct the original text. It is small wonder, therefore, that Cappel's philological approach incurred the animosity of those who believed in divine inspiration (*theopneustia*). Both the Protestant and the Catholic orthodox parties accused Cappel of impiety. The reactionary *Consensus Helveticus*, concocted by the Swiss orthodox Calvinist pastors in 1675, was not only aimed at crushing late Arminianism and Amyraldism but also at reproving Cappel's historicocritical method. The *Consensus* was so retrograde that it claimed that even the Hebrew vowel points were divinely inspired. Eventually, Cappel was vindicated by eighteenth-century biblical scholarship.

The followers of Filippo Neri, the Oratorians, had in the meanwhile gained a wide reputation for erudition. One of them, Richard Simon (1638–1712), educated by the Jesuits and the Oratorians, studied at the Sorbonne of Paris. His magnum opus, *Critical History of the Old Testament*, was released in 1678 among outcries of indignation. Bishop Bossuet, the defender of Tridentine orthodoxy, the Port Royal party, the Oratory, and Calvinist ministers all joined in condemning Simon's scientific reconstruction of the literary history of the Israelites. Simon was duly ousted from the Oratory that same year. Why such a hatred? Simply because on scientific grounds Simon had dared to maintain that Moses could not have written all that has been attributed to him. In 1702 Simon's *New Testament Translated into French* met with equal reprobation. Poor Simon, abandoned by his few friends and having made no discipline, was now assimilated into the heretics, schismatics, and unbelievers, even in spite of his genuine efforts to show his attachment to the Catholic church. Although one can hardly speak of a true historicocritical method prior to J. G. Eichhorn (1752–1827), Richard Simon may rightly be regarded as the originator of biblical criticism.

In 1670 Jews and Christians leafed through an anonymous Latin theological and political treatise with utmost repugnance. The *Tractatus Theologico-Politicus* sundered philosophy from revealed theology, denounced superstition, prejudice, and religious intolerance, pled for freedom of thought and the separation of church and state in the age of absolutism, and worst of all, evidenced that the bible, written about the law of God by the prophets, was meant only to provide guidance to untutored minds. What could have been more subversive than the assertion that the laws revealed to Moses by God were nothing else than Hebrew state legislation? What could have been less welcome to Amsterdam Jews, Dutch Calvinists, French Catholic monarchists, and Anglican and Lutheran divines than an invitation to disclaim temporal power? Who was the author of this book that Jews and Christians alike rejected as the "most plagueful book" (*liber pestilentissimus*)? His name was Baruch Spinoza (1632–1677), the son of Jewish Portuguese immigrants to the United Provinces. Was Spinoza, an excommunicated Jew, actually a despiser of religion? Who was right, the Anglican rationalist apologist Samuel Clarke (1675–1729), who detected atheism, or the German Romantic poet Frederick von Hardenberg-Novalis, who praised the God-intoxicated philosopher? Spinozism resulted from the encounter of two opposite lines of thought: the dualism of the newly emerged Cartesianism (separation of thought and matter) and the monism of the traditional immanental metaphysics, which is traceable back to Giordano Bruno, Thomas Bradwardine of Oxford, Boetius of Dacia, Chasdai Crescas, Maimonides, and Plotinus. It was John Toland (*Pantheisticon*, 1720), who first coined the term "pantheism" to characterize Spinoza's key concept: God or nature (*Deus sive Natura*). In the posthumously released *Ethics* (1677), Spinoza geometrically demonstrated the existence of God as an ultimate necessity, as the unique substance of the universe (*Deum esse unicum*). Monism does not, however, preclude internal distinction. Although the substance is unique—God and nature at the same time—God is called "naturing nature" (*natura naturans*) and nature "natured nature" (*natura naturata*).

What were the implications of this "excessive Cartesianism," as Leibniz called it, from the vantage point of Christian orthodoxy? There were ten of them, as follows:

1. There is neither a transcendent nor a personal God but a universal theism.
2. There is no special revelation because nature reveals God.
3. The Holy Scriptures are not essential to religion.
4. Creation out of nothing (*Creatio ex nihilo*) is denied.
5. There is a general and special divine providence.
6. Predestination is universal; everything is determined.
7. Miracles are inconceivable.
8. Good and evil pertain to nature; the Christian view of sin is absurd.
9. Self-preservation constitutes the essence of human nature.
10. Self-contentment through virtue is the ultimate goal of life.

So as Pascal has been called the last grand apologist of Christian belief, his contemporary, Spinoza, may be considered the first radical critic of the biblical and ecclesiastical tradition. Instead of either Judaism or Christianity and in order to remedy the misappropriation of religious belief *(vana religio)* by rulers and priests, Spinoza proposed a religion based on the intellectual love of God. True philosophy, so he believed, is true religion. Spinoza, the theophile and the heretic par excellence who designed an alternative way to salvation, has exerted a tremendous influence on many unorthodox thinkers of the past two centuries. Kant, Goethe, Hegel, Marx, Freud, Nietzsche, and even Einstein—all shared in some respect the fundamentals of Spinoza's philosophy of immanence.

Natural Law Political Theorists

The third damaging blow to orthodox Christianity was delivered by political philosophers. And here again, Spinoza played a crucial part. The offensive, which in the end discredited the Old Regime in the eyes of the intelligentsia, had been prepared by a political theorist of the Spanish Low Countries: Johannes Althusius (1557–1638). Following Jean Bodin (1530–1596) and prefiguring Thomas Hobbes, Althusius focused his political reflection on the concept of sovereignty. At a time of civil disorder and religious antagonisms, Jean Bodin had argued in *Six Books of the*

Commonwealth (1577) that sovereignty was absolute, indivisible, untransferable, and the sole prerogative of the prince, and that the absolutist monarchy was the best guaranty of a well-ordered society or commonwealth. Theorizing within the context of the Belgian guilds, Althusius instead expressed the political aspirations of the mercantile bourgeoisie. In *Methodical Political Digest* (1603), he thus defined the state as a corporate body, a federation of autonomous groups bound together by free consent. Because it is the contract that makes the state, the state is no more than a society of societies. Unlike his predecessor Bodin and his successor Hobbes, Althusius held that sovereignty emanated from the will of the people and therefore rulers were responsible before the people, not merely before the law of nature and God, as at first Bodin and later Hobbes had contended. In addition, Althusius's further demand that church and state should be kept separate anticipated Spinoza, Locke, and Rousseau.

A hitherto famous plea for natural law and popular sovereignty was made by the Dutch publicist and statesman Hugo Grotius (1583–1645) in 1625. After having justified the rebellion of the United Provinces against Spanish rule, Grotius wrote one of the earliest treatises on national and international jurisprudence. *The Right of War and Peace* argued that because the human being is endowed with reason and moral virtues, natural law is a sufficient basis for jurisprudence in war time. Grotius did not, however, discard the divine law: It rules the realm of conscience. In other respects of life, it is the prerogative of the state to enact a body of positive laws by which citizens naturally abide.

The most significant breakthrough in the field of jurisprudence, as regards natural law and the notion of contract, was carried out by the son of a Lutheran pastor of Saxony, Samuel Pufendorf (1632–1692), who occupied at Heidelberg the chair of the Law of Nature and Nations—the first ever to exist in the world. The German school of law was the heir of Grotius, Hobbes, and the French school of law of Bourges. Pufendorf's masterpiece, *The Law of Nature and Nations* (1672), which had authority in Germany until Kant, anticipated Locke's treatises on government, inspired the theorists of American independence, and paved the way for Rousseau's *Social Contract*. Pufendorf's modernity appears in that the method is philosophical, social ethics is given a prominent role, and the idea of social contract is central. By no means a denier of divine revelation, Pufendorf nevertheless differentiated between levels of authority. Revelation and rationality are not on the same level. There are duties imposed by natural reason at a given level and others by the Holy Scriptures at another level. Pufendorf's doctrine of the state significantly contributed to the creation of enlightened despotism in central and eastern Europe.

Spinoza upheld his thesis—that of all forms of government, democracy was the best—in both the *Theological-Political Treatise* (1670) and the *Political Treatise* (1677). Whereas in the former he adduced evidence from the history of the Israelites, in the latter he reflected on contemporary historical events. Spinoza, the first secular European, stunned the world by contending that the state, to which citizens have forfeited some of their rights in exchange for protection, should guarantee freedom of thought, abstain from controlling the universities, and regulate religious institutions by supporting only those that further justice and love.

John Locke formulated his political theory in the wake of two huge political turns: the revocation of the Edict of Nantes (1685), which was the apogee of the Counter-Reformation, absolutism, and intolerance in France; and the Glorious Revolution (1688), which marked the triumph of constitutional monarchism in England. Set against the dual background of French royal tyranny and English parliamentary oligarchy, Locke's *Two Treatises on Government* (1690) take their fullest meaning. His intention was on the one hand to vindicate the restored and extended parliamentary regime (convention Parliament) and on the other to refute the divine-right theories of Thomas Hobbes and Robert Filmer. Against Hobbes, Locke argued that the "state of nature" in the human being is not harmful but merely imperfect, and that it is the purpose of the social state to remedy this imperfection. Therefore, individuals must surrender some of their rights to the state. Advocate of personal freedom, equality, and private property, and defender of the notion of contract—which can be traced back to Richard Hooker's *Of the Laws of Ecclesiastical Polity* (1594–1597)—Locke distinguished between the natural law from which the legislative and the executive power are separately derived, and the social laws, which expand the natural law. Montesquieu's theory of the Three Orders (legislative, executive, and judicial), expounded in the *Spirit of the Laws* (1748) and implemented by the French revolutionaries of 1789 had largely been inspired by Locke and the English constitutional monarchy.

The Reign of Critique

A Huguenot immigrant to the United Provinces struck the fourth disruptive blow at the seventeenth-century worldview. His name was Pierre Bayle (1647–1706). Skeptic philosopher and passionate publicist, Bayle devised two most effective weapons: the *News from the Republic of Letters* (1682), which popularized and diffused new controversial ideas and the *Historical and Critical Dictionary* (1695–1697), which submitted every area of knowledge to critical evaluation. Bayle promoted the permanent exercise of criticism as an art of attaining conclusive insights. Mainly influential on the continent, Bayle stands at the turning point of European mentality. He inaugurated the "reign of the critique," and showed the advantages of nonpartisanship.

Doctrine of Knowledge

Another substantial blow to the prevailing worldview came unavoidably from a thorough revision of epistemology. John Locke's 1690 *Essay Concerning Human Un-*

derstanding, which rose to favorite bedside-table-book for a century, profoundly changed people's perception of reality. Refuting Descartes's theory of innate ideas and carefully avoiding Bayle's skepticism, Locke unfolded a new theory of knowledge as a result of an introspective analysis of consciousness. Experience is the source of all certainty. Our ideas are derived either from perception (the five senses) or from reflective consciousness. Lockean epistemology engendered Berkeley, Condillac, and Hume and influenced Rousseau and Kant. As for the proofs of the existence of God, Locke predictably preferred the cosmological argument, also favored by Leibniz, to the Anselmian and Cartesian ontological argument. Eighteenth-century philosophers and theologians learned the relevance of facts and consciousness from Locke, and thereafter they tempered their initial rationalism with empiricism.

Against Prejudice

A general offensive against forms of irrationalism that are particularly repugnant to reason and common sense delivered the sixth fatal blow to the old concepts. A forerunner of the German *Aufklärung*, the jurist Christian Thomasius (1655–1728) declared war against prejudice in 1689. In *About Prejudices* (*De Praejudiciis*), Pufendorf's most illustrious disciple denounced the tyrannical tutelage under which the authorities keep people by means of prejudices. Prejudices reign as a result of an excessive liking for institutions and dogmas. As symptoms of dependence, prejudices hinder autonomous thinking. *About Prejudices* highlighted the specific difference in mentality between the seventeenth and the eighteenth century. Autonomy is the principal aspiration of eighteenth-century people. In a similar vein, a Reformed church minister in Amsterdam and disciple of Descartes declared his intention to disenchant *The World Bewitched* (*De Betoverde Weereld*) in 1690. Balthazar Bekker's (1634–1698) hefty book, translated into several languages, earned him some notoriety. Self-appointed supreme exorcist of a bewitched universe, Bekker attempted to convince credulous people that belief in the action of the devil, the supernatural power of sorcerers, and the influence of planets and comets on destiny was utterly groundless.

In previous centuries, religious enthusiasm had engendered mystics and reformers of all sorts. Some clerics and laypeople still claimed supernatural inspiration at the turn of the eighteenth century. Their activity mainly consisted in clairvoyance and prophecy. The Camisard movement, which emerged in France in the Cevennes shortly after the revocation of the Edict of Nantes, is a striking illustration of alleged spiritual possession. The Camisards (armed Huguenots in active resistance) claimed to be possessed by the Holy Spirit. There also were several enthusiastic sects in London at the time. It was in this context that a pupil of Locke, the moral and aesthetic philosopher Shaftesbury (1671–1713), wrote his *Letter Concerning Enthusiasm* (1708). Shaftesbury observed that there is a true and a false enthusiasm. True enthusiasm is regulated by reason, unlike false enthusiasm, which being unbridled usually ends in either fanaticism or superstition. Consequently, Shaftesbury advised people to learn to master their enthusiasm. By denouncing excesses, he also largely contributed to the secularization and demythologizing of seventeenth-century religiosity.

The Emancipation of History

A last blow, insidious yet far-reaching, was struck by historians. The old-fashioned chronicle and myth-history died in splendor with Bishop Bossuet's 1681 *Discourse on Universal History*, which drew from history lessons in the art of morality and politics. What has been called the historiographical revolution began with a Belgian school of Benedictine critical hagiographers, the Bollandists, in the early seventeenth century. The *Acts of the Saints* purged the lives of the saints of all exaggerated miraculous accounts. The first attempt at writing Roman history on a critical basis was made by a Port Royalist historian, Le Nain de Tillemont (1637–1698). His *History of the Roman Emperors* was released to the public in 1690, but the historiographical revolution came from Naples. The first historian to lay down the principles of historical method was Giambattista Vico (1668–1744). His *New Science* (*Scienza nuova*, 1725) did for history what Bacon's *Advancement of Learning* had done for science. In line with Bacon and Locke, Vico based knowledge on the convergence of truth and data (*verum et factum convertuntur*). His modernity is manifest in the conviction that history is built by human beings and not by God and that therefore the task of the historian is to analyze the birth and development of human societies and their institutions (customs, laws, governments, languages, etc.).

Historians of the Enlightenment took over the methods of historical research. They did not improve them significantly but turned them into a sophisticated weapon against religion and the church. Voltaire's 1731 *History of Charles XII* of Sweden and the *Age of Louis XIV* (1751–1768), David Hume's *History of England* (1754–1762), and Edward Gibbon's *Decline and Fall* (1776–1788) played a significant part in the overall crusade of the modern spirit of commerce, industry, and enlightened despotism against backwardness, barbarism, and religion. Initially serving a religious purpose, historiography swerved to a philosophical aim under the influence of the new ideas. Eventually, the alliance of history with philosophy—both sciences being liberated from the tutelage of theology—gave birth to philosophy of history. A first attempt was made by Voltaire in 1754 (*Essay on the Mores and Spirit of Nations*). Shortly afterward, Herder disclosed his teleological vision of history in *Ideas of a Philosophy of the History of Humanity* (1784–1791). The pinnacle was attained with Hegel's idea-impregnated history (*Philosophy of History*, 1822–1823), against which Karl Marx reasserted eighteenth-century historical naturalism. In the 1820s, the German historian Leopold Ranke advocated an objective history based on the establishment of facts and the study of sources. With the rise of positivism and the natural sciences by the mid-nineteenth century, the differentiation of the historical from the scientific method became a much debated issue (F. H. Bradley; W. Windelband; G. Simmel; W. Dilthey). At the close of the century, an Italian philosopher, Benedetto Croce, delivered a vigorous plea for the independence of history from both science and philosophy. Meanwhile, the human sciences had grown powerful. In the 1930s, a cluster of French historians, Lucien Febvre, Marc Bloch, and Fernand Braudel, outlined in their journal, *Annals of Social and Economic History*, a new approach to culture history that integrated social and economic analyses into a "history of mentalities." They attempted to recapture the scientific, technological, economic, social, political, and cultural conjunctures which constitute the framework of vast chronological expanses called the "lougue durée".

Apologists of Infallible Nature

Who better than a poet could celebrate the novel passion for nature?

> Know then thyself, presume not God to scan;
> The proper study of mankind is Man. . . .
> Go, wondr'ous creature! Mount where science guides;
> Go measure earth, weigh air, and state the tides,
> Show by what laws the wand'ring planets stray,
> Correct old Time, and teach the Sun his way. . . .
> Yes, Nature's road must ever be prefer'd;
> Reason is here no guide, but still a guard;
> 'Tis her's to rectify, not overthrow,
> And treat this passion more as friend than foe.[1]

Alexander Pope's *Essay on Man* (1733) beautifully encapsulated the idealized program of the enlighteners, whose ambition was to ensure human beings' happiness by a subtle blend of the natural and the virtuous. "That Virtue only makes our bliss below" appropriately concludes Pope's philosophical poem.

With the Civil War, the Restoration, and the Glorious Revolution, the British Isles passed through the seventeenth century amid recurring political and religious hurricanes. William III's 1689 Bill of Rights and 1690 Toleration Act eventually laid the basis for political and religious stability. Worn out, fanaticism gave way to moderation and common sense. Within the Church of England, which had unfortunately swayed between bibliolatry and popery, some moderate clerics had emerged as a

---

[1] *The Complete Poetical Works of Alexander Pope*, Cambridge Edition (Boston and New York: Houghton Mifflin Company, 1903), p. 142.

third party, distant from both the Puritan party and the high church party (Laudi-ans). Because of their attachment to the liturgy and organization of the Anglican church and their aversion to Puritan and medieval scholasticism alike, they were called Latitude Men. Two luminaries deserve mention: John Tillotson (1630–1694), consecrated archbishop of Canterbury in 1691, and Bishop Edward Stillingfleet (1635–1699).

Along with Herbert of Cherbury and William Chillingworth (1602–1644), an anti-Catholic polemicist, Tillotson and Stillingfleet were among the true precursors of eighteenth-century English religious mentality, which can be best characterized as reasonable belief. That burning desire for an acceptable compromise between the church and the sects, reason and belief, which repudiated dogmatic parochialism on the one hand and avoided the perils of atheism and skepticism on the other, enthralled clerics of all sorts and ranks for a century from Locke and Toland to Butler and Hume. Tillotson's *Sermons* (1704) were widely read in the eighteenth century. They served as a mine of arguments to the rationalist divines and deists alike. Educated at Cambridge, Stillingfleet steered a middle path between fideism and rationalism. A formidable polemicist, Stillingfleet used his impressive erudition as an arsenal of weapons against Romanism, dissent, and atheism. As early as 1677, he warned the English against the perils of Spinozism in a *Letter to a Deist*. It was the first attack on the nascent deist movement.

Locke

Like Isaac Newton, who in his later days wrote a commentary on the Book of Daniel, John Locke was fascinated by the interpretation of the Bible. Having already gained a considerable repute throughout Europe in the fields of epistemology, political phi-losophy, and pedagogy (*Thoughts Concerning Education*, 1693), and having made several well-received pleas for religious freedom (*Letters on Toleration*, 1666, 1690, 1691, 1704 and *Epistola de Tolerantia*, 1685), Locke made a most conspicuous entry on the theo-logical stage with *The Reasonableness of Christianity* in 1695. The hefty tome caused much controversy. Some judged his view on revelation and the person of Jesus to be dangerous; others thought it not radical enough. In the 1690 *Essay Concerning Human Understanding*, Locke had differentiated reason (as instrument of knowledge) from faith (as assent to propositions disclosed by some extraordinary means). Re-vealed propositions can be either "above, contrary, or according to reason." What is above or according to reason is acceptable; what is contrary to reason is not. Such were the conditions Locke fixed for a reasonable Christianity. The The *Reasonableness of Christianity* became a classic for three reasons. First, Locke precluded any dogmatic method of interpretation and read the bible without any support other than his own senses. His rejection of doctrinal partisanship was aimed at rendering biblical teach-ings more objectively and thereby making them universally acceptable. Second,

Locke set forth that Christianity consisted in acknowledging Christ, king and Savior, and the teachings known to come from him. Locke's simple Christocentrism represented a radical departure from the obsessive complexity of Puritan scholasticism and had the unmatchable advantage of providing a solid basis on which all parties could meet. Third, Locke shifted the center of gravity from piety to morality. Stoicism, Jansenism, and Puritanism had impregnated society with an urge for virtue. Virtue was so much in fashion in the seventeenth century that it shaped three new models of humanity: the Spanish picaresque hero immortalized by Baltasar Gracian's *El Heroe* (1637); the French classically bred "honest man" (*honnête homme*) celebrated by the moralist La Bruyere; and the English gentleman whose moral and social values were propagated by the *Tatler* and the *Spectator*. Epitome of the gentleman, Locke set the standards of a gentleman's religion. Similarly, Archbishop Synge's *A Gentleman's Religion* (1695) was aimed at helping gentlemen avoid the perils of enthusiasm and the avant garde.

Moreover, seventeenth-century awareness of non-Christian cultural values and beliefs had brought upsetting questions to the force: Is a virtuous Chinese doomed because he never heard of Christ? Or, conversely, do all beliefs equally open the gates of heaven? Acknowledging the universal fact of religious belief, Locke steered a middle course between relativism and exclusivism. He maintained that Christianity was morally useful to the human being and superior to any religion or philosophy in ethical matters. Christian revelation is the ultimate promulgation of the moral law. This conciliatory line of thought was later successfully exploited by the German Enlighteners from Lessing to Schleiermacher.

The Deists Compete in Audacity

In 1696 a radical book, *Christianity Not Mysterious*, came out amid much indignation. Its author claimed that Christ "fully and clearly preached the purest Morals," that "he taught that reasonable Worship, and those just Conceptions of Heaven and Heavenly Things, which were more obscurely signified or designed by the Legal Observations" (Jewish Law), and held the priesthood responsible for making "the plainest things in the world appear mysterious" in order to "increase the Splendor" of their status and make people "believe they were in good earnest Mediators between God and Men."

Born a Catholic in Ireland, converted to Protestantism, self-declared disciple of Locke and critical admirer of Spinoza, familiar with biblical criticism and in agreement with the antitrinitarian current, John Toland (1670–1722) concocted a most persuasive rationalization and demythologizing of Christian belief. His ambition was to reform the Reformation. In his opinion, Locke's *Reasonableness* did not carry out its promise to the full. Therefore, another more radical attempt was needed. Toland built his cathedral of criticism on four pillars: (1) Lockean epistemology; (2) Socinian rationalism; (3) biblical criticism; and (4) noncontradictory logic, which dismisses all illogicalness. On account of this fourfold basis, propositions that were above reason were treated like those which were against reason. No theological proposition can embody a mystery and still be true. The result of Toland's treatment of Christian dogmas was unmistakable:

1. Revelation became just another means to convey rational truth: Although different in form, natural and revealed religion convey an identical content.

2. The God of reason and nature is identical with the God of revelation and history (against Pascal).

3. "Vulgar faith" is sharply distinguished from true religion: The former holds mysteries to be things imperfectly knowable, whereas the latter liberates belief from the mysterious and denies any substitution of adoration for comprehension.

4. Mysteries and ceremonies are additions invented by the self-serving priesthood.

5. The authentic substance of Christianity is morality; Jesus is the "perfect rule of life."

In sum, Toland's *Christianity Not Mysterious* sapped the very foundations of orthodoxy.

A philosophical heir of Herbert of Cherbury, Charles Blount (1654–1693) strengthened the case for the sufficiency of natural religion by adducing proofs from writers of classical antiquity. His 1697 *Soul of the World* (*Anima Mundi*), which betrays leanings toward Hobbes and Spinoza, made a stand on naturalism, disproved immortality, and denounced priestcraft.

At the close of the seventeenth century, Cambridge produced the greatest polymath of the Church of England: Samuel Clarke (1675–1729). Born of wealthy parents, endowed with a versatile and luminous mind, and open to novelty, rector of St. James, Westminster, Samuel Clarke acquired a wide repute in sciences, classics, and theology. As a natural philosopher, he defended Newtonianism against Leibniz's criticism. Clarke was a friend of William Whiston, author of a Newtonian *New Theory of the Earth* (1696). As a preacher, he impressed both Samuel Johnson and James Boswell.

Besides numerous scholarly works, Clarke is best remembered for two famous series of Boyle Lectures that he delivered at St. Paul's, London, in 1704 and 1705, and for *The Scripture Doctrine of the Trinity* (1712), in which he stressed the supremacy of God the Father and the subserviency of the Son and the Spirit. The first series of Boyle Lectures dealt with the existence and attributes of God and were aimed at refuting Hobbes and Spinoza. Against the deists, the second series unfolded Clarke's view on natural and revealed religion. As expected, Clarke's father-centered doctrine of the Trinity got him in trouble with the convocation of the Church of England. He was suspected of Arianism. It was mainly against him that Daniel Waterland, the renowned Cambridge divinity professor, directed his orthodox *Vindication of Christ's Divinity*.

What did Clarke stand for? A man of reason, though not a deist, Clarke had a deep aversion to any kind of religion that stimulates excesses in emotion or action. He disliked Calvinism and abhorred enthusiasm and sectarianism. A reasonable Christianity was the right alternative. He firmly believed in a harmonious encounter of reason with Christian revelation, and therefore he pled for a constructive alliance of natural with revealed religion. Like Locke, he also taught that obedience to the moral and eternal law of God was the essence and purpose of true religion. Clarke truly was the epitome of Latitudinarianism.

While in London the deist circle of the Grecian Coffee House was debating about free inquiry, rationality, and toleration, one of their members published in 1713 what has since been considered the manifesto of the Free Thinker's club: *Discourse of Free-Thinking*. Anthony Collins (1676–1729) was a wealthy dilettante, a layman who had been educated at Cambridge and had befriended Locke. A pamphlet that was pro–natural religion and anticlerical, *Priestcraft in Perfection* (1709) had already gained him some notoriety among the deists. However, it was his audacious 1713 *Discourse* which propelled him to the heights of fame in Europe. It was even translated into French and Dutch. The kind of Protestantism that appealed to Collins was a liberal one: subordination of revealed religion to natural religion, or of revelation to reason.

A forerunner of Voltaire, Holbach, Helvetius, Marx, and Nietzsche, Collins cynically remarked in the *Discourse of Free-Thinking:*

> If any Man presumes to think for himself, and in consequence of that departs from the Sentiments of the Herd of Mankind among whom he lives, he is sure to draw upon himself the whole Malice of the Priest, (. . .). Whereas any profligate Fellow is sure of Credit, Countenance and Support, in any Sect or Party whatsoever, tho he has no other quality to recommend him than the worst of all Vices, a blind Zeal to his Sect or Party.[2]

As the reign of Queen Anne was nearing its close, political tension was building between the Tories and the Whigs. The Tories naturally attacked what they saw as a Whig tract, whereas the Whigs repudiated their fellow writer as being too radical to their taste. In the *Guardian*, the famous Irish metaphysician, George Berkeley, later bishop of Cloyne, launched a notable offensive by a series of *Essays against Free-Thinking* (1714). Yet the fatal blow was struck by none other than the formidable theologian and classical scholar, Richard Bentley, master of Trinity College at Cam-

[2]Anthony Colins, *A Discourse of Free-Thinking, Occasioned by The Rise and Growth of a Sect Call'd Free-Thinkers* (London, 1713), p. 120.

bridge. Bentley ruined Collins's reputation in England. He skillfully demonstrated how defective Collins's scholarship was and concluded that he was little else than a mere atheist. Who would want to trust a careless, ignorant, godless, and self-styled interpreter of the bible? Bentley made sure nobody would.

Owing to two well-argued apologies of natural religion, the deist movement reached its zenith around the 1730s. *The Religion of Nature Delineated* (1724) and *Christianity as Old as the Creation* (1730) dignified the otherwise impetuous deist cause. The former apology, well balanced in its argumentation, came closer to Clarke's Latitudinarianism than to Toland's radicalism, whereas the latter, more insidious, was reminiscent of Collins. An imposing fruit of thirty years of reclusive meditation, William Wollaston's (1660–1724) masterpiece, *The Religion of Nature Delineated*, established the necessary existence of a deity, underscored morality, acknowledged prayer, the immortality of the soul and particular providence. Wollaston asserted that his defense of natural religion was not intended to undermine revealed religion but, on the contrary, to pave the way for its reception. Like most of his contemporaries, Wollaston more frequently cited classical rather than biblical authors. Although his lifework was reprinted several times, it was soon overshadowed by Matthew Tindal's (1655–1733) majestic dialogue on the tenets of deism.

As a fellow of All Soul's College at Oxford, Tindal spent most of his uneventful life compiling *Christianity as Old as the Creation*, which was an overt attack on the principle of authority of orthodoxy:

> To receive Religion on the account of Authority supposes, that if the Authority promulgated a different Religion, we should be obliged to receive it; and indeed, it's an odd Jumble, to prove the Truth of a Book by the Truth of the Doctrines it contains, and at the same time conclude those Doctrines to be true, because contained in that Book.[3]

Clearer than any deist before him, Tindal defined God as the great artificer. Since his avowed goal was not to dispose of historical religion but to reconcile the immutable and infinitely just, wise, and good God of reason and nature with the God of Moses and the Thirty-Nine Articles of Religion, Tindal convincingly argued that the historical revelation is but a replication of the law of nature written in the human heart by God since creation. Revealed religion is a duplicate of natural religion; it is the law of nature conveyed otherwise. Both Confucius and Jesus taught simple truths that encapsulated the substance of natural religion. Like so many of his contemporaries, Tindal preferred Chinese wisdom to Judaic prophecies. His natural and ahistorical rationalism led to three consequential emphases: (1) an elitist Christian moralism; (2) an antidoctrinalism and anticlericalism; (3) an antibiblicism and anti-Judaism. There were not many replies that matched Tindal's polemical essay. In

---

[3]Matthew Tindal, *Christianity as Old as the Creation* (London, 1730), p. 186.

1731 Daniel Waterland (*Scripture Vindicated*) and William Law (*The Case of Relgion and Reason*) attempted without much avail to vindicate the biblical picture of God.

Ever since Spinoza, prophecies and miracles had become the favorite targets of the deists. Two deists focused their attack on the miraculous: Thomas Woolston dealt with the bible and Conyers Middleton with the early church fathers. Woolston (1669–1733), dismissed as a Cambridge don, produced a sensation by releasing a series of six *Discourses on Miracles* between 1727 and 1730. Woolston upheld the view that the biblical miracles were allegories, thereby implying their lack of historical authenticity. An ineffective Cambridge don and librarian, Middleton (1683–1750) channeled his resentment against Christianity through a skillful and insidious assault on the early church fathers, so highly valued in the Anglican church. His 1748 *Free Enquiry into the Miraculous Powers*, solidly grounded in historical criticism, demonstrated the supernatural deceits of early Christianity.

The Anticlimax

Shortly after reaching its zenith, deism was confronted by its fate. For diametrically opposed reasons, Christian apologetics and philosophical skepticism independently achieved the downfall of deism. Whereas the Pascalian Butler argued the probability of Christianity, the Pyrrhonist Hume argued the improbability of the deist God. Under cross fire, deism eventually collapsed in England by the mid-eighteenth century.

Often considered the definitive Anglican answer to deism, *The Analogy of Nature, Natural and Revealed, to the Constitution and Course of Nature* (1736) ranked Joseph Butler (1692–1752) among the luminaries of the Church of England at the time, men such as Clarke, Bentley, and Berkeley. Since the Latitude men and Locke, moral theology had gained considerable popularity among theologians. The emphasis on the moral law was urged by all moderate parties as a suitable means to counter the rise of libertinism, exemplified by Mandeville's *Fable of the Bees* (1714), and to quench religious fanaticism. It was also at that time that Francis Hutcheson (1694–1746) unfolded his moral sense philosophy. Small wonder that Butler aspired to a reasonable Christianity that would enhance the practice of virtue. His heart was set on promoting Christian moralism. The *Analogy of Nature* was aimed at defending the tenets of Christianity against Toland, Collins, and particularly Tindal, on the basis of Lockean epistemology and common-sense philosophy. By comparing Christianity as a whole to nature, Butler established that God actually governs nature and human existence in accordance with the tenets of Christian belief. There are so many analogies between nature and Christianity that one may conclude it to be probable that, like nature, Christianity was originated by God. The probability that the deist God (argument from design), the God of the rationalists (Anselm and Descartes), and the biblical God are one and the same is very high. Natural and revealed religion are similar, yet the latter is not a mere duplicate of the former. As a set of religious theories—Herbert's five principles—natural religion evidently is a part, although not the whole, of revealed religion.

Butler, the Engish "Pascal," who intended to salvage Christianity by encouraging moral people to practice religion, believed that there was no difference between leading a moral life and being a Christian.

An apparent ally, David Hume (1711–1776), the British "Pyrrho," ironically turned out to be the worst enemy of the deist cause. The Scottish philosopher and historian not only maintained that any reasonable religion should deny any divine intervention in the world but also that any causal connection between the two in the mind was merely an association supported by repetition.

Closer to Pierre Bayle than to the deists, Hume's skepticism prefigured the momentous destruction of traditional metaphysics by Kant. Just as Hume's assault on the apologetic arguments could not have pleased the deists more, so his conclusion in the *Enquiry Concerning Human Understanding* (1758) and in the posthumous *Dialogues Concerning Natural Religion* (1779) that the existence of God was a void hypothesis could not have displeased them less. As a description of the birth and development of religious belief, Hume's 1759 *Natural History of Religion* had a shattering effect. The criticisms of religion by Toland, Collins, and Tindal seemed harmless by comparison. Hume differentiated the philosopher's theism from the theism of common believers. The former is derived from the inconclusive design argument, whereas the latter results from ignorance and emotions. The origin of religion lies in the fear of suffering and death, the need for security and happiness, and a tendency to anthropomorphize. As a product of barbarism, religion tends to nurture ignorance. Religious tenets are but a collection of superstitions.

At the close of the eighteenth century, a Cambridge man, William Paley (1743–1805), resuscitated the design argument regardless of Hume and Kant (*Evidences of Christianity*, 1794 and *Natural Theology*, 1802, respectively). A late Latitudinarian and a staunch believer in the power of reason in a disillusioned age, Paley more successfully propounded a utilitarian view of the church that deeply marked his generation (*Principles of Moral and Political Philosophy*, 1785).

In the meantime, an antirational and proevangelical revival had taken place within the Church of England. It had started in the 1680s, as religious societies were proliferating, had gained a powerful identity under the leadership of George Whitefield and the Wesley brothers, and after considerable trouble with the established church, consolidated into an independent society in the 1750–1770s. The members of that society were called Methodists.

Early Ecumenical Endeavors

Almost half a century after the welcome conclusion of the Thirty Years' War and just eight years after the infamous revocation of the Edict of Nantes, an optimistic

German jurist, mathematician, and philosopher, Gottfried Wilhelm Leibniz (1646–1716), ventured the incredible opinion that when all Protestants will have turned Catholic, the Catholics will have become Protestant. For some time, ecumenical dialogue between Lutherans and Calvinists and between Protestants and Catholics had been flourishing at the University of Helmstädt in the Lutheran principality of Braunschweig. Rapprochements among Lutherans, Calvinists, and Catholics had been promoted in the 1620s by the syncretistic theologian George Calixt and further encouraged by the Hanoverian dynasty.

In the 1680s, the Holy See, the Viennese Hapsburg dynasty, and the Protestant Hanoverian dynasty had a political interest in the matter. The Catholic party was led by Cristobal de Rojas y Spinola, a Dutch-born bishop, and the Helmstädt delegation was chaired by a disciple of Calixtus, Gerhard Wolter Molanus. Each leader had presented a project. Molanus's project, called *Method for the Return of Ecclesiastical Unity*, outlined the progressive steps toward the convocation of a new universal council. First, the Catholic church was required not only to recognize the Protestant churches as Christian churches—thereby lifting the current excommunication—but also to concede communion in two species and some issues pertaining to justification. Next, the Protestant churches were called to acknowledge papal primacy. Once these preliminary agreements were sealed, easy matters of controversy could be cleared at an initial meeting that all heads of state might attend. On the strength of its results, a universal council would then be convened to settle the more delicate questions regarding faith, the bible, and the tradition. Molanus's project aroused much criticism in the Lutheran ranks and failed to gain the sanction of either Vienna or Rome in spite of Spinola's mediatory efforts. It would have fallen into oblivion had it not been rescued in 1688 by Leibniz, a Lutheran layperson who skillfully captured the attention of the leader of the Gallican church, the formidable Bishop Bossuet.

Leibniz was no ordinary thinker. Born in an academic milieu, he was a thorough polymath. With a ravenous appetite for novelty, an unquenchable passion for universal harmony, and a boundless love for God, in addition to a discursive and innovative mind, Leibniz was predisposed to the titanic task of reconciling irreconcilables. An avid reader, he was familiar not only with classical and contemporary philosophies but also with patristic, scholastic, Protestant, and Tridentine literatures, and heterodoxies as well. Against Arianism and Socinianism, he wrote an *Apology of the Trinity*. Fascinated by alchemy, he joined the Rosicrusians. Through his friendship with a Catholic statesman, he was introduced to an open-minded Catholicism, which he honestly planned to render comprehensible to his reluctant coreligionists in the unfinished *Catholic Demonstrations*. From traveling widely throughout Europe, mostly in the service of the elector of Mainz, he acquired a cosmopolitan perspective quite ahead of his time. Leibniz became acquainted with luminaries so diverse as the pietist Spener, the Jansenist Arnauld, the Oratorian Malebranche, the Jesuit La Chaise (Louis XIV's confessor), and Spinoza, the other "God-besotted" metaphysician.

Open to non-Christian civilizations, Leibniz fully supported the Jesuit mission to China by showing the compatibility of the Chinese cultural legacy with Christianity. That Christian revelation should complete and not eradicate Confucianism was the message of his *Discourse on the Natural Theology of the Chinese*. Beyond their theological variance, the Lutheran Leibniz and the Catholic Malebranche entertained a comparable conception of missionary activity.

It was during the decades spent at Hanover and Wolfenbüttel that Leibniz produced the masterpieces which propelled him to the philosophical firmament. At the same time, he engaged in constructive ecumenical dialogue with Calvinists, Anglicans, and Catholics. As a metaphysician who elucidated the harmony of a pluralistic universe and framed the idea of a best possible world to solve the riddle of evil, Leibniz foresaw that the future of Christianity lay in the reconciliation between northern and southern Europe, between a Protestantism that regenerated Christian belief and a Roman Catholicism that provided authority and unity—in brief, between dynamism and statism. As the axis of Leibniz' multifarious endeavors, the love of God had made that demand on him. Luther had given priority to faith over love; Leibniz prioritized love. Love makes all humans, Christian or pagan, members of the invisible church, or the body of Christ.

Already corresponding with noted Catholic divines, Leibniz initiated a correspondence with Bishop Bossuet in 1692, raising the crucial issue: Can church unity nonetheless tolerate diversity? Interrupted in 1694, because Leibniz disputed the alleged ecumenical character of the Council of Trent, the correspondence resumed in 1699 after the Helmstädt theologians made new proposals for unity, and ended with Bossuet's stern refusal of any concession in 1702. Why did Leibniz and Bossuet fail to reach any agreement? The whole discussion focused on doctrine and discipline. In spite of a common goal, Leibniz and Bossuet were and remained at odds on method and priorities. Their conceptions of truth and authority were too far apart ever to meet. Leibniz showed that the Catholic tradition varied and evolved throughout history and that at the present time, far from being monolithic, Catholicism was quite diverse. In his rejoinder, Bossuet sought refuge under the umbrella of absolute and unnegotiable principles in total disregard of any historical perspective. As advocate of an orthodox interpretation of the Tridentine Reformation, Bossuet was calling for submission and obedience to the infallible church. In addition, he was engaged in a fierce struggle against biblical criticism (Simon) and quietism (Fénelon) and was counterattacking the Calvinist Pierre Jurieu's ferocious anti-Romanist propaganda. Therefore, he was adamant to any doctrinal concession of significance. Leibniz's proposal to consider Lutheranism one of the "variations" of Catholicism alongside Jesuitism, Jansenism, quietism, and Gallicanism was unacceptable to Bossuet because it imperiled his upcompromising stand within the Catholic church. Likewise, the suggestion of restricting the infallibility of the church to matters of faith, so as to secure room for disciplinary and doctrinal diversity, met with unqualified reprobation. Although they both were equally dedicated to the glory of God, they could not agree on how best to serve it. Humanistic and conciliatory, Leibniz naively believed faith and love sufficed. Authoritarian and doctrinaire, Bossuet obstinately insisted on a submissive assent to a perennial and immutable transmitted truth.

So pioneering had been Leibniz's vision of a worldwide Christian church that would embrace all churches regardless of their particularism that until only recently has it becomes less of a dream. The *aggiornamento*, or updating, of the Catholic church, at the Second Council of the Vatican (1962–1965), indirectly vindicated Leibniz's vision. By acknowledging the existence of non-Catholic churches and promoting Christian unity, Vatican II acceded to some clauses of Molanus's forgotten project. It took the Catholic church four centuries to withdraw the Tridentine excommunication of the Protestants.

In the meantime, the unity of Protestantism had slowly taken form. At Königsberg, where the elector of Brandenburg had been crowned king of Prussia, a first interdenominational service (Lutheran and Calvinist) had taken place in 1707. A century later, the Prussian Union was created (1817) on the basis of another of Molanus's projects. The unity, doctrinal and ritual, of Lutheranism and Calvinism was finally achieved in nineteenth-century Prussia. The intensification of ecumenical dialogue led to the World Missionary Conference of Edinburgh in 1910. The non-Catholic churches—Protestant and Orthodox—together began to advance church unity. Several world conferences were launched: Life and Work at Stockholm in 1925–1930; Faith and Order at Lausanne in 1927; Christian Youth at Amsterdam in 1939. At Utrecht in 1938, the foundations were laid for a World Council of Churches based primarily on the confession of Jesus Christ as Lord and Savior.

Protestant Revivals of Piety

In eighteenth-century Lutheran Germany and Anglican England, the religion of the heart blossomed afresh in response to the ascending religion of reason. Originally a peripheral phenomenon, Methodism and Moravian Pietism grew in importance in the nineteenth century, especially in the United States.

The Lord's Shelter

Heterodox sects, such as the Paracelsans, Weigelans, Anabaptists, Schwenkfeldians, and Socinians, had traditionally found refuge on the borders between Germany, Poland, and Bohemia, where, under the protection of empathetic landlords, they escaped persecution by mainstream orthodoxies. In 1721 a group of Moravian refugees under the guidance of a carpenter, Christian David, requested the hospitality of a Saxon landowner who was known for his unorthodox Pietism and caring open-mindedness. Soon a village was built on his estate at Berthelsdorf and populated with Brethren from Bohemia and Poland as well as Pietist, Calvinist, and Roman

Catholic refugees. Called *Herrnhut* ("the Lord's Shelter"), the Christian commune became an exemplary institution comparable with the Jesuit colonies, or reductions, in Paraguay. The landlord revealed himself to be an extraordinary leader. Social life was organized so as to nurture continuously the relationship of the believer with God. Bible reading, hymn singing, and prayer paced daily life. The old and the very young were well cared for. Marriages were arranged, and male and female elders were in charge of pastoral care. Worship was disciplined yet allowed for free expression. Religious professions were common. Many early Christian practices were unearthed: footwashing, love feasts, the kiss of peace, and the casting of lots in decisive matters. Religious fervor also had its morbid side with its devotion to the wounds of Christ. The physical agony of their Savior was stressed in a manner reminiscent of Spanish and French Catholic mysticism. Naturally, the Lutheran church of Saxony became suspicious of these devotional extravagances, and the Herrnhut community fell under sharp criticism.

Who was the community leader and what were his beliefs? Count Nikolaus Ludwig von Zinzendorf (1700–1760) was born in Dresden, the capital of Saxony, and was educated at Halle, where he came under Francke's influence. At the age of fourteen he founded the Order of the Grain of Mustard Seed, a boys' group whose members pledged themselves "to love the whole human race." An avid reader of Fénelon and Madame Guyon, Zinzendorf, who had been blessed in his youth by Spener himself, believed in love and harmony. Destined by his guardians to a career in the Saxon higher civil service, he completed his education by visiting Holland, France, and Switzerland, where he became acquainted with religious luminaries and socialites. On his return, he married a Pietist noblewoman, acquired the Berthelsdorf estate from his grandmother, and unexpectedly started on an ecclesiastical career. Zinzendorf wrestled with the ascending Enlightenment and especially Pierre Bayle, whom he greatly admired. The result was an anti-Enlightenment pamphlet, *The Socrates of Dresden* (1725).

The Herrnhut community received its official statutes in 1727. It remained within the Lutheran communion yet preserved its Bohemian and Moravian traditions. The clerical organization of the *Unitas Fratrum* ("Unity of the Brethren") was revived and posed a legal problem to the officially Lutheran state of Saxony. Nonetheless, in 1734 Zinzendorf qualified for ordination and was consecrated bishop of the Moravian church by the son-in-law of Amos Comenius, the erstwhile bishop of the Polish Brethren. Banished from Saxony from 1736 to 1747, Bishop Zinzendorf undertook a systematic visitation of worldwide Moravian settlements. Energetic settlers and ardent missionaries, the Moravians had established communities in Berlin, Amsterdam, London, Greenland, Georgia, Pennsylvania, and the West Indies, and had even sent Brethren to Persia, Ethiopia, and Ceylon. Already by the end of the 1740s, the Moravian diaspora formed a powerful denomination. Eventually, the state of Saxony granted the Moravians religious freedom in 1749.

Zinzendorf's theology can best be characterized as a Lutheran theology of the heart. Equally rejecting orthodoxy and the Enlightenment, Zinzendorf focused on the personal experience of Christ. He internalized Luther's theology of the Cross, and counterbalanced the Reformers' theology of the Word of God with a sensualist-spiritualist theology of the Holy Spirit. According to Zinzendorf, the true essence of religion is the union of the soul with God. Using the metaphor of marriage, he compared God or Christ to a bridegroom and the believer to a bride. His innovative interpretation of the Trinity as Father, Mother, and Son sounded heretical to the orthodox. In addition, Zinzendorf worked on a new translation of the bible and produced a collection of daily devotional mottoes and some very fine Christian poetry and hymns.

William Law

In eighteenth-century Anglicanism, inward religion was revived by a follower of the Desert Fathers (i.e., Pachomius and Anthony of Egypt) and the Dutch-German mystical tradition: William Law (1686–1761). Jan van Ruysbroeck, Thomas à Kempis, Johannes Tauler, and Jacob Böhme all molded William Law's mystical moralism. A fellow of Emmanuel College, Cambridge, as much a devout and a moral rigorist as a detractor of Deism and Latitudinarianism, William Law rose to fame with masterpieces of devotional prose literature, a *Treatise on Christian Perfection* (1726) and *A Serious Call to a Devout and Holy Life* (1729). Christianity is understood as a "godly life," which is attained by prayer, meditation on the bible, self-denial, and obedience to the divine will. By contrast with Protestant orthodoxy, Law stressed the indwelling Christ (Christ in us) instead of the justifying Christ (Christ for us). William Law influenced the revivalist John Wesley, the writer Samuel Johnson, Cardinal John Henry Newman of the Oxford Movement, and the Christian novelist C. S. Lewis.

Methodist Christians

The prominent apostles of the Evangelical Revival, which in the long run gave birth to a new denomination, Methodism, were two Oxford men, John Wesley (1703–1791) and his pupil George Whitefield (1714–1770). Three sons of an Anglican rector—Samuel, a minor poet, John, an indefatigable preacher, and Charles Wesley, a prolific hymn writer—had their hearts bent on invigorating the drowsy body of their church. In 1729, Charles Wesley and a few intimate friends, Robert Kirkham and William Morgan, formed at Oxford a small religious society known as the Holy Club, which John Wesley and later George Whitefield joined. The members had adopted a Rule or a methodical way of nurturing their spiritual life (prayer, devotional readings, self-examination, fasting, frequent communion, and good works), which won them the nickname of "Methodists."

After having received the holy orders in 1725, John Wesley spent several years at Oxford deepening his understanding of the bible and exploring mystical and Quietist writings. In 1735 he sailed to the new colony of Georgia with his brother Charles and a small team of Holy Club members. They intended to evangelize the Indians. There he met August Gottlieb Spangenberg, who was later to succeed Zinzendorf as leader of Herrnhut, and was impressed by the piety of the Moravian settlers. The Georgia venture failed lamentably. On the ship bound to England, John Wesley entered in his *Journal*: "I went to America to convert the Indians: but oh, who shall convert me?" Thereupon he underwent a long religious crisis and sought the spiritual guidance of the London Moravian community. Finally, in May 1738, he experienced the gift of grace and recorded in his *Journal*: "I felt my heart strangely warmed. I felt I did trust in Christ, Christ alone for my salvation: and an assurance was given me that He had taken away my sins, even mine and saved me from the law of sin and death." Upon his return from a pilgrimage to Germany's Moravian communities, "where the Christians live," and where he held fruitful conversations with Zinzendorf, he eventually embarked on his lifelong evangelical activity, cease-lessly preaching salvation by faith, a somewhat forgotten theme among the Anglican clergy.

What happened in the Bristol area in 1739 truly launched the Evangelical Revival. It was the first of many of John Wesley's "field preachings," which attracted masses of common people (coal miners, weavers, artisans) in Wales, Northumberland, Corn-wall, Ireland, and Scotland. Because he failed to enlist more clergy, such as George Whitefield, to meet the needs of a widening preaching itinerancy, Wesley began to appoint lay preachers whom he put in charge of "circuits." A first annual conference of lay preachers took place in London in 1744. In England alone in 1760, there were already 50 circuits totaling 30,000 members.

The spectacular spread and growth of Methodist societies, the concession of clerical prerogatives to laypeople, Wesley's own unconventional ministry, and the awakening of religious exuberance or enthusiasm aroused the suspicion of the An-glican hierarchy. Soon the churches closed their doors to Methodist preachers. Separatist sentiments grew among the Methodists. Unshakably loyal to the Thirty-Nine Articles of Religion, John Wesley succeeded all his life in maintaining the Methodist societies within the fold of the Church of England. He was less an original thinker than a practical reformer. His theology was eclectic, as the varied selection of texts of his *Christian Library* shows. His four volumes of *Sermons* and his *Explanatory Notes upon the New Testament* (1755), which laid the foundation of Methodist preach-ing, are profoundly Arminian. John Wesley believed salvation was offered to every human being, and thus he rejected the Puritan doctrine of predestination.

In the wake of the independence of thirteen English North American colonies, American Methodists became eager to sever their ties with Anglicanism. A revised edition of *The Book of Common Prayer* was issued for their use in 1784 with Wesley's approval. At the famous Christmas Conference of 1784 in Baltimore, the Methodist

Episcopal church was established. By the time of Wesley's death in 1791, the American Methodist church numbered more than 57,000 members with 227 itinerant preachers, and the English Methodist societies were more than 76,000 members strong with 313 itinerant preachers. The social impact of Wesley's Methodism had been paramount. By bringing the gospel to the common people, the Methodists had awakened their sense of responsibility and enhanced their dignity. By praying together, singing hymns, and guarding each other from lapsing into sin, the Methodist people acquired a sense of spiritual equality and social fraternity, which undoubtedly preserved English society from breaking apart during the European revolutionary earthquakes of the close of the century.

In England the Methodist societies organized themselves in new denominations in the second half of the nineteenth century. Because of the example set by the Methodists, Presbyterians and Anglicans had begun their own evangelical revival.

Despisers of Christianity

In 1764 Voltaire wrote as follows:

> What is toleration? It is the appurtenance of humanity. We are all full of weakness and errors; let us mutually pardon each other our follies,—it is the first law of nature. (. . .) Of all religions, the Christian ought doubtless to inspire the most toleration, although hitherto the Christians have been the most intolerant of all men.[4]

With the death of Louis XIV of France, a devout in his later days, the most flamboyant symbol of a theocratic society vanished in 1715. His immediate successor, Duke Philip of Orleans, who assumed the regency until Louis XV's majority, was a freethinker and a libertine. For some time libertinism had pervaded cultural circles, yet remained peripheral and weak. The period spanning the 1715s and the 1750s saw a dramatic change. Increasingly, the freethinkers, who then called themselves "philosophes," were able to remold public opinion, even in spite of a still watchful censorship. Center of classical Christianity for almost a century, Paris soon shifted to being the center of an alternative culture, thoroughly humanistic and profoundly irreligious: the Enlightenment. From Paris, the new intellectual climate spread eastward to Prussia, Austria, and Russia, and westward to the American colonies. Most "philosophes" optimistically propounded that the categories of human understanding were universal and timeless and that the principles of reason and morality were common to all people regardless of time, space, race and social class. This utopian

[4]Article on Toleration, M. de Voltaire, *A Philosophical Dictionary*, Vol. VI (London: J. & H. L. Hunt, 1824), pp. 272, 274.

belief led to a remodeling of the system of religion and morality; they also devised a social and political order that would be free from prejudice and superstition. The mathematician Jean Le Rond d'Alembert (1751–1772), who was immortalized by his *Preliminary Discourse* to Diderot's *Encyclopedia*, believed that science had come of age and held the elitist opinion that it was the mission of the scientists to be the legislators of society.

Voltaire

"Crush the infamous" was the battle cry against Christianity of the self-styled "pope" of continental Enlightenment, Voltaire. A frail man with a sharp mind and a biting sense of humor, the son of a Parisian notary, Francois-Marie Arouet (1694–1776) adopted the name Voltaire on social grounds and was the most prolific, versatile, elegant writer of his age. Initially a much celebrated lyric poet and neoclassical tragedian, he gained an even greater repute as a novelist, a historiographer, a literary critic, a philosopher, and a profuse correspondent. By the mid-century, his mighty pen had altered the course of European civilization like no other. His writings were commented on by men of letters and rulers of all persuasion from Naples to St. Petersburg. Educated by the Jesuits and exposed to the classics and the freethinkers at an early age, Voltaire masterfully struck a balance between French conformism and English nonconventionalism.

As an insolent young poet, he offended the crown and some powerful aristocrats and was imprisoned several times. He spent three philosophically formative years (1726–1729) in London and for a time worked for the French crown as a historiographer. In 1750 he emigrated to Brandenburg. At the palace of Sans Souci at Potsdam near Berlin, he spent three years conversing with Frederick the Great, the "king-philosopher." A bitter argument broke their friendship. A couple of years later, Voltaire found in the hideousness of life a fresh reason to deny metaphysical optimism. Indeed, the destruction of Lisbon by an earthquake in 1755 deeply shocked most "philosophers," especially Voltaire. They were reminded of the magnitude of evil and pain in the world and were confirmed in their distrust of the biblical God whom they held responsible. The last twenty years of Voltaire's life were spent in the comfortable and wealthy seclusion of his estate of Ferney near the Swiss border. In the meantime he had become a legend. He died at the height of glory and was secretly buried in an abbey in Champagne after a last-minute convenient adhesion to the Catholic faith.

What can be said of Voltaire's advocacy of the Enlightenment? First, he propagated English culture on the Continent. In his *Philosophical Letters on the English* (1734), he praised England for her political, intellectual, and religious freedom and for her entrepreneurial spirit of commerce. This praise was an indirect condemnation of French and most Continental societies. Second, he diffused Newtonianism—*Elements of Newton's Philosophy*, 1738—and advocated Baconian and Lockean empiricism against Cartesian rationalism. Every eighteenth-century *philosophe* was a follower of a sort of English philosophy and science. Third, Voltaire promoted the cause of deism. Next to the current historical argument against Christianity, much in use since Bayle, Voltaire especially emphasized the moral argument borrowed from the radical English deists. In the *Ignorant Philosopher* (1766), Voltaire observed that the necessary idea of a Watchmaker does not conclusively lead to that of a provident and Infinite Being, a Creator.

Voltaire took the leadership of the crusade of the Continental intelligentsia against established religion and above all against the Roman Catholic church. Although he showed much respect for the person of Jesus, to whom however he denied divine status and also praised the Quakers for their integrity and moral lifestyle, he despised organized religion for all the evil it brings about. His most famous play, *Zaïre*, attacked superstition. The worst aspect of orthodoxy is religious fanaticism, which breeds intolerance. Voltaire demolished every Christian dogma, mystery, and sacrament as fraud and imposture. Like any other revealed religion, Christianity is founded on unreliable sources, and therefore it deserves utter destruction. Anti-Pascal, Voltaire, the apologist of freethinking, rejected any supernatural truth. Voltaire did not, however, favor agnosticism. Albeit hard to prove the existence of God, it is absurd to deny it. Voltaire believed that atheism was even more threatening than religious fanaticism because it dismantles the social structure. "If God did not exist, it would be necessary to invent him" was one of Voltaire's most famous dicta.

According to Voltaire, a skeptic and pessimist at heart, the overwhelming presence of evil in the world disproves the naive, pious, and confident view that there is a greater good to be gained in the end—*Poem on the Disaster of Lisbon*, 1756. In the philosophical tale *Candide* (1759), a masterpiece of subversive literature, Voltaire portrayed Leibniz under the features of Candide's preceptor, the optimistic philosopher Pangloss, who in the face of repeated adversity and recurrent despair, glibly observes, "Nevertheless this is the best of all possible worlds!" The lesson the young Candide draws from his tribulations is that all is for the worst in the best of possible worlds, but that life continues in spite of all. Candide's closing observation is that there is little else to do other than "to cultivate one's garden." Fatalistic detachment is the answer to unfathomableness and powerlessness.

The Encyclopedia

On the Continent, Roman Catholic and Protestant authorities joined in banning and burning Voltaire's sacrilegious works. His 1764 anonymously published *Philosophical Dictionary* was burned by all the upholders of orthodox belief—Rome, Geneva, Paris, and even the United Provinces. Nonetheless, Voltaire had sapped the religious foundations of the Old Regime irredeemably, and the so-called Voltairian spirit, much in favor among progressive intellectuals, triumphed in the secular and anticlerical world of the late nineteenth century.

Lockean epistemology in a radicalized version reached its zenith in Continental Europe in the 1740s and 1750s with the publication of La Mettrie's materialistic *Machine Man* (1748), the basic tenet of which consisted in a reduction of the human being to the animal level, and of Condillac's sensationalist *Treaty of Sensations* (1754), in which an entire generation of freethinkers found its inspiration. The physician La Mettrie held religion for an unproductive illusion. Quite naturally, the Roman Catholic church refused to tolerate works which either furthered a materialistic point of view or drew antireligious conclusions from sensationalist premises. These works were banned by the Sorbonne of Paris, and the personal freedom of their authors was under serious threat. Amazingly, however, the Roman Catholic church did not oppose the printing of Denis Diderot's *Encyclopedia* (1751–1772), a repository of contemporary science, technology, art, moral philosophy, and social science, because it was believed to advocate harmless sensationalist views. The *Encyclopedia* became the landmark of the Enlightenment. Very much in the spirit of Chambers, the aim was "to gather all the lights of nations in one work" according to the laws of reason. The focus of investigation was the achievements of humanity in every field. There was no longer any concern about God.

Did Diderot (1713–1784) believe in God? Son of a cutler, follower of Seneca and Shaftesbury, protégé of Empress Catherine II of Russia who offered him temporary hospitality in St. Petersburg, Diderot shared with his fellow Enlighteners a vivid aversion to Christianity, which he held responsible for superstition, fanaticism, and intolerance. By far he preferred atheism to religious tyranny, sensuality to asceticism (his eroticopsychological novel *The Nun* depicts perversions in a nunnery), and reason and nature to dogmatic "truth" (*Philosophical Thought*, 1746). In a *Letter to the Blind for the Use of Those who See* (1749), Diderot repudiated both theism and deism and turned to the law of nature. Above all, what matters in life is to attain the supreme virtue of humanity. Diderot's alternative to Christian religion was a combination of naturalism and humanism.

Helvetius and Holbach

Long before the Germans Ludwig Feuerbach and Karl Marx, two "philosophes" carried naturalism and materialism to the extreme: Claude Adrien Helvetius (1715–1771) and Baron Paul Thiry von Holbach (1723–1789). With perhaps the exception of Rousseau's *Emile* (1762), no work aroused such an outcry from religious and civil authorities during the entire eighteenth century than Helvetius's *Of the Spirit* (1758). As soon as the treatise appeared, its sale was prohibited and its author was compelled to retract. The Jesuits, the Jansenists, the Archbishop of Paris, the Sorbonne, the Parlement, and the Pope all condemned the work as blasphemous and subversive. Had it not been for the protection of the king's mistress, Madame de Pompadour, Helvetius would not have escaped imprisonment.

Why was Helvetius the victim of clerical repression? Basically unoriginal, *Of the Spirit* openly published views mostly shared by the philosophic movement and was taken to be symbolic of its intrinsic irreligiosity. Six antireligious conclusions may be drawn from Helvetius's sensationalism:

1. The human being is said to be exclusively material. The denial of the spirituality of the soul directly led to the denial of its immortality, which in turn led to a disinterest in life after death.

2. Since all ideas, as copies of impressions, come to us from outside through the senses, human actions are thoroughly determined by external circumstances.

3. Self-love is the rule of all action and the motive of all learning. Because the purpose of life is life itself, earthly happiness is all there is to hope for. Earthly happiness results from the largest possible amount of pleasure. Yet to prevent selfishness from being destructive, social laws must regulate human selfishness. Above all, there is no need to be a Christian to lead a virtuous life. An atheist is capable of virtue.

4. Social utility is the criterion of truth, beauty, and morality. Private and public virtue must coalesce. It is the function of society, and no longer of the church, to ensure that human egoism serve public welfare.

5. Human education and progress are of primary importance. It is the philosopher's task to inform the public of the truth. Legislation, and not revolution, is the way to free human beings from intellectual, religious, and political oppression.

6. The clergy is to blame for being self-serving, for exploiting human gullibility and ignorance, and for using religion as a means to preserve its privileged position in society. As a handiwork of ambitious opportunists, the church is detrimental to the happiness of the human race. Every dogma derives from a desire for wealth and power. Therefore, the church must be eradicated from society.

In a similar vein, a German-born Parisian socialite, a friend of Diderot, Voltaire, and Rousseau and a collaborator on the notorious *Encyclopedia*, Baron Paul Thiry von Holbach anonymously published *Christianity Unveiled* in 1756 and *System of Nature* in 1770. The latter treatise soon became a landmark of eighteenth-century atheism. Holbach's anti-Christianism was based on the antimony of nature, the true reality, and religion, the pseudoreality. *Christianity Unveiled* demolished Christian revelation, miracles, prophecies, mysteries, dogmas, and rites as mythological and illogical. Biblical inerrancy is absurd. Christian ethics is blamed for encouraging fanaticism and cruelty and for arousing a persecutor mentality. In a pre-Nietzschean fashion, Holbach repudiated Christian virtues—obedience, humility, sacrifice, and resignation—as antinatural and suicidal. Instead, he stressed natural goodness and love for humanity. He attacked clerical immorality, imperialism, and totalitarianism. With a wealth of examples, Holbach evidenced that Christianity destroys every dimension of life, be it personal, social, or economic. As a conclusion, he invited every ruler to dispose of religion in his or her realm, for, he said, religion is merely mythology and alienation. In the *System of Nature*, after having observed that truth and virtue were always persecuted, Holbach disproved every argument for the existence of God, refuted theism, deism, and pantheism, rejected metaphysical dreams and otherworldly optimism, and declared theology to be a hindrance to human progress. Anticipating Karl Marx's famous slogan "religion, opium of the people," Holbach defined religion as the art of intoxicating people with enthusiasm. Christian religion is nothing but a monstrous plague. Materialism and humanism are the true remedy to the Christian plague. And so sounded Holbach's conclusive advice: "Be reasonable, this is your religion; be virtuous, this is your path to blissfulness."

For all eighteenth-century despisers of Christianity, experience, reason, and nature were the exclusive guides to a self-fulfilled humanity.

How far did the philosophic movement contribute to the dechristianization of Continental Europe? Considerably in France, marginally in other countries. The plea for freedom of expression and religious toleration could no longer be ignored. Civil authorities either strengthened or softened their policy regarding censorship and religious pluralism. So much criticism had been cast on powerful religious orders such as the Jesuits that rulers and the pope had to surrender to public opinion. The separation of morality and society from religion accelerated the process of political centralization and cultural secularization. Along with social and political libellers, anticlerical pamphleteers created a climate of discontent and rebellion that in the long run partly caused the 1789 revolution. As a result of popular skepticism and institutional ossification, religious devotion waned, religious vocations declined, theological studies lost their appeal, and mysticism fell under suspicion. Monasticism sharply declined; contemplative life was viewed as useless and idle. Conversely, atheism became fashionable and respectable. However, the philosophic movement, which fuelled nineteenth-century irreligiosity, provoked various reactions because of its excesses that in most cases amounted to salvaging Christianity. Indirectly, the Enlightenment produced a revival of piety and irrationality.

The Quest for an Enlightened Christianity

The most prominent figure of the Enlightenment in German-speaking countries, Gotthold Ephraim Lessing, encapsulated the new cultural idea in the disquieting opinion that anyone who in good faith argues untruth is superior to anyone who out of prejudice defends the highest truth. He further audaciously contended that the quest for truth and not the possession of it was what truly exalted the human being (*Ein Duplik*, 1778).

What was the state of Christianity when the stream of new ideas, flowing from England and France, reached German soil? The religious clauses of the peace treaties of Westphalia (1648) had culturally and religiously divided Protestants and Catholics along political lines. A century later, Catholic Bavaria and Austria differed sharply from Protestant Prussia. Austrian and German Catholicism had closed itself to any external intellectual influence. Cultural insularity thus strengthened religious uniformity. Unchallenged, the Tridentine Reformation met with complete success. The Roman Catholic church in Austria took the religious leadership of German Catholicism. Religious orders prospered.

On the whole, the Jesuits had become the most influential religious order in the Austrian Empire. They were in charge of education, directed culture toward religious goals, and in politics achieved a close union of church and state. The cultural expression of their theology was altogether colorful and dramatic, essentially visual and sensual. Apart from the Benedictine University of Salzburg, where strict Thomism was kept alive, the theology taught in colleges and seminaries was largely derived from Spanish-Jesuit scholasticism. Religious practice was unilaterally enforced in Catholic lands. Attendance at Mass, fast-keeping, participation in processions and pilgrimages were expected from state officials, just as belief in the Immaculate Conception was expected from academics. In Hungary, however, the Hapsburg regime conceded religious freedom to the Protestants in 1691 and even tolerated the presence of a Greek Orthodox church. A first breach in the Austrian symbiosis of religious and political values appeared during the reign of Emperor Joseph I (1678–1711). It was caused by the deterioration of papal-imperial relations. By the 1720s, a new phenomenon appeared that was comparable to that of the seventeenth-century Gallican and Spanish "Liberties." The breach steadily widened under the growing pressure of the Enlightenment. The final disruption followed the anticlerical policy of Emperor Joseph II (1741–1790).

By contrast, German Protestantism offered a varied picture. Protestantism was divided into a Calvinist minority and a Lutheran majority. Lutheranism was further divided into an orthodox minority and a Pietist majority. Dominant in the seventeenth century, Lutheran orthodoxy, learned and scholastic, had lost considerable ground in the eighteenth century. At the outset of the Enlightenment, Pietism had become the strongest ferment in the religious and cultural life of German Protestant principalities. Because of its anti-worldly, anti-intellectual, and anti-institutional disposition, Pietism gave rise to a sharp sociopolitical criticism of feudal society, the late echo of which can be heard in *Intrigue and Love*, the third drama written by the Romantic poet, Friedrich Schiller, in 1783.

The Takeoff of the German Enlightenment

How did the Enlightenment, or *Aufklärung*, take off in Germany? Christian Thomasius, Gottfried Wilhelm Leibniz, and Christian Wolff were the forefathers of the *Aufklärung*, Moses Mendelssohn and Gotthold Ephraim Lessing its prominent luminaries, and Immanuel Kant its last and most critical interpreter. The jurist Thomasius (1655–1728) had openly denounced witchcraft, superstition, and the barbarism of torture. A century before Kant, he upheld that reasonableness should be the motive of human actions. A quiet mystic, Leibniz had promoted the refreshing vision of a friendly God, architect and guarantor of the order of the universe. Often called "preceptor of Germany," Wolff was to Leibniz what Melanchthon had been to Luther. Wolff systematized and popularized Leibnizianism, thereby creating the first great German academic philosophy since the demise of Aristotelianism. Just as Luther had molded German piety and language, Wolff shaped the German philosophical mind and language. As a consequence, the leadership of European thought, which had been assumed by France in the seventeenth century and by Britain in the eighteenth, passed to Germany in the nineteenth century.

A professor at the University of Halle, Christian Wolff (1679–1754) was proficient in mathematics and sciences and well versed in scholastic and Cartesian philosophies. His life ambition was to build an encyclopedic synthesis on the Thomist model, a modern *Summa*, which would achieve the harmony between rational inquiry and Christian belief. In the Philippist vein (Melanchthon's brand of Lutheranism), Wolff advocated a "philosophical Christianity." He believed in rediscovering by rational means the God revealed in the Bible by supernatural means. His philosophical works established his reputation, while also arousing suspicion among his Pietist colleagues. Wolff's assumption that heathens were capable of genuine morality repelled the Pietists of Halle.

The clash with the Pietists followed a public lecture Wolff delivered at Halle in 1721. Wolff's *Speech on the Practical Philosophy of the Chinese*, which favorably echoed Malebranche's and Leibniz's positive attitude toward Confucianism, stressed the similarities between Christian and Chinese ethics. Wolff's colleague Joachim Lange launched the Pietist offensive, and a virulent and learned controversy raged for several years. Eventually, the Pietist cabal succeeded in obtaining from the head of state, the devout Frederick William I of Prussia, Wolff's dismissal in 1723. When Wolff's *Natural Theology*, his chief refutation of atheism, was published in 1736, his influence in Protestant theological schools became overwhelming. It is no wonder, then, that Frederick II, the king-philosopher who highly praised Wolff in his correspondence with Voltaire, invited Wolff to resume his teaching at Halle in 1740. At Halle and other German theological schools, the Pietist movement by then was in steady recession.

Wolff's philosophical theology was culturally and religiously influential in four respects:

- Wolff's moralism, rational and natural, suited bourgeois intellectualism.

- By adopting the doctrine of being (ontology) as a basis for every discipline, Wolff directed Protestantism along a metaphysical course.

- His distinction between theoretical knowledge (ontology, epistemology) and practical knowledge (economics, ethics, politics) had a long-lasting effect on German philosophy and theology.

- In reaction to the anti-Christian potential of the Cartesian divorce of reason and faith, Wolff cleared the path for a fruitful reconciliation of Christian revelation and human reason, of faith and culture. To both those who denied faith and those who denied reason, Wolff opposed a reasonable Christianity.

Secular Enlighteners: Mendelssohn and Lessing

When dealing with the German Enlightenment, or *Aufklärung*, one may distinguish between a secular and a clerical Enlightenment. Closer to English deism than to the French philosophic movement, the secular Enlightenment was more radical than the clerical, which tempered rationalism and naturalism with the rising historicism.

The new ideas, ranging from philosophy to politics, were mainly debated in Masonic lodges and in informal clubs such as the Society of the Friends of the Enlightenment, and they were diffused in the upper and middle classes by journals such as the *General German Library* (*Allgemeine Deutsche Bibliothek*, 1765–1806) and the *Berlin Monthly Magazine* (*Berlinische Monatsschrift*, 1783–1811).

One of the foremost German Enlighteners was a Berlin Jew, a disciple of Wolff, and Lessing's friend, Moses Mendelssohn (1729–1786). Mendelssohn unfolded the first Jewish philosophy of religion in modern times. He takes rank among such luminaries of Jewish thought as Philo of Alexandria, Maimonides, and Spinoza. Influenced by Locke, Shaftesbury, and Leibniz, Mendelssohn believed in the rationality of religious truth and, repudiating miracles and supernatural revelation, upheld that natural reason established the existence and unity of God, the reality of Providence, and the immortality of the soul (*Phädon*, 1767; *Morgenstunden*, 1785). In his chief contribution to Jewish thought, *Jerusalem or On Religious Power and Judaism* (1783), Mendelssohn denied the Torah to be a set of revealed truths and required freedom of conscience, religious toleration, and separation of church and state as well as civil rights for the Jews.

Mendelssohn's influence on the course of the *Aufklärung* cannot be overlooked for four reasons:

- Along with his friend Lessing, he was a brilliant advocate of toleration, understanding, and mutual recognition between the religions.

- He initiated the first Jewish-Christian dialogue in modern times with two noted Protestant divines.

- In the already most tolerant of German states, Prussia, he stood up for the further emancipation of the Jews. He promoted Germanization and social integration in order to remedy the Jewish spiritual and cultural isolation.
- Christian Wilhelm von Dohm's famous treatise *On the Civic Improvement of the Jews* was published in 1781 with Mendelssohn's warmest support. Dohm called on German governments to grant the Jewish community the same rights already given to other minorities in society. His appeal was heard.

Poet, playwright, critic, publicist, philosopher, theologian, and occasional secretary and librarian, Lessing excelled in whatever he undertook. The son of a Lutheran minister, Lessing studied theology and philosophy at Leipzig. He was, however, deterred from entering into the Christian ministry by the growing awareness of a poetic vocation. At Berlin, where he first lived, he started a journalistic and literary career, became Mendelssohn's friend, and wrote his first theological work (*Thoughts on the Moravians*, 1750), which propounded an ethically oriented deism. In 1767 Lessing revealed his views on esthetics in *Laocoön or On the Limits of Painting and Poetry* and laid the foundation of the modern German stage with the drama *Ninna von Barnhelm*. In the same year, he joined the national theater of Hamburg as critic and playwright and made the acquaintance of the family of the orientalist and radical Enlightener Hermann Samuel Reimarus (1694–1768). There he also met the German "Milton," Friedrich Gottlieb Klopstok, whose *Messias* (first three cantos) had won little acclaim outside conservative religious circles.

The 1770 decade saw the apogee of Lessing's creativity. He journeyed in Austria and Italy and eventually married at forty-seven. The most important of his publications of this period are a collection of considerations on history and literature (1773–1781); the *Fragments of an Unknown* (1774—1778), which were selected from Reimarus's controversial and unpublished manuscript *Apology for Reasonable Worshippers of God*; Freemason dialogues (*Ernst und Falk*, 1778–1780); his finest play *Nathan the Wise* (1779), a tribute to Mendelssohn, which unveiled Lessing's own vision of himself (he unfortunately never saw it performed); and the highest monument to the ideal of the *Aufklärung*, the *Education of the Human Race* (1780), which conveyed the message that religion was a device planned by God to educate humanity. On the whole, Lessing's philosophical and theological views reflected those of his enlightened contemporaries.

As an enlightened critic, Lessing persistently fought for freedom of conscience and unqualified toleration. He respected otherness and believed in unity beyond plurality. As the fable of the ring in *Nathan the Wise* illustrates, Christianity, Judaism, and Islam are individuations of a single original religion. And the true goal of any religious belief is the achievement of humanity.

In theological issues, Lessing finally took a moderate stand after having been somewhat of a radical in his early years. He repudiated Reimarus's deism and was as distant from pure rationalism (e.g., Johann Christoph Edelmann's *The Divinity of*

Reason, 1741) as from Lutheran orthodoxy. The main challenge was for Lessing to determine whether the foundation of religious belief was rational and eternal or historical and temporal. Are natural religion and revealed (i.e., historical) religion mutually exclusive? Lessing's answer prefigured Idealism and Romanticism. To bridge the "ugly, wide ditch" between the rational and the historical, Lessing upheld religion to be both necessary and accidental inasmuch as it is the manifestation of timeless rationality in a dynamic temporal process. In the play, God so created the world that Nathan's rational religion and the revealed religion of the monks can live together in peace and harmony.

The Lessing-Goeze virulent polemic, which followed the release of the *Fragments* and raged in the winter of 1777–1778, is another illustration of the tension between two religious mentalities: one that values free inquiry and the other that relies on dogmatic certainty. A champion of scriptural inspiration and infallibility, Pastor Johann Melchior Goeze of Hamburg accused Lessing in a newspaper article of up-setting simple believers. Against Lessing's distinction between the bible and religion, Goeze argued that the bible was religion solely and entirely, and that Christian belief was incontrovertibly true because God spoke to the biblical authors through the Holy Spirit. Lessing responded in several short pieces that he, and not the Lutheran ministers, stood on Luther's side, fighting for the progress of Christianity. By hin-dering scriptural research and prohibiting its diffusion, and thereby keeping believers in ignorance, Lutheran ministers act like little popes and by contrast make the real pope look attractive, concluded Lessing.

Clerical Enlightenment

The clerical Enlightenment was the prodigal son of an unlikely *ménage à trois*, a triple union of reason, history, and revelation. The diffusion of Leibnizo-Wolffianism, the emancipation of the historical sciences and the resiliency of revealed knowledge to-gether produced an array of theologies ranging from unyielding rationalism to pure historicism. Two prominent schools deserve mention. First was the neologist School, the towering figures of which were Johann Joachim Spalding (1714–1804) and Wilhelm Abraham Teller (1734–1804). Second was the school of historical criticism of the bible, which included the most formidable Lutheran divines of the second half of the eighteenth century: Johann August Ernesti (1707–1781), Johann David Michaelis (1717–1791), and Johann Salomo Semler (1725–1791), whose four-volume *Treatise on the Free Investigation of the Canon* (1771–1775) epitomized unprejudiced historical and critical research.

The author of a very controversial *Attempt at a Free Theological Teaching* (1777), Semler revolutionized the making of theology by applying the yardstick of history to religious truth. Hence he debunked the orthodox confidence in biblical inerrancy and canonical authority. The bible is the human and historical witness of a divine revelation, he said. Expanding Calvin's doctrine of a dual knowledge of God, Semler distinguished in a Wolffian fashion between a natural and a special revelation of God. The natural revelation is given to every rational being, whereas the special revelation is exclusively confined to the bible. The aim of special revelation is to certify and complement natural revelation. Semler's interpretation of scripture was based on the theory of accommodation. The special revelation of God in the bible has been accommodated to the then human cognitive and moral capacity. In summary, Semler's promotion of the historical critical method was a pioneering research in the fields of New Testament textual criticism (e.g., Johann Jakob Griesbach, 1745–1812) and church history (e.g., Gottlieb Jakob Planck, 1751–1833).

One of the major preoccupations of enlightened biblicists was formulated in 1787 in a public address at Altorf by Johann Philipp Gabler, a pupil of the Old Testament scholar Eichhorn. Gabler masterfully divorced biblical theology from dogmatic theology. He thereby secured the nascent emancipation of biblical disciplines.

The theologies of the German *Aufklärung* can be characterized by the following ten major features:

1. Their basic intent was apologetical, inasmuch as they refuted naturalism and abstract Deism.

2. Biblical to the core, they were closer to the English than to the French mode of Enlightenment.

3. They provided the church with a theology adapted to contemporary culture.

4. They also aimed at liberating Christian belief from the alternative confinements of orthodoxy and Pietism.

5. They claimed to achieve the incomplete Lutheran Reformation by disclosing the "true religion of Jesus."

6. They drafted a full program of historical research (bible, history, doctrine).

7. They advocated the demythologization of the New Testament.

8. They revised the classical doctrine of Christ (Chalcedonian Christology), especially emphasizing the humanity of Jesus.

9. They gave preference to morality over worship and piety.

10. They reinterpreted the doctrine of faith into a doctrine of happiness (*eudaemonism*), for the true goal of religion is the completion of human nature.

Biblical criticism attained full maturity by the close of the nineteenth century with the scholarly works of Julius Wellhaussen (1844–1918) and Alfred Loisy (1857–1940). In the twentieth century, biblical criticism developed in five directions: literary criticism (e.g., K. H. Graff); comparative religion (e.g., G. Kittel); tradition history and literary genres (e.g., H. Gunkel); form criticism (e.g., R. Bultmann);

and redaction criticism (e.g., H. Conzelmann). A good deal of nineteenth- and twentieth-century biblical theology was devoted to the burning issues of biblical inerrancy, interpretation of scriptures (i.e., hermeneutics), canonical authority, and the relationship of the Old Testament to the New.

In 1783, a Berlin minister, Johann Friedrich Zöllner, raised the crucial question in the *Berlin Monthly Magazine* of the meaning of the *Aufklärung*. Theodor Adorno and Max Horkheimer of the Frankfurt School have thus mistakenly argued that the Enlightenment lacked critical self-reflection (*Dialectic of Enlightenment*, 1942–1944). As Mendelssohn's 1784 response in the same journal shows, Enlighteners had become acutely aware of the potential threat to personal and social life posed by egoism, irreligion, and anarchy, and they thereafter began to appraise the causes, goals, and limits of their enterprise. Later in the year, the *Berlin Monthly Magazine* published another response by an East Prussian philosopher. In *Answer to the Question: What Is Enlightenment?*, Immanuel Kant saw the whole matter in terms of an exercise of the will and not, like Mendelssohn, as a social and cultural phenomenon. Just as idleness and cowardice are to blame for human immaturity, so maturity demands resolution and courage. "Dare to know," exhorted Kant. Freedom is the condition of personal enlightenment.

Yet another East Prussian pointed out that the self is also related to and dependent on others. Therefore, however bold free inquiry might be, it must be counterpoised by the demand of the common good lest it destroy the social and political structure. Enlightened though he was, Johann Gottfried Herder approved of only a mode of Enlightenment that would produce a true humanity by improving understanding and by strengthening organic ties (*Letters on the Advancement of Humanity*, 1793–1797).

Königsberg, the Last Beacon of the Enlightenment

The third and last phase of the *Aufklärung* was launched in the last two decades of the eighteenth century from the northeastern boundaries of enlightened Europe. Owing to Johann Georg Hamann, Johann Gottfried Herder, and above all, Immanuel Kant, Königsberg, the metropolis of East Prussia, became the new beacon of the *Aufklärung*. Both critical of the Enlightenment, Hamann and Herder anticipated the Romantics, whereas Kant inaugurated the age of encyclopedic philosophical systems, called German Idealism, by reinterpreting the cultural legacy of the century.

Of Pietist and lower-middle-class stock, Immanuel Kant (1724–1804) was born and schooled in Wolffianism at Königsberg, where he lived and died as a staunch bachelor. When at the age of forty-six he was finally appointed to a chair of logic and metaphysics, he began to reflect critically on rationalism (Descartes, Leibniz, Wolff), empiricism (Locke, Newton, Hume), and moralism (Rousseau, Lessing). As a result, ten years later came a stream of incomparable masterpieces: the *Critique of Pure Reason* (1781), the *Critique of Practical Reason* (1788), and the *Critique of Judgment*

(1790). A philosophy of religion, *Religion within the Limits of Reason Alone* (1793), was among the most influential writings of Kant's later years.

Kant's philosophy has often been compared with Platonism because of its inherent dualism, and time and again Kant has been claimed by Lutheran thinkers as Luther's philosophical heir. Indeed, Kant fulfilled the potentialities of Reformation thought: the autonomy of human consciousness, antidogmatism, and the moral dimension. Kantian philosophy or criticism was an attempt at answering three crucial questions: What can I know? What should I do? What may I hope for?

For this fulfillment to take place, Kant achieved what has been described as a "Copernican revolution." In search of norms, he directed his investigation, not to the outer world, like Galileo, but to the inner world of human consciousness. Kant placed the thinking person at the center of the universe, like the Sun, and then defined the process of the cognitive faculty in terms that combine empiricist with rationalist theories. Knowledge is limited to the world of sense. However, without the mediation of rational concepts there would not be any knowledge. It follows first that what we actually know is the object as it appears to us and not as it is in itself, and second that anything that claims reality must either come by or be certified by experience. Thereupon, Kant became, as Mendelssohn deplored, the "great demolisher" of classical metaphysics. Until Kant, only the skeptics, materialists, and radical naturalists had refuted the classical arguments for the existence of God. Kant masterly demonstrated that none of the various proofs, however logical they may be, can actually be certified by experience. In sum, they are groundless.

Was Kant yet another Helvetius or Holbach? Did he also aim at destroying the Christian metaphysical tradition, so close to the churches' teachings, in order to free humanity from superstition and religious fanaticism? After all, Kantianism was temporarily prohibited at the University of Marburg by a 1786 princely decree. Although not a real Christian, Kant nevertheless aimed at salvaging ethics and metaphysics by securing their basis against any potential attack by modern science. He therefore unfolded a moral worldview that functionally replaced the classical metaphysical worldviews. Thus, he is counted with Jean-Jacques Rousseau, who came before him, and Friedrich Schleiermacher, who came after him, among the momentous rebuilders of European thought. By differentiating between the mediating activity of cognitive reason and the free postulating activity of moral reason, Kant pulled knowledge and belief apart and thereby proved that both science and morality (or religion) were legitimate in their respective spheres.

How did Kant influence the course of Christianity? As it was to be expected, Kant predominantly and variously influenced Continental Protestantism, above all German Lutheranism, but only marginally and more recently Anglo-Saxon Protestantism. Although most Roman Catholic thinkers refuted him, as did many orthodox Lutherans, a few assimilated some tenets of Kantianism. Kant's overall legacy may be summarized in the following seven observations.

1. Kant demonstrated that natural theology, so much in vogue since the early

days of the Enlightenment, no longer functioned. The concept of nature was an unreliable basis for religion. He put an end to both classical theism and the Enlighteners' favorite type of religion, and unwittingly gave fideism (reliance on faith instead of reason) a fresh chance.

2. Kant refuted the dominant morality of the Enlightenment. He replaced eudaemonism, based on the self-quest for happiness, with a rational version of Lutheran-Pietist ethics. True morality is obedience to the general moral law, which springs from individual consciousness. With Kant the moral component of the Enlightenment gained a metaphysical status. Kantian moral legalism largely contributed to the shaping of the mentality of the nineteenth-century central European middle class.

3. Kant advocated a rational religion of morality. In order to be, morality also demands the immortality of the soul as well as the existence of a Supreme Being who primarily is holy lawgiver, benevolent ruler, and just judge. Thus, neither nature nor revelation but the moral law is the threshold of "pure religion." A moral life, and not devotional practice, is the right way to please God. The moral commonwealth is the kingdom of God. Both nineteenth-century culture and Protestantism are deeply rooted in Kant's ethical idealism.

4. Like any Enlightener, Kant denounced the blatant anthropomorphism of traditional religions. He leveled all religions to mere external and contingent manifestations of moral religion, the best of which is Christianity.

5. Kant offered a moral interpretation of Christian Scripture and dogma that stands as another summit of enlightened Christianity. He framed the theory of radical evil and denied every dogma that did not serve an ethical purpose. Although he did not repudiate revelation, he did not consider it necessary to religion. Miracles, mysteries, means of grace, rituals, prayers, and sacraments are illusions and instruments of superstition. The ethical and rationalist theologies of the end of the century derived from Kant's drastic reduction of Christian doctrine.

6. Kant adumbrated a philosophy of nature and art in order to overcome his philosophical dualism. The faculty of judgment mediates between cognitive and moral reason because there is an ultimate purpose to organic nature and art. Germany's greatest poets, Friedrich Schiller (1759–1805) and Wolfgang Goethe (1749–1832) found some inspiration in the *Critique of Judgment*. An admirer of Greek culture, Schiller transformed ethical idealism into estheticism. Goethe's 1790 *Metamorphosis of the Plants* expressed the affinity between natural history and poetry in a Kantian fashion.

7. Like Pufendorf and Leibniz, Kant outlined a political philosophy which reflected the changes of the time. He glorified the transforming moment of the 1789 French revolution and pled for liberty, equality, and popular sovereignty. After Kant, German philosophers took an ever greater part in the drafting of the political program.

As Kantianism began to supplant Wolffianism in German universities, Christian belief increasingly became identified with morality. In reaction to the newly emerging ethical school, Pietists and upholders of orthodoxy joined in the defense of super-natural revelation and formed the supernaturalist school. Meanwhile, a more radical trend appeared, rationalism, which crystallized the highest achievements of the En-lighteners' ambitious quest for a reasonable religion.

The Emancipation of the Jews

Although undoubtedly one of the highest achievements of the Enlightenment, the religious, cultural, and civil emancipation of the Jews in Europe should not be over-estimated. Anti-Semitism had been a permanent feature of western Christianity and still was very much alive throughout the eighteenth century. Voltaire's and Holbach's crusade against organized religion did not spare Jewish religious practices. To appease anti-Semitic sentiment, 70,000 Jews were expelled from Prague in 1745, and a bill authorizing the naturalization of foreign-born Jews had to be repealed in 1753 by the English Parliament. In northeastern Europe (Poland and Lithuania), there had been and still were regular outbursts of anti-Semitism (pogroms) for religious, ethnic, and economic reasons. Social outcasts, the Ashkenazic Jews lived by rabbinic precepts, paid heavy taxes, and were at the mercy of the prince's benevolence.

Since the Middle Ages, European Jews had survived and often prospered as traders and moneylenders. Expelled from Spain in the fifteenth century, Sephardic Jews settled in rising economic centers such as Frankfurt, London, Amsterdam, Bordeaux, and Venice. In the sixteenth century, they were rivalled by Protestant merchants and bankers who practiced lending at interest. On the whole, Protes-tantism and Tridentine Catholicism still promoted a negative image of the Jew as someone who bore responsibility for the deicide and who obstinately refused to convert to Christian belief. Martin Luther's infamous pamphlet *Concerning Jews and Their Lies* (1534) has been surpassed in hatred only by the ignominious Nazi (i.e., National Socialist) anti-Semitic propaganda. By prescribing the burning of syn-agogues, schools, houses, and holy books, the silencing of rabbis, and the reduction of all Jews to misery and captivity, Luther substantially nurtured Western anti-Semitism, particularly among the lower and middle classes. Fortunately, bigotry and intolerance were often counterpoised in the churches by evangelical eirenism, so that the Jews were never completely eradicated from Christian lands, at least not before the National Socialist dictatorship of Hitler.

The Enlighteners succeeded in changing the image of the Jew. In the play *Nathan the Wise*, Lessing argued that Moslems, Jews, and pagans were equals of the Chris-tians and deserved equal rights. In another play, *The Jews*, Lessing portrayed a Jew who is so cultured, mannered, virtuous, and affluent that a Christian nobleman considered him worthy of his daughter's hand. Dohm's 1781 plea for the civic eman-cipation of the Jews raised great expectations in central Europe.

Although Prussia was the most tolerant state of central Europe, it was the Austrian emperor, Joseph II, who issued in 1781 a toleration patent for all non-Catholics, including Jews. Similarly in France in 1787, a royal edict recognized the religious and civic rights of non-Catholics. It was the French Revolution, however, that, defeating a last anti-Semitic coalition, finally granted every human being equal political rights regardless of her or his religious persuasion. The revolutionary leader Mirabeau (1749–1791) had been the Jews' most committed advocate. Following the French pattern, the Jews were granted full citizenship in the United Provinces in 1796 and in Prussia in 1812. As the Prussian edict stipulated, the Jews no longer formed a segregated community.

The western and central European Jewish emancipation affected only a small portion of the global European Jewish population. Nineteenth-century social and political changes furthered Jewish emancipation in the remainder of Europe, apart from Russia. The Jews obtained full political rights in 1858–1860 in England under Queen Victoria, in 1859–1870 in united Italy and Rome under Victor-Emanuel II, and in Calvinist Switzerland by the 1874 constitution. For the masses of Askenazic Jews who lived miserably in ghettos under Russian jurisdiction, things had changed for the worse. The May Laws of 1892 rendered their existence more precarious than ever. Until the 1917 Bolshevik Revolution, pogroms were the too-familiar episodes of the tragic Jewish saga.

The Ordeal of the Roman Catholic Church

In spite of the Enlighteners' widely publicized anticlericalism, the established churches, whether Roman Catholic, Anglican, Lutheran, Calvinist, or Eastern Orthodox, showed amazing resiliency and thus preserved almost unimpaired their privileged position in society. On the Continent, their conservative function overall remained unchanged, at least until the diffusion of revolutionary ideals by the Napoleonic army. Popular piety even rebounded in eighteenth-century Protestantism. The Roman Catholic church continued to reflect and strengthen the political system and the social hierarchy of the Old Regime. Major religious festivals were still well attended, and pious and charitable organizations, such as the Confraternity of the Rosary, a women's group, were very much alive, even in spite of a tangible falling-off of popular religiosity. Recent research showed that popular piety declined more in town than in country, more among men than among women, and more in the bourgeoisie than in the aristocracy. Monasticism suffered most from popular disaffection toward contemplative life. However, just before the 1789 revolution, the Roman Catholic church witnessed a rise in religious vocations, in contrast with the decline of the 1750s.

The eighteenth century incontrovertibly accelerated the process of the dechristianization of Europe that began with the Renaissance. However, what was lost quantitatively was gained qualitatively. In the general population, religious conformism decreased notably, yet the Christian message was better understood and practiced by those who confessed it. The care and integrity of many poor parish priests were the sole redeeming features of an institution that had grown dysfunctional from top to bottom. The parish priest celebrated Mass, administered the other sacraments, kept the records of births, marriages, and deaths, monitored charitable activities, and often served as schoolmaster as well as mediator between the parishioners and the civil authorities. Even the Enlighteners, who stigmatized clerical ignorance, praised the parish clergy for its contribution to the life of the community.

No significant changes in popular superstitious religiosity actually occurred in the eighteenth century. Pilgrimages, processions, and devotions to saints, images, and relics remained the main external expression of popular Catholic piety. In Spain, Italy, France, and Poland, the devotion to the Virgin Mary was as strong as ever. The Enlighteners' crusade against superstition failed to reach the masses, at least before the French Revolution.

The fear of the church as well as its moral authority were, however, severely eroded as is evident in the libertine lifestyle of the upper class and the dramatic rise of prostitution and of the abandonment of children in public places. The new moral plague devastated Paris, Milan, London, and Amsterdam.

The reforming policies of Catholic rulers and the incompetence of the church's leadership were more detrimental to the institution than the novel ideas of the Enlightenment. For a century, from 1700 to 1800, the institution was left without any pope of stature. There was no one to contain the secularizing tide.

The wealth of the Roman Catholic church was colossal. In Spain, France, and Austria, for example, the church owned a sizable part of the land. Bishops and heads of religious houses and cathedral chapters, most of whom were nobles, enjoyed huge revenues and led a worldly life, whereas the parish clergy, mostly of a lower-middle-class origin, lived on a small income and labored hard. The disparity in lifestyle between an opulent, despotic, and uncaring upper clergy and a poor and dedicated lower clergy dissolved cohesion and solidarity in critical times.

As an ideological and economic power, the Roman Catholic church could no longer afford resisting the expansion of the absolutist state and variously fell under secular control. In France, Louis XIV's successors held the Gallican church under close supervision. In Spain, the devout Charles III took control of the Spanish Inquisition and of episcopal appointments and subjected the proclamation of papal bulls to royal sanction. In the Austrian empire, Maria Theresa and her son, Joseph II, proceeded to a radical and comprehensive reform of the church that was surpassed only by the French 1790 *Civil Constitution of the Clergy*.

The fate of the Society of Jesus points out the weakness of the Holy See. Rome surrendered to the combined pressures of suspicious governments, envious bishops, and hostile religious orders. Too powerful as European educators and overseas missionaries, too competitive in colonial trade, too influential in state affairs, too lax in their moral teaching, the Jesuits were sacrificed to public opinion by Clement XIV in 1773, regardless of their unique contribution to the success of the Tridentine Reformation. The Enlighteners celebrated the downfall of the Jesuits as a triumph of their cause, overlooking how much they had in common.

As regards constitutional theory, the Roman Catholic church traditionally swayed between the supremacy of councils or synods (Conciliarism) and papal supremacy (Ultramontanism). The 1682 *Declaration of the French Clergy* had initiated a conciliar phase. The assertion of the "Liberties" of the Gallican church, followed by those of the Spanish church, was later imitated by the German clergy. A German bishop, Nikolaus von Hontheim, better known as Febronius, defended in 1763 the rights of the German episcopate against the despotism of the Roman curia in his *On the State of the Church and the Lawful Power of the Roman Pontiff*. Febronius was compelled to recant, yet his denial of papal supremacy found much support among leading German bishops. Conciliarism and episcopalism were widespread throughout the German episcopate.

The worst blow to Ultramontanism, however, was struck by the enlightened despot Joseph II and his chancellor, Kaunitz. Like Frederick II of Prussia and Catherine II of Russia, Joseph II of Austria had adopted the Enlighteners' political theories. Continuing Empress Maria Theresa's reforming policy, Joseph II hastened the process of modernization of the Hapsburg state. He reorganized education, amended civil and criminal law, abolished serfdom, softened censorship, and introduced an extensive agrarian reform. The lethargic body of the church, which formed a state within the state, could not be spared if efficiency was to be enhanced in the realm. Unlike his neighbor Frederick II, who was officially Calvinist yet truly a deist, Joseph II was a real Christian. A staunch orthodox believer with Masonic sympathies, he despised superstition, mysticism, and Jansenism as much as Voltairianism. Joseph II upheld the supremacy of the state over the church. In a 1782 pamphlet, *What Is the Pope?*, Joseph II argued that the emperor is sovereign by divine right, whereas the pope, the spiritual leader of the church, is merely the bishop of Rome.

At an extravagant pace, Joseph II and Kaunitz altered the face of Catholicism in Austria and the southern Low Countries: A 1781 toleration patent legalized religious pluralism; the 1783 Edict on Idle Institutions suppressed all contemplative monastic orders; and an edict of 1786 ordered the Mass to be said in German. The imperial government rationalized the church's activities, redefined diocesan boundaries, took control of financial resources as well as clerical training, and required the simplification of religious services. Joseph II and Kaunitz envisioned the priest as a civil servant in charge of public morality.

Joseph II, the modern leader in whose honor Mozart had composed a Masonic cantata in 1785, was informed shortly before his death in January 1790 that he had failed to rally public opinion. As a romantic hero, he died misunderstood and forsaken. Too dictatorial, his caesaro-papalism had aroused popular discontent: too hasty, his political reforms had fueled nationalism and separatism in Hungary, Bohemia, and the Low Countries.

Meanwhile in France, a dramatic sequence of events portended disaster on a European scale. The traditional social order was brutally overthrown and the administrative monarchy was disestablished by the inadequacies of mercantilism, chronic financial and agrarian crises, and the Enlighteners' social and political ideas (e.g., Rousseau's 1755 *Discourse on the Origin of Inequality*). On July 14, 1789, a Parisian mob stormed the Bastille, a fortress-prison, which symbolized absolutism. The next month, the Constituent Assembly—the National Assembly with constitutional powers—voted the abolition of feudal privileges and passed the famous Declaration of the Rights of Man, the apex of the Enlightenment. In the following autumn, church lands were nationalized and auctioned. On July 12, 1790, the church-state relations were radically altered: The 1517 concordat between Francis I and Pope Leo X, still in force, was replaced by the Civil Constitution of the Clergy. More Gallican than Louis XIV, far more anti-Roman than anti-Christian, Honoré de Mirabeau (1749–1791) and the Constituent Assembly reorganized the church in France. At the height of the revolution in 1790, the feast of *Corpus Christi* ("Body of Christ") was celebrated throughout the realm with the usual enthusiasm. And yet the revolution turned against the church in France. Voltairianism among the bourgeoisie and the association of the church with royal despotism and feudal privileges in the mind of the populace were together fatal to the church. In November 1790, the French clergy was compelled to take an oath of loyalty to the constitution. Because more than half the clergy refused to comply, the Gallican church plunged into a schism of an oath-taking and an oath-refusing church. When the papal condemnation of the Civil Constitution of the Clergy fell in the spring of 1791, the revolutionaries toughened their position against the church. Oath-refusing or refractory clergy became suspect of counterrevolutionary activities. Rome reacted by excommunicating oath-taking clergy.

In an attempt to curb the revolutionary process, Austria and Prussia sent an army to France in 1792. The revolutionaries thereupon declared "the fatherland in danger" and mobilized the nation against the enemy from within and without. In the wake of the German defeat at Valmy, which salvaged the revolution and augured the eclipse of Europe's Old Regimes, the revolutionaries abolished the monarchy and proclaimed the republic; beheaded the monarch, Louis XVI, who had been found guilty of high treason; and expelled, deported, or executed all oath-refusing clergy. An estimated 30,000 priests fled abroad. It was under the Reign of Terror, however, launched in 1793 by the Committee of Public Safety, that dechristianization reached its peak. A zealous follower of Rousseau, Maximilien de Robespierre (1758–1794), as much fanatic as virtuous and incorruptible, instituted the worship of the Supreme Being, Reason, over which ceremony he presided in Paris in June 1793. The new cult was meant to replace Catholicism nationwide.

After another spell of anti-Christian terror, under the government of the Directory, which in 1794 enforced the cult of the Supreme Being, the assumption to power in 1799 of a brilliant young general, Napoleon Bonaparte (1769–1821), once again altered the destiny of French Catholicism. Negotiations started between the Consulate, the new French government, and the Holy See, and concluded in 1801 with a new concordat. The Ultramontanist tendency of the concordat was, however, counterbalanced by the ultragallicanism of the Organic Articles, which were released at the same time by the first consul, Napoleon Bonaparte. This led to an unequaled revival of Catholic worship in France. Henceforth, the conclusion of a concordat became the Holy See's basic European strategy in church-state relations.

The "Third Rome" Reformed

In 1589 Moscow, the so-called third Rome, took rank among the ancient patriarchates of Christendom—Rome, Alexandria, Antioch, Constantinople, and Jerusalem—when its metropolitan, Bishop Job, was elevated to the patriarchate by Jeremias II, patriarch of Constantinople. The Muscovite partriarchate was abolished in 1721 by the enlightened czar Peter the Great and restored in 1918 after the Bolshevik Revolution.

Since the conversion in 988 of Prince Vladimir I of Kiev, in the lands of Rus', and his marriage with a Byzantine princess, the Russians had adopted Greek or Eastern Christianity and looked to Constantinople as a beacon of religious beliefs and cultural values. Byzantine or orthodox Christianity blossomed in the Ukraine until the Tartars' invasion in the thirteenth century. The monastery of the Caves, founded in Kiev by Antony and Theodosius, was the heart of Ukrainian spiritual and cultural life. By the mid-thirteenth century, Moscow took over as political, religious, and cultural center and remained so until Peter the Great transferred the seat of government to St. Petersburg in the early eighteenth century.

The founder and abbot of the Holy Trinity monastery, near Moscow, Sergius of Radonezh (ca. 1314–1392), a mystic and reformer of monastic life, is considered to be one of the nation's earliest luminaries. For centuries Holy Trinity monastery produced the nation's creative minds, artists, missionaries, and ecclesiastical and political leaders. After the fall of Constantinople in 1453, the Greek or orthodox clergy began to look to Moscow as the last bastion of Christianity in an Ottoman-dominated southeastern Europe and framed the "third Rome" theory. In the seventeenth century, Russian orthodoxy underwent further changes. Whereas in the Ukraine a process of Latinization had begun under Peter Moghila (ca. 1596–1647), metropolitan of Kiev, in Muscovy Patriarch Nikon (1605–1681) undertook in the 1650s a thorough pro-Byzantine liturgical reform. A former student of the University of Paris, Moghila promoted an Orthodox Confession and brought numerous doctrines and practices from the Latin or western church into the Ukrainian church. Nikon's reform of the Muscovite church, sanctioned by the synods of 1654 and 1656, put the Russian liturgy back in line with the Byzantine rite. Service books were revised and the icons remodeled according to the Constantinople pattern. Nikon's anti-Slavic reform, implemented by force, antagonized many believers who then formed a schismatic church of Old Ritualists.

In the eighteenth century, the accession to power of Czar Peter the Great (1672–1725) again changed the physiognomy of the Russian Orthodox church. Since 1613 the Romanov dynasty, especially Czar Alexis (1645–1676), had unrelentingly strengthened the state, borrowing ideas from abroad, mainly from Poland, Germany, and the United Provinces. At the outset of Peter the Great's reign, besides an established church, there were in Moscovy an absolute monarchy, an army, and a bureaucracy. The czar and the patriarch both resided in the Kremlin.

In the wake of an instructive European grand tour, from Sweden and Prussia to England and France, Peter the Great introduced a string of reforms mostly inspired by what he had observed in Sweden and France. He established a senate after the Swedish model, built up the army, created a navy, reorganized the bureaucracy after the French pattern, initiated a mercantilist economic policy (Colbertism), and started industrialization. Taking control of the Russian Orthodox church, he radically altered its system of government. Guided by a Protestant polity, he abolished the patriarchate and instead instituted a collegial Holy Synod, of which the czar's representative was the convener.

The modernization of Russia was completed by the wife of Peter the Great's grandson, Catherine II (1729–1796), known as Catherine the Great. Born a Lutheran, orthodox by political convenience, yet an atheist at heart, Catherine II, praised by the Enlighteners—Diderot especially—as the "Semiramis of the North," endeavored to actualize the social and political ideals of the Enlightenment. Her voracious reading of the *Philosophes*, and especially of Cesare Bonesana Beccaria (1738–1794), whose 1764 *On Crimes and Punishments* was a European best-seller, led her to prescribe in 1766 a radical program of enlightened government: the *Nakaz* or *Instructions to the Commission in Charge of the New Civil Code*. Comprised of more than 500 articles, the *Nakaz* advocated the happiness of the people, the prominence of the state, and the glory of the sovereign. Its major themes were moderation in government, public education, freedom of conscience, religious toleration, respect for the law, and crime prevention. Unfortunately, not much of this magnificent program was implemented. Catherine's cultural and economic policies were undeniably a success: She embellished the city of St. Petersburg and generously sponsored the letters and the arts; she created financial facilities and industrialized the country. However, her social policy was a disaster. As the Pugachev rebellion of 1773–1774 illustrates, there was a great deal of discontent in Russian society. Emelyn Ivanovich Pugachev (ca. 1741–1775), an Old Ritualist Cossack, who posed as a protector of the people, a sort of "redeemer czar," rallied Cossacks (nomads like the Tartars), peasants, industrial serfs, and religious dissenters in the steppes between Moscow and the Caspian Sea. They rebelled against the modernization and centralization of enlightened despotism as well as against the oppressiveness of the ruling class (i.e., the nobility). The uprising was crushed by Catherine II's army, and Pugachev was executed in 1775. In religious affairs, Catherine II ruled the Holy Synod; no decision was taken without her sanction.

Western influence on ecclesiastical institutions was, however, counterpoised by a revival of the ascetical and mystical tradition of Russian orthodoxy with Paisy Velichkovsky (1722–1794) and Tikhon of Zadonsk (1724–1783). Born in the Ukraine, trained at the theological Academy of Kiev, Velichkovsky became a monk on Mount Athos in northern Greece, where he undertook the translation into Russian of the devotional and ascetical writings of the eastern fathers. His *Writings from Philokalia (Dobrotolubie)*, a collection of extracts on prayer from Greek church fathers, became extremely popular. A holy man, Tikhon was consecrated in 1763 bishop of Voronezh, near Cossack territory. In 1767 he withdrew to the monastery of Zadonsk and was canonized by the Russian Orthodox church in 1861. Father Zosima of *The Brothers Karamazov* and Bishop Tikhon in *The Possessed* are characters drawn by Dostoevsky from this exemplary monastic figure.

The main tenets of Eastern orthodoxy are as follows:

- The orthodox church emphasizes the mystical aspect of theology. Prayer is essential.
- The bible and tradition (the creed, the decrees of the seven ecumenical councils, the eastern fathers, liturgical books, and icons) are the sources of orthodox doctrine and worship.
- The doctrine of God and the doctrine of the human being are trinitarian.
- "Ingodding," or deification, describes the process of salvation, in which the human being cooperates by decision of the free will.
- Devotion to the Holy Virgin and veneration of icons are given a special place.
- Easter (Pascha) is the most important festival of the liturgical year.
- Eschatology—the return of Christ in glory, the resurrection of the dead, and the Last Judgment—gives Christian life its final meaning. As Platon, a metropolitan of Moscow, put it in his 1814 *Present State of the Greek Church in Russia:* Dwelling "with the most holy angels, with the prophets, with the glorious apostles, with triumphant martyrs, with all the holy saints" is the reward of the righteous.

The Irrational Revisited

Rousseau: The Primacy of Conscience

In an age overpowered by the desire to dispose of God or at least to prevent God from interfering in human affairs, spell-breaking voices rose in defense of the human-divine relation within the church and without, even among some of the Enlighteners. The first voice to be heard on the Continent was that of Jean-Jacques Rousseau (1712–1778). As early as 1750, his *Discourse on Sciences and Arts* refuted the current optimistic view that progress in sciences and arts purify morals, and instead he pled for a return to moral and religious values. His works made a tremendous impression on the young generation in France and Germany by stirring personal emotions, thereby engendering literature, poetry, and philosophy based on the authors' inner experiences.

What was Rousseau's religious belief? A Geneva-born and Calvinist-bred philosopher, a convert to Catholocism yet an adherent of the Enlightenment, a foremost utopian social theorist (*The Social Contract*, 1762), and a didactic novelist and friend of Diderot and Voltaire, Jean-Jacques Rousseau adopted a paradoxical position halfway between an evangelical Christianity and the deist religion of nature. For that reason, he was hounded as a contemptible freethinker by Calvinists and Catholics alike, while being reproached by the Enlighteners for being a "party-pooper."

Rousseau framed a dual definition of religion as both natural and civil religion. Religion as natural religion was mainly exposed by him in *The Profession of Faith of the Savoyard Vicar*, in *Emile Or On Education* (1762). The latter delineates a pedagogy of autonomous growth mostly through personal experience, whereas he unveiled religion as civil religion in the last chapter of *The Social Contract* (1762).

As distant from eighteenth-century materialism and atheism as from seventeenth-century dogmatism, Rousseau propounded the sublime simplicity of the religion of the gospels as the perfect crystallization of natural religion. Such a religion is solely derived from the inward teachings of conscience. Our conscience teaches us right action and presupposes an otherworldly reality. Against Bayle and Diderot, Rousseau associated morality, religion, and virtue with faith and hope. If God did not exist and if the soul died with the body, the righteous would then have to renounce happiness. Rousseau prefigured Kant. In his *Letter to Voltaire*, in reply to Voltaire's *Poem on the Disaster of Lisbon*, Rousseau made a stand of faith in divine providence and in the immortality of the soul. His vision of divine providence was broader than Voltaire's. God is not merely a clockmaker, whose providence is confined to the natural laws. God is also a personal God, whose providence is manifest in people's lives.

In sum, Rousseau understood religion above all as a means to "re-nature" the denatured, or corrupted, human being. Jesus Christ is not the Redeemer, but as the perfect example of the human being in the state of nature, he is a model and a guide for the recovery of one's original nature. In addition, Rousseau envisioned a catechism of the citizen composed of social maxims and imposed by the state. In Rousseau's mind, natural religion and civil religion were identical although aimed at different goals.

Swedenborg the Visionary

In 1758 Swedenborg wrote as follows:

> Truths are of threefold order, civil, moral, and spiritual. Civil truths relate to matters of judgement and government. . . . Moral truths pertain to the matters of every one's life which have regard to companionships and social relations. . . . But spiritual truths relate to matters of heaven and the church, and in general to the good of love and the truth of faith.[5]

An eminent Swedish scientist and natural philosopher, a precursor of Darwin and Teilhard de Chardin (*On Cult and the Love of God*, 1745), Emanuel Swedenborg (1688–1772), son of a Lutheran bishop, had reached the height of his fame with theosophic works in the line of Jakob Böhme and the mystical and prophetic traditions: *Heavenly Mysteries* (1747–1758), *New Jerusalem and Its Heavenly Doctrine* (1757–1758), *Heaven and Its Wonders and Hell* (1757–1758), all released in London. A synthesis of his thought was published in Amsterdam under the title *True Christian Religion* (1769–1771). Increasingly subjected to parapsychological sensations, Swedenborg saw a vision in 1745. The apparition, Jesus Christ himself, called him to reveal the inner meaning of the scriptures to the world. From that time until his death, he indefatigably wrote hefty biblical commentaries and theological treatises, reinterpreting the central tenets of Christianity through his own mystical experiences. Swedenborg actually believed that God spoke a new revelation through him and that his prophesying marked the second advent. Most of his speculations concerned life after death. Upon death people receive a real spiritual body and live a genuine life in the spiritual world, he thought. The invisible or spiritual world—an actual world—is divided into three kingdoms: heaven, hell, and the world of the spirits between them.

Swedenborg's conception of a progressive revelation in five stages, expounded in the *Heavenly Mysteries*, counts among his most original ideas. The first revelation, an oral one, created the Adamic church; the second, written and now lost, started the Noetic church; the third or the Old Testament produced the Israelite church; the fourth or the New Testament launched the Christian church; and the fifth and last, through Swedenborg, announced the new Christian church.

In spite of the condemnation of his writings on the charge of Socinianism, Swedenborg's influence steadily grew. In England Swedenborgians founded in 1788 the New Jerusalem church. Swedenborgian societies and churches appeared in continental Europe, in America, and in Australia, and they proselytized extensively. Swedenborg's influence on European literature was not negligible either. Although

---

[5]Emanuel Swedenborg, *Heaven and its Wonders and Hell*, Vol. 21, Rotch Edition (Boston and New York: Houghton Mifflin Company, 1976) p. 328.

critical, the Anglican revivalist John Wesley still saw in the visionary a man inspired by God. Even Emanuel Kant, his strongest detractor, could not refrain from admiring him in his critical appraisal, *Dreams of a Spirit-Seer* (1766).

Romantics

Just as Rousseau associated religion with feeling or conscience and Swedenborg associated it with clairvoyance and prophecy, William Blake related Christianity to art. A London lyrical poet, painter, and book illustrator endowed with a mystical and imaginative mind, William Blake (1757–1827) is mostly remembered for the *Visions of the Daughters of Albion* (1793), the *Vision of the Last Judgment* (1810), and *Jerusalem*, his grand symbolical poem adorned with a hundred magnificent etchings. Blake identified art and religion and held that art revealed through beauty the same truth that Christianity did through the Incarnation. Christ calls us to be imaginative and adventurous in order to express esthetically both truth and beauty. A "traveller to heaven" and intimate of God, who proclaimed in *The Laocoon Group* (1820), that "Christianity is art" and "Jesus and his Apostles and Disciples were all Artists," Blake could not but feel as much contempt for an established church indifferent to art as he felt abhorrence for the deism and materialism of the Enlighteners. In *There Is No Natural Religion* (1788), Blake denied that reason was natural revelation, arguing in *All Religions Are One* that all religions and philosophies originated from God, the universal "Poetic Genius."

Switzerland had her foremost Protestant mystic in Johann Kaspar Lavater (1741–1802). A close friend of the German Catholic revivalist and biblical ethicist Johann Michael Sailer, author of a *Handbook of Christian Ethics* (1817), Lavater believed in the miraculous power of prayer, practiced Christocentric devotions, promoted ecumenical dialogue, and speculated on the nature of the otherworldly reality in *Outlooks on Eternity* (1768–1778).

In Germany the antirationalist trend was above all represented by another philosopher from Königsberg, commonly known as "Magus of the North": Johann Georg Hamann (1730–1788). An opponent of the Enlightenment and of the orthodoxy as well, Hamann emphasized the irrational, equivocal, and existential dimensions of religion and brought emphatically to the fore both life and paradox. He prefigured Goethe and Kierkegaard and was known to Schelling and Nietzsche. Yet his greatest contribution to European thought was the unfolding of a philosophy of language. Hamann understood language as a manifestation of the unity of body, soul, spirit, and sensibility (*Zwei Scherflein*, 1780), and interpreted the biblical revelation as the spoken word of the Creator. God revealed himself as an author (*Schriftsteller*). In post-revolutionary France, at the turn of the nineteenth century, the Catholic renascence was led by Francois-René de Chateaubriand (*The Genius of Christianity*, 1802).

As a political, social, cultural, and religious movement, Romanticism blossomed in the period that spanned the publication in 1761 of Rousseau's *Julia or the New Heloise* and the European revolutions of 1848. In political matters, the Romantics were the heirs of the French Revolution of 1789 and promoted the concept of nation and peoplehood (the organic body of the people as defined by Herder). They inspired people's liberation from foreign rule. Their social views were progressive, sometimes even utopian.

In philosophy, the Romantics craved for harmony and totality, and therefore they refused the polarizations of the Enlightenment. They attempted a subjective synthesis of reason and faith, freedom and necessity, subject and object, the historical and the universal, the human and the divine, and of paganism and Christianity (e.g., Fichte, Schelling, Hegel, and the Schlegels). In religion, the Romantics repudiated the God of the Enlightenment and returned to the biblical God. They denied tradition as well as the dogmatism of orthodoxy, and instead valued personal religious experience. Above all, they celebrated the closeness to the Beyond, analyzed the relatedness of the self, soul, and conscience to the Infinite. They strove to merge human subjectivity into divine eternity. The religion of the Romantics was an infinite emotion of the human soul. *Faith and Love or the King and the Queen* (1789) and *Christendom or Europe* (1799) by the German poet Friedrich von Hardenberg-Novalis (1772–1801) crystallized the religion of the Romantics. The Romantic predilection for Asian civilization was best exemplified by Joseph von Görres' *History of the Myths of the Asian World* (1810), which traced the origin of monotheism back to primal Indian myths. A fervent nationalist, an Ultramontane Catholic, and a disciple of Schelling, Görres (1776–1848) also framed the most impressive system of Catholic mysticism (*The Christian Mystic*, 4 vols., 1836–1842).

Friedrich Schleiermacher

The Romantic theologian and eclectic philosopher Friedrich Schleiermacher (1768–1834) has rightly been considered the towering figure in the history of Protestant thought between the triad of the Reformation (i.e., Luther, Zwingli, Calvin) and Karl Barth, the protagonist of neo-orthodoxy after World War I. There are three reasons for Schleiermacher's paramount position. First, Schleiermacher absorbed the gains of the Enlightenment and overcame the dualism of rationalism and supernaturalism by ascribing a special domain to religion. Second, he made religious consciousness the new foundation for the making of theology, thereby clearing a path for psychologism. Third, he strengthened historicism by promoting the historical dimension of the religious phenomenon.

Schleiermacher was educated by the Moravian Brethren, from whom he retained the assimilation of religion to life, the idea of a pious community clustering around Christ, and the belief in inner religious experience. During his stay at the Seminary of Barby, he discovered the Enlightenment and consequently underwent a spiritual crisis. In 1787 he matriculated at the University of Halle, where Wolffianism was still prominent, and sided with the Kantians againt the Wolffians. A crucial shift to Spinozism dates from 1793. Schleiermacher acknowledged in *A Short Exposition of the Spinozian System* his affinity to Spinoza, in whom the Romantics had found a philosophical redeemer.

After several years of academic and pastoral activities in various parts, Schleiermacher was eventually appointed pastor of Trinity Church in 1809 and given in 1810 the Chair of Reformed Theology at the new University of Berlin, where Hegel held the chair of philosophy.

One may divide Schleiermacher's mature theological production into three periods: (1) the Romantic period represented by *On Religion: Speeches Addressed to Its Cultured Despisers* (1799) and the *Soliloquies* (1800); (2) the period of refutation of ethical idealism (Kant, Fichte) marked by *Outlines of a Critique of Previous Moral Philosophy* (1803) and *The Celebration of Christmas: A Dialogue* (1806); and (3) the period of ethical and dogmatic construction culminating with *The Christian Faith* (1821–1822) and his Berlin lectures on ethics and dialectics.

When Schleiermacher released the *Speeches* in 1799, he was thirty years old; it had taken him ten years to free himself from the confines of Moravian Pietism. The *Speeches* comprise five discourses and an epilogue. The first speech, entitled, *Defence*, defines the issues. Religion is not very popular among educated people, explains Schleiermacher, who are "saturated with the wisdom of the centuries" and continue to raise questions about the Deity, rewards and punishments, happiness and morality, and religiosity. Religion, he argues, has little to do with doctrines and systems; nor is it necessary for morality. "You can only understand religion," writes Schleiermacher, "if you look inside the soul of a religious person, i.e., a person surrendered to the Universe (the All)."

The second speech, the most important, entitled *The Essence of Religion*, defines the nature of religion. Religion is neither a set of truths about God and the world (metaphysics) nor a set of precepts for life (ethics), but "immediate consciousness of the universal existence of all finite things, in and through the Infinite, and of all temporal things in and through the Eternal." To allow oneself to be affected by the Infinite is the beginning of religious activity. Very much like music, religion is a "sense of and taste for the Infinite," and "intuitive contemplation and feeling" that every single reality is part of the Whole, the Universe, the All, or God. Against the "cultured despisers," Schleiermacher argued that as the "highest philosophy" only religion actualizes the synthesis of thought and action. As "intuition of the Universe" and "feeling of the Infinite," religion provides access to the Absolute or harmony of immanence and transcendence, subjectivity and objectivity, and of the creativity and receptivity of human consciousness. Schleiermacher's eclectic definition of religion shows the combined influences of Zinzendorf, Kant, Fichte, Spinoza, Nikolaus von Kues (Cusanus) and the Greek Presocratic philosoher Anaxogoras.

Called *The Cultivation of Religion*, the third speech stated in utter contrast to orthodoxy, ethicism, and rationalism that religion cannot be taught, only experienced. The fourth speech, *Association in Religion, Or: Church and Priesthood*, deals with the social dimension of religion. The church is the place where people exchange their religious intuitions and feelings. In the last speech, entitled *The Religions*, Schleiermacher divorced himself strongly from the English, French, and German Enlighteners by preferring the positive or historical religions to natural religion. Since religion is the sum of the relations of the human being to God, every religion is a different individuation of that sum. Of all religions, Christianity is the highest and noblest; however, it is not a perfect religion. In the person of the founder of Christianity, Schleiermacher found another opportunity to diverge from the Enlighteners' main line by maintaining that Jesus had become the axis of the mediation between the human and the divine, that is, of redemption and reconciliation, because of his unique consciousness of God. In spite of all, Schleiermacher remained profoundly Christocentric.

Just as the *Speeches* focused on the Absolute, the *Soliloquies* concentrated on human nature. Asserting the unity of sensuousness and reason, nature and morality, Schleiermacher saw human nature as a whole, which he defined as 'individuality." Shaped by the community and shaping it in return, individuality is the supreme achievement of humanity. Against orthodoxy and rationalism alike, but in line with Hamann, Herder, and the Romantics, Schleiermacher stressed the importance of love and imagination in human nature.

Schleiermacher's masterpiece, *The Christian Faith*, represented a radical departure from any previous formulation of Christian doctrine. *The Christian Faith* calls for eleven observations.

1. The theological thinking process proceeds from the universal (ethics and philosophy of religion) to the particular (apologetics and dogmatics).

2. In utter contrast to German idealism, theology is not speculation but a description of a given historical and ecclesiastical belief.

3. As the basis of all theological statements, the consciousness of God arises from immediate self-consciousness or the feeling of absolute dependence provoked by the impact of the universe, or the All.

4. There are three types of theological statements: those about the states of the self; those about God's attributes and actions; and those about the world.

5. The Christian doctrine is divided into two parts: a general and a particular. The general or first part expounds the doctrines that arise directly from the experience of absolute dependence (creation, providence, God). The particular, or the second part, unfolds the doctrines that arise from the inner experience of the antithesis of sin and grace. In the latter part, Schleiermacher reinterprets the cardinal tenet of Pauline and Lutheran theology.

6. Creation and Providence are inseparable. Yet Providence prevails over creation, because it is the origin and guarantee of the feeling of absolute dependence.

Miraculous or supernatural occurrences are acceptable only as part of the course of nature.

7. Moral evil, whether natural or social, is imperfection or refusal to cooperate with God.

8. There is an original and universal revelation of God in human self-consciousness (natural religion) and a particular and historical revelation in and through Jesus Christ (positive religion).

9. Schleiermacher's Christology combines the rationalist with the supernaturalist view of Christ, the enlightened conception of a teacher and an example with the orthodox definition of high priest and mediator (Calvin). Incarnation means that the consciousness of God in Christ was so perfect that Christ became the true indwelling of God in human nature. As such, Christ embodies the ideal humanity. The doctrines of the Trinity, the two natures of Christ (Council of Chalcedon), and the divine condescension, all essential to orthodoxy, are superfluous. Belief in the resurrection, the ascension, and the second coming of Christ is equally irrelevant. On the whole, Schleiermacher's Christology was on the edge between Docetism and Hebionism.

10. Redemption or regeneration is the transformation of the relationship between the human being and God under Christ's influence. This renovation, or rebirth, is called *conversion* from the human perspective and *justification* from the divine perspective.

11. Schleiermacher called into question both the authority of the scriptures and the integrity of the biblical canon. The bible is no longer the ultimate authority in religious matters, though still normative. The Old and New Testaments are of an unequal value because of a "considerable difference" between them. The Christian is neither a pagan nor a Jew but a new human being. Thus, the Mosaic law is discarded as Judaic legalism. Schleiermacher also outlined a new interpretation of the scriptures that inspired many contemporary hermeneutists like Hans-Georg Gadamer (*Truth and Method*, 1960). Schleiermacher focused on the relationship between the reader and the text in the search for meaning.

What can be said about Schleiermacher's infuence on Protestant thought? It was so overpowering that it even survived the rise of neo-orthodoxy after World War I. More than a school and far more than a generation, Schleiermacher had actually infuenced an entire age of Continental Protestant theological production.

Chapter 27

THE PARADOX: ECCLESIASTICAL BELIEF AMID SECULAR AMBIGUITY

Toward a Europeanized World

The combined influence of a prodigious population growth with an unparalleled economic, cultural, and colonial expansion gave birth to a period of European world domination that gathered momentum at the turn of the twentieth century and ended in the wake of World War II. After the ordeal of the eighteenth century, which climaxed with the French Revolution of 1789, the Christian churches were given a fresh chance comparable in some respects to the religious explosion of the sixteenth century. Whereas liberal and conservative Christianity regained the upper and middle classes, social Christianity failed to win the working class.

European Preponderance

From 1815 to 1914—that is, from the second abdication of Napoleon I, emperor of the French, after the battle of Waterloo, to the crisis that provoked World War I— Europe progressively assumed world leadership economically, politically, militarily, culturally, and religiously. European powers rivaled one another in controlling the largest part of the four remaining continents as well as strategic axes and in imposing their particular cultural and religious values. European languages (French, German, Dutch, Italian, in addition to English, Portuguese, and Spanish), beliefs (Roman Catholicism and Protestantism), modes of government (monarchical or republican), types of administration (centralized or decentralized), architectural traditions, and

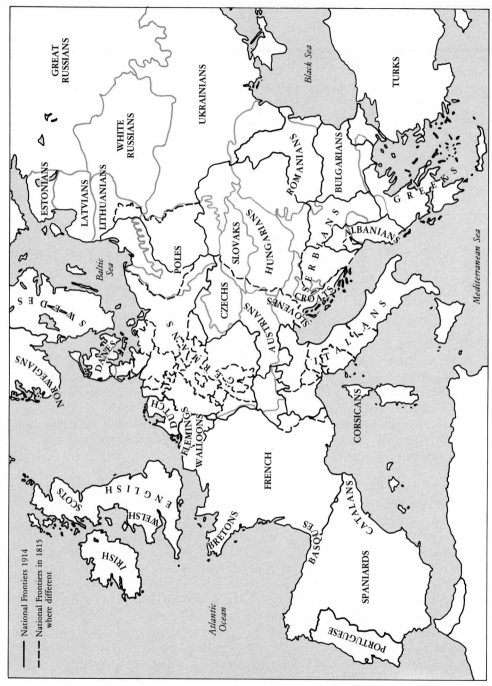

Figure 27.1 The Nationalities of Europe (1800–1914)

lifestyles began to spread throughout the globe. World history entered the age of European imperialism.

The decline of European leadership began with World War I and was accelerated by World War II, which brought physical destruction and necessitated extensive rebuilding. The emergence of the United States and the Soviet Union as superpowers and the division of the world in their respective spheres of influence, the sweep of decolonization, and the rebirth of Asia (the emancipation of India, the awakening of China, and the modernization of Japan and Southeast Asia) also contributed to that acceleration. Ironically, the Achilles heel of European imperialism lay in its achievement: the Europeanization of the world.

Between the collapse of the Napoleonic empire and the present, the political geography of Europe was substantially reshaped three times. These changes had a considerable impact on the status of the Christian churches. First, at the Congress of Vienna in 1815, the legitimate Protestant and Catholic monarchies were restored and the former Holy Roman Empire of the German Nation, a mosaic of 350 principalities, was replaced by a German confederation of thirty-nine autonomous states, among which an extended kingdom of Prussia and a powerful Austrian empire rivaled each other in influence. Second, World War I (1914–1918) brought about the destruction of four continental empires, the Austro-Hungarian, the German, and the Ottoman (these three forming the central powers during the war) and the Russian, which though an allied power, collapsed because of the Bolshevik Revolution of November 1917. Third, at the conclusion of World War II (1939–1945), the Allies' leaders—Churchill (Britain), Stalin (USSR), and Roosevelt (USA)—redefined the borders of European states and divided the Continent into two spheres of influence, a democratic West under American influence and a communist East under Soviet influence. The new order lasted until 1990.

Among the many political transformations, one may single out the following five of overriding importance.

1. Instigated by the prime minister of the kingdom of Piedmont-Sardinia, Camille de Cavour (1810–1861), the unification of Italy was achieved in 1870 with the annexation of the papal states. In spite of the anticlerical storm, the 1871 Law of Guarantees secured religious freedom for every citizen and autonomy for the Roman Catholic church in the new kingdom of Italy. However, the reconciliation of the Holy See with the Italian regime was sealed much later, in February 1929, by the Lateran Treaty, which recognized the Vatican as an independent state.

2. The unification of Germany, presided over by the Prussian prime minister, Otto von Bismarck (1815–1898), was officially marked after the Franco-Prussian war by the proclamation of William I of Prussia, the German emperor, in the Hall of Mirrors at Versailles in January 1871. In the new Reich, Lutheranism and Calvinism formed a powerful evangelical church through the Prussian Union (founded in 1817), and Protestantism and Catholicism consolidated their competitive stand.

551

3. The progressive dismemberment of the Ottoman Empire created a mosaic of Balkan states and gave eastern orthodoxy a fresh chance.

4. The Bolshevik Revolution, which established communism in Russia, outlawed freethinking and drastically cut religious freedom. Church-state relations became tense and even sometimes bellicose. Nonetheless, the Russian Orthodox church survived and even experienced a revival in the last decades of the twentieth century, while the Marxist ideology began to lose its appeal.

5. The economic instability of the Weimar Republic, the post–World War I German democracy, cleared the path for the most dehumanizing dictatorship in European history. In January 1933, the founder and leader of the National Socialist party (Nazi), Adolf Hitler (1889–1945), became German chancellor and shortly afterward concentrated all legislative and executive power into his demonic hands through the Enabling Law of March 1933. Europe had entered the age of totalitarianism, best illustrated by Charlie Chaplin's first talking picture, *The Great Dictator* (1940). The Spanish Civil War in 1939, won by a fascist general, Francisco Franco, occasioned three antitotalitarian works of art of notoriety: two novels, *Man's Hope* (1937) by André Malraux and *For Whom the Bell Tolls* (1940) by Ernest Hemingway, and a colossal cubist painting by Pablo Picasso, *Guernica*, which represents the destruction of the Basque town of Guernica by three German bombers in April 1937.

The Second Wave of Colonialism

Colonialism goes far back into the fifteenth century. The Portuguese and the Spanish at first, and the British, French, and the Dutch afterward, formed the first wave of colonialism.

The second wave of colonialism began in 1830 and reached its peak at the turn of the twentieth century, as European states divided up the remnants of the unconquered world. Almost the entire African continent, the Pacific, Southeast Asia, India, and the Celestial Empire (China) after the repression of the 1900 Boxer Rebellion had passed under European control.

What aroused the second wave of colonialism? The Bolshevik leader, Vladimir Ilich Lenin (1870–1924), contended in *Imperialism: The Highest Stage of Capitalism* (1916) that imperialism unavoidably grew out of capitalism. The rate of profit is lowered by the emergence of new technologies, and the market becomes so saturated that to survive, capitalism must expand and thus move abroad. Although right, Lenin's explanation is incomplete. If the growing need for raw materials; the search for new markets for primary products, manufactured goods, and high-yield financial investments; and the creation of new jobs (in, e.g., the Civil Service) gave a major impulse to expansion, there were more than mere economic reasons.

Other causes include the following:

- Psychological (needs stemming from national pride or the desire of a nation to secure its greatness).
- Political goals of international leadership.
- Strategic control of straits and isthmuses, including the Suez and Panama Canals.
- Demographic pressures caused by surplus population and a need to deal with convicts.
- Scientific expeditions sponsored by geographic societies.
- Philanthropic and humanitarian programs of the Clapham Sect and others.
- The perceived civilizing task of the highly civilized Europeans.
- The propagation of Christian religion by Roman Catholic orders such as the Jesuits, the Lazarists, and the so-called White Fathers organized in 1874 by Cardinal Charles Lavigerie (1825–1892), and by Protestant missionaries sent by the Church Missionary Society and the London Missionary Society among others.

Socioeconomic Life

Demography after 1800

World population increased by 77 percent between 1800 and 1900, going from an estimated 906 million to 1.608 billion. Then it doubled between 1930 and 1975, passing from 2 billion to 4 billion. From the time of the French Revolution to the Belle Epoque at the turn of the twentieth century, European population grew from 187 million to 401 million. Even more spectacularly, North American population rose thirteen times—from 6 million to 81 million. In 1800 one out of four persons was a European; in 1900 it was one out of three; and in 1988 only one out of seven. Owing to two devastating world wars and to birth control (by abstinence, coitus interruptus, condoms, and much later, chemical contraception), European population increased by only 52 percent between 1900 and 1988 (690 million).

Urban population skyrocketed at the cost of rural population following the tremendous development of industrial capitalism. Migration from country to town involved 85 percent of the population in the second half of the nineteenth century, so that Europe passed from being a mostly rural to a mostly urban society. Industrial centers became magnets and developed a large working-class population. Urban population explosion dislocated traditional social ties, transformed cultural habits, shifted the shape of politics, and offered a formidable challenge to the Christian churches.

Steady population growth alarmed many who believed they saw the specter of overpopulation looming ahead. The "surplus" population naturally found an outlet in massive emigration to the United States, Argentina, Brazil, Canada, South Africa, Australia, and New Zealand. The causes of emigration varied from one country to another; mostly they were economic yet sometimes political or religious.

As British, Swedish, and French statistics show, the lowering of the mortality rate was the main feature of nineteenth-century European demography. Sharper in northern and western than in southern and eastern Europe, and in the upper and middle classes than in the lower class, the decline of the mortality rate had five causes: (1) the progressive disappearance of massively deadly diseases such as the plague; (2) some decisive breakthroughs in hygiene and medicine (e.g., vaccination); (3) the revolution of transportation and communication; (4) the greater availability of quality food owing to the cultivation of new crops and to crucial improvements in the methods of agricultural production and distribution; and (5) extensive urban renewal.

A New Economic Era

Before the nineteenth century, there was no continuous economic growth, no steady material progress, and no mass civilization. The new era began in the 1780s in Great Britain with the industrial revolution, which then embraced first western Europe (France, Low Countries), next central and northern Europe (Germany, Sweden), then eastern and southern Europe (Russia, Italy, Spain), lasting through depressions and financial crashes (1818–1819, 1836, 1845–1847, 1859, 1873, 1893–1895, 1913, 1929), world wars, postwar decolonization, and the communist assumption of power in eastern Europe.

Just as the steam engine, completed by James Watt in the 1760s, gave impetus to the first industrial revolution, so the internal combustion engine, built by Gottlieb Wilhelm Daimler in 1883, launched the second. A host of discoveries, inventions, and technological advances propelled Europe, the old industrial countries as well as the others, into the age of industrialization.

After a long period of free trade, championed by Great Britain since Adam Smith's 1776 *Inquiry into the Nature and Causes of the Wealth of Nations*, continental European countries adopted protectionist policies in the latter part of the nineteenth century. Thus, the second industrial revolution modified international relations.

Economic historians have endeavored to account for the fluctuations of European economic expansion. An early prominent theory of economic development was the hypothesis of long waves, or long cycles, set forth in 1922–1925 by the Russian economist and statistician Nikolai Dmitrievich Kondratieff, founder of the Moscow Business Conditions Institute. Analyzing the trend of annual prices in capitalist economies, Kondratieff singled out three long waves or cycles—from 1787 to 1849; from 1850 to 1896; and from 1897 to 1920—each with an upward and a downward phase (i.e., 1928). Kondratieff's hypothesis has been much criticized, yet it found a following in Joseph Schumpeter's three-cycle pattern of economic fluctuations (*Business Cycles*, 1939), as well as in Ulrich Weinstock's 1964 interpretation of economic cycles. An Austro-Hungarian, Joseph Alois Schumpeter (1883–1950) observed that economic fluctuations, or business cycles, consisted in four phases—upswing, recession, depression, and recovery. He predicted the triumph of socialism, not communism, as the final outcome of a capitalism that would have achieved miracles.

Recently, Walt Whitman Rostow framed the famous, yet controversial "five-stages-of-growth" theory in *The Stages of Economic Growth* (1960): (1) originally every society is traditional (limited productivity); (2) a transitional period then takes place which creates "the preconditions for takeoff"; (3) the takeoff occurs next; (4) this is followed by a "drive to maturity"; (5) which finally culminates in the age of high mass consumption (in most cases occurring after 1914).

New Modes in Arts and Sciences

In the course of the nineteenth century, just as the opera surpassed the concerto and the symphony as the most popular form of musical expression, so also in literature the novel outdistanced poetry and drama, and in painting the Impressionist school took center stage after the scandal caused by Edouard Manet's *Olympia* (1863). Whereas poetry endeavored to embrace pure and supreme beauty through symbolism, prominent novelists, of the like of Dickens and Zola, attempted to be as realistic as any scientist would be in their description of human nature and the social condition. In music, romantic emotions and nationalist sentiments became supreme. *The Flowers of Evil* (*Les Fleurs du Mal*), a collection of poems by Charles Baudelaire, marked in 1857 the beginning of modern literature. Similarly, Richard Wagner's musical drama *Tristan und Isolde* (1865) initiated modern music.

Much of nineteenth- and twentieth-century science depended on the fascination of late eighteenth-century scientists with electricity. Nineteenth-century science dawned with the discovery of electromagnetism and ended with the discovery of X rays, the electron, and natural radioactivity. The atomic age began with Einstein's theory of relativity, Planck's quantum theory, and further discoveries regarding subatomic particles. Quantum mechanics developed in the 1920s and quantum electrodynamics after World War II. Nuclear fission was achieved for the first time in 1938. Just as Newtonian physics had changed the way philosophers and theologians perceived the universe in the seventeenth century, so did quantum physics in the interwar period. It heralded the dawning of the so-called postmodern age.

The nineteenth century was a period in which many new fields of science were successfully explored—anthropology, archaeology, psychology, sociology, cell biology, and organic chemistry—and older fields such as medicine, geology, chemistry, and mathematics expanded and matured considerably.

Three scientific minds deserve mention for their exceptional influence: Wilhelm von Humboldt, Auguste Comte, and Charles Darwin. In charge of the department of education in the kingdom of Prussia, Wilhelm von Humboldt (1767–1835), the founder of the University of Berlin in 1809, enunciated the new ideals of higher education—academic freedom and freedom to choose the topics of study and research for both teachers and students alike—which promoted the advancement of the humanities as much as that of the natural sciences. Owing to Humboldt, German universities became centers of pure learning (*Wissenschaft*) as well as of culture (*Bildung*). Every systematic discipline thus received a fresh impetus. Thereafter, theological disciplines came to full maturity.

An heir to Hume's empiricism, to the French encyclopedists and to Condorcet's doctrine of progress, and a disciple of Claude de Saint-Simon, Auguste Comte (1798–1857) unfolded a theory of society in *Lectures in Positive Philosophy* (1830–1842) and advocated a new order of society in the *System of Positive Polity* (1851–1854). Comte's chief idea, expressed in the Law of the Three States, was that every field of human knowledge passes through three different states: the theological or fictitious, the metaphysical or abstract, and the scientific or positive. Establishing a hierarchy of sciences, Comte placed psychology and sociology at the top and elevated the ethical principle of altruism—to live for others—into a religion of humanity.

With Charles Darwin's (1809–1882) theories of evolution and of natural selection, made public in 1859 by *On the Origin of Species by Means of Natural Selection*, the Christian churches were faced with a scientific refutation of the biblical account of the creation and with a view of human nature as a part of the animal kingdom. Darwinism appeared to undermine Christian morality. Unfairly branded with atheism, Darwinism came under the fire of ignorant and conservative clergy as well as talented yet partisan writers such as Samuel Butler and George Bernard Shaw. An offshoot of Darwin's theory of the survival of the fittest, social Darwinism gave a scientific guise to socially conservative, nationalistic, and racist political theories. Evolution stirred up a virulent and long-lasting controversy on both sides of the Atlantic. Not surprisingly, conservative Christians sought refuge in creationism. Of the many theologians who addressed the crucial issue of evolution (for instance, Henry Drummond [*Natural Law in the Spiritual World*, 1883]), none has been more innovative and optimistic than the French Jesuit and geologist Pierre Teilhard de Chardin (1881–1955). Following the lead of Henri Bergson's evolutionism (*Creative Evolution*, 1907), Teilhard de Chardin conceived of a revolutionary symbiosis of modern cosmology, geology, and biology with the Logos theology of Christocentric Catholicism. With unmatched flair, Teilhard de Chardin envisioned an evolutionary universe in which the creative, redemptive, unifying, and sanctifying role was attributed to a cosmic Christ (*The Phenomenon of Man*, 1938–1940). The dynamic kernel of the cosmogenesis, Teilhard de Chardin's Christ was at the same time the world-originating alpha and the world-culminating omega.

The Challenge of New Ideologies

Counterrevolutionary Theories

Just as the 1789 French Revolution made a tabula rasa of Europe's old regimes, so the 1815 restoration made a tabula rasa of the recently established rational, egalitarian, and democratic societies. The counterrevolution disestablished the revolution; legitimacy, tradition, and history recovered their former place, which had been temporarily usurped by the principle of the sovereignty of the people. Those who were heard were no longer the Enlighteners and the *philosophes* but the theorists of the counterrevolution: Edmund Burke (1719–1797), Joseph de Maistre (1753–1821), and Karl Ludwig von Haller (1768–1854).

In his 1790 *Reflections on the Revolution in France*, the Irishman Burke attacked the eighteenth-century concepts of nature and reason and repudiated liberty, equality, and the rights of man as antinatural. Burke's *Reflections* were extremely well received in Britain and on the Continent, ironically even by an enthusiastic patroness of the *philosophes*, Empress Catherine II of Russia. A French emigrant, a conservative Catholic, and an Ultramontanist, Joseph de Maistre, who abominated Rousseauism, argued in the 1796 *Consideration on France* that moral and religious decadence was responsible for the "satanic" revolution, and that Christianity and philosophy were now engaged in a fight to the death. He strongly believed in the final victory of Catholicism and urged rulers to re-establish the Old Regime, yet on a firmer basis as a renovated theocratic society. Austro-Hungarian and Roman Catholic by choice, the Swiss-born Karl Ludwig von Haller expounded the doctrine of the patriarchal state in the *Restoration of Politic or Theory of the Natural-Social Order against the Chimera of the Artificial Bourgeois Order* of 1816. An admirer of medieval society, Haller denied Rousseau's idea of a social contract and instead propounded a patriarchal society in which people are bound together by personal consent. The sovereign as a *pater familias*, the family, and the guild are the pillars of Haller's ideal society.

The Enlighteners, the theologians who followed them, and the revolutionists proclaimed the rights of man. Conversely, the leaders of the counterrevolution and the reactionary theologians proclaimed the rights of God. The history of nineteenth-century Christianity, and to a large extent of contemporary Christianity, is the story of the unresolved tension between both rights.

The spread of sectarianism is to be counted among the most fascinating conservative reactions in nineteenth-century Christianity. In addition to the central and eastern rites (Uniats, Catholic Byzantine rite, Old Believers, etc.) and the long-established sectarian movements (Bohemian and Polish Brethren, Dutch Mennonites, English Dissenters), a wealth of free Protestant churches, autonomous institutions (Old Catholics who denied papal infallibility), and dynamic and proselytizing sects (Adventists, Christian Scientists, Jehovah's Witnesses, and Pentecostals) emerged and modified the scope of European Christianity.

The Dawn of Liberalism

Although eventually crushed, the 1789 French Revolution continued, like a ferment, to stimulate social unrest and political turmoil. Europe had embarked on a revolutionary course. Like the pangs of birth of a new age, revolutions broke out at intervals throughout Europe: the liberal revolution of 1830 in France; the democratic revolutions of 1848 in France, Germany, Italy, and Austria-Hungary; the 1871 socialist "Commune" of Paris; the 1909 Tragic Week of Barcelona in Spain; the Bolshevik Revolution of 1917 in Russia; and the socialist uprisings of 1918 and 1919 in Germany.

The French Revolution had irreversibly altered European social structure—serfdom, privileges, and ecclesiastical oversight were abolished, and the industrial revolution had secured the economic power of the bourgeoisie, which had gained full social and political emancipation. An heir of eighteenth-century enlightened and aristocratic cosmopolitanism and a precursor of international socialism, nineteenth-century bourgeois liberalism developed into a preponderant international ideology and gave the impetus to a rich variety of currents in the Christian churches. The most influential of these currents were the Broad Church Party in Anglicanism in the 1830s (S. J. Coleridge and T. Arnold), Culture-Protestantism in German-speaking Protestantism in the 1870s–1890s, and modernism in Roman Catholicism in the 1900s.

What are the main features of standard liberalism? (1) Above all, liberalism is an optimistic world view. (2) Its epistemology gives priority to the power of reason over the authority of tradition. (3) It is a political philosophy built on the concept of freedom. (4) As an economic philosophy, it advocates free enterprise and mainly serves the goals of the middle class. (5) Its social philosophy emphasizes the individual over and against the masses. (6) Last, liberalism understands history as a process in which the crucial role is played by the individual.

Just as feudalism had been the means of domination by the aristocracy, so liberalism became the means of domination by the bourgeoisie. As a middle way between feudalism and democracy, liberalism inevitably entailed some ambiguity. Further social progress and wider political emancipation advocated by progressive liberals, democrats, and socialists, eventually disrupted liberal society. Both a product of the demographic explosion, the industrial revolution, the liberalization of politics, and the democratization of education, democracy and socialism claimed to embody the rule of the people by the people, respectively. The democratic age began in 1848 and lasted until World War I; socialism emerged as a political force in the 1870s. Notwithstanding its purpose, socialism eventually turned out to be little else than the means of domination of the working class.

Liberalism considerably improved the status of religious minorities. In England, for instance, the pressure for Catholic emancipation and for the removal of the disabilities of the Dissenters (Congregationalists, Baptists, Independents, Presbyterians, and Quakers) progressively gathered momentum in the first quarter of the nineteenth century. For the first time, Roman Catholics gained access to public schools and universities by the University Act of 1820. The Test Act was repealed in 1828, and Dissenters and Catholics, often called the "Romish dissenters," were given the right to hold public office and to sit in Parliament. The newly founded London University received its charter in 1836. It was free from any religious affiliation. Eventually in 1865 the clergy of the Church of England and the dons of the Universities of Oxford and Cambridge were no longer compelled to subscribe to the Thirty-Nine Articles of Religion of 1571.

Liberal Anticlericalism

An eminent pathologist and an active liberal, Rudolf Virchow (1821–1902) defined in 1872 the struggle against the Roman Catholic Church as a "great struggle for civilization in the interest of humanity." The struggle for civilization known as *Kulturkampf* raged from 1872 to 1878 and was mainly carried out in Prussia, Baden, and Hessen. Three factors precipitated the conflict: a psychological, a political, and a theological factor. Since medieval times the Germans had a deep prejudice against the Holy See, and that distrust intensified during the Reformation. Moreover, the recent victory of the Germans in the Franco-Prussian War (1870) was perceived by many as the victory of the champion of Protestantism over the champion of Catholicism (Napoleon III). The Protestant majority in Prussia feared the interference of the Vatican in home affairs through the powerful center party (*das Zentrum*), which was openly backed by the Roman Catholic hierarchy. The antiliberal and ultramontane stand of the Holy See epitomized religious conservatism and cultural backwardness to the heirs of the Enlightenment.

Although he was a pious Lutheran, the German chancellor Otto von Bismarck supported the liberals because of his dislike of the center party. Anticlerical, the liberals waged the struggle against Rome in their field of predilection, namely, education. To outlaw Roman Catholic influence on the school system, the liberals passed several laws in the Prussian parliament that were understandably denied by the Roman Catholic hierarchy. The Prussian government reacted by threatening to expel recalcitrant clerics (the May Laws of 1874), causing the Holy See to retaliate in 1875 by threatening to excommunicate compliant clerics. The Prussian government struck back by suspending financial support and by suppressing most monastic orders. A persecution followed, the inhumanity of which was a blatant violation of the liberal spirit. Recalcitrant bishops and priests were expelled or imprisoned. Eventually, the anti-Roman crusade, which left about 1,400 Catholic parishes without an incumbent, recoiled against both the liberals and the conservatives, whose popularity had dropped dramatically. Stronger than ever, the center party was more than ever before an embarrassment to Bismarck's politics. Fortunately, the election in 1878 of a new pope, Leo XIII, facilitated a much craved for reconciliation with Rome. The barbarian struggle for civilization ended with Bismarck's radical change of heart signified by the dismissal of the Prussian minister of culture and the repeal of most of the anticlerical legislation (the May Laws).

The Socialist Utopia

In England melodramatic frescos of the fate of the needy and the outcast in Charles Dickens' *Oliver Twist* (1837–1838) glamorized the underworld, just as in France Victor Hugo's *Les Miserables* (1862) vindicated the social and humanitarian ideals of the 1830 and 1848 revolutions. The 1848 revolutionaries believed in a more democratic society and struggled for freedom of the press, universal manhood suffrage, and the right to work. The 1848 ideals even reached eastern Europe, where they inspired Alexander Herzen (1812–1870), the founder of the revolutionary movement in Russia.

The first industrial revolution generated a class of illiterate, exploited, and starving workers: the proletariat. The second industrial revolution expanded the proletariat, and cyclical economic crises aggravated its desperate condition. In the second half of the nineteenth century, peasants and proletarians comprised as much as 75 to 90 percent of the European population. Social reformers began to realize that democracy was insufficient to meet the vital needs of the proletariat, and therefore they organized trade unions and engaged in radical political action. It was owing to the First International (1864), which reflected eclectic socialist views, and more specifically to the predominantly Marxist Second International (1889), that the European working classes eventually gained political consciousness. Labor parties were created in most European democracies. In addition, in the wake of the Bolshevik Revolution, a Third International (1919) established communism as a radical alternative to social democracy. Socialism had become messianic because the working class was now convinced of working and suffering for humanity.

Among the various schools of socialism, the most typical were the following:

- The school of Claude de Saint-Simon (1760–1825), an aristocrat with a sincere social concern who argued in *The Reorganization of European Society* (1814) and in *On the Industrial System* (1821) that the state should take control of all means of production. In his *The New Christianity* (1825), Saint-Simon advocated a religion of love in a society organized for the benefit of the poor. It is noteworthy that Saint-Simon's most illustrious disciple, the positivist philosopher Auguste Comte (1798–1857), founded sociology. Both Saint-Simon and Comte had adopted Condorcet's doctrine of progress.

- A second school of socialism was that of Charles Fourier (1772–1837), a utopian socialist who envisioned a kind of cooperative settlement called *Phalanstere*, as the expression of the true religion of Jesus in *The New Industrial and Societal World* (1829).

- The school of Pierre Joseph Proudhon (1809–1865), a libertarian humanist who contended that property was theft in *What Is Property?* (1840) and recommended the dispersion of productive property among owner-producers.

- The school of Michael Bakunin (1814–1876), a Russian counterpart of Proudhon, who founded collectivistic anarchism.

- The school of the Left Wing Hegelians, Karl Marx (1818–1883) and Friedrich Engels (1820–1895), whose historical materialism, as expounded in *The Communist Manifesto* (1847–1848) and in *The Capital*, vols. I–IV (1867–1927) became supreme in socialist ranks.

- The school of Vladimir Ilich Lenin (1870–1924) and his prominent disciple Joseph Stalin (1879–1953), both Soviet rulers who adapted dialectical materialism to the Russian political tradition and economic needs. Stalin's 1924 *The Foundations of Leninism* sums up their special brand of Marxism.

- The School of Leon Trotsky (1879–1939), an unfortunate opponent of Stalin, who is mainly remembered for having framed the permanent revolutionary theory (*Our Revolution*, 1918; and *The Revolution Betrayed*, 1931).

- The school of Robert Owen, a Welsh philanthropist who devised a socialist society based on mutual cooperation in *A New View of Society* (1813).

The Social Concern of the Churches

The spread of socialism forced the Christian churches to frame their own social theories in response. Though rejecting socialism, Pope Leo XIII's encyclical *De Rerum Novarum* (1891) invited the state to promote social and economic justice and supported the creation of Catholic trade unions. In the interwar period, Pope Pius XI's encyclical *Quadragesimo Anno* (1931) attempted to win back the masses gained to socialism. Shortly afterward, the French Catholic philosopher Jacques Maritain (1882–1973) cleared a path for a Christian social democracy in *Integral Humanism* (1936).

Urbanization, industrialization, and the rise of socialism awakened social consciousness in Protestantism to a higher extent than in Catholicism, as the four following examples illustrate. In the Church of England, a group of clergymen (J. M. Ludlow, C. Kingsley, F. D. Maurice, and T. Hugues) launched in the mid-1800s an unsuccessful Christian Socialist movement that was intended to address the social issue in a more suitable manner than that used by the official church. Born out of Chartism, which was a late offspring of Robert Owen's (1771–1858) socialist and cooperative movement, the Christian Socialist movement laid a special emphasis on the universal brotherhood and fought liberal individualism as much as the crude utilitarianism of the age. As expected in the conservative Victorian age, the message was barely heard in the Church of England. However, the social issue finally caught the attention of Tractarian clergy, and the Guild of St. Matthew was founded in 1877 by Steward D. Headlam (1847–1924). In the ensuing decade, the Christian Social Union was established in 1889 under the inspiration of T. H. Green's social ethics. Both movements combined high and low church social concerns.

In the Netherlands, the Calvinist theologian Abraham Kuyper (1837–1920), who founded the Free University of Amsterdam in 1880 and created a secessionist Calvinist church, outlined a theology of creation that rejected both capitalist individualism and socialist collectivism and instead focused on the role of the state as guardian of social justice.

The main social achievement of Protestantism in Restoration Germany was the Inner Mission started in 1848 by Johann Heinrich Wichern (1808–1881). Wichern combined pietistic orthodoxy with social concern. At the height of the Bismarck era, a court chaplain endowed with a social conscience yet showing deplorable anti-Semitic feelings, Adolf Stöcker (1835–1909), founded in the late 1870s the Christian Social Labor Party, which promoted extensive social reforms and launched the Protestant Social Conference in 1890. Notwithstanding the German emperor's 1890 appeal to the clergy to help resolve the social issue, further social progress was blocked in the Reich by Bismarck's antisocialist laws. The social gospel was furthermore heralded by Friedrich Naumann (1860–1919) and by some leading figures of Culture-Protestantism such as Adolf von Harnack and Wilhelm Herrmann. A man of action, an admirer of Wichern, and a successor to Stöcker, Naumann propounded that Marx and Christ gave the answer to the social problem (*Jesus, the Man of the People*, 1894). In 1896 Naumann organized the National Social Union, which failed to rally the masses, then turned left-liberal and joined the Radical Association in 1903. At the end of his life, he was first president of the German Democratic Party in the post-World War I German Republic. Another prominent leader of the Protestant social crusade was Christoph Blumhardt (1842–1919), the son of Johann Christoph Blumhardt, a much celebrated Pietist pastor. Christoph Blumhardt enthusiastically believed that the social movement was bringing forth the kingdom of God, and he became a socialist member of Parliament in 1900. His influence on the young Karl Barth was not negligible, as the 1919 *Epistle to the Romans* evidences.

Switzerland was not sheltered from social turmoil either. A social-democratic party increasingly took part in Swiss political life. The two chief figures of the Swiss religious-socialist school were Herman Kutter (1863–1931), author of *They Must* (1904) and of *The Revolution of Christianity* (1908), and Leonhard Ragaz (1868–1921), who founded in 1907 the Religious-Socialist Conference. Both Kutter and Ragaz demanded social justice and believed the kingdom of God to be looming at the horizon of socialism.

The Nationalist Credo and the Churches

The 1789 principle of the sovereignty of the people, the rally of European Jacobins to the patriotic messianism of the "Great Nation" so enthusiastically embodied in the military anthem *La Marseillaise,* and the people's rebellion against the Napoleonic hegemony as illustrated by Leon Tolstoy's epic novel *War and Peace* (1863–1869), awakened national self-consciousness on the Continent from Spain to Russia. Directly or indirectly propagated by writers, philologists, grammarians, historians, and composers, nationalism grew into an overpowering ideological force in nineteenth-century Europe, moving minorities as well as political giants. The national principle won recognition in the 1850s–1870s with the unification of Italy and of Germany, the reorganization of Austria-Hungary, and the independence of the Balkan states. Having gained momentum by blending with hero worship (Thomas Carlyle's 1840 *On Heroes, Hero Worship, and the Heroic in History*) and/or with race worship (Arthur de Gobineau's 1853 *Essay on the Inequality of Human Races*), nationalism competed with socialist internationalism. Nationalism stimulated religious and cultural imperialism, through the creation of movements such as Panislamism (by Djemal al-Din al-Afghani in the Ottoman Empire), Pan-Slavism (by Aksakov and Katkov in Russia), and Pan-Germanism (by Treitschke, Hasse, and Lehr in Germany); it was twisted into exclusivism and xenophobia (by Barrès and Maurras in France) as well as into anti-Semitism (the notorious Dreyfus affair in France and Wilhelm Marr's 1873 *The Victory of Jewry over Germanness*); and it was finally deformed into Fascism and National Socialism after World War I.

In Germany in the interwar period, the encounter of Lutheranism with the national principle gave birth to right-wing political theologies (P. Althaus, F. Gogarten, and E. Hirsch) that essentially focused on the natural order created by God (theology of creation and ordinances), and produced the multiform and pluridoctrinal conservative and racist movements of the German Christians. The Church Movement German Christians was founded in 1927 in Thuringia by Siegfried Leffler and Julius Leutheusser, and the Faith Movement German Christians was begun by Wilhelm Kube and Joachim Hossenfelder in 1932 in the Old Prussian Union while National Socialism was overwhelming German democracy. Among the numerous German Christian confessional documents, the *Twenty-Eight Theses of the Folkchurch of Saxony regarding the Establishment of the German Evangelical Church* of 1933 best exemplify their endeavor to revive the medieval alliance of the spiritual with the temporal by attuning the Christian message to the National Socialist ideology of blood and race. The peculiarity of the 1920s–1930s conservative Lutheranism lay in the focus on the concept of people, or folk. The idea originated with Johann Gottfried Herder, who maintained in *Reflections on the Philosophy of the History of Mankind* (1776–1803) that every nation had a unique folk spirit (*Volksgeist*), a common ingredient composed of kinship, social solidarity, cultural affinity such as language, and history, and that this spirit expressed the divine will of the Creator. Often celebrated as the "Magna

Charta" of German nationalism, Johann Gottlieb Fichte's *Address to the German Nation* (1807–1808) elevated the concept of nation to the status of a historical, divine revelation.

If both Protestantism and Catholicism failed to take an open stand against the National Socialist regime as well as to denounce the violation of basic human rights and cultural freedom, they were, however, relatively successful in withstanding the state's attempt to control them. They resisted Josef Goebbels's policy of bringing culture and belief in line with National Socialism (*die Gleichschaltung*). It is notable, for instance, that the Roman Catholic church prevented the Nazi subversion of its youth organizations and firmly protested the state's euthanasia policy (e.g., Cardinal Galen of Münster, and Archbishop Gröber of Freiburg). Among the Protestants, the movement known as the Confessing Church (*die Bekennende Kirche*) was persecuted by both the state and the German Evangelical church because of its refusal to conform. Individual clergymen paid for their resistance activities with either their freedom or their lives. The Berlin Domprobst Lichtenberg was sentenced to prison for offering prayers for persecuted Jews. A former head of the Inner Mission, Martin Niemöller (1892–1984), who founded in 1933 the Pastors' Emergency League (*Pfarrernotbund*) and launched the Confessing Church in 1934, was sent to a concentration camp in 1937 for speaking against the racial and judicial policies of the regime. His associate Dietrich Bonhoeffer (1906–1945) was executed in April 1945 for having participated in an attempt to assassinate the Führer. Religious socialists such as Gunther Dehn and Paul Tillich were also the victim of political repression. Tillich emigrated to the United States in 1933. Similarly, the Swiss theologian Karl Barth was forced to leave the University of Bonn because of his unwelcome support for the Confessing Church (*Theological Existence Today*, 1933; *Barmen Declaration*, 1934).

Reactionary Protestantism

In 1845 in the Canton of Vaud in Switzerland Alexandre Vinet wrote as follows:

> The sole concern of the church should be to exist; that is to exist as a church; namely to take birth. For, what we have hitherto called church was not a church. . . . Time has come to have one. Dissident or not, this new church will be a church of the multitude.[1]

The Enlightenment, the French Revolution, and industrialization, which together eventually weakened the orthodoxies, provoked by reaction in the nineteenth century a variety of religious revivals of medieval and pre-Enlightenment dogmatic certain-

---

[1] Alexandre Vinet, *Religious Freedom and Ecclesiastical Matters* (Paris, 1854), p. 459.

ties. Even in the Jewish communities of Poland, the Hasidic tradition was heightened by an unprecedented growth of popular piety.

The evangelical awakening and neo-orthodoxy in Switzerland, Scotland, France, and the Netherlands, confessionalism in Germany and Scandinavia, and ritualism in the Church of England formed the major reactionary trends within European Protestantism.

The Evangelical Revival and the Rebound of Reformed Orthodoxy

The evangelical awakening, known as the *réveil*, was initiated in Geneva in 1816 by an antirationalist pastor, César Malan (1812–1894), who preached the Calvinist doctrines of sin, grace, and predestination. Influenced by the local Moravian community, Malan formed his own congregation (the Chapel of Witness) after having been ousted from the Genevan church by the prorationalist Company of Pastors. Malan wrote hymns (*Songs of Sion*) and undertook missionary journeys to France and the Netherlands. As happened elsewhere, in the Swiss Cantons, the evangelical revival clashed with the civil and ecclesiastical authorities and resulted in the organization of independent bible and missionary societies and free churches. The foremost champion of the liberty of the church in French-speaking Switzerland was Alexandre Vinet (1797–1847), whose affinity with Blaise Pascal earned him the appellation of the "Protestant Pascal" (*Moral and Social Philosophy, Religious Philosophy*, 1837). Indeed, Vinet believed in a personal religion anchored in human consciousness, a religion of the heart, an active faith that reconciles God with humanity beyond all disparity. In his most famous work, *New Discourses on Some Religious Topics* (1841) and *Essay on the Manifestation of Religious Convictions* (1842), Vinet combines the enthusiasm of the revival with the dogmatism of Reformed orthodoxy. In the 1820s, he had been a fervent auditor of Wilhelm Leberecht de Wette at Basel.

In Great Britain in the first half of the nineteenth century, the evangelicals had two luminaries, Charles Simeon (1759–1836), a popular biblical scholar, and Thomas Chalmers (1780–1847), who grappled with natural theology and social economy in his *Bridgewater Treatises* (1833–1834) and instigated the disruption of the Scottish established church (or kirk), which resulted in the creation of the Free Church of Scotland. Often associated and identified with the low church party, English evangelicalism received in the second half of the nineteenth century a fresh impulse from the American revivalists Dwight Lyman Moody (1837–1899) and Ira David Sankey (1840–1908). The social concern of English evangelicalism was mainly voiced by William Wilberforce (1759–1833), a leader of the Clapham Sect, who obtained from the government the abolition of slave trade, and by the seventh earl of Shaftesbury (1801–1885), a philanthropist and social reformer whose legislation alleviated the fate of the poor.

In France by mid-century, the Huguenots were divided into an evangelical and a rationalist faction. The victory of Calvinism over liberalism was sealed at the Synod of 1872 by the adoption of a Reformed confession of faith (*Confession of La Rochelle*, 1559). It was the strength of the evangelical party to have revived Calvinist orthodoxy and to have given its final shape to the doctrine of scripture of Turrettini's 1675 *Formula Consensus Helveticus*. A blatant denial of current biblical criticism, Louis Gaussen's 1840 *Theopneustia or Literal Inspiration of Holy Scriptures* raised theopneustia to the "dogma of all dogmas." Among the many luminaries of the evangelical party, two men stand out, Frédéric Monod and Adolphe Monod, the orator. Both were products of British evangelicalism and Swiss revivalism.

Likewise, in the Netherlands, the revival that began in the 1820s under the influences of German Romanticism and Swiss awakening focused on theological renewal (Calvinist orthodoxy), church autonomy (William I's 1816 *Reglement* placed the church under state tutelage), and on education by demanding a confessional, private school system. Eventually, it resulted in the creation of a secessionist Calvinist church.

Uncritically bound to the inerrancy of scriptures, the evangelicals denied the value of biblical criticism. Too doctrinaire, they were ill prepared to respond adequately to the vexing challenge of modern science. Overridingly focused on religious conversion, they were handicapped in their promotion of social betterment. And far too puritanical, they lamentably failed to appreciate visual arts, music, and the pleasures of life.

In September 1919, Karl Barth (1886–1968), a Swiss pastor, delivered an epochal lecture, *The Christian in Society*, at a religious-socialist conference at Tambach in Thuringia. A former religious-socialist won over to Christoph Blumhardt's millennarian eschatology, Barth deprecated altogether Stöcker's Christian-social movement, Naumman's Protestant-social era, and Ragaz's religious-social program. All these attempts, charged Barth, built a "hyphenated Christianity" that merges religion with socialism and disregards revelation and the Beyond. Instead, Barth demanded that the otherworldliness of God be taken seriously. On the whole, Barth's speech marked a return to sixteenth- and seventeenth-century Protestant orthodoxy. World War I had shattered Barth's confidence in Culture-Protestantism, which in spite of its emphasis on the religious, moral, and social commitments of the Christian, had failed to prevent a resurgence of barbarism of such magnitude. That same year, 1919, Barth's *Commentary on the Epistle to the Romans* heralded a new era. Emil Brunner, a Swiss colleague who joined Barth, praised this first victory over the platitudes of nineteenth-century Protestantism while a dismayed Adolf von Harnack, the renown church historian, diagnosed it as a typical illness of the time. Within a couple of years the "new theology" had found outstanding advocates: Eduard Thurneysen (*Dostoevsky*, 1921), Friedrich Gogarten (*The Religious Decision*, 1921), Emil Brunner (*Experience, Knowledge, and Faith*, 1921), and Rudolf Bultmann, from whom the school received the name "dialectical theology." In 1923 the dialectical theologians began a journal, *Zwischen den Zeiten* (*Between the Times*), which lasted until the disruption of the school in 1933. By the time of Adolf Hitler's accession to power, the dialectical theologians had gone separate routes: Barth had discovered Anselm and had begun to unfold a theology of the Word of God (*Church Dogmatics*, 1932–1959); Brunner had rediscovered natural theology and was promoting a new Christian apologetic (*Nature and Grace*, 1934); Gogarten had joined the nationalist Lutherans; and Bultmann was striving to Christianize Martin Heidegger's existential philosophy. In the meantime, the dialectical theologians had orchestrated a massive return to pre-Enlightenment theological patterns. Protestant lay people and ministers on both sides of the Atlantic increasingly turned away from both the Enlightenment and its heir, Culture-Protestantism, accusing both of having historicized, anthropologized, psychologized, and secularized Christian revelation.

Confessionalism

Unlike other revivals, the German awakening and confessionalism, though stimulated by talented minds, had a harder task in countervailing the overwhelming influence of liberal or progressive theological giants. Nevertheless, like the other revivals, the German reactionary Protestantism found its full expression in biblicism and confessionalism. It all began at the tricentennial celebration of the Reformation in 1817 with the publication of Luther's *95 Theses* by Claus Harms. The purpose was to proclaim that faith rested on revelation and not reason, and that the Word of God and the sacraments made the church. The notable advocates of the return to orthodoxy were the following:

- The former orientalist and Halle biblical and practical theologian August Gottreu Tholuck (1799–1877).
- The Germanist and Marburg divine August Friedrich Christian Vilmar (1800–1868), who censured scientific theology in *The Theology of Facts against the Theology of Rhetoric* (1856).
- The Tübingen biblicist Johann Tobias Beck (1808–1878).
- The neo-Lutherans of Erlangen, Adolf Harless (1806–1879), who framed the theory of kenosis (self-emptying of God in Christ), Franz Hermann Reinhold von Franck (1827–1877), and Johann Christian Konrad von Hofmann (1810–1877), who emphasized personal conversion and "salvation history."
- The leader of the Prussian revival, the Berlin Old Testament scholar Ernst Wilhelm Hengstenberg (1802–1869).

A fierce enemy of the Enlightenment, idealism, and the principles of the 1848 revolution, Hengstenberg believed in the authenticity of the bible, advocated theism, acknowledged the 1530 Augsburg Confession, and defended the alliance of throne and altar.

Closely related to the rebirth of cultural identity, the Danish revival was dominated by the rival figures of Nicolai Grundtvig (1783–1872) and Hans Lassen Martensen (1808–1884), whose Hegelianism was vigorously attacked in 1855 by Søren Kierkegaard. In Sweden and Norway, the revival came from Pietist circles.

Tractarianism

The 1829 Catholic emancipation in Britain provoked by Ricochet in the Church of England a renascence of high church doctrines against current liberalism and the intrusion of the secular government into church affairs. A group of Oriel College scholars, who disdained the evangelicals, despised the Dissenters, and held the Reformation in utter contempt, launched in 1833 at Oxford an unexpected series of tracts that initiated a unique reactionary Christianity: the Oxford Movement. The movement was inspired by four outstanding personalities: John Keble (1792–1866), much admired for his sacred poetry (*The Christian Year*, 1827), whose sermon of July 14, 1833 on national apostasy instigated Tractarianism; Richard Hurrell Froude (1803–1836), a devotee of the medieval church; John Henry Newman (1801–1890), a Patristic scholar, who was received in the Roman Catholic church in 1845 and was made cardinal in 1879; and the Regius Professor of Hebrew, Edward Bouverie Pusey (1800–1882), a brilliant exponent of Anglo-Catholicism, who valued disciplined devotion, believed in divine incarnation and meditation, and championed a high doctrine of the sacraments, the ministry, and the church with a special emphasis on the apostolic succession in the episcopate.

It was the interference of a Whig Parliament (Liberal) in the internal affairs of the Church of Ireland in 1833 that precipitated Keble's offensive against Liberalism and Erastianism. He was soon followed by Froude and Newman and later joined by Pusey. The Oriel group voiced its reactionary views through a series of pamphlets entitled *Tracts of the Time*, which appeared from September 1833 to January 1841. The last pamphlet, *Tract 90*, written by Newman, offered a Romanist interpretation of the 1571 Thirty-Nine Articles of Religion. Having antagonized the Anglican hierarchy, Newman, who in the meantime had begun to publish a *Library of the Fathers* in English and a *Library of Anglo-Catholic Theology*, completely disillusioned and closer to Rome than ever, recanted the Anglican faith. The Tractarian period of the Oxford Movement had come to a close. Under the ensuing leadership of Pusey, the movement became by the mid-century, an Anglo-Catholic revival, later known as Ritualism. The Ritualists revived monastic life, and active work among the poor was carried on by such groups as Miss Sellon's Sisterhood of Mercy, John Leycester Syne's Anglican Benedictine Order, and Charles Gore's Community of the Resurrection.

What was the aim of the Oxford Movement? No less than generating "a new Reformation," as Newman remarked in his 1864 *Apologia pro Vita sua*. However, unlike the evangelical revival, it was a return not to the sixteenth century but to seventeenth-century high Anglicanism. If the strength of the Oxford Movement lay in the rediscovery of the specificity of Anglicanism as a middle course (*via media*) between Catholicism and Protestantism, and if its originality resided in its emphasis on the antiquity and catholicity of the Church of England, its modernity, however, became apparent at the Anglo-Catholic symposium, *Lux Mundi*, of 1889, which acknowledged the validity of biblical criticism and evolutionary science.

Closely related to early nineteenth-century religious revival, the Gothic architectural style of the Middle Ages was variously revived throughout Europe and especially in Britain, where it reached its fullest dimension. Art historians have often considered Gothic Revival as the only purely English architectural movement. Another purely English movement in painting was the pre-Raphaelite brotherhood that clustered in the 1850s around John Everett Millais (1829–1896), William Holman Hunt (1827–1910), and Dante Gabriel Rossetti (1828–1882). It marked a revival of the style of Italian art that was prevalent before the time of Raphael. Rossetti's *The Girlhood of Mary Virgin* (1849), Millais's *Christ in the House of His Parents* (1850), and Hunt's *The Light of the World* (1854) rendered a moral and religious solemnity close to both the Oxford Movement and the Catholic renascence.

On the Cutting-Edge of Religion and Culture

Hegel's Absolute Idealism

On October 28, 1816, in an inaugural address at Heidelberg University, Georg Wilhelm Friedrich Hegel (1770–1831) defined the philosopher's First Commandment as "courage for truth, belief in the power of the spirit." Hegel saw the philosophical task as a mission of a mystical, religious, quasi-divine nature. Like Spinoza and Leibniz before him, Hegel was possessed with the idea of God. God, as the whole, the absolute, and the unconditional, is at the principle and conclusion of his system. Therefore, he claimed that to think is to worship, and he showed in his lectures on *Philosophy of Religion* (1840) that philosophy, the highest of all sciences, embodied the purest form of religion, the conceptual.

Of his monumental production, the most significant works are the *Phenomenology of the Spirit* (1807), which retraces the experience of consciousness from the world of sense to the self-consciousness of the absolute; the *Science of Logic* (1812–1816), which unfolds God's thought before the creation; the *Encyclopedia of Philosophical Sciences* (1817), composed of a logic, a philosophy of nature, and a philosophy of the mind; the *Philosophy of Right* (1821), on law and state; and the posthumously released Berlin lectures on philosophy of religion (1840). In short, like Fichte and Schelling, Hegel took up the matter where Kant had left off. A pupil of the age, Hegel craved for harmony and unity, and as a matter of course sought to resolve the Kantian dualism. Helped by neo-Platonism, Spinoza's pantheism, and Jakob Boehme's theosophy, Hegel framed a monistic system, panlogical and panentheistic, in which the dialectic (thesis, antithesis, synthesis) functioned as the instrument of differentiation and unification. Hegel's speculative or absolute idealism implied trust in the speculative power of reason and the identification of thought with being (the real is rational and the rational is real). As a result, Hegel reconciled the human being with God, the finite with the infinite spirit. This reconciliation means that human self-consciousness is ultimately God's self-consciousness, that the free, rational, and finite being is at the same time an instrument and a modification of the absolute and infinite spirit.

It is noteworthy that many twentieth-century Christologies, Protestant or Catholic, drew inspiration from Hegel's view on Christ.

In the lectures on philosophy of religion, from which the right-wing and the left-wing Hegelian schools drew opposing conclusions, Hegel set forth the principle that philosophy and religion have the same content—the consciousness of God—yet express it in different ways. Philosophy renders in a conceptual form what religion does in the form of representation.

Five Innovative Schools

From Schleiermacher and Hegel to Ernst Troeltsch and Karl Barth, German Protestantism produced an impressive array of eminent scholars and powerful thinkers who may be divided into five schools.

1. At the outset of the nineteenth century, the theology of the Enlightenment and Kantianism together crystallized into rationalism. The rationalist school, which pervaded the Protestant churches for a couple of decades, had three prominent advocates: the biblical scholar Heinrich Eberhard Paulus (1761–1851); the Weimar superintendent Johann Friedrich Röhr (1777–1848), whose notorious *Letters on Rationalism* (1813) outlined the program of the school that Julius August Wegscheider (1771–1849) had implemented in his 1815 *Theological Institutions of Christian Dogmatics*.

2. In the first half of the nineteenth century, two schools rivaled in influence: the right-wing Hegelians and the school of mediation. Firmly anchored in speculative idealism, the leaders of the Hegelian school were Karl Daub (1765–1836), a former Kantian; Philipp Konrad Marheineke (1780–1846), who contended in *Fundamental Doctrines of Christian Dogmatics* (1819) that the biblical doctrine of reconciliation, the church tradition, and speculative idealism were one and the same; Ferdinand Christian Baur (1792–1860), the founder of the new Tübingen school and Strauss's teacher, an advocate of the historical approach to the bible, whose controversial work *About the So-called Pastoral Letters of Apostle Paul* (1835) disproved the authority of scriptures; and the lesser known Karl Rosenkranz (1805–1879). The absoluteness of Christianity

was among the characteristic themes of Hegelian dogmatics. Rosenkranz organized his *Encyclopedia of Theological Sciences* (1831) into three parts: the first part, or speculative theology, demonstrates the truth of Christian tenets on the basis of the dialectical self-revelation of God in the divine-human relationship; the second, or historical theology, treats the bible and ecclesiastical texts as objectifications of the Christian idea in the finite world; and the third, or practical theology, defines the institutions and activities of Christianity.

3. The school of mediation, mostly in line with Schleiermacher, was led by Karl Immanuel Nitzsch, August Twesten, Schleiermacher's successor at Berlin University; Wilhelm Martin Leberecht de Wette, whose theology of feeling brings knowledge into harmony with faith (*On Religion and Theology*, 1815; *Christian Ethics*, 1819; *The Essence of Christian Faith*, 1846); and Richard Rothe, renowned for an epochal *Theological Ethics* (1845). With Rothe, dogmatics became ethics. Divided into three comprehensive doctrines—goods, virtues, and duties—Rothe's *Theological Ethics* rests on the Schleiermacherian assumption that self-consciousness is at the same time consciousness of God. As moral beings, argued Rothe, it is our duty to form a moral community on earth as it is our retribution to partake in the moral kingdom of God.

4. For half a century, from the Kantian renascence of the mid-1860s that was orchestrated by Otto Liebmann's 1815 *Kant and the Epigones* to the formation of the dialectical school (Barth, Bultmann, Brunner) in the early 1920s, Culture-Protestantism dominated the theological spectrum in Germany, Switzerland, the Netherlands, and France. It all began at Göttingen, where an apostate of the Tübingen school, Albrecht Ritschl (1822–1889), exhumed the true design of the Protestant Reformation in *The Christian Doctrine of Justification and Reconciliation* (1870–1886). Ritschl was a staunch Lutheran, although not a reactionary one. Bibliocentric and Christocentric, he nonetheless disparaged Pietism as crypto-Catholicism (*History of Pietism*, 1880–1886). Like most of his contemporaries, Ritschl had grown disillusioned with absolute idealism. The Hegelian conception of history favored by his teacher Baur no longer quenched his thirst for historical truth (see the second edition of *The Origin of the Old Catholic Church*, 1857). At Göttingen in the late 1860s, he befriended Hermann Lotze in whose philosophy of value he found some inspiration. A Kantian to the core, Ritschl associated eschatology with ethics and advocated an alliance of Christian theology with the historical sciences as a replacement for the misalliance of theology and metaphysics (*Theology and Metaphysics*, 1881). For instance, God's historical revelation in Jesus Christ was selected as the foundation stone of Christian theology. Ritschl had an impressive following. The Ritschlians occupied leading chairs in divinity schools throughout the country and launched several journals that propagated their variegated opinions (*Theologische Literaturzeitung*, *Zeitschrift für Theologie und Kirche*, and *Die christliche Welt*). In sum, the Ritschlians were successful in promoting the synthesis of Christian belief with modern German culture. One distinguishes among the Ritschlians between the old generation, who were closer to Ritschl, conservative in theology and liberal in politics

though with social convictions, and the new generation, who were progressive and essentially attuned to the history of religion. Some of the luminaries of the old generation deserve mention because of the considerable influence they exerted: the social-liberal activist Martin Rade (1857–1940); Julius Kaftan, a powerful advocate of the uniqueness of Christianity among world religions (*The Essence of Christian Religion*, 1881); the Christocentric dogmatician and Luthero-Kantian ethicist Wilhelm Herrmann (1846–1922), who taught both Karl Barth and Rudolf Bultmann; and the church historian Adolf von Harnack, immensely famous not only for his radical onslaught on Hellenized Christianity in his monumental *History of Dogmas* (1886–1889) but for reducing in *The Essence of Christianity* (1900) Jesus's message to three themes: the kingdom of God is coming; the fatherhood of God and the eternal value of the human soul; and a higher righteousness.

5. The new generation of Ritschlians, better known as the school of history of religion, assumed the momentous shift in theology from dogmatism to history and sociology. Ritschl was still too speculative for their taste. In an epoch-making article, *On Historical and Dogmatical Method in Theology* (1896), the founder of the school, Ernst Troeltsch (1865–1923), a historian and a sociologist of Lutheran stock, contrasted the historian's method with that of the dogmatician. In spite of the difference between them, Troeltsch did not, however, consider them incompatible. On the contrary, aware that modern science was shattering orthodox faith, he had the ambition to lay a new foundation for theology, a scientific one. And it was his belief that the historian of religion should collaborate with the dogmatician to achieve this goal. Indeed, only a philosophy or metaphysics of religion that was drawn from an analysis of the history and development of religious consciousness could, as a scientific foundation, strengthen the standing of the science of religion among other sciences and additionally facilitate the Christian strategy against materialism, naturalism, skepticism, estheticism, and pantheism. Troeltsch was an apologist in disguise. From his studies at Erlangen, Göttingen, and Berlin, he gained historical expertise and retained the influences of Schleiermacher (*The Religious Apriori*, 1904), German Idealism (*The Absoluteness of Christianity*, 1909), and neo-Kantianism (the school of Baden—Wilhelm Windelband and Heinrich Rickert). He was close to the sociologist Max Weber, with whom he often disagreed, and grappled with some of Wilhelm Dilthey's issues concerning historiography and relativism in *Historicism and Its Problems* (1922). Troeltsch embarked on his academic career at Heidelberg as a theologian and concluded it as a philosopher in Berlin. After World War I, as a committed democrat, he took an active part in the establishment of the new regime, the Weimar Republic.

Troeltsch's foremost historical study, *Protestantism and Progress* (1906), argued that early Protestantism marked a retreat to the church-civilization of the Middle Ages. By holding to the principle of authority and by perpetuating medieval asceticism, at least inwardly, early Protestantism delayed the development of modern culture, which had been initiated by the Renaissance. Early Protestantism was merely a modified medieval Catholicism. Of little impact on European culture, the Reformation, however, gave the impetus to "a religion of conscience and conviction, without compulsorily imposed dogma." Troeltsch's controversial thesis was rebutted by Karl Holl, a Lutheran scholar of note, in *The Cultural Significance of the Reformation* (1911). As a sociologist, Troeltsch posed the twofold question of whether the development of religious beliefs and movements has been conditioned by external factors and whether, in turn, they have affected society and culture. His masterpiece, *The Social Teaching of the Christian Churches* (1912) deals with these issues. Troeltsch inferred from a detailed study of Christian social history that there were three types of "sociological self-formation of the Christian idea": the church, the sect, and the mystic, and concluded that "the history of the Christian Ethos becomes the story of a constantly renewed search for this compromise, and of fresh opposition to this spirit of compromise." The fate of Culture-Protestantism is a perfect illustration of Troeltsch's thesis. Culture-Protestantism and the spirit of compromise it embodied collapsed in the 1920s under the pressure of the dialectical school, a neo-orthodox resurgence that denied any form of compromise with modern secular culture.

The Religion of Humanity

In utter contrast to the high speculative road of the right-wing Hegelians, which was built on the supernaturalist foundation of absolute idealism, the program of the left-wing Hegelian school dechristianized Hegel's worldview, promoted naturalism and humanism, and demanded historical action or change. David Friedrich Strauss's (1808-1874) *Life of Jesus* came out in 1835 amidst outcries of indignation. Theodor Fontane, a German poet and novelist, saluted Strauss's *Life of Jesus* as one of the most influential books of the age, along with Lessing's *Nathan* and Goethe's *Faust*. Strauss's ambition was to reveal the making of the Christ-image. He repudiated all prior Christologies and taught instead that the unity of both natures, divine and human, was not exclusively embodied in the historical Jesus, the true God-man, but inclusively comprehended in humanity as a species in development. Strauss's vehemently controverted Christology resulted from an alliance of Hegelianism with biblical criticism. It rested on the merging of two concepts: the Hegelian concept of representation and the exegetical concept of myth. By myth, Strauss understood a process that clothed religious ideas with historical apparel. True to the exegetical tradition of the Enlightenment, Strauss demythologized in order to divest of its mythical clothing the self-objectification of human essence into divine transcendence. It was Strauss's belief that the Jewish messianic expectation produced the image of a savior that then was projected upon Jesus because of his person and fate.

Later in his life, Strauss took his position to the extreme and fulfilled the shift from Christian culture to modern consciousness, that is, from transcendence to immanence. This was how Strauss envisioned his contribution to the advancement of Protestantism. In *The Life of Jesus for the German People* (1864), Strauss aimed at shifting the religion of Christ to a religion of humanity. Humanity, not the historical Jesus, is now the true God-man. Redemption is the reconciliation of the human being not with God but with the idea of humanity. However much reduced the function of Christ's atonement in human salvation had become, Jesus remained, so Strauss conceded, useful as a historical embodiment of the idea of humanity.

In a similar vein, Bruno Bauer (1809–1882) released in 1838 *The Religion of the Old Testament in the Historical Development of its Principles*, in which he described the concept of religion as it took historical form among the Hebrews, in the self-consciousness of Christ, and in the religious representations of early Christians. Eventually, refuting Strauss's mythical interpretation and reading Hegel's philosophy as an atheistic system, Bauer maintained in his *Critique of the Synoptic Gospels* and in *The Trumpet of Doom for Hegel*, both of 1841, that God was dead for philosophy since the religious relationship was nothing other than an internal relationship of human consciousness with itself.

The reduction of theology to anthropology and the substitution of nature for the supernatural were completed by Ludwig Feuerbach, whose *Essence of Christianity* (1841) and *Essence of Religion* (1845) cleared the path for a post-Christian age. In the revolutionary year 1848, Ludwig Feuerbach delivered a series of lectures on religion in the townhall in Heidelberg and enunciated the following doctrine:

> Our world—not only our political and social world, but our learned, intellectual world as well—is a world upside down. . . . It is a universal principle of this upside-down world that God manifests Himself in nature, whereas we should say the opposite, namely, that originally at least nature manifests itself to man as a God, that nature makes on man an impression which he calls God, which he becomes conscious of and objectifies under the name of God. It is a universal doctrine in our upside-down world that nature sprang from God, whereas we should say the opposite, namely, that God was abstracted from nature and is merely a concept derived from it; for all the predicates, all the attributes or determinations, all the realities, as the philosophers say, that is, all the essence or perfections which are summed up in God, or whose totality is, or is called, God—in short, all those divine predicates that are not borrowed from man are derived from nature, so that they objectify, represent, illustrate nothing other than the essence of nature, or nature pure and simple. The difference is only that God is an abstraction, that is, a mere notion, while nature is concrete, that is, real; but the essence, the substance, the content are the same; God is nature in the abstract, . . .[2]

What was the substance of Feuerbach's antireligious argument? First of all, it

[2]Ralph Manheim, trans., Ludwig Feuerbach, *Lectures on the Essence of Religion* [1848–1849] (New York: Harper & Row, 1967), pp. 103–104.

must be said in all fairness that Feuerbach's ambition was not to destroy but to purify religion of falsehood and to restore its truth. The crux of Feuerbach's argument was that the secret of religion lay in self-alienated, objectified, and mystified anthropology. Religion exists because the human being has consciousness of the infinite, namely, one experiences a feeling of dependence. And it is not a dependence on a transcendent being, as Schleiermacher believed, but a dependence on immanent nature. In religion, the human being relates to the very essence of humanity. God is not a transcendent subject relating to his creatures but a projection of the human "species being" onto a transcendent, personal, and deified being. Therefore, to speak about God is to speak about human nature indirectly. To say that God is omnipotent, omniscient, eternal, infinite, love, just, and holy is merely to concentrate and project upon a single imaginary being that which constitutes the essence of humanity. If religion originates in the needs and desires of the human being as an emotional and sensuous being who craves for comforting images and thereby shows a deficiency of human knowledge, then true human bliss begins with the recognition of the origin of religious illusion and is achieved by the emancipation from the tutelage of religious dogmas. Hence, with Feuerbach, the philosopher's task shifted from that of rationalizing Christian belief to that of liberating humanity from the alienating authority of the supernatural. As Feuerbach concluded in *The Essence of Christianity*, the more one invests in God, the less one keeps for oneself, and for that reason, as Karl Marx and Sigmund Freud later concurred, "the end of religion is the welfare, the salvation, and the ultimate felicity of man."

The Ascent of Ultraconservative Catholicism

Throughout the nineteenth century, Roman Catholicism swayed from Ultramontanism to liberalism and modernism and eventually settled on the most conservative course. In France, Italy, and Germany, whose political, social, and religious systems had been subverted by the principles of the 1789 revolution, no church offered the counterrevolutionaries and the Romantics, such as François-René de Chateaubriand and Friedrich von Schlegel, a higher sense of authority, tradition, immutable truth, and beauty, than the Roman Catholic church. For that reason, no other church underwent a more comprehensive and triumphant renewal, whether in matters of doctrine, devotion, or discipline. New religious orders were founded in numbers, new dogmas were promulgated, new churches were erected in old rural and new urban areas in some kind of Gothic revival, pro-Catholic political parties were organized, and new rights were acquired by Catholics in non-Catholic countries such as England and the Netherlands.

Moreover, the Catholic renascence benefited from a line of formidable popes: Pius VII (1800–1823), who restored in 1814 the Society of Jesus by the bull *Sollicitudo Omnium Ecclesiarum*, the Holy Office and the *Index* (where Descartes, Spinoza, Locke,

Bayle, Voltaire, Rousseau, Lessing, and Kant were listed among prohibited authors); Leo XII (1823–1829), whose achievement was the Catholic emancipation in the British Isles; Gregory XVI (1831–1846), an adversary of liberal Catholicism (freedom of conscience, of speech, and of the press) and of the separation of church and state; Pius IX (1846–1878), a liberal turned ultraconservative following the 1848 revolution, who promulgated the dogmas of Immaculate Conception by the 1854 bull *Ineffabilis Deus*, condemned the so-called errors of the time in the 1864 encyclical *Quanta Cura* and its appended *Syllabus of Errors*, and finally convened the First Vatican Council; and Leo XIII (1878–1903), an advocate of social justice whose encyclical *Rerum Novarum* of 1891 boldly restricted liberal economy by supporting state intervention.

The Catholic Renascence

At the forefront of the Catholic renascence stood Bavaria, France, and Italy. In Bavaria, Johann Michael Sailer (1751–1832), consecrated bishop of Regensburg in 1822 and often praised as the Bavarian church father, bridged the chaotic revolutionary era by restoring the church and by reconstructing its moral and pastoral theology. Trained by the Jesuits and nurtured by Spanish and German mysticism, Sailer, an admirer of Archbishop Fénelon and a friend of the Swiss mystic pastor Johann Caspar Lavater, wrote a *Complete Prayer Book for Catholic Christians* (1785), proscribed the fashionable "Werther disease" aroused by Goethe's 1774 *The Sorrows of Young Werther*, grappled with Kantianism, denounced eighteenth-century eudemonism, and laid the new foundations of ethics in *Fundamental Doctrine of Religion* (1805) and *Handbook of Christian Ethics* (1817). Beyond the limits of Kant's ethico-theology and in a manner reminiscent of Schleiermacher and de Wette, although more metaphysical, Sailer unfolded a Roman Catholic theology of religious consciousness. For it was his aim to bring knowledge, morality, and Christian revelation together. Combining the subjectivism of the Enlightenment and of the Romantics with the inwardness of mystical spirituality, Sailer propounded an immediate knowledge of God in reason and of the divine law in conscience. As a religious faculty, conscience opens access to transcendence. For the Christian, the path to salvation is obedience to conscience. As a Christian educator, Sailer believed in agreement with Rousseau in the harmony of nature and supernature. He therefore conceived of education as a means of fulfilling the free religious identity of youth by developing the intellectual, moral, and religious aptitudes together (*On Education for Educators*, 1807).

With Johann Adam Möhler (1796–1838) and Johann Joseph von Görres (1776–1848), Munich rose to be the center of Roman Catholic culture in Germany. Möhler's major works, *The Unity in the Church or the Principle of Catholicism* (1825) and *Symbolic or Description of the Dogmatic Differences between the Catholics and the Protestants* (1832), both upheld a high view of the church that later found expression at the

Second Vatican Council. As incarnation of the spirit of history, as dynamic body and lively unity, as symbol of the unique truth and Son of God, and as synthesis of all opposites, the church is best embodied in the Roman Catholic church. Once a supporter of the French Revolution, Görres, a historian and publicist who as a disciple of Schelling had taken part in the Romantic movement, became a devout Catholic in his later years and rehabilitated the belief in the supernatural in a skillful historical study entitled *Christian Mysticism* (1836–1842). Another historian who worked for the regeneration of the Bavarian church was Ignaz von Döllinger (1799–1890), who, however, had the misfortune of opposing the dogma of papal infallibility on historical grounds and suffered the humiliation of being excommunicated in April 1871.

French postrevolutionary Catholicism was divided between a Gallican hierarchy, which gave its full support to the renewed alliance of throne and altar and sanctioned the royal authority over the church, and a liberal and Ultramontane party that demanded freedom for the church (an independent school system, for instance) and looked to the Holy See for guidance and authority. The latter party was dominated in the first half of the century by the tragic figure of Félicité de Lamennais (1780–1854). Initially an ally of the counterrevolutionary theorists, Lamennais began his career by blaming the French Revolution for all the ills of the age and by defending the church against secular intrusion in *Reflections on the State of the Church of France in the Eighteenth Century and on Its Present Condition* (1809).

In 1817, Lamennais's *Essay on Indifference in Matters of Religion* came out and brought him immediate fame. Attacked by the Jesuits, Lamennais's *Essay* was, however, praised by the French Romantics and by the high church party of the Church of England. Against the *philosophes*, Lamennais demanded human submission to the authority of God, the church, the tradition, and the state. In the wake of the 1830 revolution, Lamennais accentuated his Ultramontanism and substituted liberalism for royalism. The restored Bourbon dynasty had failed, and Lamennais decided to "baptize the Revolution." Encouraged by the successful alliance of liberals and Catholics in Belgium and Ireland, Lamennais became the champion of the freedom of the church and was joined by the politician Charles de Montalembert (1810–1870), the future founder of a Catholic party, and by Henri Lacordaire (1802–1861), a magnificent preacher who delivered noted revivalist lectures at Notre Dame of Paris from 1835 to 1851 and restored the Dominican Order in France. With the purpose of separating the church from the state, Lamennais and his associates launched a newspaper, *The Future* (*L'Avenir*), which antagonized the state, the pro-Gallican Catholic hierarchy, and the Holy See.

Pope Gregory XVI condemned Lamennais's program, at first indirectly in 1832 (encyclical *Mirari vos*), then explicitly in 1834 (encyclical *Singulari nos*) after Lamennais had reiterated his commitment to freedom and humanism in *Words of a Believer* (1834). Praised though he was by Engels and Proudhon, yet still embittered, Lamennais repudiated the Catholic church. More democratic and humanistic than ever, he denied in *Outline of a Philosophy* (1840–1846) sin, grace, and redemption, advocating instead a philosophy of evolution. Eventually, in the second half of the century, the issue of state supervision of private, confessional education became the catalyst to the fatal divorce between the liberal Catholics, often pro-Gallican, and the Ultra-montanists, who found a talented spokesman in Louis Veuillot, journalist at the newspaper *The Universe*. After the collapse of the second empire in 1870 (Napoleon III), the radicals who governed the Third Republic denounced the Catholic church's interference in church affairs. Fiercely anticlerical, the radicals made in 1880 an issue of the role of the church in public education. An accidental political scandal, the famous Dreyfus Affair, crystallized in the 1890s the current anti-Semitic sentiments and further drew the divide between the forces of progress (the radicals) and the conservatives (nationalists, monarchists, Catholics). Eventually, the long-standing and acrimonious dispute culminated in 1905 to the advantage of the liberals with the promulgation of the *Law of Separation of Church and State*, which definitively disestablished the church and removed state support and supervision, yet guaranteed freedom of worship.

The Roman Pontiff Becomes Infallible

The story of the reign of Pius IX is that of a reforming pope who, alarmed by the 1848 revolution and by the threat to his temporal power by the growing desire for a unification of the Italian peninsula, sought refuge in ultraconservativism. Afraid of being dragged into what he intended to avoid by being openminded and liberal, Pius IX gave the first warning of the coming repression in the encyclical *Qui Pluribus* of 1846, in which he condemned indifferentism, communism, liberal philosophy, and the belief in progress. The attempt by some Italian theologians to reconcile the tenets of Catholicism with the philosophy of the movement for the unification of Italy, the *risorgimento* was severely repressed by the Holy See. The works of Antonio Rosmini (1797–1855) and Vincenzo Gioberti (1801–1852) were put on the *Index* in 1849 and 1852, respectively. Since the Renaissance, no pope had shown more generosity and understanding. The Jews were allowed to live outside the ghetto; the laws of censorship and of the press were softened; scientific conferences were authorized in the Eternal City; and, above all, a constitution was granted to the papal states in March 1848. Nonetheless, no pope had held firmer to the past in utter defiance of the age. It is likely that Pius IX finally deemed that in the end the sense of history might imperil the church.

In mid-December 1864, the encyclical *Quanta Cura* and its appended *Syllabus*, or catalogue of doctrines, theories, and views condemned by the church, caused a sensation. *Quanta Cura* proscribed the principles of secular society, of freedom of conscience and worship, and of the sovereignty of the people, and prescribed the autonomy of the church, its right to educate and guide people, and the full authority of the Roman pontiff. As for the *Syllabus*, it condemned every opinion that under-mined Catholic orthodoxy: rationalism, pantheism, naturalism, indifferentism, utili-tarianism, Gallicanism, statism, liberalism, socialism, and communism. Aghast, Ger-man newspapers branded this the return to the age of the Inquisition. On the morning of December 8, 1869, the twentieth ecumenical council was solemnly opened by Pius IX. The last council had taken place at Trent three hundred years before. Besides a renewed condemnation of all the "isms," the question of papal infallibility was debated at length. On July 18, 1870, while France and Prussia were on the eve of war, an overwhelming majority of council fathers voted the infallible magister of the Roman pontiff (*De Romani Pontificis Infallibili Magisterio*). Ultramontanism, trium-phant over liberal Catholicism, strengthened orthodoxy. Conservativism had become so powerful in the church of Rome that it was able to defeat the Modernist trend at the turn of the twentieth century. The Modernist crisis began in the early 1890s when Alfred Loisy (1857–1940) of the Catholic Institute of Paris, who had been won over to biblical criticism by Ernest Renan of the *College de France*, seriously questioned the inerrancy of the bible. Just as retrograde as the evangelicals, Pope Leo XIII responded by asserting the doctrine of biblical inerrancy in the encyclical *Providen-tissimus Deus* of 1893. His successor, Pius X, followed suit. His imperious condem-nation of Modernism in the 1907 encyclical *Pascendi*, however, was a Pyrrhic victory, inasmuch as Modernism eventually rebounded after World War II and even more so in the wake of the Second Vatican Council.

The spectacular success of the Catholic renascence was inseparable from a massive return to Thomas Aquinas under the impulse of Leo XIII's encyclical *Aeterni Patris* (1879). For the first time, at the University of Louvain in Belgium, a chair of Thomist philosophy was established in 1882, which Mgr. Désiré Mercier later transformed into the Superior Institute of Philosophy. There, neoscholastic thinkers engaged in constructive dialogue with the positive sciences and modern philosophies. Hence, neoscholasticism spread throughout the Catholic world from Paris and Milan to Sao Paulo. In 1903 near Tournai in Belgium, a Dominican school (Le Saulchoir) was founded to promote a more progressive Thomism (i.e., A. D. Sertillanges). Among the many scholastics, three outstanding figures deserve mention: Fathers Chenu, Congar, and de Lubac.

"Aggiornamento"

On St. Paul's Day, January 25, 1959, Pope John XXIII declared his intention to convene an ecumenical council in order to invigorate the church and to accommodate its structure and mission to the needs of the modern world, which were both plural and changing. The council convened in four sessions from December 1962 to De-cember 1965. Upon John XXIII's death in 1963, the *Aggiornamento* was continued by his successor Paul VI. Unlike the Council of Trent and Vatican I, the new council dealt primarily with pastoral issues and consciously avoided matters of doctrinal controversy. In the constitution *Lumen Gentium*, the council fathers, closer to the bible than ever, defined the church as the people of God, body of Christ, and temple of the Holy Spirit and stressed its service to the world. The council revised the inner organization of the church, highlighted the leading role of the bishops, acknowledged the responsibility of the laity, and promoted the diffusion of the bible and the use of the vernacular (mother tongue) in the liturgy. In a true ecumenical spirit, Vatican II called for a Christian unity based on the acceptance of pluralism. Furthermore, the Roman Catholic church adopted a more positive attitude toward the secular world and philosophical pluralism, as the constitution *Gaudium and Spes* and the Decree on Religious Freedom both illustrate. Having finally abandoned the citadel mentality in vogue since the eighteenth century, the Roman Catholic church was at last able to enter into a constructive dialogue with non-Christian religions and especially with Judaism.

Knights of Faith

Since 1815, in spite of secularization and dechristianization, many writers, composers, and artists found in Christianity a source of inspiration. For instance, in Britain the leading figure of his generation, Thomas Carlyle (1795–1881), a Presbyterian Scot who was much indebted to German Idealism and Romanticism, envisioned a Christianity altogether social, brave, and medieval (*Past and Present*, 1843). An Anglican, anti-Tractarian clergyman, Charles Kingsley (1819–1875) devoted his literary talent to the cause of the working class and to the propagation of the virtues of manliness (*The Saint's Tragedy*, 1848). Some of Anthony Trollope's (1815–1882) novels, *The Warden* (1855) and *Barchester Towers* (1857), offer a humorous depiction of rural Christianity in the Victorian age. A friend of Ezra Pound, the American-born T. S. Eliot (1888–1965) settled in England and became a brilliant advocate of Anglo-Catholicism (*The Idea of a Christian Society*, 1940). Christian themes appeared in some of Graham Greene's best novels: *Brighton Rock* (1938) and *The Power and the Glory* (1940).

Joan of Arc was canonized in 1920 at the time when France produced a cluster of outstanding Catholic writers. Fighting against the materialism and skepticism of the interwar period, they revived the sense of sin that modern humanity had lost. It was his symbolist poetry and his Christians plays (*Break at Noon*, 1906; *The Tidings Brought to Mary*, 1912; *The Satin Slipper*, 1924) that brought world fame to Paul Claudel (1868–1955), a career diplomat who experienced a mystical conversion at Notre Dame of Paris on Christmas 1886. Claudel also wrote the libretto for Arthur Honegger's 1939 oratorio *Joan at the Stake*. No French Catholic novelist reflected more intensely on the presence of evil in human spiritual life than George Bernanos (1888–1948). *The Star of Satan* (1927), and *Diary of a Country Priest* (1936) bear witness that in the end "everything is grace." A Catholic journalist, essayist, and novelist, François Mauriac (1885–1970) of the Bordeaux region belonged to the Jansenist tradition of Pascal and Racine. His best novels, *A Kiss to the Leper* (1922), *The Desert of Love* (1925), *Therese Desqueyroux* (1927), and *Vipers' Tangle* (1932), express the tensions between religious beliefs and the desires of human nature.

The lyric poets Stephan George (1868–1933) and Rainer Maria Rilke (1875–1926) aided in the assimilation of Catholicism into German culture. Almost exclusively lyrical, George's poetry (*Books of Eclogues and Poems of Praise*, 1895; *The Year of the Soul*, 1897; *The Carpet of Life*, 1899) praised beauty and the splendor of the human spirit. A member of the German-speaking minority of Prague, in the Austro-Hungarian Empire, Rilke rebelled against Catholic faith, converted to the religion of art, and produced lyric poems that are among the greatest of the twentieth century (*The Book of Pictures*, 1902; *The Book of Hours*, 1905; *Sonnets to Orpheus*, 1923). In Rilke's mystical universe, poets and painters are the true revealers of the deity, and art is the means by which they unveil the mystery and wonder of nature and life. Beyond estheticism, the poet's mission is thus of a religious nature.

Although nineteenth- and twentieth-century music was primarily secular and is best remembered for symphonic and operatic compositions, sacred music was far from being neglected and in most instances was composed for splendid occasions or concert halls. Impressive masses and requiems were written by the greatest composers—from Luigi Cherubini and Beethoven to Igor Stravinsky and Benjamin Britten. The oratorio genre was continued by Felix Mendelssohn, Liszt (*Christus*, 1862–1867), Camille Saint-Saëns (*The Flood*, 1875), Gounod (*Redemption*, 1882), Edward Elgar (*The Dream of Gerontius*, 1900), Arnold Schoenberg (*Jacob's Ladder*, 1917–1922), Arthur Honegger (*King David*, 1923), and William Walton (*Belshazzar's Feast*, 1931). Even the librettos of some operas were still inspired by either the bible or religious history. Rossini's *Moses in Egypt* (1818), Arnold Schoenberg's unfinished opera *Moses and Aaron* (1932), Darius Milhaud's *David* (1954), and Olivier Messiaen's *St. Francis of Assisi* (1983) shine as flamboyant gems of sacred operatic music.

Denmark: the Cradle of Existentialism

Of the many knights of faith in the nineteenth century, three deserve to be singled out for their originality: Søren Aabye Kierkegaard, Fyodor Dostoevsky, and Lev Nikolayevich Tolstoy. The recoil against Hegelianism, much in vogue in Danish Lutheranism, found in Kierkegaard a formidable spokesman. A melancholy and imaginative Dane, Kierkegaard (1813–1855), who described himself as a poet and a thinker of a sort, carried on the legacy of Eckhart, Cusanus, Böhme, Bruno, Arndt, Pascal, Fénélon, Hamann, and Jacobi. Of little influence in his own time, Kierkegaard's philosophy attained prominence in the early part of the twentieth century, inspiring writers, philosophers, and theologians. Franz Kafka's sense of the ordinary and the sinister (*The Trial*, 1925) and Albert Camus's revolt against the meaninglessness of life (*The Stranger*, 1942) take root in Kierkegaard's conception of absurdity, anxiety, and despair. Existentialist philosophers like Martin Heidegger (*Being and Time*, 1927), Karl Jaspers, Jean-Paul Sartre, and Maurice Merleau-Ponti, and the Jewish philosopher Martin Buber (1878–1965), an advocate of personalism (*I and Thou*, 1923), further theorized on the Kierkegaardian themes of selfhood, authenticity, and temporality. Kierkegaard's conception of faith and transcendence achieved full expression in the 1920s neo-orthodox school called dialectical theology.

The substance of Kierkegaard's philosophy of existence, mainly set out in pseudonymous works—*Either–Or* (1843), *Fear and Trembling* (1843), *The Concept of Anxiety* (1844), *Philosophical Fragments* (1844), *Stages of Life's Way* (1845), and *The Sickness unto Death* (1849)—may be summed up in ten points.

1. There were three determining experiences in Kierkegaard's life: his relationship to his father, a tradesman who cultivated guilt-ridden piety based on the impression that God had forsaken his family; his broken engagement to Regina Olsen, essentially due to his own tormented nature; and a bitter controversy over a Copenhagen scandal sheet, which ended in his being exposed to public ridicule.

2. Originally destined for the ministry in the established Lutheran Church of Denmark, yet leading a dilettante existence for a while, Kierkegaard finally came to understand his vocation as that of a prophet, a reformer, and a pedagogue.

3. Kierkegaard's attack on Hegelianism, which was championed in Denmark by Hans Martensen (*Christian Dogmatics*, 1849), was prompted by his emphasis on personal experience and on the false security of all philosophical and theological systems. Instead of providing answers to the problems of selfhood, Hegelianism annihilated individuality and personal responsibility by embracing everything—good and evil, God and humanity—into a global system that abolished all differences.

4. Kierkegaard's attack on the Church of Denmark, which further isolated him, expressed his deep aversion to hypocrisy, bourgeois respectability, and religious conformism.

5. An unsystematic thinker, Kierkegaard was at his best in psychological analyses. He unveiled the role of anxiety and despair in the discovery by the self of the possibility, through freedom, of an authentic existence.

6. Just as Kierkegaard stressed human sinfulness, he also claimed that deliverance from sin or authentic human existence demands a leap of faith, that is, a qualitative spring into the beyond. Faith is neither knowledge nor morality, but, like an either-or, faith is a radical life decision.

7. Against Hegel, Kierkegaard argued for the absolute otherworldliness of God. There is a discontinuity between the divine and the human, between eternity and time, which Kierkegaard called "an infinite qualitative difference." Although God is unknowable and inaccessible, we subjectively experience him amidst the personal crises of their own existence.

8. Like Luther and even more so like Hamann, Kierkegaard defined Christianity

as paradox (Cusanus's and Bruno's coincidence of opposites). Incarnation, or God becoming human, is the absolute paradox, beyond understanding, as Pascal enunciated earlier.

9. In receiving grace, the believer becomes Jesus Christ's contemporary. In faith, time is abolished.

10. The final touchstone of Kierkegaard's apology for true Christianity was the identification of three fundamental stages of existence: esthetic, ethical, and religious. At the esthetic stage, life is very much like that of Mozart's *Don Giovanni*—an unreflective indulgence in the pleasures of this world. Autonomy and responsibility start at the ethical stage with the discovery of freedom and the possibility of a genuine existence. At the third and highest stage, where the dependence of the self on God has been acknowledged, the human being undergoes the transforming experience of faith, which opens up access to authentic existence.

The Religion of Love: Dostoevsky and Tolstoy

The epileptic son of a murdered hospital doctor, the Russian novelist Fyodor Dostoevsky (1821–1881) was, as Eduard Thurneysen observed in his 1921 monograph, a witness to the presence of divine love in abysses of human vice. In all his major works, *Crime and Punishment* (1866), *The Idiot* (1868), *The Possessed* (1871–1872), and *The Brothers Karamazov* (1879–1880), the main characters contend with moral and religious issues. His novels depict the social and intellectual situation of Russia in the 1860s, stressing its irreconcilable contradictions. Dostoevsky's own life was so eventful that it even upstaged that of his fictional characters. The nationalist journalist and the populist writer had gained such an acclaim that he was honored with a state funeral, although he had once been sent to a prison camp in Siberia for subversive activities (*Notes from the House of the Dead*, 1860–1861).

What was Dostoevsky's version of Christianity? Like Pascal and Kierkegaard, Dostoevsky dreaded living in a meaningless universe; however, unlike them, he did not believe that human redemption demanded a special gift of grace. Brought up in Eastern orthodoxy, he was confident in human free will and firmly believed that the divine incarnation was sufficient to redeem the human being from sin and death. Dostoevsky was eminently aware that, as Dimitri Karamazov professed in *The Brothers Karamazov*, God and the devil were waging war in the human heart. A child of his century, Dostoevsky struggled with the current tension between faith and reason, between the humble belief of the common people and the arrogant rationalism of the Russian intellectual elite, and like Pascal left it unresolved, siding with Christianity though not denying the conclusions of reason. A passionate advocate of the values of the Russian people, he combated every Western idea, almost to the extent of lapsing into a vindictive sort of Slavism. He had no sympathy for liberalism or utilitarianism and showed a profound antipathy to materialism. The social question and the question of egoism were much debated in some Russian cultural circles. Egoism had become fashionable in the wake of the publication of *The Ego and Its Own* (1845) by the left-wing Hegelian Max Stirner. The tension between the right of the individual ego and the Christian law of love thus became a burning issue in Dostoevsky's novels. One of his fictional characters, Father Zosima, the true Russian monk, personified Christian love, which is forgiveness and self-sacrifice. Like Saint-Simon and Proudhon before him, Dostoevsky also held that the law of love was the solution to all social problems. However, unlike the utopian socialists, the left-wing Hegelians, and the Russian anarchists such as Herzen and Bakunin, Dostoevsky distrusted any form of sociopolitical realization of that love. The victory over evil, egoism, and the social plague was to take place in "the paradise of Christ." In that eschatological kingdom of God, personal sufferings, intellectual uncertainty, and social injustice would disappear at last. "True philosophy," as Dostoevsky called his own version of Christianity, reconciled the individual with the community in the harmony of love.

Whereas Dostoevsky was a middle-class townsman, his compatriot and contemporary Leo Tolstoy (1828–1910) belonged to the landed aristocracy. Tolstoy's life falls into two parts: first, the novelist of genius who wrote such immortal masterpieces as *Family Happiness* (1859), *The Cossacks* (1863), *War and Peace* (1863–1869), and *Anna Karenina* (1873–1877); then, after his conversion in the 1880s, the vastly influential prophet of personal and social renewal, the dogmatic, pessimistic, partial, arrogant, perverse, self-deceived yet spiritual and moral mentor of the human race. His favorite writers were Rousseau and Schopenhauer, and he especially admired the wisdom of Solomon, Buddha, Socrates, and Jesus's Sermon on the Mount. Tolstoy sojourned twice in western Europe, which he considered to be decaying rapidly, and took part in the Crimean War (1853–1856). He reared thirteen children and ruled over his household and estate like a medieval tyrant. In the autumn of 1869, in a provincial Russian inn where he was staying overnight, he was assailed by a vision of death that terrified him, obsessed him for years, and spurred him on his religious quest. In *A Confession* (1879–1882), reminiscent of that of Augustine and Rousseau, Tolstoy narrates the long crisis that led to his conversion. Moralistic and religious works followed: *Translation and Harmony of the Four Gospels* (1880–1881), *A Criticism of Dogmatic Theology* (1880–1881), *What I Believe* (1882–1884), *On Life* (1887), and *The Kingdom of God Is within You* (1892–1893), and a series of long, gloomy, puritanical stories (*The Kreutzer Sonata*, 1889; *The Devil*, 1889).

When a thinker places truth above all considerations, inconsistencies and contradictions are unavoidable. Tolstoy did not unfold a coherent Christian worldview. He held Western society in contempt, yet unlike Dostoevsky, he was no Slavophile. He had profound affinities with the modern Russian metaphysicians such as Nicholas Fyodorov (1828–1903) and Vladimir Solovyov (1853–1900), yet drew inspiration from Western thinkers and writers. Like de Maistre, Burke, and Haller, he was a political reactionary, yet denied his support for the Christian and nationalist crown of Russia. He detested democracy, liberalism, and secularism, yet repudiated the conservative parties of his time. He believed in individual freedom, social justice, and progress, yet disdained political reformers. He was a utopian anarchist, yet held the Russian revolutionaries in abomination. He grappled with philosophical, ethical, and theological issues, yet had an unyielding aversion to intellectualism. As a critical mind, he had much in common with the eighteenth-century French *philosophes*, especially Helvetius, yet was contemptuous of historians and sociologists who were the true heirs of the Enlightenment. As a devout Eastern Christian, he assumed the legacy of Gregory of Nyssa, a leading church father of the Russian Orthodox church, and espoused the Platonism of the Eastern tradition, yet ruthlessly attacked his church and its dogmas in *Resurrection* (1899) and was excommunicated by the Holy Synod in 1901. In radical Russian circles, Tolstoy was perceived as a reactionary aristocrat and army officer, while he passed for a dangerous nihilist among his peers. A Russian peasant to the core, regardless of his aristocratic background, Tolstoy never overcame his distrust of the new values of the modern world.

What were the main tenets of Tolstoy's ambiguous Christian worldview? In *War and Peace*, Tolstoy's reflections on history and knowledge highlighted the contrast between natural and historical determinism and individual free will. As a theologian, like Dostoevsky's father Zosima, Tolstoy believed in redemption through love, in salvation through self-perfection, which is active human collaboration with God. As a moralist, he propounded that the true way to love is to offer no resistance to evil. The doctrine of nonresistance to evil became famous with Mohandas K. Gandhi. As an educator, he denounced coercive education in *Education and Culture* (1862) and instead advocated a rearing and education that awaken the sense of freedom and release the inner power. Finally, as a social and political reformer, he was averse to any form of coercion and dreamed of an anarchistic community freed from church and state control, governed only by God.

The Deity before Humanity's Tribunal

At the time at which the Hegelian school sought to explain why the French Revolution, this "great mental dawn," had failed to realize an ideal world governed by moral and natural philosophers, and instead culminated in tyranny and dictatorship, the Russian revolutionist Alexander Ivanovitch Herzen (1812–1870) incisively remarked in *From the Other Shore* that people "will be cured of idealism as they have been of other historical diseases—chivalry, Catholicism, Protestantism."[3]

In Herzen's opinion, any universal principle or magical formula, such as progress, history, humanity, equality, eternal salvation, national security, the church, the state, or the proletariat, in the end sacrifices individual freedom; it destroys human

---

[3]*Collected Writings in Thirty Volumes*, Moscow, 1954–1965, Vol. VI.

dignity. A political heir of French utopians and philosophical heir of German idealism, Herzen, skeptical like Voltaire and as pessimistic as Tolstoy, upheld an overt and unqualified purposelessness, prefiguring both Jean-Paul Sartre and Albert Camus.

To be the executioner of God was the dream of both Alexander Herzen and Michael Bakunin. Both were leading Russian anarchists; both repudiated any form of authority and coercion, and instead promoted the absolute value of personal freedom. Michael Bakunin, who was evicted from the First International in 1882 under Marx's pressure, enunciated in *God and the State* (1871):

> Christianity is precisely the religion par excellence, because it exhibits and manifests, to the fullest extent, the very nature and essence of every religious system, which is the impoverishment, enslavement, and annihilation of humanity for the benefit of divinity.
>
> God being everything, the real world and man are nothing. God being truth, justice, goodness, beauty, power, and life, man is falsehood, iniquity, evil, ugliness, impotence, and death. God being master, man is the slave. Incapable of finding justice, truth, and eternal life by his own effort, he can attain them only through a divine revelation. But whoever says revelation says revealers, messiahs, prophets, priests, and legislators inspired by God himself; and these, once recognized as the representatives of divinity on earth, as the holy instructors of humanity, chosen by God himself to direct it in the path of salvation, necessarily exercise absolute power. All men owe them passive and unlimited obedience; for against the justice of God no terrestrial justice holds. Slaves of God, men must also be slaves of Church and State, insofar as the State is consecrated by the Church.[4]

A charismatic champion of the spirit of revolt, Bakunin stigmatized the "credo quia absurdum," the principle of theology, as "the triumph of credulous stupidity over the mind"; he described priests as licentious, gluttonous, ambitious, greedy, selfish, and grasping; he called his "two bêtes noires"—the church and the state—the fundamental institutions of human enslavement; and he concluded by inverting Voltaire's notorious dictum, saying that "if God really existed, it would be necessary to abolish him," because "the idea of God implies the abdication of human reason and justice; it is the most decisive negation of human liberty, and necessarily ends in the enslavement of mankind, both in theory and practice."[5]

[4]Michael Bakunin, *God and the State*, introduction by Paul Avrich (New York: Dover Publications, Inc., 1970), p. 24.
[5]Ibid., pp. 77, 53, 34, and 25.

Dialectical Materialism and Christianity

The integration of German idealism, French utopian socialism, and British economics into a radical critique of political economy was Karl Marx's unrivaled achievement. Of Jewish ancestry yet raised in the Protestant faith, Marx, a graduate in philosophy of the University of Berlin, spent most of his nomadic existence in exile because of his subversive views. In Brussels he wrote, in collaboration with Friedrich Engels, the famous *Communist Manifesto* (1848) for the newly founded Communist League. And it was finally in London, where he died in 1883, that his major works reached completion: *Contribution to the Critique of Political Economy* (1859), and *Das Kapital* (1867)—*Capital*, Vols. II, III, and IV or *Theories of Surplus Value* were all released posthumously.

Hegel's *Philosophy of Right* (1821) set the groundwork for Marx's identification of the revolutionary proletariat with social transformation. Critical of Hegel, Marx placed his hopes for social justice not in the liberal state but in the oppressed and alienated working class. The unfortunate proletariat became the prospective bearer of the moral community or kingdom of ends. Marx's analysis of the forces and relations of production and his interpretation of class antagonism—the theory of class struggle—led him to the conclusion that the worker has been dehumanized, alienated from real humanity (*National Economy and Philosophy*, 1844). To restore the worker's true humanity, it is essential, prescribed Marx, to overthrow the capitalist and classist state, to eliminate religion, that "opium of the people," and to establish instead a communist society. As much as Marx praised the left-wing Hegelians, especially Feuerbach, for starting a new religion corresponding to a new humanity and a new society, he nonetheless reproached them for failing to understand that the socio-economic structures were the primary factors in the shaping of political, cultural, and religious ideas. Therefore, he claimed in the *Theses on Feuerbach* (1845), that "the philosophers have only interpreted the world in different ways, yet what matters is to transform the world."

Why should religion be eliminated? Marx had read not only Strauss, Bauer, and Feuerbach but also Paul Thiry von Holbach. To their criticisms, Marx subjoined that religion provided a mythical justification for a social frustration, satisfying an artificial need in the lives of alienated people. Human beings do not merely produce material goods to stay alive but also create works of art, ideas, and beliefs to understand their lives. These productions form a superstructure that is artificially super-imposed on the real structure of life or the socioeconomic reality. Marx professed the following:

1. God is nothing other than a production of the human mind (*Capital*, I).

2. Religion substitutes an illusory happiness in heaven for real happiness on earth.

3. Religion deprives humanity of its legitimate right to rule and to control nature by transferring it upon an imaginary autocratic being.

4. Religion inhibits basic human qualities, replacing reason by faith, freedom by obedience, actual love by the love of God, and real willpower by "will in Christ" (*The Holy Family*, 1845).

5. Religion creates a mortal enemy, God, to whom the exercise of reason and sexuality is a crime and who keeps humanity at his mercy.

6. Religion produces a class of exploiters, the priesthood or divine agents, who impoverish people financially and intellectually to enrich themselves, taking advantage of every human weakness, especially guilt.

Can the need for religious alienation actually be overcome? Yes, it can, but only in a communist society, answered Marx. In such a society, the practical relations of everyday life will be perfectly reasonable and intelligible, the sensual and the spiritual will be reconciled, and the question of God's existence will naturally vanish. The sacrilegious motto, which opens Marx's 1841 dissertation for Jena University, perfectly summarizes a lifelong struggle against God: "Philosophy does not conceal it. Prometheus' Confession 'in one word, I hate all the gods' is its own confession, its own maxim against all celestial and terrestrial gods."

Reconciliation between Marxism and Christianity became a crucial issue, in the East as well as in the West, not only among church officials in socialist countries and religious-socialists in capitalist countries but also among soul-searching communist intellectuals, such as Nikolai Berdiaev (1874–1948), author of *The Origin of Russian Communism* (1937), who expounded a philosophy based on the concept of freedom and a communal view of Christianity in his *Spiritual Autobiography*; Sergej Bulgakov (1871–1944), a convert to Christianity who grappled with the problem of the salvation of the world, focusing on the revelation of the wisdom of God (*Investigations in the Nature of Social Ideals*, 1911; *The Duskless Light*, 1917); and Leszek Kolakowski of Warsaw University, whose famous book *Toward a Marxist Humanism* (1968) defined Marxism and Christianity as alternative living, philosophical ways of apprehending the world.

Among the many Protestant theologians who sought to make the best of Marxism, four names stand out: Georg Wünsch, Paul Tillich, Josef L. Hromádka, and Jürgen Moltmann.

An heir of the theological left of the Ritschlian school, Georg Wünsch (1887–1964), the first to hold a chair of social ethics in Germany, related during the "twenties socialism" to the ethics of Jesus's Sermon on the Mount (*Evangelical Economic Ethics*, 1925). In the last years of the Weimar Republic, Wünsch contended that only plain socialism could remedy the failure of charity in an age of high inflation and mass unemployment. As a this-worldly realism, Marxism had the threefold advantage of making room for God by requiring a religious and metaphysical basis, of disencumbering Christianity from useless clericalism and churchiness, and of focusing Christian love on the demand of the moment, that is, the suppression of the class system (*Our Task*, 1929; *The Christian Task at a Turn of an Era*, 1933).

Similarly, Paul Tillich (1886–1965), a member of the Religious-Socialist League, along with Günther Dehn and Carl Mennicke, claimed at the time of Hitler's accession to power that only socialism could salvage European society from a relapse into barbarism. In his quest for a renewed socialism, Tillich combined the Marxist theory of class and class struggle with the Christian spirit of prophecy within a philosophy of history that stressed the *Kairos* (the crisis of the experience of the unconditioned in the conditioned, *The Socialist Decision*, 1933). Moreover, Tillich endeavored to provide Marx's critique of capitalist society with a new philosophical foundation derived from a Christian ontology and anthropology.

The Czech theologian, Josef L. Hromádka (1889–1969), who bore the legacy of the Bohemian Brethren, contended that the church had failed in its mission because it identified Christ's message with the liberal economic, social, and political order. Emphasizing the positive goals of Marxism—the elimination of human exploitation, the conquest of poverty, the belief in human dignity and in communal life— Hromádka urged the church to acknowledge them and to make its contribution by arousing faith and obedience to God. Even a classless society needs the message of the forgiving grace and reconciling love of God, since beyond the social and economic conditions the real root of human misery lies in human sinfulness (*Theology between Yesterday and Tomorrow*, 1957; *The Gospel for Atheists*, 1960).

In the sixties in Germany, Jürgen Moltmann's *Theology of Hope* (1964) rose to the theological firmament. Among the influences that shaped Moltmann's theology, two were dominant: Karl Barth's theology of the Word of God, which initiated his reappraisal of the revelation, and Ernst Bloch's *Principle Hope* (1954–1959), which treated the future of humanity in terms of a passage from order and necessity to freedom. A Marxist humanist, the German philosopher Bloch showed that Marxism fell within a tradition that had its origin in Exodus, Jesus's vision of the kingdom of God, Marcion, Joachim de Fiore, and the Anabaptist reformer Thomas Münster. Bloch defined God as the embodiment of the liberating spirit of the Hebrews' exodus from Egypt. God is a projection of utopian hope. And the true goal of history is the constitution of a free and atheistic humanity, that is, a humanity liberated from the existing order. By interpreting the mystery of Easter as the revelation of a promise, that of the future of truth, Moltmann described the faith in Easter as hope in the future of the world, namely in justice, life, and freedom in the kingdom of God. Such a hope arouses an exodus mentality and creates a community which fulfills the personal and communal truth of the future.

Attending God's Funeral

In Christianity pessimism variously found expression in Augustinianism, Calvinism, Jansenism, and Puritanism. However, no Western thinker has more radically exploited this line of thought than Arthur Schopenhauer (1788–1860). The son of an East Prussian banker and a graduate in philosophy of the University of Berlin, Schopenhauer found no pleasure in teaching and turned to writing. He was a care-worn and embittered young man, an unappreciated genius, who scorned both the world and the philosophy of his time, especially Hegelianism. Ironically, he gained notoriety with a masterpiece of pessimism, *The World as Will and Representation* (1819), and became vastly influential. Both Friedrich Nietzsche and Jean-Paul Sartre were significantly indebted to him. Schopenhauer's whole philosophy is sustained by three pillars: (1) the will, a legacy of Kant, (2) pessimism, directed against Spinoza's, Leibniz's, and Hegel's optimism, and (3) self-denial, borrowed from Buddhism. Schopenhauer argued that we essentially experience ourselves as will, that the will is the reality of human nature. By will, he did not merely mean the free will but also the passions of the heart (emotions, desires, love, hatred). Furthermore, the will is the essence of nature. Natural forces and natural laws are its expression. By positing a thoroughly blind, irrational, purposeless, and senseless will at the core of both the universe and the self, Schopenhauer not only repudiated capital Christian tenets; he also denied any fundamental spiritual principle, especially the Romantic and Idealist idea of a World-Spirit (Hegel and Schleiermacher).

Enthusiastic and optimistic, Leibniz had proclaimed that we live in the best possible world. What could, in revenge, a pessimistic witness of pain in a meaningless universe draw for a conclusion but that we live in the *worst* possible world? If there is any escape from "the playground of tormented and terrified beings," it must be, argued Schopenhauer, by suppressing the source of pain. Self-denial and withdrawal from the world are all that Schopenhauer sees in Christianity.

It is not surprising that the two most controversial figures of nineteenth-century Germany, the composer Richard Wagner and the philosopher Friedrich Nietzsche, both influenced by Schopenhauer, were once friends (see Nietzsche's 1888, *The Case of Wagner*). They were kindred spirits. Born in Leipzig in 1813, Richard Wagner died in Venice in 1883. Thomas Mann's novel, *Death in Venice* (1912) magnificently encapsulates the tragic tension between middle-class values and artistic talent. Wagner rose to the musical firmament at first with romantic operas like *The Flying Dutchman* (1843) and then with large-scale musical dramas (*Tristan und Isolde*, 1865; *Die Meistersinger von Nürnberg*, 1868; *Der Ring der Nibelungen*, 1869–1876; and *Parsifal*, 1882). What gave Wagner a unique position in nineteenth-century music was not only a matter of style—the ideas of leitmotif, infinite melody or unchanged recurrence, harmonic style, and musical prose—and of themes such as German legends and myths, but also an unequaled synthesis of poetry, philosophy, and music. Wagner had adopted Schopenhauer's bleak worldview, yet he avoided pessimistic conclusions. Obsessed as he was with the desire to relieve humanity from pain and despair, Wagner employed his pioneering musical esthetics to convey his belief in remission, redemption, and regeneration.

The son of a Lutheran minister from Saxony, Friedrich Nietzsche (1844–1900), an unsystematic philosopher, envisioned his task as that of a physician who diagnoses the ailments of his culture and prescribes the remedy. Trained in literature, theology, and philosophy at the Universities of Bonn and Leipzig, Nietzsche began an academic career teaching classical philology at the University of Basel in 1869 and, as a victim of a mental and physical breakdown in 1889, concluded his life under the care of his sister Elizabeth Förster-Nietzsche. She published his posthumous works and is largely responsible for the misappropriation of his thought by the National Socialists.

The essentials of Nietzsche's apparently incoherent thought may be summarized with ten observations.

1. Nietzsche's perception of life as a tragic contest between harmonious beauty (Apollo) and drunken frenzy (Dionysius) was inspired by Wagner and the ancient Greeks (*The Birth of Tragedy*, 1872). His nihilistic belief in the purposelessness and meaninglessness of the universe comes from Schopenhauer, his emphasis on creativity from Wagner, and his naturalism and immanentism from Spinoza. In 1881 in a letter to a friend, Nietzsche avowed that he had discovered in Spinoza, the Jewish philosopher, a precursor and a true soul-mate who, like himself, was mystically bound to something beyond good and evil.

2. Like Descartes and Kant, Nietzsche's philosophy is two-sided. There is a deconstructive aspect, or devaluation of values ("no-saying"), which reveals the lack of foundations of traditional metaphysical and ethical values as well as the indigence of modern science. And there is a reconstructive aspect or revaluation of values ("yes-saying"), which propounds new values and a new type of human being, the superman (*der Übermensch*).

3. However, unlike Descartes and Kant, Nietzsche thoroughly rejected the tyranny of either revelation or reason. Instead of either God or reason, Nietzsche called for freedom and acknowledged only the superior drive of instinct (*Beyond Good and Evil*, 1886).

4. The sole remedy to the age of nihilism in which we live is a "transvaluation of all values."

5. Nietzsche drew a sharp distinction between master-morality (strong impulses and passions) and slave-morality (weak impulses and passions). Discarding the morality of the herd, suited only to the mediocre, he stressed the higher and more severe master-morality, which beyond good and evil corresponds to the creativity of life.

6. Essentially a creative force, the will-to-power articulates in Nietzsche's thought the natural tendency of the living being to overcome itself. The will-to-power conditions every human behavior.

7. Nowhere is the will-to-power more potent than in the superman. First appearing in *Thus Spoke Zarathustra* (1883–1885), the idea of a superman crystallizes the overcoming of mere humanity and the possible attainment of a higher human being who is better attuned to life.

8. To express the meaninglessness of things, Nietzsche unfolds in *The Gay Science* (1882) and *Zarathustra* the theme of eternal recurrence. Our lives find meaning only in joyfully overcoming ourselves while eternally doing whatever our task may be.

9. The criticism that Nietzsche leveled against religion is reminiscent of that of

Holbach. With the single exception of the religion of the ancient Greeks, religious activity on the whole has a destructive effect on life. Nietzsche saw religion as the instrument of revenge that the weak, the sick, the life-weary, and the resentful had discovered. Thus, the priests, who most resented the master-morality and vitality, transvalued all naturalistic values and forced the slave-morality on the master. It is by arousing a bad conscience that the priest poisons the master's heart and thereby achieves the slave's revenge. Hatred, denial, and demand for conformity are the essential features of the slave, and by extension, of the religious morality (*The Genealogy of Morals*, 1887).

10. In *The Gay Science*, Nietzsche affirms that "God is dead." Unlike the atheists, he did not deny God's existence, but merely stated that God, once alive, was now dead, thereby signifying that we humans create and de-create our moral valuations (*Twilight of the Idols*, 1889; *The Antichrist*, 1895).

After his death, Nietzsche became widely influential in central European political, literary, and artistic circles. Unfortunately, his sophisticated and ambiguous thought was often reduced to simplistic misconceptions. In both philosophy and theology, Nietzsche gained an important following. He is regarded by many as the founder of the "philosophy of life" (*Lebensphilosophie*) and as one of the inspirers of existential philosophy. Martin Heidegger saluted in him the man who dealt the death blow to Western metaphysics. An opponent of metaphysics though he was, Karl Jaspers acknowledged in a Nietzschean fashion the human search for transcendence and prescribed a philosophic faith as a better alternative than Christian faith (*Philosophic Faith*, 1848). The critical theory of society and culture developed by the Frankfurt School (Horkheimer and Adorno) is a legacy of both Marx and Nietzsche. In the wake of Nietzsche's onslaught on Christianity, theologians were forced to frame new doctrines of God and human nature. The post-World War I dialectical theology is to some extent a response to the death of God. Its attack on Culture-Protestantism was partly motivated by the repugnance that Nietzsche felt toward bourgeois religion and morality.

The road to freedom, Jean-Paul Sartre claimed, implied "missing God." Just as Orestes discovered in *The Flies* (1943) that human freedom makes both the gods and the tyrants powerless, so also Goetz, in *The Devil and the Good Lord*, rejoiced in the sudden awareness that God is dead:

> I alone. I supplicated, I demanded a sign, I sent messages to Heaven, no reply. Heaven ignored my very name. Each minute I wondered what I could be in the eyes of God. Now I know the answer: nothing. God does not see me, God does not hear me. God does not know me. You see this emptiness over our heads? That is God. You see this gap in the door? It is God. You see that hole in the ground? That is God again. Silence is God. Absence is God. God is the loneliness of man.[5]

[5] K. Black, Trans. (New York: A. A. Knopf, 1960), p. 141.

Secular Faith or "Religionless Christianity"?

After the horror of Auschwitz, the genocide perpetrated by the National Socialists, it is no longer possible to believe naively in the provident God of traditional Christianity, contended the theologians of the "death of God." Sensible to the meaninglessness of existence, evil, and human suffering, they expressed in the 1960s their despondency and powerlessness in a secular world beyond Christendom, emphasized the hiddenness or absence of God, and started on a quest for a new concept and a new manifestation of God. In a manner which calls to mind Pascal, Harvey Cox in *The Secular City* (1965) contrasted the God of Abraham, Isaac, and Jacob with the delusory gods created by human religious needs.

More than two centuries after Balthazar Beker's plea for a desacralization of the world in *The World Bewitched*, Max Weber characterized the process of secularization, which steadily divested natural phenomena of their magical and religious apparel, as "disenchantment of the world" (*Collected Essays in the Sociology of Religion*, 1920). A long-term historical trend, secularization goes far back into the Renaissance and the Reformation. The disruption of medieval Christendom, the fragmentation of the religious geography of Europe, the introduction of pluralism, the rationalization and internalization of Christian doctrine and practice, as well as the association of confessional affiliation with political identity—all gave impetus to the secularizing process. A late offspring of the Renaissance, the Enlightenment claimed the right of reason to rule human existence and to test freely any idea or belief, and thereby it denied any form of religious tutelage and demanded the autonomy of the social and political system. Thereafter, the path was cleared for the laicization of the state, the secularization of society, the divorce of the religious from the profane in the realm of culture, and the emergence of a secular Christianity that reduced the relevance of the gospel to earthly existence and personal relationships.

Historically, secularization began with the French Revolution. Although the revolutionists did not envisage a nation deprived of a common religious belief, they affranchised religious minorities (Jews and Huguenots) and legalized atheism. The laicization of the state and the secularization of society were carried out in Europe in a climate of quasi-religious warfare, involving the forces of progress on one side and the reactionaries on the other.

The prodigious development of secularization in nineteenth- and twentieth-century Europe was caused by four factors: psychological, cultural, social, and political.

1. The psychological factor was the uprooting of masses of people from their traditional social and religious environment. The dramatic rise of migration, voluntary or forced, for economic, political, cultural, or religious reasons, enhanced the spirit of individualism.

2. The cultural factor consisted in the confidence in empirical enquiry that became supreme in the age of science and technology. Newspapers and scientific pe-

riodicals spread the idea that true knowledge demanded verification by experimentation and observation. Materialistic science and evolutionary philosophy invalidated the principle of authority and irretrievably undermined the hold of tradition (Ludwig Büchner's 1855 *Force and Matter*; Claude Bernard's 1865 *Introduction to Experimental Medicine*; and Thomas Henry Huxley's illustrious 1893–1894 *Essays*).

3. The social factor became decisive as the working class gained self-consciousness and voiced its demand for social betterment through trade unions and labor parties. Already by the mid-nineteenth century, anticlericalism, indifferentism, and atheism had descended from the higher sphere of eighteenth-century educated freethinkers to the lowest social scale, where the social cause was paramount (F. Engels's *Condition of the Working Classes in England in 1844*).

4. The political factor was a necessary offshoot of the growing role of the state in everyday life. In spite of the prevailing liberal tenet of nonintervention, it was increasingly expected of the state to protect individual freedom and initiative, to introduce social reform, and to regulate the economy. Cataclysms, wars, epidemics, and economic crises prompted state intervention and expanded state control. Health, education, research, housing, labor relations, and the exercise of skilled or learned professions gradually passed under state control. At the outset of World War I, the state had already become overwhelmingly present in people's lives, whereas the Christian churches' influence had receded to personal piety and morality.

Among contemporary theologians, Ernst Troeltsch was the first to reflect objectively on the place of Christianity in the modern secular world. Diagnosing the disintegration of Christendom, Troeltsch predicted in the 1910s the dawning of a new religious mentality attuned to modern individualistic culture, which he characterized as "churchless Christianity." He envisaged the future of Christianity as a "free Christianity," namely as a religion of conviction and conscience emancipated from ecclesiastical authority (*Collected Writings: On the Religion Situation, Philosophy of Religion, and Ethics*, Vol. 2, 1913). One of his pupils, Friedrich Gogarten (1886–1967), who deserted him after World War I by joining Karl Barth, opposed secularism to secularization. Secularism, or false secularization, claims control over the realm of faith, whereas secularization in the true sense remains within the confines of secularity. On the strength of Luther's distinction between law (the secular) and gospel (the realm of faith), Gogarten advocated secularization inasmuch as it gives the churches a fresh chance to proclaim the otherworldliness of revelation and faith, to divest Christianity of its worldliness, and to ensure human freedom for God. To want to Christianize the world is to ruin salvation. In secularized Christianity or Christian secularism, Luther's justifying faith is deformed into an objectifying faith (*The Doom and Hope of the Modern Age: Secularization as Theological Problem*, 1953).

While Gogarten acknowledged secularization of life but denied secularization of faith, Dietrich Bonhoeffer (1906–1945), a pupil of Harnack and a member of the German resistance, hailed "the world come of age," and from Tegel, where he was imprisoned by the Nazis, warned against the temptation of escaping from the world.

As his political commitment evidenced, Bonhoeffer truly believed that the Christian must live in the secular world "without the working hypothesis of God" (*etsi deus non daretur*). In other words, the Christian is called to be as real and incarnate as Jesus was (*The Cost of Discipleship*, 1950–51; *Ethics*, 1962). In a world beyond Christendom, a world come to adulthood and further progressing toward a religionless time, the only suitable apologetics is to let the "religionless Christianity" be. In our secular world, Christianity finds its identity as a personal and secret discipline (*Arkandiszi-plin*). The God of religion is dead; more than ever is the God of Christianity alive. In the summer of 1944, Bonhoeffer was executed by the Nazis. His courageous death testified to the truth that "before God and with God we live without God."

Religion as a Human Phenomenon

In nineteenth-century European secularized universities, the triumph of positive knowledge and the collapse of dogmatic certainty transformed religion into an object of study by the human sciences. Philosophy of religion, psychology of religion, sociology of religion, anthropology of religion, and history of religion offered a variety of explanations and interpretations of the religious phenomenon, which has recently been enriched by the linguistic approach of the semiologists who assumed the legacy of Ferdinand de Saussure (*Course in General Linguistics*, 1915) in the field of religion.

Philosophy of Religion

Philosophy of religion developed along four lines of thought: (1) the Cartesian-Humean—the relation of religion to reason and empirical facts; (2) the Kantian—the relation of religion to personal and social ethics; (3) the Schleiermacherian—the relation of religion to intuition; and (4) the Hegelian—the relation of religion to wholeness. The positivist Auguste Comte, the evolutionary philosopher Herbert Spencer, the utilitarian John Stuart Mill (*Three Essays on Religion*, 1875), the neo-Lockean Matthew Arnold (*Literature and Dogma*, 1873), and the Vienna-born Cambridge professor of philosophy Ludwig Wittgenstein are among the prominent figures of the Cartesian-Humean tradition.

In a posthumously released writing, *Philosophical Investigations* (1953), Wittgenstein highlighted the natural history and social context of all concepts. As does any concept, religion reflects a form of life whose meaning is to be determined by the linguistic use of its concepts.

The Kantian approach was much in favor in Culture-Protestantism. Best illustrated by Feuerbach, Marx, Kierkegaard, and Nietzsche, the ethical critique and reinterpretation of religion were continued by the neo-Kantians, Wilhelm Windelband, Heinrich Rickert, Paul Natorp, and Hermann Cohen, and more recently by Rudolf Bultmann (*Kerygma and Mythos*, published from 1948 to 1966).

A legacy of the Romantics, the third approach analyzes the religious representation of history and reality (myths and symbols), and determines the moment of religious mediation. Rudolf Otto's definition of the sacred as *mysterium tremendum et fascinosum* (*The Idea of the Holy*, 1917) and Anders Nygren's conception of a religious *apriori* (*Religiöst Apriori*, 1921) exemplifies the Schleiermacherian tradition.

Last, the Hegelian approach was variously revived by Martin Heidegger, Karl Jaspers, and A. N. Whitehead.

Psychology of Religion

Owing to the works of the Vienna Psychological Society, psychology of religion gained immense popularity not only in learned but also in popular religious circles. At the turn of the twentieth century, a Viennese physician, Sigmund Freud (1859–1939), who promoted psychoanalysis in collaboration with his colleagues Alfred Adler, Carl Jung, and Otto Rank, revealed in *The Interpretation of Dreams* (1900) the power of the unconscious (the libido) and framed the theory of repression as unfulfilled sexual instincts (*Three Essays on the Theory of Sexuality*, 1905). *Totem and Taboo* (1913), his most popular work, brought the Oedipus complex to the fore. Freud used the mythological figure of Oedipus, a Greek who ignorantly killed his father and married his mother, to explain the dependence of religious emotions on feelings of guilt. In *The Future of an Illusion* (1927), Freud characterized religion as "the universal obsessional neurosis of humanity."[6] Religious belief answers a need for protection against death and natural threats like earthquakes, floods, and storms. Familiar with the Judeo-Christian tradition, which highlights the fatherhood of God, Freud demonstrated how illusory the feeling of fatherly, divine protection was. He claimed that positive knowledge will at last dissipate the belief in mysterious powers behind nature. A disciple of Freud, the Swiss psychiatrist Carl Gustav Jung (1875–1961) emphasized by contrast the positive aspect of religious belief. No longer regarded as a neurosis, religion was said to be the symbolic expression of ageless mysterious experiences of life and of the world. Another follower of Freud, Erich Fromm, recently argued in *Psychoanalysis and Religion* (1966) that all great religions, whether Western or Eastern, share a common ethical nucleus that has been conditioned by identical human needs.

Sociology of Religion

Sociology was founded by Auguste Comte in the first half of the nineteenth century. At the outset of the twentieth century, two sociologists, one French and the other

[6]J. Strachey, trans., Sigmund Freud, *Psychological Works*, Vol. XXI (Basic Books: New York, 1961), p. 44.

German, gave birth to the sociology of religion: Emile Durkheim (1858–1917) and Max Weber (1864–1920). Both were indebted to the models of the innovative social theorist, Ferdinand Tönnies (*Community and Society*, 1887). As it appears in *The Division of Labor in Society* (1893) and in the *Rules of Sociological Method* (1895), Durkheim was primarily concerned with the structure of society. From his study of primitive forms of religion, mostly done in collaboration with his disciple and nephew Marcel Mauss (*Primitive Classification*, 1903), Durkheim drew the conclusion that primitive culture did not differentiate between the social and the religious. Durkheim argued in his masterpiece of sociology of religion, *The Elementary Forms of the Religious Life* (1912), that our beliefs are molded by society. Sacredness is crucial to the life of societies. It is the way by which societies claim unconditional loyalty from their members; in a word, they sacralize themselves. The contribution of the German sociologist Max Weber to the field of comparative religion has been considerable, inasmuch as he drew ample material from a plurality of religious traditions (e.g., Confucianism, Hinduism) to substantiate his theses on the relationship between religion and culture. Better than any of his predecessors, Weber understood the interplay between economic situations and religious beliefs (*Collected Essays in Sociology of Religion*, 1920).

Anthropology of Religion

It is now agreed that the term *totemism* was coined by an eighteenth-century American trader, John Long, in his travel account *Voyages and Travels of an Indian Interpreter and Trader* (1791). Nonetheless, it was not before the second half of the nineteenth century that anthropology of religion made its official debut with the Scottish amateur anthropologist John Ferguson McLennan (1827–1881). His seminal work *Primitive Marriage* (1857) is based on the now famous distinction between endogamy (marriage within the clan) and exogamy (marriage outside the clan). In the early 1870s, anthropological and ethnological research received a decisive impetus with epoch-making studies of prehistoric people and cultures, namely John Lubbock's *The Origin of Civilisation and the Primitive Condition of Man* (1870) and Edward Burnett Tylor's *Primitive Culture* (1871). Tylor framed the theory of animism. In his view, animism was at the origin of all religion, ancient or modern. A friend of McLennan, the Scottish Semitic philologist William Robertson Smith largely contributed to the development of this new discipline with a major study: *Lectures on the Religion of the Semites* (1889). His disciple and fellow-Scot James George Frazer (1854–1951) gained much notoriety with the now classic work *The Golden Bough* (1890), which dealt with magic, divine kingship, and gods and goddesses of vegetation.

Two prominent French anthropologist-philosophers of the twentieth century deserve mention: Lucien Lévy-Bruhl (1857–1939), who studied the "prelogical" and "mystical" modes of thought of primitive people in *Primitive Mentality* (1922); and the chief exponent of structuralist anthropology, Claude Lévy-Strauss, whose *Tristes Tropiques* (1955) and *Structural Anthropology* (1958) are among the literary and anthropological masterpieces of the century.

History of Religion

An Italian Jesuit Roberto de Nobili settled in 1606 in Madure in India and discovered Brahman Hinduism. He thereupon became one of the first missionaries to empathize with a non-Christian religion. With the exception of Islam, the reflective encounter of Christianity with other religions goes back only to the early colonial conquest. In the aftermath of the spectacular missionary effort of Tridentine Catholicism, European divines and freethinkers, from Herbert of Cherbury to Friedrich Schelling (*Philosophy of Mythology*, 1828), engaged in an ongoing discussion about the features, the essence, and the truth of non-Christian religions. Primarily informed by traders' and missionaries' accounts, the Enlighteners progressively dispelled the religious prejudice of European Christians against non-Christian cultures. Herbert, Grotius, Malebranche, Leibniz, Wolff, Voltaire, and Lessing brought to light some analogies among world religions.

The earlies attempts at a descriptive and comparative approach date from the eighteenth century: *Mores of American Savages Compared to the Mores of Early Times* (1724) by the Jesuit missionary Lafitau; *On the Cult of Fetishist Gods* (1760) by Charles de Brosses, who studied West African fetishism; and *The Origin of the Gods of Paganism* (1767), a study of Greek polytheism by Nicolas Sylvestre Bergier. Further steps toward comparative religion were made by the translation into English of the Bhagavad Gita (1785), of Shakuntala (1789), and the Upanishads (1802). The Egyptologist Jean François Champollion's colossal *Description of Egypt* (1808–1822) and Josef Görres's description of Asian myths in his seminal *History of the Myths in Asia* (1810) were further contributions. However, it was not until Friedrich Max Müller (1823–1900), a German philologist who spent most of his career at Oxford, that comparative religion gained academic recognition. His epochal *Introduction to the Science of Religion* (1873) laid the foundation of this novel human science. Henceforth, chairs of history of religions were created throughout Europe. One of the most significant innovations was the creation in France in 1886 of the Section of Religious Sciences at the École Pratique des Hautes-Études at the Sorbonne in Paris by the anticlerical Third Republic.

History of religion is less a discipline than a field that offers a variety of methodological approaches to religious phenomena. Philologists, philosophers, sociologists, anthropologists, ethnologists, psychoanalysts, and recently semiologists have all brought and continue to bring their indispensable contributions to the successful enterprise of historians of religion. Although any classification remains ultimately arbitrary, one may nonetheless distinguish among five main trends or schools of thought.

1. There is the *German philosophical school* of Ernst Cassirer, a neo-Kantian who propounded a symbolic interpretation of mythical thought in a famous book *Philosophy of Symbolic Forms* (1923). In this direction, the French philosopher Paul Ricoeur recently advocated a semiological interpretation of myths.

2. The *functionalist school* was founded by Bronislaw Malinowski (1884–1942) and A. R. Radcliffe-Brown (1881–1955) and dominated the English-speaking world in the first half of the century. Malinowski's books include *Myth in Primitive Psychology* (1926), *Crime and Custom in Savage Society* (1926), and *Sex and Repression in Savage Society* (1927).

3. The *phenomenological school* was started by the Dutch scholar P. D. Chantepie de la Saussaye, whose *Handbook of the History of Religion* (1887) became a landmark. Another Dutch scholar, Gerardus van der Leeuw published in 1933 a masterpiece of phenomenology of religion: *Religion in Essence and Manifestation*. The Scandinavian countries produced a triad of prominent phenomenologists: Nathan Söderblom, Edvard Lehmann, and William Brede Kristensen who was van der Leeuw's teacher.

4. The greatest exponent of the *psychoanalytical school* in the Jungian line was a Romanian who wrote in French and taught at Chicago: Mircea Eliade (*Myth of the Eternal Return*, 1955; *Patterns in Comparative Religion*, 1958; *The Sacred and the Profane*, 1959; *Myths, Dreams, and Mysteries*, 1960).

5. The *structuralist school* of Paris was led by the formidable scholar George Dumézil, who made a comprehensive inventory of Indo-European mythologies. His masterpiece *The Indo-European Ideology of Tripartition* (1958) set forth that all Indo-European societies were divided into three classes: the working class, the warrior class, and the priestly class.

A contemporary historian of religion reflected on his task and wisely concluded the following:

> It may be well to repeat . . . that the phenomenological approach to religious studies does not deny the importance of ultimate questions, but it deliberately holds them at bay in the interest of better illuminating a less important but still significant area in the foreground, the area of human religious experience.[8]

[8]John Carman, *The Theology of Ramnauja* (New Haven/London: Yale University Press, 1974), p. 23.

Part Five

Christianity and Culture in America

The story of Christianity in America is the story of both Christianity and America. From the start of European colonization, conditions in the New World exerted an influence on the shape of Christian faith. Sometimes that influence was subtle and took decades, or even centuries, to be discerned. Such was the bond between Christianity and "the common people" of North America in contrast to the traditional European bond between the faith and the ruling institutions of society. Sometimes the new environment exerted its influence with sudden and abrupt force, impressing both residents and visitors from the Old Country with the novelty of religious life in America. Such was the influence of the nearly limitless space on those who first brought Christianity to the western hemisphere. So much land with so little governmental or ecclesiastical supervision opened up a freedom both intimidating and exhilarating. From the start, Christianity in America was stamped with the image of its new environment.

At the same time, the faith in the New World was very much part of the worldwide Christian movement. European patterns dominated the earliest periods of colonial settlement. Later on, ties to third-world Christians grew stronger as missionaries from America circled the globe and as Christian immigrants from many regions swarmed into the United States. The "peculiar institution" of slavery also meant that Christianity in America would carry the imprint of Africa. This thorough mixture of universal Christian faith and the particular American environment is the justification for a separate section here on the history of Christianity in America, but it is also the reason for including this section with the whole. Moreover, as throughout the world so also in America, Christianity has always sustained dynamic and shifting relations with public life, the political sphere, ethnic distinctives, and the world of thought.

A final introductory word must be said about the words "America" and "American." Historically, the noun and the adjective belong to all peoples and lands in the Western hemisphere, from Hudson's Bay in Canada to Tierra del Fuego off the southern coast of Argentina. In the early pages of this section, however, the word *America* will be used in a stricter sense as a collective word for the major regions of the North American continent. Later on, the word will sometimes appear as a synonym for the United States, but such usage implies no covert imperialism, merely the absence of a convenient adjective for the United States of America.

Mark A. Noll

Chapter 28

CHRISTIANITY IN EUROPEAN AMERICA (1492–1740)

Almost as soon as there were European settlers in North America, there were also several varieties of Christianity in the New World. Despite our legends, the English Puritans did not dominate settlement. Even in the territory that would become the United States, the Puritans were preceded by their near, but not very dear, fellow Englishmen, the state-church Episcopalians. Representatives of the Dutch Reformed Church were also fairly well established in New York before the main body of Puritans first glimpsed Boston in 1630. Soon German-speaking believers of many types joined English Quakers in William Penn's Pennsylvania, Swedish Lutherans came to Delaware, and Presbyterians from Scotland and the north of Ireland had established a foothold on Long Island, in New Jersey, and in Pennsylvania. Well before any Protestants appeared on the scene, moreover, Roman Catholic priests from Spain had already been working for generations to convert the Native Americans of the great Southwest. Also in advance of the Protestants, other Catholic missionaries from France had pursued their missionary tasks in the North and along the Mississippi River. Well into the eighteenth century, the infusion of religious energy from Europe defined the course of Christianity in America. But that energy was always present in many types and varieties. The history of Christian diversity in America begins, therefore, with European events before the sailing of Columbus in 1492.

Roman Catholicism in Early America

The first Christians in the New World were Roman Catholics. Before the English settled permanently at Jamestown in 1607, thousands of Indians had become at least nominal Christians under Catholic missionaries in the New Mexico territories. The first printed hymn book in America was not the Puritans' *Bay Psalm Book* of 1640 but the *Ordinary of the Mass* published in Mexico City in 1556, and it had music printed with the words, something the British-Americans would not do in New England until the eighteenth century. The Protestant impact on the United States has been great in nearly every way, but even in the states, names like St. Augustine, San Antonio, and Los Angeles, or Vincennes, Dubuque, and Louisville testify to the fact that Spanish and French Catholics were here first.

New Spain

Spanish Christianity lasted in North America from the early sixteenth century to the mid-nineteenth. Unfortunately for the Native Americans conquered by the Spanish, Christian ideals in the Old World were difficult to translate into practical realities in the New. Conquistadors like Cortez in Mexico or Pizzaro in Peru were accompanied by priests, but the priests were not able to prevent the invaders from brutalizing the native population. Spanish priests sometimes protested when military rulers treated the Indians like animals. One such protest by the Dominicans Bernardio de Minaya and Julian Garces led Pope Paul III to issue in 1537 a formal declaration *(Sublimis Deus)* affirming that Indians were people indeed and could become Christians.

Colonial administration in New Spain was heavy-handed and often displayed anything but the ideals of Jesus. Yet Spanish Catholicism had a notable history in the early days of European interest in America. In 1542 the Franciscan priest, Juan de Padilla, became the first of the American missionary martyrs when he left the company of Vasquez Coronado to make a preaching tour among natives in what is now Kansas. In New Mexico, as many as 35,000 Christian Indians had gathered around twenty-five missionary stations by the year 1630.

Over the next two centuries dedicated missionary activity continued in the American southwest and in California. Franciscans like Junipero Serra (1713–1784) took the lead in establishing a Christian presence in California. From 1769 to 1845, 146 Franciscans helped found twenty-one mission stations in that future state. Together they baptized nearly 100,000 Indians. Serra was patient in teaching habits of settled agriculture to his converts, fervent in promoting spiritual discipline among his fellow-workers and their converts, and sharp with Spanish officials who impeded his work.

Spanish mission work was seriously compromised by the callousness of Spain's grip on the colonies, however. Priests and friars were not immune from European ethnocentricism, even if they tried to preserve the spiritual priorities of the faith. On the other hand, viceroys and generals who were sometimes sincere in personal faith regarded the Indians as potential workers much more than as potential converts. The situation in the Spanish settlements was complicated by the fact that the popes had granted complete authority over the church in New Spain to the Spanish government. This meant that civil officials controlled church finances and church appointments. The general result was to impede seriously the long-range effectiveness of the mission work.

In addition, conversions among the Indians tended to be opportunistic. With a few exceptions, the Native Americans remained Christian so long as Spanish colonial rule was secure. When the chance appeared, as during the uprising by the Puebloes in August 1680, the Indians often lashed out at the missionaries. That revolt led to the destruction of Sante Fe and the death of more than one-tenth of the Spanish in the city. Significantly, however, the Puebloes killed two-thirds of the missionaries in that rebellion. Despite valiant efforts by Spanish missionaries, in other words, the message of an inclusive faith was not able to bridge the cultural divide separating the Spanish and the Native Americans. The Spanish did leave a distinct style of church architecture as a permanent legacy in what would become the American southwest. Their religious legacy was more ambiguous.

New France

With variations, the history of Spanish missionary effort was mostly the same in territories settled by the French and the English. From the founding of Quebec by Samuel de Champlain in 1608 to 1759, when a British army defeated the French forces on the Plains of Abraham outside the same city, the government of France held sway in Canada and what would later become the midwestern United States. Thereafter, the province of Quebec remained a center of French-Catholic culture. As such, its presence in Canada would be one of the most significant features differentiating that society from the emerging nation to its south. Where Roman Catholics in significant numbers came relatively late to what would be the United States, they were present as the first permanent settlers of Canada and so provided a foundational contribution to later Canadian civilization.

As in New Spain, French traders, trappers, and settlers were accompanied by Catholic priests and brothers. Missionary work among the Indians in Canada had been going on for two generations when the most famous French explorations of what was to be the United States took place. But the way they combined secular and religious purposes had been typical throughout the course of French exploration. When Louis Jolliet traversed the upper Mississippi River valley in 1673, a Jesuit, Father Jacques Marquette, was his companion. Jolliet wanted to find trade and establish claim to the region. Marquette was seeking souls. He had long heard of the Illinois Indians, rumored to be a vast multitude inhabiting the midlands of the continent, and Jolliet's expedition gave him the chance to seek them out. As Marquette put it, he wanted "to seek toward the south sea [Gulf of Mexico] nations new and unknown to us, in order to make them know our great God of whom they have been up to now ignorant."[1] His initial contacts with these and other Native American groups were promising. But worn out by years of arduous travel, Marquette died the next year, still short of his thirty-eighth birthday.

Franciscan missionaries made a significant contribution to the colonization of New France. One of them, Louis Hennepin, explored modern Minnesota with René de La Salle. The county in which Minneapolis is now located was named in his memory. But most of the Canadian missionary work was carried on by the Jesuits. Jesuits, whose missionary service in the Far East had been marked by an effort to adapt the faith to Asian cultures, showed some of the same cultural sensitivity in North America.

The best example of that sensitive spirit was probably Jean de Brebeuf, who came to Canada in 1626 when he was thirty-two. Brebeuf helped found mission stations near Georgian Bay, where he enjoyed considerable success at winning the friendly Huron Indians to Christianity. In his capacity as a senior missionary, he regularly counseled his fellows to adopt, as far as possible, the ways of the potential converts. Louis Hennepin would later write that "the way to succeed in converting the Barbarians, is to endeavour to make them men before we go about to make them Christians."[2] Brebeuf's attitude was different. He wrote in 1637:

> You must have sincere affection for the Savages, looking upon them as ransomed by the blood of the son of God, and as our Brethren with whom we are to pass the rest of our lives. . . . You should try to eat their sagamite or salmagundi in the way they prepare it, although it may be dirty, half-cooked, and very tasteless. As to the other numerous things which may be unpleasant, they must be endured for the love of God, without saying anything or appearing to notice them.[3]

Brebeuf and his fellows enjoyed considerable success with the friendly Hurons for more than a decade. But then warfare among the Indians forced the Hurons to move, and many of the leading missionaries, including Brebeuf, were killed by the Hurons' ancient enemies, the Iroquois. Brebeuf's martyrdom came in 1649 when he was captured by a band of Iroquois. It says something of the stature he had gained among the Native Americans that when he was finally killed, after excruciating torture, the killers ate his heart and drank his blood so that they might possess the courage he had displayed through this ordeal.

French Canada was also the scene of significant Christian endeavor by women. Marie Guyart (1599–1672), who came to be known as Marie of the Incarnation, was a French widow from Tours in France, who joined the Ursuline order and eventually

---

[1]Mark Noll, ed., *Eerdmans' Handbook to Christianity in America* (Grand Rapids, MI: Eerdmans, 1983), p. 13.
[2]John Tracy Ellis, ed., *Documents of American Catholic History* (Milwaukee: Bruce, 1962), p. 75.
[3]Edna Kenton, ed., *The Jesuit Relations and Allied Documents* (New York: Harcourt Brace and Co., 1927), p. 118.

came to Canada as the first woman missionary in the New World. From her residence in Quebec, Marie took an active interest in the Indian groups of the region and played a major part in writing grammars, liturgies, and catechisms in Huron and Algonquin for the native converts. She also wrote thousands of letters to France in which she poured out her concern for family in the Old Country and gave expression to a deep, mystical faith. By the time of her death she had been joined by several younger women in religious orders who continued her work.

French colonial officials were considerably more enlightened than their Spanish counterparts. They encouraged mission work and also saw that the church was given a large measure of latitude in established areas of European settlement. Francis Xavier de Montmorency Laval, who became the first bishop of Quebec in 1674, was an especially forceful personality, well able to defend the prerogatives of the church. Laval directed his diocese firmly, promoted formal education (including a seminary for training priests), and tried to make French contact with the Indians more humane (by opposing, for example, the liquor traffic).

A few Indian groups in Canada trace their Christian convictions to the pioneering work of the French Jesuits. Even more important for Christianity in the Western hemisphere, however, was the firm presence that the Roman Catholic church established among the families and other permanent settlers who eventually came to Canada from France. From that day to this, the Catholic civilization of French-Canada would offer a prominent and sometimes deeply disquieting contrast to the Protestants who were busy with the task of subduing the areas that would become the rest of Canada and the United States.

The Reformation in English and the First English Settlements

The English who played the major part in settling British North America were Protestants of a distinct type. When the youthful Protestant Edward VI succeeded his father Henry VIII in 1547, his advisors greatly accelerated the pace of religious change in England. Protestant reform came to a rapid halt, however, when Edward, never a healthy youth, died in 1553 and was succeeded by his ardently Catholic half-sister, Mary Tudor.

Until this time, the English Reformation had been a mixture of Lutheran influences, elements from other Protestant movements in Europe, and native English tendencies. When Protestants fled England during the reign of Mary, however, they were not able to go to Lutheran lands. Defeats in warfare and intramural disputes after Luther's death in 1546 made it difficult for Lutheran regions in Germany and Scandinavia to accept the English refugees. The situation was much different in Reformed or Calvinist regions. John Calvin had secured a thoroughly Protestant settlement in Geneva early in the 1550s, and he welcomed the English refugees eagerly. Similar hospitality was extended by the Reformed of other Swiss cities and of southwestern Germany. In these Reformed regions, many of the English refugees caught a vision of how they would like to see their native land renewed if ever the opportunity presented itself again. What Calvin and other Reformed leaders were attempting was a systematic restructuring of society on the basis of their understanding of the bible. Under such influence, some of the English refugees began to wonder if the eclecticism of England's previous reform had been enough.

When Mary Tudor died in 1558 after a short reign, the English refugees were able to return home. The more advanced of their number, joined by many who had remained in England, pressed forward under the new monarch, Queen Elizabeth I, to seek a more systematic reform of England's religion. That drive led to the rise of Puritanism in England, with all the momentous consequences that we have seen. It was also a major impetus behind the settlement of the English colonies in North America.

Virginia

England's first permanent settlement in the New World was the Virginia colony, which established a foothold at Jamestown in 1607. Historians have customarily contrasted the secular character of Virginia's founding with the overtly religious settlements of Puritans to the north in Plymouth and Massachusetts Bay. It is true that the Virginia Company of London was more interested in turning a profit than was the Massachusetts Bay Company that settled Boston and its environs. It is also true that the dispersed patterns of settlement in Virginia were not conducive to the close spiritual fellowship that was possible in the northern English colonies. Still, if the Virginians were never Puritans, they did make room for a remarkable degree of religion.

As soon as the first settlers arrived on Virginia soil in May 1607, they joined the Reverend Robert Hunt ("an honest, religious, and courageous Divine" according to Captain John Smith) in holding a service of communion. When Lord De La Warr, a new governor, arrived in 1610 as the colony teetered on the brink of collapse, his first action was to organize a worship service in order to issue a biblical call for sacrifice and industry. Virginia's earliest legal code made attendance at Sunday services compulsory and contained harsh laws against violations of the Sabbath, adultery, and excessive dress. All of these were also concerns of the Puritans. Even the missionary motive was not absent in Virginia. John Rolfe married the legendary Pocahontas in part to share the Christian faith as well as to secure her love. "I will never cease," he wrote of his desire to have Pocahontas become a Christian, "untill I have accomplished, & brought to perfection so holy a worke, in which I will daily pray God to blesse me, to mine, and her eternall happiness."[4] Alexander Whitaker,

---

[4] Edwin S. Gaustad, ed., *A Documentary History of Religion in America*, Vol 1. (Grand Rapids, MI: Eerdmans, 1982), p. 96.

the leading minister in Virginia's early history, never lost his desire to convert the Indians, even as he maintained a regular ministry among the English settlers.

As part of Virginia's incorporation, the Church of England was made the colony's established church. This establishment would eventually lend a very different flavor to religion in the Chesapeake region than it had in New England. Other circumstances of Virginia's early history also contributed to its differences from New England, especially its early turn to growing tobacco for export and its early introduction of black chattel slavery. Still, it is possible to glimpse in the early years of the colony some of the same devotional fervor that would play such a large part in the settlement of New England to the north.

Plymouth

England's next permanent colony bore the stamp of Puritanism much more completely. The settlers who arrived in 1620 at Plymouth in southeastern Massachusetts were even in some senses more "Puritan" than the Puritans. Where others were still contending in England for the thorough reform of the church and the religious life of the nation, the Plymouth settlers had largely abandoned that effort in order to carve out a separate society for themselves. Among the more extreme Protestants who were deeply disappointed when the Scottish James I, successor in 1603 to Queen Elizabeth, did not embrace the Puritan cause, were local congregations who met together beyond the jurisdiction of the national church. One of these in Scrooby, Nottinghamshire, grew so uneasy with the course of religious events in England that it resolved to migrate to a more friendly environment. Under its pastor John Robinson, this congregation chose first to go to Holland. But in that land they were disappointed. The Dutch allowed them to worship as they pleased, but the English migrants found the Dutch culture unappealing. They were also worried that their children were being led astray from their religious principles by the desire for economic gain and by alternative faiths. So after a dozen years they resolved to move much farther afield to find the space they needed to worship and live as they thought best. As their chronicler William Bradford wrote of that move: "So they left the godly and pleasant city which had been their resting place . . . ; but they knew they were pilgrims and looked not much on those things but lifted their eyes to the heavens, their dearest country, and quieted their spirits."[5]

These "pilgrims" secured the sponsorship of English merchants and eventually surmounted an unremitting series of difficulties to board the *Mayflower* on September 6, 1620, for the New World. They sailed for Virginia but were blown off course to Cape Cod, where they arrived in early November. They decided to stay. But before leaving the ship, the male passengers (not all of whom were members of the congre-

---

[5]William Bradford, *Of Plymouth Plantation, 1620–1647* (New York: Modern Library, 1981), p. 50.

gation) signed an agreement, or compact, in which they pledged to uphold the solidarity of the group and to forsake the individual pursuit of gain. William Bradford, who would soon become the governor of the colony, left a deeply moving record of the ravages of the first winter. Half of the Pilgrims died. Heroic toil by Captain Miles Standish, Elder William Brewster, Bradford, and a few others pulled them through to the spring. Despite that bleak beginning, these humble settlers soon established a secure dwelling. After their first harvest, they enjoyed a special feast of Thanksgiving lasting several days with their Native American friends, a feast that bequeathed a pattern for many later celebrations.

The Plymouth colony remained small, with only 300 residents by 1630. But it prospered. And it enjoyed the liberty to plant a congregational form of worship and a deeply pious sense of community. William Bradford lived long enough (he died in 1657) to wonder if the colony's very success had not distracted it from its early spiritual commitments. But at least he and a few others among the aging original settlers never lost the wonder of their experience. In his history of Plymouth Plantation, Bradford wrote:

> Thus out of small beginnings, great things have been produced by His hand that made all things of nothing, and gives being to all things that are; and as one small candle may light a thousand, so the light here kindled hath shone to many, yea in some sort to our whole nation; let the glorious name of Jehovah have all the praise.[6]

The Puritans

As significant as early Christian experience was in New Spain, New France, Virginia, and Plymouth, it is the record of the Puritans in New England that has dominated modern perceptions of America's early Christian history. There are a number of reasons why this is so. The early American Puritans were blessed—or cursed, from some points of view—with dominant personalities. From the leaders of the first settlements, like Governor John Winthrop or the Reverend John Cotton, to the last defenders of "The New England Way," like the Reverend Cotton Mather (himself a descendant of John Cotton and Richard Mather, another famous minister of the first generation), Puritans enjoyed a long stream of vigorous guides. These leaders, moreover, were often involved in obviously important and sometimes sensational events. The religious influence, for example, was very strong in the governments of early New England where, without necessarily intending it to be so, Massachusetts and its fellow Puritan colonies advanced the cause of democracy. It was

[6]Francis Dillon, *A Place for Habitation: The Pilgrim Fathers and Their Quest* (London: Hutchinson, 1973), p. 225.

equally strong in the Salem witch scare of 1692, an event that ever after has been a source of shame to the friends of the Puritans and a proof of hysterical instability to their enemies. The Puritans were also a highly verbal people who left a full written record of their thoughts and actions. Well beyond the founding of the United States, Boston was the publishing capital of North America. Until after the Civil War, most educational programs in the United States, from grade schools through universities, were modeled on patterns established by the first generations of New England's Puritans.

Most important, the Puritan moral vision was so strenuous that almost all Americans since their day have been forced to react to it in some way. Throughout the mid-nineteenth century Puritan morality was widely thought to provide the foundation for the great success of the United States. Then for the next century or so it was thought that Puritan morality was the great nemesis to be exorcised from the American past. Not all have agreed with the judgment of Perry Miller, one of the twentieth century's great historians, that "many amenities of social life have increased in New England and in America, in direct proportion as Puritanism has receded. But while we congratulate ourselves upon these ameliorations, we cannot resist a slight fear that much of what has taken the place of Puritanism in our philosophies is just so much failure of nerve."[7] Yet almost all who have investigated the Puritans agree with Miller that their moral energy was indeed unusual.

Puritanism in England

Puritanism arose as the "advanced" or "precise" party among English Protestants. Defined negatively, the Puritans wanted to wipe out the vestiges of Roman Catholic worship and habits that survived within the Church of England as fashioned by Queen Elizabeth I, James I, and their clerical advisors. Defined positively, the Puritans wanted to finish the Reformation and to finish it now. One of their most extreme representatives, the congregationalist Robert Browne, published a stirring tract, *Reformation Without Tarrying for Any*, in 1582. Its sentiments spoke for many others whose views were not quite as radical.

The main Puritan convictions can be summarized under four categories. First, Puritans believed that humankind must depend entirely on God for salvation. They held that humans were sinners who would not choose to be reconciled with God unless God initiated the process of their salvation. Second, the Puritans emphasized the authority of the bible. Moreover, they believed that the bible exerted a "regulative" authority, which meant that Christians so far as possible should do only what the Scriptures explicitly directed. Puritans, third, believed, as did almost all Euro-

---

[7]Perry Miller, "Introduction," in *The Puritans: A Sourcebook of Their Writings*, Vol. I (New York: Harper & Row, 1963), p. 63.

peans of the day, that God had created society as a unified whole. Church and state, the individual and the public sphere, were not unrelated spheres of life but complementary areas, intimately related by God's acts of creation and by his continuing Providence. This conviction lay behind the Puritan effort to fashion colonies in the New World in which all parts of colonial life would reflect the glory of God. Finally, Puritans believed that God worked with peoples through covenants, or solemn agreements. Especially the congregationalist Puritans of the New World emphasized that local churches arose when individual believers covenanted together to serve God as a unit and to follow his will. Almost all varieties of Puritans also held that God entered into covenant with nations, especially those that had been granted special insight into the truths of the bible.

Puritanism derived much of its strength from the subtle interweaving of these covenants. John Cotton claimed, for example, that God had appointed humans to "live in Societies, first, of Family, Secondly, Church, Thirdly, Common-Wealth."[8] And another early leader drew the bonds even tighter: "The Covenant of Grace is cloathed with Church-Covenant in a Political visible Church-way."[9] The secret of understanding the Puritans is realizing not only that energies from private religious life flowed readily into church and society but also that they flowed in the opposite direction.

The great Puritan migration to the New World took place when it looked as if opportunities for reform were closed off in England. Charles I, who succeeded his father James I in 1625, not only had Roman Catholic proclivities. He also seemed determined to rule England by divine right. Charles quarreled with several Parliaments and then from 1629 tried to rule England without calling Parliament into session. He also commissioned his archbishop of Canterbury, William Laud, to root out Puritanism from the Anglican Church. In 1628 a group of Puritans leaning toward congregational church organization purchased a controlling interest in the New England Company. After the company was reorganized to emphasize colonization instead of commerce, and after it obtained a new charter from the king providing for more self-government, the first migration to Massachusetts Bay (more than 1,000 settlers) took place in 1630. During the next decade, while leading Puritans in England continued to resist the programs of Charles and Laud and while some future leaders of Puritan England like Oliver Cromwell wondered if they should go to Massachusetts, more than 20,000 more settlers actually made the hazardous trip to America. By no means all of these early settlers were heartfelt Puritans in a religious sense. But their leaders were, and few came to Massachusetts and its sister colonies who were not content with a society ordered by Puritan beliefs.

[8]Edmunt S. Morgan, *The Puritan Family*, rev. ed. (New York: Harper, 1966), p. 18.
[9]Perry Miller, *The New England Mind: From Colony to Province* (Boston: Beacon, 1961) p. 70.

Puritan Life and Faith

Puritanism was the dominant religion in four American colonies: Plymouth, settled as we have seen by separatistic congregationalists; Massachusetts, the main Puritan colony, which absorbed Plymouth in 1691; New Haven, founded in 1638 under the leadership of the Reverend John Davenport and Governor Theophilus Eaton, and probably the strictest experiment in New World Puritanism; and Connecticut, which came into existence in 1636 when several ministers under the direction of the Rev. Thomas Hooker led settlers from Massachusetts to new homes on the Connecticut River near modern Hartford. In 1662 a new charter from England joined New Haven and Connecticut into a single unit.

For the first generation of settlement, it seemed as if the New England Puritans could achieve the total reform of life that had eluded them in old England. The three other colonies did not follow the Massachusetts system in every particular, but its New England Way set a standard for them all. Almost as soon as they arrived, the Massachusetts ministers and magistrates agreed to a somewhat more visible measure of conversion than they had practiced in England. Now a new stress was placed on the experience of conversion as a criterion for full church membership. Prospective members were to accept Puritan doctrines and live moral lives, but they were also to confess before their fellows that they had experienced God's saving grace. Those who could testify credibly to their redemption in this way formed the churches by covenanting with one another. The stroke of genius that transformed ecclesiastical purity into social purity was to open the franchise to men who had become full members of covenanted churches. (Women in New England had somewhat more rights in law and, generally speaking, more privileges than in England, but nowhere in the world in the seventeenth century did women as a class take a direct part in political life.)

To put it in the Puritans' own terms, the covenant of grace qualified a person for church membership and a voting role in the colony's public life. This public life fulfilled the social covenant with God since the leaders selected by the church members promoted laws that honored the scriptures. Moreover, the church covenant linked converted individuals to the social project without requiring the burden of a church-state machinery like that bedeviling the church in England. New England was, thus, no theocracy where the clergy exercised direct control of public life. It was, however, a place where magistrates frequently called on ministers for advice, including how best they might promote the religious life of the colonies. And the churches were nonseparating. Local congregations had responsibilities for the good of the whole, not just for themselves.

For a while, the system worked. John Winthrop, a man of unusual self-restraint and public-spirited faith, served as Massachusetts's governor for most of its first two decades. Under his direction, Massachusetts saw up to half of the colony's male citizens join the churches and participate in government. (The Puritans did not set out to promote democracy, but they ended by doing it inadvertently.) The churches by and large flourished. The colony's laws provided for all healthy-bodied individuals to attend church, a stipulation against which almost no one complained. The tumults in England during the 1640s, when Puritans in league with Parliamentarians made war on the king, provided an occasion for the New Englanders to compose a Cambridge Platform (1648) that reaffirmed their Reformed theology and their church order of nonseparating congregationalism.

Early on as well, the Puritans worked hard to construct an educational system that would preserve their experiment. In 1636 the Massachusetts legislature authorized a college, which got underway two years later when a young minister, John Harvard, left a library of 400 volumes to the new institution. (By contrast, the first college in Virginia, William and Mary, was not founded until 1693). The purposes of Harvard College from the beginning were broader than the training of ministers, although Harvard remained the prime source of New England's Congregational clergy well into the eighteenth century. Lower levels of education did not escape the attention of the Puritan leaders. The legislature in 1642 threatened towns with fines if they did not see that all children come to "read & understand the principles of religion & the capitall lawes of this country." Five years later it passed an act requiring each town of at least fifty households to appoint a teacher. Later in the century, Boston publishers would issue *The New-England Primer*, a book that taught basic reading and writing through a presentation of the Lord's Prayer, the Ten Commandments, and the Apostles' Creed. It became the most popular textbook in all the colonies for much of the next century. This attention to learning made New England one of the most literate places in the world.

Apart from notable dissenters in its early days, to whom we turn shortly, the major opponent of the Puritan system was time itself. As the 1640s gave way to the 1650s, more and more children of the earliest settlers were failing to experience God's grace in the same fashion as their parents, and hence were not seeking full membership in the churches. The problem became extreme when these children began to marry and produce children of their own. Under the Puritans' Reformed theology, converted people had the privilege of bringing their infant children to be baptized as a seal of God's covenant grace. Now many of those who had been baptized as infants were not stepping forth on their own to confess Christ. Yet they still wanted to have their children baptized. The Puritan dilemma was delicate: Leaders wished to preserve the church for genuine believers, but they also wanted to keep as many people as possible under the influence of the church. Their solution was to propose a "half-way" covenant whereby second-generation New Englanders could bring their third-generation children for baptism and half-way membership. Participation in the Lord's Supper and other privileges were, however, reserved for those who could testify to a specific work of God's grace in their lives. This plan was formalized by a special synod of ministers in 1662. Its implementation, though opposed by some important leaders as a dilution of Puritan spirituality, did preserve the interlocking covenants of person, church, and society. And so with this adjustment the Puritans continued on through the middle decades of the seventeenth century.

Even more severe crises seemed to impend, however, toward the end of the century. Warfare with Indians in 1675 and 1676 wrought great havoc on outlying towns and left several thousand colonists dead. In 1685 the New England colonies were deprived of their representative assemblies and placed with New York and New Jersey into the Dominion of New England. This expedient was an effort by the Roman Catholic James II, who had become England's king in 1685, to rein in the extreme Protestants of the New World. The Dominion did not last long, for a measure of self-rule was returned to the colonies after Parliament replaced James II with new monarchs, William and Mary, in 1688. But Massachusetts's new charter of 1691 was much more secular then the colony's original basis for government. It stipulated that the governor would be appointed by the king. Even more important, the right to vote for the colonial legislature was now determined by property rather than by church membership. The New England Way was beginning to dissolve.

At a "Reforming Synod" in 1679 Massachusetts ministers suggested "that God hath a controversy with his New-England People." The ministers thought they saw an increase in Sabbath-breaking and other forms of ungodliness. Although they called on New Englanders to repent and to seek again the spiritual fervor that drove their predecessors into the wilderness, they were preparing for the worst.

But no one was prepared for the devastation that broke out in Salem Village north of Boston in 1692. Prosecution and execution for witchcraft was by no means unknown in New England, but the alarm at Salem went much further than previous incidents. A number of factors fueled the alarm: political strife between Salem Village and the larger town of Salem, voodoo practices associated with a West Indian slave, the recent republication of an ancient book presenting ways to combat witchcraft, tension with marauding Native Americans and their French allies, judges and ministers nervous about the colony's spiritual decline and eager to find ways of checking it, simmering community hostility against a few lonely old women and a few new families, a wide range of occult practices, and adolescent hysteria in a few teenage girls along with judicial hysteria among a few old men. The result was several months of anguished excitement and the execution of twenty souls (nineteen hanged, one pressed to death with weights for refusing to testify). Finally, when accusations began to be presented against individuals of spotless character and when leading citizens, such as the Boston minister Increase Mather, spoke out against the proceedings, the incident came quickly to an end.

Even including the supposed witches executed in Salem, the number of executions for witchcraft in New England was considerably lower than in most of the countries of western Europe. New England suffered nonetheless from this wild outburst. Its own citizens came to the conclusion that the devil had been extraordinarily active in the incident, not so much in the accused witches as in those who had accused them and those that harkened to the accusations. Several years after the trial in 1697, one of the judges at Salem, Samual Sewall, publicly confessed his guilt for "the Blame and shame of it" in a moving statement read aloud in his church. But such repentance has not effaced the blot that the Salem witch trials left on the Puritans' public record.

Historians have long argued whether, or in what ways, Puritan New England "declined" in the late seventeenth and early eighteenth centuries. A judgment from the twentieth century might be mixed. It would note, as some ministers and lay people also did, that the pursuit of prosperity was becoming more important than the pursuit of godliness for at least some merchants in Boston and some common people on the land. At the same time, however, the church still exerted the central role in the society, defining the grand questions and orienting life in the daily round. It still set the norms for public speech (with rich use of biblical language), for architecture (the simplicity of the meeting house), and for much else. And the church's basic message was still the same: that God saves individuals by his grace and calls them together into the nurturing fellowship of the church. On one item, the Puritan leaders and later observers might have come to different conclusions. This was the fact that by the end of the century New England had definitely become an easier place to live for those who did not share the Puritan faith.

Dissent from Puritanism

Early New England dissent was often more Puritan than the colonial establishments. By the mid-seventeenth century, a number of individuals and groups had challenged the New England Way. Some of these were shunted off to the colony of Rhode Island, which soon became a byword for eccentricity and extremism to the leaders of Puritan New England. From another view, however, some of the features of Rhode Island life that the Puritans so despised anticipated more general characteristics of religious life in what later would become the United States.

Baptists, who shared a number of beliefs with the Puritans, appeared in Massachusetts soon after the first migrations. The earliest Baptist congregation in England, established by John Smyth near London in 1612, combined the Puritans' basic Calvinism with baptismal practices acquired from the Dutch Mennonites, who baptized adult believers on profession of their own faith. The Puritans felt threatened by the Baptists, especially by the Baptist insistence that the state had no role to play in the churches, as well as by the way their baptismal practices sundered the bond between personal faith, church guidance, and participation in the wider society. The leading Baptist in early New England, John Clarke, arrived in Rhode Island in 1639 to found the town of Newport. He and his followers made frequent forays into Plymouth and Massachusetts over the next several decades. They were able to convince some there of the correctness of the Baptist beliefs, including a president of Harvard College, Henry Dunster, who in 1654 made public his criticism of the baptism of infants. On the whole, however, the Puritan colonies remained suspicious of the Baptists and even briefly imprisoned several of their advocates, including laymen, for spreading Baptist ideas.

One of the reasons Massachusetts authorities may have distrusted the Baptists was that they had received help in settling in Rhode Island from one of the Puritans' great nemeses, Roger Williams (1603?–1683). Williams was born in England around 1603 and came to Massachusetts in 1631 after establishing a reputation as a faithful Puritan preacher. Yet Williams's Puritanism was always so excruciatingly thorough that he had great difficulty fitting into the closely regulated Massachusetts system. Although called to serve churches in both Boston and Salem, Williams refused, choosing rather to settle in Plymouth, which he felt had largely escaped the errors of the Massachusetts settlers. All who knew Williams testified to his gentle spirit and Christian demeanor, but many who came to disagree with him wished he had kept his opinions to himself. These were disquieting in the extreme: The Puritans, he held, had no right to the Indian lands in the New World, since the lands were simply plundered, and so the colonial charters were invalid. Moreover, individuals who had not confessed Christ could not be held accountable to a social covenant. It was simply wrong in principle for magistrates to enforce attendance at church and other spiritual duties, since true Christian action proceeds from the heart. "Christening makes not Christians," he repeated, and so attempts to make nonbelievers act like believers were simply self-defeating. Williams was a separatist who saw no future in a Christian faith compromised by attempts to rule in the world.

Such views perhaps could have been ignored when whispered in a Plymouth corner. But when Williams in 1633 finally accepted the repeated call from the Salem church to serve as its minister, these views drew the immediate wrath of the Massachusetts authorities. Such views imperiled nearly every aspect of the colony's life. And so in relatively short order, Williams was expelled from the colony as a threat to its continued existence. John Winthrop arranged for Williams's banishment to take place in the spring, when conditions for migration would be better, but Williams chose to leave Massachusetts in October 1635. After a brutal winter, he finally arrived at the head of Narragansett Bay in April 1636, where he founded the city of Providence to honor the power that had carried him through the winter.

Roger Williams is known as America's greatest early "democrat," and that reputation is partly justified. Under his direction, Rhode Island became the first place in the North American colonies where freedom of religious worship was defined as a human right for (almost) all groups. It was also the first American colony to attempt a separation between the institutions of religion and the institutions of the state. Even more than a democrat, however, Williams was a thorough-going Puritan. His reasons for favoring soul liberty and the separation of church and state were themselves religious. Only God knew the heart, and only God could promote a truly spiritual life. Since that was so, ministers and magistrates must protect with greatest respect the relationship between God and his servants on the earth.

Just as unsettling to the Puritan authorities but also just as Puritan was the challenge of Anne Hutchinson (1591–1643). Mrs. Hutchinson migrated to Massachusetts in order to remain under the ministry of her English pastor, John Cotton, who had come to Boston in 1633. In particular, she hung on his message of God's free grace. Once in New England, Hutchinson began a mid-weekly meeting to discuss Coton's sermon of the previous Sunday and also to take up other spiritual matters. All went well until it came to be feared that her views were edging toward Antinomianism (the error, in Puritan eyes, that Christians do not need the Ten Commndments to show them how to live). In her meetings she argued that a believer possessed the Holy Spirit and thus was not bound by the requirements of law. In addition, simply because a person obeyed the laws of society (of Massachusetts, for example) did not mean that the person was really a Christian. As John Cotton taught so clearly, salvation was by grace and not by works of the law.

Hutchinson's views were in fact a legitimate if unusual extension of basic Puritan theology. The difficulty came in the clash of such notions with the Puritan Way in New England. If individuals were left on their own even as Christians, where would the godly society be for which the Puritans longed so dearly? The Massachusetts authorities were displeased and demanded an accounting. Through many days of a formal judicial proceeding, Mrs. Hutchinson held her own, citing scripture and reasoning carefully against the colony's leaders. When Winthrop ran out of arguments, he groused that Mrs. Hutchinson's theologizing was somehow unnatural for a woman. Just when it seemed as if she had finally silenced her opponents, however, she made a fatal mistake. She claimed that the Holy Spirit communicated directly to her apart from scripture, and this the leaders could not tolerate. As a result of her rash assertion, she and those who followed her were banished from Massachusetts in 1638. After stopping briefly in Rhode Island and Long Island, she settled in the colony of New York, where she and most of her family were killed shortly thereafter in an Indian attack. Massachusetts Puritans nodded grimly on hearing the news. Less involved observers can regret that this woman of unusual spiritual intelligence did not live longer to promote her distinctive interpretation of the Puritan faith, for it was an interpretation that would be echoed time and again in the American experience.

Other Beginnings

Outside of New England, the Church of England was the major religious presence in the early British colonies. It was the established church in Virginia, the Carolinas, Georgia, Maryland (after 1691), and parts of New York City after 1693. Yet in the American environment that establishment was often very thin. English experience could not prepare ministers for the size of New World parishes (Virginia's averaged 550 square miles each in 1724). And it offered precious few resources to stand up against the rough, individualistic, honor-driven, slave-holding society of the southern colonies.

Difficulties of communication with the mother country were also a persistent problem. Anglicans in the colonies never enjoyed the services of their own bishop. At first the failure to name a bishop for America seemed to be more of an oversight, a failure of creativity in the face of new opportunities, rather than anything deliberate. After 1700 another difficulty stood in the way, for talk of a colonial bishop began to arouse fears that Parliament wanted to rein in the political freedom of its colonies. The absence of a bishop created severe strain. In the polity of the Church of England, it took a bishop to confirm (that is, to make a baptized person into a full member of the church) and to ordain new candidates for the ministry. In England, furthermore, bishops provided the very cohesion and sense of overall purpose that were conspicuous by their absence in the colonies. A final problem for colonial Anglicans involved their ministers. At least a few of the Anglican clergymen who came to the New World were failures at home for whom service in America was a desperate last chance. Though never a majority of the Anglican ministers, a few of these wastrels gave the entire ministerial corps an evil reputation that has taken historians of colonial Anglicanism literally centuries to remove.

This is not to say that the Church of England was an insignificant or flighty body in the colonies. It did enjoy the services of many faithful leaders. James Blair (1655–1743), for example, served with considerable effect as the commissary (or administrator) of the Virginia church for over half a century. Blair's achievements included the founding of a college (William and Mary in 1693), determined advocacy of the church's position before the Virginia legislature, and faithful support of the colony's clergy. Similarly effective was Thomas Bray (1656–1730), the commissary for the Church of England in Maryland from 1696 to 1700. During his short stay in the colonies, he founded two agencies that would have a continued effect long after he left America. The Society for Promoting Christian Knowledge (SPCK) provided books for ministers and interested lay people. The Society for the Propagation of the Gospel in Foreign Parts (SPG) sponsored missionary work on behalf of the Church of England, first among the Native Americans but then later (to the great consternation of the Puritans) in settled areas like New England.

Other Anglican ministers, who made a sincere effort at their tasks, were simply overwhelmed by American ways. Such a one was John Wesley, the founder of Methodism, who during the mid-1730s spent a frustrating eighteen months in Georgia as a young missionary. Wesley was earnest, perhaps to a fault; he diligently preached to Indians and the local settlers. But his mission—complicated by a miscarried affair of the heart, by strident controversy with local leaders, and by the indifference of both Indians and colonists to his message—was an abject failure.

Ironically, the Church of England eventually had its greatest successes in regions where it was not the established church. During the great revivals of the mid-eighteenth century, New Englanders seeking a church of more repose and less enthusiasm turned in considerable numbers to Anglicanism. Without the protection of an establishment, Anglican missionaries eventually established a limited number of strong churches in Pennsylvania, New Jersey, and Long Island.

The Church of England's great importance in early America did not depend primarily on its intrinsic strength or weakness. What mattered most was that it was still England's established church. So long as the colonies remained English, the Church of England would be a major factor in its religious life—for some an example of Old World corruption, for others a point of stability in the hurly-burly of the New World.

Roman Catholics in Maryland

George Calvert (1580?–1632) and his son Cecil (1605–1675), first and second Lords Baltimore, were the founders of Maryland, the only one of the original American colonies with significant Roman Catholic influence. George Calvert, who converted to Catholicism in 1625, was secretary of state under James I of England. Calvert was forced to resign his post because he was unable to swear allegiance to the Church of England when Charles I succeeded his father as king later that same year. Charles I was, however, eager to repay the Calverts for loyal service rendered to his father and to himself, a desire he fulfilled by giving the family a large proprietary grant in the New World. The colony that resulted was named after Charles I's Catholic queen, Maria Henrietta of France. The Calverts wanted to do two things with this grant: provide a heaven for English Catholics and increase the family fortune through rents on the proprietary lands. In spite of the Catholicism of the Calverts, many Protestants were included among the original settlers. English Catholics were reluctant to leave England at a time when Charles I was looking more favorably on their religion. Cecil Calvert also wanted to reassure Protestants in England that Maryland would not become a hostile Catholic enclave. Soon after the arrival of the first settlers in 1634, Catholic missionaries began work among the Native Americans in the colony, while most of the other settlers turned to the raising of tobacco. In 1649 Cecil Calvert issued a justly famous "Act Concerning Religion" for Maryland. It provided freedom of belief for all who called themselves Christian, whether Catholic, Anglican, or Puritan. It was an advanced step for that day. Yet it was proposed more to protect Catholic interests against the Puritan parliament in England than out of theoretical commitment to freedom of religion. In 1691 the original Maryland charter was stripped from the Calvert family, only to be returned in 1715 when the fourth Lord Baltimore entered the Church of England. Maryland remained a proprietary possession of the Calverts until the American Revolution. It was the center of American Catholicism for an even longer time thereafter.

Quakers

As an English area of settlement, it could only be expected that other varieties of British Christianity would also soon find their way to the New World. Quakers, or Friends as they called themselves under the inspiration of George Fox (1624–1691), appeared in New England within a generation of the founding of Massachusetts. In July 1656 two Quaker women, Ann Austin and Mary Fisher, arrived in Boston with their message of the Inner Light of Christ and their criticism of formal, external religion. The Puritan authorities immediately sent these Quaker missioners packing. But the Quakers kept coming to Massachusetts despite the fines and whippings they endured at the hand of the authorities. Eventually, the patience of Massachusetts's leaders ran out, and in the years 1659 to 1661 (at a time of unusual political unrest in England and almost no attention to the colonies), four Quakers were hanged in Massachusetts for sedition, blasphemy, and persistent disturbance of the peace. Rhode Island offered much more freedom for beliefs that the Puritans judged to be deviant, so it soon became the site of a considerable Quaker settlement. Roger Williams had no love for Quaker doctrines and said so in unmistakeable terms to George Fox himself when the latter visited Rhode Island in 1672. But grudgingly he still gave them room.

The colonial settlement that put the Quakers permanently on the American map was Pennsylvania. And the man who accomplished the deed was William Penn (1644–1718). Penn was born in London, raised there and in Ireland, and given all the privileges befitting his station as the eldest son of Admiral Sir William Penn, who had captured Jamaica from the Dutch in 1655. By 1661, however, a very worldly William Penn had begun to fall under the influence of the Friends, and by 1666 he had joined their number. A prolific writer throughout his life, Penn ran afoul of the law in 1668 for a tract attacking the doctrines of the Church of England. While in prison in 1669, he wrote the devotional classic, *No Cross, No Crown*, an exposition concerning Christian suffering that has rarely been out of print. After his release from prison, he grew steadily disillusioned about the prospects for Quakers in England.

Penn took his first step toward finding a refuge for the Friends by backing a Quaker expedition to New Jersey in 1677 and 1678. In 1681 he acquired a huge tract of land from King Charles II to settle a large debt owed to his father. Pennsylvania ("Penn's Woods") thereafter became the most secure home for religious toleration in the world. In 1682 the city of Philadelphia was laid out and, of certainly equal importance, Pennsylvania's "Frame of Government" was published. This constitution set out the terms of Penn's "Holy Experiment" in the new world. It allowed unprecedented freedom of religion to any who believed in one God; it was also a liberal document politically for its times. Although Penn realized very little profit from his colony, Pennsylvania flourished from the start. One of the reasons for this was Penn's vigorous promotion of the colony on the European continent; another was Pennsylvania's spreading reputation for toleration. The source of many of the early immigrants was memorialized in the name chosen for a town founded in 1683, Germantown, as a grant from Penn to a group of German Mennonites and Dutch Quakers. One of the most appealing features of the Penn administration was its fair and just treatment of the Indians.

Penn was able to remain in his colony for only two brief periods (1682–1684, 1699–1701). And his later life was filled with constant troubles. But modern historians have written correctly in calling Penn a "compassionate humanitarian, mystic, theologian, and profound political theoriest"—or more simply "the Renaissance Quaker."

Quaker religion remained an important counterweight to the dominant faiths of colonial America. In the eighteenth century, the Quaker John Woolman (1720–1772) became one of the most effective advocates for peace and the abolition of slavery in North America. Woolman's family helped settle Quaker West Jersey, where Woolman earned his living as a tailor. After 1746 he embarked on a series of colonial tours to argue against slave-holding and war. His diplomacy was mild but firm. He retained compassion for the slaver as well as for the slave. But he would brook no compromise with the evils of the slave system, insisting, for example, on paying slaves when they performed personal services for him, or, eventually, rejecting food that they grew or cloth that they dyed. His antislavery efforts had an impact on Rhode Island, where wealthy Quaker shipowners had long taken part in the slave traffic, but especially in Pennsylvania. Woolman's tract *Considerations on the Keeping of Negroes* (1754, 1762) contended that slavery affronted common humanity as well as the "inner light of Christ." Woolman also played a role in the withdrawal of Pennsylvania Quakers from the government of their colony during the French and Indian War (1756–1763), when they chose to follow the Quaker "peace testimony" rather than promote the conflict.

Woolman's mystical piety represented an important development in Quaker thought as well as in Quaker social action. His *Journal* reveals one who saw physical life as an intimate reflection of the spiritual world, and one who devoutly reverenced the work of God in both nature and other humans. He was a man of rare spiritual sensitivity who exerted more of an influence on public moral values, at least among the Quakers, than many of the would-be reformers who have so filled America throughout its history.

Presbyterians

With migration to America growing from Scotland and the north of Ireland, the colonies were also soon home to increasing numbers of Presbyterians. Francis Makemie (1658–1708), born in Ireland, educated in Scotland, and commissioned in

Northern Ireland to serve as a missionary in America, was the individual most responsible for their early organization. Makemie evangelized throughout the English-speaking New World—in New England, New York, Maryland, Virginia, and North Carolina, as well as in Barbados. He established the first Presbyterian congregation in America at Snow Hill, Maryland, in 1684. The Mathers of New England spoke highly of his work, and Congregationalists in general wished him well. In 1706 he succeeded in bringing together Presbyterians of different backgrounds (English, Welsh, Scotish, Scotch-Irish, and from New England) into the Presbytery of Philadelphia. Its purpose was "to meet yearly and oftener, if necessary, to consult the most proper measures for advancing religion and propagating Christianity in our various stations." In spite of differences in emphasis and custom, these Presbyterians could agree to take their stand on the Westminster Confession's statement of Calvinist theology. In 1707 Makemie was arrested by New York's governor, Lord Cornbury, for preaching without a license in a private home on Long Island. Makemie defended himself by appealing to the English Toleration Act of 1689, which granted religious freedom to Quakers, whose views were much further from the Establishment's than those of the Presbyterians. He was acquitted, but he did have to pay the high costs of his trial. This event solidified the image of Presbyterians as defenders of freedom in the public mind and won new respect for the denomination in America.

Dutch and German Reformed

The spaciousness of what would later be the United States also made room very early on for religious groups from other places in Europe. The Dutch, who controlled New York until 1664, brought their hereditary Calvinistic, or Reformed, faith with them to that colony. As an established church, the Dutch Reformed in New Amsterdam, as it was then called, labored under many of the same difficulties besetting the established Church of England in other colonies. Only after the colony was taken over by the British did vigorous Dutch churches emerge in New York and New Jersey. These more vital beginnings were fueled both by fresh waves of immigration and a more vigorous clergy.

Hard on the heels of the Dutch came immigrants with similar Reformed views from southern Germany. Civil war, strife with France, and intolerant rule by Lutherans and Roman Catholics drove considerable numbers of the German Reformed to the New World, where by 1740 they were gathered into fifty congregations, mostly in Pennsylvania.

The Dutch and German Reformed were part of a little-noticed trend. Especially in Pennsylvania but soon in other colonies as well, it was apparent that the New World offered space for religious life that settled European circumstances often did not afford. To other European bodies North America was a ripened mission field, ready to be harvested. So it was that before the mid-eighteenth century a number of Continental Christian groups, drawn especially by a desire for religious liberty, began to wend their way to America. Included were Mennonites, German Baptists, Schwenkfelders, French Huguenots, and Moravians (who would become the most successful Protestant missionaries to Native Americans in North America). The European Pietist movement inspired many of these groups and lent its flavor also to several sectarian establishments (for example, the Ephrata community in Pennsylvania) and the growing numbers of German Lutherans. (In the seventeenth century a small colony of Swedish Lutherans had settled in Delaware.)

Native Americans and Slaves

Before the first century of British colonization was over, the diversity that would later flower into American religious pluralism had gained a secure foothold in North America. What had not yet been established, however, was a significant Christian presence among Native Americans and Black slaves in the British colonies. Compared to French efforts among the Native Americans of Canada, English missions were largely ineffectual. The seal of the charter of the Massachusetts Bay Company was emblazoned with the image of an Indian and words the Apostle Paul had heard in a dream from Macedonia, "Come Over and Help Us." But, with exceptions, British contact with the Indians was more a harm than a help to the spread of the faith.

Two early Massachusetts pastors, John Eliot (1604–1690) of Roxborough and Thomas Mayhew, Jr. (1621–1657) of Martha's Vineyard, did make a significant effort at evangelizing Native Americans. Eliot succeeded in gathering a number of converts into "praying towns," which he organized after models provided by the Pentateuch. With the help of several Native Americans, Eliot also translated the bible into Algonquian. On Martha's Vineyard and the nearby islands of Nantucket and Chappaquiddick, Mayhew, his father (when the son died), and other members of the Mayhew family had even more success than Eliot, perhaps because they allowed a little more Indian culture to remain in the Christian civilization they established.

King Philip's War of 1675–1676 proved the undoing of the Indian mission on the mainland. Conversions had been tenuous before then, especially because of the rigidness with which the English missionaries imposed their conceptions of settled order on potential converts. Eliot, for example, held that the Indians must "have visible civility before they can rightly enjoy visible sanctities in ecclesiastical communion." The problem was not racism as such, for John Eliot could be every bit as unbending in treating what he considered sins among his white congregation as in attacking what he saw as barbarism among the Indians. The problem lay rather in an inability to conceive of an "Indian Christianity" as something equal to "English Christianity." This prospect would not be explored until centuries later, especially among the Cherokee in the southeast during the early nineteenth century and in several twentieth-century groups. The result was that when warfare broke out between colonists and Indians in 1675, all Native Americans, including Eliot's converts (and Eliot too) fell under suspicion. The Christianized Indians were quarantined on Deer Island in Boston Harbor, and bad blood colored future attempts at bringing the Christian message to the native Americans. Only on Martha's Vineyard, relatively secure because of its physical distance from the conflict, did considerable numbers of Indians retain their alligiance to the church.

Slaves from Africa were brought to Virginia in 1619. Soon slavery had become a major element in southern ways of life. It was also a major economic factor throughout the colonies, since the slave trade enriched many merchants in New York, Newport, Boston, and other trading centers of the North. At first, virtually no individuals or denominations questioned the propriety of slavery. Only at the end of the seventeenth century did a few Quakers and a small band of German Mennonite immigrants speak out against slavery as a violation. The first known American protest appeared in 1688 from Quakers and Mennonites at Germantown, Pennsylvania. After referring to the biblical principle—"there is a saying that we should do to all men like as we will be done ourselves"—they asked pointedly, "Have these poor negers not as much right to fight for their freedom, as you have to keep them slaves?"[10] But such voices were very few and far between in the first century of British colonization.

From their side, there is scant record of slaves adopting Christianity in this early period. Into the eighteenth century, differences of language and culture, not to speak of the immense barriers erected by the slave system itself, effectively prevented the transmission of Christianity to slaves. The great expansion of Christian belief among black Americans still lay in the future.

What then may we conclude about Christianity in North America after a century or so of British colonization? First, European patterns continued to dominate Christian religious life. Whether Puritan in New England, Anglican in Virginia, Quaker or Mennonite in Pennsylvania, most Christians in British North America sought to find in their religious lives what they had been instructed to find by European religious traditions. Second, the new environment was already working changes in that European deposit. The goal of religious hegemony, even in restricted areas, was harder and harder to achieve. The open environment of the New World was beginning to encourage a larger role for lay people in religious leadership. Early efforts to combine the civilization and Christianization of non-European groups (Native Americans, Blacks) were not particularly successful, but the presence of such groups had already begun to receive serious Christian attention.

Third, although evidence is fragmentary, it does seem that most colonists re-

[10]Lester B. Scherer, *Slavery and the Churches in Early America, 1619–1819* (Grand Rapids, MI: Eerdmans, 1975), p. 42.

mained in contact with traditional forms of Christian faith. Full church membership in the colonies was indeed quite low, never higher than a third of adult New Englanders, perhaps as low as 5 percent of adults in the South. But "adherence," or relatively regular participation in religious activities and churchgoing, seems to have been quite high. Detailed study of diaries, missionary reports back to England, and other fragmentary evidence suggest that in 1700 as many as 80 percent of colonists attended some kind of religious service with some regularity. The situation, then, was the reverse of the more recent situation in the United States where formal church membership, around 60 percent in the 1980s, has been considerably higher than actual church attendance (which stands at roughly 40 percent).

Finally, the distribution of churches reflected the ethnic and denominational heritage of the early settlements. In 1740 three of the four denominations with the most churches were English and Protestant—Congregationalists (423 churches), Anglicans (246), and Baptists (96)—and the fourth was Scottish (or Scotch-Irish) and Protestant—Presbyterians (160). Then came three largely continental groups: Lutherans, largely from Germany (95 churches), the Dutch Reformed (78), and the German Reformed (51). At the time there were twenty-seven Roman Catholic churches, largely in Maryland. A wide scattering of smaller Continental bodies could be found in Pennsylvania and adjoining territories. Alone among American urban centers, New York, with its nine churches in eight denominations, reflected in one place the Christian pluralism that the colonies as a whole were beginning to exhibit.

Chapter 29

THE AMERICANIZATION OF CHRISTIANITY (1720–1820)

During the second century of British colonization, "the American circumstance" began more decisively to shape the character of Christian life and faith. From the early eighteenth century to the early nineteenth, three such circumstances were especially important. First, the loosely connected revivals of the 1730s and 1740s, known as the Great Awakening, gave colonial piety a distinctive American cast. Second, the War for Independence from Great Britain, which attracted the energies and contributions of almost all churches, drew Christianity into an intimate bond with the political life of the new United States. Third, the Christian churches were also chief players in applying the cultural meaning of the American Revolution: What *did* the newly won freedoms couched in the language of republicanism actually mean for day-to-day life? In and through these events the American churches helped define what it meant to be "American," while at the same time what it meant to be "American" had much to do with the development of the churches. Nowhere is it easier to see this interplay between inherited faith and the new national environment than in a comparison between the United States and Canada. Whereas the states marched onto a path of self-government and so defined themselves over against Europe, Canada chose to remain with Britain. As a result, its religious development, although not unaffected by life in the New World, remained much closer to European patterns and so offers a sharp contrast to the development of Christianity in the United States.

To be sure, in the eighteenth century the influence of Europe never slackened throughout North America. Immigration continued from many parts of western Europe. England continued to exert a powerful cultural sway (in fact, intellectual elites in the colonies were becoming more English in their tastes and habits even as they broke from the rule of king and Parliament). And Americans still spoke of religious life in terms largely defined by British and Continental debates, whether

627

formal theology, general conceptions of the church, or practical Christian experience. Yet the situation that Alexis de Tocqueville would describe in the 1830s—with Christianity unusually prominent in America and the principles of America's political self-definition unusually prominent in American Christianity—had begun to emerge several generations before.

A Renewal of Piety

The colonial revival was called a great and general awakening because it touched so many regions and so many aspects of colonial life. Although the Great Awakening represented more a general upsurge of revivalistic piety than a distinct event, it was massively important for both the churches and American society. In New England the revival brought new life to many Congregational churches and greatly stimulated the growth of the Baptists. In the middle colonies the Presbyterians and the Dutch Reformed, after initial divisions over revival practices, ended by growing rapidly because of its emphases. In the southern colonies, which were affected in the last phases of the Awakening, the revival led to new growth for Baptists and began to prepare the way for the great Methodist movement of the postrevolutionary period. The Awakening was made up of local revivals, but it did have two "national" leaders, an English preacher, George Whitefield, and a New England theologian, Jonathan Edwards.

George Whitefield and Jonathan Edwards

George Whitefield (1714–1770) may have been the best-known Protestant in the whole world during the eighteenth century. Certainly he was the best-known religious leader in America of that century and the most widely recognized figure of any sort in North America before George Washington. Whitefield was an ordained minister of the Church of England, who shared membership with John and Charles Wesley in the Holy Club at Oxford during the 1720s and 1730s. Whitefield later introduced the Wesleys to some of the practices that would characterize their Methodist movement, including preaching out-of-doors and aiming the message of salvation at common people with weak ties to the churches. Whitefield visited Georgia briefly in 1738 to aid in the founding of an orphanage. When he returned to the colonies in 1739, his reputation as a dramatic preacher went before him. His visit became a sensation. When he preached in New England during the fall of 1740, Whitefield addressed crowds of up to 8,000 people nearly every day for over a month. (In 1740 the whole population of New England was only 290,000). Whitefield's tour, one of the most remarkable episodes in the whole history of American Christianity, was the key event in New England's Great Awakening. (See Figure 29.1.) Whitefield

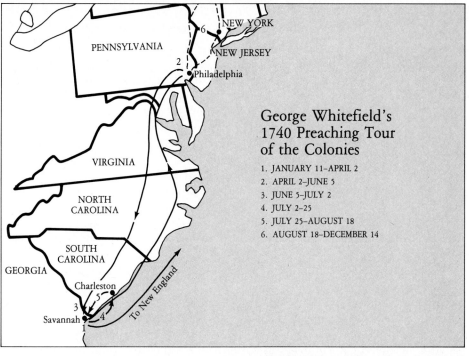

George Whitefield's
1740 Preaching Tour
of the Colonies

1. JANUARY 11–APRIL 2
2. APRIL 2–JUNE 5
3. JUNE 5–JULY 2
4. JULY 2–25
5. JULY 25–AUGUST 18
6. AUGUST 18–DECEMBER 14

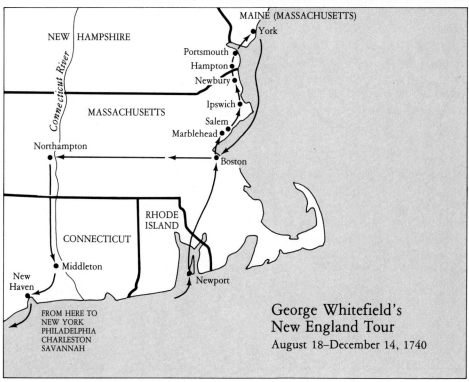

George Whitefield's
New England Tour
August 18–December 14, 1740

FROM HERE TO
NEW YORK
PHILADELPHIA
CHARLESTON
SAVANNAH

Figure 29.1 George Whitefield's Preaching Tour of Colonial America (1740)

returned often to the American colonies, where in 1770 he died as he had wished, in the midst of yet another preaching tour.

Unlike later American revivalists, Whitefield was a Calvinist who stressed the power of God in salvation. He broke with John Wesley over theological matters in 1741, with Wesley holding to a moderate Armininianism that gave more sway to human free will. (Later Wesley and Whitefield were reconciled as friends, though not in theological opinion, and Wesley preached a warm memorial sermon after Whitefield's death.) At the same time, Whitefield was much more interested in preaching than in theology. Although he believed in predestination, election, and other themes of traditional Calvinism, Whitefield confessed in a letter to Wesley early in his career that "I never read anything Calvin wrote; my doctrines I had from Christ and His apostles: I was taught (by) them of God." It was this sense of divine purpose that made him an effective preacher and a model to other aspiring revivalists in America.

Whitefield's greater cultural significance was his innovative approach to the sermon. He was not a good organizer, as the Wesleys were, so those quickened through his preaching found their own ways to Anglican or Methodist congregations in England or to Congregational, Presbyterian, and Baptist churches in America. Whitefield did, however, know how to address plain people in plain language. And he did so much more freely than was customary. He appealed to the heart, he knew how to play on emotions, and he was casual in the extreme about denominational differences. Besides these innovations, he also preached almost all his sermons *ex tempore*, speaking directly without notes and depending on the strength of his own charisma and the force of his message. In all these ways he contributed to the more democratic and popular style of Christianity in America. And these qualities made him a much-respected figure in his own day. Benjamin Franklin, for example, was an admirer of Whitefield, if not necessarily of his message. Franklin, skeptical about reports of great crowds coming out for the traveling preacher, once conducted an experiment during one of Whitefield's sermons out-of-doors in Philadelphia that convinced him that Whitefield could be heard by up to 30,000 people at one time. Many others in America and Britain also had a chance to hear Whitefield, for it is estimated that he preached 15,000 times in a career of thirty-three years.

If Whitefield was the most important preacher of the Great Awakening who inspired many others by his preaching, Jonathan Edwards was the most important apologist for the revival, who set the standard for theology in America for well over a century. Many of Edwards's theological works grew out of his efforts to defend the colonial revivals as real works of God. His sermon, "Sinners in the Hands of an Angry God," preached at Enfield, Connecticut, in 1741, is his best known work, but he expended most of his time and energy preparing more formal studies, including a major examination of revival phenomena published in 1746 as *A Treatise Concerning Religious Affections*. This book argued that true Christianity is not revealed by the quantity or intensity of religious emotions. Rather, true Christianity is manifest when a heart has been changed to love God and seek God's pleasure. After his death, Edwards's friends published his work *The Nature of True Virtue* (1765), which suggested that an experience of God's grace was the only basis of ultimate and long-lasting morality (ordinary human experience could account for ordinary human good-ness, but not for "true virtue").

Earlier, Edwards's book *Freedom of the Will* (1754) presented traditional Calvinistic ideas on the nature of salvation in a powerful new shape. Its basic argument was that the will is not a real entity but an expression of the strongest motive in a person's being. Sinful nature, in other words, cannot want to please God unless God, by an infusion of his grace, changes the sinner's character. Edwards supported the thrust of this work with another book, *Original Sin* (1758). In it he argued that all mankind was present in Adam when he sinned. Consequently, all people share the sinful character and the guilt that Adam brought upon himself.

Jonathan Edwards was a theologian overwhelmed by the majesty and the splendor of the divine. The major themes of his theology were the greatness and glory of God, the utter dependence of sinful humanity on God for salvation, and the supernal beauty of the life of holiness. Edwards was not only a fervent Christian person; he was also a theological genius who studied the best philosophy and science of his day, including both the Platonism of Cambridge philosophers and the new science of Isaac Newton and John Locke, in order to explore the workings of the physical world that he believed God made for his own glory. In later generations, American revivalists were more likely to follow Edwards in appealing for the new birth than were Amer-ican theologians in defending the broadly Calvinistic themes so central to his concern.

Religious Effects of the Revivals

The revivals that Whitefield and Edwards encouraged led, at least for a time, to a rapid increase in the number of people making personal profession of their faith and joining a church. In Connecticut, for which good records remain, an average of eight people had joined each of the colony's congregations each year from 1730 to 1740. But in 1741 and 1742, at the height of the Awakening, the average reached thirty-three a year. Similar rates of growth could be found elsewhere—for example, in the Carolinas as a result of vibrant Baptist preaching in the 1750s.

One must be careful not to claim too much for these statistics, however, for the same church records in Connecticut show that the number of new members declined rapidly in the late 1740s to levels below that of the 1730s. For the whole period 1730 to 1750 in Connecticut, about the same proportion of the population joined the churches through a profession of faith as had joined during the preceding thirty years. And throughout the colonies responses to revival preaching represented surges in formal church membership rather than a whole new wave of members. Accurate information on church membership and attendance is very hard to come by for the colonial period, but it does seem as if both church membership and church "adherence" (i.e., reasonably regular attendance) declined gradually from 1700 to the time of the American Revolution. At the same time, periods of revival, inspired by preachers who imitated Whitefield and interpreted along theological lines suggested by Edwards, measurably strengthened many churches in all colonial regions, especially in those areas closest to the Atlantic.

Numbers, however, tell only part of the story. In communities visited by revival, it became customary for laypeople to gather for prayer, bible reading, and personal exhortation. In Jonathan Edwards's Northampton, Massachusetts, from 1735 through 1742, renewal rolled through the community in a series of waves. The result was a population that at least temporarily set aside personal quarrels, practiced its businesses more diligently and more honestly, and took greater delight in the exercises of religion. Again, it is necessary to observe long-term results to obtain a balanced picture of the awakening. Before the 1740s were over, Jonathan Edwards lost favor with his congregation when he altered the long-standing Northampton practice of allowing all members of the community to participate in the Lord's Supper even if they had not yet joined the church by a profession of faith. Edwards's new proposal, that only the "professedly regenerate" be allowed to take communion, upset some of the town's leading citizens, and after a period of bitter debate, he was dismissed from his pulpit. The dismissal was a blessing in disguise for theology in America, since Edwards spent most of his last years as a pastor to small Indian and white congregations in Stockbridge, Massachusetts, where he was able to give nearly all his time to study and writing.

Also as a result of the revivals, the Christian message came more directly to the downtrodden and despised of society. Some readers still find inspiration in the spiritual diary of David Brainerd (1718–1747), which Jonathan Edwards edited for publication. Brainerd was just one of a number of ardent souls who were led by the revival spirit to become missionaries among the Native Americans. Brainerd's own work with the Delaware of eastern New Jersey was not particularly successful, but other sons of the Awakening like Brainerd's brother John, who also worked among the Delaware, had much more success in bringing religious and humanitarian aid to Native Americans.

The Awakening also stimulated evangelism among slaves, a work in which the Presbyterian Samuel Davies (1723–1761) took an especially important part in Virginia. Whitefield also was concerned about preaching to Black slaves, but in the first generation of leading revivalists, little attention was paid to the institution of slavery itself.

That situation changed when some of the younger followers of Jonathan Edwards themselves became pastors. In particular, they broadened out spiritual notions of the revival concerning the essential dignity of all created beings as ones who shared the "Being" of their Creator (a theme from Edwards's *Nature of True Virtue*). With such notions, a distinct movement of social reform grew from the Awakening. Samuel

Hopkins (1721–1803), who had studied personally with Edwards, eventually spoke out against the practice of slavery in America. By the time of the Revolution, Hopkins had become a minister in Newport, Rhode Island, where he had the chance to view the slave trade firsthand. Increasingly, he came to feel that slavery violated the essential "being" of the kidnapped Africans and that the practice of slave trading made a mockery of Christian efforts to spread the gospel among Blacks. In 1776 he published a pamphlet that he sent to all members of the Continental Congress. How could the Congress complain about "enslavement" from Parliament when it so casually overlooked the real slavery imposed on hundred of thousands of Blacks in America? Hopkins further asked his readers to "behold the *sons of liberty*, oppressing and tyrannizing over many thousands of poor blacks, who have as good a claim to liberty as themselves."[1] In this attack on slavery, Hopkins was joined by other followers of Edwards, like Levi Hart in Connecticut, Jacob Green in New Jersey, and Edward's own son, Jonathan, Jr., a minister in New Haven, Connecticut.

The Awakening also stimulated a greater interest in education, both to prepare ministers to spread the gospel and to train laymen (women did not yet attend college) in a Christian setting for careers in politics, law, medicine, farming, or business. Although links to the revivals were sometimes indirect, several important colleges were founded as a result of its general inspiration—Princeton by Presbyterians in 1746, Brown by Baptists in 1760, Queens (later Rutgers) by the Dutch Reformed in 1764, and Dartmouth in 1769 by Congregationalists with a special interest in providing higher education for Indian converts.

In sum, the series of local revivals known collectively as the Great Awakening stimulated considerable renewal in the American churches. To be sure, they did not halt the general trends of secularization in colonial society, trends that accelerated with great loss to the churches during the trying days of the 1770s and 1780s. Yet they provided new energy, new recruits, new concern for preaching to the unconverted, and new impetus for dealing with marginalized members of society.

The Awakening and America

The revivals of the 1740s and 1750s, along with the general turn to a more pietistic religion, also had significant results for American society more generally. The revival, for instance, was America's first truly national event. Whitefield and his exploits were common matters for discussion from Maine to Georgia. Ministers throughout the colonies corresponded with each other to encourage revival. Similarly, ministers opposed to revivalistic enthusiasm, such as Charles Chauncy of Boston, gathered information from a wide network to bring the movement into discredit. The end

---

[1]Samuel Hopkins, *A Dialogue Concerning the Slavery of the Africans* (Norwich, CT: J. P. Spooner, 1776), p. 30.

result was the same. Events with a local significance were transformed into events linking wider and wider sections of the continent together.

The revivals also served as something of a melting pot to give immigrant communities more contact with other colonists. The career of Gilbert Tennent (1703–1764), a prominent Presbyterian evangelist from New Jersey, shows how the revival joined different groups together. Tennent was born in northern Ireland of Scottish descent, he was trained by his own father in upstate New York, his Presbyterian congregation in New Jersey included some settlers from New England, his preaching tours took him as far away as Piscataqua, Maine, and Hanover County, Virginia, and Tennent's own apprehension of Christianity was influenced by Theodore Frelinghuysen (a German-born, Dutch-educated minister pastoring a church of immigrants from the Netherlands in New Jersey). The process that would lead to European immigrants' identifying themselves as Americans had begun.

The other side of the process that led to greater self-identification as Americans was a propensity to harbor suspicions against Europe. During the Awakening and under its influence in later decades, religious leaders among Dutch, Scottish, and German immigrants came into conflict with European leaders who had not grasped the dynamics of North American piety. As might be expected, sources of tension were most ready to hand against the Church of England, already suspect for its close ties with crown officials. After the Awakening, the Church of England was the focus of even more suspicion because of its indifference to revivals. Especially when the suggestion again rose about a bishop of colonial Anglicans, many colonists were distressed by the prospect of losing religious freedoms practiced during the revivals. Such feelings had more than casual implications when political tensions rose between the colonists and Parliament. Suspicion of the Church of England was one more reason for simply distrusting England.

The Great Awakening also gave more energy to a set of phrases with multiple levels of meaning. Terms such as *liberty*, *virtue*, and *tyranny* were most often applied to spiritual realities during the 1740s and 1750s. In addition, when revivalists and their hearers spoke of the millennium, they mostly had in mind the spread of religious liberation as a result of the spread of Christianity. But the time soon came when, for example, Whitefield's appeal to seek "everlasting Liberty" from "Bondage and Servitude" would take on different shading. It became relatively easy, when the tyrant on the horizon was Parliament rather than sin, to make fruitful use of the capital that these terms had acquired in the revival.

Perhaps most important for later American history, however, was the new model of leadership that emerged during the mid-century revivals. The Awakening was sustained by traveling evangelists; they encouraged lay people to perform religious responsibilities for themselves and not to rely on elite clergy or magistrates. As we noted, Whitefield did not read his sermons like so many ministers of his century but, rather, spoke directly to his hearers. His style drove home the message that it was not formal education or prestige in society that mattered most. Rather, it was the choice of the individual for or against God. Whitefield seems not to have thought about the political implications of such a style. But his form of public speaking and the implicit message of his ministry moved in a democratic direction. Whitefield, as a symbol for a new form of piety, became also an agent for new forms of social order. His ministry represented the sharpest demonstration of a new confidence in the religious powers of the people. Whitefield was a Calvinist who did not believe in natural human capacity to choose God. But he did believe that God's grace made it possible for even the humblest individual to take a place alongside the greatest of the saints. This spirit—a frank expression of popular democracy and the sharpest attack yet on inherited privilege in colonial America—had much to do with the rise of a similar spirit in politics later on.

In light of such connections, one of the most bizarre incidents early in the revolution begins to make more sense. In 1775, colonial troops were mustered near Newburyport, Massachusetts, in preparation for an expedition to Canada. The hope was that a show of force to the North would draw Canadians into the struggle for independence from Britain. Before the troops set out, however, they paused for a sermon from a young chaplain, the Reverend Samuel Spring. After the message, Spring and some of the officers visited a nearby crypt. It was the tomb of George Whitefield, who had died in Newburyport only five years before. Together the minister and officers pried open the coffin and removed the clerical collar and wrist bands from the revivalist's skeleton. Somehow it was thought that the spirit of America's greatest preacher of spiritual freedom would assist them in this struggle for political freedom. Whatever powers the living Whitefield enjoyed, his relics did not work. The expedition ultimately failed. For reasons that receive attention at the end of this chapter, the Canadians were not impressed.

The Churches in the Revolution

Public spokesmen for Christianity played a significant role in promoting the movement for independence from Great Britain in the 1770s, and they rendered great service to the patriot cause during the Revolutionary War itself. Christian leaders commented less directly on public affairs between the end of the conflict with Great Britain in the early 1780s and the reorganization of the United States government under the Constitution at the end of the decade. Yet believers regularly offered moral and religious contributions to the political process during the entire period that witnessed the break from Britain and the establishment of the Constitution. At every stage in that momentous era, American Christians were present, involved, and even in the forefront of promoting an independent United States of America.

Before and during the Revolutionary War, Christian faith played a political role at two levels. It first contributed to the content of the period's dominant political ideology. It was also a significant force in the actual outworking of the war.

Two crises dominated the political history of this era. The first was a crisis of the British Empire and was resolved by the American Revolution. The second was a crisis of government in the new United States and was resolved by the delegates who convened in Philadelphia during the summer of 1787 to write the Constitution. Both crises represented an effort by Americans to preserve the virtues of *republican* government.

Christians and the Christian faith had played a substantial, if ambiguous, role in the shaping of republicanism. In eighteenth-century Britain and America, republicanism was an ideal rather than a sharply defined system. It arose with what could be called the political theorists of the Italian Renaissance, of whom Machiavelli is best known. Republicanism took on a particular British cast during the English civil wars of the seventeenth century. While the Puritan Oliver Cromwell and the armies of Parliament waged war against King Charles I for corrupting and oppressing the English people, theorists struggled to define the way good government related to social well-being.

Republicanism and democracy are not the same. In simple terms, republicanism was the conviction that power defined the political process and that unchecked power led to corruption even as corruption fostered unchecked power. Furthermore, the arbitrary exercise of unchecked power must by its very nature result in the demise of liberty, law, and natural rights. Republicans, therefore, tended to favor separation of power in government rather than its concentration. They usually held that a good government must mix elements of popular influence, aristocratic tradition, and executive authority, rather than be simply democratic, simply aristocratic, or simply monarchical.

Christians contributed their fair share to the formation of republicanism, though that process involved numerous individuals and groups over a long period. The Puritans who supported Cromwell or the Scottish Calvinists who agitated for the independence of their Presbyterian kirk linked republican values with scripture. They felt that republicanism represented a political recognition of the bible's realistic teaching about human sinfulness and the ongoing struggle between Christ (who promoted true liberty) and Satan (who defined the worst possibly tyranny). Others who contributed to the rise of republicanism, however, were deists or agnostics. These included some of Britain's "real Whigs" of the early eighteenth century who had given up traditional Christian faith for a religion of nature with no place for miracles, the Incarnation, or special revelation.

Republicanism was critical for the bond between religion and politics in the revolutionary era because the beliefs of American Christians paralleled republican principles in many particulars. This in turn led to the widespread assumption that republican principles expressed Christian values and that they could be defended with Christian fervor.

The republican and the Puritan traditions shared many formal similarities. In the first place, the Puritan and republican traditions both held to a view of human

636

nature that recognized the human capacity for evil as well as for good. Puritans dwelt at length on the natural tendency toward evil that arose as a consequence of Adam's fall. Republicans dwelt at length on the natural tendency to abuse official power as a consequence of the corrupting nature of power itself.

Puritans and republicans also defined virtue, freedom, and social well-being in very similar terms. Both saw virtue primarily as a negative quality: Puritans as the absence of sin, republicans as the absence of corrupt and arbitrary power. Puritans looked on freedom as liberation from sin, republicans as liberation from tyranny. The Puritans defined a good society as one in which sin was vanquished and in which people stood vigilantly on guard against its reappearance. Similarly, republicans defined a good society as one in which political freedom from tyranny was preserved and in which citizens resolutely resisted any tendencies toward the corruption of power.

With similar views on virtue, freedom, and social well-being, it is not surprising that republican and Christian points of view began to merge during the revolution, especially since a general Puritan influence remained strong in America. It was only a small step, for example, to expand concern for the glorious liberty of the children of God into concern for the glorious freedoms imperiled by Parliament.

Republicans and the heirs of the Puritans also shared a common view of history. Both regarded the record of the past as a cosmic struggle between good and evil. To American Christians good and evil were represented by Christ and the Antichrist; to republicans, by liberty and tyranny. Both republicans and Puritans longed for a new age in which righteousness and freedom would flourish. Both hoped that the revolution would play a role in bringing such a golden age to pass.

A lively tradition of millennialism also helped to forge a link between political freedom and Christian liberty. Millennialism came in many variations, but at its heart was the belief, taken from biblical prophecy (especially the Book of Revelation), that at the end of time there would be a 1,000-year period of triumphant goodness. Then Satan would be "bound," and Christ would rule the entire world. Speculation of this sort had been applied to social and political conditions before. Now it encouraged the notion that the great conflict between God and Satan was somehow being played out in the struggle with Britain, and that a victory over Parliament might signal the near approach of God's rule on earth, the millennium.

Millennial speculation in the revolutionary era fit comfortably with many shades of theology, from Samuel Hopkins's orthodox Calvinism to the biblical Universalism of the Philadelphia minister, Elhanan Winchester. It could be expressed by those who promoted radical restructuring of American society and those who backed a conservative revolution. Throughout the period, millennial speculation remained primarily spiritual. Only in their most heated moments did ministers and lay theologians apply their millennial theories directly to political events. At the same time, during the revolution itself an established tradition of millennialism, hitherto largely apolitical, may have become the most important vehicle for melding evangelical Christianity and republican political theory into the morally charged ideology that fueled the War for Independence. Later on, several varieties of biblical millennialism may have made a more important contribution to the egalitarian ideology of Thomas Jefferson's Democratic-Republican party than is usually recognized.

Republican and Christian points of view began to grow closer together after the French and Indian Wars (1756–1763) when Britain and the Church of England replaced France and Roman Catholicism as the great terrors in colonial eyes. For many Americans, republican and Christian perspectives soon became almost indistinguishable as the crisis with the British Parliament grew more intense.

During the actual conflict, Christian political action played a leading role in the achievement of independence. On the most general level, a broadly Puritan ethic set the tone for the patriots' political exertions. From the Puritan heritage, patriots took a seriousness about the vocation of "public servants," individuals who sacrificed private gain for the public good. The same source provided an example of perseverance in the face of adversity—just as the earliest American settlers had continued to work and trust God when their enterprise was threatened by the forces of nature, so too could patriots labor on and pray when the tide of battle ran against them. Similarly, the Puritan link between personal virtue, the exercise of frugality, and the enjoyment of liberty served as a model for how the same qualities could be joined together in an independent United States. On this level, Christian values shaped political behavior quite generally but still with telling effect.

In other ways Christian political action was more direct. New England preachers had long stressed the special relationship between God and that region. As war approached, many of them cast the conflict with Great Britain in cosmic terms. God had called his people to religious and political freedom in the New World; certainly he would now sustain them as they fought off the tyrannical grasp of Parliament. New England was the scene of the sharpest early tensions with Britain, Boston patriots led in resisting parliamentary efforts to sustain a tax on tea (the Boston Tea Party), and the first actual battles of the war took place in Massachusetts (Lexington and Concord, and Bunker Hill). It was thus of great significance for the whole American effort against Great Britain that a long New England tradition had perceived God as the Lord of Battles actively intervening on behalf of "his people."

Sermons encouraging a defense of political liberty, however, were by no means restricted to New England. Presbyterians in New Jersey and the South preached a similar message, as did representatives of the Baptists and other smaller denominations. Even some clergymen of the Church of England, contradicting the official stance of their denomination, denounced the tyranny of Parliament.

The services of religion to the patriot cause were great and multiform. Ministers preached rousing sermons to bands of militia as they met for training or embarked for the field. Many ministers served as chaplains. Clergy joined Christian laymen on the informal committees of correspondence that preceded the formation of new state governments. Other ministers served gladly as traveling agents of the new governments, which wanted them to win the support of settlers in outlying areas to the patriot cause. Throughout the conflict, common soldiers were urged to their duty by the repeated assertion that Britain was violating divine standards.

This direct political activity of Christians had consequential results. Opponents recognized the importance of the Christian element immediately. A Hessian captain wrote of his experiences in Pennsylvania, "Call this war . . . by whatever name you may, only call it not an American Rebellion, it is nothing more or less than an Irish-Scotch Presbyterian Rebellion."[2] Joseph Galloway, a moderate opponent of Parliament who eventually chose loyalty to Great Britain over colonial independence, wrote that the colonial insurrection was led by "Congregationalists, Presbyterians, and Smugglers."[3] From the patriot side the connotations were different, but the message was largely the same. John Adams (thinking of their clerical gowns) called the New England clergy a "Black Regiment" that provided critical support in winning the war.

Loyalists and Pacifists

Not all Christians in America supported the push toward independence so completely, or even supported it at all. A substantial number remained loyal to Great Britain. Throughout the colonies, especially in Pennsylvania, the population also included many Christian pacifists who felt both sides were wrong to take up arms.

Somewhere between a fifth and a third of the colonists either remained loyal to Great Britain during the War for Independence or harbored Loyalist sentiments of some sort. Among these were many individuals who felt a religious duty to remain faithful to the mother country. The most visible spokesmen for a Christian loyalism were members of the Church of England, but at least a few Loyalists could also be found among Congregationalists, Presbyterians, and Baptists (mostly cultural conservatives who thought the revolution would drift into anarchy), and even Roman Catholics (some of whom were grateful for the relative toleration they enjoyed in the New World). Loyalist arguments sometimes stressed a different understanding of the bible than that which the patriots displayed. Jonathan Boucher, an Anglican minister in Maryland, for example, preached a sermon in 1775 entitled, "On Civil Liberty, Passive Obedience, and Nonresistance." His text was Galatians 5:1, which speaks of "the liberty wherewith Christ hath made us free." Boucher denied that this verse justified political self-determination but argued instead that the New Testament taught clearly that "Obedience to Government is every man's duty . . . it is

---

[2] Leonard J. Kramer, "Muskets in the Pulpit, 1776–1783," in *Journal of the Presbyterian Historical Society* 31 (December 1953), p. 320.

[3] Leonard J. Kramer, "Presbyterians Approach the American Revolution," in *Journal of the Presbyterian Historical Society* 31 (September 1953), p. 176.

enjoined by the positive commands of God."[4] Other Anglican Loyalists worried more generally about what would happen to religious life and the orders of society supported by religion if the revolution should prevail. Miles Cooper, the president of King's College (later Columbia University) expressed such a sentiment after the fighting had begun: "When once [the People] conceive the governed to be superior to the Governors and that they may set up their pretended Natural Rights in Opposition to the positive law of the state, they will naturally proceed to despise dominion and speak evil of dignities and to open a door for Anarchy, confusion, and every evil work to enter."[5]

The several groups of Christian pacifists in the colonies joined the Loyalists in questioning the American recourse to arms but went beyond them to criticize all resort to military coercion. The most vocal pacifists during the war were the Quakers, but these sentiments were shared also by Mennonites, Moravians, and members of the Church of the Brethren. Where pacifists lived together in fairly large communities, they were usually able to work out some kind of peaceful agreement with the new patriotic authorities to avoid military service. But where pacifists were isolated, or where they refused to submit payment in lieu of military duty, they were sometimes forced to pay large fines or to forfeit their property. Despite unfriendly treatment from both Loyalists and patriots, pacifists several times offered notable service to prisoners, to soldiers wounded in battle, or to refugees from the fighting. The Philadelphia Quaker, Anthony Benezet, was the most outspoken public critic of warfare during America's struggle for independence. A tract published in 1778, for example, stated his position with great economy: "[Christ] positively enjoins us, to love our enemies, to bless them that curse us; to do good to those that hate us, and pray for them which despitefully use and persecute us. . . . On the other hand, War requires of its votaries that they kill, destroy, lay waste, and to the utmost of their power distress and annoy, and in every way and manner deprive those they esteem their enemies of support and comfort."[6]

The record of Christian Loyalists and pacifists during the Revolutionary War is instructive. Not only does it offer an alternative voice on warfare itself. It also testifies to the plurality of Christian positions that were present even at a time when one sentiment (the patriots') seemed to prevail so widely.

The Faith of the Founders

The relationship of Christianity to the founding of the United States goes beyond what the churches did in the revolution. Also relevant is the factor of what Chris-

---

[4]Jonathan Boucher, *A View of the Causes and Consequences of the American Revolution* (London: G.G. and J. Robinson, 1797), pp. 503–506.
[5]Raymond W. Albright, *A History of the Protestant Episcopal Church* (New York: Macmillan, 1964), p. 116.
[6]Anthony Benezet, *Some Considerations on Several Important Subjects* (Philadelphia: Joseph Crukshank, 1778), p. 2.

tianity meant to the leading patriots, the men who founded the new nation. On this matter, it is important to advance with care. Most of the leading founders were in fact sincerely religious. At the same time, the most important of their number practiced decidedly nontraditional forms of religion that did not conform to traditional Christian patterns. In addition, even the more traditional Christians among the founders do not seem to have viewed the crisis with Britain as a cause for special religious reflection. It was, rather, a political struggle to be adjudicated by natural political axioms, not by the special insights of faith.

To be sure, a number of the leading patriots were also well known as Christian leaders. Among signers of the Declaration of Independence, John Witherspoon (president of Princeton College) was a Presbyterian clergyman who had won a reputation in his native Scotland as a defender of evangelical Protestantism. Roger Sherman of Connecticut was a faithful member of the Congregational church pastored by Jonathan Edwards, Jr. Both John Jay of New York, an important diplomat and the first chief justice of the Supreme Court, and Patrick Henry of Virginia, famous for his "Liberty or Death" speech before the war, were low-church Anglicans whose personal faith could be characterized as evangelical. Elias Boudinot of New Jersey, who carried out important civilian tasks for General Washington during the war and who played an important part in the early national legislature, was a dedicated Christian layman who eventually came to devote almost all his time and energy to the promotion of Christian causes, including his service as first president of the American Bible Society. The presence of these patriots and a few more like them suggest that faithful believers played no small role in the founding of the new nation.

At the same time, however, the leading founders were much less traditional in their religion. Benjamin Franklin appreciated a good sermon and had an especially warm spot in his heart for George Whitefield. But for Franklin, Jesus was a model for humility rather than God's incarnate Son. If humans were to improve, Franklin thought, they would pretty much have to do it for themselves. George Washington served faithfully on the vestry of his local Anglican parish, but his faith was mostly a social convention. In the words of a recent biographer, Marcus Cunliffe: "He was a Christian as a Virginia planter understood the term. He seems never to have taken communion; he stood to pray, instead of kneeling; and he did not invariably go to church on Sundays."[7] Thomas Jefferson was a deeply religious man who late in life contributed money to bible societies. But he was also a freethinker who considered New England Congregationalists dangerous dogmatists and who twice edited the New Testament to take out the parts testifying to the deity of Christ, his resurrection, or the Trinity (the "*deliria* of crazy imaginations," Jefferson called such notions). James Madison, always an intensely private person, remained to study theology with John Witherspoon after he finished his undergraduate course at Princeton. But Madison also expressed utmost distaste for any religious belief that upset public peace

---

[7]Marcus Cunliffe, *George Washington: Man and Monument* (New York: NAL, 1958).

in any way. Although he defended religious liberty to the hilt, his own religion seems to have been cool, detached, and very much his own affair.

The God of the Founding Fathers was a distant deity, more like the God of eighteenth-century deism or nineteenth-century Unitarians than of the early Puritans or later American revivalists. This God had made the world an orderly and understandable place. He was "nature's God," as the Declaration of Independence put it, who had created humankind with nearly infinite potential. The men who put the nation together were sincere moralists and great humanitarians. They were entirely convinced that human exertion and goodwill could make America into a nearly ideal place, perhaps even a millennial place. What Daniel Boorstin, formerly Librarian of Congress, once wrote about Jefferson and his friends applies more generally to most of the Founders: They had found in God what they most admired in humanity. In short, the religious views of the founders were quite different from those of America's sincerest Christians of the period. But unlike the revolutionary situation in France a few years later, there were still enough shared morality and common political values between traditional believers and Enlightenment deists to establish a common national tradition.

The Founders were a noble group. Many of their actions were clearly compatible with traditional Christian values. Some of those actions on the other hand, like the continuation of racial chattel slavery in a "free" United States, were incompatible with those values.

The Religious Problem of Slavery in the American Revolution

From the very beginning of agitation against Britain for American "freedom," at least a few Christians sensed a great hypocrisy. How was it that so much moral indignation could flow against Britain for the threat of "slavery" suggested (perhaps) by Parliamentary actions (often misguided, even stupid, but rarely deliberately malicious) when white Americans calmly continued to enslave hundreds of thousands of Black Africans? Founding Fathers such as Thomas Jefferson may have been secretly troubled by such a question. To the extent that a protest existed at this time, it was mounted by religious leaders, however. The arguments that Samuel Hopkins and other followers of Jonathan Edwards directed to the Continental Congress on slavery were echoed by abolitionist actions from other Christian leaders, including Methodists Francis Asbury, James O'Kelly, Freeborn Garrettson, and William McKendree; Presbyterians Jacob Green and David Rice; Baptist David Barrow; and the poet and publicist Thomas Branagan.

After Christian antislave agitation had begun to die down, two Christian veterans of the revolutionary struggle paused to regret their part in enshrining slavery in the Constitution. John Jay of New York and Elias Boudinot of New Jersey had both been active in the effort to secure passage of the Constitution. In addition, both shared an active Christian faith that led them to promote a wide variety of mission and reform activities. In 1819 Boudinot sent Jay a brochure describing the work of a New Jersey antislave society. Jay responded by ruminating on the clause in the Constitution that spoke of the enslaved as "other persons" to be counted as three-fifths of a person for the sake of congressional representation. Jay confessed sadly that "the word *slaves* was avoided, probably on account of the existing toleration of slavery, and of its discordancy with the principles of the Revolution; and from a consciousness of its being repugnant to . . . the Declaration of Independence."[8]

What John Jay and others could see clearly enough as whites was even more sharply etched in the perception of Blacks. The principles of America's founding documents, just as the principles of Christianity, could be put to use for human liberation, but they also could easily be twisted to justify the status quo between masters and slaves. It was an exslave, Frederick Douglass, who perhaps best captured the hypocrisy, for both national and religious principles, in a memorable address from 1852. It was given on Independence Day to the Ladies Anti-Slavery Society of Rochester, New York. It was a vision of America's founding in relation to religion that few of the whites in attendance had ever faced before.

> What, to the American slave, is your 4th of July? I answer; a day that reveals to him, more than all other days in the year, the gross injustice and cruelty to which he is the constant victim. . . . You boast of your love of liberty, your superior civilization and your pure Christianity, while the whole political power of the nation . . . is solemnly pledged to support and perpetuate the enslavement of three millions of your countrymen. . . . You can bare your bosom to the storm of British artillery to throw off a three-penny tax on tea; and yet wring the last hard-earned farthing from the grasp of the black laborers of your country. You profess to believe 'that, of one blood, God made all nations of men to dwell on the face of all the earth' [Acts 17:26], and hath commanded all men, everywhere, to love one another; yet you notoriously hate (and glory in your hatred) all men whose skins are not colored like your own. . . . The existence of slavery in this country brands your republicanism as a sham, your humanity as a base pretense, and your Christianity as a lie.[9]

Douglass's message was a painful one. He was pointing out that in the history of nations as well as in the history of the Christian church, the noblest ideals are not able by themselves to overcome the human bent to self-serving moral blindness.

[8]Philip B. Kurland and Ralph Lerner, eds. *The Founders' Constitution*, Vol. III (Chicago: University of Chicago Press, 1987), p. 298.
[9]Philip S. Foner, ed., *The Life and Writings of Frederick Douglass*, Vol. II (New York: International, 1950), pp. 192, 200–201.

The Revolution in the Churches

The third major "circumstance" of the eighteenth century that, after the Great Awakening and the War for Independence, did so much to make Christianity more American was the aftermath of the revolution. At issue was how the church would adjust to the political freedom from England, but even more how they would adjust to the ideology of democratic republicanism that had undergirded the war with England. The answer involved formal arrangements of church and state, new aspirations among "the people," and far-reaching changes in religious thought.

The Separation of Church and State

The First Amendment to the United States Constitution, with its provision that "Congress shall make no law respecting an establishment of religion, or prohibiting the free exercise thereof," took effect in 1791. At the time, five of the nation's fourteen states (Vermont had joined the Union in 1791) provided for tax support of ministers, and those five plus seven others had continued religious tests for state office. Only Virginia and Rhode Island enjoyed the sort of separation of church and state that Americans now take for granted, that is, where government provides no tax money for churches and poses no religious conditions for participation in public life. With less than a handful of exceptions, even the defenders of religious liberty in Rhode Island and Virginia did not object when Congress or the president proclaimed national days of prayer, when the federal government began its meetings with prayer, or when military chaplains were appointed and funded by law.

In light of these conditions, a natural question is how the First Amendment came to coexist with what, from a modern vantage point, looks like a thorough intermingling of religion and state. The answer involves matters of principle and of practical concerns. As part of the era's great fears about the potential for governmental tyranny, more and more Americans came to affirm that religion was a matter of conscience between God and the individual and should be exempt from the meddling of government at any level. A growing number also spoke out much more strongly for the spiritual need to separate church and state. Such a one was the leader of New England's Baptists, Isaac Backus (1724–1806). During the revolution, which he supported, Backus asked Massachusetts and Connecticut why they maintained establishments of religion that forced Baptists and other non-Congregationalists to support forms of Christianity that these others conscientiously opposed. If the colonists were fighting Britain for liberty, Backus asked, why do the colonies themselves not grant religious liberty to their own residents?

More practically, the possibility of establishing a national government seemed increasingly to hinge on leaving religious matters with the states. At both the Constitutional Convention and the first Congress, which was responsible for the First

Amendment, leaders like James Madison realized both how explosive and how complicated the question of religion was. Any effort to establish one particular faith would have drawn violent protests from adherents to other denominations. Any effort to deny the importance of religion would have deeply offended the substantial numbers who still believed that the health of a nation depended on the health of its faith. The compromise chosen by the Founding Fathers was to disengage the issue. If they were going to have a Constitution for all the people, they somehow were going to have to get the government out of the religion business. By leaving such matters to the states, it was hoped, they could establish a government for the nation without being forced to decide what the nation's religion should be.

At the same time, however, the colonial background of all the new states was so overwhelmingly Protestant that it was simply assumed that Sunday legislation, laws prohibiting atheism and promoting public morals, as well as the regular use of Christian language by governmental officials were appropriate. The distance between the new United States and our modern period is suggested by the fact that during the Constitutional period Catholics and Jews protested against the form, but not the existence, of religious tests for office-holding in the states. When the new state constitution in Pennsylvania required legislatures to "acknowledge the Scriptures of the old and new Testaments to be given by divine inspiration," the Philadelphia Synagogue protested by noting that "Jews are as fond of liberty as their religious societies can be."[10] In the light of such protests, it was becoming very difficult to see how religious tests of any sort could accompany the determined promotion of "freedom."

On the related question of how religion in general might come to bear on public life, the Founders were divided. What Thomas Jefferson thought the First Amendment meant is well known. As he put it to the Danbury Baptist Association in 1802, there was to be "a wall of separation between Church and State." Jefferson also felt that debate over the famous Virginia Statute for Religious Freedom in 1785 formed the essential background to the First Amendment, and that the Virginia Statute was consciously written to guarantee full participation in public life on equal terms, as he put it, by "the Jew and the Gentile, the Christian and Mahometan, the Hindoo, and Infidel of every denomination."[11]

Other founders interpreted the words differently. In 1812 Joseph Story at age thirty-two became the youngest judge ever to be appointed to the Supreme Court. Over the course of his lengthy tenure on the bench (1812–1845) he was John Marshall's right hand in defining the role of the court itself and its jurisdiction over state and national laws. Story's influential 1833 commentary on the First Amendment showed how he read the Founders' intent. He began by asserting that "the promulgation of the great doctrines of religion . . . [can] never be a matter of indifference

[10]Kurland and Lerner, *The Founders' Constitution*, Vol. IV, p. 635.
[11]Kurland and Lerner, *The Founders' Constitution*, Vol. V, pp. 96, 85.

to any well ordered community." "A republic" in particular required "the Christian religion, as the great basis, on which it must rest for its support and permanence." The First Amendment therefore allowed "Christianity . . . to receive encouragement from the state, so far as was not incompatible with the private rights of conscience, and the freedom of religious worship." Moreover, "the whole power over the subject of religion is left exclusively to the state governments," but to the end that "the Catholic and the Protestant, the Calvinist and the Arminian, the Jew and the Infidel, may sit down at the common table of the national councils, without any inquisition into their faith, or mode of worship."[12]

James Madison, the individual most influential in the drafting of both the Constitution and the First Amendment, offered an interpretation more like Jefferson's. On the basis of the First Amendment as well as the general principles of the Constitution, Madison opposed public payment for chaplains in Congress and the military, spoke out against national proclamations of days of prayer (though as president he did "recommend" them), and while president vetoed congressional efforts to incorporate churches in the District of Columbia. At the same time, Madison frequently opined that it was appropriate for private citizens to support chaplains and other kinds of semiorganized public religion through voluntary contributions.

Whose "intention" among the Founders defines the real "meaning" of the First Amendment? On particular questions, it is difficult to say, but on general matters there was agreement. None of the Founders interpreted the First Amendment as prohibiting religiously grounded arguments for general public policies. Nor did they seem to worry about incidental benefits accruing to religious institutions from government measures designed for the benefit of all citizens. On the other hand, they also clearly indicated their belief that the federal government could not support religion in general without edging toward the legal establishment of something like a church.

A New Era of Democracy

The American Revolution stimulated social changes almost as dramatic as the political changes it brought about. As much as the winds of war offered a marvel to the world—an upstart band of provincials defying the greatest power in western civilization—even more did the libertarian spirit—self-evident truths, inalienable rights, the equal creation of all—harvest a democratic whirlwind at home. Historian Nathan Hatch has succinctly noted that the two generations after 1776 witnessed a "cultural ferment over the meaning of freedom."[13] What was true for America at large was no less true for its Christian churches.

---

[12]Ibid., pp. 108–110.
[13]Nathan O. Hatch, *The Democratization of American Christianity* (New Haven: Yale University Press, 1989), p. 6.

The new prominence given to "the sovereignty of the people" no doubt had something to do with the gradual decline of Calvinism and its insistence on the jealous sovereignty of God. The revival spirit that would transform the American landscape in the early decades of the nineteenth century also drew on the spirit of the Revolution. Revivalists called on individuals to exert themselves for God. They found traditional church structures largely irrelevant. They encouraged the formation of *ad hoc* voluntary societies to reform the nation. The revival became the dominant religious force in American Protestantism and an underappreciated infuence among American Catholics, in part because it was so effective in winning the unaffiliated, but also because it so effectively expressed the country's democratic spirit.

The social changes of the revolutionary period had much to do with a universal passion for liberty. Restraint—whether political from a corrupt Parliament, ecclesiastical from denominational traditions, or professional from the special prerogatives of lawyer, minister, physician—was everywhere a cause for resentment. A Presbyterian minister in 1781 put it bluntly: "This is a time in which civil and religious liberty is attended to. . . . It is a time in which a spirit of liberty prevails, a time in which the externals of religion may properly be new modeled, if needful, and fixed upon a gospel plan."[14]

One of the things this passion for liberty affected most was bible reading. So many new denominations sprang to life in America between the War for Independence and the Civil War—Disciples of Christ, and "Christians" of several varieties, Adventists, Mormons, Cumberland Presbyterians, offshoots of the Methodists, and more—in large part because there were so many unfettered interpretations of scripture. Americans in the early nineteenth century took to an earlier battle cry of the Reformation, "the Bible alone," with a vengeance. The result was a blend of Christian fervor and democratic fragmentation.

This blend brought a Christian message adapted to the shape of American social realities to a wide circle of the previously unchurched. Leaders of the Restoration Movement, for example, like Barton Stone, or Thomas and Alexander Campbell, sought to roll back what they perceived as the corruptions of the centuries to restore the purities of primitive Christianity. Their message in addition, however, was thoroughly imbued with an American spirit. Barton Stone wrote as an old man that "from my earliest recollection I drank deeply into the spirit of liberty, and was so warmed by the soul-inspiring draughts, that I could not hear the name of British, or Tories, without feeling a rush of blood through the whole system."[15] When he and his followers broke with the Presbyterians of Kentucky, he called the move their "declaration of independence." For his part, Alexander Campbell, in an effort to encourage the hearts of his "Christian" followers, would one day write that July 4,

[14]Jacob Green, *A View of a Christian Church and Church Government* (Chatham, N.J.: Shepard Kollock, 1781), p. 56.
[15]Nathan Hatch, *Democratization of American Christianity*, pp. 70–71.

1776, was "a day to be remembered as with the Jewish Passover. . . . This revolution, taken in all its influences, will make men free indeed."[16] The Disciples of Christ, the Christian churches, and the Churches of Christ founded by these leaders effectively evangelized America because they had translated the Christian message into an indigenous American idiom. Their adjustment of the Christian message to the themes of the revolution's ideology also characterized many leaders in more traditional groups as well.

Theology in an American Key

The themes of the American Revolution also marked a crucial turning in religious thought. They led to the establishment of a Christianized form of the Enlightenment as the dominant intellectual force in the country. Almost all Americans, to be sure, repudiated skeptical or radical forms of the European Enlightenment. The philosophical doubts of Scotland's David Hume or the sneers at religion from the French savant Voltaire found little sympathy in the new nation. Yet important principles of the Enlightenment, as these had been refined especially by great Scottish thinkers of the eighteenth century, came to exert a near universal domination in America.

Following the lead of such eighteenth-century Scottish philosophers as Francis Hutcheson and Thomas Reid, Americans became "realists" in questions of ethics and knowledge. That is, they defended the ability of human common sense to grasp accurately the genuine structure of the world, whether the world revealed by our physical senses or the moral world revealed by our "moral sense" (or conscience). Americans in general had great faith in the ability of human reason, unaided by experts, tradition, or religious institutions, to perceive reality. In addition, they believed that an appeal to reason could provide adequate defenses for morality and for public order. They were convinced that the scientific triumphs of Sir Isaac Newton could be repeated in epistemology, ethics, jurisprudence, and other spheres if only practitioners in those fields could be as rigorous as Newton had been in his scientific work. Although earlier theological emphases did not disappear entirely in this new intellectual orientation, much from former days was set aside because of its influence. For example, most Americans who thought about such things in the wake of the revolution no longer held with the Puritans that a revelation from God was the first necessity in understanding life (instead, it was important to show that a rigorous, "scientific" chain of reasoning demonstrated the truth of revelation). Again, most had moved beyond Jonathan Edwards's belief that the inclinations of the heart infallibly determined human choices. Instead, our own self-consciousness showed us that we were free to choose between various inclinations that might compete within

[16]Ibid., p. 71.

648

us. This new intellectual system, often called Scottish Common Sense Realism, was widely shared. Jefferson put it to use in writing the Declaration of Independence, Madison called on it to argue for the Constitution, and the leading educators of America's colleges used it to structure their curricula.

What makes this system of thought so important for the history of Christianity is that most of the leading thinkers in America's most visible Protestant churches embraced some variety of Scottish Common Sense for expressing their own views. The Scottish Presbyterian John Witherspoon had brought philosophical Common Sense with him as the new president of Princeton College in 1768. At Princeton such ideas would flourish for over a century, with Witherspoon and his successors at the college and with the first generation of theologians at the Presbyterian seminary founded at Princeton in 1812. Other religious leaders soon adapted it for their own uses as well, including Congregationalists Timothy Dwight at Yale College and Nathaniel W. Taylor at Yale Divinity School, Unitarians Henry Ware, Sr., and Henry Ware, Jr,. at Harvard, Baptist Francis Wayland at Brown, Alexander Campbell of the Disciples, as well as many others.

For most of these leading religious thinkers, it was the American Revolution that cemented the bond between Protestant theology and the philosophy of Scottish Common Sense Realism. The ethics of Francis Hutcheson had provided a solid moral basis for resisting British tyranny (it was self-evident "common sense," he wrote, that a distant mother country should not exercise absolute rule over a colony, when the colony became populous and economically self-sufficient). In addition, when the patriotic fear of Old World political traditions broadened out into a more general fear of Old World traditions in all areas, Christians in America needed new ways to defend their own faith. No longer would it do to appeal blindly to authority or to affirm that religious practice had always been done a certain way. American believers shared fears about Old World corruptions, but they still wanted to rescue Christianity itself and conceptions of social order allied with Christianity from the revolutionary assault on tradition. The Scottish philosophy of Common Sense provided an ideal way to defend the traditional faith without needing to rely on discredited European traditions. With such a system, Christian apologists could appeal to the beliefs they thought were common to all human minds—that, for example, a First Cause had brought the world into existence, or that individual moral judgments presuppose a Perfect Morality. From these axioms of the mind, then, sound arguments could be found for more traditional Christian beliefs. The result was that as American Christians called on principles of the philosophy of Common Sense to defend their faith and promote social order, they were able to keep in step with more general national feelings about personal liberty, self-determination, and the need for all men (and soon women too) to think for themselves.

The changes wrought in theology by this accommodation to the ideology of the revolution were subtle but far-reaching, but they did not affect all groups the same.

A number of German-speaking bodies, for example, continued to stress ideals of personal piety and community cohesion that they had brought with them from Europe. These included the Moravians, the Church of the Brethren (or Dunkers, so-called because of their practice of threefold, face-forward baptism), the Mennonites, and to some extent the German Reformed. Where these ethic communions were concentrated, as in Pennsylvania, American theology retained more the flavor of European piety than of the American Enlightenment.

Developments among the theologians of New England, on the other hand, were more closely watched at the time because of that region's leadership in the nation's intellectual life. They illustrate clearly the changes associated with the eighteenth century's major theological shifts. Jonathan Edwards's own students, Joseph Bellamy and Samuel Hopkins, writing during the revolutionary period with its concerns for fairness in government and self-responsibility in citizens, talked of God as "the infinitely wise and good Governor of the world" and concluded that humans suffer the penalty of only their own sins, not those supposedly inherited from Adam. A generation later, Timothy Dwight at Yale, at a time still preoccupied with the dangers of unregulated power, defined God's sovereignty in terms palatable to a republican environment. God rules, wrote Dwight, "by motives, addressed to the understanding and affections of rational subjects, and operating on their minds, as inducements to voluntary obedience. No other government is worthy of God: there being, indeed, no other, beside that of mere force and coercion."[17] At Princeton, Dwight's contemporary, Samuel Stanhope Smith, used principles of Common Sense Philosophy to defend the unity of humanity against suggestions from Europe that the different races might indicate a plural origin for human begins. To Smith, these notions were repugnant, not primarily because they contradicted the bible, but because it was necessary for all people to learn common moral principles from studying their own moral natures if there was to be any hope for a well-ordered society or any hope for arguing toward the specific truths of Christianity.

In the next generation, a host of capable theologians carried on these themes. N. W. Taylor at Yale, Edwards Amasa Park at Andover Theological Seminary, Charles Hodge at Princeton Theological Seminary, and J. H. Thornwell from South Carolina might debate fiercely with each other on major theological questions. But what they shared—as believers in the ability of common sense to provide an underpinning for more specific religious beliefs—was every bit as important as the matters over which they differed.

Changes in religious thought brought about by the revolution did not change Christianity in its essence, but they did lead to major adjustments. A country convinced of the innate capacities of the individual naturally preferred a theology with at least modest curbs on the all-encompassing power of God.

---

[17]Timothy Dwight, *Theology: Explained and Defended, Vol. I* (Middletown, CT: 1818), p. 182.

Another Way: Colonial Canada

Nothing draws into sharper relief the changes worked in American Christianity by the revolution than a comparison with Canada. For a number of reasons, Christianity in Canada has had a different history from that of the states. But one of the most important reasons is that, as noted earlier, the colonies to the north chose to remain loyal to the mother country whereas the thirteen from New Hampshire to Georgia broke away.

Many elements in Canada's early Christian history are similar to those in the states. A diversity of early settlements eventually came under the control of Britain. European forms of religious practice and belief were imported to the New World, where they underwent a process of accommodation to the new environment. Protestant denominations of British background were the major shapers of Canadian religious life during the period before the region gained dominion status as part of the British Empire in 1867. Significant as these similarities were, the differences were even more important.

The first major difference was the entrenched position of the Roman Catholic church in the province of Quebec. During its early history, Canada was divided roughly into thirds. Beginning in the east, the Atlantic provinces of Nova Scotia, New Brunswick, Prince Edward Island, and Newfoundland were populated thinly and late. Once settlement occurred, there was a measure of religious diversity. Lower Canada, or Quebec, was and is overwhelmingly Catholic. Even after Britain triumphed in the French and Indian War and took control of Quebec, the Catholic church remained the dominant religious presence in that region. Further west in Upper Canada, or Ontario, British Protestant denominations, especially the Church of England, prevailed from the start.

The presence of a large and active Catholic enclave between the Protestant Atlantic provinces and Protestant Ontario made Canada religiously pluralistic from the start. When the French ceded Quebec to Britain by treaty in 1763, there were 180 priests in the province. To secure its control of Quebec, Britain chose to accommodate itself to Catholicism, even though Catholics in Great Britain would continue to suffer civil handicaps well into the next century. Britain's mildness with religion in Quebec even became a stimulus to the American Revolution. The Quebec Act of 1774 granted the Catholic citizens of Quebec full citizenship and the right to hold public office. It also allowed the church to continue the European practice of collecting a tithe from its members. To some ardent anti-Catholics in the lower colonies, these measures seemed to prove Britain's eagerness to promote tyranny, since nothing wsa more obvious to America's strictest Protestants than that the Catholic church was a foe of liberty. Given these sentiments in the southern colonies, it is little wonder that Quebec looked very coldly on the suggestion from the Continental Congress that it join the revolution against Britain. Nor is it surprising that thousands of individuals loyal to Great Britain would migrate to Canada from the new United States.

The presence of a major Catholic province in Canada situated between Ontario and the Maritimes also restricted communications and fellowship between the two Protestant regions. In the Atlantic provinces, a thin Anglican settlement was disrupted by an active revival in the 1770s and 1780s. Led by a preacher of great spiritual energy, Henry Alline, the Atlantic provinces rapidly developed a revivalistic tradition. These provinces also provided a home for many other groups as well, including Baptists of several kinds, Presbyterians, German Reformed, Methodists, Lutherans, Quakers, Moravians, and eventually many Roman Catholics. In Ontario, Methodism grew rapidly toward the end of the eighteenth century when strong ties developed between Methodists in Canada and in the states. The War of 1812, however, disrupted those connections. As in the previous conflict with Great Britain, Canadians as a whole wanted nothing to do with armed struggle against their mother country. As a result, the Methodists and most other Protestant groups developed independently from their American cousins, at least until the twentieth century.

Differences between Christianity in Canada and the United States are just as evident in cultural areas as in demography. Almost all Canadian churches throughout the nineteenth century remained closer to their European roots than did churches in the United States. Morever, in comparison with the states, Canadian Christianity tended to be, in the words of historian Robert Handy, "more cautious, traditional, and church-oriented." Nineteenth-century Canadians did not feel, as many did to the south, that God had singled out their country in a unique way. Very few Canadian believers felt that it was necessary to revise inherited ways to accommodate the spirit of either the American or the French Revolutions. And since a republican fear of governmental tyranny was conspicuous by its absence, very few Canadians worried about the separation of church and state. Controversy did arise in the 1830s over the use of income from public land designated as "clergy reserves." But the issue was more over sharing that income among the denominations than about its propriety as such. The general Canadian solution to church-state issues was to guarantee rights of minorities over against the majority, rather than to do away with all governmental support for reilgious institutions. Finally, though Canada was huge in extent, it simply did not at first have the great number of Christian denominations that had come to exist in the states by the early nineteenth century. In 1842, out of a total population of under 2.5 million, Canada had only four denominations with a considerable population: Catholics (640,000), Church of England (150,000), Presbyterians (130,000), and Methodists (100,000). With 20,000 adherents, the Baptists were the largest of the smaller bodies.

In a word, when we set Canadian religious history beside that of the United States, the chief contrast lies between the revolution that altered the shape of Christianity in the states with the revolution that did not take place to the north.

The fortitude with which Father Jean Brebeuf and his fellow Jesuit missionaries met their deaths in 1648 awed their Indian captors and has been a treasured memory in French Canada ever since. (National Archives of Canada [Neg. No. C 73709])

The Pilgrims who embarked from Holland on a journey that would eventually lead to Plymouth in the New World were in fact almost as laudably pious as they appear in this picture. (Architect of the Capitol)

William Penn, who offered unusual religious freedom to Pennsylvania's first settlers, also thought it was a religious duty to establish cordial relations with native Americans. (Library of Congress)

George Whitefield (1714–1770) (Library of Congress)

Charles Grandison Finney (1792–1875) (Library of Congress)

Billy Sunday (1862–1935) (Library of Congress)

Martin Luther King, Jr. (1929–1968) (Library of Congress)

The spellbinding "man of God" has been a fixture in American religious life. George Whitefield was the prototype, Charles Finney the embodiment of zeal in the years before the Civil War, Billy Sunday the best known preacher at the turn of the century, and Martin Luther King, Jr., a voice of conscience for all America in the 1950s and 1960s.

Christian connections with wider social and political worlds have assumed many shapes during the course of American history. Three representative specimens are illustrated here.

After the Civil War, the Northern churches supported a whole range of schools established for the freed slaves. This one was in Vicksburg, Mississippi. (Library of Congress)

D. L. Moody (1837–1899) became a well-known evangelist, but he got his start organizing Sunday school classes for urban vagabonds. Moody is the bearded man on the left in this 1876 lithograph. (Library of Congress)

A New York City parade from 1908 hints at the importance which the Roman Catholic church had assumed in the public life of Northern cities. Here Cardinal Logue and Archbishop John Murphy Farley are bracketed between the author Samuel Clemens and the politician James Farley. (Library of Congress)

While the forms have been as different as can be imagined, gathering for church has always been a permanent feature of American life.

During the nineteenth century the camp meeting was the most important vehicle for bringing the Christian message to America's rapidly expanding frontier. (Library of Congress)

This baptism from a Greek Orthodox church took place in Portland, Oregon, in 1925. It is a symbol of the continuing power of the churches to mark the transitional stages of human life. (Oregon Historical Society)

Worshippers at the Reverend George Stalling's Imani Temple (July 1989) "raise holy hands in prayer." (© Eli Reed/Magnum Photos)

Chapter 30

THE CHRISTIANIZING OF AMERICA
(1789–1880)

When in 1835 the Frenchman Alexis de Tocqueville published *Democracy in America*, a book growing out of a lengthy tour in the states, he expressed the opinion that "there is no country in the world where the Christian religion retains a greater influence over the souls of men than in America." Tocqueville was struck, however, not just by the simple fact of Christianity in the United States but by its character. "In France," he wrote, "I had almost always seen the spirit of religion and the spirit of freedom marching in opposite directions. But in America I found they were intimately united and that they reigned in common over the same country."[1] Generations of historians have seconded Tocqueville's themes. Antebellum America was a distinctly religious land, but it was religious in a distinctly American way. How that situation came about is the subject of this chapter.

From the vantage point of 1789, the year in which government began under the United States Constitution, it would have been difficult to foresee Tocqueville's conclusions fifty years later. To be sure, Christian groups had contributed substantially to the War of Independence, both practically and ideologically. In addition, the Christian faith enjoyed vast reservoirs of support among the population. Where religious assumptions, presuppositions, convictions, or conventions of whatever sort existed, they were almost all Christian in some sense. Still, the churches were definitely disorganized in the wake of the war, and the role of Christianity in the new national culture was anything but secure. Although church adherence remained high at least into the 1770s (perhaps as many as 60 percent of the population attending church with some regularity), formal church membership was sinking, and in the

---

[1] Thomas Bender, ed., Alexis de Tocqueville, *Democracy in America* (New York: Modern Library, 1981), pp. 182, 185.

1790s reached an all-time low (somewhere between 5 and 10 percent of the adult population).

The causes of this unsettled situation were many. They included new notions about separation of church and state, new religious convictions related to revolutionary standards of democracy, and the vast new spaces of the frontier. As it happened, the churches rapidly overcame the confusion of the revolutionary era to mount vigorous campaigns aimed at evangelizing the populace and christianizing the civilization. Prominent in these campaigns were representatives of the colonial-era churches and dynamic leaders of new denominations. Together they created an evangelical Protestant phalanx that came to dominate the public perception of religion in the United States. At the same time that this phalanx was exerting its greatest sway, however, the prehistory of the next significant era in American Christian history was being written. That era would be marked by a pluralism of Christian experience broadening well beyond evangelical Protestantism, and a cultural diversity seriously undermining "Christian America." But in the century after the American Revolution, it was the evangelical empire that stood at center stage.

Evangelical Mobilization

The Second Great Awakening was the most influential revival of Christianity in the history of the United States. Its very size and its many expressions have led some historians to question whether *a* single Second Great Awakening can be identified as such. Yet from about 1795 to about 1810 there was a broad and general rekindling of interest in Christianity throughout the country. This movement in turn provided a pattern and an impetus for similar waves of revival that continued throughout the nation until after the Civil War.

The state of Christianity in the United States after the American Revolution was not good. The tide of warfare itself had disrupted many local congregations, particularly in New Jersey, New York City, the Philadelphia area, and the Carolinas where fighting had been most intense. The revolution had dealt an especially hard blow to the Episcopal church, whose ties with England made it particularly suspect. The disestablishment of the churches in the southern states and attacks on the tie between states and the church in New England also led to uncertainty.

Interest in religion more generally also seemed on the decline. Concern for creating a new nation, for populating the open lands west of the Appalachians, for overcoming the ravages of inflation, and for staying clear of foreign entanglements left little time for church. In addition, a well-publicized attack on traditional Christianity convinced some that the old faith was not worth preserving. This attack was led by the deists Ethan Allen, who had captured Fort Ticonderoga during the war "in the name of the Great Jehovah and the Continental Congress," and Tom Paine, whose book, *The Age of Reason* (1794–1796) with its questioning of traditional supernaturalism, was almost as widely discussed as his earlier rouser against British rule, *Common Sense* (1776). As a result of these varied influences, allegiance to the churches wavered.

To be sure, scattered outbursts of Christian renewal had continued during the war and afterward. Immigrant communities nourished a variety of faiths from the Old World. The Congregational heirs of Jonathan Edwards in New England, Presbyterians in the middle states, and Baptists in the South had some encouraging successes. These local revivals did "awaken" a few individuals who later come to the fore as new leaders—for example, Barton W. Stone in Virginia. But they did not yet amount to a major change of religious direction.

The western phase of the revival movement had its genesis in the dedicated missionary work of Presbyterians like James McGready and itinerants from the Baptist and Methodist churches. McGready's church in Logan County, Kentucky, began in 1797 to pray regularly "for the conversion of sinners in Logan County, and throughout the world." In 1801 the efforts of McGready and like-minded leaders bore spectacular fruit. In August of that year a great camp meeting convened at Cane Ridge, Kentucky. Thousands streamed to this gathering, as several preachers—Black and white; Presbyterian, Baptist, and Methodist—fervently proclaimed the Good News.

The results were electrifying. Some of the unusual bodily effects—the jerks, dancing, laughing, running, and "the barking exercise"—may be attributed to powerful psychological release. Isolated families, subject to a hard and perilous life, were responding with their emotions to a message from stirring, charismatic leaders. Other effects—such as the rapid organization of churches that followed the camp meeting—were more clearly religious. The renewed interest in the faith touched off at Cane Ridge and similar camp meetings led to a rapid growth in Presbyterian churches in the South. By comparison, however, Presbyterian efforts paled beside the accomplishments of the Methodists and Baptists. Methodist circuit riders and Baptist farmer-preachers fanned out throughout the South and the opening West in unprecedented numbers. By the 1830s these groups had replaced the Congregationalists and Presbyterians as the largest denominations, not only in the South but in the whole country.

In the East, concern for revival gripped several local Congregational ministers in Connecticut during the first years of the 1790s. By the turn of the century, a considerable network of these ministers was passing information back and forth among one another on signs of religious vitality. The work of Timothy Dwight, a grandson of Jonathan Edwards, who became president of Yale College in 1795, was the most visible symbol of this activity. When he arrived in New Haven, Dwight found many of his students at least superficially attached to the deistical fashions of the French Enlightenment. To meet the challenges of "infidelity," Dwight launched a two-pronged effort. He labored by forthright argument to restore confidence in the bible, and he began a four-year cycle of sermons designed to communicate the essentials of the faith. Progress was slight at first, but in 1802 revival swept the Yale campus. One-third of the 225 students were converted, and many of these became agents for revival and reform in New England, upstate New York, and the West. From Connecticut, concern for revival spread up and down the East Coast. Soon there was hardly a locale in which Christians were not praying for revival or thanking God for giving them one.

One of Timothy Dwight's pupils, Lyman Beecher (1775–1863), was particularly active in organizing the forces of the revival into permanent organizations designed to evangelize and reform America. Through the efforts of Beecher and people with his vision, the country saw the founding of the American Board for Foreign Missions (1810), the American Bible Society (1816), the Colonization Society for Liberated Slaves (1817), the American Tract Society (1823), the American Sunday School Union (1824), the American Education Society (1826), the American Society for the Promotion of Temperance (1826), the American Home Missionary Society (1826), and many more. These agencies gave the Second Great Awakening the kind of long-lived institutional influence that the first had never enjoyed.

The theology of the Second Great Awakening, particularly in the expression of another of Dwight's pupils, Nathaniel Taylor (1786–1858), differed from the theology of the colonial revival. To preserve God's sovereignty in salvation, Edwards and Whitefield had stressed the inability of sinful people to save themselves. The theology of the leading revivalists in the South and of Taylor stressed more the ability that God had bestowed on all people to come to Christ. The Second Awakening thus played an important role in the process by which the dominant Calvinism of the eighteenth century gave way to the more Arminian faith of the nineteenth.

Francis Asbury and Charles Finney

Two individuals more than any others embodied the major thrusts of the revival impulse. The first was the Methodist Francis Asbury, an Englishman who eventually traveled over more of America than probably any other person in his generation. The second, a Presbyterian-become-Congregationalist who may have had a greater impact on the public life of antebellum America than most of the nation's politicians, was Charles Grandison Finney.

Francis Asbury (1745–1816) was born in Birmingham, England, where his parents were among the early followers of John Wesley, founder of Methodism. Their son was converted at the age of thirteen and began lay preaching three years later. When John Wesley asked for volunteers to go to America as missionaries in 1771, Asbury responded eagerly. Upon his arrival in America, Asbury rapidly assumed leadership of the four Methodist workers already here. Where his colleagues favored a settled clergy located in populous areas, Asbury was convinced that preachers should go where the gospel most needed to be heard. His example set the style for the itinerating, or traveling, Methodist minister in early America. Later he would exhort his associates to "go into every kitchen and shop; address all, aged and young, on the salvation of their souls."[2] Asbury's desire to spread the gospel kept him on the move the rest of his life. Before he died, he traveled nearly 300,000 miles, mostly on horseback. He crossed the Appalachians more than sixty times to reach the un-reached Americans. He saw more of American countryside than any other person of his generation. He may have been the best-known person in North America.

In the 1780s American Methodists set up an organization to bind established eastern centers with missionary outposts on the frontier. In 1784 Wesley appointed Asbury a general superintendent of the Methodists in the United States. In December of that year at the famous Christmas Conference in Baltimore, the Methodist Episcopal church in America was officially organized, with Asbury as its guiding force. From that time on the church grew rapidly, particularly west of the mountains where the roughness of life and the near-barbarism of the population discouraged representatives of more traditional denominations.

Asbury's message in city and wilderness alike was a traditional Christian one, with the special Wesleyan emphases: God's free grace, mankind's liberty to accept or reject that grace, and the Christian's need to strive for "perfection," an end to willful sin after conversion. Asbury used the Methodist pattern of organization— local classes, preaching circuits, and general conferences—to further the growth of the church and in the process to civilize the frontier.

Asbury's normal activities were strenuous. "My present mode of conduct is . . . to read about one hundred pages a day; to preach in the open air every other day; and to lecture in prayer meeting every evening." His journeys were often difficult, but Asbury remained undaunted: "The water froze as it ran from the horse's nos-trils. . . . I have suffered a little by lodging in open houses this cold weather; but this is a very small thing when compared to what the dear Redeemer suffered for the salvation of precious souls."[3] His vision of Christianity reached beyond the inner life to take in also social responsibilities. Asbury established educational institutions, he willed his very modest estate to the Methodist "Book Concern," he argued against slavery, and he urged abstinence from hard liquor.

Statistics can never tell a whole story. But when Francis Asbury came to America in 1771, four Methodist ministers were caring for about 300 lay people. When he died in 1816, there were 2,000 ministers and more than 200,000 Methodists devoted, as he put it, to "the dear Redeemer . . . of precious souls."

Charles Grandison Finney (1792–1875) was the best-known revivalist in the two generations after Asbury. Finney's range was breathtaking. He created powerful yet controlled revivalistic methods for the frontier (upstate New York, Ohio) at the same

[2] Elmer T. Clark, ed., *The Journal and Letters of Francis Asbury*, 3 vols. (Nashville, TN: Abingdon, 1958), May 24, 1795.
[3] Clark, *Francis Asbury*, February 21 and February 22, 1773; July 29, 1776.

time that he orchestrated successful evangelism in the nation's major cities (especially Boston and New York) and overseas in Britain. More than any other individual of his day he succeeded in joining evangelical religion to social reform. Although other interests never superseded evangelism, Finney always was an effective promoter of benevolence, as an abolitionist, a pioneer of coeducation at Oberlin College, and a protean reformer (temperance, peace, sabbatarianism, care for the retarded, as well as phrenology, the whole-wheat diet of Sylvester Graham, and anti-Masonry). In addition, he formalized ties between conservative theology and industrial wealth that still characterize evangelical culture. If this were not enough, Finney's theological emphases on the moral government of God, the powers of the human will, and the state of complete holiness played a key role in the evolution of American Protestant theology.

Finney experienced a dramatic conversion in 1821 while a legal apprentice in Adams, New York. He began preaching almost immediately and soon acquired a local reputation for vigorous, confrontational sermons. In 1827 he met ecclesiastical opponents from New England at a famous gathering in New Lebanon, New York, where Finney successfully defended his "new measures" against charges of innovation and anarchy. A great revival in Rochester over the winter of 1830–1831 catapulted him to national renown. Soon Philadelphia, Boston, and New York were scenes of his extended preaching campaigns. During the early 1830s, he completed his break from traditional Presbyterianism, which to Finney labored under burdensome organizational handicaps and a theology unappreciative of native human ability. By the mid-1830s, Finney had as well become the mentor to a growing number of ardent young reformers who wished to see Christianity as they understood it shaping society as well as individuals. Some of these reformers became leading abolitionists. Some of their older associates were influential in convincing Finney that he should go to Oberlin College in Ohio, which they planned as a center of both evangelism and social reform. From Oberlin, Finney later traveled to Great Britain and mounted other social campaigns like his fulminations against the Masons in the 1860s. At Oberlin as well, Finney fully supported the admission of women as regular students (the first college in the country to do so). His major works spread his views even further, especially the *Lectures on Revivals* (1835) and his *Systematic Theology* (1846/47).

A good case could be made that Finney deserves to be ranked with Andrew Jackson, Abraham Lincoln, and Andrew Carnegie (or some other representative industrialist) among the most important public figures in nineteenth-century America and that he stands by himself as *the* crucial figure in American evangelicalism after Jonathan Edwards. It is, for example, entirely possible that Ralph Waldo Emerson, Daniel Webster, Horace Mann, and Henry Adams did not exert the influence on American life, and certainly on American religion, that Finney did.

Finney was an Arminian who went beyond Wesley by not seeing a particular need for divine grace to make the will capable of choosing God. He was a perfectionist who felt that a permanent stage of higher spiritual life was possible to one who sought it wholeheartedly. He held a governmental view of the atonement in which Christ's death was thought to be a public demonstration of God's willingness to forgive sins rather than a payment for sin itself. And he tended toward a belief that emotions were the culprits that kept reason and will from following God's purposes.

Asbury and Finney were representatives of the most visible religious movements between the revolution and the Civil War. They were both willing to modify a hereditary Calvinism to fit more easily into the ethos of the new republic. They were both charismatic figures who relied on their own native abilities instead of inherited status or educational certification to convince others to heed their message. They were both great communicators with the common people who gave the American faith a distinctly populist tone. They both had broad visions of Christian society, not extending to questions about the structures of economic life but nonetheless defining Christian social responsibilities as clearly as they defined personal spiritual duties. Together with like-minded leaders of only slightly less influence, they established the revival and the voluntary society as the foundational elements of American Protestant faith.

Historians of a previous generation were prone to contend that leaders such as Asbury and Finney, along with Timothy Dwight, Lyman Beecher, N. W. Taylor, and other revival leaders, were driven by an urge to control an American society that seemed about to pass from the dominion of clergymen. To some extent this interpretation is correct. The revivalists and voluntary organizers did want to see American life ordered by the precepts of their religion. The process, however, was rarely manipulative. In their minds, the Christian faith was true and as such, deserved everyone's allegiance. It had also been shown to be an effective shaper of society and as such, particularly useful for helping to organize a fragmenting, far-flung civilization. The burgeoning frontier (population in Tennessee, Kentucky, and Ohio went from barely 100,000 in 1790 to nearly a million in 1810) and the restructuring of urban life by the advance of capitalism created immensely unsettling conditions. More than any other group, it was the Protestant revivalists who brought order into the near chaos of American life before the Civil War.

A New Visibility for Women

The revivals of the early nineteenth century were also the occasion for bringing women to the forefront of American religious life, even to some extent to the forefront of public life in general. Women had always been the mainstay of the churches in North America. In Puritan New England, men and women had joined churches in roughly equal proportions during the first years of settlement and at the time of the Great Awakening. But for most of New England's Puritan history, women consistently outnumbered men, so much so that by the end of the seventeenth century three-quarters of the people joining some of the major churches in the region were women. Ratios are hard to determine exactly in other colonies, but a predominance of female membership seems to have been the case elsewhere as well.

In the new republic women continued to make up the majority of those who took most active part in the churches, but now changing social conditions and new theological agendas allowed for greater public ministry. A more fluid social setting, the thinly populated spaces newly opened to settlement, and the rhetoric of democracy from the revolution all served to advance women in the public practice of religion. In many areas of the country, it soon became conventional to look on women as the prime support for the nation's republican spirit. Mothers, it was thought, were the ones who could most effectively inculcate the virtues of public-spiritedness and self-sacrifice that were so essential to the life of the republic. Increasingly as well, such notions were linked to the idea that women had a special capacity for the religious life as persons who could understand intuitively the virtues of sacrifice, devotion, and trust that were so important to the Christian faith.

Perhaps most important in the emergence of women as public figures was a new emphasis from revivalists, especially the Methodists, on the holiness of life. John Wesley's doctrine of "Christian perfection," or freedom from all known sin, had always been a main element of Methodist teaching in America. To that emphasis, revivalists like Charles Finney added exhortations to go on to "perfect love" or "entire sanctification." The result was new expectations about the work of the Holy Spirit in converted individuals. Those who had been brought to Christ should go on with the Spirit to seek the perfection that the Father promised to those who sought him with their whole hearts. In such exhortations there were no barriers of gender. Women as well as men could find "the second blessing" of the Holy Spirit. Once found, it seemed only natural to promote the work of godliness as energetically as possible. With this theological orientation, it became increasingly common to see women involved in revivals and soon also in works of social reform growing from the revivals, especially temperance and abolition.

The career of one of the leading holiness advocates illustrates the power of this teaching. Phoebe Worrall Palmer (1807–1874) was raised in New York in a conventionally Christian home. Her husband Walter Palmer was a physician with whom she enjoyed close spiritual as well as domestic accord. During the early years of her married life, Phoebe Palmer was active as a bible teacher, but she longed for a deeper experience of the faith. This was given to her on July 26, 1837, which she always called thereafter "the day of days." After receiving a special sense of the Holy Spirit's indwelling power, she began to share the experience with others. The forum she employed was a weekly gathering established by her sister Mrs. Sarah Lankford, who had experienced the indwelling of the Spirit in 1835. This Tuesday Meeting for the Promotion of Holiness became a magnet for a distinguished group of New York believers and soon for prominent Holiness teachers from throughout the English-speaking world. Mrs. Palmer was at first reluctant to share her experiences with men present, but after Thomas Upham, a prominent Congregational minister, received the fullness of the Spirit under her guidance, she set aside social convention and talked to whoever would listen about her experience. Soon she began to write for the religious press. The first set of her essays in the *Christian Advocate and Journal* were published in 1843 as *The Way of Holiness*. The book was an immediate success and enjoyed many reprintings at home and abroad.

In an age like hers when women were not often forthcoming in public, Mrs. Palmer proclaimed her message winsomely and without attempting to draw attention to herself. She even published several of her books without putting her name on the title page. At the same time, she did insist that God's grace was poured out on women and men alike, and that all who tasted the heavenly gift had the obligation to pass it on to others. In 1859 she published *The Promise of the Father*, a vigorous defense of women's right to preach, a work that made much of such biblical passages as Galatians 3:28 ("There is neither . . . male nor female; for you are all one in Christ Jesus") and Joel 2:28 ("Your sons and daughters will prophesy"). These had also been the passages used by the Reverend Luther Lee in presiding over the ordination of Antoinette Brown to the ministry of the Congregational Church in 1853. This was the first formal ordination of a woman in America, although women, both Black and white, among Quakers and Methodists especially, had been active as regular preachers before this time. Such ordinations were rare in the nineteenth century (Antoinette Brown herself resigned ministerial service when she left the Congregationalists for the Unitarians shortly thereafter). But they testified to a growing involvement of women in the public life of America's churches.

The revivalistic faith led women to play a more active part not only in spiritual matters but also in the larger arenas of social reform inspired by the revivals. Women strove mightily against slavery (Harriet Beecher Stowe, Sarah and Angelina Grimké), for better treatment of the mentally ill (Dorothea Dix), and for women's educational opportunities (Catherine Beecher). Later, women were leaders of the temperance crusade (Frances Willard) and in urban social work (Jane Addams). Intense female involvement especially on behalf of temperance (to liberate from the bondage of drink) and abolition (to liberate from the bondage of slavery) seemed almost naturally to spill over into growing concern for the social bondage of women themselves.

The religious factor in that move was also prominent. The first formal call for fuller women's rights in society, including the right to vote, went forth from Seneca Falls, New York, where active abolitionists, men and women, white and Black, gathered in July 1848 to appeal for public justice for women. Conveners of the meeting were Lucretia Coffin Mott (1793–1880) and Elizabeth Cady Stanton (1815–1902), both of whom had been nurtured in centers of religious reform, Mott having served as an "acknowledged minister" in the Society of Friends and Stanton whose route to social reform came through more conventional evangelical nurturing. Significantly, the Seneca Falls meeting took place in the town's Wesleyan Methodist

Church, the local gathering place for a denomination that had broken from the main group of Methodists precisely because of its leaders' desire to promote both holiness and abolition more vigorously.

The new spheres opened up for women in America even came to include the leadership of religious movements. Ann Lee (1736–1784), founder of the "Shakers," had immigrated from her native Manchester, England, to the colonies in 1774. By the Civil War, about 6,000 adherents in nineteen communities were following the way of celibacy, frugality, communalism, millennialism, pacifism, vegetarianism, spiritualism, and industriousness she had marked out. Mary Baker Eddy (1821–1910) founded the Christian Science movement after years of spiritual questing and repeated bouts of sickness. Her book *Science and Health, with Key to the Scriptures* (1875) set out a picture of mental and spiritual harmonies that she skillfully transformed into a church and long-lasting auxiliary enterprises. Ellen White (1827–1915) helped found the Seventh-Day Adventist Church, a body growing out of the apocalyptic biblical interpretations of William Miller (who is described later). As leader of the Seventh-Day Adventists, Ellen White helped promote health reforms, including the use of dried grain as breakfast food, which were taken up widely in the nation as a whole.

During the nineteenth century women did not yet participate in the churches on an equal footing with men. The opportunities offered by a combination of revival and the opening of American society, however, gave women a remarkable new visibility in the nation's religious life.

A Missionary Vision

One feature of the evangelical mobilization that would have dramatic long-range consequences for Christianity in America was a new thrust in missionary endeavor. Protestant missions from English-speaking lands had begun only shortly before with the sailing of William Carey from England to India in 1793. Soon thereafter, Americans followed their English co-religionists in organizing missionary agencies. As significant as the beginnings of active religious work overseas were, however, it is important to remember that the great achievement of American missions in the nineteenth century was the conversion of the citizenry of the United States. Asbury, Finney, and like-minded leaders inspired Americans to go abroad with the Christian message, but the work done by those who stayed at home was the truly great missionary story of the century.

A revival at Williams College in 1806 led to the first overseas missionary venture. That revival soon spilled over into the student body of Andover Theological Seminary, the nation's first full-fledged theological seminary, which had been founded in 1807 by a coalition of New England's Trinitarian Congregationalists to combat the drift of Harvard College toward Unitarianism.

In 1810 the American Board of Commissioners for Foreign Missions (ABCFM) was established as an agency to send young evangelists overseas. Among the first contingent of five to set out for India in 1812 was Adoniram Judson (1788–1850), who would become a greatly revered figure among American Protestants. Judson's conversion to Baptist convictions on board ship to the East estranged him from the ABCFM but led in 1814 to the establishment of a Baptist missionary society. Judson worked for nearly forty years in Burma, where his efforts were followed diligently by a host of Americans eager for news of the progress of the gospel. Americans also took a great interest in the women who served with Judson, especially the first of his four successive wives, Ann Hasseltine Judson (1789–1826). Books on the work of the Judsons were best-sellers in antebellum America. Confidence in the spread of the faith in America was broadening out to eager anticipation of its spread elsewhere.

Innovations in missionary work on the North American continent were well illustrated by efforts to bring Christianity to the Cherokee of Georgia and neighboring states. The tragedy of this story speaks also of the general ambiguity of American missions during this era when evangelization often involved an indiscriminate mingling of Christian and national values. After the Revolutionary War, the United States punished the old Cherokee Nation for aligning with the British and for blocking national expansion to the southwest. A peace treaty of 1794 stimulated a cultural revival among the Cherokee and also opened the way for white missionaries to begin their work. Moravians, who maintained single-minded religious purposes, were among the first. Presbyterians and Congregationalists soon arrived in greater numbers; they also more thoroughly mingled evangelization and Americanization. What followed was painfully slow but steady progress in gaining converts for the Christian faith. Some of the Native Americans resisted and contributed to the periodic revivals of tribal religion that so distressed the missionaries. Some became all-out converts and took their cues entirely from the white evangelists. Still others became Christians and Americans but exercised considerable discretion in the process, retaining selective elements of Native American religion in their new faith and using the symbols and doctrines of Christianity to resist total assimilation into white culture.

During the administration of Andrew Jackson (1829–1837), the evangelical work of the missionaries and the work of selective cultural adaptation by the Cherokee both received a fatal blow. White settlers wanted the Indian land, and Jacksonian Indian officials were eager to give it to them. The result was a forced removal of the Cherokee from Georgia to the West that became known as the "Trail of Tears." Despite the fact that the Indians had adapted to American ways with remarkable skill, the removal proceeded with ruthless finality. The missionaries who had come to the Indians as bearers of civilization as well as of Christianity faced a terrible dilemma. They now were forced to watch their country, supposedly the embodiment of Christian civilization, turn violently against the Indians who had responded to their message.

667

Some of the missionaries vigorously protested, even to the point of civil disobedience. Some forfeited standing in their denominations by persisting in their advocacy of Indian rights. Some eventually forged stronger bonds of Christian fellowship with their converts, whom they had at first patronized, than with the "sending churches." Yet missionary support for the Cherokee was not enough, and the brutal removal went on. The United States, touting the gifts of Christian faith and republican politics, destroyed a tribal people who were working to accept those gifts. Christian leaders, more often in the churches than on site with the Cherokee, played a signal part in that destruction. Such spokesmen were good culture Christians. The agents of Andrew Jackson's Indian policy were good democrats. Together they did an evil work in the name of God and of what they claimed was his chosen country.

Insiders and Outsiders

The mobilization of public-minded evangelical Protestants was far from the whole picture in antebellum America. If the "insiders" in American religion were the evangelical revivalists, a whole host of "outsiders," each with an important story, also inhabited the American landscape. Among the most significant outsiders were the aggressive new Protestant denominations that sprang up in the early years of the republic. Groups like the Disciples of Christ and Christians, or even the Baptists and Methodists, self-consciously set themselves apart from the older denominations that had dominated the colonial period, but they were not too distinct. They did gain ground by presenting themselves as denominations of "the people," opposed to inherited privilege and fiercely democratic in their views of religious life. At the same time, once they had achieved a certain measure of success, they themselves moved easily into the mainstream. Their Protestantism was more an extension of the dominant evangelical trends than a contrast to them. For other groups, however, the open spaces of America made it possible to create newer religious patterns, although these groups also made use of themes from the history of Christianity or the history of the nation that were common to groups on the inside.

Millerites and Mormons

Perhaps the two most significant of the new bodies were the followers of William Miller and the followers of Joseph Smith. The Millerites, who eventually formed several Adventist denominations, were closer to the inside groups than the Mormons, who came into existence through the work of Joseph Smith, but both were expressions of notable new developments in American religious life.

William Miller (1782–1849) was a self-educated farmer from Low Hampton, New York, who was converted as an adult after service in the War of 1812 and a long career of serious reading in the important religious (and skeptical) writers of his day. From the vigorous study of the bible that followed his conversion, Miller came to the conclusion that the return of Christ and the end of the world as foretold in scripture, would occur sometime "around 1843." Miller's exegesis paid detailed attention to the minutest parts of the bible, including its numbers, and thus fit well into the American zeal for scientific demonstration that loomed so large before the Civil War. Miller's interests were in many ways typical for antebellum American Protestants, including as they did biblical literalism, revivalism, and millennialism. For his followers, Miller was only following the logic announced by countless bible-preaching revivalists in the early United States.

Miller's message was promoted in ways that were also typical for the period. Joseph V. Himes (1805–1895), a communications genius who popularized Miller's opinions in something more than 5 million pieces of literature, led the way. In response to the media barrage, thousands (perhaps tens of thousands) waited expectantly on March 21, 1843, and then on the postponed date, October 22, 1844, for the Lord's return. Many of those who believed were transplanted Yankee Pietists for whom Millerism was a natural extension of mainstream American themes of optimistic expectation, confidence in the scriptures, and great belief in the human ability to understand the deepest mysteries of the sacred writings. When the end was not manifest, some of those who had accepted Miller's interpretation of the bible returned to their previous religious commitments, but others persevered to become Advent Christians or Seventh-Day Adventists.

If the Millerites lived on the border between evangelical Protestant insiders and sectarian Protestant outsiders, the Mormons under Joseph Smith went even further toward the outside. Joseph Smith (1805–1844) seemed an unlikely candidate for the founding of a major religious movement. He was born to New Englanders who could never quite succeed in making a comfortable living in either their native Vermont or in upper New York State to which they moved in 1816. Yet the family was intensely religious, and Joseph Smith received powerful spiritual direction from his mother, Lucy Mack Smith, a seeker who despite considerable effort could not find in the traditional denominations the spiritual energy she sought. Joseph Smith later reported that he began to receive visions from heavenly beings in the early 1820s, a few years before the angel Moroni revealed to him a unique *Book of Mormon* that detailed God's special dealings with prehistoric settlers in America and long-lost tribes of Israel.

When Smith published his translation of the Book of Mormon in 1830, it sparked considerable interest among others in upper New York state, sometimes called a "burned-over district" because of the intensity of revival and reform movements that had swept over it for the previous generation. It also sparked considerable opposition because of how Mormon views—for example, that God has a material body, or that people existed as spirits before entering this life—differed from traditional Christian teachings. The move of Smith and his followers to Kirtland, Ohio in 1831 began the series of migrations that would eventually lead to the great migration of the main body of Mormons to the basin of the Great Salt Lake in 1847. Before that last migration, Smith was killed by an angry mob in Carthage, Illinois. Brigham Young (1801–1877), an organizational genius, succeeded him and masterminded the move to Utah. Also before the migration, a segment of Smith's earlier followers, made apprehensive by Smith's later visions and the autocratic nature of his leadership, had broken away to form the Reorganized Church of Jesus Christ of Latter Day Saints.

Joseph Smith's religion drew on themes prominent in the early national period, including a republican conception of world order and a democratic belief in the ability of common people to grasp religious truth. Even more, however, Mormonism represented a new religious movement, dependent on but also transcending the traditions of Jews and Christians. The *Book of Mormon* presupposed the Judeo-Christian scriptures yet amounted to a new contribution to the canon. Joseph Smith was a new prophet who reenacted the deeds of prophets in past times. The gathering of the Latter-day Saints constituted a re-forming of the church of Jesus Christ. The trek to Utah became a kind of New Exodus, and Utah a Promised Land for the Saints. The result was a religious movement that arose out of specific conditions in the early national period but that also laid the foundation for the worldwide movement that Mormonism has become.

Black Christianity

Although the conversion of slaves was one of the often-stated purposes of those who supported the institution of slavery, white slaveholders did little to promote the evangelization of Blacks throughout the whole history of slavery. By the time of the American Revolution, some slaves and free Blacks had begun to accept the Christian faith, but they did so much more in opposition to the main trends of their society than in conformity with them.

The evangelical revivals in the 1740s did make a bridgehead of Christianity among slaves, from which Blacks themselves carried on most of the work. Revivalistic preaching, with its appeal to all people to turn to Christ, and the evangelical conversion experience, with its emotional intensity, won some converts among southern slaves and northern free Blacks. Black religious ecstasy was able to make use of African religious patterns, especially rhythmic singing and dancing, but it was acceptable to revivalist Christianity as an indication of the Holy Spirit's work. The rapid rise of the Methodists and Baptists also broadened the appeal for Christianity among Blacks. Methodists and Baptists aimed their message at ordinary people, they were often quite egalitarian, and for a few years during the 1780s and 1790s they even made noises against the slave system itself. In the wake of revivals led by itinerants of these denominations and of increased preaching by Blacks to Blacks, the number of Black Americans adhering to churches rose dramatically from the

1770s to the 1830s. During this period, most Christian Blacks were formally attached to white congregations and denominations, even though informal meetings organized by themselves often provided the deepest sustenance for their religious faith. This was also the period when Blacks began to organize their own churches.

One of the earliest and most important groups to be formed in this way was the African Methodist Episcopal Church. Its story, along with the story of its founder Richard Allen (1760–1831), tells much about the lengths to which Black Christians could go to express the faith for themselves. Allen was born a slave and was converted at the age of seventeen under Methodist influence. Immediately he began to preach, first to his family, then to his master, and finally in much wider circles. Allen taught himself to read and write; then after much hard work he was able to purchase his freedom. After pursuing several trades—all the time preaching as a layman—he finally arrived in Philadelphia at the age of twenty-six. With several other Blacks he worshipped regularly at St. George's Methodist Church.

Then a distressing incident in 1787 drove them from that congregation. While Allen's friend, Absalom Jones, was praying publicly in a Sunday service, white trustees of the church forced him to his feet in an effort to make him keep quiet. In response, Jones, Allen, and the other Blacks left the church. Shortly thereafter Allen and Jones founded the Free African Society, America's first organization established by Blacks for Blacks. This nonsectarian society provided mutual aid and spiritual encouragement to Philadelphia's Black community. It also became a prototype for other Black fraternal organizations, which would also be supported by religious motives. Four years later in 1791 Jones and Allen left the Society, and Jones in 1794 became the minister of St. Thomas Episcopal Church in Philadelphia, the nation's first Black Episcopal congregation. In 1793 Jones and Allen led other Blacks in providing aid to the entire population of Philadelphia during a dreadful epidemic of yellow fever. Also in 1793 Allen established Bethel Church for Negro Methodists, and he himself was ordained a Methodist minister in 1799. In a long dispute not finally settled by the Pennsylvania Supreme Court until 1816, Allen and his colleagues successfully survived an effort by trustees of the white St. George's to claim control of the Bethel property and structure that the Blacks had bought and constructed for themselves. Owing to uneasiness over such efforts by the predominantly white Methodist church, Allen's congregation and other Black Methodist churches in 1814 organized their own denomination, the African Methodist Episcopal Church (Bethel). Richard Allen became its first bishop in 1816. He served this growing body of Black Methodists as its widely respected leader until his death in 1831. The year before he died Allen was elected president of the first national Black political organization, the National Negro Convention, which grew from the forty delegates who met at Allen's Bethel Church to protest the systematic discrimination of Blacks in America.

By that time, other northern Blacks had also begun to organize for themselves. Local congregations of Methodists, Baptists, and Presbyterians could be found in the major urban areas. Black churches sent members as missionaries to Liberia, Sierra Leone, and Haiti. Black ministers also soon became important leaders of the abolitionist movement. They lent their energies to other reforming causes like temperance. Although they did not ordain women, at least some Black women, like Richard Allen's associate, Jarena Lee, did exercise wide ministries as exhorters and lay preachers. (In 1827 she traveled more than 2,000 miles and preached nearly 180 sermons.)

For slaves in the South opportunities to organize churches or voluntary societies were much fewer. Yet such institutions did come into existence, like the First African Baptist Church of Savannah, Georgia, where Andrew Bryan, an able former slave, overcame white opposition to establish one of the largest congregations in the region. Despite the notorious "slave codes," which prohibited a wide range of meetings and created barriers to literacy, Christianity made progress among the slaves. Some masters encouraged their slaves to attend church with them. Others permitted supervised religious meetings on the plantations. Still others gave grudging approval to white missionaries to work among the slaves. Methodist William Capers and Presbyterian Charles Colcok Jones faced the daunting task of evangelizing Blacks while assuring owners that slavery could be Christianized. Even when owners forbade religious meetings, slaves were often able to meet in secret for prayer, exhortation, and preaching from fellow Blacks.

At such meetings and on other occasions, songs added immeasurably to Black American spirituality. Narratives about Abraham, David, Daniel, and Jesus were sung with fervor, both as signs of spiritual assurance for the age to come and encouragement to persevere for the present. When possible, these songs were also acted out, often in the "shout," a counterclockwise, circular dance that recalled African ritual. One of the best known, with its fully intended double meaning, was recorded as follows by a New York visitor to the South in 1861:

> When Israel was in Egypt's land,
>   O let my people go!
> Oppressed so hard they could not stand,
>   O let my people go!
> CHORUS—O go down, Moses,
>   Away down to Egypt's land.
> And tell King Pharoah
> To let my people go! . . .

Christianity could be a source of comfort, reconciling slaves to their fate in bondage. But it could also feed rebellion. In some form or other, whether through redemptive images from the bible or Christian patterns of organization, Christianity contributed to the major slave revolts under Gabriel Prosser in Richmond in 1800, Denmark Vesey in Charleston in 1822, and Nat Turner in Virginia in 1831. Much more commonly, Christianity nerved slaves to disobey masters in order to meet together for worship and song, to labor diligently with an eye toward freedom at least for coming generations, and even to escape. In this determination to find freedom—in Christ and in this world—the southern slaves shared the commitments of their northern peers, some of whom were leaders in the struggle against slavery.

No group stood as far outside America's dominant patterns of religion between the Revolution and the Civil War as the slaves. Yet few groups promoted themes as close to the heart of traditional Christian belief. It is a testimony to Black resilience, as well as to the transforming power of Christianity itself, that a religion used so often to support the system of bondage could become a means for counteracting its inhuman influence.

Roman Catholics in the United States

An increasingly important outsider in American religion during the nineteenth century was the Roman Catholic church. Numbers alone cannot tell the whole story, but they are nonetheless of great significance. In 1789 when the election of the first Catholic bishop for the United States was confirmed by the pope, there were approximately 35,000 Catholics, with 60 percent of these in Maryland. By 1830 the total number of Catholics had grown to over 300,000. Within the next thirty years, while the nation's population increased two and a half times from 13 million to 31½ million, the Catholic population leaped nearly tenfold to over 3,100,000. The addition of new territory contributed marginally to Catholic growth, with about 40,000 Catholics added through the purchase of Louisiana and the cessions after the Mexican War. Healthy natural increase also contributed substantially to the rise. The most important reason was immigration, however, first from Ireland and then from Germany. During the 1840s, when blight ruined several successive potato crops in Ireland, nearly 800,000 immigrants came to America. The next decade the total climbed to over 900,000. From Germany, for a variety of political, economic, and religious reasons, came nearly 400,000 immigrants in the 1840s and almost 1 million in the 1850s. Most of the Irish immigrants were Catholic, as were many of the Germans. The result of this great growth was to transform the character of Roman Catholicism in the United States and also to alter greatly the picture of American Christianity.

The early history of Catholicism in the United States was centered in Maryland and was guided by aristocratic representatives of old English-origin families. The career of the first Roman Catholic bishop in the United States illustrates that lineage and also how the revolution and democracy affected early attempts at organizing the church. John Carroll (1735–1815), son of a wealthy Maryland merchant, was educated by English Jesuits in France. After entering the Catholic priesthood, he taught in France before returning to North America in 1774. His cousin, Charles Carroll, was an ardent Maryland patriot and the only Catholic signer of the Declaration of Independence. With this cousin and Benjamin Franklin, John Carroll reluctantly undertook a trip in 1776 to Quebec in the vain effort to persuade the Catholic French Canadians to enter the Revolutionary War on the side of the Americans. Although that effort did not succeed, general Catholic support for independence, combined with the help of the Catholic French in winning the war, led to much greater tolerance for Catholics in the new United States. Some of the state constitutions did discriminate against non-Protestants, but in general Catholics enjoyed as much latitude in the states as in any other Protestant area of the world.

After the war, John Carroll took the leadership in strengthening the tiny bands of Catholics in the new country. His *Address to the Catholics of the United States* (1784) was really written for Protestants, defending Catholics against charges of being unpatriotic and sub-Christian. As Catholic leaders in the United States gained a measure of control over their own affairs, Carroll was the official to whom they looked, first in 1784 as Perfect Apostolic and superior of missions in the United States. Then in 1789 Carroll was made the bishop of Baltimore, the first American bishop. In 1808 Carroll became the archbishop of Baltimore when four suffragan bishops were appointed to new dioceses in Boston, New York, Philadelphia, and (reflecting active western expansion) Bardstown, Kentucky. Although the denomination would soon become an immigrant church, most of the bishops throughout the nineteenth century who succeeded Carroll in the metropolitan see of Baltimore were descendants of Maryland's colonial English elite.

Carroll's major accomplishment was to enlist European priests and teachers to staff schools, churches, and mission societies in America. Many of these Europeans came from France. Like most of his Protestant counterparts in early United States history, Carroll was deeply committed to education, an interest that led to the founding of Georgetown College for the training of future priests.

Within a generation of Carroll's death, the American bishops met for their First Provincial Council in 1829, an occasion that enabled them to solidify much of the work of his pioneering generation. The council regularized the authority of bishops over all priests in their dioceses, including those in religious orders. Despite Protestant stereotypes about Catholic suspicion of the bible, it also declared that the scriptures, "when used with due care, and an humble and docile spirit," should be read by lay people "for the edification and instruction of the faithful."[4] (A later archbishop of Baltimore, Francis Patrick Kenrick, published his own English translation of the bible in an effort to provide a more modern alternative to the older Douay-Rheims English translation for American Catholics.) In addition, the 1829 council also declared that all church property was to be held in deed by the bishops.

This last measure spoke to the one issue where Carroll had largely failed. In the free American atmosphere, with heady talk of rights and individual liberties, as well

---

[4]Gerald F. Fogarty, S.J., "The Quest for a Catholic Vernacular Bible in America," in N. O. Hatch and M. A. Noll, eds., *The Bible in America: Essays in Cultural History* (New York: Oxford University Press, 1982), p. 167.

as in an atmosphere where Protestant varieties of congregational autonomy abounded, Catholics too tended to think that local communities could and should control their churches, including their property. In the early years of Catholic settlement, when priests were not always present, lay trustees had often had no choice but to organize for themselves and take in hand the construction and maintenance of church buildings. But trusteeism, as it came to be called, clashed with traditional patterns of Catholic authority, where bishops maintained close control over all aspects of a diocese's life, including property. Disputes between lay trustees and bishops usually centered on who could name new priests. Bishops claimed the privilege exclusively for themselves, while trustees claimed a veto power over episcopal appointments. As the church grew both in numbers and conformity to Rome, trusteeism died away as a movement, but lay protests against seemingly un-American ways of wielding episcopal power could still be heard as late as the 1840s and 1850s.

The presence of ever larger numbers of Roman Catholics did not always sit well with Protestants who had grown accustomed to thinking of the nation as their special preserve. After Lyman Beecher moved to Cincinnati from his native New England, he published in 1835 a strongly worded tract, *A Plea for the West*, outlining the dangers to freedom and true Christianity if Roman Catholicism should increase its already substantial influence in the opening American frontier. But the greatest clashes between Protestants and Catholics occurred in the cities of the East. There immigrant Catholic labor seemed to threaten Protestant jobs, and there able bishops, solicitous for the well-being of their flocks, spoke out against what they saw as favoritism to Protestants. In 1834 a Boston mob burned the Ursuline Convent of Charlestown, and Boston Protestants backed the publication of scandalmongering books allegedly by ex-Catholics—for example, *Six Months in a Convent* (1835) and Maria Monk's forgery, *Awful Disclosures of the Hotel Dieu Nunnery in Montreal* (1836). In 1844 Protestant and Catholic disputes over labor issues led to violent clashes in the Philadelphia suburbs of Kensington and Southwark. Four years before, New York's Bishop John Hughes had petitioned the city's Public School Society to provide money for Catholic schools in a manner similar to its support for Protestant establishments. The result was a bitter, long-lasting quarrel that provided no subsidies to the Catholics, but did lead to the demise of the society and the emergence of a nonsectarian program for New York public education.

The most concerted resistance to the rise of the Catholic church came, however, when Protestants, worried about the tide of European and specifically Catholic immigration, organized a fraternal-political organization to resist the tide. The new body was founded in 1849 as The Order of the Star-Spangled Banner and reorganized in 1852 as the American Party. But its members were styled "Know Nothings" from their habit of saying they did not "know anything" when questioned about the group's principles or activities. It had simplistic convictions—immigrants were damaging the Anglo-Saxon stock of "native" Americans; Roman Catholics were minions of a despotic foreign power, the pope. The American Party enjoyed a brief day in the sun, winning heavily in local and congressional contests in 1854, when the party elected seventy-five members of the House of Representatives and in Massachusetts numbered 376 of the 378 state legislators. It declined very rapidly, however, as a new party (the Republicans) arose to challenge the Democrats and as a new issue (the North-South conflict) arose to replace fear of Catholic immigration.

This kind of opposition disconcerted but did not materially effect the effort by Catholics to organize, instruct, and mobilize their growing numbers. Traveling Catholic missioners even copied a page or two from evangelical itinerants by adopting strategies to energize nominal Catholics and inspire the committed to more dedicated service. Thus, French brothers of the Society for the Propagation of the Faith, Germans of the Leopoldine Foundation, and eventually American Paulists traveled from congregation to congregation, held extended meetings during the evenings for a week or more, featured stirring music and affecting oratory, and called on individuals to make spiritual decisions to advance the work of the church.

As it did also for Protestants, the American environment opened up a full sphere for the religious work of women, although American Catholics also were able to draw on a long tradition of women's religious orders. In 1818, Rose Philipine Duchesne from France established the first convent of the Sacred Heart in America. Even earlier an indigenous American Catholic women's order had come into being through the efforts of Elizabeth Ann Seton (1774–1821). A trip to Italy for the recuperation of her husband's health had unexpected results when Elizabeth Seton found the worship of local Catholics and especially firsthand experience with the Catholic Eucharist unexpectedly meaningful. After she returned to her native New York City and an extended period of discussion with her Episcopalian bishop, Elizabeth Seton finally entered the Catholic Church in March 1805. Friends and family expressed such sharp disapproval that Mrs. Seton, after consulting with Bishop John Carroll and French Sulpician Fathers, moved to Baltimore. There, with the assistance of the Sulpicians, she opened a school for girls. Then when several young women came to assist in her work, she was able to secure property near Emmitsburg, west of Baltimore. On this site she established an order for women, the Sisters of Charity, who carried out a wide variety of tasks in education and care for orphans. (In 1975 Mother Seton became the first person born in the United States to be made a saint by the Roman Catholic church.) Mother Seton was not alone in her work, however, for by the Civil War fifty-one communities of religious women had been established in the United States. Over the next forty years another fifty-nine would be added. The result was that in 1900 over 40,000 Catholic sisters were active in a great number of services in the church, especially in education, where almost all of the Catholic church's nearly 4,000 parochial schools, as well as nearly 700 academies for young women, were staffed by the sisters.

Well before 1900, however, it was clear that the Catholic church had become a major presence in America. When Prince Napoleon, cousin of the French emperor, visited the United States in 1861, his entourage included a Corsican officer, Camille

Ferri-Pisani, who wrote a series of letters on his travels that were eventually published. He was much impressed with the strength of Catholicism in America, but he could not tell if that strength derived from the church's internal circumstances or its rapid adjustment to America. His conclusion was that "from a theoretical point of view, the application of the *voluntary* system to the Catholic religion offers a system of balanced forces, an intimate alliance of symmetrical principles, and that this conception is very appealing to the mind."[5] The adjustment of the principal church of traditional Europe to the open spaces and cultural innovations of the American New World was by no means complete by 1860. What could be said even then, nonetheless, was that the Catholic Church was destined to make an ever-increasing impact on its new environment, just as that new environment was bound in some measure to make an impression on the church.

Immigrant Protestants

Yet another important group of outsiders in the antebellum period were immigrants from Europe who, although they were Protestants, differed at many points from the Protestants of British stock already in America. Migrants from Ireland at this time were mostly Catholic, but from Germany came thousands of Lutherans and Protestant Pietists along with many Catholics. Much of the migration from the Netherlands was Reformed, and most of the migrants from Scandinavia were Lutheran. Between 1800 and 1920, the United States received about 40 million immigrants, among whom a substantial minority were Protestant. As with Catholics, some of the Protestant immigrants never reestablished church ties on this side of the Atlantic, or they maintained only the sort of religion to be found in ethnic fraternal organizations. Others, representing groups that had been intensely religious, nearly sectarian, within the state churches of Europe, spun off into separate American organizations that retained only general connections with Old World faiths. Examples of such bodies were the Church of the Lutheran Brethren in America, the Evangelical (originally Swedish) Covenant church, and the Swedish Evangelical Free Mission (which in 1950, when supplemented by other Scandinavian "Free" denominations, became the Evangelical Free Church of America). Still other immigrants formed American churches that were at first simply offshoots of European bodies but that later became self-standing denominations. In this category were most of the Reformed and Lutheran churches.

The large Lutheran immigrations of the nineteenth century illustrate how a process of indigenization, in which a European tradition comes closer and closer to American patterns, could be reversed by the tide of migrants from abroad. The

[5]Milton B. Powell, ed., *The Voluntary Church: American Religious Life, 1740–1860, Seen Through the Eyes of European Visitors* (New York: Macmillan, 1967), pp. 187–88.

Lutheran churches in the United States during the first decades of the nineteenth century were largely the product of organizing efforts by Henry Melchior Muhlenberg (1711–1789), who had been sent from the Pietist center in Halle to provide guidance for the German Lutheran immigrants in colonial Pennsylvania. As these earlier settlers learned English and took on other American characteristics, their religion also assumed an American cast.

A leading figure in the creation of this "more American" Lutheranism was Samuel Simon Schmucker (1799–1873), a graduate of the Presbyterians' Princeton Seminary, who worked throughout his life for causes that he felt would benefit both Lutherans and other Protestants in the United States. It was Schmucker's conviction that New World Lutherans could profitably link characteristics of American Protestantism with traditional European distinctions. From these convictions, he worked on behalf of the General Synod of Lutheran churches (formed in 1820), became a mainstay at Gettysburg Lutheran Seminary, and pledged himself to fight rationalism and religious indifference with the weapons of the Augsburg Confession and Luther's Small Catechism. At the same time, Schmucker's concerns moved beyond Lutheranism. He supported revivalism. He favored the development of interdenominational agencies, such as the Sunday School movement, to spread Christianity and to improve national morality. He spoke out on American national issues—by expressing fears, for example, concerning immigrants and Roman Catholics. He also was a founder of the American branch of the interdenominational Evangelical Alliance (1846). What became most upsetting to traditional Lutherans, however, was Schmucker's plan to modify the historic Augsburg Confession—he did not believe in a Real Presence of Christ's body in the Lord's Supper; he rejected private confession; he wondered if baptism really brought regeneration; and (in keeping with American "Puritan" opinions) he desired a much stronger emphasis on keeping the Sabbath. These opinions represented distinct innovations for traditional Lutherans.

Schmucker's point of view came close to prevailing in his denomination until about the time of the Civil War. Then, however, the growing numbers of immigrants from Germany and Scandinavia and a revival of interest in the roots of the Reformation combined to lessen his influence. Schmucker's books, like *A Fraternal Appeal to the American Churches* (1838), pleased his friends and worried immigrants by combining traditionally Lutheran and modern American convictions. The anonymous *Definite Synodical Platform* of 1855, which proposed a revision of the Augsburg Confession along lines favored by Schmucker, precipitated a clash of interests that eventually led to the mobilization of "European" Lutheranism against the trends favored by Schmucker.

In the struggle between "American" and "European" Lutherans, defenders of old ways also enjoyed capable leaders. One of these was the American-born Charles Porterfield Krauth (1823–1883), whose book *The Conservative Reformation and Its Theology* provided a forthright rationale for maintaining strict Old World standards for Lutheran teaching, even in the confines of the New World. Another was Carl Ferdinand Wilhelm Walther (1811–1887), a native of Saxony who migrated to the United States in 1838. Walther was every bit as active as an American revivalist, but the goal of his activity was the strengthening of the German Lutheran community. He pastored a church in St. Louis, helped start a training institute for ministerial candidates, founded a publishing house, a newspaper, and a theological journal, and he worked to unite the many different bodies of Lutherans in the United States. He was the president of the German Evangelical Lutheran Synod of Missouri, Ohio, and Other States (the forerunner of the modern Lutheran Church-Missouri Synod), and he was a leading figure in the Evangelical Lutheran Synodical Conference of North America that came into existence in 1872. Although Walther leaned toward a congregational form of church government and proclaimed such high views of God's grace that he was called a "crypto-Calvinist," he shared with Krauth the conviction that the main task for Lutherans in the New World was to maintain their Old World distinctiveness rather than adjusting to the ways of America. Following Krauth, Walther, and like-minded individuals, American Lutheranism turned back toward Europe. With other ethnic Protestants like the Dutch Reformed who settled especially in Michigan and Iowa, the Lutherans also established their own system of private schools at a time when most other American Protestants were strong supporters of public education. Lutheranism in America remained a largely self-contained, European outsider in contrast to American insiders until the 1930s and the end of large-scale immigrations from the European centers of Lutheran strength.

In nineteenth-century America, great space existed for religious groups to establish their own identity and to preserve their distinctive character as new American faiths or old European religions. For all of these groups, the evangelical Protestantism that predominated in the public sphere was a problem of some sort. Sometimes that Protestantism caused real hardship for the outsiders (especially the Catholics but also occasionally other groups like the Mormons), sometimes it merely ignored the existence of groups different from itself (as was often the case with the Lutherans). For their part, some of the religious outsiders would grow over time, establish more formal norms of organization, assume characteristics of the public faiths, and themselves begin to look as much like insiders as outsiders. That process has clearly taken place in the twentieth century for Roman Catholics, Mormons, and Lutherans. Both the space for new groups to find a haven as outsiders and the tendency to move toward the inside are characteristic of the cultural circumstances of Christianity in America, where fluidity and change have always been much more the order of the day than stability and tradition.

"Evangelical America"

By the end of the Civil War, the Roman Catholic church had surpassed the Methodists to become the largest American denomination. In addition, the large influx of

German and Scandinavian Lutherans further diluted the British-Protestant character of American religion. Yet for public purposes, for the perceptions that loomed largest for Americans and that first struck foreign visitors, the nation still seemed mostly to be a Protestant country dominated by denominations of British origin.

Membership figures, though again not as accurate as could be wished, tell a revealing story. By 1870, in a total population of nearly 40 million, there were about 4 million Catholics and another 430,000 Lutherans. The Methodists were the largest of the Protestant denominational families of British heritage with well over 2 million adherents. Another million and a half or so were Baptists and Disciples of Christ, there were about 700,000 in the various Presbyterian bodies, and about 300,000 Congregationalists. The last of the major groups with origins in the colonial period, the Episcopalians, numbered around 220,000. The Universalists were the largest of the new denominations that had sprung up after the Revolution, with approximately 140,000 adherents. Other bodies with substantial numbers included the German Reformed and the Quakers (each between 90,000 and 100,000), and the Dutch Reformed (about 55,000). Unitarians, who had separated from the Trinitarian Congregationalists in the first decades of the century, numbered about 30,000. Mennonites, the Church of the Brethren, Winebrennarians, Swedenborgians, and Shakers were among the groups at about 10,000.

The diversity of churches was great, and there were also many of them. In 1860 the census counted 38,183 church buildings, or an average of one house of worship for every 608 Americans. These churches were served by over 26,000 professional ministers and priests, while well over 10,000 others worked as part-time local preachers. The Methodists alone had 19,883 churches in that year. Church-going was most regular along the Atlantic coast and along the northern tier of states in which New England influence was pronounced. In 1870, for example, between 35 and 40 percent of the population in New England, the Atlantic states, and the eastern belt of southern states were regular adherents of a church. Farther west the rate dropped to about 25 percent but then climbed to eastern levels in the sparsely populated regions of the Far West.

The View from Abroad

Visitors from overseas were often struck by the vitality of America's faiths. Andrew Reed, an English Congregationalist active in establishing voluntary societies for charitable purposes, visited the states in the mid-1830s and came away marveling at the energy of the churches. He took pains in comparing the number of churches, ministers, and communicants in British and American cities of similar size (that is, Liverpool and New York, Edinburgh and Philadelphia, Glasgow and Boston), where he found the Americans ahead on nearly every account. In comparison to Nottingham, an English city of 50,000 inhabitants with twenty-three churches and 4,864 communicants, he was flabbergasted to find that Cincinnati, "a city only forty years old, and in the forests," with only 30,000 citizens, had nearly as many churches (twenty-one) and almost twice as many communicants (8,555).

Other foreign visitors interpreted all this American energy differently. Frances Trollope, mother of the novelist, lived in Cincinnati from 1827 to 1831 and was definitely not impressed by what she had seen of the country's religious life. "The whole people appear to be divided into an almost endless variety of religious factions," she wrote on returning to England. To her, America's wild regions were simply a mirror of its wild society. "The vehement expressions of insane or hypocritical zeal, such as were exhibited during 'the Revival,' can but ill atone for the want of village worship, any more than the eternal talk of the admirable and unequalled government can atone for the continual contempt of social order. Church and State hobble along, side by side, notwithstanding their boasted independence." She further reported that a stranger in the western United States, who was looking for regular worship, prayer, or preaching, would likely find only "that most terrific saturnalia, 'the camp meeting'."[6]

To yet other visitors the lack of general supervision, the absence of a governmental connection with the churches, was much more a strength than a weakness. Philip Schaff came from Germany and his native Switzerland to teach at the German Reformed seminary in Mercersburg, Pennsylvania, in 1843. When he returned to Germany for the first time in 1853, he was asked to lecture about the religious life of the United States. Schaff, who at first had doubted the wisdom of America's voluntary organization of religion, now entertained a much more favorable view:

"The nation . . . is still Christian, though it refuses to be governed in this deepest concern of the mind and heart by the temporal power. In fact, under such circumstances, Christianity, as the free expression of personal conviction and of the national character, has even greater power over the mind, than when enjoined by civil laws and upheld by police regulations. This appears practically in the strict observance of the Sabbath, the countless churches and religious schools, the zealous support of Bible and Tract societies, of domestic and foreign missions, the numerous revivals, the general attendance on divine worship, and the custom of family devotion—all expressions of the general Christian character of the people, in which the Americans are already in advance of most of the old Christian nations of Europe.[7]

Protestant Life in "Christian America"

Schaff no doubt exaggerated the comprehensive sweep of Christianity in the United States at mid-century, for in fact a majority of the population did not then have a

[6]Powell, *The Voluntary Church*, pp. 69, 71.
[7]Ibid., pp. 145–46

regular church attachment, and in some regions of the country organized religion had made only little headway. At the same time, Schaff did catch something of the evangelical Protestant tone given to much of the nation's public life. During the decades from the postrevolutionary revivals at least through the Civil War, the country's ethos was definitely evangelical. In a number of particulars, this was indeed the era of Christian America, defined as evangelical Protestants would use the term.

The most striking testimony to the evangelical sway was the conversion of the West and the South. To some extent the history of New England illustrates modern conceptions of so-called secularization theory. Its Protestantism remained strong through the mid-nineteenth century, but then it seemed to thin out doctrinally and culturally as the cities grew, capitalism took firmer hold, and intellectual innovations from Europe came to erode previous dogmatic certainties. In the South and West, however, the movement was the other way. The western frontier, a region that only recently had been devoid of European civilization as well as Christianity, was successfully evangelized and civilized by agents of the churches. In the South, where religion had always existed in some form, the problem was different. Through the early years of the nineteenth century, the dominant southern culture was confrontational, violent, self-possessed, and driven more by personal honor than by personal religion. The revivals of the Second Great Awakening did not change that system of personal values entirely. It remained, for example, as a great prop of the slave system, in which the ability to own and control slaves was regarded as a symbol of self-sufficient virility. Yet the successes of the revival, especially in linking ideals of womanhood with ideals of Christianity, dramatically altered southern culture. To honor wives and daughters was now much more clearly to respect Christianity. To act responsibly in the world at large was now much more to make room for the church. No change had more effect on the general culture of America in the antebellum period than the progress of evangelical Protestantism in the South.

The extent of evangelical influence extended much further, however. It was, for example, evangelical religion that drove the great developments in popular communications in the period between the revolution and the Civil War. In that era, evangelicals, whether as individuals or in voluntary societies, literally transformed the ground rules of print. Between 1790 and 1830, nearly 600 religious magazines were founded. Every state in the Union except Mississippi became the publishing home of at least one such effort. By 1830 two of these new journals, a Methodist weekly entitled *The Christian Advocate and Journal and Zion's Herald* and a monthly interdenominational magazine, the *American National Preacher*, each claimed a circulation of 25,000. Nowhere else in the world at the time did any journal of any kind circulate so widely. Evangelicals, like those who backed the various bible societies, pioneered in print technology (for example, cheap stereotyping, steam-powered printing, and machine papermaking). And they were leaders in conceiving innovative ways of distributing the printed word. In this matter, itinerating Methodist preachers had no peers, for they were always sellers of the written word as well as preachers of the spoken word.

Not only did evangelical religion provide ordinary Americans with their reading material. To a large extent it shaped the patterns of their thought. Insofar as it is possible to discover the popular opinions of Americans who left only letters, an occasional diary, or other fugitive records, it seems as if a deeply religious spirit imbued much of the American population in this period. It was not necessarily a spirit well-versed in formal Christian doctrine. Moreover, ordinary people do not seem to have given much thought to the messianic character of the United States or to the prospects for the soon coming of the millennium, subjects that did engage the publishing elites. Rather, the mood of common Americans was more at home in the somber universe of Nathaniel Hawthorne or Herman Melville, much closer to the melancholy of Abraham Lincoln than to the cosmic optimism of Ralph Waldo Emerson or Walt Whitman. Whatever their formal religious beliefs, ordinary Americans seemed to retain a generally Calvinistic outlook, impressed more with human limitations than with potential. Ordinary people, in a life made difficult by unexpected death, families separated by vast distances, and the unpredictability of weather and crops, tended toward personal resignation; they were earnest, wary of pretension, and above all pessimistic about human nature. They were not so much concerned about controlling other people for their own ends as controlling themselves and their immediate environments. Common people had a vital interest in order and a deep-seated fear of disorder. They dealt with these inner needs, it seems, with efforts to control the self, to find alignment with God's particular call to salvation and the more general designs of Providence. Most common people worried about controlling themselves in the face of personal guilt, anxieties due to the vicissitudes of love and marriage, the uncertainties of birth, the unknown possibilities of the West, and the ever-present reality of death. These are generalizations that would not apply to many antebellum Americans, but for the majority, it was this vision of life that shaped the daily round.

Evangelical religion also was the major influence in defining the nation's intellectual life. Very few individuals went to college (no more than 2 percent of the college-age population until the 1880s), but where colleges existed, they were almost always sponsored and staffed by evangelicals. Exceptions were the colleges founded by Roman Catholics (twenty-seven such institutions were founded before the Civil War) and a very occasional institution like Harvard, which by the early nineteenth century had drifted from its earlier evangelical orientation to a more genteel Unitarianism. Before 1820, almost 70 percent of America's colleges were sponsored by Congregationalists, Presbyterians, and Episcopalians. By the Civil War, Methodists and Baptists were sponsoring a third of the nation's institutions of higher learning, the three large colonial denominations another third, and other religious groups (mostly within a general evangelical frame) another 10 percent.

Among the nation's intellectual elite, the periodicals that were most widely distributed and influential were the theological quarterlies. It was a period when all denominations worthy of the name sponsored at least one such journal, and when Methodists, Presbyterians, Episcopalians, Congregationalists, and Unitarians patronized several weighty quarterlies each. Presbyterians, who prided themselves on the care that they devoted to religious thought, had the *Southern Presbyterian Review* and *The Cumberland Presbyterian* for readers below the Mason–Dixon line, the *American Presbyterian* and the *Presbyterian Quarterly Review*, which promoted more activistic, Americanized "New School" views, and the *Biblical Repertory and Princeton Review*, edited for forty-five years by Charles Hodge of Princeton Theological Seminary to promote more traditional and dogmatic Old School opinions. Methodists, Congregationalists, and Episcopalians enjoyed just about as wide a spectrum of learned journals. What these journals published also went well beyond normal religious fare. They gave full attention to theological questions and divergent interpretations of the bible, but they also discussed literary and historical subjects, commented extensively on current events (especially before and during the Civil War), and provided general discussions of scientific questions that were among the best informed in the country.

The country's evangelical theologians were its most respected intellectuals before the Civil War. The thought of an Emerson or a Thoreau might seem more substantive to modern Americans than the work of theologians. But it was much more Edwards Amasa Park of Andover Seminary, Nathaniel W. Taylor of Yale, Charles Hodge at Princeton, R. L. Dabney at Union Seminary in Virginia, or Charles Finney and Asa Mahan at Oberlin, who most impressed their contemporaries. And when it was not these evangelical voices that commanded intellectual attention, it was the opinions of the Unitarian William Ellery Channing or the maverick Congregationalist Horace Bushnell, both substantially evangelical in style if no longer explicitly so in dogmatic theology, to which educated Americans were likely to turn.

The influence of evangelical religion extended beyond the intellectual to the political as well. Here many other influences were also important. At the least, however, evangelical forms of voluntary organization provided a viable model for the organization of partisan political bodies that occurred in "the second party system" beginning under Andrew Jackson. Evangelical mobilization for reform also provided a forceful style adapted to American circumstances that political reformers increasingly put to use as the century wore on. In addition, evangelical values deeply shaped the formal political parties. The Anti-Masonic Party, the Liberty Party (which advocated a more rapid liberation of the slaves), and the Know-Nothing or American Party (which exploited Protestant fears of Roman Catholics) were each important third parties with considerable local (and even national) loyalties for at least an election or two in the forty years before the Civil War. All of them were direct products of evangelical worldviews, apprehensions, and aspirations. The Whig party, from its rise as the formal opposition to Jackson to its demise in the 1850s, came close to being an embodiment of evangelical public faith. The Whig sense of urgency at promoting righteousness in society, its often confusing alliances with the forces of freedom (religious, social, capitalistic), its ambiguous but persistent uneasiness with slavery—all reflected an evangelical influence. And the Democrats, though opposing the Whigs systematically, also reflected some evangelical influences as well, especially from the South and especially from theological conservatives who felt alienated from the larger, more publicly visible evangelical spokesmen.

The importance of evangelical religion for antebellum politics is indicated by the fact that denominational allegiance in conjunction with ethnic ties was the best predictor for voting behavior in the period. Congregationalists, New School Presbyterians, Methodists in the North, most Lutherans, and Black Protestants could be counted on to give three-fourths or more of their votes to the Whigs, and then (once it had been founded) the Republican party. By contrast, Baptists and Methodists in the South along with most ethnic Catholic communities could be expected to vote in the same proportion for Democrats. Other religious groups could be counted on just as predictably to lean toward the Whig/Republicans or the Democrats.

America's Book, America's Icon: The Bible

The most pervasive symbol of Christian America during the nineteenth century was the bible. Abraham Lincoln noted in his Second Inaugural Address that "both [sides] read the same Bible," and indeed they did. The complex, multidimensional story of the bible in America began well before 1800 and extends to the present, but during the century of the Awakenings and Civil War, of expansion, immigration, and industrialization, the bible was a particularly potent force on the American scene.

Throughout their entire history, Americans have sustained an incredible rate of bible publication and an even more stupendous appetite for literature about the bible. Publication of the bible has been a lucrative business in America but one not without peril. Before the Revolutionary War, the publication of English-language bibles was prohibited in America, since the king's printers in England enjoyed an exclusive copyright to printing the authorized version. This meant that the first bibles and biblical portions printed in America were in languages other than English. In 1743 Christopher Sauer published an edition of Martin Luther's bible on type carried from Frankfurt and in so doing established his family as America's leading publisher for speakers of German. Even earlier, the bible had made its appearance in native tongues. Spanish Franciscans were translating biblical liturgies and other Catholic literature for the Rimucuan Indians of Florida in the sixteenth and very early seventeenth centuries before permanent English colonies existed in New England. Decades later the Massachusetts Puritan minister John Eliot translated the bible into Algonquian (New Testament 1661, entire bible 1663). Other laborers since Eliot have translated at least parts of the bible into a whole series of Indian languages, including Apache, Cherokee, Cheyenne, Choctaw, Dakota, Hopi, Inupiat, Kuskokwim, Muskogee, Navajo, and Ojibwa.

Once American printers began producing their own editions of the Authorized King James Version, business boomed. More than 2,500 English-language editions of the bible were published in the United States between 1777 and 1957. Mason Weems, who fabricated the story of Washington and the cherry tree, made his living in the early years of the new nation selling bibles in Virginia. From there he reported to his publisher: "I tell you this is the very season and age of the Bible. Bible Dictionaries, Bible tales, Bible stories—Bibles plain or paraphrased, Carey's Bibles, Collin's Bibles, Clarke's Bibles, Kimptor's Bibles, no matter what or whose, all, all, will go down—so wide is the crater of public appetite at this time."[8] As successful as bible publishing was in general, however, that success did not extend to efforts at producing new translations. Until well into the twentieth century, the King James version for Protestants and the Douay-Rheims version for Catholics reigned supreme as the bibles of choice for Americans. Nineteenth-century publishers who underwrote efforts to translate the bible into an American idiom encountered stiff market resistance. In 1833, for example, Noah Webster, father of the American dictionary, finished his translation of a bible shorn of British spellings and archaic usages. His contemporary Andrew Comstock devised a phonetic "purfekt alfabet" for a "Filadelphia" New Testament published in 1848. But these and similar efforts met with little success. Only with the production of the American Standard version in 1901 did publishers begin to enjoy the market for newer versions.

One of the ways scripture was circulated in the early history of the United States was through bible societies. Although Britain had the first formal bible society, American groups would be even more active. The American Bible Society, the largest of the societies, has distributed nearly 4 billion complete bibles, testaments, scriptural portions, and selections since its founding in 1816. Bible societies received the support of many who held traditional Christian views on the bible's supernatural character, like the first president of the United States Congress, Elias Boudinot of New Jersey, who also became first president of the American Bible Society. The societies also were patronized by others with unconventional religious ideas, such as Thomas Jefferson.

The bible has clearly influenced the way Americans write, talk, think, and think of themselves. In 1864 a group of grateful Blacks from Baltimore presented President Lincoln with a pulpit bible bound in violet-tinged velvet, finished in gold, with a raised design depicting the emancipation of the slaves, as a token of their respect for his efforts on their behalf. In response, Lincoln called the bible "God's best gift to man." Some years before, the skeptical John Adams wrote to his even more skeptical friend, Thomas Jefferson, that the bible "contains more of my little philosophy than all the libraries I have seen."

America's common people have also reflected a pervasive respect for scripture. The use of biblical names for children continues into the late twentieth century and extends a much longer pattern of employing biblical nomenclature. As Americans

---

[8]Garry Wills, "Mason Weems, Bibliopolist," *American Heritage* (February-March 1981), p. 68.

686

in the nineteenth century settled new towns and named new features of the terrain, it was instinctive to turn to the bible for names like Zoar (from Gen. 13:10) in Ohio and Mount Tirzah (Josh. 12:24) in North Carolina, or the forty-seven variations on Bethel to be found across the country, sixty-one on Eden, and ninety-five on Salem.

In American social history, the bible has acted as both a conservative and a radical force. As we shall see, it played a large role in the circumstances leading to the Civil War. Scripture has provided a vocabulary for traditional deference but also for innovative egalitarianism. It has fueled both stability in the face of anarchy and freedom in the face of tyranny. The bible has been a charter of social liberty for many who have felt constrained by traditional boundaries or dominating cultural fashions. "The bible only" was the liberating cry of the energetic men and women who formed many of the new denominations established between the revolution and the Civil War. On the other side of the picture, the bible has also played a part in reinforcing social conformity. When the Catholic bishop of Philadelphia, Francis Patrick Kenrick, petitioned city officials in 1842 to allow school children of his faith to hear readings from the Douay version instead of the King James version, Protestant protests followed. Evangelical ministers formed national anti-Catholic organizations, and Protestant laymen vented their anger by rioting against Philadelphia's Catholic churches.

The most important instance of the bible's social liberation in America belongs to the history of Black Americans. Slaves made a sharp distinction between the bible their owners preached to them, with its emphasis on not stealing and obeying masters, and the bible they found for themselves, with a message of liberation for the captive and redemption for the oppressed. Under slavery, regulations often forbade unsupervised preaching or sometimes even the possession of bibles. With permission or not, slaves worked diligently to obtain the scriptures for themselves. Many made a special effort to hear Black preachers expound the scriptures in circumstances unsupervised by masters. One slave left a striking testimony of the difference: "A yellow [light-complexioned] man preached to us. [The slave owner] had him preach how we ought to obey our master and missy if we want to go to heaven, but when she wasn't there, he came out with straight preachin' from the Bible."[9] Blacks sang about Adam, Eve, and the Fall, about "wrestlin' Jacob" who "would not let [God] go," about Moses "going down" to Egypt, about Joshua possessing the Promised Land, about Daniel in the lion's den and Daniel's three friends in the fiery furnace, about Jonah in the whale, about the birth of Jesus, and his death and future return. The stories of the Old Testament in particular lent slave use of the bible its special social dimension. For slaves, the figure of Moses loomed especially large as the one raised up by God to free his people. To the hope of liberation in this world, the slaves added a concentration on the figure of Jesus, who suffered innocently and who

---

[9] Charles V. Hamilton, *The Black Preacher in America* (New York: William Morrow, 1972), p. 39.

ministered to the oppressed, as the source of hope for the future. The slave's profound embrace of scripture created the climate for the ongoing importance of bible reading and biblical preaching among Blacks since the Civil War.

The bible has also played an important role in efforts to define the character of the country. Borrowing liberally from Old Testament precedents, many early Americans and not a few in more recent days have regarded the United States as God's New Israel, a nation established in this New World Canaan as a land flowing with wealth and freedom. Although Canadians have never indulged such notions to the extent of their fellows in the United States, Canada too has seen ideas of a special divine covenant. In both the nineteenth and twentieth centuries, at least a few Canadian leaders have spoken of "His dominion" with the understanding that God had bestowed special blessings on that northern land. To balance the picture, however, we must also note a different perspective on the role of the United States. Black slaves before the Civil War and not a few Christian radicals in the late twentieth century have reversed the typology: America was Egypt, and *escape* from American institutions and influence was the Exodus. Particularly at moments of crisis, however, the themes of scripture have easily slid over into the terms of national identity, whether apocalypse during the Revolutionary and Civil Wars, redemption during the Civil War by the one called by some "Father Abraham," or judgment during national disasters. Late into the twentieth century, the messages of American politics still sometimes echo the words and themes of the bible.

In many other ways the bible has played a part in American culture, often shaping that culture by the power of its own message but also often shaped itself by the social, economic, and artistic patterns of life in America. The bible has informed the spirituals of Blacks and Shakers and the more formal hymnody of the churches; it has provided material for paintings both refined and primitive; it has been a primary textbook itself in many American schools and a decisive influence on the curriculum in many more; it has been a factor in legal decisions and jurisprudential reasoning; it has provided the raw material for historical novels, plays, mass art, country music, humor, broadcasting, children's literature, and much much more. In sum, the bible has been an ever-present force in American life. Americans have perhaps been more prone than people elsewhere to bend, twist, and abuse the bible for their own sometimes very un-Christian purposes. But from its pages they have also drawn insight, strength, and wisdom for life more in keeping with scripture's central themes. At no time was this more so than in the first two-thirds of the nineteenth century when evangelical Protestantism was the dominant religious force in the land.

Chapter 31

THE PASSING OF CHRISTIAN AMERICA
(1861–1925)

Between the Civil War and World War I, an important transition occurred in the history of Christianity in America. These decades witnessed the highpoint of American Protestant civilization, but they also witnessed a rapid decline of Christianity in the nation's centers of cultural influence. Two primary circumstances accounted for the transition. The first was the splintering diversity of religion in America. Not only did Roman Catholics become, through immigration and natural increase, the largest American denomination; the Catholic church also began cautiously to break from its ghettoes in order to participate in the nation's public life. In addition, Protestants of non-British background, especially the Lutherans, established an unmistakable presence in the nation. Black Christian groups, now liberated from hereditary slavery, organized for themselves. Representatives of various Eastern Orthodox churches made their first appearance on the North American continent. And beyond the Christian orbit, even more religious groups, at first Jews but then others as well, began to claim a place in the sun. A majority of Americans still identified themselves as Protestants, and most of these Protestants had some connection to the nation's traditional denominations, but the age of Protestant hegemony was nearly over.

The second circumstance was the decline of Protestant influence in the nation's culture. For a number of reasons—social, political, economic, and intellectual, as well as religious—the control of the churches over the nation's organs of communication, its centers of higher learning, and its public morality gradually receded as the nineteenth century gave way to the twentieth. These circumstances did not lead to inactivity but, rather, stimulated all sorts of Christians to action—theological as well as social, ecclesiastical as well as political. An inescapable reality had, however, become clear by the mid-1920s. The nation had moved from a situation in which most religious instincts were Christian in a Protestant form to one in which instincts were jumbled and competitive, Protestant versus Protestant, Protestant versus Catholic and Christian versus non-Christian.

The Civil War

Christianity was everywhere present in the crisis leading to civil war and in the war itself. As during the War for Independence, Christianity was not a cause, as such, of the conflict, but it did provide a network of intensifying influences for the political, social, and cultural differences that brought on the strife of arms.

The reforms inspired by revival included abolitionism, the drive to abolish slavery. One of the most effective antislave agents was Theodore Dwight Weld (1803–1895), a convert under revivalist Charles G. Finney who worked throughout the 1830s and 1840s with equal zeal to convert and liberate America. Harriet Beecher Stowe (1811–1896) was the daughter of the revivalist and social reformer Lyman Beecher and the wife of a Congregationalist minister. Her immensely influential novel *Uncle Tom's Cabin* (1852) exerted its great impact at least in part because the book was such a forceful summation of Christian revivalism, Christian domesticity, and Christian abolitionism. In similar manner, the 1858 hymn, "Stand Up, Stand Up, for Jesus," by a Presbyterian minister from Philadelphia, George Duffield, nicely combined appeals to external religious truths and to the temporal challenge to eradicate slavery. At mid-century, a growing number of northerners had come to link the future of the faith as well as the future of the country with an end to slavery. Correspondingly, in the South more and more believers came to see the northern assault on slavery as also an assault on their faith.

The "nation's book," the bible, figured large in this clash of cultures. To many southerners the bible was the sure foundation for their way of life. The Reverend Federick Ross of Hunstville, Alabama, for one, insisted that southern slavery was modeled on a biblical pattern: "Every southern planter is not more truly a slaveholder than Abraham. And the Southern master, by divine authority, may today consider his slaves part of his social and religious family, just as Abraham did."[1] From the North it was a much different story but based on the same authority. As the Presbyterian Albert Barnes from Philadelphia put it, "The principles laid down by the Saviour and his Apostles are such as are opposed to Slavery, and if carried out would secure its universal abolition."[2]

---

[1]Eugene D. Genovese, *"Slavery Ordained of God": The Southern Slaveholders' View of Biblical History and Modern Politics* (Gettysburg, PA: Gettysburg College, 1985), p. 19.
[2]Albert Barnes, *An Inquiry into the Scriptural Views of Slavery* (Philadelphia: Pickens and Purves, 1846), p. 340.

Crises in the denominations also contributed to the weakening of the Union. The main body of American Presbyterians divided in 1837 for reasons that were largely theological and ecclesiastical, but a secondary source of contention did involve sectional politics. The more conservative Old School party held that slavery was a secular topic that the church should not address directly. The more revivalistic New School group took the opposite view and wanted to see the church act more aggressively on slavery and other social problems. Not surprisingly, the New School was strongest in the North, and the Old School derived much of its strength from the South. Sectional conflict was not the major issue at stake for the Presbyterians in 1837, but it soon became the key to even larger Protestant divisions.

In the mid-1840s, the Baptists and the Methodists, who by that time had become the nation's largest Protestant denominations, both divided over the issue of slavery. The issue among Methodists concerned the propriety of bishops' holding bondsmen. Among the Baptists, the specific question was the appointment of slaveholders as missionaries. In both cases, negotiations gave way to recriminations; standoff gave way to schism. For Baptists in the South, the contention over slave-holding missionaries led in 1845 to the formal organization of the Southern Baptist Convention. At the time, however, the major consequence of intradenominational strife over slavery was to weaken cultural ties between North and South. The result was a break at the Mason–Dixon line between not just large and influential religious bodies but also between significant forces for social cohesion. In the phrases of historian C. C. Goen, the "broken churches" led to a "broken nation."

A deep longing for the millennium also played its part in heightening the stakes of sectional conflict. Visions of the End of the Age, when Christ would rule the world in a 1,000-year kingdom of righteousness and peace, drove revivalists and social reformers to unpredecented personal sacrifices in pursuit of converts and social righteousness. It also lent a sacred aura to the fabric of national civilization that northerners felt the South was threatening and southerners felt the North imperiled. The increasing strife between North and South inspired not only loyalty to section but also apocalyptic conceptions of the nation, as in a work published in 1854 under the title, *Armageddon: or the . . . existence of the United States Foretold in the Bible, its . . . expansion into the millennial republic, and its dominion over the whole world.*

The by now standard American identification of the United States as "God's New Israel" served only to heighten religious conceptions of the conflict. After Abraham Lincoln's assassination at the very end of the war, a great outpouring of sermons mourned his passing. Many of these rehearsed the notion of God's special plan for America. Ministers, for example, affirmed that the meaning of Psalm 147:20 ("He hath not dealt so with any nation") still was "as true of us as of ancient Israel."[3] They expressed their belief that "the Hebrew Commonwealth, 'in which all the families of the earth were to be blest,' was not more of the whole world's concern

[3]T. R. Howlett, *The Dealing of God with Our Nation* (Washington, D.C.; 1865), p. 1.

than is this Republic."[4] Even Isaac Wise, a rabbi, could use this language of the Old Testament in calling on the American "Israel" to repent of its sins and to obey God's law.

The war itself was the occasion for a great deal of Christian activity. In the public sphere, Christianity rapidly became a prop for the efforts of both sides. During the conflict, Jefferson Davis called for nine national days of fasting in the Confederacy, and Abraham Lincoln proclaimed four days of thanksgiving in the Union. The bible, moreover, was the lens through which it all was viewed. Early in the war, a southern Presbyterian teased II Chronicles 6:34–35, King Solomon's prayer for success in battle for Israel, into a biblically worded analysis of the current crisis: "Eleven tribes sought to go forth in peace from the house of political bondage, but the heart of our modern Pharoah is hardened, that he will not let Israel go."[5] In the North, one of the more than 400 sermons published after the assassination of Lincoln was an exposition of II Samuel 18:32, in which David learns about the treacherous slaying of his son Absalom. After an examination of the text, the minister concluded that no one "will be able to separate in thought the murder of the president from Jefferson Davis' persistent effort to murder the Union."[6]

During the war, Christians and Christian institutions were also active in more strictly spiritual, less overtly ideological areas. Revivals were common in the camps of both the Blue and the Gray. In the field, if not always at the home front, preaching focused more directly on the spiritual needs of individuals before God, less on a supposedly biblical mandate to win the war. The result was a series of deeply moving conversions. In the South, fervor increased along with the tide of northern advance. Some southerners apparently expected a supernatural intervention to come from the turn to piety. Others like Captain Daniel Hundley, who was a prisoner of the Union forces, were learning something else: "Adversity has its lessons," he wrote at the time, "and those who will take the trouble patiently to master them will in the end be forced to acknowledge that it is oftentimes better to go up to the house of mourning than to the house of rejoicing."[7]

The voluntary tradition also flourished during the conflict when thousands enlisted not to fight the enemy but to assist soldiers and others thrown into difficulty by the war. In the North, the Sanitary Commission looked to material needs of the combatants, and groups like the Christian Commission and the American Tract Society ministered directly to spiritual concerns. Nursing care for the wounded was often a product of specific religious concern, as with the 640 Catholic sisters who served in military hospitals and the numerous nurses from Episcopalian sisterhoods.

---

[4]Treadwell Walden, *The National Sacrifice* (Philadelphia, 1865), p. 17.
[5]James W. Silver, *Confederate Morale and Church Propaganda* (Gloucester, MA: Peter Smith, 1964), p. 27.
[6]Henry A. Nelson, *The Divinely Prepared Ruler, and the Fit End of Treason* (Springfield, IL: 1865), p. 32.
[7]Gardiner H. Shatuck, Jr., *A Shield and Hiding Place: The Religious Life of the Civil War Armies* (Macon, GA: Mercer University Press, 1987).

In addition, more general appeals to religious motives helped the war's nursing leaders—Clara Barton, director of a large volunteer network, who had been raised a Universalist, and the Unitarian Dorothea Dix, superintendent of Nurses for the Union Army—to enlist volunteers for this very necessary service. The immense job of assisting released slaves fell largely on the agents of the Freedman's Bureau. In the face of considerable local resistance, its workers provided shelter, began education, trained for employment, and encouraged spiritually the former slaves. All of these voluntary societies were built on models earlier pioneered by evangelicals for purposes of revival and reform.

In a word, the Civil War was a religious event because it consumed the energies of a religious people. The economic and social ramifications of the conflict certainly did stimulate forces that led to a more secular America. The war acted as a spur to large-scale industrialization, intensive bureaucratic efficiency, and the mass movement of rural dwellers out of their customary environments—all factors working against the settled harmonies of republican Christianity and small-town morality that prevailed so widely in the antebellum period. At the same time, the most important long-term effects of the war on the churches may have come from its very religiosity. In both the North and the South, believers were tempted to equate success in a battle with basic religious concern. To the extent this took place, the stage was set for other consuming national interests to exert a similar shaping influence on the churches. Only occasionally did participants in the war step back from the pressure of the moment and reflect more generally on the mysteries of Providence. The great example of such reflection came from a most unlikely source, the Union's president from Illinois, Abraham Lincoln.

Abraham Lincoln

Abraham Lincoln (1809–1865), sixteenth president of the United States, has become a mythic figure in America's civil religion. Born into relative poverty on the midwestern frontier, he rose from humble origins through self-discipline, honesty, common sense, a ready wit, and considerable ambition to shepherd the nation through the black days of the Civil War. After his death, Americans found it irresistible to view his achievement in a religious light. It was soon noted, for example, that Lincoln—the "Savior" of the Union—was shot on Good Friday (April 14, 1865), that his efforts to liberate the bondslave and to bind up the wounds of war were cut short by "martyrdom," and that his very name—Abraham—speaks of one who was the father of his people. Although Lincoln himself originally saw the Civil War as a political struggle to preserve the Union, he came to regard it as a crusade for truth and right. He could speak of the United States as "the last, best hope of the earth," of its citizens as "the almost chosen people," and of the war as a test to see if a nation "conceived in liberty . . . can long endure."

Considerable uncertainty arises, however, when Lincoln's own religious beliefs and practices are examined. It is obvious that Christianity exerted a profound influence on his life. His father was a member of Regular Baptist churches in Kentucky and Indiana. Lincoln himself read the bible throughout his life, quoted from it extensively, and made very frequent use of biblical images (as in the "House Divided" speech of 1858). It was said of him, perhaps with some exaggeration, that he knew by heart much of the Psalms, the book of Isaiah, and the entire New Testament. His life also exhibited many Christian virtues. He was scrupulously honest in repaying debts from ill-fated business ventures of the 1830s. He offered tender sympathy to the widows and orphans created by the Civil War. He pardoned numerous sleeping sentries and other soldiers condemned to death for relatively minor lapses. And he kept his head concerning the morality of the contending sides in the war, refusing to picture the North as entirely virtuous and the South as absolutely evil. In addition, during his years as president he regularly attended the New York Avenue Presbyterian church in Washington.

On the other hand, Lincoln never joined a church nor ever made a clear profession of standard Christian beliefs. And his early views on race were quite conventional—he was always disturbed about slavery but not committed to the full rights of citizens for Blacks. Although Lincoln read the bible in the White House, he was not in the habit of saying grace before meals. Lincoln's friend, Jesse Fell, noted that the president "seldom communicated to anyone his views" on religion but went on to suggest that those views were not orthodox: "On the innate depravity of man, the character and office of the great head of the Church, the Atonement, the infallibility of the written revelation, the performance of miracles, the nature and design of . . . future rewards and punishments . . . and many other subjects, he held opinions utterly at variance with what are usually taught in the church."[8] It is probable that Lincoln was turned against organized Christianity by his experiences as a young man in New Salem, Illinois, where the ministry of traveling preachers and the yearly camp meetings were marked by excessive emotion and bitter sectarian quarrels. Yet, although Lincoln was not a church member, he did ponder the eternal significance of his own life, marked as it was by tragedy (the early death of two sons) and difficulty (the occasional mental instability of his wife). And he took to heart the carnage of war over which he presided.

Whether it was from these experiences or from other sources, Lincoln came to express a spiritual perception far above the ordinary. It is one of the great ironies of the history of Christianity in America that the most profoundly religious analysis of the nation's deepest trauma came not from a clergyman or a theologian but from a politician who was self-taught in the ways of both God and man. The source of Lincoln's Christian perception will probably always remain a mystery, but the un-

[8]William J. Wolf, *The Almost Chosen People: A Study of the Religion of Abraham Lincoln* (Garden City, N.Y.: Doubleday, 1959), p. 107.

usual depth of that perception none can doubt. Nowhere was that depth more visible than in his Second Inaugural Address of March 1865:

> Both [North and South] read the same Bible and pray to the same God; and each invokes His aid against the other. It may seem strange that any men should dare to ask a just God's assistance in wringing their bread from the sweat of other men's faces; but let us judge not that we be not judged. The prayers of both could not be answered; that of neither has been answered fully. The Almighty has His own purposes.[9]

Even more to the point was his reply when a minister from the North told the president that he "hoped the Lord is on our side." Responded Lincoln: "I am not at all concerned about that. . . . But it is my constant anxiety and prayer that I and this nation should be on the Lord's side."[10]

Protestantism on the March

The most visible Protestantism to emerge from the Civil War was considerably simpler than Abraham Lincoln's complex faith. In the North, triumph in war encouraged an optimism about the prospects of religion and American civilization. In the South, where the experience of defeat lent a solemn tinge to religion, a no less active faith emerged. The conditions of American life in which Protestants of British background had flourished were in fact changing rapidly. But still the eyes of the nation's "public Protestants" were fixed on lofty goals—in evangelism and missions, moral and political reform, the rescue of the cities, and the reunification of Christianity.

Evangelism at Home and Abroad

The drive to spread the Christian message to those who had not yet embraced it grew even stronger after the war. At home, it led to great energy in evangelism. Abroad, it was the impetus behind a dramatic rise in missionary endeavor.

During the second half of the nineteenth century, no one figure symbolized this evangelistic appeal more completely than Dwight Lyman Moody (1837–1899). After moving from his native New England to Chicago shortly before the Civil War, Moody took an active part in the work of the Young Men's Christian Association.

[9]Roy P. Basler, ed., *The Collected Works of Abraham Lincoln*, Vol. VIII (New Brunswick, N.J.: Rutgers University Press, 1953), p. 333.
[10]William Wolf, *Almost Chosen People*, p. 128.

In 1873 Moody and a song-leader friend, Ira Sankey, embarked on a modestly conceived preaching tour of Great Britain that changed the course of their lives. The meetings proved unexpectedly successful. When, after two years, they returned, Moody was everywhere in demand.

Moody's manner as a preacher nicely fit the character of his age. He was not as intense as Charles Finney, his famous predecessor, nor did he engage in the theatrical antics of Billy Sunday, his best-known successor. Rather, Moody tried to talk sense to his audiences about God and the need for a Savior. He dressed like a conventional businessman and spoke calmly and plainly. Moody's message was a basic Christian one, which he summarized as the "Three R's": Ruin by Sin, Redemption by Christ, and Regeneration by the Holy Ghost. Increasingly his concerns turned away from the reform of society. He saw himself first and foremost as a winner of souls. In his most famous statement about his own work, Moody said, "I look upon this world as a wrecked vessel. God has given me a lifeboat and said to me, 'Moody, save all you can.' "

Moody's personal influence was extended through his founding of important institutions. These included a bible training center for lay workers in Chicago (later the Moody Bible Institute) and the summer missions conferences held near his home in Northfield, Massachusetts. From these meetings came the founding in 1876 of the Student Volunteer Movement, a great effort that encouraged thousands of students to seek "the evangelization of the world in this generation."

Joining Moody as promoters of efforts to take the Christian message around the world were a host of capable and earnest promoters of the missionary enterprise. The Presbyterian A. T. Pierson (1837–1911) organized conferences throughout the 1880s that led to the recruitment of 3,000 young men and women for missionary service. A Baptist from New England A. J. Gordon (1836–1895) founded the Boston Missionary Training Institute (later Gordon College and Seminary) in 1889 to prepare laity, esepcially women, for missionary service. In the 1890s A. B. Simpson (1844–1919) established a missionary network for foreign service and then a stateside fellowship to support the missionary endeavor, two bodies that eventually merged to become a new denomination, The Christian and Missionary Alliance. John R. Mott (1865–1955), who had been recruited for missionary service by Pierson, traveled extensively in America and around the world throughout his long life to promote the cause of missions. And perhaps the most visible promoter of missionary service at this time was a Presbyterian layman, Robert Elliott Speer (1867–1947), who was an early administrator of the Student Volunteer Movement, and then from 1891 to 1937 the secretary of the Board of Foreign Missions for the northern Presbyterian church.

The rise of Protestant missions from America was very much a part of the expansion of the United States. In this respect it paralleled the expansion of Europe, since Britain, France, and Germany were also colonizing and sending out missionaries with enthusiasm during the era. President William McKinley, who led the nation to war against Spain for control of the Philippines in 1898, felt that he was acting as much from missionary as from national motivation. As he told a delegation of Methodists in 1899, he came to a decision to enter the conflict with largely religious motives: "There was nothing left for us to do but to take them all, and to educate the Filipinos, and uplift and civilize and Christianize them, and by God's grace do the very best we could by them, as our fellow-men for whom Christ died."[11]

A major factor in the rising missionary interest was the participation of women. When denominational officials expressed ambivalence about giving women full recognition as missionaries, the response was to found missionary societies staffed, directed, and funded by women. Abbie Child led other American women in establishing the World's Missionary Committee of Christian Women, one of the earliest bodies attempting to coordinate the missionary activities in scattered fields of service. Single women in their own missionary societies combined with the wives of male missionaries to make up 60 percent of the nation's missionary force in the late nineteenth century. By the turn of the century, forty-one women's missionary societies supported more than 1,200 missionaries. On the field itself, women often enjoyed opportunities for authority, for public speaking, and for institutional leadership that were not yet available in the states. In many missionary compounds throughout China, for example, women took the lead in providing schooling and medical care for Chinese women and children, they supervised often large staffs of men and women helpers, and they represented both Christianity and western culture in public gatherings.

At the start of the twentieth century, Americans played central roles in bringing together large groups of missionaries to discuss the state of the world and their common purposes in spreading the Christian faith. In 1900 President McKinley himself addressed the Ecumenical Missionary Conference in New York, which assembled representatives from more than 200 missionary agencies. It was the largest such gathering of its kind ever held. Ten years later the World Missionary Conference in Edinburgh, with a vast array of participants from a wide variety of denominational and theological persuasions, marked the highpoint of expectant missionary zeal. The conference heard from many Americans, including John R. Mott and Robert Speer. Mott was later appointed chairman of a continuation committee that evolved into the International Missionary Conference, which itself became part of the World Council of Churches in 1961.

To many American Protestants at the end of the nineteenth century and in the early years of the twentieth, it seemed as if the evangelization of the world was within reach. Atlantic civilization was at its peak, and the United States was at the forefront of Christian endeavors in that rising civilization. Clouds of war might be gathering in Europe, economic and political strife might distract the attention of

---

[11]George M. Marsden, "The Era of Chrisis: From Christendom to Pluralism," in Mark Noll, *Eerdmans' Handbook to Christianity in America* (Grand Rapids, MI: Eerdmans, 1983), pp. 292–93.

some church members, and the relationship of Christianity to modern learning might pose a problem. Still it seemed that the rising tide of America marked also the rising tide of Christian expansion at home and throughout the world.

The Moral Reform of Society

The older Protestant bodies continued to dominate conceptions of public moral reform at the end of the nineteenth century. The drive to renovate society that had bulked so large with the antebellum revivalists continued as a potent force in American life at least through World War I. For most Protestant reformers, the conversion of individuals leading on to the reordering of private life was the key to changing society. The organization of life was now more complicated—with new industries, new systems of transportation such as the railroad, and new types of immigrants adding to the population—but the key to a better life together was still personal moral reform.

The campaign against the use of alcohol provides the best example of how such assumptions led to a vast outpouring of energy designed to alter the moral structure of American life. The various temperance and prohibition movements may appear somewhat quixotic or extreme, but they were the direct successor of such antebellum movements as abolition. Just as Christians led the fight to win freedom for the slave, now great efforts were exerted to free the nation from slavery to alcohol.

Religious reaction to drinking began with the Second Great Awakening at a time when Americans really had begun to drink a great deal more than in previous generations. After the Civil War, opposition to drink became a national cause. In 1869 a number of temperance advocates called a convention in Chicago to promote their cause. To show how progressive such a reform was at that time, this meeting was the nation's first political convention in which women participated on an equal basis with men. The Prohibitionists, strongly embued with religious ardor, ran a candidate for president in 1872, as they have every four years since. Yet even in an America energized by reforming zeal, Prohibition was simply too narrow a platform on which to build a successful political party.

If the Prohibition party had its political difficulties, however, there were triumphs to be gained by working through other channels. These included the denominations as well as a multitude of voluntary societies. For most of the century before 1919, the Methodist church, with its strong perfectionist theology, spearheaded the drive to outlaw all forms of alcoholic beverages, and most of the other major denominations contained temperance caucuses to promote the cause. The most dynamic special purpose group was the Women's Christian Temperance Union (WCTU) under the dynamic leadership of Frances Willard (1839–1898) from Evanston, Illinois, who campaigned for women's rights as well as against alcohol. The Anti-Saloon League, organized on a national basis in 1895 by an Iowa Methodist Alpha J. Kynett, joined the WCTU in combining moral suasion and political lobbying to support the drive for temperance reform. These largely Protestant organizations also received considerable assistance from some members of the Roman Catholic hierarchy, who wished both to prove themselves good Americans and to disabuse their fellow citizens of the notion that Catholics were anti-American and loose-living.

The events of World War I heightened American fears of social disorder and paved the way for the prohibition amendment to the Constitution. Americans of this period were joined by Canadians and many from Europe, who also successfully promoted temperance measures of some sort in their countries.

When the Eighteenth Amendment and its prohibition of "the manufacture, sale, or transportation of intoxicating liquors" took effect on January 17, 1920, some Christians heralded the bright dawning of a new era. In Norfolk, Virginia, the revivalist Billy Sunday staged a funeral service for "John Barleycorn." His speech summed up the aspirations that had led to so much Christian political action against the trade in alcohol. "Good-by, John," the revivalist said, "the reign of tears is over. . . . The slums will soon be only a memory. We will turn our prisons into factories and our jails into storehouses and corncribs. Men will walk upright now, women will smile, and the children will laugh. Hell will be forever rent."[12]

Prohibition did bring marginal improvements in the nation's health and welfare but nothing like the utopia its promoters had foreseen. If the results of national Prohibition did not achieve its lofty goals, however, the movement still illustrated the power of the nation's public Protestants—generally evangelical, almost all white, largely of British Isles background—in translating its moral vision into the law of the land.

Protestant Politics

Christian efforts in politics were not so sharply focused as efforts at moral reform, but the period between the Civil War and World War I also saw in politics a high tide of Protestant influence. Where the nation's earliest political leaders had, like Jefferson, turned aside from traditional Christianity, or, like Lincoln, practiced a traditional faith in unconventional ways, many of the nation's political leaders of this period saw public service as a generally Christian enterprise. So it was with the Methodist Rutherford Hays and the Disciples of Christ lay minister, James A. Garfield. (The wives of these Republican presidents lent the temperance crusade their support by refusing to serve alcoholic beverages at White House functions.) So it was with William McKinley, who saw victory in the Philippines as an opportunity for spreading Christian civilization, and to some extent with McKinley's successor,

[12]Herbert Asbury, *The Great Illusion: An Informal History of Prohibition* (Westport, CT: Greenwood, 1968), pp. 144–45.

Theodore Roosevelt, whose robust vision of life made some room for a masculine embrace of Christian faith. The most notable expressions of Protestant political aspiration came in the public careers of the era's leading Democrats, William Jennings Bryan and Woodrow Wilson.

Woodrow Wilson (1856–1924), the professional academic who went from the presidency of Princeton University to the governorship of New Jersey and then to the White House in the three brief years from 1910 to 1913, was a reforming Democrat who won the nation's highest office in large part because of his record at cleaning up corruption in New Jersey. When the United States then entered World War I, Wilson defined the nation's effort in noble terms as "making the world safe for democracy." After the war, in the crowning moment of his career, he attempted to establish a new standard for international justice through The Fourteen Points submitted to the Peace Conference at Versailles and especially through his plan for a League of Nations.

Wilson's ideals for both national and international affairs were based on the assumption that general principles of Christian morality could be translated fairly easily into national policy and that they also could serve as the direct model for international agreement. With this attitude toward political life, Wilson experienced a considerable measure of success in domestic affairs. He was, however, much less successful in international dealings where his ideals fell foul of the intransigent realities of Europe's conflicting interests. When Wilson traveled to the peace convention in 1919, great crowds in England and France hailed him as the savior of western democracy. The leaders of the other European states spoke of him in private as a naive amateur who could not cope with the realities of historic antagonisms and the practicalities of postwar needs. Wilson's efforts as a crusader for public morality also failed in the effort to secure Senate confirmation for the League of Nations. When Republican leaders in the Senate balked at approving the treaty, Wilson took to the stump to campaign for ratification of the Treaty of Versailles and the League of Nations. And so Wilson wore himself out crisscrossing the country, making reasoned but also impassioned addresses in halls and from railroad platforms on behalf of the treaty, but he did not succeed. The Senate rejected the treaty. What Wilson had attempted in public life was the political equivalent of what the abolitionist Theodore Dwight Weld or the temperance reformer Frances Willard had undertaken in their efforts to remake the character of America according to a largely religious vision.

Something of the same effort with something of the same results marked the public career of Wilson's contemporary, William Jennings Bryan (1860–1925). Bryan was a Democratic populist from Nebraska who three times was his party's standard-bearer in presidential campaigns (1896, 1900, 1908) and who then served as secretary of state during Wilson's first term. Like Wilson, Bryan was a dedicated believer who had been converted as a young man and who saw politics as a forum for promoting the general principles of Christian morality. Bryan took a special interest in the welfare of the American farmers and workers who were suffering from the grasp of manipulating financiers and overweening industrialists. His great speech against the tight gold standard at the Democratic convention in 1896 ("You shall not press down upon the brow of labor this crown of thorns, you shall not crucify mankind upon a cross of gold") summed up both his economic policies and the Christian overtones of his thought. Bryan's reformist campaigns on behalf of ordinary American citizens never succeeded, but he was a valiant political warrior who left his mark on a whole generation of American politics.

Bryan's goals were undoubtedly worthy. With only a few other leading politicians of his day, he argued for justice to the working classes, fairness (including the vote) to women, and respect for the values of common American citizens. While other Americans hastened toward war, he held out for peaceful means of resolving international conflict. With a commitment to principle that has been rare in American political history, Bryan even resigned his high office under Wilson when he felt that the president's policies were needlessly pushing the country toward war with Germany. After he left Washington, Bryan turned his energies increasingly to the campaign against the teaching of biological evolution in the nation's schools. In his mind, this effort was only an extension of earlier efforts to preserve the rights of common citizens (against the imperialism of the elite) and the values of traditional America (against the encroaching naturalism of an alien moral system). Unlike Wilson, Bryan never lapsed into disillusionment when his projects were defeated. Yet like Wilson he too illustrated the power of the public Protestantism when its ideals and its revivalistic style were put to use in the political sphere.

The Cities and the Social Gospel

During this last American era of Protestant dominance, the reforming impulse extended even to the nation's new and rapidly expanding cities. In an era of incredible business expansion, the cities had become scenes of great wealth but also of great squalor. In the sixty years between 1860 and 1920, the nation's population more than tripled, but its number of businesses increased eightfold and its net national product became thirty times as large. Urban areas showed the greatest effects of these changes. They were places of employment for immigrants from Europe and migrants from farms and rural villages. They were places to make a fortune. They were also places where social services often broke down, where incredible deprivation lurked just beyond the boundaries of prosperity, and where rootlessness and alienation could become a way of life.

The most prevalent Protestant attempts to reform urban life were based on principles of private action and personal responsibilities. Many older churches developed programs of social outreach to supplement more traditional services. The Salvation Army, which arrived in the states from Britain in 1880, was a pioneer in providing social services from religious motivation. Founded in the 1860s when William Booth came into contact with the slums of East London, the Army balanced evangelistic and social zeal in its English work as well as in its stations overseas. William's daughter Evangeline (1865–1950) eventually came to head the Army's work in the United States, where she promoted the same range of activities that her father had advanced in England—provision of food, shelter, and medical assistance; vocational training, elementary schooling, internships in manufacturing and in farming; visits to prisons, legal aid for the indigent, and inexpensive coal in the winter. By 1904 the Army had more than 900 stations, or corps, in the states. It was (and remains) the most comprehensive Christian outreach to the cities.

Better known, however, was an informal, loosely organized movement known as the Social Gospel, which existed from roughly 1890 to the start of the Great Depression in 1929. Its leaders also attempted a Christian response to the rapid social changes of the period, but one in which an analysis of corporate entities and structural evil supplemented the appeal to individuals. They may have received some inspiration from prominent Christian socialists in England like F. D. Maurice and Charles Kingsley, but their most immediate antecedents were American.

The Social Gospel was in part a product of the strong link in the revival tradition between personal holiness and social reform. It also arose from the newer scientific study of social problems that accompanied the rise of the modern American university after the Civil War. Early expressions of the Social Gospel included the work of Washington Gladden (1836–1918), a Congregationalist minister in Springfield, Massachusetts, and Columbus, Ohio. While still in Massachusetts he had published *Working People and Their Employees* (1876), an appeal for fairness to laborers. In his Ohio congregation were mine owners whose laborers struck twice in the mid-1880s for better wages and working conditions. Gladden's belief in the justice of their demands led to a more insistent appeal for the rights of labor and the application of the Golden Rule to industrial organization. A different expression of the Social Gospel appeared in the work of a clergyman from Topeka, Kansas, Charles Sheldon, whose best-selling novel *In His Steps* (1897) presented a picture of what could happen in a community torn by social dissension if Christians would only ask themselves at every moment, "What would Jesus do?"

The most important exponent of the Social Gospel was Walter Rauschenbusch (1861–1918), a German-American Baptist who ministered for ten years in New York City's Hell's Kitchen before becoming a professor of church history at Rochester Seminary in upstate New York. Rauschenbusch's firsthand experiences with industrial exploitation and governmental indifference to workers made him a convinced critic of the established order. His fruitful relationships with New York City socialists like Henry George offered alternative models for social organization. Rauschenbusch's main concern, however, was to search the scriptures for a message to fit the troubled circumstances of industrial society. The results were published in 1907 as *Christianity and the Social Crisis*, a work that recalled the prophetic denunciations of Old Testament prophets against social callousness as well as New Testament injunctions about the dangers of Mammon. Rauschenbusch followed this work with other influential volumes, including *Prayers of the Social Awakening* (1910), *Christianizing the Social Order* (1912), and *A Theology for the Social Gospel* (1917). In these works Rauschenbusch combined a prophetic ideal of justice with a commitment to building the kingdom of God through the power of Christ.

The Social Gospel is often associated with more liberal trends in theology. Gladden, for example, was a popularizer of biblical higher criticism, and Rauschenbusch, though more realistic about the intractably fallen character of human nature, yet reinterpreted some traditionally supernatural elements of Christian doctrine. At the same time, however, themes of social service associated with the Social Gospel were also prominent among more evangelical bodies like the Salvation Army. With the Army and many local efforts scattered from coast to coast, leaders of the Social Gospel were trying to solve an American dilemma: How can we adapt the Protestant tradition of an earlier rural America to the changing demands of a newly industrialized society?

The Ecumenical Movement and World War I

As Protestants attempted the reform of their own society, moreover, they also seemed poised to make a notable advance in the reconciliation of Christian bodies. Interest in cooperation among Christian, and especially Protestant groups had been rising throughout the nineteenth century. Americans formed a branch of the British-inspired Evangelical Alliance in 1867, and before the end of the century Americans were playing significant roles in several other notable ecumenical bodies, including the Young Mens' and Young Womens' Christian Associations, Christian Endeavor, the World Student Christian Federation, a number of missionary cooperative bodies, and the worldwide fellowships of the Methodists, Baptists, and Reformed. In addition, inter-Protestant cooperation in the vast panoply of American voluntary societies was a well-established feature of American religious experience.

Two events during the first decade of the twentieth century gave further impetus to ecumenical efforts. The first was the formation of the Federal Council of Churches of Christ, established in 1908 to coordinate social efforts and provide a forum for the discussion of religious questions. The second was the Edinburgh Missionary Conference of 1910, which proved to be even more significant by showing Americans how their own efforts at cooperation could expand the worldwide ecumenical effort.

World War I also promoted ecumenical cooperation among Christians. Although church leaders were at first divided over whether the United States should enter that conflict, when Congress did declare war in April 1917, virtually all major church bodies—Catholic as well as Protestant—joined in enthusiastic support of the effort. Only the peace churches, Quakers and Mennonites especially, who were joined by members of a new group, the Jehovah's Witnesses, protested the recourse to arms.

But the consensus was overwhelmingly in the other direction. Support for the conflict came from all positions on the political spectrum. The revivalist Billy Sunday, for example, claimed that "Christianity and Patriotism are synonymous terms"; similarly, "hell and traitors are synonymous." No less direct was a doyen of American religious liberalism, Shailer Mathews of the University of Chicago Divinity School: "For an American to refuse to share in the present war . . . is not Christian."[13] Exigencies of war led to fresh Protestant cooperation in agencies like the YMCA, which sent many ministers and young seminarians to Europe to staff canteens for the soldiers. The war also led Roman Catholics to organize a National Catholic War Council, which later evolved into the National Catholic Welfare Conference, one of the first major cooperative ventures of Catholics as a national body.

After the war ambitious Christian leaders, backed by seed money from the Rockefellers, established the Interchurch World Movement of North America. Its grand scheme to raise nearly $400 million for the relief of war-torn Europe and to advance social renewal in the states fell far short of its goal, but it did draw further attention to spheres of activity in which churches could cooperate instead of competing against themselves.

The failure of the Interchurch World Movement, however, was also indicative of deeper trends in American church life. The buoyant spirit that had been driving reform efforts in social and political life was passing away. Problems both in the churches and in the churches' relation to society that once seemed manageable suddenly looked intractable. If the Interchurch World Movement marked a highpoint of Protestant aspirations for leading and shaping American culture, its failure suggested that the day for public Protestantism of this sort was almost past. Why that was so requires us to step back to observe a different range of circumstances that had been undercutting the cohesion and strength of the nation's traditional Protestants even as they reached the apex of their influence.

Protestantism Shaken

A simple statistic highlights the great changes underway in American society after the Civil War. In 1870, 9.9 million Americans (or 26 percent) lived in towns and cities with 2,500 people or more. By 1930, the absolute number had risen to 69 million Americans and the national proportion to 56 percent. The shift in population to the cities did not mean that revivalistic, evangelical, voluntaristic Protestantism passed away, but it did mean that the small towns and rural settlements in which that Protestantism had dominated culture were no longer so important in the nation as a whole. The urban environment, with more intense commercial pressure, greater access to higher education, more opportunities for contact with representa-

[13]Marsden, "Era of Crisis," in Noll, *Eerdmans' Handbook*, pp. 369–70.

tives of diverse religious and ethnic groups—all worked in some degree or other to undercut the evangelical character of the nation. It may have been that these sorts of social changes, to which we give some further attention later, were the primary reasons for the shaking of white Protestantism in the period between the Civil War and World War I. These social changes were matched, however, by intellectual developments that left no doubt about the fragmentation of the energies that once dominated public perception of Christianity in America.

Intellectual Challenge

The intellectual challenge to the old Protestantism was both external and internal. Externally, the reshaping of American universities in response to changing intellectual conventions from abroad and changing demands for higher education at home made a great difference. Internally, the gathering momentum of new ideas eventually made it possible for unbelief to become as respectable in America's new intellectual culture as belief.

The origins of the modern American university can be found in the decade after the Civil War. Convenient starting points are 1869, when the innovative Charles Eliot became president of Harvard, and 1876, when the Johns Hopkins University was founded in Baltimore with the express intent of providing specialized, graduate instruction on the model of the German seminar. In the generation that followed, important new universities such as Stanford and the University of Chicago, the most substantial older American schools such as Yale, Princeton, and Columbia, and many of the newer state universities joined Harvard in transforming older patterns of education. Money for this academic revolution came from the federal government in the form of land grants. Even more important, it came also from the nation's new class of fabulously wealthy entrepreneurs. Ezra Cornell (telegraph, banking), Johns Hopkins (banking, railroads), Cornelius Vanderbilt (steamships, railroads), Leland Stanford (railroads), James Duke (tobacco), and John D. Rockefeller (oil) were only a few of the prominent business men who poured vast sums into the creation of modern universities. As more money came to the unversities, so also did more students. Where less than 2 percent of the nation's 18 to 21 year olds attended college in 1870, the number had risen to over 12 percent by 1930.

A nearly unnoticed change with the great influx of dollars and students to the new universities was the rapid weakening of traditional Christian marks of American higher education. At Harvard, compulsory chapel came to an end in 1886. As money from businessmen increased, so also did the concern that boards of trustees and college administrators function in a businesslike way. Businessmen increasingly replaced clergymen as trustees, and professional educators replaced ministers as presidents. In 1839 fifty-one of the fifty-four presidents of America's largest colleges were clergymen (forty either Presbyterian or Congregational). By 1900 that number was greatly reduced.

Another part of the academic revolution was the growing appeal of the German model of academic life that was initiated early in the century by Emperor Frederick on an appeal by scholar Wilhelm von Humboldt at the University of Berlin. Education in America, as also in Britain, had traditionally stressed character formation. In the last half of the century, however, the German emphasis on specialized, advanced scholarship became increasingly attractive. Under the influence of the German model, the new university laid increasing stress on freedom from sectarian control. Andrew Dickinson White, the founding president of Cornell, for example, affirmed that his university would above all "afford an asylum for Science—where truth shall be sought for truth's sake, where it shall not be the main purpose of the Faculty to stretch or cut sciences exactly to fit 'Revealed Religion'."[14] White himself wrote an influential book, *A History of the Warfare of Science with Theology in Christendom* (1895) that described the way he felt organized western religion had stymied the advance of science.

Leaders of the new universities were confident they could slip free of traditional sectarian control because they enjoyed a vast new technique with immeasurable reliability. The new technique was science, and the champion of the new science, who stood for everything positive in the disinterested pursuit of truth, was Charles Darwin. Darwin's *Origin of Species* published in 1859 seemed to offer a model for rigorous, critical pursuits of all sorts. But Darwin's science, summarized by a recent scholar as "a scientifically credible theory of random and purposeless change," sharply contradicted traditional habits in American intellectual life. In particular it seemed to call into question a treasured proof for God's existence, the Argument from Design. Protestant and Roman Catholic theologians alike had long argued that the world with all its splendor and complexity could not be explained except by the kind of creating and sustaining God of which the bible spoke. Protestant educators in America for decades had grounded their religious instruction on the proposition that the Argument from Design showed that belief in God was intellectually as well as spiritually respectable. Especially as backed by the Scottish Philosophy of Common Sense Realism—a school of conservative Enlightenment thought making much of what all people could know about the external world and about morals through self-examination—the Argument from Design had been a mainstay of American higher education.

When applied more generally, the evolutionary perspective appeared devastating to these traditional Christian ideas. Darwin's British popularizers, such as Herbert Spencer and T. H. Huxley, were suggesting that evolutionary theories could provide a whole philosophy of life. Humanity, indeed all of life, was progressing from simpler

---

[14]Henry Warner Bowden, *Church History in the Age of Science: Historiographical Patterns in the United States, 1876–1918* (Chapel Hill, N.C.: University of North Carolina Press, 1971), p. 7.

to more complex forms, from primitive to sophisticated states of existence. Christianity, some who held such views concluded, may have been helpful in aiding primitives to cope with life. But because life in all its variety is always at its highest and best stage of evolution, primitive notions, including traditional Christianity, now must be carefully reconsidered.

If general notions about science and evolution affected America's traditional higher education, more specific ideas about the bible seemed even more revolutionary. Advanced scholarship from the Continent increasingly called into question the traditional certainty that most American Christians had enjoyed in the veracity of the bible. The German scholar Julius Wellhausen, for instance, was gaining wide acceptance for his view that most of the Old Testament books were composed much later than traditional views held. (Protestant Americans had long been notorious for their inability to interpret the bible in anything like a harmonious fashion, but only a very few Christians in America before the 1870s had doubted the fact that, however interpreted, the bible was true in largely commonsensical ways.) In addition, a rapid increase in knowledge about the ancient world led some scholars to consider Christianity as merely one of many similar religions in the ancient Near East. If—as the British anthropologist James Frazer pointed out in *The Golden Bough* (first published 1890)—other cultures had their stories about great floods or the appearance of gods on earth, why should Christianity be considered unique? An increased willingness to regard historical writing as a product of the historians' worldviews and habits of mind as well as of the actual events reported led other academics to question some or all of the miracle stories in the bible. And advances in the study of texts and their transmission convinced still other scholars that many writings in the bible were actually composed, or at least collected, centuries later than Christians had traditionally thought was the case.

Evolutionary assumptions, dedication to the new science, and a willingness to question traditional views of the bible did not lead to uniform responses from Christians. Some academics of conservative theological bent, like the distinguished Harvard botanist Asa Gray, thought it was possible to reconcile traditional Christian ideas with Darwin's evolutionary theory. Other thinkers, both clergy and laity, felt that minor adjustments in received Christian teaching could make it possible easily to accommodate aspects of the new learning into traditional belief. In a word, responses to new ideas and the new academic structures ranged very widely. Often the results were unpredictable. Benjamin B. Warfield of Princeton Theological Seminary was at the end of the nineteenth century the nation's most forceful defender of the bible's inerrancy, the view that all of scripture's statements are truthful if interpreted according to the intention of the biblical authors. At the same time, Warfield also felt that such a view of the bible could accommodate theories of evolution accounting for the development of all life, including human beings.

If Christian responses to the new learning were not always predictable, the new learning itself was doubtless disruptive. It ended the Protestant control of American higher education. It opened the doorway to secular interpretations of life. And it contributed to something very new in American public life: the willingness of some leading intellectuals to question publicly whether God existed or not.

Protestant Responses

Protestants responded to the combination of challenges—social in the shifting character of American society and intellectual in the scientific assumptions of the new universities—in a wide variety of ways. Some leading voices thought the Christian faith should make a conscious adjustment to the ideas defining modern culture. These Modernists held that God is best understood as working within human culture, and so they were convinced that the evolving shape of society as well as the new developments in learning were somehow related to the realization of God's work in the world. Thinkers of this sort drew some inspiration from the theology of Horace Bushnell (1802–1876), a Connecticut minister who had held that scripture and the Christian creeds were closer to poetry than to precisely descriptive language. Bushnell wanted to revise traditional doctrines into language that emphasized intuition, human potential, social progress, and the redemptive potential of the world. In his own times these ideas had attracted more opposition than support, but at the end of the century there were many who followed in his train. Theodore Munger, a pastor and theologian from New Haven, Connecticut, championed the idea that modern views amounted to revisions in older forms of thought rather than their rejection. He thought it should be possible to see Christian faith and the laws of nature coming together into one form of truth. On this basis, old Christian doctrines like "reconciliation" or "atonement" began to take on new meanings, much more the divine development of the human spirit than supernatural views of God's activity over against humanity.

Somewhat later, Shirley Jackson Case (1872–1947) at the University of Chicago spoke for other Modernists when he urged that a proper understanding of how religion fits into society and history would offer a more realistic and more naturalistic view of the bible and Christian faith. The New Testament could still be regarded as true but truth seen as valid religious expression, not direct revelation of God. "Everything [in the Gospels] was genuine," Case wrote in 1914, "insofar as it was the expression of genuine convictions . . . and answered a real religious need of . . . the time."[15]

Other Protestant responses were very different from those of the Modernists. Evangelicals of a more conservative theological and more sectarian ecclesiastical bent found in the late nineteenth century a new theological emphasis and a new form of spirituality with which to absorb the shocks of the times. The new theology was

[15]William J. Hynes, *Shirley Jackson Case and the Chicago School* (Chico, CA: Scholars Press, 1981), p. 43.

premillennial dispensationalism, which figuratively speaking dug in its heels at every point against the new ideas of the academy. Dispensationalism arose in modern form from the work of John Nelson Darby (1800–1882), a minister who left the Church of England to help found the movement eventually known as the Plymouth Brethren. Partially as a result of the influence of Darby, who traveled to America in the mid-nineteenth century, but also from a native desire to understand the subject better, major conferences examining the bible's teachings on End times took place in the late 1880s. The emphasis on biblical prophecy may be seen as a natural culmination of concern for the End that had been prominent in various ways throughout American Protestant history and also as a defensive reaction to the realization that American culture was slipping away from evangelical Protestant control. Those who attended these conferences generally held a premillennial view of Christ's return to earth, or the belief that Christ would come again before (pre-) establishing a literal, 1,000-year reign (millennium) of righteousness on the earth. Not all the premillennialists at these conferences or among later Protestants were dispensationalists, for proponents of dispensationalism stressed more literal interpretations of the bible and sharper divisions between periods of history said to be taught in scripture than did other Protestants who shared the conservative bent of the dispensationalists.

The most influential formulation of dispensational teaching appeared in 1909 when the Oxford University Press published a bible annotated by C. I. Scofield (1843–1921). Scofield, a lawyer before becoming a Congregational minister, had undertaken a long period of private study in preparing this edition of the scriptures, which was intended more as a portable guide for missionaries than as a polished theological system. The impact of the *Scofield Reference Bible* (published in a revised edition in 1967) has extended well beyond the early centers of dispensationalism to influence a wide spectrum of American Protestants. Dispensationalism, which places great stress on biblical prophecy, has remained a potent force in American religious life. In fact, the best-selling trade book *of any kind* published in the United States in the decade of the 1970s was a popular dispensational description of the end of the world, *The Late Great Planet Earth* by Hal Lindsey. For the purposes of understanding the late nineteenth century, however, dispensationalism was most important as a theological system that provided some beleaguered Protestants with intellectual ballast in the roiling seas of modern thought.

A counterpart in spirituality to the theology of dispensationalism was a movement known among more conservative Protestants as Higher Life, or Victorious Living. Often associated with the English Keswick movement, which stressed prayer and triumphant living in the Holy Spirit, an American version of Higher Life approached from a more Calvinistic angle the perfectionist tendencies of Arminian Holiness.

As with dispensationalism, the Higher Life movement may be regarded in two perspectives. In one sense, it represented only another stage in the development of a spirituality that can be traced back through the Holiness movement of Mrs. Phoebe Palmer, the rigorous spirituality of David Brainerd, the arduous piety of the Puritans, to more general founts of mysticism in the medieval and early church. But from another angle, Higher Life and its variations may have been ways of adjusting to the shifting character of American religious life—or as historian Douglas Frank has recently put it, "a certain partial letting go of temporal history and a disillusionment with American history in particular" in order to seek "perfect victory centered in a subjective inner kingdom."[16]

Whatever the correct interpretation, proponents of the Higher Life and of dispensational theology were making their own adjustments to the ongoing course of American religious life, just as Protestant Modernists had done, albeit with a very different strategy.

Fundamentalist-Modernist Controversy

Conservative discontent with the course of Christianity in American life came to a head early in the twentieth century in a movement known as *fundamentalism*. The word itself first came into prominence when a widely circulated set of booklets called *The Fundamentals: A Testimony to the Truth* was published between 1910 and 1915. Together the booklets contained nearly 100 articles defending the "fundamentals," or basics of the faith, which newer forms of thought called into question. The quality of the articles varied greatly; some were balanced and judicious, others frightened and petty. Together, however, they reasserted a common set of fundamentals: The bible was the inspired Word of God. Jesus Christ was God in human flesh and had been born of a virgin. He lived a sinless life. He died on the cross for the salvation of souls. He rose from the dead. He ascended into heaven and would return at the end of the age in great glory. Sin was real and not the product of fevered imaginations. God's grace and not human effort was the source of salvation. Authors of these articles included some of the leading evangelicals alive at the start of the twentieth century: the Scottish theologian James Orr, the Princeton Presbyterian B. B. Warfield, the Anglican bishop H. C. G. Moule, the American dispensationalist C. I. Scofield, evangelist R. A. Torrey, and the Southern Baptist scholar E. Y. Mullins.

A more sharply defined Fundamentalist movement arose shortly after the publication of *The Fundamentals* especially among the northern Baptists and the northern Presbyterians. This fundamentalism was a direct descendant of nineteenth-century Protestant revivalism as fortified by belief in the inerrancy of scripture, a premillennial eschatology, conventions of Victorian morality, and the epistemology of Scottish Common Sense philosophy. World War I, with its sense of crisis about the fate of Western civilization, mobilized the movement and gave it its initial energy. Those

[16]Douglas W. Frank, *Less Than Conquerors: How Evangelicals Entered the Twentieth Century* (Grand Rapids, MI: Eerdmans, 1986).

who spearheaded the movement—such as the Presbyterian J. Gresham Machen (a New Testament scholar at Princeton Theological Seminary) and the populist William Jennings Bryan (who in the 1920s took a growing interest in the concerns of his own Presbyterian denomination) and Baptist leaders such as Minneapolis minister William Bell Riley and Curtis Lee Laws, editor of the *Watchman-Examiner* (who in 1920 first used the word *fundamentalist* in its modern sense)—agreed that the time had come to halt a drift into theological indifferentism or liberalism. They were deeply offended by the efforts of moderate and liberal Protestants to promote accommodation with the newer shapes of modern learning or American culture.

The Fundamentalists who battled liberals and moderates in the 1920s had an ambiguous attitude toward the United States. Sometimes they spoke of it as "Babylon," far gone in its sins. Sometimes it was "God's New Israel," still at least potentially a light to the nations. Often in the 1920s Fundamentalists affirmed both. In this regard, William Jennings Bryan's emergence as a Fundamentalist spokesman makes a good deal of sense. In his person Bryan embodied a link with nineteenth-century efforts to establish a Christian America. Bryan's campaign against evolution culminated in 1925 with a celebrated clash in Dayton, Tennessee, with Clarence Darrow at the trial of John Scopes, a teacher who had tested a state law by teaching evolution in a high school classroom. It was not so much a fight against new ideas itself as a fight against what Bryan and other Fundamentalists felt the new ideas were doing to destroy the nation's Christian heritage.

For their part, leaders in the churches who opposed the Fundamentalist movement often minced no words in stating their case. The best such example came from the well-known Baptist minister, Harry Emerson Fosdick (1878–1969), who with Billy Sunday was probably the nation's best-known preacher between Dwight L. Moody and Billy Graham. On May 22, 1922, Fosdick, filling the pulpit of New York City's First Presbyterian Church as regular pulpit supply, preached a famous sermon, "Shall the Fundamentalists Win?" Fosdick had been educated at Colgate University and Union Seminary, where he came under the influence of liberal theologians W. Newton Clark and A. C. McGiffert. After his tiff with the Fundamentalists, he went on to a long association with the Park Avenue Baptist Church, which became after an infusion of Rockefeller funds New York's world-renowned Riverside Church (1925–1946).

When Fosdick's sermon of 1922 was quickly distributed throughout the country to 130,000 ordained Protestants by John D. Rockefeller, Jr.'s associate Ivy Lee, it created a sensation. The sermon's message was by that date not unusually different from moderate or liberal voices: Christianity did not need the intolerance of the Fundamentalists but the tolerance of diverse belief practiced by enlightened Modernists. Fosdick had experienced some of the theological tensions of his era firsthand in New York. He was kept abreast of strains among both Baptists and Presbyterians through a far-flung correspondence, and he had traveled to the Far East in an effort (vain, as it turned out) to mediate disputes between contending theological parties among American missionaries. His sermon, coming as it did from a person of his stature, from an ordained Baptist in a Presbyterian pulpit who seemed not so subtly to be condemning the confessionalism of the Westminster Standards, led to an extended controversy. The events that followed—tangles in the New York Presbytery, bitter battles at three consecutive Presbyterian General Assemblies, momentary triumphs for conservatives but longer-term gains for Presbyterian moderates and liberals, and Fosdick's lingering separation from the First Presbyterian Church (finally completed in March 1925)—were played out before an eager national audience. Fosdick's Fundamentalist opponents won many small battles in their struggle. But with the swing of northern white denominations away from militance and toward toleration, the Fundamentalists lost the war.

Pentecostalism: A New Departure

While Fundamentalists were gearing to do battle with Modernists, an event in the Far West heralded a major new force on the American religious scene. In 1906 an abandoned Methodist church at 312 Azusa Street in the industrial section of Los Angeles became the founding site for modern Pentecostalism. William J. Seymour, a mild-mannered Black Holiness preacher, founded the Apostolic Faith Gospel Mission on Azusa Street, where a new emphasis on the work of the Holy Spirit rapidly became a local sensation and eventually a worldwide phenomenon. Before coming to Los Angeles, Seymour had been influenced by the ministry of Charles Fox Parham, who had grown up in Methodist and Holiness circles. In his schools in Kansas and Texas, Parham taught that a baptism of "the Holy Ghost and fire" should be expected among those who had been converted and who had also gone forward to the perfect sanctification proclaimed by John Wesley and American Holiness bodies. Parham had also pioneered the teaching that a special sign of the Holy Spirit baptism would be "speaking with other tongues." With many others in the Methodist and Holiness traditions at the end of the nineteenth century, he also placed a stronger emphasis generally on the gifts of the Spirit, including that of healing.

The revival that began on Azusa Street in 1906 rapidly attracted attention from secular media like the *Los Angeles Times*. More important, it soon became the center of attraction for thousands of visitors from around the world who often went back to their homelands proclaiming the need for a special postconversion baptism of the Holy Spirit. These included Florence Crawford, founder of the Apostolic Faith movement in the northwestern United States; missionary T. B. Barratt, who is credited with the establishment of Pentecostalism in Scandanavia and northwestern Europe; William H. Durham of Chicago, early spokesman for Pentecostalism in the Midwest; and Eudorus N. Bell of Fort Worth, first chairman of the Assemblies of God.

Meetings at Azusa Street, which went on daily for three years, were marked by spontaneous prayer and preaching, a nearly unprecedented cooperation between Blacks and whites, and the active participation of women. Observers at the time linked Azusa Street with the great Welsh revival of 1904 and 1905 and the Latter Rain movement that had enjoyed pockets of influence throughout the United States. ("Latter Rain" referred to a prophecy in Joel 2:23 of an outpouring from God of special power.) Azusa Street remains a potent symbol for the activity of the Holy Spirit to the now more than 300 million Pentecostals and charismatics worldwide.

At the start of the century, well-known Fundamentalists and Modernists were offered considerable public opportunity to explain their reactions to the major changes in American society. In the end, however, the most significant development of the era may have been the rise of Pentecostalism, a movement that from next to nothing by the end of the 1980s had a far greater impact on world Christianity than the concerns of either Fundamentalists or Modernists.

Nonwhite, Non-Protestant

The triumphs and turmoils of white Protestants were America's main public religious concern through the time of World War I. As distinct from perception, however, the story of white Protestantism was no longer the only major Christian story in America. The Civil War is a convenient place from which to begin those other stories, for it marked a period of new beginnings for America's Black Christians. It also occurred near the start of major new migrations from Europe that introduced into America an ancient form of Christianity, the Eastern Orthodox. And it was a time after which the Roman Catholic church was transformed from a large curiosity into a dominant national force.

Black Americans in Control of Their Own Destinies

The ending of slavery had immediate consequences for church life among people of color. Despite the failure of Reconstruction to secure the civil rights of Blacks and despite the intensifying racism of the half century after the Civil War, Black Christians seized control of their own religious lives. Blacks in previously white denominations abandoned those organizations in great numbers, and new opportunities arose for expanding previously existing Black denominations and for forming new bodies.

Three important developments occurred in the organization of separate Black churches. The first was the establishment of new denominations, primarily in the South. Between the end of the war and 1870, for example, exslaves founded the Colored Methodist Episcopal Church and the Colored Cumberland Presbyterian Church as entities separate from denominations under white control. Baptist organization was more fragmented, but of even greater long-lasting significance. State conventions of Blacks in the South formed slowly but then looked to even broader venues of fellowship. The result was the establishment of the National Baptist Convention in 1895. The two groups that emerged from this body, after a split in 1907 (the National Baptist Convention of the U.S.A., Inc. and the National Baptist Convention) have been the largest Afro-American clusters of Christians in the United States.

A second development after the war was the expansion of previously existing northern denominations into the South. Here the Methodists took the lead, especially the African Methodist Episcopal Church. In 1865 Bishop Daniel Alexander Payne, who thirty years before had been forced out of South Carolina, returned in triumph to Charleston to establish his church in that area. Soon other northern bodies followed suit, which added to the number of national Black denominations.

The third development was the establishment of numerous independent congregations, at first mostly rural, in which locally supported preachers created and maintained their own congregations. These groups, usually Baptist in practice, have continued to be a mainstay of Black Christian experience in the South. In later decades, with the vast migrations of Blacks into cities both North and South, this pattern of independent congregations led to some of the largest and most influential urban churches as well as to an array of smaller congregations.

Blacks also played prominent roles in the development of Holiness and Pentecostal denominations. The Church of God in Christ, for example, was organized in Memphis in 1897 by two ministers, C. H. Mason and C. P. Jones, who had been urging their Baptist constituencies to seek a postconversion experience of God's grace as a path to holiness. Later, after Mason journeyed to Azusa Street in Los Angeles to explore the Pentecostal vision of special charismatic gifts, he and his followers divided from Jones and others who rejected tongues-speaking. The result was division in which those who followed Mason kept the name Church of God in Christ, which eventually became the largest of the Black Pentecostal churches. Jones and his supporters became known as the Church of Christ (Holiness) U.S.A.

The constitutional end of slavery meant also that Blacks were freer to organize their own institutions of culture and religious outreach. Most of the Black colleges founded immediately after the war were organized, funded, and directed by white churches, but after 1880 Black Christians began to establish colleges for their own youth. The Colored Methodist Episcopal Church (Lane College), the African Methodist Episcopal Church Zion (Livingstone College), and the African Methodist Episcopal Church (Morris Brown College) took the lead in this venture, but other groups participated as well, with the result that by 1900 more than twenty-five such church-connected colleges had come into being in the South.

Church groups also took the lead in providing book and periodical literature for the Black community. The Sunday School Union of the African Methodist Episcopal church began its own publishing house in 1887, but well before then other local churches and national denominations had brought out books, published magazines, and even begun weekly newspapers. These forms of publication continued to flow from the Black churches well into the twentieth century. They were sources of religious information and spiritual direction, but they also often contained more general news and intellectual culture.

Once freed from slavery, Blacks added a significant contribution to the missionary eagerness of the age. The European partitioning of Africa into spheres of influence incited American Blacks to send their own missionaries to Africa with the hope that the message of the gospel could prevent in their ancestral homeland the sort of white exploitation that they had known in America. A Baptist Foreign Mission Convention was organized in 1880 and was later absorbed into the work of the National Baptist Convention. The major Methodist denominations also established a significant missionary presence in Africa, with especially strong works in Liberia and Sierra Leone. Like their white counterparts, Black women also organized their own missionary societies and sent out energetic workers (though usually not ordained), such as Amanda Smith, who toured India in 1880 and labored for the rest of that decade in Liberia.

Black Christianity advanced as much against the wishes of whites, including many church leaders, as with their blessing. Even on the mission fields of Africa, Black missionaries often won only suspicion from white colonial officials for their efforts to evangelize the native peoples. Persistent shortages of funds also hampered Blacks in efforts to strengthen churches and their outreach. Still, if the period between the Revolutionary War and the Civil War was a time in which Blacks turned to Christianity in unprecedented numbers, so the period between the Civil War and World War I was a time in which Blacks began to control their own religious lives.

In sum, after the Civil War the Black churches rapidly became the center for Black culture more generally as well as for Black religious life. Some persons have accused these churches and their leaders of offering a pious expectation of spiritual riches in heaven in place of social resistance to the systematic racism of American society. It comes closer to the mark, however, to say that Black Christians in the generations after the Civil War found in the churches stability and direction for this life as well as consolation for the life to come.

The Eastern Orthodox in America

Problems involved in the establishment of a strong Eastern Orthodox presence in America were much different from those of Black Christians, but the difficulties were almost as daunting. Not systematic racial prejudice but a bewildering array of ethnic divisions, complicated by ambiguous ties to European homelands, created great obstacles for the Orthodox Christians to overcome in establishing a foothold in the new world.

Orthodoxy is the hereditary Christian faith of the eastern Mediterranean and much of eastern Europe. It is a faith distinguished from both Roman Catholicism and Protestantism by its adherence to the seven ecumenical councils of the early church (through the Second Council of Nicaea in 787), by fidelity to the liturgies of the church of the first centuries, and by a concept of spirituality in which material forms (the Incarnation of Christ and then churches, chants, icons) become the means through which God communicates aspects of his divine nature to humans. The patriarch of Constantinople (later Istanbul) was long the leading primate among the Orthodox because of Constantinople's central place in the ancient Roman Empire. Later major Orthodox churches, quasi-independent (or *autocephalous*), developed in Greece, many of the countries of southeastern Europe, the Middle East, and especially Russia. When in the last decades of the nineteenth century, immigration on a large scale brought to the United States millions of new residents from these parts of the world, their numbers included many Orthodox Christians.

Continued immigration and natural increase have made the Orthodox family of churches an important part of the story of Christianity in America. By the 1980s, the various Orthodox groups in the United States and Canada numbered about 3.5 million, or more than the Presbyterians, the Episcopalians, or the Congregationalists. Still, the relatively recent arrival of the Orthodox, as well as the bewildering diversity of Orthodox groups (what one historian has called "a crazy quilt that defies telling"), makes it difficult to relate a coherent account of their American experience.

Russian Orthodox monks had been active as early as the 1790s in what is now Alaska, where sporadic missionary efforts continued among the Eskaleutian tribes through 1867, when Alaska was sold to the United States. These early efforts had some success, in part because of the dedicated work of leaders like the saintly monk Herman and the energetic Bishop Innocent, both of whom were later canonized by the Russian Church.

The immigration of the late nineteenth century led to the establishment of many Orthodox congregations, first in large port cities and then in other major urban areas. Early in the migration, conflict over Byzantine rites practiced by the Uniates, who followed traditional Orthodox practices but who recognized the authority of the Roman Catholic pope, led to tensions between the Orthodox and Roman Catholics. As a result, some Uniates in America returned to Orthodoxy, and relations with the Catholic church were strained.

A leader in establishing Russian Orthodoxy in the states was Bishop Tikhon Bellavin, who in 1905 transferred his see from San Francisco to New York in order to minister more effectively to the centers of Russian settlement. Tikhon encouraged greater lay participation in the councils of the church and in 1907 convened the first All-American Council, an initial step toward broader cooperation among the Orthodox Christians in America. Tikhon was later called to Russia, where in 1917 he was elected the patriarch of Moscow.

The Russian Revolution of that same year brought about a division of loyalties among the Russian Orthodox in the states. One small body, known as the Russian

Orthodox church, became fiercely anticommunist and tenaciously ethnic. Another somewhat larger group, the Patriarchial Exarchate, remained completely loyal to the patriarch of Moscow, who was forced to hew to a line drawn by the Kremlin. The third and largest Russian body, whose allegiance to the Moscow patriarchy was always ambiguous, became known as the Metropolia. In 1970 it was conceded an independent status (*autocephaly*) by the patriarch of Moscow. Soon thereafter this group, which had proceeded furthest of all Orthodox bodies along the road of cultural adaptation, changed its name to the Orthodox Church in America. Subsequently it has sought to provide a home for Orthodox believers from beyond the Russian immigrant community.

The largest Orthodox body in America is the Greek Orthodox Archdiocese of North and South America, which in the 1980s numbered about 2 million adherents. It came into existence as a separate church early in the twentieth century through the efforts of Meletios Metaxakes, a Greek bishop who traveled and worked in the states from 1918 to 1921, and by Athenagoras Sperou, who served as the head of the Greek Orthodox Christians in the states from 1930 to 1949. Like the Russian Tikhon, Athenagoras also became head of a world communion when he was elected the ecumenical patriarch of Constantinople in 1949.

Political and religious conflicts in Old World countries and regions—for example, the Ukraine, Byelorussia, Syria, Albania, Bulgaria, Romania, Serbia, Egypt—have often disrupted Orthodox immigrant communities in the states. The upshot is a tangled network of small and sometimes aggressively competitive churches and related institutions. In more recent years, however, a measure of common Orthodox cooperation has been achieved. A Standing Conference of Canonical Bishops in the Americas (founded 1960) provides for dialogue and a measure of cooperative action (as in the provision of military chaplains). Leading emigré theologians, Georges Florovsky (1893–1979) and Alexander Schmemann (1921–present) helped transform the Russian St. Vladimir's Seminary in New York into an institution serving a broader Orthodox constituency.

For the Orthodox, as for other immigrant groups, the irreversible process of Americanization offers both perils and prospects. The perils concern threats that American culture poses to the distinctives of Orthodox spirituality and ecclesiology. The prospects involve the challenge of enlightening American Protestants and Roman Catholics with the unique insights of the Orthodox tradition, about which most Americans know very little.

Catholics

Roman Catholics became ever more important in American life between the Civil War and World War I for two compelling reasons. First, their numbers grew dramatically, from about 4.5 million in 1870 to well over 16 million by 1910. Second, not just an increase in numbers but an increasing attention to broader American culture made Catholics more of a force in the nation. Catholics in the nineteenth century underwent a process of assimilation just as Protestants of British background had in earlier centuries, and as non-British Protestants, the Orthodox, Jews, and members of other immigrant groups did at the same time as the Catholics. Catholic assimilation, however, had a distinct character because of the bond that tied American Catholics to their co-religionists throughout the world.

A great surge in immigration in the last third of the nineteenth century brought millions of Catholics to the United States from Italy, Poland, and other places in southern and central Europe. The new Catholics created both problems (simple survival in an alien society as well as a clash of ethnic communities) and opportunities (especially for organizing Catholic social institutions) for the American hierarchy, in which the Irish, followed by Germans, were now most prominent. With much struggle, the immigrant church developed its own educational institutions. After trying unsuccessfully to secure some rights for Catholic students in government-sponsored schools, Catholics developed an extensive system of parochial education. Catholic higher education, already well in place before the Civil War, was strengthened even further by efforts to establish in 1889 the Catholic University of America in Washington, D.C. Despite some uneasiness in the hierarchy, Catholic laymen and laywomen worked actively to organize workers and promote their rights. Bishops objected to oaths of secrecy standard among some labor organizations, and they worried lest labor organizing drift into violence or promote socialism. But when prominent labor organizations like the Knights of Labor renounced the use of violence, they continued to attract widespread support from the Catholic laity and eventually won approval from the hierarchy as well.

In America, Catholic laity were especially active in establishing their own organizations. Ethnic church groups founded almost as many fraternal organizations, with almost as many purposes, as had the Protestant voluntarists before the Civil War. The laity also patronized a wide range of spiritual activities associated directly with the churches, including sodalities of prayer and service devoted to Our Lady or the Holy Spirit and societies of the Rosary or the Sacred Heart of Mary. Lay congresses were held in Baltimore in 1889 and Chicago in 1893 to encourage broader participation in the church. Reading circles, magazines of every description, and special courses during summer vacations added to the variety of Catholic lay experience. In a word, Catholics were not just present in increasing numbers but were establishing the social and religious infrastructures that would sustain a vital church life once the crises of immigration had become only a family memory.

One of the signals that the Catholic faith was adjusting to the new world environment was its ability to attract the interest of Americans raised in Protestant traditions. The most notable of many hereditary Protestants to make the spiritual journey to Rome was Isaac Hecker, whose life itself is an important gauge of Catholic influence in America. Even more, the uses to which lessons from Hecker's life were put after his death precipitated a major debate between the Vatican and Roman Catholics in America, in which the question of Catholic adjustment to the New World was probed even more intensively.

Isaac Hecker (1819–1888) was born in New York City into a home that was nominally Dutch Reformed. The shaping religious influence of Hecker's early life was his mother's Methodism, however, which she turned to fervently and diligently when Isaac was a child. Although Hecker came to appreciate Methodist zeal, the Methodist rejection of Calvinism, and Methodist optimism concerning natural human capacities, he did not find his mother's faith satisfying. It took him, however, some time to find one that was. As a young adult he explored Unitarianism, he poured himself into the reformist activities of New York's Equal Rights Party (these were the "Loco-Focos" whom one historian has styled "Methodists of Democracy"), he felt the tug of Mormonism and its vision of radical social reorganization, and eventually he fell under the spell of the New England romantic, Orestes Brownson (1803–1876). Through Brownson, Hecker came into the orbit of the Transcendentalists, with whom he spent nearly two years. From January through June 1843, he lived at George Ripley's Brook Farm, and in July of that same year he spent two weeks at Bronson Alcott's Fruitlands.

Hecker finally found a satisfying form of spirituality when he became Roman Catholic in 1844. He devoted the rest of his life to accommodating his expansive vision of the divine to Catholicism and to ardent labors on behalf of his new faith. In 1845 he joined the Redemptorists, an order that had recently arrived in the United States to work with German immigrants and—of special attraction to Hecker—to evangelize in Catholic churches and in the American population at large. When Hecker sensed a slackening of missionary zeal among the Redemptorists in the late 1850s, he founded the Paulist order and directed it especially toward the conversion of Americans. The Paulists also reflected Hecker's emphasis on the immediate work of the Holy Spirit and were thus less rigid in structure than traditional Catholic orders. Until his health broke in 1871, Hecker performed prodigious amounts of work for the Paulists—traveling extensively to lecture before Catholics and Protestants, organizing evangelistic forays, publishing books, launching periodicals (e.g., *The Catholic World* in 1865), and overseeing a large parish in New York City.

Hecker was the most influential churchman among the substantial number of Transcendentalists who turned to Catholicism, a group that included also Brownson and Mrs. George Ripley. These Americans had grown up in the democratic Protestantism of the early national period. This Protestantism had largely set aside Calvinistic convictions on original sin and sovereign grace and was full of enthusiasm for the spiritual potential of individuals and the religious significance of America. Hecker never lost the perfectionist bent, the reformist utopianism, the American messianism, the belief in the extraordinary activity of the Spirit, and the reliance on infused grace that characterized the egalitarian evangelicalism of the antebellum period. Yet he was not content with the ecclesiastical anarchy, the excessive individualism, and the rampant anti-intellectualism that this form of Protestantism also nurtured. And so he turned to Rome because Catholic spirituality, especially in its mystical expressions, offered a resting place for his own romanticism. It is, thus, no surprise that after Hecker's death his approach to Catholicism—or at least what was perceived to be his approach in its extreme form—became the center of controversy between the papacy and Roman Catholics in the United States.

That affair came to be known as the Americanist Controversy because it raised the question of how far the traditions of the ancient church could be accommodated to New World notions of freedom, evangelism, and spiritual illumination. After Hecker's death (1888), a Paulist father Walter Elliott wrote a book *The Life of Father Hecker*, which praised his goals and methods highly. When it was translated into French (1898), European Catholics were upset. It seemed as if the liberal soil of the New World was nourishing a break from Catholic traditions. The upshot was a clash, or at least the appearance of a clash, between Pope Leo XIII (1878–1903) and leaders of the American hierarchy.

That hierarchy had come to include capable spokesmen arguing for the compatibility between the church and American patterns of life. Among its leading representatives were Bishops John Ireland and James Gibbons, whose careers illustrate the way in which leading Catholics were attempting to balance fidelity to their inherited faith with sensitivity to the American situation.

John Ireland (1838–1918) was the influential archbishop of St. Paul, Minnesota, who spent his active life campaigning for full Catholic participation in American education, politics, and society. Born in Ireland, the archbishop maintained a lifelong commitment to aiding the immigrants and laborers whose experiences in the New World matched those of his own family. Ireland aligned himself with other "Americanizing" leaders against German, Polish, and conservative Irish Catholics who wanted to see a European-style Catholicism established in the United States. With the other Americanists Ireland argued for strong Catholic education in both public schools and a separate parochial system. He supported the Catholic University of America in Washington but also took an active interest in public higher education. He urged American Catholics to take part in politics. Unlike many of his fellow religionists, he leaned toward the Republican party, in large measure so that the Democrats would not take the immigrant Catholic vote for granted. His enthusiasm for America led him to work with the railroads in bringing immigrants to the upper Midwest. He summed up his feelings on the place of Catholics in the United States with these words in 1894: "There is no conflict between the Catholic Church and America. . . . the principles of the church are in thorough harmony with the interests of the Republic."

James Gibbons (1834–1921), archbishop of Baltimore, was for many years the leading figure in the American Catholic hierarchy. Faced with both internal and external difficulties, Gibbons wanted to bring Catholic practice into the mainstream of American life without at the same time forsaking traditional Catholic teaching.

Gibbons, as archbishop of the leading archdiocese in America and after 1886 a cardinal, was known as a liberal because of his views on the church-state issue. Unlike traditionalists, he thought Catholics could flourish in a society without the official support of the state. Gibbons was the son of immigrants from Ireland; he spent much of his career working to assimilate the millions of Roman Catholic immigrants who came to this country after the Civil War. He also labored to rebut virulent anti-Catholic opposition to the new waves of immigration. His willingness to support "American" reforms such as Prohibition and to cooperate on a limited basis with Protestants earned him the scorn of Catholic conservatives. Yet his own works, such as *The Faith of Our Fathers* (1877), presented traditional Catholic doctrine in a winsome fashion.

Pope Leo XIII took note of American developments in several important actions. In 1895 he addressed American Catholics in the encyclical *Longinqua Oceani* which praised them for what they had accomplished in the New World, but he also cautioned against making American church-state relations the norm for all places. Four years later he issued another encyclical *Testem Benevolentiae* in which he attacked notions alleged to have been spread abroad in America, such as the idea that church teaching may be altered to appeal to special local conditions. Leo said that if American Catholics did indeed teach certain doctrines—such as that the church should "show some indulgence to modern popular theories" or that more freedom should be given to individuals in interpreting the faith—they must stop. Conservative Catholics in America and in Europe were satisfed that the pope had halted dangerous experimentation. For his part, Cardinal Gibbons responded in a famous letter of March 17, 1899, that American Catholics were in fact loyal children of the Roman church and that no such heresies as the pope described were tolerated in America. Confusion reigned for a brief period. No American Roman Catholics left the church specifically over this controversy, even if it did lend extra caution to efforts by leaders such as Gibbons and Ireland to promote Roman Catholic traditions in America.

The Christian Map in 1926

For about fifty years surrounding the turn of the twentieth century, the United States government took a decennial census of the American churches. The census of 1926 provided cold, statistical evidence for what a more general account has already demonstrated. Church life in America had become pluralistic in the extreme. In addition, the age of Protestant domination was over.

In 1926 the largest denomination of Christians by far was the Roman Catholic church, with nearly 19 million members in nearly 20,000 churches. The largest Protestant bodies at the time were the Methodists and the Baptists, each with slightly more than 8 million members and 60,000 churches. Among the Methodists, the largest denominations were the white bodies that had divided before the Civil War

(North, about 4 million; South, about 2.5 million), and the Black African Methodist Episcopal and the African Methodist Episcopal Zion churches (each with about half a million). About 1,290,000 Baptists belonged to the Northern Baptist Convention, and the Southern Baptist Convention and the Black Baptist denominations each numbered about 3.5 million. Other Protestant families with more than 1 million members were the Lutherans (3,966,000 in twenty-one different bodies), the Presbyterians (2,625,000 with about three-quarters of that number in the largest northern denomination), the Protestant Episcopal church (1,859,000), and the Disciples of Christ (1,378,000). Many bodies reflecting broad ethnic and theological diversity numbered more than 100,000 (including Adventists, the German Church of the Brethren, the Christian Church, Churches of Christ, Congregationalists, Eastern Orthodox, the Evangelical church, the Evangelical Synod of North America, the Society of Friends, Latter-day Saints, Reformed Dutch, and the United Brethren). And literally scores with even more extensive diversity in origin, belief, and practice had at least 10,000 members, including the Assemblies of God, Plymouth Brethren, Christian and Missionary Alliance, Church of God, Church of God (Anderson, Indiana), Church of the Nazarene, Mennonites-Amish, Moravians, Old Catholics, Pilgrim Holiness, Polish National Catholic church, Salvation Army, Unitarians, and the Scandinavian Evangelical "Free" churches.

About 43 percent of Americans were members of churches in 1926, with about 37 percent of the church members being Roman Catholic, about 16 being Methodist, and 16 percent Baptist. Even with the precision aspired to by the Census Department, these figures are but solid estimates. What they show in the aggregate, however, is that America had provided a lush soil for the flourishing of many different Christian groups. No longer could it be said, however, that any one of those groups, or even any one family of those groups, defined *the* history of Christianity in the United States.

Chapter 32

CHRISTIANITY IN POST-CHRISTIAN AMERICA (1925–1988)

Since World War I, it has become ever more difficult to relate the history of Christianity in America as a single, unified story. For one thing, we are so close to the recent past that its truly important patterns are difficult to separate from more ephemeral circumstances. The very nature of recent history also contributes to that difficulty. America has become more pluralistic in its religions, and that pluralism extends to its Christian faiths. In a nation where there are now more Black Baptists than white Methodists, more Orthodox of Greek, Russian, and other eastern European stock than either of the colonial period's leading denominations (Episcopalians and Congregationalists), where families of denominations that did not exist in 1900 (like the Pentecostals) are now larger than historic Amerian groups like the Presbyterian and Reformed deonominations, it becomes increasingly difficult to find a single thread on which to hang a history. Likewise, the major events of the twentieth century—including two global wars, the Great Depression of the 1930s, the United States's wholehearted engagement with the world economy, several revolutions in communications, and the cultural upheavals of the 1960s and 1970s—have restructured patterns of ordinary life to such a degree that they bear less and less resemblance to life at the time of the Civil War. Such a list does not even include the much debated question of whether the United States has undergone a systematic secularization of life in which religion is either ignored or shunted to the side. In such a national environment, it is little wonder that the rapid shifts and sallies of religious life present what psychologist William James once called a "bloomin', buzzin' confusion."

At the same time, the kaleidescopic permutations of modern America still do reveal what seem to be observable patterns in the history of Christianity. For one, a decades-long process of consensus, which involved Jews as well as Catholics and

723

Protestants, seemed to culminate in the 1950s, only then to give way to renewed outbursts of public strife among Christians and between certain groups of Christians and nonreligious elements in the society. For another, a consistent pattern can be glimpsed in church adherence. In general, previously marginal groups have become much more important, whereas previously central groups have moved to the margins. One thing, however, has not changed. Throughout the twentieth century, American Christians have remained intensely involved in America, often with some of the same ambiguities that marked early periods, sometimes through new experiments undreamt of in previous generations.

Turbulent Decades

It is an intellectual trick to think that the dynamics of lived human experience can be neatly packaged into discrete decades. Yet it may still be valuable, as an effort to capture something of the recent development of Christianity in America, to attempt a rough decade-by-decade account of that history.

The Great Crash of the stock market in October 1929 provided a dramatic symbol to end an era. In the churches, the 1920s had been the decade of highly publicized controversy between Fundamentalists and those designated by them as Modernists. It was the decade of the Scopes trial, which seemed to show traditional Christianity reeling from the blows of modern science. It was the era of great hopes from the Interchurch World Movement, as well as the era in which those hopes were dashed. It was the era in which for the first time one of the major political parties nominated a Roman Catholic for president. If Al Smith did not defeat Herbert Hoover in 1928, he did receive 60 percent more votes than any Democratic candidate had ever garnered before, and he had shown the increasing political strength of non-Protestants (Catholics, Jews, the unchurched) in several of the nation's major cities. Smith's candidacy pointed to perhaps the most important religious development of the decade: the growing awareness that American life was no longer exclusively dominated by white, Anglo-Saxon, Protestants.

The 1930s proved to be a difficult decade for the older Protestant denominations. With the traumas of Fundamentalist-Modernist debate behind them, these denominations did display considerable internal unity, but they also suffered greatly from the difficulties of the era, especially economic uncertainty and theological indecision. They struggled and often failed to maintain numbers and contributions on a par with the 1920s. They were the gorups that experienced an institutional "religious depression" to match the nation's economic one.

Other, newer Protestant bodies knew better how to redeem the times. The Fundamentalists, although vanquished in the old denominations, sustained a thriving variety of evangelistic, educational, and missionary activities. And some of the traditionally more sectarian denominations excelled throughout the decade in providing a religious home for ordinary people and in offering a convincing Christian inter-pretation of daily life. The Southern Baptist Convention, for instance, grew in the 1930s from fewer than 4 million members to well over 5 million; Seventh-Day Ad-ventists went from about 112,000 to 181,000. Some urban Black churches, several Holiness denominations, and many newer Pentecostal groups, both Black and white, experienced similar growth as well.

Protestant theologians struggled during the decade to express a convincing Chris-tian faith. Fundamentalists became a cognitive minority largely content with the anti-intellectual label with which they had been identified in the 1920s. More liberal Protestants bent under the pressure of events—especially economic collapse and the rise of the Nazis—to propound a theology more realistic about the limits of human nature and more open to the notion of divine transcendence. The continental neo-orthodox theology of Karl Barth and Emil Brunner made considerable inroads among such Protestants during this period.

In the Catholic church, which continued its steady rise in numbers and (despite the Depression) economic resources, a different theological climate prevailed. During the 1930s, a neoscholastic synthesis rooted in the thought of Thomas Aquinas became the dominant influence among Catholic thinkers. Neo-Thomism, which stressed the church's authority, the value of disciplined reasoning, and the unifying spirituality of the sacraments, provided ballast for a vast intellectual exercise in which academics from many disciplines organized societies to explore the religious implications of their work. Catholic thought of the age was formally similar to Fundamentalistic thought. The two groups differed markedly, but both were practicing the life of the mind on their own without addressing the larger intellectual community.

Social and economic strain no doubt contributed to the rise of sensational, apoc-alyptic voices in the churches. Premillennialist evangelist Gerald B. Winrod from Kansas saw a plot behind Franklin Roosevelt's "Jewish New Deal" and tried to rally Fundamentalists to oppose the president. The most noticeable public religious voice, however, probably belonged to a Detroit Catholic priest, Father Charles Coughlin. After first supporting FDR on his regular radio broadcast, Coughlin then turned against him for yielding too much influence to bankers, Jews, and defenders of tight money. Father Coughlin's vitriolic campaign soon became an embarrassment to his Catholic superiors.

The Depression era also saw the beginning of more significant involvement by immigrant churches in American life. The immigration legislation passed by Con-gress in the 1920s greatly restricted fresh infusion of Old World culture as well as actual immigrants. Some former enclaves actually began to reach out to the wider society—for example, the heavily German Luthean Church-Missouri Synod, which sponsored a successful radio program, "The Lutheran Hour," on which the scholarly Walter Maier preached effectively in English. The immigrant churches were not yet part of mainstream American life, but the assimilation process was accelerating.

For the decade of the 1940s, the dominant influence in American religion, as in

725

almost everything else in the nation, was World War II. Social change was the major legacy of the war for the churches. The movement of troops and economic mobilization of the home front loosened traditional patterns of gender, family, place, and occupation. When a grateful government made it easier through the G.I. Bill for veterans to attend college, change was only accelerated. The war brought women and Blacks especially more centrally into the public view. Women, who had managed factories and other traditionally masculine domains for the duration, were not always eager to return to traditional roles after the peace. Blacks, who served in great numbers fighting for the freedom of the West, became more aggressive in asking what freedom within American society might be like.

During the war itself, the churches through chaplains and social agencies offered consistent ministry to troops at home and abroad. The war was also a harbinger of ecumenical movements because it drew together in common tasks, often for the first time, representatives of most of the nation's denominations. The economic prosperity that unexpectedly followed in the wake of the war also provided denominations and local churches with resources long denied by the Depression and the war.

The decade of the 1950s was a period of booming growth for the nation and also for the churches. The vast surge in the population—the postwar Baby Boom—created countless new families for whom attachment to church became as normal as increased personal prosperity and a move to the suburbs. Church membership and the building of churches both increased dramatically throughout the decade. Expenditures for church construction were only $68 million in 1946, but had reached over a third of a billion by 1950. In that same year the number of seminarians was double what it had been before the war. And between 1940 and 1960 membership more than doubled in the Assemblies of God, the Catholics, the Christian Reformed church, the Church of the Nazarene, the Mormons, Southern Baptists, and several other denominations.

Also on the increase was interdenominational, or parachurch, cooperation among Christians. Theologically conservative Protestants had organized the National Association of Evangelicals in 1942, and they continued after the war with myriads of new organizations for evangelism, missions, publishing, and youth work. For their part, the older Protestant churches took the lead in the creation of the National Council of Churches in 1950. These same churches were also in the forefront of interdenominational mergers, including a major union among Presbyterians in 1958 and the formation of the United Church of Christ from Congregational and Evangelical and Reformed denominations in 1959.

The postwar period also witnessed a notable increase in concern for the psychological dimensions of religion. The national effort to adjust to postwar conditions as well as continual uncertainty internationally, given the atomic bomb and the perceived threat of communism, fostered a climate in which religion was enlisted in the search for psychological repose. Beginning with Rabbi Joshua Loth Liebman's *Peace of Mind* in 1946, a whole series of influential best-sellers showed how religion could lead to a fuller and more settled existence. The most widely distributed of these books came from some of the era's major religious figures: Norman Vincent Peale, *Guide to Confident Living* (1948) and *The Power of Positive Thinking* (1952), Bishop Fulton J. Sheen, *Peace of Soul* (1949), and Billy Graham, *Peace with God* (1953).

Christianity of different sorts also had much to do with reactions to the Cold War. The fall of China to Mao Tse Tung seemed especially tragic for many Americans in both liberal and Fundamentalist camps, for a wide spectrum of Protestant missionaries had invested decades of work (evangelizing, teaching, healing) in that corner of the world. At the start of the 1950s, Senator Joseph McCarthy from Wisconsin grabbed headlines and wrenched hearts with sensational charges about communists in the state department.

The fact that Senator McCarthy was a Catholic pointed to the increasing visibility of that denomination in the nation's public life. Postwar affluence increased Catholic ability to mobilize for the strengthening of their communities. Catholic schools, colleges, service organizations, publishers, and learned societies all came into existence or were strengthened in the postwar period. At the end of the decade, the election of the nation's first Catholic president, John F. Kennedy, signaled how far this most influential Christian community had come in moving out of its earlier ghettoes.

If the 1950s represented a decade of wide-ranging growth and diversification for the churches, the 1960s was simply a shock. The rapid shift from the settled order of the 1950s (symbolized by a grandfatherly President Eisenhower) to the tumults of the 1960s (symbolized by the assassination of President Kennedy) seems to have defined the course of Christianity in America since that time. During the 1960s, marked by moral revolution, older mainline churches seemed to seek accommodation with the times. During the next decade, marked by moral reaction, Fundamentalist churches seized the initiative in attempting to exert a conservative influence on the society. During the 1980s, a pervasive split between liberal and conservative Christians reflected divided attitudes on both public issues and the life of faith.

The 1960s were tumultuous in many particulars. Black Americans, long frustrated by the painfully slow progress in realizing the nation's vaunted freedom for themselves, agitated for new civil rights in a movement in which clergymen played the central roles. Violence broke in on the public with unprecedented force with the assassination of John F. Kennedy in 1963 and of both Robert Kennedy and Martin Luther King, Jr., in 1968. The death of 50,000 less-well-known Americans in Vietnam left perhaps an even more permanent scar. Disarray in public life seemed also to be matched by disarray in private life. Whether an actual sexual revolution occurred in the 1960s or more simply a new frankness about practices already habitual in secret, the public became ineluctably aware of shifting values. More and more people talked about a relaxation of sexual standards, and less and less restraint hindered public discussion of sexual issues. The feminist movement, the increased participation of women in the job market, the rising divorce rate, the widespread availability of pornography, and the public advocacy of homosexuality were symptoms of upheaval in family and sexual ethics.

Christian voices in sympathy with the revolutionary character of the times were the ones most frequently heard in the 1960s. Although many religious figures supported the Vietnam War, those who opposed it made a larger public impact. The Vietnam conflict also seemed to stimulate other questions of national military policy and to feed directly into a trend that saw representatives of mainline Protestant churches and some Catholics join traditional pacifists like the Mennonites and Quakers in agitating against nuclear armaments. Socially progressive denominations were also in the forefront in opening leadership ranks to women. Early in the century it had been Pentecostal, Holiness, and other sectarian evangelicals who gave women more scope for preaching and leadership. After mid-century it was the United Church of Christ, the Methodists, the Presbyterians, the American Lutheran Church, and, somewhat later, the Episcopalians who took the lead in ordaining women for the ministry.

Among Catholics, the great event of the 1960s was the Second Vatican Council (1962–1965). Whether American understanding of the council was the same as that held by later popes and their advisors, for America the council was unquestionably a liberalizing event. In response to Pope John XXIII's call for the opening of windows into the church, the council appealed for greater collegiality, more scope for the laity, and more interaction with modern scholarship. Since the council, American Catholics have found it much more acceptable to carry on conversations with Protestants and members of other faiths. The more accepting attitude toward American democracy, which was still not completely in favor among the hierarchy as late as the 1950s, now prevailed in almost all corners of the church. The council's attitude toward the bible encouraged a contrasting pair of developments. Catholic biblical scholars began to look more like liberal Protestants as they put to use conventional critical approaches to scripture. But groups of Catholic laity began to look more like evangelical Protestants as they adopted patterns and habits of small-group bible study. Among this latter group, the Catholic charismatics were especially important. A thorny development after the council was the publication in 1968 of Pope Paul VI's encyclical *Humanae Vitae*, which forbade any form of artificial birth control. For perhaps the first time in American history, large numbers of Catholics, lay and cleric, chose to ignore a major teaching of the church and in practice sanctioned the use of artificial forms of family planning. Because of events in the 1960s, in other words, Roman Catholics came much more rapidly to resemble their Protestant counterparts than almost anyone in the 1950s could have predicted.

During the 1970s, considerable reaction took place against the main developments of the 1960s (these were breakthroughs or disasters, depending on point of view). Most visible was the rise of a political movement known as the New Religious Right. Three events seemed to have stimulated a renewal of the sort of evangelical political participation that had been standard in the nineteenth century but that had diminished since the 1930s. The first was the 1973 ruling of the Supreme Court on abortion. Its decision in Roe v. Wade, which legalized abortion on demand, angered many religious conservatives as an explicit affront to Judeo-Christian reverence for life as well as an implicit sanction of the morally reprehensible sexual revolution. The second was the nation's bicentennial in 1976, an event exploited by many aggrieved conservatives to issue appeals for returning the nation to its Christian heritage. The third event was the election as president at the end of the decade of Ronald Reagan, a conservative voice who won overwhelming approval from theologically conservative Protestants and who also had unprecedented success, as a Republican, among Roman Catholics. With spokesmen skillful in the use of the media, such as Jerry Falwell of the Moral Majority, conservative Christians rallied to the cause of what they regarded as traditional values. At the same time that these conservatives made a new effort in politics, they also geared up for new initiatives in education. Hundreds of new academies were founded to protect traditional American values and to save children from the religion of secular humanism, thought to be rampant in the public schools. In public schools, aroused conservatives campaigned against the teaching of evolution or sought to exert some control over the books assigned to their children.

In the 1980s, the American religious landscape was sharply divided between those who favored a civil religion of tolerance, expressiveness, and civility and those who favored a civil religion of tradition, restraint, and moral resolution. A spectacular rise in the number of religious voluntary associations has provided virtually every interest group in the nation with an organization and platform for promoting its cause. Most of these groups are low-key (such as neighborhood bible studies or local partnerships to feed the homeless), but some (such as gay caucuses or antiabortion groups) are aggressively public. The fact that these special interest groups usually divide between conservative and liberal, often in alignment with other voluntary associations drawing on similar constituencies, reinforces the depth of the division in recent public religion. A deep disagreement over the role of government in areas of moral, family, and economic life—with conservatives generally opposed and liberals generally in favor—adds to the systematic tension that began in the 1980s and continues into the 1990s.

The cluster of volatile family and sexual controversies drives a particularly deep wedge among Americans in the churches. Although some denominations offer formal opinions on abortion and AIDS, many are split down the middle. Most of the nation's Christian groups agree on the undesirability of abortion, but they remain deeply divided on what to do about it. Some, the more liberal theologically, consider free access to abortion a lesser evil than the social cost of undesired pregnancies or any restriction of womens' right to control reproduction. Others, the more conservative theologically, consider abortion on demand an affront to moral law and to the fabric of civilization itself. Advocates of the latter view, however, have considerable difficulty agreeing on tactics to halt abortion. Constitutional amendments, normal legislation, and a judicial reversal of *Roe v. Wade* have all been called for. One of the most important results of controversy over abortion has been to yoke together members of different religious groups whose hereditary theological differences had once kept them apart. In the not too distant past, for example, some Fundamentalists looked on the pope as the Antichrist and on Mormons as pernicious cultists. Now at least some of these same Fundamentalists willingly march in front of abortion clinics with Catholics and Mormons as valued comrades in arms.

The 1980s was also a decade for controversy within the denominations, nowhere more spectacularly than in the Southern Baptist Convention where strife continues into the 1990s. As had happened often in American history, the growth in size, wealth, and social influence of a formerly separated group led to increasing contacts between Southern Baptists and the national culture. Especially after World War II, the Southern Baptists gave the lie to their own name by moving aggressively into northern and western states. One sign of the more general shift was new support for the Republican party among Southern Baptist clergy and laity. This strengthening pattern represented a major change from earlier in the century when this southern and populist denomination had regularly voted for Democrats in state and national elections. Another sign of the new situation was a sometimes bitter struggle over theological issues, especially in the seminaries and in the church's publications. Southern Baptist "conservatives" were especially distressed by what they saw as too much willingness on the part of Southern Baptist "moderates" to accept principles of biblical higher criticism. In response, the conservatives effectively mobilized their constituencies to elect like-minded individuals as chief officers of the convention, which in turn led to many more conservatives being placed on boards and agencies of the denomination. Because of the size and influence of the Southern Baptists, the internal story of the organization was a major matter for the religious life of the whole nation.

A survey of the decades since World War I hardly does justice to the complexity of Christian experience in the United States over those years. It does, however, provide some sense of the scope of that complexity during these tumultuous years.

Denominations and Leaders

Along with the social and political changes in modern America have come also major shifts in the configuration of its churches. Some of these changes represent major breaks with past American experience, some present the last stage of long, evolutionary development. One conclusion drawn from examining the rise and decline of Christian groups relates to a denomination's ability to speak the language of the moment but with some sort of distinctive Christian accent. Groups that attune their voice completely to the spirit of an age, as well as those who present their vision of Christian faith in a foreign language (either actual or conceptual), do not enjoy widespread allegiance. Something similar could be said about the major public spokespersons for Christianity since the 1920s. The most widely respected have had an uncannny ability to communicate on the level of the American masses, but they have also known how to do so without reducing the Christian content of their message to simple mass appeal.

Rises and Declines

In general terms, the denominations that have grown most rapidly in the twentieth century are those that are newest in America. Thus, the Roman Catholic church is now beyond question the major Christian presence in a once overwhelmingly Protestant nation. The Southern Baptists, once marginalized because of region and Protestant pecking order, are the largest Protestant body in the country. Groups that once seemed to be but pesky sects—like the Mormons, the Adventists, and various Pentecostal and Fundamentalist groups—are booming. On the other hand, most of the denominations that dominated America's religious life before the Civil War (Congregationalists, Episcopalians, Presbyterians, and Methodists) are in decline. Since the 1940s, public polling has given a more accurate picture of the nominal religious allegiance of Americans. (See Table 32–1.) For the most general categories, results from 1947 and 1986 show a considerable growth for Catholics (from 20 to 27 percent of the population), a corresponding loss for Protestants (from 69 to 59 percent), a serious decline for Jews (5 to 2 percent), and considerable enlargement in the categories of "Other" (1 to 4 percent) and "None" (6 to 8 percent).

Between 1940 and 1986, the population of the United States increased by 83 percent from somewhat more than 130 million to more than 240 million. Religious groups whose growth has greatly exceeded the general population rise in that time include a number of Pentecostal, Holiness, and sectarian bodies as well as the Catholic church. Denominations defined by their European origins—for example, Lutherans and Mennonites—have grown at rates roughly comparable to the rise in population. Most of the older Protestant denominations have had rates of growth considerably below the rise in population, and some of the mainline denominations actually lost membership in the 1970s and 1980s.

Interpreting these changes is more difficult than noting them. Catholic growth comes in part from continued immigration (most recently, Hispanic) as well as from relatively good success at retaining the allegiance of those who grow up in that church. Some analysts plausibly ascribe the growth of Southern Baptists, Mormons, the Pentecostals and other evangelical or Fundamentalist groups to a combination of factors. These churches often define doctrine firmly and make high demands of commitment and conformity in daily practice (and so counter the culture's general trends toward permissiveness and "value neutrality"). At the same time, their very numbers communicate an aura of success and sometimes even socioeconomic opti-

Table 32-1   Denominational Size, 1940–1986

	1940	1960	1980	1986	Percentage of change
(U.S. population, millions)	(132)	(178)	(227)	(241)	+83

Growth Substantially above Rise in Population

	1940	1960	1980	1986	Percentage of change
Assemblies of God	199,000	509,000	1,064,000	2,135,000	+973
Christian & Missouri Alliance	23,000	60,000	190,000	239,000	+904
Church of God (TN)	63,000	170,000	435,000	n.a.	+590
Mormons	724,000	1,487,000	2,811,000	3,860,000	+433
Seventh-Day Adventists	176,000	318,000	571,000	666,000	+278
Jehovah's Witnesses	n.a.	250,000	565,000	752,000	

Growth above Rise in Population

	1940	1960	1980	1986	Percentage of change
Church of the Nazarene	166,000	308,000	484,000	531,000	+220
Southern Baptists	4,949,000	9,732,000	13,600,000	14,614,000	+195
Roman Catholics	21,284,000	42,105,000	50,450,000	52,893,000	+149

Growth Near Rise in Population

	1940	1960	1980	1986	Percentage of change
Lutheran Church, Missouri Synod	1,277,000	2,391,000	2,262,000	2,631,000	+106
Salvation Army	238,000	318,000	417,000	433,000	+82

Table 32-1   Denominational Size, 1940–1986 (Continued)

	1940	1960	1980	1986	Percentage of change
Growth Near Rise in Population (Continued)					
Christian Reformed Church	122,000	236,000	212,000	220,000	+80
Mennonite Church	51,000	73,000	100,000	91,000	+78
Evangelical Lutheran Church (ALC + LCA)	3,118,000	5,296,000	5,276,000	5,216,000	+67
Wisconsin Evangelical Lutherans	257,000	348,000	407,000	416,000	+62
Growth Less Than Rise in Population					
Reformed Church in America	255,000	355,000	346,000	340,000	+33
Episcopal Church	1,996,000	3,269,000	2,786,000	2,505,000	+26
United Methodist	8,043,000	10,641,000	9,519,000	9,192,000	+14
Presbyterian U.S. (No. + So.)	2,691,000	4,162,000	3,362,000	3,007,000	+12
United Church (Congregational)	1,708,000	2,241,000	1,736,000	1,676,000	−2
Disciples of Christ	1,659,000	1,802,000	1,178,000	1,107,000	−33

From C. H. Jacquet, Jr., ed., *Yearbook of American and Canadian Churches: 1988*, (Nashville, TN: Abingdon, 1988).

mism (and so conform well to American myths of progress and improvement). The difficulties of the older Protestant denominations may stem from their willingness to embrace ideas and trends as defined by the nation's media and educational elites, elites that are remarkably unrepresentative of the religion, politics, and values of the nation's population. From one perspective, the promotion of causes or the acceptance of mores from these sources can be regarded as a prophetic effort to keep the Christian message relevant to a changing world. From another angle, it can be seen as simply selling out. Whatever lies behind the different rates of denominational expansion in recent decades, the result is a major shift in the center of gravity in American church life.

Finally, it is important to take note of the large number of Black Christians in their own denominations for which statistics are usually not so precise as for the groups already listed. Estimates for the major Black Baptist groups range up to a total of 10 to 11 million (National Baptist Convention USA Inc., from 5.5 to 7 million; National Baptist Convention of America [unincorporated], about 2.5 million; and the Progressive National Baptist Convention, between 500,000 and 1 million). The three largest Black Methodist denominations likewise include a large number of members (African Methodist Episcopal Church at about 2.2 million, the African Methodist Episcopal Church Zion at about 1.2 million, and the Christian Methodist Episcopal Church at about 800,000). In addition, the largest black Pentecostal body, the Church of God in Christ, numbers between 3.5 to 4 million members. And several other Holiness and Pentecostal bodies have substantial membership as well.

The Lutherans: An Emerging Ethnic Enclave

A most important general development in recent American Christianity is the public emergence of groups previously segregated by the immigrant experience. The prime cases of this process are found within the Catholic church and include its Irish, southern European, and now Hispanic subcommunities. But it has also been a process at work among ethnic Protestants. The best example of ethnic Protestant consolidation is the Lutherans, an impressively large body of Christians in America who, however, are still known more as the descendants of German and Scandinavian immigrants than as major players in the public Christian life of the United States.

The story of Lutherans in America is the story of unification following on the heels of fragmentation. The waves of German and Scandinavian immigration, which grew especially strong after the 1840s, led to the creation of myriad small Lutheran bodies, as many as sixty-six independent organizations at one time. During the nineteenth century, a General Synod (which leaned in the direction of adjusting to American ways), a General Council (staunchly defending European ways), and eventually in 1872 a Synodical Conference provided a measure of cooperation. It was not until the twentieth century—not, that is, until two generations had passed from the start of massive Lutheran immigration—that real consolidation took place. World War I, with its intense anti-German feelings and its forced cooperation in many spheres, set the backdrop for important mergers. In 1917 most of the Norwegian bodies joined to form the Norwegian Lutheran church. The next year the United Lutheran Church came into existence through the merger of several different bodies. In the same year the influential Iowa and Ohio Synods established fellowship for preaching and communion. In 1930, the Ohio, Buffalo, Texas, and Iowa Synods joined to form the American Lutheran Church (ALC), a body that served as the base for an expanded denomination of the same name that came into existence in 1960 through the addition of the Norwegian Lutheran Church and two large Danish bodies. The creation of the ALC in 1960 was significant as the first major merger of American Lutherans involving both German and Scandinavian churches. Two years later the United Lutheran Church joined the Augustana Lutherans (Swedish), a smaller Danish church, and the largest of the Finnish Lutheran bodies to form the Lutheran Church in America (LCA). From 1967 a Lutheran Council in the United States of America provided a forum for discussion among the ALC, the LCA, and the Lutheran Church—Missouri Synod, the latter a more conservative body that was itself the product of smaller synods. In 1987 the process of consolidation reached a climax when the ALC and the LCA joined to create the Evangelical Lutheran Church in America. With its more than 5 million members, this new entity has become the third largest predominantly white Protestant denomination in the country.

Meanwhile, the Missouri Synod Lutherans underwent a traumatic internal dispute that in some particulars resembled the nineteenth-century clash between Samuel Schmucker and his European opponents. Throughout the postwar period, some of the leading academics in the Missouri Synod had urged the denomination, which with the 400,000-strong Wisconsin Evangelical Lutheran Synod was the most traditionalist of the Lutherans, to take a more open attitude toward modern biblical scholarship. With this proposal, in its own way an effort to bring the denomination into closer contact with main movements in American religious thought, a number of influential leaders were not pleased. It seemed at once too much a concession to contemporary academic conventions and too obvious a deviation from the traditional positions on scripture contained in historic Lutheran confessions. The result was a major struggle in the early 1970s in which the majority of the denomination backed the traditionalists. As a consequence, a small group (the Evangelical Lutheran Church in Mission) broke from Missouri and eventually took part in the creation of the Evangelical Lutheran Church in America. Weighty differences over the nature and use of scripture were at the heart of the Missouri Synod's strife, but an additional factor was cultural. The majority, perhaps in keeping with the strength of conservative cultural forces in the 1970s, concluded it was simply not necessary to take their cue from larger developments in American religious or academic life. Whatever the drift in other Lutheran bodies, they were resolved to make the sacrifices required to keep the denomination in line with what its leaders felt was its Old World heritage.

American Lutherans have not yet contributed to American public or religious life in proportion to the numbers. There are, to be sure, Lutheran academics who have become American leaders in the interpretation of Christianity to the wider American public. At the start of the 1990s, for example, the Lutheran Martin Marty at the University of Chicago is the most knowledgeable and most often quoted commentor on religion in contemporary America, and the Lutheran Jaroslav Pelikan of Yale University is widely regarded as the nation's leading historian of Christian doctrine. At the same time, however, no Lutheran has ever been the nominee of a major political party for president; Lutheran efforts in publication are with some exceptions directed mostly to Lutherans; and Lutheran literary voices though often outstanding have been, like Ole Rolvaag, chroniclers of the immigrant experience rather than shapers of more general American perceptions.

Leaders

The revolution in communications media has meant that radio, television, satellite, and cable can carry messages from and stories about leading figures in all walks of life to unprecedented numbers. In such an age, it is almost inevitable that religious leaders too would take on a larger-than-life status, especially those with the savvy to exploit the media for the causes they champion. Religion, like politics and commerce, has had its share of charlatans and quacks exploiting the potentials of this media revolution, but it has also had a number of exemplary figures who have maintained the integrity of their message even while putting the media to use. Three of those individuals—Martin Luther King, Jr., Bishop Fulton J. Sheen, and William Franklin ("Billy") Graham—have consistently ranked among the most admired Americans since World War II. Brief sketches of their lives show something of their personal contributions as well as how each became the voice of a significant segment of the Christian community in the United States.

Martin Luther King, Jr. (1929–1968) was America's most visible civil rights leader fom 1955 until his assassination in April 1968. The son of a prominent Black Baptist pastor in Atlanta, King studied at Morehouse College, Crozer Theological Seminary, and Boston University (where he took his Ph.D.) before becoming the pastor of the Drexler Avenue Baptist Church in Montgomery, Alabama. He vaulted into national prominence when he led the successful Montgomery bus boycott (1955–1956), which sought an end to racial segregation in that city's public transportation. In 1957 King helped organize the Southern Christian Leadership Conference (SCLC), which rapidly became one of the foremost civil rights groups in the country. Its leaders were, like King, mostly Black Baptist ministers.

Dr. King's own personal prestige was at its height in the early and middle 1960s. He keynoted a massive march on Washington in August 1963 with a moving speech from which the following extract is taken:

Even though we face the difficulties of today and tomorrow, I still have a dream. It is a dream deeply rooted in the American dream. I have a dream that one day this nation will rise up and live out the true meaning of its creed, 'We hold these truths to be self-evident, that all men are created equal.' I have a dream that one day on the red hills of Georgia, sons of former slaves and the sons of former slave owners will be able to sit down together at the table of brotherhood.[1]

He also helped to organize the well-publicized march from Selma to Montgomery in the spring of 1965. The first of these events provided major support for the Civil Rights Act of 1964, the second for the federal Voter Registration Act of 1965. King was in direct communication with the White House and was awarded the Nobel Prize for Peace in 1964. Toward the end of his life, however, King's influence was in jeopardy. His excursions into the North (Chicago, 1966, for example) cost him the support of those who saw civil rights as strictly a southern problem. His criticism of the Vietnam War angered other Americans. And he was caught in the ideological crossfire caused by the rioting in American cities during the middle and late 1960s. Some whites assigned to King the responsibility for these outbursts because of his promotion of Black civil rights. Some Blacks felt that King betrayed their cause by continuing to repudiate the use of violence to attain racial justice.

During the 1950s and 1960s, King was a living example on American television screens of Black preaching at its best. His speeches and writings drew heavily on the vocabulary provided by the rich reservoirs of Black Christian history. His ideology was constructed on an evangelical realism concerning the nature of human evil and a scriptural defense of nonviolence ("love your enemies"). In classic Black fashion, he made little distinction between spiritual and social problems involved in the civil rights struggle. Other elements also entered his thinking—the pacifism of Gandhi, the civil disobedience of Thoreau, the philosophical idealism that he had studied at Boston University, and the American public faith in democratic equality. In the moving words of Dr. King it was often hard to tell where, if at all, the Christian substratum of his thought left off and the superstructure of his social theory began. In any case, he was beyond question the most important Christian voice in the postwar drive for civil rights.

For millions of Americans in the first decdes of electronic mass communication, Fulton J. Sheen (1895–1979) embodied the Christian message. He was the first individual to conduct a televised religious service (1940). Ten years before that he had

---

[1]James M. Washington, ed., *A Testament of Hope: The Essential Writings of Martin Luther King, Jr.* (San Francisco: Harper & Row, 1986), p. 219.

become the regular speaker on the "Catholic Hour," a Sunday evening radio program over the National Broadcasting Company that eventually reached 4 million listeners a week. In 1951 he added a regular appearance on television to an already full schedule when he began the weekly series "Life is Worth Living." From these broadcasts Bishop Sheen received a great correspondence that once reached 30,000 letters in a single day and averaged 40,000 a week. The bishop's message went out even further through his newspaper columns in both the Catholic and secular press, his many speaking engagements in this country and abroad, and his nearly seventy books.

Casual observers of the American scene who equated popular preaching with a lack of formal education and a surplus of mindless emotion could not fathom Bishop Sheen or his popularity. He was born in El Paso, Illinois, where he took his part at chores on the family farm before moving with his parents and three brothers to Peoria. He excelled in the local Catholic schools as he would also later at St. Viator's College (Illinois), St. Paul Seminary (Minnesota), the Catholic University of America, the Sorbonne in Paris, the University of Louvain in Belgium, and the Collegio Angelico in Rome. He held earned doctorates in philosophy and theology and taught philosophy for a quarter century at the Catholic University of America. He was an influential delegate to the Second Vatican Council, an auxiliary bishop of New York from 1951, bishop of Rochester from 1966, and titular archbishop of Newport (Wales) from 1969. Honors came to him from around the world and in the United States, including an Emmy for his television work.

On radio and television or in person, Bishop Sheen was a compelling presence. His habit was to speak without notes after hours of rigorous preparation, a practice that enabled him to communicate informally while still having something to say. Bishop Sheen followed time-honored missionary strategy by attempting to move his audience from the known to the unknown, from significant circumstances in everyday life to the church's message of hope in God. His tapes still circulate and continue to attract individuals to Christian faith.

For all his fame, however, Bishop Sheen never lost the common touch; throughout his life religious devotion was an anchor. Nearly every day of his adult life he set aside an hour to meditate on scripture and the teachings of the church. On October 2, 1979, in New York's St. Patrick's Cathedral, two months before the bishop's death, Pope John Paul II embraced Fulton Sheen and said, "You have written and spoken well of the Lord Jesus. You are a loyal son of the Church."[2]

Through more than forty years of evangelistic campaigns in the states and abroad, Billy Graham (b. 1918) has become one of the most widely known Protestants in the twentieth century. Graham was raised in North Carolina in a conventionally Fundamentalist environment. He attended Wheaton College in Illinois at a time when

[2]*Fulton Sheen, Treasure in Clay: The Autobiography of Fulton J. Sheen* (Garden City, N.Y.: Doubleday, 1980), p. 356.

that institution was cautiously shifting its self-designation from aggressive Fundamentalism to a more open neoevangelicalism. An impressive preacher from an early age, Graham became in 1944 the first full-time employee of the Youth for Christ movement, a recently founded effort to evangelize the young people of the nation. He traveled extensively on behalf of that organization, was briefly president of an evangelical bible college, and conducted periodic tent crusades. In the summer of 1949, Graham and associates planned such a gathering in Los Angeles, thinking it would last three weeks. Spectacular conversions of athletes, mobsters, and entertainers toward the close of the third week led to the extension of the campaign. Publisher William Randolph Hearst got wind of the event and instructed his newspapers to cover the meetings and promote the young evangelist. The results were spectacular. The meetings were extended for another nine weeks; crowds jammed the 6,000-seat "Canvas Cathedral"; and a new star had risen on the nation's religious horizon.

Graham's Christian message has been remarkably consistent throughout his career. He has boldly proclaimed what, in a trademark phrase, "the bible says" about human sin and the need for divine redemption. His gospel message is a simple one of the need for faith in Christ, but it does not deny the reality of struggle in the life of faith. What has set Graham apart is his winning charisma and his freedom from the eccentricities and incivilities with which other revivalists have so often been marked in American history. In addition, Graham has been eager to cooperate with a wide range of Christian groups. A major campaign in New York City in 1957 marked something of a turning point in his career. When Graham insisted on including representatives of old Protestant, or mainline, churches in the planning for the crusade and on directing some who made decisions for Christ at his meetings to these same churches, he won the undying wrath of more separatistic Fundamentalists. In subsequent years, Graham has even gained the guarded support of various Catholic bishops for his work. Earlier he had been a pioneer in integrating Blacks and whites in his crusades, even in the South.

Graham's conventional evangelical faith was matched in his early career by a conventional faith in America. In 1950 the first broadcast of his long-running radio program, "The Hour of Decision," offered what was then a typical mixture of evangelical and anticommunist fervor. "The Battle Hymn of the Republic" provided the backdrop for an appeal for spiritual repentance, and the evangelist's message was filled with alarm about "the tragic end of America" and the "hour of tragic crisis all across the world." Graham has been invited to the White House by every president since Harry Truman, but he enjoyed a particularly close relationship with conservative political leaders, especially Richard Nixon. Only last-minute intervention by Bobby Kennedy kept Graham from publishing an endorsement of then Vice President Nixon on the eve of the 1960 election. The resignation of President Nixon in 1974, and even more the earlier revelations of sordid doings in the Nixon White House, sobered Graham politically. Since then, he has been more circumspect and more determinedly nonpartisan in his political associations. He has also advanced well beyond the conventional views of his evangelical constituency to advocate greater controls on nuclear arms and increased efforts to establish world peace. In the 1980s he also made several well-received visits to China and the Soviet Union, during which he went out of his way to cooperate with local officials and to encourage the Christian churches in these countries. Almost as remarkable as the constancy of Graham's preaching, therefore, is the evolution of his politics, from aggressive cold warrior to widely respected advocate for world peace and internal toleration.

Like Martin Luther King, Jr., and Fulton J. Sheen, Graham also knew how to exploit the media. He early used radio, television, and motion pictures to promote the gospel. Several of his books have sold in the millions, and *Decision* magazine, which he supervises, is the most widely circulated religious periodical in the world. The Billy Graham Evangelistic Association has also been a leader in office efficiency and has offered guidelines to other organizations—religious and nonreligious both— on maintaining connections with a far-flung constituency.

Graham does not speak authoritatively for American Protestant evangelicals any more than King did for Blacks or Sheen for Catholics. Yet each was, and continues to be, a respected voice, summing up in his own person those qualities by which those large constituencies would like themselves to be judged by the wider world.

Life and Thought

In twentieth-century America the profusion of Christian styles of life and thought is as broad as the nation itself. Twentieth-century American Christianity includes applications of the faith drawn from both hot tubs and picket lines. It includes a population whose artistic tastes range from Bach to popular songwriter Bill Gaither, from the cerebral Simone Weil to the best-selling Majorie Holmes, from Rembrandt to Charles Schultz. Theologically, its ranks are well populated with intense conservatives and radical liberals, as well as countless variations in between. Old standoffs, like that between Protestants and Catholics, still count in some venues, but so also do new ones such as prolife versus prochoice. Even with this diversity, it is possible to provide something of the flavor of twentieth-century Christianity in America by sketching salient apsects of its experience. Ecumenical developments, the expanding role of women Christian leaders, and important voices in theology do not by any means exhaust the scope of recent Christian experience, but they do illustrate some important matters.

Ecumenism

The most visible intra-Christian groups have been interdenominational agencies aiming directly at increased ecumenical cooperation. In this regard, the National Council of Churches of Christ has been the most visible. With a record of support to causes others have deemed radical, it is also the most controversial. Not surprisingly, with the relative decline of the older Protestant denominations, the National Council of Churches in which those groups have been prominent has also suffered through difficult times in the 1970s and 1980s. A combination of decreased funding and continuing ire from social and political conservatives has made for ongoing strain within the organization. At the same time, however, other ecumenical groups have begun to take on some of the tasks that the National Council may have once wished it could include within its famework. The Baptist Joint Committee on Public Affairs, the Christian Holiness Association, the National Association of Evangelicals, the Pentecostal Fellowship of North America, and, above all, the Catholic Council of Bishops are examples of organizations that have carved out niches for themselves. They promote cooperation among bodies of similar backgrounds or belifes, lobby governments on issues of special concerns to constituencies, and provide national meetings for fellowship and encouragement.

A much more significant ecumenical breakthrough has come, however, in the cooling of previous antagonism between Roman Catholics and Protestants. No one group is responsible for this improved state of affairs, but it may be the most important ecumenical story of the century.

As late as the post-World War II era, feelings between Catholics and Protestants were still very sensitive. In 1945, for example, a fundamentalist radio preacher Carl McIntire argued publicly that the Catholic church posed a greater threat to America than even the communists. "If one had to choose between the two [communism or Catholicism]," he wrote, "one would be much better off in a communistic society than in a Roman Catholic Fascist set-up."[3] When in the next year President Truman proposed assigning a formal representative to the Vatican, it was the Protestant establishment, led by G. Bromley Oxnam, president of the Federal Council of Churches, who protested the loudest. Such a move, he said, would encourage an "un-American policy of a union of church and state" of the sort favored by Catholics. All suspicion was not on one side either. The second General Assembly of the World Council of Churches was held at Evanston, Illinois, in 1954, and Chicago's influential Cardinal Samuel Strich forbade Catholic priests from attending its sessions. A year earlier, Catholics had protested, as a scurrilous attack on their faith, the release of a motion picture depicting the life of Martin Luther.

Then the situation changed with lightning speed. The most visible public signal of a shift was the election of a Catholic president in 1960. John F. Kennedy's victory was itself a milestone. To be sure, his candidacy did split voters to an unprecedented degree along religious lines. Catholics had given Democratic presidential candidate Adlai Stevenson 51 and 45 percent of their vote in 1952 and 1956, respectively. In 1960, 82 percent of Catholics voted for Kennedy. White Protestants who regularly

[3]James Morris, *The Preachers* (New York: St. Martin's Press, 1973), p. 199.

741

attended church had given Stevenson a little more than 30 percent of their vote in 1952 and 1956. In 1960 they gave Richard Nixon 75 percent of their vote. Even Black Protestants, who since World War II had usually voted overwhelmingly Democratic, split their votes almost evenly between Nixon and Kennedy. But Kennedy proved adept at allaying Protestant fears. During his campaign, he used a speech before Protestant ministers in Houston to pledge strict fidelity to American traditions of separating church and state. And when he became president, he scrupulously held to his word, even to the point of working against any sort of governmental aid to parochial schools. As a result, the issue of Catholics in politics was greatly defused. (Indeed, some Catholics and even a few Protestants were disappointed that Kennedy's religion seemed to manifest so little influence on his policy or style of government.)

Even more important for improved Catholic-Protestant relations were events coming from Rome and the Second Vatican Council convened by Pope John XXIII in 1962. In the wake of the Council's Decree on Ecumenism, which "commends this work to the bishops everywhere in the world for their diligent and prudent guidance," the Conference of American Bishops in November 1964 set up its own Ecumenical Commission. This agency sponsored subcommissions that very soon were deep in discussion with the Eastern Orthodox as well as with several of the major Protestant bodies. Catholic-Protestant discussions, dialogue, and interaction continue to occur at almost every imaginable level.

Other religious antagonisms have grown up to replace traditional differences. American Christians in the 1980s differ sharply, for example, on some political questions (budget for defense versus budget for social programs), on social issues (support for traditional families and traditional marriages versus support for alternative lifestyles), and on general approaches to ethical behavior itself (believing that they are grounded in timeless truths versus believing that they are adjustable according to the circumstances of the times). Even the growth of such differences, however, should not be allowed to diminish the significance of more peaceful relations between Catholics and Protestants.

Women and the Faith

The changes in American society since World War II have also made a great deal of difference for the practice of Christianity by women. By the 1980s, women were active at every level of Christian life, including personal and domestic spheres where women have traditionally taken the lead but also more public spheres of responsibility that had once been regarded as the preserve of men. The careers of exemplary leaders in the twentieth century do not satisfactorily describe the range and extent of those activities, but it does give some sense of the achievements in public venues by Christian women in this century. Four examples of women who worked with very different constituencies suggest something of these opportunities.

Aimee Semple McPherson (1890–1944) was one of America's most flamboyant revivalists in the 1920s and 1930s. She married first the man who had been influential in her conversion, Robert Semple, a Pentecostal preacher with whom she went to China as a missionary in 1908. When Semple died, his wife returned to the United States with their son Robert. She then married Harold McPherson from whom she was subsequently divorced. A third marriage and another divorce came later, as did many rumors about other affairs with men. With her mother as companion, Aimee Semple McPherson began after World War I a very successful series of revival tours across the United States. "Sister Aimee," as she was known to her followers, was a physically attractive woman who knew how to exploit her good looks and vibrant personality to capture the attention of the media. She pioneered in radio evangelism (1922) and may have participated in a staged kidnapping of herself in 1926, a case that remains a mystery. Her teaching was probably not as important as her personality in her great success, but it did include standard Fundamentalist and Pentcostal emphases: sanctification, baptism of the Holy Spirit, the gift of tongues, Christ as savior and healer (hence faith healing), and the imminent return of Christ. In 1922 she settled in Los Angeles, where she preached to thousands each week at her $1.5 million Angelus Temple. The International·Church of the Foursquare Gospel arose as a result of her ministry in 1927. It continued under the direction of her son after she died and now numbers around 100,000 members. Part of the sensation surrounding McPherson's career arose from allegations linking her romantically to other men. Even her death in 1944 was not free from sensation, some ascribing it to a heart attack, others to an overdose of sleeping pills.

Very different in style from Sister Aimee but equal in visibility, was Dorothy Day (1897–1980), whom historian David O'Brien called at her death "the most significant, interesting, and influential person in the history of American Catholicism." The editor of her selected writings Robert Ellsberg continues that "such a statement is all the more extraordinary considering that it refers to someone who occupied no established position of authority, and whose views, after all, met with virtually universal rejection throughout most of her career."[4]

For almost fifty years, Dorothy Day directed the Catholic Worker movement, a lay ministry that she and fellow Catholic Peter Maurin founded in 1931. Her commitment to the Catholic Worker's cause came only several years after her conversion to Catholicism. In *From Union Square to Rome* (1938), she tells the story of a tempestuous adolescence and early adulthood, which included first an affair and an abortion, and then a common-law marriage that was over by the time of her conversion. In their work together in the 1930s, Day and Maurin sought to develop an alternative Catholic social philosophy in the pages of the *Catholic Worker* and a network of "Houses of Hospitality," in which Christ's acts of mercy—feeding the hungry, cloth-

---

[4]Robert Ellsberg, ed., *By Little and By Little: The Selected Writings of Dorothy Day* (New York: Knopf, 1983), p. xvii.

ing the naked, sheltering the homeless—would be carried out by his contemporary disciples. She sustained her commitment to the Catholic Worker movement through the Depression, World War II, the Korean and Vietnam conflicts, and the civil rights upheavals of the 1950s and 1960s. Throughout those years, Day sought to retain the simple program of the movement, whose spiritual sensibility she defined as, "Sacrifice, worship, a sense of reverence."

Like Dorothy Day, Flannery O'Connor (1925–1964) was a Catholic, but unlike the leader of the Catholic Workers, O'Connor made her mark by pursuing the solitary tasks of a writer. The spirit of O'Connor's life is suggested by a conversation in which she took part during a visit from her home in Milledgeville, Georgia, to New York City. She reported the incident as follows:

> Mrs. Broadwater said when she was a child and received the Host, she thought of it as the Holy Ghost, He being the "most portable" person of the Trinity. Now she thought of it as a symbol and implied that it was a pretty good one. I then said, in a very shaky voice, "Well, if it's a symbol, to hell with it." That was all the defense I was capable of but I realize now that this is all I will ever be able to say about it . . . except that it is the center of existence for me; all the rest of life is expendable.[5]

Flannery O'Connor received her training at the Georgia State College for Women and in the renowned writing workshop at the University of Iowa. She quickly distinguished herself, winning a certain degree of critical acclaim and several awards and fellowships. Then at the age of twenty-five, she was diagnosed as having lupus, a virulent form of arthritis that was to claim her life before the age of forty.

In her brief career O'Connor wrote some of the most distinguished fiction of the postwar era. Among her best known works are the novels *Wise Blood* (1952) and *The Violent Bear It Away* (1960) and two collections of short stories, *A Good Man Is Hard to Find* (1955) and *Everything That Rises Must Converge* (1965). Her fiction has been acclaimed by Christian and non-Christian readers alike for its eerie fidelity to experience, for its masterful depiction of character, and for its troubling moral implications. O'Connor set almost all her stories in her native South. She claimed that this region was, if not Christ-centered, then at least still "Christ-haunted" in a way that the rest of the nation was not.

O'Connor's stories often dealt with individuals on the fringe. Some were itinerant laborers who, although illiterate and inarticulate, acted according to deeply felt reasons of the heart. Others were "respectable" people whose time had come and gone and who clung to dead patterns of belief and behavior in a frightening world. O'Connor forced her characters, whatever their makeup, to confront a truth that consumes before it consoles. Most of her stories contain a moment when a character's expec-

[5]Sally Fitzgerald, ed., Flannery O'Connor, *The Habit of Beings: Letters* (New York: Vintage, 1979), p. 125.

tations or fortunes are shockingly overturned. It is this moment of judgment that serves also as the prelude to the Word of grace and forgiveness.

A very different sort of widely read author was Catherine Marshall (1914–1983), like O'Connor from the South but unlike her a Presbyterian of traditional Protestant sentiments. Born into the home of a Presbyterian minister in Tennessee, her rural upbringing later provided material for an inspirational novel *Christy* (1967). Before this book appeared, however, she had become widely known as the editor of her husband's sermons and the author of his biography. When Catherine Ambrose married Peter Marshall in 1936, she entered immediately into the public eye. Peter Marshall was an eloquent Presbyterian minister and immigrant from Scotland who eventually became the minister of the New York Avenue Presbyterian Church in Washington, DC and, in the the last years of his life, chaplain of the United States Senate.

Peter Marshall's death in 1949 was a crushing blow, but it did not undermine his wife's pluck and determination. In that same year she published a collection of her husband's sermons *Mr. Jones, Meet the Master*, which achieved great popularity. And soon she was at work on the story of his life. The book that resulted *A Man Called Peter: The Story of Peter Marshall* was not an "objective" biography but neither was it a sanitized and predictable memorial. It proved successful at a very difficult task: showing that a pious man of God could also be a knowledgeable man of this world.

Aimee Semple McPherson, Dorothy Day, Flannary O'Connor, and Catherine Marshall were very different in gifts, audiences, and specific religious convictions. What they shared, however, was noteworthy influence on the expression of Christianity in twentieth-century America. Although none of them had this as her main concern, all contributed to the expanding voice and the deepening contribution of women to the public religion of the nation.

Theology

Formal religious thought has never been of utmost importance in the history of Christianity in America. Faith has been more active than contemplative, more pragmatic than intellectual. Still, with the rise of the modern university in addition to the growing attention paid by almost all religious groups to higher education, notable theological voices have emerged. If no recent American theologian has had the general influence of the Swiss Karl Barth or worked so provocatively at the borders between philosophy and theology as did England's Alfred North Whitehead, or succeeded in conveying solid popular theology to a broad audience as did C. S. Lewis from Britain, a number of capable individuals have nonetheless articulated forceful theological statements.

Of a long list of such theologians, at least a few should be mentioned. John

Courtney Murray gave Catholics a reasoned defense of more democratic procedures in state and church. The German emigré, Paul Tillich, gained a wide following after the War by describing God as the "being beyond being" who transcends all human efforts at description. Following in Tillich's train, Thomas J. J. Altizer was only one of many who propounded a parodoxical "theology of Christian atheism" during the 1960s. From a very different perspective, Elton Trueblood for more than half a century has applied a theology compounded of Quaker and more traditional Protestant elements to discussions of family, education, and formal philosophy. James Cone provided a "Black theology" built from his race's experiences of suffering and resistance. Rosemary Radford Ruether has expounded forcefully on the anti-Semitic, patriarchal, and antifeminist tendencies in traditional Christian thought. Thomas Merton showed how much a silent Trappist monk could contribute to public discussion by constructing a spiritual theology that drew on both oriental influences and the monastic tradition. The Canadian Bernard Lonergan gave Catholics a sophisticated interpretation of their faith based both in the certainties of neo-Thomism and the subtleties of phenomenology. Carl F. H. Henry has provided evangelical Protestants a sturdy defense of propositional revelation. Harvey Cox regularly charts the theological implications of new social trends in the United States and Latin America. And a number of theologians associated with Yale Divinity School (Hans Frei, Brevard Childs, George Lindbeck) have argued in different ways for the integrity of Christian life and thought as opposed to merely cultural understandings of the bible or Christian history. Theology in America since World War II has also been enriched by a whole host of sociologists, philosophers, historians, and even political scientists and economists who want to illuminate their own fields with Christian reasoning, and vice versa.

The most significant American theology since the 1920s, however, has probably been the work of two brothers, Reinhold and H. Richard Niebuhr, whose histories also reveal something about the contribution of immigrant perspectives to the ongoing task of conceiving the Christian faith. They are not necessarily the best theologians of the last half century, but their work has had broad influence and so is worth more extended consideration.

Reinhold (1892–1971) and H. Richard (1894–1962) Niebuhr were sons of a pastor in the German Evangelical church. After attending denominational institutions of higher learning (Elmhurst College and Eden Seminary), both did graduate work at Yale. In 1915 Reinhold accepted the pastorate of Bethel Evangelical church in Detroit, where he served for thirteen years. Niebuhr came of age theologically in this urban church as the liberalism of his formal training encountered the harsh realities of industrial America. He was particularly upset with what industrial life did to the laborers. And he wondered what hope there was for American civilization when "naive gentlemen with a genius for mechanics suddenly become the arbiters over the lives and fortunes of hundreds of thousands." While still in Detroit, Niebuhr began to advocate radical solutions to the human crisis as he saw it—socialism and pacifism for life in society, a new Christian Realism for theology. For his part, Richard served three years as a pastor in St. Louis, then taught theology at Eden Seminary, pursued his doctoral studies at Yale University, served as president of Elmhurst, and again was theological professor at Eden. In 1931 he accepted a position at Yale Divinity School, where he remained until his death.

When Reinhold Niebuhr moved to New York's Union Theological Seminary in 1928, he carried with him the commitments formed in Detroit. The coming of World War II led him to abandon his socialism and pacifism, but he remained a dedicated social activist—serving on scores of committees in the 1930s and 1940s, helping to form Americans for Democratic Action and New York's Liberal Party, editing the journal *Christianity and Crisis*, and writing prolifically for newspapers and magazines.

His theological ethics were developed more systematically in a long string of major books. The two most important were *Moral Man and Immoral Society* (1932) and *The Nature and Destiny of Man* (1941, 1943). The first criticized severely the liberal optimism concerning humanity, pointing out that social groups are selfish almost by their very definition. It sharply rebuked the notion that human beings were perfectible as individuals or inherently good in groups. The second book provided a more systematic discussion of what Niebuhr called mankind's "most vexing problem. How shall he think of himself?" In this work and elsewhere Niebuhr proposed a series of dialectical relationships to answer his own question: humans as sinners and saints, humans as subject to history and social forces but also as shapers of history and society, humans as creatures of the Creator but potential lords of the creation, humans as egotistical but capable of living for others.

In making these judgments, Niebuhr was considerably less interested in theology as such than the European neo-orthodox thinkers with whom he is often associated. To be sure, he did make use of scripture. What he called the biblical "myth" of creation helped show the human potential (made in the image of God) for both true good and radical evil. Niebuhr also felt scripture supported his contention that people sin inevitably but not by moral necessity. In the person of Christ, Niebuhr found a unique example of one who used power only for good and not—as all other people—for evil. The cross of Christ was a particularly important theme for Niebuhr because it revealed the great paradox of powerlessness turned into power. At the same time, Niebuhr showed little interest in traditional doctrines of Christ and salvation. In response, some critics held that he was more concerned about the paradoxes of human life than about the church's historic picture of salvation offered through Christ. Whatever final judgments may be made, it is noteworthy that Reinhold Niebuhr was read with appreciation in very wide circles. A few post-Christian secular academics (such as the Harvard historian Perry Miller) even called themselves "atheists for Niebuhr."

Richard Niebuhr was driven by some of the same concerns as his brother, but he was also more directly interested in theology and less captivated by issues thrown up in contemporary experience. A diversity of influences shaped his theology. From the older liberalism, Niebuhr took a commitment to the essentially experiential nature of religion. From the same source, he took the view that humanity, immersed in history, can never transcend that history to see truth unbiased and whole. From European neo-orthodoxy he took a sharply critical view of liberal optimism concerning the human potential. From the classical orthodoxy of Augustine, the Reformers, and Jonathan Edwards, he took a high conception of the divine sovereignty and a firm belief in the utter dependency of all existence on God.

These influences combined with Niebuhr's own creativity to produce a stimulating flow of influential books. One group of them dealt broadly with the church in society. *The Kingdom of God in America* (1937), for example, provided a brilliant portrait of the way in which the idea of God's kingdom had shifted content throughout American history—from God's sovereignty in the time of Jonathan Edwards, to the kingdom of Christ during the 1800s, and finally, to the coming kingdom for twentieth-century liberals. The book has sharp criticisms to make of each period but looks most fondly on the earliest period when some Americans truly believed in the ultimacy of God. It also contains the best short critical description of theological liberalism ever written: "A God without wrath brought men without sin into a kingdom without judgment through the ministrations of a Christ without a cross."[6] *Christ and Culture* (1951) provided a classic schematization for the various ways in which believers over the centuries have interacted with their surrounding worlds. Its five categories—Christ against culture, the Christ of culture, Christ above culture, Christ and culture in paradox, and Christ the transformer of culture—have become standard ways to describe Christian approaches to political, economic, and social affairs.

Niebuhr's more directly theological works have not been so widely read but have exerted a special influence on American religious thought. *The Meaning of Revelation* (1941) argued that when God reveals himself to people, all other events and questions become relative. The work has been criticized for making revelation overly subjective, but here and elsewhere Niebuhr pointed to the Christian community as a body providing standards (though they are relative also) for describing and communicating God's revelation. *Radical Monotheism and Western Culture* (1960) was Niebuhr's last full statement. In it he looked to God as the source of all being, as Being itself, and decried all that would detract from his all-sufficiency.

The concerns of America's formal Christian theologians, including the Niebuhrs and all their colleagues, by no means encompass the thought of all Christians in America. They remain, nonetheless, important efforts at spelling out what an ancient faith might continue to mean in the American corner of the modern world, and for what the conditions of that world might mean for the ancient faith.

[6]H. Richard Niebuhr, *The Kingdom of God in America* (New York: Harper & Row, 1973), p. 193.

Christianity in America, Christianity in the World

The twentieth century has registered seismic shocks in American society, including two world wars, a great economic depression followed by unprecedented (if unevenly distributed) affluence, and a major cultural upheaval at the time of the Vietnam War. As integral parts of society, America's Christian churches felt the effects of those shocks as fully as did any institutions. In this chapter we have sketched some of the major developments and reactions in the churches. In closing, it is fitting once again to raise our sights to ask how Christian experience in recent America relates to Christian experience more generally in the world. A comparison with Canada is again useful for that purpose, as is also an overview of American missionary efforts in this tumultuous century.

Canadian Counterpoint

Religious developments in Canada show revealing contrasts with the American situation in both their early and later Christian history. From the time of Canada's confederation as a dominion in 1867 through the 1920s, the main Protestant bodies pursued a course of consolidation. At almost the same time, however, the arrival of many new groups of immigrants as well as continuing tensions between Catholics and Protestants, between the settled East and the rapidly opening prairie, and between theological polarities within the denominations led to a far greater religious pluralism than Canada had known in its earlier history.

With Canada's new status of a dominion, Protestant groups took the lead in seeking to Christianize Canadian civilization, both in existing settlement and in the opening West. The Canadian population was small enough and (except for Quebec) Protestant enough to think that a concentrated effort could provide a religious bonding for the needs of the new nation. Presbyterians and Methodists, with national mergers in 1874 and 1884, took the lead in consolidating their own efforts. For their part, the Anglican church was a leader in work among Indians and Eskimoes, providing considerably more latitude for indigenous expression of the faith than was customary in the United States or even in Canada's own earlier history. Baptists were never as successful at creating a national denomination, but strong regional associations of Baptist churches were formed about this time in the Maritimes, Ontario, and the western provinces. The movement toward Protestant consensus culuminated in 1925 with the formation of Canada's United Church, which brought together 4,800 Methodist congregations, 3,700 Presbyterian, and 166 Congregationalist. A substantial number of Presbyterians remained out of the union to continue their own denomination, but it was still a signal event emblematic of the movement for national unity and purpose.

By the 1920s, however, the migrations had begun that would lead to a many-hued pattern of sects and denominations. Ukrainian Catholics, Greek Orthodox, Lutherans (from the United States as well as Europe), German-speaking Mennonites from Russia, Salvationists from Britain, and Dutch Christian Reformed migrated to Canada, settling usually in Ontario or the prairie provinces. From the states, smaller numbers of Adventists, Pentecostals, Christian and Missionary Alliance, and other American denominations also entered Canada's religious life. The result by the 1980s was something approaching an American-style patchwork. Even more than in the United States, however, the Catholic church was the dominant religious presence. In the 1981 census, Roman Catholic adherents made up over 47 percent of the population, with a primary concentration in Quebec (where four out of five residents were Catholics). The Catholic church was also the largest Christian denomination in each of the Maritime provinces, in Ontario, the Yukon, and the Northwest Territories, and it was the second largest denomination in each of Canada's other provinces. The United Church, Canada's second largest Christian body, had consistent strength in all provinces, but like the old Protestant denominations in the United States, it was struggling to maintain its membership. The Anglican church was next largest, at about 10 percent of the population, with greatest strength in Ontario, Newfoundland, and missionary regions in the Northwest. Presbyterians, Baptists, and Lutherans each registered 3 to 4 percent of the nation's population, with Baptists and Presbyterians strongest in the Maritimes and Ontario, Lutherans in the West. The many other Christian bodies were distributed in smaller numbers. As in the states, major interfaith associations have come into existence, with the Canadian Council of Churches (from 1944) coordinating discussion among most of the major groups. In 1964 the formation of the Evangelical Fellowship of Canada signaled a new self-consciousness about bonds tying together Canada's more conservative Protestant bodies.

The most startling statistic from the 1981 religious census was the growth in Canadians registering "no religious preference," up to over 7 percent from 4.3 percent in 1971. Secular trends influencing the states have been at work north of the border as well, especially in the Far West, where in British Columbia more than a fifth of the residents put themselves in the category of "no religion."

Larger patterns of religion and culture continue to be different in Canada from those in the United States. Religion, for example, is much more a backdrop than a public presence in politics. Party leaders do not hide their religious affiliations, and significant themes from the Canadian equivalent of the Social Gospel contributed to the rise of Canada's third major party, the New Democrats. Yet it has been rare in Canada for religious issues to become central themes in political campaigns, which have for decades been dominated by issues of national self-definition, trade with the United States, and constitutional questions about relations between provinces and the federal government. Canadian legal traditions continue to make it easier for Christian groups to sponsor schools and to maintain ongoing relationships with the universities. Tighter government control of radio and television broadcasting also means that Canadians do not have as ready access to televangelists and religious entrepreneurs as in the states. In general, Canada has fostered a mosaic of Christian groups rather than a melting pot. Compared to the United States, the national government is weaker, and local institutions are stronger. Relaxed trade barriers and greater contact between Canada and the United States may move Canadian churches closer to American models. It is also possible that Canada's distinctive Christian traditions will continue to make a religious point of contrast to developments in the United States.

Twentieth-Century American Missions

One of the most striking developments in the history of Christianity has occurred in the twentieth century. It is the shift in the centers of world Christianity from the West to the nonwestern world. In 1900 something like 85 percent of Christians lived in the West. It has been predicted that by the year 2000 nearly 60 percent of world Christians will live in the Third World. The story of Christian missions from America since World War I has played a part in that redistribution. It is, however, also a story illuminating important changes in domestic religion as well.

The major twentieth-century shifts in American denominational strength have been reflected also in the size of missionary populations. American Catholics have become the main financial supporters of the missionary effort of their church. Although the recruitment of Catholic personnel has lagged somewhat behind the raising of funds, by the mid-twentieth century, American Catholics led by the Catholic Foreign Mission Society (Maryknoll) and by the Jesuits contributed several thousand overseas missionaries to their church, about a third of the total. Among Protestants the highpoint of missionary work from the older, or ecumenical, denominations came in the 1920s. At the time of the 1910 Edinburgh Conference, workers from the United States and Canada made up about one-third of the world's 21,000 Protestant missionaries. By 1925 half of the world's 29,000 missionaries were Americans or Canadians. (In 1925 there were more than 3,300 American missionaries in China alone.) By the mid-1950s, that proportion had reached two-thirds. It has subsequently declined, with the rise in missionary activity among Third World Protestants, but the contribution of North America to Protestant missions remains very great.

By the 1950s, however, a significant change was taking place in the source of these Protestant missionaries. Whereas mainline, ecumenical denominations had taken the lead between Edinburgh and World War II, independent evangelical mission agencies grew rapidly in size after the war. As late as 1953 about half the nearly 19,000 American Protestant missionaries were affiliated with the National Council of Churches or the Canadian Council of Churches. By 1985 only slightly more than 10 percent of the nearly 40,000 American career missionaries were so affiliated. Instead, most were members of independent mission agencies, some of which had been established around the turn of the century (e.g., the Africa Inland Mission, the China Inland Mission, the Sudan Interior Mission), while some were part of the postwar surge of evangelical voluntary agencies (e.g., Missionary Aviation Fellowship, Far Eastern Gospel Crusade, Greater European Mission). More than 3,000 were at work translating the scriptures or supporting such work with the Wycliffe Bible Translators. In addition, very substantial numbers of missionaries were being sponsored by the Southern Baptists (more than 3,000 in 1984) and the Assemblies of God (more than 1,500 in 1986).

The evangelical surge of mission efforts reflected in part the general growth of this segment of American church life, but it also came about as a result of significant institutional developments. Since 1946 the Inter-Varsity Christian Fellowship has held a missionary conference for students every two years at the University of Illinois in Urbana, with upward of 20,000 young people attending to receive a missionary challenge. In 1974 American evangelicals were leaders in holding an International Congress on World Evangelization in Lausanne, Switzerland, a meeting that has led to an active continuing committee engaged especially in bringing Third World evangelists to the fore as leaders of such panevangelical gatherings. At meetings after Lausanne, sponsored also by the World Evangelical Fellowship, Third World evangelicals have pressed their American counterparts to expand the notion of evangelism to include redress of economic and racial injustice, in addition to maintaining an emphasis on personal salvation.

Similar discussions have gone much further in the ecumenical denominations that once were leaders in world evangelization. They were anticipated by the 1927 meeting of the Student Volunteer Movement, which repudiated its slogan concerning "the evangelization of the world in this generation." They could also be glimpsed in the controversial report *Re-Thinking Missions* (1932) written by Harvard philosopher William Hocking after an extensive study funded by John D. Rockefeller, Jr. This report, to the great chagrin of more conservative groups, called on Christians to work alongside the forces of justice and peace to be found in all religious systems. Since World War II, the general theological uncertainty in the mainline denominations has been matched by an increasing uncertainty about the idea of evangelization itself. Voices still may be heard in such bodies defending the need to proclaim the gospel as the sole hope of the world. More typical, however, are two other stances. One is the growing conviction that, although Christianity enjoys a unique status as God's fullest revelation, other world religions share part of that truth. The other is the belief that Christianity is an important expression of human religion but not one that should necessarily be promulgated as a replacement for the religions practiced by the other peoples of the world. An ecumenical spokesman, W. Richey Hogg, put it like this: "The shift marks a move away from a Western Christian evangelistic crusade to the world and toward an engagement with the world in what is regarded as a total evangelistic response to the world's needs and the religious beliefs of the people."[7]

Missionary efforts by American Catholics had always nurtured a two-pronged approach, seeking to draw non-Christians into the church while also working extensively at social tasks such as education, medicine, and the care of orphans. Because the Second Vatican Council expressed views that many persons have interpreted as showing a greater acceptance of non-Christian faiths, Catholics have had some of the same debates as their Protestant ecumenical associates about traditional understandings of the need for world evangelization.

The engagement of American Christians through missions with the rest of the world is nearly two centuries old. Previous certainties now appear less secure—that, for example, the United States enjoys a distinctly Christian civilization that should be exported alongside the Christian message. In addition, the rapid spread of secular opinions and secular habits of life in the West has created a situation in which Christian efforts at conversion may be more urgently required in the western countries than in the countries of the Third World. When, for example, more Koreans are practicing Christians than in most of the western European countries and when Catholicism advances much more rapidly in the Third World than in the West, the missionary picture is bound to change. Still, it would be wrong to de-emphasize the great importance of American mission efforts in the twentieth century. They have brought American visions of the Christian faith to millions around the world. They have also enlightened both missionaries and believers remaining in North America. Especially instructive has been the ability of the missionary message to take on a life of its own once it has been integrated into cultures with very little similarity to the West.

American Christianity and Christianity in America

Christianity is a worldwide movement that obviously existed long before the United States came into existence. Although the Christian faith has played an important role in the development of America, it has never been the case—even at the height of the United States's world influence—that a majority of Christians lived in America, that worldwide habits of Christian worship and devotion were dictated by Americans, or that the most dominant patterns of Christian thought even in the twentieth century have uniformly followed American approaches. At the same time, American versions of the ancient faith have been unusually influential. Pentecostalism, which began humbly on Los Angeles's Azusa Street, is the most dynamic, most rapidly growing style of Christianity in the world. American Catholics contributed substantially to

[7]Gerald H. Anderson, "American Protestants in Pursuit of Mission: 1886–1986," *International Bulletin of Missionary Research* 12 (July 1988), p. 111.

the discussions at the Second Vatican Council that saw this ancient church adjust to modern conditions. America may be the place where the Eastern Orthodox break through the barriers of their historic ethnic divisions. America's old-line Protestants have been key supporters of the World Council of Churches. More recently, Americans have taken the lead in promoting greater fellowship and communication among Protestant evangelicals around the globe. The significance of Americans in the history of modern times makes it all the more important to differentiate what has been American and what has been Christian in their history.

Such discrimination, however, is immensely difficult. It might be easy to label some expressions of the faith as mere "culture Christianity"—that is, merely the veneering of indigenous social patterns with traditional Christian language or symbolism. Such, we might think, were such phenomena as the scriptural defense of the slave system, the Christianized resistance to immigration, or the hyper-Christian patriotism that seems to crop up during most of the nation's wars. The analysis is really much more complicated, however. Christian abolitionism, Christian one-worldism, Christian antipatriotism could in fact be just as much culturally conditioned as the religious movements they opposed. Religion and culture do not in fact coexist like pieces of bread in a sandwich. They are, rather, interwoven deeply into one another.

If we wish to see Christianity in America rather than simply American Christianity, it is far better to look for signs of contradiction, moments when the faith seemed to infuse something unexpected into the culture of a person, a region, or a movement. Such moments might have existed when slave owners, against their better judgment, gave bibles to their slaves. They might be illustrated by the conversion of a few social radicals, like Dorothy Day, from left-wing politics to Christian faith during the traumatic 1930s. They were moments like Abraham Lincoln's Second Inaugural when he chose to meditate on the secrets of divine Providence rather than on the depths of Confederate evil. They are illustrated supremely by the Black acceptance of Christianity, offered as it was with a whip.

Such signs of contradiction suggest that the story of American Christianity verges over into the story of Christianity in America at unexpected moments, or better yet, that there is really only one story, the cultural and the religious mixed well beyond easy disentangling. The story simply *is* American Christianity even as it simply *is* Christianity in America. In words from the Founder, the one "with eyes to see" may sometimes detect the difference.

Epilogue

Dana L. Robert

Chapter 33

CHRISTIANITY IN ASIA, AFRICA, AND LATIN AMERICA

The most startling aspect of church history in the twentieth century has been the breaking of the European domination of Christianity. The typical Christian in 1900 was a European or a descendent of Europeans. By 2000, however, the profile of the typical Christian will have undergone a radical change: The continent with the largest number of Christians will be Africa. Christianity, a religion that began in a Jewish world, spread into Greco-Roman culture, and from there into Europe, is now undergoing its third massive cultural shift—a shift to the southern hemisphere and to the Third World.[1]

A powerful illustration of the shift from western Christian to southern Christian dominance is the composition of the Lambeth Conference, the decennial meeting of the bishops of the Anglican Communion.[2] Whereas in 1897 the vast majority of the bishops at the Lambeth Conference were from England or the United States, in 1988 only 30 percent were from those two countries. The Church of England, one of the most venerable of the mission-sending churches, is now a minority among its Third World children. The nonwestern contingent of the Anglican Communion was so powerful that at Lambeth 1988 it reversed a centuries-old Anglican prohibition against the baptism of polygamists. This example shows that at the dawn of the twenty-first century, new forms of the Christian faith are taking their place alongside traditional European assumptions about the nature of Christianity.

[1] In this essay, the term "Third World" is being used as shorthand for Africa, Asia, and Latin America.
[2] The Anglican Communion is composed of churches descended from the Church of England who recognize the Archbishop of Canterbury as their titular head.

The European Missionary Legacy

The European dominance of Christianity began because the spread of Islam in the seventh century helped to eliminate or to isolate the early Christian communities of Asia and Africa. By the 1400s, Christianity, hemmed in by Islam, had retreated to northern Europe. But the age of exploration in the early 1500s meant that Portugal and Spain, strong Roman Catholic powers, could sail past the Islamic barrier between Europe and the rest of the world. Christianity traveled with the European merchants and the military, and the great age of European foreign missions had begun. Ironically, although they were the result of European imperialist expansion, foreign missions began the process that led to the twentieth-century development of Christianity as a Third World religion.

In 1493 Pope Alexander VI promulgated the *Padroado*, an arrangement by which Portugal and Spain divided the world beyond Europe into respective spheres of influence. According to the *Padroado*, Spain and Portugal agreed to evangelize all non-Christians with whom they came into contact. On his second voyage to America, Christopher Columbus took a Catholic priest. Ferdinand Magellan took a chaplain when he rounded South America, crossed the Pacific, and discovered the Philippines in 1521. Missionary priests accompanied the explorers to America, Africa, and Asia, and said Mass on arriving at their destinations. European orders, notably the Franciscans, Dominicans, and Jesuits, conducted missions in newly conquered Spanish and Portuguese territories as well as in independent countries such as China and India.

As other European countries began to explore the world, they too tried to export their particular brands of Christianity. The first Protestant foreign missionaries Bartholomew Ziegenbalg and Henry Plutschau were pietistic German Lutheran college students who went to India in the employ of the Danish king in 1706. Puritans conducted missions among the American Indians throughout the 1600s and 1700s. British Baptists, inspired by the visionary shoemaker William Carey, launched the modern British Protestant missionary movement in 1792. American Congregationalists sent the first American foreign missionaries in 1812. The Russian Orthodox church conducted a successful mission among native Alaskans during the eighteenth and nineteenth centuries. By 1900, 600 foreign mission agencies were in operation with a combined income of $200 million.

By the beginning of the twentieth century, the western missionary enterprise was well established around the world. Missionaries conducted evangelistic work and bible translation projects in many parts of Asia, Africa, and Latin America. Mission organizations founded thousands of schools ranging from kindergartens up to the major colleges of China and India. One of the greatest contributions of Christian missions was the introduction of western medicine, sanitation, and nursing techniques into the Third World. Missions ran orphanages, literacy programs, agricultural cooperatives, and other social services. A phalanx of women missionaries worked to elevate the status of women throughout the world. In 1910 all the major Protestant mission agencies met at Edinburgh, Scotland, to conduct the first international survey of the emerging world church. "Edinburgh 1910" marked the realization that the Christian church was beginning to overflow its European cultural boundaries and that a number of "younger churches" had been successfully planted in the Third World.

Scripture Translation

The twentieth-century explosion of Christianity into Africa, Asia, and Latin America has been directly related to the translation of the bible, prayer books, and catechisms into vernacular languages. Christian scriptures have been translated into approximately 2,000 languages, and most of this work has been accomplished in the twentieth century. From the first, Protestant missionaries saw their primary task to be the translation of the bible. Protestants believed that having the scriptures in one's own language was the prelude to founding a healthy church. Pioneer missionaries painstakingly compiled dictionaries and wrote grammars of non-European languages in preparation for the all-important task of bible translation. William Carey, pioneer British missionary to India, set up a translation house, hired indigenous people as translators, and succeeded in translating the bible, in whole or in part, into forty-four Indian languages by 1832. Currently, more than 100 national and regional bible societies are affiliated with the United Bible Societies, a worldwide interdenominational organization for bible translation and distribution. The UBS staff cooperates with scholars around the world who are now at work on translations of the bible into 558 different languages. Many of these are first-time translations into regional languages spoken by large numbers of people. The largest nondenominational mission agency today is the Wycliffe Bible Translators, whose primary concern is translating the bible into new languages.

Mission scholar Lamin Sanneh has argued that the translatability of Christianity was the key to its success in the Third World.[3] By adopting vernacular languages as the means of transmitting the Christian message, missionaries were forced to employ indigenous modes of thought. Whether it was of the bible or the catechism and liturgy, translation meant that indigenous concepts of God and human nature were carried over into Christianity. The fact of translatability gave every language group a sense of ownership over Christian theology and tradition. An additional benefit of translatability is that it helped to preserve many native languages from destruction. Just as Martin Luther's translation of the bible became the basis for modern German,

[3]See Lamin Sanneh, *Translating the Message* (Maryknoll, New York: Orbis, 1989).

so has bible translation become the basis for a number of African and Asian languages.

With the assistance of translated scriptures or catechisms, indigenous Christians became powerful evangelists to their own people. The nation becoming Christianized the fastest today is Korea, where the bible was translated into "Hangul," the script of the common people, in the 1870s. One of the reasons for the growth of Christianity in Korea was the decision of early missionaries to concentrate on indigenous bible study as a mission method; and the Korean church continues to spread as Christians evangelize each other through drawing people into small bible study groups. In 1864 the Church of England ordained the African Samuel Ajayi Crowther as its first nonwestern bishop and appointed him head of the mission in western Africa. Crowther presided over a group of indigenous mission agents who attempted to create a self-governing and self-supporting church that relied on the native languages. Although Crowther himself had a difficult career because of British racists who resented his authority, his followers sustained a spiritual independence that encouraged indigenous-led revivals involving thousands of people well into the twentieth century. The ability of Christianity to become a living force among every people is directly related to the way that translation helps it to cross cultural boundaries and to empower its followers.

Nationalism

The earliest indication that Christianity was successfully making the transition into nonwestern cultural milieus was the advent of Christian-inspired nationalism. The mission school, the linchpin of the missionary presence, educated people not only in the bible but in western political and scientific ideas as well. Patriotic intellectuals, especially from China, India, Japan, and Korea, believed that Christian ideals were the basis of western democratic thought and that the adoption of western learning, including western religion, would hasten the process of modernization. Many intellectuals, especially in the Far East, believed that modernization would help their nations to throw off European imperialism and to develop independence and economic prosperity. Mission schools, where modernistic ideas were taught, thus became the cradle for eastern nationalism.

The first nation to experience a Christian-inspired nationalistic revolution was the Philippines, also the first Asian nation to become predominantly Christian (Roman Catholic). When Magellan arrived, the Philippines were not a nation but a group of 7,000 largely unconnected islands. The process of Christianization followed in the wake of military conquest. The Catholic church provided a common set of experiences that helped to create a unified nation within the boundaries of the Spanish political administration. By the nineteenth century, however, unjust Spanish rule led to Filipino attempts to overthrow Spanish domination in both church and state.

After a Filipino revolt in 1872, the colonial government executed three Filipino friars who had been leaders in church reform. The memory of those three and other nationalist Christian martyrs inspired the Filipino people to revolt again in 1896 and to declare themselves independent of Spain in 1898. During the twentieth century, Filipino Catholics continued in the forefront of protest against the American colonialism that replaced the Spanish.

In the Far East, Christian-educated intellectuals led in twentieth-century nationalist movements. When Koreans protested against Japanese imperialism by writing a declaration of independence in 1919, sixteen of the thirty-three signers were Christians, even though Christians comprised only 1 percent of the total population. Christianity had a greater impact on Chinese nationalism than its tiny numbers suggested: The founder of the 1911 republic was Sun Yat-sen, a Christian, as were many of the nationalist martyrs buried in the Mausoleum of Revolutionary Heroes. The first Protestants in Japan were student members of the displaced samurai (warrior) class. These intellectuals used the western scientific knowledge they gained in the mission schools to make Japan the first eastern nation to modernize itself industrially and militarily.

Perhaps the clearest connection between Christian education and nationalism occurred following World War II when the nations of Africa became independent of European colonialist control, beginning with Ghana in 1954. Many of the fathers of nationalism in independent Africa had attended mission schools. Leaders such as Leopold-Sedar Senghor of Senegal, Tom Mboya and Jomo Kenyatta of Kenya, Kwame Nkrumah of Ghana, Kenneth Kaunda of Zambia, and Julius Nyerere of Tanzania were Christians at a time when most Africans were not. Mission education in western philosophy and political thought had produced Christians equipped to lead their peoples into modern statehood.

Inculturation

According to Pedro Arrupe, former head of the Society of Jesus, the most powerful mission order in the Roman Catholic church, inculturation is "the incarnation of Christian life and of the Christian message in a particular cultural context."[4] The success of Christianity in becoming meaningful to people in the Third World is related to its degree of inculturation. Travelers can see the record of the missionary presence in the western-style churches and the western hymnody that characterizes much of Christianity from Korea to Tonga. But increasingly, the churches of Asia, Africa, and Latin America are moving beyond the stage of being western transplants and are being truly inculturated. Indigenous liturgies, theologies, and forms of

---

[4]Quoted in Peter Schineller, *A Handbook on Inculturation* (New York: Paulist Press, 1990).

church life are appearing with increasing frequency as Christianity gains strength in Third World cultures.

The theological development in the Third World that most signifies the successful inculturation of Christianity in the twentieth century is "liberation theology." Liberation theology began in Latin America, but its influence has spread to the Philippines, Sri Lanka, South Africa, and other places that have experienced similar colonial oppression. The Second Vatican Council (1962–1965) opened the church to liberation theology: It approved the saying of Mass in the vernacular and emphasized the importance of the laity. The Latin American bishops who attended Vatican II returned home and attempted to put its ideals into practice with a meeting of their own in Medellin, Colombia, in 1968. The Medellin meeting shifted the church's emphasis from the hierarchy to the laity, it recognized the political oppression and poverty in which most Latin Americans lived, and it called for physical and spiritual liberation. Medellin, along with Father Gustavo Gutierrez's book *A Theology of Liberation* (1971), gave birth to liberation theology.

During the 1970s, liberation theology spread throughout Latin America and to the rest of the world. Liberation theology was appealing because it began with the context in which people lived rather than with abstract metaphysics. The theology developed within Base Christian Communities, small groups of lay people who met for reflection on their situation, bible study, and action aimed at improving their lives. Catholicism in Latin America has suffered a shortage of priests ever since it was introduced by the Conquistadors, but the Base Christian Communities have served a vital function in re-evangelizing and educating the Catholic laity within small groups.

As Catholic laity became empowered in the Base Christian Communities, however, government oppression of the church increased in Latin America. Nuns, priests, lay catechists, and community workers became the targets of military death squads who sought to silence liberation theology. In 1980 Archbishop Oscar Romero of El Salvador, defender of the poor, became the most famous martyr to a theology of liberation when he was assassinated while saying Mass.

Another powerful example of the inculturation of Christianity in the twentieth century has been the emergence of more than 7,000 indigenous African denominations in at least forty-three countries. In most cases, these churches were founded by an African who saw a vision, broke away from a mission church, and founded an independent congregation that combined Christian theology with African cultural practices such as dancing, healing, and the defeat of witchcraft. The African Independent Churches differ widely in their theologies and practices.

The largest African Independent Church is the Church of Jesus Christ on Earth Through the Prophet Simon Kimbangu, with approximately 3 million members. Located in Zaire, the Kimbanguist Church began among the followers of the Baptist Simon Kimbangu. In 1921 the Belgian colonial authorities arrested and imprisoned Kimbangu until his death in 1953 for conducting a six-month-long healing and preaching ministry. Kimbanguists have their own schools, sacred sites, cooperatives, medical facilities, and theological seminary. The church is a member of the World Council of Churches. As did other independent churches, the Kimbanguist church emerged as a way for Africans to express nationalist sentiments as well as to reemphasize traditions opposed by foreign missionaries. For many members, the independent churches have provided a bridge between African tradition and western-style modernization.

Church Growth and Vitality

With the passing of European colonialism after World War II, the Christian churches in Africa, Asia, and Latin America entered a period of great expansion. As necessary as was the missionary presence to plant Christianity around the world, the connection of that presence with western imperialism hindered the growth of the church. When imperialism disappeared and a trained, indigenous church leadership replaced the missionaries, the church in the Third World exploded with vitality. Within Catholicism, the Second Vatican Council unleashed an era of liturgical experimentation and inculturation that fostered Catholic expansion. Among Protestants, Pentecostalism became the most powerful vehicle of church growth from Singapore to Brazil.

Following a period in the 1970s when Christians in Africa and the South Pacific called for a moratorium on western missionaries, Christians around the world reaffirmed a need for Christian missionaries in a spirit of partnership. Hundreds of Third World mission societies came into being. American missionaries work in Korea, and Korean missionaries work in Thailand; British missionaries work in India, and Kenyan missionaries work in Great Britain. The age of a world church marked by missions to and from every continent was a reality by the late twentieth century.

One sign of vitality among Third World churches has been leadership in the modern ecumenical movement. In 1912 the Anglican church consecrated its first Indian bishop V.S. Azariah, who had a vision of a Christian church undivided by imported western denominational divisions. In 1947 his dream came true, and the Church of South India was founded as the first church union that successfully combined episcopal and nonepiscopal denominations. The Church of South India and other union churches in Asia showed that western divisions of Christianity need not continue to divide the rest of the world.

The growth of the church in China was another impressive sign of health in the world church of the late twentieth century. Despite China's being the largest mission field during the first half of the twentieth century, very few Chinese became Christians. After the communist revolution succeeded in 1949, most missionaries left the country. In 1950 the Chinese Protestants founded the "Three Self Patriotic Movement," designed to make the Chinese church independent from the West, both financially and organizationally. Western analysts forecast the demise of Christianity in China once its western support structure was repudiated by the Chinese. From 1966 to 1976, China was plunged into the Cultural Revolution, and public worship was abolished and Christians persecuted. But when the Chinese church reemerged in 1979, observers discovered that there were millions of Chinese Christians where only 700,000 had existed in 1949. Its period of suffering during the Cultural Revolution convinced many Chinese that Christianity was no longer a foreign religion and that it had a spiritual contribution to make to China. Today a growing church, independent of western support and with its own house churches, seminaries, and bishops, thrives in China.

In diverse ways, the church in the Third World witnesses to its vitality. The largest congregation in the world is the Yoido Full Gospel Church of Seoul, Korea, pastored by Paul Yong-gi Cho, with 600,000 members. Cho's ministry has become a model for churches in America that desire to grow numerically. The largest women's university in the world, Ewha Women's University, founded by missionaries, is also in Korea. In South Africa, church leaders such as the Anglican Archbishop Desmond Tutu and Methodist minister Frank Chikane lead the fight against apartheid. For his continued stand against apartheid, Tutu received the Nobel Peace Prize in 1984. In Argentina, Adolfo Perez Esquivel, secretary of the Service for Latin American Nonviolent Activity, received the Nobel Peace Prize in 1980 for his attempts to reform society through nonviolent means. In India, although Christians comprise only a tiny percentage of the population, a large proportion of health care workers are Christians—people who are often willing to cross caste barriers to care for others' physical needs.

At no time in its 2,000-year history has Christianity flourished in so many different cultures. The third millennium of Christian history begins with an explosion of Christianity in Asia, Africa, and Latin America that not only challenges the historical European domination of the church but promises to diversify Christian practice and belief as never before.

SELECTED BIBLIOGRAPHY

Part I. The Context, Birth, and Early Growth of Christianity
Howard Clark Kee

Analyses of the social and cultural history of the period down to the fourth century:

Alfoldy, Geza. *The Social History of Rome.* Baltimore: Johns Hopkins University Press, 1988.
Brown, Peter. *The World of Late Antiquity.* New York: Harcourt-Brace-Jovanovich, 1975.
Frend, W. H. C. *The Rise of Christianity.* Philadelphia: Fortress Press, 1984.

Analysis of the New Testament and the period of its origins:

Kee, H. C. *Understanding the New Testament.* Englewood Cliffs, NJ: Prentice-Hall, Inc., 1983.

English translations of basic ancient Jewish and Christian writings:

Chadwick, Henry, ed. *Alexandrian Christianity.* Philadelphia: Westminster, 1964.
———, ed. *Origen: Contra Celsum.* Cambridge: Cambridge University Press, 1965.
Charlesworth, J. H., ed. *Apocrypha and Pseudepigrapha of the Old Testament.* 2 vols. Garden City, NY: Doubleday, 1983, 1985.
Frend, W. H. C., ed. *The New Eusebius: Documents Illustrating the History of the Church to A.D. 377.* London: SPCK, 1987.
Hennecke-Schneemelcher, E., and W. McL. Wilson. *New Testament Apocrypha.* 2 vols. Philadelphia: Westminster, 1963, 1964.
Jurgens, W. A., ed. & trans. *The Faith of the Early Fathers.* Collegeville, MN: Liturgical Press, 1970.
Layton, Bentley, ed. *The Gnostic Scriptures.* Garden City, NY: Doubleday, 1987.

Part II. The Christian Empire and Early Middle Ages
Emily Albu Hanawalt

Alexander, Paul J. *The Patriarch Nicephorus of Constantinople: Ecclesiastical Policy and Image Worship in the Byzantine Empire*. Oxford: Clarendon Press, 1958. A classic work on Byzantine iconoclasm.

Bolton, Brenda. *The Medieval Reformation*. London: Edward Arnold, 1983. Introduces the turmoil of twelfth-century Western Christendom and the achievements of Pope Innocent III, who recreated medieval European civilization by channeling the energy produced by religious crisis.

Bowersock, G. W. *Julian the Apostate*. Cambridge, MA: Harvard University Press, 1978. Presents and interprets the evidence for Julian's brief life and his attempted rejuvenation of paganism in the late Roman empire.

Brown, Peter. *Augustine of Hippo: A Biography*. Berkeley, CA: University of California Press, 1967. A dazzling study of Augustine and his world.

Brown, Peter. *The Cult of the Saints. Its Rise and Function in Latin Christianity*. Chicago: University of Chicago Press, 1981. A provocative essay exploring the devotion to saints in late antiquity and the battle for control of the cult.

Brown, Peter. *The World of Late Antiquity, A.D. 150–750*. London: Thames and London Ltd., 1971. A pioneering work on Mediterranean society. Richly illustrated.

Bryer, Anthony, and Judith Herrin, eds. *Iconoclasm: Papers Given at the Ninth Spring Symposium of Byzantine Studies*. Birmingham, G. B.: Centre for Byzantine Studies, 1977. Groundbreaking and influential articles on Byzantine iconoclasm.

Burns, Thomas S. *A History of the Ostrogoths*. Bloomington, IN: Indiana University Press, 1984. Though somewhat spare in its study of Germanic religion and Ostrogothic Christianity, this book does make good use of archaeological evidence to follow changes in Ostrogothic society from the presettlement stage to the end of the kingdom in Italy.

Frend, W. H. C. *The Rise of Christianity*. Philadelphia: Fortress Press, 1984. An authoritative study.

Holum, Kenneth G. *Theodosian Empresses: Women and Imperial Dominion in Late Antiquity*. Berkeley, CA: University of California Press, 1982. Sheds precious insight on the influence of imperial women, which extended even to the shaping of Christian dogma and practice.

Jones, A. H. M. *Constantine and the Conversion of Europe*. New York: Macmillan Company, 1962; revised edition, New York: Collier Books, 1962. Religious, political, economic, and military history from the accession of Diocletian (284 C.E.) to the death of Constantine (337 C.E.).

Jones, A. H. M. *The Later Roman Empire (284–602): A Social, Economic, and Administrative Survey*. 3 vols. Oxford: Basil Blackwell, 1964. Indispensable guide to the administrative and social structures of the late Roman world.

Kitzinger, Ernst. *Byzantine Art in the Making: Main Lines of Stylistic Development in Mediterranean Art, 3rd–7th Century*. Cambridge, MA: Harvard University Press, 1977. A superb overview of pictorial art, with over 200 monochrome and eight color plates.

Mango, Cyril. *Byzantium: The Empire of New Rome*. New York: Scribner's, 1980. Surveys Byzantine Christian society, with intriguing discussions of Byzantine worldviews, monasticism, and dissenters, including pagans, Christian heretics, and Jews.

Momigliano, Arnaldo, ed. *The Conflict between Paganism and Christianity in the Fourth Century*.

Oxford: Clarendon Press, 1963. Contains important essays by internationally renowned scholars.

Ostrogorsky, George. *History of the Byzantine State*, 2nd ed., trans. Joan Hussey. New Brunswick, NJ. Rutgers University Press, 1968. Still the best single volume on Byzantine political history.

Pelikan, Jaroslav. *The Christian Tradition: A History of the Development of Doctrine;* I: *The Emergence of the Catholic Tradition (100–600);* II: *The Spirit of Eastern Christendom* (600–1700); III: *The Growth of Medieval Theology (600–1300).* Chicago: University of Chicago Press, 1971, 1974, 1978. A masterly study of dogma.

Riché, Pierre. *Education and Culture in the Barbarian West, Sixth through Eighth Centuries.* Columbia, SC: University of South Carolina Press, 1976. Translated from the third French edition by John J. Contreni. An introduction to Carolingian society.

Southern, R. W. *Western Society and the Church in the Middle Ages* (The Pelican History of the Church, vol. 11). Grand Rapids, MI: Eerdmans, 1970. Briefly treats the period from 700 to 1050, but focuses on church and society from 1050 to 1550.

Strayer, Joseph R., ed. *Dictionary of the Middle Ages.* 13 vols. New York: Charles Scribner's Sons, 1982–1989. The latest scholarship on medieval subjects, from Aachen to Zwart Noc. Excellent bibliographies.

Wemple, Suzanne Fonay. *Women in Frankish Society: Marriage and the Cloister, 500–800.* Philadelphia: University of Pennsylvania Press, 1981. An important early contribution to the recent flowering of studies on medieval women.

Zarnecki, George. *The Monastic Achievement.* New York: McGraw-Hill Book Company, 1972. A slim volume that surveys monasticism and monastic art. Contains many illustrations, including some in color.

Part III. The Late Middle Ages and the Reformations of the Sixteenth Century
Carter Lindberg

Comprehensive Resources

Anderson, Charles. *Augsburg Historical Atlas of Christianity in the Middle Ages and the Reformation.* Minneapolis, MN: Augsburg Press, 1967.

Cross, F. L. and E. A. Livingstone, eds. *The Oxford Dictionary of the Christian Church.* New York: Oxford University Press, 1984. A one-volume encyclopedia containing over 6,000 entries on all aspects of the history of Christianity.

Jedin, Herbert and John Dolan, eds. *History of the Church.* 10 vols. New York: Crossroad, 1987. A multi-author, scholarly resource with emphasis on the theological and institutional aspects of Christianity in their cultural and political contexts; extensive bibliographies for each chapter.

The Middle Ages

Boswell, John. *The Kindness of Strangers.* New York: Vintage Books, 1990. A study of the abandonment of children and societal responses in the Middle Ages.

Cantor, Norman F. *The Meaning of the Middle Ages: A Sociological and Cultural History.* Boston: Allyn & Bacon, 1973. A cultural history focusing on the significance of the leading ideas of the Middle Ages for social life and personal behavior.

Cook, William R. and Ronald B. Herzman. *The Medieval World View.* New York: Oxford University Press, 1983. An undergraduate text that attempts "to understand and appreciate the Middle Ages from the inside, that is, as the people of the Middle Ages saw themselves" (p. xviii).

Deanesly, Margaret. *A History of the Medieval Church, 590–1500.* London & New York: Methuen, 1981. An emphasis upon the social and personal aspects of the history of Christianity, as well as the actual working of the church system.

Herlihy, David. *Medieval Households.* Cambridge, MA: Harvard University Press, 1985. An overview of the medieval family and its relations.

Mollat, Michel. *The Poor in the Middle Ages: An Essay in Social History,* trans. A. Goldhammer. New Haven, CT: Yale University Press, 1986. An examination of how successive medieval generations understood poverty and responded to the poor.

Morris, Colin. *The Discovery of the Individual, 1050–1200.* Toronto: University of Toronto Press, 1987. A study of medieval history, theology, literature, and art that places the discovery of the individual in the twelfth century.

Oakley, Francis. *The Medieval Experience: Foundations of Western Cultural Singularity.* Toronto: University of Toronto Press, 1988. An interpretive essay on medieval life arranged by topics such as church, economics, politics, sentiment, etc.

Petry, Ray C., ed. *A History of Christianity: Readings in the History of the Early and Medieval Church.* Englewood Cliffs, NJ: Prentice-Hall, Inc., 1962. A comprehensive collection of sources in translation.

Southern, Richard W. *Western Society and the Church in the Middle Ages.* Baltimore: Penguin Books, 1973. A master scholar's view of the relations between ecclesiastical development and social change.

Tierney, Brian, and Sidney Painter. *Western Europe in the Middle Ages, 300–1475.* New York: Alfred A. Knopf, 1983. A standard textbook with a vigorous narrative style.

Ullmann, Walter. *A Short History of the Papacy in the Middle Ages.* London: Methuen, 1974. A historical account for the general reader of the intellectual, constitutional, legal, theological, and administrative development of the papacy.

Reformation

DeMolen, Richard L., ed. *Leaders of the Reformation.* Selinsgrove, PA: Susquehanna University Press, 1984. Eleven essays on major Reformation figures by their respective scholars.

Hsia, R. Po-Chia, ed. *The German People and the Reformation.* Ithaca, NY, & London: Cornell University Press, 1988. A collection of twelve essays by leading Reformation scholars on such topics as cities, communication and the media, women and family, and the impact of the Reformation.

Manschreck, Clyde, L., ed. *A History of Christianity: Readings in the History of the Church from the Reformation to the Present.* Englewood Cliffs, NJ: Prentice-Hall, Inc., 1965. A comprehensive collection of sources in translation.

Oberman, Heiko A. *The Dawn of the Reformation: Essays in Late Medieval and Early Reformation*

Thought. Edinburgh: T. & T. Clark Ltd., 1986. A collection of seminal essays by the leading proponent of the medieval context for the Reformation.

O'Malley, John, S.J., ed. *Catholicism in Early Modern History: A Guide to Research*. St. Louis, MO: Center for Reformation Research, 1988. Essays by leading scholars on the major issues of their fields.

Ozment, Steven. *The Age of Reform, 1250–1550: An Intellectual and Religious History of Late Medieval and Reformation Europe*. New Haven, CT, & London: Yale University Press, 1980. A lively, well-written textbook on the Reformation by a leading scholar.

Ozment, Steven, ed. *Reformation Europe: A Guide to Research*. St. Louis, MO: Center for Reformation Research, 1982. Essays by leading scholars on the major issues of their fields; includes essays on social history, witchcraft, popular religion, and women.

Scribner, R. W. *Popular Culture and Popular Movements in Reformation Germany*. London: The Hambledon Press, 1987. A collection of essays by a provocative social historian.

Sessions, Kyle, and Phillip Bebb, eds. *Pietas et Societas: New Trends in Reformation Social History* (Sixteenth Century Essays and Studies IV). Kirksville, MO: The Sixteenth Century Journal Publishers, 1985. Essays by leading scholars from the perspectives of social history.

Spence, Jonathan D. *The Memory Palace of Matteo Ricci*. New York: Elisabeth Sifton Books, Penguin Books, 1986. A stimulating study of a Counter-Reformation mission to Ming China.

Spitz, Lewis W. *The Protestant Reformation, 1517–1559*. San Francisco: Harper & Row, 1985. A very well-written narrative with an extensive annotated bibliography.

Strauss, Gerald, ed. & trans. *Manifestations of Discontent in Germany on the Eve of the Reformation*. Bloomington, IN, and London: Indiana University Press, 1971. A collection of documents in translation.

Zuck, Lowell, H., ed. *Christianity and Revolution: Radical Christian Testimonies, 1520–1650*. Philadelphia: Temple University Press, 1975. A collection of documents in translation ranging from the Peasants' War to the Puritan Revolution.

Part IV: European Christianity Confronts the Modern Age
Jean-Loup Seban

Arnold, Duane W. H. *The Way, the Truth and the Life: an Introduction to Lutheran Christianity*. Grand Rapids, MI: Baker Book House, 1982. A clear exposition of the history and doctrine of the Lutheran Church.

Barth, Karl. *From Rousseau to Ritschl*. London: SCM Press, 1959. A critical presentation of nineteenth-century Protestant thought from a neo-orthodox perspective.

Bangert, William V. *A History of the Society of Jesus*. St. Louis, MO: Institute of Jesuit Sources, 1972. A fair historical account.

Berlin, Isaiah. *Karl Marx, His Life and Environment*, 4th ed. Oxford: Oxford University Press, 1978. A fascinating account of the life and thought of the author of *Das Kapital*.

Berlin, Isaiah. *Russian Thinkers*. Harmondsworth, U.K.: Penguin Books, 1978. A superb introduction to nineteenth-century Russian intellectual life.

Bokenkotter, Thomas. *A Concise History of the Catholic Church*. New York: Doubleday, 1977. A basic history.

Bokenkotter, Thomas. *Essential Catholicism*. New York: Doubleday, 1985. On Roman Catholic doctrines.

Braudel, Fernand. *Civilization and Capitalism, 15th–18th Century*, trans. Sian Reynolds. 3 vols. Vol. 1, *The Structures of Everyday Life*; vol. 2, *The Wheels of Commerce*; vol. 3, *The Perspective of the World*. New York: Harper & Row, 1981, 1982, 1984. A masterpiece of the history of the human condition by a leading member of the *Annales School*.

Breunig, Charles. *The Age of Revolution and Reaction, 1789–1850*. New York: Norton, 1977. An excellent textbook.

Byrnes, J.F. *The Psychology of Religion*. New York & London: Free Press and Collier Macmillan, 1984. A basic book on the subject.

Caraman, Philip. *The Lost Paradise: An Account of the Jesuits in Paraguay, 1607–1768*. London: Sidwick & Jackson, 1975. A fine study of a unique political-religious venture.

Cassirer, Ernst. *The Myth of the State*. New Haven, CT, & London: Yale University Press, 1946. A reflective analysis of the history of political theories.

Cassirer, Ernst. *The Philosophy of the Enlightenment*, trans. F. C. A. Keolln & J. P. Pettegrove. Princeton, NJ: Princeton University Press, 1979. A classic work.

Chadwick, Owen. *The Secularization of the European Mind in the Nineteenth Century*. Cambridge: Cambridge University Press, 1975. Challenging reflections on liberalism, socialism, anticlericalism, history, and the moral nature of the human being.

Collingwood, R.G. *The Idea of History*. Oxford: Oxford University Press, 1961. A magisterial study and interpretation of the history of historiography and the philosophy of history.

Collins, James D. *The Mind of Kierkegaard*. Princeton, NJ: Princeton University Press, 1983. A helpful introduction to the Danish philosopher.

Cragg, Gerald R. *Reason and Authority in the Eighteenth Century*. Cambridge: Cambridge University Press, 1964. A classic work on the Enlightenment.

Davies, Horton. *Worship and Theology in England from Cranmer to Hooker, 1534–1603*. Princeton, NJ: Princeton University Press, 1970. *Worship and Theology in England from Andrewes to Baxter and Fox, 1603–1690*. Princeton, NJ: Princeton University Press, 1975. *Worship and Theology in England from Watts and Wesley to Maurice, 1690–1850*. Princeton, NJ: Princeton University Press, 1961. *Worship and Theology in England from Newman to Martineau, 1850–1900*. Princeton, NJ: Princeton University Press, 1962. *Worship and Theology in England: The Ecumenical Century, 1900–1965*. Princeton, NJ: Princeton University Press, 1965. The most comprehensive account.

Davies, Rupert Eric. *Methodism*. London: Epworth Press, 1976. A very useful introduction.

Davies, R. E. and E. G. Rupp. *A History of the Methodist Church in Great Britain*. 4 vols. London: Epworth Press, 1965–1988. The definitive history of British Methodists.

Drummond, A. L. *German Protestantism Since Luther*. London: Epworth Press, 1951. A still helpful introduction to German Protestant theology.

Dunn, Richard S. *The Age of Religious Wars, 1559–1715*. 2nd ed. New York: Norton, 1979. Comprehensive introductory coverage of the period.

Dunne, George H. *Generation of Giants: The Story of the Jesuits in China in the Last Decade of the Ming Dynasty*. Notre Dame, IN: University of Notre Dame Press, 1962. An exciting account of Roman Catholic missionary efforts in Asia.

Frank, Joseph. *Dostoevsky: The Years of Ordeal, 1850–1859*. Princeton, NJ: Princeton University Press, 1983. *Dostoevsky: The Stir of Liberation, 1860–1865*. Princeton, NJ: Princeton University Press, 1986. Both books offer a fascinating literary biography.

Gay, Peter. *The Enlightenment: An Interpretation*. 2 vols. Vol. 1, *The Rise of Modern Paganism;* vol. 2, *The Science of Freedom*. New York: Norton, 1966 & 1969. A remarkable achievement.

Gerrish, B. A. *A Prince of the Church: Schleiermacher and the Beginnings of Modern Theology*. Philadelphia: Fortress Press, 1984. A brilliant book which offers a perceptive approach to the relevance of Schleiermacher's thought.

Gilbert, Felix. *The End of the European Era, 1890 to the Present*. 3rd ed. New York: Norton, 1984. A useful introduction.

Hazard, Paul. *The European Mind, 1680–1715*, trans. J. Lewis May. London: Hollis & Carter, 1953. Still a classic on cultural history.

— — —, *The European Thought in the Eighteenth Century: From Montesquieu to Lessing*, trans. J. Lewis May. London: Hollis & Carter, 1954. Still the best intellectual history of the period.

Hick, John H. *Philosophy of Religion*. Englewood Cliffs, NJ: Prentice-Hall, Inc., 1973. A useful textbook on the subject.

Hill, Christopher. *Puritanism and Revolution: Studies in Interpretation of the English Revolution of the 17th Century*. London: Secker & Warburg, 1958. A superb narration of the Puritan revolution.

Hill, Christopher. *The World Turned Upside Down*. New York: Viking Press, 1972. On seventeenth century English intellectual life.

Howse, E.M. *Saints in Politics: The Clapham Sect and the Growth of Freedom*. Toronto: University Press of Toronto, 1952. A book on late eighteenth-century British social history.

Koyre, Alexandre. *From the Closed World to the Infinite Universe*. Baltimore: Johns Hopkins Press, 1968. Indispensable for the understanding of the scientific revolution.

Lefebvre, George. *The Coming of the French Revolution*, trans. R.R. Palmer. Princeton, NJ: Princeton University Press, 1989. A Marxist interpretation.

Mandrou, Robert. *From Humanism to Science: 1480–1700*, trans. B. Pearce. Harmondsworth, U.K.: Penguin Books, 1978. A basic intellectual history.

McLellan, David. *Ideology*. Minneapolis, MN: University of Minnesota Press, 1986. A brief history of the concept.

Neill, Stephen Charles. *Anglicanism*. Harmondsworth, U.K.: Penguin Books, 1958. A basic coverage.

Neill, Stephen Charles. *Christian Missions*. Grand Rapids, MI: Eerdmans, 1965. On the history of Christian missions.

Okey, Robin. *Eastern Europe: Feudalism to Communism, 1740–1985*. Minneapolis, MN: University of Minnesota Press, 1987. An excellent sociopolitical history of Eastern Europe.

Pelikan, Jaroslav. *The Christian Tradition*. Vol. 4, *Reformation of Church and Dogma, 1300–1700;* vol. 5, *Christian Doctrine and Modern Culture Since 1700*. Chicago & London: University of Chicago Press, 1985, 1989. On the developments of Christian dogmas throughout history.

Popkin, Richard H. *The History of Scepticism from Erasmus to Spinoza*. Berkeley, CA: University of California Press, 1979. Outstanding book.

Rich, Norman. *The Age of Nationalism and Reform, 1850–1890*, 2nd ed. New York: Norton, 1977. A helpful introduction.

Rupp, Ernst Gordon. *Religion in England, 1688–1791*. Oxford: Clarendon Press, 1986. A superb book on the subject.

Russell, Jeffrey Burton. *A History of Witchcraft, Sorcerers, Heretics, and Pagans*. London: Thames & Hudson, 1980. The best history of witchcraft by an authority in the field.

Schattenschneider, Allen W. *Through Five Hundred Years: a Popular History of the Moravian*

Church Beginning with the Story of the Ancient Unitas Fratrum. Bethlehem, PA: Comenius Press, 1956. An illustrated account.

Sedgwick, Alexander. *Jansenism in Seventeenth-Century France*. Charlottesville, VA: University of Virginia Press, 1977. A fair account of French Jansenism.

Sharpe, Eric J. *Comparative Religion, A History*. London: Duckworth, 1975. Perhaps the best history of the field.

Stoeffler, Ernst. *The Rise of Evangelical Pietism*. Leiden, Brill, 1965. A solid study.

Tillich, Paul. *Perspectives on 19th and 20th Century Protestant Theology*. New York: Harper & Row, 1967. A modern and challenging view.

Troeltsch, Ernst. *The Social Teaching of the Christian Churches*, trans. Olive Wyon. 2 vols. New York: Scribner's, 1954.

Vidler, A.R. *A Century of Social Catholicism, 1820–1920*. London: SPCK, 1964. A detailed account of the social concern of the Roman Catholic Church.

Visser't Hooft, Willem Adolph. *The Genesis and Formation of the World Council of Churches*. Geneva: World Council of Churches, 1982. An account by a leading participant.

Wade, Ira. *The Structure and Form of the French Enlightenment*. 2 vols. Princeton, NJ: Princeton University Press, 1977. A brilliant book.

Ward, W.R. *Theology, Sociology and Politics: The German Protestant Social Conscience, 1890–1933*. Berne, Lang, 1979. An essential book on social Protestantism in Germany.

Ware, Timothy. *The Orthodox Church*. Baltimore: Penguin Books, 1964. A helpful introduction to Eastern Orthodoxy.

Watts, M.R. *The Dissenters*, vol. 1. Oxford: Oxford University Press, 1978. Essential on English Church history.

Weber, Max. *The Protestant Ethic and the Spirit of Capitalism*, trans. T. Parsons. New York: Scribner's, 1958. A vastly influential book.

Welch, Claude. *Protestant Thought in the Nineteenth Century*. 2 vols. New Haven, CT: Yale University Press, 1972. An excellent coverage.

Woloch, Isser. *Eighteenth-Century Europe, Tradition and Progress, 1715–1789*. New York: Norton, 1982. An excellent introduction.

Part V. Christianity and Culture in America
Mark Noll

Ahlstrom, Sydney E. *A Religious History of the American People*. New Haven, CT: Yale University Press, 1972. Still the fullest single-volume coverage.

Brumberg, John J. *Mission for Life: The Story of the Family of Adoniram Judson*. Glencoe, IL: Free Press, 1980. America's "first family" of missionaries.

Carey, Patrick W., ed. *American Catholic Religious Thought*. New York: Paulist, 1987. Outstanding introduction plus representative documents.

Ellis, John Tracy, ed. *Documents of American Catholic History*, 2nd ed. Milwaukee: Bruce, 1962. The best general collection for its subject.

Frazier, E. Franklin. *The Negro Church in America*, rev ed., with C. Eric Lincoln. *The Black*

Church Since Frazier. New York: Schocken, 1973. An updated perspective on a central theme in American religious history.

Gaustad, Edwin S. *A Documentary History of Religion in America.* 2 vols. Grand Rapids, MI: Eerdmans, 1982, 1983. Helpfully representative sources.

Genovese, Eugene D. *Roll, Jordan, Roll: The World the Slaves Made.* New York: Pantheon, 1974. A book in which slave religion figures large.

Grant, John Webster, ed. *A History of the Christian Church in Canada*: H. H. Walsh. *The Church in the French Era.* Toronto: McGraw-Hill Ryerson, 1966; John S. Moir. *The Church in the British Era.* Toronto: McGraw-Hill Ryerson, 1972; John Webster Grant. *The Church in the Canadian Era*, rev. ed. Burlington, Ontario: Welch, 1988. The basic history.

Handy, Robert T. *A History of the Churches in the United States and Canada.* New York: Oxford University Press, 1977. A solid narrative that is strengthened by the inclusion of Canada.

Harrell, David Edwin. *All Things Are Possible: The Healing and Charismatic Renewal in Modern America.* Bloomington, IN: Indiana University Press, 1975. Excellent introduction to pentecostal renewal in modern America.

Hatch, Nathan O. *The Democratization of American Christianity.* New Haven, CT: Yale University Press, 1989. How the churches chose democracy.

———, and Mark A. Noll, eds. *The Bible in America.* New York: Oxford University Press, 1982. Preliminary essays on a very important subject.

———, and Harry S. Stout, eds. *Jonathan Edwards and the American Experience.* New York: Oxford University Press, 1988. A wide-ranging updating of the burgeoning scholarship on Edwards.

Hennesey, James J. *American Catholics: A History of the Roman Catholic Community in the United States.* New York: Oxford University Press, 1982. One of the best one-volume histories of its subjects.

Hill, Samuel S., ed. *Encyclopedia of Religion in the South.* Macon, GA: Mercer University Press, 1984. Regional history at its best.

Holifield, E. Brooks. *A History of Pastoral Care in America.* Nashville, TN: Abingdon, 1983. A perceptive history of a multifaceted subject.

Hudson, Winthrop S. *Religion in America*, 4th ed. New York: Macmillan, 1987. Probably the best short, one-volume history.

Hutchison, William R. *The Modernist Impulse in American Protestantism.* Cambridge, MA: Harvard University Press, 1976. A fine study of what was at the end of the nineteenth century the "new liberalism."

Kuklick, Bruce. *Churchmen and Philosophers from Jonathan Edwards to John Dewey.* New Haven, CT: Yale University Press, 1985. A book that goes far to restoring the centrality of theology to American intellectual history.

Lippy, Charles H. and Peter W. Williams, eds. *Encyclopedia of the American Religious Experience.* 3 vols. New York: Scribner's, 1988. One hundred outstanding essays by acknowledged authorities.

Marsden, George M. *Fundamentalism and American Culture: The Shaping of Twentieth-Century American Evangelicalism, 1870–1925.* New York: Oxford University Press, 1980. Magisterial account of an important stream of American religion.

Marty, Martin E. *A Nation of Behavers.* Chicago: University of Chicago Press, 1976. Perceptive mapping of modern religious patterns.

Mathews, Donald G. *Religion in the Old South*. Chicago: University of Chicago Press, 1977. Outstanding on the paradoxes of its subject.

May, Henry F. *The Enlightenment in America*. New York: Oxford University Press, 1976. Excellent study of religion and the mind in the Revolutionary era.

Miller, Perry. *The New England Mind*. 2 vols. Cambridge, MA: Harvard University Press, 1939, 1953. Brilliant, pace-setting volumes.

Moorhead, James H. *American Apocalypse: Yankee Protestants and the Civil War, 1860–1869*. New Haven, CT: Yale University Press, 1978. Full account of the complicated role of religion in the Union North.

Noll, Mark A., ed. *Religion and American Politics from the Colonial Period to the 1980s*. New York: Oxford University Press, 1989. Wide-ranging coverage of a central relationship in American history.

Raboteau, Albert. *Slave Religion: The "Invisible Institution" in the Antebellum South*. New York: Oxford University Press, 1978. The essential book on a once neglected subject.

Smith, Timothy L. *Revivalism and Social Reform: American Protestantism on the Eve of the Civil War*, 2nd ed. Baltimore: Johns Hopkins University Press, 1980. A solid book on the activism of evangelicals.

Stout, Harry S. *The New England Soul: Preaching and Religious Culture in Colonial New England*. New York: Oxford University Press, 1986. A comprehensive treatment of a subject central to American religion.

Turner, James. *Without God, Without Creed: The Origin of Unbelief in America*. Baltimore: Johns Hopkins University Press, 1985. A brilliant study of how Christians paved the way for atheism.

Wells, Ronald A., ed. *The Wars of America: Christian Views*. Grand Rapids, MI: Eerdmans, 1981. A story mostly of churches supporting war.

Wilson, John F., ed. *Church and State in America*. 2 vols. New York: Greenwood, 1986, 1987. Outstanding bibliographical essays.

Wuthnow, Robert. *The Restructuring of American Religion: Society and Faith Since World War II*. Princeton, NJ: Princeton University Press, 1988. A sociologist's perceptive reading of the last half-century.

Epilogue.
Dana Robert

Barrett, David B., ed. *World Christian Encyclopedia: A Comparative Study of Churches and Religions in the Modern World, A.D. 1900–2000*. Oxford: Oxford University Press, 1982.

Berryman, Phillip. *Liberation Theology*. Oak Park, IL: Meyer Stone Books, 1987.

Clark, Donald H. *Christianity in Modern Korea*. Lanham, MD: University Press of America, 1986.

Cleary, Edward L. *Crisis and Change: The Church in Latin America Today*. Maryknoll, NY: Orbis, 1985.

Daneel, Inus. *Quest for Belonging: Introduction to a Study of African Independent Churches*. Gweru, Zimbabwe: Mambo Press, 1987.

Deats, Richard L. *Nationalism and Christianity in the Philippines*. Dallas, TX: Southern Methodist University Press, 1968.

DeGruchy, John. *The Church Struggle in South Africa*. Grand Rapids, MI: Eerdmans, 1979.

Drummond, Richard H. *A History of Christianity in Japan*. Grand Rapids, MI: Eerdmans, 1971.

Dussel, Enrique. *A History of the Church in Latin America*, trans. Alan Neely. Grand Rapids, MI: Eerdmans, 1981.

Firth, Cyril. *An Introduction to Indian Church History*. Serampore: Christian Literature Society, 1961.

Hastings, Adrian. *African Christianity*. New York: Seabury Press, 1976.

Hastings, Adrian. *A History of African Christianity, 1950–1975*. Cambridge: Cambridge University Press, 1979

Neill, Stephen. *A History of Christian Missions*. Harmondsworth, U.K.: Penguin Books, 1964.

Sanneh, Lamin. *Translating the Message. The Missionary Impact on Culture*. Maryknoll, NY: Orbis, 1989.

Sanneh, Lamin. *West African Christianity*. Maryknoll, NY: Orbis, 1983.

Sitoy, T. Valentino. *A History of Christianity in the Philippines*. Vol 1. Quezon City, Philippines: New Day Philippines 1985.

Thekkedath, Joseph. *History of Christianity in India, 1542–1700*. Vol. 2. Bangalore, India: St. Peter's Seminary, 1982.

INDEX

ABCFM. *See* American Board of Commissioners for
    Foreign Missions
Abelard, Peter, 261, 264–267
Abortion, 729–730
About Prejudices (De Praejudiciis), 503
Absolutism, 487–489
Absolutist state, rise of, 430
Academies of science, 493
Academy of Sedan, 498
Acropolis, 194
Act of Supremacy, 387
Act of Toleration, 393
Act of Uniformity, 392
Acts and Monuments of matters happening in the Church, 392
The Acts of the Martyrs, 141
Admonition for the Reformation of Church Discipline,
    455
Admonition to Peace, 348
Adrian II, 234
Adrian VI, 407
Adventure of Simplicius Simplicissimus, 442
African Christianity
    nationalism and, 761
    scripture translation and, 759–760
African Independent Church, 762–763
African Methodist Episcopal Church, 671
Age of Bede, 218
Aggiornamento, 579–580
Alain of Lille, 277
Alberti, Salomon, 422
Albigenses, 292
ALC. *See* American Lutheran Church
Alcuin of York, 224
Alexander II, 246–247
Alexander V, 315–316
Alexander VI, 327–328, 756
Alexandria, 149, 191
Alexius Commenus, 237, 255
Alfonso VI, 242, 253
Alfred the Great, 241
Alighieri, Dante, 312
Allen, Richard, 671
Almsgiving, 276–277
Althusius, Johannes, 500
Ambrose of Milan, 154, 160
Ameaux, Pierre, 380
America. *See* United States
American Bible Society, 686
American Board of Commissioners for Foreign Missions
    (ABCFM), 667

Americanist Controversy, 720
American Lutheran Church (ALC), 735
American Missions, of twentieth century, 751–753
American Revolution
    Christian churches and, 627–628, 635–643
    democracy and, 646–648
    slavery in, 642–643
    theology and, 648–650
Americans, native, Christianity and, 624–626
Ames, William, 455
Amyraut, Moise, 445
Anabaptists
    multiplicity of, 367–368
    refusal to bear arms, 364
    refusal to pay tithes, 364–365
    See also Radical reformers
*The Analogy of Nature, Natural and Revealed, to the
    Constitution and Course of Nature*, 511
Anastasius, 178
Anglicanism, first systematic statement, 392
Anglicans, in colonial America, 618–619
Anne of Cleves, 388
Annunciation, 251
Anonymity, of Middle Ages, 272
Anselm, 261–264, 302
Anthemius, 179
Anthony of Bourbon, 398
Anthropocentric theory of the Atonement, 266
Anthropology of religion, 597–598
Antichrist, 306
Anticlericalism, liberal, 559–560
Antinomianism, 618
Antioch, 149
Anti-Semitism, 534
Antony, 161–162, 163
Apocalyptic writings
    Christian, 130
    growth of, 115–117
    impact on Christianity and Judaism, 117
    Jewish, 129
Apology for the Anglican Church, 392
Apostles, Acts of, non-canonical, 125
"Apostolic Pilgrim," 246
Aquinas, Thomas, 280, 300–304
Arcadius, 170
Architecture, Jesuit style, 438
Arian Germans, 154–156
Arians, 151–154
Aristotelian logic, 261, 300, 305–306, 421
Aristotle, 300, 303

Arius, 152
Arminius, Jacob, 444
Arnauld, Antoine, 470–472
Arndt, Johann, 473
Art
  Carolingian, 224
  Christian, 129
  in nineteenth century, 555–556
  Reformation and, 422–423
Asbury, Francis, 660–661
Asceticism, 281
Asian Christianity, scripture translation and, 759–760
Assertio Septem Sacramentorum, 386
Assumption, 251
Athanasius, 153, 161
Attrition, 281
Attritionists, 469
Auctoritas, 284
Augusta, Aelia Pulcheria, 166
Augustine, 160, 165, 259, 260, 274
Augustine (monk), 185
Augustine of Hippo, 167
Authoritative scriptures, 122–126
Avarice, as vice, 273, 276
Averroës (Ibn-Rushd), 267
Avicenna (Ibn Sina), 267
Avignonese papacy, 312

Baby boom, 726
"Babylonian captivity" of the church, 311–313, 323
Bach, Johann Sebastian, 354, 423, 434, 435
Backus, Isaac, 644–645
Bacon, Francis, 421
Bakunin, Michael, 561
Bañez, Dominic, 437
Baptism, 222, 279, 280, 415
Baptists
  in Canada, 749
  Puritanism and, 616–617
  in the South, 691
Barbarians, 170–171
Baronius, Caesar, 422–423
Baroque music, 453–454
Baroque period, 434
Baroque style, 452–454
Barth, Karl, 566–567
Barton, Clara, 693
Baruch, 116
Base Christian Communities, 762
Basileia ton Romaion (Empire of the Romans), 189
Basileus, 199
Basilian Rule, 163
Basil of Caesarea, 153, 163
Basil II the Bulgar-Slayer, 232, 235, 254
Bastille, 538
Bauer, Bruno, 574
Baxter, Richard, 455
Bayle, Pierre, 479, 502
Beccaria, Cesare Bonesana, 540
Bede, Venerable, 217–219
Beecher, Lyman, 660, 675
Beguines, 290–291
Belgian Confession of 1561, 444

Bellarmino, Roberto, 439
Bellavin, Tikhon, 716
Benedict Biscop (Biscop Baducing), 217
Benedictine monasteries, 242
Benedictines, 164, 275–276
Benedict of Nursia, 164
Benedict's Rule, 164
Benedict XI, 310
Benedict XIII, 314, 317
Benezet, Anthony, 640
Bengel, Johann Albrecht, 477
Bentley, Richard, 509–510
Berdiaev, Nikolai, 588
Bernard of Clairvaux, 243, 250, 261, 268–269
Berno, 242
Berulism, 447
Beza, Theodore, 373, 399
Bible
  American Christianity and, 685–688
  publishing, 685–688
  translations, for Africa, Asia, and Latin America,
    759–760
Biblical criticism, birth of, 498–500
Bill of Rights (1689), 487, 505
Bishops, in late antiquity, 160–161
  See also specific bishops
Black Americans
  book and periodical literature for, 714–715
  Christianity and, 670–673, 689, 734
  in 1960s, 727
  non-Protestant, 713–715
  social liberation of Bible and, 687–688
Black Cloister (Black Augustinians), 339
Black theology, 746
Blair, James, 619
Blake, William, 544
Blount, Charles, 508
Blumhardt, Christoph, 562
Boccaccio, 325, 408
Bodin, Jean, 500–501
Body, Christian society as, 270
Boethius, 177
Bogomilism, 236–237
Böhme, Jakob, 473, 474–475
Boleyn, Anne, 386, 387
Bolshevik Revolution, 551, 552
Bonaparte, Napoleon, 539
Bonaventure, 304
Bonhoeffer, Dietrich, 594–595
Boniface, 219–220
Boniface III, 304
Boniface VIII, 307–311
Boniface IX, 313–314
Book of Common Prayer, 388, 392, 453
Book of Concord, 432
Book of Mormon, 669–670
Boris, 235–236
Bosch, Hieronymous, 337
Bossuet, Jean Bénigne, 450
Bothwell, James, 395
Boucher, Jonathan, 639
Boudinot, Elias, 642–643
Boyle, Robert, 463

Brahe, Tycho, 422
Brainerd, David, 632
Brant, Sebastian, 327
Bray, Thomas, 619
Brebeuf, Jean de, 606
British Protestant missionary movement, 758
Brownson, Orestes, 719
Brunner, Emil, 566–567
Bryan, William Jennings, 700–701, 711
Bubonic plague, 321–322
Bucer, Martin, 377
Bugenhagen, Johannes, 346
Bulgakov, Sergem, 588
Bull, 287
Bunschuh, 348
Burke, Edmund, 557
Bushnell, Horace, 708
Butler, Joseph, 511
Buxtehude, Dietrich, 434
Byzantine Christianity, 194–195, 235
Byzantine churches, 230
Byzantine cities, seventh century, 194
Byzantine iconoclasm, 196–201
Byzantine missions, to Slavs, 232–237
Byzantium
    after Justinian, 189–190
    Constantine and, 150–151
    Muslim advances and, 202
    post-iconoclast, 229–232
    See also Constantinople

Caecilian, 141
Caliph Jazid II, 197
Calixt, Georg, 442
Calvert, Cecil, 620
Calvert, George, 620
Calvin, John
    autobiographic information, 372–373
    consolidation of his authority, 380–381
    Gallican Confession and, 397
    journey to Geneva, 373–375
    leadership in Geneva, 378–380, 396
    predestination and, 420
    Reformation in Geneva and, 375–378
    Servetus case and, 381–383
    social welfare and, 421
Calvinism
    in crisis, 443–446
    in France, 397
Cambridge Platform, 614
Cambridge Platonists, 463
Camisard movement, 503–504
Campanella, Tommaso, 433
Canadian Christianity
    colonial, 651–652
    from 1925–1988, 749–751
Candlemas, 251
Canon, as primary instrument of unity, 126–127
Canon law, 161
Canons of Dort, 432
Cappadocia, 153
Cappadocian Fathers, 153–154, 160
Cappel, Louis, 498

Caracalla, 132
Caraffa, Cardinal, 408–409
Caravaggio, 434
Caravaggio-Carracci controversy, 434
Carissimi, Giacomo, 434
Carlyle, Thomas, 580
Carnival, 281–282
Carolingian Renaissance, Charlemagne and, 220–225
Carolingian rulers, 212–215
Caroloman, 219, 221
Carolus Magnus. *See* Charlemagne
Carroll, John, 673–674
Cartesianism, 445, 451, 499, 500
Carthage, 136, 174
Cartwright, Thomas, 455
Case, Shirley Jackson, 708
Cassiodorus, 175–176
Cathars, 290, 291
Cathedral of Intellect, 300–304
Cathedrals, European, 259, 260
Catherine, 403
Catherine of Aragon, 386
Catherine II (Catherine the Great), 540
Catholic Epistles, 124
Catholic Foreign Mission Society (Maryknoll), 751
Catholicism, ultraconservative, ascent of, 575–580
Catholic Piety and Letters, 446–447
Catholic reform movement, 416
Catholic Renascence, 576–578
Catholic renewal movement, 406
Catholic worker movement, 743–744
Cechy, 233
Cecil, William (Lord Burghley), 391
Celestine V, 306–307
Celibacy of priests, 420
Celtic church, English Monasticism and, 215–220
Chalcedonian Orthodoxy, 170
Chalmers, Thomas, 565
Charity
    doctrine of, 274
    salvation and, 276
Charlemagne (Carolus Magnus), 212–215, 220–225,
    242, 285
Charles I, 457, 477–478, 612
Charles III, 375, 467
Charles V, 351, 386, 389, 390, 398, 415
Charles IX, 398
Charles of Anjou, 305
Charles the Great, 221
Charles the Simple, 226, 240–241
Charpentier, Marc Antoine, 438
Charter of Anglicanism, 432
Chikane, Frank, 764
Childeric I, 208
Chillingworth, William, 506
Chilperic, 212
China, 467–468, 762
Chlothar I, 210, 212
Chosroes I, 178, 191
Christ, as divine judge, 279
Christendom
    Eastern, 237
    Western, 237–240

Christian art, 167–168
Christian commonwealth. *See Corpus Christianum*
Christian denominations
  in Africa, Asia, and Latin America, 763–764
  in America, strength of in twentieth century, 751
  in Canada, 750
  Nationalist credo and, 563–564
  rises and declines in post-Christian America, 731–734
  socialism and, 561–562
  See also specific denominations
Christian doctrine, Schleiermacher and, 547–548
Christian groups, 729–730
Christianity
  in America from 1925 to 1988, 753–754
  antagonism with Islam, 267
  apocalyptic view of, 115–118
  as central expression of Medieval life, 186–188
  classical Greco-Roman culture and, 159–160
  dialectical materialism and, 587–589
  early strength of, 136–137
  Gnosticism challenge and, 122
  Immanuel Kant and, 532–533
  map of, in 1926, 721–722
  regional hierarchical structure of, 129–130
  "religionless," 593–595
  Roman imperial hostility and, 137–140
  Roman opposition to, 133–136
  in southern hemisphere and Third World, 757
Christian of Anhalt, 440
Christian society, as body, 270
Christian Topography, 187
Chronicle of John Malalas, 186–187
Chrysostom, John, 160, 166, 167
Chu-Hsi, 452
Churches, in America, distribution of, 626
Church of England, colonial America and, 618–620
Church of God in Christ, 714
Church of Jesus Christ of Latter Day Saints, 670
Church-state issues, in Canada, 652
Cistercians, 243, 268
Cities
  in late antiquity, 160–161
  rise of, in Middle Ages, 271–274
  See also specific cities
City of God, 171, 245, 259
Civil War. *See* United States
Clare of Assisi, 296
Clarke, Samuel, 499, 508–509
Claudel, Paul, 580
Clement of Alexandria, 124, 196, 274
Clement V, 310–311
Clement VII, 313, 314, 386, 406, 407
Clergy, marriage of, 237, 238
Clericis Laicos, 308
Clotilda, 208–209
Clovis, 207, 208, 284
Cluny, abbey of, 242–243
Cluny monastery, 240
Cnut, 241
Codex Bezae, 400
Codex Sinaiticus, 125
Codex Vaticanus, 125
Cold War, 727

Collection of Seventy-Four Titles, 246
Colleges
  in America, 683
  Black Christian, 714
  See also Universities
Collins, Anthony, 509
Colloquy of Poissy, 399–401
Colonialism, second wave of, 552–553
Colonial trade, in eighteenth century, 490
Colonna, Odo, 318
Colonna, Sciara, 310
Colonna family, 308
Colossus of Rhodes, 193
Columba, 215
Columbanus, 215
Comenius, 433
Commerce, in seventeenth century, 431
Commodus, 132
Communicatio idomatum, 354
Communist Manifesto, 561, 587
Comte, Auguste, 556, 596–597
Conciliarism, 315–318, 537
Concomitance, doctrine of, 280
Concordat of Worms, 249
Concordats, 318
Confessionalism, 567–568
Confession of Westminster, 457
Confirmation, 415
Confucianism, 438
Congregational churches, 659
Connecticut, church membership in 1700s, 631–632
Conrad II, 240
Conrad of Gelnhausen, 315
Consistory, 379–380
Consolamentum, 291–292
Constans II, 201
Constantine
  death of, 153
  invasion of Italy, 139
  Licinius and, 147
  "New Rome" of, 150–151
  ninth-century Byzantine missionary success and, 232–234
  revision of Roman Empire, 149
  transformation of Church and, 140–143
Constantine V, 198–199, 214
Constantine VII, 231
Constantinople
  Avar-Slav-Persian reign in 626, 174
  early Christendom and, 151, 200–201, 229
  Heraclius' return to, 192
  iconoclast controversy and, 201
  Muslim conquests and, 202
  post-iconoclast Byzantine state and, 231
  versus Rome, 237–238
  from 398–407, 160
  See also Byzantium
Constitutio Westphalia, 441
Contarini, Gasparo, 407
Contritionists, 469
Conventicle Acts, 461
Conventual Franciscans, 306
Coppe, Abiezer, 459

Corpus Christianum, 278, 305–306, 319, 320, 323, 332
Cosmas, 187–188
Cosmic redemption, stages of, 119–120
Cosmocentric theory of atonement, 264
Cossa, Baldassare, 316
Council at Ephesus, 167
Council of Basel, 319–321
Council of Chalcedon, 170
Council of Constance, 280, 314, 316, 318
Council of Constantinople, 179
Council of Ephesus, 168–170
Council of Ferrara-Florence, 319–321
Council of Florence, 278–279
Council of Pisa, 315
Council of Trent, 327, 408, 411, 413–416, 432
Council of Trullo (*Quinisext* Synod), 183, 185, 196, 237
Counter-Reformation
  Catholic renewal movement and, 406
  Council of Trent and, 413–416
  Edict of Nantes and, 502
  Ignatius Loyola and, 409–413
  Mary Tudor and, 389
  popes of, 408
Counterrevolutionary theories, 557
Cranmer, Thomas, 385, 388
Creation, Gnostic account of, 119–120
Cromwell, Oliver, 458
Cromwell, Thomas, 385
Crops, pagan protection of, 210–211
Crusades, 267
Cudworth, Ralph, 463
Culture
  Reformation and, 419–421
  of seventeenth century, 432–433
  vital revolution, 492
Cur deus homo, 263, 264
Cyprian, 137
Cyran, 468–470
Cyril, 168
Cyrillic alphabet, 235

d'Albret, Jeanne, 398
D'Alembert, Jean Le Rond, 520
Damascus, John of, 198
Damasus, 184
Damian, Cardinal Peter, 280–281
Darby, John Nelson, 709
Darwin, Charles, 556, 706–707
Daub, Karl, 570
Davies, Samuel, 632
Day, Dorothy, 743
Dead Sea Scrolls, 116
de Bergerac, Cyrano, 493
de Bérulle, Pierre, 448
Decameron, The, 325, 408
Decet Romanum, 343
de Chateaubriand, François-René, 451
Decius, 136
de Clairvaux, Bernard, 448
Declaration of Rights of Man, 538
de Coligny, Gaspard, 397
de Condorcet, Antoine-Nicolas Caritat, 494
Decretum, 298

Defenestration of Prague, 440
Deism
  Anglican answer to, 511
  rise of, 497–498
de Labadie, Jean, 476
de Lamennais, Félicité, 577
de la Mothe Fénelon, François, 450
de Machault, Guillaume, 434
De Maistre, Joseph, 557
de Medici, Catherine, 398
De Mirabeau, Honoré, 538
Democracy
  after American Revolution, 646–648
  republicanism and, 636
Demography
  after 1800, 553–554
  between 1600 and 1740, 430–431
  between 1680 and 1800, 489
de Molina, Luis, 437
de Molinos, Miguel, 450
De Montalembert, Charles, 577
de Montesquieu, Charles, 485, 487
Denmark, existentialism and, 581–583
De Robespierre, Maximilien, 538
Descartes, René, 433, 451, 474
de Tocqueville, Alexis, 657
de Xavier, Francisco, 436
Dialectical materialism, Christianity and, 587–589
Dialectical school, 571
Dictatus papae, 247
Diderot, Denis, 522
Diet of Speyer, 351
Diet of Worms, 418
Dietrich of Niem, 316
Diocletian, 137–139
Discourse of Free-Thinking, 509
Dispensationalism, theology of, 709
Dix, Dorothea, 693
Dominicans, 292–297
Dominic Guzman, 292–297
Domitian, 130, 131
Donation of Constantine (Pseudo-Isadorian Decretals), 214–215, 286, 310
Donation of Pepin, 214, 285
Donatists, 478
Donatus, 141
Dostoevsky, Fyodor, 583–584
Douglass, Frederick, 643
Dreyfus Affair, 578
Dudley, John, 388
Dudley, Robert, 391
Dürer, Albrecht, 324, 326–327
Durkheim, Emile, 597
Dutch Reformed Church, 623–624
Dwight, Timothy, 659

Eastern Orthodoxy
  in America, 715–717
  tenets of, 541
Ecclesiastical History of the English People, 143, 163, 218
Ecclesiastical Ordinances, 378–379
Eckhard, Meister, 300
Economics, after 1800, 554–555

Economy
  in the eighteenth century, 489–490
  of Middle Ages, 272–273
Ecthesis, 201
Ecumenical council
  seventh (787), 237
  twentieth (1869), 579
Ecumenical Movement, and World War I, 703
Ecumenism, 740–742
Eddy, Mary Baker, 666
Edict of Fontainebleu, 478
Edict of Nantes, 405, 477–479, 502
Edict of Restitution, 442
Edict of Toleration, 401
Edict of Union, 179
Edict of Worms, 344
Edinburgh Missionary Conference of 1910, 703
Education, Reformation and, 421–422
Edward III, 323
Edward VI, 385, 388
Edward Lord Herbert of Cherbury, 463, 497–498
Edwards, Jonathan, 630–631
Eichhorn, J.G., 499
Eighteenth century
  European monarchies, 487
  "long" (1680–1815), 494–495
  socioeconomic life of, 489–491
El Cid (Rodrigo Diaz de Vivar), 253
Eligius of Noyen, 211
Elijah, 116
Eliot, John, 624
Elizabeth I (Elizabeth Tudor), 388, 390–393
Elliott, Walter, 720
Encyclopedia, 521–522
Engels, Friedrich, 587
England
  in early Middle Ages, 240–241
  Monarchic, religious and cultural restoration, 461
  Puritanism in, 611–612
  Reformation in, 384–387, 607–610
English Church, 454–456
English Masons, 495
English Monasticism, Celtic church and, 215–220
English Peasants' Revolt (1381), 314
English Protestantism, 387
Enlightened despotism, 487–489
Enlighteners
  anticlimax of reign, 511–512
  early ecumenical endeavors, 512–515
  emancipation of Jews and, 534–535
  John Locke, 506–507
  Methodist Christians and, 517
  Protestant revivals of piety and, 515–519
  reign of
    deists compete in audacity, 507–511
    despisers of Christianity and, 519–524
    quest for Christianity and, 524–534
  Roman Catholic Church ordeal and, 535–539
  secular, 527–529
  William Law and, 517
Enlightenment
  clerical, 529–531
  Königsberg and, 531–534

Enoch, 116
Ephesus, 149
Episcopal congregation, first Black, 671
Episcopius, Simon, 444, 445
Eroticism, eighteenth century, 496
Esdras. *See* Ezra
Essay Concerning Human Understanding, 502–503
Eucharist, 279, 415
  controversies, 279–280
Eugene IV, 318, 319–320
Europe
  economic recovery of, during Medieval times, 252–253
  political transformations, modern, 551–552
  world leadership of
    decline of, 551
    from 1815–1914, 549–551
European Missionary legacy, 758–759
European politics
  in the Enlightened Age, 485–489
  at the turn of the seventeenth century, 427–430
European universities, of the twelfth through the
    sixteenth centuries, 297–300
Eusebius of Caesarea, 143
Evangelical Alliance, 678
Evangelical religion
  in America, 679–688
  antebellum politics and, 685
  at home and abroad, 695–698
  intellectual life and, 683
Evolutionary theory, 706–707
Evolutionism, 556
Ewha Women's University, 764
Execrabilis, 318
Exilit qui Seminat (1279), 306
Existentialism, 581–583
Exsurge Domine, 343
Ezra, 116

Falwell, Jerry, 729
Famine, in mid-fourteenth century, 321
Farel, William (Guillaume), 374–377
Fasting, on Saturdays in Lent, 237, 238
Felix V, 320
Feminist movement, 727–728
Fénlon, 451
Ferdinand of Hapsburg, 440
Ferdinand VI, 467
Feudalism
  dissolution of Frankish Realm and, 225–228
  lord, vassal and, 271
  merchant class and, 272
"Feudal" system, 271
Feuerbach, Ludwig, 574–575
Filioque, 234, 237, 238
Finaliter, 287
Fine Arts, of seventeenth century, 433–434
Finney, Charles Grandison, 661–664
First Amendment, 644–645
First Crusade (1095–1099), 249–250
First Vatican Council, 576
Five Mile Act (1664), 461
Five Remonstrant Articles, 444
Flacilla, 166

Flacius, Matthew, 422
Florovsky, Georges, 717
Fosdick, Harry Emerson, 711–712
Four Books of Sentences, 298
Fourier, Charles, 560–561
Fourth Lateran Council (1215), 274, 281, 289, 298
Fox, George, 460, 621
Foxe, John, 392–393
France
    age of Enlightenment and, 535–539
    Calvinism in, 445–446
    colonization of New France, Roman Catholicism and,
        605–607
    in early Middle Ages, 240–241
    postrevolutionary Catholicism, 577
    Protestant Reformation of, 396–399
Franciscans
    Conventual, 306
    in early America, 604–605
    founding of, 292–297
    missionaries, 606
    Spiritual, 306
Francis I, 396
Francis II, 394, 398
Francis of Assisi, 275, 292, 295–297
Francke, August Hermann, 476
Frankish Realm, dissolution of, 225–228
Franks, and Merovingian Gaul, 207–210
Frederick II, 288
Frederick V of Palatinate, 440
Free African Society, 671
Freemasonry, 495
French Masons, 495
French Revolution, secularization and, 593
Frequens, 318, 319
Freud, Sigmund, 596
Frondes, 478
Functionalist school of religion, 599
Fundamentalists
    popes and, 730
    in Post-Christian America, 731
    versus modernists, 710–712

Gaetani, 307
Galerius, 139
Galileo (Galileo Galilei), 433
Gallican Confession, 397
Gallicanism, 320, 396
Gallican Liberties, 439
Gaul, Paganism in, 210–212
Gautier de Coinci, 250
Gelasius I (Pope), 284
Geneva
    John Calvin and, 384
    Reformation in, 375–378
Geneva Company of Pastors (Venerable Company), 379
George, Stephan, 581
George I, 487
Gerbert of Aurillac, 261
Gerhard, Johann, 473
German *Aufklärung*, theologies of, 530–531
German Christians, racist movements of, 563

German Enlightenment, takeoff of, 526–527
Germanic social customs, 220
German Illuminati, 495
Germanos I, 197
German philosophical school of religion, 599
German Protestantism, schools of, 570–573
German Reformed Church, 623–624
Germans
    Arian, 154–156
    conversion to Christianity, 222
    settlement in Roman territory, 174
Germany
    confessionalism and, 567–568
    culture, nineteenth and twentieth century, 581
    in late Middle Ages, 249
    Nationalist credo and churches, 563–564
    pietism and, 476–477
    Restoration, Protestantism in, 562
    unification of, 551
Gibbons, James, 720–721
Giberti, Gian Matteo, 406
Gladden, Washington, 702
Glagolitic, 233
Glorious Revolution (1688), 487, 502
Gnosticism, 118–122
God
    death of, 589–592
    existence of, 263
Goethe, Wolfgang, 533
Gogarten, Friedrich, 594
Golden Bull of 1356, 342
Gomar, Franz, 444
Gomarians, 444
Gordon, A. J., 696
Gospels
    addressed to special groups, 125
    linked with an apostle or early follower, 125
Graham, Billy, 738–740
Great Awakening
    America and, 632–635
    second, 658–660, 698
    See also Revival movement
"Great charter of the medieval papacy," 284
Great Depression, 702, 725–726
Great Peasants' War, 332
Grebel, Conrad, 365
Greco-Roman culture, Christianity and, 159–160
Greco-Roman paganism, 157–159
Greco-Roman World (324), 147–150
Greek Orthodox Christians, 717
Gregorian chant, 185
Gregorian papal reform movement, 246
Gregorian reform, 286
Gregory of Nazianzus, 153–154
Gregory of Nyssa, 153–154
Gregory of Tours, 164, 207–208
Gregory I (Gregory the Great), 184–185, 334
Gregory II, 197–198, 202
Gregory III, 220
Gregory VII (Pope), 245–248, 286–287, 307–308
Gregory XI, 313
Gregory XII, 314, 317
Gregory XIII, 404

Gregory XVI, 576, 577–578
Grey, Jane, 389
Grotius, Hugo, 501
Gruet, Jacques, 380
Guise-Lorraine family, 397
Guyart, Marie (Marie of the Incarnation), 606–607
Guyon du Chesnoy, Jeanne-Marie, 448–449

Hadrian, 131
Haec sancta, 316
Hagia Sophia of Constantinople, 181–182, 198–199, 230
Hamann, Johann Georg, 544–545
Handel, George Frederick, 435, 462
Hanoverian dynasty, 487
Hapsburg regime, 430, 525
Hapsburg–Valois wars, 398
Harrington, James, 462
Haydn, Joseph, 435
Headlam, Steward D., 562
Hecker, Isaac, 718–720
Hegel, Georg Wilhelm Friedrich, 569–570, 587
Hegelianism, Kierkegaard and, 582
Hegira, 192
Heidelberg Catechism of 1563, 444
Heleniana, 169
Hellenized, 152
Helvetius, Claude Adrien, 522–523
Henoticon, 179
Henry, Carl F. H., 746
Henry of Anjou, 404
Henry of Guise, 405
Henry of Langenstein, 315
Henry of Navarre, 404, 405
Henry I, 248–249
Henry II, 397, 398
Henry III, 240, 245, 304, 405
Henry II of Bavaria, 240
Henry IV, 248, 286
Henry V, 249
Henry VI, 287, 288
Henry VII, 386
Henry VIII, 385, 386–387
Heraclius, 190–193, 201
Herbert of Cherbury, 506
Herder, Johann Gottfried, 531, 563–564
"Heresy of the three languages," 233–234
Heretical and protest movements, of sixteenth century, 289–292
Heretics, fictions by, 125
Herzen, Alexander Ivanovitch, 585–586
Higher education in America, traditional Christian marks of, 705–706
Higher Life movement, 709–710
Hildebrand, 246, 286
  See also Gregory VII
Himes, Joseph V, 669
Hippolytus of Rome, 133
History of religion, 598–599
History of the Abbotts of Wearmouth and Jarnow, 218
Hitler, Adolf, 552
Hobbes, Thomas, 260, 462, 492
Hocking, William, 752
Hofmann, Melchior, 368

Hohenzollern, 342
Holy Cross, 191
Holy Liturgy, 231
Holy orders, 415
Homosexuality, male, 496
Honorius, 170
Hooker, Richard, 392
Hooper, John, 388
Hopkins, Samuel, 632–633
Hosios Loukas, 230
Hospitalitas, 174
Howard, Catherine, 388
Hromádka, Josef L., 589
Hrotsvitha, 239–240
Hugh, Abbot, 242
Huguenots
  Edict of Nantes and, 405, 478
  Edict of Toleration and, 401
  factions of, 565–566
  formation of, 375, 396
  French Reformed Church and, 446
Humanism, devout, 447–448
Humanity, religion of, 573–575
Humbert of Silva Candida, Cardinal, 238
Hume, David, 512
Humiliati, 290
Hundred Years' War, 308, 322, 323
Hus, John, 314, 318
Hutcheson, Francis, 511, 648
Hutchinson, Anne, 618
Hutterite Anabaptists, 371

Ibn Jubayr, 254
Iconoclasm
  Byzantine, 196–201
  Byzantium after, 229–232
  definition of, 195
  schism between Eastern and Western Christendom and, 201–202
Iconodules, 196
Icons, 195
Ignatius of Loyola, 436
Illuminati, 436
Immaculate Conception, 250, 251
Immanence, 500
Immigrant Protestants, 677–679
Immigration, American, Roman Catholicism and, 718
Impersonalism, of Middle Ages, 272
Inculturation of Christianity, in twentieth century, 759–761
Index librorum prohibitorum (Index of Prohibited Books), 408
Indians, American, Christianity and, 624–626
Individual, discovery of, 266
Infancy Gospels, 126
Infant baptism, radical reformists and, 363–364
Innocent III, 283–289, 307–308, 311
Innocent VII, 314
Innocent XI, 472
Inquisition
  Roman, 409
  Spanish, 408
Institutes of the Christian Religion, 374

Interchurch World Movement of North America, 704
International Church of the Foursquare Gospel, 743
Inter-Varsity Christian Fellowship, 752
Investiture conflict, 240, 247
Ireland, early Christianity in, 215
Ireland, John, 720
Irenaeus, 134
Irene, 199, 229
Isador of Mercator, 286
Isaiah, 116
Islam, 192, 197, 267
Italy
    Ostrogothic, 175–177
    unification of, 551
Ivan III, 320

Jackson, Andrew, 667
James I, 395
James II, 463
James VI, 395, 456
Jansen, Cornelius, 468–470
Jansenism, 469–470, 472
Japan, Protestants in, 761
Japanese Christendom, 467
Jay, John, 642–643
Jefferson, Thomas, 641, 645
Jehovah's Witnesses, 703
Jerome, 167
Jerusalem, 149, 191
Jesuits (Society of Jesus)
    fate of, 534
    Jansenism and, 472
    Loyola and, 411
    motto of, 452
    response to Reformation, 413
    of seventeenth century, 435–439
    success of, 468
Jesus, as fully God and fully human, 152
Jewel, John, 392
Jewish Bible, 116
Jewish revolt, 131
Jews
    emancipation of, 534–535
    usury and, 273–274
Joachim of Fiore, 306
Joan I of Anjou, 315
Joan of Arc, 323, 580
John, King of England, 288
John of Ephesus, 182
John of the Cross, 416, 437
John VIII, 234
John XII, 239, 241
John XXII, 311
John XXIII, 316, 317, 579–580, 742
Jolliet, Louis, 605
Jones, Absalom, 671
Joseph I, 525
Joseph II, 525, 537–538
Judaism
    Christianity as branch of, 128–130
    versus Christianity, Roman view of, 129–130
Judson, Adoniram, 667

Judson, Ann Hasseltine, 667
Julia Domna, 132
Julia Mamaea, 132–133
Julian, 157–158
Julius II, 327–328, 406
Julius III, 408, 415
Jung, Carl Gustav, 596
Jurieu Pierre, 479
Jurisprudence, natural law and, 501
Jus Reformandi, 439, 442
Justin, 178
Justinian age, Christian culture in, 186–189
Justinian, 177–183
Justinian II, 196–197, 202

Kaftan, Julius, 572
Kant, Immanuel, 531–534
Karlstadt, 352
Kastron, 194
Keble, John, 568
Kedwick movement, 709
Kennedy, John F., 727, 741–742
Kepler, Johannes, 422
Kierkegaard, S. A., 581–582
Kiev, 235
King, Martin Luther, Jr., 727, 736–737
Kinglets, 310
Kings, Christian, rights and duties of, 247–248
Kingsley, Charles, 580
Knights of Faith, 580–585
Knights of St. John of Jerusalem (Knights Hospitalers),
    244
Knox, John, 372, 388, 391, 394
Kolde, Dietrich, 338–339
Komensky, Jan Amos (Comenius), 465–466
Königsberg, Enlightenment and, 531–534
Kontakion, 185
Koran, Latin translation of, 267
Korea, 759, 762
Krauth, Charles Porterfield, 678
Kutter, Herman, 562
Kuyper, Abraham, 562

Labarum, 147
Lacordaire, Henri, 577
Laicization, 460
Lainez, 414
Lamb, Christ as, 237
Lambeth Conference, 757–758
Languages, for liturgy, 233–234
Latern Council, 246
Latin, 234
Latin American Christianity, scripture translation and,
    759–760
Latin Bible, Vulgate version, 167
Latin liturgy, 234
Latitude-men. *See* Cambridge Platonists
Laud, William, 457, 612
Lavater, Johann Kaspar, 544
Lay investiture, 239, 248
Lazarists, 468
League of Nations, 700
Lee, Ann, 666

Index

Legend of St. Sylvester, 285
Leibniz, Gottfried Wilhelm, 513–514
Le Nain de Tillemont, 504
Lenin, Vladimir Ilyich, 552–553, 561
Lent, 281
Leo I, 184, 283–284
Leo III, 197, 221, 285
Leo IX, 238, 245–246
Leo X, 329
Leo XIII, 576, 720, 721
Lessing, Gotthold Ephraim, 524–529
Letter of Phileas, 141–142
Levellers, 459
Liberalism, 558–559
Liberation theology, 762
Libertines, 380
Licinius, 147
Lincoln, Abraham, 693–695
Lipsius, Justus, 438
Literature
    Reformation and, 422–423
    vernacular, 234
Liudprand (bishop of Cremona), 238
Liudulf, 239
Locke, John, 392, 502, 506–507
Logic, 260–261
Loisy, Alfred, 530–531, 579
Lombard, Peter, 298
Long Rules, 163
Longsword, Duke William, 241
Lord, vassal and, 271
Lord Darnley, 395
Lord's Shelter, 515–517
Lord's Supper, Luther-Zwingli debate,
    352–355
Lorraine-Guise family, 403
Louis the Pious, 227
Louis IX, 301, 304, 308
Louis XIV, 405, 477, 478, 487–488
Love
    Christianity and, 449
    heavenly vs. earthly, 274–275
    perfect, 446–447
    religion of, 583–585
Loyalists, 639–640
Loyola, Ignatius, 409–413
Luke, 123
Luther, Martin
    anti-Semitism of, 534
    autobiographic details, 330–331, 335–337
    decision to become monk, 339–340
    Diet of Worms and, 341–344
    Karlstadt and, 352
    Peasants' War and, 348–349
    social welfare and, 344–347, 421
    theological reform, 407
    University of Wittenberg and, 421–422
    Zwingli and, 354–355
Lutheranism
    divisions of, 525
    in seventeenth century, 473–477
    Spener's reform program for, 475–476
Lutheran Mysticism, 473

Lutherans
    in America, after Civil War, 689
    in England, 385
    immigrations of, in nineteenth century, 677–678
    in post-Christian America, 734–736

Macedonian dynasty, 231
Macedonian Renaissance, 229
Madison, James, 646
Magdeburg Centuries, 422
Magisterium, 414
Magna carta liberatum, 288
Magnus, Albertus, 295, 300, 301–302
Magnus, Carolus (Charlemagne), 212–215
Magnus Magnentius, 157
Maimonides (Moses ben Maimon), 267
Makemie, Francis, 622–623
Malalas, John, 186–187
Malan, César, 565
Malebranche, Nicolas, 451–452
Mannerism, 453
Mantz, Felix, 365–366
Marburg Colloquy, 355
Marcellus II, 408
Marcion, 123
Marcus Aurelius, 132
Margaret of Valois, 404
Marheineke, Philipp Konrad, 570–571
Marie of the Incarnation (Marie Guyart), 606–607
Mark, Gospel of, versions of, 124
Marquette, Jacques, 605–606
Marriage
    of clergy, 237, 238
    in eighteenth century, 495–496
    Martin Luther and, 420
    Reformation and, 335
    as sacrament, 415
Marshall, Catherine, 745
Marsilius of Padua, 312
Martel, Charles, 212, 214, 219
Martin IV, 305
Martin V, 314, 318, 319
Martyrdom, 131, 133–136, 141–142
Marx, Karl, 561, 587–588
Mary, Mother of God, 169, 188, 250
Maryknoll (Catholic Foreign Mission Society), 751
Maryland, Roman Catholics in, 620
Mary of Guise, 394
Mary Queen of Scots (Mary Stuart), 393–395
Mass, 281, 400
    for the dead, 325–326
Massachusetts Bay Colony, 456, 608
Mathijs, Jan, 369–370
Matrimony. *See* Marriage
Mauriac, François, 581
Mausoleum of Galla Placidia, 168
Maximian, 138–140
Maximinus, 133
Mayhew, Thomas Jr., 624
May Laws of 1874, 559
May Laws of 1892, 535
McCarthy, Senator Joseph, 727
McGready, James, 659

McPherson, Aimee Semple, 743
Mechanism, 452
Mediation, school of, 571
Medieval Christendom
    popular religion of, 250–252
    rise of towns and commerce, 252–253
Medieval era, late, crisis of, 324–329
Medina, 192
Melanchthon, 421–422
Melchiorites, 368
Mendelsshon, Moses, 527–529
Mendicant movement, 276
Mennonite Anabaptists, 371
Mennonites, 361, 625
Menurius, 141
Merchant class, rise of, 272
Merovingian dynasty, 208–210, 284
Merovingian Gaul, Franks and, 207–210
Methodist Christians, 517–519
Methodists, 512, 691
Methodius (of Thessalonica), ninth-century Byzantine
        missionary success and, 232-234
Metropolitan, 165, 235
Michaelmas, 188
Middle Ages
    cities, rise of, 271–274
    life during, 259–260
    money and, 272–273
    penance during, 280–281
    role of church, 269–270
Millenary Petition, 456
Millennialism, 637–638
Miller, William, 668–669
Millerites, 668–670
Milton, John, 458
The Miseries and Ills of the War, 442
Mishnah, 129
Missionary agencies, 666–668
Missionary movement, European legacy, 758–759
Missouri Synod Lutherans, 735–736
Mocius, 151
Möhler, Johann Adam, 576–577
Molanus, Gerhard Wolter, 513
Moltmann, Jürgen, 589
Monasteries, 271
Monasticism
    in early Middle Ages, 161–165
    English, Celtic church and, 215–220
    Pachomian, 163
Money, during Middle Ages, 272–273
Monologion argument, 262–263
Monophysitism, 170
Montanus of Phrygia, 117–118, 123
Monte Cassino, 242
Moody, Dwight Lyman, 565, 695–696
Moody Bible Institute, 696
Moral-influence, 266
Moral Majority, 729
Moravia (Bohemia), 233, 234
More, Henry, 463
More, Thomas, 386
Mormons, 668–670, 731
Moscow, as "third Rome," 539–541

Moses Maimonides, 254
Mott, Lucretia Coffin, 665
Mozarabs, 253
Muhammed, 192–193
Muhlenberg, Henry Melchior, 678
Münster debacle, 368–371
Müntzer, Thomas, 346–347
Muratorian Canon, 124
Muret, battle of, 289
Music
    nineteenth and twentieth century, 581
    of seventeenth century, 433–434
Muslim conquests, 193–195, 202
Mysticism, 448–451

National Association of Evangelicals, 726
National Council of Churches, 740–741
Nationalism, Christian-inspired, 760–761
Natural law political theorists
    doctrine of knowledge, 502–503
    emancipation of history and, 504–505
    orthodox Christianity and, 500–505
    against prejudice, 503–504
    reign of critique, 502
Natural religion, essence of, 497
Nature, medieval view of, 260–261
Neo-Thomism, 725
Neri, Filippo, 499
Nerva, 131
Nestorianism, 169–170, 190
Nestorius, 168
New England, Puritan life and faith in, 613–616
New France, Roman Catholicism in, 605–607
New Religious Right, 728
News from the Republic of Letters (1682), 502
New Spain, Roman Catholicism in, 604–605
New Testament canon, 123–125
Newton, Isaac, 463
Nicaea, 289
Nicene Creed, 152, 234
Nicholas I, 233, 241, 286
Nicholas II, 246
Nicholas III, 306
Nicodemites, 373
Nicolaites, 245
Nicolaitism, 247
Nicole, Pierre, 472
Niebuhr, H. Richard, 746–748
Niebuhr, Reinhold, 746–747
Niemöller, Martin, 564
Nietzsche, Friedrich, 590–592
Nihilism, 591
95 Theses, 341–342
Nixon, Richard, 742
Nogaret, William, 310
Normandy, 240–241

O'Connor, Flannery, 744–745
Odilo of Cluny, 242, 245
Odo of Cluny, 242, 244
Of the Laws of Ecclesiastical Polity (1594–1597), 502
Old Testament, 123
Oleg, 234

Olivi, Peter John, 306
Oracles, revelations and, 115–118
Oratorians, 499
Ordericus Vitalis, 243–244
Order of Preachers (Dominicans), 292–297
The Order of the Star-Spangled Banner, 675
Origen, 133, 134
Origen of Alexandria, 143
Original sin, 167
Origin of Species, 706
Orthodox Christianity, 234
Orthodox missions, Logos and, 233–234
Ostrogothic Italy, 175–177
Otto I, 239
Otto III, 240
Otto IV, 287–288
Ottoman Empire, 427–429, 485
Ottonian Empire, Church and, 238–240
Ottonianum, 239
Owen, Robert, 561–562
Oxford movement, Tractarian period of, 568–569

Pachomius, 163
Pacifists, 639–640
Padroado, 758
Paganism
  in Gaul, 210–212
  Greco-Roman, 157–159
Palaeologus, Manuel II, 319
Paley, William, 512
Palmer, Phoebe Worrall, 664–665
Pantheism, 499
Pantokrator, Monastery of, 244
Papacy
  decline of, Boniface VIII and, 307–310
  infallibility of, 306
  Innocent III and, 283–289
  in Medieval Christendom, 249
  reform movement and, 241–250
  of Renaissance, 326–329
  and Roman Catholics in the United States, 720
  self-perception of, in sixteenth century, 286–287
  supremacy of, 286
Paracelsus, Theophrastus, 421, 473
Parker, Matthew, 391
Parliamentary system, 487
Parr, Catherine, 388
Pascal, Blaise, 471
Pastorals, 124
Patrarch, Francesco, 312
Patriarchial Exarchate, 717
Paul, 131
  letters of, 123
Paul I, 202
Paul III, 407, 409, 415
Paul IV, 408, 409
Paul VI, 728
Paulus, Heinrich Eberhard, 570–571
Pax Romana, 149
Peace treaty of Karlowitz, 485
Peasants' War, 273, 347–349
Peasant uprisings, 332

Peire Cardenal, 250
Pelagius, 167
Penance, 280–281, 415
Penn, William, 621–622
Pentecostalism
  blacks and, 714
  in Christian America, 712–713
  in Post-Christian America, 731, 753
Pepin, 284–285
Pepin III, 219, 221
Pepin III the Short, 214
Pepin II of Heristal, 212–213
Periodicals, theological, 683–684
Perkins, William, 418, 455
Peter of Murrone, 307
Peter the Great, 539–540
Peter the Venerable, 253–254, 267
Petrine Succession, 184, 284
Peucer, Casper, 422
Phenomenological school of religion, 599
Philip, 136, 311
Philip Augustus of France, 288
Philip of France, 304
Philip of Hesse, 352
Philip I, 248–249
Philip II, 390, 391
Philip II of Spain, 389
Philip IV, 308
Philippines, Christian-inspired nationalistic revolution, 760–761
Philip VI, 322–323
"Philosophes," 519–524
Philosophy of religion, 595–596
Phocas, 190
Photian schisms, 237–238
Photius, 233
Pierson, A. T., 696
Pietism, 473, 476, 525
Piety
  in colonial America, 628–635
  in late middle ages, 278–282
  Protestant revivals of, 515–519
Pilgrims, 609–610
Pitt, William, 487
Pius II, 318
Pius IV, 415
Pius V, 393, 408
Pius VII, 575–576
Pius IX, 576, 578–579
Plato, 119
Pliny, 130, 131
Plymouth, English Reformation and, 609–610
Plymouth Brethren, 709
Poland, 464–466
Politics, Reformation and, 418–419
Polycarp, 131–132
Polygamy, 370
Pomponazzi, Pietro, 498
Poor Clares, 296
Pop Bogomil, 236
Pope, lineage of, 184
Popes. *See* individual names
Potestas, 284

Poverty
  Reformation and, 332, 345
  salvation and, 274
  theology of, 274–278
Preaching, letters and reports of, non-canonical, 125
Presbyterian churches, 659
Presbyterians, 470, 622–623, 691
Pride, as vice, 275–276
Priesthood, doctrine of, 419
Priests
  celibacy of, 245
  nicolaites, 245
Prignano, Bartolomeo, 313
Primary Chronicle, 235
Principaliter, 287
Probabilism, 437
Procopius, 180
Prohibitionists, 698
Prohibition movement, 698
Proletariat, 491
Pronocracy, Reform movement and, 241–250
Proslogion argument (ontological), 263
Protestant denominations
  in Christian America, 691
  of 1930s, 724–725
    See also specific denominations
Protestant influence in the nation, decline of, 689–690
Protestantism
  after Civil War, 695–704
  between Civil War and World War I, 704–713
  evolution theory and, 708–710
  German, 525
  moral reform of society, 698
  politics and, 699–701
  reactionary, 564–569
Protestant life, in Christian America, 681–685
Protestant missionaries, 751–752
Protestant missions, from America, 696–697
Protestant Reformation. *See* Reformation
Protestants
  in 1950s, 726–727
  post-World War II feelings toward Catholics, 741–742
Proudhon, Pierre Joseph, 561
Pseudo-Clementine Epistle IV, 369
Pseudo-Isadorian Decretals (Donation of Constantine),
  214–215, 286, 310
Psychoanalytical school of religion, 599
Psychology of religion, 596
Pufendorf, Samuel, 501
Pugachev, Emelyn Ivanovich, 540–541
Pulcheria, 169
Purcell, Henry, 462
Purgatory, 237, 326
Puritan interregnum, features of, 458
Puritanism
  in American colonies, 613–616
  convictions of, 611–612
  dissent from, 616–618
  emergence of, 392, 454
  republicanism and, 636–637
Puritans
  in early America, 610–618
  in England, 457–461

  missions of, 758
  world review, 458–461
Pusey, Edward Bouverie, 568

Quakers, 460, 621–622
Quanta Cura, 578–579
Quarrel of the rites, 468
Quesnel, Pasquier, 472
Quietism, 447, 448–451
Quinisext Synod (Council in Trullo), 183, 185, 196, 237

Rade, Martin, 572
Radegund, 211
Radical reformers, 361–371
Radical reformists, Münster debacle and, 368–371
Ragaz, Leonhard, 562
Rastislav, 233
Rauschenbusch, Walter, 702–703
Reconquista, 251, 253
Reed, Andrew, 680
Reformation
  artistic legacy of, 422–423
  cultural legacy of, 419–421
  early, everyday life during, 330–335
  educational legacy of, 421–422
  in France, 396–399
    coloquy of Poissy and, 399–401
  in Geneva, 375–378
  left wing of, 362
  literacy legacy of, 422–423
  major battles of, 402
  Martin Luther and, 335–337
  political legacy of, 418–419
  scientific legacy of, 421–422
  social change and, 344–347
  Theological legacies of, 417–418
  in Zurich, Zwingli and, 349–356
Reformed Orthodoxy, Evangelical revival and, 565–567
Réformés ("the Reformed"), 396
Regensburg Colloquy (1541), 408
Reid, Thomas, 648
Reimarus, Hermann Samuel, 528
Religion
  anthropology of, 597–598
  history of, 598–599
  philosophy of, 595–596
  psychology of, 596
  sociology of, 596–597
    See also specific religions
la Religion Déformée, 396
Religious fronts, in seventeenth century, 432
Religious literary works, orthodox but not canonical,
  125
Religious toleration, 460
Religious writings, non-canonical, 125–126
Renaissance papacy, 326–329
Republicanism, Christianity and, 636
Revelation of Methodius of Patara, 193–194
Revelations, oracles and, 115–118
Revival movement
  of the early nineteenth century, women and, 663–666
  of Whitefield and Edwards, religious effects of,
    631–633

western phase, 659
See also Great Awakening
Ricci, Matteo, 436
Riccio, David, 395
Richer, Edmond, 439
Rilke, Rainer Maria, 581
Ritschlians, 572
Robert of Geneva, 313
Rococco style, 453
Roe v. Wade, 729–730
Röhr, Johann Friedrich, 570
Rollo, 240–241
Roman bishops, lineage of, 184
Roman Catholic orders
Jesuits, 553
Lazarists, 553
White Fathers, 553
Roman Catholics
after Civil War, 679–680
between the Civil War and World War I, 717–721
in early America, 603–607
Enlightenment and, 535–539
inculturation, 761
in Maryland, 620
in post-Christian America, 731
post-World War II feelings toward Protestants,
741–742
in the United States, 673–677, 689
Roman Empire
Christians and, 128–143
fall of, Mediterranean world after, 172–175
state cult, Christian nonparticipation in, 130–133
Romantics, 544–545, 596
Rome
from Episcopate to papacy, 183–186
versus Constantinople, 237–238
Romulus Augustulus, 175
Roosevelt, Franklin, 725
Roosevelt, Theodore, 700
Rosenkranz, Karl, 570–571
Rothmann, 369, 370
Rousseau, Jean-Jacques, 451, 541–542
Rudolf of Rheinfelden, 248
Rudolf II, 440
Rule of Saint Francis, 296
Rulers, Roman vs. Christian concept of, 130–131
Rus, 234
Rus church, 235
Russia
during age of Enlightenment, 539–541
socialism of, 560–561
Russian Orthodox church, 716, 758
Russian Revolution, 716–717

Sacraments, 278–279, 415
Sacrifices, 129
Sailer, Johann Michael, 576
Sailic Law, 207
Saint Clement of Rome, relics of, 234
Saints
veneration of, 337
See also individual names
Saint-Simon, Claude de, 560

St. Bartholomew's Day Massacre, 401, 403–405
St. Paul's monastery at Jarrow, 217
St. Peter's monastery at Wearmouth, 217
St. Sophia Cathedral at Kiev, 235
Salem witch trials, 615–616
Salesianism, 447
Salmerón, 414
Salvation
charity and, 276
insecurity, theological and pastoral responses, 337–341
Reformation and, 346
Salvation Army, 701–702
Sankey, Ira David, 565
Santiago de Compostella, 251
Sartre, Jean-Paul, 592
Sattler, Michael, 367
Savonarola, Girolamo, 328
Scarlatti, Alessandro, 434
Schiller, Friedrich, 533
Schleiermacher, Friedrich, 545–548
Schleitheim Confession, 361, 367
Schmemann, Alexander, 717
Schmucker, Samuel Simon, 678
Scholasticism, Father of. *See* Anselm
Schopenhauer, Arthur, 590
Science
Charles Darwin and, 706
of the eighteenth century, 494–493
in nineteenth century, 555–556
Reformation and, 421–422
Scientific revolutions, 493
Scofield, C. I., 709
Scofield Reference Bible, 709
Scottish Common Sense Realism, 649
Scottish Episcopal church, 456
Scotus, Duns, 300
"Second Jansenism," 472
Second Vatican Council, 515, 728, 742, 754, 762
Secret revelations, non-canonical, 125
Sectarianism, 557
Secular faith (secularization), 593–595
Secularization, in nineteenth- and twentieth-century
Europe, 593–594
Secularization theory, 682
Septimius Severus, 132
Septuagint, 123
Serfdom, 240
Sergius of Radonezh, 539
Servetus, Michael, 381–383
Servetus case, 381–383
Seton, Elizabeth Ann, 676
Seventeenth century
the religious cultural climate, 432–433
socioeconomic life, 430–431
Seventh-Day Adventists, 669, 725, 731
Seventh Ecumenical Council, 199
Severus Alexander, 133, 135
Sexuality, eighteenth century, 496
Seymour, Edward, 388
Seymour, Jane, 387
Shaftesbury, 503–504
Sheen, Fulton J., 737–738
Shepherd of Hermas, 117

Shrove Tuesday, 281–282
Sibylline oracles, 117, 130
Sic et Non, 266
Sicilian Vespers, 305
Sigismund, 316
Simeon, Charles, 565
Simon, Richard, 490
Simon Magus, 121–122
Simons, Menno, 371
Simony, 247
Sirach, 276–277
Sixteenth Century
    Avignon and Western Schism, 310–315
    conciliarism, 315–318
Slave codes, 672
Slavery
    in American Revolution, religious problem of,
        642–643
    Christianity and, 624–626
    Civil War, 690–695
    justification of, 244–245
    social liberaton of Bible and, 687–688
    women and, 665
Slavic liturgy, 234
Slavic territory, 234
Smith, Joseph, 669–670, 678
Sobieski, John III, 464
Social Gospel, 702–703
Socialism, 560–562
Social liberty, Bible and, 687
Social structure, of eighteenth century, 491
Social transformations, in seventeenth century, 431
Society for Promoting Christian Knowledge (SPCK), 619
Society for the Propagation of the Gospel in Foreign
        Parts (SPG), 619
Society of Friends, 460
Society of Jesus. *See* Jesuits
Socioeconomic life, after 1800, 553–555
Solway Moss, battle of, 394
Southern Baptist Convention, 691, 725, 730
Sozzini, Fausto (Socinus), 465–466
Spain
    colonization of New Spain, Roman Catholicism and,
        604–605
    in first decade of the seventeenth century, 427
Spalding, John Joachim, 529
Spanish Inquisition, 408
SPCK. *See* Society for Promoting Christian Knowledge
Speer, Robert Elliott, 696
Spener, Philipp Jakob, 475–477
SPG. *See* Society for the Progagation of the Gospel in
        Foreign Parts
Spinoza, Baruch, 466, 499–500, 501–502
Spinozism, 506
Spiritual Exercises, 410, 411, 437
Spiritual Franciscans, 306
Stalin, Joseph, 561
Stanton, Elizabeth Cady, 665
Stephen II, 214, 284
Stöcker, Adolf, 562
Stock market crash of October 1929, 724
Stone, Barton W., 659
Stowe, Harriet Beecher, 690

Strauss, David Friedrich, 573–574
Structuralist school of religion, 599
Stuart, Henry, 395
Stuart, Mary, 393–395
Student Volunteer Movement, 752
Sturm, Jean, 377
Suarez, Francisco, 439
Subjectivism, 306
Summae, 261
Summa theologica, 298
Superstition, in the seventeenth century, 435
Supplication for Beggars, 385
Swabian Syngramma, 353
Swedenborg, Emanuel, 543–544
Syllabus, 578–579
Sylvester, 261
Symeon the Stylite, 162
Symmachan forgeries, 285
Symmachus, 158–159
Synagogue worship, local peculiarities of, 129
Synod of 1872, 566
Synod of Rome, 279
Synod of Whitby, 217

Tarasius, 229
Taylor, Nathaniel, 660
Technological developments
    of eighteenth century, 492–493
    of sixteenth century, 336
Te Deum, 343
Telemann, Georg Philipp, 434
Teller, Wilhelm Abraham, 529
Temperance crusade, 665, 698
Tennent, Gilbert, 634
Teresa of Avila, 416
Tertullian, 133, 196
Test Act of 1673, 463
Tetrapolitan Confession (Zwinglian confession),
        355
Tetzel, John, 341
Theodora, 178–179, 199
Theodosius, 154, 160–161, 169
Theodosius II, 172
Theology, Reformation and, 417–418
Theophilus of Antioch, 124
Theotokos, 169, 269
Third Ecumenical Council at Ephesus, 188
"Third Rome" theory, 539–541
Third World churches, vitality of, 763–764
Third World evangelicals, 752
Thirty-Nine Articles, 457
Thirty Years' War, 439–442
Thomas, Gospel of, 121
Thomasius, Christian, 503, 526
Three Orders, theory of, 244
"Three Self Patriotic Movement," 762–763
Tiepolo, Giambattista, 453
Tikhon of Zadonsk, 541
Tillich, Paul, 589, 746
Tillotson, Johns, 506
Tindal, Matthew, 510
Tobit, 276
Toland, John, 507–508

Toledo
  capture of, 253
  school of translation, 253–254
Toleration Act (1690), 505
Tolstoy, Leo, 584–585
Tonsure, Celtic, 215, 217
"Tonsure of St. Peter," 215
Tories, 509
Tours, battle of, 193
Tractarianism, 568–569
Trajan, 130, 131
Transsubstantiation, 280
Treaties of Westphalia, 441
Treatise on the Laws of Ecclesiastical Polity, 392
Treaty of Cateau-Cambrésis (1559), 398
Treaty of Sensations, 522
Trent, 289
Tribonian's Code, 182
Tridentine Catholicism, 413, 432, 439, 442, 466
Troeltsch, Ernst, 572–573, 594
Trollope, Frances, 681
Trotsky, Leon, 561
Truce of God, 244
True Levellers (Diggers), 459
Tudor, Mary, 386, 388–390
Turretini, Francis, 446
Tutu, Desmond, 764
"The Twelve Articles of the Peasants" (1525), 348
  Luther's reply, *Admonition to Peace*, 348–349
Typika (foundation documents), 195
Typus, 201

Ulfila, 155
Ultramontanism, 470, 472, 537, 579
Unam sanctam, 309, 310
Unction, extreme, 415
United Provinces, Calvinism in, 443–445
United States
  Christianity in, between the Civil War and World
    War I, 689–722
  Civil War, 690–695
  early, Roman Catholicism in, 603–607
  founding fathers, faith of, 640–642
  Loyalists, 639–640
  pacifists, 639–640
  post-Christian (1925–1988), theology of, 745–748
  Roman Catholics, 673–677
  separation of church and state, 644–646
  urban life from 1860 to 1920, 701–703
Universalists, 680
Universities
  creation of, 705
  Medieval, rise of, 297–300
  See also Colleges
University of Wittenberg, 333, 340
Urban II, 245, 254, 267
Urban VI, 313, 315
Usury, 273
Usus pauper, 306

Valdimir, 234
Valens, 171
Valentinus, 120–121

Valerian, 137
Varangians, 234
Vasari, Giorgio, 453
Vassal, lord and, 271
Vatican I (1869–1870), 320, 327
Vatican II (1962–1965), 754, 762
Velichkovsky, Paisy, 541
Venerabilem, 287
Vergentis in senium, 288
Vico, Giambattista, 504
Vikings, first recorded attacks of, 226
Vinet, Alexandre, 565
Virchow, Rudolf, 559
Virginia, English Reformation and, 608–609
Virgin of Consolation, 326
Visitation, 251
Vital Revolution, 492
Vivaldi, Antonio, 434
Vivarium, 164
Voltaire, 504, 519, 520–521
Voltairianism, 538
Von Bismarck, Otto, 559–560
Von Görres, Johann Joseph, 576–577
von Grimmelshaussen, Hans, 442
Von Haller, Karl Ludwig, 557
Von Holbach, Paul Thiry, 522, 523–524
Von Hontheim, Nikolaus, 537
Von Humboldt, Wilhelm, 556
von Swedenborg, Emmanuel, 477
Von Zinzendorf, Nikolaus Ludwig, 516

Wagner, Richard, 590
Waldeneses, 290–291
Walpole, Robert, 487
Walsingham, Francis, 391
Walther, Wilhelm, 679
War of 1812, 652
War of the Three Henrys, 405
Wars of Religion (1562–1598), 401
WCTU. *See* Women's Christian Temperance Union
Weber, Max, 597
Weigel, Valentin, 473, 474
Weld, Theodore Dwight, 690
Wellhaussen, Julius, 530–531
Wesley, John, 517–519
Western schism of the church, 313
Whichcote, Benjamin, 463
Whigs, 509, 684–685
White, Ellen, 666
Whitefield, George, 517, 628, 630, 641
Wichern, Johann Heinrich, 562
Wilberforce, William, 565
Willard, Frances, 698
Willhausen, Julius, 707
William I, 241
William III, 505
William IV of Hesse, 442
William Law, 517
William of Ockham, 300, 312
William of Orange, 464
William Rufus, 248–249
Williams, Roger, 617
William the Conqueror, 248

William the Pious, 242
Willibrord, 219
Wilson, Woodrow, 700
Winstanley, Gerrard, 459
Winthrop, John, 613, 617
Witchcraft, in seventeenth century, 435
Witherspoon, John, 649
Wittenberg disturbances of 1521–1522, 361
Wolff, Christian, 526–527
Wollaston, William, 510
Wolsey, Thomas, 385
Women
  in American colonies, 613
  Catholic religious orders of, 676
  in Christian chain of command, 165–166
  feminist movement and, 727–728
  in missionary movement, 759
  Nestorius and, 169
  in 1980s, Christian faith and, 742–745
  participation in Protestant missions, 697
  support for icons, 199–200
Women's Christian Temperance Union (WCTU),
  698–699
Woolman, John, 622
Woolston, Thomas, 511
Work of God, 164

World Council of Churches, second General Assembly
  of, 741
World Missionary Conferences, 515, 697
World War I, ecumenical movement, 703
Wren, Christopher, 461
Wünsch, Georg, 588–589
Wyclif, John, 314, 318
Wynfrith, 219

Xavier, Francis, 467

Yaroslav, 235

Zacharias, 191
Zacharias I, Pope, 214
Zöllner, Johann Friedrich, 531
Zoroastrianism, 178, 192–193
Zurbarán, Francisco, 453
Zurich, Anabaptist beginnings in, 363–366
Zurich Reformation, Zwingli and, 349–356
Zwingli, Ulrich
  Anabaptist movement in Zurich and, 363–367
  Martin Luther and, 330, 354–355
  Reformation in Zurich and, 349–356
  Swiss Reformation and, 356
Zwinglian confession (Tetrapolitan Confession), 355